AMERICAN HISTORY
A Survey

"The American Environment"
essays by William Cronon, University of Wisconsin–Madison

NINTH EDITION

AMERICAN HISTORY

A Survey

ALAN BRINKLEY

Columbia University

McGraw-Hill, Inc.

New York   St. Louis   San Francisco   Auckland   Bogotá   Caracas   Lisbon   London   Madrid
Mexico City   Milan   Montreal   New Delhi   San Juan   Singapore   Sydney   Tokyo   Toronto

AMERICAN HISTORY
A Survey

This book is printed on acid-free paper.

    5 6 7 8 9 0 DOW DOW 9 0 9 8 7

P/N 007955-2
PART OF
ISBN 0-07-912114-4

This book was set in Palatino by York Graphic Services, Inc.
The editors were Peter Labella and Larry Goldberg;
the designer was Wanda Siedlecka;
the production supervisor was Elizabeth J. Strange.
The photo editor was Elyse Rieder.
R. R. Donnelley & Sons Company was printer and binder.

Cover Painting

Childe Hassam. *Winter in Union Square,* (detail) 1894.
Oil on canvas, 18¼ x 18 in. (46.4 x 45.7 cm).
The Metropolitan Museum of Art, New York,
Gift of Mrs. Ethelyn McKinney, in memory of her brother,
Glenn Ford McKinney, 1943   43.116.2

Library of Congress Cataloging-in-Publication Data

American history: a survey / Alan Brinkley. —9th ed.
        p.   cm.
    Includes bibliographical references and index.
    ISBN 0-07-912114-4 (set)
    1. United States—History.   I. Brinkley, Alan.
E178. 1.A492   1995
973—dc20   94-12795

ABOUT THE AUTHOR

Alan Brinkley is Professor of History at Columbia University. He is the author of *Voices of Protest: Huey Long, Father Coughlin, and the Great Depression,* for which he won the 1983 American Book Award; *The Unfinished Nation: A Concise History of the American People*; and *The End of Reform: New Deal Liberalism in Recession and War*. He has held Guggenheim, National Endowment for the Humanities, Woodrow Wilson Center, and National Humanities Center fellowships and has written many articles, essays, and reviews for both scholarly and nonscholarly publications.

CONTENTS

CHAPTER THREE
LIFE IN PROVINCIAL AMERICA 63

CHAPTER FOUR
THE EMPIRE UNDER STRAIN 95

CHAPTER EIGHT
VARIETIES OF AMERICAN NATIONALISM   219

CHAPTER FOURTEEN
THE CIVIL WAR   381

PREFACE

HE PAST, OF COURSE, can never change. But our understanding of the past changes constantly. Perhaps at no time has that been more evident than in the last two decades, when historical scholarship has experienced something close to a revolution. Once historians viewed the past largely through the experiences of great men and great events. Today, they attempt to tell a much more complicated story—one that includes private as well as public events, ordinary people as well as celebrated ones, difference as well as unity. The new history is fragmented at times, because it attempts to embrace so many more areas of human experience than the older narrative. It is often disturbing, because it reveals failures and injustices as well as triumphs. But it is also richer, fuller, and better suited to helping us understand our own diverse and contentious world.

This book began its life several decades ago; and like most general histories of its time, it concentrated at first primarily on America's political development and on its expanding role in the world. Nine editions later, it continues to tell those important stories. But it tells many other stories as well. This newest version continues a process of change stretching now over more than a decade. It attempts to present not only the traditional stories of great public events, but also the many areas of the nation's past that historians have more recently revealed.

Despite the many changes, I have tried to retain what I believe has long been the most important strength of this book: a balanced picture of the American past that attempts to connect the newer histories of society, culture, and ordinary people with the more traditional stories of politics, diplomacy, and great public events. The United States is a nation of extraordinary diversity, and we cannot understand its history without understanding the experience of the many different groups that have shaped its society and of the particular worlds that have developed within it based on race, gender, ethnicity, religion, class, or region. But America is not just a collection of different cultures. It is also a nation, whose people share a common political system, a connection to a vast national economy, and a familiarity with a powerful public culture. To understand the American past, it is necessary to examine not just the nation's considerable diversity, but also the powerful forces that have drawn it together and allowed it to survive and flourish despite division.

The process of revision usually means adding things, and this book—like many books that experience periodic revisions—has tended to grow steadily longer. In this edition, I have tried to reverse that process. I have substantially rewritten the entire narrative to make it clearer and more compact, and to make it possible for me to add substantial new material without increasing the length of the book as a whole. I have reorganized several sections to provide a more coherent picture of various elements of the past. Chapters 7 through 11, in particular, have been reorganized to allow for an extended discussion of the social and economic development of antebellum America and to permit considerable expansion of the descriptions of the Old South and slavery. Chapter 15 has been restructured to link the extended description of the New South to the account of the Reconstruction process that did so much to shape it. Chapter 16 is now devoted entirely to the history of the trans-Mississippi West in the late nineteenth century and contains a considerably expanded account of that important area of American history. There is a new chapter (27) on the diplomacy of the period between the two world wars, and a new and expanded chapter (28) on World War II itself. There is a new final chapter (34), which contains an account of events since the publication of the previous edition and a significantly expanded discussion of some of the issues that have emerged to shape contemporary society and culture.

There are many other important changes in this edition as well. Throughout the book, there is considerably expanded coverage of the history of the American West (beginning with an extended discussion of early Spanish settlement in what is now the American Southwest and continuing through the rise of the modern "Sunbelt") and substantially increased attention to the history of Hispanic and Asian people in the United States. There is important new material derived from recent scholarship in women's history. There is a much-expanded discussion of the complicated social and cultural history of the 1950s, a greatly extended account of the origins and impact of the Vietnam War, and a major new section on the rise of the right in the 1970s and 1980s. There are also two new essays in the series entitled "Where Historians Disagree": one on the history of the West (Chapter 16) and the other on women's history (Chapter 32). There are many new illustrations, and there are expanded and updated bibliographies.

*

The first edition of *American History: A Survey* was the work of three distinguished historians: Richard N. Current, Frank Freidel, and T. Harry Williams. I have had the great privilege of inheriting this book from them and trying to keep alive in a very different time the high standards they established more than thirty years ago. It has now been over fifteen years since I assumed sole responsibility for this book; and as I have attempted to adapt it to the many changes in historical scholarship of the last several decades, it has now evolved into something very different from the book the original authors bequeathed me. Consequently, it now seems to us time for me to accept sole public responsibility for the result. This book will always reflect the extraordinary talents and enduring contributions of its three original authors. But beginning with this edition, it will carry my name alone.

As always, I am grateful to many people for their help in producing this new edition. John Alexander, Sonya Michel, Gary Okihiro, and George Sanchez were among the scholars who read and commented on the previous edition. Their suggestions were of great value. I owe a particular debt to Richard White, both for his thoughtful critique of the coverage of western history in the previous edition of this book, and for his excellent history of the American West (*"It's Your Misfortune and None of My own"*), which introduced me to much of the new work in this rapidly changing field of scholarship. My research assistants Yanek Mieczkowski, Thaddeus Russell, and Charles Forcey made enormous contributions to this edition. So did the many people at McGraw-Hill who steered it through production, among them Peter Labella, Larry Goldberg, Joan Benham, Kathy Bendo, Elyse Rieder, and Sandra Topping. Finally, I am grateful, as always, to the students, teachers, and other readers of this book who have sent me unsolicited comments, criticisms, and corrections. I hope they will continue to offer their reactions by sending them to me in care of the Department of History, Columbia University, New York, N.Y. 10027.

Alan Brinkley

AMERICAN HISTORY

A Survey

INDIANS FISHING
The English explorer John White visited areas of the Atlantic coast in the 1580s and created
a series of watercolors of native life there—among them this scene of Woodland Indians
fishing from a canoe. *(British Museum)*

CHAPTER ONE

THE MEETING OF CULTURES

THE DISCOVERY OF AMERICA did not begin with Christopher Columbus. It began many thousands of years earlier when human beings first crossed an ancient land bridge over the Bering Strait into what is now Alaska and—almost certainly without realizing it—began to people a new continent. No one is certain when these migrations began; recent estimates suggest between 14,000 and 16,000 years ago, but some scholars believe the first crossings were much earlier. They were probably a result of the development of new stone tools—spears and other hunting implements—with which it became possible to pursue the large animals that regularly crossed between Asia and North America. Year after year, a few at a time, these nomadic peoples—all of them apparently from a Mongolian stock similar to that of modern-day eastern Siberia—entered the new continent and moved ever deeper into its heart. Ultimately, perhaps as early as 8,000 B.C., the migrations reached the southern tip of South America. By the end of the fifteenth century A.D., when the first important contact with Europeans occurred, America was the home of many millions of men and women. Scholars estimate that well over 10 million people lived in South America by 1500 and that perhaps 4 million lived in the territory that now constitutes the United States.

AMERICA BEFORE COLUMBUS

As settlement spread, the peoples of the different regions of America began to adapt themselves to their surroundings and to create distinctive civilizations appropriate to their climates and resources. There was as much variety among the civilizations of the Americas as among the civilizations of Europe, Asia, and Africa.

The Civilizations of the South

The most elaborate of these societies emerged in South and Central America and in Mexico. In Peru, the Incas created a powerful empire of perhaps 6 million people. They developed a complex political system and a large network of paved roads that welded together the populations of many tribes under a single rule. In Central America and on the Yucatán peninsula of Mexico, the Mayas built a sophisticated culture with a written language, a numerical system similar to the Arabic (and superior to the Roman), an accurate calendar, and an advanced agricultural system. They were succeeded by the Aztecs, a once-nomadic warrior tribe from the north. In the late thirteenth century, the Aztecs established a precarious rule over much of central and southern Mexico and built elaborate administrative, educational, and medical systems comparable to the most advanced in Europe at the time. The Aztecs also developed a harsh religion that required human sacrifice. Their Spanish conquerors discovered the skulls of 100,000 victims in one location when they arrived in 1519—one reason why many Europeans came to consider the Aztecs "savages" despite their impressive accomplishments (and despite the holy wars and witch burnings in the Christian world, which demonstrate that the Aztecs were not alone in finding religious justification for killing).

Principal Subsistence Patterns of Early Native Peoples of North America

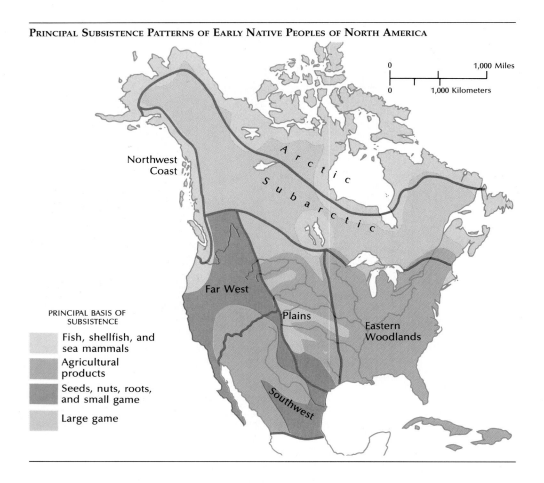

PRINCIPAL BASIS OF
SUBSISTENCE

- Fish, shellfish, and sea mammals
- Agricultural products
- Seeds, nuts, roots, and small game
- Large game

The economies of these societies were based primarily on agriculture, but there were also substantial cities in which lived, among others, many of the warriors and priests who ruled the empires and formed their hereditary elites. Some of these cities were as large as the greatest capitals of Europe. Tenochtitlán, the Aztec capital built on the site of present-day Mexico City, had a population of over 100,000 in 1500 and an impressive complex of majestic public buildings—including temples equal in size to the great pyramids of Egypt. The Mayas (at Mayapán and elsewhere) and the Incas (in such cities as Cuzco and Machu Picchu) produced similarly elaborate settlements with striking religious and ceremonial structures of their own. These achievements are all the more remarkable for their having been attained without some of the important technologies that Asian and European civilizations possessed. The Incas, for example, never had any system of writing or any equivalent for paper. And as late as

the sixteenth century, no American society had yet developed wheeled vehicles.

The Civilizations of the North

The peoples north of Mexico—in the lands that became the United States and Canada—did not develop empires as large or political systems as elaborate as those of the Incas, Mayas, and Aztecs. They did, however, build complex civilizations of great variety. In the northern regions of the continent emerged societies that subsisted on hunting, gathering, fishing, or some combination of the three: the Eskimos of the Arctic Circle, who fished and hunted seals and whose civilization spanned thousands of miles of largely frozen land, which they traversed by dog sled; the big-game hunters of the northern forests, who led nomadic lives based on pursuit of moose and caribou; the tribes of

INDIANS OF NEW FRANCE
The drawing is by the cartographer
Charles Bécard de Granville, who was
employed by the French government to
make maps of their territories in North
America. Granville also produced drawings of the flora and fauna of the region
and of the natives he encountered. This
depiction of Indian hunters traveling by
river dates from approximately 1701.
(Gilcrease Institute)

the Pacific Northwest, whose principal occupation was salmon fishing, who created substantial permanent settlements along the coast, and who engaged in constant and often violent competition with one another for access to natural resources; and a group of tribes spread through relatively arid regions of the Far West who developed successful communities, many of them quite wealthy and densely populated, based on fishing, hunting small game, and gathering.

Other societies in North America were primarily agricultural. Among the most developed were those in the Southwest. The people of that region built large irrigation systems to allow farming on their relatively dry land, and they constructed substantial towns that became centers of trade, crafts, and religious and civic ritual. Their densely populated settlements at Chaco Canyon and elsewhere consisted of stone and adobe terraced structures, known today as pueblos, many of which resembled large apartment buildings in size and design. In the Great Plains region, too, most tribes were engaged in sedentary farming (corn and other grains) and lived in substantial permanent settlements, although there were some small nomadic tribes that subsisted by hunting buffalo. (Only in the eighteenth century, after Europeans had introduced the horse to North America, did buffalo hunting begin to support a large population in the region; at that point, many once-sedentary farmers left the land to pursue the great migratory buffalo herds.)

The eastern third of what is now the United States—much of it covered with forests and inhabited by people who have thus become known as the Woodland Indians—had the greatest food resources of any region of the continent. It supported many tribes, most of whom simultaneously engaged in farming, hunting, gathering, and fishing. In the South there were for a time substantial permanent settlements and large trading networks based on the corn and other grains grown in the rich lands of the Mississippi River valley. As in the Southwest, cities emerged as trading and political centers. Among them was Cahokia (near present-day St. Louis), which at its peak in 1200 A.D. had a population of 40,000 and contained a great complex of large earthen mounds comparable to those found in the Aztec empire in Mexico.

The agricultural societies of the Northeast were more mobile than those in other regions. Farming techniques there were designed to exploit the land quickly rather than to develop permanent settlements. Natives often cleared the land by setting forest fires or cutting into trees to kill them. They then planted crops—corn, beans, squash, pumpkins, and others—among the dead or blackened trunks. After a few years, when the land became exhausted or the filth from a settlement began to accumulate, they moved on and established themselves elsewhere. In some parts of eastern North America, villages dispersed every winter and families foraged for themselves in the wilderness until warm

weather returned; those who survived then reassembled to begin farming again.

Many of the tribes living east of the Mississippi
River were linked together loosely by common linguistic roots. The largest of the language groups was
the Algonquin tribes, which lived along the Atlantic
seaboard from Canada to Virginia. More elaborately
organized was the Iroquois Confederation, which
emerged in the mid-fifteenth century, centered in what
is now upstate New York. The Iroquois included at
least five distinct northern "nations"—the Seneca,
Cayuga, Onondaga, Oneida, and Mohawk—and had
links as well with the Cherokees and the Tuscaroras
farther south, in the Carolinas and Georgia. The third
largest language group—the Muskogean—included
the tribes in the southernmost region of the eastern
seaboard: the Chickasaws, Choctaws, Creeks, and
Seminoles. Alliances among the various Indian societies (even among those with common languages)
were fragile, since the peoples of the Americas did not
think of themselves as members of a single civilization.
When Europeans arrived and began to threaten their
way of life, Indians generally viewed the threat in
terms of how it affected their own community and
tribe, not how it affected any larger "Indian nation."
Only rarely did tribes unite in opposition to challenges
from whites.

Given the enormous diversity of economic, social,
and political structures among the North American Indians, large generalizations about their cultures are difficult. But in the last centuries before the arrival of Eu-

ropeans, Native Americans—like peoples in other areas of the world—were experiencing an agricultural
revolution. In all regions of the United States (if in
varying degrees from place to place), tribes were becoming more sedentary and were developing new
sources of food, clothing, and shelter. Most regions
were experiencing significant population growth. And
virtually all were developing the sorts of elaborate social customs and rituals that only relatively stationary
societies can produce. Religion was as important to Indian society as it was to most other cultures and was
usually closely bound up with the natural world on
which the tribes depended. Native Americans worshiped many gods, whom they associated variously
with crops, game, forests, rivers, and other elements
of nature. Some tribes created elaborate, brightly colored totems as part of their religious ritual; most staged
large festivals on such important occasions as harvests
or major hunts.

Also as in other parts of the world, the societies of
North America tended to divide tasks according to
gender. All tribes assigned women the jobs of caring
for children, preparing meals, and gathering certain
foods. But the allocation of other tasks varied from one
society to another. Some tribal groups (notably the
Pueblos of the Southwest) reserved farming tasks almost entirely for men. Among others (including the
Algonquins, the Iroquois, and the Muskogees), women
tended the fields, while men engaged in hunting, warfare, or clearing land. Iroquois women and children
were often left alone for extended periods while men

THE INDIAN VILLAGE OF SECOTON (C. 1585), BY JOHN WHITE
John White created this illustration of life among the Eastern Woodland Indians in coastal North Carolina. It shows the diversified agriculture practiced by the natives: squash, tobacco, and three varieties of corn. The hunters shown in nearby woods suggest another element of the native economy. At bottom right, Indians perform a religious ritual, which White describes as "strange gestures and songs." *(British Museum)*

were away hunting or fighting battles. As a result, women tended to control the social and economic organization of the settlements and played powerful roles within families (which in many tribes were traced back "matrilineally," or through the mother's line).

EUROPE LOOKS WESTWARD

Europeans were almost entirely unaware of the existence of the Americas before the fifteenth century. A few early wanderers—Leif Ericson, an eleventh-century Norse seaman, and perhaps others—had glimpsed parts of the New World and had demonstrated that Europeans were capable of crossing the ocean to reach it. But even if their discoveries had become common knowledge (and they did not), there would have been little incentive for others to follow. Europe in the Middle Ages (roughly 500–1500 A.D.) was not an adventurous civilization. Divided into innumerable small duchies and kingdoms, its outlook was overwhelmingly provincial. Subsistence agriculture predominated, and commerce was limited; few merchants looked beyond the boundaries of their own regions. The Roman Catholic Church exercised a measure of spiritual authority over most of the continent, and the Holy Roman Empire provided at least a nominal political center. Even so, real power was for the most part widely dispersed; only rarely could a single leader launch a great venture. Gradually, however, conditions in Europe changed so that by the late fifteenth century interest in overseas exploration had grown.

Commerce and Nationalism

Two important and related changes provided the first incentive for Europeans to look toward new lands. One was a result of the significant growth in Europe's population in the fifteenth century. The Black Death, a catastrophic epidemic of the bubonic plague that began in Constantinople in 1347, had decimated Europe, killing (according to some estimates) more than a third of the people of the continent and debilitating its already limited economy. But a century and a half later, the population had rebounded. With that growth came a rise in land values, a reawakening of commerce, and a general increase in prosperity. Affluent landlords were becoming eager to purchase goods from distant regions, and a new merchant class was emerging to meet their demand. As trade increased, and as advances in navigation and shipbuilding made long-distance sea travel more feasible, interest in developing new markets, finding new products, and opening new trade routes rapidly increased.

Paralleling the rise of commerce in Europe, and in part responsible for it, was the rise of new governments that were more united and powerful than the feeble political entities of the feudal past. In the western areas of Europe in particular, where the authority of the distant pope and the even more distant Holy Roman Emperor was necessarily weak, strong new monarchs were emerging and creating centralized nation-states, with national courts, national armies, and—perhaps most important—national tax systems. As these ambitious kings and queens consolidated their power and increased their wealth, they became eager to enhance the commercial growth of their nations.

Ever since the early fourteenth century, when Marco Polo and other adventurers had returned from Asia bearing exotic goods (spices, cloths, dyes) and even more exotic tales, Europeans who hoped for commercial glory had dreamed above all of trade with the East. For two centuries, that trade had been limited by the difficulties of the long, arduous overland journey to the Asian courts. But in the fourteenth century, as the maritime capabilities of several western European societies increased, there began to be serious talk of finding a faster, safer sea route to Asia. Such dreams gradually found a receptive audience in the courts of the new monarchs. By the late fifteenth century, some of them were ready to finance daring voyages of exploration.

The first to do so were the Portuguese. Their maritime preeminence in the fifteenth century was in large part the work of one man, Prince Henry the Navigator. Henry's own principal interest was not in finding a sea route to Asia, but in exploring the western coast of Africa—where he dreamed of establishing a Chris-

tian empire to aid in his country's wars against the Moors of northern Africa and where he hoped to find new stores of gold. But the explorations he began, while they did not fulfill his own hopes, ultimately led farther than he had dreamed. Some of Henry's mariners went as far south as Cape Verde, on Africa's west coast. In 1486 (six years after Henry's death), Bartholomeu Dias rounded the southern tip of Africa (the Cape of Good Hope); and in 1497–1498 Vasco da Gama proceeded all the way around the cape to India. In 1500, the next fleet bound for India, under the command of Pedro Cabral, was blown westward off its southerly course and happened upon the coast of Brazil. But by then another man, in the service of another country, had already encountered the New World.

Christopher Columbus

Christopher Columbus, who was born and reared in Genoa, Italy, obtained most of his early seafaring experience in the service of the Portuguese. As a young man, he became intrigued with the possibility, already under discussion in many seafaring circles, of reaching Asia by going not east but west. Columbus's hopes rested on several basic misconceptions. He believed that the world was far smaller than it actually is. He also believed that the Asian continent extended farther eastward than it actually does. He assumed, therefore, that the Atlantic was narrow enough to be crossed on a relatively brief voyage. It did not occur to him that anything lay to the west between Europe and Asia.

Columbus failed to win support for his plan in Portugal, so he turned to Spain. The Spaniards were not yet as advanced a maritime people as the Portuguese, but they were at least as energetic and ambitious. And in the fifteenth century, the marriage of Spain's two most powerful regional rulers, Ferdinand of Aragon and Isabella of Castile, had produced the strongest monarchy in Europe. Like other young monarchies, it would soon grow eager to demonstrate its strength by sponsoring new commercial ventures.

Columbus appealed to Queen Isabella for support for his proposed westward voyage. In 1492, having consolidated the monarchy's position within Spain itself, Isabella agreed to Columbus's request. Commanding ninety men and three ships—the *Nina*, the *Pinta*, and the *Santa Maria*—Columbus left Spain in August 1492 and sailed west into the Atlantic on what he thought was a straight course for Japan. Ten weeks later, he sighted land and assumed he had reached his target. In fact, he had landed on an island in the Bahamas. When he pushed on and encountered Cuba, he assumed he had reached China. He returned to Spain

BALBOA DISCOVERING THE PACIFIC
The Spanish historian Herrera created this engraving to commemorate Vasco de Balboa's discovery of the Pacific Ocean, which he encountered after fighting his way across the Isthmus of Panama. Balboa's contemporaries called the Pacific "El Mar del Sur," the "South Sea." *(Bettmann)*

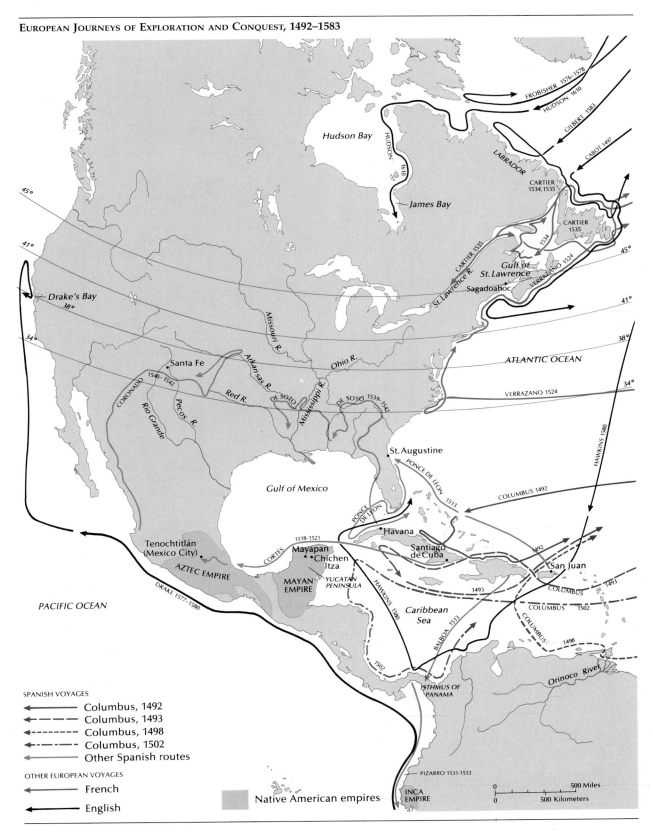

SPANISH VOYAGES
- Columbus, 1492
- Columbus, 1493
- Columbus, 1498
- Columbus, 1502
- Other Spanish routes

OTHER EUROPEAN VOYAGES
- French
- English

Native American empires

0   500 Miles
0   500 Kilometers

COLUMBUS'S THIRD VOYAGE TO AMERICA, 1498
This engraving is a sixteenth-century re-creation by the Flemish engraver Theodore DeBry of an earlier drawing. It shows Columbus's third expedition to the New World as it encountered natives near the island of Margarita, off the coast of Venezuela. Columbus's men received three pounds of pearls from the natives (the Indian canoes are shown here filled with pearl oysters) in exchange for some pieces of pottery, and then sailed on. *(New York Public Library)*

in triumph, bringing with him several captured natives as evidence of his achievement. (He called the natives "Indians" because he believed they were from the East Indies in the Pacific.)

But Columbus had not, of course, encountered the court of the great khan in China or the fabled wealth of the Indies. And so a year later, he tried again, this time with a much larger expedition. As before, he headed into the Caribbean, discovering several other islands and leaving a small and short-lived colony on Hispaniola. On a third voyage, in 1498, he finally reached the mainland and cruised along the northern coast of South America. When he passed the mouth of the Orinoco River (in present-day Venezuela), he concluded for the first time that what he had discovered was not in fact an island off the coast of China, as he had assumed, but a separate continent; such a large freshwater stream, he realized, could emerge only from a large body of land. Still, he remained convinced that Asia was only a short distance away. And although he failed in his efforts to sail around the northeastern coast of South America to the Indies (he was blocked by the Isthmus of Panama), he returned to Spain believing that he had explored at least the fringes of the Far East. He continued to believe that until the day he died.

Columbus's celebrated accomplishments made him a popular hero for a time, but he ended his life in obscurity. When Europeans at last gave a name to the New World, they ignored him. The distinction went instead to a Florentine merchant, Amerigo Vespucci, member of a later Portuguese expedition to the New World who wrote a series of vivid descriptions of the lands he visited and who recognized the Americas as new continents.

Columbus has been celebrated for centuries as the "Admiral of the Ocean Sea" (a title he struggled to have officially bestowed on him during his lifetime) and as a representative of the new, secular, scientific impulses of Renaissance Europe. But Columbus was also a deeply religious man, even something of a mystic, and his voyages were inspired as much by his conviction that he was fulfilling a divine mission as by his interest in geography and trade. A strong believer in biblical prophecies, he came to see himself as a man destined to advance the coming of the millennium. "God made me the messenger of the new heaven and the new earth," he wrote near the end of his life, "and he showed me the spot where to find it." A similar combination of secular and religious passions lay behind many subsequent efforts at exploration and settlement of the New World.

Partly as a result of Columbus's initiative, Spain began to devote greater resources and energy to maritime exploration and gradually replaced Portugal as the foremost seafaring nation. The Spaniard Vasco de Balboa fought his way across the Isthmus of Panama (1513) and became the first European to gaze westward upon the great ocean that separated America from China and the Indies. Seeking access to that ocean, Ferdinand Magellan, a Portuguese in Spanish employ, found the strait that now bears his name at the southern end of South America, struggled through the stormy narrows and into the ocean (so calm by contrast that he christened it the Pacific), then proceeded to the Philippines. There Magellan died in a conflict with the natives, but his expedition went on to complete the first known circumnavigation of the globe (1519–1522). By 1550, Spaniards had explored the coasts of North America as far north as Oregon in the west and Labrador in the east as well as some of the interior regions of the continent.

The Conquistadores

In time, Spanish explorers in the New World stopped thinking of America simply as an obstacle to their search for a route to the East. They began instead to consider it a possible source of wealth rivaling and even surpassing the original Indies. On the basis of Columbus's discoveries, the Spanish claimed for themselves the whole of the New World, except for a piece of it (today's Brazil) that was reserved by a papal de-

CORTÉS IN THE NEW WORLD
An Aztec artist created this image of Hernando Cortés in Mexico. Cortés is visible at upper left, on horseback, wielding a sword. Other images suggest the destruction his arrival produced among the Aztecs. One of the most brutal and successful of the Spanish conquistadores, Cortés burned his ships upon landing at Vera Cruz (where he founded a city) in 1519 to prevent his men from turning back. In 1521, he captured the Aztec capital, Tenochtitlán, after a long siege. *(Apostolic Library, Vatican City)*

cree for the Portuguese. By the mid-sixteenth century, the Spanish were well on their way to establishing a substantial American empire.

The early Spanish colonists, beginning with those Columbus brought on his second voyage, settled on the islands of the Caribbean, where they tried to enslave the Indians and find gold. They had little luck at either endeavor. But then, in 1518, Hernando Cortés, who had been a Spanish government official in Cuba for fourteen years and who had to that point achieved little success, decided to lead a small military expedition (about 600 men) into Mexico after hearing stories of great treasures there. He met strong and resourceful resistance from the Aztecs and their powerful emperor Montezuma; the first Spanish assault on Tenochtitlán, the Aztec capital, failed. But Cortés and his army had, unknowingly, unleashed an assault on the Aztecs far more devastating than military attack: they had exposed the natives to smallpox. An epidemic of that disease decimated the population and made it possible for the Spanish to triumph in their second attempt at conquest. Through his ruthless suppression of the surviving natives, Cortés established a lasting reputation as the most brutal of the Spanish "conquistadores" (conquerors).

The news that silver was to be found in Mexico turned the attention of other Spaniards to the mainland. From the island colonies and from the mother country, a wave of conquistadores descended on Mexico in search of fortune—a movement comparable in some ways to the nineteenth-century gold rushes elsewhere in the world, but much more vicious. Francisco Pizarro, who conquered Peru (1532–1538) and revealed to Europeans the wealth of the Incas, opened the way for other advances into South America. His one-time deputy Hernando De Soto, in a futile search for gold, silver, and jewels, led several expeditions (1539–1541) through Florida west into the continent and became the first white man known to have crossed the Mississippi River. Francisco Coronado traveled north from Mexico (1540–1542) into what is now New Mexico in a similarly fruitless search for gold and jewels; in the process, he opened the Southwest of what is now the United States to Spanish settlement.

The story of the Spanish warriors is one of great military daring and achievement. It is also a story of remarkable brutality and greed. The conquistadores subjugated and, in some areas, virtually exterminated the native populations. In this horrible way, they made possible the creation of a vast Spanish empire in the New World.

The Spanish Empire

Spanish exploration, conquest, and colonization in America was primarily a work of private enterprise, carried on by individual leaders, with little direct support from the government at home. Those who wished to launch expeditions to the New World had first to get licenses from the crown. Those who obtained licenses received titles to large estates or land grants (*encomiendas*) and the right to exact tribute (and often labor) from the natives, a system the Spanish had first imposed on the Moors in Spain itself.

A license did no more than confer rights; colonizers had to equip and finance their expeditions on their own and assume the full risk of loss or ruin. They might succeed and make a fortune; they might fail—through shipwreck, natural disaster, incompetence, or bad luck—and lose everything, including their lives, as many adventurers did. The New World did not always attract good or intelligent immigrants, but in the beginning it seldom attracted the fainthearted.

The first Spaniards to arrive in the New World, the conquistadores, were interested in only one thing: getting rich. And in that they were fabulously successful. For three hundred years, beginning in the sixteenth century, the mines in Spanish America yielded more than ten times as much gold and silver as the rest of the world's mines put together. These riches made Spain for a time the wealthiest and most powerful nation on earth.

PIZARRO IN PERU
A European artist depicted Pizarro's arrival on the coast of Peru in the early 1530s, where he was greeted by crowds of hostile Indians. By 1538, Pizarro had conquered the empire of the Incas. *(British Museum)*

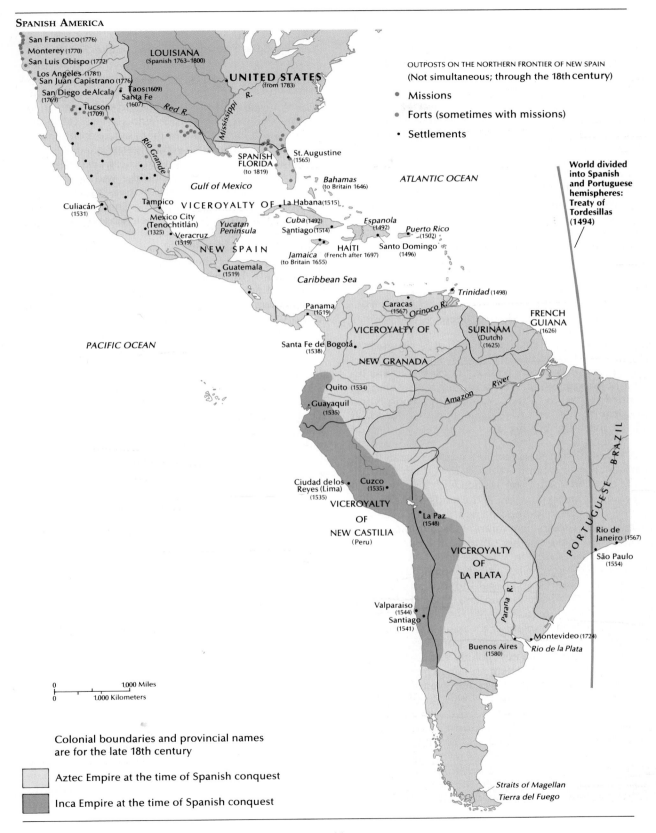

After the first wave of conquest, however, most Spanish settlers in America traveled to the New World for other reasons. Many went in hopes of creating a profitable agricultural economy. And unlike the conquistadores, who left little but destruction behind them, they helped establish elements of European civilization in America that permanently altered both the landscape and the social structure. Other Spaniards went to America to spread the Christian religion. Indeed, after the era of the conquistadores came to a close in the 1540s, the missionary impulse became one of the principal motives for European emigration to America, and priests or friars accompanied all colonizing ventures. Through the work of zealous missionaries, the gospel of the Catholic Church ultimately extended throughout South and Central America, Mexico, and into the South and Southwest of the present United States.

Northern Outposts

The Spanish fort established in 1565 at St. Augustine, Florida, became the first permanent European settlement in the present-day United States. But it was little more than a military outpost and a headquarters for unsuccessful missionary campaigns among North American natives that were ultimately abandoned. It did not mark the beginning of a substantial effort at colonization in the region.

A more substantial colonizing venture began thirty years later in the Southwest. In 1598, Don Juan de Oñate traveled north from Mexico with a party of 500 and claimed for Spain some of the lands of the Pueblo Indians that Coronado had passed through over fifty years before. The Spanish migrants began to establish a colony, modeled roughly on those the Spanish had created farther south, in what is now New Mexico. Oñate created *encomiendas*, and the Spanish began demanding tribute from the local Indians (and at times commandeering them as laborers). Spanish colonists founded Santa Fe in 1609.

Oñate's harsh treatment of the natives (who greatly outnumbered the small Spanish population) threatened the stability of the new colony and led to his recall in 1606. But the settlement remained precarious for decades. That was not only because of continuing tensions between the Spanish and the Pueblo Indians whose lands they were attempting to control. In fact, the Spanish and the Pueblos learned to cooperate in many ways and even profited at times from each other's presence. Substantial numbers of Pueblos converted to Christianity under the influence of Spanish missionaries. Others entered into important trading relationships with the Spanish. The greater danger to the colony came from Apache and Navajo raiders, who

threatened the Spanish and Pueblos alike. But the New Mexico settlement continued to grow. By 1680, there were over 2,000 Spanish colonists living among about 30,000 Pueblos. The economic heart of the colony was not the gold and precious metals the early Spanish explorers had tried in vain to find. It was cattle and sheep, raised on the *ranchos* that stretched out around the small towns Spanish settlers established.

In 1680, the colony was nearly destroyed when the Pueblos rose in revolt. Despite the widespread conversions to Catholicism, most natives (including the converts) continued also to practice their own religious rituals—rituals that sustained their sense of tribal identity. In 1680, Spanish priests and the colonial government, which was closely tied to the missionaries, were engaged in one of their periodic efforts to suppress these rituals. In response, Pope, an Indian religious leader, led an uprising that killed hundreds of European settlers (including 21 priests), captured Santa Fe, and drove the Spanish temporarily from the region. But twelve years later the Spanish returned, resumed seizing Pueblo lands, and crushed a last revolt in 1696.

Spanish exploitation of and brutality toward the Indians did not end. But after the revolts, many Spanish colonists seemed to understand that they could not hope to prosper in New Mexico in constant conflict with a native population that greatly outnumbered them. On the one hand, the Spanish intensified their efforts to assimilate the Indians—baptizing Indian children at birth and enforcing observance of Catholic rituals. On the other hand, they now permitted the Pueblos to own land; they stopped commandeering Indian labor; they replaced the *encomienda* system with a less demanding and oppressive one; and they tacitly tolerated the survival of tribal religious rituals. There was significant intermarriage between Europeans and Indians. And increasingly, the Pueblos came to consider the Spanish their allies in the continuing battles with the Apaches and Navajos. By 1750, the Spanish population had grown modestly to about 4,000. The Pueblo population had declined (through disease, war, and migration) to about 13,000, less than half what it had been in 1680. New Mexico had by then become a reasonably stable but still weak and isolated outpost of the Spanish empire.

The Empire at High Tide

By the end of the sixteenth century, the Spanish empire had become one of the largest in the history of the world. It included the islands of the Caribbean and the coastal areas of South America that had been the targets of the first Spanish expeditions. It extended to Mexico and southern North America, where a second wave of colonizers had established outposts.

The empire spread southward and westward as well: into the land mass of South America—Chile, Argentina, and Peru—which was the target of a third Spanish military thrust. In 1580, when the Spanish and Portuguese monarchies temporarily united, Brazil came under Spanish jurisdiction as well.

It was, however, a colonial empire very different politically from the one the English would establish in North America beginning in the early seventeenth century. Although the earliest Spanish ventures in the New World had been largely independent of the throne, by the end of the sixteenth century the monarchy had established an elaborate hierarchical system by which its authority extended directly into the governance of local communities. Colonists had few opportunities to establish political institutions independent of the crown. The British administration of North America, by contrast, would be far looser and more casual; and European settlers there would quickly develop a political system in which the monarch often played an indirect, even a nominal, role.

There was also a significant economic difference. The Spanish were far more successful than the British would be in extracting great surface wealth—gold and silver—from their American colonies. But for that very reason, they concentrated relatively less energy on making agriculture and commerce profitable in their colonies. The problem was compounded by the strict and inflexible commercial policies of the Spanish government. To enforce the collection of duties and to provide protection against pirates, the government required all trade with the colonies to go through a single Spanish port and only a few colonial ports, in fleets making but two voyages a year. The system stifled the economic development of the Spanish areas of the New World. The British colonies, in contrast, faced fewer restrictions and ultimately produced a large, flexible, and flourishing commercial economy that would sustain prosperity in North America long after the depletion of the gold and silver supplies had begun to debilitate the economies to the south.

Above all, perhaps, there was a demographic difference between the Spanish empire in America and the colonies to the north. Almost from the beginning, the English, Dutch, and French colonies in North America were centered on farming and permanent settlement and emphasized family life. Hence, the Europeans in North America reproduced rapidly after their first difficult years and in time came to outnumber the natives. The Spanish, by contrast, ruled their empire but did not people it. In the first century of settlement, fewer than 250,000 settlers in the Spanish colonies were from Spain itself or from any other European country. Only about 200,000 more arrived in the first half of the seventeenth century. Many settlers came from various

outposts of Spanish civilization in the Atlantic—the Azores, the Cape Verde Islands, and elsewhere; but even with these additional sources, the number of European settlers in Spanish America remained relatively small. Despite the ravages of disease and war, the vast majority of the population continued to consist of natives. The Spanish, in other words, imposed a small ruling class upon a much larger existing population; they did not create a self-contained European society in the New World as the English would attempt to do in the north. The story of the Spanish empire, therefore, is the story of a collision between and then a commingling of two cultures that had been developing for centuries along completely different lines.

Biological and Cultural Exchanges

Even in the Spanish empire, where the lines separating the races grew less distinct than they were in the English colonies to the north, European and native cultures never entirely merged. Indeed, significant differences remain today between European and Indian cultures throughout South and Central America. Nevertheless, the arrival of whites launched a process of interaction between different peoples that left no one unchanged.

That Europeans were exploring the Americas at all was in large part a result of their early contacts with the natives, from whom they gained their first knowledge of the rich deposits of gold and silver. From that moment on, the history of the Americas became one of increasing levels of exchanges—some beneficial, some catastrophic—among different peoples and cultures. (See "The American Environment," pp. 57–60.)

The first and perhaps most profound result of this exchange was the importation of European diseases to the New World. It would be difficult to exaggerate the consequences of the exposure of Native Americans to such illnesses as influenza, measles, typhus, and above all smallpox—diseases to which Europeans had over time developed at least a partial immunity but to which Native Americans were tragically vulnerable. Millions died. Native groups inhabiting some of the large Caribbean islands and some areas of Mexico were virtually extinct within fifty years of their first contact with whites; on Hispaniola—where the Dominican Republic and Haiti are today and where Columbus landed and established a small, short-lived colony in the 1490s—the native population quickly declined from approximately 1 million to about 500. In the Mayan areas of Mexico, as much as 95 percent of the population perished within a few years of their first contact with the Spanish. Some groups fared better than others; some (although far from all) of the tribes

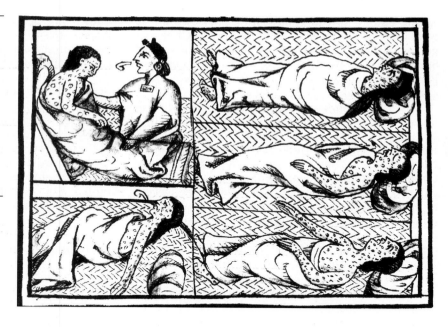

north of Mexico, whose contact with European settlers
came later and was often less intimate, were spared
the worst of the epidemics. But for most areas of the
New World, this was a demographic catastrophe at
least as grave as, and in many places far worse than,
the Black Death that had killed at least one-third of the
population of Europe two centuries before.

The decimation of native populations in the southern regions of the Americas was not, however, purely
a result of this inadvertent exposure to infection. It was
also a result of the conquistadores' quite deliberate policy of subjugation and extermination. Their brutality
was in part a reflection of the ruthlessness with which
Europeans waged war in all parts of the world. It was
also a result of their conviction that the natives were
"savages"—uncivilized peoples whom they considered somehow not fully human. Paradoxically, the brutality was also a consequence of the high level of development of some native societies. Had the natives
truly been as primitive as Europeans wanted to believe, there would have been little need to decimate
them. But organized into substantial empires, they
posed a threat to the conquistadores' ambitions. That,
more than anything else, accounts for the thorough-
ness with which the Spanish set about obliterating native cultures. They razed cities and dismantled temples and monuments. They destroyed records and
documents (one reason why modern scholars have
been able to learn so little about the histories of these
native societies). They systematically killed Indian
warriors, leaders, priests, and organized elites. They

tried, in short, to eliminate the underpinnings of existing civilizations so as to bring the native population
fully under Spanish control and to remove all obstacles to the spread of Christianity. By the 1540s, the combined effects of European diseases and European military brutality had all but destroyed the empires of
Mexico and South America and had largely eliminated
native resistance to the Spanish.

Not all aspects of the exchange were so disastrous
to the natives. The Europeans introduced to America
important new crops (among them sugar and ba-
nanas), domestic livestock (cattle, pigs, and sheep),
and perhaps most significantly the horse, which had
disappeared from the Western Hemisphere in the Ice
Age and now returned aboard Spanish ships in the sixteenth century. These imports were generally intended
for the use of the Europeans themselves. But Indian
tribes soon learned to cultivate the new crops, and European livestock proliferated rapidly and spread
widely among tribes that in the past had possessed virtually no domesticated animals other than dogs. The
horse, in particular, became central to the lives of many
natives and transformed their societies.

The exchange was at least as important (and more
beneficial) to the Europeans. In both North and South
America, the arriving white peoples learned new agricultural techniques from the natives, techniques often
better adapted to the demands of the new land than
those they had brought with them from Europe. They
discovered new crops, above all maize (corn), which
Columbus took back to Europe from his first trip to

America and which soon became an important staple in Europe itself as well as among European settlers in the New World. Such American foods as squash, pumpkins, beans, sweet potatoes, tomatoes, peppers, and potatoes all found their way into European diets and in the process revolutionized European agriculture. Agricultural discoveries ultimately proved more important to the future of Europe than the gold and silver the conquistadores valued so highly.

In South America, Central America, and Mexico, a society emerged in which Europeans and natives lived in intimate, if unequal, contact with one another. As a result, Indians adopted many features of European civilization, although those features seldom survived the transfer to America unchanged. Many natives gradually came to speak Spanish or Portuguese, but in the process they created a range of dialects, fusing European words with their own linguistic traditions. European missionaries—through a combination of persuasion and coercion—spread Catholicism through most areas of the Spanish empire. But native Christians tended to combine the new religion with features of their old ones, creating a hybrid of faiths that was, while essentially Christian, nevertheless distinctively American.

Colonial officials were expected to take their wives with them to America, but among the ordinary settlers—the majority—European men outnumbered European women by at least ten to one. Not surprisingly, therefore, the Spanish immigrants had substantial sexual contact with native women. Intermarriage became frequent, and before long the population of the colonies came to be dominated (numerically, at least) by people of mixed race, or mestizos. Through much of the Spanish empire, as a result, an elaborate racial hierarchy developed, with Spanish at the top, natives at the bottom, and people of mixed races distributed in between. Racial categories, however, were much more fluid than the Spanish wanted to believe and could not long remain fixed. Over time, the wealth and influence of a family often came to define its place in the "racial" hierarchy more decisively than race itself. A successful or powerful person could become "Spanish" regardless of his or her actual racial ancestry.

The frequency of intermarriage suggests a number of important aspects of the emerging society of the Spanish empire. It reveals, of course, that men living alone in a strange land craved female companionship and the satisfactions of family life and that they sought those things in the only places they could—among the native population. It reflects the desperate need for labor among the white settlers, including the domestic labor that native wives could provide; in some cases, therefore, intermarriage was a form of labor recruitment. And it suggests why the lines separating the races in the areas of Spanish settlement did not remain as distinct as they did in the later English colonies, which were peopled largely by families and in which intermarriage was consequently rare.

Intermarriage was not just a result of the needs and desires of white men. It required, too, at least some measure of acquiescence among native women. Some Indian women entered marriages to white men only under coercion. But the extent of intermarriage suggests that not all women resisted. That may have been in part because of the depleted populations of Indian societies, and the particular shortage of native men (many of whom had died in warfare or been enslaved by the Spaniards). There were also long-established customs of intermarriage among some Indian tribes as a way of forming or cementing alliances. Since many Indians considered the white settlers little more foreign than some rival native groups, that custom probably contributed to the frequency of intermarriage as well.

Natives were the principal labor source for the Europeans. Virtually all the commercial, agricultural, and mining enterprises of the Spanish and Portuguese colonists depended on an Indian work force. Different forms of labor recruitment emerged in different areas of the empire. In some places, Indians were sold into slavery. More often, colonists used a coercive wage system closely related, but not identical, to slavery, by which Indians worked in the mines and on the plantations under duress for fixed periods, unable to leave without the consent of their employers. These indentured work forces survived in some areas of the South American mainland for many centuries. So central was the need for native labor that European settlers requesting *encomiendas* from imperial authorities generally asked for title not to vacant tracts of territory but to particular Indian villages, which could become a source of labor and tribute to the usually absentee landlords.

Yet even that was not, in the end, enough to meet the labor needs of the colonists—particularly since the native population had declined (and in some places virtually vanished) because of disease and war. As early as 1502, therefore, European settlers began importing slaves from Africa.

Africa and America

Most of the black men and women who were taken forcibly to America came from a large region in west Africa below the Sahara Desert, known as Guinea. It was the home of a wide variety of peoples and cultures. And since over half of all the new arrivals in the New World between 1500 and 1800 were Africans, those cultures greatly affected the character of American civilization. Europeans and white Americans came to portray African society as primitive and uncivilized (in part to justify the enslavement of Africa's people). But most Africans were, in fact, civilized peoples with well-developed economies and political systems.

Humans began settling in west Africa at least 10,000 years ago. By the fifteenth century, they had developed extensive civilizations and complex political systems. The residents of upper Guinea had substantial commercial contact with the Mediterranean world—trading ivory, gold, and slaves for finished goods—and, largely as a result, became early converts to Islam. After the collapse of the ancient kingdom of Ghana around 1100 A.D., they created the even larger empire of Mali, which survived well into the fifteenth century and whose great city, Timbuktu, became fabled as a trading center and a seat of education.

Southern Africans were more isolated from Europe and the Mediterranean. They were also more politically fragmented. The central social unit in much of the south was the village, which usually consisted of members of an extended family group. Some groups of villages united in small kingdoms—among them Benin, Congo, and Songhay. But no large empires emerged in the south comparable to the Ghana and Mali kingdoms farther north. Nevertheless, these southern societies developed extensive trade—in woven fabrics, ceramics, wooden and iron goods, as well as crops and livestock—both among themselves and, to a lesser degree, with the outside world.

The African civilizations naturally developed economies that reflected the climates and resources of their lands. In upper Guinea, fishing and rice cultivation, supplemented by the extensive trade with Mediterranean lands, were the foundation of the economy. Farther south, Africans grew wheat and other food crops, raised livestock, and fished. There were some more nomadic tribes in the interior, which subsisted largely on hunting and gathering and developed less elaborate social systems. But most Africans were sedentary people, linked together in elaborate networks of political, economic, and familial relationships.

Like many Native American societies, but in contrast to those in Europe, African societies tended to be matrilineal. People traced their heredity through and inherited property from their mothers. When a couple married, the husband left his own family to join the family of his wife. Like virtually all other peoples, Africans divided work by gender, but the nature of that division varied greatly from place to place. Women played a major role, often the dominant role, in trade; in many areas they were the principal farmers (while the men hunted, fished, and raised livestock); and everywhere, they managed child care and food preparation. Most tribes also divided political power by gender, with men choosing leaders and systems for managing what they defined as male affairs and women choosing parallel leaders to handle female matters. Tribal chiefs generally were men (although in some places there was a female counterpart), but the position customarily passed down not to the chief's son but to the son of the chief's eldest sister. African societies, in short, were characterized by a greater degree of sexual equality than those of most other parts of the world.

THE GREAT MOSQUE OF DJENNÉ, MALI Djenné emerged in the Middle Ages as one of the two principal urban centers of Mali. (The other was Timbuktu.) It was a center of scholarship and commerce, "large, flourishing and prosperous," one African writer of the time wrote, "rich, and blessed and favoured by heaven. God has granted this spot all his favours, as a natural and innate thing." After Islam spread into northern and central Africa, Djenné also became a religious center and the site of this striking mosque, which still stands today. *(Eugene Gordon)*

original

In those areas of west Africa where indigenous religions had survived the spread of Islam (which included most of the lands south of the empire of Mali), people worshiped many gods, whom they associated with various aspects of the natural world and whose spirits they believed lived in trees, rocks, forests, and streams. Most Africans also developed forms of ancestor worship and took great care in tracing family lineage; the most revered priests (who were often also important social and political leaders as well) were generally the oldest people.

African societies were elaborately hierarchical. Small elites of priests and nobles stood at the top. Most people belonged to the large middle group of farmers, traders, crafts workers, and others. At the bottom of society were slaves—men and women who were put into bondage after being captured in wars or because of criminal behavior or as a result of unpaid debts. Slavery was not usually permanent; people were often in bondage for a fixed term, and in the meantime retained certain legal protections (including the right to marry). Their children, moreover, did not inherit their parents' condition of bondage. The slavery that Africans would experience at the hands of the Europeans was to be very different; but the existence of slavery among Africans themselves facilitated their enslavement by Europeans.

The African slave trade long preceded European settlement in the New World. As early as the eighth century, west Africans began selling slaves to traders from the Mediterranean. They were responding to a demand from elite families who wanted black men and women as domestic servants as well as to more general labor shortages in some areas of Europe and north Africa. When Portuguese sailors began exploring the coast of Africa in the fifteenth century, they too bought slaves—usually criminals and people captured in war—and took them back to Portugal, where there was a small but steady demand.

In the sixteenth century, however, the market for slaves grew dramatically as a result of the rising European demand for sugar cane. The small areas of sugar cultivation in the Mediterranean were proving inadequate, and production soon moved to the island of Madeira off the African coast, which became a Portuguese colony. Not long after that, it moved to the Caribbean islands and Brazil. Sugar was a labor-intensive crop, and that increased the demand for black workers in these new areas. European slave traders found a ready supply along the coast of west Africa (and some areas of east Africa as well), where kingdoms warred with one another in an effort to capture potential slaves to exchange for European goods. At first the slave traders were overwhelmingly Portuguese and, to a lesser extent, Spanish. By the seventeenth century, the Dutch had won control of most of the market. In the eighteenth century, the English dominated it. By then, slavery had spread well beyond its original locations in the Caribbean and South America and into the English colonies to the north.

THE ARRIVAL OF THE ENGLISH

England's first documented contact with the New World came only five years after Spain's. In 1497, John Cabot (like Columbus a native of Genoa) sailed to the northeastern coast of North America on an expedition sponsored by King Henry VII. Other English navigators, continuing Cabot's unsuccessful search for a northwest passage through the New World to the Orient, explored other areas of North America during the sixteenth century. But while England claimed dominion over the lands its explorers surveyed, nearly a century passed before the English made any serious efforts to establish colonies there. Like other European nations, England had to experience an internal transformation before it could begin settling new lands. That transformation occurred in the sixteenth century.

The Commercial Incentive

Part of the attraction of the New World to the English was its newness, its contrast to their own troubled land. America seemed a place where human settlement could start anew, where a perfect society could be created without the flaws and inequities of the Old World. Such dreams began to emerge in England only a few years after Columbus's voyages. They found classic expression in Sir Thomas More's *Utopia* (published in Latin in 1516, translated into English thirty-five years later), which described a mythical and nearly perfect society on an imaginary island supposedly discovered by a companion of Amerigo Vespucci in the waters of the New World.

More's picture of an ideal community was, among other things, a comment on the social and economic evils of the England of his own time. The people of Tudor England suffered from frequent and costly European wars, from almost constant religious strife, and above all from a harsh economic transformation of the countryside. Because the worldwide demand for wool was growing rapidly, many landowners were finding it profitable to convert their land from fields for crops to pastures for sheep. The result was a significant growth in the wool trade. But that meant land worked at one time by serfs and later by rent-paying tenants was steadily enclosed for sheep runs and taken away from the farmers.

Thousands of evicted tenants roamed the countryside in gangs, begging from (and at times robbing) the more fortunate householders through whose communities they passed. The government passed various laws designed to halt enclosures, relieve the worthy poor, and compel the able-bodied or "sturdy beggars" to work. Such laws had little effect. The enclosure movement continued unabated, and relatively few of the dislocated farmers could find reemployment in raising sheep or manufacturing wool. By removing land from cultivation, the enclosure movement also limited England's ability to feed its population, which grew from 3 million in 1485 to 4 million in 1603. Both because of the dislocation of farmers and the restriction of the food supply, therefore, the nation had a serious problem of surplus population.

Amid this growing distress, a rising class of merchant capitalists was prospering from the expansion of foreign trade. At first, England had exported little except raw wool; but new merchant-capitalists helped create a domestic cloth industry that allowed them to begin marketing finished goods at home and abroad. At first, most exporters did business almost entirely as individuals. In time, however, some merchants joined forces and formed chartered companies. Each such enterprise operated on the basis of a charter acquired from the monarch, which gave the company a monopoly for trading in a particular region. Among the first of these were the Muscovy Company (1555), the Levant Company (1581), the Barbary Company (1585), the Guinea Company (1588), and the East India Company (1600). Investors in these companies often made fantastic profits from the exchange of English manufactures, especially woolens, for exotic goods; and they felt a powerful urge to continue the expansion of their profitable trade.

Central to this drive was the emergence of a new concept of economic life known as mercantilism, which was gaining favor throughout Europe. Mercantilism rested on the assumption that the nation as a whole was the principal actor in the economy, not the individuals within it. The goal of economic activity should be to increase the nation's total wealth. Mercantilists believed that the world's wealth was finite. One person or nation could grow rich only at the expense of another. A nation's economic health depended, therefore, on extracting as much wealth as possible from foreign lands and exporting as little wealth as possible from home.

The principles of mercantilism guided the economic policies of virtually all the European nation-states in the sixteenth and seventeenth centuries. It greatly enhanced the position of the new merchant-capitalists, whose overseas ventures were thought to benefit the entire nation and to be worthy of government assistance. It also increased competition among nations. Every European state was trying to find markets for its exports while trying to limit its imports. One result was the increased attractiveness of acquiring colonies, which could become the source of goods that a country might otherwise have to buy from other nations.

In England, the mercantilistic program thrived at first on the basis of the flourishing wool trade with the European continent, and particularly with the great cloth market in Antwerp. Beginning in the 1550s, however, that glutted market collapsed, and English merchants found themselves obliged to look elsewhere for overseas trade. The establishment of colonies seemed to be a ready answer to that and other problems. Richard Hakluyt, an Oxford clergyman and the outstanding English propagandist for colonization, argued that colonies would not only create new markets for English goods, they would also help alleviate poverty and unemployment by siphoning off the surplus population. For the poor who remained in England "idly to the annoy of the whole state," there would be new work as a result of the prosperity the colonies would create. Perhaps most important, colonial commerce would allow England to acquire products from its own new territories for which the nation had previously been dependent on foreign rivals—products such as lumber, naval stores, and, above all, silver and gold.

The Religious Incentive

In addition to these economic motives for colonization, there were also religious ones, rooted in the events of the European and English Reformations. The Protestant Reformation began in Germany in 1517, when Martin Luther openly challenged some of the basic practices and beliefs of the Roman Catholic church—until then, the supreme religious authority and also one of the strongest political authorities throughout western Europe. Luther, an Augustinian monk and ordained priest, challenged the Catholic belief that salvation could be achieved through good works or through loyalty (or payments) to the church itself. He denied the church's claim that God communicated to the world through the pope and the clergy. The Bible, not the church, was the authentic voice of God, Luther claimed, and salvation was to be found not through "works" or through the formal practice of religion, but through faith alone. Luther's challenge quickly won him a wide following among ordinary men and women in northern Europe. He himself insisted that he was not revolting against the church, that his purpose was to reform it from within. But when the pope excommunicated him in 1520, Luther defied him and began to lead his followers out of the Catholic Church entirely. A schism within European Christianity had begun that was never to be healed.

As the spirit of the Reformation spread rapidly throughout Europe, creating intellectual ferment and (in some places) war, other dissidents began offering other alternatives to orthodox Catholicism. The Swiss theologian John Calvin was, after Luther, the most influential reformer and went even further than Luther had in rejecting the Catholic belief that human institutions could affect an individual's prospects for salvation. Calvin introduced the doctrine of predestination. God "elected" some people to be saved and condemned others to damnation; each person's destiny was determined before birth, and no one could change that predetermined fate. But while individuals could not alter their destinies, they could strive to know them. Calvinists believed that the way people led their lives might reveal to them their chances of salvation. A wicked or useless existence would be a sign of damnation; saintliness, diligence, and success could be signs of grace. Calvinism created anxieties among its followers, to be sure; but it also produced a strong incentive to lead virtuous, productive lives. The new creed spread rapidly throughout northern Europe and produced (among other groups) the Huguenots in France and the Puritans in England.

The English Reformation began, however, less as a result of these doctrinal revolts than because of a political dispute between the king and the pope. In 1529 King Henry VIII, angered by the refusal of the pope to grant him a divorce from his Spanish wife (who had failed to bear him the son he desperately wanted), broke England's ties with the Catholic Church and established himself as the head of the Christian faith in his country. He made relatively few other changes in English Christianity, however, and after his death the survival of Protestantism remained in doubt for a time. When Henry's Catholic daughter Mary ascended the throne, she quickly restored England's allegiance to Rome and harshly persecuted those who refused to return to the Catholic fold. Many Protestants were executed (the origin of the queen's enduring nickname, "Bloody Mary"); others fled to the European continent, where they came into contact with the most radical ideas of the Reformation. Mary died in 1558, and her half-sister, Elizabeth, became England's sovereign. Elizabeth once again severed the nation's connection with the Catholic Church (and, along with it, an alliance with Spain that Mary had forged).

The Church of England, as the official religion was now known, satisfied the political objectives of the

JOHN CALVIN
Next to Martin Luther, John Calvin was the most important figure of the European reformation. His belief in predestination was central to the Puritan faith of early New England. *(Bettmann)*

queen, but it failed to satisfy the religious desires of many English Christians. Large groups of Catholics continued to claim allegiance to the pope. Others, affected by the teachings of the European Reformation, believed the new church had abandoned Rome without abandoning Rome's offensive beliefs and practices. Under Elizabeth, the church began to incorporate some of the tenets of Calvinism, but never enough to satisfy its critics—particularly the many exiles who had fled the country under Mary and who now returned, bringing their new, more radical religious ideas with them. They continued to clamor for reforms that would "purify" the church; as a result, they became known as "Puritans."

A few Puritans took what were, by the standards of the time, genuinely radical positions. They were known as Separatists, and they were determined to worship as they pleased in their own independent congregations, a determination that flew in the face of English law—which outlawed unauthorized religious

Elizabeth - Anglican
James I - Catholics

meetings, required all subjects to attend regular Anglican services, and levied taxes to support the established church. Their radicalism was visible in other ways as well, including their rejection of prevailing assumptions about the proper religious roles of women. Many Separatist sects, perhaps most prominently the Quakers, permitted women to serve as preachers and to assume a prominence in other religious matters that would have been impossible in the established church.

Most Puritans resisted separatism. Still, their demands were by no means modest. They wanted to simplify Anglican forms of worship. They wanted to reduce the power of the bishops, who were appointed by the crown and who were, in many cases, openly corrupt and highly extravagant. Perhaps above all they wanted to reform the local clergy, a group composed in large part of greedy, uneducated men with little interest in (or knowledge of) theology. The more moderate Puritans wished, in short, to see the church give more attention to its spiritual role and less to its temporal ambitions. No less than the Separatists, they grew increasingly frustrated by the refusal of either the political or ecclesiastical hierarchies to respond to their demands.

Puritan discontent, already festering, grew rapidly after the death of Elizabeth, the last of the Tudors, and the accession of James I, a Scotsman and the first of the Stuarts, in 1603. James believed kings ruled by divine right, and he felt no obligation to compromise with his opponents. He quickly antagonized the Puritans, a group that included most of the rising businessmen, by resorting to arbitrary taxation, by favoring English Catholics in the granting of charters and other favors, and by supporting "high church" forms of ceremony. By the early seventeenth century, some religious nonconformists were beginning to look for places of refuge outside the kingdom. Along with the other economic and social incentives for colonization, such religious discontent helped turn England's gaze to distant lands.

ELIZABETH I

The flemish artist Marcus Gheeraerts the younger moved to England in 1568 (along with his father, also a painter) as a Protestant refugee from his homeland. In approximately 1593 he painted this portrait of the English queen, portraying her as she was seen by many of her contemporaries: a strong, confident ruler presiding over an ambitious, expansionist nation. She stands here on a map of England. *(National Portrait Gallery, London)*

The English in Ireland

England's first experience with colonization came not in the New World, but in a land separated from Britain only by a narrow stretch of sea: Ireland. The English had long laid claim to the island and had for many years maintained small settlements in the area around Dublin. But it was only in the second half of the sixteenth century that serious efforts at large-scale colonization began. Through the 1560s and 1570s, would-be colonists moved through Ireland, capturing territory and attempting to subdue the native population. In the process they developed many of the assumptions that would guide later English colonists in America.

The most important of these assumptions was that the native population of Ireland—approximately 1 million people, loyal to the Catholic Church, with their own language (Gaelic) and their own culture—was a collection of wild, vicious, and ignorant "savages." The Irish lived in ways that the English believed crude and wasteful ("like beasts"), and they fought back against the intruders with a ferocity that the English considered barbaric. Such people could not be tamed, the English concluded. They certainly could not be assimilated into English society. They must, therefore, be suppressed, isolated, and if necessary destroyed. Eventually, they might be "tamed" and "civilized," but only after they were thoroughly subordinated.

Whatever barbarities the Irish may have inflicted on the colonizers the English more than matched in return. Sir Humphrey Gilbert, who was later to establish the first British colony in the New World (an unsuccessful venture in Newfoundland), served for a time as governor of one Irish district and suppressed rebellions by the natives with extraordinary viciousness. Gilbert was an educated and supposedly civilized man; yet because he considered the natives somehow less than human, and therefore not entitled to whatever decencies civilized people reserved for their treatment of one another, he managed to justify, both to himself and to others, such atrocities as beheading Irish soldiers after they were killed in battle. Gilbert himself, Sir Walter Raleigh, Sir Richard Grenville, and others active in Ireland in the mid-sixteenth century derived from their experiences there an outlook they would take to America, where they made similarly vicious efforts to subdue and subjugate the natives.

The Irish experience led the English to another important (and related) assumption about colonization: that English settlements in distant lands must retain a rigid separation from the native populations. In Ireland, English colonizers established what they called "plantations," transplantations of English society to a foreign land. Unlike the Spanish in America, the English in Ireland did not try simply to rule a subdued native population; they tried to build a complete society of their own, peopled with emigrants from England itself. The new society would exist within a "pale of settlement," an area physically separated from the natives. That concept, too, they would take with them to the New World, even though in Ireland, as later in America, the separation of peoples and the preservation of "pure" English culture proved impossible.

The French and the Dutch in America

English settlers in North America, unlike those in Ireland, were to encounter not only natives but also other Europeans who were, like them, driven by mercantilist ideas to establish economic outposts abroad. To the south and southwest was the Spanish empire. Spanish ships continued to threaten English settlements along the coast for years. But except for Mexico and scattered outposts such as those in Florida and New Mexico, the Spanish made little serious effort to colonize North America.

More formidable North American rivals in the early sixteenth century were the French. France founded its first permanent settlement in America at Quebec in 1608, less than a year after the English started their first colony at Jamestown, but the French colony's population grew very slowly. Few French Catholics felt any inclination to leave their homeland, and French Protestants who might have wished to emigrate were excluded from the colony. The French, however, exercised an influence in the New World disproportionate to their numbers, largely because of their relationships with Native Americans.

Unlike the English, who for many years hugged the coastline and traded with the Indians of the interior through intermediaries, the French forged close, direct ties with natives deep inside the continent. French Jesuit missionaries were among the first to penetrate Indian societies, and they established some of the first contacts between the two peoples. More important still were the *coureurs de bois*—adventurous fur traders and trappers—who also penetrated far into the wilderness and developed an extensive trade that became one of the underpinnings of the French colonial economy.

The fur trade was, in fact, more an Indian than a French enterprise. The *coureurs de bois* were, in many ways, little more than agents for the Algonquins and the Hurons, who were the principal fur traders among the Indians of the region and from whom the French purchased their pelts. The French traders were able to function only to the degree that they could form partnerships with the Indians. That they succeeded was often a result of their ability to become virtually a part of native society, living among the Indians and at times marrying Indian women. The fur trade helped open the way for the other elements of the French presence in North America—the agricultural estates (or *seignuries*) along the St. Lawrence River, the development of trade and military centers at Quebec and Montreal, and the creation of an alliance with the Algonquins and others—that enabled the French to compete with the more numerous British in the contest for control of North America. That alliance also brought the French into conflict with the Iroquois, the Algonquins' ancient enemies, who assumed the central role in the English fur trade. An early result of these tensions was a 1609 attack led by Samuel de Champlain, the founder of Quebec, on a band of Mohawks, apparently at the instigation of his Algonquin trading partners.

The Dutch, too, were establishing a presence in North America. Holland had won its independence from Spain in the early seventeenth century and was one of the leading trading nations of the world. Its merchant fleet was larger than England's, and its traders were active not only in Europe but also in Africa, Asia, and—increasingly—America. In 1609 an English explorer in the employ of the Dutch, Henry Hudson,

A CATHOLIC CONVENT IN QUEBEC
Catholic missionaries were an important part of the French civilization in North America. The Ursuline Convent in Quebec, built in 1642, was one of the central institutions of the city. Its nuns worked as teachers and nurses, ministering both to French settlers and to Indian converts to Christianity. *(National Gallery of Canada)*

sailed up the river that was to be named for him in what is now New York State. Because the river was so wide, he believed for a time that he had found the long-sought water route through the continent to the Pacific. He was wrong, of course, but his explorations led to a Dutch claim on territory in America and to the establishment of a permanent Dutch presence in the New World.

For more than a decade after Hudson's voyage, the Dutch maintained an active trade in furs in and around New York. In 1624, the Dutch West India Company established a series of permanent trading posts on the Hudson, Delaware, and Connecticut Rivers. The company actively encouraged settlement of the region—not just from Holland itself, but from such other parts of northern Europe as Germany, Sweden, and Finland. It transported whole families to the New World and granted vast feudal estates to patroons on condition that they bring still more immigrants to America. The result was the colony of New Netherland and its principal town, New Amsterdam, on Manhattan Island. Its population, diverse as it was, remained relatively small; the colony was only loosely united, with chronically weak leadership.

The First English Settlements

The first permanent English settlement in the New World was established at Jamestown, in Virginia, in 1607. But for nearly thirty years before that, English merchants and adventurers had been engaged in a series of failed efforts to create colonies in America.

Through much of the sixteenth century, the English had mixed feelings about the New World. They knew of its existence and were intrigued by its possibilities. And under the strong leadership of Elizabeth I, they were developing a powerful sense of nationalism that encouraged dreams of expansion. At the same time, however, England was leery of Spain, which remained the dominant force in America and, it seemed, the dominant naval power in Europe.

ROANOKE
A drawing by one of the English colonists in the ill-fated Roanoke expedition of 1585 became the basis for this engraving by Theodore DeBry, published in England in 1590. A small European ship carrying settlers approaches the island of Roanoke, at left. The wreckage of several larger vessels farther out to sea and the presence of Indian settlements on the mainland and on Roanoke itself suggest some of the perils the settlers encountered.   *(New York Public Library)*

But much changed in the 1570s and 1580s. English "sea dogs" such as Sir Francis Drake staged successful raids on Spanish merchant ships and built confidence in England's ability to challenge Spanish sea power. More important was the attempted invasion of England by the Spanish Armada in 1588. Philip II, the powerful Spanish king, had recently united his nation with Portugal. He was now determined to end England's challenges to Spanish commercial supremacy and to bring the English back into the Catholic Church. He assembled one of the largest military fleets in the history of warfare—known to history as the "Spanish Armada"—to carry his troops across the English Channel and into England itself. Philip's bold venture turned into a fiasco when the smaller English fleet dispersed the Armada and, in a single stroke, ended

Spain's domination of the Atlantic. The English now felt much freer to establish themselves in the New World.

The pioneers of English colonization were Sir Humphrey Gilbert and his half-brother Sir Walter Raleigh—both friends of Queen Elizabeth, and both veterans of the earlier colonial efforts in Ireland. In 1578 Gilbert obtained from Elizabeth a patent granting him the exclusive right for six years "to inhabit and possess at his choice all remote and heathen lands not in the actual possession of any Christian prince."

After numerous setbacks, Gilbert led an expedition to Newfoundland in 1583 and took possession of it in the queen's name. He proceeded southward along the coast, looking for a good place to build a military outpost that might eventually grow into a profitable

SIGNIFICANT EVENTS

14,000–12,000 B.C.   Asians begin migrating to North America across the Bering Strait

1000 A.D.   Scandinavian explorers establish temporary settlement in Newfoundland

1347   Black Death begins in Europe

1420s   Portuguese explorers travel down west coast of Africa in search of sea route to Asia

1492   Columbus sails west from Spain in search of Asia, reaches Bahama Islands in the Caribbean

1494   Treaty of Tordesillas divides New World between Spain and Portugal

1497   John Cabot establishes first English claim in North America

1502   First African slaves arrive in Spanish America

1517   Martin Luther challenges Catholic Church, sparking Protestant Reformation in Europe

1518–1530   Smallpox epidemic ravages Indian societies of Central and South America

1519–1522   Magellan expedition circumnavigates globe

1521   Cortés captures Tenochtitlán and conquers Aztec Empire in Mexico

1533   Pizarro captures Cuzco and conquers Incas in Peru

1558   Elizabeth I ascends English throne

1565   St. Augustine founded in Florida

1566   English conquest of Ireland begins

1587   "Lost Colony" established on Roanoke Island

1598   Don Juan de Oñate establishes Spanish colony in present-day New Mexico

1603   James I succeeds Elizabeth I in England

1606   James I establishes Virginia Company, divided between groups at London and Plymouth

1608   French establish Quebec, their first permanent settlement in America

1609   Spanish colonists found Santa Fe

1624   Dutch establish permanent settlements in what is now New York

1680   Pueblos revolt and drive Spanish colonists from present-day New Mexico

1692   Spanish return to New Mexico

1696   Spanish crush last Pueblo revolt in New Mexico

colony. But a storm sank his ship, and he was lost at sea.

Roanoke

Raleigh was undeterred. The next year, he secured from Elizabeth a six-year grant similar to Gilbert's and sent a small group of men on an expedition to explore the North American coast. They returned with two captive Indians and glowing reports of what they had seen. They were particularly enthusiastic about an island the natives called Roanoke and about the area of the mainland just beyond it (in what is now North Carolina). Raleigh asked the queen for permission to name the entire region "Virginia" in honor of Elizabeth, "the Virgin Queen." But while Elizabeth granted the permission, she did not offer the financial assistance Raleigh had hoped his flattery would produce. So he turned to private investors to finance another expedition.

In 1585 Raleigh recruited his cousin, Sir Richard Grenville, to lead a group of men (most of them from the English plantations in Ireland) to Roanoke to establish a colony. Grenville deposited the settlers on the island, remained long enough to antagonize the natives by razing an Indian village as retaliation for a minor theft, and returned to England. The following spring, Sir Francis Drake unexpectedly arrived in Roanoke. With supplies and reinforcements from England long overdue, the beleaguered colonists boarded Drake's ships and left.

Raleigh tried again in 1587, sending an expedition carrying ninety-one men, seventeen women (two of them pregnant), and nine children—the nucleus, he hoped, of a viable "plantation." The settlers landed on Roanoke and attempted to take up where the first group of colonists had left off. (Shortly after arriving, one of the women—the daughter of the commander of the expedition, John White—gave birth to a daughter, Virginia Dare, the first American-born child of English parents.) White returned to England after several weeks (leaving his daughter and granddaughter behind) in search of supplies and additional settlers; he hoped to return in a few months. But the hostilities with Spain intervened, and White did not return to the island for three years. When he did, in 1590, he found the island utterly deserted, with no clue to the settlers' fate other than the cryptic inscription "Croatoan" carved on a post. Some have argued that the colonists were slaughtered by the Indians in retaliation for Grenville's (and perhaps their own) hostilities. Others have contended that they left their settlement and joined native society, ultimately becoming entirely assimilated. But no conclusive solution to the mystery of the "Lost Colony" has ever been found.

The Roanoke disaster marked the end of Sir Walter Raleigh's involvement in English colonization of the New World. In 1603, when James I succeeded Elizabeth to the throne, Raleigh was accused of plotting against the king, stripped of his monopoly, and imprisoned for more than a decade. Finally (after being released for one last ill-fated maritime expedition) he was executed by the king in 1618. No later colonizer would receive grants of land in the New World as vast or undefined as those Raleigh and Gilbert had acquired. But despite the discouraging example of these early experiences, the colonizing impulse remained alive.

In the first years of the seventeenth century, a group of London merchants to whom Raleigh had assigned his charter rights decided to renew the attempt at colonization in Virginia. A rival group of merchants, from Plymouth and other West Country towns, were also interested in American ventures and were sponsoring voyages of exploration farther north, up to Newfoundland, where West Country fishermen had been going for many years. In 1606 James I issued a new charter, which divided America between the two groups. The London group got the exclusive right to colonize in the south, and the Plymouth merchants received the same right in the north. Through their efforts, the first enduring English colonies were planted in America.

SUGGESTED READINGS

Pre-Columbian America and Indian Societies.   James Axtell, *The European and the Indian: Essays in the Ethnohistory of Colonial North America* (1981); *The Invasion Within: The Contest of Cultures in Colonial North America* (1985); *After Columbus: Essays in the Ethnohistory of Colonial North America* (1988). John Bierhorst, *The Mythology of North America* (1985). Henry Warner Bowden, *American Indians and Christian Missions* (1982). Alfred W. Crosby, Jr., *The Columbian Exchange: Biological and Cultural Consequences of 1492* (1972); *Ecological Imperialism: The Biological Expansion of Europe, 900–1900* (1986). Harold E. Driver, *Indians of North America*, 2nd ed. (1969). Stuart Fiedel, *The Prehistory of the Americas* (1987). Francisco Guerra, *The PreColumbian Mind* (1971). Ake Hultkrantz, *The Religions of the American Indians* (1979). Francis Jennings, *The Invasion of America: Indians, Colonialism, and the Cant of Conquest* (1975). J. D. Jennings, ed., *Ancient North America* (1983). Alvin M. Josephy, Jr., *America in 1492* (1992); *The Indian Heritage of America* (1968). Kenneth MacGowan and J. A. Hester, Jr., *Early Man in the New World* (1950). James H. Merrell, *The Indians' New World* (1989). Christopher L. Miller, *Prophetic Worlds: Indians and Whites on the Columbia Plateau* (1985). Gary B. Nash, *Red, White, and Black*, rev. ed. (1982). Neal Salisbury, *Manitou and Providence: Indians, Europeans, and the Making of New England* (1982). Carl Sauer, *Sixteenth-Century North America* (1985). R. F. Spencer, J. D. Jennings, et al., *The Native Americans* (1978). William C. Sturtevant, et. al., eds., *Handbook of North American Indians* (1986). Bruce G. Trigger, *Natives and Newcomers* (1985). Bruce G. Trigger and Wilcomb Washburn, eds., *Cambridge History of the Native Peoples of the New World*, vol. 3: *North America* (1993). Nathan Wachtel, *The Vision of the Vanquished* (1977). Wilcomb E. Washburn, *The Indian in America* (1975).

European Explorations and Spanish America.   J. H. Elliott, *The Old World and the New, 1492–1650* (1970). Charles Gibson, *Spain in America* (1966). Thomas D. Hall, *Social Change in the Southwest, 1350–1880* (1989). James Lang, *Conquest and Commerce: Spain and England in the Americas* (1975). James Lockhart, *Spanish Peru, 1532–1560: A Colonial Society* (1968). Samuel Eliot Morison, *Admiral of the Ocean Sea*, 2 vols. (1942); *The European Discovery of America: The Northern Voyages* (1971); *The European Discovery of America: The Southern Voyages* (1974).

J. H. Parry, *The Age of Reconnaissance* (1963). William H. Prescott, *History of the Conquest of Mexico*, 3 vols. (1843). David B. Quinn, *North America from Earliest Discovery to First Settlements* (1977). Kirkpatrick Sale, *The Conquest of Paradise: Christopher Columbus and the Columbian Legacy* (1990). Donald J. Weber, *The Spanish Empire in North America* (1992). Eric Wolf, *Europe and the People Without History* (1982).

Africa and America. J. F. A. Ajayi and Michael Crowder, eds., *History of West Africa*, vol. 1 (1972). Philip Curtin, *The Atlantic Slave Trade* (1969). J. S. Fage, *A History of Africa* (1978). Patrick Manning, *Slavery and African Life: Occidental, Oriental, and African Slave Trades* (1990). Walter Rodney, *A History of the Upper Guinea Coast* (1970).

England Looks West. Carl Bridenbaugh, *Vexed and Troubled Englishmen*, 1590–1642 (1968). Nicholas Canny, *The Elizabethan Conquest of Ireland* (1976); and *Kingdom and Colony: Ireland in the Atlantic World* (1988). Patrick Collinson, *The Elizabethan Puritan Movement* (1967). C. H. George and Katherine George, *The Protestant Mind of the English Reformation* (1961). Christopher Hill, *The Century of Revolution*, 1603–1714 (1961). Peter Laslett, *The World We Have Lost* (1965). W. H. McNeill, *The Rise of the West* (1963). D. W. Meinig, *The Shaping of America*, vol I: *Atlantic America*, 1492–1800 (1986). Wallace Notestein, *The English People on the Eve of Colonization*, 1603–1630 (1954). J. H. Parry, *Europe and the New World*, 1415–1715 (1949); *The Age of Reconnaissance* (1963). David B. Quinn, *The Elizabethans and the Irish* (1966); and *North America from Earliest Discoveries to First Settlements* (1977). Margaret Spufford, *Contrasting Communities* (1974). Lawrence Stone, *The Crisis of the Aristocracy* (1965). Keith Thomas, *Religion and the Decline of Magic* (1971). David Underdown, *Pride's Purge* (1985). Michael Walzer, *The Revolution of the Saints* (1965).

First English Colonies. Karen Ordahl Kupperman, *Roanoke: The Abandoned Colony* (1984). David B. Quinn, *The Roanoke Voyages, 1584–1590*, 2 vols. (1955); *Raleigh and the British Empire* (1947); *Set Fair for Roanoke* (1985). Keith Wrightson, *English Society, 1580–1680* (1982).

THE MARYLAND PROPRIETOR, C. 1670
In a detail of a portrait by the court painter to King Charles II, the young Cecilius Calvert reaches for a map of Maryland. His grandfather and namesake, the second Lord Baltimore (1606–1675), holds it out to him. George Calvert, the father of the elder Cecilius, began negotiations to win a royal charter for Maryland; his son completed them in 1632 and became the first proprietor of the colony. He published the map shown here in 1635 as part of an effort to attract settlers to the colony. By the time this portrait was painted, Lord Baltimore's son, Charles, was governor of Maryland. The boy Cecilius, the heir apparent, died in 1681 before he could assume his title. *(Enoch Pratt Free Library)*

CHAPTER TWO

THE ENGLISH
"TRANSPLANTATIONS"

HE ROANOKE FIASCO DAMPENED the colonizing enthusiasm in England—for a time. But
the lures of the New World—the presumably vast riches, the abundant land, the opportunities for religious freedom, the chance to begin
anew—were too strong to be suppressed for very long.
Propagandizers such as Richard Hakluyt kept the
image of America alive in English society, and by the
early seventeenth century, the effort to establish permanent colonies in the New World resumed.

The first few of these new efforts were much like
the earlier, failed ones. They were largely private ventures, with little planning or direction from the English government. They were small, fragile, and generally unprepared for the hardships they were to face.
And although, unlike the Roanoke experiment, they
survived, they at first met with similar disasters.

Three things in particular characterized the first
English settlements. First, the colonies were business
enterprises, financed by private companies and, in
most cases, expected to produce a profit for them. Second, as in Ireland, there were few efforts to blend English society with the society of the natives. The Europeans attempted, as far as they could, to isolate
themselves from the Indians and create enclosed societies that would be entirely their own—"transplantations" of the English world they had left behind. And
third, nothing worked out as they had planned.

Most colonies made few if any profits for their corporate sponsors until years, even decades, after their
founding; and when they did, the profits usually came
from sources no one had anticipated. European settlers
generally found it impossible to isolate themselves entirely from the native population; their lives were
shaped in crucial ways by their relationships with Indians, and the tribes were transformed in turn by their
relationships with the white immigrants. And however
much the settlers tried to re-create English society in
the New World, American society very quickly began
to develop its own habits and institutions.

THE EARLY CHESAPEAKE

Once James I issued his 1606 charters to the London
and Plymouth Companies, the principal obstacle to
founding new American colonies was, as usual,
money. The Plymouth group made an early, unsuccessful attempt to establish a colony at Sagadoahoc, on
the coast of Maine; but in the aftermath of that failure,
it largely abandoned its colonizing efforts. The London
Company, by contrast, moved quickly and decisively.
Only a few months after receiving its charter, it
launched a colonizing expedition headed for Virginia—a party of 144 men aboard three ships: the *God-
speed*, the *Discovery*, and the *Susan Constant*.

29

JAMESTOWN
This aerial view of seventeenth-century Jamestown, a semi-imaginative but generally realistic creation of a later artist, shows the colony as it appeared after having survived its first disastrous decades: a modest but reasonably stable town located on a narrow neck of land between two rivers. *(Colonial National Historical Park)*

The Founding of Jamestown

Only 104 men survived the journey. They reached the American coast in the spring of 1607, sailed into the Chesapeake Bay and up a river they named the James, and established their colony on a peninsula extending from the river's northern bank. They named it Jamestown.

They had chosen their site poorly. In an effort to avoid the mistakes of Roanoke (whose residents were assumed to have been killed by Indians) and select an easily defended location, they chose an inland setting that they believed would offer them security. But the site was low and swampy, hot and humid in the summer, and prey to outbreaks of malaria. It was surrounded by thick woods, which were difficult to clear for cultivation. And it encroached on the territories of powerful local Indians, a confederation led by the imperial chief Powhatan.

The result could hardly have been more disastrous. For seventeen years, one wave of English settlers after another attempted to make Jamestown a habitable and profitable colony. Every effort failed. The town became instead a place of misery and death; and the London Company, which had sponsored it in the hope of vast profits, saw itself drained of funds and saddled with endless losses. All that could be said of Jamestown at the end of this first period of its existence was that it had survived.

The initial colonists, too many of whom were adventurous gentlemen and too few of whom were willing laborers, ran into serious difficulties from the moment they landed. Much like the Indians to the south, who had succumbed quickly to European diseases when first exposed to them, these English settlers had had no prior exposure, and thus no immunity, to the infections of the new land. Malaria, in particular, debilitated the colony, killing some and weakening others so they could do virtually no work. Because the promoters in London demanded a quick return on their investment, the colonists spent much of their limited and dwindling energy on futile searches for gold and only slightly more successful efforts to pile up lumber, tar, pitch, and iron for export. Growing food was a second priority.

The London Company promoters had little interest in creating a family-centered community, and at first they sent no women to Jamestown. The absence of English women made it difficult for the settlers to establish any semblance of a "society." The colonists were seldom able (and also seldom willing) to intermarry with native women, and hence Jamestown was at first an entirely male settlement. Without women, settlers could not establish real households, could not order their domestic lives, and had difficulty feeling any sense of a permanent stake in the community.

Greed and rootlessness contributed to the failure to grow sufficient food; inadequate diets contributed to the colonists' vulnerability to disease; the ravages of disease made it difficult for the settlers to recover from their early mistakes. The result was a community without the means to sustain itself. By January 1608, when ships appeared with additional men and supplies, all but 38 of the first 104 colonists were dead. Jamestown, now facing extinction, survived the crisis largely as a result of the efforts of twenty-seven-year-old Captain John Smith, a famous world traveler, hero of his own implausible travel narratives, but a capable organizer. Leadership in the colony had been divided among the several members of a council who quarreled continually until the fall of 1608, when Smith, as council president, asserted his will. He imposed work and order on the community. He also organized raids on neighboring Indian villages to steal food and kidnap natives. During the colony's second winter, fewer than a dozen (in a population of about 200) died. By the summer of 1609, when Smith was deposed from the council and returned to England for the treatment of a serious powder burn, the colony was showing promise of survival.

Reorganization

The London Company (now calling itself the Virginia Company) was, in the meantime, dreaming of bigger things. In 1609 it obtained a new charter from the king, which increased its power over the colony and enlarged its area. It raised additional capital by selling stock to "adventurers," who would remain in England but share in future profits. It attracted new settlers by offering additional stock to "planters" who were willing to migrate at their own expense. And it provided free passage to Virginia for poorer people who would

agree to serve the company for seven years. The company itself would hold title to all land in Jamestown and would control all trade with the colony. In the spring of 1609, confident that it was now poised to transform Jamestown into a vibrant, successful venture, the company launched a "great fleet" of nine vessels with about 600 people (including some women and children) aboard—headed for Virginia.

More disaster followed. One of the Virginia-bound ships was lost at sea in a hurricane. Another ran aground on one of the Bermuda islands and was unable to free itself for months. Many of those who reached Jamestown, still weak from their long and stormy voyage, succumbed to fevers before winter came. The winter of 1609–1610 became known as the "starving time," a period worse than anything before. The local Indians, antagonized by John Smith's raids and other hostile actions by the early English settlers, killed off the livestock in the woods and kept the colonists barricaded within their palisade. The Europeans lived on what they could find: "dogs, cats, rats, snakes, toadstools, horsehides," and even the "corpses of dead men," as one survivor recalled. When the migrants who had run aground and been stranded on Bermuda finally arrived in Jamestown the following May, they found only about 60 people (out of 500 residents the previous summer) still alive—and those so weakened by the ordeal that they seemed scarcely human. There seemed no point in staying on. The new arrivals took the survivors onto their ship, abandoned the settlement, and sailed downriver for home.

That might have been the end of Jamestown had it not been for a strange twist of fate. As the refugees proceeded down the James toward Chesapeake Bay, they met an English ship coming up the river—part of a fleet bringing supplies and the colony's first governor, Lord De La Warr. The departing settlers agreed to return to Jamestown. New relief expeditions with hundreds of colonists soon began to arrive, and the effort to turn a profit in Jamestown resumed.

De La Warr and his successors (Sir Thomas Dale and Sir Thomas Gates) imposed a harsh and rigid discipline on the colony. They organized settlers into work gangs; they sentenced offenders to be flogged, hanged, or broken on the wheel. But this communal system of labor did not function effectively for long. Settlers often evaded work, "presuming that howsoever the harvest prospered, the general store must maintain them." Governor Dale soon concluded that the colony would fare better if the colonists had personal incentives to work. He began to permit the private ownership and cultivation of land. Landowners would repay the company with part-time work and contributions of grain to its storehouses.

Under the leadership of these first governors, Virginia was not always a happy place. But it survived and even expanded. New settlements began lining the river above and below Jamestown. That was partly because of the order and discipline the governors at times managed to impose and because of increased military assaults on the local Indian tribes to protect the new settlements. But it was also because the colonists had at last discovered a marketable crop: tobacco.

Europeans had become aware of tobacco soon after Columbus's first return from the West Indies, where he had seen the Cuban natives smoking small cigars *(tabacos),* which they inserted in the nostril. By the early seventeenth century, tobacco from the Spanish colonies was already in wide use in Europe. Some critics denounced it as a poisonous weed, the cause of many diseases. King James I himself led the attack with *A Counterblaste to Tobacco* (1604), in which he urged his people not to imitate "the barbarous and beastly manners of the wild, godless, and slavish Indians, especially in so vile and stinking a custom." Other critics were concerned because England's tobacco purchases meant a drain of English gold to the Spanish importers. Still, the demand for tobacco soared.

Then in 1612, the Jamestown planter John Rolfe began to experiment in Virginia with a harsh strain of tobacco that local Indians had been growing for years and produced crops of high quality. He found ready buyers in England. Tobacco cultivation quickly spread up and down the James. The character of this tobacco economy—its profitability, its uncertainty, its land and labor demands—transformed Chesapeake society in fundamental ways.

Of most immediate importance, perhaps, was the pressure tobacco cultivation created for territorial expansion. Tobacco growers needed large areas of farmland to grow their crops; and because tobacco exhausted the soil after only a few years, the demand for land increased even more. English farmers began establishing plantations deeper and deeper in the interior, isolating themselves from the center of European settlement at Jamestown and encroaching on territory the natives considered their own.

Expansion

Even the discovery of tobacco cultivation was not enough to help the Virginia Company. By 1616, there were still no profits, only land and debts. Nevertheless, the promoters continued to hope that the tobacco trade would allow them finally to turn the corner. In 1618, they launched a last great campaign to attract settlers and make the colony profitable.

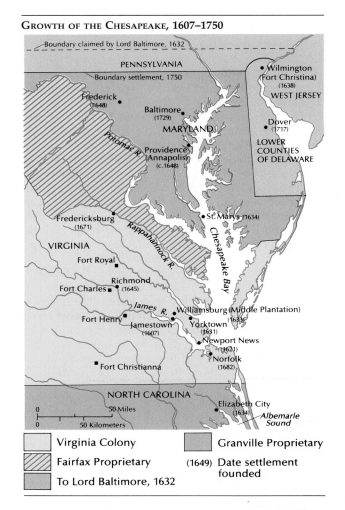

GROWTH OF THE CHESAPEAKE, 1607–1750

The tobacco economy created a heavy demand not only for land but for labor. To entice new laborers to the colony, the company established what they called the "headright" system. Headrights were fifty-acre grants of land, which settlers could acquire in a variety of ways. Those who already lived in the colony received 100 acres apiece. Each new settler received a single headright for himself or herself. This system encouraged family groups to migrate together, since the more family members traveled to America, the larger the landholding the family would receive. In addition, anyone (new settler or old) who paid for the passage of other immigrants to Virginia would receive an additional headright for each new arrival—thus, it was hoped, inducing the prosperous to import new laborers to America. Some colonists were able to assemble sizable plantations with the combined headrights they received for their families and their servants. In return,

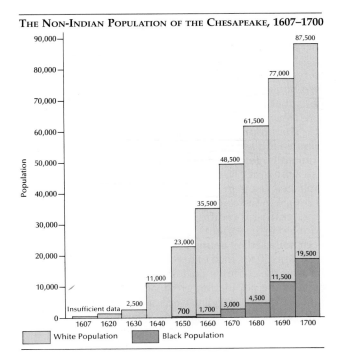

THE NON-INDIAN POPULATION OF THE CHESAPEAKE, 1607–1700

with whom the planters were already familiar. For a time, moreover, the use of black labor remained limited. Although Africans continued to trickle steadily into the colony, planters continued to prefer European indentured servants until at least the 1670s, when such servants began to become scarce and expensive. But whether or not anyone realized it at the time, the small group of black people who arrived in 1619 marked a first step toward the enslavement of Africans within what was to be the American republic.

The expansion of the colony was able to proceed only because of effective suppression of the local Indians, who resisted the expanding English presence. For two years, Sir Thomas Dale led unrelenting assaults against the Powhatan Indians and in the process kidnapped the great chief Powhatan's daughter Pocahontas. When Powhatan refused to ransom her, she converted to Christianity and in 1614 married John Rolfe. (Pocahontas accompanied her husband back to England, where, as a Christian convert and a gracious woman, she stirred interest in projects to "civilize" the Indians. She died while abroad.) At that point, Powhatan ceased his attacks on the English in the face of overwhelming odds. But after his death several years later, his brother, Opechancanough, became head of the native confederacy and resumed the effort to defend tribal lands from European encroachments. On a March morning in 1622, tribesmen called on the white settlements as if to offer goods for sale, then suddenly attacked. Not until 347 whites of both sexes and all ages (including John Rolfe) lay dead or dying were the Indian warriors finally forced to retreat. The surviving English struck back mercilessly at the Indians and turned back the threat for a time, although it was only after Opechancanough led another unsuccessful uprising in 1644 that the Powhatans finally ceased to challenge the eastern regions of the colony.

By then the Virginia Company in London was defunct. The company had poured virtually all its funds into its profitless Jamestown venture and in the aftermath of the 1622 Indian uprising faced imminent bankruptcy. In 1624, James I revoked the company's charter, and the colony came under the control of the crown and would remain so until 1776.

Maryland and the Calverts

Maryland was founded under circumstances very different from those of Virginia, but it developed in ways markedly like its neighbor to the south. The new colony was the dream of George Calvert, the first Lord Baltimore, a recent convert to Catholicism and a shrewd businessman. Calvert envisioned establishing

they contributed a small quitrent (one shilling a year for each headright) to the company.

The company added other incentives as well. To diversify the colonial economy, it transported ironworkers and other skilled craftsmen to Virginia. In 1619, it sent 100 Englishwomen to the colony (which was still overwhelmingly male) to become the wives of male colonists. (The women could be purchased for 120 pounds of tobacco and enjoyed a status somewhere between indentured servants and free people, depending on the good will—or lack of it—of their husbands.) It promised the colonists the full rights of Englishmen (as provided in the original charter of 1606), an end to the strict and arbitrary rule of the communal years, and even a share in self-government. On July 30, 1619, in the Jamestown church, delegates from the various communities met as the House of Burgesses. It was the first meeting of an elected legislature, a representative assembly, within what was to become the United States.

A month later, another event in Virginia established a very different but no less momentous precedent. As John Rolfe recorded, "about the latter end of August" a Dutch ship brought in "20 and odd Negroes." The status and fate of these first Africans in the English colonies remains obscure. There is some reason to believe that the colonists did not consider them slaves, that they thought of them as servants to be held for a term of years and then freed, like the white servants

a colony both as a great speculative venture in real estate and as a retreat for English Catholics, many of whom felt oppressed by the Anglican establishment at home. He died before he could receive a charter from the king. But in 1632, his son Cecilius, the second Lord Baltimore, received a charter remarkable not only for the extent of the territory it granted to Calvert—an area that encompassed parts of Pennsylvania, Delaware, and Virginia, in addition to present-day Maryland—but for the powers it bestowed on him. He and his heirs were to hold their province as "true and absolute lords and proprietaries," and were to acknowledge the ultimate sovereignty of the king only by paying an annual fee to the crown.

Lord Baltimore named his brother, Leonard Calvert, governor and sent him with another brother to oversee the settlement of the province. In March 1634, two ships—the *Ark* and the *Dove*—bearing 200 to 300 passengers entered the Potomac River and turned into one of its eastern tributaries. On a high and dry bluff, these first arrivals laid out the village of St. Mary's (named, diplomatically, for the queen). The neighboring Indians, threatened by rival tribes in the region, befriended the settlers, provided them with temporary shelter, sold them land, and provided them with stocks of corn. The early Marylanders experienced no Indian assaults, no plagues, no starving time.

The Calverts had invested heavily in their American possessions, and they needed to attract many settlers to make the effort profitable. As a result, they had to encourage the immigration of Protestants as well as their fellow English Catholics, who were both relatively few in number (about 2 percent of the population of England) and generally reluctant to emigrate. The Protestant settlers (mostly Anglicans) outnumbered the Catholics from the start, and the Calverts quickly realized that Catholics would always be a minority in the colony. They prudently adopted a policy of religious toleration. To appease the non-Catholic majority, Lord Calvert appointed a Protestant as governor in 1648. A year later, he sent from England the draft of an "Act Concerning Religion," which assured freedom of worship to all Christians.

Nevertheless, politics in Maryland remained plagued for years by tensions between the Catholic minority (including the proprietor) and the Protestant majority. Zealous Jesuits and crusading Puritans frightened and antagonized their opponents with their efforts to establish the dominance of their own religion. At one point, the Protestant majority barred Catholics from voting and repealed the Toleration Act. There was frequent violence; and in 1655 a civil war temporarily unseated the proprietary government and replaced it with one dominated by Protestants. The English in

Maryland were spared serious conflict with Indians, but they made up for that by inflicting decades of conflict and instability on themselves.

Although Maryland's government ultimately came to resemble those of other American colonies, with a two-house assembly and a governor appointed from abroad, the distribution of real power in the colony differed sharply from that in other parts of English America. The proprietor retained absolute authority to distribute land as he wished, and Lord Baltimore initially granted large estates to his relatives and to other English aristocrats, so that a landed aristocracy quickly established itself in Maryland. By 1640, a severe labor shortage in the colony had forced a modification of the land grant procedure; and Maryland, like Virginia, adopted a "headright" system—a grant of 100 acres to each male settler, another 100 for his wife and each servant, and 50 for each of his children. But the great landlords of the colony's earliest years remained powerful even as the population grew larger and more diverse. Like Virginia, Maryland became a center of tobacco cultivation; and like Virginia, planters worked their land with the aid, first, of indentured servants imported from England and then, beginning late in the seventeenth century, with black slaves imported from Africa. Settlement and trade remained dispersed, centered on scattered large plantations, and few towns of any significance emerged.

Turbulent Virginia

By the mid-seventeenth century, the Virginia colony had survived its early disasters, and both its population and the complexity and profitability of its economy were increasing. It was also growing more politically contentious, as emerging factions within the province began to compete for the favor of the government. Perhaps the most important dispute involved policy toward the natives. As settlement moved west and encroached still further on Indian lands, border conflicts grew increasingly frequent. Much of the tension within English Virginia in the late seventeenth century revolved around how to respond to those conflicts.

Sir William Berkeley arrived in Virginia in 1642 at the age of thirty-six with an appointment from King Charles I as governor, and with but one interruption he remained in control of the government until the 1670s. Berkeley was popular at first as he sent explorers across the Blue Ridge Mountains to open up the western interior of Virginia. He organized the force that put down the 1644 Indian uprising, captured Opechancanough, and (against Berkeley's orders) shot and killed him. The defeated Indians ceded a large area of land to the English, but Berkeley agreed to prohibit white settlement west of a line he agreed upon with the tribes.

This attempt to protect Indian territory—like many such attempts later in American history—was a failure from the start, largely because of the rapid growth of the Virginia population. Oliver Cromwell's victory in 1649 in the English civil war (see p. 45) and the flight of many of his defeated opponents to the colony contributed to what was already a substantial population increase. Between 1640 and 1650, Virginia's population doubled from 8,000 to 16,000. By 1660, it had more than doubled again, to 40,000. As the choice lands along the tidewater became scarce, new arrivals and indentured servants completing their terms or escaping from their masters pressed westward into the piedmont. By 1652, English settlers had established three counties in the territory promised to the Indians. Unsurprisingly, there were frequent clashes between natives and whites.

By the 1660s, Berkeley had become a virtual autocrat in the colony. When the first burgesses were elected in 1619, all men aged seventeen or older were entitled to vote. By 1670, the vote was restricted to landowners, and elections were rare. The same burgesses, loyal and subservient to the governor, remained in office year after year. Each county continued to have only two representatives, even though some of the new counties of the interior contained many more people than the older ones of the tidewater area. Thus the more recent settlers in the "backcountry" were underrepresented or (if living in areas not yet formally organized as counties) not represented at all.

Bacon's Rebellion

In 1676, backcountry unrest combined with factional political rivalries to create a major conflict. Nathaniel Bacon, a wealthy young graduate of Cambridge University, arrived in Virginia in 1673. He purchased a substantial farm in the west and won a seat on the governor's council. He established himself, in other words, as a member of the backcountry gentry—an influential, propertied elite that was emerging in the western region of the state just as other elites had emerged earlier in the east.

But the new backcountry gentry was at odds with its tidewater counterpart on many issues, and above all on policies toward the natives. Their settlements were in constant danger of attack from the Indians, on whose lands (reserved to the tribes by treaty) they were encroaching. They had long chafed at the governor's attempts to hold the line of settlement steady so as to avoid antagonizing the natives. It was, they believed, an effort by the eastern aristocracy to protect its dominance by restricting western expansion. (In reality, it was in part an effort by Berkeley to protect his own lucrative fur trade with the Indians.)

Bacon, an aristocratic man with great political ambitions, had additional reasons for unhappiness with Berkeley. He chafed at his exclusion from the inner circle of the governor's council (the so-called Green Spring group, whose members enjoyed special access to patronage). Bacon resented, too, Berkeley's refusal to allow him a piece of the Indian fur trade. He was developing grievances that made him a natural leader of an opposition faction.

Bloody events thrust him into that role. In 1675, some Doeg Indians—chafing at the European intrusions into their lands—raided a western plantation and killed a white servant. Bands of local whites retaliated indiscriminately, attacking not only the small Doeg tribe but the powerful Susquehannock as well. The Indians responded with more raids on plantations and killed many more white settlers. As the fighting escalated, Bacon and other concerned landholders demanded that the governor send the militia out to pursue and destroy the Indian warriors. Berkeley, however, took a more cautious route and ordered the construction of several new forts along the western line of settlement.

When Berkeley rejected an offer from Bacon to organize his own army to fight the Indians, Bacon ignored him and launched a series of vicious but generally unsuccessful pursuits of the Indian challengers. Berkeley dismissed Bacon from the governor's council and proclaimed him and his men rebels. At that point what had been an unauthorized assault on the Indians became a military challenge to the colonial government, a conflict known as Bacon's Rebellion. It was the largest and most powerful insurrection against established authority in the history of the colonies, one that would not be surpassed until the Revolution.

Twice, Bacon led his army east to Jamestown. The first time he won a temporary pardon from the governor; the second time, after the governor reneged on the agreement, he burned the city and drove the governor into exile. In the midst of widespread social turmoil throughout the colony, Bacon stood on the verge of taking command of Virginia. Instead, he died suddenly of dysentery; and Berkeley, his position bolstered by the arrival of British troops, soon managed to regain control. In 1677, the Indians (aware of their inability to defeat the white forces militarily) reluctantly signed a new treaty that opened additional lands to white settlement.

Bacon's Rebellion was significant for several reasons. It was evidence of the continuing struggle to define the Indian and white spheres of influence in Virginia—of the English settlers' unwillingness to abide by earlier agreements with the natives and the Indians' unwillingness to tolerate further encroachments into their territory. It revealed the bitterness of the competition among rival elites—and between easterners and westerners in particular—in the still half-formed society of the colonies. But it also revealed something that Bacon himself had never intended to unleash: the potential for instability in the colony's large population of free, landless men. These men—most of them former indentured servants, propertyless, unemployed, with no discernible prospects—had formed the bulk of Bacon's constituency during the rebellion. They had come to constitute a large, unstable, floating population eager above all for access to land. Bacon had for a time maintained his popularity among them by exploiting their hatred of Indians, but ultimately he found himself, without really meaning to, leading a movement that reflected their animosity toward the landed gentry of which Bacon himself was a part.

One result was that landed elites in both eastern and western Virginia began to recognize a common interest in quelling social unrest from below. That was one of several reasons for their turning increasingly to the African slave trade to fulfill their need for labor. Enslaved blacks might pose dangers too, but the events of 1676 suggested that the perils of importing a large white subordinate class were even greater.

CARIBBEAN COLONIZATION

The Chesapeake was the site of the first permanent English settlements in the New World. But throughout the first half of the seventeenth century, the most important destinations for English immigrants were the islands of the Caribbean and the northern way station of Bermuda. These Caribbean societies had close ties to English North America from the beginning and influenced the development of the mainland colonies in several ways.

The West Indies

Most of the Caribbean islands had substantial native populations—the Arawaks, the Caribs, and the Ciboney—before the arrival of the Europeans. But beginning with Christopher Columbus's first visit in 1492, and accelerating after the Spanish established their first colony on Hispaniola in 1496, the native population was all but wiped out by European epidemics.

The Spanish Empire claimed title to the islands in the Caribbean, but there was substantial Spanish set-

tlement only on the largest of the islands: Cuba, Hispaniola, and Puerto Rico. English, French, and Dutch traders began settling on some of the smaller islands early in the sixteenth century, although these fledgling colonies were always vulnerable to Spanish attack. After Spain and the Netherlands went to war in 1621 (distracting the Spanish navy and leaving the English in the Caribbean relatively unmolested), the pace of English colonization increased. By midcentury, there were several substantial English settlements on the islands, the most important of them on Antigua, St. Kitts, Jamaica, and Barbados.

The Caribbean colonies built their economies on raising crops for export. In the first years of the seventeenth century, English settlers experimented unsuccessfully with tobacco and cotton. But they soon discovered that the most lucrative crop was sugar, for which there was a substantial and growing market in Europe. Because sugar was a labor intensive crop, and because the native population (ravaged by epidemics) was too small to provide a work force, English planters quickly found it necessary to import laborers. As in the Chesapeake, they began by bringing indentured servants from England. But the arduous work discouraged white laborers; many found it impossible to adapt to the enervating tropical climate—so different from that of England. By midcentury, therefore, the English planters in the Caribbean (like the Spanish colonists who preceded them) were relying more and more heavily on an enslaved African work force, which soon substantially outnumbered them.

On Barbados and other islands where a flourishing sugar economy developed, the English planters were a tough, aggressive, and ambitious breed. Some of them grew enormously wealthy; and since their livelihoods depended on their work forces, they created a rigid slave system remarkably quickly. By the late seventeenth century, African slaves outnumbered white settlers by better than four to one. By then the West Indies had ceased to be an attractive destination for English immigrants; most now went to the colonies on the North American mainland instead.

Masters and Slaves

A small white population, much of it enjoying great economic success, and a large African population, all of it in bondage, was a potentially explosive combination. As in other English colonies in the New World in which Africans came to outnumber Europeans, whites in the Caribbean—fearful of slave revolts—monitored their labor force closely and often harshly. The English West Indians devised, therefore, a rigid set of laws and practices to ensure control over their black labor force.

Beginning in the 1660s, all the islands enacted legal codes to regulate relations between masters and slaves and to give white people virtually absolute authority over Africans. A master could even murder a slave with virtual impunity.

There was little in either the law or the character of the economy to compel planters to pay much attention to the welfare of their workers. Many concluded it was cheaper to buy new slaves periodically than to protect the well-being of those they already owned, and it was not uncommon for masters literally to work their slaves to death. Few African workers survived more than a decade in the brutal Caribbean working environment. Even whites, who worked far less strenuously, often succumbed to the harsh climate; most died before the age of forty—often from tropical diseases to which they had no immunity.

Establishing a stable society and culture was extremely difficult for people living in such harsh and even deadly conditions. Many of the whites were principally interested in getting rich and had no long-term commitment to the islands. Those who could returned to England with their fortunes and left their estates in the hands of overseers. A large proportion of the European settlers were single men, and many of them either died or left at a young age. Those who remained, many of them common white farmers and laborers living in desperate poverty, were unable to contribute to the development of a flourishing society. The society of Europeans in the Caribbean lacked many of the institutions that gave stability to the North American settlements: church, family, community. And it is perhaps not surprising, therefore, that the white population never became a majority on the islands. Like much of the Spanish Empire, the Caribbean colonies of England were governed by a small white elite ruling over a much larger population of Africans and natives. But as in the English colonies on the mainland, there was little intermarriage in the Caribbean.

Africans in the Caribbean faced even greater difficulties, but they managed to create a world of their own despite the hardships. They started families (although many of them were broken up by death or the slave trade); they sustained African religious and social traditions (and resisted Christianity); and within the rigidly controlled world of the sugar plantations, they established patterns of resistance.

The Caribbean settlements were important to the North American colonies in many ways. They were an important part of the Atlantic trading nexus in which many Americans became involved. They were the principal source of African slaves for the mainland colonies. And because Caribbean planters established an elaborate plantation system earlier than planters in North America, they provided models that many mainland people consciously or unconsciously emulated. In the American South, too, planters grew wealthy at the expense of poor whites and, above all, of African slaves.

THE GROWTH OF NEW ENGLAND

The first enduring settlement in New England—the second in English America—resulted from the discontent of a congregation of Puritan Separatists in England. For years, Separatists had been periodically imprisoned and even executed for defying the government and the Church of England; some of them, as a result, began to contemplate leaving England altogether in search of freedom to worship as they wished.

Plymouth Plantation

It was illegal to leave the realm without the consent of the king, but in 1608 a congregation of Separatists from the hamlet of Scrooby began emigrating quietly, a few at a time, to Leyden, Holland, where they could worship without interference. Holland, however, was unsatisfying to them in other ways. As foreigners, they were barred from the Dutch craft guilds and had to work at unskilled and poorly paid jobs. They were troubled by the effects of the tolerant atmosphere of Dutch society, which seemed to pose as much of a threat to their dream of a close-knit Christian community as had the repression in England. They watched with alarm as their children began to drift away from their families and their church and into Dutch society. As a result, some of the Separatists decided to move again, this time across the Atlantic, where they hoped to create the kind of community they wanted and where they could spread "the gospel of the Kingdom of Christ in those remote parts of the world."

Leaders of the Scrooby group obtained permission from the Virginia Company to settle in Virginia. From the king, they received informal assurances that he would "not molest them, provided they carried themselves peaceably." (This was a historic concession by the crown, for it opened English America to settlement not only by the Scrooby group but by other dissenting Protestants.) Several English merchants agreed to advance the necessary funds in exchange for a share in the profits of the settlement at the end of seven years.

The migrating Puritans "knew they were pilgrims" even before they left Holland, their leader and histo-

Mayflower Compact

rian, William Bradford, later wrote. In September 1620 they left Plymouth on the English coast, in the *Mayflower* with thirty-five "saints" (Puritan Separatists) and sixty-seven "strangers" aboard. By the time they sighted land in November, it was too late in the year to go on. Their original destination was probably the mouth of the Hudson River, in the northeast corner of the London Company's Virginia grant. But they found themselves instead on Cape Cod. After a few explorations of the region, they chose a site for their settlement in the area just north of the cape, an area Captain John Smith had named "Plymouth" during an exploratory journey years before. Plymouth lay outside the London Company's territory, and the settlers realized they had no legal basis for settling there. As a result, forty-one of the "saints" signed a document, the Mayflower Compact, which established a civil government and proclaimed their allegiance to the king.

Then, on December 21, 1620, the Pilgrims stepped ashore at Plymouth Rock.

They settled on cleared land that had once been an Indian village until, four years earlier, a smallpox epidemic (known as "the plague" and probably brought to the region by earlier European explorers) had swept through the region and depopulated it. (See "The American Environment: The Other Pilgrims," pp. 57–60.) The Pilgrims' first winter was a difficult one; half the colonists perished from malnutrition, disease, and exposure. Those who survived, however, managed to keep the colony alive.

The Pilgrims' experience with the Indians was, for a time at least, markedly different from the experiences of the early English settlers farther south. That was in part because the few remaining natives in the region were significantly weaker than their southern neighbors and realized they had to conciliate the Europeans.

THE FIRST THANKSGIVING
Pilgrims gather in Plymouth for a blessing at a feast in celebration of their first harvest in America—a celebration that became an annual event ultimately known as Thanksgiving. This much later painting was based on contemporary descriptions of the event. *(The Pilgrim Society)*

It was also, perhaps, because the Pilgrims were less actively hostile. In the end, the survival and growth of the colony depended crucially on the assistance they received from natives. Important Indian friends—Squanto and Samoset, among others—showed them how to gather seafood and cultivate corn. Squanto, a Pawtuxet who had earlier been captured by an English explorer and taken to Europe, spoke English and was of particular help to the settlers in forming an alliance with the local Wampanoags, under Chief Massasoit. But the relationship between settlers and natives was never an equal one. The Pilgrims were few and weak, but the smallpox-ravaged Wampanoags were even weaker, particularly in the face of the firearms the English had brought with them. After the first harvest, in 1621, the settlers marked the alliance by inviting the Indians to join them in an October festival, the first Thanksgiving.

The Pilgrims could not aspire to rich farms on the sandy, marshy soil, and their early fishing efforts produced no profits. In 1622, the colony became semimilitarized (through the efforts of the military officer Miles Standish) and eventually the Pilgrims began to grow enough corn and other crops to provide them with a modest trading surplus. They also developed a small fur trade with the Abenaki Indians of Maine. From time to time new colonists arrived from England, and in a decade the population reached 300.

The people of "Plymouth Plantation" chose William Bradford again and again to be their governor. As early as 1621, he won them title to their land by securing a patent from the Council for New England (the successor to the old Plymouth Company, which had charter rights to the territory). He terminated the communal labor plan Standish had helped create, distributed land among the families, and thus, as he explained it, made "all hands very industrious." He and a group of fellow "undertakers" assumed the colony's debt to its original financiers in England and, with earnings from the fur trade, finally paid it off—even though the financiers had repeatedly cheated them and had failed to send them promised supplies.

The Pilgrims were always a poor community. As late as the 1640s, they had only one plow among them. But they clung to the belief that God had put them in the New World to live as a truly Christian community; and they were, on the whole, content to live their lives in what they considered godly ways. At times, they spoke of serving as a model for other Christians. Governor Bradford wrote in retrospect: "As one small candle may light a thousand, so the light here kindled hath shone to many, yea in some sort to our whole nation." But the Pilgrims were less committed to grand designs, less concerned about how they were viewed by others, than the Puritans who settled the larger and more ambitious English colonies to their north.

The Massachusetts Bay Experiment

Turbulent events in England in the 1620s (combined with the example of the Plymouth colony) generated a strong interest in colonization among other groups of Puritans. James I had been creating serious tensions for years between himself and Parliament through his effort to claim the divine right of kings and by his harsh, repressive policies toward the Puritans. The situation worsened after his death in 1625, when he was succeeded by his son, Charles I. By trying to restore Roman Catholicism to England and to destroy religious nonconformity, he launched the nation on the road that in the 1640s would lead to civil war. The Puritans were particular targets of Charles's policies. Some were imprisoned for their beliefs, and many began to consider the climate of England intolerable. The king's dissolution of Parliament in 1629 (it was not to be recalled until 1640) ensured that there would be no political redress.

In the midst of this political and social turmoil, a group of Puritan merchants began organizing a new enterprise designed to take advantage of opportunities in America. At first their interest was largely an economic one. They obtained a grant of land in New England for most of the area now comprising Massachusetts and New Hampshire; they acquired a charter from the king (who was evidently unaware of their religious inclinations) allowing them to create the Massachusetts Bay Company and to establish a colony in the New World; and they bought equipment and supplies from a defunct fishing and trading company that had attempted (and failed) to establish a profitable enterprise in North America. In 1629, they were ready to dispatch a substantial group of settlers to New England.

Among the members of the Massachusetts Bay Company, however, were a number of Puritans who saw the enterprise as something more than a business venture. They began to consider emigrating themselves and creating a refuge for Puritans in New England. Members of this faction met secretly in Cambridge in the summer of 1629 and agreed to buy out the other investors and move en masse to America.

For governor, the new owners of the company chose John Winthrop, an affluent, university-educated gentleman with a deep piety and a forceful character. Winthrop had been instrumental in organizing the migration, and he commanded the expedition that sailed for New England in 1630: seventeen ships and 1,000

Boston Harbor

The founders of Boston (and of the Massachusetts Bay colony, of which it was the capital) envisioned the town as a peaceful, harmonious, religious community. But they also hoped to create a thriving commercial center that would contribute to their own and the empire's prosperity. This early view of Boston harbor, showing the north battery built in 1646, suggests the growing commercial orientation of the city even in its early years. *(Library of Congress)*

people (who were, unlike the earlier migrants to Virginia, mostly family groups). It was the largest single migration of its kind in the seventeenth century. Winthrop carried with him the charter of the Massachusetts Bay Company, which meant that the colonists would be responsible to no company officials in England, only to themselves.

Unlike the two previous English settlements in America—Jamestown and Plymouth—the Massachusetts migration quickly produced several different new settlements. The port of Boston, at the mouth of the Charles River, became the company's headquarters and the colony's capital. But in the course of the next decade colonists moved into a number of other new towns in eastern Massachusetts: Charlestown, Newtown (later renamed Cambridge), Roxbury, Dorchester, Watertown, Ipswich, Concord, Sudbury, and others.

The Massachusetts Bay Company soon transformed itself into a colonial government. According to the original company charter, the eight stockholders (or "freemen") were to meet as a general court to choose officers and adopt rules for the corporation. But this commercial definition of government, which concentrated authority in what was in effect a corporate board of directors, quickly gave way to a more genuinely political system. The definition of "freemen" changed to include all male citizens, not just the stockholders. John Winthrop dominated colonial politics just as he had dominated the original corporation, but after 1634 he and most other officers of the colony had to face election each year.

Unlike the Separatist founders of Plymouth, the founders of Massachusetts had no intention of breaking away from the Church of England. Yet if they continued to feel any real attachment to the Anglican establishment, they gave little sign of it in their behavior. In every town, the community church had (in the words of the prominent minister John Cotton) "complete liberty to stand alone." Each congregation chose its own minister and regulated its own affairs. In both Plymouth and Massachusetts, this form of parish organization eventually became known as the Congregational Church.

The Massachusetts Puritans were not grim or joyless, as many observers would later come to believe. But they were serious and pious people. They strove to lead useful, conscientious lives of thrift and hard work, and they honored material success as evidence of God's favor. "We here enjoy God and Jesus Christ," Winthrop wrote to his wife soon after his arrival; "is this not enough?" He and the other Massachusetts founders believed they were founding a holy commonwealth—a "city upon a hill"—that could serve as a model for the rest of the world. They were not the last to define American society in such terms.

But if Massachusetts was to become a beacon to others, it had first to maintain its own "holiness." The clergy and the government worked closely together to ensure that it did. Ministers had no formal political power, but they exerted great influence on church members, who were the only people who could vote or hold office. The government in turn protected the ministers, taxed the people (members and nonmembers alike) to support the church, and enforced the law requiring attendance at services. Dissidents had no more freedom of worship in America than the Puritans themselves had had in England. Colonial Massachusetts was, in effect, a "theocracy," a society in which the church was almost indistinguishable from the state.

Like other new settlements, the Massachusetts Bay colony had early difficulties. During their first winter, an unusually severe one, nearly a third of the colonists died; others left in the spring. But more rapidly than Jamestown, the colony grew and prospered. The Pilgrims and neighboring Indians helped with food and advice. Incoming settlers, many of them affluent, brought needed tools and other goods, which they exchanged for the cattle, corn, and other produce of the established colonists and the natives. The large number of family groups in the colony (a sharp contrast to the early years at Jamestown) helped ensure a feeling of commitment to the community and a sense of order among the settlers. It also allowed the population to reproduce itself more rapidly. And the strong religious and political hierarchy ensured a measure of social stability.

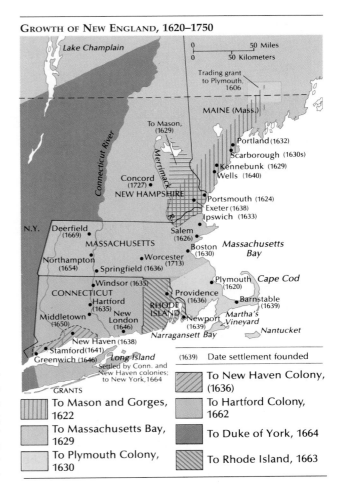

GROWTH OF NEW ENGLAND, 1620–1750

(1639) Date settlement founded

To Mason and Gorges, 1622

To Massachusetts Bay, 1629

To Plymouth Colony, 1630

To New Haven Colony, (1636)

To Hartford Colony, 1662

To Duke of York, 1664

To Rhode Island, 1663

The Expansion of New England

As the population grew, more and more people arrived in Massachusetts who did not accept all the religious tenets of the colony's leaders or who were not Puritan "saints" and hence could not vote. The theocratic Massachusetts government considered religious dissent as much a threat to the community as heresy or treason. Newcomers had a choice of conforming to the religious practices of the colony or leaving. Many left, helping to begin a process that would spread settlement throughout present-day New England and beyond.

The Connecticut Valley, about 100 miles west of the edge of European settlement around Boston, began attracting English families as early as the 1630s, despite claims to those lands by the Dutch. The Connecticut settlers were attracted by the valley's fertile lands (a

contrast to the stony, unproductive soil around Boston) and by its isolation from the intensely religious character of Massachusetts Bay. The valley appealed in particular to Thomas Hooker, a minister of Newtown (Cambridge), who defied the Massachusetts government in 1635 and led his congregation through the wilds to establish the town of Hartford. Four years later, the people of Hartford and of two other newly founded upriver towns, Windsor and Wethersfield, established a colonial government of their own and adopted a constitution known as the Fundamental Orders of Connecticut. This created a government similar to that of Massachusetts Bay but gave a larger proportion of the men the right to vote and hold office. (Women were barred from voting virtually everywhere.)

Another Connecticut colony, the project of a Puritan minister and a wealthy merchant from England,

THE WHITE POPULATION OF NEW ENGLAND, 1620–1700

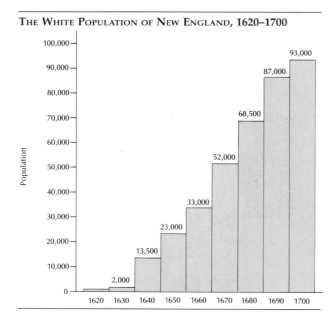

grew up around New Haven on the Connecticut coast. It reflected impatience not with the orthodoxy of Massachusetts Bay, but with what its founders considered the increasing religious laxity in Boston. The Fundamental Articles of New Haven (1639) established a religious government even stricter than that in Boston. New Haven remained independent until 1662, when a royal charter combined it with Hartford to create the colony of Connecticut.

Rhode Island had its origins in the religious and political dissent of Roger Williams, an engaging but controversial young minister who lived for a time in Salem, Massachusetts. Even John Winthrop, who considered Williams a heretic, called him a "sweet and amiable" man, and William Bradford described him as "a man godly and zealous, having many precious parts." But he was, Bradford added, "very unsettled in judgment." Williams, a confirmed Separatist, argued that the Massachusetts church should abandon all allegiance to the Church of England. More disturbing to the clergy, he called for a complete separation of church and state—to protect the church from the corruption of the secular world. The colonial government, alarmed at this challenge to its spiritual authority, banished him. During the bitter winter of 1635–1636, he took refuge with Narragansett tribesmen; the following spring he bought a tract of land from them and, with a few followers, created the town of Providence on it. Other communities of dissidents followed him to Rhode Island, and in 1644 Williams obtained a charter

from Parliament permitting him to establish a government. Rhode Island's government gave no support to the church and allowed "liberty in religious concernments." For a time, it was the only colony in which members of all faiths (including Judaism) could worship without interference.

An even greater challenge to the established order in Massachusetts Bay emerged in the person of Anne Hutchinson, an intelligent and charismatic woman from a substantial Boston family. Hutchinson had come to Massachusetts with her husband in 1634 as part of a community led by the minister John Cotton. She shared Cotton's belief that only the "elect" were entitled to any religious or political authority. Living a righteous life was not enough to earn a place among the "elect"; to be a saint, it was necessary to have undergone a conversion experience.

Hutchinson antagonized the leaders of the colony by arguing much more vehemently than Cotton that the many members of the Massachusetts clergy who were not among the elect (including her own uninspiring minister) had no right to spiritual office. Such teachings (which her critics called "Antinomian," from the Greek meaning "hostile to the law") were a serious threat to the spiritual authority of the established clergy. Hutchinson also created alarm by affronting prevailing assumptions about the proper role of women in Puritan society. She was not a retiring, deferential wife and mother, but a powerful religious figure in her own right.

Hutchinson developed a large following among women, who chafed at their limited role in religious affairs. She also attracted support from others (merchants, young men, and dissidents of many sorts) who resented the oppressive character of the colonial government. As her influence grew, and as she began to deliver open attacks on some members of the clergy, the Massachusetts hierarchy mobilized to stop her. Hutchinson's followers were numerous and influential enough to prevent Winthrop's reelection as governor in 1636, but the next year he returned to office and put her on trial for heresy. Hutchinson embarrassed her accusers by displaying a remarkable knowledge of theology; but because she continued to defy clerical authority (and because she claimed she had herself communicated directly with the Holy Spirit—a violation of the Puritan belief that the age of revelations had passed), she was convicted of sedition and banished as "a woman not fit for our society." With her family and some of her followers, she moved to Rhode Island. Later still, she moved south into New Netherland, where in 1643 she died during an Indian uprising.

The Hutchinson affair had an important impact on the role of women within the Massachusetts church.

Alarmed by Hutchinson's heresy, male clergy began to restrict further the already limited public activities of women within congregations. But Hutchinson's followers had an even greater effect on settlements north of Massachusetts Bay, in New Hampshire and Maine.

Colonies were established there in 1629 when two English proprietors, Captain John Mason and Sir Ferdinando Gorges, received a grant from the Council for New England and divided it along the Piscataqua River to create two separate provinces. But despite their lavish promotional efforts, few settlers moved into these northern regions until the religious disrup-

tions in Massachusetts Bay. In 1639, John Wheelwright, a disciple of Anne Hutchinson, led some of his fellow dissenters to Exeter, New Hampshire. Other groups—of both dissenting and orthodox Puritans—soon followed. New Hampshire became a formal colony in 1679. Maine remained a part of Massachusetts until 1820.

Settlers and Natives

Indians were less formidable rivals to the early New England immigrants than to their counterparts further south. By the mid-1630s, the native population, small to begin with, had been almost extinguished by the epidemics. The survivors sold much of their land to the English (a great boost to settlement, since much of it had already been cleared); some—known as "praying Indians"—even converted to Christianity and joined Puritan communities.

Indians provided crucial assistance to the early settlers in adapting to the land. Whites learned from the natives about vital food crops: corn (which Indians had adapted from a Mexican strain to the colder, damper climate of the northern regions), beans, pumpkins, and potatoes. They also learned such crucial agricultural techniques as annual burning for fertilization and planting beans to replenish exhausted soil.

Natives also served as important trading partners to European immigrants, particularly in the creation of the thriving North American fur trade. They were an important market for such manufactured goods as iron pots, blankets, metal-tipped arrows, eventually guns and rifles, and (often tragically) alcohol. Indeed, commerce with the Indians was responsible for the creation of some of the first great fortunes in British North America and for the emergence of elite families who would exercise influence in the colonies (and later the nation) for many generations. The relationship between whites and Indians, in New England as throughout the areas of European settlement in the Americas, was one of constant interaction, in which each group influenced the other in crucial ways.

But as in other areas of white settlement, there were also conflicts, and the early peaceful relations between whites and Indians did not last. That tensions soon developed was primarily a result of the white colonists' insatiable appetite for land and their steady encroachments into territories such as the Connecticut Valley, where the natives were more numerous and more powerful than they had been along the Massachusetts coast. But the character of those conflicts—and the brutality with which whites assaulted their Indian foes—emerged as well out of changing Puritan attitudes toward the natives. At first, many white New Englanders

ANNE HUTCHINSON PREACHING IN HER HOUSE IN BOSTON
Anne Hutchinson was alarming to many of Boston's religious leaders not only because she openly challenged the authority of the clergy, but also because she implicitly challenged norms of female behavior in Puritan society. *(Bettmann)*

had looked at the Indians with a somewhat bemused admiration. Before long, however, they came to view them primarily as heathen, and hence as a constant threat to the existence of a godly community in the New World. Some Puritans believed the solution to the Indian "problem" was to "civilize" the natives by converting them to Christianity and European ways, and some English missionaries had modest success in producing converts. One such missionary, John Eliot, even translated the Bible into an Algonquian language. Other Puritans, however, envisioned a harsher "solution": displacing or, if that failed, exterminating the natives.

To the natives, the threat from the English was more direct. European settlers were penetrating deeper and deeper into the interior, seizing land, clearing forests, driving away much of the wild game on which the tribes depended for food. English farmers often let their livestock run wild, and the animals often destroyed natives' crops. The Indian population in the region had been declining for years as a result of epidemic disease. Now land and food shortages worsened their plight. There had been more than 100,000 Indians in New England at the beginning of the seventeenth century. By 1675, only 10,000 remained. This decline created despair among New England natives. It drove some Indians to alcoholism and others to con-

version to Christianity. But it also produced conflict.

The first major conflict came in 1637, when hostilities broke out between English settlers in the Connecticut Valley and the Pequot Indians of the region. Competition between the white settlers and the Pequots over trade with the Dutch in New Netherland, combined with friction over land, produced what became known as the Pequot War. English settlers allied in the conflict with the Mohegan and Narragansett Indians (who were also rivals of the Pequots), but the greatest savagery of the conflict was the work of the English. In the most brutal act of the war, white raiders under Captain John Mason marched against a palisaded Pequot stronghold and set it afire. Hundreds of Indians died, burned to death in the flaming stockade or killed as they attempted to escape. Those who survived were hunted down, captured, and sold as slaves. The Pequot tribe was almost wiped out.

The bloodiest and most prolonged encounter between whites and Indians in the seventeenth century began in 1675, a conflict that whites would remember for generations as King Philip's War. As in Connecticut nearly forty years before, an Indian tribe—in this case the Wampanoags, under the leadership of a chieftain known to the white settlers as King Philip and among his own people as Metacomet—rose up to resist English encroachment on their lands. The Wam-

A PEQUOT VILLAGE DESTROYED
An English artist drew this view of a fortified Pequot village in Connecticut surrounded by English soldiers and their allies from other tribes during the Pequot War in 1637. The invaders massacred more than 600 residents of the settlement. *(Rare Book Division, New York Public Library)*

panoags had not always been hostile to the settlers; indeed, Metacomet's grandfather had once forged an alliance with the English. But by the 1670s, they had become convinced that only armed resistance could protect them from the movement of the English into their lands and, more immediately, from the efforts by a colonial government to impose English law on the natives. (A court in Plymouth had recently tried and hanged several Wampanoags for murdering a member of their own tribe.)

For three years, the natives—well organized and armed with guns—terrorized a string of Massachusetts towns, destroying or depopulating twenty of them and causing the deaths of as many as a thousand people (including at least one-sixteenth of the white males in the colony). The war greatly weakened both the society and economy of Massachusetts. But the white settlers gradually prevailed, beginning in 1676 when Massachusetts leaders joined forces with the Mohawks, long-time rivals of the Wampanoags, and recruited guides, spies, and soldiers from among the so-called praying Indians of the region. While white militiamen attacked Indian villages and destroyed native food supplies, a group of Mohawks ambushed Metacomet and shot and killed him, then bore his severed head to Boston to present to the colonial leaders. After that the fragile alliance that Metacomet had managed to forge among local tribes collapsed. Europeans were soon able to crush the uprising. Some Wampanoag leaders were executed; others were sold into slavery in the West Indies. The Wampanoags and their allies, their populations depleted and their natural resources reduced, were now powerless to resist the English.

Yet these victories by the white colonists did not end the danger to their settlements. This was in part because other Indians in other tribes survived, capable of attacking English settlements. It was also because the New England settlers faced competition not only from the natives but also from the Dutch and the French, who claimed the territory on which some of the outlying settlements were established. The French, in particular, would pose a constant threat to the English through their alliance with the Algonquins. In later years, they would join forces with Indians in their attacks on the New England frontier.

THE RESTORATION COLONIES

By the end of the 1630s, then, English settlers had established the beginnings of what would eventually become six of the thirteen original states of the American republic: Virginia, Massachusetts, Maryland, Connecticut, Rhode Island, and New Hampshire. But for nearly thirty years after Lord Baltimore received the charter for Maryland in 1632, the English government launched no additional colonial ventures. It was preoccupied with troubles of its own at home.

The English Civil War

England's problems had begun during the rule of James I, who attracted widespread opposition before he died in 1625 but never openly challenged Parliament. His son, Charles I, was not so prudent. After he dissolved Parliament in 1629 and began ruling as an absolute monarch, he steadily alienated a growing number of his subjects—and the members of the powerful Puritan community above all. Finally, desperately in need of money, Charles called Parliament back into session and asked it to levy new taxes. But he antagonized the members by dismissing them twice in two years; and in 1642, some of them organized a military challenge to the king, thus launching the English Civil War.

The conflict between the Cavaliers (the supporters of the king) and the Roundheads (the forces of Parliament, who were mostly Puritans) lasted seven years. Finally, in 1649, the Roundheads defeated the king's forces, captured Charles himself, and—in an action that horrified not only much of continental Europe at the time but future generations of English men and women—beheaded the monarch. To replace him, they elevated the stern Roundhead leader Oliver Cromwell to the position of "protector," from which he ruled for the next nine years. When Cromwell died in 1658, his son and heir proved unable to maintain his authority. Two years later, King Charles II, son of the beheaded monarch, returned from exile and claimed the throne.

Among the many results of the Stuart Restoration was the resumption of colonization in America. Charles II quickly began to reward faithful courtiers with grants of land in the New World; and in the twenty-five years of his reign, he issued charters for four additional colonies: Carolina, New York, New Jersey, and Pennsylvania. The new colonies were all proprietary ventures (modeled on Maryland rather than on Virginia and Massachusetts), thus exposing an important change in the nature of American settlement. No longer were private companies interested in launching colonies, realizing at last that there were no quick profits to be had in the New World. The goal of the founders of the new colonies was not so much quick commercial success as permanent settlements that would provide proprietors with land and power.

The Carolinas

Carolina (a name derived from the Latinate form of "Charles") was, like Maryland, carved in part from the original Virginia grant. Charles II awarded the territory to a group of eight court favorites, all prominent politicians already active in colonial affairs. In successive charters issued in 1663 and 1665, the eight proprietors received joint title to a vast territory stretching south to the Florida peninsula and west to the Pacific Ocean. Like Lord Baltimore, they received almost kingly powers over their grant.

Also like him, they expected to profit as landlords and land speculators. They reserved large estates for themselves, and they proposed to sell or give away the rest in smaller tracts (using a headright system similar to those in Virginia and Maryland) and to collect annual payments ("quitrents") from the settlers. Although committed Anglicans themselves, they wel-comed any settlers they could get, whatever their faith. Indeed, the charter of the colony guaranteed religious freedom to everyone who would worship as a Christian. The proprietors also promised a measure of political freedom; laws were to be made by a representative assembly. With these incentives, they hoped to attract settlers from the existing American colonies and thus to avoid the expense of financing expeditions from England.

Their initial efforts failed dismally, and some of the original proprietors gave up. But one man—Anthony Ashley Cooper, soon to become the earl of Shaftesbury—persisted. Cooper convinced his partners to finance migrations to Carolina from England themselves. And in the spring of 1670, the first of these expeditions—a party of 300—set out from England. Only 100 people survived the difficult voyage; those who did established a settlement in the Port Royal area of the Carolina coast. Ten years later they founded a city

CHARLES TOWN IN 1739
An English engraver produced this prospect of the harbor at Charles Town (now Charleston), South Carolina, as it looked six decades after the city was founded in 1680. It was by then the principal port of the southern colonies. The city's original waterfront (or battery), pictured here, looks much the same today as it did in the eighteenth century. *(I.N. Phelps Stokes Collection of American Historical Prints, New York Public Library)*

at the junction of the Ashley and Cooper rivers, which in 1690 became the colonial capital. They called it Charles Town. (It was later renamed Charleston.)

The earl of Shaftesbury, troubled by the instability in England, wanted a planned and well-ordered community. With the aid of the English philosopher John Locke, he drew up the Fundamental Constitution for Carolina in 1669, which created an elaborate system of land distribution and a rigidly hierarchical social order. In fact, however, Carolina developed along lines quite different from the almost utopian vision of Shaftesbury and Locke. For one thing, the colony was never really united in anything more than name. The northern and southern regions remained widely separated and were socially and economically distinct from one another. The northern settlers were mainly backwoods farmers, largely isolated from the outside world, scratching out a meager existence at subsistence agriculture. They developed no important aristocracy and for many years imported virtually no African slaves. In the south, fertile lands and the good harbor at Charles Town promoted a more prosperous economy and a more stratified, aristocratic society. Settlements grew up rapidly along the Ashley and Cooper rivers, and colonists established a flourishing trade in corn, lumber, cattle, pork, and (beginning in the 1690s) rice—which was to become the colony's principal commercial crop. Traders from the interior used Charles Town to market furs and hides they had acquired from Indian trading partners; some also marketed Indian slaves, generally natives captured by rival tribes and sold to the white traders.

Southern Carolina very early developed close ties to the large (and now overpopulated) European colony on the island of Barbados. For many years, Barbados was Carolina's most important trading partner. And during the first ten years of settlement, most of the new settlers in Carolina were Barbadians, some of whom arrived with large groups of African workers and established themselves quickly as substantial landlords. African slavery had taken root on Barbados earlier than in any of the mainland colonies (see pp. 36–37); and the white Caribbean migrants—tough, uncompromising profit seekers—established a similar slave-based plantation society in Carolina. (The proprietors, too, encouraged the importation of Africans; four of them had a financial interest in the African slave trade.)

For several decades, Carolina remained one of the most factious of all the English colonies in America. There were tensions between the small farmers of the Albemarle region in the north and the wealthy planters in the south. And there were conflicts between the rich Barbadians in southern Carolina and the smaller landowners around them. After Lord Shaftesbury's death, the proprietors proved unable to establish order, and in 1719 the colonists seized control of the colony from them. Ten years later, the king divided the region into two royal colonies, North and South Carolina.

New Netherland and New York

In 1664, one year after he issued the Carolina charter, Charles II granted to his brother James, the duke of York, all the territory lying between the Connecticut and Delaware Rivers. But much of the territory included in the grant was already claimed by the Dutch, who had established substantial settlements at New Amsterdam and other strategic points.

The emerging conflict between the English and the Dutch in America was part of a larger commercial rivalry between the two nations in the seventeenth century throughout the world. But the English particularly resented the Dutch presence in America, because it served as a wedge between northern and southern English colonies and because it provided bases for Dutch smugglers evading English customs laws. And so in 1664, an English fleet under the command of Richard Nicolls sailed into the lightly defended port of New Amsterdam and extracted a surrender from the arbitrary and unpopular Dutch governor, Peter Stuyvesant, who had failed to mobilize resistance to the invasion. Under the Articles of Capitulation, the Dutch colony surrendered to the British and received in return assurances that the Dutch settlers would not be displaced. Several years later, in 1673, the Dutch briefly reconquered New Amsterdam. But they lost it for good in 1674.

The duke of York, his title to New Netherland now clear, renamed the colony New York and prepared to govern a colony of extraordinary diversity. New York contained not only Dutch and English, but Scandinavians, Germans, French, Africans (imported as slaves by the Dutch West India Company), and members of several different Indian tribes. There were, of course, many different religious faiths among these groups. James made no effort to impose his own Roman Catholicism on the colony. Like other proprietors before him, he remained in England and delegated powers to a governor and a council. But he provided for no representative assembly, perhaps because a parliament had executed his own father, Charles I. The laws did, however, establish local governments and guarantee religious toleration.

Despite these concessions, there were immediate tensions over the distribution of power in the colony. The great Dutch "patroonships" survived with their economic and political power largely intact. James granted

NEW AMSTERDAM
The small Dutch settlement on Manhattan Island, known before 1664 as New Amsterdam, fell to the English in 1664.
(Bettmann)

large estates as well to some of his own political supporters in an effort to create a class of influential landowners loyal to him. Power in the colony thus remained widely and unequally dispersed—among wealthy English landlords, Dutch patroons, fur traders (who forged important alliances with the Iroquois), and the duke's political appointees. Like Carolina, New York would for many years be a highly factious society.

It was also a growing and generally prosperous colony. By 1685, when the duke of York ascended the English throne as James II, New York contained approximately 30,000 people, about four times as many as when he had received his grant twenty years before. Most of them still lived within the Hudson Valley, close to the river itself, with the largest settlement at its mouth, in the town of New York (formerly New Amsterdam).

Originally, James's claims in America extended south of the Hudson to the Delaware Valley and beyond. But shortly after receiving his charter, he gave a large portion of that land to a pair of political allies, Sir John Berkeley and Sir George Carteret, both of whom were also Carolina proprietors. Carteret named the territory New Jersey, after the island in the English channel on which he had been born. In 1702, after nearly a decade of political squabbling and economic profitlessness, the proprietors ceded control of the territory back to the crown and New Jersey became a royal colony.

Like New York (from which much of the population had come), New Jersey was a place of enormous ethnic and religious diversity. But unlike New York, New Jersey developed no important class of large landowners; most of its residents remained small farmers. Nor did New Jersey (which, unlike New York, had no natural harbor) produce any single important city.

The Quaker Colonies

Pennsylvania, like Massachusetts, was born out of the efforts of dissenting English Protestants to find a home for their own distinctive social order. The Society of Friends originated in mid-seventeenth-century England and grew into an important force as a result of the preachings of George Fox, a Nottingham shoemaker, and Margaret Fell. Their followers came to be known as Quakers from Fox's admonition to them to "tremble at the name of the Lord." Unlike the Puritans, Quakers rejected the concept of predestination and original sin. All people had divinity within themselves (an "Inner Light," which could guide them along the path of righteousness), and all who cultivated that divinity could attain salvation. Also unlike the Puritans, Quakers granted women a position within the church generally equal to that of men. Women and men alike could become preachers and define church doctrine. A symbol of that sexual equality was the longtime partnership between Fox and Fell.

Of all the Protestant sectarians of the time, the Quakers were the most anarchistic and the most democratic. They had no church government, only periodic meetings of representatives from congregations. They had no paid clergy, and in their worship they spoke up one by one as the spirit moved them. Disregarding distinctions of gender and class, they addressed one another with the terms "thee" and "thou," words then commonly used in other parts of English society only in speaking to servants and social inferiors. And as confirmed pacifists, they refused to fight in wars. The Quakers were unpopular enough in England as a result of these beliefs and practices. They increased their unpopularity by occasionally breaking up other religious groups at worship. Many were jailed.

As a result, like the Puritans before them, the Quakers looked to America for asylum. A few went to New England. But except in Rhode Island, they were greeted there with fines, whippings, and banishment; three men and a woman who refused to leave were actually put to death. Others migrated to northern Carolina, and there became the fastest-growing religious community in the region. They were soon influential in colonial politics. But most Quakers wanted a colony of their own. As a despised sect, they had little chance of getting the necessary royal grant without the aid of someone influential at court. But fortunately for Fox and his followers, a number of wealthy and prominent men had become attracted to the faith. One of them was William Penn—the son of an admiral in the Royal Navy who was a landlord of valuable Irish estates—who received a gentleman's education but could not

A QUAKER MEETING
An anonymous artist painted this view of a Quaker meeting in approximately 1790. Because the Society of Friends (or Quakers) believed that all people were equal in the eyes of God, they appointed no ministers and imposed no structure on their religious services. Members of the congregation stood up to speak at will. *(Museum of Fine Arts, Boston)*

overcome his dissenting inclinations despite his father's efforts to force him to do so. Converted to the doctrine of the Inner Light, the younger Penn took up evangelism. With George Fox he visited the European continent and found Quakers there who, like Quakers in England, longed to emigrate to the New World. He set out to find a place for them to go.

Penn turned his attention first to New Jersey, half of which belonged to two fellow Quakers after 1764. Penn himself became an owner and proprietor of part of the colony. But in 1681, after the death of his father, he received from the king an even more valuable grant of lands. Penn had inherited his father's Irish lands and also his father's claim to a large debt from the king. Charles II, short of cash, paid the debt with a grant of territory between New York and Maryland—an area larger than England and Wales combined and which (unknown to him) contained more valuable soil and minerals than any other province of English America. Penn would have virtually total authority within the province. At the king's insistence, the territory was named Pennsylvania, after Penn's late father.

Like most proprietors, Penn wanted Pennsylvania to be profitable for him and his family. And so he set out to attract settlers from throughout Europe through informative and honest advertising in several languages. Pennsylvania soon became the best known of all the colonies among ordinary people in England and on the continent. It also became the most cosmopolitan. Settlers flocked to the province from throughout Europe, joining several hundred Swedes and Finns who had been living in a small trading colony—New Sweden—established in 1638 at the mouth of the Delaware River. But the colony was never profitable for Penn and his descendants. Indeed, Penn himself, near the end of his life, was imprisoned in England for debt and died in poverty in 1718.

Penn was more than a mere real estate promoter, however, and he sought to create in Pennsylvania what he called a holy experiment. He helped create a liberal Frame of Government with a representative assembly. In 1682, he sailed to America and personally supervised the laying out of a city between the Delaware and the Schuylkill Rivers, which he named Philadelphia ("Brotherly Love"). With its rectangular streets, like those of Charles Town, Philadelphia helped set the pattern for most later cities in America. Penn believed, as had Roger Williams, that the land belonged to the Indians, and he was careful to see that they were reimbursed for it, as well as to see that they were not debauched by the fur traders' alcohol. Indians respected Penn as an honest white man, and during his lifetime the colony had no major conflicts with the natives. More than any other English colony, Pennsylvania

prospered from the outset (even if its proprietor did not), because of Penn's successful recruitment of emigrants, his thoughtful planning, and the region's mild climate and fertile soil.

But the colony was not without conflict. By the late 1690s, some residents of Pennsylvania were beginning to chafe at the nearly absolute power of the proprietor. Residents of the southern areas of the colony, in particular, complained that the government in Philadelphia was unresponsive to their needs. As a result, a substantial opposition emerged to challenge Penn. Pressure from these groups grew to the point that in 1701, shortly before he departed for England for the last time, Penn agreed to a Charter of Liberties for the colony. The charter established a representative assembly (consisting, alone among the English colonies, of only one house), which greatly limited the authority of the proprietor. The charter also permitted "the lower counties" of the colony to establish their own representative assembly. The three counties did so in 1703 and as a result became, in effect, a separate colony: Delaware—although until the American Revolution, it had the same governor as Pennsylvania.

The Founding of Georgia

By the mid-1680s, English settlements extended along the Atlantic Coast from New England to South Carolina. But while the European presence continued to spread steadily westward, there were no attempts to enlarge English North America farther north or south for nearly fifty years. Not until 1733 did another new colony emerge: Georgia, the last English colony on the mainland of what would become the United States.

Georgia was unique in its origins. Its founders were a group of unpaid trustees led by General James Oglethorpe, a member of Parliament and military hero. They were not uninterested in economic success, but they were driven primarily by military and philanthropic motives. They wanted to erect a military barrier against the Spanish lands on the southern border of English America, and they wanted to provide a refuge for the impoverished, a place where English men and women without prospects at home could begin anew.

The need for a military buffer between South Carolina and the Spanish settlements in Florida was growing urgent in the first years of the eighteenth century. There had been tensions between the English and the Spanish ever since the first settlement at Jamestown. In a 1676 treaty, Spain had recognized England's title to lands already occupied by English settlers. But conflict between the two colonizing powers continued. In 1686, a force of Indians and Creoles from Florida, directed by Spanish agents, attacked and destroyed an outlying South Carolina settlement south of the treaty line. And when hostilities broke out again between Spain and England in 1701 (known in England as Queen Anne's War and on the continent as the War of the Spanish Succession), the fighting renewed in America as well. That war ended in 1713, but another European conflict with repercussions for the New World was continually expected.

Oglethorpe, himself a veteran of the most recent Spanish war, was keenly aware of the military advantages of an English colony south of the Carolinas. Yet his interest in settlement rested even more on his philanthropic commitments. As head of a parliamentary committee investigating English prisons, he had grown appalled by the plight of honest debtors rotting in confinement. Such prisoners, and other poor people in danger of succumbing to a similar fate, could, he believed, become the farmer-soldiers of the new colony in America.

In 1732, King George II granted Oglethorpe and his fellow trustees control of the land between the Savannah and Altamaha Rivers. Their colonization policies reflected the vital military purposes of the colony. They limited the size of landholdings to make the settlement compact and easier to defend against Spanish and Indian attacks. They excluded Africans, free or slave; Oglethorpe feared slave labor would produce internal revolts, and that disaffected slaves might turn to the Spanish as allies. The trustees prohibited rum (both because Oglethorpe disapproved of it on moral grounds and because the trustees feared its effects on the natives). They strictly regulated trade with the Indians, again to limit the possibility of wartime insurrection. They also excluded Catholics for fear they might collude with their coreligionists in the Spanish colonies to the south.

Oglethorpe himself led the first colonial expedition to Georgia, which built a fortified town at the mouth of the Savannah River in 1733 and later constructed additional forts south of the Altamaha. In the end, only a few debtors were released from jail and sent to Georgia. Instead, the trustees brought hundreds of impoverished tradesmen and artisans from England and Scotland and many religious refugees from Switzerland and Germany. Among the immigrants was a small group of Jews. English settlers made up a lower proportion of the European population of Georgia than of any other English colony.

The strict rules governing life in the new colony stifled its early development and ensured the failure of Oglethorpe's vision. Settlers in Georgia—many of whom were engaged in labor-intensive agriculture—needed a work force as much as those in other southern colonies. Almost from the start they began demanding the right to buy slaves. Some opposed the restrictions on the size of individual property holdings. Many resented the nearly absolute political power of Oglethorpe and the trustees. As a result, newcomers to the region generally preferred to settle in South Carolina, where there were fewer restrictive laws.

Oglethorpe (whom some residents of Georgia began addressing rhetorically as "our perpetual dictator") at first bitterly resisted the demands of the settlers for social and political reform. But over time, he wearied of the conflict in the colony and grew frustrated at its failure to grow. He also suffered military disappointments, such as a 1740 assault on the Spanish outpost at St. Augustine, Florida, that ended in failure. Oglethorpe, now disillusioned with his American venture, began to loosen his grip. Even before the 1740 defeat, the trustees had removed the limitation on individual landholdings. In 1750, they removed the ban on slavery. A year later they ended the prohibition of rum and returned control of the colony to the king, who immediately permitted the summoning of a representative assembly. Georgia continued to grow more slowly than the other southern colonies, but in other ways it now developed along lines roughly similar to those of South Carolina. By 1770, there were over 20,000 non-Indian residents of the colony, nearly half of them African slaves.

THE DEVELOPMENT OF EMPIRE

The English colonies in America had originated as quite separate projects, and for the most part they grew up independent of one another. But by the mid-seventeenth century, the growing commercial success of the colonial ventures was producing pressure in England for a more rational, uniform structure to the empire.

The Drive for Reorganization

Imperial reorganization, many people in England claimed, would increase the profitability of the colonies and the power of the English government to supervise them. Above all, it would contribute to the success of the mercantile system, the foundation of the English economy. Colonies would provide a market for England's manufactured goods and a source of supply for raw materials it could not produce at home, thus promoting the principal goal of the mercantile system—increasing the total wealth of the nation. But for the new possessions truly to promote mercantilist

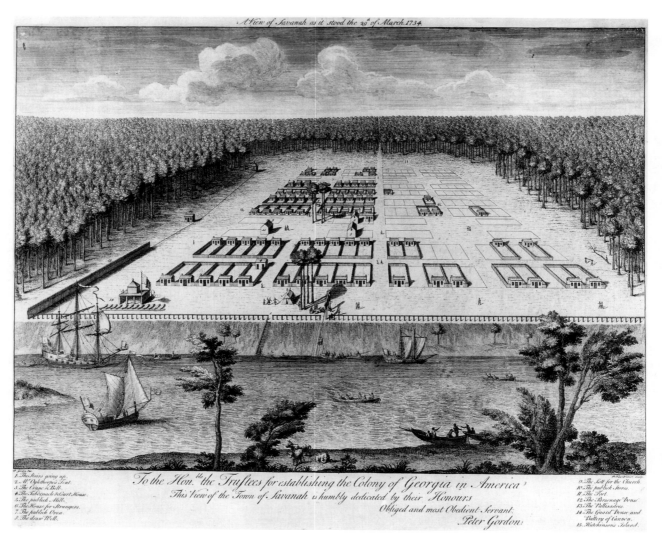

A View of Savanah as it stood the 29ᵗʰ of March 1734

To the Honᵇˡᵉ the Trustees for establishing the Colony of Georgia in America
This View of the Town of Savanah is humbly dedicated by their Honours
Obliged and most Obedient Servant.
Peter Gordon.

SAVANNAH IN 1734
This early view of the English settlement at Savannah by an English artist shows the intensely orderly character of Georgia in the early moments of European settlement there. As the colony grew, its residents gradually abandoned the rigid plan created by Georgia's founders. *(I.N. Phelps Stokes Collection of American Historical Prints, New York Public Library)*

goals, England would have to exclude foreigners (as Spain had done) from its colonial trade. According to mercantilist theory, any wealth flowing to another nation could come only at the expense of England itself. Hence the British government sought to monopolize trade relations with its colonies.

In theory, the mercantile system offered benefits to the colonies as well by providing them with a ready market for the raw materials they produced and a source for the manufactured goods they did not. But some colonial goods were not suitable for export to England, which itself produced wheat, flour, and fish and had no interest in obtaining them from America. Colonists also found it more profitable at times to trade with the Spanish, French, or Dutch even in goods that England did import. Thus, a considerable trade soon developed between the English colonies and non-English markets.

For a time, the English government made no serious efforts to restrict this challenge to the principles of mercantilism, but gradually it began passing laws to regulate colonial trade. During Oliver Cromwell's "Protectorate," in 1650 and 1651, Parliament passed laws to keep Dutch ships out of the English colonies. After the Restoration, the government of Charles II adopted three Navigation Acts designed to regulate colonial commerce even more strictly. The first of them, in 1660, closed the colonies to all trade except that carried in English ships. This law also required the colonists to export certain items, among them tobacco, only to England or English possessions. The second act, in 1663, provided that all goods being shipped from Europe to the colonies had to pass through England on the way; they could be subject to English taxation in the process. The third act, in 1673, was a response to the widespread evasion of the first two laws by the colonial shippers, who frequently left port claiming to be heading for another English colony but then sailed to a foreign port. It imposed duties on the coastal trade among the English colonies, and it provided for the appointment of customs officials to enforce the Navigation Acts. These acts formed the legal basis of England's mercantile system in America for a century.

The system created by the Navigation Acts had obvious advantages for England. But it had some advantages for the colonists as well. By restricting all trade to British ships, the laws encouraged the colonists (who were themselves legally British subjects) to create an important shipbuilding industry of their own. And because the English wanted to import as many goods as possible from their own colonies (as opposed to importing them from other, rival nations), they encouraged—and at times subsidized—the development of American production of goods they needed, among them iron, silk, and lumber. Despite the bitter complaints the laws provoked in America in the late seventeenth century, and the even more bitter conflicts they would help to provoke decades later, the system of the Navigation Acts served the interests of the British and the Americans alike reasonably well through most of the eighteenth century.

The Dominion of New England

Enforcement of the Navigation Acts required not only the stationing of customs officials in America, but the establishment of an agency in England to oversee colonial affairs. In 1679, Charles II attempted to increase his control over Massachusetts (which behaved at times as if its leaders considered it an independent nation) by stripping the colony of its authority over New

Hampshire and chartering a separate, royal colony there whose governor he would himself appoint. Five years later, after the Massachusetts General Court defied instructions from Parliament to enforce the Navigation Acts, he revoked the Massachusetts corporate charter and made it a royal colony.

Charles II's brother and successor, James II, who came to the throne in 1685, went much further. In 1686, he created a single Dominion of New England, which combined the government of Massachusetts with the governments of the rest of the New England colonies and, in 1688, with those of New York and New Jersey as well. He eliminated the existing assemblies within the new Dominion and appointed a single governor, Sir Edmund Andros, to supervise the entire region from Boston. Andros was an able administrator but a stern and tactless man; his rigid enforcement of the Navigation Acts, his brusque dismissal of the colonists' claims to the "rights of Englishmen," and his crude and arbitrary tactics made him quickly and thoroughly unpopular. He was particularly despised in Massachusetts, where he tried to strengthen the Anglican Church.

The "Glorious Revolution"

James II was not only losing friends in America; he was making powerful enemies in England by attempting to exercise autocratic control over Parliament and the courts. He was also appointing his fellow Catholics to high office, inspiring fears that he would try to reestablish Catholicism as England's official religion. By 1688, his popular support had all but vanished.

Until 1688, James's heirs were two daughters—Mary and Anne—both whom were Protestant. But in that year the king had a son and made clear that the boy would be raised a Catholic. Some members of Parliament were so alarmed that they invited the king's daughter Mary and her husband, William of Orange, ruler of the Netherlands and Protestant champion of Europe, to assume the throne. When William and Mary arrived in England with a small army, James II (perhaps remembering what had happened to his father, Charles I) offered no resistance and fled to France. As a result of this bloodless coup, which the English called "the Glorious Revolution," William and Mary became joint sovereigns.

When Bostonians heard of the overthrow of James II, they moved quickly to unseat his unpopular viceroy in New England. Andros managed to escape an angry mob, but he was arrested and imprisoned as he sought to flee the city dressed as a woman. The new sovereigns in England chose not to contest the toppling of Andros and quickly acquiesced in what the colonists

SIGNIFICANT EVENTS

1607 Jamestown founded

1609 Pilgrims flee to Holland from England

1612 Tobacco production established in Virginia

1619 First African workers arrive in Virginia

Virginia House of Burgesses meets for first time

1620 Pilgrims found Plymouth colony

1620s English colonization accelerates in the Caribbean

1622 Powhatan Indians attack English colony in Virginia

1624 Dutch establish settlement on Manhattan Island

1629 New Hampshire and Maine established

1630 Puritans establish Massachusetts Bay colony at Boston

1634 First English settlements founded in Maryland

1635 Roger Williams founds settlement in Rhode Island

1636 Connecticut colony founded

1637 Anne Hutchinson expelled from Massachusetts Bay colony

Pequot War fought

1638 Swedes and Finns establish New Sweden on the Delaware River

1642–1648 English Civil War

1644 Last major Powhatan uprisings against English settlers in Virginia

1649 Charles I executed

1655 Civil War in Maryland temporarily unseats Catholic proprietor

1660 English Restoration: Charles II becomes king

First Navigation Act passed

1663 Carolina colony chartered

Second Navigation Act passed

1664 English capture New Netherland

New Jersey chartered

1673 Third Navigation Act passed

1675–1676 King Philip's War in New England

1676 Bacon's Rebellion in Virginia

1681 William Penn receives charter for Pennsylvania

1685 James II becomes king

1686 Dominion of New England established

1688 Glorious Revolution in England: William and Mary ascend throne

1689 Glorious Revolution in America: rebellion breaks out against Andros in New England

Leisler leads rebellion in New York

1732 Georgia chartered

had, in effect, already done: abolishing the Dominion of New England and restoring separate colonial governments. They did not, however, accede to all the colonists' desires. In 1691, they combined Massachusetts with Plymouth and made it a royal colony. The new charter restored the General Court, but it gave the crown the right to appoint the governor. It also replaced church membership with property ownership as the basis for voting and officeholding and required the Puritan leaders of the colony to tolerate Anglican worship.

Andros had been governing New York through a lieutenant governor, Captain Francis Nicholson, who enjoyed the support of the wealthy merchants and fur traders of the province—the same groups who had dominated the colony for years. Other, less favored colonists—farmers, mechanics, small traders, and shopkeepers—had a long accumulation of grievances against both Nicholson and his allies. The leader of the New York dissidents was Jacob Leisler, a German immigrant and a prosperous merchant who had married into a prominent Dutch family but had never won acceptance as one of the colony's ruling class. Much like Nathaniel Bacon in Virginia, the ambitious Leisler chafed at his exclusion and eagerly grasped the opportunity to challenge the colonial elite. In May 1689, when news of the Glorious Revolution in England and the fall of Andros in Boston reached New York, Leisler raised a militia, captured the city fort, drove Nicholson into exile, and proclaimed himself the new head of government in New York. For two years, he tried in vain to stabilize his power in the colony amid fierce factional rivalry. In 1691, when William and Mary appointed a new governor, Leisler briefly resisted this challenge to his authority. Although he soon yielded, his hesitation allowed his many political enemies to charge him with treason. He and one of his sons-in-law were hanged, drawn, and quartered. Fierce rivalry between what became known as the "Leislerians" and the "anti-Leislerians" dominated the politics of the factious colony for many years thereafter.

In Maryland, many people erroneously assumed when they heard news of the Glorious Revolution that their proprietor, the Catholic Lord Baltimore, who was living in England, had sided with the Catholic James II and opposed William and Mary. So in 1689, an old opponent of the proprietor's government, John Coode, started a new revolt as head of an organization calling itself "An Association in Arms for the Defense of the Protestant Religion, and for Asserting the Right of King William and Queen Mary to the Province of Maryland and All the English Dominions." The insurgents drove out Lord Baltimore's officials. Through an elected convention, they chose a committee to run the government and petitioned the crown for a charter as a royal colony. In 1691, William and Mary complied, stripping the proprietor of his authority. The colonial assembly established the Church of England as the colony's official religion and forbade Catholics to hold public office, to vote, or even to practice their religion in public. Maryland became a proprietary colony again in 1715, but only after the fifth Lord Baltimore joined the Anglican Church.

As a result of the Glorious Revolution, the colonies revived their representative assemblies and successfully thwarted the plan for colonial unification. In the process, they legitimized the idea that the colonists had some rights within the empire, that the English government needed to consider their views in making policies that affected them. But the Glorious Revolution in America was not, as many Americans later came to believe, a clear demonstration of American resolve to govern itself or a clear victory for colonial self-rule. In New York and Maryland, in particular, the uprisings had more to do with local factional and religious divisions than with any larger vision of the nature of the empire. And while the insurgencies did succeed in eliminating the short-lived Dominion of New England, their ultimate results were governments that increased the crown's potential authority in many ways. As the first century of English settlement in America came to its end and as colonists celebrated their victories over arbitrary British rule, they were in fact becoming more a part of the imperial system than ever before.

SUGGESTED READINGS

General Histories. Charles M. Andrews, *The Colonial Period in American History*, 4 vols. (1934–1938). John E. Pomfret and F. M. Shumway, *Founding the American Colonies, 1583–1660* (1970). Clarence L. Ver Steeg, *The Formative Years, 1607–1763* (1964).

Jamestown. Philip L. Barbour, ed., *The Complete Works of Captain John Smith*, 3 vols. (1986); *The Three Worlds of Captain John Smith* (1964). Bradford Smith, *Captain John Smith* (1953). Alden T. Vaughn, *American Genesis* (1975).

The Chesapeake. T. H. Breen, *Tobacco Culture* (1985). T. H. Breen and Stephen Innes, *"Myne Owne Ground": Race and Freedom on Virginia's Eastern Shore, 1640–1676* (1980). Lois G. Carr and David W. Jordan, *Maryland's Revolution of Government,* *1689–1692* (1974). Wesley Frank Craven, *The Dissolution of the Virginia Company* (1932); *The Southern Colonies in the Seventeenth Century* (1949); *White, Red, and Black: The Seventeenth Century Virginian* (1971). David W. Jordan, *Foundations of Representative Government in Maryland, 1632–1715* (1988). Allan Kulikoff, *Tobacco and Slaves: The Development of Southern Cultures in the Chesapeake, 1680–1800* (1986). Aubrey Land et al., *Law, Society, and Politics in Early Maryland* (1977). Suzanne Lebsock, *A Share of Honour* (1984). Gloria L. Main, *Tobacco Colony: Life in Early Maryland, 1650–1720* (1982). Edmund S. Morgan, *American Slavery, American Freedom* (1975). Richard L. Morton, *Colonial Virginia*, 2 vols. (1960). James R. Perry, *The Formation of a Society on Virginia's Eastern Shore, 1615–1655* (1990). David B. Quinn, ed., *Early Maryland in a Wider World* (1982). Darrett B. and Anita H. Rutman, *A Place* *in Time* (1984). Fredrick F. Siegel, *The Roots of Southern Distinctiveness: Tobacco and Society in Danville, Virginia 1780–1865* (1987). Thad Tate and David L. Ammerman, eds., *The Chesapeake in the Seventeenth Century* (1979). Wilcomb E. Washburn, *The Governor and the Rebel* (1958).

The West Indies. Hilary M. Beckles, *White Servitude and Black Slavery in Barbados, 1627–1715* (1989). Richard S. Dunn, *Sugar and Slaves: The Rise of the Planter Class in the English West Indies, 1624–1713* (1972). Richard B. Sheridan, *Sugar and Slavery: An Economic History of the West Indies* (1973).

Plymouth and Massachusetts Bay. Bernard Bailyn, *The New England Merchants in the Seventeenth Century* (1955). William Bradford, *Of Plymouth Plantation* (1952). David Cressy, *Coming Over: Migration and Communication Between England and New England in the Seventeenth Century* (1987). William Cronon, *Changes in the Land: Indians, Colonists, and the Ecology of New England* (1983). John Demos, *A Little Commonwealth* (1970). George Langdon, *Pilgrim Colony* (1966). John Frederick Martin, *Profits in the Wilderness: Entrepreneurship and the Founding of New England Towns in the Seventeenth Century* (1991). Edmund S. Morgan, *The Puritan Dilemma: The Story of John Winthrop* (1958). Samuel Eliot Morison, *Builders of the Bay Colony* (1930). Darrett Rutman, *Winthrop's Boston* (1965). Alden T. Vaughn, *New England Frontier: Puritans and Indians* (1965). R. E. Wall, *Massachusetts Bay: The Crucial Decade, 1640–1650* (1972).

New England Puritanism. Sacvan Bercovitch, *The American Jeremiad* (1978); *The Puritan Origins of the American Self* (1975). Andrew Delbanco, *The Puritan Ordeal* (1989). Kai Erikson, *Wayward Puritans* (1966). Stephen Foster, *Their Solitary Way: The Puritan Social Ethic in the First Century of Settlement in New England* (1971); *The Long Argument: English Puritanism and the Shaping of New England Culture, 1570–1700* (1991). Edwin S. Gaustad, *Liberty of Conscience: Roger Williams in America* (1991). Philip F. Gura, *A Glimpse of Sion's Glory* (1984). David Hall, *The Faithful Shepherd* (1972); *Worlds of Wonder, Days of Judgement* (1989). Charles Hambrick-Stowe, *The Practice of Piety* (1982). J. V. James, *Colonial Rhode Island* (1975). M. J. A. Jones, *Congregational Commonwealth: Connecticut, 1636–1662* (1968). Paul R. Lucas, *Valley of Discord* (1976). Robert Middlekauff, *The Mathers* (1971). Perry Miller, *The New England Mind: The Seventeenth Century* (1939); *The New England Mind: From Colony to Province* (1953); *Orthodoxy in Massachusetts* (1933); *Errand into the Wilderness* (1956). Edmund S. Morgan, *Visible Saints* (1963); *The Puritan Family* (1966); *Roger Williams:*

The Church and the State (1967). Norman Pettit, *The Heart Prepared: Grace and Conversion in Puritan Spiritual Life* (1989). Kenneth Silverman, *The Life and Times of Cotton Mather* (1984). W. K. B. Stoever, *A Faire and Easy Way to Heaven* (1978). Harry S. Stout, *The New England Soul* (1986). Larzer Ziff, *Puritanism in America* (1973).

The Restoration Colonies. Thomas J. Archdeacon, *New York City, 1664–1710* (1976). Van Cleaf Bachman, *Peltries or Plantations* (1969). Patricia Bonomi, *A Factious People* (1971). Edwin B. Bronner, *William Penn's Holy Experiment* (1962). Kenneth Coleman, *Colonial Georgia* (1976). Thomas J. Condon, *New York Beginnings* (1968). Mary Maples Dunn, *William Penn: Politics and Conscience* (1967). Roger Ekirch, *Poor Carolina* (1981). Christopher Hill, *The World Turned Upside Down* (1972). Michael Kammen, *Colonial New York* (1975). James T. Lemmon, *The Best Poor Man's Country* (1972). Barry Levy, *Quakers and the American Family* (1988). H. T. Merrens, *Colonial North Carolina* (1964). Donna Merwick, *Possessing Albany, 1630–1710: The Dutch and English Experiences* (1990). Gary B. Nash, *Quakers and Politics: Pennsylvania, 1681–1726* (1968). J. E. Pomfret, *The Province of East and West New Jersey, 1609–1702* (1956); *The Province of East New Jersey* (1962). T. R. Reese, *Colonial Georgia: A Study in British Imperial Policy in the Eighteenth Century* (1963). Oliver A. Rink, *Holland on Hudson* (1986). Robert C. Ritchie, *The Duke's Province: A Study of New York Politics and Society, 1664–1691* (1977). M. E. Sirmans, *Colonial South Carolina* (1966). George L. Smith, *Religion and Trade in New Netherland* (1973). Alan Tully, *William Penn's Legacy* (1977). Clarence L. Ver Steeg, *Origins of a Southern Mosaic* (1975). Robert M. Weir, *Colonial South Carolina* (1983). Peter H. Wood, *Black Majority* (1974).

The Development of Empire. Viola Barnes, *The Dominion of New England* (1923). Thomas C. Barrow, *Trade and Empire* (1967). Lawrence Gipson, *The British Empire Before the American Revolution,* 15 vols. (1936–1970). Michael Hall, *Edward Randolph and the American Colonies* (1960). Lawrence Harper, *The English Navigation Laws* (1939). James Henretta, *Salutary Neglect* (1972). Richard R. Johnson, *Adjustment to Empire: The New England Colonies, 1675–1715* (1981). Michael Kammen, *Empire and Interest* (1970). Leonard Labaree, *Royal Government in America* (1964). David S. Lovejoy, *The Glorious Revolution in America* (1972). J. M. Sosin, *English America and the Revolution of 1688* (1982); and *English America and the Restoration Monarchy of Charles II* (1980). I. K. Steele, *The Politics of Colonial Policy* (1968). Stephen S. Webb, *The Governors-General* (1979); *1676: The End of American Independence* (1984).

THE AMERICAN ENVIRONMENT

THE OTHER PILGRIMS

T HE STORY OF THE Pilgrims and the first Thanksgiving remains one of the oldest and best known in American history. Schoolchildren still learn about the Pilgrims' flight from religious persecution in England, their efforts to make a new home at Plymouth, and their first celebration with their Indian neighbors to give thanks for their survival, as one of the great symbolic events of the American past.

But there is another pilgrim story that is much less familiar. The colonists at Plymouth, like those up and down the Atlantic seaboard, did not travel alone. Along with themselves and their worldly goods, they brought to North America a host of other organisms, plants, and animals that were familiar to Europeans but completely unknown to the Indians. The colonization of America was as much a biological invasion as a cultural one, and its long-term result was a subtle but radical transformation of the American landscape.

Most devastating to the Indians were the Old World diseases. Among these were the childhood illnesses—chicken pox, measles, mumps—that were so common in Europe as to be an expected part of growing up. Others were more serious epidemics like smallpox or debilitating illnesses like tuberculosis. All had been absent from North America, which meant that the Indians' immune systems were not equipped with antibodies that could defend against them. The area around Plymouth had experienced a mysterious European epidemic just three years before the Pilgrims arrived. The illness had depopulated the area's Indian villages. Sixteen years later, equally large numbers of Indians fell victims to a devastating smallpox epidemic. In Plymouth as in most parts of North America, Indian communities experienced population declines of 50 to 90 percent as a result of these epidemics, which would continue for centuries.

The disappearance of so many Indians was itself a profound change in the American landscape, but Indians who survived the epidemics soon helped European colonists bring about many other changes. Among the most important ecologically was the fur trade. Indian demand for trade goods encouraged tribes to hunt native animals much more intensively than before. Animal populations declined as hunting pressure increased, so much so that areas like New England had lost most of their large mammals within two centuries of the first settlements. By 1800, such animals as deer, moose, turkeys, and wolves had vanished from the lands around Plymouth, and were fast disappearing elsewhere as well.

Their departure made room for the domesticated grazing animals that colonists brought with them. Cattle, sheep, hogs, and horses were among the most important members of colonial society, furnishing such diverse items as meat, leather, milk, cheese, textile fibers, and animal power for doing work. Most of these animals had been entirely absent from Indian America. Increasing their livestock became one of the colonists' overriding goals. As the herds expanded, so did the colonists' need for new land. They cut down forests to create new pastures, which they planted with imported European species like clover and bluegrass. Wherever the animals grazed, they encouraged the spread of European weeds that thrived on disturbed soils. Thus dozens of plant migrants made their way to America and eventually became some of its most common in-

THE AMERICAN ENVIRONMENT

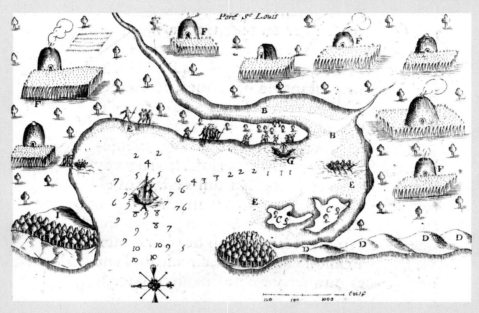

CHAMPLAIN'S MAP OF PLYMOUTH PLANTATION, 1605
When Samuel de Champlain visited Plymouth, Massachusetts, in 1605, he drew this map of the bay showing numerous Indian settlements in the vicinity. The many cornfields suggest what a prosperous community this was. Fifteen years later, when the Pilgrims arrived, most of these Indians would be dead from European diseases. *(Houghton Library, Harvard University)*

habitants: dandelions, stinging nettles, chickweeds, mulleins, and others. The Indians went so far as to call plantain "Englishman's foot" because of the way it sprang up wherever the Europeans settled or grazed animals.

Cattle and horses were critical to colonial agriculture because they made it possible to plant crops using plows. Indians had depended for their farming on hoes, which required more human labor and limited the amount of land that one person or family could tend. Although some of the crops the colonists planted with their plows were in fact Indian—corn being the most important—many were brought across the Atlantic as seeds. Wheat, rye, barley, and oats soon appeared in colonists' fields and quickly spread wherever the colonists went. Such grains furnished colonists with bread and helped feed their animals.

But not all colonial crops involved plows. In their gardens, colonial women used metal-edged hoes to tend vegetables and herbs that were a mixture of Indian and European crops. Cabbages, peas, and potatoes (a Caribbean plant reimported from Eu-

THE AMERICAN ENVIRONMENT

rope) lent variety to the colonial diet. Herbs added flavorings to otherwise bland meals, furnished medicines for healing, and supplied the color in homespun fabrics. In the orchards around their homesteads, colonists planted apples, pears, plums, cherries, and other fruit trees. From apples came one of the colonists' favorite beverages, cider, and from orchards generally came fresh fruit, preserves, and others sweeteners of colonial tables.

Everywhere, European migrants brought with them the species with which they were most familiar and on which they most depended for their livelihoods. To enable those plants and animals to thrive, colonists sought to re-create the ecological conditions under which they had lived on the other side of the Atlantic. Toward that end, they divided their lands into the familiar functional units of a peasant agricultural system: grain fields, pastures, hay meadows, woodlots, orchards, gardens, barnyards. They built

---

DOMESTICATED ANIMALS AT PLYMOUTH
Among the most important Eurasian species that colonists like the Pilgrims introduced to North America were domesticated grazing animals. Goats ate almost anything and supplied their owners with dairy products; horses, although rare at first, helped pull plows and wagons. Even more important to the colonists were cattle, pigs, and sheep. *(Plimoth Plantation Photo)*

THE AMERICAN ENVIRONMENT

fences to separate the places reserved for animals from the places where crops grew, lest the animals eat the crops. And so the fence—a construction almost entirely absent from Indian America—became for the colonists a symbol of "improvement," a sign that the landscapes of the New World were becoming more like those of the Old.

The changing landscape was in many ways a reproduction of the agricultural world they had left behind in England, and it was familiar precisely because it contained so many of the plants and animals that lay at the foundation of English society. When the Pilgrims celebrated their first November harvest, they were partly thanking their Indian neighbors for the corn and wild meat they had shared. But they gave thanks too for their own crops and animals, on which not just their survival but their sense of safety, familiarity, and home depended. Those other, nonhuman, pilgrims were in fact the foundation on which the whole of colonial society would be built. Without them, the English colonies would never have succeeded as they did.

DETAIL FROM *THE FISHING LADY*, C. 1750
This embroidered sampler depicts scenes of upper-class life in colonial New England. Its style reflects the continuing dominance of English culture in American life. *(Museum of Fine Arts, Boston)*

CHAPTER THREE

LIFE IN PROVINCIAL AMERICA

A S THE EUROPEAN AND African populations of North America grew, and as the economies of the colonies began to flourish, several distinctive ways of life emerged. The new American societies differed considerably from the society that many settlers had attempted to re-create in the New World—the society of England. They differed as well from one another.

There were many reasons for the divergence between the culture of the colonies and that of England. The physical environment was very different—vaster and less tamed. The population was more diverse as well. Beginning with the Dutch settlements in New York, the area that would become the United States was a magnet for immigrants from many lands other than England: Scotland, Ireland, the European continent. And beginning with the first importation of slaves into Virginia, English North America became the destination for thousands of forcibly transplanted Africans.

At least equally important, Europeans and Africans were interacting constantly with a native population that for many years outnumbered them. For all the efforts of the colonists to isolate themselves from Indian society and create a culture all their own, the European and Native American worlds could not remain entirely separate.

Just as the colonies were becoming increasingly different from England, so were they different from one another. Indeed, the pattern of society in some areas of North America seemed to resemble that of other ar-

eas scarcely at all. And although Americans would ultimately discover that they had enough in common to join together to form a single nation, these regional differences continued to affect their society well beyond the colonial period.

THE COLONIAL POPULATION

Not until long after the beginning of European colonization did Europeans and Africans in North America outnumber the native population. But after uncertain beginnings at Jamestown and Plymouth, the non-native population grew rapidly and substantially, through continued immigration and through natural increase, until by the late seventeenth century Europeans and Africans became the dominant population group along the Atlantic coast.

The Early Population

A few of the early English settlers were members of the upper classes—usually the younger sons of the lesser gentry, men who stood to inherit no land at home and aspired to establish estates for themselves in America. For the most part, however, the early English population was decidedly unaristocratic. It included some members of the emerging middle class, businessmen who migrated to America for religious or

AMERICA IN 1700

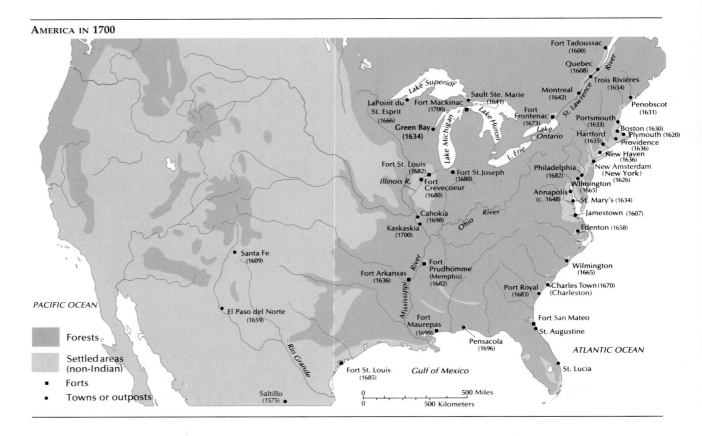

commercial reasons, or (like John Winthrop) both. But the dominant element was English laborers. Some came to the New World independently. The religious dissenters who formed the bulk of the population of early New England, for example, were men and women of modest means who arranged their own passage, brought their families with them, and established themselves immediately on their own land.

Others came as indentured servants. At least three-fourths of the immigrants to the Chesapeake in the seventeenth century, and a majority in the southern and mid-Atlantic colonies as a whole, arrived as indentures. The system of temporary servitude in the New World developed out of existing practices in England. Young men and women bound themselves to masters for a fixed term of servitude (usually four to five years). In return they received passage to America, food, and shelter. Upon completion of their terms of service, male indentures were supposed to receive such benefits as clothing, tools, and occasionally land; in reality, however, many left service without anything approaching adequate preparation or resources to begin earning livings on their own. Roughly one-fourth of the inden-

tures in the Chesapeake were women, most of whom worked as domestic servants and expected to marry when their terms of servitude expired. Because men greatly outnumbered women in the region in the seventeenth century, those expectations were nearly always fulfilled.

Most indentured servants came to the colonies voluntarily, but not all. Beginning as early as 1617, the English government occasionally dumped shiploads of convicts in America to be sold into servitude, although some criminals, according to Captain John Smith, "did chuse to be hanged ere they would go thither, and were." The government also transported prisoners taken in battles with the Scots and the Irish in the 1650s, as well as other groups deemed undesirable: orphans, vagrants, paupers, and those who were "lewd and dangerous." Other involuntary immigrants were neither dangerous nor indigent but simply victims of kidnapping, or "impressment," by aggressive and unscrupulous investors and promoters.

It was not difficult to understand why the system of indentured servitude proved so appealing to those in a position to employ servants in colonial America—

THE NON-INDIAN POPULATION OF THE COLONIES, 1700–1780

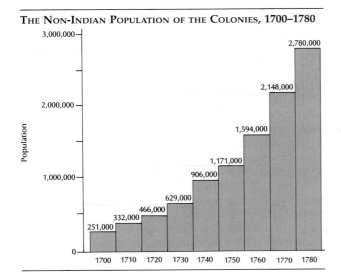

Indentured servitude remained an important source of population growth well into the eighteenth century, but beginning in the 1670s the flow began to decline substantially. A decrease in the English birth rate and an increase in English prosperity reduced the pressures on many men and women who might otherwise have considered emigrating. After 1700, those who did travel to America as indentured servants generally avoided the southern colonies, where working conditions were arduous and prospects for advancement were slim, and settled in the mid-Atlantic colonies, especially Pennsylvania and New York, where they could anticipate better opportunities. In the Chesapeake, landowners themselves began to find the indenture system less attractive, in part because they were facing challenges and competition from former servants. That was one reason for the increasing centrality of African slavery in the southern agricultural economy.

Birth and Death

At first, new arrivals in most colonies, whatever their background or status, could anticipate great hardship: inadequate food, frequent epidemics, and in an appalling number of cases, early death. Gradually, however, conditions of settlement improved enough to allow the population to begin to expand. By the end of the seventeenth century, the European population in the English colonies of North America had grown to over a quarter of a million.

Although immigration remained for a time the greatest source of population increase, the most important long-range factor in the growth of the colonial population was its ability to reproduce itself. Marked improvement in the reproduction rate began in New England and the mid-Atlantic colonies in the second half of the seventeenth century, and after the 1650s natural increase became the most important source of population growth there. The New England population more than quadrupled through reproduction alone in the second half of the seventeenth century. This was less a result of unusual fertility (families in England and in other colonies were probably equally fertile) than of exceptional longevity. Indeed, the life spans of residents of some areas of New England were nearly equal to those of people in the twentieth century. In the first generation of American-born colonists, according to one study, men who survived infancy lived to an average age of seventy-one, women to seventy. The next generation's life expectancy declined somewhat—to sixty-five for men who survived infancy—but remained at least ten years higher than the

particularly once it became clear, as it quickly did, that the Indian population could not easily be transformed into a servile work force. The indenture system provided a means of coping with the severe labor shortage in the New World. And in the Chesapeake, the headright system (by which masters received additional land grants for every servant they imported) offered another incentive. For the servants themselves, the attractions were not always so clear. Those who came voluntarily often did so to escape troubles in England; others came in the hope of establishing themselves on land or in trades of their own when their terms of service expired. Yet the reality usually differed sharply from the hope.

By the late seventeenth century, indentured servants had become one of the largest elements of the population. Some former indentures managed to establish themselves successfully as farmers, tradespeople, or artisans. Others (mostly males) found themselves without land, without employment, without families, and without prospects; and there grew up in some areas a large floating population of young single men—such as those who supported Bacon's Rebellion—who traveled restlessly from place to place in search of work or land and who were a potential (and at times actual) source of social unrest, particularly in the Chesapeake. Even those free laborers who did find employment or land and settled down with families often did not stay put for very long. The phenomenon of families simply pulling up stakes and moving to another, more promising location every several years was one of the most prominent characteristics of the colonial population.

English equivalent and approximately twenty years higher than life expectancy in the South. Scholars disagree on the reasons for these remarkable life spans, but contributing factors probably include the cool climate and the relatively disease-free environment it produced, clean water (a stark contrast to England in these years), and the absence of large population centers that might breed epidemics.

Conditions improved much more slowly in the South. The mortality rates in the Chesapeake region did not begin to match those elsewhere until nearly a hundred years later. Throughout the seventeenth century, the average life expectancy for men in the region was just over forty years, and for women slightly less. One in four children died in infancy, and fully half died before the age of twenty. The high death rate among adults meant that only about a third of all marriages lasted more than ten years; thus those children who survived infancy often lost one or both of their parents before reaching maturity. Widows, widowers, and orphans formed a substantial proportion of the Chesapeake population. The continuing ravages of disease (particularly malaria) and the prevalence of salt-contaminated water kept the death rate high in the South; only after the settlers developed immunity to the local diseases (a slow process known as "seasoning") did life expectancy increase significantly. Population growth was substantial in the region, but this was largely a result of immigration.

Natural increases in the population, wherever they occurred, were in large part a result of a steady improvement in the sex ratio through the seventeenth century. In the early years of settlement, more than three-quarters of the white population of the Chesapeake consisted of men. And even in New England, which from the beginning had attracted more families (and thus more women) than the southern colonies, 60 percent of the inhabitants in 1650 were male. Gradually, however, more women began to arrive in the colonies; and increasing birth rates, which of course produced roughly equal numbers of males and females, contributed to shifting the sex ratio as well. Not until well into the eighteenth century did the ratio begin to match that in England (where women were a slight majority), but by the late seventeenth century, the proportion of males to females in all the colonies was becoming more balanced.

Women and Families in the Chesapeake

The importance of reproduction in the labor-scarce society of seventeenth-century America had significant effects on both the status and the life cycles of women.

The high sex ratio meant that few women remained unmarried for long. The average European woman in America married for the first time at twenty or twenty-one years of age, considerably earlier than in England; in some areas of the Chesapeake, the average bride was three to four years younger.

In the Chesapeake, the most important factor in shaping the structure of families and the role of women remained, until at least the mid-eighteenth century, the extraordinarily high mortality rate. Under those circumstances, the traditional patriarchal family structure of England—by which husbands and fathers exercised firm, even dictatorial control over the lives of their wives and children—was difficult to maintain. Because so few families remained intact for long, rigid patterns of familial authority were constantly undermined. Sexual mores were also more flexible than in England or other parts of America. Because of the large numbers of indentured servants who were forbidden to marry until their terms of service expired, premarital sexual relationships were frequent. Female servants who became pregnant before the expiration of their terms could expect harsh treatment: heavy fines, whippings if no one could pay the fines, an extra year or two of service added to their contract, and loss of their children after weaning. Bastard children were themselves bound out as indentures at a very early age. On the other hand, a pregnant woman whose term of service expired before the birth of her child or whose partner was able to buy her remaining time from her master might expect to marry quickly. Over a third of Chesapeake marriages occurred with the bride already pregnant.

Women in the Chesapeake could anticipate a life consumed with childbearing. The average wife became pregnant every two years. Those who lived long enough bore an average of eight children apiece (up to five of whom typically died in infancy or early childhood). Since childbirth was one of the most frequent causes of female death, few women survived to see all their children grow to maturity.

For all the hardships women encountered in the seventeenth-century South, they also enjoyed more power and a greater level of freedom than women in other areas (or than southern women in later years). Because men were plentiful and women scarce, females had considerable latitude in choosing husbands. (They also often had no fathers or other male relatives nearby trying to control their choices.) Because women generally married at a much younger age than men, they also tended to outlive their husbands (even though female life expectancy was somewhat shorter than male). Widows were generally left with several children and with responsibility for managing a farm or plantation, a circumstance of enormous hardship but one that also gave them significant economic power.

Widows seldom remained unmarried for long, however. Those who had no grown sons to work the tobacco farms and plantations had particular need for male assistance, and marriage was the surest way to secure it. Since many widows married men who were themselves widowers, complex combinations of households were frequent. With numerous stepchildren, half brothers, and half sisters living together in a single household, women often had to play the role of peacemaker—a role that may have further enhanced their authority within the family.

The high mortality rate in the seventeenth-century Chesapeake also created large numbers of orphans, many with no property and no extended family on which to rely. Much earlier than in England or in the northern American colonies, therefore, Maryland and Virginia created special courts and other institutions to protect and control orphaned children.

By the early eighteenth century, the demographic character of the Chesapeake was beginning to change, and with it the nature and structure of the typical family. Life expectancy was increasing, and indentured servitude was in decline. Hence natural reproduction was becoming the principal source of white population increase. The sex ratio was becoming more equal. One result of these changes was that life for white people in the region became less perilous and less arduous. Another result was that women lost some of the power that their small numbers had once given them. As families grew more stable, traditional patterns of male authority revived. By the mid-eighteenth century, southern families were becoming highly patriarchal.

Women and Families in New England

In New England, where many more immigrants arrived with family members and where death rates declined far more quickly, family structure was much more stable than in the Chesapeake and hence much more traditional. Because the sex ratio was reasonably balanced, most men could expect to marry. But women remained in the minority; as in the Chesapeake, they married young, began producing children early, and continued to do so well into their thirties. In contrast to the South, however, northern children were more likely to survive (the average family raised six to eight children to maturity), and their families were more likely to remain intact. Fewer New England women

A Boston Woman and Her Baby, c. 1674
This oil portrait by an unknown Boston artist is of Elizabeth Freake and her daughter Mary. The lives of most New England women in the seventeenth century were largely consumed by childbearing and child rearing, although women also performed other important functions in the home-centered economies of the time. *(Worcester Art Museum)*

became widows, and those who did generally lost their husbands later in life. Hence women were less often cast in roles independent of their husbands. Young women, moreover, had less control over the conditions of marriage, both because there were fewer unmarried men vying for them and because their fathers were more often alive and able to exercise control over their choice.

Among other things, increased longevity meant that, unlike in the Chesapeake (where three-fourths of all children lost at least one parent before the age of twenty-one), parents in New England usually lived to see their children and even their grandchildren grow to maturity. Still, the lives of most New England women were nearly as consumed by childbearing and child rearing as those of women in the Chesapeake. Even women who lived into their sixties spent the vast majority of their mature years with young children in the home.

The longer lives in New England also meant that parents continued to control their children far longer than did parents in the South. Although they were less likely than parents in England actually to "arrange" marriages for their children, few sons and daughters could choose spouses entirely independent of their parents' wishes. Men usually depended on their fathers for land to cultivate—generally a prerequisite for beginning families of their own. Women needed dowries from their parents if they were to hope to attract desirable husbands. Stricter parental supervision of children meant, too, that fewer women became pregnant before marriage than in the South (although even in Puritan New England the premarital pregnancy rate was not insubstantial—as high as 20 percent in some communities).

For New Englanders more than for residents of the Chesapeake, family relationships and the status of women were defined in part by religious belief. In the South, established churches were relatively weak. But in New England the Puritan church was a powerful institutional and social presence. In theory, the Puritan belief that men and women were equal before God and hence equally capable of interpreting the Bible created possibilities for women to emerge as spiritual leaders. But in reality, religious authority remained securely in the hands of men, who used it in part to reinforce a highly patriarchal view of society. The case of Anne Hutchinson—a woman who became an important religious figure only to be disciplined and expelled by the male church hierarchy—is an example of both the possibilities and the limits of female spiritual power.

Puritanism placed a high value on the family, which was not only the principal economic unit but the principal religious unit within every community. In one sense, then, Puritan women played important roles within their families because their culture valued the position of wife and mother. At the same time, however, Puritanism reinforced the idea of nearly absolute male authority and the assumption of female weakness and inferiority. Women were expected to be modest and submissive. (Such popular girls' names as Prudence, Patience, Chastity, and Comfort suggest something about Puritan expectations of female behavior.) A wife was expected to devote herself almost entirely to serving the needs of her husband and household.

Women were of crucial importance to the New England agricultural economy. Not only did they bear and raise children who at relatively young ages became part of the work force, but they themselves were continuously engaged in tasks vital to the functioning of the farm—gardening, raising poultry, tending cattle, spinning, and weaving, as well as cooking, cleaning, and washing. Northern women also played an important role in influencing the spending of family resources. Homes in New England were larger, better built, and more comfortably furnished than those in the southern colonies. Given the Puritan definition of the home as the woman's sphere, it is reasonable to assume that wives and mothers were in part responsible.

While family life in the Chesapeake colonies grew more patriarchal in the late seventeenth and early eighteenth centuries, New England families were growing somewhat less so. As settlement spread beyond the early Puritan centers, as the authority of the church began gradually to decline, and as sons began increasingly to chafe under the control of their fathers, family life became somewhat more fluid—although only by the rigid standards of seventeenth-century New England. Patriarchal forms remained dominant, and the status of women remained intimately bound to their roles as wives and mothers.

The Beginnings of Slavery in British America

There was a demand for black servants to supplement the always-scarce southern labor supply from very near the beginning of European settlement, and the demand grew rapidly once tobacco cultivation became a staple of the Chesapeake economy. But the supply of African laborers was limited during much of the seventeenth century, because the Atlantic slave trade did not at first serve the English colonies in America. Portuguese slavers, who had dominated the trade since the sixteenth century, shipped captive men and women from the west coast of Africa to the new European colonies in South America and the Caribbean. Gradually, however, Dutch and French navigators joined the slave trade. A substantial commerce in slaves grew up within the Americas, particularly between the Caribbean islands and the southern colonies of English America. By the late seventeenth century, the supply of black workers in North America was becoming plentiful.

As the commerce in slaves grew more extensive and more sophisticated, it also grew more horrible. Before it ended in the nineteenth century, it was responsible for the forced immigration of as many as 11 million Africans to North and South America and the Carib-

AFRICANS BOUND FOR AMERICA
Shown here are the below-deck slave quarters of a Spanish vessel en route to the West Indies. A British warship captured the slaver, and a young English naval officer (Lt. Francis Meynell) made this watercolor sketch on the spot. The Africans seen in this picture appear somewhat more comfortable than prisoners on some other slave ships, who were often chained and packed together so tightly that they had no room to stand or even sit. *(National Maritime Museum, London)*

bean. (Until the late eighteenth century, the number of African immigrants to the Americas was higher than that of Europeans.) Native chieftains captured members of enemy tribes in battle, tied them together in long lines, or "coffles," and sold them in the flourishing slave marts on the African coast. Then, after some haggling on the docks between the European traders and the African suppliers, the terrified victims were packed into the dark, filthy holds of ships for the horrors of the "middle passage"—the journey to America. For weeks, sometimes even months, the black prisoners were kept chained in the bowels of the slave ships. Conditions varied from one ship to another. Some captains took care to see that their potentially valuable cargo remained reasonably healthy. Others accepted the deaths of numerous Africans as inevitable and tried to cram as many as possible into their ships to ensure that enough would survive to yield a profit at journey's end. On such ships, the African prisoners were sometimes packed together in such close quarters that they were unable to stand, hardly able to breathe. Some ships supplied them with only minimal food and water. Women were often victims of rape and other sexual abuse. Those who died en route were simply thrown overboard. Upon arrival in the New World, slaves were auctioned off to white landowners and transported, frightened and bewildered, to their new homes.

The first black laborers arrived in English North America before 1620, and as English seamen began to establish themselves in the slave trade, the flow of Africans to the colonies gradually increased. But North America was always a much less important market for Africans than other parts of the New World, especially the islands of the Caribbean and Brazil, whose labor-intensive sugar economies created a large demand for slaves. Fewer than 5 percent of the blacks imported to the Americas arrived initially in the English colonies on the mainland. In the beginning, those blacks who did end up in what became the United States came not directly from Africa, but from the West Indies. Not until the 1670s did traders start importing blacks directly from Africa to North America. Even then, however, the flow remained small for a time, mainly because a single group, the Royal African Company of England, maintained a monopoly on the trade and managed as a result to keep prices high and supplies low.

A turning point in the history of the African population in North America came in the mid-1690s, when the Royal African Company's monopoly was finally broken. With the trade now opened to English and colonial merchants on a competitive basis, prices fell and the number of Africans arriving in North America greatly increased. By the end of the century, about 25,000 slaves lived in the English colonies. That was approximately 10 percent of the population, but because Africans were so heavily concentrated in a few southern colonies, they were already beginning to outnumber Europeans in some areas. The high ratio of men to women among African immigrants (there

THE BLACK POPULATION, 1620–1780

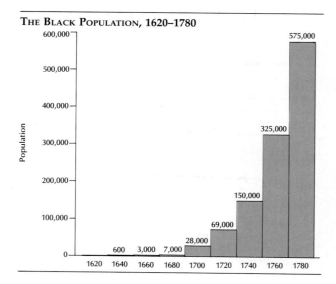

were perhaps two males to one female in most areas) retarded the natural increase of the black population. But in the Chesapeake at least, more new slaves were being born by 1700 than were being imported from Africa. In South Carolina, by contrast, the arduous conditions of rice cultivation ensured that the black population would barely be able to sustain itself through natural increase until much later.

Between 1700 and 1760, the number of Africans in the colonies increased tenfold to approximately a quarter of a million. A relatively small number (16,000 in 1763) lived in New England; there were slightly more (29,000) in the middle colonies. The vast majority, however, continued to live in the South. By then the flow of free white laborers to that region had all but stopped, and blacks had become securely established as the basis of the southern work force.

It was not entirely clear at first that the status of black laborers in America would be fundamentally different from that of white indentured servants. In the rugged conditions of the seventeenth-century South, it was often difficult for Europeans and Africans to maintain strictly separate roles. In some areas—South Carolina, for example, where the number of African arrivals swelled more quickly than anywhere else—whites and blacks lived and worked together for a time on terms of relative equality. Some blacks were treated much like white hired servants, and some were freed after a fixed term of servitude. A few Africans themselves became landowners, and some apparently owned slaves of their own.

But by the early eighteenth century, a rigid distinction had become established between black and white. (See "Where Historians Disagree," pp. 72–73.) Masters were contractually obliged to free white servants after a fixed term of servitude. There was no such necessity to free black workers, and the assumption slowly spread that blacks would remain in service permanently. Another incentive for making the status of Africans rigid was that the children of slaves provided white landowners with a self-perpetuating labor force.

White assumptions about the inferiority of people of color contributed further to the growing rigidity of the system. Most whites considered Africans a lesser breed, capable of little more than manual labor. Indeed, many whites convinced themselves that they were actually helping the Africans by "civilizing" and Christianizing them; conversion to Christianity did not, however, entitle slaves to freedom. Assumptions of racial inferiority came naturally to the English settlers. Whites had already defined themselves as a superior race in their relations with the native Indian population. The idea of subordinating a supposedly inferior race was, therefore, already established in the European imagination by the time substantial numbers of Africans appeared in America.

In the early eighteenth century, colonial assemblies began to pass "slave codes," limiting the rights of blacks in law and ensuring almost absolute authority to white masters. One factor, and one factor only, determined whether a person was subject to the slave codes: color. And in contrast to the colonial societies of Spanish America, where people of mixed race were granted a different (and higher) status than pure Africans, English America recognized no such distinctions. Any African ancestry was enough to classify a person as black.

Changing Sources of European Immigration

The diverse character of the American population was a result of the mingling of the English with Indians and Africans. But it was also a result of substantial immigration from other parts of Europe. By the early eighteenth century, the flow of immigrants from England itself began to decline substantially—a result of better economic conditions there and of new government restrictions on emigration in the face of massive depopulation in some regions of the country. But as English immigration declined, French, German, Swiss, Irish, Welsh, Scot, and Scandinavian immigration continued and increased.

The earliest, although not the most numerous, of these non-English European immigrants were the

DOMINANT IMMIGRANT GROUPS IN COLONIAL AMERICA, c. 1760

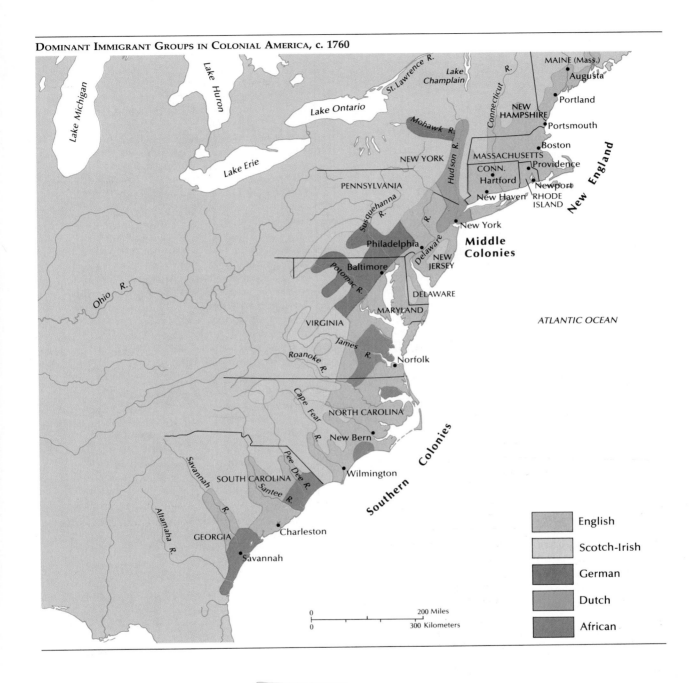

French Calvinists, or Huguenots. The Edict of Nantes of 1598 had granted them liberties and privileges that enabled them to constitute practically a state within the state in Roman Catholic France. In 1685, however, the French government revoked the edict. Soon thereafter, the Huguenots began leaving the country. A total of about 300,000 left France in the following decades; a small proportion of them traveled to the English colonies in North America.

Many German Protestants suffered similarly from the arbitrary religious policies of their rulers; and all Germans, Catholics as well as Protestants, suffered from the devastating wars between their principalities and King Louis XIV of France (the "Sun King"). The

WHERE HISTORIANS DISAGREE

THE ORIGINS OF SLAVERY

THE DEBATE AMONG HISTORIANS over how and why white Americans created a system of slave labor in the seventeenth century—and how and why they determined that people of African descent and no others should populate that system—has been an unusually lively one. At its center is the question of whether slavery was a result of white racism or helped to cause it.

In 1950, Oscar and Mary Handlin published an influential article, "Origins of the Southern Labor System," which noted that many residents of the American colonies (and of England) lived in varying degrees of "unfreedom" in the seventeenth century, although none resembling slavery as it came to be known in America. The first Africans who came to America lived for a time in conditions not very different from those of white indentured servants. But slavery came ultimately to differ substantially from other conditions of servitude. It was permanent bondage, and it passed from one generation to the next. That it emerged in America, the Handlins argued, resulted from efforts by colonial legislatures to increase the available labor force. White laborers needed an incentive to come to America; black laborers, forcibly imported from Africa, did not. The distinction between the conditions of white workers and the conditions of black workers was, therefore, based on legal and economic motives, not on racism. Racism emerged to justify slavery; it did not cause slavery.

In 1959, Carl Degler became the first of a number of important historians to challenge the Handlins. In his essay "Slavery and the Genesis of American Race Prejudice," he argued that blacks had never been like other servants in the Chesapeake; "the Negro was actually *never* treated as an equal of the white man, servant or free." Racism was strong "long before slavery had come upon the scene." It did not result from slavery, but helped cause it. Nine years later, Winthrop D. Jordan argued similarly that white racism, not economic or legal conditions, produced slavery. In *White Over Black* (1968) and other, earlier writings, Jordan argued that Europeans had long viewed people of color—and black Africans in particular—as inferior beings appropriate for serving whites. Those attitudes migrated with white Europeans to the New World, and white racism shaped the treatment of Africans in America—and the nature of the slave labor system—from the beginning.

George Frederickson has echoed Jordan's emphasis on the importance of racism as an independent factor reinforcing slavery; but unlike Jordan, he has argued that racism did not precede slavery. "The treatment of blacks," he wrote, "engendered a cultural and psycho-social racism that after a certain point took on a life of its own . . . . Racism, although the child of slavery, not

---

Rhineland of southwestern Germany, the area known as the Palatinate, experienced particular hardships. Its proximity to France exposed its people to slaughter and its farms to ruin at the hands of invaders. And the unusually cold winter of 1708–1709 dealt a final blow to the precarious economy of the region. More than 12,000 Palatinate Germans sought refuge in England, and approximately 3,000 of them soon found their way to America. They arrived in New York and tried at first to make homes in the Mohawk Valley, only to be ousted by the powerful landlords of the region. Some of the Palatines moved farther up the Mohawk, out of reach of the patroons; but most made their way to Pennsylvania, where they received a warm welcome (and where they ultimately became known to English settlers as the "Pennsylvania Dutch," a corruption of "Deutsch"). After that, the Quaker colony became the most common destination of Germans, who sailed for America in growing numbers. (Among them were Moravians and Mennonites, with religious views similar to those of the Quakers.) Many German Protestants went to North Carolina as well, especially after

WHERE HISTORIANS DISAGREE

only outlived its parent but grew stronger and more independent after slavery's demise."

Peter Wood's *Black Majority* (1974), a study of seventeenth-century South Carolina, moved the debate back away from racism and toward social and economic conditions. Wood demonstrated that blacks and whites often worked together on relatively equal terms in the early years of settlement. But as rice cultivation expanded, finding white laborers willing to do the arduous work became more difficult. The forcible importation of African workers, and the creation of a system of permanent bondage, was a response to a growing demand for labor and to fears among whites that without slavery a black labor force would be difficult to control. Similarly, Edmund Morgan's *American Slavery American Freedom* (1975) argued that the southern labor system was at first relatively flexible and later grew more rigid. In colonial Virginia, he claimed, white settlers did not at first intend to create a system of permanent bondage. But as the tobacco economy grew and created a high demand for cheap labor, white landowners began to feel uneasy about their dependence on a large group of dependent white workers, since such workers were difficult to recruit and control. Thus slavery was less a result of racism than of the desire for whites to find a reliable and stable labor force. Racism, Morgan contended, was a result of slavery, an ideology created to justify a system that had been developed to serve other needs. And David Brion

Davis, in *The Problem of Slavery in the Age of Revolution* (1975), argued that while prejudice against blacks had a long history, racism as a systematic ideology was the invention of the American Revolution—part of the effort to explain the paradox of slavery existing in a republic committed to individual freedom.

The debate continues. Alden Vaughan, in a 1989 essay "The Origins Debate," called racism a "necessary precondition" for the emergence of slavery in America. White Virginians enslaved Africans for many reasons; but among those reasons was their belief "that Africans were an inherently inferior branch of humankind, suited by their God-given characteristics and the circumstances of their arrival in America to be slaves forever." Barbara Fields, in "Slavery, Race and Ideology in the United States of America" (1990) sharply disagreed. Racism cannot be an independent cause of anything, she argues; "race" itself is a biologically meaningless concept, and racism, therefore, is simply an ideology invented to reinforce some other human endeavor. An ideology cannot "take on a life of its own," she argued. It "must be constantly created and verified in social life." Like Davis, she concludes that racism in the United States was not an ideology (and hence not a cause of slavery) until the American Revolution.

---

the founding of New Bern in 1710 by a company of 600 German-speaking Swiss.

The most numerous of the newcomers were the so-called Scotch-Irish—Scottish Presbyterians who had settled in northern Ireland (in the province of Ulster) in the early seventeenth century. The Ulster colonists had prospered for a time despite the barren soil and the constant, never wholly successful struggle to suppress the Catholic natives. But in the first years of the eighteenth century, Parliament prohibited Ulster from exporting to England the woolens and other

products that had become the basis of the northern Irish economy; at the same time, the English government virtually outlawed the practice of the Presbyterian religion in Ulster and insisted on conformity with the Anglican church. After 1710, moreover, the long-term leases of many Scotch-Irish expired; English landlords doubled and even tripled the rents. Thousands of tenants embarked for America.

Often coldly received at the colonial ports, most of the Scotch-Irish pushed out to the edges of European settlement. There they occupied land without much regard for who actually claimed to own it, whether absentee whites, Indians, or the colonial governments. They believed that, as one colonist said "it was against the laws of God and nature that so much land should be idle while so many Christians wanted it to labor on and to raise bread." They were as ruthless in their displacement and suppression of the Indians as they had been with the native Irish Catholics.

Immigrants from Scotland itself and from southern Ireland added other elements to the colonial population. Scottish Highlanders, some of them Roman Catholics who had been defeated in rebellions in 1715 and 1745, immigrated into several colonies, North Carolina above all. Presbyterian Lowlanders, faced in Scotland with high rents in the country and unemployment in the towns, left for America in large numbers shortly before the American Revolution. The Irish migrated steadily over a long period, and by the time of the Revolution they were almost as numerous as the Scots, although less conspicuous. Many of them had by then abandoned their Roman Catholic religion and with it much of their ethnic identity.

Continuing immigration and natural increase contributed to a rapid population growth in the colonies in the eighteenth century. In 1700, the non-Indian population of the colonies totaled less than 250,000; by 1775, it was over 2 million—a nearly tenfold increase. Throughout the colonial period, the non-Indian population nearly doubled every twenty-five years.

THE COLONIAL ECONOMY

To those who remained in Europe, and even to some who settled in North America, the English colonies often appeared so isolated as to seem virtually at the end of the world. But from the beginning, almost all the colonies were commercial ventures and were tied in crucial ways to other economies. They developed substantial trade with the native population of North America, with the French settlers to the north, and, to a lesser extent, with Spanish colonists to the south and west. And over time they developed an even more substantial trade within the growing Atlantic economy of the sixteenth and seventeenth centuries, of which they became a critical part.

American colonists engaged in a wide range of economic pursuits. But except for a few areas in the West where the small white populations subsisted largely on the fur and skin trade with the Indians, farming dominated all areas of European and African settlement throughout the seventeenth and eighteenth centuries. Some farmers engaged in simple subsistence agriculture; but whenever possible American farmers attempted to grow crops for the local, intercolonial, and export markets.

The Southern Economy

In the Chesapeake region, tobacco early established itself as the basis of the economy. A strong European demand for the crop enabled some planters to grow enormously wealthy and at times allowed the region as a whole to prosper. But production frequently exceeded demand, and as a result the price of tobacco periodically suffered severe declines. The first major bust in the tobacco economy occurred in 1640, and the boom-and-bust pattern continued throughout the colonial period and beyond. Growing more tobacco only made the problem of overproduction worse, but Chesapeake farmers never understood that. Those planters who could afford to do so expanded their landholdings, enlarged their fields, and acquired additional laborers. After 1700, tobacco plantations employing several dozen slaves or more were common.

The staple of the economies of South Carolina and Georgia was rice production. By building dams and dikes along the low-lying coastline with its many tidal rivers, farmers managed to create rice paddies that could be flooded and then drained. Rice cultivation was arduous work, performed standing knee-deep in the mud of malarial swamps under a blazing sun, surrounded by insects. It was a task so difficult and unhealthful that white laborers generally refused to perform it. Hence the far greater dependence of planters in South Carolina and Georgia on slaves than was true of their northern counterparts. Yet it was not only because blacks could be compelled to perform these difficult tasks that whites found them so valuable. It was also because they were much better at the work than whites. They showed from the beginning a greater resistance than whites to malaria and other local diseases (although the impact of disease on black workers was by no means inconsiderable). And they proved more adept at performing the basic agricultural tasks required. That was in part because some of them had come from rice-producing regions of west Africa (a fact that has led some historians to argue that blacks were responsible for introducing rice cultivation to America in the early seventeenth century). It was also because most Africans were more accustomed to the hot and humid climate of the rice-growing regions than were the Europeans.

In the early 1740s, another staple crop contributed to the South Carolina economy: indigo. Eliza Lucas, a young Antiguan woman who managed her family's American plantations, experimented with cultivating the West Indian plant (which was the source of a blue dye in great demand in Europe) in America. She discovered that it could grow on the high ground of South Carolina that was unsuitable for rice planting, and that its harvest came while the rice was still growing. It became an important complement to rice and a popular import in England.

Because of the South's early dependence on large-scale cash crops, the southern colonies developed less of a commercial or industrial economy than the colonies of the North. The trading in tobacco and rice was handled largely by merchants based in London and, later, in the northern colonies. Few cities of more than modest size developed in the South. No substantial local merchant communities emerged. A pattern was established that would characterize the southern economy, and differentiate it from that of other regions, for more than two centuries.

The Northern Economy

The economies of the northern colonies—the settlements stretching from Pennsylvania into Maine—were more varied than those of their southern counterparts. In the North, as in the South, agriculture continued to dominate, but it was agriculture of a more diverse kind. In addition to farming, there gradually emerged an important commercial sector of the economy.

One reason why the Northern economy developed nonagricultural sectors was that conditions for farming were less favorable than in the South. In most of New England, in particular, colder weather and hard, rocky soil made it difficult for colonists to develop the kind of large-scale commercial farming system that southerners were creating. Instead, most settlers culti-vated relatively small areas of land, growing food, rais-ing animals, and in general attempting to serve their own families' needs. Modest cash crops—livestock, apples, and corn—enabled New Englanders to trade for those things they could not grow or make for them-selves. But most New Englanders did not produce a staple crop that could become a major export item.

Conditions for agriculture were far better in south-ern New England and the middle colonies, where the soil was fertile and the weather slightly more temper-ate. Farmers in New York, Pennsylvania, and the Con-necticut River valley cultivated staple crops for sale both at home and abroad. The region was the chief supplier of wheat to much of New England and to parts of the South. In Pennsylvania, in particular, Ger-man immigrants succeeded in greatly increasing pro-duction by applying methods of intensive cultivation they had practiced in Europe. The sex ratio in the Ger-man communities was relatively even, and women commonly worked alongside the men in the fields—a practice that other immigrant groups on occasion found appalling.

From time to time, entrepreneurs in New England and the middle colonies (particularly New Jersey and Pennsylvania) attempted to augment their agricultural economy with industrial enterprises. Many such ven-tures failed (beginning with an unsuccessful iron works in Saugus, Massachusetts, in the mid-seven-teenth century), but the colonists did manage to es-tablish a wide range of industrial activities on a mod-est scale. At the simplest level, almost every colonist engaged in a certain amount of industry at home. Women, in particular, were active in spinning, weav-ing, making soap and candles, and other tasks basic to the life of the family. Men engaged in carpentry. Oc-casionally these home industries provided families with goods they could trade or sell. Beyond these domestic efforts, craftsmen and artisans established themselves in colonial towns as cobblers, blacksmiths, rifle makers, cabinetmakers, silversmiths, and printers. In some areas, entrepreneurs harnessed the water power of the many streams and rivers to run small mills—some for grinding grain, others for processing cloth, still others for milling lumber. And in several places, large-scale shipbuilding operations began to flourish.

The largest industrial enterprise anywhere in Eng-lish North America was that of the German ironmas-ter Peter Hasenclever in northern New Jersey. Founded in 1764 with British capital, it employed several hun-dred laborers, many of them imported from ironworks in Germany. There were other, smaller ironmaking en-terprises in every northern colony (with particular con-centrations in Massachusetts, New Jersey, and Penn-sylvania), and in several of the southern colonies as well. But these and other growing industries did not become the basis for the kind of explosive industrial growth that Great Britain experienced in the late eigh-teenth century. That was in part because of restrictions such as those imposed by the Iron Act of 1750, a mea-sure passed by Parliament that barred the colonists from engaging in metal processing (and thus stifled the development of a steel industry in America). Sim-ilar prohibitions applied to the manufacture of woolens (the Woolen Act of 1699) and hats (the Hat Act of 1732), although Americans often disregarded such legisla-tion. The real obstacles to industrialization, however, were more basic: an inadequate labor supply, an in-adequate domestic market, and an inadequate infra-structure of transportation facilities, energy supplies, and other necessities. Americans would not overcome such obstacles until the mid-nineteenth century.

More important than manufacturing to the econ-omy of the northern colonies were industries that ex-ploited the natural resources of the continent. The flourishing fur trade of the first decades of settlement did not survive for long; by the mid-seventeenth cen-tury, the supply of fur-bearing animals along the At-lantic seaboard had been nearly exhausted, and the in-terior fur trade was largely in the hands of the Algonquins and their French allies. For the next cen-tury and more, the colonists relied instead on lumber-ing, which took advantage of the vast forests of the New World; mining, which exploited iron and other mineral reserves throughout the colonies; and fishing, particularly in the waters off the New England coast. These extractive industries provided what manufac-turing and agriculture often failed to give the north-ern colonists: commodities that could be exported to England in exchange for manufactured goods. And they helped, therefore, to produce the most distinctive feature of the northern economy: a thriving commer-cial class.

The Rise of Colonial Commerce

Perhaps the most remarkable feature of colonial com-merce in the seventeenth century was that it was able to survive at all. American merchants faced such be-wildering and intimidating obstacles, and lacked so many of the basic institutions of trade, that they man-aged to stay afloat only with great difficulty. There was, first, no commonly accepted medium of exchange. The colonies had almost no specie (gold or silver coins). They experimented at times with different forms of pa-

OVERSEAS TRADE DURING THE COLONIAL PERIOD

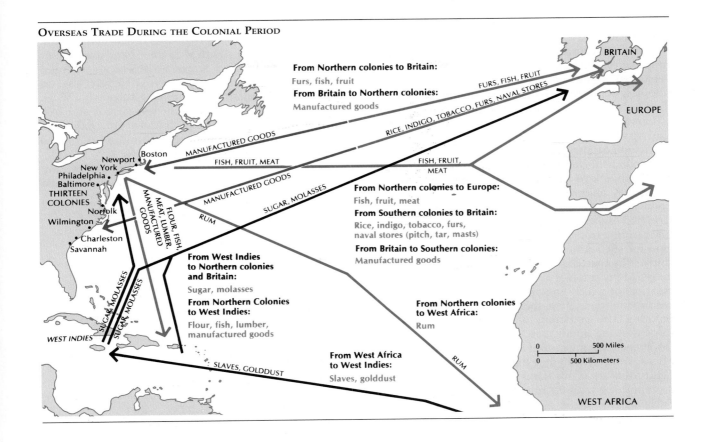

From Northern colonies to Britain:
Furs, fish, fruit

From Britain to Northern colonies:
Manufactured goods

From Northern colonies to Europe:
Fish, fruit, meat

From Southern colonies to Britain:
Rice, indigo, tobacco, furs, naval stores (pitch, tar, masts)

From Britain to Southern colonies:
Manufactured goods

From West Indies to Northern colonies and Britain:
Sugar, molasses

From Northern Colonies to West Indies:
Flour, fish, lumber, manufactured goods

From Northern colonies to West Africa:
Rum

From West Africa to West Indies:
Slaves, golddust

per currency—tobacco certificates, for example, which were secured by tobacco stored in warehouses; or land certificates, secured by property. Such paper was not, however, acceptable as payment for any goods from abroad; and it was in any case ultimately outlawed by Parliament. For many years, colonial merchants had to rely on a haphazard system of barter or on crude money substitutes such as beaver skins.

A second obstacle was the near impossibility of rationalizing trade. In the fragmented, jerry-built commercial world of colonial America, no merchants could be certain that the goods on which their commerce relied would be produced in sufficient quantity; nor could they be certain of finding adequate markets for them. Few channels of information existed to inform traders of what they could expect in foreign ports; vessels sometimes stayed at sea for several years, journeying from one market to another, trading one commodity for another, attempting to find some way to turn a profit. Engaged in this chaotic commerce, moreover, were an enormous number of small, fiercely competitive companies, which made the problem of rationalizing the system even more acute.

Despite these and other problems, commerce in the colonies not only survived but grew. There was an elaborate coastal trade, through which the colonies did business with one another and with the West Indies, largely in such goods as rum, agricultural products, meat, and fish. The mainland colonies received sugar, molasses, and slaves from the Caribbean markets in return. There was as well an expanding transatlantic trade, which linked the North American colonies in an intricate network of commerce with England, continental Europe, and the west coast of Africa. This commerce has often been described, somewhat inaccurately, as the "triangular trade," suggesting a neat process by which merchants carried rum and other goods from New England to Africa, exchanged their merchandise for slaves, whom they then transported to the West Indies (hence the term "middle passage" for the dread journey—it was the second of the three legs of the voyage), and then exchanged the slaves for sugar and molasses, which they shipped back to New England to be distilled into rum. In fact, the system was almost never so simple. The "triangular" trade in rum, slaves, and sugar was in fact a maze of highly diverse trade routes: between the northern and southern colonies, America and England, America and Africa, the West Indies and Europe, and other combinations.

Out of this complex and highly risky trade emerged a group of adventurous entrepreneurs who by the mid-eighteenth century were beginning to constitute a distinct merchant class. Concentrated in the port cities of the North (above all, Boston, New York, and Philadelphia), they enjoyed protection from foreign competition within the English colonies; the British Navigation Acts had excluded all non-British ships from the colonial carrying trade. They had access to a market in England for such American products as furs, timber, and ships. But that did not satisfy all their commercial needs. Many colonial products—fish, flour, wheat, and meat, all of which England could produce for itself—required markets altogether outside the British empire. Ignoring laws restricting colonial trade to England and its possessions, many merchants developed markets in the French, Spanish, and Dutch West Indies, where prices were often higher than in the British colonies. The profits from this commerce enabled the colonies to import the manufactured goods they needed from Europe.

In the course of the eighteenth century, the colonial commercial system began to stabilize. In some cities, the more successful merchants expanded their operations so greatly that they were able to dominate some sectors of trade and curb some of the destabilizing effects of competition. Merchants managed, as well, to make extensive contacts in the English commercial world, securing their positions in certain areas of transatlantic trade. But the commercial sector of the American economy remained open to newcomers, largely because it—and the society on which it was based—was expanding so rapidly.

PATTERNS OF SOCIETY

Although there were sharp social distinctions in the colonies, the well-defined and deeply entrenched class system of England failed to reproduce itself in America. In England, where land was scarce and the population large, the relatively small proportion of people who owned property had enormous power over the great majority who did not; the imbalance between land and population became a foundation of the English economy and the cornerstone of its class system. In America, the opposite was true. Land was abundant, and people were scarce. Aristocracies emerged there, to be sure. But they tended to rely less on landownership than on control of a substantial work force, and they were generally less secure and less powerful than their English counterparts. Far more than in England, there were opportunities in America for social mobility—both up and down.

There emerged, too, new forms of community whose structure reflected less the British model than

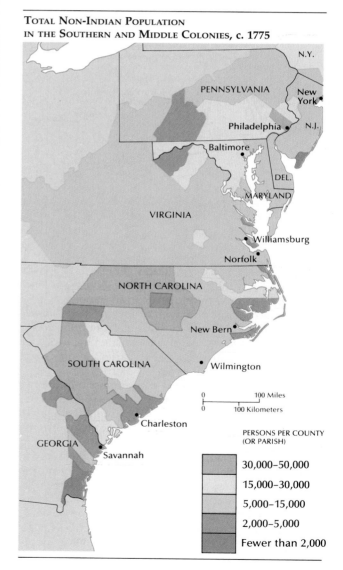

TOTAL NON-INDIAN POPULATION
IN THE SOUTHERN AND MIDDLE COLONIES, c. 1775

PERSONS PER COUNTY
(OR PARISH)

30,000–50,000

15,000–30,000

5,000–15,000

2,000–5,000

Fewer than 2,000

the realities of the American environment. These forms varied greatly from one region to another, but several basic—and distinctly American—types emerged.

The Plantation

The plantation defined a distinctive way of life for many white and black southerners that would survive, in varying forms, until the Civil War. The first plantations emerged in the early settlements of Virginia and Maryland, once tobacco became the economic basis of the Chesapeake.

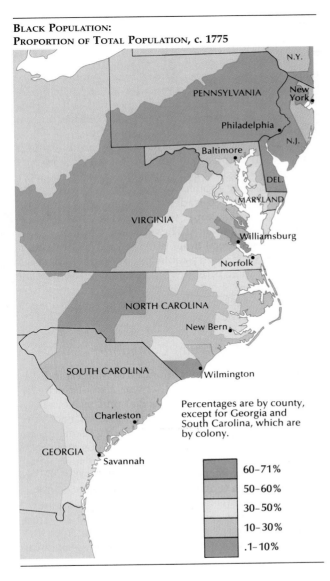

BLACK POPULATION:
PROPORTION OF TOTAL POPULATION, c. 1775

Percentages are by county, except for Georgia and South Carolina, which are by colony.

60–71%
50–60%
30–50%
10–30%
.1–10%

In a few cases, plantations were of enormous size—much like some of the great estates of England. The Maryland plantation of Charles Carroll of Carrollton, reputedly the wealthiest man in the colonies, covered 40,000 acres and contained 285 slaves. On the whole, however, seventeenth-century colonial plantations were rough and relatively small estates. In the early days in Virginia, they were little more than crude clearings on the edges of settlement, where landowners and indentured servants worked side by side in conditions so horrible that death was an everyday occurrence. Even in later years, when the death rate declined and the landholdings became more established, plantation work forces seldom exceeded thirty people. Most landowners lived in rough cabins or houses, with their servants or slaves nearby. Relatively few lived in anything resembling aristocratic splendor.

The economy of the plantation, like all agricultural economies, was a precarious one. In good years, successful growers could earn great profits and expand their operations. But since they could not control their markets, even the largest planters were constantly at risk. When prices for their crops fell—as tobacco prices did, for example, in the 1660s—they faced ruin.

Because plantations were often far from cities and towns—which were, in any case, relatively few in the South—they tended to become self-contained communities. Residents lived in close proximity to one another in a cluster of buildings that included the "great house" of the planter himself (a house that was usually, although not always, far from great), the service buildings, the barns, and the cabins of the slaves. Wealthier planters often created something approaching a full town on their plantations, with a school (for white children only), a chapel, and a large population. Smaller planters lived more modestly, but still in a relatively self-sufficient world.

On the larger plantations, the presence of a substantial slave work force altered not only the economic, but the family lives of the planter class. Plantation mistresses, unlike the wives of small farmers, could rely on servants to perform ordinary household chores and could thus devote more time to their husbands and children than their counterparts in other parts of colonial society. But there were also frequent sexual liaisons between their husbands or sons and black women of the slave community. Southern women generally learned to pretend not to notice these relationships, but they were almost certainly a source of anxiety and resentment. Black women, naturally, had even greater cause to resent such liaisons.

Southern society was highly stratified. Even though the fortunes of planters could rise and fall quickly, at any given time there were always wealthy landowners who exercised much greater social and economic influence than their less prosperous neighbors. Within given areas, great landowners not only controlled the lives of those who worked their own plantations but also the livelihoods of independent farmers who could not effectively compete with the wealthy planters and thus depended on them to market crops and receive credit. Independent farmers, working small plots of land with few or no slaves to help them, formed the majority of the southern agrarian population, but it was the planters who dominated the southern agrarian economy.

African slaves, of course, lived very differently. On the smaller farms with only a handful of slaves, there was not always a rigid social separation between whites and blacks. But by the mid-eighteenth century, over three-fourths of all blacks lived on plantations of at least ten slaves; nearly half lived in communities of fifty slaves or more. And in these larger establishments, Africans developed a society and culture of their own—influenced by their white masters, to be sure, but also partly independent of them.

Although whites seldom encouraged formal marriages among slaves, blacks themselves developed a strong and elaborate family structure. Slaves attempted to construct nuclear families, and they managed at times to build stable households, even to work together growing their own food in gardens provided by their masters. But such efforts were in constant jeopardy. Any family member could be sold at any time to another planter, even to one in another colony. As a result, the black family evolved along lines in many ways different from its white counterpart. Blacks placed special emphasis on extended kinship networks. They even created surrogate "relatives" for blacks separated entirely from their own families. They adapted themselves, in short, to difficult conditions over which they had limited control.

Blacks also developed languages of their own. In South Carolina, for example, the early slaves communicated with one another in Gullah, a hybrid of English and African tongues, that not only reinforced a sense of connection with their African ancestry but enabled them to engage in conversations their white masters could not understand. There emerged, too, a distinctive slave religion, which blended Christianity with African folklore and which became a central element in the emergence of an independent black culture.

Nevertheless, black society was subject to constant intrusions from and interaction with white society. Black house servants, for example, at times lived in what was, by the standards of slavery, great luxury; but they were also isolated from their own community and under constant surveillance from whites. Black women were subject to usually unwanted sexual advances from owners and overseers and hence to bearing mulatto children, who were rarely recognized by their white fathers but who were generally accepted as members of the slave community. On some plantations, black workers received kindness and even affection from their masters and mistresses and at times displayed genuine devotion in return. On others, they encountered physical brutality and occasionally even sadism, against which they were virtually powerless.

There were occasional acts of individual resistance by slaves against masters, and at least twice during the colonial period there were actual slave rebellions. In the most important such revolt, the so-called Stono Rebellion in South Carolina in 1739, about 100 blacks rose up, seized weapons, killed several whites, and attempted to escape south to Florida. Whites quickly crushed the uprising and executed most participants. The most frequent form of resistance was simply running away, but for most slaves that provided no real solution either. There was nowhere to go.

Most slaves, male and female, worked as field hands (with women shouldering the additional burdens of cooking and child rearing). But on the larger plantations that aspired to genuine self–sufficiency, some slaves learned trades and crafts: blacksmithing, carpentry, shoemaking, spinning, weaving, sewing, midwifery, and others. These skilled craftsmen and craftswomen were at times hired out to other planters. Some set up their own establishments in towns or cities and shared their profits with their owners. On occasion, they were able to buy their freedom. There was a small free black population living in southern cities by the time of the Revolution.

The Puritan Community

A very different form of community emerged in Puritan New England, but one that was also distinctively American. The characteristic social unit in New England was not the isolated farm, but the town. Each new settlement drew up a "covenant" among its members, binding all residents together in a religious and social commitment to unity and harmony. Some such settlements consisted of people who had immigrated to America together (occasionally, entire Puritan congregations who had traveled to the New World as a group). More often, they consisted of people who had met during their voyage or after their arrival in America.

The structure of the towns reflected the spirit of the covenant. Colonists laid out a village, with houses and

THE NEW ENGLAND TOWN: SUDBURY, MASSACHUSETTS, 17TH CENTURY

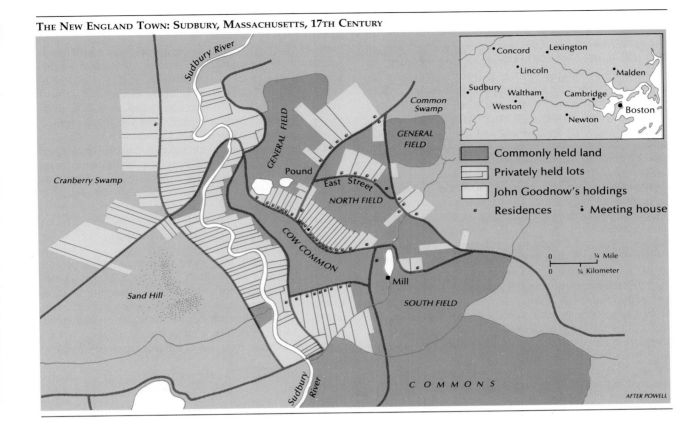

a meetinghouse arranged around a central pasture, or "common." They also divided up the outlying fields and woodlands of the town among the residents; the size and location of a family's field depended on the family's numbers, wealth, and social station. But wherever their lands might lie, families generally lived in the village with their neighbors close by, reinforcing the strong sense of community.

Once established, a town was generally able to run its own affairs, with little interference from the colonial government. Residents held a yearly "town meeting" to decide important questions and to choose a group of "selectmen," who governed until the next meeting. Only adult males were permitted to participate in the meeting. But even among them, important social distinctions remained, the most crucial of which was membership in the church. Only those residents who could give evidence of grace, of being among the elect (the "visible saints") assured of salvation, were admitted to full membership, although other residents of the town were still required to attend church services.

The English system of primogeniture—the passing of all property to the firstborn son—did not take root in New England. Instead, a father divided up his lands among all his sons. His control of this inheritance was one of the most effective means of exercising power over the male members of his family. Often a son would reach his late twenties before his father would allow him to move into his own household and work his own land. Even then, sons would usually continue to live in close proximity to their fathers. Young women were generally more mobile than their brothers, since they did not stand to inherit land; their dowries and their inheritances consisted instead of movable objects (furniture, household goods, occasionally money or precious objects) and thus did not tie them to a particular place.

The early Puritan community, in short, was a tightly knit society. The town as a whole was bound together by the initial covenant, by the centralized layout of the village, by the power of the church, and by the town meeting. The family was held together by the rigid patriarchal structure that limited opportunities for younger members (males in particular) to strike out on their own. Yet as the years passed and the communities grew, this communal structure experienced strains. This was partly because of the increasing commercialization of New England society. But it was also a result of other pressures that had been developing within even purely agricultural communities, pressures that were a result primarily of population growth.

As towns grew larger, residents tended to cultivate lands farther and farther from the community center and, by necessity, to live at increasing distances from the church. Often, groups of outlying residents would eventually apply for permission to build a church of their own, usually the first step toward creation of a wholly new town. Such applications were frequently the occasion for bitter quarrels between the original townspeople and those who proposed to break away.

The practice of distributing land through the patriarchal family structure also helped create tensions in the Puritan community. In the first generations, fathers generally controlled enough land to satisfy the needs of all their sons. After several generations, however, when such lands were being subdivided for the third or fourth time, there was often too little to go around, particularly in communities surrounded by other towns, with no room to expand outward. The result was that in many communities, groups of younger residents began breaking off and moving elsewhere—at

times far away—to form towns of their own where land was more plentiful.

Even within the family, economic necessity often undermined the patriarchal model to which most Puritans, in theory at least, subscribed. It was not only the sons who needed their fathers (as a source of land and wealth); fathers needed their sons, as well as their wives and daughters, as a source of labor to keep the farm and the household functioning. Thus, while in theory men had nearly dictatorial control over their wives and children, in reality relationships were more contractual, with patriarchal authority limited by economic necessity (and, of course, bonds of affection).

The Witchcraft Phenomenon

The gap between the expectation of a cohesive, united community and the reality of an increasingly diverse and fluid one was difficult for early New Englanders to accept. At times, such tensions could produce bizarre and disastrous events. One example was the widespread hysteria in the 1680s and 1690s over supposed witchcraft—the human exercise of Satanic powers—in New England.

The most famous outbreak (although by no means the only one) was in Salem, Massachusetts, where adolescent girls began to exhibit strange behavior and lev-

ACCUSATION OF A WITCH
This nineteenth-century inlaid wood version of an earlier painting conveys something of the terror that witchcraft accusations produced in Puritan communities in the 1690s and earlier.
(Peabody Essex Museum)

eled accusations of witchcraft against several West Indian servants steeped in voodoo lore. The hysteria they produced spread throughout the town, and before it was over, hundreds of people (most of them women) were accused of witchcraft. As the crisis in Salem grew, accusations shifted from marginal women like the West Indians to more prominent and substantial people. Nineteen residents of Salem were put to death before the trials finally ended in 1692; the girls who had been the original accusers later recanted and admitted that their story had been fabricated.

In Salem, at least, the witchcraft crisis seems to have been in part a reflection of social strains peculiar to the community. The character of the accused and the accusers there suggests that it emerged out of tensions between those who were gravitating toward the new commercial economy of the town's thriving seaport and those who remained tied to the languishing agricultural economy of the community's western areas. Residents of the outlying areas of the town resented the favored position of their eastern neighbors. The accusations were usually made by the relatively isolated and unsuccessful members of the community against people associated with its more prosperous segments—perhaps reflecting a jealousy that could not be openly expressed in a "godly" community and that hence found other, more dangerous expressions.

But the Salem experience was only one of many. Accusations of witchcraft spread through many New England towns in the early 1690s (and indeed had emerged regularly in Puritan society for many years before). Research into the background of accused witches reveals that most were middle-aged women, often widowed, with few or no children. Many accused witches were of low social position, were often involved in domestic conflicts, had frequently been accused of other crimes, and were considered abrasive by their neighbors. Others were women who, through inheritance or enterprise, had come into possession of substantial land and property on their own and hence also challenged the gender norms of the community. Puritan society had little tolerance for "independent" women. That so many "witches" were women who were not securely lodged within a patriarchal family structure (and that many seemed openly to defy the passive, submissive norms society had created for them) suggests that tensions over gender roles played a substantial role in generating the crisis.

The witchcraft controversies were also a reflection of the highly religious character of these societies. New Englanders believed in the power of Satan and his ability to assert his power in the world. Belief in witchcraft was not a marginal superstition, rejected by the mainstream. It was a common feature of Puritan religious conviction.

Cities

To call the commercial centers that emerged along the Atlantic coast in the eighteenth century "cities" would be to strain the modern definition of that word. Even the largest colonial community was scarcely bigger than a modern small town. Yet by the standards of the eighteenth century, cities did indeed exist in America. In the 1770s the two largest ports—Philadelphia and New York—had populations of 28,000 and 25,000, respectively, which made them larger than most English urban centers. Boston (16,000), Charles Town (later Charleston), South Carolina (12,000), and Newport, Rhode Island (11,000), were also substantial communities by the standards of the day.

Colonial cities served as trading centers for the farmers of their regions and as marts for international trade. Their leaders were generally merchants who had acquired substantial estates. Disparities of wealth were features of almost all communities in America, but in cities they seemed particularly glaring. Wealthy merchants and their families moved along crowded streets dressed in fine imported clothes, often riding in fancy carriages, coming in and out of large houses with staffs of servants. Moving beside them were the numerous minor tradesmen, workers, and indigents, dressed simply and living in crowded and often filthy conditions. More than in any other area of colonial life (except of course in the relationship between masters and slaves), social distinctions were real and visible in urban areas.

There were other distinctive features of urban life as well. Cities were the centers of much of what industry there was in the colonies, such as distilleries for turning imported molasses into exportable rum. They were the locations of the most advanced schools and sophisticated cultural activities and of shops where imported goods could be bought. In addition, they were communities with peculiarly urban social problems: crime, vice, pollution, epidemics, traffic. Unlike smaller towns, cities were required to establish elaborate governments. They set up constables' offices and fire departments. They developed systems for supporting the urban poor, whose numbers grew steadily and became especially large in times of economic crisis.

Cities were also particularly vulnerable to fluctuations in trade. When a market for a particular product became glutted and prices fell, the effects on residents of a town—merchants and those whose livelihoods de-

BALTIMORE IN 1752
Baltimore remained a small and relatively quiet port even two decades after its founding in 1729. Most Maryland tobacco growers shipped their crops from their own wharves along the river and had little need for a central harbor. *(Maryland Historical Society, Baltimore)*

rived from commerce—could be severe. In the countryside, the impact was generally more muted. Finally, and of particular importance for the political future of the colonies, cities became places where new ideas could circulate and be discussed. Because there were printers, it was possible to have regular newspapers. Books and other publications from abroad introduced new intellectual influences. And the taverns and coffeehouses of cities provided forums in which people could gather and debate the issues of the day. It was not surprising that when the revolutionary crisis began to build in the 1760s and 1770s, it manifested itself in the cities.

THE COLONIAL MIND

Two powerful forces were competing in American intellectual life in the eighteenth century. One was the traditional outlook of the sixteenth and seventeenth centuries, with its emphasis on a personal God, intimately involved with the world, keeping watch over

individual lives. The other was the new spirit of the Enlightenment, a movement that was sweeping both Europe and America, which stressed the importance of science and human reason. The old views supported such phenomena as the belief in witchcraft, and they placed great value on a stern moral code in which intellect was less important than faith. The Enlightenment, by contrast, suggested that people had substantial control over their own lives and the course of their societies, that the world could be explained and therefore could be structured along rational scientific lines. Much of the intellectual climate of colonial America was shaped by the tension between these two impulses.

The Pattern of Religions

American colonists brought their religions with them from abroad. But like so many other imported institutions, religion took on a new and distinctive pattern in the New World. In part, this was because there were so many different faiths, making America an ecclesiastical patchwork. Toleration of religious diversity, although limited by later standards, flourished to a degree unmatched in any European nation, not because Americans deliberately sought to produce it, but because conditions virtually required it.

The experience of the Church of England illustrated how difficult the establishment of a common religion would be in the colonies. By law, Anglicanism was established as the official faith in Virginia, Maryland, New York, the Carolinas, and Georgia. In these colonies everyone, regardless of belief or affiliation, was supposed to be taxed for the support of the church. But except in Virginia and Maryland, the Church of England only succeeded in maintaining its position as the established church in certain localities. To strengthen Anglicanism, in America and elsewhere, the Church of England set up the Society for the Propagation of the Gospel in Foreign Parts in 1701; but SPG missionaries never succeeded in making Anglicanism a dominant force in America.

Even in areas where a single faith had once predominated, the forces of denominationalism soon began to be felt. In New England, for example, Puritans had believed themselves all to be part of a single faith: Calvinism. In the course of the eighteenth century, however, there was a growing tendency for different congregations to affiliate with different denominations. Some became Congregationalists; others identified themselves as Presbyterians. In belief, these two groups were essentially the same, but they differed in ecclesiastical organization. Each Congregationalist church was virtually autonomous; the Presbyterians had a more highly centralized government.

In parts of New York and New Jersey, Dutch settlers established their own Calvinist denomination, Dutch Reformed, which survived long after the colonies became part of the British empire. The American Baptists (of whom Roger Williams is considered the first) were also originally Calvinistic in their theology. Then, in Rhode Island and in other colonies, a bewildering variety of Baptist sects sprang up. They had in common a belief that infant baptism did not suffice and that rebaptism, usually by total immersion, was necessary when believers reached maturity. Some Baptists remained Calvinists, believers in predestination; others came to believe in salvation by free will.

Protestants extended toleration to one another more readily than to Roman Catholics. To strict Puritans, the pope seemed no less than the Antichrist. They viewed their Catholic neighbors across the border in New France (Canada) not only as commercial and military rivals, but as agents of the devil bent on frustrating the divine mission of the Puritans in New England. In most of the English colonies, however, Roman Catholics were too small a minority to occasion serious conflict. They were most numerous in Maryland, and even there they numbered no more than 3,000. Ironically, they suffered their worst persecution in that colony, which had been founded as a refuge for them and had been distinguished by its Toleration Act of 1649. According to Maryland laws passed after 1691, following the overthrow of the original proprietors, Catholics not only were deprived of political rights but also were forbidden to hold religious services except in private houses. In the American Southwest, still part of the Spanish Empire, Catholicism was considerably stronger, but the small group of Spanish settlers had only partial success in converting the Indian majority to their faith.

Jews in provincial America totaled no more than about 2,000 at any time. The largest community lived in New York City. Smaller groups settled in Newport and Charleston, and there were scattered Jewish families in all the colonies. Nowhere could they vote and hold office. Only in Rhode Island could they practice their religion openly. Such restrictions survived in some communities until after the American Revolution.

Substantial numbers of Americans embraced religious traditions that were not part of the Judeo-Christian tradition. Although some Indians converted to Christianity, most clung to traditional tribal faiths, which deified various elements of nature and placed great importance on tradition and genealogy. Black slaves brought their African religious traditions with them to America, traditions similarly rooted in a sensitivity to nature and lineage; and while most African Americans eventually converted to Christianity, elements of African faith remained part of their religious life for generations.

The Decline of Piety

By the beginning of the eighteenth century, some Americans were troubled by the apparent decline in religious piety in their society. In part, this was a result of the rise of denominationalism. With so many diverse sects existing side by side, some people were tempted to doubt whether any particular denomination, even their own, possessed a monopoly on truth and grace. More important, however, were other changes in colonial society. The movement of the population westward and the wide scattering of settlements had caused many communities to lose touch with organized religion. The rise of towns and the multiplication of material comforts led to an increasingly secular outlook in densely settled areas. The progress of science and free thought in Europe—and the importation of Enlightenment ideas to America—caused at least some colonists to adopt a rational and skeptical view of the world.

Concerns about declining piety surfaced as early as the 1660s in New England, where the Puritan oligarchy warned of a deterioration in the power of the church. As the first generation of American Puritans died, the number of church members rapidly declined, for few of the second generation seemed to harbor enough religious passion to demonstrate the "saving grace" that was a prerequisite for membership. The children of "saints" had generally been baptized and had attended services, but in the absence of a true "conversion experience," many had never become full members of the church. When these people began to have children of their own, the clergy was faced with a dilemma. Should the infants of these unconverted churchgoers be baptized? In 1662, a conference of ministers attempted to solve the problem by instituting the Halfway Covenant, which gave people of the third and later generations the right to be baptized but not the right to partake of communion or vote in church affairs.

As time passed, this carefully drawn distinction between full and half members was often forgotten, and in many communities the church came to include the families of all who could take part in colonial politics as voters and officeholders. Qualification for membership in the church, in other words, became largely secular. Orthodox Puritans, however, continued to oppose the transformation that was enveloping the erstwhile land of the saints. Sabbath after Sabbath, ministers preached sermons of despair (known as "jeremiads"), deploring the signs of waning piety. "Truly so it is," one minister lamented in 1674, "the very heart of New England is changed and exceedingly corrupted with the sins of the times." Only in relative terms was religious piety actually declining in New England. By the standards of later eras (or by the standards of other societies of the seventeenth century), the Puritan faith remained remarkably strong. So did the communal character of the New England town and the patriarchal character of the Puritan family. But New Englanders measured their faith by their own standards, not by those of other times and places, and to them the "declension" of religious piety was a serious problem.

The Great Awakening

By the early eighteenth century, similar concerns were emerging in other regions and among members of other faiths. Everywhere, colonists were coming to believe, religious piety was in decline and opportunities for spiritual regeneration were dwindling. The result was the first great American revival.

It was known as the Great Awakening. Although the first stirrings (or "freshenings") began in some places early in the century, the Great Awakening began in earnest in the 1730s and reached its climax in the 1740s. Then, for a time, a new spirit of religious fervor seemed to reverse the trend away from piety for thousands of Americans.

GEORGE WHITEFIELD
Whitefield succeeded John Wesley as leader of the Calvinistic Methodists in Oxford, England. Like Wesley, he was a major force in promoting religious revivalism in both England and America. He made his first missionary journey to the New World in 1738 and returned in the mid-1740s for a celebrated journey through the colonies that helped spark the Great Awakening. *(National Portrait Gallery, London)*

That the movement was not purely religious in origin is suggested by the identity of those who responded most frequently to it: residents of areas where social and economic tensions were greatest; women (who constituted the majority of converts) frustrated by their social and familial subjugation; younger sons of the third or fourth generation of settlers—those who stood to inherit the least land and who thus faced the most uncertain futures. The social origins of the revival were evident too in much of its rhetoric, which emphasized the potential of every person to break away from the constraints of the past and start anew in his or her relationship to God (and, implicitly, to the world). But social tensions were not alone responsible for the revival. At work, too, was a powerful desire among people of all backgrounds for an intense religious experience.

Wandering exhorters from England did much to stimulate the revivalistic spirit. John and Charles Wesley, the founders of Methodism (which had begun as a reform movement within the Church of England), visited Georgia and other colonies in the 1730s with the intention of revitalizing religion and converting Indians and blacks. George Whitefield, a powerful open-air preacher from England and for a time an associate of the Wesleys, made several evangelizing tours through the colonies. Everywhere he went, Whitefield drew tremendous crowds.

But the Wesleys, Whitefield, and other evangelizers from abroad were ultimately less important than the colonial ministers themselves. Theodore Frelinghuysen, of the Dutch Reformed Church, and Gilbert Tennent, a Presbyterian, were important native voices of evangelism. But the outstanding preacher of the Great Awakening was the New England Congregationalist Jonathan Edwards—a deeply orthodox Puritan but also one of the most original theologians in American history. From his pulpit in Northampton, Massachusetts, Edwards attacked the new doctrines of easy salvation for all. He preached anew the traditional Puritan ideas of the absolute sovereignty of God, the depravity of man, predestination, the necessity of experiencing a sense of election, and salvation by God's grace alone. His vivid descriptions of hell could terrify his listeners. Day after day agonized sinners crowded his parsonage to seek his aid; at least one committed suicide in despair at his inability to experience grace.

The Great Awakening spread over the colonies like a religious epidemic. It was most successful in frontier areas and was strongest of all in the southern backcountry. The Awakening created a sharp division in the Presbyterian Church between a large and rapidly growing group of revivalistic "New Light" Presbyterians and the traditional "Old Lights." New Methodist and Baptist sects attracted other converts.

Education

Many colonists placed a high value on education, despite the difficulties they confronted in gaining access to it. Some families tried to teach their children to read and write at home, although the heavy burden of work in most agricultural households limited the time avail-

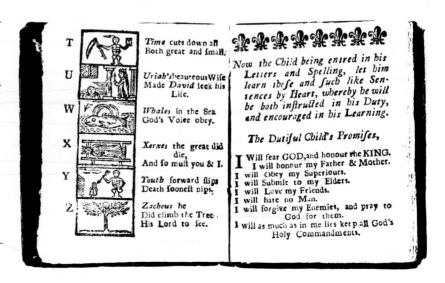

A "DAME SCHOOL" PRIMER
More than the residents of any other region of North America (and far more than those of most of Europe), the New England colonists strove to educate their children and achieved perhaps the highest level of literacy in the world. Throughout the region, young children attended institutions known as "dame schools" (because the teachers were almost always women) and learned from primers like this one. Puritan education emphasized both basic skills (the alphabet and reading) and moral and religious precepts, as this sample page suggests. (*American Antiquarian Society*)

able for schooling. In Massachusetts, a 1647 law required every town to support a public school, and while many communities failed to comply, a modest network of educational establishments emerged as a result. Elsewhere, the Quakers and other sects operated church schools. And in some communities, widows or unmarried women conducted "dame schools" by holding private classes in their homes. In cities, master craftsmen set up evening schools for their apprentices; at least a hundred such schools appeared between 1723 and 1770.

Only a relatively small number of children received education beyond the primary level; but white male Americans, at least, achieved a high degree of literacy. By the time of the Revolution, well over half of all white men could read and write, a rate substantially higher than in most European countries. The literacy rate for women lagged behind that of men until the nineteenth century; and while opportunities for further education were scarce for males, they were almost nonexistent for females. Nevertheless, in their early years colonial girls often received the same home-based education as boys, and their literacy rate too was substantially higher than that of their European counterparts.

African slaves had virtually no access to education. Occasionally a master or mistress would teach slave children to read and write, but they had few real incentives to do so. Indeed, as the slave system became more firmly entrenched, strong social (and ultimately legal) sanctions developed to discourage any efforts to promote black literacy, lest it encourage slaves to question their station. Indians, too, remained largely outside the white educational system—to a large degree by choice; most tribes preferred to educate their children in their own way. But some white missionaries and philanthropists established schools for Native Americans and helped create a small but significant population of Indians literate in spoken and written English.

Nowhere was the intermingling of the influences of traditional religiosity and the new spirit of the Enlightenment clearer than in the colleges and universities that grew up in colonial America. Of the six colleges in operation by 1763, all but two were founded by religious groups primarily for the training of preachers. Yet in almost all, the influences of the new scientific, rational approach to knowledge could be felt. Harvard, the first American college, was established in 1636 by the General Court of Massachusetts at the behest of Puritan theologians, who wanted to create a training center for ministers. Two years later, in 1638, instruction began in Cambridge. In that same year the college was named for a Charlestown minister, John Harvard, who had died and left his library and half his estate to the college. Decades later, in 1693, William and Mary College (named for the English king and queen) was established in Williamsburg, Virginia, by Anglicans; like Harvard, it was conceived as an academy to train clergymen. In 1701, conservative Congregationalists, dissatisfied with what they considered the growing religious liberalism of Harvard, founded Yale (named for one of its first benefactors, Elihu Yale) in New Haven, Connecticut. Out of the Great Awakening emerged the College of New Jersey, founded in 1746 and known later as Princeton (after the town in which it is located). One of its first presidents was Jonathan Edwards.

Despite the religious basis of these colleges, students at most of them could derive something of a liberal education from the curricula, which included not only theology, but logic, ethics, physics, geometry, astronomy, rhetoric, Latin, Hebrew, and Greek. From the beginning, Harvard attempted not only to provide an educated ministry but also to "advance learning and perpetuate it to posterity." King's College, founded in New York in 1754 and later renamed Columbia, was even more devoted to the spread of secular knowledge. It had no theological faculty and was interdenominational from the start. The Academy and College of Philadelphia, which became the University of Pennsylvania, was a completely secular institution, founded in 1755 by a group of laymen under the inspiration of Benjamin Franklin. It offered courses in utilitarian subjects—mechanics, chemistry, agriculture, government, commerce, and modern languages—as well as in the liberal arts.

The Allure of Science

The clearest indication of the spreading influence of the Enlightenment in America was an increasing interest in scientific knowledge. Most of the early colleges established chairs in the natural sciences and introduced some of the advanced scientific theories of Europe, including Copernican astronomy and Newtonian physics, to their students. But the most vigorous promotion of science in these years occurred outside the colleges, through the private efforts of amateurs and the activities of scientific societies. Leading merchants, planters, and even theologians became corresponding members of the Royal Society of London, the leading English scientific organization. Benjamin Franklin, the most celebrated amateur scientist in America, won international fame through his ex-

THE MAGNETIC DISPENSARY
In this 1790 painting, artist Samuel Collings caricatured the popular enthusiasm that Benjamin Franklin and others had produced for scientific experiments. The men and women shown here are rubbing iron rods with silk cloth to produce static electricity. A popular pastime was to place the charged rods over people's heads to watch their hair stand on end. *(Library Company of Philadelphia)*

periments with electricity (and most notably through his 1752 demonstration, using a kite, that lightning and electricity were the same).

The high value that influential Americans were beginning to place on scientific knowledge was clearly demonstrated by the most daring and controversial scientific experiment of the eighteenth century: inoculation against smallpox. The Puritan theologian Cotton Mather had learned of experiments in England by which people had been deliberately infected with mild cases of smallpox in order to immunize them against the deadly disease. Despite strong opposition from many of his neighbors, he urged inoculation on his fellow Bostonians during an epidemic in the 1720s. The results confirmed the effectiveness of the technique. Other theologians (including Jonathan Edwards) took up the cause, along with many physicians. By the mid-eighteenth century, inoculation had become a common medical procedure in America.

Concepts of Law and Politics

In seventeenth- and eighteenth-century law and politics, as in other parts of their lives, Americans of European descent believed that they were re-creating in the New World the practices and institutions of the Old. But as in other areas, they managed, without meaning to or even realizing it, to create something very different.

Changes in the law in America resulted in part from the scarcity of English-trained lawyers, who were al-

SIGNIFICANT EVENTS

1636   Harvard College founded in Massachusetts

1640   Instability in tobacco markets begins

1647   Massachusetts law requires a public school in every town

1662   Halfway Covenant established in New England

1650   Population of New England begins to grow by natural increase

1670s   Flow of indentured servants declines

Slave traders begin importing slaves directly from Africa to North America

1685   Edict of Nantes revoked in France;

Huguenots begin migrating to North America

1690s   Rice production becomes central to South Carolina economy

Slave trade expands as prices decline

1691   Official toleration of Catholics ends in Maryland

1692   Witchcraft trials begin in Salem

1693   College of William and Mary founded in Virginia

1697   Royal African Company monopoly of slave trade broken

Slave importations begin to increase

1701   Yale College founded in Connecticut

1708–1709   First major migration of Palatinate Germans to North America begins

1710   Major Scotch-Irish migrations to North America begin

German Swiss establish settlements in North Carolina

1720   Cotton Mather initiates smallpox inoculations in Massachusetts

1734   Great Awakening begins in Massachusetts

Zenger tried in New York

1739   George Whitefield arrives in North America

Great Awakening intensifies

1739   Stono slave rebellion in South Carolina

1740s   Indigo production begins in South Carolina

1746   College of New Jersey founded at Princeton

1754   King's College (later Columbia University) founded in New York

1755   Academy and College of Philadelphia (later University of Pennsylvania) founded

1764   Major ironworks established in New Jersey

---

most unknown in the colonies until after 1700. Not until well into the eighteenth century did authorities in England try to impose the common law and the statutes of the realm upon the provinces. By then, it was already too late. Although the American legal system adopted most of the essential elements of the English system, including such ancient rights as trial by jury, significant differences had already become well established.

Pleading and court procedures were simpler in America than in England, and punishments were different. Instead of the gallows or prison, colonists more commonly resorted to the whipping post, the brand-ing iron, the stocks, and (for "gossipy" women) the ducking stool. In a labor-scarce society, it was not in the interests of communities to execute or incarcerate potential workers. Crimes were redefined. In England, a printed attack on a public official, whether true or false, was considered libelous. In the 1734 trial of the New York publisher John Peter Zenger, who was powerfully defended by the Philadelphia lawyer Andrew Hamilton, the courts ruled that criticisms of the government were not libelous if factually true—a verdict that removed some restrictions on the freedom of the press. There was a subtle but decisive transformation in legal philosophy: colonists came to think of law as a reflection of the divine will or the natural order, not as an expression of the power of an earthly sovereign.

Even more significant for the future of the relationship between the colonies and England were important differences that were emerging between the American and British political systems. Because the royal government was so far away, Americans created a group of institutions of their own that gave them—in reality, if not in theory—a large measure of self-government. In most colonies, local communities grew accustomed to running their own affairs with minimal interference from higher authorities. Communities also expected to maintain strict control over their delegates to the colonial assemblies, and those assemblies came to exercise many of the powers that Parliament exercised in England (even though in theory Parliament remained the ultimate authority in America). Provincial governors appointed by the crown had broad powers on paper, but in fact their influence was sharply limited. They lacked control over appointments and contracts; such influence resided largely in England or with local colonial leaders. They could never be certain of their tenure in office; because governorships were patronage appointments, a governor could be removed any time his patron in England lost favor. And in many cases, governors were not even familiar with the colonies they were meant to govern. Some governors were native-born Americans, but most were Englishmen who came to the colonies for the first time to assume their offices.

The result of all this was that the focus of politics in the colonies became a local one. The provincial governments became accustomed to acting more or less independently of Parliament, and a set of assumptions and expectations about the rights of the colonists began to take hold in America that policy makers in England did not share. These differences caused few problems before the 1760s, because the British did little to exert the authority they believed they possessed. But when, beginning in 1763, the English government began attempting to tighten its control over the American colonies, a great imperial crisis developed.

SUGGESTED READINGS

General Social Histories. David Hackett Fischer, *Albion's Seed* (1989). James A. Henretta and Gregory Nobles, *The Evolution of American Society, 1700–1815*, rev. ed. (1987). Richard Hofstadter, *America at 1750: A Social Portrait* (1971).

Population and Family. John Putnam Demos, *Past, Present, and Personal: The Family and Life Course in American History* (1986). J. William Frost, *The Quaker Family in Colonial America* (1972). Philip Greven, *Four Generations* (1970); *The Protestant Temperament: Patterns of Child-Rearing, Religious Experience, and the Self in Early America* (1977). Christopher Jedrey, *The World of John Cleaveland: Family and Community in Eighteenth-Century New England* (1979). Joan M. Jensen, *Loosening the Bonds: Mid-Atlantic Farm Women, 1750–1850* (1986). Lyle Koehler, *A Search for Power: "The Weaker Sex" in Seventeenth-Century New England* (1982). Judith Walzer Leavitt, *Brought to Bed: Child Bearing in America, 1750–1950* (1986). Edmund S. Morgan, *The Puritan Family* (1966). Daniel Blake Smith, *Inside the Great House: Planter Family Life in Eighteenth Century Chesapeake Society* (1980). Roger Thompson, *Women in Stuart England and America* (1974). Laura Thatcher Ulrich, *Good Wives: Image and Reality in the Lives of Women in Northern New England, 1650–1750* (1982). Robert V. Wells, *The Population of the British Colonies in America Before 1776* (1975).

Immigration. Bernard Bailyn, *The Peopling of British North America: An Introduction* (1986); *Voyagers to the West: A Passage in the Peopling of America on the Eve of the Revolution* (1986). R. J. Dickson, *Ulster Immigration to the United States*, (1966).

Albert B. Faust, *The German Element in the United States*, 2 vols. (1909). Ian C. C. Graham, *Colonists from Scotland: Emigration to North America, 1707–1783* (1956). Marcus L. Hanson, *The Atlantic Migration, 1607–1860* (1940). James Kettner, *The Development of American Citizenship* (1978). Frederic Klees, *The Pennsylvania Dutch* (1950). James G. Leyburn, *The Scotch-Irish: A Social History* (1962).

Society and Slavery in the Colonial South. T. H. Breen, *Tobacco Culture* (1985). T. H. Breen and Stephen Innes, *"Myne Owne Ground": Race and Freedom on Virginia's Eastern Shore* (1980). Jay Coughtry, *The Notorious Triangle: Rhode Island and the African Slave Trade, 1799–1807* (1981). Philip D. Curtin, *The Atlantic Slave Trade* (1969). David Brion Davis, *The Problem of Slavery in Western Culture* (1966). David Eltis, *Economic Growth and the Ending of the Transatlantic Slave Trade* (1987). Jean E. Friedman, *The Enclosed Garden: Women and Community in the Evangelical South* (1985). David W. Galenson, *Traders, Planters, and Slaves: Market Behavior in Early English America* (1986). Eugene Genovese, *From Rebellion to Revolution* (1979). Jack P. Greene, *Pursuits of Happiness: The Social Development of Early Modern British Colonies and the Formation of American Culture* (1988). Rhys Isaac, *The Transformation of Virginia, 1740–1790* (1982). Winthrop D. Jordan, *White over Black* (1968); *The White Man's Burden* (1974). Charles Joyner, *Down by the Riverside: A South Carolina Slave Community* (1984). Allan Kulikoff, *Tobacco and Slaves* (1986). Daniel Littlefield, *Rice and Slaves: Ethnicity and the Slave Trade in Colonial South Carolina* (1981). Edmund S. Morgan, *American Slavery, American Freedom: The Ordeal of*

Colonial Virginia (1975). Gerald Mullin, *Flight and Rebellion* (1972). Gary B. Nash, *Red, White, and Black*, rev. ed. (1982). James R. Perry, *Formation of a Society on Virginia's Eastern Shore, 1615–1655* (1990). Darrett B. Rutman and Anita H. Rutman, *A Place in Time: Middlesex County, Virginia, 1659–1750* (1984). Abbot E. Smith, *Colonists in Bondage* (1947). Mechal Sobel, *The World They Made Together: Black and White Values in Eighteenth-Century Virginia* (1987). Julia C. Spruill, *Women's Life and Work in the Southern Colonies* (1972). James Titus, *The Old Dominion at War: Society, Politics, and Warfare in Late Colonial Virginia* (1991). Daniel H. Usner, Jr., *Indians, Settlers, and Slaves in a Frontier Exchange Economy: The Lower Mississippi Valley Before 1783* (1992). Peter Wood, *Black Majority* (1974). J. Leitch Wright, Jr., *Anglo-Spanish Rivalry in North America* (1971); *The Only Land They Knew: The Tragic Story of the American Indians of the Old South* (1981).

Society and Town in Colonial New England.   Paul Boyer and Stephen Nissenbaum, *Salem Possessed* (1974). Richard Bushman, *From Puritan to Yankee* (1967). John Camp, *Out of the Wilderness: The Emergence of an American Identity in Colonial New England* (1990). E. M. Cook, Jr., *The Fathers of Towns* (1975). John Putnam Demos, *Entertaining Satan: Witchcraft and the Culture of Early New England* (1982). Charles Grant, *Democracy in the Connecticut Frontier Town of Kent* (1961). Paul Robert Gross, *The Minutemen and Their World* (1976). David D. Hall, *Worlds of Wonder, Days of Judgment: Popular Religious Belief in Early New England* (1990). Carol Karlsen, *The Devil in the Shape of a Woman: Witchcraft in Colonial New England* (1987). Kenneth Lockridge, *A New England Town* (1970). Teresa Anne Murphy, *Ten Hours Labor: Religion, Reform, and Gender in Early New England* (1992). Carla Gardina Pestana, *Quakers and Baptists in Colonial Massachusetts* (1991). Sumner Chilton Powell, *Puritan Village* (1963). Darrett B. Rutman, *Winthrop's Boston* (1965). Michael Zuckerman, *Peaceable Kingdoms* (1970).

The Colonial Economy.   Carl Bridenbaugh, *Myths and Realities: Societies of the Colonial South* (1963). Stuart Bruchey, *Roots of American Economic Growth, 1607–1861* (1965). Paul G. E. Clemens, *The Atlantic Economy and Colonial Maryland's Eastern Shore: From Tobacco to Grain* (1980). David W. Galenson, *White Servitude in Colonial America: An Economic Analysis* (1982). Stephen Innes, *Labor in a New Land: Economy and Society in Seventeenth Century Springfield* (1983). Stephen Innes, ed., *Work and Labor in Early America* (1988). Alice Hanson Jones, *Wealth of a Nation to Be* (1980). Jackson Turner Main, *The Social Structure of Revolutionary America* (1965). John J. McCusker and Russell R. Menard, *The Economy of British America, 1607–1787* (1985). Harry R. Merrens, *Colonial North Carolina in the Eighteenth Century* (1964). Edmund S. Morgan, *Virginians at Home* (1952). Jacob M. Price, *France and the Chesapeake*, 2 vols. (1973); *The Tobacco Adventure to Russia* (1961); and *Capital and Credit in the British Overseas Trade: The View from the Chesapeake, 1700–1776* (1980). Sharon U. Salinger, *"To Serve Well and Faithfully": Labor and Indentured Servants in Pennsylvania, 1692–1800* (1987).

Cities and Commerce.   Bernard Bailyn, *The New England Merchants in the Seventeenth Century* (1955). Carl Bridenbaugh, *Cities in the Wilderness* (1938); and *Cities in Revolt* (1955). Stuart Bruchey, *The Colonial Merchant* (1966). Thomas M. Doerflinger, *A Vigorous Spirit of Enterprise: Merchants and Economic Development in Revolutionary Philadelphia* (1986). Joyce D. Goodfriend, *Before the Melting Pot: Society and Culture in New York City, 1664–1730* (1992). James B. Hedges, *The Browns of Providence Plantation*, vol. 1 (1952). Arthur Jensen, *The Maritime Commerce of Colonial Philadelphia* (1963). Randolph S. Klein, *Portrait of an Early American Family* (1975). Gary B. Nash, *The Urban Crucible* (1979); and *Forging Freedom: The Formation of Philadelphia's Black Community, 1720–1840* (1988). Marcus Rediker, *Between the Devil and the Deep Sea: Merchant Seamen, Pirates, and the Anglo-American Maritime World, 1700–1750* (1987). J. F. Shepherd and G. M. Walton, *The Economic Rise of Early America* (1979). Frederick B. Tolles, *Meeting House and Counting House: The Quaker Merchants of Colonial Philadelphia, 1682–1763* (1948). G. B. Warden, *Boston, 1687–1776* (1970). Stephanie G. Wolf, *Urban Village* (1976).

Colonial Religion.   (For studies of Puritanism, see bibliography for Chapter 2.) Sidney Ahlstrom, *A Religious History of the American People* (1972). Patricia U. Bonomi, *Under the Copy of Heaven: Religion, Society, and Politics in Colonial America* (1986). Carl Bridenbaugh, *Mitre and Sceptre: Transatlantic Faiths, Ideas, Personalities, and Politics, 1689–1775* (1962). J. T. Ellis, *Catholics in America* (1965). J. R. Marcus, *Early American Jewry* (1951). William C. McLoughlin, *New England Dissent, 1630–1833*, 2 vols. (1971). Sidney Mead, *The Lively Experiment: The Shaping of Christianity in America* (1963). W. W. Sweet, *Religion in Colonial America* (1942). Marilyn Westerkamp, *Triumph of Laity* (1988). Janet Whitman, *John Woolman, American Quaker* (1942).

The Great Awakening.   J. M. Bumsted and John E. Van de Wetering, *What Must I Do to Be Saved? The Great Awakening in Colonial America* (1976). J. W. Davidson, *The Logic of Millennial Thought* (1977). Edwin S. Gaustad, *The Great Awakening in New England* (1957). Alan Heimert, *Religion and the American Mind* (1966). Perry Miller, *Jonathan Edwards* (1949). Patricia Tracy, *Jonathan Edwards: Pastor* (1980). Ola Winslow, *Jonathan Edwards* (1940). Conrad Wright, *The Beginnings of Unitarianism in America* (1955).

Education.   James Axtell, *The School upon a Hill: Education and Society in Colonial New England* (1974). Bernard Bailyn, *Education in the Forming of American Society* (1960). Lawrence A. Cremin, *American Education: The Colonial Experience, 1607–1783* (1970). Jurgen Herbst, *From Crisis to Crisis* (1982). Kenneth Lockridge, *Literacy in Colonial New England* (1974). Robert Middlekauff, *Ancients and Axioms* (1963). Samuel Eliot Morison, *The Founding of Harvard College* (1935).

Culture and the Enlightenment.   Jean-Christophe Agnew, *Worlds Apart: The Market and the Theater in Anglo-American*

Thought, 1550–1750 (1986). Daniel J. Boorstin, *The Americans: The Colonial Experience* (1958). V. W. Crane, *Benjamin Franklin and a Rising People* (1954). Richard Beale Davis, *Intellectual Life in the Colonial South*, 2 vols. (1978). Brook Hindle, *The Pursuit of Science in Revolutionary America* (1956). Howard Mumford Jones, *O Strange New World* (1964). H. Leventhal, *In the Shadow of Enlightenment* (1976). Henry May, *The Enlightenment in America* (1976). Carl Van Doren, *Benjamin Franklin* (1941). Louis B. Wright, *The Cultural Life of the American Colonies* (1957).

Law & Politics.   Bernard Bailyn, *The Origins of American Politics* (1968). Thomas Curry, *The First Freedoms: Church and State in America to the Passage of the First Amendment* (1986). Robert Ferguson, *Law and Letters in American Culture* (1984). Gerald W. Gawalt, *The Promise of Power: The Emergence of the Legal Profession in Massachusetts, 1760–1840* (1979). Jack P. Greene, *The Quest for Power* (1963). Charles Hoffer, *Law and People in Colonial America* (1992). Michael Kammen, *Spheres of Liberty: Changing Perceptions of Liberty in American Culture* (1986). Leonard W. Labaree, *Royal Government in America* (1930). J. G. A. Pocock, *The Machiavellian Moment* (1975). J. R. Pole, *Political Representation in England and the Origins of the American Republic* (1966). A. G. Roeber, *Faithful Magistrates and Republican Lawyers: Creators of Virginia Legal Culture, 1680–1810* (1981). Caroline Robbins, *The Eighteenth-Century Commonwealthman* (1959). Marylynn Salmon, *Women and the Law of Property in Early America* (1986). Robert Zemsky, *Merchants, Farmers, and River Gods* (1971).

THE BOSTON MASSACRE (1770), BY PAUL REVERE

This is one of many engravings, by Revere and others, of the conflict between British troops and Boston laborers that became important propaganda documents for the Patriot cause in the 1770s. Among the victims of the massacre listed by Revere was Crispus Attucks, probably the first black man to die in the struggle for American independence. *(American Antiquarian Society)*

CHAPTER FOUR

THE EMPIRE UNDER STRAIN

salutary neglect

A S LATE AS THE 1750s, few Americans saw any reason to object to their membership in the British Empire. The imperial system provided them with many benefits: opportunities for trade and commerce, military protection, political stability. And those benefits were accompanied by few costs; for the most part, the English government left the colonies alone. While Britain did attempt to regulate the colonists' external trade, those regulations were usually so laxly administered that they could be easily circumvented. Some Americans predicted that the colonies would ultimately develop to a point where greater autonomy would become inevitable. But few expected such a change to occur soon.

By the mid-1770s, however, the relationship between the American colonies and their British rulers had become so strained, so poisoned, so characterized by suspicion and resentment that the once seemingly unbreakable bonds of empire were on the verge of dissolution. And in the spring of 1775, the first shots were fired in a war that would ultimately win America its independence.

The revolutionary crisis emerged as a result of both longstanding differences between the colonies and England and particular events in the 1760s and 1770s. Ever since the first days of settlement in North America, the ideas and institutions of the colonies had been diverging from those in England in countless ways. Only because the relationship between America and Britain had been so casual had those differences failed to create serious tensions in the past. Beginning in 1763,

however, the British government embarked on a series of new policies toward its colonies—policies dictated by changing international realities and new political circumstances within England itself—that brought the differences between the two societies into sharp focus. In the beginning, most Americans reacted to the changes with relative restraint. Gradually, however, as crisis followed crisis, a large group of Americans found themselves fundamentally disillusioned with the imperial relationship. By 1775, that relationship was, for all practical purposes, damaged beyond repair.

A LOOSENING OF TIES

After the Glorious Revolution of 1688 in England and the collapse of the Dominion of New England in America, the English government (the British government after 1707, when Great Britain emerged out of the union of England and Scotland) made no serious or sustained effort to tighten its control over the colonies for over seventy years. During those years, it is true, an increasing number of colonies were brought under the direct control of the king. New Jersey in 1702, North and South Carolina in 1729, Georgia in 1754—all became royal colonies, bringing the total to eight; in all of them, the king had the power to appoint the governors and other colonial officials. During those years, Parliament also passed new laws supplement-

ENGLISH MONARCHS, 1702–1820	
Anne	1702–1714
George I	1714–1727
George II	1727–1760
George III	1760–1820

ing the original Navigation Acts and strengthening the mercantilist program—laws restricting colonial manufactures, prohibiting paper currency, and regulating trade. On the whole, however, the British government remained uncertain and divided about the extent to which it ought to interfere in colonial affairs. The colonies were left, within broad limits, to go their separate ways.

A Tradition of Neglect

In the fifty years after the Glorious Revolution, the British Parliament established a growing supremacy over the king. During the reigns of George I (1714–1727) and George II (1727–1760), both of whom were German born and unaccustomed to English ways, the prime minister and his fellow cabinet ministers began to become the nation's real executives. They held their positions not by the king's favor but by their ability to control a majority in Parliament.

These parliamentary leaders were less inclined than the seventeenth-century monarchs had been to try to tighten imperial organization. They depended heavily on the support of the great merchants and landholders, most of whom feared that any such experiments would require large expenditures, would increase taxes, and would diminish the profits they were earning from the colonial trade. The first of the prime ministers, Robert Walpole, deliberately refrained from strict enforcement of the Navigation Acts, believing that relaxed trading restrictions would stimulate commerce.

Meanwhile, the day-to-day administration of colonial affairs remained decentralized and inefficient. There was no colonial office in London. The nearest equivalent was the Board of Trade and Plantations, established in 1696—a mere advisory body that had little role in any actual decisions. Real authority rested in the Privy Council (the central administrative agency for the government as a whole), the admiralty, and the treasury. But those agencies were responsible for administering laws at home as well as overseas; none could concentrate on colonial affairs alone. To compli-

cate matters further, there was considerable overlapping and confusion of authority among the departments.

Few of the London officials, moreover, had ever visited America; few knew very much about conditions there. What information they did gather came in large part from agents sent to England by the colonial assemblies to lobby for American interests, and these agents, naturally, did nothing to encourage interference with colonial affairs. (The best known of them, Benjamin Franklin, represented not only his own colony, Pennsylvania, but also Georgia, New Jersey, and Massachusetts.)

It was not only the incoherence of administrative authority in London and the ministerial policy of salutary neglect that weakened England's hold on the colonies. It was also the character of the royal officials in America—the governors and other officers of the royal colonies and (in all the colonies) the collectors of customs and naval officers. Some of these officeholders were able and intelligent men; most were not. Appointments generally came as the result of bribery or favoritism, not in response to merit. Many appointees remained in England and, with part of their salaries, hired substitutes to take their places in America. Such deputies received paltry wages and thus faced great temptations to augment their incomes with bribes. Few resisted the temptation. Customs collectors, for example, routinely waived duties on goods when merchants

AN APPEAL FOR COLONIAL UNITY
This sketch, one of the first American editorial cartoons, appeared in Benjamin Franklin's Philadelphia newspaper, the *Pennsylvania Gazette,* on May 9, 1754. It was meant to illustrate the need for intercolonial unity and, in particular, for the adoption of Franklin's Albany Plan. *(Library Company of Philadelphia)*

paid them to do so. Even honest and well-paid officials usually found it expedient, if they wanted to get along with their neighbors, to yield to the colonists' resistance to trade restrictions.

Resistance to imperial authority centered in the colonial legislatures. By the 1750's the American assemblies had claimed the right to levy taxes, make appropriations, approve appointments, and pass laws for their respective colonies. Their legislation was subject to veto by the governor or the Privy Council. But the assemblies had leverage over the governor through their control of the colonial budget, and they could circumvent the Privy Council by repassing disallowed laws in slightly altered form. The assemblies came to look upon themselves as little parliaments, each practically as sovereign within its colony as Parliment itself was in England. In 1754, the Board of Trade reported to the king, regarding the members of the New York assembly, that they "have wrested from Your Majesty's governor the nomination of all offices of government, the custody and direction of the public military stores, the mustering and direction of troops raised for Your Majesty's service, and in short almost every other part of executive government."

The Colonies Divided

Despite their frequent resistance to the authority of London, the colonists continued to think of themselves as loyal English subjects. In many respects, in fact, they felt stronger ties to England than they did to one another. "Fire and water," an English traveler wrote, "are not more heterogeneous than the different colonies in North America." New Englanders and Virginians viewed each other as something close to foreigners. A Connecticut man denounced the merchants of New York for their "frauds and unfair practices," while a New Yorker condemned Connecticut because of the "low craft and cunning so incident to the people of that country." Only an accident of geography, it seemed, connected these disparate societies to each other.

Yet for all their differences, the colonies could scarcely avoid forging connections with one another. The growth of the colonial population produced an almost continuous line of settlement along the seacoast and led to the gradual construction of roads and the rise of intercolonial trade. The colonial postal service helped increase communication. In 1691, it had operated only from Massachusetts to New York and Pennsylvania. In 1711, it extended to New Hampshire in the North; in 1732, to Virginia in the South; and ultimately, all the way to Georgia.

Still, the colonists were loath to cooperate even when, in 1754, they faced a common threat from their old rivals, the French, and France's Indian allies. A conference of colonial leaders—with delegates from Pennsylvania, Maryland, New York, and New England—was meeting in Albany in that year to negotiate a treaty with the Iroquois. The delegates stayed on to talk about forming a colonial federation for defense against the Indians. Benjamin Franklin proposed, and the delegates tentatively approved, a plan by which Parliament would set up in America "one general government" for all the colonies. Each colony would "retain its present constitution," but would grant to the general new government such powers as the authority to govern all relations with the Indians.

War with the French and Indians was already beginning when this Albany Plan was presented to the colonial assemblies. None approved it. "Everyone cries, a union is necessary," Franklin wrote to the Massachusetts governor, "but when they come to the manner and form of the union, their weak noodles are perfectly distracted."

THE STRUGGLE FOR THE CONTINENT

In one sense, the war that raged in North America through the late 1750s and early 1760s was but one part of a larger struggle between England and France for dominance in world trade and naval power. The British victory in that struggle, known in Europe as the Seven Years' War, confirmed England's commercial supremacy and cemented its control of the settled regions of North America.

In another sense, however, the conflict was the final stage in a long battle among the three principal powers in northeastern North America: the English, the French, and the Iroquois. For more than a century prior to the conflict—known in America as the French and Indian War—these three groups had maintained an uneasy balance of power. The events of the 1750s upset that balance, produced a prolonged and open conflict, and established a precarious dominance for the English societies throughout the region.

The French and Indian War had additional significance for the English colonists in America. By bringing the Americans into closer contact with British authority than ever before, it raised to the surface some of the underlying tensions in the colonial relationship.

English = better terms   *French = tolerance*

New France and the Iroquois Nation

The French and the English had coexisted relatively peacefully in North America for nearly a century. But by the 1750s, as both English and French settlements expanded, religious and commercial tensions began to produce new frictions and new conflicts. The crisis began in part because of the expansion of the French presence in America in the late seventeenth century—a result of Louis XIV's search for national unity and increased world power. France began to devote new attention to the development of its North American territories, and French settlement rapidly expanded. The lucrative fur trade drew immigrant peasants deeper into the wilderness. Missionary zeal drew large numbers of Jesuits into the interior in search of potential converts. The bottomlands of the Mississippi River valley attracted farmers discouraged by the short growing season in Canada.

By the mid-seventeenth century, the French Empire in America comprised a vast territory. Louis Joliet and Father Jacques Marquette, French explorers of the 1670s, journeyed together by canoe from Green Bay on Lake Michigan as far south as the junction of the Arkansas and Mississippi Rivers. A year later, René Robert Cavelier, Sieur de La Salle, began the explorations that in 1682 took him to the delta of the Mississippi, where he claimed the surrounding country for France and named it Louisiana in the king's honor. Subsequent traders and missionaries wandered to the southwest as far as the Rio Grande, and the explorer Pierre Gaultier de Varennes, Sieur de La Verendrye, pushed westward in 1743 from Lake Superior to a point within sight of the Rocky Mountains. The French had by then revealed the outlines of, and laid claim to, the whole continental interior.

To secure their hold on these enormous claims, they founded a string of widely separated communities, strategically located fortresses, and far-flung missions and trading posts. Fort Louisbourg, on Cape Breton Island, guarded the approach to the Gulf of St. Lawrence. Would-be feudal lords established large estates (*seigneuries*) along the banks of the St. Lawrence River; and on a high bluff above the river stood the fortified city of Quebec, the center of the French Empire in America. To the south was Montreal, and to the west Sault Sainte Marie and Detroit. On the lower Mississippi emerged plantations much like those in the southern colonies of English America, worked by black slaves and owned by "Creoles" (white immigrants of French descent). New Orleans, founded in 1718 to service the French plantation economy, soon was as big as some of the larger cities of the Atlantic seaboard; Biloxi and Mobile to the east completed the string of French settlement.

But the French were not, of course, alone in the continental interior. They encountered there a large and powerful Indian population, and their relations with the natives were crucial to the shaping of their empire. Both the French and the English were aware that the battle for control of North America would be determined in part by which group could best win the allegiance of native tribes—as trading partners and, at times, as military allies. The Indians, for their part, were principally concerned with protecting their independence, and what alignments they formed with the European societies growing up around them were generally marriages of convenience, determined by which group offered the most attractive terms. The English—with their more advanced commercial economy—could usually offer the Indians better and more plentiful goods. But the French offered something that was often more important: tolerance. Unlike the English settlers, most of whom tried to impose their own social norms on the Indians they encountered, the French settlers in the interior generally adjusted their own behavior to Indian patterns. French fur traders frequently married Indian women and adopted tribal ways; Jesuit missionaries interacted comfortably with the natives and converted them to Catholicism by the thousands without challenging most of their social customs. By the mid-eighteenth century, therefore, the French had better and closer relations with most of the Indians of the interior than did the English.

The most powerful native group, however, had a rather different relationship with the French. The Iroquois Confederacy—the five Indian nations (Mohawk, Seneca, Cayuga, Onondaga, and Oneida) that had formed a defensive alliance in the fifteenth century—had been the most powerful native presence in the Northeast since the 1640s, when they had fought—and won—a bitter war against the Hurons. With their major competitors now largely exterminated or driven from the region, the Iroquois formed an important commercial relationship with the English and Dutch along the eastern seaboard.

The Hurons had been the principal trading partners of the French in the early seventeenth century, and their disappearance pushed French traders farther into the interior in search of furs and native partners to help trap them. For nearly a century, however, neither the French nor the English raised any serious challenge to Iroquois dominance. The Iroquois maintained their autonomy in part by avoiding too close a relationship with either group. They traded successfully with both the English and the French and astutely played the two groups off against each other. As a result, they managed to maintain an uneasy balance of power in the Great Lakes region.

The principal source of conflict among these three groups was the Ohio Valley, which the French claimed and which was the home of a number of competing Indian tribes (many of them refugees from lands farther east, driven into the valley by the English expansion). As English settlement expanded westward, as France's ambitions grew, as the Iroquois began to establish a presence as traders, the Ohio Valley became a potential battleground.

Anglo-French Conflicts

As long as England and France remained at peace in Europe, and as long as the precarious balance in the North American interior survived, English and French colonists coexisted with each other and with the Iroquois without serious difficulty. But after the Glorious Revolution in England, the English throne passed to one of Louis XIV's principal enemies, William III, who was also the *stadholder* (chief magistrate) of the Netherlands and who had long opposed French expansionism. William's successor, Queen Anne (the daughter of James II), ascended the throne in 1702 and carried on the struggle against France and its new ally, Spain. The result was a series of Anglo-French wars that continued intermittently in Europe for nearly eighty years.

The wars had important repercussions in America. King William's War (1689–1697) produced only a few, indecisive clashes between the English and French in northern New England. Queen Anne's War, which began in 1701 and continued for nearly twelve years, generated more substantial conflicts: border fighting with the Spaniards in the South as well as with the French and their Indian allies in the North. The Treaty of Utrecht, which brought the conflict to a close in 1713, transferred substantial areas of French territory in North America to the English, including Acadia (Nova Scotia) and Newfoundland.

Two decades later, European rivalries led to still more conflicts in America. Disputes over British trading rights in the Spanish colonies produced a war between England and Spain and led to clashes between the British in Georgia and the Spaniards in Florida. (It was in the context of this conflict that the last English colony in America, Georgia, was founded in 1733; see pp. 50–51.) The Anglo-Spanish conflict soon merged with a much larger European war, in which England

and France lined up on opposite sides of a territorial dispute between Frederick the Great of Prussia and Maria Theresa of Austria. (France supported Prussia, in the hope of seizing the Austrian Netherlands; England supported Austria, to keep Holland from the French.) The English colonists in America were soon drawn into the struggle, which they called King George's War; and between 1744 and 1748 they engaged in a series of conflicts with the French. New Englanders captured the French bastion at Louisbourg on Cape Breton Island; but the peace treaty that finally ended the conflict forced them (in bitter disappointment) to abandon it.

In the aftermath of King George's War, relations among the English, French, and Iroquois in North America quickly deteriorated. The Iroquois (in what in retrospect appears a major blunder) began for the first time to grant trading concessions in the interior to English merchants. In the context of the already-tense Anglo-French relationship in America, that decision set in motion a chain of events disastrous for the Iroquois Confederacy. The French, fearful that the English were using the concessions as a first step toward expansion into French lands (which to some extent they were), began in 1749 to construct new fortresses in the Ohio Valley. The English, interpreting the French activity as a threat to their western settlements, protested and began making military preparations and building fortresses of their own. The balance of power that the Iroquois had carefully and successfully maintained for so long rapidly disintegrated, and the five Indian nations had little choice now but to ally themselves with the British and assume an essentially passive role in the conflict that ensued.

For the next five years, tensions between the English and the French increased, until in the summer of 1754 the governor of Virginia sent a militia force (under the command of an inexperienced young colonel, George Washington) into the Ohio Valley to challenge French expansion. Washington built a crude stockade (Fort Necessity) not far from Fort Duquesne, the larger outpost the French were building on the site of what is now Pittsburgh. After the Virginians staged an unsuccessful attack on a French detachment, the French countered with an assault on Fort Necessity, trapping Washington and his soldiers inside. After a third of them died in the fighting, Washington surrendered.

The clash marked the beginning of the French and Indian War, the American part of a much larger conflict that spread to Europe and became known as the Seven Years' War. It was the climactic event in the long Anglo-French struggle for empire.

Impressment

The Great War for the Empire

1st phase

The French and Indian War lasted nearly nine years, and it proceeded in three distinct phases. During the first of these phases, from the Fort Necessity debacle in 1754 until the expansion of the war to Europe in 1756, it was primarily a local, North American conflict. The English colonists managed the war largely on their own. The British provided modest assistance during this period, but they provided it so ineptly that it had little impact on the struggle. The British fleet failed to prevent the landing of large French reinforcements in Canada; and the newly appointed commander in chief of the British army in America, General Edward Braddock, failed miserably in a major effort in the summer of 1755 to retake the crucial site at the forks of the Ohio River where Washington had lost the battle at Fort Necessity. A French and Indian ambush a few miles from the fort left Braddock dead and what remained of his forces in disarray. The local colonial forces, meanwhile, were preoccupied with defending themselves against raids on their western settlements by the Indians of the Ohio Valley. Virtually all of them (except the Iroquois) were now allied with the French, having interpreted the defeat of the Virginians at Fort Duquesne as evidence of British weakness. Even the Iroquois, who were nominally allied with the British, remained fearful of antagonizing the French. They engaged in few hostilities and launched no offensive into Canada, even though they had, under heavy English pressure, declared war on the French. By late 1755, many English settlers along the frontier had withdrawn to the east of the Allegheny Mountains to escape the hostilities.

The second phase of the struggle began in 1756, when the governments of France and England formally opened hostilities and a truly international conflict (the Seven Years' War) began. In Europe, the war was marked by a realignment within the complex system of alliances. France allied itself with its former enemy, Austria; England joined France's former ally, Prussia. The fighting now spread to the West Indies, India, and Europe itself. But the principal struggle remained the one in North America, where so far England had suffered nothing but frustration and defeat.

2nd phase

Beginning in 1757, William Pitt, the English secretary of state (and future prime minister), began to transform the war effort in America by bringing it for the first time fully under British control. Pitt himself began planning military strategy for the North American conflict, appointing military commanders, and issuing orders to the colonists. Military recruitment had slowed dramatically in America after the defeat of Braddock, and to replenish the army British commanders began forcibly enlisting colonists (a practice known as "impressment"). Officers also began to seize supplies and equipment from local farmers and tradesmen and to compel colonists to offer shelter to British troops—all generally without compensation. The Americans, who had long ago become accustomed to running their own affairs and who had been fighting for over two years without much assistance or direction from the British, resented these new impositions and firmly resisted them—at times, as in a 1757 riot in New York City, violently. By early 1758, the friction between the British authorities and the colonists was threatening to bring the war effort to a halt.

3rd phase

Beginning in 1758, therefore, Pitt initiated the third and final phase of the war by relaxing many of the policies that Americans had found obnoxious. He agreed to reimburse the colonists for all supplies requisitioned by the army. He returned control over recruitment to the colonial assemblies (which resulted in an immediate and dramatic increase in enlistments). And he dispatched large numbers of additional troops to America.

Finally, the tide of battle began to turn in England's favor. The French, who had always been outnumbered by the British colonists and who, after 1756, suffered from a series of poor harvests, were unable to sustain their early military successes. By mid-1758, the British regulars in America (who did the bulk of the actual fighting) and the colonial militias were seizing one French stronghold after another. Two brilliant English generals, Jeffrey Amherst and James Wolfe, captured the fortress at Louisbourg in July 1758; a few months later Fort Duquesne fell without a fight. The next year, at the end of a siege of Quebec, supposedly impregnable atop its towering cliff, the army of General James Wolfe struggled up a hidden ravine under cover of darkness, surprised the larger forces of the Marquis de Montcalm, and defeated them in a battle in which both commanders died. The dramatic fall of Quebec on September 13, 1759, marked the beginning of the end of the American phase of the war. A year later, in September 1760, the French army formally surrendered to Amherst in Montreal.

Not all aspects of the struggle were as romantic as Wolfe's assault on Quebec. The British resorted at times to such brutal military expedients as population dispersal. In Nova Scotia, for example, they uprooted several thousand French inhabitants, whom they suspected of disloyalty, and scattered them throughout the English colonies. (Some of these Acadians eventually made their way to Louisiana, where they became the ancestors of the present-day Cajuns.) Elsewhere, English and colonial troops inflicted even worse atrocities on the Indian allies of the French—for example,

THE SIEGE OF LOUISBOURG, 1758
The fortress of Louisbourg, on Cape Breton Island in Nova Scotia, was one of the principal French outposts in eastern Canada during the French and Indian War. It took a British fleet of 157 ships nearly two months to force the French garrison to surrender. "We had not had our Batteries against the Town above a Week," wrote a British soldier after the victory, "tho we were ashore Seven Weeks; the Badness of the Country prevented our Approaches. It was necessary to make Roads for the Cannon, which was a great Labour, and some Loss of Men; but the spirits the Army was in is capable of doing any Thing." *(New Brunswick Museum)*

offering "scalp bounties" to those who could bring back evidence of having killed a native. The French and their Indian allies retaliated, and hundreds of families along the English frontier perished in brutal raids on their settlements.

Peace finally came after the accession of George III to the British throne and the resignation of Pitt, who, unlike the new king, wanted to continue hostilities. The British achieved most of Pitt's aims nevertheless in the Peace of Paris, signed in 1763. Under its terms, the French ceded to Great Britain some of their West Indian islands and most of their colonies in India. They also transferred Canada and all other French territory east of the Mississippi, except New Orleans, to Great Britain. They ceded New Orleans and their claims west of the Mississippi to Spain, thus surrendering all title to the mainland of North America.

The French and Indian War had profound effects on the British Empire and the American colonies. It greatly expanded England's territorial claims in the New World. At the same time, it greatly enlarged Britain's debt; financing the vast war had been a major drain on the treasury. And it generated substantial resentment toward the Americans among British leaders. Officials in England were contemptuous of the colonists for what they considered American military ineptitude during the war; they were angry that the colonists had made so few financial contributions to a struggle waged largely for American benefit; they were particularly bitter that some colonial merchants had been selling food and other goods to the French in the West Indies throughout the conflict. All these factors combined to persuade many English leaders that a major reorganization of the empire, giving London increased authority over the colonies, would be necessary in the aftermath of the war.

The war had an equally profound but very different effect on the American colonists. It forced them, for the first time, to act in concert against a common foe. The friction of 1756–1757 over British requisition and impressment policies, and the 1758 return of authority to the colonial assemblies, established an important precedent in the minds of the colonists: it seemed to confirm the illegitimacy of English interference in local affairs. And for thousands of Americans—the men who served in the colonial armed forces—the war was an important socializing experience. The provincial troops, unlike the British regiments, had generally viewed themselves as part of a "people's army." The relationship of soldiers to their units was, the soldiers believed, in some measure voluntary; their army was a communal, not a coercive or hierarchical organization. The contrast with the British regulars, whom the colonists widely resented for their arrogance and arbitrary use of power, was striking; and in later years, the memory of that contrast helped to shape the American response to British imperial policies.

For the Indians of the Ohio Valley, the third major party in the French and Indian War, the British victory was disastrous. Those tribes that had allied themselves with the French had earned the enmity of the victorious English. The Iroquois Confederacy, which had allied itself with Britain, fared only slightly better. English officials saw the passivity of the Iroquois during the war (a result of their effort to hedge their bets and avoid antagonizing the French) as evidence of duplicity. In the aftermath of the peace settlement, the Iroquois alliance with the British quickly unraveled, and the Iroquois Confederacy itself began to crumble from within. The Iroquois Nations would continue to contest the English for control of the Ohio Valley for another fifty years; but increasingly divided and increasingly outnumbered, they would seldom again be in a position to deal with their white rivals on terms of military or political equality.

THE NEW IMPERIALISM

With the treaty of 1763, England found itself truly at peace for the first time in more than fifty years. But the difficult experiences of the previous decade had convinced many English leaders that they could no longer govern their empire as casually as they had in the past. Saddled with enormous debts from the many years of fighting, England was desperately in need of new revenues from its empire. And responsible for vast new lands in the New World, the imperial government could not long avoid expanding its involvement in its colonies.

Burdens of Empire

The experience of the French and Indian War, however, suggested that such increased involvement would not be easy to achieve. Not only had the colonists proved so resistant to British control that Pitt had been forced to relax his policies in 1758, but the colonial assemblies had continued after that to respond to British needs slowly and grudgingly. Unwilling to be taxed by Parliament to support the war effort, the colonists were generally reluctant to tax themselves as well. Defiance of imperial trade regulations and other British demands continued, and even increased, through the last years of the war.

The problems of managing the empire were compounded after 1763 by a basic shift in Britain's imperial design. In the past, the English had viewed their colonial empire primarily in terms of trade; they had opposed acquisition of territory for its own sake. But by the mid-eighteenth century, a growing number of English and American leaders (including both William Pitt and Benjamin Franklin) were beginning to argue that land itself was of value to the empire—because of the population it could support, the taxes it could produce, and the imperial splendor it would confer. The debate between the old commercial imperialists and the new territorial ones came to a head at the conclusion of the French and Indian War. The mercantilists wanted England to return Canada to France in exchange for Guadeloupe, the most commercially valuable of the French "sugar islands" in the West Indies. The territorialists, however, prevailed. The acquisition of the French territories in North America was a victory for, among others, Benjamin Franklin, who had long argued that the American people would need these vast spaces to accommodate their rapid and, he believed, limitless growth. But Franklin and his supporters in the colonies were soon to discover that the new acquisitions brought with them unexpected problems.

With the territorial annexations of 1763, the area of the British Empire was suddenly twice as great as it had been, and the problems of governing it thus became considerably more complex. Some argued that the empire should restrain rapid settlement and the development of the western territories. To do otherwise

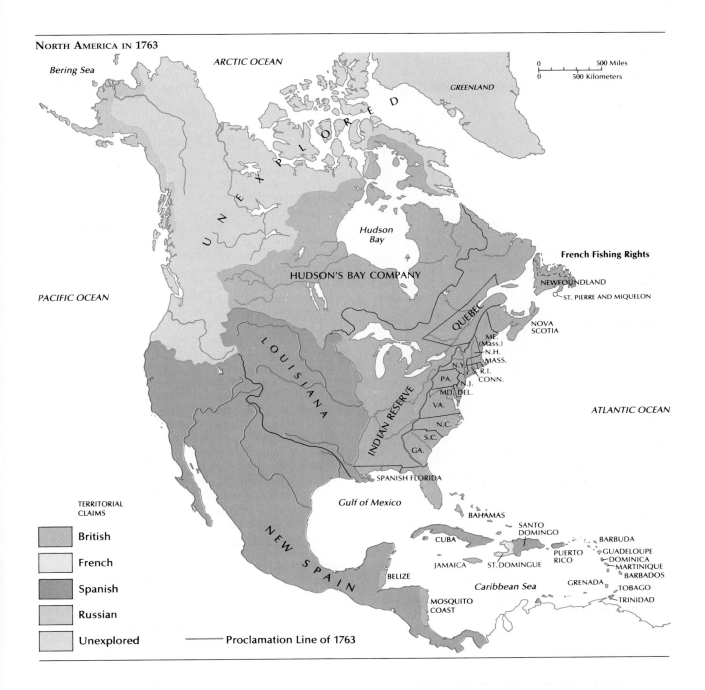

NORTH AMERICA IN 1763

TERRITORIAL CLAIMS

- British
- French
- Spanish
- Russian
- Unexplored

—— Proclamation Line of 1763

would be to risk further costly conflicts with the Indians and might encourage France to launch a new attack somewhere in America in an effort to recover some of its lost territories and prestige. And restricting settlement would keep the land available for hunting and trapping. Others wanted to see the new territories opened for immediate development, but they disagreed among themselves about who should control the western lands. Colonial governments made fervent, and often conflicting, claims of jurisdiction. Others argued that control should remain in England, and that the territories should be considered entirely new

GEORGE III

This portrait by the Scottish artist Allan Ramsay shows the twenty-two-year-old English king in his coronation robes as he ascended the throne in 1760. American patriots during the long revolutionary crisis came to consider George III a vicious and brutal tyrant. In reality, the king was a man of limited ability who tried desperately, stubbornly, and generally unsuccessfully to play a role for which he was fundamentally ill-suited. As early as 1780, he began to suffer intermittently from insanity. After 1810, he was blind and permanently deranged and spent the last decade of his sixty-year reign as an invalid, barred from all official business by the Regency Act of 1811. His son (later King George IV) served as regent in those years. *(Colonial Williamsburg Foundation)*

in England itself were objecting strenuously to increases in what they already considered excessively high taxes. The colonies, many British believed, had contributed virtually nothing to the support of a war fought in large part for their benefit. The necessity of stationing significant numbers of British troops on the Indian border after 1763 was adding even more to the cost of defending the American settlements. And the halfhearted response of the colonial assemblies to the war effort had suggested that in its search for revenue, England could not rely on any cooperation from the colonial governments. Only a system of taxation administered by London, the leaders of the empire believed, could effectively meet England's needs.

At this crucial moment in Anglo-American relations, with the imperial system in desperate need of redefinition, the government of England experienced a series of changes as a result of the accession to the throne of a new king. George III assumed power in 1760 on the death of his grandfather. And he brought two particularly unfortunate qualities to the office. First, he was determined, unlike his two predecessors, to be an active and responsible monarch. In part because of pressure from his ambitious mother, he removed from power the longstanding and relatively stable coalition of Whigs, who had (under Pitt and others) governed the empire for much of the century and whom the new king mistrusted. In their place, he created a new coalition of his own through patronage and bribes and gained an uneasy control of Parliament. Yet the new ministries that emerged as a result of these changes were inherently unstable, each lasting in office an average of only about two years.

The king had serious intellectual and psychological limitations that compounded his political difficulties. He suffered, apparently, from a rare disease that produced intermittent bouts of insanity. (Indeed, in the last years of his long reign he was, according to most accounts, a virtual lunatic, confined to the palace and unable to perform any official functions.) Yet even when George III was lucid and rational, which in the 1760s and 1770s was most of the time, he was painfully immature (he had been only twenty-two when he ascended the throne) and insecure—striving constantly to prove his fitness for his position but time and again finding himself ill equipped to handle the challenges he seized for himself. The king's personality, therefore, contributed to both the instability and the intransigence of the British government during these critical years.

More immediately responsible for the problems that soon emerged with the colonies, however, was George Grenville, whom the king made prime minister in 1763.

colonies, unlinked to the existing settlements. There were, in short, a host of problems and pressures that the British could not ignore.

At the same time, the government in London was running out of options in its effort to find a way to deal with its staggering war debt. Landlords and merchants

Grenville, a brother-in-law of William Pitt, did not share Pitt's sympathy with the American point of view. He agreed instead with the prevailing opinion within Britain that the colonists had been too long indulged and that they should be compelled to obey the laws and to pay a part of the cost of defending and administering the empire. He promptly began trying to impose a system upon what had been a loose collection of colonial possessions in America.

The British and the Tribes

The western problem was the most urgent. With the repulse of the French, settlers and traders from the English colonies had begun immediately to move over the mountains and into the upper Ohio Valley. Objecting to this intrusion into their land and their commerce, an alliance of Indian tribes, under the Ottawa chieftain Pontiac, struck back. To prevent an escalation of the fighting that might threaten western trade, the British government issued a ruling—the Proclamation of 1763—forbidding settlers to advance beyond a line drawn along the Appalachian mountains.

The Proclamation of 1763 was appealing to the British for several reasons. It would allow London, rather than the provincial governments and their land-hungry constituents, to control the westward movement of the white population. Hence, westward expansion would proceed in an orderly manner, and conflicts with the tribes, which were both militarily costly and dangerous to trade, might be limited. Slower western settlement would also slow the population exodus from the coastal colonies, where England's most important markets and investments were. And it would reserve opportunities for land speculation and fur trading for English rather than colonial entrepreneurs.

Although the Indians had few illusions about the Proclamation, which required them to cede still more land to the white settlers, many tribal groups supported the agreement as the best bargain available to them. The Cherokee, in particular, worked actively to hasten the drawing of the boundary, hoping to put an end to white encroachments for good. Relations between the western tribes and the British improved in at least some areas after the Proclamation, partly as a result of the work of the Indian superintendents the British appointed. John Stuart was in charge of Indian affairs in the southern colonies and Sir William Johnson in the northern ones. Both were sympathetic to Native American needs and lived among the tribes; Johnson married a Mohawk woman, Mary Brant, who was

later to play an important role in the American Revolution.

In the end, however, the Proclamation of 1763 failed to meet even the modest expectations of the Indians. It had some effect in limiting colonial land speculation in the West and in controlling the fur trade, but on the crucial point of the line of settlement it was almost completely ineffective. White settlers continued to swarm across the boundary and to claim lands farther and farther into the Ohio Valley. The British authorities tried repeatedly to establish limits to the expansion. In 1768, Stuart and Johnson negotiated new agreements with the western tribes creating a supposedly permanent boundary (which, as always, increased the area of white settlement at the expense of the Indians). But these treaties (signed respectively at Hard Labor Creek, South Carolina, and Fort Stanwix, New York) also failed to stop the white advance. Within a few years, the 1768 agreements were replaced with new ones, which pushed the line of settlement still farther West.

The Colonial Response

The Grenville ministry soon moved to increase its authority in the colonies in more direct ways. Regular British troops, London announced, would now be stationed permanently in the provinces; and under the Mutiny Act of 1765 the colonists were required to assist in provisioning and maintaining the army. Ships of the British navy were assigned to patrol American waters and search for smugglers. The customs service was reorganized and enlarged. Royal officials were ordered to take up their colonial posts in person instead of sending substitutes. Colonial manufacturing was to be restricted, so that it would not compete with the rapidly expanding industry in Great Britain.

The Sugar Act of 1764, designed in part to eliminate the illegal sugar trade between the continental colonies and the French and Spanish West Indies, raised the duty on sugar and established new vice-admiralty courts in America to try accused smugglers—thus depriving them of the benefit of sympathetic local juries. The Currency Act of 1764 required the colonial assemblies to stop issuing paper money (a widespread practice during the war) and to retire on schedule all the paper money already in circulation. Most momentous of all, the Stamp Act of 1765 imposed a tax on most printed documents in the colonies: newspapers, almanacs, pamphlets, deeds, wills, licenses.

The new imperial program was an effort to reapply to the colonies the old principles of mercantilism. And

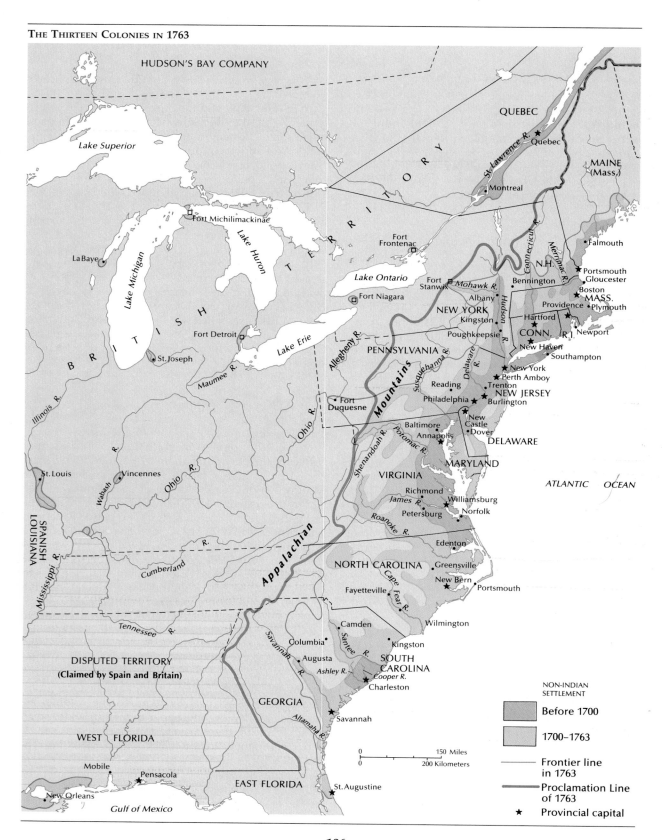

THE THIRTEEN COLONIES IN 1763

HUDSON'S BAY COMPANY

QUEBEC

Lake Superior

MAINE
(Mass.)

St. Lawrence R.
Quebec

Montreal

Fort Michilimackinae

Lake Huron

Fort Frontenac

B R I T I S H   T E R R I T O R Y

Lake Michigan

Lake Ontario

Fort Stanwix

Mohawk R.

N.H.

Connecticut R.

Merrimac R.

Falmouth

LaBaye

Portsmouth
Gloucester

Fort Niagara

Albany

Bennington

Boston

Fort Detroit

Lake Erie

NEW YORK

Kingston

Hudson R.

Providence
Hartford

MASS.

Plymouth

St. Joseph

Maumee R.

Allegheny R.

PENNSYLVANIA

Poughkeepsie

CONN.

R.I.

Newport

New Haven

Southampton

Mountains

Susquehanna R.

Delaware R.

New York

Reading

Perth Amboy

Illinois R.

Ohio R.

Fort Duquesne

Philadelphia

Trenton

NEW JERSEY

Burlington

St. Louis

Vincennes

Ohio R.

Baltimore

New Castle

Dover

DELAWARE

R.

Annapolis

Wabash R.

Shenandoah R.

Potomac R.

MARYLAND

ATLANTIC   OCEAN

SPANISH
LOUISIANA

VIRGINIA

Mississippi R.

Cumberland

Richmond

James R.

Williamsburg

Petersburg

Norfolk

Tennessee R.

Roanoke R.

Edenton

NORTH CAROLINA

Greensville

Cape Fear R.

New Bern

Portsmouth

DISPUTED TERRITORY
(Claimed by Spain and Britain)

Fayetteville

Wilmington

Camden

Santee R.

Kingston

Columbia

Augusta

Savannah R.

SOUTH
CAROLINA

Ashley R.

Cooper R.

Charleston

GEORGIA

R.

Appalachian

WEST   FLORIDA

Altamaha R.

Savannah

NON-INDIAN
SETTLEMENT

Before 1700

1700–1763

Mobile

Pensacola

EAST FLORIDA

St. Augustine

Frontier line
in 1763

Proclamation Line
of 1763

New Orleans

Gulf of Mexico

★ Provincial capital

0   150 Miles

0   200 Kilometers

in some ways, it proved highly effective. British officials were soon collecting more than ten times as much annual revenue in America as before 1763. But the new policies created many more problems than they solved.

The colonists may have resented the new imperial regulations, but they found it difficult to resist them effectively. For one thing, Americans continued to harbor as many grievances against one another as against the authorities in London. Often, the conflicts centered around tensions between the established societies of the Atlantic coast and the newer, more precarious areas of white settlement further west—areas often known as the "backcountry." Residents of the backcountry often felt isolated from, and underrepresented in, the colonial governments. And they sometimes felt beleaguered because their world was much closer to the worlds of the Indian tribes than the societies of the East. In 1763, for example, a band of people from western Pennsylvania known as the Paxton Boys descended on Philadelphia with demands for relief from colonial (not British) taxes and for money to help them defend themselves against Indians; the colonial government averted bloodshed only by making concessions to them.

In 1771, a small-scale civil war broke out as a result of the so-called Regulator movement in North Carolina. The Regulators were farmers of the Carolina upcountry who organized politically to oppose the high taxes that local sheriffs (appointed by the colonial governor) collected. The western counties were badly underrepresented in the colonial assembly, and the Regulators failed to win redress of their grievances there. Finally they armed themselves and began resisting tax collections by force. To suppress the revolt, Governor William Tryon raised an army of militiamen, mostly from the eastern counties, who defeated a band of 2,000 Regulators in the Battle of Alamance. Nine on each side were killed and many others wounded. Afterward, six Regulators were hanged for treason.

The bloodshed was exceptional, but bitter conflicts within the colonies were not. After 1763, however, the new policies of the British government began to create common grievances among virtually all colonists that to some degree counterbalanced these internal divisions. For under the Grenville program, as the Americans saw it, all people—in all classes, in all colonies—would suffer.

Northern mechants would suffer from restraints on their commerce, from the closing of opportunities for manufacturing, and from the increased burden of taxation. Backcountry settlers resented the closing of the West to land speculation and fur trading. Southern

planters, in debt to English merchants, would now have to pay additional taxes and would be unable to ease their debts by speculating in western land. Professional men—ministers, lawyers, professors, and others—depended on merchants and planters for their livelihood and thus shared their concerns about the effects of English law. Small farmers, the largest group in the colonies, would suffer from increased taxes and from the abolition of paper money, which had been the source of most of their loans. Workers in towns faced the prospect of narrowing opportunities, particularly because of the restraints on manufacturing and paper money.

The new restrictions came, moreover, at the beginning of an economic depression. The British government, by pouring money into the colonies to finance the fighting, had stimulated a wartime boom; that flow stopped after the peace in 1763. Now the authorities in London proposed to aggravate the problem by taking money out of the colonies. The imperial policies would, many colonists feared, doom them to permanent economic stagnation and a declining standard of living.

In reality, most Americans soon found ways to live with (or circumvent) the new British policies. The American economy was not, in fact, being destroyed. But economic anxieties were rising in the colonies nevertheless, and they created a growing sense of unease, particularly in the cities—the places most directly affected by British policies and the places where resistance first arose. The periodic economic slumps that were occurring with greater and greater frequency, the frightening depression of the early 1760s, the growth of a large group within the population who were unemployed or semi-employed, and who were in either case a destabilizing element in the community: all combined to produce a feeling in some colonial cities—and particularly in Boston, the city suffering the worst economic problems—that something was deeply amiss.

Whatever the economic consequences of the British government's programs, the political consequences were—in the eyes of the colonists, at least—far worse. Nowhere else in the world did so large a proportion of the people take an active interest in public affairs. Anglo-Americans were accustomed (and deeply attached) to a wide latitude in self-government. The keys to self-government, they believed, were the provincial assemblies; and the key to the power of the provincial assemblies was their long-established right to give or withhold appropriations for the colonial governments. By attempting to circumvent the colonial assemblies, raise extensive revenues directly from the public, and

PATRICK HENRY AND THE PARSON'S CAUSE, 1763
A dispute over ministerial salaries in the 1750s and early 1760s, known as the "Parson's Cause," became the occasion for some of the earliest colonial challenges to British authority. In 1759 the Privy Council in England responded to appeals from Anglican ministers in Virginia and overturned a colonial law regulating (and limiting) their salaries. As a result, ministers were able to sue for back pay. In a 1763 trial in Hanover County, the young Virginia attorney Patrick Henry persuaded a jury to rule against the Rev. James Maury in one such suit on the grounds that the king and his government had exceeded their authority. This painting by George Cooke (c. 1830) portrays Henry addressing the court as a large crowd of onlookers presses at the doors. *(Virginia Historical Society)*

provide salaries directly and unconditionally to royal officials in America, the British government was challenging the basis of colonial political power: control over public finance.

Home rule, therefore, was not something new and different that the colonists were striving to attain. It was something old and familiar that they desired to keep. The movement to resist the new imperial policies, a movement for which many would ultimately fight and die, was thus at the same time democratic and conservative. It was a movement to conserve liberties Americans believed they already possessed.

STIRRINGS OF REVOLT

By the mid-1760s, therefore, a hardening of positions had begun in both England and America that would bring the colonies into increasing conflict with the mother country. The victorious war for empire had given the colonists a heightened sense of their own importance and a renewed commitment to protecting their political autonomy. It had given the British a strengthened belief in the need to tighten administration of the empire and a strong desire to use the colonies as a source of revenue. The result was a series of events that, more rapidly than anyone could imagine, shattered the English empire in America.

The Stamp Act Crisis

If he had tried, Prime Minister Grenville could not have devised a better method for antagonizing and unifying the colonies than the Stamp Act of 1765. The Sugar Act of a year earlier had affected few people other than the New England merchants whose trade it hampered. But the new tax fell on all Americans, of whatever section, colony, or class. And it evoked particular opposition from some of the most powerful members of the population. Merchants and lawyers were obliged to buy stamps for ships' papers and legal documents. Tavern owners, often the political oracles of their neighborhoods, were required to buy stamps for their licenses. Printers—the most influential group in distributing information and ideas in colonial society—had to buy stamps for their newspapers and other publications.

The actual economic burdens of the Stamp Act were, in the end, relatively light. What made the law obnoxious to the colonists was not so much its immediate cost as the precedent it seemed to set. In the past, Americans had rationalized the taxes and duties on colonial trade as measures to regulate commerce, not raise money. Some Americans had even managed to persuade themselves that the Sugar Act, which was in fact designed primarily to raise money, was not fundamentally different from the traditional imperial duties. The Stamp Act, however, they could interpret in only one way. It was a direct attempt by England to raise revenue in the colonies without the consent of the colonial assemblies. If this new tax passed without resistance, the door would be open for more burdensome taxation in the future.

Few colonists believed that they could do anything more than grumble and buy the stamps—until the Virginia House of Burgesses sounded a "trumpet of sedition" that aroused Americans to action almost everywhere. The "trumpet" was the collective voice of a group of young Virginia aristocrats. They hoped, among other things, to challenge the power of tidewater planters who (in alliance with the royal governor) dominated Virginia politics. Foremost among the malcontents was Patrick Henry, who had already achieved fame through his fiery oratory and his defiance of British authority. Henry made a dramatic speech to the House in May 1765, concluding with a vague prediction that if present policies were not re-

vised, George III, like earlier tyrants, might lose his head. There were shocked cries of "Treason!" and, according to one witness, an immediate apology from Henry (although many years later he was quoted as having made the defiant reply: "If this be treason, make the most of it"). Henry introduced a set of resolutions declaring that Americans possessed the same rights as the English, especially the right to be taxed only by their own representatives; that Virginians should pay no taxes except those voted by the Virginia assembly; and that anyone advocating the right of Parliament to tax Virginians should be deemed an enemy of the colony. The House of Burgesses defeated the most extreme of Henry's resolutions, but all of them were printed and circulated as the "Virginia Resolves" (creating an impression in other colonies that the people of Virginia were more militant than they actually were).

In Massachusetts at about the same time, James Otis persuaded his fellow members of the colonial assembly to call an intercolonial congress for action against the new tax. In October 1765, the Stamp Act Congress met in New York with delegates from nine colonies and decided to petition the king and the two houses of Parliament. Their petition conceded that Americans owed to Parliament "all due subordination," but it denied that the colonies could rightfully be taxed except through their own provincial assemblies.

Meanwhile, in several colonial cities mobs began taking the law into their own hands. During the summer of 1765 serious riots broke out up and down the coast, the largest of them in Boston. Men belonging to the newly organized Sons of Liberty terrorized stamp agents and burned the stamps. The agents, themselves Americans, hastily resigned, and the sale of stamps in the continental colonies virtually ceased. In Boston, a mob also attacked such pro-British "aristocrats" as the lieutenant governor, Thomas Hutchinson (who had privately opposed passage of the Stamp Act but who, as an officer of the crown, felt obliged to support it once it became law). The protestors pillaged Hutchinson's elegant house and virtually destroyed it.

The action of the Stamp Act mobs raises the question of whether the protests in the colonies represented more than opposition to British policy. That the mobs seemed often to target symbols of affluence (such as Hutchinson's lavish home) as well as symbols of authority suggests that resentment of disparities of wealth (which had grown increasingly visible in colonial cities) played at least some role in fueling the anger among ordinary citizens. But opposition to British policy and protests against it were widespread, embracing rich and poor alike. Whatever class basis there may have been to the protests was almost certainly less important in the end than the larger political and ideological foundation.

The Stamp Act crisis was a dangerous moment in the relationship between the colonies and the British government. But the crisis subsided, largely because England backed down. It was not the legislative resolutions, the petitions, or the riots that deterred the authorities in London. What changed their attitude was economic pressure. Even before the Stamp Act, many New Englanders had stopped buying English goods to protest the Sugar Act of 1764. Now the colonial boycott spread, and the Sons of Liberty intimidated those colonists who were reluctant to participate in it. The merchants of England, feeling the loss of much of their colonial market, begged Parliament to repeal the Stamp Act, while stories of unemployment, poverty, and discontent arose from English seaports and manufacturing towns.

The Marquis of Rockingham, who succeeded Grenville as prime minister in July 1765, tried to appease both the English merchants and the American colonists, and he finally convinced the king to kill the Stamp Act. On March 18, 1766, Parliament repealed it. Rockingham's opponents were strong and vociferous, and they insisted that unless England compelled the colonists to obey the Stamp Act, they would soon cease to obey any laws of Parliament. So on the same day, to satisfy such critics, Parliament passed the Declaratory Act, asserting Parliament's authority over the colonies "in all cases whatsoever." In their rejoicing over the repeal, most Americans paid little attention to this sweeping declaration of power.

The Townshend Program

The English reaction to the Rockingham government's policy of appeasement was less enthusiastic than the American one. English landlords, a powerful political force, angrily protested that the government had "sacrificed the landed gentlemen to the interests of traders and colonists." They feared that backing down from taxing the colonies would lead the government to increase taxes on them. The king finally bowed to their pressure and dismissed the Rockingham ministry. To replace it, he called upon the aging but still powerful William Pitt to form a government. Pitt had been a strong critic of the Stamp Act and had a reputation in America as a friend of the colonists (even though his acceptance of a peerage in 1766 had disillusioned some of his American admirers). Once in office, however, Pitt (now Lord Chatham) was so hobbled by gout and at times so incapacitated by mental illness that the actual leadership of his administration fell to the chancellor of the exchequer, Charles Townshend—a brilliant, flamboyant, and at times reckless politician known to his contemporaries variously as "the Weathercock" and "Champagne Charlie."

Among Townshend's first challenges was dealing with the continuing American grievances against Parliament. The greatest of them, now that the Stamp Act had failed, involved the Mutiny (or Quartering) Act of 1765, which required the colonists to provide quarters and supplies for the British troops in America. The British considered this a reasonable requirement. The troops were stationed in North America to protect the colonists from Indian or French attack and to defend the frontiers; lodging the troops in coastal cities was simply a way to reduce the costs of supplying them. To the colonists, however, the law was another assault on their liberties. They did not so much object to quartering the troops or providing them with supplies; they had been doing that voluntarily ever since the last years of the French and Indian War. They resented that these contributions were now mandatory, and they considered it another form of taxation without consent. They responded with defiance. The Massachusetts Assembly refused to vote the mandated supplies to the troops. The New York Assembly soon did likewise, posing an even greater challenge to imperial authority, since the army headquarters were in New York City.

To enforce the law and to try again to raise revenues in the colonies, Townshend steered two measures through Parliament in 1767. The first disbanded the New York Assembly until the colonists agreed to obey the Mutiny Act. (By singling out New York, Townshend thought he would avoid Grenville's mistake of arousing all the colonies at once.) The second levied new taxes (known as the Townshend Duties) on various goods imported to the colonies from England—lead, paint, paper, and tea. The colonists could not logically object to taxation of this kind, Townshend reasoned, because it met standards they themselves had accepted. Benjamin Franklin, as a colonial agent in London trying to prevent the passage of the Stamp Act, had long ago argued for the distinction between "internal" and "external" taxes and had denounced the stamp duties as internal taxation. Townshend himself had considered the distinction laughable; but he was now imposing duties on what he believed were clearly external transactions.

But Townshend's efforts to satisfy colonial grievances were to no avail. The new duties were no more acceptable to Americans than the stamp tax. Townshend might call them external taxes, but colonial mer-

THE BRITISH IN BOSTON, 1768

British troops arrived in Boston on September 30, 1768, marched into the city, and pitched tents on the Boston common. The soldiers were charged with ensuring the safety of British customs officers, who three months earlier had been driven from the city by local residents and had appealed to England for protection. The presence of the troops became a continuing irritant in relations between the colonists and the British government. This 1770 engraving by Paul Revere shows troops embarking from British naval vessels at Long Wharf and marching "with insolent Parade" up King Street into the city. *(Henry Francis du Point Winterthur Museum)*

chants and, indirectly, colonial consumers would have to pay them. Their purpose was the same as that of the Stamp Act: to raise revenue from the colonists without their consent. And the suspension of the New York Assembly, far from isolating New York, aroused the resentment of all the colonies. They considered this assault on the rights of one provincial government a precedent for the annihilation of the rights of all of them.

The Massachusetts Assembly took the lead in opposing the new measures by circulating a letter to all the colonial governments urging them to stand up against every tax, external or internal, imposed by Parliament. At first, the circular evoked little response in some of the legislatures (and ran into strong opposition in Pennsylvania's). Then Lord Hillsborough, secretary of state for the colonies, issued a circular letter of his own from London in which he warned that as-

semblies endorsing the Massachusetts letter would be dissolved. Massachusetts defiantly reaffirmed its support for the circular. (The vote in the Assembly was 92 to 17, and for a time "ninety-two" became a patriotic rallying cry throughout British America.) The other colonies, including Pennsylvania, promptly rallied to the support of Massachusetts.

In addition to his other unpopular measures, Townshend tried to strengthen enforcement of commercial regulations in the colonies by, among other things, establishing a board of customs commissioners in America. Townshend hoped the new board would stop the rampant corruption in the colonial customs houses, and to some extent his hopes were fulfilled. The new commissioners virtually ended smuggling in Boston, their headquarters, although smugglers continued to carry on a busy trade in other colonial seaports.

The Boston merchants—accustomed, like all colonial merchants, to loose enforcement of the Navigation Acts and doubly aggrieved now that the new commission was diverting the lucrative smuggling trade elsewhere—were indignant, and they took the lead in organizing another boycott. In 1768, the merchants of Philadelphia and New York joined them in a nonimportation agreement, and later some southern merchants and planters also agreed to cooperate. Colonists boycotted British goods subject to the Townshend Duties; and throughout the colonies, American homespun and other domestic products became suddenly fashionable, while English luxuries fell from favor.

Late in 1767, Charles Townshend suddenly died—before the consequences of his ill-conceived program had become fully apparent. The question of dealing with colonial resistance to the Townshend Duties fell, therefore, to the new prime minister, Lord North. Hoping to break the nonimportation agreement and divide the colonists, Lord North secured the repeal in March 1770 of all the Townshend Duties except the tea tax.

The Boston Massacre

The withdrawal of the Townshend Duties never had a chance to pacify colonial opinion. Before news of the repeal reached America, an event in Massachusetts raised colonial resentment to a new level of intensity. The harassment of the new customs commissioners in Boston had grown so intense that the British government had placed four regiments of regular troops within the city. The presence of the "redcoats" was a constant affront to the colonists' sense of independence and a constant reminder of what they considered British oppression. Everywhere they went, Bostonians encountered British soldiers—often arrogant and intrusive, sometimes coarse and provocative. There was particular tension between the redcoats and Boston laborers. Many British soldiers, poorly paid and poorly treated by the army, wanted jobs in their off-duty hours; and they competed with local workers in an already tight market. Clashes between them were frequent.

On the night of March 5, 1770, a few days after a particularly intense skirmish between workers at a ship-rigging factory and British soldiers who were trying to find work there, a mob of dockworkers, "liberty boys," and others began pelting the sentries at the customs house with rocks and snowballs. Hastily, Captain Thomas Preston of the British regiment lined up several of his men in front of the building to protect it. There was some scuffling; one of the soldiers was knocked down; and in the midst of it all, apparently, several British soldiers fired into the crowd, killing five

people (among them a mulatto sailor, Crispus Attucks).

This murky incident, almost certainly the result of panic and confusion, was quickly transformed by local resistance leaders into the "Boston Massacre"—a graphic symbol of British oppression and brutality. The victims became popular martyrs; the event became the subject of such lurid (and inaccurate) accounts as the widely circulated pamphlet *Innocent Blood Crying to God from the Streets of Boston*. A famous engraving by Paul Revere, widely reproduced and circulated, portrayed the massacre as a carefully organized, calculated assault on a peaceful crowd. A jury of Massachusetts colonists found the British soldiers guilty of no more than manslaughter and sentenced them to no more than a token punishment. Colonial pamphlets and newspapers, however, convinced many Americans that the soldiers were guilty of official murder. Year after year, resistance leaders marked the anniversary of the massacre with demonstrations and speeches.

The leading figure in fomenting public outrage over the Boston Massacre was Samuel Adams, the most effective radical in the colonies. Adams (a distant cousin of John Adams, second president of the United States) was born in 1722 and was thus somewhat older than other leaders of colonial protest. As a member of an earlier generation with strong ties to New England's Puritan past, he was particularly inclined to view public events in stern moral terms. A failure in business, he had occupied several political and governmental positions, but his real importance was as a publicist, an unflagging voice expressing outrage at British oppression. England, he argued, had become a morass of sin and corruption; only in America did public virtue survive. He spoke frequently at Boston town meetings; and as one unpopular English policy followed another—the Townshend Duties, the placement of customs commissioners in Boston, the stationing of British troops in the city (with its violent results)—his message attracted increasing support. In 1772, he proposed the creation of a "committee of correspondence" in Boston to publicize the grievances against England throughout the colony, and he became its first head. Other colonies followed Massachusetts's lead, and there grew up a loose network of political organizations that kept the spirit of dissent alive through the 1770s.

The Philosophy of Revolt

"The Revolution was effected before the war commenced," John Adams later remarked. "The Revolution was in the minds and hearts of the people."

Adams exaggerated. Few Americans were willing to consider complete independence from England until after the war had begun, and even those few (among them Samuel Adams) generally denied that independence was their goal. But John Adams was certainly correct in arguing that well before the fighting began in 1775, a profound ideological shift had occurred in the way many Americans viewed the British government and their own.

The ideas that would support the Revolution emerged from many sources. Some were indigenous to America, drawn from religious (particularly Puritan) sources or from the political experiences of the colonies. But powerful arguments from abroad enriched and enlarged these native ideas. Particularly important were the "radical" ideas of those in Great Britain who stood in opposition to their government. Some were Scots, who viewed the English government as tyrannical. Others were embittered "country Whigs," who considered the existing system (from which they were largely excluded) corrupt and oppressive. Drawing from some of the great philosophical minds of earlier generations—among them John Locke—these English dissidents framed a powerful argument against their government; and while that argument had only limited appeal in England, it found a ready audience in the troubled colonies.

Central to this argument was a new concept of what government should be. Because humans were inherently corrupt and selfish, government was necessary to protect individuals from the evil in one another. But corruptible people ran government; and so it too needed safeguards against abuses of power.

In the eyes of most Englishmen and most Americans, the English constitution was the best system ever devised to meet these necessities. By distributing power among the three elements of society—the monarch, the aristocracy, and the common people—the English political system ensured that no individual or group could exercise authority unchecked by another. Yet by the mid-seventeenth century, dissidents in both England and America were becoming convinced that this noble constitution was in danger. The king and his ministers were exercising such corrupt and autocratic authority that they were undermining the independence of the various elements of government. A single center of power was emerging, and the system was thus threatening to become a dangerous tyranny.

The English constitution was not a written document, nor was it a fixed set of unchangeable rules. It was—and remains—a general (and flexible) sense of the "way things are done." Americans, however, thought of a consitution in terms of their colonial charters, which set out permanently, on paper, the shape and powers of government. They had difficulty accepting the idea of a flexible, changing set of basic principles. Many argued that the English constitution should itself be written down, to prevent fallible politicians from tampering with its essence.

Part of that essence, Americans believed, was their right to be taxed only with their own consent. When Townshend levied his "external" duties, the Philadelphia lawyer John Dickinson published a widely circulated pamphlet *Letters of a Pennsylvania Farmer,* which argued that even external taxation was legal only to regulate trade, not to raise a revenue. Gradually, most Americans ceased to accept even that distinction and took an unqualified stand: "No taxation without representation." Whatever the nature of a tax—whether internal or external, whether designed to raise revenue or to control trade—Parliament could not levy it without the consent of the colonists themselves.

This clamor about "representation" made little sense to the English. Only about 4 percent of the population of Great Britain could vote for members of Parliament, and some populous boroughs in England had no representatives at all. According to the prevailing English theory, such apparent inequities were of no importance. Members of Parliament did not represent individuals or particular geographical areas. Instead, each member represented the interests of the whole nation and indeed the whole empire, no matter where he happened to come from. The unenfranchised boroughs of England, the whole of Ireland, and the colonies thousands of miles away—all were thus represented in the Parliament at London, even though they elected no representatives of their own.

This was the theory of "virtual" representation. But Americans, drawing from their experiences with their town meetings and their colonial assemblies, believed in "actual" representation. Every community was entitled to its own representative, elected by the people of that community and directly responsible to them. Since they had none of their own representatives in Parliament, it followed that they were not represented there. But even having representatives in Parliament, many believed, would not resolve the problem, because their representatives would be outnumbered and outvoted and would be so isolated from the people who had elected them that they would not be able to perform as true representatives. Thus most colonists reverted to the argument that they could be fairly represented only in their own colonial assemblies.

According to the emerging American view of the empire, these assemblies played the same role within the colonies—had the same powers, enjoyed the same rights—that Parliament did within England. By the mid-1770s, some Americans were arguing that the empire was a sort of federation of commonwealths, each with its own legislative body, all tied together by common loyalty to the king (a view that augured the structure of the British Commonwealth in the twentieth century). This concept allowed them to vent their anger not at the empire itself, but at the English Parliament, which was presumptuously exerting authority to which it was not entitled over the colonies. Not until very late did they begin to criticize the king himself. And not until the colonies were ready to declare their independence in 1776 were they ready to repudiate the English constitution.

What may have made the conflict between England and America ultimately insoluble was a fundamental difference of opinion over the nature of sovereignty. By arguing that Parliament had the right to legislate for England and for the empire as a whole, but that only the provincial assemblies could legislate for the individual colonies, Americans were in effect arguing for a division of sovereignty. Parliament would be sovereign in some matters; the assemblies would be sovereign in others. To the British, such an argument was untenable and absurd. Sovereignty, they believed, was by definition unitary. In any system of government there must be a single, ultimate authority. And since the empire was, in their view, a single, undivided unit, there could be only one authority within it: the English government of king and Parliament. And so the Anglo-American crisis ultimately presented the colonists with a stark choice. In the eyes of the English, there was, in effect, no middle ground between complete subordination (at least in theory) and complete independence. Slowly, cautiously, Americans found themselves moving toward independence.

That movement began with resistance, not open revolt. Opposition to British policies in the 1760s had taken the form of refusal to obey certain unjust laws. Colonists justified that resistance by citing biblical and Lockean justifications for opposing tyranny. But those justifications included within them a rationale for actual rebellion as well. The Bible suggested that people had a right not only to resist but to overthrow unjust rulers. And Locke had argued that if a government should persist in exceeding its rightful powers, the people would be free not only from their obligation to obey particular laws but from their obligation to obey the government at all. They would have the right to dissolve the "compact" and make a new one, to establish another government. The right to resist was, in other words, only the first step. If resistance proved ineffective, if a government proved to be so thoroughly corrupt and tyrannical that it could not be reformed, then citizens were entitled to revolt against it. They had a "right of revolution."

By the early 1770s, the relationship between America and England had become poisoned by resentment and mutual suspicion. Many Americans had become convinced that a "conspiracy against liberty" existed within the British government. And they had articulated a philosophy that seemed to them to justify whatever measures might be necessary to protect themselves from that conspiracy. Only a small distance remained between resistance and revolution, before the colonists would be ready to break their ties with the empire. They crossed that distance quickly, beginning in 1773, when a new set of British policies shattered the imperial relationship forever.

The Tea Excitement

The apparent calm in America in the first years of the 1770s disguised a growing sense of resentment at the increasingly heavy-handed British enforcement of the Navigation Acts. The customs commissioners, who remained in the colonies despite the repeal of the Townshend Acts, were mostly clumsy, intrusive, and arrogant officials. They harassed colonial merchants and seamen constantly with petty restrictions, and they also enriched themselves through graft and through illegal seizures of merchandise. The popular anger lying just beneath the surface was visible in occasional acts of rebellion. At one point, colonists seized a British revenue ship on the lower Delaware River. And in 1772, angry residents of Rhode Island boarded the British schooner *Gaspée,* set it afire, and sank it in Narragansett Bay. The British response to the *Gaspée* affair further inflamed American opinion. Instead of putting the accused attackers on trial in colonial courts, the British sent a special commission to America with power to send the defendants back to England for trial.

What finally revived the revolutionary fervor of the 1760s, however, was a new act of Parliament—one that the English government had expected to be relatively uncontroversial. It involved the business of selling tea. In 1773, Britain's East India Company (which had an official monopoly on trade with the Far East) was sitting on large stocks of tea that it could not sell in England. It was on the verge of bankruptcy. In an effort to save the company, the government passed the Tea Act of 1773, which gave East India the right to export its merchandise directly to the colonies without paying any of the regular taxes that were imposed on the colonial merchants, who had traditionally served as the middlemen in such transactions. With these privileges,

Monday Morning, December 27, 1773.

THE Tea-Ship being arrived, every Inhabitant who wishes to preserve the Liberty of America, is desired to meet at the STATE-HOUSE, This Morning, precisely at TEN o'Clock, to advise what is best to be done on this alarming Crisis.

To the P U B L I C.

THE Sense of the City relative to the Landing the India Company's Tea, being signified to Captain Lockyer, by the Committee, nevertheless, it is the Desire of a Number of the Citizens, that at his Departure from hence, he should see, with his own Eyes, their Detestation of the Measures pursued by the Ministry and the India Company, to enslave this Country. This will be declared by the Convention of the People at his Departure from this City; which will be on next Saturday Morning, about nine o'Clock, when no Doubt, every Friend to this Country will attend. The Bells will give the Notice about an Hour before he embarks from Murray's Wharf.

By Order of the COMMITTEE.

NEW YORK, APRIL 21st, 1774.

THE BOSTON TEA PARTY

The artist Ramberg produced this wash drawing of the Boston Tea Party in 1773. A handbill in a Philadelphia newspaper ten days later and another distributed in New York the following April illustrate how quickly the spirit of resistance spread to other colonies. *(Left, Metropolitan Museum of Art;* Upper Right, *Chicago Historical Society;* Bottom Right, *Bettmann)*

the company could undersell American merchants and monopolize the colonial tea trade.

The act angered many colonists for several reasons. First, it enraged influential colonial merchants, who feared being replaced and bankrupted by a powerful monopoly. The East India Company's decision to grant franchises to certain American merchants for the sale of their tea created further resentments among those excluded from this lucrative trade. More important, however, the Tea Act revived American passions about the issue of taxation without representation. The law provided no new tax on tea. But the original Townshend duty on the commodity—the only one of the original duties that had not been repealed—survived. It was the East India Company's exemption from that duty that put the colonial merchants at such a grave competitive disadvantage. Lord North assumed that most colonists would welcome the new law because it would reduce the price of tea to consumers by removing the middlemen. But resistance leaders in America argued that it was another insidious example of the results of an unconstitutional tax. Many colonists responded by boycotting tea.

The boycott was an important event in the history of colonial resistance. Unlike earlier protests, most of which had involved relatively small numbers of people, the boycott mobilized large segments of the population. It also helped link the colonies together in a common experience of mass popular protest. Particularly important to the movement were the activities of colonial women, who were among the principal consumers of tea and now became leaders of the effort to boycott it.

Women had played a significant role in resistance activities from the beginning. Several women (most prominently Mercy Otis Warren) had been important in writing the dissident literature—in Warren's case satirical plays—that did much to fan colonial resentments in the 1760s. Women had participated actively in anti-British riots and crowd activities in the 1760s; they had formed an informal organization—the Daughters of Liberty—that occasionally mocked their male counterparts as insufficiently militant. The Sons of Liberty, they wrote in a 1768 poem, were "Supinely asleep, and depriv'd of their Sight . . . strip'd of their Freedom, and rob'd of their Right." Now, as the sentiment for a boycott grew, some women mobilized as never before, determined (as the Daughters of Liberty

PAYING THE EXCISEMAN
This eighteenth-century satirical drawing by a British artist depicts Bostonians forcing tea down the throat of a customs official, whom they have tarred and feathered. In the background, colonists are dumping tea into the harbor (presumably a representation of the 1773 Boston Tea Party); and on the tree at right is a symbol of the Stamp Act, which the colonists had defied eight years earlier. *(Metropolitan Museum of Art)*

had written) "that rather than Freedom, we'll part with our Tea."

In the last weeks of 1773, with strong popular support, leaders in various colonies made plans to prevent the East India Company from landing its cargoes in colonial ports. In Philadelphia and New York, determined colonists kept the tea from leaving the company's ships. In Charleston, they stored it away in a public warehouse. In Boston, after failing to turn back the three ships in the harbor, local patriots staged a spectacular drama. On the evening of December 16, 1773, three companies of fifty men each, masquerading as Mohawks, passed through a tremendous crowd of spectators (which served to protect them from official interference), went aboard the three ships, broke open the tea chests, and heaved them into the harbor. As the electrifying news of the Boston "tea party" spread, other seaports followed the example and staged similar acts of resistance of their own.

When the Bostonians refused to pay for the property they had destroyed, George III and Lord North decided on a policy of coercion, to be applied only against Massachusetts—the chief center of resistance. In four acts of 1774, Parliament closed the port of Boston, drastically reduced the powers of self-government in the colony, permitted royal officers to be tried in other colonies or in England when accused of crimes, and provided for the quartering of troops in the colonists' barns and empty houses.

Parliament followed these Coercive Acts—or, as they were more widely known in America, Intolerable Acts—with the Quebec Act, which was separate from them in origin and quite different in purpose. Its object was to provide a civil government for the French-speaking Roman Catholic inhabitants of Canada and the Illinois country. The law extended the boundaries of Quebec to include the French communities between the Ohio and Mississippi Rivers. It also granted political rights to Roman Catholics and recognized the legality of the Roman Catholic church within the enlarged province. In many ways it was a tolerant and long overdue piece of legislation. But in the inflamed atmosphere of the time, many people in the thirteen colonies considered it a threat. They were already alarmed by rumors that the Church of England was scheming to appoint a bishop for America who would impose Anglican authority on all the various sects. And since the line between the Church of England and the Church of Rome had always seemed to many Americans dangerously thin, the passage of the Quebec Act convinced some of them that a plot was afoot in London to subject Americans to the tyranny of the pope. Those interested in western lands, moreover, believed that the act would hinder westward expansion.

The Coercive Acts, far from isolating Massachusetts, made it a martyr to residents of other colonies and sparked new resistance up and down the coast. Colonial legislatures passed a series of resolves supporting Massachusetts. Women's groups throughout the colonies mobilized to extend the boycotts of British goods and to create substitutes for the tea, textiles, and other commodities they were shunning. In Edenton, North Carolina, fifty-one women signed an agreement in October 1774 declaring their "sincere adherence" to the anti-British resolutions of their provincial assembly and proclaiming their duty to do "every thing as far as lies in our power" to support the "publick good."

COOPERATION AND WAR

Revolutions do not simply happen. They need organizers and leaders. Beginning in 1765, colonial leaders developed a variety of organizations for converting popular discontent into direct action—organizations that in time formed the basis for an independent government.

New Sources of Authority

The passage of authority from the royal government to the colonists themselves began on the local level, where the tradition of autonomy was already strong. In colony after colony, local institutions responded to the resistance movement by simply seizing authority on their own. At times, entirely new, extralegal bodies emerged semi-spontaneously and began to perform some of the functions of government. In Massachusetts in 1768, for example, Samuel Adams called a convention of delegates from the towns of the colony to sit in place of the General Court, which the governor had dissolved. The Sons of Liberty, which Adams had helped organize in Massachusetts and which sprang up elsewhere as well, became another source of power. Its members at times formed disciplined bands of vigilantes who made certain that all colonists respected the boycotts and other forms of popular resistance. And in most colonies, committees of prominent citizens began meeting to perform additional political functions.

The most effective of these new groups were the committees of correspondence, which Adams had inaugurated in Massachusetts in 1772. Virginia later established the first intercolonial committees of correspondence, which made possible continuous cooperation among the colonies. And Virginia took the greatest step of all toward united action in 1774 when, after the royal governor dissolved the assembly, a rump session met in the Raleigh Tavern at Williamsburg, declared that the Intolerable Acts menaced the liberties of every colony, and issued a call for a Continental Congress.

Variously elected by the assemblies and by extralegal meetings, delegates from all the thirteen colonies except Georgia were present when, in September 1774,

the First Continental Congress convened in Carpenter's Hall in Philadelphia. They made five major decisions. First, in a very close vote, they rejected a plan (proposed by Joseph Galloway of Pennsylvania) for a colonial union under British authority (much like the earlier Albany Plan). Second, they endorsed a statement of grievances, whose tortured language reflected the conflicts among the delegates between moderates and extremists. The statement reflected the influence of the moderates by seeming to concede Parliament's right to regulate colonial trade and by addressing the king as "Most Gracious Sovereign"; but it included a more extreme demand for the repeal of all the oppressive legislation passed since 1763. Third, they approved a series of resolutions that a Suffolk County, Massachusetts, convention had passed recommending, among other things, that the colonists make military preparations for defense against possible attack by the British troops in Boston. Fourth, they agreed to nonimportation, nonexportation, and nonconsumption as means of stopping all trade with Great Britain, and they formed a "Continental Association" to enforce the agreements. And fifth, when the delegates adjourned, they agreed to meet again the next spring, thus indicating that they considered the Continental Congress a continuing organization.

Through their representatives in Philadelphia the colonies had, in effect, reaffirmed their autonomous status within the empire and declared economic war to maintain that position. The more optimistic of the Americans supposed that economic warfare alone would win a quick and bloodless victory, but the more pessimistic had their doubts. "I expect no redress, but, on the contrary, increased resentment and double vengeance," John Adams wrote to Patrick Henry; "we must fight." And Henry replied, "By God, I am of your opinion."

During the winter, the Parliament in London debated proposals for conciliating the colonists. Lord Chatham (William Pitt), the former prime minister, urged the withdrawal of troops from America. Edmund Burke called for the repeal of the Coercive Acts. But their efforts were in vain. Lord North finally won approval early in 1775 for a series of measures known as the Conciliatory Propositions, but they were in fact far less conciliatory than the approaches Burke or Chatham had urged. Parliament now proposed that the colonies, instead of being taxed directly by Parliament, would tax themselves at Parliament's demand. With this offer, Lord North hoped to divide the American moderates, who he believed represented the views of the majority, from the extremist minority. But his offer was probably too little and, in any case, too late. It

THE FIRST BATTLES OF THE REVOLUTION

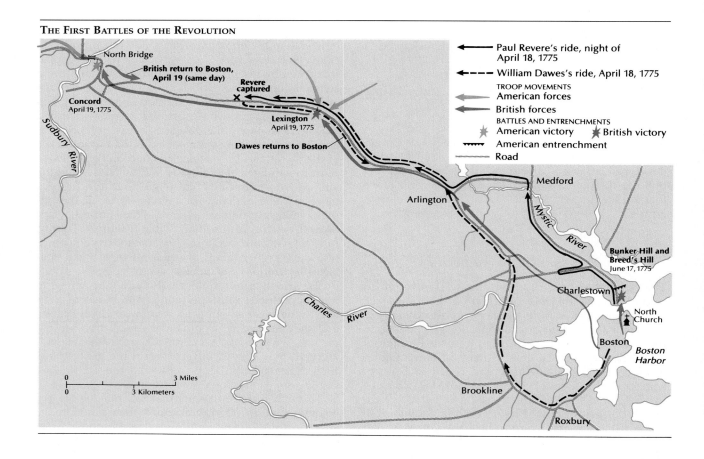

did not reach America until after the first shots of war had been fired.

Lexington and Concord

For months, the farmers and townspeople of Massachusetts had been gathering arms and ammunition and training as "minutemen," preparing to fight on a minute's notice. The Continental Congress had approved preparations for a defensive war, and the citizen-soldiers awaited an aggressive move by the British regulars in Boston.

In Boston, General Thomas Gage, commanding the British garrison, knew of the military preparations in the countryside but considered his army too small to do anything until reinforcements arrived. He resisted the advice of less cautious officers, who assured him that the Americans would never dare actually to fight, that they would back down quickly before any show of British force. Major John Pitcairn, for example, insisted that a single "small action," such as the burning of a few towns, would "set everything to rights."

When General Gage received orders from England to arrest the rebel leaders Sam Adams and John Hancock, known to be in the vicinity of Lexington, he still hesitated. But when he heard that the minutemen had stored a large supply of gunpowder in Concord (eighteen miles from Boston), he at last decided to act. On the night of April 18, 1775, he sent a detachment of about 1,000 soldiers out from Boston on the road to Lexington and Concord. He intended to surprise the colonials and seize the illegal supplies without bloodshed.

But patriots in Boston were watching the British movements closely, and during the night two horsemen, William Dawes and Paul Revere, rode out to warn the villages and farms. When the British troops arrived in Lexington the next day, several dozen minutemen awaited them on the town common. Shots were fired and minutemen fell; eight of them were killed and ten more wounded. Advancing to Concord,

The Retreat

From Concord to Lexington of the Army of Wild Irish Asses Defeated by the Brave American Militia

Mr Deacon Mr Loeings Mr Mulikens Mr Bonds Houses and Barn all Plunder'd and Burnt on April 19th.

THE BRITISH RETREAT FROM CONCORD, 1775

This American cartoon satirizes the retreat of British forces from Concord after the battle there on April 19, 1775. Patriot forces are lined up on the left, and the retreating British forces (portrayed with dog heads, perhaps because many of the soldiers were "wild" Irish) straggle off at right—some fleeing in panic, others gloating over the booty they have plundered from the burning homes above. In its crude and exaggerated way, the cartoon depicts the success of Patriot forces at the Old North Bridge in Concord in repulsing a British contingent under the command of Lord Percy. As the redcoats retreated to Lexington and then to Boston, they continued to encounter fire from colonial forces, not arrayed in battle lines as shown here, but hidden along the road. One British soldier described the nightmarish withdrawal: "We were fired on from Houses and behind Trees . . . the Country was . . . full of Hills, Woods, stone Walls . . . which the Rebels did not fail to take advantage of." *(Brown University Library)*

the British discovered that the Americans had hastily removed most of the powder supply, but the British burned what was left of it. All along the road from Concord back to Boston, farmers hiding behind trees, rocks, and stone fences harassed the British with continual gunfire. By the end of the day, the British had lost almost three times as many men as the Americans.

The first shots—the "shots heard round the world," as Americans later called them—had been fired. But who had fired them? According to one of the minutemen at Lexington, Major Pitcairn had shouted to the colonists on his arrival, "Disperse, ye rebels!" When the Americans ignored the command, he had given the order to fire. British officers and soldiers told a different story. They claimed that the minutemen had fired first, that only after seeing the flash of American guns had the British begun to shoot. Whatever the truth, the rebels succeeded in circulating their account well ahead of the British version, adorning it with lurid tales of British atrocities. The effect was to rally to the rebel cause thousands of colonists, north and south, who previously had had little enthusiasm for it.

It was not immediately clear to the British, and even to many Americans, that the skirmishes at Lexington and Concord were the first battles of a war. Many saw them as simply another example of the tensions that had been afflicting Anglo-American relations for years. But whether they recognized it at the time or not, the British and the Americans had taken a decisive step. The War for Independence had begun.

SIGNIFICANT EVENTS

1713 Treaty of Utrecht concludes Queen Anne's War

1718 New Orleans founded to serve French plantation economy in Louisiana

1744–1748 King George's War

1749 French construct fortresses in Ohio Valley

1754 Albany Plan for intercolonial cooperation rejected

Battle of Fort Duquesne begins French and Indian War

1756 Seven Years' War begins in Europe

1757 British policies provoke riots in New York

1758 Pitt returns authority to colonial assemblies

British capture Louisbourg fortress and Fort Duquesne

1759 British forces under Wolfe capture Quebec

1760 George III becomes King

French army surrenders to Amherst at Montreal

1763 Peace of Paris ends Seven Years' (and French and Indian) War

Grenville becomes prime minister

Proclamation of 1763 restricts western settlement

Paxton uprising in Pennsylvania

1764 Sugar Act passed

Currency Act passed

1765 Stamp Act crisis

Mutiny Act passed

1766 Stamp Act repealed

Declaratory Act passed

1767 Townshend duties imposed

1768 Boston, New York, and Philadelphia merchants make nonimportation agreement

1770 Boston Massacre

Most Townshend Duties repealed

1771 Regulator movement quelled in North Carolina

1772 Committees of correspondence established in Boston

Gaspée incident in Rhode Island

1773 Tea Act passed

Bostonians stage tea party

1774 Intolerable Acts passed

First Continental Congress meets at Philadelphia

North Carolina women sign Edenton Proclamation calling for boycott of British goods

1775 Clashes at Lexington and Concord begin American Revolution

SUGGESTED READINGS

General Histories. J. R. Alden, *A History of the American Revolution* (1969). Charles M. Andrews, *The Colonial Background of the American Revolution* (1924, rev. 1931). Ian R. Christie, *Crisis of Empire* (1966). Ian R. Christie and Benjamin W. Labaree, *Empire or Independence, 1760–1776* (1976). Edward Countryman, *The American Revolution* (1985). Lawrence Henry Gipson, *The Coming of the Revolution, 1763–1775* (1954). Merill Jensen, *The Founding of a Nation* (1968). Robert Middlekauff, *The Glorious Cause: The American Revolution, 1763–1789* (1982). John C. Miller, *Origins of the American Revolution* (1957). Edmund S. Morgan, *The Birth of the Republic* (1956). Alfred E. Young, Jr., ed., *The American Revolution* (1976).

The British Imperial System. John Brewer, *Party Ideology and Popular Politics at the Accession of George III* (1967). John Brooke, *King George III* (1972). Richard L. Bushman, *King and People in Colonial Massachusetts* (1987). Bernard Donoughue, *British Politics and the American Revolution: The Path to War, 1773–1775* (1965). Sylvia R. Frey, *The British Soldier in America* (1981). Lawrence Henry Gipson, *The British Empire Before the American Revolution*, 15 vols. (1936–1970). Michael Kammen, *A Rope of Sand* (1968). Lewis B. Namier, *England in the Age of the American Revolution*, rev. ed. (1961); *The Structure of Politics at the Accession of George III*, rev. ed. (1961). Robert C. Newbold, *The Albany Congress and Plan of Union of 1754* (1955). Robert R. Palmer, *The Age of the Democratic Revolution: Vol. 1, The Challenge* (1959). Richard Pares, *War and Trade in the West Indies, 1739–1763* (1936). Howard H. Peckham, *The Colonial Wars, 1689–1762* (1963). Alan Rogers, *Empire and Liberty* (1974). John Shy, *Toward Lexington: The Role of the British Army in the Coming of the American Revolution* (1965).

The French and the Indians. Thomas P. Abernethy, *Western Lands and the American Revolution* (1937). Fred Anderson, *A People's Army: Massachusetts Soldiers and Society in the Seven Years War* (1984). David H. Corkran, *The Cherokee Frontier* (1962); and *The Creek Frontier* (1967). R. S. Cotterill, *The Southern Indians* (1954). Francis Jennings, *Empire of Fortune* (1988); and *The Ambiguous Iroquois Empire* (1984). Howard H. Peckham, *Pontiac and the Indian Uprising* (1947). William Pencak, *War, Politics, and Revolution in Provincial Massachusetts* (1981). Harold E. Selesky, *War and Society in Early Connecticut* (1990). J. M. Sosin, *Whitehall and the Wilderness* (1961). Richard White, *The Middle Ground: Indians, Empires, and Republics in the Great Lakes Region, 1650–1815* (1991).

Merchants and the Empire. Thomas C. Barrow, *Trade and Empire: The British Customs Service in Colonial America* (1967). Oliver M. Dickerson, *The Navigation Acts and the American Revolution* (1951). Thomas Doerflinger, *A Vigorous Spirit of Enterprise: Merchants and Economic Development in Revolutionary Philadelphia* (1986). Joseph Ernst, *Money and Politics in America, 1755–1775* (1973). Michael Kammen, *Empire and Interest: The American Colonies and the Politics of Mercantilism* (1970). Arthur M. Schlesinger, *The Colonial Merchants and the American Revolution* (1917). John W. Tyler, *Smugglers and Patriots: Boston Merchants and the Advent of the American Revolution* (1986).

American Resistance. David Ammerman, *In the Common Cause* (1974). Marc Egnal, *A Mighty Empire: The Origins of the American Revolution* (1988). Paul A. Gilje, *The Road to Mobocracy: Popular Disorder in New York City, 1763–1834* (1987). Dirk Hoerder, *Crowd Action in Revolutionary Massachusetts* (1977). Peter C. Hoffer, *Revolution and Regeneration: Life Cycle and the Historical Vision of the Generation of 1776* (1983). Benjamin W. Labaree, *The Boston Tea Party* (1964). Pauline Maier, *From Resistance to Revolution* (1972). Edmund S. Morgan and Helen M. Morgan, *The Stamp Act Crisis*, rev. ed. (1953). Peter D. G. Thomas, *The Townshend Duties Crisis* (1987). Hiller B. Zobel, *The Boston Massacre* (1970).

Revolutionary Ideology. Bernard Bailyn, *The Ideological Origins of the American Revolution* (1967). Ian R. Christie, *Wilkes, Wyvil, and Reform* (1962). Nathan Hatch, *The Sacred Cause of Liberty* (1977). Rhys Isaac, *The Transformation of Virginia, 1740–1790* (1982). Isaac Kramnick, *Bolingbroke and His Circle* (1968). Richard Merritt, *Symbols of American Community, 1735–1775* (1966). Gary B. Nash, *The Urban Crucible: The Northern Seaports and the Origins of the American Revolution* (1979). Clinton Rossiter, *Seedtime of the Republic* (1953). George Rudé, *Wilkes and Liberty* (1962).

Revolutionary Politics. Carl Becker, *The History of Political Parties in the Province of New York* (1909). R. E. Brown and B. K. Brown, *Virginia, 1705–1786* (1964). Richard D. Brown, *Revolutionary Politics in Massachusetts* (1970). L. R. Gerlach, *Prologue to Independence* (1976). Ronald Hoffman, *A Spirit of Dissension* (1973). David Lovejoy, *Rhode Island Politics and the American Revolution* (1958). Neil R. Stout, *The Perfect Crisis: The Beginning of the Revolutionary War* (1976). Charles S. Sydnor, *Gentlemen Freeholders* (1952). Theodore Thayer, *Pennsylvania Politics and the Growth of Democracy* (1953).

PULLING DOWN THE STATUE OF GEORGE III
In the immediate aftermath of independence, many Americans sought to destroy symbols of their colonial past. In this updated painting, Patriots in New York City topple a statue of King George III, as fires and chaos erupt around them.   *(New-York Historical Society)*

CHAPTER FIVE

THE AMERICAN REVOLUTION

WO STRUGGLES OCCURRED SIMULTANEOUSLY during the seven years of war that began in April 1775. One was the military conflict with Great Britain. The second was a political conflict within America. The two struggles had profound effects on each other.

The military conflict was, by the standards of later wars, a relatively modest one. Battle deaths on the American side totaled fewer than 5,000. The technology of warfare was so crude that cannons and rifles were effective only at very close range, and fighting of any kind was virtually out of the question in bad weather. Yet the war in America was, by the standards of its own day, an unusually savage conflict, pitting not only army against army, but at times the population at large against a powerful external force. This shift of the war from a traditional, conventional struggle to a new kind of conflict—a revolutionary war for liberation—made it possible for the new American army finally to defeat the vastly more powerful British.

At the same time, Americans were wrestling with the great political questions the conflict necessarily produced: first, whether to demand independence from Britain; then, how to structure the new nation they had proclaimed. Only the first of these questions had been resolved when the British surrendered at Yorktown in 1781. But by then the United States had already established itself—both in its own mind and in the mind of much of the rest of the world—as a new kind of nation, one with a special mission and dedicated to enlightened ideals. Thomas Paine, an impor-

tant figure in shaping the Revolution, reflected the opinion of many when he claimed that the American War for Independence had "contributed more to enlighten the world, and diffuse a spirit of freedom and liberality among mankind, than any human event . . . that ever preceded it." And if the subsequent history of the United States did not always fulfill those ideals, the belief that it should exercised a continuing influence on the nation's behavior.

THE STATES UNITED

Although many Americans had been expecting a military conflict with Britain for months, even years, the actual beginning of hostilities in 1775 found the colonies generally unprepared for the enormous challenges awaiting them. America was a still-unformed nation, with a population less than a third as large as the 9 million of Great Britain, and with vastly inferior economic and military resources. It faced the task of mobilizing for war against the world's greatest armed power. Americans faced that task, moreover, deeply divided about what they were fighting for.

Defining American War Aims

Three weeks after the battles of Lexington and Concord, the Second Continental Congress met in the State

House in Philadelphia, with delegates from every colony except Georgia, which sent no representative until the following autumn. The members agreed to support the war. But they disagreed, at times profoundly, about its purpose.

At one extreme was a group led by the Adams cousins (John and Samuel), Richard Henry Lee of Virginia, and others, who favored complete independence from Great Britain. At the other extreme was a group led by such moderates as John Dickinson of Pennsylvania, who hoped for modest reforms in the imperial relationship that would permit an early reconciliation with Great Britain. Most of the delegates tried to find some middle ground between these positions. They demonstrated their uncertainty in two very different declarations, which they adopted in quick succession. They approved one last, conciliatory appeal to the king, the so-called Olive Branch Petition. Then, on July 6, 1775, they adopted a Declaration of the Causes and Necessity of Taking Up Arms. It proclaimed that the British government had left the American people with only two alternatives, "unconditional submission to the tyranny of irritated ministers or resistance by force."

The attitude of much of the public mirrored that of the Congress. At first, most Americans believed they were fighting not for independence but for a redress of grievances within the British Empire. During the first year of fighting, however, many of them began to change their minds, for several reasons. First, the costs of the war—human and financial—were so high that the original war aims began to seem too modest to justify them. Second, what lingering affection American Patriots retained for England greatly diminished when the British began trying to recruit Indians, black slaves, and foreign mercenaries (the hated "Hessians") against them. Third, and most important, colonists came to believe that the British government was forcing them toward independence by rejecting the Olive Branch Petition and instead enacting the Prohibitory Act, which closed the colonies to all overseas trade and made no concessions to American demands except an offer to pardon repentant rebels. The British enforced the Prohibitory Act with a naval blockade of colonial ports.

But the growing support for independence remained to a large degree unspoken until January 1776, when an impassioned pamphlet appeared that galvanized many Americans. It was called, simply, *Common Sense*. Its author, unmentioned on the title page, was Thomas Paine, who had emigrated from England to America less than two years before (with letters of introduction from Benjamin Franklin, whom he had met in London). Long a failure in various trades, Paine now

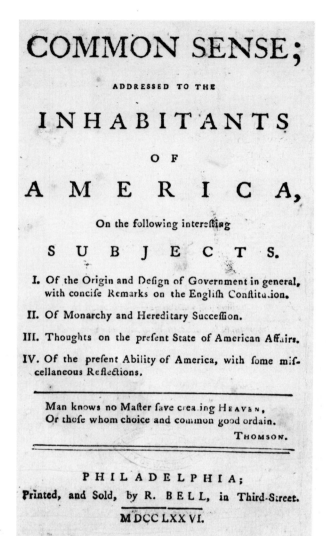

COMMON SENSE
Shown here is the title page of the first edition of Thomas Paine's influential pamphlet, published anonymously in Philadelphia on January 10, 1776. Paine served in Washington's army during the campaigns in New Jersey and at the same time wrote a series of essays designed to arouse support for the Patriot cause. They were collectively titled *The Crisis* (the first of them contains the famous phrase "These are the times that try men's souls"). In later years Paine took an active part in the French Revolution, on behalf of which he published *The Rights of Man* (1791–1792). He also wrote *The Age of Reason* (1794–1796), which attacked conventional Christian beliefs and promoted his own "deist" philosophy. He returned to America in 1802 and spent the last years before his death in 1809 in poverty and obscurity. *(Library of Congress)*

proved a brilliant success as a revolutionary propagandist. His pamphlet helped change the American outlook toward the war. Paine wished to expose the folly of continuing to believe reconciliation with Britain was possible. He wanted to turn the anger of Americans away from the specific parliamentary measures they were resisting and toward what he considered the root of the problem—the English constitution itself. It was not enough, he argued, for Americans to continue blaming their problems on particular ministers, or even on Parliament. It was the king, and the system that permitted him to rule, that was to blame. It was, he argued, simple common sense for Americans to break completely with a government that could produce so corrupt a monarch as George III, a gov-

ernment that could inflict such brutality on its own people, a government that could drag Americans into wars in which America had no interest. The island kingdom of England was no more fit to rule the American continent, he claimed, than a satellite was fit to rule the sun.

The Decision for Independence

Common Sense sold more than 100,000 copies in its first few months. To many of its readers it was a revelation. Although sentiment for independence was still far from unanimous, support for the idea grew rapidly in the first months of 1776.

VOTING FOR INDEPENDENCE
The Continental Congress actually voted in favor of independence from Great Britain on July 2, 1776. July 4, the date Americans now celebrate as Independence Day, is when the Congress formally approved the Declaration of Independence. This painting by Edgar Pine-Savage re-creates the scene in Philadelphia as delegates from the various colonies made their momentous decision.   *(Historical Society of Pennsylvania)*

In the midst of all this, the Continental Congress (meeting again in Philadelphia) was moving slowly and tentatively toward a final break with England. It opened American ports to the ships of all nations except Great Britain, entered into communication with foreign powers, and recommended to the various colonies that they establish governments without the authority of the empire, as in fact most already were doing. Congress also appointed a committee to draft a formal declaration of independence. On July 2, 1776, it adopted a resolution: "That these United Colonies are, and, of right, ought to be, free and independent states; that they are absolved from all allegiance to the British crown, and that all political connexion between them and the state of Great Britain is, and ought to be, totally dissolved." Two days later, on July 4, Congress approved the Declaration of Independence itself, which provided the formal justifications for the actions the delegates had in fact taken two days earlier.

Thomas Jefferson, a thirty-three-year-old delegate from Virginia, wrote most of the Declaration, with some help from Benjamin Franklin and John Adams. As Adams later observed, Jefferson said little in the document that was new. Its virtue lay in the eloquence with which it expressed beliefs already widespread in America.

The document was in two parts. In the first, Jefferson restated the familiar contract theory of John Locke: that governments were formed to protect the rights of life, liberty, and property; Jefferson gave the theory a more idealistic tone by referring instead to the rights of "life, liberty and the pursuit of happiness." In the second part he listed the alleged crimes of the king, who, with the backing of Parliament, had violated his "contract" with the colonists and thus had forfeited all claim to their loyalty.

The Declaration's ringing endorsement of the idea that "all men are created equal" was to help movements of liberation and reform of many kinds in the United States; abroad it helped inspire the French Revolution's own Declaration of the Rights of Man. More immediately, the Declaration—and its claim of American sovereignty—led to increased foreign aid for the struggling rebels and prepared the way for France's intervention on their side. It steeled American Patriots, as those opposing the British called themselves, to fight on, to reject the idea of a peace that stopped short of winning independence. And at the same time it created deep divisions within American society.

At the news of the Declaration of Independence, crowds in Philadelphia, Boston, and other places gathered to cheer, fire guns and cannons, and ring church bells. But there were many in America who did not rejoice. Some had disapproved of the war from the beginning. Others had been willing to support it only so long as its aims did not conflict with their basic loyalty to the king. Such people were a minority, but a substantial one. They called themselves Loyalists; supporters of independence called them Tories.

In the aftermath of the Declaration of Independence, the colonies began to call themselves states—a reflection of their belief that each province was now in some respects a separate and sovereign entity. And as states, they had to create new governments to replace the royal governments that independence had repudiated. By 1781, most states had produced written constitutions that established republican governments; some of these governments survived, with only minor changes, for decades to come.

At the national level, however, the process was more halting and less successful. For a time, Americans were uncertain whether they even wanted a real national government; the Continental Congress had not been much more than a coordinating mechanism, and virtually everyone considered the individual colonies (now states) the real centers of authority. Yet fighting a war required a certain amount of central direction. Americans began almost immediately to do something they would continue to do for more than two centuries: balance the commitment to state and local autonomy against the need for some centralized authority.

In November 1777, Congress adopted the Articles of Confederation (which were not finally ratified until 1781). They did little more than confirm the weak, decentralized system already in operation. The Continental Congress would survive as the chief coordinating agency of the war effort, but its powers over the individual states would be very limited. Indeed, the Articles did not make it entirely clear that the Congress was to be a real government at all. The new nation would fight a war for its survival with a weak and uncertain central government, never sure of its own legitimacy.

Mobilizing for War

The new governments of the states and the nation faced a series of overwhelming challenges: raising and organizing armies, providing them with the supplies and equipment they needed, and finding a way to pay for it all. Without access to the British markets on which the colonies had come to depend, finding nec-

REVOLUTIONARY SOLDIERS
Jean Baptiste de Verger, a French officer serving in America during the Revolution, kept a journal of his experiences illustrated with watercolors. Here he portrays four American soldiers carrying different kinds of arms: a black infantryman with a light rifle, a musketman, a rifleman, and an artilleryman. *(Brown University Library)*

essary supplies was exceptionally difficult. Shortages persisted to the end.

America had many gunsmiths, but they could not come close to meeting the wartime demand for guns and ammunition, let alone the demand for heavy arms. Although Congress created a government arsenal at Springfield, Massachusetts, in 1777, the Americans managed to manufacture only a small fraction of the equipment they used. They relied heavily on weapons and materiel they were able to capture from the British. But they got most of their war materials from European nations, mainly from France.

Financing the war proved in many ways the most nettlesome problem. Congress had no authority to levy taxes directly on the people; it had to requisition funds from the state governments. But hard money was scarce in America, and the states were little better

equipped to raise it than Congress was. None of them contributed more than a small part of their expected share. Congress tried to raise money by selling long-term bonds, but few Americans could afford them and those who could generally preferred to invest in more profitable ventures, such as privateering. In the end, the government had no choice but to issue paper money. Continental currency came from the printing presses in large and repeated batches. The states printed sizable amounts of paper currency of their own.

The result, predictably, was inflation. Prices rose to fantastic heights, and the value of paper money plummeted. Many American farmers and merchants began to prefer doing business with the British, who could pay for goods in gold or silver coin. (That was one reason why George Washington's troops suffered from severe food shortages at Valley Forge in the winter of

1777–1778; many Philadelphia merchants would not sell to them.) Congress tried repeatedly to stem the inflationary spiral. But all such efforts failed. In the end, the new American government was able to finance the war effort only by borrowing heavily from other nations.

After the first great surge of patriotism ebbed in 1775, few Americans volunteered for military service. As a result, the states had to resort to persuasion and force, to bounties and the draft. Even when it was possible to recruit substantial numbers of militiamen, they remained under the control of their respective states. Congress recognized the disadvantages of this decentralized system and in 1775 created a Continental army with a single commander in chief. George Washington, a forty-three-year-old Virginia planter-aristocrat who had commanded colonial forces during the French and Indian War, possessed more experience than any other American-born officer available. He had also been an early advocate of independence. Above all, he was admired, respected, and trusted by nearly all Patriots. He was the unanimous choice of the delegates, and he took command in June 1775.

Congress had chosen well. Throughout the war, Washington kept faithfully at his task, despite difficulties and discouragements that would have daunted a lesser man. He had to deal with serious problems of morale among soldiers who consistently received short rations and low pay; open mutinies broke out in 1781 among the Pennsylvania and New Jersey troops. The Continental Congress, Washington's "employers," always seemed too little interested in supplying him with manpower and equipment and too much interested in interfering with his conduct of military operations. During the discouraging winter of Valley Forge, some congressmen and army officers apparently even conspired unsuccessfully (in the so-called Conway Cabal, named for Thomas Conway, one of its alleged leaders) to replace Washington as commander in chief.

Washington was not without shortcomings as a military commander. But he was, in the end, a great war leader. With the aid of foreign military experts such as the Marquis de Lafayette from France and Baron von Steuben from Prussia, he succeeded in building and holding together an army of fewer than 10,000 men that, along with the state militias, ultimately prevailed against the greatest military power in the world. Even more important, perhaps, in a new nation still unsure of either its purposes or its structure, with a central government both weak and contentious, Washington provided the army—and the people—with a symbol of stability around which they could rally. He may not have been the most brilliant of the country's early leaders. But in the crucial years of the war, at least, he was the most successful in holding the new nation together.

THE WAR FOR INDEPENDENCE

On the surface, at least, all the advantages in the military struggle between America and Great Britain appeared to lie with the British. They possessed the greatest navy and the best-equipped army in the world. They had access to the resources of an empire. They had a coherent structure of command. The Americans, by contrast, were struggling to create an army and a government at the same time that they were trying to fight a war.

Yet the United States had advantages that were not at first apparent. Americans were fighting on their own ground, while the English were far from their own land (and their own resources). The American Patriots were, on the whole, deeply committed to the conflict; the British people only halfheartedly supported the war. And beginning in 1777, the Americans had the benefit of substantial aid from abroad, when the American war became part of a larger world contest in which Great Britain faced the strongest powers of Europe—most notably France—in a struggle for imperial supremacy.

But the American victory was not simply the result of these advantages, or even of the remarkable spirit and resourcefulness of the people and the army. It was a result, too, of a series of egregious blunders and miscalculations by the British in the early stages of the fighting, when England could (and probably should) have won. And it was, finally, a result of the transformation of the war—through three different phases—into a new kind of conflict that the British military, for all its strength, could not win.

The First Phase: New England

For the first year of the fighting—from the spring of 1775 to the spring of 1776—the British remained uncertain about whether or not they were actually engaged in a war. Many English authorities continued to believe that what was happening in America was a limited, local conflict and that British forces were simply attempting to quell pockets of rebellion in the contentious area around Boston. Gradually, however, colonial forces took the offensive and made almost the entire territory of the American colonies a battleground.

THE REVOLUTION IN THE NORTH, 1775–1776

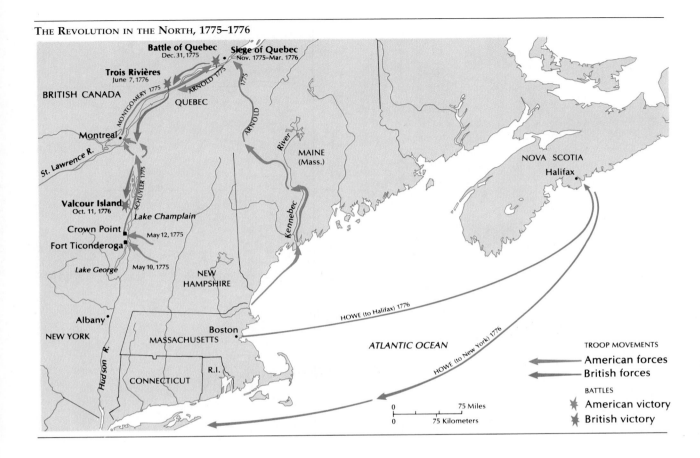

After the British withdrawal from Concord and Lexington in April 1775, American forces besieged the army of General Thomas Gage in Boston. The Patriots suffered severe casualties in the Battle of Bunker Hill (actually fought on Breed's Hill) on June 17, 1775, and were ultimately driven from their position there. But they inflicted much greater losses on the enemy (indeed, the heaviest casualties the British were to suffer in the entire war) and thereafter continued to tighten the siege. By the first months of 1776, the British had concluded that Boston was not the best place from which to wage war. Not only was it in the center of the most fervently anti-British region of the colonies, it was also tactically indefensible—a narrow neck of land, easily isolated and besieged. By late winter, in fact, Patriot forces had surrounded the city and occupied strategic positions on the heights. And so, on March 17, 1776 (a date still celebrated in Boston as Evacuation Day), the British departed Boston for Halifax in Nova Scotia with hundreds of Loyalist refugees. Less than a year after the firing of the first shots, the Massachusetts colonists had driven the British—temporarily—from American soil.

Elsewhere, the war proceeded fitfully and inconclusively. To the south, at Moore's Creek Bridge in North Carolina, a band of Patriots crushed an uprising of Loyalists on February 27, 1776, and in the process discouraged a British plan to invade the southern states. The British had expected substantial aid from local Tories; they realized now that such aid might not be as effective as they had hoped. To the north, Americans launched an invasion of Canada—hoping to remove the British threat and to win the Canadians to their cause. Benedict Arnold, the commander of a small American force, threatened Quebec in late 1775 and early 1776 after a winter march of incredible hardship. Richard Montgomery, coming to his assistance, combined his forces with Arnold's and took command of both. Montgomery died in the assault on the city; and although a wounded Arnold kept up the siege for a time, the Quebec campaign ended in frustration. A civilian commission sent to Canada by Con-

THE BATTLE OF BUNKER HILL, 1775
British troops face Patriot forces outside Boston on June 17, 1775, in the first great battle of the American Revolution. The British ultimately drove the Americans from their positions on Breed's Hill and Bunker Hill, but only after suffering enormous casualties. General Gage, the British commander, reported to his superiors in London after the battle: "These people show a spirit and conduct against us they never showed against the French." This anonymous painting reveals the array of British troops and naval support and also shows the bombardment and burning of Charlestown from artillery in Boston. *(National Gallery of Art, Washington)*

gress and headed by the seventy-year-old Franklin also failed to win the allegiance of the northern colonists. Canada was not to become part of the new nation.

The British evacuation in 1776 was not, therefore, so much a victory for the Americans as a reflection of changing English assumptions about the war. By the spring of 1776, it had become clear to the British that the conflict was not a local phenomenon in the area around Boston. The American campaigns in Canada, the agitation in the South, and the growing evidence of colonial unity all suggested that England must be prepared to fight a much larger conflict. The departure

of the British, therefore, marked a shift in strategy more than an admission of defeat.

The Second Phase: The Mid-Atlantic Region

The next phase of the war, which lasted from 1776 until early 1778, was when the British were in the best position to win. Indeed, had it not been for a series of blunders and misfortunes, they probably would have crushed the rebellion then. For during this period the

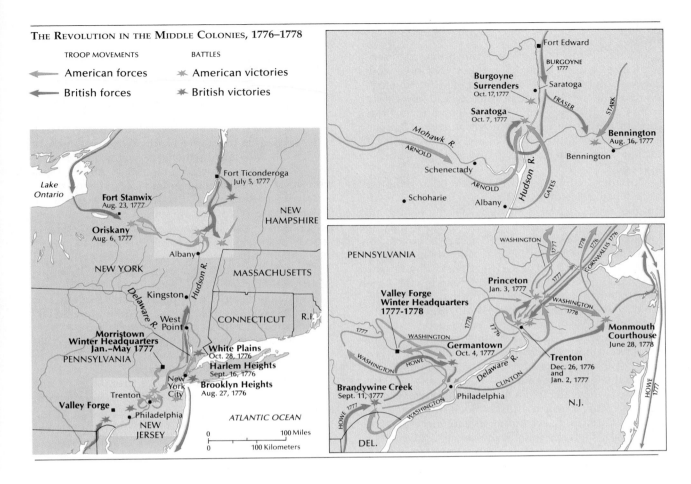

THE REVOLUTION IN THE MIDDLE COLONIES, 1776–1778

TROOP MOVEMENTS
- American forces
- British forces

BATTLES
- American victories
- British victories

struggle became, for the most part, a traditional, conventional war. And in that, the Americans were woefully overmatched.

The British regrouped quickly after their retreat from Boston. During the summer of 1776, in the weeks immediately following the Declaration of Independence, the waters around New York City grew crowded with the most formidable military force Great Britain had ever sent abroad. Hundreds of men-of-war and troopships and 32,000 disciplined soldiers arrived, under the command of the affable William Howe. Howe felt no particular hostility toward the Americans. He hoped to awe them into submission rather than fight them, and he believed that most of them, if given a chance, would show their loyalty to the king. In a meeting with commissioners from Congress, he offered them a choice between submission with royal pardon and a battle against overwhelming odds.

To oppose Howe's impressive array, Washington could muster only about 19,000 poorly armed and trained soldiers, even after combining the Continental army with state militias; he had no navy at all. Even so, the Americans quickly rejected Howe's offer and chose to continue the war—a decision that led inevitably to a succession of rapid defeats. The British pushed the defenders off Long Island, compelled them to abandon Manhattan, and then drove them in slow retreat over the plains of New Jersey, across the Delaware River, and into Pennsylvania.

For eighteenth-century Europeans, warfare was a seasonal activity. Fighting ceased in cold weather. The British settled down for the winter at various points in New Jersey, with an outpost of Hessians (German mercenaries) at Trenton on the Delaware. But Washington did not sit still. On Christmas night 1776, he boldly recrossed the icy river, surprised and scattered the Hessians, and occupied the town. Then he advanced to Princeton and drove a British force from their base in the college there. But Washington was unable to hold either Princeton or Trenton, and he finally took refuge for the rest of the winter in the hills around Morristown.

For the campaigns of 1777 the British devised a strategy to cut the United States in two. Howe would move north from New York City up the Hudson to Albany, while another British force would come south from Canada to meet him. One of the younger British officers, the dashing John Burgoyne, secured command of this northern force and planned a two-pronged attack along both the Mohawk and the upper Hudson approaches to Albany.

But after setting this plan in motion, Howe himself abandoned it. He decided instead to launch an assault on the rebel capital Philadelphia—an assault that would, he hoped, discourage the Patriots, rally the Loyalists, and bring the war to a speedy conclusion. He removed the bulk of his forces from New York by sea, landed at the head of the Chesapeake Bay, brushed Washington aside at the Battle of Brandywine Creek on September 11, and proceeded north to Philadelphia, which he was able to occupy with little resistance. Meanwhile, Washington, after an unsuccessful October 4 attack at Germantown (just outside Philadelphia), went into winter quarters at Valley Forge. The Continental Congress, now dislodged from its capital, reassembled at York, Pennsylvania.

Howe's move to Philadelphia left Burgoyne to carry out the campaign in the north alone. Burgoyne sent Colonel Barry St. Leger up the St. Lawrence River toward Lake Ontario and the headwaters of the Mohawk, while Burgoyne himself advanced directly down the upper Hudson Valley. He got off to a flying start. He seized Fort Ticonderoga easily and with it an enormous store of powder and supplies; this caused such dismay in Congress that the delegates removed General Philip Schuyler from command of American forces in the north and replaced him with Horatio Gates.

By the time Gates took command, Burgoyne had already experienced two staggering defeats. In one of them—at Oriskany, New York, on August 6—a Patriot band of German farmers led by Nicholas Herkimer held off a force of Indians and Tories commanded by St. Leger. That gave Benedict Arnold time to go to the relief of Fort Stanwix and close off the Mohawk Valley to St. Leger's advance.

In the other battle—at Bennington, Vermont, on August 16—New England militiamen under the Bunker Hill veteran John Stark severely mauled a detachment that Burgoyne had sent out to seek supplies. Short of materials, with all help cut off, Burgoyne fought several costly engagements and then withdrew to Saratoga, where Gates surrounded him. On October 17, 1777, Burgoyne ordered what was left of his army, nearly 5,000 men, to surrender.

The campaign in upstate New York was not just a British defeat. It was a setback for the ambitious efforts of several Iroquois leaders, who hoped to involve Indian forces in the English military effort, believing that a British victory would help stem white encroachments on tribal lands. Although the Iroquois Confederacy had declared its neutrality in the Revolutionary War in 1776, not all Native Americans were content to remain passive in the northern campaign. Among those who worked to expand the Indian role in the war were a Mohawk brother and sister, Joseph and Mary Brant. Both were people of stature within the Mohawk nation: Joseph was a celebrated warrior; Mary was a magnetic woman and the widow of Sir William Johnson, the British superintendent of Indians, who had achieved wide popularity among the tribes. The Brants persuaded their own tribe to contribute to the British cause and attracted the support of the Seneca and Cayuga as well. They played an important role in Burgoyne's unsuccessful campaigns in the north.

But the alliance was also a sign of the growing divisions within the Iroquois Confederacy. Only three of the six nations of the Confederacy supported the British. The Oneida and the Tuscarora backed the Americans; the Onondaga split into several factions. The three-century-old Confederacy, weakened by the aftermath of the French and Indian War, continued to unravel.

The alliance had other unhappy consequences for the Iroquois. A year after Oriskany, Indians joined British troops in a series of raids on outlying white settlements in upstate New York. Months later, Patriot forces under the command of General John Sullivan harshly retaliated, wreaking such destruction on Indian settlements that large groups of Iroquois fled north into Canada to seek refuge. Many never returned.

To the Patriots, however, the New York campaign was a remarkable victory. News of it reverberated throughout the new nation and through Europe as well. The British surrender at Saratoga became a major turning point in the war—above all, perhaps, because it led directly to an alliance between the United States and France.

The British failure to win the war during this period, a period in which they had overwhelming advantages, was in large part a result of their own mistakes. And in assessing them, the role of William Howe looms large. He abandoned his own most important strategic initiative—the northern campaign—leaving Burgoyne to fight alone. And even in the south, where he chose to engage the enemy, he refrained from moving in for a final attack on the weakened Continental army, even though he had several opportunities. Instead, he repeatedly allowed Washington to retreat and regroup; and he permitted the American army to spend a long winter unmolested in Valley Forge, where—weak and hungry—they might have been easy prey for British attack. Some believed that Howe did not want to win the war, that he was secretly in sympathy with the American cause. His family had close ties to the colonies, and he himself was linked politically to those forces within the British government that opposed the war. Others pointed to personal weaknesses: Howe's apparent alcoholism, his romantic attachment (he spent the winter of 1777–1778 in Philadelphia with his mistress when many were urging him to move elsewhere). But the most important problem, it seems clear, was lack of judgment.

Whatever the reasons, the failure of the British to crush the Continental army in the mid-Atlantic states, combined with the stunning American victory at Saratoga, transformed the war and ushered it into a new and final phase.

Securing Aid from Abroad

Central to this transformation of the war was American success in winning support from abroad—indirect support from several European nations, and direct support from France. Even before the Declaration of Independence, Congress dispatched representatives to the capitals of Europe to negotiate commercial treaties with the governments there; if America was to leave the British empire, it would need to cultivate new trading partners. Such treaties would, of course, require European governments to recognize the United States as an independent nation.

"Militia diplomats," John Adams called the early American representatives abroad; and unlike the diplomatic regulars of Europe, they had little experience with the formal art and etiquette of Old World diplomacy. Since transatlantic communication was slow and uncertain (it took from one to three months to cross the Atlantic), they had to interpret the instructions of Congress very freely and make crucial decisions entirely on their own.

The most promising potential ally for the United States was France. King Louis XVI, who had come to the throne in 1774, and his astute foreign minister, the Count de Vergennes, were eager to see Britain lose a crucial part of its empire. Through a series of covert bargains, facilitated by the creation of a fictional trading firm and the use of secret agents on both sides (among them the famed French dramatist Caron de Beaumarchais), France began supplying the Americans large quantities of much-needed supplies. But the French government remained reluctant to provide the United States with what it most wanted: diplomatic recognition.

Finally, Benjamin Franklin himself went to France to represent the United States. A natural diplomat, Franklin became a popular hero among the French—aristocrats and common people alike. His popularity helped the American cause. Of even greater help was the news of the American victory at Saratoga, which arrived in London on December 2, 1777, and in Paris two days later. On February 6, 1778—in part to forestall a British peace offensive that Vergennes feared might persuade the Americans to abandon the war—France formally recognized the United States as a sovereign nation and laid the groundwork for greatly expanded assistance to the American war effort.

France's intervention made the war an international conflict. In the course of the next two years, France, Spain, and the Netherlands all drifted into another general war with Great Britain in Europe, and all contributed both directly and indirectly to the ultimate American victory. But France was America's truly indispensable ally. Not only did it furnish the new nation with most of its money and munitions, it also provided a navy and an expeditionary force that proved invaluable in the decisive phase of the revolutionary conflict.

The Final Phase: The South

The last phase of the military struggle in America was very different from either of the first two. The British government had never been fully united behind the war in the first place; after the defeat at Saratoga and the intervention of the French, it imposed new limits on its commitment to the conflict. Instead of a full-scale military struggle against the American army, therefore, the British decided to enlist the support of those elements of the American population—a majority, they continued to believe—who were still loyal to the crown; in other words, they would work to undermine the Revolution from within. Since the British believed Loyalist sentiment was strongest in the southern colonies, the main focus of their effort shifted there; and so it was in the South, for the most part, that the final stages of the war occurred.

The new strategy was a dismal failure. British forces spent three years (from 1778 to 1781) moving

THE REVOLUTION IN THE SOUTH, 1778–1781

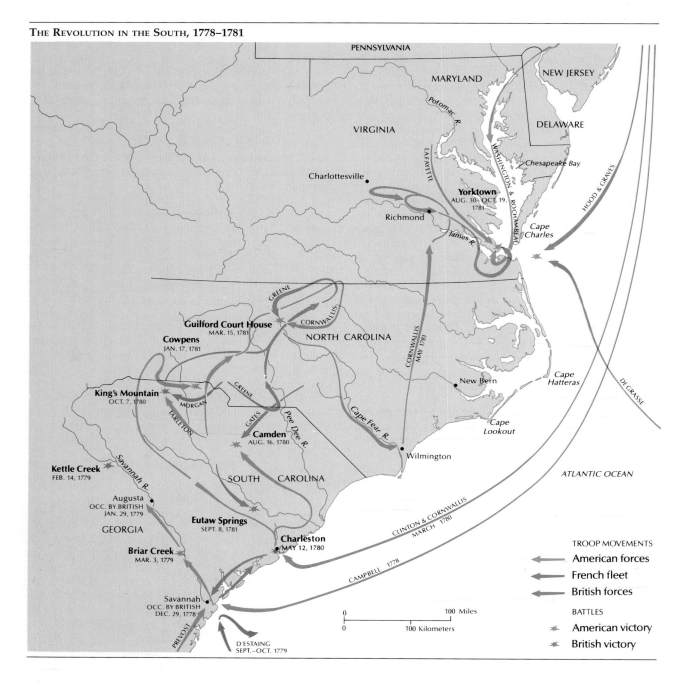

TROOP MOVEMENTS
→ American forces
→ French fleet
→ British forces

BATTLES
✳ American victory
✳ British victory

through the South, fighting small battles and large, and attempting to neutralize the territory through which they traveled. All such efforts ended in frustration. The British badly overestimated the extent of Loyalist sentiment. There were many Tories in Georgia and the Carolinas, some of them disgruntled members of the Regulator movement. But there were also many more Patriots than the British had believed. In Virginia, support for independence was as fervent as in Massachusetts. And even in the lower South, Loyalists often refused to aid the British because they feared reprisals from the Patriots around them. The British also faced severe logistical problems in the South. Patriot forces could move at will throughout the region, living off the resources of the countryside, blending in with the civilian population and leaving the British unable to distinguish friend from foe. The British, by contrast, suffered all the disadvantages of an army in hostile territory.

It was this phase of the conflict that made the war truly "revolutionary"—not only because it introduced a new kind of warfare, but because it had the effect of mobilizing and politicizing large groups of the population who had previously remained aloof from the struggle. With the war expanding into previously isolated communities, with many civilians forced to involve themselves whether they liked it or not, the political climate of the United States grew more heated than ever. And support for independence, far from being crushed as the British had hoped, greatly increased.

That was the context in which the important military encounters of the last years of the war occurred. In the North, where significant numbers of British troops remained, the fighting settled into a relatively quiet stalemate. Sir Henry Clinton replaced the hapless William Howe in 1778 and moved what had been Howe's army from Philadelphia back to New York. There the British troops stayed for more than a year, with Washington using his army to keep watch around them. The American forces in New York did so little fighting in this period that Washington sent some troops west to fight hostile Indians who had been attacking white settlers. During that same winter, George Rogers Clark, under orders from the state of Virginia—not from either Washington or Congress—led a daring expedition over the mountains and captured settlements in the Illinois country from the British and their Indian allies.

During this period of relative calm, General Benedict Arnold shocked the American forces—and Washington in particular—by becoming a traitor. Arnold had been one of the early heroes of the war, but now, convinced that the American cause was hopeless, he conspired with British agents to betray the Patriot stronghold at West Point on the Hudson River. The scheme unraveled before Arnold could complete it, and he fled to the safety of the British camp, where he spent the rest of the war.

In the meantime, the decisive fighting was in progress in the South. The British did have some significant military successes during this period. On December 29, 1778, they captured Savannah, on the coast of Georgia; and on May 12, 1780, they took the port of Charleston, South Carolina. They also inspired

some Loyalists to take up arms and advance with them into the interior. But although the British were able to win conventional battles, they were constantly harassed as they moved through the countryside by Patriot guerrillas led by such resourceful fighters as Thomas Sumter, Andrew Pickens, and Francis Marion, the "Swamp Fox."

Penetrating to Camden, South Carolina, Lord Cornwallis (Clinton's choice as British commander in the South) met and crushed a Patriot force under Horatio Gates on August 16, 1780. Congress recalled Gates, and Washington gave the southern command to Nathanael

---

CORNWALLIS ENTERS PHILADELPHIA, SEPTEMBER 26, 1777
After defeating General Anthony Wayne's forces outside the city, the British general Lord Cornwallis led his army into Philadelphia, where jubilant loyalists greeted them with enthusiasm. "Some of the older spectators," the British historian Trevelyan later wrote, "could not avoid comparing that brilliant and martial procession with the destitute and dilapidated army which, trying hard to look its best, had traversed the same line of streets a few weeks before." *(New York Public Library)*

Greene, a former Quaker blacksmith from Rhode Island and probably the ablest of all the American generals of the time next to Washington himself.

Even before Greene arrived in the war theater, the tide of battle began to turn against Cornwallis. At King's Mountain (near the North Carolina–South Carolina border) on October 7, 1780, a band of Patriot riflemen from the backwoods killed, wounded, or captured an entire force of 1,100 New York and South Carolina Tories that Cornwallis was using as auxiliaries. Once Greene arrived, he confused and exasperated Cornwallis by dividing the American forces into small, fast-moving contingents while refraining from a showdown in open battle. One of the contingents inflicted what Cornwallis admitted was "a very unexpected and severe blow" at Cowpens on January 17, 1781. Finally, after receiving reinforcements, Greene combined all his forces and maneuvered to meet the British on ground of his own choosing, at Guilford Court House, North Carolina. After a hard-fought battle there on March 15, 1781, Greene withdrew from the field; but Cornwallis lost so many men that he decided at last to abandon the Carolina campaign.

Cornwallis withdrew to the port town of Wilmington, North Carolina, to receive supplies being sent to him by sea; later he moved north to launch raids in the interior of Virginia. But Clinton, concerned for the army's safety, ordered him to take up a position on the peninsula between the York and James rivers and wait for ships to carry his troops to New York or Charleston. So Cornwallis retreated to Yorktown and began to build fortifications there.

George Washington—along with the Count Jean Baptiste de Rochambeau, commander of the French expeditionary force in America, and Admiral François Joseph Paul de Grasse, commander of the French fleet in American waters—set out to trap Cornwallis at Yorktown. Washington and Rochambeau marched a French-American army from New York to join other French forces under Lafayette in Virginia, while de Grasse sailed with additional troops for Chesapeake Bay and the York River. These joint operations, perfectly timed and executed, caught Cornwallis between land and sea. After a few shows of resistance, he capitulated on October 17, 1781 (four years to the day after the capitulation of Burgoyne at Saratoga). Two days later, as a military band played the old tune "The World Turn'd Upside Down," he formally surrendered his army of more than 7,000 men.

Except for a few skirmishes, the fighting was now over; but the United States had not yet won the war. British forces continued to hold the seaports of Savannah, Charleston, Wilmington, and New York. Before long, a British fleet met and defeated Admiral de Grasse's fleet in the West Indies, ending Washington's hopes for further French naval assistance. For more than a year, although there was no significant further combat between British and American forces, it remained possible that the war might resume and the struggle for independence might still be lost.

Winning the Peace

Cornwallis's defeat provoked outcries in England against continuing the war. Lord North resigned as prime minister; Lord Shelburne emerged from the political wreckage to succeed him; and British emissaries appeared in France to talk informally with the American diplomats there, of whom the three principals were Benjamin Franklin, John Adams, and John Jay.

The Americans were under instructions to cooperate fully with France in their negotiations with England. But Vergennes insisted that France could not agree to any settlement of the war with England until its ally Spain had achieved its principal war aim: winning back Gibraltar from the British. There was no real prospect of that happening soon, and the Americans began to fear that the alliance with France might keep them at war indefinitely. As a result, Franklin, Jay, and Adams began proceeding on their own, without informing Vergennes, and signed a preliminary treaty with Great Britain on November 30, 1782. Franklin, in the meantime, skillfully pacified Vergennes and avoided an immediate rift in the French-American alliance.

The British and Americans signed a final treaty on September 3, 1783, when both Spain and France agreed to end hostilities. It was, on the whole, remarkably favorable to the United States in granting a clear-cut recognition of independence and a generous, though ambiguous cession of territory—from the southern boundary of Canada to the northern boundary of Florida and from the Atlantic to the Mississippi. With good reason Americans celebrated in the fall of 1783 as the last of the British occupation forces embarked from New York and General Washington, at the head of his troops, rode triumphantly into the city.

WAR AND SOCIETY

Historians have long debated whether the American Revolution was a social as well as a political revolution. Some have argued that the colonists were strug-

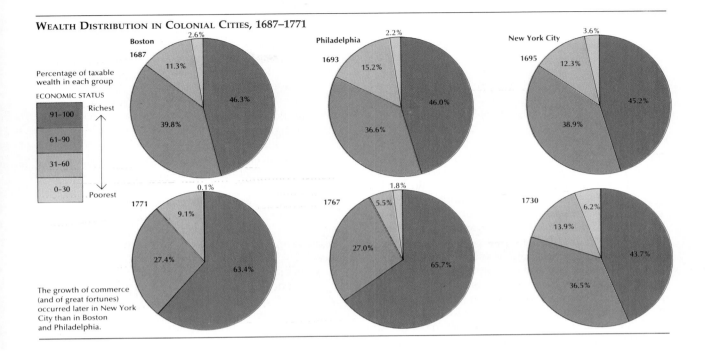

WEALTH DISTRIBUTION IN COLONIAL CITIES, 1687–1771

Percentage of taxable wealth in each group

ECONOMIC STATUS

91–100	Richest
61–90	
31–60	
0–30	Poorest

Boston 1687: 2.6%, 11.3%, 39.8%, 46.3%
Philadelphia 1693: 2.2%, 15.2%, 36.6%, 46.0%
New York City 1695: 3.6%, 12.3%, 38.9%, 45.2%

Boston 1771: 0.1%, 9.1%, 27.4%, 63.4%
Philadelphia 1767: 1.8%, 5.5%, 27.0%, 65.7%
New York City 1730: 6.2%, 13.9%, 36.5%, 43.7%

The growth of commerce (and of great fortunes) occurred later in New York City than in Boston and Philadelphia.

gling not only over the question of home rule, but over "who should rule at home." Others claim that domestic social and economic concerns had little to do with the conflict. (See "Where Historians Disagree," pp. 138–139.) Whatever the motivations of Americans, however, there can be little doubt that the War for Independence had important effects on the nature of American society.

Loyalists and Minorities

Any war produces both winners and losers. The losers in the American Revolution included not only the British but American Loyalists. There is no way to be sure how many Americans remained loyal to England during the Revolution, but it is clear that there were many—at least a fifth (and some estimate as much as a third) of the white population. Their motivations were varied. Some were officeholders in the imperial government, who stood to lose their positions as a result of the Revolution. Others were merchants engaged in trade closely tied to the imperial system. (Most merchants, however, supported the Revolution.) Still others were people who lived in relative isolation and who thus had not been exposed to the wave of discontent

that had turned so many Americans against Britain; they had simply retained their traditional loyalties. There were cultural and ethnic minorities who feared that an independent America would not offer them sufficient protection. And there were those who, expecting the British to win the war, were simply currying favor with the anticipated victors.

What happened to these men and women during the war is a turbulent and at times tragic story. Hounded by Patriots in their communities, harassed by legislative and judicial actions, the position of many of them became intolerable. Up to 100,000 fled the country. Those who could afford to—for example, the hated Tory governor of Massachusetts, Thomas Hutchinson—fled to England, where many lived in difficult and lonely exile. Others of more modest means moved to Canada, establishing the first English-speaking community in the province of Quebec. Some returned to America after the war and, as the earlier passions and resentments faded, managed to reenter the life of the nation. Others remained abroad for the rest of their lives.

Most Loyalists were people of average means, but a substantial minority consisted of men and women of wealth. They left behind large estates and vacated important positions of social and economic leadership.

WHERE HISTORIANS DISAGREE

THE AMERICAN REVOLUTION

T HROUGH MOST OF ITS long life, the debate over the origins of the American Revolution has tended to reflect two broad schools of interpretation. One sees the Revolution largely as a political and intellectual event and argues that the revolt against Britain was part of a defense of ideals and principles. The other views the Revolution as a social and economic phenomenon and contends that material interests were at its heart.

The Revolutionary generation itself portrayed the conflict as a struggle over ideals, and their interpretation prevailed through most of the nineteenth century. For example, George Bancroft wrote in 1876 that the Revolution "was most radical in its character, yet achieved with such benign tranquillity that even conservatism hesitated to censure." Its aim, he argued, was to "preserve liberty" against British tyranny.

But in the early twentieth century, historians influenced by the reform currents of the progressive era began to identify social and economic forces that they believed had contributed to the rebellion. In a 1909 study of New York, Carl Becker wrote that two questions had shaped the Revolution: "The first was the question of home rule; the second was the question . . . of who should rule at home." The colonists were not only fighting the British; they were also engaged in a kind of civil war, a contest for power between radicals and conservatives that led to the "democratization of American politics and society."

Other "progressive" historians elaborated on Becker's thesis. In *The American Revolution Considered as a Social Movement* (1926), J. Franklin Jameson argued that "the stream of revolution, once started, could not be confined within narrow banks, but spread abroad upon the land. . . . Many economic desires, many social aspirations, were set free by the political struggle, many aspects of society profoundly altered by the forces thus let loose." In a 1917 book Arthur M. Schlesinger maintained that colonial merchants, motivated by their own interest in escaping the restrictive policies of British mercantilism, aroused American resistance in the 1760s and 1770s.

Beginning in the 1950s, a new generation of scholars began to re-emphasize the role of ideology and to de-emphasize the role of economic interests. Robert E. Brown (in 1955) and Edmund S. Morgan (in 1956) both argued that most eighteenth-century white Americans, regardless of station, shared basic political principles and that the social and economic conflicts the progressives had identified were not severe. The rhetoric of the Revolution, they suggested, was not pro-

Even some who remained in the country saw their property confiscated and their positions forfeited. The result was new opportunities for Patriots to acquire land and influence, a situation that produced significant social changes in many communities.

It would be an exaggeration, however, to claim that the departure of the Loyalists was responsible for anything approaching a social revolution or that the Revolution created a general assault on the wealthy and powerful in America. When the war ended, those who had been wealthy at its beginning were, for the most part, still wealthy. Most of those who had wielded social and political influence (which often accompanied the possession of wealth) continued to wield it. Indeed,

the distribution of wealth became more uneven in the aftermath of the war than it had been in the decades preceding it.

The war had a significant effect on other minorities as well, and on certain religious groups in particular. No sect suffered more than the Anglicans, many of whose members were Loyalists and all of whom Patriots identified with England. In Virginia and Maryland, where the colonial governments had recognized Anglicanism as the official religion and had imposed a tax for its maintenance, the new Revolutionary regimes disestablished the church and eliminated the subsidy. In other states, Anglicans had received aid from England, which also ceased with the outbreak of

paganda, but a real reflection of the colonists' ideas. Bernard Bailyn, in *The Ideological Origins of the American Revolution* (1967), demonstrated the complex roots of the ideas behind the Revolution and argued that this carefully constructed political stance was not a disguise for economic interests but a genuine ideology that itself motivated the colonists to act. The Revolution, he claimed, "was above all else an ideological, constitutional, political struggle and not primarily a controversy between social groups undertaken to force changes in the organization of the society or the economy."

By the late 1960s, however, a group of younger historians—many of them influenced by the New Left—were challenging the ideological interpretation again by illuminating social and economic tensions within colonial society that they claimed helped shape the Revolutionary struggle. Jesse Lemisch and Dirk Hoerder pointed to the actions of mobs in colonial cities as evidence of popular resentment of both American and British elites. Joseph Ernst re-emphasized the significance of economic pressures on colonial merchants and tradesmen. Gary Nash, in *The Urban Crucible* (1979), emphasized the role of growing economic distress in colonial cities in creating a climate in which Revolutionary sentiment could flourish. Edward Countryman and Rhys Isaac both pointed to changes in the nature of colonial

society and culture, and in the relationship between classes in eighteenth-century America, as a crucial prerequisite for the growth of the Revolutionary movement.

Some newer social interpretations of the Revolution attempt to break free of the old debate pitting ideas against interests. The two things are not in competition with, but rather reinforce one another, more recent scholars argue. "Everyone has economic interests," Gary Nash has written, "and everyone . . . has an ideology." Only by exploring the relationships between the two can historians hope fully to understand either. Also, as Linda Kerber has written, newer interpretations have "reinvigorated the Progressive focus on social conflict between classes and extended it to include the experience not only of rich and poor but of a wide variety of interest groups, marginal communities, and social outsiders."

Finally, Gordon Wood, in *The Radicalism of the American Revolution* (1992), helped revive an interpretation of the revolution that few historians have embraced since the nineteenth century: that it was a genuinely radical event, which led to the breakdown of such longstanding patterns of society as deference, patriarchy, and traditional gender relations. Class conflict and radical goals may not have caused the Revolution; but it had a profound, even radical impact on society nevertheless.

war. By the time the fighting ended, many Anglican parishes no longer even had clergymen, for there were few ministers to take the place of those who had died or who had left the country as Loyalist refugees. Anglicanism survived in America, but the losses during the Revolution permanently weakened it. The Revolution also weakened the Quakers in Pennsylvania and elsewhere. They incurred widespread unpopularity because of their pacifism. Their refusal to support the war destroyed much of the social and political prestige they had once enjoyed, and the church never fully recovered.

While the war was weakening the Anglicans and the Quakers, it was improving the position of the Ro-

man Catholic church. On the advice of Charles Carroll of Carrollton, a Maryland statesman and Catholic lay leader, most American Catholics supported the Patriot cause during the war. The French alliance brought Catholic troops and chaplains to the country, and the gratitude with which most Americans greeted them did much to erode old hostilities toward Catholics, whom Americans had in the past often denounced as agents of the devil. The church did not greatly increase its numbers as a result of the Revolution, but it did gain considerable strength as an institution. Not long after the end of the war, the Vatican provided the United States with its own Catholic hierarchy. (Until then, English bishops had controlled the American church.) Father John Carroll (also of Maryland) was named head of Catholic missions in America in 1784 and, in 1789, the first American bishop. In 1808 he became archbishop of Baltimore. Hostility toward Catholics had not disappeared forever from American life, but the church had established a solid footing from which to withstand future assaults.

For the largest of America's minorities—the African-American population—the war had limited, but nevertheless profound, significance. For some, it meant freedom. Because so much of the fighting occurred in the South during the last years of the war, many slaves came into contact with the British army, which—in the interests of disrupting and weakening the American cause—emancipated thousands of slaves and led them out of the country. For other blacks, the Revolution meant an increased exposure to the idea, although seldom the reality, of liberty. Most black Americans could not read, but few could avoid exposure to the new and exciting ideas circulating through the towns and cities where many of them lived. At times, they attempted to apply those ideas to themselves. The results included incidents in several communities in which blacks engaged in open resistance to white control. In Charleston, South Carolina, for example, Thomas Jeremiah, a free black, was executed after white authorities learned of elaborate plans for a slave uprising.

That was one reason why revolutionary sentiment was more restrained in South Carolina and Georgia than in other colonies. Blacks constituted a majority in South Carolina and almost half the population in Georgia, and whites in both places feared that revolution would foment slave rebellions. The same fears helped prevent English colonists in the Caribbean islands (who were far more greatly outnumbered by black slaves) from joining with the continental Americans in the revolt against Britain.

Native Americans and the Revolution

Most Indians viewed the American Revolution with considerable uncertainty. The American Patriots tried to persuade them to remain neutral in the conflict, which they described as a "family quarrel" between the colonists and Britain that had nothing to do with the tribes. The British, too, generally sought to maintain Indian neutrality, fearing that native allies would prove unreliable and uncontrollable. Most tribes ultimately chose to stay out of the war.

To some Indians, however, the Revolution threatened to replace a ruling group in which they had developed at least some measure of trust (the British)

with one they considered generally hostile to them (the Patriots). The British had consistently sought to limit the expansion of white settlement into Indian land (even if unsuccessfully); the Americans had spearheaded the encroachments. Thus some Indians, among them those Iroquois who participated in the Burgoyne campaign in upper New York, chose to join the English cause. Still others took advantage of the conflict to launch attacks of their own.

In the western Carolinas and Virginia, the Cherokee, led by Chief Dragging Canoe, launched a series of attacks on outlying white settlements in the summer of 1776. Patriot militias responded with overwhelming force, ravaging Cherokee lands and forcing the chief and many of his followers to flee west across the Tennessee River. Those Cherokee who remained behind agreed to a new treaty by which they gave up still more land. Not all Indian military efforts were so unsuccessful. Some Iroquois, despite the setbacks at Oriskany, continued to wage war against Americans in the West and caused widespread destruction in large agricultural areas of New York and Pennsylvania—areas whose crops were of crucial importance to the Patriot cause. And although the retaliating American armies inflicted heavy losses on the Indians, the attacks continued throughout the war.

In the end, however, the Revolution generally weakened the position of Native Americans in several ways. The Patriot victory increased the white demand for western lands; many American whites associated restrictions on settlement with British oppression and expected the new nation to remove the obstacles. At the same time, white attitudes toward the tribes, seldom friendly in the best of times, took a turn for the worse. Many whites deeply resented the assistance such nations as the Mohawk had given the British and insisted on treating them as conquered people. Others adopted a paternalistic view of the tribes that was only slightly less dangerous to them. Thomas Jefferson, for example, came to view the Indians as "noble savages" uncivilized in their present state but redeemable if they were willing to adapt to the norms of white society.

Among the Indians themselves, the Revolution both revealed and increased the deep divisions that made it difficult for them to form a common front to resist the growing power of whites. In 1774, for example, the Shawnee Indians in western Virginia had attempted to lead an uprising against white settlers moving into the lands that would later become Kentucky. They attracted virtually no allies and (in a conflict known as Lord Dunmore's War) were defeated by the colonial militia and forced to cede more land to white settlers. The Cherokee generated little support from surrounding tribes in their 1776 battles. And the Iroquois, whose power had been eroding since the end of the French and Indian War, were unable to act in unison in the Revolution; the nations that chose to support the British attracted little support from tribes outside the Confederacy (many of whom resented the long Iroquois domination of the interior) and even from other tribes within the Iroquois nation.

Nor did the conclusion of the Revolutionary War end the fighting between white Americans and Indians. Bands of Native Americans continued to launch raids against white settlers on the frontier. And white militias, often using such raids as pretexts, continued to attack Indian tribes who stood in the way of expansion. Perhaps the most vicious massacre of the era occurred in 1782, after the British surrender, when white militias slaughtered a peaceful band of Delaware Indians at Gnadenhuetten in Ohio. They claimed to be retaliating for the killing of a white family several days before, but few believed this band of Delaware (who were both Christian converts and pacifists) had played any role in the earlier attack. The white soldiers killed ninety-six people, including many women and children. Such massacres did not become the norm of Indian-white relations. But they did reveal how little the Revolution had done to settle the basic conflict between the two peoples.

Women's Rights and Women's Roles

The long Revolutionary War, which touched the lives of almost every region, naturally had a significant effect on American women. The departure of so many men to fight in the Patriot armies left wives, mothers, sisters, and daughters in charge of farms and businesses. Some women handled these tasks with great success. In other cases, inexperience, inflation, the unavailability of male labor, or the threat of enemy troops led to failures and dislocations. Some women whose husbands or fathers went off to war did not have even a farm or shop to fall back on. Many cities and towns developed significant populations of impoverished women, who on occasion led popular protests against price increases. On a few occasions, hungry women rioted and looted for food. On several other occasions (in New Jersey and Staten Island), women launched attacks on occupying British troops, whom they were required to house and feed at considerable expense.

Not all women, however, stayed behind when the men went off to war. Sometimes simply by choice, more often out of economic necessity or because they had been driven from their homes by the enemy (and by the smallpox and dysentery the British army car-

ABIGAIL ADAMS
When this portrait was painted in the mid-1780s, Abigail Adams was living in London, where her husband, John Adams, was serving as the first American ambassador. Harboring strong political opinions, she was outspoken on public issues, and critics often charged John Adams with being "under the sovereignty of his wife." But she was generally more a fierce defender of her husband's policies than an active force in shaping them. During much of her married life, she lived apart from her husband, who spent many years traveling on diplomatic assignments. As a result, she became a tireless letter writer. Her correspondence survives today as one of the most important sources of information about her extraordinary family. *(New York State Historical Association, Cooperstown)*

ried with it), women flocked in increasing numbers to the camps of the Patriot armies to join their male relatives. George Washington looked askance at these female "camp followers," convinced that they were disruptive and distracting (even though his own wife, Martha, spent the winter of 1778–1779 with him at Valley Forge). Other officers were even more hostile, voicing complaints that reflected a high level of anxiety over this seeming violation of traditional gender roles (and also, perhaps, over the generally lower-class backgrounds of the camp women). One described them in decidedly hostile terms: "their hair falling, their brows beady with the heat, their belongings slung over one shoulder, chattering and yelling in sluttish shrills as they went and spitting in the gutters." In fact, however, the women were of significant value to the new army, which had not yet developed an adequate system of supply and auxiliary services and which profited greatly from the presence of women who increased army morale and who performed such necessary tasks as cooking, laundry, and nursing.

But female activity did not always remain restricted to "women's" tasks. In the rough environment of the camps, traditional gender distinctions proved difficult to maintain. Considerable numbers of women became involved, at least intermittently, in combat—including the legendary "Molly Pitcher" (so named because she carried pitchers of water to soldiers on the battlefield), who watched her husband fall during one encounter and immediately took his place at a field gun. A few women even disguised themselves as men so as to be able to fight.

After the war, of course, the soldiers and the female camp followers returned home. The experience of combat had little visible impact on how society (or on how women themselves) defined female roles in peacetime. The Revolution did, however, call certain assumptions about women into question in other ways. The emphasis on liberty and the "rights of man" led some women to begin to question their position in society as well. "By the way," Abigail Adams wrote to her husband John Adams in 1776, "in the new code of laws which I suppose it will be necessary for you to make, I desire you would remember the ladies and be more generous and favorable to them than your ancestors. Do not put such unlimited power into the hands of the Husbands."

Adams was calling for a very modest expansion of women's rights: for new protections against abusive and tyrannical men. A few women, however, went further. Judith Sargent Murray, one of the leading essayists of the late eighteenth century, wrote in 1779 that women's minds were as good as men's and that girls as well as boys therefore deserved access to education. Murray later was one of the leading defenders of the works of the English feminist Mary Wollstonecraft, whose *Vindication of the Rights of Women* was published in the United States in 1792. After reading it, Murray rejoiced that Americans were beginning to understand "the Rights of Women" and that future generations of women would inaugurate "a new era in female history."

But in most respects the new era did not arrive. Some political leaders—among them Benjamin Franklin and Benjamin Rush—voiced support for the education of women and for other feminist reforms. Yale students in the 1780s debated the question "Whether women ought to be admitted into the magistracy and government of empires and republics." And there was for a time wide discussion of the future role of women in the new republic. But few concrete reforms became either law or common social practice.

In colonial society, under the doctrines of English common law, an unmarried woman had some legal rights (to own property, to enter contracts, and others), but a married woman had virtually no rights at all. She could own no property and earn no independent wages; everything she owned and everything she earned belonged to her husband. She had no legal authority over her children; the father was, in the eyes of the law, the autocrat of the family. Because she had no property rights, she could not engage in any legal transactions (buying or selling, suing or being sued, writing wills). She could not vote. Nor could she obtain a divorce; that too was a right reserved almost exclusively to men. That was what Abigail Adams (who herself enjoyed a very happy marriage) meant when she appealed to her husband not to put "such unlimited power into the hands of the Husbands."

The Revolution did little to change any of these legal customs. In some states, it did become easier for women to obtain divorces. And in New Jersey, women obtained the right to vote (although that right was repealed in 1807). Otherwise, there were few advances and some setbacks—including widows' loss of the right to regain their dowries from their husbands' estates. That change left many widows without any means of support and was one of the reasons for the increased agitation for female education: such women needed a way to support themselves.

The Revolution, in other words, far from challenging the patriarchal structure of American society, actually confirmed and strengthened it. Not even many American women ever doubted that they should continue to occupy a sphere distinct from men, that their place remained in the family. Abigail Adams, in the same letter in which she asked her husband to "remember the Ladies," urged him to "regard us then as Beings placed by providence under your protection and in imitation of the Supreme Being make use of that power only for our happiness." Nevertheless, the revolutionary experience did contribute to an alteration of women's expectations of their status within the family. In the past, they had often been little better than servants in their husbands' homes; men and women both had generally viewed the wife as a clear subordinate, performing functions in the family of much less importance than those of the husband. But the Revolution encouraged people of both genders to reevaluate the contribution of women to the family and the society.

Part of this change was a result of the participation of women in the revolutionary struggle itself. And part was a result of the reevaluation of American life during and after the revolutionary struggle. As the republic searched for a cultural identity for itself, it began to place additional value on the role of women as mothers. The new nation was, many Americans liked to believe, producing a new kind of citizen, steeped in the principles of liberty. Mothers had a particularly important task, therefore, in instructing their children in the virtues the republican citizenry was expected now to possess. Wives were still far from equal partners in marriage, but their ideas, interests, and domestic roles received increased respect.

The War Economy

Inevitably, the Revolution produced important changes in the structure of the American economy. After more than a century of dependence on the British imperial system, American trade suddenly found itself on its own. No longer did it have the protection of the great British navy; on the contrary, English ships now attempted to drive American vessels from the seas. No longer did American merchants have access to the markets of the empire; those markets were now hostile ports—including, of course, the most important source of American trade: England itself.

Yet while the Revolution disrupted traditional economic patterns, in the long run it strengthened the American economy. Well before the war was over, American ships had learned to evade the British navy with light, fast, easily maneuverable vessels. Indeed, the Yankees began to prey on British commerce with hundreds of privateers. For many shipowners, privateering proved to be more profitable than ordinary peacetime trade. More important in the long run, the end of imperial restrictions on American shipping opened up enormous new areas of trade to the nation. Colonial merchants had been violating British regulations for years, but the rules of empire had nevertheless inhibited American exploration of many markets. Now, enterprising merchants in New England and elsewhere began to develop new commerce in the Caribbean and in South America. By the mid-1780s, American merchants were developing an important

BANNER OF THE SOCIETY OF PEWTERERS Members of the American Society of Pewterers carried this patriotic banner when they marched in a New York City parade in July 1788. Its inscription celebrates the adoption of the new federal Constitution and predicts a future of prosperity and freedom in "Columbia's Land." The banner also suggests the growing importance of American manufacturing, which had received an important boost during the Revolution when British imports became unavailable. *(New York Historical Society)*

new pattern of trade with Asia; and by the end of that decade, Yankee ships were regularly sailing from the eastern seaboard around Cape Horn to California, there exchanging manufactured goods for hides and furs, and then proceeding across the Pacific to barter for goods in China. There was also a substantial increase in trade among the American states.

When English imports to America were cut off—first by the prewar boycott, then by the war itself—there were desperate efforts throughout the states to stimulate domestic manufacturing of certain necessities. No great industrial expansion resulted, but there were several signs of the economic growth that was to come in the next century. Americans began to make their own cloth—"homespun," which became both patriotic and fashionable—to replace the now-unobtainable British fabrics. It would be some time before a large domestic textile industry would emerge, but the nation was never again to rely exclusively on foreign sources for its cloth. There was, of course, pressure to build factories for the manufacture of guns and ammunition. And there was a growing general awareness that America need not forever be dependent on other nations for manufactured goods.

The war stopped well short of revolutionizing the American economy; not until the nineteenth century would that begin to occur. But it did serve to release a wide range of entrepreneurial energies that, despite the temporary dislocations, encouraged growth and diversification.

THE CREATION OF STATE GOVERNMENTS

At the same time that Americans were struggling to win their independence on the battlefield, they were also struggling to create new institutions of government for themselves, to replace the British system they had repudiated. That effort continued for more than fifteen years, culminating in the federal Constitution of 1789. But its most crucial phase occurred during the war itself, and at the state, not the national, level.

The formation of state governments began early in 1776, even before the adoption of the Declaration of Independence. At first, the new state constitutions reflected primarily the fear of bloated executive power that had become so pronounced during the 1760s and early 1770s. Gradually, however, Americans began to become equally concerned about the instability of a government too responsive to the popular will. In a second phase of state constitution writing, therefore,

they gave renewed attention to the idea of balance in government.

The Assumptions of Republicanism

If Americans agreed on nothing else when they began to build new governments for themselves, they agreed that those governments would be republican. To them, that meant a political system in which all power came directly from the people, rather than from some supreme authority (such as a king) standing above them. The success of any government, therefore, depended on the nature of its citizenry. If the population consisted of sturdy, virtuous, independent property owners, then the republic could survive. If it consisted of a few powerful aristocrats and a great mass of dependent workers, then it would be in danger. From the beginning, therefore, the ideal of the small freeholder became basic to American political ideology.

Another crucial part of that ideology was the concept of equality. The Declaration of Independence had given voice to that idea in its most ringing phrase: "all men are created equal." It was a belief that stood in direct contrast to the old European assumption of an inherited aristocracy. Every citizen, Americans believed, was born in a position of equality with every other citizen. It would be the innate talents and energies of individuals that would determine their roles in society, not their position at birth. The republican vision did not, in other words, envision a society without social gradations. Some people would inevitably be wealthier and more powerful than others. But all people would have to earn their success. There would be no equality of condition, but there would be full equality of opportunity.

In reality, of course, these assumptions could not always be sustained. The United States was never to become a nation in which all (or even most) people were independent property holders. From the beginning, there was a large dependent labor force—of which the white members were allowed many of the privileges of citizenship and the black members had virtually no rights at all. American women remained both politically and economically subordinate, with few opportunities for advancement independent of their husbands. Native Americans were systematically exploited and displaced by whites hungry for land and impatient with legalities. Nor was it possible to ensure full equality of opportunity. American society was more open and more fluid than that of most European nations, but it remained true that wealth and privilege were often passed from one generation to another. The conditions of a person's birth survived as a crucial determinant of success.

Nevertheless, in embracing the assumptions of republicanism, Americans were adopting a powerful, even revolutionary new ideology, one that would enable them to create a form of government never before seen in the world. Their experiment in statecraft became a model for many other countries and made the United States the most admired and studied nation on earth.

The First State Constitutions

Two of the original thirteen states saw no need to produce new constitutions. Connecticut and Rhode Island already had corporate charters which provided them with governments that were republican in all but name; they simply deleted references to England and the king from their charters and adopted them as constitutions. The other eleven states, however, chose to create entirely new governments. In doing so, they set out to avoid the problems of the British system they were repudiating.

The first and perhaps most basic decision was that the American constitutions, unlike the English one, were to be written down. Americans believed that the vagueness of the English system had opened the way to the corruption of the British government. To avoid a similar fate, they insisted that their own governments rest on clearly stated and permanently inscribed laws, so that no individual or group could pervert them.

The second decision was that the power of the executive, which Americans believed had grown bloated and threatening in England (and even, at times, in the colonies), must be limited. Only one state—Pennsylvania—went so far as to eliminate the executive altogether. But most states inserted provisions sharply limiting the power of the governor over appointments, reducing or eliminating his right to veto bills, and preventing him from dismissing or otherwise interfering with the legislature. Above all, every state forbade the governor or any other executive officer from holding a seat in the legislature, thus ensuring that (unlike in England) the two branches of government would remain wholly separate. The constitutions also added provisions protecting the judiciary from executive control, although in most states the courts did not yet emerge as fully autonomous branches of government.

In limiting the executive and expanding the power of the legislature, the new constitutions were moving in the direction of direct popular rule. They did not, however, move all the way. Only in Georgia and Pennsylvania did the legislature consist of one house. In all the other states there was an upper and a lower chamber, and in most cases, the upper chamber was designed to represent the "higher orders" of society. In all states, there were property requirements for voters—in some states, only the modest amount that would qualify a person as a taxpayer, in other states somewhat greater requirements. Such restrictions often had limited impact, since property ownership was widespread among the white male population. But universal suffrage (even among white men) was not yet an accepted part of American government.

The initial phase of constitution writing proceeded rapidly. Ten of the states completed the process before the end of 1776. Only Georgia, New York, and Massachusetts delayed. Georgia and New York completed the task by the end of the following year, but Massachusetts did not finally adopt its version until 1780. By then, the construction of state governments had moved into a new phase.

Revising State Governments

By the late 1770s, Americans were already growing concerned about what they perceived as the excessive factiousness and instability of their new state governments. Legislatures were the scene of constant squabbling. Governors were unable to exercise sufficient power to provide any real leadership. It was proving extraordinarily difficult to get the new governments to accomplish anything at all. Many observers began to believe that the problem was one of too much democracy. By placing so much power in the hands of the people (and their elected representatives in the legislature), the state constitutions were inviting disorder and political turbulence.

As a result, most of the states began to revise their constitutions to cope with what they considered to be their problems. Massachusetts—which had waited until 1780 to ratify its first constitution—became the first state to act on the new concerns. It produced a constitution that was to serve as a model for the efforts of others.

Two changes in particular characterized the Massachusetts and later constitutions. The first was a change in the process of constitution writing itself. In the first phase, the documents had usually been written by state legislatures. As a result, they could easily be amended (or violated) by those same bodies. By 1780, sentiment was growing to find a way to protect the constitutions from the people who had written them, to make it difficult to change the documents once they were approved. The solution was the constitutional convention: a special assembly of the people that would meet only for the purpose of writing the constitution and that would never (except under extraordinary circumstances) meet again. The constitution would, therefore, be the product of the popular will; but once approved, it would be protected from the whims of public opinion and from the political moods of the legislature.

The second change was similarly a reflection of the new concerns about excessive popular power: a significant strengthening of the executive. In Massachusetts, the governor under the 1780 constitution became one of the strongest in any state. He was to be elected directly by the people; he was to have a fixed salary (in other words, he would not be dependent on the good will of the legislature each year for his wages); he would have expanded powers of appointment; and he would be able to veto legislation. Other states soon followed. Those states that had weak or nonexistent upper houses strengthened or created them. Most states increased the powers of the governor; and Pennsylvania, which had had no executive at all at first, now produced a strong one. By the late 1780s, almost every state had either revised its constitution or drawn up an entirely new one to accommodate the belief in the need for stability.

Toleration and Slavery

The new states moved far and quickly in the direction of complete religious freedom. Most Americans continued to believe religion should play some role in government, but they did not wish to give special powers to any particular denomination. So they stripped away the privileges they had once given particular churches. New York and the southern states, in which the Church of England had received public support, disestablished the church, and the New England states stripped the Congregational Church of its special status. Boldest of all was Virginia. In 1786, it enacted a Statute of Religious Freedom, written by Thomas Jefferson, which called for the complete separation of church and state.

More difficult to resolve was the question of slavery. In areas where slavery was weak—in New England, where there had never been many slaves, and in Pennsylvania, where the Quakers were outspoken in their opposition to slavery—state governments abolished it. Pennsylvania passed a general gradual-emancipation act in 1780, and the supreme court of Massachusetts ruled in 1783 that the ownership of slaves was impermissible under the state's bill of rights. Even in the South, there were some pressures

to amend the institution (a result, in part, of the activities of the first antislavery society in America, founded in 1775). Every state but South Carolina and Georgia prohibited the further importation of slaves from abroad, and even South Carolina placed a temporary wartime ban on the slave trade. Virginia passed a law encouraging manumission (the freeing of slaves), and other states encountered growing political pressures to change the institution.

In the end, however, slavery survived in all the southern and border states, for several reasons: racist assumptions about the natural inferiority of African Americans; the enormous economic investments many white southerners had in their black laborers, investments they were unwilling to give up; and the inability of most southerners—including such men as Washington and Jefferson, who expressed deep moral misgivings about slavery—to envision any alternative to it. If slavery were abolished, what would happen to the black people in America? Returning the slaves to Africa, as some urged, was clearly unrealistic; the black population was too large, and many slaves felt little identification with Africa and had no wish to go there. Few whites believed that blacks could be integrated into American society as equals. In maintaining slavery, Jefferson once remarked, Americans were holding a "wolf by the ears." However unappealing it was to hold on to it, letting go would be even worse. Jefferson himself, for all his qualms, never let go. He continued to own slaves until he died, and unlike George Washington, he made no provision for their freedom on his death.

There was, finally, a more subtle obstacle to the elimination of slavery. The economy of the South depended, most southerners believed, on a large, servile labor force. Yet the ideals of republicanism required a homogeneous population of independent, property-owning citizens. Were slavery to be abolished, the South would find itself with a substantial population of unpropertied free people; and whether that class were black or white, its existence would raise troubling implications for the future of democracy. The social tensions that would inevitably ensue would, southerners feared, ultimately destroy the stability of society.

THE SEARCH FOR A NATIONAL GOVERNMENT

Americans were much quicker to agree on the proper shape of their state institutions than they were to decide on the form of their national government. At first, most believed that the central government should remain relatively weak and unimportant. Each state would be virtually a sovereign nation, and national institutions would serve only as loose, coordinating mechanisms, with little independent authority. Such beliefs reflected the assumption that a republic operated best in a relatively limited, homogeneous area; that were a republican government to attempt to administer too large and diverse a nation, it would founder. It was in response to such ideas that the Articles of Confederation emerged.

The Confederation

No sooner did the Continental Congress appoint a committee to draft a declaration of independence in 1776 than it appointed another to draft a plan of union. After much debate and many revisions, the Congress adopted the committee's proposal in November 1777 as the Articles of Confederation.

The Articles provided for a national political structure very similar to the one already in operation. Congress was to survive as the central—indeed the only—institution of national authority. But its powers were to be somewhat expanded. It was to have the authority to conduct wars and foreign relations, and to appropriate, borrow, and issue money. But it could not regulate trade, draft troops, or levy taxes directly on the people. For troops and taxes it would have to make formal requests to the state legislatures, which could and often did refuse them. There was to be no separate executive (the "president of the United States" was merely the presiding officer at the sessions of Congress). Each state would have a single vote in Congress, and at least nine of the states would have to approve any important measure. All thirteen state legislatures would have to approve the Articles before they could be ratified or amended.

The ratification process revealed broad disagreements over the plan. The small states had insisted on equal state representation, but the larger states wanted representation based on population. More important, the states claiming western lands wished to keep them, but the rest of the states demanded that all such territory be turned over to the Confederation government. When New York and Virginia finally agreed to give up their western claims, Maryland (the only state still holding out) approved the Articles of Confederation. They went into effect in 1781.

The Confederation, which existed from 1781 until 1789, was not the complete failure that subsequent accounts often described. But it was far from a success. Lacking adequate powers to deal with interstate issues or to enforce its will on the states, and lacking sufficient stature in the eyes of the world to be able to negotiate effectively, it suffered a series of damaging setbacks.

Diplomatic Failures

Evidence of the low esteem in which the rest of the world held the Confederation was its difficulty in persuading Great Britain (and to a lesser extent Spain) to live up to the terms of the peace treaty of 1783.

The British had promised to evacuate American soil, but British forces continued to occupy a string of frontier posts along the Great Lakes within the United States. Nor did the British honor their agreement to make restitution to slaveowners whose slaves the British army had confiscated. There were also disputes over the northeastern boundary of the new nation and over the border between the United States and Florida, which Britain had ceded back to Spain in the treaty. And there were diplomatic problems involving American commerce. Freed from imperial regulations, it was expanding in new directions, but most American trade remained within the British empire. Americans wanted full access to British markets; England, however, placed sharp postwar restrictions on that access.

In 1784, Congress sent John Adams as minister to London to resolve these differences, but Adams made no headway with the English, who could never be sure whether he represented a single nation or thirteen different ones. Throughout the 1780s, the British government refused even to return the courtesy of sending a minister to the American capital.

In dealing with the Spanish government, the Confederation demonstrated similar weakness. Its diplomats agreed to a treaty with Spain in 1786 that accepted the American interpretation of the Florida boundary in return for American recognition of Spanish possessions in North America and an agreement that the United States would limit its right to navigate the Mississippi for twenty years. But the southern states, incensed at the idea of giving up their access to the Mississippi, blocked ratification.

The Confederation and the Northwest

The Confederation's most important accomplishment was its resolution of some of the controversies involving the western lands—although even this was a partial and ambiguous achievement.

STATE CLAIMS TO WESTERN LANDS AND CESSIONS TO NATIONAL GOVERNMENT, 1782–1802

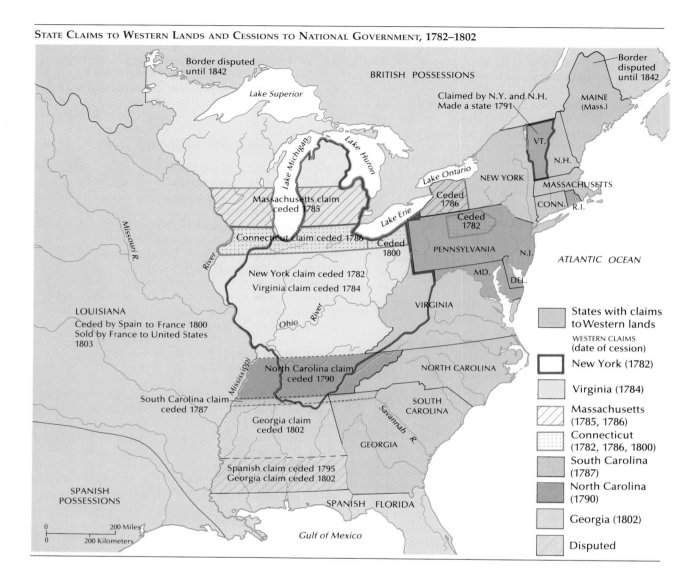

When the Revolution began, only a few thousand whites lived west of the Appalachian divide; by 1790 their numbers had increased to 120,000. The Confederation had to find a way to include these new settlements in the political structure of the new nation. The western settlers were already often in conflict with the established centers of the East over Indian policies, trade provisions, and taxes. At times, in fact (as with the Paxton Boys uprising in Pennsylvania in 1763 and the Regulator movements in North Carolina in 1771), there had been overt hostilities between eastern and western peoples. And Congress faced the additional difficulty of competing with state governments for jurisdiction over the trans-Appalachian region. With Virginia's cession of its western territory to Congress in 1781, the landed states began to yield their claims to the Confederation, and by 1784 the states had ceded enough land to the Confederation to permit Congress to begin making policy for the national domain.

The Ordinance of 1784, based on a proposal by Thomas Jefferson, divided the western territory into ten self-governing districts, each of which could petition Congress for statehood when its population equaled the number of free inhabitants of the smallest existing state. Then, in the Ordinance of 1785, Congress created a system for surveying and selling the western

LAND SURVEY: ORDINANCE OF 1785

The Seven Ranges—first area surveyed

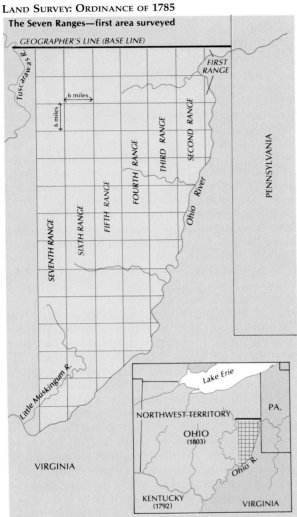

One township (six miles square)

36	30	24	18	12	6
35	29*	23	17	11*	5
34	28	22	16	10	4
33	27	21	15	9	3
32	26*	20	14	8*	2
31	25	19	13	7	1

Section 16 reserved for school funds

*Four sections reserved for subsequent sale

6 miles

One section = 640 acres (1 mile square)
A Half section = 320 acres
B Quarter section = 160 acres
C Half-quarter section = 80 acres
D & E Quarter-quarter section = 40 acres

1 mile

lands. The territory north of the Ohio River would be surveyed and marked off into neat rectangular townships. (This grid system established a pattern that would leave an indelible mark on the American landscape and, through it, the American economy. See "The American Environment," pp. 155–159.) In every township four sections would be reserved for the national government; the revenue from the sale of one of the others would support the creation of a public school (the first example of federal aid to education). Sections were to be sold at auction for no less than one dollar an acre. Since there were 640 acres in a section, the prospective buyer of government land had to have at least $640—a very large sum by the standards of the day.

The original ordinances proved highly favorable to land speculators and less so to ordinary settlers, many of whom could not afford to buy the land. Congress compounded the problem by selling much of the best land to the Ohio and Scioto companies (land speculation operations) before making it available to anyone else. Criticism of these policies led to the passage in 1787 of another law governing western settlement— legislation that became known as the "Northwest Ordinance." The 1787 Ordinance abandoned the ten districts established in 1784 and created a single Northwest Territory out of the lands north of the Ohio; the territory might subsequently be divided into three to five territories. It also specified a population of 60,000 as a minimum for statehood, guaranteed freedom of religion and the right of trial by jury to residents of the Northwest, and prohibited slavery throughout the territory.

The western lands south of the Ohio River received less attention from Congress, and development was more chaotic there. The region that became Kentucky and Tennessee developed rapidly in the late 1770s, and in the 1780s speculators and settlers began setting up governments and asking for recognition as states. The Confederation Congress was never able to resolve the conflicting claims in that region successfully. But in the Northwest territory, the western land policies of the Confederation created a system that—on paper at least—brought order and stability to the process of white settlement.

Indians and the Western Lands

That order and stability came slowly, and at great cost. That was because the lands the Confederation was taking from the states, neatly subdividing, and offering for sale consisted in large part of territory the Indians

LITTLE TURTLE

Little Turtle led the Miami confederacy in its wars with the United States in what is now Ohio and Indiana in the early 1790s. For a time he seemed almost invincible, but in 1794 Little Turtle was defeated in the Battle of Fallen Timbers. In this sketch (a rough copy of a painting attributed to Gilbert Stuart), Little Turtle wears a medal bearing the likeness of George Washington, awarded him by the United States after the signing of the treaty of Greenville. *(Bettmann)*

ously resisted white movement into their lands in Georgia and South Carolina for five years until 1790 when their leader, Alexander McGillivray (who had fought with the British during the Revolution), negotiated a treaty with the federal government settling the dispute for a time. Other tribes—among them the Miami, Shawnee, Delaware, Ottawa, and Chippewa—some of whom had once been represented in negotiations with whites by the Iroquois, formed new confederations of their own in an effort to strengthen their hand in dealings with the U.S. government.

Violence between whites and Indians on the Northwest frontier reached a crescendo in the early 1790s. The first governor of the new Northwest Territory, General Arthur St. Clair, tried and failed in 1789 to force an agreement on the Miami, Shawnee, and Delaware, whose refusal to cede their lands threatened plans by the Ohio Company and others to extend white settlement north of the Ohio River. In 1790 and again in 1791, the Miami, led by the famed warrior Little Turtle, defeated United States forces in two major battles near what is now the western border of Ohio; in the second of those battles, on November 4, 1791, 630 white Americans died in fighting at the Wabash River—the greatest military victory Indians had ever or would ever achieve in their battles with whites. Efforts to negotiate a settlement foundered on the Miami insistence that no treaty was possible that did not forbid white settlement west of the Ohio River.

In 1794, General Anthony Wayne cautiously moved 4,000 soldiers into the Ohio Valley toward the Maumee River, and built forts as he went. British officials in Canada, who were providing supplies to the Indians, themselves constructed a fort about twenty miles from the mouth of the river, well within the boundaries of the United States. In the summer of 1794, Wayne met and decisively defeated the Indians in a battle fought near the British fort: the Battle of Fallen Timbers (so named because it occurred at a place where trees had been blown over by a wind storm). The British garrison prudently stayed out of the fight. A year later, the Miami unhappily signed the Treaty of Greenville. It ceded substantial new lands to the United States. In exchange, the Miami received a formal acknowledgment of their claim to the territory they retained. This was the first recognition by the United States government of the sovereignty of Indian nations; in doing so, the U.S. was repudiating its earlier position (that the tribes had no binding legal claim to land) and affirming that Indian lands could be ceded only by the tribes themselves. That hard-won assurance, however, proved a frail protection against the pressure for white expansion westward in later years.

of the region already occupied. Congress tried to resolve that problem in 1784, 1785, and 1786 by pressuring Iroquois, Choctaw, Chickasaw, and Cherokee leaders to sign several treaties ceding substantial western lands in the North and South to the United States. But those agreements proved largely ineffective. Even the Indian nations that agreed to the treaties did so unwillingly. In 1786, the leadership of the Iroquois Confederacy repudiated the treaty it had signed two years earlier and threatened to attack white settlements in the disputed lands (although by then the Six Nations were too weak and divided to mount an effective resistance). Other tribes had never agreed to the treaties affecting them. One of those tribes, the Creek, strenu-

The conflicts in the Ohio Valley in the aftermath of the Northwest Ordinance suggested the continuing tenuousness of the American claim to control of its western territories. Large areas of the region remained highly unstable, and hence unreceptive to white settlement, until the first decades of the nineteenth century.

Debts, Taxes, and Daniel Shays

At the end of the Revolutionary War, foreign ships crowded into American seaports with cargoes of all kinds, and the American people bought extravagantly with cash or credit—satisfying a desire for foreign goods that had found few outlets during the Revolution. As a result, there was a rapid and substantial flow of hard currency out of the country. Consumer indebtedness to importing merchants increased greatly, which intensified an already severe postwar depression that had begun in 1784 and lasted until 1787. The depression increased the perennial American problem of an inadequate money supply, a problem that bore particularly heavily on debtors. It was in dealing with this increasingly serious problem of debts that the Confederation Congress failed most conspicuously.

The Confederation itself had an enormous outstanding debt, and few means with which to pay it. It had borrowed large sums of money from American citizens and foreign governments during the war, and it owed back pay to its Revolutionary soldiers. Its powers of taxation, in the meantime, were limited; Congress received only about one-sixth of the money it requisitioned from the states—barely enough to meet the government's ordinary operating expenses. The nation was faced with the prospect of defaulting on its obligations, a possibility that threatened to destroy the fragile new government.

This alarming prospect brought to the fore a group of leaders who would play a crucial role in the shaping of the republic for the next several decades. Committed nationalists, they were looking for ways to increase the powers of the central government and to permit it to meet its financial obligations. Robert Morris, the head of the Confederation's treasury; Alexander Hamilton, his young protégé; James Madison of Virginia; and others were soon lobbying for a "continental impost"—a 5 percent duty on imported goods, to be levied by Congress and used to fund the debt. The impost, the nationalists believed, would not only preserve the financial integrity of the new nation; it would strengthen the national government by making it principally responsible for the nation's debts.

But their proposals encountered substantial opposition. Many Americans feared that the impost plan was the first step toward the creation of a corrupt center of privilege, that it would concentrate too much financial power in the hands of Robert Morris and his allies in Philadelphia. The first effort to secure the impost, in 1781, received the approval of twelve state delegations in Congress, but Rhode Island's refusal to agree killed the plan. A second effort in 1783 also failed to win the necessary unanimous approval. Angry and discouraged, the nationalists largely withdrew from any active involvement in the Confederation.

In the absence of any effective action by Congress, the domestic debt problem remained in the hands of the states, which generally relied on increased taxation to deal with their financial difficulties. To the state creditors—that is, the bondholders—this was sound, honest public finance, which protected their legitimate interests. But poor farmers, already burdened by debt and now burdened again by taxes on their lands, considered such policies unfair, even tyrannical. They demanded that the state governments issue paper currency to increase the money supply and make it easier for them to meet their obligations. Resentment ran especially high among farmers in New England, who felt that the states were extorting money from them to swell the coffers of wealthy bondholders in Boston and other towns. Debtors who failed to pay their taxes found their mortgages foreclosed and their property seized; sometimes they found themselves in jail.

Throughout the late 1780s, therefore, mobs of distressed farmers rioted periodically in various parts of New England. They caused the most serious trouble in Massachusetts. Dissidents in the Connecticut Valley and the Berkshire Hills, many of them Revolutionary veterans, rallied behind Daniel Shays, himself a former captain in the Continental army. Shays demanded paper money, tax relief, a moratorium on debts, the removal of the state capital from Boston to the interior, and the abolition of imprisonment for debt. He organized his followers into a military force. During the summer of 1786, the Shaysites concentrated on preventing the collection of debts, private or public, and traveled from place to place in armed bands to keep courts from sitting and to prevent sheriffs from selling confiscated property. In Boston, members of the legislature, including Samuel Adams, denounced Shays and his men as rebels and traitors.

When winter came, the rebels advanced on Springfield hoping to seize weapons from the arsenal there. An army of state militiamen, financed by a loan from wealthy merchants who feared a new revolution, set out from Boston to confront them. In January 1787, this

SIGNIFICANT EVENTS

1774   Shawnee defeated by Virginia militia in Lord Dunmore's War

1775   Second Continental Congress meets

George Washington appointed to command American forces

Battle of Bunker Hill

Montgomery assault on Quebec fails

1776   Thomas Paine's *Common Sense* published

British troops leave Boston

Declaration of Independence debated and signed (July 2–4)

Howe routs Americans on Long Island

Battle of Trenton

First state constitutions written

1777   Articles of Confederation adopted

Battles of Princeton, Brandywine, and Germantown

Howe occupies Philadelphia

Washington camps at Valley Forge for winter

Burgoyne surrenders to Gates at Saratoga

1778   French-American alliance concluded

Clinton replaces Howe

British leave Philadelphia

War shifts to the South

British capture Savannah

1779   British capture Charleston

1780   Cornwallis defeats Gates at Camden, South Carolina

Patriots defeat Tories at King's Mountain, South Carolina

Massachusetts constitution ratified

Slavery abolished in Pennsylvania

1781   Battles of Cowpens and Guilford Court House

Cornwallis surrenders at Yorktown

Articles of Confederation ratified

Continental impost proposed

1782   American militiamen massacre Delaware Indians in Ohio

1781–1784   States cede western lands to Confederation

1783   Treaty of Paris with Great Britain recognizes American independence

Slavery abolished in Massachusetts

1784   Postwar depression begins, aggravating currency problems

1784–1785   First ordinances establishing procedures for settling western lands enacted

1786   Virginia Statute of Religious Liberty passed

1786–1787   Shays's Rebellion in Massachusetts

1787   Northwest Ordinance enacted

1789   John Carroll named first bishop of Catholic Church of United States

1792   Mary Wollstonecraft's *Vindication of the Rights of Women* published in the United States

1794   Anthony Wayne defeats Indians in Ohio

army met Shays's ragged troops, killed several of them, captured many more, and scattered the rest to the hills in a blinding snowstorm.

As a military enterprise, Shays's Rebellion was a fiasco. But it had important consequences for the future of the United States. In Massachusetts, it resulted in a few immediate gains for the discontented groups.

Shays and his lieutenants, at first sentenced to death, soon received pardons and even some economic concessions: tax relief and postponement of debt payments. Much more significant, however, the rebellion added urgency to a movement already gathering support throughout the new nation—the movement to produce a new, national constitution.

SUGGESTED READINGS

General Studies. Edward Countryman, *The American Revolution* (1985). Jack P. Greene, ed., *The American Revolution: Its Character and Limits* (1987). Merrill Jensen, *The Founding of a Nation, A History of the American Revolution, 1763–1789* (1968). Michael Kammen, *A Season of Youth: The American Revolution and the Historical Imagination* (1978). Robert Middlekauff, *The Glorious Cause: The American Revolution, 1763–1789* (1985). Edmund S. Morgan, *The Birth of the Republic, 1763–1789* (1956). Gordon S. Wood, *The Radicalism of the American Revolution* (1992). Alfred E. Young, Jr., ed., *The American Revolution* (1976).

The Road to Independence. Carl Becker, *The Declaration of Independence* (1922). Eric Foner, *Tom Paine and Revolutionary America* (1976). David Hawke, *Paine* (1974). John R. Howe, Jr., *The Changing Political Thought of John Adams* (1966). Edmund S. Morgan, *The Meaning of Independence* (1976). Peter Shaw, *The Character of John Adams* (1976); *American Patriots and the Rituals of Revolution* (1981). Morton White, *The Philosophy of the American Revolution* (1978). Gary Willis, *Inventing America: Jefferson's Declaration of Independence* (1978).

The War. John R. Alden, *The American Revolution* (1964). G. W. Allen, *Naval History of the American Revolution*, 2 vols. (1913). Richard Buel, Jr., *Dear Liberty: Connecticut's Mobilization for the Revolutionary War* (1980). E. Wayne Carp, *To Starve the Army at Pleasure: Continental Army Administration and American Political Culture, 1775–1783* (1984). Lawrence D. Cress, *Citizens in Arms: The Army and the Militia in American Society to the War of 1812* (1982). James T. Flexner, *George Washington in the American Revolution* (1968). Douglas Southall Freeman, *George Washington*, 7 vols. (1948–1957). T. G. Frothingham, *Washington: Commander in Chief* (1930). Ronald Hoffman and Thad W. Tate, eds., *An Uncivil War: The Southern Backcountry During the American Revolution* (1985). Don Higginbotham, *The War of American Independence* (1983); *George Washington and the American Military Tradition* (1985). Piers Mackesy, *The War for America* (1964). Samuel Eliot Morison, *John Paul Jones* (1959). Howard H. Peckham, *The War for Independence* (1958). Steven Rosswurm, *Arms, Country, and Class: The Philadelphia Militia and the "Lower Sort" in the Era of the American Revolution* (1987). Charles Royster, *A Revolutionary People at War: The Continental Army and American Character* (1979); *Light-Horse Larry Lee and the Legacy of the American Revolution* (1981). John Shy, *A People Numerous and Armed* (1976); *The American Revolution* (1973). Willard Wallace, *Appeal to Arms* (1950). Christopher Ward, *The War of the Revolution*, 2 vols. (1952).

Revolutionary Diplomacy. Samuel F. Bemis, *The Diplomacy of the American Revolution* (1935). Jonathan R. Dull, *A Diplomatic History of the American Revolution* (1985). E. J. Ferguson, *The Power of the Purse* (1961). L. S. Kaplan, *Colonies into Nation: American Diplomacy, 1763–1801* (1972). Richard B. Morris, *The Peacemakers* (1965). Gerald Stourzh, *Benjamin Franklin and American Foreign Policy*, rev. ed. (1969). Clarence L. Ver Steeg, *Robert Morris* (1954).

The Loyalists. Bernard Bailyn, *The Ordeal of Thomas Hutchinson* (1974). Wallace Brown, *The King's Friends* (1965). Robert M. Calhoon, *The Loyalists in Revolutionary America* (1973). Mary Beth Norton, *The British Americans: The Loyalist Exiles in England 1774–1789* (1972). William H. Nelson, *The American Tory* (1962). Anne M. Ousterhout, *A State Divided: Opposition in Pennsylvania to the American Revolution* (1987). Paul H. Smith, *Loyalists and Redcoats* (1964). James W. St. G. Walker, *The Black Loyalists* (1976).

Women, Family, and the Revolution. Joy Day Buel and Richard Buel, Jr., *The Way of Duty: A Woman and Her Life in Revolutionary America* (1984). Linda Grant DePauw, *Founding Fathers* (1975). Ronald Hoffman and Peter J. Albert, eds., *Women in the Age of the American Revolution* (1989). Joan Jensen, *Loosening the Bonds: Mid-Atlantic Farm Women, 1750–1850* (1986). Linda K. Kerber, *Women of the Republic: Intellect and Ideology in Revolutionary America* (1980). Mary Beth Norton, *Liberty's Daughters: The Revolutionary Experience of American Women, 1750–1800* (1980).

Indians and Blacks in the Revolution. Ira Berlin and Ronald Hoffman, eds., *Slavery in the Revolutionary Era* (1982). David Brion Davis, *The Problem of Slavery in the Age of Revolution* (1975). Sylvia R. Frey, *Water from the Rock: Black Resistance in a Revolutionary Age* (1991). Barbara Graymount, *The Iroquois in the American Revolution* (1973). Isabel T. Kelsay, *Joseph Brant, 1743–1807* (1984). Duncan McLeod, *Slavery, Race and the American Revolution* (1974). Edmund S. Morgan, *American Slavery American Freedom: The Ordeal of Colonial Virginia* (1975). Gary B. Nash and Jean R. Soderlund, *Freedom by Degrees: Emancipation in Pennsylvania and Its Aftermath* (1991). Gary B. Nash, *Race and Revolution* (1990). James H. O'Don-nell, III, *Southern Indians in the American Revolution* (1973). Benjamin Quarles, *The Negro in the American Revolution* (1961). Anthony F. C. Wallace, *The Death and Rebirth of the Seneca* (1969). Arthur Zilversmit, *The First Emancipation* (1967).

Social and Economic Effects. Edward Countryman, *A People in Revolution* (1981). Jeffrey J. Crow and Larry E. Tise, *The Southern Experience in the American Revolution* (1978). Robert Gross, *The Minutemen and Their World* (1976). J. F. Jameson, *The American Revolution Considered as a Social Movement* (1962). Merrill Jensen, *The American Revolution Within America* (1974). Rachel N. Klein, *Unification of a Slave State: The Rise of the Planter Class in the South Carolina Backcountry, 1760–1808* (1990). Staughton Lynd, *Class Conflict, Slavery and the United States Constitution* (1968). Jackson Turner Main, *The Social Structure of Revolutionary America* (1965). Cathy D. Matson and Peter S. Onuf, *Union of Interests: Political and Economic Thought in Revolutionary America* (1990). Richard P. McCormick, *Experiment in Independence* (1950). Jerome J. Nadlehaft, *The Disorders of War: The Revolution in South Carolina* (1981). Billy G. Smith, *"The Lower Sort": Philadelphia's Laboring People, 1750–1800* (1990). Charles G. Steffen, *The Mechanics of Baltimore: Workers and Politics in the Age of Revolution, 1763–1812* (1984). Gordon S. Wood, *The Radicalism of the American Revolution* (1992).

State Governments. Willi Paul Adams, *The First American Constitutions* (1980). Richard Beeman et al., eds., *Beyond Confederation: Origins of the Constitution and American National Identity* (1987). Donald S. Lutz, *Origins of American Constitutionalism* (1988). Jackson Turner Main, *Political Parties Before the Constitution* (1973); *The Sovereign States, 1775–1783* (1973); and *The Upper House in Revolutionary America, 1763–1788* (1967). Stephen E. Patterson, *Political Parties in Revolutionary Massachusetts* (1973). Irwin Polishook, *Rhode Island and the Union, 1774–1795* (1969). Gordon S. Wood, *The Creation of the American Republic* (1969).

The Articles of Confederation. Andrew R. L. Cayton, *The Frontier Republic: Ideology and Politics in the Ohio Country, 1780–1825* (1986). Jack Eblen, *The First and Second United States Empires* (1968). John Fiske, *The Critical Period of American History, 1783–1789* (1883). H. James Henderson, *Party Politics in the Continental Congress* (1974). Merrill Jensen, *The New Nation* (1950); and *The Articles of Confederation*, rev. ed. (1959). Jack N. Rakove, *The Beginnings of National Politics* (1979). David Szatmary, *Shays' Rebellion: The Making of an Agrarian Insurrection* (1980). Steven Watts, *The Republic Reborn: War and the Making of Liberal America, 1790–1800* (1987).

THE AMERICAN ENVIRONMENT

THE GRID

AMONG THE MANY ENVIRONMENTAL changes that people have wrought upon the American landscape is one so familiar that we inhabit it every day without recognizing its significance. Only when we board an airplane and see our world from above do we grasp the extraordinary transformations it entailed. Everywhere there are lines on the land, boundaries that divide one person's property from another's. In those lines is an intricate story of environmental change.

When European colonists first arrived in North America, one of their earliest tasks was to divide up the land around their settlements into tracts that individuals could own. The pattern of property boundaries they established is called a *cadastral system*, and different versions of such systems have profoundly different consequences for the way colonial lands and societies developed.

The Spanish, for instance, had given a few of their most prominent colonists in New Mexico, Texas, and California vast estates (*encomiendas*) with the right to claim payments in labor or produce from the people who lived there. Such grants became a means of subjugating Indian inhabitants, but they also shaped the European society that developed upon them. Class differences were reinforced by the uneven distribution of land, and a semifeudal society resulted. A similar land system was imposed by the Dutch along the banks of the Hudson River in New York, though most of the tenants who lived there were European immigrants rather than Indians. In the agricultural landscape of New York, one of the landlord's most important ways of extracting rent payments was by running the estate's grain mill, earning a share of the flour it ground. In the case of both the Spanish and the Dutch, the cadastral system encouraged and reinforced social hierarchy.

The French imposed a different system in places like Louisiana, Missouri, and Illinois. Because their transportation network depended almost entirely on rivers, they aligned their property boundaries so that each tract of land fronted on the water. Long narrow fields called *rotures* were the result. Colonists built their houses to face the river, with their land stretching out behind. Long fields had the added convenience that one could plow them without having to turn one's horses around very often. The system encouraged dispersed settlement with few village centers, leading to the relative weakness of local elites and the relative strength of the few major cities towards which the rivers flowed—especially Montreal and New Orleans.

The English colonies had at least two major cadastral systems. One was the New England town system, in which a large tract of land was granted to a small group of proprietors, who then divided it up for the benefit of individual settlers. The New England town system was designed to encourage compact settlements, so all original colonists were given house lots near the church and meetinghouse in the center of town. Each also received tracts of land for traditional agricultural uses, so that each possessed croplands, pastures, meadows, and woodlots widely scattered in different parts of the town. The system had the great advantage of fitting ownership patterns to different ecological uses, but it tended to break down with time.

THE AMERICAN ENVIRONMENT

METES AND BOUNDS, NORTH CAROLINA
The lack of a standardized survey system in the southern colonies produced crazy-quilt field patterns that persist to this day. The irregular fencelines and property boundaries one sees when flying over the southern landscape reflect the metes and bounds surveys that were made centuries ago. *(Comstock)*

In the South, land was surveyed according to a system called "metes and bounds"— which in practice amounted to virtually no system at all. People wanting to buy land went to the county courthouse and purchased a claim to a given number of acres. They then went more or less wherever they chose and marked out the allotted number of acres. To describe their tract, they walked its property boundary and described its corners: a tree here, a rock there, a river on this side. The result was a crazy-quilt pattern of properties, many of them overlapping because their owners had not known a prior claim existed when they were surveyed. The southern system was cheap and initially easy to administer, but it produced so many conflicts over who owned what land that claimants were often forced to litigate their rights for decades.

When the government of the United States met in the wake of the Revolution to settle various problems of the new nation, one of their most important tasks was to decide which cadastral system was most appropriate for the republic. After the states be-

THE AMERICAN ENVIRONMENT

THE GRID, ILLINOIS
Starting at the point where the Ohio River crosses the Pennsylvania-Ohio border, government surveyors applied the Land Ordinance of 1785 to most parts of the United States. The uniform checkerboard pattern of the national grid is visible to any traveler who flies or drives across this terrain. *(Comstock)*

---

gan to cede their western lands to the national government in 1781, the United States for the first time acquired what would henceforth be called "the public domain." The issue of what to do with it would remain a major concern of American politics right down to the present day.

Clearly, a semifeudal system of large land estates like that of the Spanish or Dutch was inappropriate for a republic like the United States. Members of Congress were also eager to avoid the random irregularities and legal conflicts associated with southern metes and bounds. They therefore turned to a modified version of the New England town system. After a trial run with an act in 1784, they finally passed what would become one of the great founding laws in American history, the Land Ordinance of 1785. In terms of the future shape of the American landscape, this act was in many ways even more important than the Constitution itself.

The Ordinance originally applied only to what was then called the Northwest Territory—present-day Ohio, Indiana, Michigan, Illinois, and Wisconsin—but it became a model for all subsequent land systems administered by the federal government. One of

THE AMERICAN ENVIRONMENT

its most important features was its requirement that lands be surveyed *before* they could be purchased, thus circumventing the problems of the southern system. To make sure that surveyed tracts did not overlap, the authors of the ordinance turned to a familiar Enlightenment symbol of rationality and order: the Cartesian coordinate plane that René Descartes had offered as a foundation for his new mathematics. America would be a gridded landscape.

Lands west of the Ohio River were divided into townships six miles to a side, each containing thirty-six square miles, or "sections." Surveyors walked along each side of a section and located its four corners so that there need be no confusion about where one section ended and another began. Would-be owners located their property by identifying its township, its section number, and which corner of the section it was in. One family, for instance, might own a forty-acre farm in the northeast quarter of the southwest quarter of section 23 of the second township in the fourth range of townships in Ohio. Townships were sold in two ways: either as thirty-six-square-mile units to large proprietors who broke them up and resold them as speculations, or as one-square-mile sections to smaller landowners.

Congress had two main goals in this and subsequent land ordinances: to encourage development of the western lands and to raise funds for the federal treasury. In the absence of an income tax, the government's main sources of revenue were the tariff and the sale of public lands. Thus there was an inevitable tension between the government's desire to earn as much money as it could from land sales and settlers' desire to purchase land as cheaply as possible. Debates about the public lands for the rest of the eighteenth and nineteenth centuries revolved around how generous to be to settlers of small means. How low should the price of land be? Should the government offer credit to would-be purchasers who lacked the capital to make a purchase with their own funds? What was the smallest unit in which it could be sold? How near to frontier settlements should auctions be held? Western settlers inevitably argued for the most liberal answers to each of these questions, urging upon the government lower prices, generous credit, small unit sales, and western auctions. The end result was the Homestead Act of 1862, in which a settler could acquire 160 acres simply by filing a claim and paying a nominal entry fee.

The environmental effects of the 1785 Ordinance are almost impossible to exaggerate. The modern landscape of the West and Middle West would be unrecognizable without it. As one flies today from Pennsylvania to Ohio, one instantly recognizes the shift from random field shapes to the rigid north-south, east-west rectilinear patterns of the grid. Except for modern interstate highways, most roads still follow the edges of the original section lines. Farmers still plow their fields within the boundaries set by the original surveyors and still preserve many of the old gnarled "witness trees" the surveyors used to mark section corners. American cities and towns mimic the national grid in the rectangular layout of their streets and lots. We live in a rectilinear world.

The 1785 Ordinance accomplished its goals with great success. It surveyed the public domain according to a regular system, prevented unnecessary litigation over property rights, and speeded the development of western lands. But it was not without prob-

THE AMERICAN ENVIRONMENT

lems. It encouraged a dispersed form of settlement—each farm family often a half mile or more from its neighbors—that undermined the very community ideals that the Ordinance's model, the New England town system, had sought to promote. It led people to arrange their fields and roads according to a rigid north-south, east-west alignment, regardless of local topography. The result was roads that were hillier and harder to travel than they need have been, and fields that were more susceptible to erosion. Finally, when the surveyors eventually reached the arid West, where a dry climate made traditional eastern farming impossible, the square mile units of the grid proved inappropriate both for livestock raising and for irrigation. Settlers had to work around the grid in order to find new systems for living successfully in the very different far western environment.

Despite these social and environmental problems, however, the grid is here to stay. Once drawn, property boundaries can survive for centuries and even millennia after the society that originally drew them has disappeared. In writing the 1785 Ordinance as they did, members of Congress made an indelible mark on the American landscape.

THE AMERICAN STAR
Frederick Kemmelmeyer painted this tribute to George Washington sometime in the 1790s,
one of many efforts by artists and others to create an iconography for the new republic.
(Metropolitan Museum of Art)

CHAPTER SIX

THE CONSTITUTION AND THE NEW REPUBLIC

B Y THE LATE 1780s, most Americans had grown deeply dissatisfied with the deficiencies of the Confederation: with the government's apparent inability to deal with factiousness and instability; with its failure to handle economic problems effectively; and perhaps most of all with the frightening powerlessness it had displayed in the face of Shays's Rebellion. A decade earlier, Americans had deliberately avoided creating a genuine national government, fearing that it would encroach on the sovereignty of the individual states. Now they reconsidered. In 1787, they created a new government, under the Constitution of the United States.

The American Constitution derived most of its principles from the state documents that had preceded it. But it was also a remarkable achievement in its own right. Out of the contentious atmosphere of a fragile new nation, Americans fashioned a system of government that has survived for more than two centuries as one of the stablest and most successful in the world. William Gladstone, the great nineteenth-century British statesman, once called the Constitution the "most wonderful work ever struck off at a given time by the brain and purpose of man." The American people in the years to come generally agreed. Indeed, to them the Constitution took on some of the characteristics of a sacred document, a holy mystery. Later generations viewed its framers as men almost godlike in their wisdom. Many considered its provisions an unassailable "fundamental law," from which all public policies, all political principles, all solutions of controversies must spring.

Yet the adoption of the Constitution did not complete the creation of the republic. It only defined the terms in which debate over the future of government would continue. Americans may have agreed that the Constitution was a nearly perfect document, but they disagreed—at times fundamentally—on what that document meant. Out of those disagreements emerged the first great political battles of the new nation.

FRAMING A NEW GOVERNMENT

So unpopular and ineffectual had the Confederation Congress become by the mid-1780s that it began to lead an almost waiflike existence. In 1783, its members timidly withdrew from Philadelphia to escape from the clamor of army veterans demanding back pay. They took refuge for a while in Princeton, New Jersey, then moved to Annapolis, and in 1785 settled in New York. Through all of this, the delegates were often conspicuous largely by their absence. Only with great difficulty did Congress secure a quorum to ratify the treaty with Great Britain ending the Revolutionary War. Eighteen members, representing only eight states, voted on the Confederation's most important piece of legislation, the Northwest Ordinance. In the meantime, a major public debate was beginning over the future of the Confederation.

GEORGE WASHINGTON AT MOUNT VERNON
Washington was in his first term as president in 1790 when an anonymous folk artist painted this view of his home at Mount Vernon, Virginia. Washington appears in uniform, along with members of his family, on the lawn. After he retired from office in 1797, Washington returned happily to his plantation and spent the two years before his death in 1799 "amusing myself in agricultural and rural pursuits." He also played host to an endless stream of visitors from throughout the country and Europe. *(National Gallery of Art, Washington)*

Advocates of Centralization

Weak and unpopular though the Confederation was, it had for a time satisfied a great many—probably a majority—of the people. They believed they had fought the Revolutionary War to avert the danger of what they considered remote and tyrannical authority; now they desired to keep political power centered in the states, where they could carefully and closely control it.

But during the 1780s, some of the wealthiest and most powerful groups in the country began to clamor for a more genuinely national government capable of dealing with the nation's problems—particularly the economic problems that most directly afflicted them. Some military men, many of them members of the exclusive and hereditary Society of the Cincinnati (formed by Revolutionary army officers in 1783), were disgruntled at the refusal of Congress to fund their pensions. They began aspiring to influence and invig-

orate the national government; some even envisioned a form of military dictatorship and flirted briefly (in 1783, in the so-called Newburgh Conspiracy) with a direct challenge to Congress, until George Washington intervened and blocked the potential rebellion.

American manufacturers—the artisans and "mechanics"—wanted to replace the various state tariffs with a uniformly high national duty. Merchants and shippers wanted to replace the thirteen different (and largely ineffective) state commercial policies with a single, national one. Land speculators wanted the "Indian menace" finally removed from their western tracts. Creditors wanted to stop the states from issuing paper money. Investors in Confederation securities wanted the government to fund the debt and thus enhance the value of their securities. Large property owners in general looked for protection from the threat of mobs, a threat that seemed particularly menacing in light of such episodes as Shays's Rebellion. By 1786, such demands had grown so powerful that the issue was no longer whether the Confederation should be changed but how drastic the changes should be. Even the defenders of the existing system reluctantly came to agree that the government needed strengthening at its weakest point—its lack of power to tax.

The most resourceful of the reformers was Alexander Hamilton, political genius, New York lawyer, onetime military aide to General Washington, and illegitimate son of a Scottish merchant in the West Indies. From the beginning, Hamilton had been unhappy with the Articles of Confederation and the weak central government they had created. He now called for a national convention to overhaul the entire document.

He found an important ally in James Madison of Virginia, who persuaded the Virginia legislature to convene an interstate conference on commercial questions. Only five states sent delegates to the meeting, held in Annapolis, Maryland, in 1786; but the delegates approved a proposal drafted by Hamilton (representing New York) recommending that Congress call a convention of special delegates from all the states to gather in Philadelphia the next year and consider ways to "render the constitution of the Federal government adequate to the exigencies of the union."

At that moment, in 1786, there seemed little possibility that the Philadelphia convention would attract any more interest than the meeting at Annapolis had done. Only by winning the support of George Washington, the centralizers believed, could they hope to prevail. But Washington at first showed little interest in joining the cause. Then, early in 1787, the news of Shays's Rebellion spread throughout the nation. Thomas Jefferson, then the American minister in Paris, was not alarmed. "I hold," he confided in a letter to James Madison, "that a little rebellion, now and then, is a good thing, and as necessary in the political world as storms in the physical." But Washington took the news less calmly. "There are combustibles in every State which a spark might set fire to," he exclaimed. "I feel infinitely more than I can express for the disorders which have arisen. Good God!" In May, he left his home at Mount Vernon in Virginia for the Constitutional Convention in Philadelphia. His support gave the meeting immediate credibility.

A Divided Convention

Fifty-five men, representing all the states except Rhode Island, attended one or more sessions of the convention that sat in the Philadelphia State House from May to September 1787. These "Founding Fathers," as they would later become known, were on the whole relatively young men; the average age was forty-four, and

only one delegate (Benjamin Franklin, then eighty-one) was really aged. They were well educated by the standards of their time. Most represented the great propertied interests of the country, and many feared what one of them called the "turbulence and follies" of democracy. Yet all were also products of the American Revolution and retained the Revolutionary suspicion of concentrated power.

The convention unanimously chose Washington to preside over its sessions and then closed its business to the public and the press. The members then ruled that each state delegation would have a single vote, but that major decisions would not require unanimity, as they did in Congress, but only a simple majority.

Virginia, the most populous state, sent the best-prepared delegation to Philadelphia. James Madison (thirty-six years old) was its intellectual leader. He had devised a detailed plan for a new "national" government, and the Virginians used it to control the agenda from the moment the convention began.

Edmund Randolph of Virginia began the discussion by proposing that "a national government ought to be established, consisting of a supreme Legislative, Executive, and Judiciary." Despite its vagueness, it was a drastic proposal. It called for the creation of a government very different from the existing Confederation, which, among other things, had no executive branch. But so committed were the delegates to fundamental reform that they approved this resolution after only perfunctory debate. Then Randolph introduced the details of Madison's plan. The Virginia Plan (as it came to be known) called for a new national legislature consisting of two houses. In the lower house, the states would be represented in proportion to their population; thus the largest state (Virginia) would have about ten times as many representatives as the smallest (Delaware). Members of the upper house were to be elected by the lower house under no rigid system of representation; thus some of the smaller states might at times have no members at all in the upper house.

The proposal aroused immediate opposition among delegates from Delaware, New Jersey, and other small states. Some responded by arguing that Congress had called the convention "for the sole and express purpose of revising the Articles of Confederation" and had no authority to do more than that. Eventually, however, William Paterson of New Jersey submitted a substantive alternative to the Virginia Plan, a proposal for a "federal" as opposed to a "national" government. The New Jersey Plan preserved the existing one-house legislature, in which each state had equal representation, but it gave Congress expanded powers to tax and to regulate commerce. The delegates voted to table Paterson's proposal.

The Virginia Plan remained the basis for discussion. But its supporters now realized they would have to make concessions to the small states if the convention was ever to reach a general agreement. They soon conceded an important point by agreeing to permit the members of the upper house to be elected by the state legislatures rather than by the lower house of the national legislature. Thus each state would be sure of always having at least one member in the upper house.

But many questions remained. Would the states be equally represented in the upper house, or would the large states have more members than the small ones? Would slaves be counted as part of the population in determining the size of a state's representation in Congress, or were they to be considered simple property? Delegates from states with large and apparently permanent slave populations—especially those from South Carolina—wanted to have it both ways. They argued that slaves should be considered persons in determining representation. But they wanted slaves to be considered property if the new government were to levy taxes on each state on the basis of population. Representatives from states where slavery had disappeared or was expected soon to disappear argued that slaves should be included in calculating taxation but not representation. No one argued seriously for giving slaves citizenship or the right to vote.

Compromise

The delegates bickered for weeks. By the end of June, as both temperature and tempers rose to uncomfortable heights, the convention seemed in danger of collapsing. Benjamin Franklin, who remained a calm voice of conciliation through the summer, warned that if they failed, the delegates would "become a reproach and by-word down to future ages. And what is worse, mankind may hereafter, from this unfortunate instance, despair of establishing governments by human wisdom, and leave it to chance, war and conquest." Partly because of Franklin's soothing presence, the delegates refused to give up.

Finally, on July 2, the convention agreed to create a "grand committee," with a single delegate from each state (and with Franklin as chairman), to resolve the disagreements. The committee produced a proposal that became the basis of the "Great Compromise." Its most important achievement was resolving the difficult problem of representation. The proposal called for a legislature in which the states would be represented in the lower house on the basis of population, with each slave counted as three-fifths of a free person in determining the basis for both representation and di-

rect taxation. (The three-fifths formula was based on the false assumption that a slave was three-fifths as productive as a free worker and thus contributed only three-fifths as much wealth to the state.) And the committee proposed that in the upper house, the states should be represented equally with two members apiece. The proposal broke the deadlock. On July 16, 1787, the convention voted to accept the compromise.

Over the next few weeks, while several committees worked on the details of various parts of the emerging constitution, the convention as a whole agreed to another important compromise on the explosive issue of slavery. The representatives of the southern states feared that the power to regulate trade might interfere with slavery. The convention agreed that the new legislature would not be permitted to tax exports; it would be forbidden to impose a duty of more than $10 a head on imported slaves; and it would have no authority to stop the slave trade for twenty years. To those delegates who viewed the continued existence of slavery as an affront to the principles of the new nation, this was a large and difficult concession. They agreed to it because they feared that without it the Constitution would fail.

Other differences of opinion the convention was unable to harmonize, and it disposed of them by evasion or omission—leaving important questions alive that would surface again in later years. The Constitution provided no definition of citizenship. Most important was the absence of a list of individual rights, which would restrain the powers of the national government in the way that bills of rights restrained the state governments. Madison opposed the idea, arguing that specifying rights that were reserved to the people would, in effect, limit those rights. Others, however, feared that without such protections the national government might abuse its new authority.

The Constitution of 1787

Many people contributed to the creation of the American Constitution, but the single most important person in the process was James Madison, the most creative political thinker of his generation. Madison devised the Virginia Plan, from which the final document ultimately emerged, and he did most of the drafting of the Constitution itself. But Madison's most important achievement was in helping resolve two important philosophical questions that had served as obstacles to the creation of an effective national government: the question of sovereignty and the question of limiting power.

The question of sovereignty had been one of the chief sources of friction between the colonies and Great

THE SIGNING OF THE CONSTITUTION, 1787
This mural by Albert Herter, depicting the final moments of the Constitutional Convention in Philadelphia, is in the Supreme Court chamber in the Wisconsin State Capitol. It shows George Washington seated behind the desk. In the right foreground are James Madison (holding his cloak) and Alexander Hamilton. Benjamin Franklin stands in the foreground at left. *(Brent Nicastro/Third Coast Stock Source)*

Britain, and it continued to perplex Americans as they attempted to create their own government. How could a national government exercise sovereignty concurrently with the states? Where did ultimate sovereignty lie? The answer, Madison and his contemporaries decided, was that all power, at all levels of government, flowed ultimately from the people. Thus neither the federal government nor the state governments were truly sovereign. All of them derived their authority from below. The opening phrase of the Constitution (devised by Robert Morris) was "We the people of the United States"—an expression of the belief that the new government derived its power not from the states but from its citizens.

Resolving the problem of sovereignty made possible one of the distinctive features of the Constitution—its distribution of powers between the national and state governments. It was, Madison wrote at the time, "in strictness, neither a national nor a federal Constitution, but a composition of both." The Constitution and the government it created were to be the "supreme law" of the land; no state would have the authority to defy it. The federal government was to have broad powers, including the power to tax, to regulate commerce, to control the currency, and to pass such laws as would be "necessary and proper" for carrying out its other responsibilities. Gone was the stipulation of the Articles that "each State shall retain every power, jurisdiction, and right not expressly delegated to the United States in Congress assembled." On the other hand, the Constitution accepted the existence of separate states and left important powers in their hands.

In addition to solving the question of sovereignty, the Constitution produced a solution to a problem that was particularly troubling to Americans: the problem of concentrated authority. Nothing so frightened the leaders of the new nation as the prospect of creating a tyrannical government. Indeed, that fear had been one of the chief obstacles to the creation of a national government at all. Drawing from the ideas of the French philosopher Baron de Montesquieu, most Americans had long believed that the best way, perhaps the only way, to avoid tyranny was to keep government close to the people. A republic must remain confined to a relatively small area; a large nation would breed corruption and despotism because the rulers would be so distant from most of the people that there would be no way to control them. In the new American nation,

THE BACKGROUND OF THE CONSTITUTION

THE DEBATE AMONG HISTORIANS about the motives of those who framed the American Constitution mirrors in many ways the debate about the causes of the American Revolution. To some scholars, the creation of the federal system was an effort to preserve the ideals of the Revolution by eliminating the disorder and contention that threatened the new nation. To others, supporters of the Constitution appear to have been men attempting to protect their own economic interests, even at the cost of betraying the principles of the Revolution.

The first and most influential exponent of the former view was John Fiske, whose book *The Critical Period of American History* (1888) painted a grim picture of political life under the Articles of Confederation. The nation, Fiske argued, was reeling under the impact of a business depression; the weakness and ineptitude of the national government; the threats to American territory from Great Britain and Spain; the inability of either the Congress or the state governments to make good their debts; the interstate jealousies and barriers to trade; the widespread use of inflation-producing paper money; and the lawlessness that culminated in Shays's Rebellion. Only the timely adoption of the Constitution, Fiske claimed, saved the young republic from disaster.

Fiske's view met with little dissent until 1913, when Charles A. Beard published a powerful challenge to it in *An Economic Interpretation of the Constitution of the United States.* According to Beard, the 1780s had been a "critical period" not for the nation as a whole but only for certain conservative business interests who feared that the decentralized political structure of the republic imperiled their financial position. Such men, he claimed, wanted a government able to promote industry and trade, protect private property, and perhaps most of all, make good the public debt—much of which was owed to them. The Constitution was, Beard claimed, "an economic document drawn with superb skill by men whose property interests were immediately at stake" and who won its ratification over the opposition of a majority of the people. Were it not for their impatience and determination, he argued in a later book (1927), the Articles of Confederation might have formed a perfectly satisfactory, permanent form of government. The Beard view of the Constitution influenced more than a generation of historians. As late as the 1950s, for example, Merrill Jensen argued in *The New Nation* (1950) that the 1780s were not years of chaos and despair, but a time of hopeful striving. He agreed with Beard that only the economic interests of a small group of wealthy men could account for the creation of the Constitution.

But the 1950s also produced a series of powerful and persuasive challenges to the Beard thesis. Robert E. Brown, for example, argued in 1956 that "absolutely no correlation" could be shown between the wealth of the delegates to the Constitutional Convention and their position on the Constitution. Forrest McDonald, in *We the People*

these assumptions had led to the belief that the individual states must remain sovereign and that a strong national government would be dangerous.

Madison, however, helped break the grip of these assumptions by arguing that a large republic would be less, not more, likely to produce tyranny, because it would contain so many different factions that no single group would ever be able to dominate it. (In this, he drew from—among other sources—the Scottish philosopher David Hume.) This idea of many centers of power "checking each other" and preventing any single, despotic authority from emerging not only made possible the idea of a large republic. It also helped shape the internal structure of the federal government. The Constitution's most distinctive feature was its "separation of powers" within the government,

(1958), looked beyond the convention itself to the debate between the Federalists and the Antifederalists and concluded similarly that there was no consistent relationship between wealth and property on the one hand and support for the Constitution on the other. Instead, opinion on the new system was far more likely to reflect local and regional interests. Areas suffering social and economic distress were likely to support the Constitution; states that were stable and prosperous were likely to oppose it. There was no intercolonial class of monied interests operating in concert to produce the Constitution.

The cumulative effect of these attacks greatly weakened Beard's argument; few historians any longer accepted his thesis without reservation. By the 1960s, however, a new group of scholars was beginning to revive an economic interpretation of the Constitution—one that differed from Beard's in important ways but that nevertheless emphasized social and economic factors as motives for supporting the federal system. Jackson Turner Main argued, in *The Antifederalists* (1961), that supporters of the Constitution, while not perhaps the united creditor class that Beard described, were nevertheless economically distinct from critics of the document. The Federalists, he argued, were "cosmopolitan commercialists," eager to advance the economic development of the nation; the Antifederalists, by contrast, were "agrarian localists," fearful of centralization. Gordon Wood's important study, *The Creation of the American Republic* (1969), de-emphasized economic grievances but nevertheless suggested that the debate over the state constituting in the

1770s and 1780s reflected profound social divisions and that those same divisions helped shape the argument over the federal Constitution. The Federalists, he suggested, were largely traditional aristocrats. They had become deeply concerned by the instability of life under the Articles of Confederation and were particularly alarmed by the decline in popular deference toward social elites. The creation of the Constitution was part of a larger search to create a legitimate political leadership based on the existing social hierarchy; it reflected the efforts of elites to contain what they considered the excesses of democracy.

Other historians have stressed not so much class divisions or economic interests as regional or generational differences. H. James Henderson argued in 1974, in *Party Politics in the Continental Congress*, that the debate over the Constitution was part of a larger argument over the integration of different regions into a single nation. Stanley Elkins and Eric McKitrick contended in a 1961 article ("The Founding Fathers," *Political Science Quarterly*) that the Federalists tended to be younger men than the Antifederalists and saw the development of a strong, united nation as the key to their own future. Pauline Maier, in *The Old Revolutionaries* (1980), offered portraits of early leaders of the resistance to Britain toward the end of their lives and argued that their passage from the scene made it possible for new ideas about the nature of the Revolution—ideas that found reflection in the Constitution—to emerge among the leaders of the next generation.

its creation of "checks and balances" between the legislative, executive, and judicial branches. The array of forces within the government would constantly compete with (and often frustrate) one another. Congress would have two chambers, the Senate and the House of Representatives, each with members elected in a different way and for different terms, and each checking the other, since both would have to agree before any

law could be passed. The president would have the power to veto acts of Congress. The federal courts would have protection from both the executive and the legislature because judges and justices, once appointed by the president and confirmed by the Senate, would serve for life.

The "federal" structure of the government, which divided power between the states and the nation, and the system of "checks and balances," which divided power among various elements within the national government itself, was designed to protect the United States from the kind of despotism Americans believed had emerged in England. But it was also designed to protect the nation from another kind of despotism, perhaps equally menacing: the tyranny of the people. Fear of the "mob," of an "excess of democracy," was at least as important to the framers as fear of a single tyrant. Shays's Rebellion had been only one example, they believed, of what could happen if a nation did not defend itself against the unchecked exercise of popular will. Thus in the new government, only the members of the House of Representatives would be elected directly by the people. Senators, the president, federal judges—all would be insulated in varying degrees from the public.

On September 17, 1787, thirty-nine delegates signed the Constitution, doubtless sharing the feelings that Benjamin Franklin expressed at the end: "Thus I consent, Sir, to this Constitution, *because I expect no better, and because I am not sure it is not the best.*"

Federalists and Antifederalists

The delegates at Philadelphia had greatly exceeded their instructions from Congress and the states. Instead of making simple revisions in the Articles of Confederation, they had produced a plan for a completely different form of government. They feared, therefore, that the Constitution might never be ratified under the rules of the Articles of Confederation, which required unanimous approval by the state legislatures. So the convention changed the rules. The Constitution specified that the new government would come into existence among the ratifying states when any nine of the thirteen had ratified it. The delegates recommended to Congress that special state conventions, not state legislatures, consider the document.

Overshadowed by the events in Philadelphia, the old Congress passively accepted the convention's work and submitted it to the states for approval. All the state legislatures except Rhode Island's elected delegates to ratifying conventions, most of which had begun meeting by early 1788. Even before the ratifying conventions adjourned, however, a great national debate on the new Constitution had begun—in the legislatures, in mass meetings, in the columns of newspapers, and in ordinary conversations. Occasionally, passions rose to the point that opposing factions came to blows. In at least one place—Albany, New York—such clashes resulted in injuries and death.

Supporters of the Constitution had a number of advantages. They were better organized than their opponents, and they had the support of the two most em-

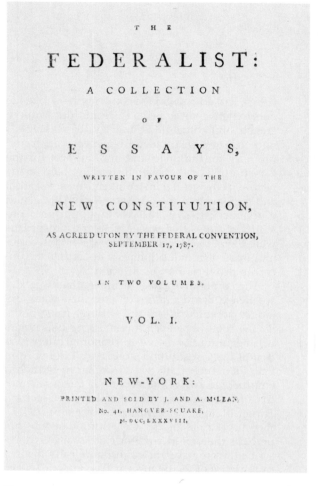

THE FEDERALIST PAPERS
James Madison, John Jay, and Alexander Hamilton would later become antagonists. But in 1788, they collaborated on one of the most important political documents ever created by Americans—a defense of and justification for the new federal Constitution. Originally published as separate essays in newspapers around the new nation, the *Federalist* was later published as a book. *(New York Public Library)*

inent men in America, Franklin and Washington. (Washington, for example, had declared that the nation faced a choice between the Constitution and disunion.) And they seized an appealing label for themselves: "Federalists"—the term that opponents of centralization had once used to describe themselves—thus implying that they were less committed to a "nationalist" government than in fact they were. The Federalists also had the support of the ablest political philosophers of their time: Alexander Hamilton, James Madison, and John Jay. Those three men, under the joint pseudonym "Publius," wrote a series of essays—widely published in newspapers throughout the nation—explaining the meaning and virtues of the Constitution. The essays were later issued as a book, and they are known today as *The Federalist Papers*. They are among the greatest American contributions to political theory.

The Federalists called their critics "Antifederalists," implying that their rivals had nothing to offer except opposition and chaos. But the Antifederalists had serious and intelligent arguments of their own. They presented themselves as the defenders of the true principles of the Revolution. The Constitution, they believed, would betray those principles by establishing a strong, potentially tyrannical center of power in the new national government. The new government, they claimed, would increase taxes, obliterate the states, wield dictatorial powers, favor the "well born" over the common people, and put an end to individual liberty. But their biggest complaint was that the Constitution lacked a bill of rights, a concern that revealed one of the most important sources of their opposition: a basic mistrust of human nature and of the capacity of human beings to wield power. (Some contemporaries, and some later scholars, described them as "men of little faith.") The Antifederalists argued that any government that centralized authority in the hands of the powerful would inevitably produce despotism. Their demand for a bill of rights was a product of this belief: no government could be trusted to protect the liberties of its citizens; only by enumerating the natural rights of the people could there be any assurance that those rights would be preserved.

At its heart, then, the debate between the Federalists and the Antifederalists was a battle between two fears. The Federalists were afraid, above all, of disorder, anarchy, chaos; they feared the unchecked power of the masses, and they sought in the Constitution to create a government that would function at some distance from popular passions. The Antifederalists were not anarchists, of course. But they were much more afraid of the state than they were of the people, much more concerned about the dangers of concentrated power than about the dangers of popular will. They opposed the Constitution for some of the same reasons the Federalists supported it: because it placed obstacles between the people and the exercise of power.

Despite the Antifederalist efforts, ratification proceeded quickly (although not without occasional difficulty) during the winter of 1787–1788. The Delaware convention was the first to act. It ratified the Constitution unanimously, as did New Jersey and Georgia. In the larger states of Pennsylvania and Massachusetts, the Antifederalists put up a more determined struggle but lost in the final vote. New Hampshire ratified the document in June 1788—the ninth state to do so. It was now theoretically possible for the Constitution to go into effect.

A new government could not hope to succeed, however, without the participation of Virginia and New York, the two biggest states, whose conventions remained closely divided. But by the end of June, first Virginia and then New York had consented to the Constitution by narrow margins. The New York convention yielded to expediency—even some of the most staunchly Antifederalist delegates feared that the state's commercial interests would suffer if, once the other states gathered under the "New Roof," New York were to remain outside. Massachusetts, Virginia, and New York all ratified, on the assumption that a bill of rights would be added to the Constitution. The North Carolina convention adjourned without taking action, waiting to see what happened to the amendments. Rhode Island, whose leaders had opposed the Constitution almost from the start, did not even call a convention to consider ratification.

Completing the Structure

The first elections under the Constitution took place in the early months of 1789. Almost all the newly elected congressmen and senators had favored ratification, and many had served as delegates to the Philadelphia convention. There was never any real doubt about who would be the first president. George Washington had presided at the Constitutional Convention, and many who had favored ratification did so only because they expected him to preside over the new government as well. Washington received the votes of all the presidential electors. John Adams, a leading Federalist, became vice president. After a journey from Mount Vernon marked by elaborate celebrations along the way, Washington was inaugurated on April 30, 1789.

The first Congress served in many ways almost as a continuation of the Constitutional Convention, because its principal responsibility was filling in the various gaps in the Constitution. Its most important task was drafting a bill of rights. By early 1789, even Madison had come to agree that some sort of bill of rights was essential to legitimize the new government in the eyes of its opponents. Congress approved twelve amendments on September 25, 1789; ten of them were ratified by the states by the end of 1791. What we know as the Bill of Rights is these first ten amendments to the Constitution. Nine of them placed limitations on Congress by forbidding it to infringe on certain basic rights: freedom of religion, speech, and the press; immunity from arbitrary arrest; trial by jury; and others. The Tenth Amendment reserved to the states all pow-

CONGRESSIONAL BRAWLERS
This cartoon lampoons a celebrated fight on the floor of the House of Representatives in 1798 between Matthew Lyon, a Republican from Vermont, and Roger Griswold, a Federalist from Connecticut. The conflict began when Griswold insulted Lyon by attacking his military record in the Revolutionary War. Lyon replied by spitting in Griswold's face. Two weeks later, Griswold attacked Lyon with his cane, and Lyon seized a pair of fire tongs and fought back. That later scene is depicted (and ridiculed) here. Other members of Congress are portrayed as enjoying the spectacle. On the wall is a picture entitled "Royal Sport," showing animals fighting. *(New York Public Library)*

ers except those specifically withheld from them or delegated to the federal government.

On the subject of the federal courts, the Constitution said only: "The judicial power of the United States shall be vested in one Supreme Court, and in such inferior courts as the Congress may from time to time ordain and establish." It was left to Congress to determine the number of Supreme Court judges to be appointed and the kinds of lower courts to be organized. In the Judiciary Act of 1789, Congress provided for a Supreme Court of six members, with a chief justice and five associate justices; thirteen district courts with one judge apiece; and three circuit courts of appeal, each to consist of one of the district judges sitting with two of the Supreme Court justices. In the same act, Congress gave the Supreme Court the power to make the final decision in cases involving the constitutionality of state laws.

The Constitution referred indirectly to executive departments but did not specify what or how many there should be. The first Congress created three such departments—state, treasury, and war—and also established the offices of the attorney general and postmaster general. To the office of secretary of the treasury, Washington appointed Alexander Hamilton of New York, who at age thirty-two was an acknowledged expert in public finance. For secretary of war he chose a Massachusetts Federalist, General Henry Knox. As attorney general he named Edmund Randolph of Virginia, sponsor of the plan on which the Constitution had been based. As secretary of state he chose another Virginian, Thomas Jefferson, who had served as minister to France.

FEDERALISTS AND REPUBLICANS

The resolution of these initial issues, however, did not resolve the disagreements about the nature of the new government. On the contrary, for the first twelve years under the Constitution, American politics was characterized by a level of acrimony seldom matched in any period since. The framers of the Constitution had dealt with many disagreements not by solving them but by papering them over with a series of vague compromises; as a result, the disagreements survived to plague the new government.

At the heart of the controversies of the 1790s was the same basic difference in philosophy that had lain at the heart of the debate over the Constitution. On one side stood a powerful group that believed America required a strong, national government: that the country's mission was to become a genuine nation-state, with centralized authority, a complex commercial economy, and a proud standing in world affairs. On the other side stood another group—a minority at first, but one that gained strength during the decade—that envisioned a far more modest central government. American society should not, this group believed, aspire to be highly commercial or urban. It should remain predominantly rural and agrarian. The centralizers became known as the Federalists and gravitated to the leadership of Alexander Hamilton. Their opponents acquired the name Republicans and gathered under the leadership of James Madison and Thomas Jefferson.

Hamilton and the Federalists

For twelve years, control of the new government remained firmly in the hands of the Federalists. That was in part because George Washington had always envisioned a strong national government and as president had done little to discourage those who were attempting to create one. But Washington believed the presidency should remain above political controversies, and so he avoided any personal involvement in the deliberations of Congress. As a result, the dominant figure in his administration became his talented secretary of the treasury, Alexander Hamilton, who exerted more influence on domestic and foreign policy than anyone else both during his term of office and, to an almost equal extent, after his resignation in 1794.

Of all the national leaders of his time, Hamilton was one of the most aristocratic in personal tastes and political philosophy—ironically, perhaps, since his own origins had been humble. Far from embracing republican ideals of the virtue of the people, he believed that a stable and effective government required an enlightened ruling class. Thus, the new government needed the support of the wealthy and powerful; and to get that support it needed to give these elites a stake in its success. Hamilton proposed, therefore, that the existing public debt be "funded." Many of the miscellaneous, uncertain, depreciated certificates of indebtedness that the old Congress had issued during and after the Revolution were now in the hands of wealthy speculators; the government should call them in and exchange them for uniform, interest-bearing bonds, payable at definite dates. He also recommended that the federal government "assume" (or take over) the Revolutionary state debts, to encourage state as well as federal bondholders to look to the central government for eventual payment. Hamilton did not, in other words, envision paying off and thus eliminating the debt. He wanted instead to create a large and permanent national debt, with new bonds being issued as old ones were paid off. The result, he believed, would be that creditors—the wealthy classes most likely to lend money to the government—would have a permanent stake in seeing the government survive.

Hamilton also wanted to create a national bank. At the time, there were only a few banks in the country,

located principally in Boston, Philadelphia, and New York. A new, national bank would help fill the void that the absence of a well-developed banking system had created. It would provide loans and currency to businesses. It would give the government a safe place to deposit federal funds. It would help collect taxes and disburse the government's expenditures. It would keep up the price of government bonds through judicious bond purchases. The bank would be chartered by the federal government, would have a monopoly of the government's own banking business, and would be controlled by directors, of whom one-fifth would be appointed by the government. It would provide a stable center to the nation's small and feeble banking system.

The funding and assumption of debts required new sources of revenue for the government. Hamilton supported two kinds of taxes (in addition to the receipts to be anticipated from the sales of public land). One was an excise to be paid by distillers of alcoholic liquors, a tax that would fall most heavily on the whiskey distillers of the backcountry, especially in Pennsylvania, Virginia, and North Carolina—small farmers who converted part of their corn and rye crop into whiskey. The other was the tariff on imports, which not only would raise revenue but would also protect American manufacturing from foreign competition. In his famous "Report on Manufactures" of 1791, he laid out a grand scheme for stimulating the growth of industry in the United States and wrote glowingly of the advantages to the nation of a healthy manufacturing base.

The Federalists, in short, offered more than a vision of how to stabilize the new government. They offered a vision of the sort of nation America should become—a nation with a wealthy, enlightened ruling class, a vigorous, independent commercial economy, and a thriving industrial sector; a nation able to play a prominent role in world economic affairs.

Enacting the Federalist Program

Few members of Congress objected to Hamilton's plan for funding the national debt, but many did oppose his proposal to fund the debt "at par," that is, to exchange new bonds for old certificates of indebtedness on a dollar-for-dollar basis. The old certificates had been issued to merchants and farmers in payment for war supplies during the Revolution, or to officers and soldiers of the Revolutionary army in payment for their services. But many of these original holders had sold their bonds during the hard times of the 1780s to speculators, who had bought them at a fraction of their face value. Many members of Congress believed that the original holders deserved some consideration, and James Madison, now a representative from Virginia, proposed dividing the new bonds between the original purchasers and the speculators. But Hamilton's allies insisted that such a plan was impractical and that the honor of the government required a literal fulfillment of its earlier promises to pay. Congress finally passed the funding bill Hamilton wanted.

His proposal that the federal government assume the state debts encountered greater difficulty. Its opponents argued that if the federal government took over the state debts, the people of states with few debts would have to pay taxes to service the larger debts of other states. Massachusetts, for example, owed far more money than did Virginia. Only by striking a bargain with the Virginians were Hamilton and his supporters able to win passage of the bill.

The deal involved the location of the national capital. The Virginians wanted a new capital near them in the South. Hamilton met with Thomas Jefferson (after Jefferson's return from France) and agreed over dinner to provide northern support for placing the capital in the South in exchange for Virginia's votes for the assumption bill. The capital had moved from New York back to Philadelphia in 1790. But the new bargain called for the construction of a new capital city on the banks of the Potomac River, which divided Virginia and Maryland, on land to be selected by Washington himself. The government would move there by the beginning of the new century.

Hamilton's bank bill sparked the most heated debate, the first of many on this controversial issue. Hamilton argued that creation of a national bank was compatible with the intent of the Constitution, even though the document did not explicitly authorize it. But Madison, Jefferson, Randolph, and others argued that Congress should exercise no powers that the Constitution had not clearly assigned it. Nevertheless, both the House and the Senate finally agreed to Hamilton's bill, and although Washington initially displayed some uncertainty about its legality, he finally signed it. The Bank of the United States began operations in 1791, under a charter that granted it the right to continue for twenty years.

Hamilton also had his way with the excise tax, although protests from farmers later forced revisions to reduce the burden on the smaller distillers. He won passage, too, of a new tariff in 1792, although it raised rates less than he had wished.

Once enacted, Hamilton's program had many of the effects he had intended and won the support of influential segments of the population. It quickly restored public credit; the bonds of the United States were soon selling at home and abroad at prices even above their par value. Speculators (among them many members of Congress) reaped large profits as a result. Manufacturers profited from the tariffs, and merchants in the seaports benefited from the new banking system.

Others, however, found the Hamilton program less appealing. Small farmers, who formed the vast majority of the population, complained that they had to bear a disproportionate tax burden. Not only did they have to pay property taxes to their state governments, but they bore the brunt of the excise tax and, indirectly, the tariff. A feeling grew among many Americans that the Federalist program served the interests not of the people but of small, wealthy elites. Out of this feeling an organized political opposition arose.

The Republican Opposition

The Constitution had made no reference to political parties, and the omission was not an oversight. Most of the framers—and George Washington in particular—believed that organized parties were dangerous and should be avoided. Disagreement on particular issues was inevitable, but most of the founders believed that such disagreements need not and should not lead to the formation of permanent factions. "The public good is disregarded in the conflicts of rival parties," Madison had written in *The Federalist Papers* (in Number 10, perhaps the most influential of all the essays), "and . . . measures are too often decided, not according to the rules of justice and the rights of the minor party, but by the superior force of an interested and overbearing majority."

Yet within just a few years after ratification of the Constitution, Madison and others became convinced that Hamilton and his followers had become just such an "interested and overbearing majority." Not only had the Federalists enacted a program that many of these leaders opposed. More ominously, Hamilton himself had, in their eyes, worked to establish a national network of influence that embodied all the worst features of a party. The Federalists had used their control over appointments and the awarding of government franchises, and all the other powers of their offices, to reward their supporters and win additional allies. They had encouraged the formation of local associations—largely aristocratic in nature—to strengthen their standing in local communities. They were doing many of the same things, their opponents believed, that the corrupt British governments of the early eighteenth century had done.

Because the Federalists appeared to be creating such a menacing and tyrannical structure of power, their critics felt there was no alternative but to organize a vigorous opposition. The result was the emergence of an alternative political organization, which called itself the Republican Party. (This first "Republican"

THE JEFFERSONIAN IDYLL
American artists in the early nineteenth century were drawn to tranquil rural scenes, symbolic of the Jeffersonian vision of a nation of small, independent farmers. By 1822, when Francis Alexander painted this pastoral landscape, the simple agrarian republic it depicts was already being transformed by rapid economic growth. *(National Gallery of Art, Washington)*

Party is not the ancestor of the modern Republican Party, which was born in the 1850s.) By the late 1790s, the Republicans were going to even greater lengths than the Federalists to create an apparatus of partisan influence. In every state they had formed committees, societies, and caucuses. Republican groups were corresponding with one another across state lines. They were banding together to influence state and local elections. And they were justifying their actions by claiming that they and they alone represented the true interests of the nation—that they were fighting to defend the people against a corrupt conspiracy by the Federalists. Just as Hamilton believed that the network of supporters he was creating represented the only legitimate interest group in the nation, so the Republicans believed that their party organization represented the best interests of the people. Neither side was willing to admit that it was acting as a party; neither would concede the right of the other to exist. This institutionalized factionalism is known to scholars as the "first party system."

From the beginning, the preeminent figures among the Republicans were Thomas Jefferson and James Madison. Indeed, the two men were such intimate collaborators with such similar political philosophies that it is sometimes difficult to distinguish the contributions of one from those of the other. But Jefferson, the more magnetic personality of the two, gradually emerged as the most prominent spokesman for the Republicans. Jefferson considered himself a farmer. (He was, in fact, a substantial planter who had spent relatively little time in recent years at his estate in Virginia.) He believed in an agrarian republic, most of whose citizens would be sturdy, independent farmer-citizens tilling their own soil.

Jefferson did not scorn commercial activity; he assumed farmers would market their crops in the national and even international markets. Nor did he oppose industry; he believed the United States should develop some manufacturing capacity. But he was suspicious of large cities, feared urban mobs as "sores upon the body politic," and opposed the development of an advanced industrial economy because it would, he feared, increase the number of propertyless workers packed in cities. In short, Jefferson envisioned a decentralized society, dominated by small property owners engaged largely in agrarian activities.

The difference between the Federalist and Republican social philosophies was visible in, among other things, reactions to the French Revolution. As that revolution grew increasingly radical in the 1790s, with its attacks on organized religion, the overthrow of the monarchy, and eventually the execution of the king and queen, the Federalists expressed horror. But the Republicans generally applauded the democratic, anti-aristocratic spirit they believed the French Revolution embodied. Some even imitated the French radicals (the Jacobins) by cutting their hair short, wearing pantaloons, and addressing one another as "Citizen" and "Citizeness."

Although both parties had supporters in all parts of the country and among all classes, there were regional and economic differences. The Federalists were most numerous in the commercial centers of the Northeast and in such southern seaports as Charleston; the Republicans were most numerous in the rural areas of the South and the West.

As the 1792 presidential election—the nation's second—approached, both Jefferson and Hamilton urged Washington to run for another term. The president reluctantly agreed. But while most Americans considered Washington above the partisan battle, he was actually much more in sympathy with the Federalists than with the Republicans. And during his presidency, Hamilton remained the dominant figure in government.

ESTABLISHING NATIONAL SOVEREIGNTY

The Federalists consolidated their position—and attracted wide public support for the new national government—by dealing effectively with two problems the old Confederation had been unable fully to resolve. They helped stabilize the nation's western lands, and they strengthened America's international position.

Securing the Frontier

Despite the Northwest Ordinance, the Confederation Congress had largely failed to tie the outlying western areas of the country firmly to the government. Farmers in western Massachusetts had risen in revolt; settlers in Vermont, Kentucky, and Tennessee had toyed with the idea of separating from the Union. At first, the new government under the Constitution faced similar problems.

In 1794, farmers in western Pennsylvania raised a major challenge to federal authority when they refused to pay a whiskey excise tax and began terrorizing the tax collectors (much as colonists had done at the time of the Stamp Act). But the federal government did not leave settlement of the so-called Whiskey Rebellion to Pennsylvania, as the Confederation Congress had left Shays's Rebellion to Massachusetts. At Hamilton's urging, Washington called out the militias of three states, raised an army of nearly 15,000 (a larger force than he had commanded against the British during most of the Revolution), and personally led the troops into Pennsylvania. As the militiamen approached Pittsburgh, the center of the resistance, the rebellion quickly collapsed.

The federal government won the allegiance of the whiskey rebels through intimidation. It won the loyalties of other frontier people by accepting new states as members of the Union. The last of the original thirteen colonies joined the union once the Bill of Rights had been appended to the Constitution—North Carolina in 1789 and Rhode Island in 1790. Then Vermont, which had had its own state government since the Revolution, became the fourteenth state in 1791 after New York and New Hampshire finally agreed to give up their claims to it. Next came Kentucky, in 1792, when Virginia gave up its claim to that region. After North Carolina finally ceded its western lands to the Union, Tennessee became first a territory and, in 1796, a state.

The new government faced a greater challenge, inherited from the Confederation, in the more distant areas of the Northwest and the Southwest, where Indians (occasionally in alliance with the British and Spanish) continued to challenge the republic's claim to tribal lands. The ordinances of 1784–1787, establishing the terms of white settlement in the West, had produced a series of border conflicts with Indian tribes resisting white settlement in their lands. The new government inherited these clashes, which continued with few interruptions for nearly a decade. Although the United States eventually defeated virtually every Indian challenge (if often at great cost), it was clear that the larger question of who was to control the lands of the West—the United States or the Indian nations—remained unanswered.

These clashes revealed another issue the Constitution had done little to resolve: the place of the Indian nations within the new federal structure. The Constitution barely mentioned Native Americans. Article I excluded "Indians not taxed" from being counted in the population totals that determined the number of seats states would receive in the House of Representatives, and it gave Congress the power to "regulate Commerce with foreign Nations, and among the several States, and with the Indian tribes." Article VI bound the new government to respect treaties negotiated by the Confederation, most of which had been

AN EXCISEMAN.

with the tribes. But none of this did very much to clarify the precise legal standing of Indians or Indian nations within the United States.

On the one hand, the Constitution seemed to recognize the existence of the tribes as legal entities. On the other hand, it made clear that they were not "foreign Nations" (in the same sense that European countries were); nor were their members citizens of the United States. The tribes received no direct representation in the new government. Above all, the Constitution did not address the major issue that would govern relations between whites and Indians: land. Indian nations lived within the boundaries of the United States, yet they claimed (and the white government at times agreed) that they had some measure of sovereignty within their own land. But neither the Constitution nor common law offered any clear guide to the rights of a "nation within a nation" or to the precise nature of tribal sovereignty, which ultimately depended on control of land. Thus, the relationship between the tribes and the United States remained to be determined by a series of treaties, agreements, and judicial decisions in a process that has continued for two centuries.

Maintaining Neutrality

Not until 1791 did Great Britain send a minister to the United States, and then only because Madison and the Republicans were threatening to place special trade restrictions on British ships. That was only one symbol of the difficulty the new government had in establishing its legitimacy in the eyes of the British. A new crisis in Anglo-American relations emerged in 1793 when the new French government created by the revolution of 1789 went to war with Great Britain and its allies. Both the president and Congress took steps to establish American neutrality in that conflict. But that neutrality quickly encountered severe tests.

The first challenge to American neutrality came from revolutionary France and its first diplomatic representative to America, the youthful and brash Edmond Genet. Instead of landing at Philadelphia and presenting himself immediately to the president, Genet disembarked at Charleston. There he made plans to use American ports to outfit French warships, encouraged American shipowners to serve as French privateers, and commissioned the aging George Rogers Clark to lead a military expedition against Spanish lands to the south. (Spain was at the time an ally of Great Britain and an enemy of France.) In all of this, Genet was brazenly ignoring Washington's proclamation and flagrantly violating the Neutrality Act. His conduct infuriated Washington (who provided "Citizen Genet," as he was known, with an icy reception in Philadelphia) and the Federalists; it also embarrassed all but the most ardent Francophiles among the Republicans. Washington eventually demanded that the French government recall him, but by then Genet's party was out of power in France. (The president granted him political asylum in the United States, and he settled with his American wife on a Long Island farm.) The neutrality policy had survived its first great test.

A second and even greater challenge came from Great Britain. Early in 1794, the Royal Navy began seizing hundreds of American ships engaged in trade in the French West Indies, outraging public opinion in the United States. Anti-British feeling rose still higher at the report that the governor general of Canada had delivered a warlike speech to the Indians on the northwestern frontier. Hamilton was deeply concerned. War would mean an end to imports from England, and most of the revenue for maintaining his financial system came from duties on those imports.

This was, Hamilton believed, no time for ordinary diplomacy. He did not trust the State Department to reach a settlement with Britain. Jefferson had resigned as secretary of state in 1793 to devote more time to his political activities, but his successor, Edmund Randolph, was even more ardently pro-French than Jefferson had been. So Hamilton persuaded Washington to name a special commissioner to England: John Jay, chief justice of the United States Supreme Court and a staunch New York Federalist. Jay was instructed to secure compensation for the recent British assaults on American shipping, to demand withdrawal of British forces from the frontier posts, and to negotiate a new commercial treaty.

The long and complex treaty Jay negotiated in 1794 failed to achieve these goals. But it was not without merit. It settled the conflict with Britain and helped prevent what had seemed likely to become a war between the two nations. It established undisputed American sovereignty over the entire Northwest. And it produced a reasonably satisfactory commercial relationship with a nation whose trade was important to the United States. Nevertheless, when the terms became public in America, there were bitter public denunciations. Jay himself was burned in effigy in various parts of the country. Opponents of the treaty—nearly all the Republicans and even some Federalists, encouraged by agents of France—went to extraordinary lengths to defeat it in the Senate. The American minister to France, James Monroe, and even the secretary of state, Edmund Randolph, cooperated closely with the desperate attempt to prevent ratification. But in the end the Senate ratified what was by then known as Jay's Treaty.

Among other things, the treaty made possible a settlement of America's conflict with the Spanish by raising fears in Spain of a joint Anglo-American challenge to Spanish possessions in North America. When Thomas Pinckney arrived in Spain as a special negotiator, he had no difficulty in gaining nearly everything the United States had sought from the Spaniards for more than a decade. Under Pinckney's Treaty (signed in 1795), Spain recognized the right of Americans to navigate the Mississippi to its mouth and to deposit goods at New Orleans for reloading on oceangoing ships; agreed to fix the northern boundary of Florida where Americans always had insisted it should be, along the 31st parallel; and required Spanish authorities to prevent the Indians in Florida from launching raids across the border.

THE DOWNFALL OF THE FEDERALISTS

The Federalists' impressive triumphs did not ensure their continued dominance in the national government. On the contrary, success seemed to produce problems of its own—problems that eventually led to their downfall.

Since almost all Americans in the 1790s agreed that there was no place in a stable republic for an organized opposition, the emergence of the Republicans as powerful contenders for popular favor seemed to the Federalists a grave threat to national stability. When, beginning in the late 1790s, major international perils confronted the government as well, the Federalists could not resist the temptation to move forcefully against the opposition. Facing what they believed was a stark choice between respecting individual liberties and preserving stability, the Federalists chose stability. The result was political disaster. After 1796, the Federalists never won another election. The popular respect for the institutions of the federal government, which they had worked so hard to produce among the people, survived. But the Federalists themselves gradually vanished as an effective political force.

The Election of 1796

Despite strong pressure from his many admirers to run for a third term as president, George Washington insisted on retiring from office in 1797. But in a "Farewell Address" to the American people (actually a long letter, composed in part by Hamilton and published in a Philadelphia newsletter), he reacted sharply to the Republicans. His reference to the "insidious wiles of foreign influence" was not just a warning against international entanglements; it was also a denunciation of those Republicans who had been conspiring with the French to frustrate the Federalist diplomatic program.

With Washington out of the running, no impediment remained to an open expression of the partisan rivalries that had been building over the previous eight years. Jefferson was the uncontested candidate of the Republicans in 1796. The Federalists faced a more difficult choice. Hamilton, the personification of Federalism, had created too many enemies to be a credible candidate. So Vice President John Adams, who had been directly associated with none of the unpopular Federalist measures, became his party's nominee for president.

The Federalists were still clearly the dominant party, and there was little doubt of their ability to win a majority of the presidential electors. But without Washington to mediate, they fell victim to fierce factional rivalries that almost led to their undoing. Hamilton and many other Federalists (especially in the South) were not reconciled to Adams's candidacy and favored his running mate Thomas Pinckney instead. And when, as expected, the Federalists elected a majority of the presidential electors, some of these Pinckney support-

JOHN ADAMS
Adams's illustrious career as revolutionary leader, diplomat, and president marked the beginning of four generations of public distinction among members of his family. His son, John Quincy Adams, served as secretary of state and president. His grandson, Charles Francis Adams, was one of the great diplomats of the Civil War era. His great-grandson, Henry Adams, was one of America's most distinguished historians and writers. *(Adams National Historic Site, Quincy, Massachusetts)*

ers declined to vote for Adams; he managed to defeat Jefferson by only three electoral votes. Because a still larger number of Adams's supporters declined to vote for Pinckney, Jefferson finished second in the balloting and became vice president. (The Constitution provided for the candidate receiving the second highest number of electoral votes to become vice president—hence the awkward result of men from different parties serving in the nation's two highest offices. The Twelfth Amendment, adopted in 1804, reformed the electoral system to prevent such situations.)

Adams thus assumed the presidency under inauspicious circumstances. He presided over a divided party, which faced a strong and resourceful Republican opposition committed to its extinction. And Adams himself was not even the dominant figure in his own party; Hamilton remained the most influential Federalist, and Adams was never able to challenge him effectively. The new president was one of the country's most accomplished and talented statesmen, but he had few skills as a politician. Austere, rigid, aloof, he had little talent at conciliating differences, soliciting support, or inspiring enthusiasm. He was a man of enormous, indeed intimidating rectitude, and he seemed to assume that his own virtue and the correctness of his positions would alone be enough to sustain him. He was usually wrong.

The Quasi War with France

American relations with Great Britain and Spain improved as a result of Jay's and Pinckney's treaties. But the nation's relations with revolutionary France quickly deteriorated. French vessels captured American ships on the high seas and at times imprisoned the crews. And when the South Carolina Federalist Charles Cotesworth Pinckney, brother of Thomas Pinckney, arrived in France, the government refused to receive him as the official representative of the United States.

Some of the president's advisers favored war, most notably Secretary of State Thomas Pickering, a stern New Englander who detested France. But former Secretary of the Treasury Alexander Hamilton, who was still a major power in the Federalist Party, recommended conciliation. Adams agreed. In an effort to stabilize relations, Adams appointed a bipartisan commission—consisting of Charles Cotesworth Pinckney, the recently rejected minister; John Marshall, a Virginia Federalist, later chief justice of the Supreme Court; and Elbridge Gerry, a Massachusetts Republican but a personal friend of the president—to negotiate with France. When the Americans arrived in Paris in 1797, three agents of the French foreign minister, Prince Talleyrand, demanded a loan for France and a bribe for French officials before any negotiations could begin. Pinckney responded succinctly and angrily: "No! No! Not a sixpence!"

When Adams heard of the incident, he sent a message to Congress denouncing the French insults and urging preparations for war. He then turned the commissioners' report over to Congress, after deleting the names of the three French agents and designating them only as Messrs. X, Y, and Z. When the report was published, it created widespread popular outrage at France's actions and strong support for the Federalists' response. For nearly two years after the "XYZ Affair," as it became known, the United States found itself engaged in an undeclared war with France.

Adams persuaded Congress to cut off all trade with France, to abrogate the treaties of 1778, and to authorize American vessels to capture French armed ships on the high seas. In 1798, Congress created a Department of the Navy and appropriated money for the construction of new warships. The navy soon won a number of duels with French vessels and captured a total of eighty-five ships, including armed merchantmen. The United States also began cooperating closely with the British and became virtually a cobelligerent in the British war with France.

In the end, France chose to conciliate the United States. Adams sent another commission to Paris in 1800, and the new French government (headed now by "first consul" Napoleon Bonaparte) agreed to a treaty with the United States that canceled the old agreement of 1778 and established new commercial arrangements. As a result, the "quasi war" came to a reasonably peaceful end, and the United States at last freed itself from the entanglements and embarrassments of its "perpetual" alliance with France.

Repression and Protest

The conflict with France helped the Federalists increase their majorities in Congress in 1798. Armed with this new strength, they began to consider ways to silence the Republican opposition. The result was some of the most controversial legislation in American history: the Alien and Sedition Acts.

The Alien Act placed new obstacles in the way of foreigners who wished to become American citizens, and it strengthened the president's hand in dealing with aliens. The Sedition Act allowed the government to prosecute those who engaged in "sedition" against the government. In theory only libelous or treasonous activities were subject to prosecution; but since such ac-

PROTECTING AMERICAN SHIPPING
An American ship under the command of Gamliel Bradford engages four French privateers in the strait of Gibraltar in July 1800—part of an effort by the United States to protect its maritime commerce. Bradford beat off the privateers after a short battle, but lost his leg in the fighting. *(Naval Historical Center)*

tivities were subject to widely varying definitions, the law had the capacity to stifle virtually any opposition. The Republicans interpreted the new laws as part of a Federalist campaign to destroy them and fought back.

President Adams signed the new laws but was cautious in implementing them. He did not deport any aliens, and he prevented the government from launching a major crusade against the Republicans. But the legislation had a significant repressive effect nevertheless. The Alien Act helped discourage immigration and encouraged some foreigners already in the country to leave. And the administration made use of the Sedition Act to arrest and convict ten men, most of them Republican newspaper editors whose only crime had been to criticize the Federalists in government.

Republican leaders pinned their hopes for a reversal of the Alien and Sedition Acts on the state legislatures. (The Supreme Court had not yet established its sole right to nullify congressional legislation, and there were many who believed that the states had that power too.) The Republicans laid out a theory for state action in two sets of resolutions in 1798–1799, one written (anonymously) by Jefferson and adopted by the Kentucky legislature and the other drafted by Madison and approved by the Virginia legislature. The Virginia and Kentucky Resolutions, as they were known, used the ideas of John Locke to argue that the federal government had been formed by a "compact" or contract among the states and possessed only certain delegated powers. Whenever it exercised any undelegated powers, its acts were "unauthoritative, void, and of no force." If the parties to the contract, the states, decided that the central government had exceeded those powers, the Kentucky Resolution claimed, they had the right to "nullify" the appropriate laws.

The Republicans did not win wide support for nullification; only Virginia and Kentucky declared the congressional statutes void. They did, however, succeed in elevating their dispute with the Federalists to the level of a national crisis. By the late 1790s, the entire nation was as deeply and bitterly politicized as it would ever be in its history. State legislatures at times resembled battlegrounds. Even the United States Congress was plagued with violent disagreements. In one celebrated incident in the chamber of the House of Representatives, Matthew Lyon, a Republican from Vermont, responded to an insult from Roger Griswold, a Federalist from Connecticut, by spitting in Griswold's eye. Griswold attacked Lyon with his cane, Lyon fought back with a pair of fire tongs, and soon the two men were wrestling on the floor.

The "Revolution" of 1800

These bitter controversies shaped the 1800 presidential election. The presidential candidates were the same as four years earlier: Adams for the Federalists, Jefferson for the Republicans. But the campaign of that year was very different from the one preceding it. Indeed, it may have been the ugliest in American history. Adams and Jefferson themselves displayed reasonable dignity, but their supporters showed no such restraint. The Federalists accused Jefferson of being a dangerous radical and his followers of being wild men who, if they should come to power, would bring on a reign of terror comparable to that of the French Revolution. The Republicans portrayed Adams as a tyrant conspiring to become king, and they accused the Federalists of plotting to subvert human liberty and impose slavery on the people. There was considerable personal invective as well. For example, it was during this campaign that the story of Jefferson's alleged romantic involvement with a slave woman on his plantation was first widely aired.

The election was close, and the crucial contest was in New York. There, Aaron Burr mobilized an organization of Revolutionary War veterans, the Tammany Society, to serve as a Republican political machine. And through Tammany's efforts, the party carried the city by a large majority, and with it the state. Jefferson was, apparently, elected.

But an unexpected complication soon jeopardized the Republican victory. The Constitution called for each elector to "vote by ballot for two persons." The normal practice was for an elector to cast one vote for his party's presidential candidate and another for the vice presidential candidate. To avoid a tie, the Republicans had intended for one elector to refrain from voting for Burr. But the plan went awry. When the votes were counted, Jefferson and Burr each had 73. No candidate had a majority. According to the Constitution the House of Representatives had to choose between the two leading candidates when no one had a majority; in this case, that meant deciding between Jefferson and Burr. Each state delegation would cast a single vote.

The new Congress, elected in 1800 with a Republican majority, was not to convene until after the inauguration of the president, so it was the Federalist Congress that had to decide the question. Some Federalists hoped to use the situation to salvage the election for their party; others wanted to strike a bargain with Burr and elect him. But after a long deadlock, several leading Federalists, most prominent among them Alexander Hamilton, concluded that Burr (whom many suspected of having engineered the deadlock in the first place) was too unreliable to trust with the presidency. On the thirty-sixth ballot, Jefferson was elected.

After the election of 1800, the only branch of the federal government left in Federalist hands was the judiciary. The Adams administration spent its last months in office taking steps to make the party's hold on the courts secure. By the Judiciary Act of 1801, passed by the lame duck Congress, the Federalists reduced the number of Supreme Court justiceships by one but greatly increased the number of federal judgeships as a whole. Adams quickly appointed Federalists to the newly created positions. Indeed, there were charges that he stayed up until midnight on his last day in office to finish signing the new judges' commissions. These officeholders became known as the "midnight appointments."

Even so, the Republicans viewed their victory as almost complete. The nation, they believed, had been saved from tyranny. A new era could now begin, one in which the true principles on which America had been founded would once again govern the land. The exuberance with which the victors viewed the future—and the importance they ascribed to the Federalists' defeat—was evident in the phrase Jefferson himself later used to describe his election. He called it the "Revolution of 1800." It remained to be seen how revolutionary it would really be.

SIGNIFICANT EVENTS

1783   Continental Congress leaves Philadelphia

1785   Continental Congress settles in New York

1786   Annapolis Conference meets

1787   Constitutional Convention in Philadelphia meets

Constitution adopted (September 17)

1787–1788   States ratify Constitution

1789   First elections held under Constitution

New government assembles in New York

Washington becomes first president

Bill of Rights adopted by Congress

Judiciary Act of 1789 is passed

French Revolution begins

1791   Hamilton issues "Report on Manufactures"

First Bank of the United States chartered

Vermont becomes fourteenth state

1792   Washington reelected without opposition

Kentucky becomes fifteenth state

1793   Citizen Genet affair challenges American neutrality

1794   Whiskey Rebellion quelled in Pennsylvania

Jay's Treaty signed

1795   Pinckney's Treaty signed

1796   John Adams elected president

Tennessee becomes sixteenth state

1798   XYZ Affair precipitates state of quasi war with France

Alien and Sedition acts passed

Virginia and Kentucky resolutions passed

1800   Jefferson and Burr tie vote in electoral college

1801   Jefferson becomes president after Congress confirms election

Judiciary Act of 1801 passed

SUGGESTED READINGS

The Constitution.   Douglas Adair, *Fame and the Founding Fathers* (1974). Charles A. Beard, *An Economic Interpretation of the Constitution of the United States* (1913). Robert E. Brown, *Charles Beard and the Constitution* (1956). Christopher Collier and James Lincoln Collier, *Decision: Philadelphia: The Constitutional Convention of 1787* (1986). J. E. Cooke, ed., *The Federalist* (1961). Thomas Curry, *The First Freedom: Church and State in America to the Passage of the First Amendment* (1986). Linda G. DePauw, *The Eleventh Pillar: New York State and the Federal Constitution* (1966). Max Farrand, ed., *Records of the Federal Convention of 1787*, 4 vols. (1911–1937). Max Farrand, *The Framing of the Constitution of the United States* (1913). Michael Kammen, *A Machine that Would Go of Itself: The Constitution in American Culture* (1986). Leonard Levy, *Constitutional Opinions: Aspects of the Bill of Rights* (1986); and *Original Intent and the Framers' Constitution* (1988). Michael Lienesch, *New Order of the Ages: Time, the Constitution, and the Making of Modern American Political Thought* (1988). Donald S. Lutz, *Origins of American Constitutionalism* (1988). Jackson Turner Main, *The Anti-Federalists* (1961). Alpheus T. Mason, *The State Rights Debate* (1964). Forrest McDonald, *We the People: The Economic Origins of the Constitution* (1958); *E. Pluribus Unum: The Formation of the American Republic, 1776–1790* (1965); and *Novus Ordo Seclorum: The Intellectual Origins of the Constitution* (1985). William L. Miller, *The First Liberty: Religion and the American Republic* (1986). Edmund S. Morgan, *Inventing the People: The Rise of Popular Sovereignty in England and America* (1988). Richard B. Morris, *The Forging of the Union, 1781–1789* (1987). Clinton Rossiter, 1787: *The Grand Convention* (1965). Robert A. Rutland, *The Ordeal of the Constitution* (1966). Gerald Stourzh, *Alexander Hamilton and the Idea of Republican Government* (1970). Garry Wills, *Explaining America* (1981).

The Federalist Era.   Leland D. Baldwin, *The Whiskey Rebels* (1939). Richard Beeman, *The Old Dominion and the New Nation, 1788–1801* (1972). Irving Brant, *The Bill of Rights* (1965). Ralph Adams Brown, *The Presidency of John Adams* (1975). Jerald A. Combs, *The Jay Treaty* (1970). Manning Dauer, *The Adams Federalists* (1953). Stanley Elkins and Eric McKitrick, *The Age of Federalism* (1993). John F. Hoadley, *Origins of American Political Parties, 1789–1803* (1986). John R. Howe, *The Changing Political Thought of John Adams* (1966). Ralph Ketcham, *Presidents Above Party: The First American Presidency, 1789–1829* (1984). Richard Kohn, *Eagle and Sword: The Federalists and the Creation of the Military Establishment in America, 1783–1802* (1975). Stephen G. Kurtz, *The Presidency of John Adams* (1957). Daniel G. Lang, *Foreign Policy in the Early Republic* (1985). Leonard Levy, *Legacy of Suppression: Freedom of Speech and Press in Early American History*, rev. ed. (1985). Forrest McDonald, *The Presidency of George Washington* (1974). John C. Miller, *Crisis in Freedom* (1951); *The Federalist Era, 1789–1801* (1960). Carl E. Prince, *The Federalists and the Origins of the U.S. Civil Service* (1978). Thomas P. Slaughter, *The Whiskey Rebellion: Frontier Epilogue to the American Revolution* (1986). James M. Smith, *Freedom's Fetters: The Alien and Sedition Laws and American Civil Liberties* (1956). Wiley Sword, *President Washington's Indian War: The Struggle for the Old Northwest, 1790–1795* (1985). Mary K. B. Tachau, *Federal Courts in the Early Republic: Kentucky, 1789–1816* (1978). Leonard D. White, *The Federalists* (1948). Ann Fairfax Withington, *Toward A More Perfect Union: Virtue and the Formation of American Republics* (1991).

The Jeffersonian Republicans.   Joyce Appleby, *Capitalism and a New Social Order: The Republican Vision of the 1790s* (1984). Lance Banning, *The Jeffersonian Persuasion* (1978). Charles A. Beard, *The Economic Origins of the Jeffersonian Opposition* (1915). Richard W. Buel, Jr., *Securing the Revolution: Ideology in American Politics, 1789–1815* (1972). William N. Chambers, *Political Parties in a New Nation* (1963). Joseph Charles, *The Origins of the American Party System* (1956). Noble Cunningham, *The Jeffersonian Republicans* (1957). Richard Hofstadter, *The Idea of a Party System* (1970). Drew McCoy, *The Elusive Republic: Political Economy in Jeffersonian America* (1980); and *The Last of the Fathers: James Madison and the Republican Legacy* (1989). Thomas L. Pangle, *The Spirit of Modern Republicanism: The Moral Vision of the American Founders and the Followers of Locke* (1988). Merrill D. Peterson, *Thomas Jefferson and the New Nation* (1970). Norman K. Risjord, *Chesapeake Politics, 1781–1800* (1978). Patricia Watlington, *The Partisan Spirit* (1972). Alfred F. Young, *The Democratic-Republicans of New York* (1967). John Zvesper, *Political Philosophy and Rhetoric: A Study of the Origins of American Party Politics* (1977).

Federalist Diplomacy.   Harry Ammon, *The Genet Mission* (1973). Samuel F. Bemis, *Jay's Treaty* (1923); and *Pinckney's Treaty* (1926, rev. 1960). Alexander DeConde, *Entangling Alliance* (1958); and *The Quasi-War* (1966). Felix Gilbert, *To the Farewell Address* (1961). Lawrence S. Kaplan, *Jefferson and France* (1967). Bradford Perkins, *The First Rapprochement: England and the United States* (1967). Charles Ritcheson, *Aftermath of Revolution: British Policy Toward the United States, 1783–1795* (1969). Louis M. Sears, *George Washington and the French Revolution* (1960). Paul A. Varg, *Foreign Policies of the Founding Fathers* (1963).

The Founders.   Irving Brant, *James Madison* (1950). James T. Flexner, *George Washington*, 4 vols. (1965–1972). Douglas Southall Freeman, *George Washington*, 7 vols. (1948–1957). Milton Lomask, *Aaron Burr*, 2 vols. (1979, 1982). Dumas Malone, *Jefferson and His Time*, 6 vols. (1948–1981). John C. Miller, *Alexander Hamilton* (1959). Richard B. Morris, *Witnesses at the Creation: Hamilton, Madison, Jay, and the Constitution* (1985). Merrill Peterson, *Thomas Jefferson and the New Nation* (1970). Barry Schwartz, *George Washington: The Making of a Symbol* (1987). Page Smith, *John Adams* (1962). William Stinchecombe, *The XYZ Affair* (1980). Garry Wills, *Cincinnatus: George Washington and the Enlightenment* (1984). Esmond Wright, *Franklin of Philadelphia* (1986).

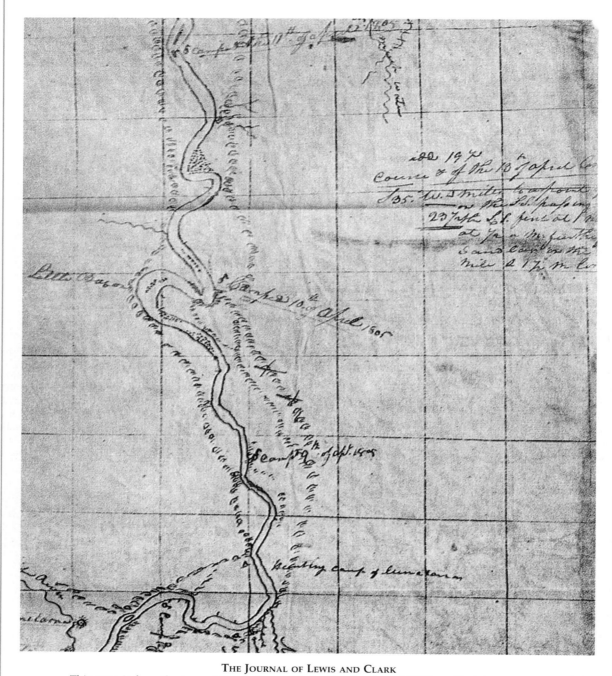

THE JOURNAL OF LEWIS AND CLARK
This page is from the journal the explorers Meriwether Lewis and William Clark kept on their
famous journey through the lands the United States had acquired in the Louisiana Purchase.
Shown here is one of the rough maps they drew to describe the lands they had seen.
(British Museum)

CHAPTER SEVEN

THE JEFFERSONIAN ERA

THOMAS JEFFERSON AND HIS followers assumed control of the national government in 1801 as the champions of a distinctive vision of America. They envisioned a society of sturdy, independent farmers, happily free from the workshops, the industrial towns, and the city mobs of Europe. They favored a system of universal education that would introduce all Americans to the scientific rationalism of the Enlightenment. They promoted a cultural outlook that emphasized localism and republican simplicity. Above all, they proposed a federal government of sharply limited power, with most authority remaining at the level of the states.

Almost nothing worked out as they planned, for during their years in power the young republic was developing in ways that made much of their vision obsolete. The American economy in the period of Republican ascendancy became steadily more diversified and complex. Growing cities, surging commerce, and expanding industrialism made the ideal of a simple, agrarian society impossible to maintain. The quest for universal education floundered, and the nation's institutions of learning remained largely the preserve of privileged elites. American cultural life, far from reflecting localism and simplicity, reflected a vigorous and ambitious nationalism reminiscent of (and often encouraged by) the Federalists. And although American religion began, as the Jeffersonians had hoped, to confront and adjust to the spread of Enlightenment rationalism, the new skepticism did not survive unchallenged. A great wave of revivalism, beginning early in the century, ultimately almost submerged the new rational philosophy.

The Republicans did manage to translate some of their political ideals into reality. Jefferson dismantled much of the bureaucratic power structure that the Federalists had erected in the 1790s, and helped ensure that in many respects the federal government would remain a relatively unimportant force in American life. Yet he also frequently encountered situations that required him to exercise strong national authority. On occasion, he used his power more forcefully and arbitrarily than his Federalist predecessors had used theirs.

The Republicans did not always like these nationalizing and modernizing trends, and on occasion they resisted them. For the most part, however, they had the sense to recognize what they could not change. In adjusting to the new realities, they began to become agents of the very transformation of American life they had once resisted.

THE RISE OF CULTURAL NATIONALISM

In many respects, American cultural life in the early nineteenth century seemed to reflect the Republican vision of the nation's future. Opportunities for education increased, the nation's literary and artistic life began to free itself from European influences, and American religion began to confront and adjust to the spread of Enlightenment rationalism. In other respects, however, the new culture was posing a serious challenge to Republican ideals.

Education and Professionalism

Central to the Republican vision of America was the concept of a virtuous and enlightened citizenry. Jefferson himself called emphatically for a national "crusade against ignorance." Republicans believed, therefore, in the creation of a nationwide system of public schools to create the educated electorate they believed a republic required. All male citizens (the nation's prospective voters) should, they argued, receive free education.

They were unable to fulfill their hopes. Although some states endorsed the principle of public education for all, none actually created a working system of free schools. A Massachusetts law of 1789 reaffirmed the colonial laws by which each town was obligated to support a school, but there was little enforcement. In Virginia, the state legislature ignored Jefferson's call for universal elementary education and for advanced education for the gifted. As late as 1815, not a single state had a comprehensive public school system.

Instead, schooling became primarily the responsibility of private institutions, most of which were open only to those who could afford to pay for them. In the South and in the mid-Atlantic states, religious groups ran most of the schools. In New England and elsewhere, private academies were usually more secular, many of them modeled on schools founded by the

THE ONE-ROOM SCHOOL
Children of many different ages came together in the one-room school. While one group recited, the others studied their lessons. A single teacher—often a recent college graduate supporting himself while preparing for a career in law or politics—had to instruct and discipline the children, tend the fire, and perform various custodial chores. *(Library of Congress)*

Phillips family at Andover, Massachusetts, in 1778, and at Exeter, New Hampshire, three years later. By 1815, there were thirty such private secondary schools in Massachusetts, thirty-seven in New York, and several dozen more scattered throughout the country. Many were frankly aristocratic in outlook, training their students to become members of the nation's elite. There were a few schools open to the poor, but not nearly enough to accommodate everyone, and the education they offered was usually clearly inferior to that provided at more exclusive schools.

Private secondary schools such as those in New England, and even many public schools, accepted only male students. The Republicans, like most of their contemporaries, clung to a patriarchal vision of society, in which virtuous white males presided benevolently over a world in which all other groups were dependents. Yet the early nineteenth century did see some important advances in female education. In the eighteenth century, women had received very little education of any kind, and the female illiteracy rate at the time of the Revolution was very high—at least 50 percent. At the same time, Americans had begun to place a new value on the contribution of the "republican mother" in training the new generation. That raised an important question: If mothers remained ignorant, how could they raise their children to be enlightened? Beginning as early as the 1770s and accelerating thereafter, such concerns led to the creation of a network of female academies throughout the nation (usually for the daughters of affluent families). In 1789, Massachusetts required that its public schools serve females as well as males. Other states, although not all, soon followed.

But there were strict limits to this new belief in education for women. Most men, at least, assumed that female education should serve only to make women better wives and mothers. Women therefore had no need for advanced or professional training; there was no reason for colleges and universities to make space for female students. Some women aspired to more. In 1784, Judith Sargent Murray published an essay defending the rights of women to education, a defense set in terms very different from those used by most men. Men and women were equal in intellect and potential, Murray argued. Women, therefore, should have precisely the same educational opportunities as men. What was more, they should have opportunities to earn their own living, to establish a role for themselves in society apart from their husbands and families. Murray's ideas became an inspiration to later generations of women, but during most of her own lifetime (1751–1820) they attracted relatively little support.

Reformers who believed in the power of education to reform and redeem ignorant and "backward" people spurred a growing interest in Indian education. Because Jefferson and his followers liked to think of Native Americans as "noble savages" (uncivilized, but unlike their view of African Americans, not necessarily innately inferior), they hoped that schooling the Indians in white culture would tame and "uplift" the tribes. Although white governments did little to promote Indian education, missionaries and mission schools proliferated among the tribes.

Higher education similarly diverged from Republican ideals. The number of colleges and universities in America grew from nine at the start of the Revolution to twenty-two by 1800 and continued to increase thereafter. None of the new schools, however, was truly public. Even those established by state legislatures (in Georgia, North Carolina, Vermont, Ohio, and South Carolina, for example) relied on private contributions and on tuition fees. Scarcely more than one white man in a thousand (and no women, blacks, or Indians at all) had access to any college education, and those few who did attend universities were almost without exception members of prosperous, propertied families.

The education that the colleges provided was, moreover, exceedingly limited—narrow training in the classics and a few other areas and intensive work in theology. Indeed, the clergy was the only profession for which college training was generally a prerequisite. A few institutions attempted to provide their students advanced training in other fields. The College of William and Mary in Virginia, the University of Pennsylvania, and Columbia College in New York all created law schools before 1800, but most lawyers continued to train for their profession simply by apprenticing themselves to practicing attorneys.

The University of Pennsylvania created the first American medical school early in the nineteenth century, under the leadership of Benjamin Rush. Most doctors, however, studied medicine by working with an established practitioner. Some American physicians believed in applying new scientific methods to medicine and struggled against age-old prejudices and superstitions. Efforts to teach anatomy, for example, encountered strong public hostility because of the dissection of cadavers that the study required. Municipal authorities had virtually no understanding of medical science and almost no idea of what to do in the face of the severe epidemics that so often swept their populations; only slowly did they respond to the warnings of Rush and others that lack of adequate sanitation programs was to blame for disease.

Individual patients often had more to fear from their doctors than from their illnesses. Even the leading advocates of scientific medicine often embraced useless and dangerous treatments. Benjamin Rush, for example, was an advocate of the new and supposedly scientific techniques of bleeding and purging, and many of his patients died. George Washington's death in 1799 was probably less a result of the minor throat infection that had afflicted him than of his physicians' efforts to cure him by bleeding and purging.

The medical profession also used its newfound commitment to the "scientific" method to justify expanding its own control to kinds of care that had traditionally been outside its domain. Most childbirths, for example, had been attended by female midwives. In the early nineteenth century, physicians began to handle deliveries themselves and to work for restrictions on the role of midwives. Among the results of that change was a narrowing of opportunities for women (midwifery was an important female occupation) and a restriction of access to childbirth care for poor mothers (who could have afforded midwives, but who could not pay the higher physicians' fees).

Education and professional training in the early republic thus fell far short of the Jeffersonian vision. Indeed, efforts to promote education and increase professionalism often had the effect of strengthening existing elites rather than eroding them. Nevertheless, the ideal of equal educational opportunity survived, and in later decades it would become a vital force behind universal public education.

"The Rising Glory of America"

Many Americans in the Jeffersonian era may have repudiated the Federalist belief in political and economic centralization, but most embraced another form of nationalism with great fervor. Having won political independence from Europe, they aspired now to a form of cultural independence. And in the process, they dreamed of an American literary and artistic life that would rival the greatest achievements of Europe. As a popular "Poem on the Rising Glory of America" had predicted as early as 1772, Americans believed that their "happy land" was destined to become the "seat of empire" and the "final stage" of civilization, with "glorious works of high invention and of wond'rous art." The United States, another eighteenth-century writer had proclaimed, would serve as "the last and greatest theatre for the improvement of mankind."

Such nationalism found expression, among other places, in early American schoolbooks. The Massachusetts geographer Jedidiah Morse, author of *Geography Made Easy* (1784), said the country must have its own textbooks to prevent the aristocratic ideas of England from infecting the people. The Connecticut

schoolmaster and lawyer Noah Webster argued similarly that the American students should be educated as patriots, their minds filled with nationalistic, American thoughts. "As soon as he opens his lips," Webster wrote, "he should rehearse the history of his own country; he should lisp the praise of liberty, and of those illustrious heroes and statesmen who have wrought a revolution in her favor."

Further to encourage a distinctive American culture and help unify the new nation, Webster insisted on a simplified and Americanized system of spelling—"honor" instead of "honour," for example. His *American Spelling Book*, first published in 1783 and commonly known as the "blue-backed speller," eventually sold over 100 million copies, to become the best-selling book (except for the Bible) in the entire history of American publishing. Webster also wrote grammars and other schoolbooks. His school dictionary, issued in 1806, was republished in many editions and was eventually enlarged to become (in 1828) *An American Dictionary of the English Language*. His speller and his dictionary established a national standard of words and usages. Although Webster's Federalist political views fell into disfavor in the early nineteenth century, his cultural nationalism remained popular and influential.

Those Americans who aspired to create a more elevated national literary life faced a number of obstacles. There was, to be sure, a large potential audience for a national literature—a substantial reading public, developed in part by the wide circulation of newspapers and political pamphlets during the Revolution. But there were few opportunities for would-be American authors to get their work before the public. Printers preferred to publish popular works by English writers (for which they had to pay no royalties); magazine publishers filled their pages largely with items clipped from British periodicals. Only those American writers willing to pay the cost and bear the risk of publishing their own works could compete for public attention.

Even so, a growing number of American authors strove to create a strong native literature so that, as the poet Joel Barlow wrote, "true ideas of glory may be implanted in the minds of men here, to take the place of the false and destructive ones that have degraded the species in other countries." Barlow himself, one of a group of Connecticut writers known as the "Hartford Wits," published an epic poem, *The Columbiad,* in 1807, in an effort to convey the special character of American civilization. The acclaim it received helped to encourage other native writers.

Among the most ambitious was the Philadelphian Charles Brockden Brown. Like many Americans, he was attracted to the new literary form of the novel, which had become popular in England in the late eighteenth century and had been successfully imported to America. But Brown sought to do more than simply imitate the English forms; he tried to use his novels to give voice to distinctively American themes, to convey the "soaring passions and intellectual energy" of the new nation. His obsession with originality led him to produce a body of work characterized by a fascination with horror and deviant behavior. Perhaps as a result, his novels failed to develop a large popular following.

Much more successful was Washington Irving, a resident of New York State who won wide acclaim for his satirical histories of early American life and his powerful fables of society in the New World. His popular folk tales, recounting the adventures of such American rustics as Ichabod Crane and Rip Van Winkle, made him the widely acknowledged leader of American literary life in the early nineteenth century and one of the few writers of that era whose works would continue to be read by later generations.

Perhaps the most influential works by American authors in the early republic were not poems, novels, or stories, but works of history that glorified the nation's past. Mercy Otis Warren, the influential playwright and agitator during the 1770s, continued her literary efforts with a three-volume *History of the Revolution,* published in 1805 and emphasizing the heroism of the American struggle. Mason Weems, an Anglican clergyman, published a eulogistic *Life of Washington* in 1806, which became one of the best-selling books of the era. Weems had little interest in historical accuracy. He portrayed the aristocratic former president as a homespun man possessing simple republican virtues. (He also invented the story of the young Washington cutting down a cherry tree.) History, like literature, was serving as a vehicle for instilling a sense of nationalism in the American people.

The Second Great Awakening

The American Revolution weakened traditional forms of religious practice by detaching churches from government and by elevating ideas of individual liberty and reason that challenged many ecclesiastical traditions. By the 1790s, only a small proportion of white Americans (perhaps as few as 10 percent) were members of formal churches, and ministers were complaining often about the "decay of vital piety." Religious traditionalists were particularly alarmed about the emergence of new, "rational" theologies that reflected modern, scientific attitudes and de-emphasized the role of God in the world. Some Americans,

including Jefferson and Franklin, embraced "deism," which had originated among Enlightenment philosophers in France. Deists accepted the existence of God, but considered Him a remote being who, after having created the universe, had withdrawn from direct involvement with the human race and its sins. Books and articles attacking religious "superstitions" attracted wide readerships and provoked much discussion, among them Thomas Paine's *The Age of Reason,* published between 1794 and 1796. Paine once declared that Christianity was the "strangest religion ever set up," for "it committed a murder upon Jesus in order to redeem mankind from the sin of eating an apple."

Religious skepticism also produced the philosophies of "universalism" and "unitarianism," which emerged at first as dissenting views within the New England Congregational Church. Disciples of these new ideas rejected the Calvinist belief in predestination, arguing that salvation was available to all. They rejected, too, the idea of the Trinity. Jesus was only a great religious teacher, they claimed, not the Son of God. So wide was the gulf between these dissenters and the Congregationalist establishment that it finally became a permanent schism. James Murray (who later married Judith Sargent Murray) founded the Universalist church as a separate denomination in Gloucester, Massachusetts, in 1779; the Unitarian church was established in Boston three years later.

Some Americans believed that the spread of rationalism marked the end of traditional, evangelistic religion in the new nation. But quite the contrary was true. In fact, most Americans continued to hold strong religious beliefs (even if the widespread popular fervor of the Great Awakening of the 1730s had largely faded). What had declined was their commitment to organized churches and denominations. Deism, Universalism, Unitarianism, and other "rational" religions seemed more powerful than they actually were because for a time traditional evangelicals were confused and disorganized. But beginning in 1801, traditional religion staged a dramatic comeback in the form of a wave of revivalism known as the Second Great Awakening.

The origins of the Second Awakening lay in the efforts of conservative theologians of the 1790s to fight the spread of religious rationalism, and in the efforts of church establishments to revitalize their organizations. Presbyterians expanded their efforts on the western fringe of white settlement, and conservatives in the church became increasingly militant in response to so-called New Light dissenters. Methodism, which John Wesley had founded in England, spread to America in the 1770s and became a formal denomination in 1784

METHODIST CAMP MEETING, 1837
Camp (or revival) meetings were popular among some evangelical Christians in America as early as 1800. By the 1820s, there were approximately 1,000 meetings a year, most of them in the South and the West. After one such meeting in 1806, a participant wrote: "Will I ever see anything more like the day of Judgement on this side of eternity—to see the people running, yes, running from every direction to the stand , weeping, shouting, and shouting for joy. . . . O! glorious day they went home singing shouting." This lithograph, dated 1837, suggests the degree to which women predominated at many revivals. *(The Granger Collection)*

under the leadership of Francis Asbury. Authoritarian and hierarchical in structure, the Methodist Church sent itinerant preachers throughout the nation to win recruits; it soon became the fastest-growing denomination in America. Almost as successful were the Baptists, who were themselves relatively new to America; they found an especially fervent following in the South.

By 1800, the revivalist energies of all these denominations were combining to create the greatest surge of evangelical fervor since the first Great Awakening sixty years before. Beginning among Presbyterians in several eastern colleges (most notably at Yale, under the leadership of President Timothy Dwight), the new awakening soon spread rapidly throughout the country, reaching its greatest heights in the western regions. In only a few years, a large proportion of the Ameri-

can people were mobilized by the movement, and membership in those churches embracing the revival—most prominently the Methodists, the Baptists, and the Presbyterians—was mushrooming. At Cane Ridge, Kentucky, in the summer of 1801, a group of evangelical ministers presided over the nation's first "camp meeting"—an extraordinary revival that lasted several days and impressed all who saw it with its size (some estimated that 25,000 people attended) and its fervor. Such events became common in subsequent years, as the Methodists in particular came to rely on them as a way to "harvest" new members. The Methodist circuit-riding preacher Peter Cartwright won national fame as he traveled from region to region exhorting his listeners to embrace the church. Even Cartwright, however, was often unprepared for the results of his efforts—a religious frenzy that manifested itself at times in convulsions, fits, rolling in the dirt, and the twitching "holy jerks."

The message of the Second Great Awakening was not entirely uniform, but its basic thrust was clear. Individuals must readmit God and Christ into their daily lives, must embrace a fervent, active piety, and must reject the skeptical rationalism that threatened traditional beliefs. Yet the wave of revivalism did not serve to restore the religion of the past. Few of the revivalist denominations any longer accepted the idea of predestination; and the belief that a person could affect his or her own destiny, rather than encouraging irreligion as many had feared, added intensity to the individual's search for salvation. The awakening, in short, combined a more active piety with a belief in God as an active force in the world whose grace could be attained through faith and good works.

Nor did the Second Awakening work to reestablish old institutional forms of religion. Instead, it reinforced the spread of different sects and denominations and helped to create a general public acceptance of the idea that men and women could belong to different Protestant churches and still be committed to essentially the same Christian faith. Finally, the new evangelicalism—by spreading religious fervor into virtually every area of the nation, including remote regions where no formal church had ever existed—provided a vehicle for establishing a sense of order and social stability in communities still searching for an identity.

One of the most striking features of the Second Great Awakening was the preponderance of women within it. Young women, in particular, were drawn to the revivalism, and female converts far outnumbered males. In some areas, church membership became overwhelmingly female as a result. One reason for this was that women were more numerous in certain regions than men. Adventurous young men often struck out on their own and moved west; women, for the most part, had no such options. Their marriage prospects thus diminished and their future plagued with uncertainty, some women discovered in religion a foundation on which to build their lives. But even where there was no shortage of men, women flocked to the revivals in enormous numbers, which suggests that they were responding to their changing economic roles as well. The movement of industrial work out of the home (where women had often contributed to the family economy through spinning and weaving) and into the factory—a process making rapid strides in the early nineteenth century (see pp. 281–282)—robbed older women, in particular, of one of their most important social roles. Younger, unmarried women with more mobility could follow the work out of the home

and into the factory with less difficulty, but that movement, too, created personal and social strains. Religious enthusiasm helped compensate for the losses and adjustments these transitions produced; it also provided access to a new range of activities associated with the churches—charitable societies ministering to orphans and the poor, missionary organizations, and others—in which women came to play important roles.

Although revivalism was most widespread within white society, it penetrated other cultures as well. In some areas of the country, revivals were open to people of all races, and many blacks not only attended but eagerly embraced the new religious fervor. Out of these revivals, in fact, emerged a substantial group of black preachers, who became important figures within the slave community. Some of them translated the apparently egalitarian religious message of the Second Awakening—that salvation was available to all—into a similarly egalitarian message for blacks in the present world. For example, out of black revival meetings in Virginia arose an elaborate plan in 1800 (devised by Gabriel Prosser, the brother of a black preacher) for a slave rebellion and attack on Richmond. The plan was discovered and the rebellion forestalled by whites, but revivalism continued to stir racial unrest in the South.

The spirit of revivalism was particularly strong in these years among Native Americans, although very different in its origins and expression from revivalism in white or black society. It drew heavily from earlier tribal experiences. In the 1760s, the Delaware prophet Neolin had sparked a widespread revival in the Old Northwest with a message combining Christian and Indian imagery and bringing to Native American religion a vision of a personal God, intimately involved in the affairs of man. Neolin had also called for Indians to rise up in defense of their lands and had denounced the growth of trade and other relationships with white civilization. His exhortations had helped stimulate the Indian military efforts of 1763 and beyond.

The dislocations and military defeats Indians suffered in the aftermath of the American Revolution created a sense of crisis among many of the eastern tribes in particular; as a result, the 1790s and early 1800s became another era of Indian religious fervor and prophecy. Presbyterian and Baptist missionaries were active among the southern tribes and sparked a great wave of conversions. But the most important revivalism came from the efforts of another great prophet: Handsome Lake, a Seneca whose seemingly miraculous "rebirth" after years of alcoholism helped give him a special stature within his tribe. Handsome Lake, like Neolin before him, called for a revival of traditional Indian ways. That meant repudiating the individualism of white society, which Handsome Lake argued had penetrated tribal life with alarming results, and restoring the communal quality of the Indian world. (He claimed to have met Jesus, who instructed him to "tell your people they will become lost when they follow the ways of the white man.") Handsome Lake's message spread through the scattered Iroquois communities that had survived the military and political setbacks of previous decades and inspired many Indians to give up whiskey, gambling, and other destructive customs derived from white society.

But the revival did not, in fact, lead to a true restoration of traditional Iroquois culture. Instead, Handsome Lake encouraged Christian missionaries to become active within the tribes, and he urged Iroquois men to abandon their roles as hunters (partly because so much of their hunting land had been seized by whites) and become sedentary farmers instead. Iroquois women, who had traditionally done the farming, were to move into more domestic roles. When some women resisted the change, Handsome Lake denounced them as witches.

The Second Great Awakening also had important effects on those Americans who did not accept its teachings. The rational "freethinkers," whose skeptical philosophies had done so much to produce the revivals, were in many ways their victims. They did not disappear after 1800, but their influence rapidly declined, and for many years they remained a small and defensive minority within American Christianity. Instead, the dominant religious characteristic of the new nation would be a fervent evangelicalism, which would survive into the mid-nineteenth century and beyond.

STIRRINGS OF INDUSTRIALISM

Not only in its cultural and religious life was the nation developing in ways unforeseen by Jefferson and his followers. Economically, the United States was taking the first, tentative steps toward a transformation that would ultimately shatter forever the vision of a simple, agrarian republic.

The Industrial Revolution in England

While Americans were engaged in a revolution to win their independence, an even more important revolution was in progress in England: the emergence of

modern industrialism. Historians differ over precisely when the industrial revolution began, but it is clear that by the end of the eighteenth century it was well under way. Its essence was relatively simple: power-driven machines were taking the place of hand-operated tools and were permitting manufacturing to become more rapid and extensive. But however simple the causes, the social and economic consequences of the transformation were complex and profound.

The factory system in England took root first in the manufacture of cotton thread and cloth. There, one invention followed another in quick succession. Improvements in weaving drove improvements in spinning, and these changes created a demand for new devices for carding (combing and straightening the fibers for the spinner). Water, wind, and animal power continued to be important in the textile industry; but more important was the emergence of steam power—which began to proliferate after the appearance of James Watt's advanced steam engine (patented in 1769). Cumbersome and inefficient by modern standards, Watt's engine was nevertheless a major improvement over the earlier "atmospheric" engine of Thomas Newcomen. England's textile industry quickly became the most profitable in the world, and it helped encourage comparable advances in other fields of manufacturing as well.

At the same time, England's social system was undergoing a wrenching change. Hundreds of thousands of men and women were moving from rural areas into cities to work in factories, and there they experienced both the benefits and the costs of industrialization. The standard of living of the new working class, when objectively quantified, was significantly higher than that of the rural poor. Most of those who moved from farm to factory, in other words, experienced some improvement in their material circumstances. But the psychological costs of being suddenly uprooted from one way of life and thrust into another, fundamentally different one could outweigh the economic gains. There was little in most workers' prior experience to prepare them for the nature of industrial labor: disciplined, routinized work on a fixed schedule, in sharp contrast to the varying, seasonal work pattern of the rural economy. Nor were many factory workers prepared for life in the new industrial towns and expanding cities. They experienced, too, a fundamental change in their relationship with their employers. Unlike the landlords and local aristocrats of rural England, factory owners and managers—the new class of industrial capitalists, many of them accumulating unprecedented wealth—were usually remote and inaccessible figures. They dealt with their workers impersonally, and the result was a growing schism between the two classes—each lacking access to or understanding of the other.

As a result, English life was changing at every level. The middle class was expanding and coming to dominate the economy, although not yet the culture or the nation's politics. Working men and women were beginning to think of themselves as a distinct class, with common goals and interests. And their efforts simultaneously to adjust to their new way of life and to resist its most damaging aspects made the late eighteenth and early nineteenth centuries a time of continuing social turbulence.

Not since the agrarian revolution thousands of years earlier, when many humans had turned from hunting to farming for sustenance, had there been an economic change of a magnitude comparable to the industrial revolution. Centuries of traditions, of social patterns, of cultural and religious assumptions were challenged and, often, shattered.

Technology in America

Nothing even remotely comparable to the English industrial revolution occurred in America in the first two decades of the nineteenth century. Indeed, it was opposition to the kind of economic growth occurring in England that had helped the Republicans defeat the Federalists in 1800; and many Americans continued to

---

PAWTUCKET BRIDGE AND FALLS
One reason for the growth of the textile industry in New England in the early nineteenth century was that there were many sources of water power in the region to run the machinery in the factories. That was certainly the case with Slater's Mill, one of the first American textile factories, which was located in Pawtucket, Rhode Island alongside a powerful waterfall. This view was painted by an anonymous artist in the 1810s. *(Rhode Island Historical Society)*

view British industrialization with deep ambivalence. Yet even while they warned of the dangers of rapid economic change, Americans of the age of Jefferson were welcoming a series of technological advances that would ultimately help ensure that the United States too would be transformed.

Americans imported some of these technological advances from England. The British government attempted to protect the nation's manufacturing preeminence by preventing the export of textile machinery or the emigration of skilled mechanics. But despite such efforts, a number of immigrants arrived in the United States with advanced knowledge of English technology, eager to introduce the new machines to America. Samuel Slater, for example, used the knowledge he had acquired before leaving England to build a spinning mill for the Quaker merchant Moses Brown in Pawtucket, Rhode Island, in 1790. It was the first modern factory in America.

But America in the early nineteenth century also produced several important inventors of its own. Among them was Oliver Evans, of Delaware, who devised a number of ingenious new machines: an automated flour mill, a card-making machine, and others. He made several important improvements in the steam engine, and in 1795 he published America's first textbook of mechanical engineering: *The Young Mill-Wright's and Miller's Guide.* His own flour mill, which began operations in 1787, required only two men to operate: one of them emptying a bag of wheat into the machinery, another putting the lid on the barrels of flour and rolling them away.

Even more influential for the future of the nation were the inventions of the Massachusetts-born, Yale-educated Eli Whitney, who revolutionized both cotton production and weapons manufacturing. The growth of the textile industry in England had created an enormous demand for cotton, a demand that planters in the American South were finding impossible to meet. Their greatest obstacle was separating the seeds from cotton fiber—a difficult and time-consuming process that was essential before cotton could be sold. Long-staple, or Sea Island, cotton, with its smooth black seeds and long fibers, was easy to clean, but it grew successfully only along the coast or on the offshore islands of Georgia and South Carolina. There was not nearly enough of it to satisfy demand. Short-staple cotton, by contrast, could grow inland through much of the South, but its sticky green seeds were extremely difficult to remove, and a skilled worker could clean no more than a few pounds a day by hand. Then, in 1793, Whitney, who was working at the time as a tutor on the Georgia plantation of General Nathanael

Greene's widow, invented a machine that performed the arduous task quickly and efficiently. It was dubbed the cotton gin ("gin" was an abbreviation for "engine"), and it transformed the life of the South.

Mechanically, the gin was very simple. A toothed roller caught the fibers of the cotton boll and pulled them between the wires of a grating. The grating caught the seeds while a revolving brush removed the lint from the roller's teeth. With the device, a single operator could clean as much cotton in a few hours as a group of workers had once needed a whole day to do. The results were profound. Soon cotton growing spread into the upland South, and within a decade the total crop increased eightfold. African-American slavery, which with the decline of tobacco production for a time some had considered a dwindling institution, regained its importance, expanded, and became more firmly fixed upon the South.

The cotton gin not only changed the economy of the South, it also helped transform the North. The large supply of domestically produced fiber was a strong incentive to entrepreneurs in New England and elsewhere to develop a native textile industry. Few northern states could hope to thrive on the basis of agriculture alone; by learning to process cotton, they could become industrially prosperous instead. The manufacturing preeminence of the North, which emerged with the development of the textile industry in the 1820s and 1830s, helped drive a wedge between the nation's two most populous regions—one becoming increasingly industrial, the other more firmly wedded to agriculture—and ultimately contributed to the coming of the Civil War. It also helped ensure the eventual Union victory.

Whitney also made a major contribution to the development of modern warfare, and with it a contribution to other industrial techniques. During the two years of undeclared war with France (1798 and 1799), Americans were deeply troubled by their lack of sufficient armaments for the expected hostilities. Production of muskets—each carefully handcrafted by a skilled gunsmith—was distressingly slow. Whitney devised a machine to make each part of a gun according to an exact pattern. Tasks could thus be divided among several workers, and one laborer could assemble a weapon out of parts made by several others. Before long, manufacturers of sewing machines, clocks, and many other complicated products were using the same system.

The new technological advances were relatively isolated phenomena during the early years of the nineteenth century. Not until at least the 1840s did the nation begin to develop a true manufacturing economy.

But the inventions of this period were crucial in making the eventual transformation possible.

Trade and Transportation

One of the prerequisites for industrialization is an efficient system for transporting raw materials to factories and finished goods to markets. The United States had no such system in the early years of the republic, and thus it had no domestic market extensive enough to justify large-scale production. But efforts were under way that would ultimately remove the transportation obstacle.

There were several ways to solve the problem of the small American market. One was to look for customers overseas, and American merchants continued their efforts to do that. Among the first acts of the new Congress when it met in 1789 were two tariff bills giving preference to American ships in American ports, helping to stimulate an expansion of domestic shipping. More important—indeed the principal reason for the growth of American trade in this period—was the outbreak of war in Europe in the 1790s, allowing Yankee merchant vessels to take over most of the carrying trade between Europe and the Western Hemisphere. As early as 1793, the young republic had a merchant marine and a foreign trade larger than those of any country except England. In proportion to its population, the United States had more ships and international commerce than any country in the world. And the shipping business was growing fast. Between 1789 and 1810, the total tonnage of American vessels engaged in overseas traffic rose from less than 125,000 to nearly 1 million. American ships had carried only 30 percent of the country's exports in 1789; they were carrying over 90 percent in 1810. The figures for imports increased even more dramatically, from 17.5 percent to 90 percent in the same period.

Another solution to the problem of limited markets was to develop new markets at home, by improving transportation between the states and into the interior. Progress was slower here than in international shipping, but some improvements were occurring nevertheless. In river transportation, a new era began with the development of the steamboat. A number of inventors began experimenting with steam-powered craft in the late eighteenth century; John Fitch exhibited a forty-five-foot vessel with paddles operated by steam to some of the delegates at the Constitutional Convention in 1787. But the real breakthrough was Oliver Evans's development of a high-pressure engine, lighter and more efficient than James Watt's, which made steam more feasible for powering boats (and, eventually, the locomotive) as well as mill machinery.

The inventor Robert Fulton and the promoter Robert R. Livingston were principally responsible for

THE LANCASTER PIKE
The growth of the American economy depended on the creation of a transportation system linking the farflung nation together. Building turnpikes, such as this one between Lancaster, Pennsylvania, and Philadelphia, was among the first major projects of the young republic. (*U.S. Department of Transportation*)

AMERICA IN 1800

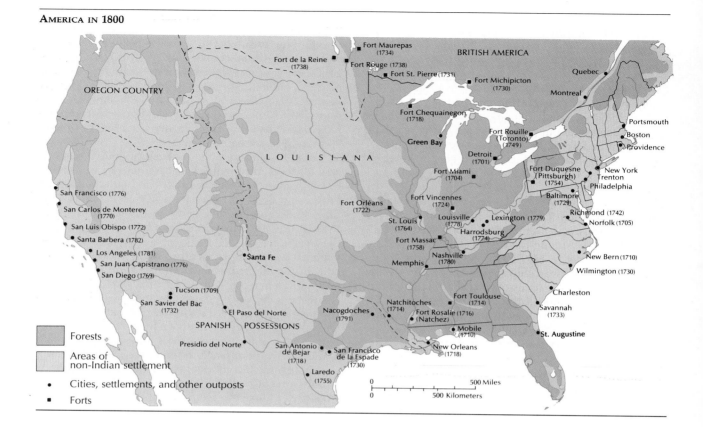

perfecting the steamboat and bringing it to the attention of the nation. Their *Clermont*, equipped with paddle wheels and an English-built engine, sailed up the Hudson in the summer of 1807, demonstrating the practicability of steam navigation (even though it took the ship thirty hours to go 150 miles). In 1811, a partner of Livingston's, Nicholas J. Roosevelt (a remote ancestor of Theodore Roosevelt), introduced the steamboat to the West by sending the *New Orleans* from Pittsburgh down the Ohio and Mississippi. The next year, this vessel began a profitable career of service between New Orleans and Natchez.

Meanwhile, what was to become known as the "turnpike era" had begun. In 1792, a corporation constructed a toll road running the sixty miles from Philadelphia to Lancaster, with a hard-packed surface of crushed rock. This venture proved so successful that several other companies laid out similar turnpikes (so named from the kind of tollgate frequently used) from other cities to neighboring towns. Since the turnpikes had to produce profits for the companies that built them, construction costs had to be low enough and the prospective traffic heavy enough to ensure an early

and ample return. As a result these roads, radiating from eastern cities, ran comparatively short distances and through thickly settled areas. Similar highways would not extend over the mountains until the state governments or the federal government began to finance the projects.

Country and City

Despite all the changes and all the advances, America in the early nineteenth century remained an overwhelmingly rural and agrarian nation. Only 3 percent of the non-Indian population lived in towns of more than 8,000 at the time of the second census in 1800. Ten percent lived west of the Appalachian Mountains, far from what urban centers there were. Much of the country remained a wilderness. Even the nation's largest cities could not begin to compare, either in size or in cultural sophistication, with such European capitals as London and Paris.

Yet here too there were signs of change. The leading American cities might not yet have become world capitals, but they were large and complex enough to rival the important secondary cities of Europe. Philadelphia, with 70,000 residents, and New York, with 60,000, were becoming major centers of commerce, learning, and a distinctively urban culture. So too were the next largest cities of the new nation: Baltimore (26,000 in 1800), Boston (24,000), and Charleston (20,000).

Much remained to be done before this small and still half-formed nation would become a complex modern society. It was still possible in the early nineteenth century to believe that those changes might not ever occur. But forces were already at work that, in time, would lastingly transform the United States. And Thomas Jefferson, for all his commitment to the agrarian ideal, found himself obliged as president to confront and accommodate them.

Jefferson the President

Privately, Thomas Jefferson may well have considered his victory over John Adams in 1800 to be what he later

termed it: a revolution "as real . . . as that of 1776." Publicly, however, he was restrained and conciliatory at the time, attempting to minimize the differences between the two parties and to calm the passions that the bitter campaign had aroused. "We are all republicans, we are all federalists," he said in his inaugural address. And during his eight years in office, he did much to prove those words correct. There was no complete repudiation of Federalist policies, no true "revolution." Indeed, at times Jefferson seemed to outdo the Federalists at their own work—most notably in overseeing a remarkable expansion of the territory of the United States.

In some respects, however, the Jefferson presidency did indeed represent a fundamental change in the direction of the federal government. The new administration oversaw a drastic reduction in the powers of some national institutions, and it forestalled the development of new powers in areas where the Federalists would certainly have attempted to expand them. Neither the executive nor the legislative branch of government was willing or able to exercise decisive authority in most ar-

WASHINGTON, D.C., IN THE EARLY NINETEENTH CENTURY

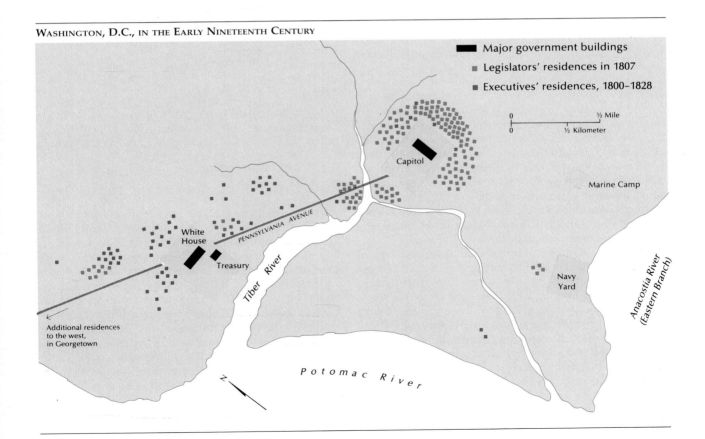

eas of national life by the end of the Jeffersonian era. Only the courts continued trying to assert federal power in the ways the Federalists had envisioned.

The Federal City

Symbolic of the relative unimportance of the federal government during the era of Jefferson was the character of the newly founded national capital, the city of Washington. John Adams had moved to the new seat of government during the last year of his administration. And there were many at that time who expected the raw, uncompleted town to emerge soon as a great and majestic city, a focus for the growing nationalism that the Federalists were promoting. The French architect Pierre L'Enfant had designed the capital on a grand scale, with broad avenues radiating out from the uncompleted Capitol building, set on one of the area's highest hills. Washington was, many Americans believed, to become the Paris of the United States.

In reality, however, throughout Jefferson's presidency—and indeed through most of the nineteenth century—Washington remained little more than a straggling, provincial village. Although the population increased steadily from the 3,200 counted in the 1800 census, it never rivaled that of New York, Philadelphia, or the other major cities of the nation. One problem was the climate: wet and cold in winter, hot and almost unbearably humid in summer, reflecting the marshy character of the site. Another problem, however, was that those in the federal government responsible for the development of the city did little to further its growth. The Republican administrations of the early nineteenth century oversaw the completion of several sections of the present-day Capitol building, of the White House, and of a few other government buildings. Otherwise, they allowed the city to remain a raw, inhospitable community. Its muddy streets were at times almost impassable. The Capitol and the White House were often cut off from each other by rising creeks and washed-away bridges.

Members of Congress viewed the city not as a home but as a place to visit briefly during sessions of the legislature and leave as quickly as possible. Few owned houses in Washington. Most lived in a cluster of simple boardinghouses in the vicinity of the Capitol. It was not unusual for a member of Congress to resign his seat in the midst of a session to return home if he had an opportunity to accept the more prestigious post of member of his state legislature. During the summers, the entire government in effect packed up and left town. The president, the cabinet, the Congress, and most other federal employees spent the hot summer months far from the uncomfortable capital.

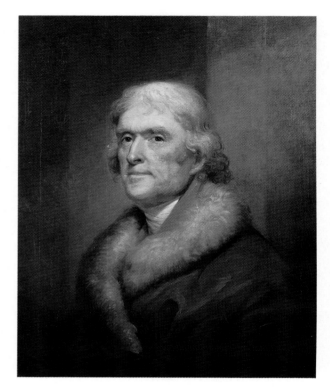

THOMAS JEFFERSON
This 1805 portrait by the noted American painter Rembrandt Peale shows Jefferson at the beginning of his second term as president. It also conveys (through the simplicity of dress and the slightly unkempt hair) the image of democratic simplicity that Jefferson liked to project as the champion of the "common man." (*New-York Historical Society*)

President and Party Leader

Jefferson set out as president to act in a spirit of democratic simplicity in keeping with the frontier-like character of the unfinished federal city. He was a wealthy and aristocratic planter by background, the owner of more than 100 slaves, and a man of rare cultivation and sophistication; but he conveyed to the public an image of plain, almost crude disdain for pretension. He walked like an ordinary citizen to and from his inauguration at the Capitol, instead of riding in a coach at the head of a procession. In the presidential mansion, which had not yet acquired the name "White House," he disregarded the courtly etiquette of his predecessors (in part, no doubt, because as a widower he had no first lady to take charge of social affairs). At state dinners, he let his guests scramble pell-mell for places at the table. He did not always bother to dress up, on one occasion prompting the fastidious British ambassador to complain of being received by the president in coat and pantaloons that were "indicative of utter slovenliness and indifference to appearances." Even when carefully dressed, the tall, freckle-faced, sandy-haired Jefferson was shy and awkward. He walked with a shambling gait. He was an ineffective public speaker.

Yet Jefferson managed nevertheless to impress most of those who knew him. He was a brilliant and charming conversationalist, a writer endowed with literary skills unmatched by any president before or since (with the possible exception of Lincoln), and undoubtedly one of the nation's most intelligent and creative men, with a wider range of interests and accomplishments than any public figure in American history. In addition to politics and diplomacy, he was an active architect, educator, inventor, scientific farmer, and philosopher-scientist. He diverted himself with such pastimes as sorting the bones of prehistoric animals and collecting volumes for one of the nation's greatest private libraries (which later became the basis of the original Library of Congress).

Jefferson was, above all, a shrewd and practical politician. On the one hand, he went to great lengths to eliminate the aura of majesty surrounding the presidency that he believed his predecessors had created. He decided, for example, to submit his messages to Congress not by delivering them in person, as Washington and Adams had done, but by sending them in writing, thus avoiding even the semblance of attempting to dictate to the legislature. (The precedent he established survived for more than a century, until the administration of Woodrow Wilson.) At the same time, however, Jefferson worked hard to exert influence as the leader of his party, giving direction to Republicans in Congress by quiet and sometimes even devious means.

To his cabinet he appointed members of his own party who shared his philosophy. His secretary of state was James Madison, his friend and neighbor; their collaboration was so close that it was often difficult to tell which of the two men was more responsible for government policy. His secretary of the treasury was Albert Gallatin, a Swiss-born politician with a French accent, whose financial expertise rivaled that of Hamilton but who was a staunch opponent of Hamilton's policies.

Although the Republicans had objected strenuously to the efforts of their Federalist predecessors to build a network of influence through patronage, Jefferson, too, used his powers of appointment as an effective political weapon. Like Washington before him, he believed that federal offices should be filled with men loyal to the principles and policies of the administra-

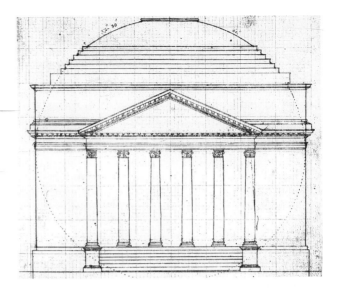

JEFFERSON THE ARCHITECT
Among his many other accomplishments, Thomas Jefferson was one of the most gifted architects in early America. This rotunda is the centerpiece of the central campus of the University of Virginia, which Jefferson designed near the end of his life. Earlier, he designed his own home near Charlottesville, Monticello; and his proposal for a president's mansion in Washington placed second in a blind competition. *(University of Virginia Library)*

tion. He did not attempt a sudden and drastic removal of Federalist officeholders, but at every convenient opportunity he replaced the holdovers from the Adams administration with his own trusted followers. By the end of his first term about half the government jobs, and by the end of his second term practically all of them, were in the hands of loyal Republicans.

When Jefferson ran for reelection in 1804, he won overwhelmingly. The Federalist presidential nominee, Charles C. Pinckney, could not even carry most of the party's New England strongholds. Jefferson won 162 electoral votes to Pinckney's 14, and the Republican majorities in both houses of Congress increased.

Dollars and Ships

Under the Federalists, the Republicans believed, the government had been needlessly extravagant. Yearly federal expenditures had nearly tripled between 1793 and 1800. Hamilton had, as he had intended, increased the public debt and created an extensive system of internal taxation, including the hated whiskey excise tax.

The Jefferson administration moved deliberately to reverse the trend. In 1802, it persuaded Congress to abolish all internal taxes, leaving customs duties and the sale of western lands as the only source of revenue for the government. Meanwhile, Secretary of the Treasury Gallatin drastically reduced government spending, cutting the already-small staffs of the executive departments to minuscule levels. Although Jefferson was unable to retire the entire national debt as he had hoped, he did cut it almost in half (from $83 million to $45 million).

Jefferson also scaled down the armed forces. He reduced the tiny army of 4,000 men to 2,500. He cut the navy from twenty-five ships to seven and reduced the number of officers and sailors accordingly. Anything but the smallest of standing armies, he argued, might menace civil liberties and civilian control of government. And a large navy, he feared, might promote overseas commerce, which Jefferson believed should remain secondary to agriculture. Yet despite his claims that "Peace is our passion," Jefferson was not a pacifist. At the same time that he was reducing the size of the army and navy, he was helping to establish the United States Military Academy at West Point, founded in 1802. And when trouble began brewing overseas, he began again to build up the fleet.

Such trouble appeared first in the Mediterranean, off the coast of northern Africa. For years the Barbary states of North Africa—Morocco, Algiers, Tunis, and Tripoli (now part of Libya)—had been demanding protection money from all nations whose ships sailed the Mediterranean. Even Great Britain gave regular contributions to the pirates. During the 1780s and 1790s the United States agreed to treaties providing for annual tribute to the Barbary states, but Jefferson was reluctant to continue this policy of appeasement. "Tribute or war is the usual alternative of these Barbary pirates," he said. "Why not build a navy and decide on war?"

In 1801, the pasha of Tripoli forced Jefferson's hand. Unsatisfied by the American response to his extortionate demands, he ordered the flagpole of the American consulate chopped down—a symbolic declaration of war. Jefferson responded cautiously, building up the American fleet in the region over the next several years. Finally, in 1805, the United States signed an agreement that ended American payments of tribute to Tripoli but required the United States to pay a substantial (and humiliating) ransom of $60,000 for the release of the American prisoners.

Conflict with the Courts

Having won control of the executive and legislative branches of government, the Republicans looked with suspicion on the judiciary, which remained largely in the hands of Federalist judges. Soon after Jefferson's first inauguration, his followers in Congress launched an attack on this last preserve of the opposition. Their first step was the repeal of the Judiciary Act of 1801, thus eliminating the judgeships to which Adams had made his "midnight appointments."

The debate over the courts led to one of the most important judicial decisions in the history of the nation. Federalists had long maintained that the Supreme Court had the authority to nullify acts of Congress (although the Constitution said nothing specifically to support the claim), and the Court itself had actually exercised the power of judicial review in 1796 when it upheld the validity of a law passed by the legislature. But the Court's authority in this area would not be secure, it was clear, until it actually declared a congressional act *un*constitutional.

In 1803, in the case of *Marbury* v. *Madison,* it did so. William Marbury, one of Adams's "midnight appointments," had been named a justice of the peace in the District of Columbia. But his commission, although signed and sealed, had not been delivered to him before Adams left office. Once Jefferson became president, his secretary of state, James Madison, was responsible for transmitting appointments. He had refused to hand over the commission. Marbury applied to the Supreme Court for an order directing Madison to perform his official duty. In its historic ruling, the Court found that Marbury had a right to his commission but that the Court had no authority to order Madison to deliver it. On the surface, therefore, the decision was a victory for the administration. But of much greater importance than the relatively insignificant matter of Marbury's commission was the Court's reasoning in the decision.

The original Judiciary Act of 1789 had given the Court the power to compel executive officials to act in such matters as the delivery of commissions, and it was on that basis that Marbury had filed his suit. But the Court ruled that Congress had exceeded its authority: that the Constitution had defined the powers of the judiciary, and that the legislature had no right to expand them. The relevant section of the 1789 act was therefore void. In seeming to deny its own authority, the Court was in fact radically enlarging it. The justices had repudiated a relatively minor power (the power to force the delivery of a commission) by asserting a vastly greater one (the power to nullify an act of Congress).

The chief justice of the United States at the time of the ruling (and until 1835) was John Marshall, one of the towering figures in the history of American law. A leading Federalist and prominent Virginia lawyer, he

WEST POINT
Creating a professional military was an important task for the leaders of the early republic. Without one, they realized, it would be difficult for the United States to win respect in the world. The establishment of the United States Military Academy at West Point (whose parade ground is pictured here) was, therefore, an important event in the early history of the republic. *(U.S. Military Academy, West Point)*

had served John Adams as secretary of state. (It had been Marshall, ironically, who had neglected to deliver Marbury's commission in the closing hours of the administration.) In 1801, just before leaving office, Adams had appointed him chief justice, and almost immediately Marshall established himself as the dominant figure on the Court, shaping virtually all its most important rulings—including, of course, *Marbury* v. *Madison*. Through a succession of Republican administrations, he battled to give the federal government unity and strength. And in so doing, he established the judiciary as a branch of government coequal with the executive and the legislature—a position that the founders of the republic had never clearly indicated it should occupy.

Jefferson recognized the threat that an assertive judiciary could pose to his policies, and even while the Marbury case was still pending he was preparing for a renewed assault on the last Federalist stronghold. He urged Congress to impeach obstructive judges, and Congress attempted to oblige him. After successfully removing from office a district judge, John Pickering of New Hampshire (on the perhaps specious grounds that he was insane and thus unfit for office), the Republicans targeted a justice of the Supreme Court itself: Justice Samuel Chase, a highly partisan Federalist. Chase had certainly been injudicious; he had, for example, delivered partisan speeches from the bench. But he had committed no crime. Some Republicans concluded, however, that impeachment was not merely a criminal proceeding and that Congress could properly impeach a judge for political reasons—for obstructing the other branches of the government and disregarding the will of the people.

At Jefferson's urging, the House impeached Chase and sent him to trial before the Senate early in 1805. But leaders of the proceeding were unable to get the necessary two-thirds' vote for conviction in the Senate. Chase's acquittal set an important precedent. It helped establish that impeachment would not become a purely political weapon, that something more than partisan disagreement would have to underlie the process. Marshall remained secure in his position as chief justice. And the judiciary survived as a powerful force within the government—more often than not on behalf of the centralizing, expansionary policies that the Republicans had been trying to reverse.

DOUBLING THE NATIONAL DOMAIN

In the same year that Jefferson became president of the United States, Napoleon Bonaparte made himself ruler of France with the title of first consul. In the year that Jefferson was reelected, Napoleon named himself emperor. The two men had little in common. Yet for a time they were of great help to each other in international politics—until Napoleon's ambitions moved from Europe to America and created conflict and estrangement.

Jefferson and Napoleon

Having failed in a grandiose plan to seize India from the British Empire, Napoleon began turning his imperial ambitions in a new direction: he began to dream of restoring French power in the New World. The territory east of the Mississippi, which France had ceded to Great Britain in 1763, was now mostly part of the United States and lost to France forever. But Napoleon decided to regain the lands west of the Mississippi, which now belonged to Spain. Under the secret Treaty of San Ildefonso of 1800, France regained title to Louisiana, which included almost the whole of the Mississippi Valley to the west of the river, plus New Orleans near its mouth. The Louisiana territory would, Napoleon hoped, become the heart of a great French Empire in America.

Also part of his prospective empire were the sugar-rich and strategically valuable West Indian islands that still belonged to France—Guadeloupe, Martinique, and above all Santo Domingo. But unrest among the Caribbean slaves posed a threat to Napoleon's hopes for the islands. Blacks in Santo Domingo (inspired by the French Revolution as some American slaves had been inspired by the American Revolution) revolted and created a republic of their own, under the remarkable black leader Toussaint L'Ouverture. Taking

advantage of a truce in his war with England, Napoleon sent an army to the West Indies. It crushed the insurrection and restored French authority; but the incident was an early sign of the problems Napoleon would have in realizing his ambitions in the New World.

Jefferson was unaware at first of Napoleon's imperial ambitions in America, and for a time he pursued a foreign policy that reflected his well-known admiration for France. He appointed as American minister to Paris the ardently pro-French Robert R. Livingston. He worked to secure ratification of the Franco-American settlement of 1800 and began observing the terms of the treaty even before it was ratified. The Adams administration had joined with the British in recognizing and supporting the rebel regime of Toussaint L'Ouverture in Santo Domingo; Jefferson assured the French minister in Washington that the American people, especially those of the slaveholding states, did not approve of the black revolutionary, who was setting a bad example for their own slaves. He even implied that the United States might join with France in putting down the rebellion (although nothing ever came of the suggestion).

But Jefferson began to reconsider his position when he heard rumors of the secret transfer of Louisiana. "It completely reverses all the political relations of the U.S.," he wrote to Livingston in April 1802. Always before, America had looked to France as its "natural friend." But there was on the earth "one single spot" whose possessor was "our natural and habitual enemy." That spot was New Orleans, the outlet through which the produce of the fast-growing western regions of the United States traveled to the markets of the world. If France should actually seize New Orleans, Jefferson said, then "we must marry ourselves to the British fleet and nation."

Jefferson was even more alarmed when, in the fall of 1802, he learned that the Spanish intendant at New Orleans (who still governed the city, since the French had not yet taken formal possession of the region) had announced a disturbing new regulation. American ships sailing the Mississippi River had for many years been accustomed to depositing their cargoes in New Orleans for transfer to oceangoing vessels. The intendant now forbade the practice—even though Spain had guaranteed Americans that right in the Pinckney Treaty of 1795—thus effectively closing the lower Mississippi to American shippers.

Westerners demanded that the federal government do something to reopen the river. The president faced a dilemma. If he yielded to the frontier clamor and tried to change the policy by force, he would run the risk of a major war with France. If he ignored the west-

EXPLORATION OF THE LOUISIANA PURCHASE, 1803–1807

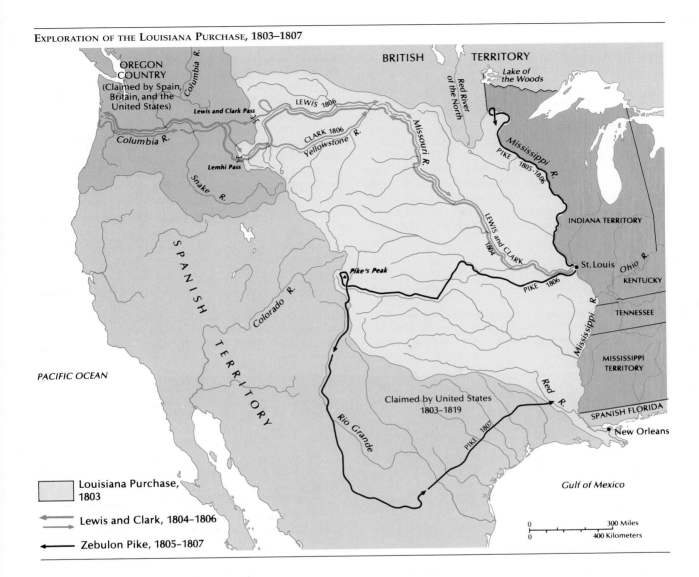

erners' demands, he might lose political support. But Jefferson saw another solution. He instructed Robert Livingston, the American ambassador in Paris, to negotiate the purchase of New Orleans. Livingston on his own authority proposed that the French sell the United States the vast western part of Louisiana as well.

In the meantime, Jefferson persuaded Congress to appropriate funds for an expansion of the army and the construction of a river fleet, and he deliberately gave the impression that American forces might soon descend on New Orleans and that the United States might form an alliance with Great Britain if the prob-

lems with France were not resolved. Perhaps that was why Napoleon suddenly decided to accept Livingston's proposal and offer the United States the entire Louisiana Territory.

Napoleon had good reasons for the decision. His plans for an American empire had already gone seriously awry, partly because a yellow fever epidemic had wiped out much of the French army in the New World and partly because the expeditionary force Napoleon wished to send to reinforce them and take possession of Louisiana had been frozen into a Dutch harbor through the winter of 1802–1803. By the time the harbor thawed in the spring of 1803, Napoleon was preparing for a renewed war in Europe. He would not, he realized, have the resources now to secure an American empire.

The Louisiana Purchase

Faced with Napoleon's startling proposal, Livingston and James Monroe, whom Jefferson had sent to Paris to assist in the negotiations, had to decide first whether they should even consider making a treaty for the purchase of the entire Louisiana Territory, since they had not been authorized by their government to do so. But fearful that Napoleon might withdraw the offer, they decided to proceed without further instructions from home. After some

haggling over the price—Napoleon's negotiator Barbe-Marbois asked for and got somewhat more than the minimum amount Napoleon had set—Livingston and Monroe signed the agreement on April 30, 1803.

By the terms of the treaty, the United States was to pay a total of 80 million francs ($15 million) to the French government. The United States was also to grant certain exclusive commercial privileges to France in the port of New Orleans and was to incorporate the residents of Louisiana into the Union with the same rights and privileges as other citizens. The boundaries of the purchase were not clearly defined; the treaty simply specified that Louisiana would occupy the "same extent" as it had when France and Spain had owned it.

NEW ORLEANS IN 1803
Because of its location near the mouth of the Mississippi River, New Orleans was the principal port of western North America in the early nineteenth century. Through it, western farmers shipped their produce to markets in the east and Europe. This 1803 painting celebrates the American acquisition of the city from France as part of the Louisiana Purchase. (*Chicago Historical Society*)

In Washington, the president was both pleased and embarrassed when he received the treaty. He was pleased with the terms of the bargain but uncertain whether the United States lacked authority to accept it, since he had always insisted that the federal government could rightfully exercise only those powers explicitly assigned to it. Nowhere did the Constitution say anything about the acquisition of new territory. But Jefferson's advisers persuaded him that his treaty-making power under the Constitution would justify the purchase of Louisiana. The president finally agreed, trusting, as he said, "that the good sense of our country will correct the evil of loose construction when it shall produce ill effects." Congress promptly approved the treaty and appropriated money to implement its provisions. Finally, late in 1803, the French assumed formal control of Louisiana from Spain just long enough to turn the territory over to General James Wilkinson, the commissioner of the United States and the commander of a small occupation force. In New Orleans, beneath a bright December sun, United States soldiers lowered the recently raised French tricolor and raised the American flag in its place.

The government organized the Louisiana Territory much as it had organized the Northwest Territory, with the assumption that its various territories would eventually become states. The first of these was admitted to the union as the state of Louisiana in 1812.

Exploring the West

Meanwhile, a series of ambitious explorations were revealing the geography of the far-flung new territory to white Americans, few of whom had ever ventured much beyond the Mississippi River. In 1803, even before Napoleon's offer to sell Louisiana, Jefferson helped plan an expedition that was to cross the continent to the Pacific Ocean, gather geographical facts, and investigate prospects for trade with the Indians. He named as its leader his private secretary and Virginia neighbor, the thirty-two-year-old Meriwether Lewis, a veteran of Indian wars skilled in the ways of the wilderness. Lewis chose as a colleague the twenty-eight-year-old William Clark, who—like George Rogers Clark, his older brother—was an experienced frontiersman and Indian fighter. In the spring of 1804, Lewis and Clark, with a company of four dozen men, started up the Missouri River from St. Louis. With the Shoshone woman Sacajawea as their guide, they eventually crossed the Rocky Mountains, descended the Snake and Columbia Rivers, and in the late autumn of 1805 camped on the Pacific coast. In September 1806, they were back in St. Louis with elaborate records of

MERIWETHER LEWIS
In 1807, when the French painter Charles de Saint-Mémin produced this watercolor, Lewis had returned from his fabled expedition through the Far West with William Clark and had been named governor of the Louisiana territory by President Jefferson. He had served earlier as a private secretary to Jefferson. *(New-York Historical Society)*

the geography and the Indian civilizations they had observed along the way.

While Lewis and Clark were still on their journey, Jefferson dispatched other explorers to other parts of the Louisiana Territory. Lieutenant Zebulon Montgomery Pike, twenty-six years old, led an expedition in the fall of 1805 from St. Louis into the upper Mississippi Valley. In the summer of 1806, he set out again up the valley of the Arkansas River and into what later became Colorado, where he encountered, but failed in his attempt to climb, the peak that now bears his name. His account of his western travels created an enduring (and inaccurate) impression among many Americans in the East that the land between the Missouri River and the Rockies was an uncultivable desert that ought to be left forever to the nomadic Indian tribes.

The Burr Conspiracy

Jefferson's triumphant reelection in 1804 suggested that most of the nation approved the new acquisition. But some New England Federalists raged against it. They realized that the more the West grew and the more new states joined the Union, the less power the Federalists and their region would retain. In Massachusetts, a group of the most extreme Federalists, known as the Essex Junto, concluded that the only recourse for New England was to secede from the Union and form a separate "Northern Confederacy." If a northern confederacy was to have any hope for lasting success as a separate nation, the Federalists believed, it would have to include New York and New Jersey as well as New England. But the leading Federalist in New York, Alexander Hamilton, refused to support the secessionist scheme. "Dismemberment of our empire," he wrote, "will be a clear sacrifice of great positive advantages without any counterbalancing good, administering no relief to our real disease, which is democracy."

Federalists in New York then turned to Hamilton's greatest political rival: Vice President Aaron Burr, a politician without prospects in his own party, because Jefferson had never forgiven him for the 1800 election deadlock. Burr accepted a Federalist proposal that he become their candidate for governor in 1804, and there were rumors (unsupported by any evidence) that he had also agreed to support the Federalist plans for secession. Hamilton accused Burr of plotting treason and made numerous private remarks, widely reported in the press, about Burr's "despicable" character. When Burr lost the election, he blamed his defeat on Hamilton's malevolence. "These things must have an end," Burr wrote. He challenged Hamilton to a duel.

Dueling had already fallen into some disrepute in America, but many people still considered it a legitimate institution for settling matters of "honor." Hamilton feared that refusing Burr's challenge would brand him a coward. And so, on a July morning in 1804, the two men met at Weehawken, New Jersey. Hamilton was mortally wounded; he died the next day.

The resourceful and charismatic Burr was now a political outcast who had to flee New York to avoid an indictment for murder. He found new outlets for his ambitions in the West. Even before the duel, he had begun corresponding with prominent white settlers in the Southwest, especially with General James Wilkinson, now governor of the Louisiana Territory. Burr and Wilkinson, it seems clear, hoped to lead an expedition that would capture Mexico from the Spanish. "Mexico glitters in all our eyes," Burr wrote; "the word is all we wait for." But there were also rumors that they wanted to separate the Southwest from the Union and create a western empire that Burr would rule. There is little evidence that these rumors were true.

Whether true or not, many of Burr's opponents—including, ultimately, Jefferson himself—chose to believe the rumors. When Burr led a group of armed followers down the Ohio River by boat in 1806, disturbing reports flowed into Washington (the most alarming from Wilkinson, who had suddenly turned against Burr and who now informed the president that treason was afoot) that an attack on New Orleans was imminent. Jefferson ordered Burr and his men arrested as traitors. Burr was brought to Richmond for trial. Determined to win a conviction, Jefferson carefully managed the government's case from Washington. But Chief Justice Marshall, presiding over the trial on circuit duty, limited the evidence the government could present and defined the charge in such a way that the jury had little choice but to acquit. Burr was free, but his political reputation was permanently destroyed. For several years, he lived in self-imposed exile in Europe. In 1812, he returned to America and established a successful legal practice in New York. He lived long enough to hail the Texas revolution of 1836 as the fruition of the movement to "liberate" Mexico that he had tried to launch.

The Burr conspiracy was in part the story of a single man's soaring ambitions and flamboyant personality. But it was also a symbol of the larger perils still facing the new nation. With a central government that remained deliberately weak, with vast tracts of land only nominally controlled by the United States, with ambitious political leaders willing, if necessary, to circumvent normal channels in their search for power, the legitimacy of the federal government, and indeed the existence of the United States as a stable and united nation, remained to be fully established.

EXPANSION AND WAR

Two very different conflicts were taking shape in the later years of Thomas Jefferson's presidency that would, together, draw the United States into a difficult and frustrating war. One was the continuing tension in Europe, which in 1803 escalated once again into a full-scale conflict (the Napoleonic Wars). As the fighting escalated, both the British and the French took steps to prevent the United States from trading with (and thus assisting) the other. The other conflict was in North America itself, a result of the ceaseless westward expansion of white settlement, which was now stretching to the Mississippi River and beyond, colliding again with native populations committed to protecting their lands and their trade from intruders. In both the North and the South, the threatened tribes mobilized to resist white encroachments. They began as well to forge connections with British forces in Canada and Spanish forces in Florida. The Indian conflict on land therefore became intertwined with the European conflict on the seas, and ultimately helped cause the War of 1812, an unpopular conflict with ambiguous results.

Conflict on the Seas

Politicians at the time and historians since have argued over whether the conflict in the West or the conflict on the seas was the real cause of the war. In fact, the war was a result of both.

The early nineteenth century saw a dramatic expansion of American shipping in the Atlantic. Britain retained significant naval superiority, but the British merchant marine was preoccupied with commerce in Europe and Asia and devoted little energy to trade with America. Thus the United States stepped effectively into the void and developed one of the most important merchant marines in the world, which soon controlled a large proportion of the trade between Europe and the West Indies.

In 1805, at the Battle of Trafalgar, a British fleet virtually destroyed what was left of the French navy. Because France could no longer challenge the British at sea, Napoleon now chose to pressure England through economic rather than naval means. The result was what he called the Continental System, designed to close the European continent to British trade. Accordingly, he issued a series of decrees (one in Berlin in 1806 and another in Milan in 1807) barring British ships and neutral ships touching at British ports from landing their cargoes at any European port controlled by France or its allies. The British government replied to Napoleon's decrees by establishing—through a series of "orders in council"—a blockade of the European coast. The blockade required that any goods being shipped to Napoleon's Europe be carried either in British vessels or in neutral vessels stopping at British ports—precisely what Napoleon's policies forbade.

American ships were caught between Napoleon's Berlin and Milan decrees and Britain's orders in council. If they sailed directly for the European continent, they risked being captured by the British navy; if they sailed by way of a British port, they risked seizure by the French. Both of the warring powers were violating America's rights as a neutral nation. But most Americans considered the British, with their greater sea power, the worse offender. British ships pounced on Yankee merchantmen all over the ocean; the French could do so only in European ports. In particular, British vessels stopped American ships on the high seas and seized sailors off the decks, making them victims of "impressment."

Impressment

The British navy—with its floggings, low pay, and terrible shipboard conditions—was a "floating hell" to its sailors. Few volunteered. Most had had to be "impressed" (forced) into the service. At every opportunity they deserted. By 1807, many of these deserters had joined the American merchant marine or the American navy. To check this loss of vital manpower, the British claimed the right to stop and search American merchantmen (although not naval vessels) and reimpress deserters. They did not claim the right to take native-born Americans, but they did insist on the right to seize naturalized Americans born on British soil. In practice, the British navy often made no such distinctions, impressing British deserters and native-born Americans alike into service.

In the summer of 1807, the British went to more provocative extremes in an incident involving a vessel of the American navy. Sailing from Norfolk, with several alleged deserters from the British navy among the crew, the American naval frigate *Chesapeake* encountered the British ship *Leopard*. When the American commander, James Barron, refused to allow the British to search the *Chesapeake,* the *Leopard* opened fire. Barron had no choice but to surrender, and a boarding party from the *Leopard* dragged four men off the American frigate.

When news of the *Chesapeake-Leopard* incident reached the United States, there was great popular clamor for revenge. If Congress had been in session, it might have declared war. But Jefferson and Madison tried to maintain the peace. Jefferson expelled all British warships from American waters, to lessen the likelihood of future incidents. Then he sent instructions to his minister in England, James Monroe, to demand that the British government renounce impressment. The British government disavowed the action of the officer responsible for the *Chesapeake-Leopard* affair and recalled him; it offered compensation for those killed and wounded in the incident; and it promised to return three of the captured sailors (one of the original four had been hanged). But the British refused to renounce impressment.

"Peaceable Coercion"

In an effort to prevent future incidents that might bring the nation again to the brink of war, Jefferson presented

---

PROTECTION FROM IMPRESSMENT

To protect American sailors from British impressment, the federal government issued official certificates of United States citizenship—known as "protection papers." But British naval officers, aware that such documents were often forged, frequently ignored them. *(Essex Institute, Salem, Massachusetts)*

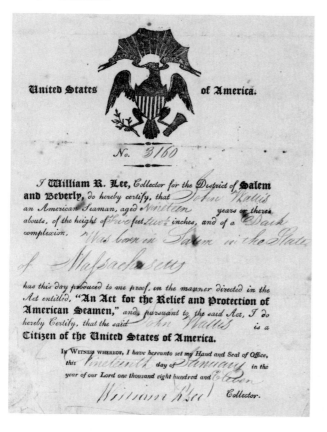

a drastic measure to Congress when it reconvened late in 1807. The Republican legislators promptly enacted it into law. It was known as the Embargo, and it became one of the most controversial political issues of its time. The Embargo prohibited American ships from leaving the United States for any foreign port anywhere in the world. (If it had specified only British and French ports, Jefferson reasoned, it could have been evaded by means of false clearance papers.) Congress also passed a "force act" to give the government power to enforce the Embargo.

The law was widely evaded, but it was effective enough to create a serious depression through most of the nation. Hardest hit were the merchants and ship-owners of the Northeast, most of them Federalists. Their once lucrative shipping business was at a virtual standstill, and they were losing money every day. They became convinced that Jefferson had acted unconstitutionally.

The election of 1808 came in the midst of the Embargo-induced depression. James Madison, Jefferson's secretary of state and political ally, won the presidency. But the Federalists ran much more strongly than they had in 1804. The Embargo was clearly a growing political liability, and Jefferson decided to back down. A few days before leaving office, he approved a bill ending his experiment with what he called "peaceable coercion."

To replace the Embargo, Congress passed the Non-Intercourse Act just before Madison took office. It reopened trade with all nations but Great Britain and France. A year later, in 1810, Congress allowed the Non-Intercourse Act to expire and replaced it with Macon's Bill No. 2, which reopened free commercial relations with Britain and France, but authorized the president to prohibit commerce with either belligerent if it should continue violating neutral shipping after the other had stopped. Napoleon, in an effort to induce the United States to reimpose the Embargo against Britain, announced that France would no longer interfere with American shipping. Madison announced that an embargo against Great Britain alone would automatically go into effect early in 1811 unless Britain renounced its restrictions on American shipping.

In time, the new, limited embargo, although less well enforced than the earlier one had been, hurt the economy of England enough that the government repealed its blockade of Europe. But the repeal came too late to prevent war. In any case, naval policies were only part of the reason for tensions between Britain and the United States.

Conflicts in the West

Given the ruthlessness with which white settlers in North America had dislodged Indian tribes to make

JAMES AND DOLLEY MADISON
James Madison may have been the most brilliant of the early leaders of the republic, but he was also one of the most serious and humorless, as this grim portrait suggests. His wife (born Dolley Payne in North Carolina and raised a Quaker in Virginia) was twenty-six when she married the forty-three-year-old Madison in 1794. Her charm and social grace made her one of her husband's greatest political assets. She acted as hostess for Thomas Jefferson, a widower, while her husband was secretary of state. And she presided over a lively social life during her eight years in the White House as first lady. *(New-York Historical Society)*

room for expanding settlement, it was hardly surprising that ever since the Revolution many Indians had continued to look to England—which had historically attempted to limit western expansion—for protection. The British in Canada, for their part, had relied on the Indians as partners in the lucrative fur trade and as potential military allies.

There had been relative peace in the Northwest for over a decade after Jay's Treaty and Anthony Wayne's victory over the tribes at Fallen Timbers in 1794. But the 1807 war crisis following the *Chesapeake-Leopard* incident revived the conflict between Indians and white settlers. Two important (and very different) leaders emerged to lead it: William Henry Harrison and Tecumseh.

The Virginia-born Harrison, already a veteran Indian fighter at age twenty-six, went to Washington as the congressional delegate from the Northwest Territory in 1799. He was a committed advocate of growth and development in the western lands, and he was largely responsible for the passage in 1800 of the so-called Harrison Land Law, which enabled white settlers to acquire farms from the public domain on much easier terms than before.

In 1801, Jefferson appointed Harrison governor of Indiana Territory to administer the president's proposed solution to the "Indian problem." Jefferson offered the Indians a choice: they could convert themselves into settled farmers and become a part of white society, or they could migrate to the west of the Mississippi. In either case, they would have to give up their claims to their tribal lands in the Northwest.

Jefferson considered the assimilation policy a benign alternative to continuing conflict between Indians and white settlers, conflict he assumed the tribes were destined to lose. But to the tribes, the new policy seemed far from benign, especially given the bludgeonlike efficiency with which Harrison set out to implement it. He played off one tribe against another and used threats, bribes, trickery, and whatever other tactics he felt would help him conclude treaties. By 1807, the United States had extracted from reluctant tribal leaders treaty rights to eastern Michigan, southern Indiana, and most of Illinois. Meanwhile, in the Southwest, white Americans were taking millions of acres from other tribes in Georgia, Tennessee, and Mississippi. The Indians wanted desperately to resist, but the separate tribes were helpless by themselves against the power of the United States. They might have accepted their fate passively but for the emergence of two new factors.

One factor was the policy of the British authorities in Canada. After the *Chesapeake* incident and the surge of anti-British feeling throughout the United States, the British colonial authorities began to expect an American invasion of Canada and took desperate measures for their own defense. Among those measures were efforts to renew friendship with the Indians—friendship badly frayed by the Battle of Fallen Timbers, in which

the British had refused to provide assistance to the tribes—and efforts to provide them with increased supplies. "Are the Indians to be employed in case of a rupture with the United States?" the lieutenant governor of upper Canada asked Sir James Craig, governor general of the province, in 1807. The governor replied: "If we do not employ them, there cannot exist a moment's doubt that they will be employed against us."

Tecumseh and the Prophet

The second, and more important, factor intensifying the border conflict was the rise of two remarkable native leaders. One was Tenskwatawa, a charismatic religious leader and orator known as the Prophet. He had experienced a mystical awakening in the process of recovering from alcoholism. Having freed himself from what he considered the evil effects of white culture, he began to speak to his people of the superior virtues of Indian civilization and the sinfulness and corruption of the white world. In the process, he inspired a religious revival that spread through numerous tribes and helped unite them. Like Neolin before him, and like his contemporary to the East, Handsome Lake, Tenskwatawa demonstrated the power of religious leaders to mobilize Indians behind political and military objectives. The Prophet's headquarters at the confluence of Tippecanoe Creek and the Wabash River

TECUMSEH
Tecumseh's efforts to unite the tribes of the Mississippi Valley against further white encroachments on their lands led him ultimately into an alliance with the British after the Battle of Tippecanoe in 1811. In the War of 1812, he was commissioned a brigadier general by the British and fought against the United States in the Battle of the Thames. He is shown in this painting (by the daughter of an English officer stationed near Detroit) wearing British military trousers. (*Fort Malden National Historical Park*)

(known as Prophetstown) became a sacred place for people of many tribes and attracted thousands of Indians from throughout the Midwest. Out of their common religious experiences, they began to consider joint political and military efforts as well.

The Prophet's brother Tecumseh—"the Shooting Star," chief of the Shawnees—emerged as the leader of these more secular efforts. Tecumseh understood, as few other Indian leaders had, that only through united action could the tribes hope to resist the advance of white civilization. Beginning in 1809, after tribes in Indiana had ceded vast lands to the United States, he set out to unite all the Indians of the Mississippi Valley, north and south. Together, he promised, they would halt white expansion, recover the whole Northwest, and make the Ohio River the boundary between the United States and the Indian country. He maintained that Harrison and others, by negotiating treaties with individual tribes, had obtained no real title to land. The land belonged to all the tribes; none of them could rightfully cede any of it without the consent of the others. "The Great Spirit gave this great island to his red children. He placed the whites on the other side of the big water," Tecumseh told Harrison. "They were not contented with their own, but came to take ours from us. They have driven us from the sea to the lakes—we can go no farther."

In 1811, Tecumseh left Prophetstown and traveled down the Mississippi to visit the tribes of the South and persuade them to join the alliance. During his absence, Governor Harrison saw a chance to destroy the growing influence of the two Indian leaders. He camped near Prophetstown with 1,000 soldiers, and on November 7, 1811, he provoked a fight. Although the white forces suffered losses as heavy as those of the natives, Harrison drove off the Indians and burned the town. The Battle of Tippecanoe (named for the creek near the fighting) disillusioned many of the Prophet's followers, who had believed that his magic would protect them. Tecumseh returned to find the confederacy in disarray. But there were still many warriors eager for combat, and by the spring of 1812 they were active along the frontier, from Michigan to Mississippi, raiding white settlements and terrifying white settlers.

The bloodshed along the western borders was largely a result of the Indians' own initiative, but Britain's agents in Canada had encouraged and helped supply the uprising. To Harrison and most white residents of the regions, there seemed only one way to make the West safe for Americans. That was to drive the British out of Canada and annex that province to the United States—a goal that many westerners had long cherished for other reasons as well.

The Lure of Florida

While white "frontiersmen" in the North demanded the conquest of Canada, those in the South looked to the acquisition of Spanish Florida, a territory that included the present state of Florida and the southern areas of what are now Alabama, Mississippi, and Louisiana. The territory was a continuing threat to whites in the southern United States. Slaves escaped across the Florida border; Indians in Florida launched frequent raids north into white settlements along the border. But white southerners also coveted Florida because through it ran rivers that could provide residents of the Southwest with access to valuable ports on the Gulf of Mexico.

In 1810, American settlers in West Florida (an area part of Mississippi and Louisiana today) seized the Spanish fort at Baton Rouge and asked the federal government to annex the territory to the United States. President Madison happily agreed and then began scheming to get the rest of Florida too. The desire for Florida became yet another motivation for war with Britain. Spain was Britain's ally, and a war might provide an excuse for taking Spanish as well as British territory.

By 1812, therefore, war fever was raging on both the northern and southern borders of the United States. The white residents of these outlying regions made up a relatively small proportion of the national population and were represented in Congress by only a few, nonvoting territorial delegates. But their demands found substantial support in Washington among a group of determined young congressmen.

In the congressional elections of 1810, voters elected a large number of representatives of both parties eager for war with Britain. They became known as the "war hawks." They represented a new generation, aggressive and impatient. The most influential of them came from the new states in the West or from the backcountry of the old states in the South. Two of their leaders, both recently elected to the House of Representatives, were Henry Clay of Kentucky and John C. Calhoun of South Carolina, men of great intellect, magnetism, and ambition who would play a large role in national politics for nearly forty years. Both were supporters of war with Great Britain.

Clay became Speaker of the House in 1811, and he filled committees with those who shared his eagerness for war. He appointed Calhoun to the crucial Committee on Foreign Affairs, and both men began agitating for the conquest of Canada. Madison still preferred peace but was losing control of Congress. On June 18, 1812, he gave in to the pressure and approved a declaration of war against Britain.

THE WAR OF 1812

Preoccupied with their struggle against Napoleon in Europe, the British were not eager for an open conflict with the United States. Even after the Americans declared war, Britain largely ignored them for a time. But in the fall of 1812, Napoleon launched a catastrophic campaign against Russia that left his army in disarray and his power in Europe diminished. By late 1813, with the French empire on its way to final defeat, Britain was able to turn its military attention to America.

Battles with the Tribes

Americans entered the War of 1812 with great enthusiasm, but events on the battlefield soon cooled their ardor. In the summer of 1812, American forces invaded Canada through Detroit. They soon had to retreat back to Detroit and in August surrendered the fort there. Other invasion efforts also failed. In the meantime, Fort Dearborn (Chicago) fell before an Indian attack.

Things went only slightly better for the United States on the seas. At first, American frigates won some spectacular victories over British warships, and American privateers destroyed or captured many British merchant ships, occasionally braving the coastal waters of the British Isles and burning vessels within sight of the shore. But by 1813, the British navy was counterattacking effectively, driving the American frigates to cover and imposing a blockade on the United States.

The United States did, however, achieve significant early military successes on the Great Lakes. First, the Americans took command of Lake Ontario, which permitted them to raid and burn York (now Toronto), the capital of Canada. American forces then seized control of Lake Erie, mainly through the work of the youthful Oliver Hazard Perry, who engaged and dispersed a British fleet at Put-In Bay on September 10, 1813. This made possible, at last, another invasion of Canada by way of Detroit, which Americans could now reach easily by water. William Henry Harrison, the American commander in the West, pushed up the river Thames into upper Canada and on October 5, 1813, won a victory notable for the death of Tecumseh, who was serving as a brigadier general in the British army. The Battle of the Thames weakened and disheartened the Indians of the Northwest and greatly diminished their ability to defend their claims to the region.

In the meantime, another white military leader was striking an even harder blow at the Indians of the Southwest. The Creeks, whom Tecumseh had aroused on a visit to the South and whom the Spanish had supplied with weapons, had been attacking white settlers near the Florida border. Andrew Jackson, a wealthy Tennessee planter and a general in the state militia, temporarily abandoned plans for an invasion of Florida and set off in pursuit of them. On March 27, 1814, in the Battle of Horseshoe Bend, Jackson's men took terrible revenge on the Indians—slaughtering women and children along with warriors—and broke the resistance of the Creeks. The tribe agreed to cede most of its lands to the United States and retreated

THE BOMBARDMENT OF FORT McHENRY
The British bombardment of Fort McHenry in Baltimore harbor in September 1814 was of modest importance to the outcome of the war of 1812. It is remembered now principally as the occasion for Francis Scott Key to write his poem "The Star-Spangled Banner," which recorded his sentiments at seeing an American flag still flying over the fort "by the dawn's early light." *(I. N. Phelps Stokes Collection of American Historical Prints, The New York Public Library)*

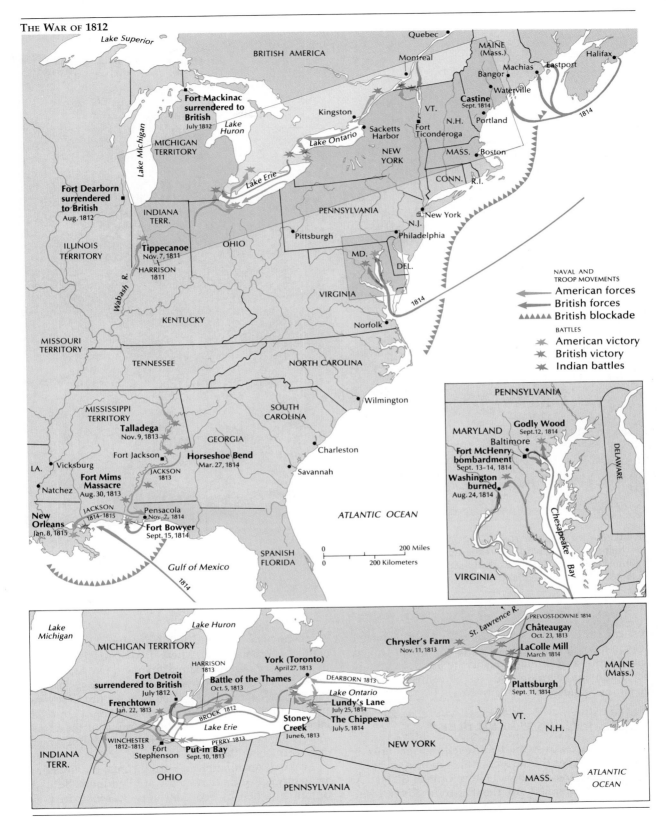

THE WAR OF 1812

Lake Superior

BRITISH AMERICA

Quebec

MAINE
(Mass.)

Montreal

Halifax

Machias — Eastport
Bangor
Waterville

Castine
Sept. 1814

1814

**Fort Mackinac
surrendered to
British**
July 1812

Kingston

Lake Huron

Lake Michigan

VT.

N.H.

Portland

MICHIGAN
TERRITORY

Sacketts
Harbor

Fort
Ticonderoga

Lake Ontario

NEW
YORK

MASS. · Boston

Lake Erie

**Fort Dearborn
surrendered
to British**
Aug. 1812

CONN.

R.I.

INDIANA
TERR.

PENNSYLVANIA

New York

ILLINOIS
TERRITORY

OHIO

N.J.

Pittsburgh

Philadelphia

Tippecanoe
Nov. 7, 1811

HARRISON
1811

MD.

Wabash R.

DEL.

VIRGINIA

1814

MISSOURI
TERRITORY

KENTUCKY

Norfolk

NAVAL AND
TROOP MOVEMENTS

→ American forces
→ British forces
▲ British blockade

BATTLES

TENNESSEE

NORTH CAROLINA

✳ American victory
✳ British victory
✳ Indian battles

Wilmington

MISSISSIPPI
TERRITORY

SOUTH
CAROLINA

Talladega
Nov. 9, 1813

GEORGIA

Fort Jackson

Horseshoe Bend
Mar. 27, 1814

PENNSYLVANIA

Charleston

MARYLAND

Godly Wood
Sept.12, 1814

JACKSON
1813

Baltimore

DELAWARE

LA.

Vicksburg

**Fort Mims
Massacre**
Aug. 30, 1813

Savannah

**Fort McHenry
bombardment**
Sept. 13–14, 1814

Natchez

JACKSON
1814–1815

Pensacola
Nov. 7, 1814

ATLANTIC OCEAN

**Washington
burned**
Aug. 24, 1814

**New
Orleans**
Jan. 8, 1815

Fort Bowyer
Sept. 15, 1814

Chesapeake Bay

SPANISH
FLORIDA

0 ____ 200 Miles

0 ____ 200 Kilometers

Gulf of Mexico

1814

VIRGINIA

Lake
Michigan

Lake Huron

St. Lawrence R.

PREVOST-DOWNIE 1814

Châteaugay
Oct. 23, 1813

MICHIGAN TERRITORY

HARRISON
1813

Chrysler's Farm
Nov. 11, 1813

LaColle Mill
March 1814

MAINE
(Mass.)

**Fort Detroit
surrendered to British**
July 1812

York (Toronto)
April 27, 1813

Battle of the Thames
Oct. 5, 1813

DEARBORN 1813

Lake Ontario

Plattsburgh
Sept. 11, 1814

Frenchtown
Jan. 22, 1813

BROCK 1812

Lundy's Lane
July 25, 1814

VT.

N.H.

**Stoney
Creek**
June 6, 1813

The Chippewa
July 5, 1814

WINCHESTER
1812–1813

Lake Erie

PERRY 1813

NEW YORK

Fort
Stephenson

Put-in Bay
Sept. 10, 1813

ATLANTIC
OCEAN

INDIANA
TERR.

OHIO

PENNSYLVANIA

MASS.

211

THE BURNING OF WASHINGTON
This dramatic engraving somewhat exaggerates the extent of the blazes in Washington when the British occupied the city in August 1814. But the invaders did set fire to the Capitol, the White House, and other public buildings in retaliation for the American burning of the Canadian capital at York. *(Bettmann)*

westward, farther into the interior. The battle also won Jackson a commission as major general in the United States Army, and in that capacity he led his men farther south into Florida and, on November 7, 1814, seized the Spanish fort at Pensacola.

Battles with the British

But the victories over the tribes were not enough to win the war. After the surrender of Napoleon in 1814, England prepared to invade the United States. A British armada sailed up the Patuxent River from Chesapeake Bay and landed an army that marched a short distance overland to Bladensburg, on the outskirts of Washington, where it dispersed a poorly trained force of American militiamen. On August 24, 1814, the British troops entered Washington and put the government to flight. Then they set fire to several public buildings, including the White House, in retaliation for the earlier American burning of the Canadian capital at York. This was the low point of American fortunes in the war.

Leaving Washington in partial ruins, the invading army proceeded up the bay toward Baltimore. But Baltimore, guarded by Fort McHenry, was prepared. To block the approaching fleet, the American garrison had sunk several ships to clog the entry to the harbor, thus forcing the British to bombard the fort from a distance. Through the night of September 13, Francis Scott Key, a Washington lawyer who was on board one of the British ships trying to secure the release of an American prisoner, watched the bombardment. The next morning, "by the dawn's early light," he could see the flag on the fort still flying; he recorded his pride in the moment by scribbling a poem—"The Star-Spangled Banner"—on the back of an envelope. The British withdrew from Baltimore. Key's words were soon set to the tune of an old English drinking song. In 1931, "The Star-Spangled Banner" became the official national anthem.

Meanwhile, American forces repelled another British invasion in northern New York at the Battle of Plattsburgh, on September 11, 1814, which turned back a much larger British naval and land force and secured the northern border of the United States. In the South, a formidable array of battle-hardened British veterans, fresh from the campaign against the French in Spain, landed below New Orleans and prepared to advance north up the Mississippi. Awaiting the British was Andrew Jackson with a motley collection of Tennesseans, Kentuckians, Creoles, blacks, pirates, and regular army troops behind earthen fortifications. On January 8, 1815, the British advanced, but their exposed forces were no match for Jackson's well-protected men. After the Americans had repulsed several waves of attackers, the British finally retreated, leaving behind 700 dead (including their commander, Sir Edward Pakenham), 1,400 wounded, and 500 prisoners. Jackson's

ATTACKING THE FEDERALISTS
A Republican cartoonist derided the secession efforts of New England Federalists at the Hartford Convention in this cartoon. It portrays timid men representing Massachusetts, Connecticut, and Rhode Island preparing to leap into the arms of George III. *(Library of Congress)*

SIGNIFICANT EVENTS

1769   James Watt patents steam engine

1778   Phillips Academy founded in Andover, Massachusetts

1779   Universalist Church founded in Gloucester, Massachusetts

1781   Phillips Exeter Academy founded in New Hampshire

1782   Unitarian Church founded in Boston

1784   Judith Sargent Murray publishes essay on rights of women

Methodist Church formally established

1789   Massachusetts law requires public schools to admit female students

1790   Samuel Slater builds textile mill, first modern factory in America, in Pawtucket, Rhode Island

1792   Toll road constructed from Philadelphia to Lancaster, beginning the turnpike era

1793   Eli Whitney invents cotton gin

1794   First black churches in America established

1794–1796   Thomas Paine's *Age of Reason* attacks traditional religion

1800   United States capital moves to Washington, D.C.

1800   Gabriel Prosser's plans for slave rebellion in Virginia foiled

1801–1805   Conflict with Tripoli

1801   Second Great Awakening begins

John Marshall appointed chief justice of the Supreme Court

1802   Jefferson administration abolishes all internal federal taxes

United States Military Academy founded at West Point

1803   Napoleonic Wars escalate in Europe

Louisiana Territory purchased from French

Supreme Court establishes power of judicial review in *Marbury* v. *Madison*

1804–1806   Lewis and Clark, and Zebulon Pike, explore Louisiana Territory

1804   Aaron Burr kills Alexander Hamilton in duel

Thomas Jefferson reelected president

1805   British defeat French at Trafalgar

1806   Burr conspiracy uncovered

1806–1807   Napoleon issues Berlin and Milan decrees

---

losses were eight killed and thirteen wounded. Only later did news reach North America that the United States and Britain had signed a peace treaty several weeks before the Battle of New Orleans.

The Revolt of New England

With a few notable exceptions, such as the Battles of Put-In Bay and New Orleans, the military operations of the United States between 1812 and 1815 consisted of a series of humiliating failures. As a result, the American government faced increasing popular opposition as the contest dragged on. In New England, opposition both to the war and to the Republican government that was waging it was so extreme that some Federalists celebrated British victories. In Congress, in the meantime, the Republicans had continual trouble with the Federalist opposition, led by a young congressman from New Hampshire, Daniel Webster, who missed no opportunity to embarrass the administration.

By now the Federalists were a minority in the country as a whole, but they were still the majority party in New England. Some of them began to dream again

SIGNIFICANT EVENTS

1807 Fulton and Livingston launch the *Clermont*, first steamboat

Burr tried for conspiracy

Chesapeake-Leopard incident nearly precipitates war with Great Britain

Embargo Act passed

Congress approves construction of National Road

1808 Economy plunges into depression

Madison elected president

1809 Embargo Act repealed

Non-Intercourse Act passed

Tecumseh establishes tribal confederacy to resist white expansion

1810 Macon's Bill No. 2 reopens trade with Britain and France

United States annexes West Florida

1811 Harrison is victorious in Battle of Tippecanoe: destroys Tecumseh's Indian confederacy

First Bank of the United States closes after charter is not renewed

1812 United States declares war on Great Britain (June 14)

Madison reelected president

Louisiana admitted to Union as state

1813 British erect naval blockade

American forces burn York (Toronto), Canadian capital

1813 Perry defeats British fleet at Put-In Bay on Lake Erie

Harrison defeats British and Tecumseh at Battle of the Thames

1814 Jackson, at Battle of Horseshoe Bend, slaughters Creek Indians

British troops capture and burn Washington

Francis Scott Key writes "The Star-Spangled Banner"

Americans win Battle of Plattsburgh

Hartford Convention meets

Treaty of Ghent signed

1815 Jackson wins Battle of New Orleans

Naval war fought with Algiers

1828 Webster's American Dictionary of the English Language published

---

of creating a separate nation in that region, which they could dominate and in which they could escape what they saw as the tyranny of slaveholders and backwoodsmen. Talk of secession revived and reached a climax in the winter of 1814–1815.

On December 15, 1814, delegates from the New England states met in Hartford, Connecticut, to discuss their grievances. Those who favored secession at the Hartford Convention were outnumbered by a comparatively moderate majority. But while the convention's report only hinted at secession, it reasserted the right of nullification and proposed seven amendments

to the Constitution (presumably as the condition of New England's remaining in the Union)—amendments designed to protect New England from the growing influence of the South and the West.

Because the war was going badly and the government was becoming desperate, the New Englanders assumed that the Republicans would have to agree to their demands. Soon after the convention adjourned, however, the news of Jackson's smashing victory at New Orleans reached the cities of the Northeast. A day or two later, reports arrived from abroad of a negotiated peace. In the euphoria of this apparent triumph, the Hartford Convention and the Federalist party came to seem futile, irrelevant, even treasonable. The failure of the secession effort was a virtual death blow to the Federalist Party.

The Peace Settlement

Peace talks between the United States and Britain had begun even before fighting in the War of 1812 began. But serious negotiations did not begin until August 1814, when American and British diplomats met in Ghent, Belgium. John Quincy Adams, Henry Clay, and Albert Gallatin led the American delegation.

Although both sides began with extravagant demands, the final treaty did little except end the fighting itself. The Americans gave up their demand for a British renunciation of impressment and for the cession of Canada to the United States. The British abandoned their call for creation of an Indian buffer state in the Northwest and made other, minor territorial concessions. The negotiators referred other disputes to arbitration. Hastily drawn up, the treaty was signed on Christmas Eve 1814.

Both sides had reason to accept this skimpy agreement. The British were exhausted and in debt from their prolonged conflict with Napoleon and eager to settle the lesser dispute in North America. The Americans realized that with the defeat of Napoleon in Europe, the British would no longer have much incentive to interfere with American commerce. Indeed, by the end of 1815, impressment had all but ceased.

Other settlements followed the Treaty of Ghent and contributed to a long-term improvement in Anglo-American relations. A commercial treaty in 1815 gave Americans the right to trade freely with England and much of the British Empire. The Rush-Bagot agreement of 1817 provided for mutual disarmament on the Great Lakes; eventually (although not until 1872) the Canadian-American boundary became the longest "unguarded frontier" in the world.

For the other parties to the War of 1812, the Indian tribes east of the Mississippi, the Treaty of Ghent was of no lasting value. It required the United States to restore to the tribes lands seized by white Americans in the fighting, but those provisions were never enforced. Ultimately, the war was another disastrous blow to the capacity of Indians to resist white expansion. Tecumseh, their most important leader, was dead. The British, their most important allies, were gone from the Northwest. The alliance that Tecumseh and the Prophet had forged was in disarray. And the end of the war served as a spur to white movement westward, into land the Indians were less than ever able to defend.

SUGGESTED READINGS

General Histories. Henry Adams, *History of the United States During the Administration of Jefferson and Adams,* 9 vols. (1889–1891). Marcus Cunliffe, *The Nation Takes Shape, 1789–1832* (1959). Charles Mayfield, *The New Nation* (1981). Marshall Smelser, *The Democratic Republicans, 1801–1815* (1968).

Society and Culture. Sydney Ahlstrom, *A Religious History of the American People* (1972). Terry D. Bilhartz, *Urban Religion and the Second Great Awakening* (1986). John Boles, *The Great Revival in the South* (1972). Jeanne Boydston, *Home and Work: Housework, Wages, and the Ideology of Labor in the Early Republic* (1990). Priscilla F. Clement, *Welfare and the Poor in the Nineteenth-Century City* (1985). Lawrence A. Cremin, *American Education: The National Experience* (1981). Whitney R. Cross, *The Burned Over District* (1950). Cathy Davidson, *The Revolution and the Word* (1986). Joseph J. Ellis, *After the Revolution: Profiles of Early American Culture* (1979). Carl F. Kaestle, *The Evolution of an Urban School System* (1973). Jan Lewis, *The Pursuit of Happiness: Family and Values in Jefferson's Virginia* (1983). William G. McLoughlin, *Revivals, Awakenings, and Reform* (1978). Russel B. Nye, *The Cultural Life of the New Nation* (1960). Kenneth Silverman, *A Cultural History of the American Revolution* (1976). Richard Slotkin, *Regeneration Through Vio-* lence (1973). William W. Sweet, *Revivalism in America* (1944). Harrry Warfel, *Noah Webster, Schoolmaster to America* (1936).

Economic Growth. W. Elliot Brownlee, *Dynamics of Ascent* (1979). Stuart Bruchey, *The Roots of American Economic Growth* (1965). Thomas C. Cochran, *Frontiers of Change: Early Industrialization in America* (1981). Arthur H. Cole, *The American Wool Manufacture,* 2 vols. (1926). C. M. Green, *Eli Whitney and the Birth of American Technology* (1956). James Henretta and Gregory Nobles, *The Evolution of American Society, 1700–1815,* (rev. ed. 1987). Douglas C. North, *The Economic Growth of the United States, 1780–1860* (1961). W. J. Rorabaugh, *The Craft Apprentice: From Franklin to the Machine Age in America* (1986). Nathan Rosenberg, *Technology and American Economic Growth* (1972). Merritt Roe Smith, *Harpers Ferry Armory and the New Technology* (1977). George R. Taylor, *The Transportation Revolution* (1951). Barbara M. Tucker, *Samuel Slater and the Origins of the American Textile Industry, 1790–1860* (1984). Anthony F. C. Wallace, *Rockdale* (1978). Caroline F. Ware, *Early New England Cotton Manufacture* (1931).

Politics and Government. Leonard Baker, *John Marshall: A Life in Law* (1974). Alexander Balinky, *Albert Gallatin: Fiscal Theories and Policy* (1958). James M. Banner, *To the Hartford Con-*

vention (1967). Morton Borden, *Parties and Politics in the Early Republic* (1967). Noble E. Cunningham, *The Jeffersonian Republicans in Power* (1963); *The Process of Government Under Jefferson* (1978). Robert Dawidoff, *The Education of John Randolph* (1979). Richard Ellis, *The Jeffersonian Crisis: Courts and Politics in the Young Republic* (1971). David Hackett Fischer, *The Revolution of American Conservatism* (1965). Ronald P. Formisano, *The Transformation of Political Culture: Massachusetts Parties, 1790s–1840s* (1983). Robert M. Johnstone, Jr., *Jefferson and the Presidency* (1978). David P. Jordan, *Political Leadership in Jefferson's Virginia* (1983). Linda Kerber, *Federalists in Dissent* (1970). Shaw Livermore, *The Twilight of Federalism* (1962). Dumas Malone, *Jefferson the President: First Term* (1970); and *Jefferson the President: Second Term* (1974). Forrest McDonald, *The Presidency of Thomas Jefferson* (1976). Merrill Peterson, *Thomas Jefferson and the New Nation* (1970). Robert W. Tucker and David C. Hendrickson, *Empire of Liberty: The Statecraft of Thomas Jefferson* (1990). Leonard White, *The Jeffersonians* (1951). James S. Young, *The Washington Community* (1966).

Jeffersonian and Madisonian Thought. Joyce Appleby, *Capitalism and a New Social Order: The Republican Vision of the 1890s* (1984). Lance Banning, *The Jeffersonian Persuasion: Evolution of a Party Ideology* (1978). Adrienne Koch, *The Philosophy of Thomas Jefferson* (1943). Leonard W. Levy, *Jefferson and Civil Liberties: The Darker Side* (1963). Drew McCoy, *The Elusive Republic: Political Economy in Jeffersonian America* (1980); *The Last of the Fathers: James Madison and the Republican Legacy* (1989). Merrill Peterson, *The Jeffersonian Image in the American Mind* (1960). Charles M. Wiltse, *The Jeffersonian Tradition in American Democracy* (1935).

Foreign Policy. Thomas P. Abernethy, *The Burr Conspiracy* (1954). Harry Ammon, *James Monroe and the Quest for National Identity* (1971). Irving Brant, *James Madison*, 6 vols. (1953–1961). George Dangerfield, *Chancellor Robert R. Livingston of New York* (1960). Alexander DeConde, *The Affair of Louisiana* (1976). Bernard De Voto, *Course of Empire* (1952). Bernard De Voto, ed., *The Journals of Lewis and Clark* (1953). Milton Lo-

mask, *Aaron Burr*, 2 vols. (1979, 1982). Bradford Perkins, *Prologue to War: England and the United States, 1805–1812* (1961). Nathan Schachner, *Aaron Burr* (1937). Arthur P. Whitaker, *The Mississippi Question* (1934).

Indians and the West. Ray Allen Billington, *Westward Expansion* (1967). Gregory Evans Dowd, *A Spirited Resistance: The North American Indian Struggle for Unity, 1745–1815* (1992). R. David Edmunds, *The Shawnee Prophet* (1983); and *Tecumseh and the Quest for Indian Leadership* (1984). Reginald Horsman, *Expansion and American Indian Policy, 1783–1812* (1962); and *Matthew Elliott, British Indian Agent* (1964). Francis S. Philbrick, *The Rise of the New West* (1965). Francis P. Prucha, *American Indian Policy in the Formative Years* (1962). James P. Ronda, *Lewis and Clarke Among the Indians* (1984). B. W. Sheehan, *Seeds of Extinction* (1973). Richard White, *The Roots of Dependency* (1983). Charles Wilkinson, *American Indians, Time, and the Law*, rev. ed. (1982).

The War of 1812. F. F. Beirne, *The War of 1812* (1949). Samuel F. Bemis, *John Quincy Adams and the Foundations of American Foreign Policy* (1949). Roger H. Brown, *The Republic in Peril: 1812* (1964). A. L. Burtt, *The United States, Great Britain, and British North America* (1940). Harry L. Coles, *The War of 1812* (1965). R. David Edmunds, *The Shawnee Prophet* (1983); and *Tecumseh and the Quest for Indian Leadership* (1984). Donald R. Hickey, *The West of 1812* (1989). Reginald Horsman, *The Causes of the War of 1812* (1962); *The War of 1812* (1969). Alfred T. Mahan, *Sea Power in Its Relation to the War of 1812*, 2 vols. (1905). John Mahon, *The War of 1812* (1975). Bradford Perkins, *Prologue to War: England and the United States, 1805–1812* (1961); *Castlereagh and Adams* (1964). Julius W. Pratt, *Expansionists of 1812* (1925). Robert V. Remini, *Andrew Jackson and the Course of American Empire* (1977). Robert Allen Rutland, *The Presidency of James Madison* (1990). J. C. A. Stagg, *Mr. Madison's War: Politics, Diplomacy, and Warfare in the Early American Republic, 1783–1830* (1983). Burton Spivak, *Jefferson's English Crisis: Commerce, Embargo, and the Republican Revolution* (1979). William Wood, *The War with the United States* (1915).

FOURTH OF JULY PICNIC AT WEYMOUTH LANDING (C. 1845), BY SUSAN MERRETT
Celebrations of Independence Day, like this one in eastern Massachusetts, became major
festive events throughout the United States in the early nineteenth century, a sign of rising
American nationalism. *(Art Institute of Chicago)*

CHAPTER EIGHT

VARIETIES OF AMERICAN NATIONALISM

L IKE A "FIRE BELL in the night," as Thomas Jefferson put it, the issue of slavery arose after the War of 1812 to threaten the unity of the nation. The debate began when the territory of Missouri applied for admission to the Union, raising the question of whether it would be a free or a slaveholding state. But the larger issue, one that would arise again and again to plague the republic, was whether the vast new western regions of the United States would ultimately move into the orbit of the North or the South.

Yet the Missouri crisis, which Congress settled by compromise in 1820, was significant at the time not only because it was a sign of the sectional crises to come but because it stood in such sharp contrast to the rising American nationalism of the years following the war. Whatever forces might be working to pull the nation apart, stronger ones were acting for the moment to draw it together. The American economy was experiencing remarkable growth. The federal government was acting in both domestic and foreign policy to assert a vigorous nationalism. Above all, perhaps, a set of widely (although never universally) shared sentiments and ideals worked to bind the nation together: the memory of the Revolution, the veneration of the Constitution and its framers, the belief that America had a special destiny in the world. These beliefs combined to produce among many Americans a vibrant, even romantic, patriotism.

Every year, Fourth of July celebrations reminded Americans of their common struggle for independence, as fife-and-drum corps and flamboyant orators appealed to patriotism and nationalism. When the Marquis de Lafayette, the French general who had aided the United States during the Revolution, traveled through the country in 1824, crowds without distinction of section or party cheered him in frenzied celebration.

And on July 4, 1826—the fiftieth anniversary of the adoption of the Declaration of Independence—an event occurred which to many seemed to confirm that the United States was a nation specially chosen by God. On that special day, Americans were to learn, two of the greatest of the country's founders and former presidents—Thomas Jefferson, author of the Declaration, and John Adams, "its ablest advocate and defender" (as Jefferson had said)—died within hours of each other. Jefferson's last words, those at his bedside reported, were "Is it the Fourth?" And Adams comforted those around him moments before his death by saying, "Thomas Jefferson still survives."

For a time, it was possible for many Americans to overlook the very different forms their nationalism took—and to ignore the large elements of their population who were excluded from the national self–definition altogether. But the vigorous economic and territorial expansion this exuberant nationalism produced ultimately brought those differences to the fore.

STABILIZING ECONOMIC GROWTH

The end of the War of 1812 allowed the United States to resume the economic growth and territorial expansion that, despite the Republicans' aspirations, had characterized the first decade of the nineteenth century. A vigorous postwar boom led to a disastrous bust in 1819. Brief though it was, the collapse was evidence that the United States continued to lack some of the basic institutions necessary to sustain long-term growth.

Banking, Currency, and Protection

The War of 1812 may have stimulated the growth of manufactures. But it also produced chaos in shipping and banking, and it exposed dramatically the inadequacy of the existing transportation and financial systems. The aftermath of the war, therefore, saw the emergence of a series of political issues connected with national economic development: reestablishing the Bank of the United States (the first Bank's charter had expired in 1811, and Congress had declined to renew it), protecting the new industries, and providing a nationwide network of roads and waterways.

THE UNITED STATES CAPITOL IN 1824
The slightly idealized view by the American artist Charles Burton shows the approach to the west front of the United States Capitol along Pennsylvania Avenue. The large, columned rotunda that today rises above the building was built in the 1860s to replace the simpler dome shown in this painting. Other later additions include the two wings containing the present chambers of the Senate and the House of Representatives. *(Metropolitan Museum of Art)*

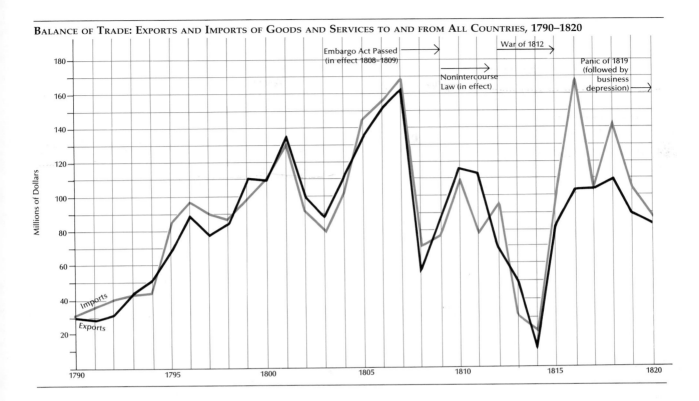

BALANCE OF TRADE: EXPORTS AND IMPORTS OF GOODS AND SERVICES TO AND FROM ALL COUNTRIES, 1790–1820

The wartime experience underlined the need for another national bank. After the expiration of the first Bank's charter, a large number of state banks had begun operations. They issued vast quantities of bank notes but did not always bother to retain a large enough reserve of gold or silver to redeem the notes on demand. The notes passed from hand to hand more or less as money, but their actual value depended on the reputation of the bank that issued them. Thus there was a wide variety of notes, of widely differing value, in circulation at the same time. The result was a confusion that made honest business difficult and counterfeiting easy.

Congress struck at the currency problem by chartering a second Bank of the United States in 1816. It was essentially the same institution Hamilton had founded in 1791 except that it had more capital than its predecessor. The national bank could not forbid state banks from issuing notes, but its size and power enabled it to dominate the state banks. It could compel them to issue only sound notes or risk being forced out of business.

Congress also acted to assist the burgeoning manufacturing capacity of the nation's economy, which the war (by cutting off imports) had greatly stimulated. Manufactured goods had been so scarce during the conflict that, even with comparatively unskilled labor and inexperienced management, new factories could start operations virtually assured of quick profits.

The American textile industry had experienced a particularly dramatic growth. The first census of manufacturing, in 1810, revealed 269 cotton and 24 woolen mills in the country. But the Embargo of 1807 and the War of 1812 had spurred a tremendous expansion. Between 1807 and 1815, the total number of cotton spindles increased more than fifteenfold, from 8,000 to 130,000. Until 1814, the textile factories—most of them in New England—produced only yarn and thread; families operating handlooms at home did the actual weaving of cloth. Then the Boston merchant Francis Cabot Lowell, after examining textile machinery in England, developed a power loom better than its English counterpart. In 1813, Lowell organized the Boston Manufacturing Company and, at Waltham, Massachusetts, founded the first mill in America to carry on the processes of spinning and weaving under a single roof. Lowell's company was an important step in revolutionizing American manufacturing. (See p. 286.)

But the end of the war suddenly dimmed the prospects for American industry. British ships—determined to recapture their lost markets—swarmed into American ports and unloaded cargoes of manufactured goods, many priced below cost. As Lord Brougham explained to Parliament, it was "well worth while to incur a loss upon the first exportation, in order, by the glut, to stifle in the cradle those rising manufactures in the United States, which war had forced into existence, contrary to the natural course of things." The "infant industries" cried out for protection against these tactics, arguing that they needed time to grow strong enough to withstand the foreign competition.

In 1816, protectionists in Congress won passage of a tariff law that effectively limited competition from abroad on a wide range of items, among the most important of which was cotton cloth. There were objec-

tions from agricultural interests, who stood to pay higher prices for manufactured goods. But the nationalist dream of creating an important American industrial economy prevailed.

Transportation

The nation's most pressing economic need in the aftermath of the war, however, was for improvements in its transportation system. Without a better transportation network, manufacturers would not have access to the raw materials they needed and would not be able to send their finished goods to markets. So an old debate resumed: Should the federal government help to finance roads and other "internal improvements"?

DECK LIFE ON THE *PARAGON*, 1811–1812
The *North River Steamboat Clermont*, launched in 1806 by the inventor Robert Fulton and propelled by an engine he had developed, traveled from Manhattan to Albany (about 150 miles) in thirty-two hours. That was neither the longest nor the fastest voyage to date, but the *Clermont* proved to be the first steam-powered vessel large enough and reliable enough to be commercially valuable. Within a few years Fulton and his partner Robert R. Livingston had several steamboats operating profitably around New York. The third vessel in their fleet, the *Paragon,* shown here in a painting by the Russian diplomat and artist Pavel Petrovich Svinin, could carry 150 people and contained an elegant dining salon fitted with bronze, mahogany, and mirrors. Svinin called it "a whole floating town," and Fulton told a friend that the *Paragon* "beats everything on the globe, for made as you and I are we cannot tell what is in the moon." *(Metropolitan Museum of Art)*

The idea of using government funds to finance road building was not a new one. When Ohio entered the Union in 1803, the federal government agreed that part of the proceeds from the sale of public lands there should finance road construction. And in 1807, Jefferson's secretary of the treasury, Albert Gallatin, proposed that revenues from the Ohio land sales help finance a National Road from the Potomac River to the Ohio. Both Congress and the president had approved. Work on the new roads did not begin until 1811 (partly because of Jefferson's doubts about the constitutionality of such expenditures). Finally, however, construction of the National Road began at Cumberland, Maryland, on the Potomac; and by 1818, this highway—with a crushed stone surface and massive stone bridges—ran as far as Wheeling, Virginia, on the Ohio River. Meanwhile the state of Pennsylvania gave $100,000 to a private company to extend the Lancaster pike westward to Pittsburgh.

Over both of these roads a heavy traffic soon moved: stagecoaches, Conestoga wagons, private carriages, and other vehicles, as well as droves of cattle. Despite high tolls, the roads made transportation costs across the mountains lower than ever before—too high still to permit the long-distance hauling of such bulky loads as wheat or flour, but low enough to justify transporting commodities with a high value in proportion to their weight. Manufactures moved from the Atlantic seaboard to the Ohio Valley in unprecedented quantities.

At the same time, on the rivers and the Great Lakes, steam-powered shipping was expanding rapidly. The development of steamboat lines was already well under way before the War of 1812, thanks to the technological advances introduced by Robert Fulton and others. The war had retarded expansion of the system for a time, but by 1816, river steamers were beginning to journey up and down the Mississippi to the Ohio River, and up the Ohio as far as Pittsburgh. Within a few years, steamboats were carrying far more cargo on the Mississippi than all the earlier forms of river transport—flatboats, barges, and others—combined. They stimulated the agricultural economy of the West and the South, by providing much readier access to markets at greatly reduced cost. And they enabled eastern manufacturers to send their finished goods west much more readily.

But despite the progress with steamboats and turnpikes, there remained serious gaps in the nation's transportation network, as experience during the War of 1812 had shown. Once the British blockade cut off Atlantic shipping, the coastal roads became choked by the unaccustomed volume of north-south traffic. Long lines of wagons waited for a chance to use the ferries that were still the only means of crossing most rivers. Oxcarts, pressed into emergency service, took six or seven weeks to go from Philadelphia to Charleston. In some areas there were serious shortages of goods that normally traveled by sea, and prices rose to new heights. Rice cost three times as much in New York as in Charleston, flour three times as much in Boston as in Richmond—all because of the difficulty of transportation. There were military consequences, too. On the northern and western frontiers, the absence of good roads had frustrated American campaigns.

In 1815, with this wartime experience in mind, President Madison called the attention of Congress to the "great importance of establishing throughout our country the roads and canals which can be best executed under the national authority," and suggested that a constitutional amendment would resolve any doubts about Congress's authority to provide for their construction. Representative John C. Calhoun promptly introduced a bill that would have used the funds owed the government by the Bank of the United States to finance internal improvements. "Let us, then, bind

FORT SNELLING
This is an 1838 sketch of Fort Snelling (at the juncture of the Minnesota and Mississippi Rivers), containing instructions for reaching it from St. Louis. It was one of a string of fortifications built along the western edges of European settlement along the Great Lakes and the upper Mississippi in the first three decades of the nineteenth century. They were designed to protect the new white communities from hostile Indians. Fort Snelling stands today in Minnesota as a "living history" site. *(Minnesota Historical Society)*

the republic together with a perfect system of roads and canals," Calhoun urged. "Let us conquer space."

Congress passed Calhoun's internal improvements bill, but President Madison, on his last day in office (March 3, 1817), vetoed it. He supported the purpose of the bill, he explained, but he still believed that Congress lacked authority to fund the improvements without a constitutional amendment. And so on the issue of internal improvements, at least, the nationalists fell short of their goals. It remained for state governments and private enterprise to undertake the tremendous task of building the transportation network necessary for the growing American economy.

EXPANDING WESTWARD

One reason for the growing interest in internal improvements was the sudden and dramatic surge in westward expansion in the years following the War of 1812. "Old America seems to be breaking up and moving westward," wrote an English observer at the time. By the time of the census of 1820, white settlers had pushed well beyond the Mississippi River, and the population of the western regions was increasing more rapidly than that of the nation as a whole. Almost one of every four white Americans lived west of the Appalachians in 1820; ten years before, only one in seven had resided there.

The Great Migration

The westward movement of the white American population was one of the most important developments of the century. It had a profound effect on the nation's economy, bringing vast new regions into the emerging capitalist system. It had great political ramifications, which ultimately became a major factor in the coming of the Civil War. And like earlier movements west, it thrust peoples of different cultures and traditions into intimate association with one another—with effects that were ultimately disastrous for some, but important on all sides. There were several important reasons for this expansion. Population pressures and economic pressures pushed many Americans from the East; the availability of new lands and the decline of Indian resistance drew them to the West.

The pressures driving white Americans out of the East came in part from the continued growth of the nation's population—both through natural increase and through immigration. Between 1800 and 1820, the population nearly doubled—from 5.3 million to 9.6 mil-

lion. The growth of cities absorbed some of that increase, but most Americans were still farmers. The agricultural lands of the East were by now largely occupied, and some of them were exhausted. In the South, the spread of the plantation system, and of a slave labor force, limited opportunities for new settlers.

Meanwhile, the West itself was becoming increasingly attractive to white settlers. The War of 1812 had helped diminish (although it did not wholly eliminate) one of the traditional deterrents to western expansion: Indian opposition. And in the aftermath of the war, the federal government continued its policy of pushing the remaining tribes farther and farther west. A series of treaties in 1815 wrested more land from the Indians. In the meantime, the government was erecting a chain of stockaded forts along the Great Lakes and the upper Mississippi, to protect the frontier. It also created a "factor" system, by which government factors (or agents) supplied the Indians with goods at cost. This not only worked to drive Canadian traders out of the region, it also helped create a situation of dependency that made the Indians themselves easier to control.

Now that fertile lands were secure for white settlement, migrants from throughout the East flocked to what was then known as the Old Northwest (now part of the Midwest). The Ohio and Monongahela Rivers were the main routes westward, until the completion of the Erie Canal in 1825. The pioneers reached the river by traveling along the turnpike to Pittsburgh or along the National Road to Wheeling, or by sailing down one of its tributaries—such as the Kanawha, the Cumberland, or the Tennessee. Once on the Ohio, they floated downstream on flatboats bearing all their possessions, then left the river (often at Cincinnati, which was becoming one of the region's—and the nation's—principal cities) and pressed on overland with wagons, handcarts, packhorses, cattle, and hogs.

White Settlers in the Old Northwest

Having arrived at their destination, preferably in the spring or early summer, most settlers built lean-tos or cabins, then hewed clearings out of the forest and put in crops of corn to supplement the wild game they caught and the domestic animals they had brought with them. It was a rough existence, plagued by loneliness, poverty, dirt, and disease. Men, women, and children worked side by side in the fields—and at times had virtually no contact for weeks or months at a time with anyone outside their own families.

Life in the western territories was not, however, as solitary and individualistic as later myth suggested. Migrants often journeyed westward in groups, and

THE RENDEZVOUS
The annual rendezvous of fur trappers and traders was a major event in the lives of the lonely men who made their livelihoods gathering furs. It was also a gathering of representatives of the many cultures that mingled in the Far West, among them Anglo-Americans, French Canadians, Indians, and Hispanics. *(Denver Public Library)*

sometimes stayed together, formed new communities, and built schools, churches, stores, and other institutions. The labor shortage in the interior led neighbors to develop systems of mutual aid, gathering periodically to raise a barn, clear land, harvest crops, or make quilts. Gradually, the settlers built a thriving farm economy based largely on family units of modest size and committed to the cultivation of grain and the raising of livestock.

Another common feature of life in the Northwest (and indeed in much of early-nineteenth-century America) was mobility. Individuals and families were constantly on the move, settling for a few years in one place, then selling their land (often at a significant profit, given the rapidly rising price of farm properties in the region) and settling again somewhere else. When new areas for settlement opened farther to the west, it was often the people already on the western

edges of white settlement—rather than those who remained in the East—who flocked to them first.

The Plantation System in the Southwest

In the Southwest, the new agricultural economy emerged along different lines—just as the economy of the Old South had long been different from that of the Northeast. The principal attraction there was cotton. The cotton lands in the uplands of the Old South had lost much of their fertility through overplanting and erosion. But the market for cotton continued to grow, and so there was no lack of ambitious farmers seeking fresh soil in a climate suitable for the crop. In the Southwest, around the end of the Appalachian range, stretched a broad zone within which cotton could thrive. That zone included what was to become known as the Black Belt of central Alabama and Mississippi, a vast prairie with a dark, productive soil of rotted limestone.

The advance of southern settlement meant the spread of cotton, plantations, and slavery. The first arrivals in an uncultivated region were usually ordinary people like the settlers farther north, small farmers who made rough clearings in the forest. But wealthier planters soon followed. They bought up the cleared or partially cleared land, while the original settlers moved farther west and started over again.

The large planters made the westward journey in a style quite different from that of the first pioneers. Over the alternately dusty and muddy roads came great caravans consisting of herds of livestock, wagonloads of household goods, long lines of slaves, and—bringing up the rear—the planter's family riding in carriages. Success in the wilderness was by no means assured, even for the wealthiest settlers. But many planters soon expanded small clearings into vast cotton fields. They replaced the cabins of the early pioneers with more sumptuous log dwellings and ultimately with imposing mansions that demonstrated the rise of a newly rich class.

The rapid growth of the Northwest and Southwest resulted in the admission of four new states to the Union in the immediate aftermath of the War of 1812: Indiana in 1816, Mississippi in 1817, Illinois in 1818, and Alabama in 1819.

Trade and Trapping in the Far West

Not many Anglo-Americans yet knew much about or were much interested in the far western areas of the continent. But a significant trade nevertheless began to develop between these western regions and the United States early in the nineteenth century, and it grew steadily for decades.

Mexico, which continued to control Texas, California, and much of the rest of the Southwest, won its independence from Spain in 1821. Almost immediately, it opened its northern territories to trade with the United States, hoping to revive an economy that had grown stagnant during the war with Spain. American traders poured into the region—overland into Texas and New Mexico, by sea into California. Merchants from the United States quickly displaced Indian traders who had dominated trade with Mexico in some areas of the Southwest. They also displaced some of the same Mexicans who had hoped this new commerce would improve their fortunes. In New Mexico, for example, the Missouri trader William Becknell began in 1821 to offer American manufactured goods for sale, priced considerably below the inferior Mexican goods that had dominated the market in the past. Mexico effectively lost its markets in its own colony, and a steady traffic of commercial wagon trains was moving back and forth along the Santa Fe Trail between Missouri and New Mexico.

Becknell and those who followed him diverted an established trade from Mexico to the United States. But fur traders created a wholly new commerce with the West. Before the War of 1812, John Jacob Astor's American Fur Company had established Astoria as a trading post at the mouth of the Columbia River in Oregon. But when the war came, Astor sold his suddenly imperiled interests to the Northwestern Fur Company, a British concern operating out of Canada; and after the war he centered his own operations in the Great Lakes area, from which he eventually extended them westward to the Rockies. Other companies carried on operations up the Missouri and its tributaries and into the Rocky Mountains.

At first, fur traders did most of their business by purchasing pelts from the Indians. But increasingly, white trappers entered the region and began to hunt beaver on their own. Substantial numbers of Anglo-Americans and French Canadians moved deep into the Great Lakes region and beyond to join the Iroquois and other Indians in pursuit of furs.

The trappers, or "mountain men," who began trading in and exploring the Far West were, without knowing it, the first wedge of a white movement into those lands that would ultimately dominate the region and transform it. But even in small numbers, they were developing important relationships with the existing residents of the West—Indian and Mexican—and altering the character of society there. White trappers were almost without exception relatively young single men. Not surprisingly, many of them entered into sexual relationships with Indian and Mexican women. They also recruited them as helpers in the difficult work of preparing furs and skins for trading. Perhaps two-thirds of the white trappers married Indian or Hispanic women while living in the West, and their marriages (according to one study) lasted an average of fifteen years and produced an average of three children.

As the trappers moved west from the Great Lakes region, they began to establish themselves in what is now Utah and in parts of New Mexico. In 1822, Andrew and William Ashley founded the Rocky Mountain Fur Company and recruited white trappers to move permanently into the Rockies in search of furs, which were becoming increasingly scarce farther east. The Ashleys dispatched supplies annually to their trappers in exchange for furs and skins. The arrival of the supply train became the occasion for a gathering of scores of mountain men, some of whom lived much of the year in considerable isolation.

But however isolated their daily lives, these mountain men were closely bound up with the expanding market economy of the United States. Some were employees of the Rocky Mountain Company (or some other, similar enterprise), earning a salary in return for providing a steady supply of furs. Others were nominally independent but relied on the companies for credit; they were almost always in debt and hence economically bound to the companies. Some trapped entirely on their own and simply sold their furs for cash, but they too depended on merchants from the East for their livelihoods. And it was to those merchants that the bulk of the profits from the trade flowed.

Many trappers and mountain men lived peacefully and successfully with the Indians and Mexicans whose lands they came to share. But some did not. Jedediah S. Smith, a trapper who became an Ashley partner, founded his own fur company to profit from trade in the northern Rockies in 1826. He also led a series of forays deep into Mexican territory that ended in disastrous battles with the Mojaves and other tribes. He escaped from an 1827 expedition to Oregon, in which sixteen members of his party of twenty died. Four years later, he set out for New Mexico and was killed by Comanches, who took the weapons he was carrying and sold them to Mexican settlers.

Eastern Images of the West

Americans in the East were only dimly aware of the world the trappers were entering and helping to reshape. Smith and others became the source of dramatic (and often exaggerated) popular stories. But the trappers themselves did not often write of their lives or draw maps of the lands they explored.

More important in increasing eastern awareness of the West were explorers, many of them dispatched by the United States government with instructions to chart the territories they visited. In 1819 and 1820, with instructions from the War Department to find the sources of the Red River, Stephen H. Long led nineteen soldiers on a journey up the Platte and South Platte Rivers through what is now Nebraska and eastern Colorado (where he discovered the peak that would be named for him), and then returned eastward along the Arkansas River through what is now Kansas. He failed to find the headwaters of the Red River. But he wrote an influential report on his trip, including an assessment of the region's potential for future settlement and development which echoed the dismissive conclusions of Zebulon Pike fifteen years before. "In regard to this extensive section of country between the Missouri River and the Rocky Mountains," Long wrote, "we do not hesitate in giving the opinion that it is almost wholly unfit for cultivation, and of course uninhabitable by a people depending upon agriculture for their subsistence." On the published map of his ex-

THE INAUGURATION OF JAMES MONROE, 1817
Monroe was the last president of the "Virginia Dynasty," which produced four of the first five presidents and occupied the White House for thirty-two of the first thirty-six years of the government under the Constitution. Monroe entered office on a wave of good feeling. By the time he left office in 1825, to be succeeded by John Quincy Adams (the son of the only non-Virginian to have held the presidency), political rivalries were growing intense and bitter. *(Bettmann)*

pedition, he labeled the Great Plains the "Great American Desert."

THE "ERA OF GOOD FEELINGS"

The expansion of the economy, the growth of white settlement and trade in the West, the creation of new states—all reflected the rising spirit of nationalism that was permeating the United States in the years following the War of 1812. That spirit found reflection, for a time, in the course of American politics. Whatever divisions and disagreements existed within American society found little expression in the nation's political life in these years. Party competition virtually disappeared; James Monroe, who became president in 1817, was elected twice almost by acclamation. Many Americans celebrated the arrival of an "Era of Good Feelings."

But beneath this surface calm, serious social and political divisions remained that, inevitably, intruded into the nation's public life. Indeed, the years of Monroe's presidency became in the end a time of very bad feelings—a time in which the dream of a harmonious republic unsullied by party and faction was shattered forever.

The End of the First Party System

Ever since 1800, the presidency seemed to have been the special possession of Virginians, passing from one to another in unvarying sequence. After two terms in office Jefferson named his secretary of state, James Madison, to succeed him; and after two more terms, Madison secured the presidential nomination for his secretary of state, James Monroe. Many in the North were expressing impatience with the so-called Virginia Dynasty, but the Republicans had no difficulty electing their candidate in the listless campaign of 1816. Monroe received 183 ballots in the electoral college; his Federalist opponent, Rufus King of New York, only 34—from Massachusetts, Connecticut, and Delaware.

Monroe was sixty-one years old when he became president, and he seemed in many respects a relic of an earlier age. Tall and dignified, he wore such old-fashioned garb as knee-length pantaloons and white-topped boots. In the course of his long and varied career, he had served as a soldier in the Revolution, as a diplomat, and most recently as a cabinet officer. He had once seemed an impulsive man, but he was now widely admired for his caution and patience.

Monroe entered office under what seemed to be remarkably favorable circumstances. With the decline of the Federalists, his party faced no serious opposition. With the conclusion of the War of 1812, the nation faced no important international threats. American politicians had dreamed since the first days of the republic of a time in which partisan divisions and factional disputes might come to an end, a time in which the nation might learn to exhibit the harmony and virtue that the founders had envisioned. The prosperity of the postwar years seemed to make that harmony possible. Monroe attempted to use his office to realize that dream.

He made that desire clear, above all, in the selection of his cabinet. For secretary of state, he chose the New Englander and former Federalist John Quincy Adams. Jefferson, Madison, and Monroe had all served as secretary of state before becoming president; Adams therefore immediately became the heir apparent, suggesting that the "Virginia Dynasty" would soon come to an end. He named John C. Calhoun of South Carolina his secretary of war. And in his other appointments, Monroe seemed to go out of his way to include both northerners and southerners, Federalists and Republicans—to harmonize the various interests and sections of the country in a government of national unity.

Soon after his inauguration, Monroe did what no other president since Washington had done: he made a goodwill tour through the country, eastward to New England, westward as far as Detroit. In New England, so recently the scene of rabid Federalist discontent, he was greeted everywhere with enthusiastic demonstrations. The *Columbian Centinel*, a Federalist newspaper in Boston, commenting on the "Presidential Jubilee" in that city, observed that an "era of good feelings" had arrived. This phrase soon spread throughout the country and became a popular label for Monroe's presidency.

On the surface, at least, it was indeed an "era of good feelings," of happy national unity. In 1820, when Monroe ran for reelection, only one elector voted against him, and he did so to ensure that Washington would remain the only unanimously elected president. For all practical purposes, the Federalist Party, which did not even offer a candidate that year, had ceased to exist. The first party system had come to an end.

John Quincy Adams and Florida

Monroe's secretary of state, John Quincy Adams, was the most important member of the cabinet. Like his father, the second president of the United States, Adams had spent much of his life in diplomatic service. He had represented the United States in Britain, Russia, the Netherlands, and Prussia. He had helped negotiate the Treaty of Ghent. And he had demonstrated in all his assignments a calmness and firmness that made him one of the great diplomats in American history.

He was also a committed nationalist, and when he assumed the office of secretary of state, he considered his most important task to be the promotion of American expansion. His first major challenge was Florida. The United States had already annexed West Florida, but most Americans still believed the nation should gain possession of the entire peninsula. Even the claim to West Florida was under dispute. Spain still claimed the whole of the province, east and west, and actually occupied most of it. In 1817, Adams began negotiations with the Spanish minister, Luis de Onís, in hopes of resolving the dispute and gaining the entire colony for the United States.

In the meantime, however, events were taking their own course in Florida itself. Andrew Jackson, now in command of American troops along the Florida frontier, had orders from Secretary of War Calhoun to "adopt the necessary measures" to put a stop to the continuing raids on American territory by the Seminole Indians south of the Florida border. Jackson (with, he later claimed, tacit encouragement from Washington) used those orders as an excuse to invade Florida, seize the Spanish forts at St. Marks and Pensacola, and order the hanging of two British subjects on the charge of supplying the Indians and inciting them to hostilities.

Instead of condemning or disavowing Jackson's raid, Adams urged the government to assume complete responsibility for it, because he saw it as a chance to win an important advantage in his negotiations with Spain. The United States, he told the Spanish, had the right under international law to defend itself against threats from across its borders. Since Spain was unwilling or unable to curb those threats, America had simply done what was necessary. And he implied that the nation might consider even more drastic action in the future.

Jackson's raid had demonstrated to the Spanish that the United States could easily take Florida by force. Onís realized, therefore, that he had little choice but to come to terms with the Americans. Under the terms of the Adams-Onís Treaty of 1819, the United States gave up its claims to Texas, but Spain gave up much more in return: all of Florida, and all of its possessions in the Pacific Northwest. Adams and Onís had concluded something more than a Florida agreement; it was a "transcontinental treaty."

The Panic of 1819

But the Monroe administration had little time to revel in its diplomatic successes. At the same time that Adams was completing his negotiations with Onís, the nation was falling victim to a serious economic crisis that helped revive many of the political disputes that the "era of good feelings" had presumably settled.

The Panic of 1819 followed a period of high foreign demand for American farm goods (a result of the disruption of European agriculture by the Napoleonic Wars) and thus of exceptionally high prices for American farmers. The rising prices for farm goods had stimulated a land boom in the western United States. Fueled by speculative investments, land prices soared well above the government-established minimum of $2 an acre; some land in the Black Belt of Alabama and Mississippi went for $100 an acre and more.

The availability of easy credit to settlers and speculators—from the government (under the land acts of 1800 and 1804), from state banks and wildcat banks, even for a time from the rechartered Bank of the United States—fueled the land boom. Beginning in 1819, however, new management at the national bank began tightening credit, calling in loans, and foreclosing mortgages. The new governors of the Bank also collected state bank notes and demanded payment in cash

from the banks, many of which could not meet the demand, and hence failed. These bank failures launched a financial panic, which many Americans, particularly those in the West, blamed on the Bank of the United States. Thus began a process that would eventually make the Bank's existence one of the nation's most burning political issues.

Six years of depression followed. Prices for both manufactured goods and agricultural produce fell rapidly. Manufacturers secured passage of a new tariff in 1824 to protect them from foreign competition. Indebted farmers won some relief through the land law of 1820 and the relief act of 1821, which lowered the price of land and reduced existing debts while extending their payment schedules.

Some Americans saw the Panic of 1819 and the widespread distress that followed as a warning that rapid economic growth and territorial expansion would destabilize the nation and threaten its survival. But by 1820 most Americans were irrevocably committed to such growth and expansion. And public debate in the future would revolve less around whether such growth was good or bad than how to encourage and control it. That debate, which the Panic of 1819 did much to encourage, created new factional divisions within the Republican party and ultimately brought the era of nonpartisanship—the "era of good feelings"—to an acrimonious end.

SECTIONALISM AND NATIONALISM

For a brief but alarming moment in 1819–1820, the increasing differences between the nation's two leading sections threatened the unity of the United States. But the Missouri Compromise averted a sectional crisis for a time. The forces of nationalism continued to assert themselves, and the federal government began to assume the role of promoter of economic growth.

The Missouri Compromise

When Missouri applied for admission to the Union as a state in 1819, slavery was already well established there. The French and Spanish inhabitants of the Louisiana Territory (including what became Missouri) had owned slaves, and in the Louisiana Purchase treaty of 1803 the American government promised to protect the human property of the inhabitants. By 1819, approximately 60,000 people resided in Missouri Territory, of whom about 10,000 were slaves.

THE MISSOURI COMPROMISE, 1820

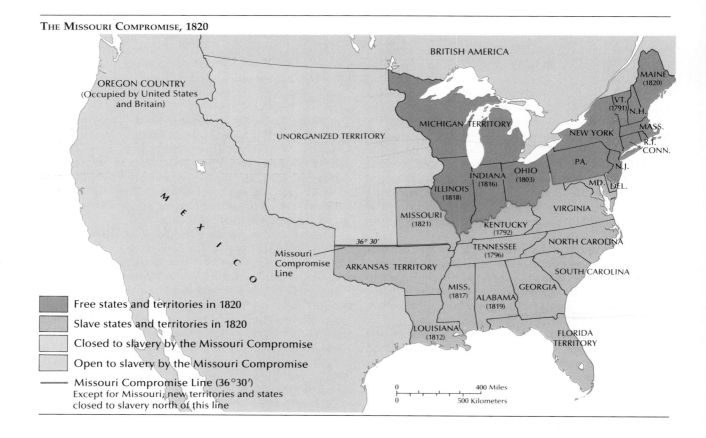

Even so, Representative James Tallmadge, Jr., of New York, proposed an amendment to the Missouri statehood bill to prohibit the further introduction of slaves into Missouri and to provide for the gradual emancipation of those already there. The Tallmadge Amendment provoked a controversy that was to rage for the next two years.

Since the beginning of the republic, partly by chance and partly by design, new states had entered the Union more or less in pairs, one from the North, another from the South. In 1819, there were eleven free states and eleven slave states; the admission of Missouri would upset that balance and establish a precedent that in the future might increase the political power of one section over another. Hence the interest of both the North and the South in the question of slavery and freedom in Missouri.

To some degree, the battle over Missouri reflected concern about slavery itself. In both the North and the South, there were groups opposed to slavery on moral grounds and committed to its destruction. On the eve of the dispute over Missouri, for example, the Manumission Society of New York was busy with attempts

to rescue runaway slaves; and Quakers were conducting a campaign to strengthen the laws against the African slave trade and to protect free blacks from kidnappers who sold them into slavery.

Northern opposition to slavery also reflected political interests. Most northern critics of slavery were affluent philanthropists and reformers associated with the Federalist Party, and for many of them, the Missouri controversy seemed to provide the opportunity some Federalist leaders had long awaited: the opportunity to revive and reinvigorate their party. In New York, the De Witt Clinton faction of the Republicans, who had joined with the Federalists in opposition to the War of 1812 and were outspoken in their hostility to "Virginia influence" and "Southern rule," were more than willing to cooperate with the Federalists again. The cry against slavery in Missouri, Thomas Jefferson wrote, was "a mere party trick." He explained: "[Rufus] King [a leading Federalist] is ready to risk the union for any chance of restoring his party to power and wriggling himself to the head of it, nor is Clinton without his hopes nor scrupulous as to the means of fulfilling them."

Complicating the Missouri question was the application of Maine (previously the northern part of Massachusetts) for admission as a new state. Speaker of the House Henry Clay informed northern members that if they blocked Missouri from entering the union as a slave state, southerners would block the admission of Maine. But Maine ultimately offered a way out of the impasse, when the Senate agreed to combine the Maine and Missouri proposals into a single bill. Maine would be admitted as a free state, Missouri as a slave state. Then Senator Jesse B. Thomas of Illinois proposed an amendment prohibiting slavery in the rest of the Louisiana Purchase territory north of the southern boundary of Missouri. The Senate adopted the Thomas Amendment, and Speaker Clay, although with great difficulty, guided the amended Maine-Missouri bill through the House.

Nationalists in both North and South hailed the Missouri Compromise as a happy resolution of a danger to the Union. Others were less optimistic. Thomas Jefferson, for example, saw in the controversy a "speck on our horizon" which might ultimately "burst on us as a tornado." And he added, "The line of division lately marked out between the different portions of our confederacy is such as will never, I fear, be obliterated." (That was one reason why Jefferson, who for all his reservations about slavery was a defender of the South's social and economic systems, devoted so much attention in his last years to the construction of the University of Virginia. It was an institution that would, he hoped, confirm southern students in the values of their own region and protect them against the taint of "anti-Missourianism" that he believed pervaded the northern universities.) The debate over Missouri had, in short, revealed a strong undercurrent of sectionalism that was competing with—although at the moment failing to derail—the powerful tides of nationalism.

Marshall and the Court

John Marshall served as chief justice of the United States for almost thirty-five years, from 1801 to 1835, and he dominated the Court as no one else before or since. Republican presidents filled vacancies with one after another Republican justice. But so influential was Marshall with his colleagues that he continued to carry a majority with him in most of the Court's decisions. More than anyone but the framers themselves, he molded the development of the Constitution: strengthening the judicial branch at the expense of the executive and legislative branches; increasing the power of the federal government at the expense of the states; and advancing the interests of the propertied and commercial classes.

John Marshall
Marshall became Chief Justice of the United States Supreme Court in 1801 after establishing himself as one of the leaders of the Federalist Party. He served as Chief Justice for thirty-five years, longer than anyone else in American history. And despite the frequent opposition of a series of Republican presidents, he used his position to make the judiciary a vigorous instrument for asserting and strengthening American nationalism. *(Boston Athenaeum)*

On the whole, though, concern about slavery itself—whether driven by moral or political concerns—was secondary to concerns about the economic competition between North and South for the western territories. The plantation system of the South and the free-labor system of the North had already taken very different forms; the futures of those systems seemed to depend in part on which of them prevailed in the West.

Committed to promoting commerce, the Marshall Court firmly strengthened the inviolability of contracts as a cornerstone of American law. In *Fletcher* v. *Peck* (1810), which arose out of a series of notorious land frauds in Georgia, the Court had to decide whether the Georgia legislature of 1796 could rightfully repeal the act of the previous legislature granting lands under shady circumstances to the Yazoo Land Companies. In a unanimous decision, Marshall held that a land grant was a valid contract and could not be repealed even if corruption was involved.

Dartmouth College v. *Woodward* (1819) further expanded the meaning of the contract clause of the Constitution. Having gained control of the New Hampshire state government, Republicans tried to revise Dartmouth's charter (granted by King George III in 1769) to convert the private college into a state university. The trustees were represented before the Court by Daniel Webster, a Dartmouth graduate. The Court, he reminded the judges, had decided in *Fletcher* v. *Peck* that "a grant is a contract." The Dartmouth charter, he went on, "is embraced within the very terms of that decision," since "a grant of corporate powers and privileges is as much a contract as a grant of land." Then, according to legend, he brought the justices to tears with an irrelevant passage that concluded: "It is, sir, . . . a small college. And yet there are those who love it." The Court ruled for Dartmouth, stating that the legislature had unconstitutionally violated the college's contract. By proclaiming that corporation charters were contracts and that contracts were inviolable, the decision also placed important restrictions on the ability of state governments to control corporations.

In overturning not only the act of the legislature but the decisions of New Hampshire courts, the *Dartmouth College* case also claimed for the Supreme Court the right to override the decisions of state courts. But some advocates of states' rights, notably in the South, continued to challenge its right to do so. In *Cohens* v. *Virginia* (1821), Marshall explicitly affirmed the constitutionality of federal review of state court decisions. The states had given up part of their sovereignty in ratifying the Constitution, he explained, and their courts must submit to federal jurisdiction; otherwise the federal government would be prostrated "at the feet of every state in the Union."

Meanwhile, in *McCulloch* v. *Maryland* (1819), Marshall confirmed the "implied powers" of Congress by upholding the constitutionality of the Bank of the United States. The Bank had become so unpopular in the South and the West that several of the states tried to drive branches out of business by outright prohibition or by confiscatory taxes. This case presented two constitutional questions to the Supreme Court: Could Congress charter a bank? And if so, could individual states ban it or tax it? Daniel Webster, one of the Bank's attorneys, argued that establishing such an institution came within the "necessary and proper" clause of the Constitution and added that the power to tax involved a "power to destroy." If the states could tax the Bank at all, they could tax it to death. Marshall adopted Webster's words in deciding for the Bank.

In the case of *Gibbons* v. *Ogden* (1824), the Court strengthened Congress's power to regulate interstate commerce. The state of New York had granted Robert Fulton and Robert Livingston's steamboat company the exclusive right to carry passengers on the Hudson River to New York City. Fulton and Livingston then gave Aaron Ogden the business of carrying passengers across the river between New York and New Jersey. But Thomas Gibbons, with a license granted under an act of Congress, began competing with Ogden for the ferry traffic. Ogden brought suit against him and won in the New York courts. When Gibbons appealed to the Supreme Court, the justices faced two questions: Did "commerce," as defined by the Constitution's commerce clause, include navigation? And did Congress alone or Congress and the states together have the authority to regulate interstate commerce? Marshall replied that "commerce" was a broad term embracing navigation as well as the buying and selling of goods, and he claimed that the power of Congress to regulate such commerce was "complete in itself" and might be "exercised to its utmost extent." Ogden's state-granted monopoly, therefore, was void.

The lasting significance of *Gibbons* v. *Ogden* was that it freed transportation systems from restraints by the states and helped pave the way for unfettered capitalist growth. But its more immediate effect was to head off a movement to weaken the Supreme Court. Influential Republicans, mostly from the South and the West, were arguing that the Marshall Court was not merely interpreting the Constitution but illegitimately changing it. In Congress, they proposed measures to curb its power. One Kentucky senator suggested making the Senate, not the Court, the agency to decide the constitutionality of state laws and to settle interstate disputes. Other members introduced bills to increase the size of the Court (from seven to ten justices) and to require more than a simple majority to declare a state law unconstitutional. Still others argued for "codification": for making legislative statutes the basis of the law, rather than the accumulation of precedent that judges used. Such a reform, codifiers argued, would limit the power of the judiciary and prevent "judge-made" law. The Court reformers failed to pass any of their measures, and after *Gibbons* v. *Ogden*, with its popular stand against monopoly power, hostility to the judicial branch of the government gradually died down.

Gibbons v Ogden → trade
McCulloch v Maryland → Bank
Fletcher v Peck → land grants

CHEROKEE LEADERS
Sequoyah (who also used the name George Guess) was a mixed-blood Cherokee who translated his tribe's language into writing through an elaborate syllabary of his own invention, pictured here. He opposed Indian assimilation into white society and saw the preservation of the Cherokee language as a way to protect the culture of his tribe. He moved to Arkansas in the 1820s and became a chief of the western Cherokee tribes. Major George Lowery, shown on the right, was also a mixed-blood Cherokee and served as assistant principal chief of the Cherokee from 1828 to 1838. He supported acculturation but remained a Cherokee nationalist. He wears a U.S. presidential medal around his neck. (Left, *National Anthropological Archives, Smithsonian;* Right, *Gilcrease Institute*)

The decisions of the Marshall Court established the primacy of the federal government over the states in regulating the economy and opened the way for an increased federal role in promoting economic growth. They protected corporations and other private economic institutions from local government interference. They were, in short, highly nationalistic decisions, designed to promote the growth of a strong, unified, and economically developed United States.

The Court and the Tribes

The nationalist inclinations of the Marshall Court were visible as well in a series of decisions concerning the legal status of Indian tribes within the United States. But these decisions did not just affirm the supremacy of the United States; they also carved out a distinctive position for Native Americans within the constitutional structure.

The first of the crucial Indian decisions was in the case of *Johnson* v. *McIntosh* (1823). Leaders of the Illinois and Pinakeshaw tribes had sold parcels of their land to a group of white settlers (including Johnson), but had later signed a treaty with the federal government ceding to the United States territory that included those same parcels. The government proceeded to grant homestead rights to new white settlers (among them McIntosh) on the land claimed by Johnson. The Court was asked to decide which claim had precedence. Marshall's ruling, not surprisingly, favored the United States. But in explaining it, he offered a preliminary definition of the place of Indians within the nation. The tribes had a basic right to their tribal lands, he said, that preceded all other American law. Individual American citizens could not buy or take land from the tribes; only the federal government could do that.

Eight years later, in *Cherokee Nation* v. *Georgia*, the Marshall Court refused to hear a case filed by the Cherokees against a Georgia law abolishing their tribal legislature and courts. The Cherokees argued that because the tribe was a "foreign nation," the Supreme Court (which had constitutional responsibility for mediating disputes between the states and foreign nations) had jurisdiction. Marshall's earlier and later rulings suggested considerable sympathy for tribal claims that states could not regulate them, but he could not accept the Cherokee argument in this case. The tribes were not foreign nations, he said. Rather, they had a special status within the nation. "The conditions of the Indians in relation to the United States is perhaps unlike that of any two people in existence," he wrote. "Their relation to the United States resembles that of a ward to his guardian." This was the origin of what became known as the "trust relationship," by which the United States claimed broad powers over the tribes but accepted substantial responsibility for protecting their welfare.

Most important was the Court's 1832 decision in *Worcester* v. *Georgia*. The Georgia state government had passed a law requiring any U.S. citizen desiring to enter Cherokee territory to obtain permission from the governor. Two missionaries (one of them named Worcester) sued, claiming the state was encroaching on the federal government's constitutionally mandated role to regulate trade with the tribes. Marshall invalidated the Georgia law, another important step in consolidating federal authority over the states (and over the tribes). In doing so, he further defined the nature of the Indian nations. The tribes, he explained, were sovereign entities in much the same way Georgia was a sovereign entity, "distinct political communities, having territorial boundaries within which their authority is exclusive." In defending the power of the federal government, he was also affirming, indeed expanding, tribal authority.

The Marshall decisions, therefore, did what the Constitution itself had not done: they defined a place for Indian tribes within the American political system. The tribes had basic property rights. They were sovereign entities not subject to the authority of state governments. But the federal government, like a "guardian" governing its "ward," had ultimate authority over tribal affairs—even if that authority was, according to the Court, limited by the government's obligation to protect Indian welfare. These provisions were seldom enough to defend Indians from the steady westward march of white civilization. But they formed the basis of what legal protections they had.

The Latin American Revolution and the Monroe Doctrine

Just as the Supreme Court was asserting American nationalism in the shaping of the country's economic life, so the Monroe administration was asserting nationalism in foreign policy. As always, American diplomacy was principally concerned with Europe. But in the 1820s, dealing with Europe forced Americans to develop a policy toward Latin America, which was suddenly winning its independence.

Americans looking southward in the years following the War of 1812 beheld a gigantic spectacle: the Spanish Empire in its death throes, a whole continent in revolt, new nations in the making. Already the United States had developed a profitable trade with Latin America and was rivaling Great Britain as the principal trading nation there. Many believed the success of the anti-Spanish revolutions would further strengthen America's position in the region.

In 1815, the United States proclaimed neutrality in the wars between Spain and its rebellious colonies, implying a partial recognition of the rebels' status as nations. Moreover, the United States sold ships and supplies to the revolutionaries, a clear indication that it was not genuinely neutral but was trying to help the insurgents. Finally, in 1822, President Monroe established diplomatic relations with five new nations—La Plata (later Argentina), Chile, Peru, Colombia, and Mexico—making the United States the first country to recognize them.

In 1823, Monroe went further and announced a policy that would ultimately be known (beginning some thirty years later) as the "Monroe Doctrine," even though it was primarily the work of John Quincy Adams. "The American continents," Monroe declared, ". . . are henceforth not to be considered as subjects for future colonization by any European powers." The United States would consider any foreign challenge to the sovereignty of existing American nations an unfriendly act. At the same time, he proclaimed, "Our policy in regard to Europe . . . is not to interfere in the internal concerns of any of its powers."

The Monroe Doctrine emerged directly out of America's relations with Europe in the 1820s. After Napoleon's defeat, the major nations of Europe combined in a "concert" to prevent future challenges to the "legitimacy" of established governments. Great Britain soon withdrew from the concert, leaving Russia and France the strongest of its four remaining members. In 1823, the four allies authorized France to intervene in Spain to restore the Bourbon dynasty, which a revolution had toppled. Some in England and the Americas feared the allies might next support a French effort to retake the lost Spanish Empire in America.

To most Americans, and certainly to the secretary of state, an even greater threat was Great Britain itself. Adams suspected that the English had designs on Cuba. He thought Cuba eventually should belong to the United States and wanted to keep it in Spanish hands until it fell to the Americans. For a time, Monroe and Adams considered making their pronouncements about Latin America part of a joint statement with Great Britain. But Adams soon came to believe that the American government should act alone instead of following along like a "cock-boat in the wake of a British man-of-war." When the British lost interest in a joint statement, they only strengthened an already growing inclination within the administration to make its own pronouncement.

Monroe and Adams hoped the message would rally the people of Latin America to resist foreign intervention. They also hoped that by appealing to national pride, the message would help arouse the United States from a business depression, divert the nation from sectional politics, and increase popular interest in the otherwise lackluster administration of Monroe. It did neither. But the Monroe Doctrine was important nevertheless for several reasons. It was an expression of the growing spirit of nationalism in the United States in the 1820s. It was an expression of concern about the forces that were already gathering to threaten that spirit. And it established the idea of American hegemony in the Western Hemisphere that later U.S. governments would invoke at will to justify policies in Latin America.

THE REVIVAL OF OPPOSITION

After 1816, the Federalist Party offered no presidential candidate and soon ceased to exist as a national political force. The Republican Party (which considered itself not a party at all but an organization representing the whole of the population) was the only organized force in national politics.

Yet the policies of the federal government continued to spark opposition. At first, criticism remained contained within the existing one-party structure. But by the late 1820s partisan divisions were emerging once again.

In some respects, the division mirrored the schism that had produced the first party system in the 1790s. The Republicans had in many ways come to resemble the early Federalist regimes in their promotion of economic growth and centralization. (That was one of the principal reasons for the Federalists' demise: the Republicans had adopted much of their program). And the opposition, like the opposition in the 1790s, opposed the federal government's expanding role in the economy. There was, however, a crucial difference. At the

JOHN QUINCY ADAMS
This photograph of the former president was taken shortly before his death in 1848—almost twenty years after he had left the White House—when he was serving as a congressman from Massachusetts. During his years as president, he was—as he had been throughout his life—an intensely disciplined and hard-working man. He rose at four in the morning and made a long entry in his diary for the previous day. He wrote so much that his right hand at times became paralyzed with writer's cramp, so he taught himself to write with his left hand as well. *(Brown Brothers)*

beginning of the century, the opponents of centralization had also often been opponents of economic growth. Now, in the 1820s, the controversy involved not whether but how the nation should continue to expand.

The "Corrupt Bargain"

Until 1820, when the Federalist Party effectively ceased operations and James Monroe ran for reelection unopposed, presidential candidates were nominated by caucuses of the two parties in Congress. In 1824, had the caucus system prevailed, Republicans in Congress would have again produced a candidate who would have run unopposed. But "King Caucus" did not prevail in 1824. The Republican caucus did nominate a candidate: William H. Crawford of Georgia, the secretary of the treasury and the favorite of the extreme states' rights faction of the party. But other candidates received nominations from state legislatures and endorsements from irregular mass meetings throughout the country.

One of them was Secretary of State John Quincy Adams, who held the office that was the traditional stepping-stone to the presidency. But as he himself ruefully understood, he was a man of cold and forbidding manners, with little popular appeal. Another contender was Henry Clay, the Speaker of the House. He had a devoted personal following and a definite and coherent program: the "American System," which proposed creating a great home market for factory and farm producers by raising the protective tariff,

strengthening the national bank, and financing internal improvements. Andrew Jackson, the fourth major candidate, had no significant political record—even though he had served briefly as a representative in Congress and was now a new member of the United States Senate. But he was a military hero and had the help of shrewd political allies from his home state of Tennessee.

Jackson received a plurality, although not a majority, of both the popular and the electoral vote. In the electoral college, he had 99 votes to Adams's 84, Crawford's 41, and Clay's 37. The Twelfth Amendment to the Constitution (passed in the aftermath of the contested 1800 election) required the House of Representatives to choose between the three candidates with the largest numbers of electoral votes. Clay was out of the running, but he was in a strong position to influence the result, both because he was speaker of the House and because thirty-seven electors were committed to him and presumably open to his advice on where to turn now.

Supporters of Jackson, Crawford, and Adams all wooed Clay as the congressional vote approached. But Clay's course was already set. Crawford was no longer a serious candidate, since he was suffering from a paralyzing disease. And Jackson was Clay's most dangerous political rival in the West and had not supported Clay's legislative program. Adams was no friend of Clay's either; but alone among the candidates, he was an ardent nationalist and a likely supporter of the American System. Clay gave his support to Adams, and the House elected him.

THE TRAIL OF TEARS
This twentieth-century painting by Robert Lindneux shows the forced evacuation of 18,000 Cherokee Indians from their ancestral lands in Georgia beginning in 1838. An epidemic of smallpox, along with starvation and exposure, cost thousands of Indians their lives. Here the Cherokees, guarded by soldiers carrying guns and bayonets, cross the Missouri River on their way to their new and unfamiliar homes in what is now Oklahoma.
(Woolaroc Museum, Bartlesville, Oklahoma)

SIGNIFICANT EVENTS

1813 Francis Lowell establishes textile factories in Waltham, Massachusetts

1815 U.S. signs treaties with tribes taking western lands from Indians

1816 Second Bank of the United States chartered

Monroe elected president

Tariff protects textile industry from foreign competition

Indiana enters Union

1817 Madison vetoes internal improvements bill

Mississippi enters Union

1818 Jackson invades Florida, ends first Seminole War

Rush-Bagot agreement signed

Illinois enters Union

1819 Commercial panic destabilizes economy

Spain cedes Florida to United States in Adams-Onís Treaty

Supreme Court hears *Dartmouth College* v. *Woodward* and *McCulloch* v. *Maryland*

Alabama enters Union

1819–1820 Stephen H. Long explores Nebraska and Colorado

1820 Missouri Compromise enacted

Monroe reelected president without opposition

1821 Mexico wins independence from Spain

William Becknell opens trade between U.S. territories and New Mexico

1822 Rocky Mountain Trapping Company established

1823 Monroe Doctrine proclaimed

1824 John Quincy Adams wins disputed presidential election

Supreme Court rules in *Gibbons* v. *Ogden*

1826 Thomas Jefferson and John Adams die on July 4

1827 Creek Indians cede lands to Georgia

1828 "Tariff of abominations" passed

Andrew Jackson elected president

The Jacksonians—who believed their large popular and electoral pluralities entitled their candidate to the presidency—were enraged enough at this. But they became much angrier when the new president announced that Clay was to be his secretary of state. The State Department was the well-established route to the presidency, and Adams thus appeared to be naming Clay as his own successor. The Jacksonians expressed outrage at this "corrupt bargain." Very likely there had been some sort of understanding between Clay and Adams, and although there was nothing corrupt, or even unusual, about it, it proved to be politically costly for both men.

The Second President Adams

Throughout Adams's term in the White House, the political bitterness arising from the "corrupt bargain"

thoroughly frustrated his policies. In his inaugural address and in his first message to Congress, Adams recommended "laws promoting the improvement of agriculture, commerce, and manufactures, the cultivation of the mechanic and of the elegant arts, the advancement of literature, and the progress of the sciences, ornamental and profound": a nationalist program reminiscent of Clay's American System. But Jacksonians in Congress prevented him from securing appropriations for most of these goals. He did win several million dollars to improve rivers and harbors and to extend the National Road westward from Wheeling—more than Congress had appropriated for internal improvements under all his predecessors together, but far less than he and Clay had envisioned.

Adams also experienced diplomatic frustrations. He appointed delegates to an international conference that the Venezuelan liberator, Simón Bolívar, had called in

ELECTION OF 1828   (57.6% of electorate voting)

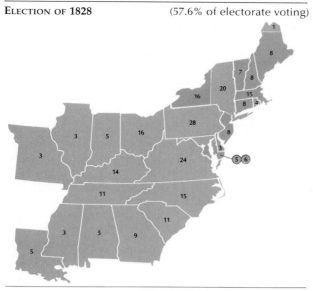

	ELECTORAL VOTE	POPULAR VOTE (%)
Andrew Jackson (Democrat)	178	647,286 (56)
John Quincy Adams (National Republican)	83	508,064 (44)

Panama in 1826. But southerners in Congress opposed the idea of white Americans mingling with black delegates from Haiti, which would be represented in Panama. And supporters of Jackson charged that Adams intended to sacrifice American interests and involve the nation in an entangling alliance. Congress delayed approving the Panama mission so long that the American delegation did not arrive until after the conference was over.

Adams also lost a contest with the State of Georgia, which wished to remove the remaining Creek and Cherokee Indians from the state to gain additional soil for cotton planters. The United States government, in a 1791 treaty, had guaranteed that land to the Creeks; but in 1825, white Georgians had extracted a new treaty from William McIntosh, the leader of one faction in the tribe and a longtime advocate of Indian cooperation with the United States. Adams believed the new treaty had no legal force, since McIntosh clearly did not represent the wishes of the tribe; and he refused to enforce the treaty, setting up a direct conflict between the president and the state. The governor of Georgia defied the president and proceeded with plans

for Indian removal. In 1827, the Creeks succumbed to pressure from Georgia and agreed to still another treaty, in which they again yielded their land, thus undercutting Adams's position further.

Even more damaging to the administration was its support for a new tariff on imported goods in 1828. This measure originated in the demands of Massachusetts and Rhode Island woolen manufacturers, who complained that the British were dumping textiles on the American market at prices with which the domestic mill owners could not compete. They won support from middle and western states, but at the cost of provisions that antagonized the original New England supporters of the bill. The western provisions placed high duties not only on woolens, as the New Englanders had wanted, but also on items the West produced. That distressed New England manufacturers; the benefits of protecting their manufactured goods from foreign competition now had to be weighed against the prospects of having to pay more for raw materials. The bill presented Adams with a dilemma, for he would lose support whether he signed or vetoed it. Adams signed it, earning the animosity of southerners, who cursed it as the "tariff of abominations."

Jackson Triumphant

By the time of the 1828 presidential election, a new two–party system had begun to emerge out of the divisions among the Republicans. On one side stood the supporters of John Quincy Adams, who called themselves the National Republicans and who supported the economic nationalism of the preceding years. Opposing them were the followers of Andrew Jackson, who took the name Democratic Republicans and who called for an assault on privilege and a widening of opportunity. Adams attracted the support of most of the remaining Federalists; Jackson appealed to a broad coalition that opposed the "economic aristocracy." But issues seemed to count for little in the end, as the campaign degenerated into a war of personal invective. The Jacksonians charged that Adams as president had been guilty of gross waste and extravagance and had used public funds to buy gambling devices (a chess set and a billiard table) for the White House. They also claimed, falsely, that when Adams had served as minister to Russia he had tried to procure a beautiful American girl for the sinful pleasures of the czar.

Adams's supporters hurled even worse accusations at Jackson. They called him a murderer and distributed a "coffin handbill," which listed, within coffin-shaped outlines, the names of militiamen whom Jackson was said to have shot in cold blood during the War of 1812. (The men had been deserters who were legally executed after sentence by a court-martial.) And they called him an adulterer, fanning rumors that Jackson had knowingly lived in sin with the wife of another man. Actually, he had married the woman, his beloved Rachel, at a time when the pair apparently believed her first husband had divorced her. (When Jackson's wife first read of the accusations against her shortly after the election, she collapsed and, a few weeks later, died; with considerable reason, Jackson blamed his opponents for her death.)

Jackson's victory was decisive, if sectional. He won 56 percent of the popular vote and an electoral majority of 178 votes to 83. Adams swept virtually all of New England, and he showed significant strength in the mid-Atlantic region. Nevertheless, the Jacksonians considered their victory as complete and as important as Jefferson's in 1800. Once again, the forces of privilege had been driven from Washington. Once again, a champion of democracy would occupy the White House and restore liberty to the people and to the economy. America had entered, some Jacksonians claimed, a new era of democracy, the "era of the common man."

SUGGESTED READINGS

Economic Growth.   George Dangerfield, *The Awakening of American Nationalism* (1965); and *The Era of Good Feelings* (1952). Bray Hammond, *Banks and Politics in America from the Revolution to the Civil War* (1957). Shaw Livermore, Jr., *The Twilight of Federalism* (1962). Murray N. Rothbard, *The Panic of 1819* (1962).

Expanding Westward.   Thomas P. Abernethy, *The South in the New Nation* (1961). Ray Allen Billington, *The Far Western Frontier* (1965); *Westward Expansion* (1974). Colin Calloway, *Crown and Calumet* (1987). John Mack Faragher, *Women and Men on the Overland Trail* (1979). John A. Hawgood, *America's Western Frontier* (1967). Julie Roy Jeffrey, *Frontier Women: The Trans-Mississippi West* (1979). Frederick Merk, *History of the Westward Movement* (1978). Francis S. Philbrick, *The Rise of the West, 1745–1830* (1965). Glenda Riley, *The Female Frontier* (1988). Malcolm J. Rohrbough, *The Land Office Business: The Settlement and Administration of American Public Lands, 1789–1837* (1968). Frederick Jackson Turner, *The Rise of the New West* (1906); and *The Frontier in American History* (1920). Dale Van Every, *The Final Challenge* (1964).

The "Era of Good Feelings".   Harry Ammon, *James Monroe: The Quest for National Identity* (1971). Samuel F. Bemis, *John Quincy Adams and the Union* (1956). Wesley Frank Craven, *The Legend of the Founding Fathers* (1956). George Dangerfield: *The Awakening of American Nationalism* (1965); *The Era of Good Feelings* (1952). Don E. Fehrenbacher, *The South and Three Sectional Crises* (1980). Shaw Livermore, *The Twilight of Federalism* (1962). Glover Moore, *The Missouri Compromise* (1953). Paul C. Nagle, *One Nation Indivisible: The Union*

in American Thought, 1815–1828 (1965). Robert V. Remini, *The Election of Andrew Jackson* (1963). Norman K. Risjord, *The Old Republicans: Southern Conservatism in the Age of Jefferson* (1965). Glyndon Van Deusen, *The Life of Henry Clay* (1937). Charles M. Wiltse, *John C. Calhoun: American Nationalist* (1944).

The Courts.   Leonard Baker, *John Marshall: A Life in Law* (1974). Albert J. Beveridge, *The Life of John Marshall*, 4 vols. (1916–1919). Alexander M. Bickel, *Justice Joseph Story and the Rise of the Supreme Court* (1971). D. O. Dewey, *Marshall Versus Jefferson: The Political Background of Marbury v. Madison* (1970). Richard E. Ellis, *The Jeffersonian Crisis: Courts and Politics in the Young Republic* (1971). Charles G. Haines, *The Role of the Supreme Court in American Government and Politics, 1789–1835* (1970). Morton J. Horowitz, *The Transformation of American Law, 1780–1865* (1977). James McClellan, *Joseph Story and the American Constitution* (1971). R. Kent Newmyer, *The Supreme Court Under Marshall and Taney* (1968). Francis N. Stites, *John Marshall: Defender of the Constitution* (1981).

The Monroe Doctrine.   Samuel F. Bemis, *John Quincy Adams and the Foundations of American Foreign Policy* (1940). Walter LaFeber, ed., *John Quincy Adams and the Continental Empire* (1965). Ernest R. May, *The Making of the Monroe Doctrine* (1975). Bradford Perkins, *Castlereagh and Adams: England and the United States, 1812–1823* (1964). Dexter Perkins, *The Monroe Doctrine* (1927); and *Hands Off: A History of the Monroe Doctrine* (1941). Frank Thistlethwaite, *The Anglo-American Connection in the Early Nineteenth Century* (1959). Arthur P. Whitaker, *The United States and the Independence of Latin America* (1941).

DETAIL FROM *THE VERDICT OF THE PEOPLE* (1855), BY GEORGE CALEB BINGHAM
This scene of an election day gathering is peopled almost entirely by white men. Women and blacks were barred from voting, but among white males political rights expanded substantially in the 1830s and 1840s. *(Boatmen's National Bank, St. Louis)*

CHAPTER NINE

JACKSONIAN AMERICA

HEN THE FRENCH ARISTOCRAT Alexis de Tocqueville visited the United States in 1831, one feature of American society struck him as "fundamental": the "general equality of condition among the people." Unlike older societies, in which privilege and wealth passed from generation to generation within an entrenched upper class, America had no rigid distinctions of rank. "The government of democracy," he wrote in his classic study *Democracy in America* (1835–1840), "brings the notion of political rights to the level of the humblest citizens, just as the dissemination of wealth brings the notion of property within the reach of all the members of the community."

Yet Tocqueville also wondered how long the fluidity of American society could survive in the face of the growth of manufacturing and the rise of the factory system. Industrialism, he feared, would create a large class of dependent workers and a small group of new aristocrats. For, as he explained it, "at the very moment at which the science of manufactures lowers the class of workmen, it raises the class of masters."

Americans, too, pondered the future of their democracy in these years of economic and territorial expansion. Some feared that the nation's rapid growth would produce social chaos and insisted that the country's first priority must be to establish order and a clear system of authority. Others argued that the greatest danger facing the nation was privilege and that society's goal should be to eliminate the favored status of powerful elites and make opportunity more widely available. Advocates of this latter vision seized control of the federal government in 1829 with the inauguration of Andrew Jackson.

Jackson and his followers were not egalitarians. They did nothing to challenge the existence of slavery; they supervised one of the harshest assaults on American Indians in the nation's history; and they accepted the necessity of economic inequality and social gradation. Jackson himself was a frontier aristocrat, and most of those who served him were people of wealth and standing. They were not, however, usually aristocrats by birth. They had, they believed, risen to prominence on the basis of their own talents and energies, and their goal in public life was to ensure that others like themselves would have the opportunity to do the same.

The "democratization" of government over which Andrew Jackson presided was permeated with the rhetoric of equality and aroused the excitement of working people. To the national leaders who promoted that democratization, however, its purpose was not to aid farmers and laborers, Jackson's greatest champions. Still less was it to assist the truly disenfranchised: African Americans (both slave and free), women, Native Americans. It was to challenge the power of eastern elites for the sake of the rising entrepreneurs of the South and the West.

ANDREW JACKSON TRAVELS TO WASHINGTON
President-elect Andrew Jackson attracted enormous crowds along his well-publicized route to Washington in 1829. Even larger crowds gathered in the capital for his inauguration, prompting some of his opponents to complain of the triumph of "King Mob."   *(Library of Congress)*

THE RISE OF MASS POLITICS

On March 4, 1829, an unprecedented throng—thousands of Americans from all regions of the country, including farmers, laborers, and others of humble rank—crowded before the Capitol in Washington, D.C., to witness the inauguration of Andrew Jackson. After the ceremonies, the boisterous crowd poured down Pennsylvania Avenue, following their hero to the White House. And there, at a public reception open to all, they filled the state rooms to overflowing, trampling one another, soiling the carpets, ruining the elegantly upholstered sofas and chairs in their eagerness to shake the new president's hand. "It was a proud day for the people," wrote Amos Kendall, one of Jackson's closest political associates. "General Jackson is their

own President." To other observers, however, the scene was less appealing. Justice of the Supreme Court Joseph Story, a friend and colleague of John Marshall, looked on the inaugural levee, as it was called, and remarked with disgust: "The reign of King 'Mob' seems triumphant."

The Expanding Electorate

What some have called the "age of Jackson" did not much advance the cause of economic equality. But it did mark a transformation of American politics that extended power widely to new groups.

Until the 1820s, relatively few Americans had been permitted to vote. Most states restricted the franchise to white males who were property owners or taxpayers or both, effectively removing a great mass of the

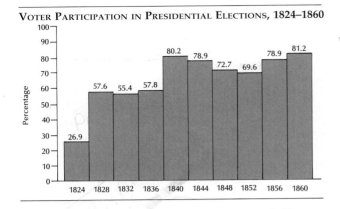

VOTER PARTICIPATION IN PRESIDENTIAL ELECTIONS, 1824–1860

less affluent from the voting rolls. But beginning even before Jackson's election, the franchise began to expand. Change came first in Ohio and other new states of the West, which, on joining the Union, adopted constitutions that guaranteed all adult white males the right to vote and permitted all voters the right to hold public office. Older states, concerned about the loss of their population to the West, began to grant similar political rights to their citizens, dropping or reducing their property ownership or taxpaying requirements. Eventually, every state democratized its electorate to some degree, although some later and less fully than others.

Change provoked resistance, and at times the democratic trend fell short of the aims of the more radical reformers, as when Massachusetts held its constitutional convention in 1820. Reform-minded delegates complained that in the Massachusetts government the rich were better represented than the poor, both because of restrictions on voting and officeholding and because of a peculiar system of property representation in the state senate. But Daniel Webster, one of the conservative delegates, opposed democratic changes on the grounds that "power naturally and necessarily follows property" and that "property as such should have its weight and influence in political arrangement." Webster and the rest of the conservatives could not prevent the reform of senate representation; nor could they prevent elimination of the property requirement for voting. But, to the dismay of the radicals, the new constitution required that every voter be a taxpayer and that the governor be the owner of considerable real estate.

More often, however, the forces of democratization prevailed in the states. In the New York convention of 1821, for example, conservatives led by James Kent in-

sisted that a taxpaying requirement for suffrage was not enough and that, at least in the election of state senators, the property qualification should survive. Kent argued that society "is an association for the protection of property as well as of life" and that "the individual who contributes only one cent to the common stock ought not to have the same power and influence in directing the property concerns of the partnership as he who contributes his thousands." But reformers, citing the Declaration of Independence, maintained that life, liberty, and the pursuit of happiness, not property, were the main concerns of society and government. The property qualification was abolished.

The wave of state reforms was generally peaceful, but in Rhode Island democratization efforts created considerable instability. The Rhode Island constitution (which was still basically the old colonial charter) barred more than half the adult males of the state from voting. The conservative legislature, chosen by this restricted electorate, consistently blocked all efforts at reform. In 1840, the lawyer and activist Thomas L. Dorr and a group of his followers formed a "People's party," held a convention, drafted a new constitution, and submitted it to a popular vote. It was overwhelmingly approved. The existing legislature, however, refused to accept the Dorr document and submitted a new constitution of its own to the voters. It was narrowly defeated. The Dorrites, in the meantime, had begun to set up a new government, under their own constitution, with Dorr as governor; and so, in 1842, two governments were claiming legitimacy in Rhode Island. The old state government proclaimed that Dorr and his followers were rebels and began to imprison them. Meanwhile, the Dorrites made a brief and ineffectual effort to capture the state arsenal. The Dorr Rebellion, as it was known, quickly failed. Dorr himself surrendered and was briefly imprisoned. But the episode helped spur the old guard to draft a new constitution, which greatly expanded the suffrage.

The democratization process was far from complete. In much of the South, election laws continued to favor the planters and politicians of the older counties and to limit the influence of more newly settled western areas. Slaves, of course, were disenfranchised by definition; they were not considered citizens and were believed to have no legal or political rights. Free blacks could not vote anywhere in the South and hardly anywhere in the North. Pennsylvania, in fact, amended its state constitution in 1838 to strip blacks of the right to vote they had previously enjoyed. In no state could women vote. Nowhere was the ballot secret, and often voters had to cast a spoken vote rather than a written one, which meant that political bosses could, and often did, bribe and intimidate them.

Despite the persisting limitations, however, the number of voters increased far more rapidly than did the population as a whole. Indeed, one of the most striking political trends of the early nineteenth century was the change in the method of choosing presidential electors and the dramatic increase in popular participation in the process. In 1800, the legislature had chosen the presidential electors in ten of the states, and the people in only six. By 1828, electors were chosen by popular vote in every state but South Carolina. In the presidential election of 1824, fewer than 27 percent of adult white males had voted. In the election of 1828, the figure rose to 58 percent and in 1840 to 80 percent.

The Legitimization of Party

The high level of voter participation was only partly the result of an expanded electorate. It was also the result of a heightening interest in politics and a strengthening of party organization.

Although party competition was part of American politics almost from the beginning of the republic, acceptance of the idea of party was not. For more than thirty years, most Americans who had opinions about the nature of government considered parties evils to be avoided and thought the nation should seek a broad consensus in which permanent factional lines would not exist. But in the 1820s and 1830s, those assumptions gave way to a new view: that permanent, institutionalized parties were a desirable part of the political process, that indeed they were essential to democracy.

The elevation of the idea of party occurred first at the state level, most prominently in New York. There Martin Van Buren led a dissident political faction (known as the "Bucktails" or the "Albany Regency"). In the years after the War of 1812, this group began to challenge the political elite—led by the aristocratic governor, De Witt Clinton—that had dominated the state for years. Factional rivalries were not new, of course. But this one was new in the way in which Van Buren and his followers posed their challenge. Refuting the traditional view of a political party as undemocratic, they argued that only an institutionalized party, based in the populace at large, could ensure genuine democracy. The alternative was the sort of closed elite that Clinton had created. In the new kind of party the Bucktails proposed, ideological commitments would be less important than loyalty to the party itself. Preservation of the party as an institution—through the use of favors, rewards, and patronage—would be the principal goal of the leadership. Above all, for a party to survive, it must have a permanent opposition. Competing parties would give each political faction a sense of purpose; they would force politicians to remain continually attuned to the will of the people; and they would check and balance each other in much the same way that the different branches of government checked and balanced one another.

By the late 1820s, this new idea of party was spreading beyond New York. The election of Jackson in 1828, the result of a popular movement that seemed to stand apart from the usual political elites, seemed further to legitimize the idea of party as a popular, democratic institution. "Parties of some sort must exist," said a New York newspaper. "'Tis in the nature and genius of our government." Finally, in the 1830s, a fully formed two-party system began to operate at the national level, with each party committed to its own existence as an institution and willing to accept the legitimacy of its opposition. The anti-Jackson forces began to call themselves Whigs. Jackson's followers called themselves Democrats (no longer Democratic Republicans), thus giving a permanent name to the nation's oldest political party.

"President of the Common Man"

Unlike Thomas Jefferson, Jackson was no democratic philosopher, and the Democratic Party, much less than Jefferson's Republicans, embraced no clear or uniform ideological position. But Jackson himself did embrace a distinct, if simple, theory of democracy. It should offer "equal protection and equal benefits" to all its white male citizens and favor no region or class over another. In practice, that meant an assault on what Jackson and his associates considered the citadels of the eastern aristocracy and an effort to extend opportunities to the rising classes of the West and the South.

Jackson's first target was the entrenched officeholders in the federal government, many of whom had been in place for a generation or more. "Office is considered as a species of property," Jackson told Congress in a bitter denunciation of the "class" of permanent officeholders, "and government rather as a means of promoting individual interests than as an instrument created solely for the service of the people." Official duties, he believed, could be made "so plain and simple that men of intelligence may readily qualify themselves for their performance." Offices belonged to the people, he argued, not to the entrenched officeholders. Or, as one of his henchmen, William L. Marcy of New York, more cynically put it, "To the victors belong the spoils."

In the end, Jackson removed a total of no more than one-fifth of the federal officeholders during his eight years in office, many of them less for partisan reasons than because they had misused government funds or engaged in other corruption. Proportionally, Jackson dismissed no more of the jobholders than Jefferson had done. But by embracing the philosophy of the "spoils system," a system already well entrenched in a number of state governments, the Jackson administration helped fix it firmly upon American politics.

Jackson's supporters also worked to transform the process by which presidential candidates won their party's nominations. They had long resented the congressional caucus, a process they believed worked to restrict access to the office to those favored by entrenched elites and a process Jackson himself had avoided in 1828. In 1832, the president's followers staged a national party convention to renominate him for the presidency—one year after the Anti-Masons (see p. 257) became the first party to hold such a meeting. In later generations, some would see the party convention as a source of corruption and political exclusivity. But those who created it in the 1830s considered it a great triumph for democracy. Through the convention, they believed, power would arise directly from the people, not from elite political institutions such as the caucus.

The spoils system and the political convention did serve to limit the power of two entrenched elites—permanent officeholders and the exclusive party caucus. Yet neither really transferred power to the people. Appointments to office almost always went to prominent political allies of the president and his associates. Delegates to national conventions were less often common men than members of local party elites. Political opportunity within the party was expanding, but much less so than Jacksonian rhetoric suggested.

JOHN C. CALHOUN
This photograph, by Matthew Brady, captured Calhoun toward the end of his life, when he was torn between his real commitment to the ideals of the Union and his equally fervent commitment to the interests of the South. The younger generation of southern leaders, who would dominate the politics of the region in the 1850s, were less idealistic and more purely sectional in their views. *(Library of Congress)*

"OUR FEDERAL UNION"

Jackson's commitment to assaulting privileged elites led him to try to reduce the functions of the federal government. A concentration of power in Washington would, he believed, restrict opportunity to the favored few with political connections. But Jackson believed, too, in forceful presidential leadership. And although he spoke frequently of the importance of states' rights, he was strongly committed to the preservation of the Union. Thus at the same time he was promoting an economic program to reduce the power of the national government, he was asserting the supremacy of the Union in the face of a potent challenge. For no sooner had he entered office than his own vice president—

John C. Calhoun—began to assert a dangerous new constitutional theory: nullification.

Calhoun and Nullification

Calhoun was forty-six years old in 1828, with a distinguished past and an apparently promising future. He had been a congressional leader during the War of 1812; he had served for eight years as head of the War Department (compiling a record as one of the few great secretaries of war); he had been vice president in John Quincy Adams's administration. And now, he was running for another term as vice president, this time with Andrew Jackson. Presumably he could look forward to the presidency itself.

But the smoldering issue of the tariff created a dilemma for him. Once he had been an outspoken protectionist, strongly supporting the tariff of 1816. But since that time many South Carolinians had changed their minds on the subject. Carolina cotton planters were disturbed because their state's economy appeared to be stagnating. One reason was the exhaustion of the South Carolina soil, which could not compete effectively with the fertile, newly opened lands of the Southwest. But most Carolinians blamed their problems on the "tariff of abominations" of 1828, which they claimed had raised the prices they had to pay for the manufactured goods they could not produce for themselves. Some exasperated Carolinians were ready to consider a drastic remedy: secession.

Calhoun's future political hopes rested on how he met this challenge in his home state. He did so by developing his theory of nullification, which he believed offered a more moderate alternative to secession. Drawing from the ideas of Madison and Jefferson and their Virginia and Kentucky Resolutions of 1798–1799, Calhoun argued that since the federal government was a creation of the states, the states themselves—not the courts or the Congress—were the final arbiters of the constitutionality of federal laws. If a state concluded that Congress had passed an unconstitutional law, it could hold a special convention and declare that law null and void within the state. The law would remain void until three-fourths of the states ratified it as an amendment to the Constitution. The nullifying state would then have to choose between submitting to the law and seceding from the Union. The South Carolina legislature published Calhoun's first statement of his theory in 1828, anonymously, in a document entitled *The South Carolina Exposition and Protest*, which attacked the "tariff of abominations" as unconstitutional and unendurable—a fit target for nullification. The nullification doctrine—and the idea of using it to kill the 1828 tariff—quickly attracted broad support in South Carolina.

What Calhoun really hoped, however, was that the nullification theory would never be put to the test, that it would simply pressure the federal government to reduce tariff rates. But he soon discovered that he did not have as much influence in the new administration as he had expected. For he had a powerful rival in Martin Van Buren.

The Rise of Van Buren

Van Buren was about the same age as Calhoun and equally ambitious. As leader of the Democratic Party organization of New York, he had helped carry the state for Jackson in 1828 while getting himself elected governor. By this time he had a reputation as a political wizard. Short and slight, with reddish-gold sideburns

MARTIN VAN BUREN
As leader of the so-called Albany Regency in New York in the 1820s, Van Buren helped create one of the first modern party organizations in the United States. Later, as Andrew Jackson's secretary of state and (after 1832) vice president, he helped bring party politics to the national level. So it was perhaps ironic that in 1840, when he ran for reelection to the presidency, he should lose to William Henry Harrison, whose Whig Party made effective use of many of the techniques of mass politics that Van Buren himself had pioneered. *(Library of Congress)*

and a quiet manner, he was known by such nicknames as "the Sage of Kinderhook," "the Little Magician," and "the Red Fox." He resigned the governorship and went to Washington in 1829 when Jackson appointed him secretary of state.

Van Buren's influence with the president was unmatched. Jackson relied for advice on an unofficial circle of allies who came to be known as the "Kitchen Cabinet." It included such Democratic newspaper editors as Isaac Hill of New Hampshire and Amos Kendall and Francis P. Blair of Kentucky. Van Buren alone was a member of both the official cabinet and this unofficial circle. He and the president grew closer still through a curious quarrel over etiquette that helped drive a wedge between the president and Calhoun.

Peggy O'Neale was the attractive and vivacious daughter of a Washington tavern keeper with whom both Andrew Jackson and his friend John H. Eaton had taken lodgings while serving as senators from Tennessee. O'Neale was married and the mother of two children, but rumors began to circulate in Washington in the mid-1820s that she and Senator Eaton were romantically involved. O'Neale's husband died in 1828, and she and Eaton were soon married. A few weeks later, Jackson named his friend Eaton secretary of war and thus made the new Mrs. Eaton a cabinet wife. The rest of the administration wives, led by Mrs. Calhoun, refused to receive her. Jackson (remembering the public slander that he believed had killed his own wife) was furious and demanded that the members of his cabinet accept Mrs. Eaton into their social world. Calhoun, however, bowed to his wife's adamant demands and refused, thus taking sides against the president. Van Buren, a widower, befriended the Eatons and thus ingratiated himself with Jackson.

By 1831, partly as a result of the Peggy Eaton affair, Jackson had settled on Van Buren as his choice to succeed him in the White House. Calhoun's dreams of the presidency had all but vanished.

The Webster–Hayne Debate

In January 1830, a great debate in the United States Senate dramatically revealed the degree to which sectional issues were intruding into national politics. The controversy grew out of a seemingly routine Senate discussion of federal policy toward the public lands in the West. In the midst of the debate, a senator from Connecticut suggested that all land sales and surveys be temporarily discontinued. Senator Thomas Hart Benton of Missouri, the Jacksonian leader in the Senate, charged that the proposal served the economic needs of the Northeast at the expense of the West.

Robert Y. Hayne, a young senator from South Carolina, took up Benton's argument. He had no direct interest in the western lands, but he and other southerners saw the issue as a way to win western support for their drive to lower the tariff. Hayne argued that the South and the West were both victims of the tyranny of the Northeast and hinted that the two regions might combine to defend themselves against that tyranny.

Daniel Webster, now a senator from Massachusetts, took the floor the day after Hayne's speech. Although once an advocate of states' rights and an opponent of the tariff, he had changed his position as the interests of his region had changed. Now he attacked Hayne, and through him Calhoun, for what he considered their challenge to the integrity of the Union. He was, in effect, challenging Hayne to a debate not on public lands and the tariff, but on the issue of states' rights versus national power. Hayne, coached by Calhoun, responded with a defense of the theory of nullification. Webster then spent two full afternoons delivering what became known as his "Second Reply to Hayne," a speech that northerners quoted and revered for years to come. He concluded with the ringing appeal: "Liberty *and* Union, now and for ever, one and inseparable!"

Calhoun's followers believed Hayne had the better of the argument, but their main concern was what President Jackson thought. The answer became clear at the annual Democratic Party banquet in honor of Thomas Jefferson. After dinner, guests delivered a series of toasts. The president arrived with a written text in which he had underscored certain words: "Our *Federal* Union—*It must be preserved.*" While he spoke he looked directly at Calhoun. The diminutive Van Buren, who stood on his chair to see better, thought he saw Calhoun's hand shake and a trickle of wine run down his glass as he responded to the president's toast with his own: "The Union—next to our liberty most dear." Sharp lines had been drawn.

The Nullification Crisis

In 1832, the controversy over nullification finally produced a genuine crisis when South Carolina responded angrily to a congressional tariff bill that offered them no relief from the 1828 "tariff of abominations." Some militant South Carolinians were ready to secede from the Union, but Calhoun persuaded them to try nullification instead. The supporters of nullification won a substantial victory in the state elections of 1832. And almost immediately, the newly elected legislature summoned a state convention, which voted to nullify the tariffs of 1828 and 1832 and to forbid the collection of duties within the state. At the same time, South Carolina elected Hayne governor and Calhoun (who resigned as vice president) to replace Hayne as senator.

Jackson insisted that nullification was treason and that its adherents were traitors. (Privately, he threat-

CHARLESTON, 1831
The little-known South Carolina artist S. Bernard painted this view of Charleston's East Battery in 1831. Then as now, residents and vistors liked to stroll along the battery and watch the activity in the city's busy harbor. But Charleston in the 1830s was a less important commercial center than it had been a few decades earlier. By then, overseas traders were increasingly avoiding southern ports and doing more and more business in New York. *(Yale University Art Gallery)*

ened to hang Calhoun.) He strengthened the federal forts in the state and ordered a warship and several revenue ships to Charleston. When Congress convened early in 1833, Jackson's followers won approval of a "force bill" authorizing the president to use the military to enforce acts of Congress. Violence seemed a real possibility early in 1833.

Calhoun faced a predicament as he took his place in the Senate. Not a single state had come to South Carolina's support. Even South Carolina itself was divided, since most realized the state could not hope to prevail in a showdown with the federal government. In the end, the timely intervention of Henry Clay, newly elected to the Senate, saved Calhoun. Clay devised a compromise that lowered the tariff gradually until in 1842 it would reach approximately the same level as in 1816. The compromise and the force bill were passed on the same day, March 1, 1833. Jackson signed them both.

In South Carolina, the convention reassembled and repealed its nullification of the tariffs. But unwilling to allow Congress to have the last word, the convention nullified the force act—a purely symbolic action, since the tariff toward which the force act was directed had already been repealed. Calhoun and his followers claimed a victory for nullification, which had, they insisted, forced the revision of the tariff. Their claim had some justification. But the episode taught Calhoun and his allies an important lesson: No state could defy the federal government alone.

THE REMOVAL OF THE INDIANS

There had never been any doubt about Andrew Jackson's attitude toward the Indian tribes that continued to live in the eastern states and territories of the United States. He wanted them to move west, beyond the Mississippi, out of the way of expanding white settlement. Jackson's antipathy toward the Indians had a special intensity because of his own earlier experiences leading military campaigns against tribes along the Southern border. But in most respects, his views were little different from those of most other white Americans.

White Attitudes Toward the Tribes

In the eighteenth century, many white Americans had considered the Indians "noble savages," peoples without real civilization but with an inherent dignity that made civilization possible among them. By the first decades of the nineteenth century, this vaguely paternalistic attitude (the attitude of Thomas Jefferson, among others) was giving way to a new and more hostile one, particularly among the whites in the western states and territories whom Jackson came to represent. Whites were coming to view Native Americans simply as "savages," not only uncivilized but uncivilizable. That was one reason for the commitment to Indian removal: the belief that whites should not be expected to live in close proximity to the "savage" Indians, that Indian cultures and societies were unworthy of respect.

BLACK HAWK AND WHIRLING THUNDER
After his defeat by white settlers in Illinois in 1832, the famed Sauk warrior Black Hawk and his son, Whirling Thunder, were captured and sent on a tour by Andrew Jackson, displayed to the public as trophies of war. They showed such dignity through the ordeal that much of the white public quickly began to sympathize with them. This portrait, by John Wesley Jarvis, was painted on the tour's final stop, in New York City. Black Hawk wears the European-style suit, while Whirling Thunder wears native costume to emphasize his commitment to his tribal roots. Soon thereafter, Black Hawk returned to his tribe, wrote a celebrated autobiography, and died in 1838. *(Bettmann)*

White westerners favored removal as well because they feared that continued contact between the expanding white settlements and the Indians would produce endless conflict and violence. Most of all, however, they favored Indian removal because of their own insatiable desire for land. The tribes possessed valuable acreage in the path of expanding white settlement. Whites wanted that territory.

Legally, the federal government alone had authority to negotiate with the Indians over land, a result of Supreme Court decisions that established the tribes as, in effect, "nations within the nation." These tribal nations were not, however, securely rooted in Indian history. The large tribal aggregations with which white Americans dealt were, in fact, relatively new entities. Most Indians were accustomed to thinking in much more local terms. They created these larger tribes when they realized they would need some collective strength to deal with whites; but as new and untested political entities, the tribes were often weak and divided. The Marshall Court had seemed to acknowledge this in declaring the tribes not only sovereign nations, but also dependent ones, for whom the federal government must take considerable responsibility. Through most of the nineteenth century, the government interpreted that responsibility as finding ways to move the Indians out of the way of expanding white settlement.

The Black Hawk War

The federal government had already taken substantial strides toward removing the Indians from the East by the time Jackson entered the White House. But substantial tribal enclaves remained. In the Old Northwest, the long process of expelling the woodland Indians culminated in a last battle in 1831–1832, between white settlers in Illinois and an alliance of Sauk (or Sac) and Fox Indians under the fabled and now aged warrior Black Hawk. An earlier treaty had ceded tribal lands in Illinois to the United States; but Black Hawk and his followers refused to recognize the legality of the agreement, which a rival tribal faction had signed. Hungry and resentful, a thousand of them crossed the river and reoccupied vacant lands in Illinois. White settlers in the region feared that the resettlement was the beginning of a substantial invasion, and they assembled the Illinois state militia and federal troops to repel the "invaders."

The Black Hawk War, as it became known, was notable chiefly for the viciousness of the white military efforts. White leaders in western Illinois vowed to exterminate the "bandit collection of Indians" and attacked them even when Black Hawk attempted to surrender. The Sauks and Foxes, defeated and starving, retreated across the Mississippi into Iowa. White troops (and some bands of Sioux whom they encouraged to join the chase) pursued them as they fled and slaughtered most of them. United States troops captured Black Hawk himself and sent him on a tour of the East, where Andrew Jackson was one of many curious whites who arranged to meet him. (Abraham Lincoln served as a captain of the militia, but saw no action, in the Black Hawk War; Jefferson Davis was a lieutenant in the regular army.)

The "Five Civilized Tribes"

More troubling to the government in the 1830s were the remaining Indian tribes of the South. In western Georgia, Alabama, Mississippi, and Florida lived the "Five Civilized Tribes"—the Cherokee, Creek, Seminole, Chickasaw, and Choctaw—most of whom had established settled agricultural societies with successful economies. The Cherokees in Georgia had formed a particularly stable and sophisticated culture, with its own written language and a formal constitution (adopted in 1827) which created an independent Cherokee Nation. They were more closely tied to their lands than many of the more nomadic tribes to the north.

Even some whites argued that the Cherokees, unlike other tribes, should be allowed to retain their eastern lands, since they had become such a "civilized" society and had, under pressure from missionaries and government agents, given up many of their traditional ways. Cherokee men had once been chiefly hunters and had left farming mainly to women. Now the men gave up most of their hunting and (like white men) took over the farming themselves; Cherokee women, also like their white counterparts, restricted themselves largely to domestic tasks.

The federal government, to which the Constitution had delegated the power to negotiate with the Indian tribes, had worked steadily through the first decades of the nineteenth century to negotiate treaties with the southern Indians that would remove them to the West and open their lands for white settlement. But the negotiating process often did not proceed fast enough to satisfy the region's whites. The State of Georgia's independent effort to dislodge the Creek Indians, over the objection of President Adams, was one example of this impatience. That same impatience became evident early in Jackson's administration, when the legislatures in Georgia, Alabama, and Mississippi began extending their laws over the tribes remaining in their states. They received assistance in these efforts from Congress, which in 1830 passed the Removal Act (with Jackson's approval), which appropriated funds for negotiating treaties with the southern tribes and relocating them to the West. The president quickly dispatched federal officials to negotiate nearly a hundred new treaties with the remaining tribes. Thus, the southern tribes faced a combination of pressures from both the state and federal governments. Most tribes were too weak to resist, and they ceded their lands in return for only token payments. Some, however, balked.

In Georgia, the Cherokees tried to stop the white encroachments by appealing to the Supreme Court. The Court's decisions in *Cherokee Nation* v. *Georgia* and *Worcester* v. *Georgia* (see p. 234) seemed at least partially to vindicate the tribe. But Jackson's longtime hostility toward the Indians and longtime commitment to their removal left him with little sympathy for the Cherokees and little patience with the Court. Eager to retain the support of southerners and westerners in the increasingly bitter partisan battles in which his administration was becoming engaged, the president had vigorously supported (and even actively encouraged) Georgia's efforts to remove the Cherokees before the Court decision. His reaction to Marshall's rulings reflected his belief that the justices were using the issue to express their hostility to the larger aims of his presidency. When the chief justice announced the decision in *Worcester* v. *Georgia*, Jackson reportedly responded with contempt. "John Marshall has made his decision," he is said to have stated. "Now let him enforce it." The decision was not enforced.

In 1835, the government extracted a treaty from a minority faction of the Cherokees, none of them a chosen representative of the Cherokee Nation, which ceded the tribe's land to Georgia in return for $5 million and a reservation west of the Mississippi. The great majority of the 17,000 Cherokees did not recognize the treaty as legitimate and refused to leave their homes. But Jackson would not be thwarted. He sent an army of 7,000 under General Winfield Scott to round them up and drive them westward at bayonet point.

Trails of Tears

About 1,000 fled across the state line to North Carolina, where the federal government eventually provided a reservation for them in the Smoky Mountains; it survives today. But most of the rest made the long, forced trek to "Indian Territory" (which later became Oklahoma) beginning in the winter of 1838. Along the way, a Kentuckian observed: "Even aged females, apparently nearly ready to drop in the grave, were travel-

THE EXPULSION OF INDIANS FROM THE SOUTH, 1830–1835

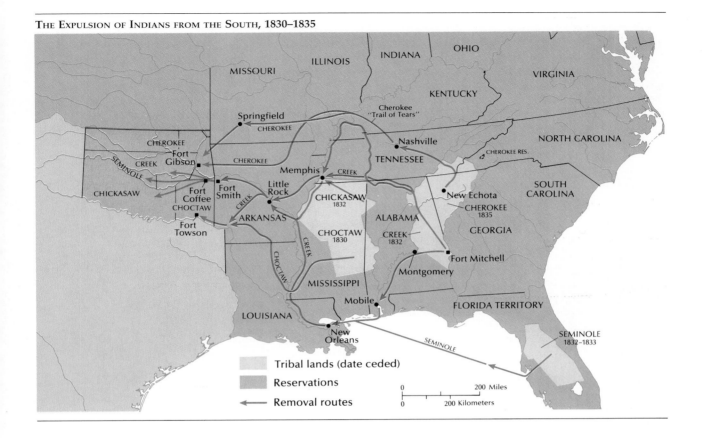

Tribal lands (date ceded)

Reservations

→ Removal routes

0   200 Miles

0   200 Kilometers

ling with heavy burdens attached to their backs, sometimes on frozen ground and sometimes on muddy streets, with no covering for their feet." Thousands, perhaps an eighth or more of the emigrés, perished before or soon after reaching their unwanted destination. In the harsh new reservations in which they were now forced to live, the survivors never forgot the hard journey. They called their route "The Trail Where They Cried," the Trail of Tears. Jackson claimed that the "remnant of that ill-fated race" was now "beyond the reach of injury or oppression," apparently trying to convince himself and others that he had supported removal as a way to protect the tribes.

The Cherokees were not alone in experiencing the hardships of the Trail of Tears. Between 1830 and 1838, virtually all the "Five Civilized Tribes" were expelled from the southern states and forced to relocate in the new Indian Territory, which Congress had officially created by the Indian Intercourse Act of 1834. The Choctaws of Mississippi and western Alabama were the first to make the trek, beginning in 1830. The army moved out the Creeks of eastern Alabama and west-

ern Georgia in 1836. The Chickasaw in northern Mississippi began the long march westward a year later, and the Cherokees, finally, a year after that.

The government thought the Indian Territory was safely distant from existing white settlements and consisted of land that most whites considered undesirable. It had the additional advantage, the government believed, of being on the eastern edge of what earlier white explorers had christened the "Great American Desert," land unfit for habitation. It seemed unlikely that whites would ever seek to settle along the western borders of the Indian Territory; and thus the prospect of whites' surrounding the reservation and producing further conflict seemed remote.

Only the Seminoles in Florida managed to resist the pressures to relocate, and even their success was limited. Like other tribes, the Seminoles had agreed under pressure to a settlement (the 1832–1833 treaties of Payne's Landing), by which they ceded their lands and agreed to move to Indian Territory within three years. Most did move west, but a substantial minority, under the leadership of the chieftain Osceola, refused to

OCEOLA'S MODE OF SIGNING THE TREATY.

OSCEOLA DEFIANT
This contemporary drawing portrays the Seminole chieftain Osceola plunging his knife through a treaty that would have paid the tribe for their land and required them to move out of Florida. The gesture was only the beginning of Osceola's defiance. In 1835, he led his people in a war against the U.S. government's efforts to remove them from the territory. *(Florida State Archives)*

leave and staged an uprising beginning in 1835 to defend their lands. (Joining the Indians in their struggle was a group of runaway black slaves who had been living with the tribe.) The Seminole War dragged on for years. Jackson sent troops to Florida, but the Seminoles with their black associates were masters of guerrilla warfare in the jungly Everglades. Even after Osceola had been treacherously captured by white troops while under a flag of truce and had died in prison; even after white troops had engaged in a systematic campaign of extermination against the resisting Indians and their black allies; even after 1,500 white soldiers had died and the federal government had spent $20 million on the struggle—even then, followers of Osceola remained in Florida. Finally, in 1842, the government abandoned the war. By then, many of the Seminoles had been either killed or forced westward. But the relocation of the Seminoles, unlike the relocation of most of the other tribes, was never complete.

The Meaning of Removal

By the end of the 1830s, virtually all the important Indian societies east of the Mississippi (with such exceptions as the Seminoles and a few Cherokee in the South and some tribal enclaves in northern Michigan and Wisconsin) had been removed to the West. The tribes had ceded over 100 million acres of eastern land to the federal government; they had received in return about $68 million and 32 million acres in the far less hospitable lands west of the Mississippi between the Missouri and Red Rivers. There they lived, divided by tribe into a series of sharply defined reservations, in a territory surrounded by a string of United States forts to keep them in (and to keep most whites out), in a region whose climate and topography bore little relation to anything they had known before. Eventually, even this forlorn enclave would face encroachments from white civilization.

What were the alternatives to the removal of the eastern Indians? There was probably never any realistic possibility that the government could stop white expansion westward. White people had already been penetrating the West for nearly two centuries, and such penetrations were certain to continue.

But there were, in theory at least, alternatives to the brutal removal policy. The West was replete with examples of white settlers and native tribes living side by side and creating a shared (if not necessarily egalitarian) world. In the pueblos of New Mexico, in the fur trading posts of the Pacific Northwest, in parts of Texas and California, settlers from Mexico, Canada, and the United States had created societies in which Indians and whites were in intimate contact with each other. Even the Lewis and Clark expedition, during its famous explorations, had combined with western Indians on terms of such intimacy that many of its members contracted venereal disease from Indian sexual partners. Sometimes these close contacts between whites and Indians were beneficial to both sides, even reasonably equal. Often they were cruel and exploitive. But the early multiracial societies of the West did not separate whites and Indians. They demonstrated ways in which the two cultures could interact, each shaping the other.

By the mid-nineteenth century, however, white Americans had adopted a different model as they contemplated westward expansion. Much as the early British settlers along the Atlantic Coast had established "plantations," from which natives were, in theory, to be excluded, so the westering whites of later years came to view the territories they were entering as virgin land, with no pre-existing civilization. Indians, they believed, could not be partners—either equal or subordinate—in the creation of new societies in the West. They were obstacles, to be removed and, as far as possible, isolated. Indians, Andrew Jackson once said, had "neither the intelligence, the industry, the moral habits, nor the desire of improvement" to be fit partners in the project of extending white civilization westward. By dismissing Indian cultures in that way, white Americans justified to themselves a series of harsh policies that they believed (incorrectly) would make the West theirs alone.

JACKSON AND THE BANK WAR

Jackson was quite willing to use federal power against the Indian tribes. Where white Americans were concerned, however, he was consistently opposed to con-

centrating power either in the federal government or in elite institutions associated with it. An early example of that was his 1830 veto of a congressional measure providing a subsidy to the proposed Maysville Road in Kentucky. The bill was unconstitutional, Jackson argued, because the road in question lay entirely within Kentucky and was not, therefore, a part of "interstate commerce." But the bill was also unwise, he believed, because it committed the government to what Jackson considered extravagant expenditures.

A similar resistance to federal power lay behind the most celebrated episode of Jackson's presidency: the war against the Bank of the United States.

Biddle's Institution

With its headquarters in Philadelphia and its branches in twenty-nine other cities, the Bank of the United States had a monopoly on the deposits of the federal government, which owned one-fifth of the bank's stock; it also did a tremendous business in general banking. It provided credit to growing enterprises; it issued bank notes, which served as a dependable medium of exchange throughout the country; and it exercised a restraining effect on the less well managed state banks. Nicholas Biddle, who served as president of the Bank from 1823 on, had done much to put the institution on a sound and prosperous basis. Nevertheless, Andrew Jackson was determined to destroy it.

Opposition to the Bank came from two very different groups: the "soft-money" faction and the "hard-money" faction. Advocates of soft money consisted largely of state bankers and their allies. They objected to the Bank of the United States because it restrained the state banks from issuing notes freely. The hard-money people believed that coin was the only safe currency, and they condemned all banks that issued bank notes, including the Bank of the United States. The soft-money advocates were believers in rapid economic growth and speculation; the hard-money forces embraced older ideas of "public virtue" and looked with suspicion on expansion and speculation. Jackson himself supported the hard-money position. Many years before, he had been involved in some grandiose land and mercantile speculations based on paper credit. His business had failed, and he had fallen deeply into debt as a result of the Panic of 1797. After that, he was suspicious of all banks and all paper currency. But as president he was also sensitive to the complaints of his many "soft-money" supporters in the West and the South. He made it clear that he would not favor renewing the charter of the Bank of the United States, which was due to expire in 1836.

Election of 1832 (55.4% of electorate voting)

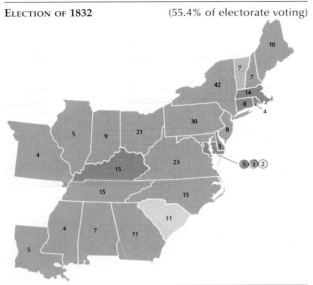

	ELECTORAL VOTE	POPULAR VOTE (%)
Andrew Jackson (Democrat)	219	687,502 (55.0)
Henry Clay (National Republican)	49	530,189 (42.4)
William Wirt (Anti-Mason)	7	33,108 (2.6)
John Floyd (Independent Democrat)	11	—
Not voted	2	—

Biddle was a Philadelphia aristocrat, unaccustomed to politics. But in his efforts to save the Bank, he began granting financial favors to influential men. In particular, he relied on Daniel Webster. He named Webster the Bank's legal counsel and director of its Boston branch; Webster was also a frequent, heavy borrower and Biddle's personal friend. He helped Biddle win the support of Henry Clay as well.

Clay, Webster, and other advisers persuaded Biddle to apply to Congress for a recharter bill in 1832, four years ahead of the expiration date. Congress passed the recharter bill; Jackson, predictably, vetoed it; and the Bank's supporters in Congress failed to override the veto. The Bank question then emerged as the paramount issue of the 1832 election, just as Clay had hoped.

In 1832, Clay ran for president as the unanimous choice of the National Republicans, who held a nominating convention in Baltimore late in 1831. But the bank war failed to provide him with the winning issue for which he had hoped. Jackson, with Van Buren as his running mate, overwhelmingly defeated Clay (and several minor party candidates) with 55 percent of the popular vote and 219 electoral votes (more than four times as many as Clay received). These results were a defeat not only for Clay, but also for Biddle.

The "Monster" Destroyed

Jackson was now more determined than ever to destroy the "monster" Bank. He could not legally abolish the institution before the expiration of its charter, but he could try to weaken it. So he decided to remove the government's deposits from the Bank. His secretary of the treasury believed that such an action would destabilize the financial system and refused to give the order. Jackson removed him and appointed a replacement. When the new secretary similarly procrastinated, Jackson named a third: Roger B. Taney, the attorney general, a close friend and loyal ally of the president. Taney began placing the government's deposits not in the Bank of the United States, as it had in the past, but in a number of state banks (which Jackson's enemies called "pet banks").

The arrogant Nicholas Biddle, whom Jacksonians derisively called "Czar Nicholas," did not give in without a fight. "This worthy President," he wrote sarcastically, "thinks that because he has scalped Indians and imprisoned Judges, he is to have his way with the Bank. He is mistaken." When the administration began to transfer funds directly from the Bank of the United States to the pet banks (as opposed to the initial practice of simply depositing new funds in those banks), Biddle called in loans and raised interest rates, explaining that without the government deposits the Bank's resources were stretched too thin. He realized his actions were likely to cause financial distress, and he hoped a short recession would persuade Congress to recharter the Bank. "Nothing but the evidence of suffering," he told a colleague, would "produce any effect in Congress."

As financial conditions worsened in the winter of 1833–1834, supporters of the Bank organized meetings around the country and sent petitions to Washington urging a rechartering of the Bank. But the Jacksonians blamed the recession on Biddle and refused to budge. When distressed citizens appealed to the president for help, he answered, "Go to Biddle."

Finally, the banker contracted credit too far even for his allies in the business community. Some of them did "go to Biddle." A group of New York and Boston merchants protested (as one of them reported) that the business community "ought not and would not sus-

"The Downfall of Mother Bank"
This 1832 Democratic cartoon celebrates Andrew Jackson's destruction of the Bank of the United States. The president is shown here driving away the Bank's corrupt supporters by ordering the withdrawal of government deposits. *(New-York Historical Society)*

tain him in further pressure, which he very well knew was not necessary for the safety of the bank, and in which his whole object was to coerce a charter." To appease the business community, Biddle at last reversed himself and began to grant credit in abundance and on reasonable terms. His vacillating tactics ended his chances of winning a recharter of the Bank.

Jackson had won a considerable political victory. But when the Bank of the United States died in 1836, the country lost a valuable financial institution and was left with a fragmented and chronically unstable banking system that would plague the economy for more than a century.

The Taney Court

In the aftermath of the Bank War, Jackson moved against the most powerful institution of economic na-

tionalism of all: the Supreme Court. In 1835, when John Marshall died, the president appointed as the new chief justice his trusted ally Roger B. Taney. Taney did not bring a sharp break in constitutional interpretation, but he did help modify Marshall's vigorous nationalism.

Perhaps the clearest indication of the new judicial mood was the celebrated case of *Charles River Bridge* v. *Warren Bridge* of 1837. The case involved a dispute between two Massachusetts companies over the right to build a bridge across the Charles River between Boston and Cambridge. One company had a longstanding charter from the state to operate a toll bridge, and claimed that this charter guaranteed it a monopoly of the bridge traffic. Another company had applied to the legislature for authorization to construct a second, competing bridge that would—since it would be toll free—greatly reduce the value of the first company's charter.

The first company contended that in granting the second charter the legislature was engaging in a breach of contract and noted that the Marshall Court, in the *Dartmouth College* case and other decisions, had ruled that states had no right to abrogate contracts. But now Taney, speaking for the Democratic majority on the Court, supported the right of Massachusetts to award the second charter. The object of government, Taney maintained, was to promote the general happiness, an object that took precedence over the rights of property. A state, therefore, had the right to amend or abrogate a contract if such action was necessary to advance the well-being of the community. Such an abrogation was clearly necessary in the case of the Charles River Bridge, he argued, because the original bridge company, by exercising a monopoly, was benefiting from unjustifiable privilege. (It did not help the first company that its members were largely Boston aristocrats and that it was closely associated with elite Harvard College; the challenging company, by contrast, consisted largely of newer, aspiring entrepreneurs—the sort of people with whom Jackson and his allies instinctively identified.) The decision reflected one of the cornerstones of the Jacksonian ideal: that the key to democracy was an expansion of economic opportunity, which would not occur if older corporations could maintain monopolies and choke off competition from newer companies.

THE EMERGENCE OF THE SECOND PARTY SYSTEM

Jackson's forceful—some claimed tyrannical—tactics in crushing first the nullification movement and then the Bank of the United States helped galvanize a growing opposition coalition that by the mid-1830s was ready to assert itself in national politics. It began as a gathering of national political leaders opposed to Jackson's use of power. Denouncing the president as "King Andrew I," they began to refer to themselves as Whigs, after the party in England that traditionally worked to limit the power of the king. As the new party began to develop as a national organization with constituencies in every state, its appeal became more diffuse. Nevertheless, both in its philosophy and in the nature of its membership, the Whig Party was different from the party of Jackson.

With the emergence of the Whigs, the nation once again had two competing political parties. What scholars now call the "second party system" had begun what turned out to be its relatively brief life.

Party Philosophies

The philosophy of the Democratic Party in the 1830s bore the stamp of Andrew Jackson, but drew from many older traditions as well. Democrats envisioned a future of steadily expanding opportunities. The function of government, therefore, was to remove artificial obstacles to that expansion and to avoid creating new obstacles of its own. The federal government should have limited power, except to the degree that it worked to eliminate social and economic arrangements that entrenched privilege and stifled opportunity. The rights of states should be protected except when state governments interfered with social and economic mobility. Jacksonian Democrats celebrated "honest workers," "simple farmers," and "forthright businessmen" and contrasted them to the corrupt, monopolistic, aristocratic forces of established wealth. As Jackson himself said in his farewell address, the society of America should be one in which "the planter, the farmer, the mechanic, and the laborer, all know that their success depends on their own industry and economy," in which artificial privilege would stifle no one's opportunity.

The Jacksonians were not hostile either to wealth or to economic growth. On the contrary, most Democrats believed in material progress, and many party leaders—including Jackson himself—were wealthy men. Yet Democrats tended to look with suspicion on government efforts to stimulate commercial and industrial growth. Such efforts, they believed, generally produced such menacing institutions of power as the Bank of the United States. Democrats were less likely than Whigs to support chartered banks and corporations, state-supported internal improvements, even public schools. They were more likely than Whigs to support territorial expansion, which would, they believed, widen opportunities for aspiring Americans. Among the most radical members of the party—the so-called Locofocos, mainly workingmen and small businessmen and professionals in the Northeast—sentiment was strong for a vigorous, perhaps even violent assault on monopoly and privilege far in advance of anything Jackson himself ever contemplated.

The political philosophy that became known as Whiggery favored expanding the power of the federal government, encouraging industrial and commercial development, and knitting the country together into a consolidated economic system. Whigs embraced material progress enthusiastically, but they were cautious about westward expansion, fearful that rapid territorial growth would produce instability. Their vision of America was of a nation embracing the industrial future and rising to world greatness as a commercial and manufacturing power. And although Whigs insisted that their vision would result in increasing opportunities for all Americans, they tended to attribute particular value to the elites they considered the enterprising, modernizing forces in society—the entrepreneurs and institutions that most effectively promoted economic growth. Thus while Democrats were inclined to oppose legislation establishing banks, corporations, and other modernizing institutions, Whigs generally favored such measures.

Party Constituencies

To some extent, the constituencies of the two major parties reflected these diffuse philosophies. The Whigs were strongest among the more substantial merchants and manufacturers of the Northeast; the wealthier planters of the South (those who favored commercial development and the strengthening of ties with the North); and the ambitious farmers and rising commercial class of the West—usually migrants from the Northeast—who advocated internal improvements, expanding trade, and rapid economic progress. The Democrats drew more support from smaller merchants and the workingmen of the Northeast; from southern planters suspicious of industrial growth; and from westerners—usually with southern roots—who favored a predominantly agrarian economy and opposed the development of powerful economic institutions in their region. Whigs tended to be wealthier than Democrats, to have more aristocratic backgrounds, and to be more commercially ambitious.

But Whigs and Democrats alike were more interested in winning elections than in maintaining philosophical purity. And both parties made adjustments from region to region in order to attract the largest possible number of voters, often at the sacrifice of party philosophy. In New York, for example, the Whigs developed a popular following through a movement known as Anti-Masonry. The Anti-Mason movement had emerged in the 1820s in response to widespread resentment against the secret and exclusive, hence supposedly undemocratic, Society of Freemasons. Such resentments increased in 1826 when a former Mason, William Morgan, mysteriously disappeared from his home in Batavia, New York, shortly before he was scheduled to publish a book purporting to expose the secrets of Freemasonry. The assumption was widespread that vengeful Masons had abducted and murdered Morgan. Whigs seized on the Anti-Mason frenzy to launch spirited attacks on Jackson and Van Buren (both Freemasons), implying that the Democrats were part of the antidemocratic conspiracy. By embracing

Anti-Masonry, Whigs were portraying themselves as opponents of aristocracy and exclusivity. They were, in other words, attacking the Democrats with the Democrats' own issues. The Anti-Masonry movement was powerful enough to become the basis of a new political party.

Religious and ethnic divisions also played an important role in determining the constituencies of the two parties. Irish and German Catholics, among the largest of the recent immigrant groups, tended to support the Democrats, who appeared to share their own vague aversion to commercial development and entrepreneurial progress and who seemed to respect their family- and community-centered values and habits. Evangelical Protestants gravitated toward the Whigs because they associated the party with constant development and improvement, goals their own religion embraced. They envisioned a society progressing steadily toward unity and order, and they looked on the new immigrant communities as a threat to that progress—as groups that needed to be disciplined and taught "American" ways. These and other ethnic, religious, and cultural tensions were often far more influential in determining party alignments than any concrete political or economic proposals.

Party Leadership

The Whig Party was more successful at defining its positions and attracting a constituency than it was in uniting behind a national leader. No single person was ever able to command the loyalties of the party in the way Andrew Jackson commanded the loyalties of the Democrats. Instead, Whigs tended to divide among three major figures: Henry Clay, Daniel Webster, and John Calhoun.

Clay won support from many of those who favored his program for internal improvements and economic development, what he called the American System; but his image as a devious operator and his identification with the West proved insuperable liabilities. He ran for president three times and never won. Daniel Webster, the greatest orator of his era, won broad support with his passionate speeches in defense of the Constitution and the Union; but his close connection with the Bank of the United States and the protective tariff, his reliance on rich men for financial support, and his excessive and often embarrassing fondness for brandy prevented him from developing enough of a national constituency to win him the office he so desperately wanted. John C. Calhoun, the third member of what became known as the Great Triumvirate, never considered himself a true Whig, and his identification with

WHERE HISTORIANS DISAGREE

THE AGE OF JACKSON

To many Americans in the 1820s and 1830s, Andrew Jackson was a champion of democracy, a symbol of a spirit of anti-elitism and egalitarianism that was sweeping American life. In the twentieth century, however, historians have disagreed sharply not only in their assessments of Jackson himself, but in their portrayal of American society in his era.

The "progressive" historians of the early twentieth century tended to see the politics of Jackson and his supporters as a forerunner of their own generation's battles against economic privilege and political corruption. Frederick Jackson Turner encouraged scholars to see Jacksonianism as the product of the democratic West: a protest by the people of the frontier against the conservative aristocracy of the East, which they believed restricted their own freedom and opportunity. Jackson represented those who wanted to make government responsive to the will of the people rather than to the power of special interests. The culmination of this progressive interpretation of Jacksonianism was the publication in 1945 of Arthur M. Schlesinger, Jr.'s *The Age of Jackson*. Schlesinger was less interested in the regional basis of Jacksonianism than the disciples of Turner had been. Jacksonian democracy, he argued, was the effort "to control the power of the capitalist groups, mainly Eastern, for the benefit of non-capitalist groups, farmers and laboring men, East, West, and South." He

portrayed Jacksonianism as an early version of modern reform efforts (in the progressive era and the New Deal) to "restrain the power of the business community."

Richard Hofstadter, in an influential 1948 essay, sharply disagreed. He argued that Jackson was the spokesman of rising entrepreneurs—aspiring businessmen who saw the road to opportunity blocked by the monopolistic power of eastern aristocrats. The Jacksonians opposed special privileges only to the extent those privileges blocked their own road to success. They were less sympathetic to the aspirations of those below them. Similarly, Bray Hammond, writing in 1957, argued that the Jacksonian cause was "one of enterpriser against capitalist," of rising elites against entrenched ones. Other historians, exploring the ideological origins of the movement saw Jacksonianism less as a democratic reform movement than as a nostalgic effort to restore a lost (and largely imagined) past. Marvin Meyer's *The Jacksonian Persuasion* (1957) argued that Jackson and his followers looked with misgivings on the new industrial society emerging around them and yearned instead for a restoration of the agrarian, republican virtues of an earlier time.

Historians of the 1960s began examining Jacksonianism in entirely new ways: looking less at Jackson himself and less at the rhetoric and ideas of his supporters and more at the nature of American society in the early nineteenth century. Lee Benson's *The Concept of Jacksonian Democracy* (1961) emphasized the role of religion and eth-

the nullification controversy in effect disqualified him from national leadership in any case. Yet he sided with Clay and Webster on the issue of the national bank. And he shared with them a strong animosity toward Andrew Jackson.

The Whigs, in other words, were able to marshal an imposing array of national leaders, each with his own powerful constituency. Yet for many years they were unable to find a way to merge those constituencies into a single winning combination. The result was that

while Whigs competed relatively evenly with the Democrats in congressional, state, and local races, they managed to win only two presidential elections in the more than twenty years of their history.

Their problems became particularly clear in 1836. The Democrats were united behind Andrew Jackson's personal choice for president, Martin Van Buren. The Whigs could not even agree on a single candidate. Instead, they ran several candidates, hoping to profit from the regional strength of each. Webster represented the

WHERE HISTORIANS DISAGREE

nicity in determining political divisions in the 1830s. If there was an egalitarian spirit alive in America in those years, it extended well beyond the Democratic Party and the followers of Jackson. Edward Pessen's *Jacksonian America* (1969) revealed that the democratic rhetoric of the age disguised the reality of an increasingly stratified society, in which inequality was growing more, not less, severe. Richard McCormick (1963) and Glyndon Van Deusen (1963) similarly emphasized the pragmatism of Jackson and the Democrats and de-emphasized clear ideological and partisan divisions.

Scholars in more recent years have also paid relatively little attention to Jackson and the Democratic Party and instead have focused on a series of broad social changes occurring in the early and mid nineteenth century which some have called a "market revolution." Those changes had profound effects on class relations, and the political battles of the era reflected only a part of their impact. Sean Wilentz, writing in 1984, identified the rise in the 1820s of a powerful class identity among workers in New York, who were attracted less to Jackson himself than to the idea that power in a republic should be widely dispersed. John Ashworth, in *"Agrarians" and "Aristocrats"* (1983), and Harry Watson, in *Liberty and Power* (1990), have also seen party politics as a reflection of much larger social changes. The party system was an imperfect reflection of a struggle between people committed to unrestricted opportunities for all white men and those committed to advancing the goals of capitalists, in part through government action.

Recent scholarship may have turned the focus of discussion away from Jackson and the Democratic Party and toward the larger society. But its success in revealing inequality and oppression in antebellum America has produced some withering reassessments of Jackson himself. In *Fathers and Children: Andrew Jackson and the Subjugation of the American Indian* (1975), Michael Rogin portrays Jackson as a man obsessed with escaping from the imposing shadow of the revolutionary generation. He would lead a new American revolution, not against British tyranny but against those who challenged the ability of white men to control the continent. He displayed special savagery toward American Indians, whom he pursued, Rogin argued, with an almost pathological violence and intensity. Alexander Saxton, in *The Rise and Fall of the White Republic* (1990), likewise points to the contradiction between the image of the age of Jackson as a time of expanding democracy and the reality of constricted rights for women, blacks, and Indians. The Democratic Party, he argues, was committed above all to defending slavery and white supremacy.

But the portrayal of Jackson as a champion of the common man has not vanished from scholarly life. The leading Jackson biographer of the postwar era, Robert V. Remini, has noted the flaws in Jackson's concept of democracy; but within the context of his time, Remini claims, Jackson was a genuine "man of the people."

---

party in New England; Hugh Lawson White of Tennessee ran in the South; and the former Indian fighter and hero of the War of 1812 from Ohio, William Henry Harrison, was the candidate in the middle states and the West. None of the three candidates could expect to get a majority in the electoral college, but party leaders hoped they might separately draw enough votes from Van Buren to prevent his getting a majority and throw the election to the House of Representatives, where the Whigs might be better able to elect one of their candidates. In the end, however, the three Whigs were no match for the one Democrat. Van Buren won easily, with 170 electoral votes to 124 for all his opponents.

POLITICS AFTER JACKSON

Andrew Jackson retired from public life in 1837, the most beloved political figure of his age. Martin Van

DANIEL WEBSTER
"The great god Webster," as he was occasionally known, was the most passionately admired public figure of his age. Crowds of up to 100,000 turned out at times for his speeches, even though many of them, in an age before amplification, presumably could not even hear him. Yet Webster inspired contempt as well as admiration among his contemporaries. His shady connections with influential businessmen tarnished his reputation among many Americans. So did his consuming (and unfulfilled) ambition for the presidency and his often embarrassing affection for brandy. *(Library of Congress)*

Buren was very different from his predecessor and far less fortunate. He was never able to match Jackson's personal popularity, and his administration encountered economic difficulties that devastated the Democrats and helped the Whigs.

The Panic of 1837

Van Buren's success in the 1836 election was a result in part of a nationwide economic boom that was reaching its height in that year. Canal and railroad builders were at a peak of activity. Prices were rising, money was plentiful, and credit was easy as banks increased

their loans and notes with little regard to their reserves of cash. The land business, in particular, was booming. Between 1835 and 1837, the government sold nearly 40 million acres of public land, nearly three-fourths of it to speculators, who purchased large tracts in hopes of reselling them at a profit. These land sales, along with revenues the government received from the tariff of 1833, created a series of substantial federal budget surpluses and made possible a steady reduction of the national debt (something Jackson had always advocated). From 1835 to 1837, the government for the first and only time in its history was out of debt, with a substantial surplus in the Treasury.

Congress and the administration now faced the question of what to do with the Treasury surplus. Reducing the tariff was not an option, since no one wanted to raise that touchy issue again. Instead, support grew for returning the federal surplus to the states. In 1836, Congress passed a "distribution" act requiring the federal government to pay its surplus funds to the states each year in four quarterly installments as interest-free, unsecured loans. No one expected the "loans" to be repaid. The states spent the money quickly, mainly to encourage construction of highways, railroads, and canals. The distribution of the surplus thus gave further stimulus to the economic boom. At the same time, the withdrawal of federal funds strained the state (or "pet") banks in which they had been deposited by the government; they had to call in their own loans to make the transfer of funds to the state governments.

Congress did nothing to check the speculative fever, with which many congressmen themselves were badly infected. Webster, for one, was buying up thousands of acres in the West. But Jackson, always suspicious of paper currency, was unhappy that the government was selling good land and receiving in return various state bank notes worth no more than the credit of the issuing bank.

In 1836, not long before leaving office, he issued a presidential order, the "specie circular." It provided that in payment for public lands the government would only accept gold or silver coins or currency backed by gold or silver. Jackson was right to fear the speculative fever but wrong in thinking the specie circular would cure it. On the contrary, it produced a financial panic that began in the first months of Van Buren's presidency. Hundreds of banks and businesses failed. Unemployment grew. There were bread riots in some of the larger cities. Prices fell, especially the price of land. Many railroad and canal projects failed. Several of the debt-burdened state governments ceased to pay interest on their bonds, and a few repudiated their debts, at least temporarily. It was the worst depression

"THE TIMES," 1837
This savage caricature of the economic troubles besetting the United States in 1837 illustrates, among other things, popular resentment of the hard-money orthodoxies of the time. A sign on the Custom House reads: "All bonds must be paid in Specie." Next door, the bank announces: "No specie payments made here." Women and children are shown begging in the street, while unemployed workers stand shoeless in front of signs advertising loans and "grand schemes." *(New-York Historical Society)*

in American history to that point, and it lasted for five years. It was a political catastrophe for Van Buren and the Democrats.

Both parties bore some responsibility for the panic. The distribution of the Treasury surplus, which had weakened the state banks and helped cause the crash, had been a Whig measure. Jackson's specie circular, which had started a run on the banks as land buyers rushed to trade in their bank notes for specie, was also to blame. But the depression was only partly a result of federal policies. England and western Europe were facing panics of their own, which caused European (and especially English) investors to withdraw funds from America, putting an added strain on American banks. A succession of crop failures on American farms

reduced the purchasing power of farmers and required increased imports of food, which sent more money out of the country. But whatever its actual causes, the Panic of 1837 occurred during a Democratic administration, and the Democrats paid the political price for it.

The Van Buren administration, which strongly opposed government intervention in the economy, did little to fight the depression. Some of the steps it took—borrowing money to pay government debts and accepting only specie for payment of taxes—may have made things worse. Other efforts failed in Congress: a "preemption" bill that would have given settlers the right to buy government land near them before it was opened for public sale, and another bill lowering the price of land. Van Buren did succeed in establishing a ten-hour workday on all federal projects, by presidential order, but he had only a few legislative achievements.

The most important and controversial of them was the creation of a new financial system to replace the Bank of the United States. Under Van Buren's plan, known as the "independent treasury" or "subtreasury" system, the government would place its funds in an independent treasury at Washington and in subtreasuries in other cities. No private banks would have the government's money or name to use as a basis for speculation; the government and the banks would be "divorced."

Van Buren called a special session of Congress in 1837 to consider the proposal, which failed in the House. In 1840, the last year of Van Buren's presidency, the administration finally succeeded in driving the measure through both houses of Congress.

The Log Cabin Campaign

As the campaign of 1840 approached, the Whigs realized that they would have to settle on one candidate for president. Accordingly, they held their first national nominating convention in Harrisburg, Pennsylvania, in December 1839. Passing over Henry Clay, who expected the nomination, the convention chose William Henry Harrison and, for vice president, John Tyler of Virginia. Harrison was a descendant of the Virginia aristocracy but had spent his adult life in the Northwest. He was a renowned soldier, a famous Indian fighter, and a popular national figure. The Democrats nominated Van Buren. But because their party was, in some respects, no more united than the Whigs, they failed to nominate a vice presidential candidate, leaving the choice of that office to the electors.

The 1840 campaign illustrated how fully the concept of party competition, the subordination of ideology to immediate political needs, had established itself in America. The Whigs—who had emerged as a party largely because of their opposition to Andrew Jackson's common-man democracy, who in most regions represented the more affluent elements of the population, and who favored government policies that would aid business—presented themselves in 1840 as the party of the common people. So, of course, did the Democrats. Both parties used the same techniques of mass voter appeal, the same evocation of simple, rustic values. What mattered now was not the philosophical purity of the party but its ability to win votes. The Whig campaign was particularly effective in portraying William Henry Harrison, a wealthy member of the frontier elite with a considerable estate, as a simple man of the people who loved log cabins and hard

WHIG HEADQUARTERS, 1840
The Whig Party in 1840 managed to disguise its relatively elite character by portraying its presidential candidate, the patrician General William Henry Harrison, as a man of the people—a man born in a log cabin who enjoyed drinking hard cider from a jug. Pictures of log cabins abounded during the Whig campaign. One of them is visible in this drawing of a party rally in Philadelphia. *(Stock Montage)*

cider. They accused Van Buren of being an aloof aristocrat who used cologne, drank champagne, and ate from gold plates. The Democrats had no defense against the combination of these campaign techniques and the effects of the depression. Harrison won the election with 234 electoral votes to 60 for Van Buren and with a popular majority of 53 percent.

The Frustration of the Whigs

Despite their decisive victory, the Whigs found their four years in power frustrating and divisive ones. In large part, that was because their popular new president, "Old Tippecanoe," William Henry Harrison, died of pneumonia one month after taking office. Vice President Tyler succeeded him. Control of the admin-

SIGNIFICANT EVENTS

1820–1840 State constitutions revised

1823 Nicholas Biddle becomes president of Bank of the United States

1826 William Morgan's disappearance inflames Anti-Masonry

1828 Calhoun's South Carolina Exposition and Protest outlines nullification doctrine

1829 Andrew Jackson inaugurated

1830 Webster and Hayne debate

Jackson vetoes Maysville Road Bill

Indian Removal Act passed

1830–1838 Indians expelled from Southeast

1831 Anti-Mason party established

Supreme Court rules in *Cherokee Nation* v. *Georgia*

1832 Democrats hold first national party convention

Jackson vetoes bill to recharter Bank of the United States

Jackson reelected president

1833 Jackson and Taney remove federal deposits from Bank of the United States

Commercial panic disrupts economy

1832–1833 Nullification crisis erupts

1834 Indian Trade and Intercourse Act renewed

1835 Roger Taney succeeds Marshall as chief justice of the Supreme Court

Federal debt retired

1835–1840 Tocqueville publishes *Democracy in America*

1835–1842 Seminole War

1836 Jackson issues "specie circular"

Martin Van Buren elected president

1837 Supreme Court rules in *Charles River Bridge* case

1837–1844 Commercial panic and depression

1838 "Aroostook War" fought in Maine and Canada

1839 Whigs hold their first national convention

1840 William Henry Harrison elected president

Independent Treasury Act passed

1841 Harrison dies

John Tyler becomes president

1842 Dorr Rebellion hastens reform in Rhode Island

---

istration thus fell to a man with whom the Whig party leadership had relatively weak ties. Harrison had generally deferred to Henry Clay and Daniel Webster, whom he named secretary of state. Under Tyler, things soon changed.

Tyler was a former Democrat who had left the party in reaction to what he considered Jackson's excessively egalitarian program and imperious methods. But there were still signs of his Democratic past in his approach to public policy. The president did agree to bills abolishing the independent treasury system and raising tariff rates. But he refused to support Clay's attempt to recharter a Bank of the United States. And he ve-

toed several internal improvement bills that Clay and other congressional Whigs sponsored. Finally, a conference of congressional Whigs read Tyler out of the party. Every cabinet member but Webster resigned; five former Democrats took their places. When Webster, too, left the cabinet, Tyler appointed Calhoun, who had rejoined the Democratic Party, to replace him.

A new political alignment was emerging. Tyler and a small band of conservative southern Whigs were preparing to rejoin the Democrats. Into the "common man's party" of Jackson and Van Buren was arriving a faction with decidedly aristocratic political ideas, who thought that government had an obligation to protect and even expand the institution of slavery, and who believed in states' rights with almost fanatical devotion.

Whig Diplomacy

In the midst of these domestic controversies, a series of incidents brought Great Britain and the United States to the brink of war in the late 1830s.

Residents of the eastern provinces of Canada launched a rebellion against the British colonial government in 1837, and some of the rebels chartered an American steamship, the *Caroline*, to ship supplies across the Niagara River to them from New York. British authorities in Canada seized the *Caroline* and burned it, killing one American in the process. The British government refused either to disavow the attack or to provide compensation for it, and resentment in the United States was high. But the British had reasons for anger as well. Authorities in New York arrested a Canadian named Alexander McLeod and charged him with the murder of the American who had died in the Caroline incident. The British government, expressing majestic rage, insisted that McLeod could not be accused of murder because he had acted under official orders. The foreign secretary, the bellicose Lord Palmerston, demanded McLeod's release and threatened that his execution would bring "immediate and frightful" war. Webster as secretary of state did not think McLeod was worth a war, but he was powerless to release him. The prisoner was under New York jurisdiction and had to be tried in the state courts, a peculiarity of American jurisprudence that the British did not seem to understand. A New York jury did what Webster could not: it defused the crisis by acquitting McLeod.

At the same time, tensions flared over the boundary between Canada and Maine, which had been in dispute since the Treaty of 1783. In 1838, groups of Americans and Canadians, mostly lumberjacks, began moving into the Aroostook River region in the disputed area, precipitating a violent brawl between the two groups that became known as the "Aroostook War."

Several years later, there were yet more Anglo-American problems. In 1841, an American ship, the *Creole*, sailed from Virginia for New Orleans with more than 100 slaves aboard. En route the slaves mutinied, took possession of the ship, and took it to the Bahamas. British officials there declared the slaves free, and the English government refused to overrule them. Many Americans, especially southerners, were furious.

At this critical juncture a new government eager to reduce the tensions with the United States came to power in Great Britain and sent Lord Ashburton, an admirer of America, to negotiate an agreement on the Maine boundary and other matters. The result was the Webster-Ashburton Treaty of 1842, under which the United States received slightly more than half the disputed area and agreed to a firm northern boundary as far west as the Rocky Mountains. Ashburton also eased the memory of the *Caroline* and *Creole* affairs by expressing regret and promising no future "officious interference" with American ships. The Webster-Ashburton treaty was popular in America, and Anglo-American relations were suddenly better than they had been for many years.

During the Tyler administration, the United States established its first diplomatic relations with China. In 1842, Britain forced China to open certain ports to foreign trade. Eager to share the new privileges, American mercantile interests persuaded Tyler and Congress to send a commissioner—Caleb Cushing—to China to negotiate a treaty giving the United States some part in the China trade. In the Treaty of Wang Hya, concluded in 1844, Cushing secured most-favored-nation provisions giving Americans the same privileges as the English. He also won for Americans the right of "extraterritoriality"—the right of Americans accused of crimes in China to be tried by American, not Chinese, officials. In the next ten years, American trade with China steadily increased.

In their diplomatic efforts, at least, the Whigs were able to secure some important successes. But by the end of the Tyler administration, the party could look back on few other victories. In the election of 1844, the Whigs lost the White House. They were to win only one more national election in their history before a great sectional crisis arose that would shatter their party and, for a time, the Union.

SUGGESTED READINGS

General Histories. James C. Curtis, *Andrew Jackson and the Search for Vindication* (1976). John Mayfield, *The New Nation, 1800–1845* (1981). Edward Pessen, *Jacksonian America*, rev. ed. (1979). Robert V. Remini, *The Jacksonian Era* (1989). Arthur M. Schlesinger, Jr., *The Age of Jackson* (1945). Charles Sellers, *The Market Revolution: Jacksonian America, 1815–1846* (1991). Glyndon Van Deusen, *The Jacksonian Era* (1959).

Democracy. Patrick T. Conley, *Democracy in Decline* (1977). Marvin E. Gettleman, *The Dorr Rebellion* (1973). Louis Hartz, *The Liberal Tradition in America* (1955). Michael Kammen, *Spheres of Liberty: Changing Perceptions of Liberty in American Culture* (1986). Moisie Ostrogorskii, *Democracy and the Organization of Political Parties*, 2 vols. (1902). Fred Somkin, *Unquiet Eagle: Memory and Desire in the Idea of American Freedom, 1815–1860* (1967). Alexis de Tocqueville, *Democracy in America*, 2 vols. (1835). Chilton Williamson, *American Suffrage from Property to Democracy, 1760–1860* (1960).

Jacksonian Society. Kenneth Cmiel, *Democratic Eloquence: The Fight over Popular Speech in Nineteenth-Century America* (1990). Nancy Hewitt, *Women's Activism and Social Change: Rochester, New York, 1822–1872* (1984). Douglas T. Miller, *Jacksonian Aristocracy* (1967). Edward Pessen, *Riches, Class, and Power Before the Civil War* (1973). Mary Ryan, *Cradle of the Middle Class: The Family in Oneida County, New York, 1790–1865* (1981). Carroll Smith-Rosenberg, *Religion and the Rise of the City* (1971). Christine Stansell, *City of Women: Sex and Class in New York, 1789–1860* (1986). Sean Wilentz, *Chants Democratic: New York City and the Rise of the American Working Class, 1788–1850* (1984).

Jacksonian Politics. Lee Benson, *The Concept of Jacksonian Democracy* (1961). Ronald P. Formisano, *The Birth of Mass Political Parties: Michigan, 1928–1861* (1971). Paul Goodman, *Towards a Christian Republic: Antimasonry and the Great Tradition in New England, 1826–1836* (1988). Richard Hofstadter, *The American Political Tradition* (1948). Morton Horwitz, *The Transformation of American Law, 1780–1860* (1977). Richard B. Latner, *The Presidency of Andrew Jackson: White House Politics, 1829–1837* (1979). Richard B. McCormick, *The Second American Party System: Party Formation in the Jacksonian Era* (1966). Marvin Meyers, *The Jacksonian Persuasion* (1960). Robert V. Remini, *The Age of Jackson* (1972); *Andrew Jackson and the Bank War* (1967). C. B. Swisher, *Roger B. Taney* (1936). John William Ward, *Andrew Jackson: Symbol for an Age* (1955). Harry L. Watson, *Jacksonian Politics and Community Conflict: The Emergence of the Second Party System in Cumberland County, North Carolina* (1981); *Liberty and Power: The Politics of Jacksonian America* (1990). Leonard White, *The Jacksonians: A Study in Administrative History* (1954).

Andrew Jackson. Marquis James, *Andrew Jackson*, 2 vols. (1933–1937). James Parton, *Life of Andrew Jackson*, 3 vols. (1860). Robert V. Remini, *Andrew Jackson and the Course of*

American Empire: 1767–1821 (1977); *Andrew Jackson and the Course of American Freedom: 1822–1832* (1981); *Andrew Jackson and the Course of American Democracy* (1984); *The Life of Andrew Jackson* (1988).

Nullification. William V. Freehling, *Prelude to Civil War: The Nullification Controversy in South Carolina* (1966). Merrill D. Peterson, *Olive Branch and Sword: The Compromise of 1833* (1983). Charles S. Sydnor, *The Development of Southern Sectionalism 1819–1848* (1948). Charles M. Wiltse, *John C. Calhoun: Nullifier* (1949).

Indian Policies. William Brandon, *The Last Americans* (1974). Angie Debo, *A History of the Indians of the United States* (1970); *The Road to Disappearance: A History of the Creek Indians* (1941); *And Still the Waters Run: The Betrayal of the Five Civilized Tribes* (1973). Arthur H. DeRosier, Jr., *The Removal of the Choctaw Indians* (1970). Cecil Elby, "*That Disgraceful Affair*" (1973). Grant Foreman, *Indian Removal: The Emigration of the Five Civilized Tribes* (1932); *Indians and Pioneers: The Story of the American Southwest Before 1830* (1936). Michael D. Green, *The Politics of Indian Removal: Cherokee Government and Society in Crisis* (1982). Daniel F. Littlefield, Jr., *Africans and Seminoles: From Removal to Emancipation* (1976); *Africans and Creeks: From the Colonial Period to the Civil War* (1979). Theda Perdue, *Slavery and the Evolution of Cherokee Society, 1540–1866* (1979). Francis P. Prucha, *American Indian Policy in the Formative Years* (1962). Michael Rogin, *Fathers and Children: Andrew Jackson and the Destruction of American Indians* (1975). Ronald N. Satz, *American Indian Policy in the Jacksonian Era* (1975). B. W. Sheehan, *Seeds of Extinction: Jeffersonian Philanthropy and the American Indian* (1973). Wilcomb E. Washburn, *The Indian in America* (1975). Richard White, *The Roots of Dependency* (1983). Thurman Wilkins, *Cherokee Tragedy* (1970).

The Bank War. T. P. Govan, *Nicholas Biddle, Nationalist and Public Banker* (1959). Bray Hammond, *Banks and Politics in America from the Revolution to the Civil War* (1957). John M. McFaul, *The Politics of Jacksonian Finance* (1972). Reginald C. McGrane, *The Panic of 1937* (1924). Robert V. Remini, *Andrew Jackson and the Bank War* (1967). William G. Shade, *Banks or No Banks: The Money Issue in Western Politics, 1832–1865* (1972). James R. Sharp, *The Jacksonians Versus the Banks* (1970). Peter Temin, *The Jacksonian Economy* (1969). J. A. Wilburn, *Biddle's Bank* (1967).

Post-Jacksonian Politics. John Ashworth, "*Agrarians*" and "*Aristocrats*": *Party Political Ideology in the United States, 1837–1846* (1983). Irving Bartlett, *Daniel Webster* (1978). Maurice C. Baxter, *One and Inseparable: Daniel Webster and the Union* (1984). John B. Brebner, *North Atlantic Triangle* (1945). Norman D. Brown, *Daniel Webster and the Politics of Availability* (1969). Thomas Brown, *Politics and Statesmanship: Essays on the American Whig Party* (1985). E. M. Carroll, *Origins of the Whig Party* (1925). Oliver P. Chitwood, *John Tyler: Cham-*

pion of the Old South (1939). Donald B. Cole, *Martin Van Buren and the American Political System* (1984). A. B. Corey, *The Crisis of the 1830–1842 in Canadian-American Relations* (1941). Richard N. Current, *Daniel Webster and the Rise of National Conservatism* (1955). James C. Curtis, *The Fox at Bay: Martin Van Buren and the Presidency* (1970). Robert Dalzell, *Daniel Webster and the Trial of American Nationalism* (1973). Clement Eaton, *Henry Clay and the Art of American Politics* (1957). Claude M. Fuess, *Daniel Webster*, 2 vols. (1930). Paul Goodman, *Toward a Christian Republic: Anti-Masonry and the Great Transition in New England, 1826–1836* (1988). R. G. Gunderson, *The Log Cabin Campaign* (1957). Daniel Walker Howe, *The Political Culture of the American Whigs* (1979). Howard Jones, *To the Webster-Ashburton Treaty* (1977). Oscar D. Lambert, *Presidential Politics in the United States, 1841–1844* (1936). Sydney Nathans, *Daniel Webster and Jacksonian Democracy* (1973). John Niven, *Martin Van Buren: The Romantic Age of American Politics* (1983). Thomas H. O'Connor, *Lords of the Loom: The Cotton Whigs and the Coming of the Civil War* (1968). Merrill D. Peterson, *The Great Triumvirate: Webster, Clay, and Calhoun* (1987). George R. Poage, *Henry Clay and the Whig Party* (1936). Robert V. Remini, *Martin Van Buren and the Making of the Democratic Party* (1959); *Henry Clay: Statesman for the Union* (1991). Alexander Saxton, *The Rise and Fall of the White Republic: Class Politics and Mass Culture in Nineteenth-Century America* (1990). William Preston Vaughn, *The Anti-Masonic Party in the United States, 1826–1843* (1983). Major L. Wilson, *The Presidency of Martin Van Buren* (1984).

THE FACTORY COMES TO NEW ENGLAND
This poster of the Bradley Fertilizer Company's factory in North Weymouth, Massachusetts, suggests both the rural character of the surrounding countryside in these early years of industrialization and the dramatic changes the factory system would soon impose on the region—and the nation. *(Bettmann)*

CHAPTER TEN

AMERICA'S ECONOMIC REVOLUTION

HEN THE UNITED STATES entered the War of 1812, it was still an essentially agrarian nation. There were, to be sure, cities in America, several of substantial size. And in some of them there was a flourishing mercantile economy, based largely on overseas trade. There was also modest but growing manufacturing activity, concentrated mainly in the Northeast. But the overwhelming majority of Americans were farmers and tradespeople, working within an economy that was still mainly local.

By the time the Civil War began in 1861, the United States had transformed itself. Most Americans were still rural people, to be sure. But even most American farmers were now part of a national, and increasingly international, market economy. Above all, perhaps, the United States had developed a major manufacturing sector and was beginning to challenge the industrial nations of Europe for supremacy. The nation had experienced the beginning of its industrial revolution; and while the changes that revolution produced were far from complete, most Americans understood that their world had changed irrevocably.

These dramatic changes—changes that affected not just the economy, but society, culture, and politics as well—did not have the same impact everywhere. The Northeast, and its new economic ally the Northwest, were rapidly developing a complex, modern economy and society, dominated by large cities, important manufacturing, and profitable commercial farming. It was in many ways an unequal society, but it was also a fluid one, firmly committed to the ideal of free labor. Relatively few white Americans yet lived west of the

Mississippi River, but parts of those western lands, too, were becoming part of large-scale commercial agriculture and other enterprises and were creating links to the capitalist economy of the Northeast.

In the South and Southwest, there were changes too. Southern agriculture, particularly cotton farming, flourished as never before in response to the growing demand from textile mills in New England and elsewhere. But while the southern states were becoming increasingly a part of the national and international capitalist economies, they also remained much less developed than their northern counterparts. And as the North became ever more committed to the fluidity and mobility of its free-labor system, the South was becoming more and more resolute in its defense of slavery.

The industrial revolution, which was doing so much to draw the nation into a single, integrated economy, was also working to isolate—and, increasingly, to alarm—the residents of one of its regions. It was transforming the nation. It was also dividing it.

FOUNDATIONS OF ECONOMIC DEVELOPMENT

The American industrial revolution was a result of many factors. Before it could occur, the United States needed a population large enough both to grow its own food and to provide a work force for the industrial economy. It needed a transportation and com-

269

POPULATION GROWTH, 1620–1860

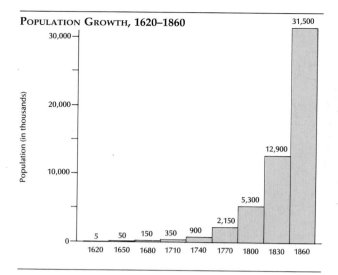

munications system capable of sustaining commerce over a large geographical area. It needed the technology to permit manufacturing on a large scale. And it needed systems of business organization capable of managing large industrial enterprises. By 1860, the northern regions of the nation had acquired at least the beginnings of all those things.

The American Population, 1820–1840

Between 1820 and 1840, not only did the population of the United States dramatically increase, but much of it became concentrated in the industrial centers of the Northeast and Northwest, where it provided a labor force for the growing factory system.

Three trends characterized the American population in these years, all of them contributing in various ways to economic growth. The population was increasing rapidly. Much of it was moving westward. And much of it was moving to towns and cities.

The American population had stood at only 4 million in 1790. By 1820, it had reached 10 million; by 1830, nearly 13 million; and by 1840, 17 million. The United States was growing much more rapidly in population than Britain or Europe and by 1860 had passed the United Kingdom and nearly overtaken Germany and France.

Public health efforts gradually improved, and the number and ferocity of epidemics (such as the great cholera plague of 1832) slowly declined, as did the mortality rate as a whole. But the population increase was also a result of a high birth rate. In 1840, the birth

rate for white women stood at 6.14, a decline from the very high rates of the eighteenth century but still substantial enough to produce rapid population increases.

Immigration, choked off by wars in Europe and economic crises in America, contributed little to the American population in the first three decades of the nineteenth century. Of the total 1830 population of nearly 13 million, the foreign-born numbered fewer than 500,000. Soon, however, immigration began to grow once again. It reached a total of 60,000 for 1832 and nearly 80,000 for 1837. Reduced transportation costs and increasing economic opportunities in America helped stimulate the immigration boom, as did deteriorating economic conditions in some areas of Europe. The migrations introduced new groups to the United States. In particular, the number of immigrants arriving from the southern (Catholic) counties of Ireland began to grow, marking the beginning of a tremendous influx of Irish Catholics that was to occur in the three decades before the Civil War.

Much of this new European immigration flowed into the rapidly growing cities of the Northeast. But urban growth was a result of substantial internal migration as well. As the agricultural regions of New England and other areas grew less profitable, more and more people picked up stakes and moved—some to more promising agricultural regions in the West, but many to eastern cities. In 1790, one person in thirty had lived in a city (defined as a community of 8,000 or more); in 1820, one in twenty; and in 1840, one in twelve. The largest such cities were in the Northeast.

The rise of New York City was particularly dramatic. By 1810 it was the largest city in the United States. That was partly a result of its superior natural harbor. It was also a result of the Erie Canal (completed

SOURCES OF IMMIGRATION, 1820–1840

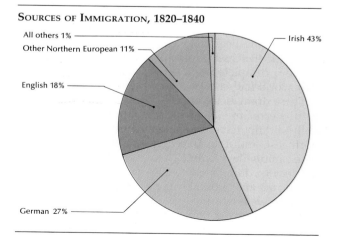

TOTAL IMMIGRATION, 1840–1860

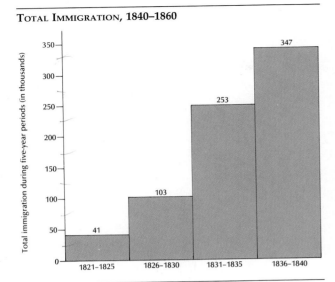

in 1825), which gave the city unrivaled access to the interior. And it was a result, too, of liberal state laws that made the city attractive for both foreign and domestic commerce.

free states?

Immigration and Urban Growth, 1840–1860

The growth of cities accelerated dramatically between 1840 and 1860. The population of New York, for example, rose from 312,000 to 805,000. (New York's population would have numbered 1.2 million in 1860 if Brooklyn, which was then a separate municipality, had been included in the total.) Philadelphia's population grew over the same twenty-year period from 220,000 to 565,000; Boston's from 93,000 to 177,000. By 1860, 26 percent of the population of the free states was living in towns (places of 2,500 people or more) or cities, up from 14 percent in 1840. That percentage was even higher for the industrializing states of the Northeast. (In the South, by contrast, the increase of urban residents was only from 6 percent in 1840 to 10 percent in 1860.)

The booming agricultural economy of the western regions of the nation produced significant urban growth as well. Between 1820 and 1840, communities that had once been small villages or trading posts became major cities: St. Louis, Pittsburgh, Cincinnati, Louisville. All of them benefited from a strategic position on the Mississippi River or one of its major tributaries. All of them became centers of the growing

carrying trade that connected the farmers of the Midwest with New Orleans and, through it, the cities of the Northeast. After 1830, however, an increasing proportion of this shipping moved from the river to the Great Lakes and created major new urban centers that gradually superseded the river ports. Among them were Buffalo, Detroit, Milwaukee, Cleveland, and—most important in the end—Chicago.

The enlarged urban population was in part simply a reflection of the growth of the national population as a whole, which rose by more than a third—from 23 million to over 31 million—in the decade of the 1850s alone. But it was also a result of the continuing, indeed increasing, flow of people into cities from the farms of the Northeast, which continued to decline because of western and European competition. Immigration from abroad continued to increase as well. The number of foreigners arriving in the United States in 1840—84,000—was the highest for any one year to that point in the nineteenth century. But in later years, even that number would come to seem insignificant. Between 1840 and 1850, more than 1.5 million Europeans moved to America, three times the number of arrivals in the 1830s; in the last years of the decade, average annual immigration was almost 300,000. Of the 23 million people in the United States in 1850, 2.2 million (almost 10 percent) were foreign born. Still greater numbers arrived in the 1850s—over 2.5 million. Almost half the

LEAVING IRELAND

A priest blesses a group of villagers as they prepare to leave Ireland for America sometime in the 1830s. The departure was a wrenching experience both for those who left and those who stayed behind; but the poverty of the Irish countryside, suggested by this somber drawing, induced many people to leave. *(Culver)*

POPULATION DENSITY OF THE UNITED STATES, 1820

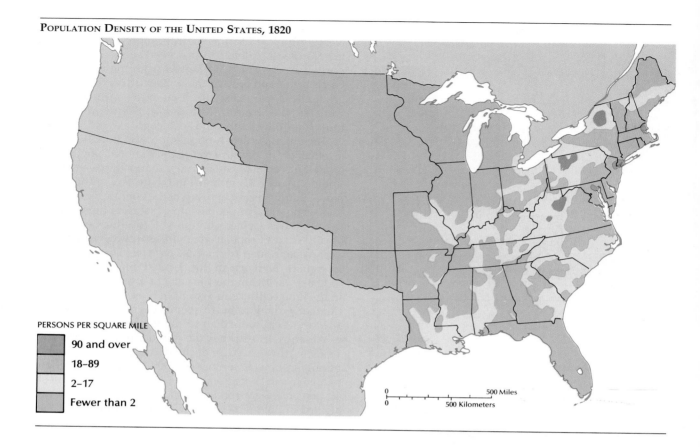

PERSONS PER SQUARE MILE

- 90 and over
- 18–89
- 2–17
- Fewer than 2

residents of New York City in the 1850s were recent immigrants. In St. Louis, Chicago, and Milwaukee, the foreign-born outnumbered those of native birth. Few immigrants settled in the South. Only 500,000 lived in the slave states in 1860, and a third of these were concentrated in Missouri.

The newcomers came from many different countries and regions: England, France, Italy, Scandinavia, Poland, and Holland. But the overwhelming majority came from Ireland and Germany. In 1850, the Irish constituted approximately 45 percent and the Germans over 20 percent of the foreign-born in America. By 1860, there were more than 1.5 million Irish-born and approximately 1 million German-born people in the United States. There were several reasons for this flood of immigration. The economic dislocations of the industrial revolution had caused widespread poverty in Germany, and the collapse of the liberal revolution there in 1848 also persuaded many Germans to emigrate. The failure of the potato and other crops had produced famine in Ireland. English rule was so oppressive and unpopular that many Irish left the country to escape it.

The Irish and German patterns of settlement in America were very different. The great majority of the Irish settled in the eastern cities, where they swelled the ranks of unskilled labor. Most Germans moved on to the Northwest, where they became farmers or went into business in the western towns. One reason for the difference was wealth: German immigrants generally arrived with at least some money; the Irish had practically none. Another important reason was gender. Most German immigrants were members of family groups or were single men, for whom movement to the agricultural frontier was both possible and attractive. Many Irish immigrants were young, single women, for whom movement west was much less plausible. They were more likely to stay in the eastern cities, where factory and domestic work was available.

The Rise of Nativism

The new foreign-born population almost immediately became a major factor in American political life. Wisconsin, after its admission to the Union in 1848, permitted aliens to become voters as soon as they had declared their intention of seeking citizenship and had resided in the state for a year. Other states followed Wisconsin's lead in liberalizing voting laws, and in most places polling officials were even more generous than the law allowed. Many politicians saw in the immigrant population a source of important potential support, and they eagerly courted the new arrivals for their ballots. Others, however, viewed the growing foreign population with alarm. Their fears led to the first important organized nativist movements in American history.

The emerging nativism took many forms. Some nativists argued that the immigrants were mentally and physically defective, that they bred urban slums, that they corrupted politics by selling their votes. Others complained that because the aliens were willing to work for low wages, they were stealing jobs from the native work force. Protestants took note of the Irish Catholics' aptitude for politics and claimed that the church of Rome was attaining an undue power in American government. Whig politicians were outraged because so many of the newcomers voted Dem-

ocratic. Many Americans of older stock feared that immigrants would inject new and radical philosophies into national thought.

Out of these tensions and prejudices emerged a number of secret societies to combat the "alien menace." Most of them originated in the Northeast. Some later spread to the West and even to the South. The first of these, the Native American Association, began agitating against immigration in 1837. In 1845, nativists held a convention in Philadelphia and formed the Native American Party. But anti-immigrant sentiment crested in the 1850s. Many of the nativist groups combined in 1850 to form the Supreme Order of the Star-Spangled Banner. It endorsed a list of demands that included banning Catholics or aliens from holding public office, more restrictive naturalization laws, and literacy tests for voting. The order adopted a strict code of secrecy, which included the secret password, used in lodges across the country, "I know nothing." Ultimately, members of the movement became known as the "Know-Nothings."

Gradually, the Know-Nothings turned their attention to party politics, and after the election of 1852 they

POPULATION DENSITY OF THE UNITED STATES, 1860

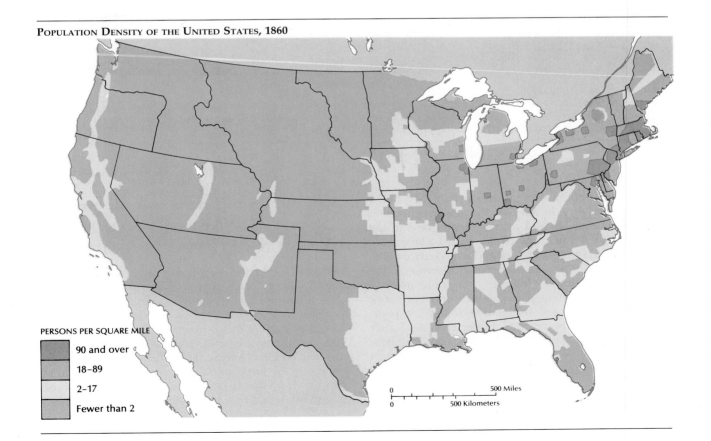

PERSONS PER SQUARE MILE

90 and over

18–89

2–17

Fewer than 2

| 0 | | 500 Miles |
| 0 | | 500 Kilometers |

THE PORT OF NEW YORK, 1828
This view of South Street in Manhattan shows the East River lined with docks. Other docks, similarly busy, lined the Hudson River on the opposite side of the island, a sign of the city's emergence as the preeminent commercial center in the nation. The population of New York City was approaching 150,000 by 1828.   *(New York Public Library)*

created a new political organization that they called the American Party. In the East, the new organization scored an immediate and astonishing success in the elections of 1854: the Know-Nothings cast a large vote in Pennsylvania and New York and won control of the state government in Massachusetts. Elsewhere, the progress of the Know-Nothings was more modest. Western members of the party, because of the presence of many German voters in the area, found it expedient to not oppose naturalized Protestants. And after 1854, the strength of the Know-Nothings declined generally. The Know-Nothing Party's most lasting impact was its contribution to the collapse of the second party system and the creation of new national political alignments.

TRANSPORTATION AND COMMUNICATIONS REVOLUTIONS

Just as the industrial revolution required an expanding population, it also required an efficient and effective system of transportation and communications. Without such a system, merchants and manufacturers would be unable to ship their goods to distant markets or communicate effectively with trading partners in other regions. And without such a system, the industrial work force would not have access to the food supplies it needed to sustain itself. The first half of the nineteenth century saw dramatic changes in both

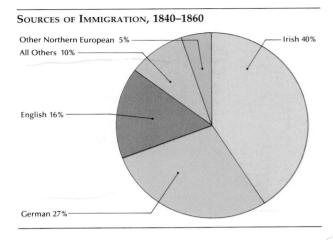

SOURCES OF IMMIGRATION, 1840–1860

Irish 40%
German 27%
English 16%
All Others 10%
Other Northern European 5%

transportation and communication in the United States.

The Canal Age

From 1790 until the 1820s, the so-called turnpike era, the United States had relied largely on roads for internal transportation. But in a country as large as the United States was becoming, roads alone (and the mostly horse-drawn vehicles that used them) were not adequate for the nation's expanding needs. And so, in the 1820s and 1830s, Americans began to turn to other means of transportation as well. The larger rivers, especially the Mississippi and the Ohio, had been important transportation routes for years, but most of the traffic on them consisted of flat barges—little more than rafts—that floated downstream laden with cargo and were broken up at the end of their journeys because they could not navigate back upstream. To return north, shippers had to send goods by land or by agonizingly slow upstream vessels that sometimes took up to four months to travel the length of the Mississippi.

These rivers became vastly more important as steamboats grew in number and improved in design. The new riverboats carried the corn and wheat of northwestern farmers and the cotton and tobacco of southwestern planters to New Orleans in a fraction of the time of the old barges. From New Orleans, ocean-going ships took the cargoes on to eastern ports. Steamboats also developed a significant passenger traffic, and companies built increasingly lavish vessels to compete for this lucrative trade (even though most passengers could not afford the luxurious amenities and slept in the hold or on the deck).

But neither the farmers of the West nor the merchants of the East were satisfied with this pattern of trade. Farmers would pay less to transport their goods (and eastern consumers would pay less to consume them) if they could ship them directly eastward to market, rather than by the roundabout river-sea route; and northeastern merchants, too, could sell larger quantities of their manufactured goods if they could transport their merchandise more directly and economically to the West. New highways across the mountains provided a partial solution to the problem. But the costs of hauling goods overland, although lower than before, were still too high for anything except the most compact and valuable merchandise.

Four horses could haul one and a half tons eighteen miles in a day on the turnpikes. But the same four horses could draw a boatload of a hundred tons twenty-four miles a day on a canal. And so, in some areas, interest grew rapidly in building new inland waterways. Canal building was too expensive for private enterprise, and the job of digging canals fell largely to the states. The ambitious state governments of the Northeast took the lead in constructing them. New York was the first to act. It had the natural advantage of a good land route between the Hudson River and Lake Erie through the only break in the Appalachian chain. But the engineering tasks were still imposing. The distance was more than 350 miles, several times

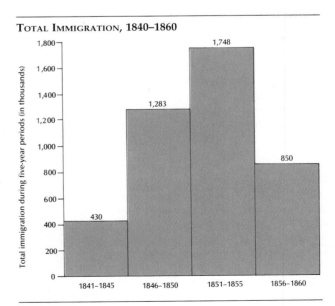

TOTAL IMMIGRATION, 1840–1860

Total immigration during five-year periods (in thousands)

Period	Immigration
1841–1845	430
1846–1850	1,283
1851–1855	1,748
1856–1860	850

as long as any of the existing canals in America. The
route was interrupted by high ridges and a wilderness
of woods. After a long public debate over whether the
scheme was practical, canal advocates prevailed when
De Witt Clinton, a late but ardent convert to the cause,
became governor in 1817. Digging began on July 4,
1817.

The building of the Erie Canal was the greatest construction project Americans had ever undertaken. The
canal itself was simple: basically a ditch forty feet wide
and four feet deep, with towpaths along the banks for
the horses or mules that were to draw the canal boats.
But hundreds of difficult cuts and fills, some of them
enormous, were required to enable the canal to pass
through hills and over valleys; stone aqueducts were
necessary to carry it across streams; and eighty-eight
locks, of heavy masonry with great wooden gates,
were needed to permit ascents and descents. The Erie
Canal was not just an engineering triumph, but an immediate financial success. It opened in October 1825,
amid elaborate ceremonies and celebrations, and traffic was soon so heavy that within about seven years
tolls had repaid the entire cost of construction. By providing a route to the Great Lakes, the canal gave New
York access to Chicago and the growing markets of
the West.

The system of water transportation extended farther when the states of Ohio and Indiana, inspired by
the success of the Erie Canal, provided water connections between Lake Erie and the Ohio River. These
canals made it possible to ship goods by inland waterways all the way from New York to New Orleans,
although it was still necessary to transfer cargoes several times between canal, lake, and river craft.

One of the immediate results of these new transportation routes was increased white settlement in the
Northwest, because it had suddenly become easier for
migrants to make the westward journey and to ship
their goods back to eastern markets. Much of the western produce continued to go downriver to New Orleans, but an increasing proportion (including most of
the wheat of the Northwest) went east to New York.
And manufactured goods from throughout the East
now moved in growing volume through New York
and then by the new water routes to the West.

Rival cities along the Atlantic seaboard took alarm
at the prospect of New York's acquiring so vast a hin-
terland, largely at their expense. But they had limited
success in catching up. Boston, its way to the Hudson
River blocked by the Berkshire Mountains, did not
even try to connect itself to the West by canal; its hin-
terland would remain confined largely to New En-

CANALS IN THE NORTHEAST, TO 1860

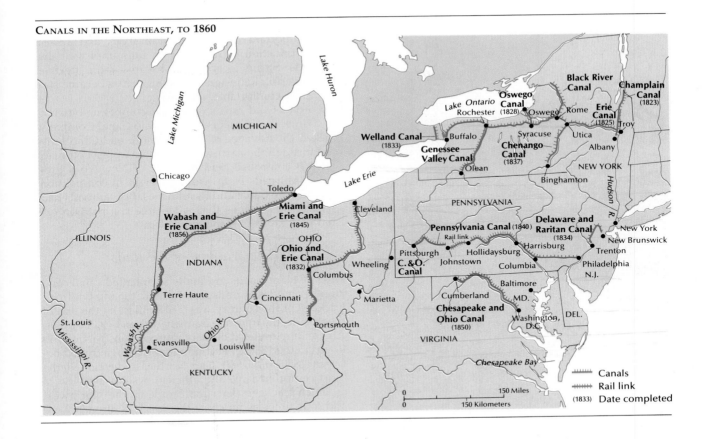

gland. Philadelphia and Baltimore had the still more formidable Allegheny Mountains to contend with. They made a serious effort at canal building, nevertheless, but with discouraging results. Pennsylvania's effort ended in an expensive failure. Maryland constructed part of the Chesapeake and Ohio Canal beginning in 1828, but completed only the stretch between Washington, D.C., and Cumberland, Maryland, and thus never crossed the mountains. In the South, Richmond and Charleston also aspired to build water routes to the Ohio Valley, but never completed them.

In the end, canals did not provide a satisfactory way to the West for any of New York's rivals. Some cities, however, saw their opportunity in a different and newer means of transportation. Even before the canal age had reached its height, the era of the railroad was already beginning.

The Early Railroads

Railroads played no more than a secondary role in the nation's transportation system in the 1820s and 1830s,

but railroad pioneers laid the groundwork in those years for the great surge of railroad building in mid-century that would link the nation together as never before. Eventually, railroads became the primary transportation system for the United States, and they remained so until the construction of the interstate highway system in the mid-twentieth century.

Railroads emerged from a combination of technological and entrepreneurial innovations: the invention of tracks, the creation of steam-powered locomotives, and the development of trains as public carriers of passengers and freight. By 1804, both English and American inventors had experimented with steam engines for propelling land vehicles. In 1820, John Stevens ran a locomotive and cars around a circular track on his New Jersey estate. And in 1825, the Stockton and Darlington Railroad in England opened a short length of track and became the first line to carry general traffic.

American entrepreneurs, especially in those northeastern cities that sought better communication with the West, quickly grew interested in the English experiment. The first company to begin actual operations was the Baltimore and Ohio, which opened a thirteen-

THE UNION CANAL
The Union Canal, shown here running through Lebanon, Pennsylvania, about 1830, was one of many such projects that attempted to connect the commercial cities of the east with the growing territories west of the Appalachians. Only New York's Erie Canal really succeeded in that goal, although shorter canals such as this one were important to local commerce. *(Pennsylvania Historical Society)*

mile stretch of track in 1830. In New York, the Mohawk and Hudson began running trains along the sixteen miles between Schenectady and Albany in 1831. By 1836, more than a thousand miles of track had been laid in eleven states.

But there was not yet a true railroad system. Even the longest of the lines was comparatively short in the 1830s, and most of them served simply to connect water routes, not to link one railroad to another. Even when two lines did connect, the tracks often differed in gauge (width), so that cars from one line often could not fit onto the tracks of another. Schedules were er-

ratic, and wrecks were frequent. But railroads made some important advances in the 1830s and 1840s. The introduction of heavier iron rails improved the roadbeds. Steam locomotives became more flexible and powerful. Redesigned passenger cars became stabler, more comfortable, and larger.

Railroads and canals were soon competing bitterly. For a time, the Chesapeake and Ohio Canal Company blocked the advance of the Baltimore and Ohio Railroad through the narrow gorge of the upper Potomac, which it controlled; and the state of New York prohibited railroads from hauling freight in competition with the Erie Canal and its branches. But railroads had so many advantages that when free competition existed they almost always prevailed.

The Triumph of the Rails

After 1840, railroads gradually supplanted canals and all other modes of transport. In 1840, the total railroad trackage of the country was 2,818 miles; by the end of the decade, the trackage figure had risen to 9,021 miles. And an unparalleled burst of railroad construction followed in the 1850s. The amount of trackage tripled between 1850 and 1860. The Northeast developed the most comprehensive and efficient system, with twice as much trackage per square mile as the Northwest and four times as much as the South. Railroads were even reaching west of the Mississippi, spanned at several points by great iron bridges. One line ran from Hannibal to St. Joseph on the Missouri River, and another was under construction between St. Louis and Kansas City.

An important change in railroad development—one that would profoundly affect the nature of sectional alignments—was the trend toward the consolidation of short lines into longer lines (known as "trunk lines"). By 1853, four major railroad trunk lines had surmounted the Appalachian barrier to connect the Northeast with the Northwest. Two, the New York Central and the New York and Erie, gave New York City access to the Lake Erie ports. The Pennsylvania road linked Philadelphia and Pittsburgh, and the Baltimore and Ohio connected Baltimore with the Ohio River at Wheeling. From the terminals of these lines, other railroads into the interior touched the Mississippi River at eight points. Chicago became the rail center of the West, served by fifteen lines and more than a hundred daily trains. The appearance of the great trunk lines tended to divert traffic from the main water routes—the Erie Canal and the Mississippi River. By lessening the dependence of the West on the Mississippi, the railroads helped weaken further the connection between the Northwest and the South.

RACING ON THE RAILROAD
Peter Cooper, who in later years was best known as a philanthropist and as the founder of the Cooper Union in New York City, was also a successful iron manufacturer. Cooper designed and built the first steam-powered locomotive in America in 1830 for the Baltimore and Ohio railroad. On August 28 of that year, he raced his locomotive (the "Tom Thumb") against a horse-drawn railroad car. This sketch depicts the moment when Cooper's engine overtook the horse-car. *(Museum of the City of New York)*

Capital to finance the railroad boom came from various sources. Private American investors provided part of the necessary funding, and railroad companies borrowed large sums from abroad. But local governments—states, counties, cities, towns—also often contributed capital, because they were eager to have railroads serve them. This support took the form of loans, stock subscriptions, subsidies, and donations of land for rights-of-way. The railroads obtained substantial additional assistance from the federal government in the form of public land grants. In 1850, Senator Stephen A. Douglas of Illinois and other railroad-minded politicians persuaded Congress to grant federal lands to aid the Illinois Central, which was building toward the Gulf of Mexico. Other states and their railroad promoters demanded the same privileges, and by 1860, Congress had allotted over 30 million acres to eleven states to assist railroad construction.

Innovations in Communications and Journalism

Facilitating the operation of the railroads was an important innovation in communications: the magnetic telegraph. Its lines extended along the tracks, connecting one station with another and aiding the scheduling and routing of the trains. But the telegraph had an importance to the nation's economic development beyond its contribution to the railroads. On the one hand, it permitted instant communication between distant cities, tying the nation together as never before. On the other hand, it helped reinforce the schism between the North and South. Like railroads, telegraph lines were far more extensive in the North than in the South, and they helped similarly to link the North to the Northwest (and thus to separate the Northwest further from the South).

The telegraph had burst into American life in 1844, when Samuel F. B. Morse, after several years of experimentation, succeeded in transmitting from Baltimore to Washington the news of James K. Polk's nomination for the presidency. The relatively low cost of constructing wire systems made the Morse telegraph system seem the ideal answer to the problems of long-distance communication. By 1860, more than 50,000 miles of wire connected most parts of the country; and a year later, the Pacific telegraph, with 3,595 miles of wire, opened between New York and San Francisco. By then, nearly all the independent lines had joined in one organization, the Western Union Telegraph Company.

New forms of journalism also drew communities together into a common communications system. In 1846, Richard Hoe invented the steam cylinder rotary press, making it possible to print newspapers rapidly and cheaply. The development of the telegraph, together with the introduction of the rotary press, made possible much speedier collection and distribution of news than ever before. In 1846, newspaper publishers from around the nation formed the Associated Press to promote cooperative news gathering by wire; no

THE GROWTH OF THE RAILROADS, 1850–1860

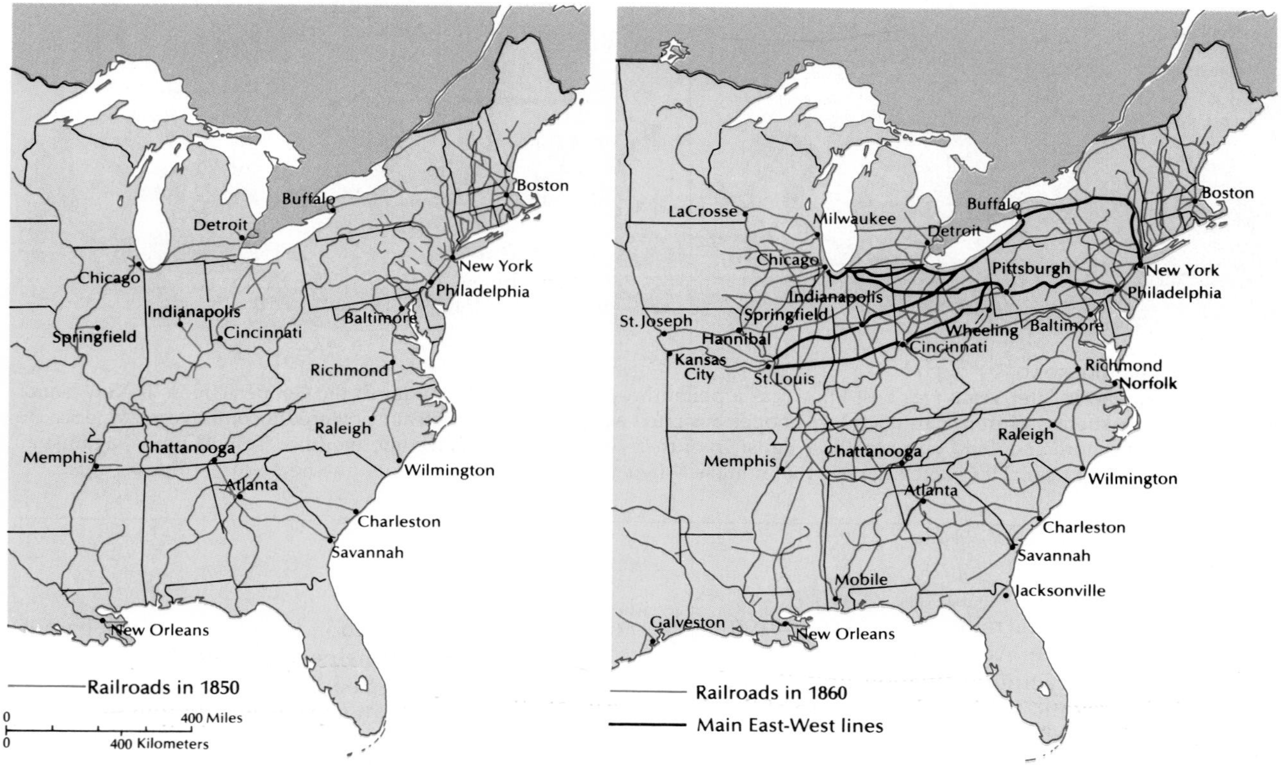

Railroads in 1850

0   400 Miles

0   400 Kilometers

Railroads in 1860

Main East-West lines

longer did they have to depend on the cumbersome exchange of newspapers for out-of-town reports.

Major metropolitan newspapers began to appear in the larger cities of the Northeast. In New York alone, there were Horace Greeley's *Tribune*, James Gordon Bennett's *Herald*, and Henry J. Raymond's *Times*. All gave serious attention to national and even international events and had substantial circulations beyond the city.

In the long run, journalism would become an important unifying factor in American life. In the 1840s and 1850s, however, the rise of the new journalism helped to feed sectional discord. Most of the major magazines and newspapers were in the North, reinforcing the South's sense of subjugation. Southern newspapers tended to have smaller budgets and reported largely local news. Few had any impact outside their immediate communities. The combined circulation of the *Tribune* and the *Herald* exceeded that of all the daily newspapers published in the South put together. Above all, the news revolution—along with the revolutions in transportation and communications that accompanied it—contributed to a growing awareness within each section of how the other sections lived and of the deep differences that had grown up between the North and the South—differences that would ultimately seem irreconcilable.

COMMERCE AND INDUSTRY

The growth of an urban population and the development of new transportation and communications systems were both causes and results of the dramatic growth of commerce and industry in nineteenth-century America. By the middle years of the nineteenth century, the United States had developed the beginnings of a modern capitalist economy and an advanced industrial capacity. But this economic development had also occurred along highly unequal lines—benefiting certain classes and certain regions far more than others.

THE CYLINDRICAL PRESS
The revolving cylindrical press revolutionized newspaper (and other) publishing in the decades before the Civil War by making possible the printing of large numbers of papers relatively quickly. This ten-cylinder model dates from about 1850. *(Bettmann)*

The Expansion of Business, 1820–1840

American business grew rapidly in the 1820s and 1830s, partly because of population growth and the transportation revolution, but also because of the daring, imagination, and ruthlessness of a new generation of entrepreneurs.

One important change came in the retail distribution of goods, which was becoming increasingly systematic and efficient. In the larger cities, stores specializing in groceries, dry goods, hardware, and other lines appeared, although residents of smaller towns and villages still depended on the general store and did much of their business by barter.

The organization of business was also changing. Individuals or limited partnerships continued to operate most businesses, and the dominating figures were still the great merchant capitalists, who generally had sole ownership of their enterprises. In some larger businesses, however, the individual merchant capitalist was giving way to the corporation. Corporations had the advantage of combining the resources of a large number of shareholders, and they began to develop particularly rapidly in the 1830s, when some legal obstacles to their formation were removed. Previously, a corporation could obtain a charter only by a special act of the state legislature—a cumbersome process that stifled corporate growth. By the 1830s, however, states were beginning to pass general incorporation laws, under which a group could secure a charter merely by paying a fee. The laws also permitted a system of limited liability, which meant that individual stockhold-ers risked losing only the value of their own investment if a corporation should fail, and that they were not liable (as they had been in the past) for the corporation's larger losses. The rise of these new corporations made possible the accumulation of much greater amounts of capital and hence made possible much larger manufacturing and business enterprises.

But investment alone still provided too little capital to meet the demands of the most ambitious businesses. They relied on credit, which often created dangerous instability. Credit mechanisms remained very crude in the early nineteenth century. The government alone could issue currency, but the official currency consisted only of gold and silver (or paper certificates backed literally by gold and silver), and there was thus too little of it to support the growing demand for credit. Under pressure from corporate promoters, many banks issued large quantities of bank notes to provide capital for expanding business ventures—some far in excess of their own reserves. As a result, bank failures were frequent and bank deposits often insecure.

The Emergence of the Factory

All of these changes—increasing population, improved transportation and communications, and the expansion of business activity—contributed to perhaps the most profound economic development in mid-nineteenth-century America: the rise of the factory.

Before the War of 1812, most of what manufacturing there was in the United States took place within households or in small, individually operated workshops. Gradually, however, improved technology and increasing demand produced a fundamental change. It came first in the New England textile industry. There, beginning early in the nineteenth century, entrepreneurs were beginning to make use of new machines driven by waterpower that allowed them to bring textile operations together under a single roof. This factory system, as it came to be known, spread rapidly in the 1820s and began to make serious inroads into the old home-based system of spinning thread and weaving cloth. It also penetrated the shoe industry, concentrated in eastern Massachusetts. Shoes were still largely handmade, but manufacturers were beginning to employ workers who specialized in one or another of the various tasks involved in production. Some factories began producing large numbers of identical shoes in ungraded sizes and without distinction as to rights and lefts. By the 1830s, factory production was spreading from textiles and shoes into other industries

CHICAGO, 1858
This photograph of the busy freight depot and grain elevators of the Illinois Central Railroad suggests the dramatic growth of Chicago in the 1850s as the great trading center of the central part of the United States. *(Chicago Historical Society)*

and from New England to other areas of the Northeast.

Machine technology advanced more rapidly in the United States in the mid-nineteenth century than in any other country in the world. Change was so rapid, in fact, that some manufacturers built their new machinery out of wood; by the time the wood wore out, they reasoned, improved technology would have made the machine obsolete. By the end of the 1830s, American technology had become so advanced—particularly in textile manufacturing—that industrialists in Britain and Europe were beginning to travel to the United States to learn new techniques, instead of the other way around.

The Expansion of Industry, 1840–1860

Between 1840 and 1860, American industry experienced even more dramatic growth. In 1840, the total value of manufactured goods produced in the United States stood at $483 million; ten years later the figure had climbed to over $1 billion; and in 1860 it reached close to $2 billion. For the first time, the value of manufactured goods was approximately equal to that of agricultural products.

Of the approximately 140,000 manufacturing establishments in the country in 1860, 74,000 were located in the Northeast. Moreover, they included most of the larger enterprises. Although the Northeast had only a little more than half the mills and factories of the nation, it produced more than two-thirds of the manufactured goods. Of the 1,311,000 workers in manufacturing in the United States, about 938,000 were employed in the mills and factories of New England and the mid-Atlantic states.

Even the most highly developed industries were still relatively immature and were far from the production levels they would later attain. Cotton manufacturers, for example, produced goods of coarse grade; fine items continued to come from England. The woolens industry suffered from a limited supply of domestic raw wool and could not even produce enough coarse goods to satisfy the home market. American industry exported little; it was not even able to meet fully the demands of American consumers. But technology and industrial ingenuity were preparing the way for future American industrial primacy.

By the 1840s, the machine tools used in the factories of the Northeast—such as the turret lathe, the grinding machine, and the universal milling machine—were already better than those in European factories. At the same time, the principle of interchangeable parts, first applied decades earlier in gun factories by Eli Whitney and Simeon North, was being introduced into many other industries. Coal was replacing wood as an industrial fuel, particularly in the smelting of iron. Coal was also generating power in steam engines, which were replacing the water power that had in the past driven most of the factory machinery in the Northeast. The production of coal, most of it mined around Pittsburgh in western Pennsylvania, leaped from 50,000 tons in 1820 to 14 million tons in 1860. The new power source made it possible to locate mills away from running streams and thus permitted industry to expand still more widely.

The great technical advances in American industry owed much to American inventors, as the patent records of the time make clear. In 1830, the number of inventions patented was 544; by 1850, the figure had risen to 993; and in 1860, it stood at 4,778. Several industries provide particularly vivid examples of how a technological innovation could produce a major economic change. In 1839, Charles Goodyear, a New England hardware merchant, discovered a method of vulcanizing rubber; by 1860, his process had found over 500 uses and had helped create a major American rubber industry. In 1846, Elias Howe of Massachusetts constructed a sewing machine; Isaac Singer made improvements on it, and the Howe-Singer machine was soon being used in the manufacture of ready-to-wear clothing. A few years later, during the Civil War, it would supply the Northern troops with uniforms.

The merchant capitalists—entrepreneurs who were engaged primarily in foreign and domestic trade and who at times invested some of their profits in small-scale manufacturing ventures—remained figures of importance in the 1840s. In such cities as New York, Philadelphia, and Boston, important and influential mercantile groups operated shipping lines to southern ports—carrying off cotton, rice, and sugar—or dispatched fleets of trading vessels to the ports of Europe and the Orient. Many of these vessels were the famous clippers, the fastest (and most beautiful) sailing ships afloat. In their heyday in the late 1840s and early 1850s, the clippers could average 300 miles a day, which compared favorably with the best time of contemporary steamships.

But merchant capitalism was declining by the middle of the century. This was partly because of the declining profitability of the export trade. The value of American exports, still largely agricultural, increased from $124 million in 1840 to $334 million in 1860; but

SPECIALIZED MANUFACTURING TOWNS: LOWELL, MASSACHUSETTS, 1832

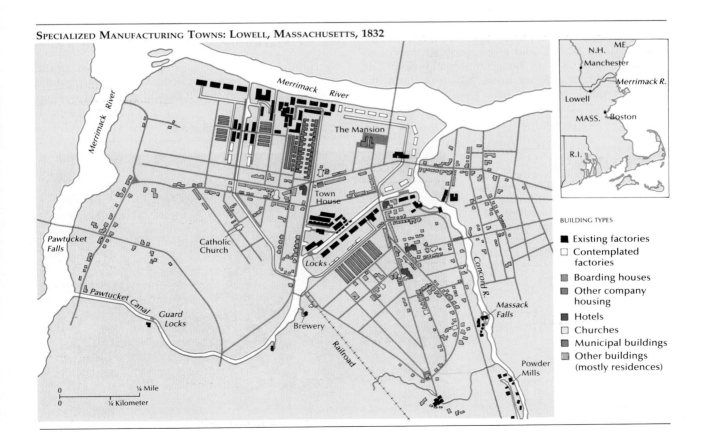

American merchants in the 1850s saw much of their carrying trade fall into the hands of British competitors, who enjoyed the advantages of steam-driven iron ships and government subsidies. The more important reason for the decline of merchant capitalism, however, was the discovery by the merchants themselves that there were greater opportunities for profit in manufacturing than in trade. They reduced their mercantile investments and invested instead in factories, at times becoming owners and operators of them. Indeed, one reason why industries developed soonest in the Northeast was that an affluent merchant class already existed there and had the money and the will to finance them.

As in the past, many business firms continued to be owned by individuals, families, or small groups of partners. But by the 1840s, particularly in the textile industry, the corporate form of organization was spreading rapidly. In their overseas ventures, merchants had been accustomed to diversifying their risks by buying shares in a number of vessels and voyages. They employed the same device when they moved their capital from trade to manufacturing, often purchasing shares in several textile companies. Ownership of American enterprise, in other words, was moving away from individuals and families and toward its highly dispersed modern form: many stockholders, each owning a relatively small proportion of the total. The discovery of new and more flexible forms of financing was, along with the technological innovations of the era, a crucial factor in the advancement of industrialization.

Whatever the form of business organization—and there continued to be many different forms—industrial capitalists soon became the new ruling class, the aristocrats of the Northeast. And just as they sought and secured economic dominance, they reached for and often achieved political influence. In local or national politics, the capitalists liked to be represented by highly literate lawyers who could articulate their prejudices and philosophy. Their ideal of a representative was Daniel Webster of Massachusetts, whom the business leaders of the section, at considerable financial cost to themselves, supported for years in the United States Senate.

MEN AND WOMEN AT WORK

However advanced industrial firms became technologically and administratively, manufacturers still relied above all on a supply of labor. In the 1820s and 1830s, factory labor came primarily from the native-born population. After 1840, the growing immigrant population became the most important new source of workers.

Recruiting a Native Work Force

Recruiting a labor force was not an easy task in the early years of the factory system. Ninety percent of the American people in the 1820s still lived and worked

WOMEN AT WORK, 1834
This engraving shows women at work in a New England textile mill, processing cotton into cloth. It illustrates the growing importance of heavy machinery in the textile industry, which made factory labor increasingly noisy, hot, and dangerous. *(The Granger Collection)*

NEW ENGLAND TEXTILE WORKERS
Women continued to constitute the majority of the work force in the cotton mills of New England even after the carefully monitored life of the "Lowell girls" became a thing of the past—as this 1868 engraving by Winslow Homer suggests. About 58 percent of the textile industry work force were female in the 1860s. Approximately 7 percent were children under twelve (shown here carrying their lunch pails alongside the adults). *(Library of Congress)*

on farms. City residents, although increasing in number, were still relatively few, and the potential workers among them even fewer. Many urban residents were skilled artisans who owned and managed their own shops as small businessmen; they were not likely to flock to factory jobs. The available unskilled workers were not numerous enough to form a reservoir from which the new industries could draw.

What did produce the beginnings of an industrial labor supply was the transformation of American agriculture in the nineteenth century. The opening of vast, fertile new farmlands in the Midwest, the improvement of transportation systems, the development of new farm machinery—all combined to increase food production dramatically. No longer did each region

have to feed itself entirely from its own farms; it could import food from other regions. And as this began to occur, some of the relatively unprofitable farming areas of the East began to decline. In the Northeast, and especially in New England, where poor land had always placed harsh limits on farm productivity, rural people began leaving the land to work in the factories.

Two systems of recruitment emerged to bring this new labor supply to the expanding textile mills. One, common in the mid-Atlantic states (especially in such major manufacturing centers as New York and Philadelphia), brought whole families from the farm to the mill. Parents tended looms alongside their children, some of whom were no more than four or five years old. The second system, common in Massachusetts, enlisted young women, mostly farmers' daughters in their late teens and early twenties. It was known as the Lowell or Waltham system, after the factory towns in which it first emerged. Many of these women worked for several years in the factories, saved their wages, and returned home to marry and raise children. Others married men they met in the factories or in town and remained part of the industrial world. But they often stopped working in the mills and took up domestic roles instead.

Labor conditions in these early years of the factory system were significantly better than those in English industry, better too than they would ultimately become in the United States. The employment of young children created undeniable hardships. But the misery was not as great as in European factories, since working children in America usually remained under the supervision of their parents. In England, by contrast, asylum authorities often hired out orphans to factory owners who showed little concern for their welfare and kept them in something close to slavery.

Even more distinct from the European labor system was the condition of working women in the mills in Lowell and factory towns like it. In England, as a parliamentary investigation revealed, women workers in the coal mines endured unimaginably wretched conditions. Some had to crawl on their hands and knees, naked and filthy, through cramped, narrow tunnels, pulling heavy coal carts behind them. It was little wonder that English visitors to America considered the Lowell mills a female paradise by contrast. The Lowell workers lived in clean boardinghouses and dormitories, which the factory owners maintained for them. They were well fed and carefully supervised. Because many New Englanders considered the employment of women to be vaguely immoral, the factory owners placed great emphasis on maintaining a proper environment for their employees, enforcing strict curfews and requiring regular church attendance. Employers quickly dismissed women suspected of immoral conduct. Wages for the Lowell workers were low, but generous by the standards of the time. The women even found time to write and publish a monthly magazine, the *Lowell Offering*.

Yet even these relatively well treated workers often found the transition from farm life to factory work difficult, even traumatic. Uprooted from everything familiar, forced to live among strangers in a regimented environment, many women suffered from loneliness and disorientation. Still more had difficulty adjusting to the nature of factory work—the repetition of fixed tasks hour after hour, day after day. That the women had to labor from sunrise to sunset was not in itself a new experience; many of them had worked similarly long days on the farm. But that they now had to spend those days performing tedious, unvarying chores, and that their schedules did not change from week to week or season to season, made the adjustment to factory work painful. But however uncomfortable women may have found factory work, they had few other options. They were barred from such manual labor as construction or from work as sailors or on the docks. Most of society considered it unthinkable for women to travel the country alone, as many men did, in search of opportunities. Work in the mills was in many cases virtually the only alternative to returning to farms that could no longer support them.

The paternalistic factory system of Lowell did not, in any case, survive for long. In the competitive textile market as it developed in the 1830s and 1840s—a market prey to the booms and busts that afflicted the American economy as a whole—manufacturers found it difficult to maintain the high living standards and reasonably attractive working conditions with which they had begun. Wages declined; the hours of work lengthened; the conditions of the boardinghouses deteriorated as the buildings decayed and overcrowding increased.

In 1834, mill workers in Lowell organized a union—the Factory Girls Association—which staged a strike to protest a 25 percent wage cut. Two years later, the association struck again—against a rent increase in the boardinghouses. Both strikes failed, and a recession in 1837 virtually destroyed the organization. Eight years later the Lowell women, led by the militant Sarah Bagley, created the Female Labor Reform Association and began agitating for a ten-hour day and for improvements in conditions in the mills. The new association not only made demands of management; it turned to state government and asked for legislative investigation of conditions in the mills. By then, however, the character of the factory work force was changing again. The mill girls were gradually moving into other occupations: teaching, domestic service, or marriage. And textile manufacturers were turning to a less contentious labor supply: immigrants.

The Immigrant Work Force

The increasing supply of immigrant workers after 1840 was a boon to manufacturers and other entrepreneurs. At last they had access to a cheap and plentiful source of labor. These new workers, because of their growing numbers and their unfamiliarity with their new country, had even less leverage than the women they at times displaced, and thus they often encountered far worse working conditions. Construction gangs, made up increasingly of Irish immigrants, performed the heavy, unskilled work on turnpikes, canals, and railroads under often intolerable conditions. Because most of these workers had no marketable skills and because of native prejudice against them, they received wages so low—and received them so intermittently, since the work was seasonal and uncertain—that they generally did not earn enough to support their families in even minimal comfort. Many of them lived in flimsy shanties, in grim conditions that endangered the health of their families (and reinforced native prejudices toward the "shanty Irish").

Irish workers began to predominate in the New England textile mills as well in the 1840s, and their arrival accelerated the deterioration of working conditions there. There was far less social pressure on owners to provide a decent environment for Irish workers than for native women. Employers began paying piece rates rather than a daily wage and employed other devices to speed up production and exploit the labor force more efficiently. By the mid-1840s, Lowell—once a model for foreign visitors of enlightened industrial development—had become a squalid slum. Similarly miserable working-class neighborhoods were emerging in other northeastern cities.

The factories themselves were becoming large, noisy, unsanitary, and often dangerous places to work; the average workday was extending to twelve, often fourteen hours; and wages were declining, so that even skilled male workers could hope to earn only from $4 to $10 per week, while unskilled laborers were likely to earn only about $1 to $6 per week. Women and children, whatever their skills, also earned less than most men. Conditions were still not as bad as in most factory towns in England and Europe, but neither were American factories the models of cleanliness, efficiency, and human concern that many people had once believed them to be.

The Factory System and the Artisan Tradition

It was not only the mill workers who suffered from the transition to the modern factory system. It was also the skilled artisans whose trades the factories were displacing. The artisan tradition was as much a part of the older, republican vision of America as the tradition of sturdy, independent, yeoman farmers. Independent craftsmen considered themselves embodiments of the American ideal; they clung to a vision of economic life that was in some ways very different from that the new capitalist class was promoting. It was a vision based not just on the idea of individual, acquisitive success (although they were not, of course, averse to profits) but also on a sense of a "moral community." Skilled artisans valued their independence; they also valued the stability and relative equality within their economic world.

The factory system threatened that world with obsolescence. Some artisans made successful transitions into small-scale industry. But others found themselves unable to compete with the new factory-made goods that sold for a fraction of the artisans' prices. In the face of this competition from industrial capitalists, craftsmen began early in the nineteenth century to form organizations—workingmen's political parties and the first American labor unions—to protect their endangered positions and to resist the new economic order in which they sensed they would have no role. As early as the 1790s, printers and cordwainers took the lead. The cordwainers—makers of high-quality boots and shoes—suffered from the competition of the new shoe factories capitalists were building in New England and elsewhere. The development of mass-production methods threatened their livelihoods; it also threatened their independence and their status in their communities. Members of other skilled trades—carpenters, joiners, masons, plasterers, hatters, and shipbuilders—felt similarly beleaguered.

In such cities as Philadelphia, Baltimore, Boston, and New York, the skilled workers of each craft formed societies for mutual aid. During the 1820s and 1830s, the craft societies began to combine on a city-wide basis and set up central organizations known as trade unions. With the widening of markets, the economies of cities were interconnected, so workers soon realized there were advantages in joining forces and established national unions or federations of local ones. In 1834, delegates from six cities founded the National Trades' Union, and in 1836, the printers and the cordwainers set up their own national craft unions.

This early craft union movement fared poorly. Labor leaders struggled against the handicap of hostile laws and hostile courts. The common law, as interpreted by the courts in the industrial states, viewed a combination among workers as, in itself, an illegal conspiracy. Adverse court decisions, however, did not alone halt the rising unions. The Panic of 1837 and the depression that followed weakened the movement further. But the failure of these first organizations did not end the efforts by workers—artisans and factory operatives alike—to gain some control over their productive lives.

Fighting for Control

Workers at all levels of the emerging industrial economy made continuous efforts to improve their lots. They tried, with little success, to persuade state legislatures to pass laws setting a maximum workday. Two states—New Hampshire in 1847 and Pennsylvania in 1848—actually passed ten-hour laws, limiting the workday unless the workers agreed to an "express contract" calling for more time on the job. Such measures were virtually without impact, however, because employers could simply require prospective employees to sign the "express contract" as a condition of hiring. Three states—Massachusetts, New Hampshire, and Pennsylvania—passed laws regulating child labor. But again, the results were minimal. The laws simply limited the workday to ten hours for children unless their parents agreed to something longer; employers had little difficulty persuading parents to consent to additional hours.

Perhaps the greatest legal victory of industrial workers came in Massachusetts in 1842, when the supreme court of the state, in *Commonwealth v. Hunt*, declared that unions were lawful organizations and that the strike was a lawful weapon. Other state courts gradually accepted the principles of the Massachusetts decision. But on the whole, the union movement of the 1840s and 1850s remained generally ineffective. Some workers were reluctant to think of themselves as members of a permanent laboring force, and so resistance to organizing remained strong. But even those unions that did manage to recruit significant numbers of industrial workers were usually not strong enough to stage strikes, and even less frequently strong enough to win them.

Artisans and skilled workers, despite their setbacks in the 1830s, had somewhat greater success. But their unions often had more in common with preindustrial guilds than with modern labor organizations. In most cases, their primary purpose was to protect the favored position of their members in the labor force by restricting admission to the skilled trades. The organizing effort that had floundered in the 1830s revived impressively in the 1850s. Among the new organizations skilled workers created were the National Typographical Union, founded in 1852, the Stone Cutters in 1853, the Hat Finishers in 1854, and the Molders and the Machinists, both in 1859.

Virtually all the early craft unions excluded women, even though female workers were numerous in almost every industry. As a result, women began establishing their own protective unions by the 1850s, often with the support of middle-class female reformers. Like the male craft unions, the female protective unions had little power in dealing with employers. They did, however, serve an important role as mutual aid societies for women workers.

Despite these persistent efforts at organization and protest, the American working class in the 1840s and

1850s was notable for its relatively modest power. In England, workers were becoming a powerful, united, and often violent economic and political force. They were creating widespread social turmoil and helping to transform the nation's political structure. In America, nothing of the sort happened.

Many factors combined to inhibit the growth of effective labor resistance. Among the most important was the flood of immigrant laborers into the country. The newcomers were usually willing to work for lower wages than native workers, and because they were so numerous, manufacturers had little difficulty replacing disgruntled or striking workers with eager immigrants. Ethnic divisions and tensions—both between natives and immigrants and among the various immigrant groups themselves—often led workers to channel their resentments into internal bickering rather than into their shared grievances against employers. There was, too, the sheer strength of the industrial capitalists, who had not only economic but political and social power and could usually triumph over even the most militant challenges. But the character of the working-class response to industrialism also reflected the emerging social structure of antebellum America.

antebellum?

Patterns of Society

The industrial revolution was making the United States—and particularly its more economically developed regions—dramatically wealthier by the year. It was also making society more unequal, and it was transforming social relationships at almost every level—from the workplace to the family.

The Rich and the Poor

The commercial and industrial growth of the United States greatly elevated the average income of the American people. But what evidence there is—and it is admittedly sketchy—suggests that this increasing wealth was being distributed highly unequally. Substantial groups of the population, of course, shared hardly at all in the economic growth: slaves, Indians, landless farmers, and many of the unskilled workers on the fringes of the manufacturing system. But even among the rest of the population, disparities of income were becoming so marked as to be impossible to ignore. Wealth had always been unequally distributed in the United States, to be sure. Even in the era of the Revolution, according to some estimates, 45 percent of the wealth was concentrated in the hands of about 10

CENTRAL PARK
To affluent New Yorkers, the construction of the city's great Central Park was important because it provided them with an elegant setting for their daily carriage rides—an activity ostensibly designed to expose the riders to fresh air but that was really an occasion for them to display their finery to their neighbors. *(Museum of the City of New York)*

percent of the population. But by the mid-nineteenth century, that concentration had become far more pronounced. In Boston in 1845, for example, 4 percent of the citizens are estimated to have owned more than 65 percent of the wealth; in Philadelphia in 1860, 1 percent of the population possessed more than half the wealth. Among the American people overall in 1860, according to scholarly estimates, 5 percent of the families possessed more than 50 percent of the wealth.

There had been wealthy classes in America almost from the beginning of European settlement. But the extent and character of wealth was changing in response to the commercial revolution of the mid-nineteenth century. Merchants and industrialists were accumulating enormous fortunes; and because there was now a significant number of rich people living in cities, a distinctive culture of wealth began to emerge. In large cities, people of great wealth gathered together in neighborhoods of astonishing opulence. They founded clubs and developed elaborate social rituals. They looked increasingly for ways to display their wealth—in the great mansions they built, the showy carriages in which they rode, the lavish household goods they accumulated, the clothes they wore, the elegant social establishments they patronized. New York, which had more wealthy families than anywhere else, developed a particularly elaborate high society. The construction of the city's great Central Park, which began in the 1850s, was in part a result of pressure from the members of high society, who wanted an elegant setting for their daily carriage rides.

There was also a significant population of genuinely destitute people emerging in the growing urban centers of the nation. These were people who were not merely poor, in the sense of having to struggle to sustain themselves; most Americans were poor in that sense. They were almost entirely without resources, often homeless, dependent on charity or crime or both for survival. Substantial numbers of people actually starved to death or died of exposure.

Some of these "paupers," as contemporaries called them, were recent immigrants who had failed to find work or to adjust to life in the New World. Some were widows and orphans, stripped of the family structures that allowed most working-class Americans to survive. Some were people suffering from alcoholism or mental illness, unable to work. Others were victims of native prejudice—barred from all but the most menial employment because of race or ethnicity. The Irish were particular victims of such prejudice.

Among the worst victims were free blacks. African-American communities in antebellum northern cities were small by later standards, but most major urban areas had significant black populations. Some of these African Americans were descendants of families that had lived in the North for generations. Others were former slaves who had escaped from the South or been released by the masters or had bought their freedom; some former slaves, once free, then worked to buy the freedom of relatives left behind. In material terms, at least, life was not always much better for them in the North than it had been in slavery. Most had access only to very menial jobs, which usually paid too little to allow a worker to support a family; in bad times many had access to no jobs at all. In most parts of the North, blacks could not vote, could not attend public schools, indeed could not use any of the public services available to white residents. Even so, most blacks preferred life in the North, however arduous, to life in the South because it permitted them at least some level of freedom.

Social Mobility

One might expect the contrasts between conspicuous wealth and conspicuous poverty in antebellum America to have encouraged more class conflict than actually occurred. But a number of factors operated to quell resentments. For one thing, however much the relative economic position of American workers may have been declining, the absolute living standard of most laborers was improving. Life, in material terms at least, was usually better for factory workers than it had been on the farms or in the European societies from which they had migrated. They ate better, they were often better clothed and housed, and they had greater access to consumer goods.

There was also a significant amount of mobility within the working class, which helped to limit discontent. Opportunities for social mobility, for working one's way up the economic ladder, were limited, but the opportunities did exist. A few workers did manage to move from poverty to riches by dint of work, ingenuity, and luck—a very small number, but enough to support the dreams of those who watched them. And a much larger number of workers managed to move at least one notch up the ladder—for example, becoming in the course of a lifetime a skilled, rather than an unskilled, laborer. Such people could envision their children and grandchildren moving up even further.

More important than social mobility was geographical mobility, which was even more extensive in the United States than in Europe, where it was considerable. America had a huge expanse of uncultivated land in the West, much of it open for settlement for the first time in the 1840s and 1850s. Some workers saved money, bought land, and moved west to farm it. The historian Frederick Jackson Turner referred to the availability of western lands as a "safety valve" for discontent, a basic explanation for the relative lack of social conflict in the antebellum United States. But few urban workers, and even fewer poor ones, could afford to make such a move or had the expertise to know how to work land even if they could have bought it. Much more common was the movement of laborers from one industrial town to another. Restless, questing, these "people in motion," as some scholars have described them, were often the victims of layoffs, looking for better opportunities elsewhere. Their search may seldom have led to a marked improvement in their circumstances, but the rootlessness of this large segment of the work force—one of the most distressed segments—made effective organization and protest far more difficult.

There was, finally, another "safety valve" for working-class discontent: politics. Economic opportunity may not have greatly expanded in the nineteenth century, but opportunities to participate in politics did. And to many working people, access to the ballot seemed to offer a way to help guide their society and to feel like a significant part of their communities.

The Changing Family

The new industrializing society of the northern regions of the United States produced profound changes in the nature and function of the family. At the heart of the transformation was the movement of families from farms to urban areas, where jobs, not land, were the most valued commodities. The patriarchal system of the countryside, where fathers controlled their children's futures by controlling the distribution of land to them, could not survive the move to a city and town.

Sons and daughters were much more likely to leave the family in search of work than they had been in the rural world.

Another important change was the shift of income-earning work out of the home and into the shop, mill, or factory. In the early decades of the nineteenth century (and for many years before that), the family itself had been the principal unit of economic activity. Family farms, family shops, and family industries were the norm throughout most of the United States. Men, women, and children worked together, sharing tasks and jointly earning the income that sustained the family.

Even among the farming population, which continued to constitute the majority of the American people, there were important changes. As farming spread to the fertile lands of the Northwest and as the size and profitability of farms expanded, agricultural work became more commercialized. Farm owners in need of labor began to rely less on their families (which often were not large enough to satisfy the demand) and more on hired male workers. These farmhands performed many of the tasks that on smaller farms had once been the jobs of the women and children of the family. As a result, farm women tended to work increasingly at domestic tasks—cooking, sewing, gardening, and dairying—a development that spared them from some heavy labor but that also removed them from the principal income-producing activities of the farm. Farm women in the new agricultural regions of the Northwest tended, therefore, to have a lower economic status within the family (and within the community) than their earlier counterparts in the East, who had been more crucial to the family economy. (See Chapter 11 for a discussion of family relations in the agrarian South.)

In the industrial economy of the rapidly growing cities, there was an even more significant erosion of the traditional economic function of the family. The urban household itself became less important as a center of production. Instead, most income earners left home each day to work elsewhere. A sharp distinction began to emerge between the public world of the workplace—the world of commerce and industry—and the private world of the family. The world of the family was now dominated not by production, but by housekeeping, child rearing, and other primarily domestic concerns.

Accompanying (and perhaps in part caused by) the changing economic function of the family was a decline in the birth rate. In 1800, the average American woman could be expected to give birth to approximately seven children during her childbearing years. By 1860, the average woman bore five children. The birth rate fell most quickly in urban areas and among middle-class women. Mid-nineteenth-century Americans had access to some birth control devices, which undoubtedly contributed in part to the change. There was also a significant rise in abortions, which remained legal in some states until after the Civil War and which, according to some estimates, may have terminated as many as 20 percent of all pregnancies in the 1850s. But the most important cause of the declining birth rate was almost certainly changes in sexual behavior—including increased abstinence.

The deliberate effort among middle-class men and women, in particular, to limit family size was a reflection of a much larger shift in the nature of society in the mid-nineteenth-century North. In a world in which the economy was becoming increasingly organized, in which production was moving out of the home, in which individuals were coming to expect more from the world, in which people placed more emphasis on calculations about the future, making careful decisions about bearing children seemed important. It expressed the increasingly secular, rationalized, and progressive orientation of the rapidly developing American North.

The "Cult of Domesticity"

The emerging distinction between the public and private worlds, between the workplace and the home, accompanied (and helped cause) increasingly sharp distinctions between the social roles of men and women. Those distinctions affected not only factory workers and farmers, but members of the growing middle class as well. There had, of course, always been important differences between the male and female spheres in American society. Women had long been denied many legal and political rights enjoyed by men; within the family, the husband and father had traditionally ruled, and the wife and mother had generally bowed to his demands and desires. It had long been practically impossible for most women to obtain divorces, although divorces initiated by men were often easier to arrange. (Men were also far more likely than women to win custody of children in case of a divorce.) In most states, husbands retained almost absolute authority over both the property and persons of their wives; wife beating was illegal in only a few areas, and the law did not acknowledge that rape could occur within marriage. Women traditionally had very little access to the worlds of business or politics. Indeed, custom in most communities dictated that women never speak in public before mixed audiences.

Most women also had much less access to education than men, a situation that survived into the mid-

MOUNT HOLYOKE
The Mount Holyoke Female Seminary, founded in 1837, was the first institution in the United States dedicated to higher education for women. It became a college in the 1880s, at about the same time that other new female colleges were emerging in the northeast. (*Mount Holyoke College Library Archives*)

nineteenth century. Although they were encouraged to attend school at the elementary level, they were strongly discouraged—and in most cases effectively barred—from pursuing higher education. Oberlin in Ohio became the first college in America to accept woman students; it permitted four to enroll in 1837, despite criticism that coeducation was a rash experiment approximating free love. Oberlin authorities were confident that "the mutual influence of the sexes upon each other is decidedly happy in the cultivation of both mind & manners." But few other institutions shared their views. Coeducation remained extraordinarily rare until long after the Civil War; and only a very few women's colleges—such as Mount Holyoke, founded in Massachusetts by Mary Lyon in 1837—emerged.

However unequal the positions of men and women were in the preindustrial era, those positions were generally defined within the context of a household in which all members played crucial roles in generating family income. In the middle-class family of the new industrial society, however, the husband was assumed to be the principal, usually the only, income producer. The wife was now expected to remain in the home and to engage in largely domestic activities.

The result was an important shift in the middle-class concept of the woman's place within the family and of the family's place within the larger society. Society in the mid-nineteenth century came to see women as guardians of the "domestic virtues." Their role as mothers, entrusted with the nurturing of the young, seemed more central to the family than it had in the past. And their role as wives—as companions and helpers to their husbands—grew more important as well. Middle-class women, no longer producers, now became more important as consumers. They learned to place a high value on keeping a clean, comfortable, and well-appointed home, on entertaining, and on dressing elegantly and stylishly.

Occupying their own "separate sphere," some women began to develop a distinctive female culture. Friendships among women became increasingly intense; women began to form their own social networks (and, ultimately, to form female clubs and associations that were of great importance to the advancement of various reforms). A distinctive feminine literature began to emerge to meet the demands of middle-class women. There were romantic novels (many of them by female writers), which focused on the private sphere that women now inhabited. There were women's magazines, of which the most prominent was *Godey's Lady's Book*, edited after 1837 by Sarah Hale, who had earlier founded a women's magazine of her own. The magazine scrupulously avoided dealing with public controversies or political issues and focused instead on fashions, shopping and homemaking advice, and other purely domestic concerns. Politics and religion were inappropriate for the magazine, Hale explained in 1841, because "other subjects are more important for our sex and more proper for our sphere."

By the standards of a later era, the increasing isolation of women from the public world seems to be a form of oppression and discrimination. And it is true that few men considered women fit for business, politics, or the professions. On the other hand, most middle-class men—and many middle-class women as well—considered the new female sphere a vehicle for expressing special qualities that made women in some ways superior to men. Women were to be the custodians of morality and benevolence, just as the home—shaped by the influence of women—was to be a refuge from the harsh, competitive world of the marketplace. It was women's responsibility to provide religious and moral instruction to their children and to counterbalance the acquisitive, secular impulses of their husbands. Thus the "cult of domesticity," as some scholars have called it, brought both benefits and costs to middle-class women. It allowed them to live lives of greater material comfort than in the past, and it placed

a higher value on their "female virtues" and on their roles as wife and mother. At the same time, it left women increasingly detached from the public world, with fewer outlets for their interests and energies.

The costs of that detachment were particularly clear among unmarried women of the middle class. By the 1840s, the ideology of domesticity had grown so powerful that few genteel women would any longer consider working (as many had in the past) in shops or mills, and few employers would consider hiring them. But unmarried women nevertheless required some income-producing activity. They had few choices. A few could become teachers or nurses, professions that seemed to call for the same female qualities that made women important within the home; and both those professions began in the 1840s and 1850s to attract sig-

---

PASTORAL AMERICA, 1848
This painting by the American artist Edward Hicks suggests the degree to which Americans continued to admire the "Peaceable Kingdom" (the name of another, more famous Hicks work) of the agrarian world. Hicks entitled this work *An Indian Summer view of the Farm w. Stock of James C. Cornell of Northampton Bucks county Pennsylvania. That took the Premium in the Agricultural Society, October the 12, 1848.* It portrays the diversified farming of a prosperous Pennsylvania family, shown here in the foreground with their cattle, sheep, and workhorses. In the background stretches a field ready for plowing and another ready for harvesting. *(National Gallery of Art, Washington)*

nificant numbers of women, although not until the Civil War did females begin to dominate them. Otherwise, unmarried females were largely dependent on the generosity of relatives.

Middle-class people gradually came to consider work by women outside the household to be unseemly, something characteristic of the lower classes—as indeed it was. Working-class women could not afford to stay home and cultivate the "domestic virtues." They had to produce income for their families. They continued to work in factories and mills, but under conditions far worse than those that the original, more "respectable" woman workers had enjoyed. They also frequently found employment in middle-class homes. Domestic service became one of the most frequent sources of female employment. In other words, now that production had moved outside the household, women who needed to earn money had to move outside their own households to do so.

THE AGRICULTURAL NORTH

Even in the rapidly urbanizing and industrializing Northeast, and more so in what nineteenth-century Americans called the Northwest (and what Americans today call the Midwest), most people remained tied to the agricultural world. But agriculture, like industry and commerce, was becoming increasingly a part of the new capitalist economy, linked to the national and international market. Where agriculture could not compete in this new commercial world—as in much of the Northeast—it declined. Where it could—as in most of the Northwest—it simultaneously flourished and changed.

Northeastern Agriculture

The story of agriculture in the Northeast after 1840 is one of decline and transformation. The reason for the decline was simple: the farmers of the section could no longer compete with the new and richer soil of the Northwest. Centers of production were gradually shifting westward for many of the farm goods that had in the past been most important to northeastern agriculture: wheat, corn, grapes, cattle, sheep, and hogs. In 1840, the leading wheat-growing states were New York, Pennsylvania, Ohio, and Virginia; in 1860 they were Illinois, Indiana, Wisconsin, Ohio, and Michigan. In raising corn, Illinois, Ohio, and Missouri supplanted New York, Pennsylvania, and Virginia. In 1840 the most important cattle-raising areas in the country were

New York, Pennsylvania, and New England; but by the 1850s the leading cattle states were Illinois, Indiana, Ohio, and Iowa in the West, and Texas in the South.

Some eastern farmers responded to these changes by moving west themselves and establishing new farms. Still others moved to mill towns and became laborers. Some farmers, however, remained on the land and managed to hold their own against, and at times even surpass, the Northwest in certain areas of agriculture. As the eastern urban centers increased in population, many farmers turned to the task of supplying food to the cities; they raised vegetables (truck farming) or fruit and sold it in nearby towns. New York, for example, led all other states in apple production. The rise of cities also stimulated the rise of profitable dairy farming. Supplying milk, butter, and cheese to local markets attracted many farmers in central New York, southeastern Pennsylvania, and various parts of New England. Approximately half the dairy products of the country were produced in the East; most of the rest came from the West, where Ohio was the leading dairy state. Partly because of the expansion of the dairy industry, the Northeast led other sections in the production of hay. New York was the leading hay state in the nation; Pennsylvania and New England grew large crops as well. The Northeast also exceeded other areas in producing potatoes.

But while agriculture in the region remained an important part of the economy, it was steadily becoming less important relative both to the agriculture of the Northwest and to the industrial growth of the Northeast itself. As a result, the rural population in many parts of the Northeast continued to decline.

The Old Northwest

Life was different in the states of the Northwest in the mid-nineteenth century. There was some industry in this region, more than in the South; and in the two decades before the Civil War, the section experienced steady industrial growth. By 1860, it had 36,785 manufacturing establishments employing 209,909 workers. There was a flourishing industrial and commercial area along the shore of Lake Erie, with Cleveland at its center. Another manufacturing region was in the Ohio River valley; the meatpacking city of Cincinnati was its nucleus. Farther west, the rising city of Chicago, destined to become the great metropolis of the section, was emerging as the national center of the agricultural machinery and meatpacking industries.

Most of the major industrial activities of the West either served agriculture (as in the case of farm ma-

S I G N I F I C A N T   E V E N T S

1813 Lowell establishes textile mill at Waltham, Massachusetts

1817–1825 Erie Canal constructed

1830 Baltimore & Ohio becomes first American railroad to begin operations

1830s Major immigration from southern (Catholic) Ireland begins

Factory system spreads in textile and shoe industries

First craft unions founded

1832 Cholera plague

1834 Women workers at Lowell mills stage strike

Cyrus McCormick patents mechanical reaper

1837 Native American Association begins efforts to restrict immigration

Oberlin becomes first American coeducational college

Mt. Holyoke College for women opens

1842 Massachusetts Supreme Court, in *Commonwealth v. Hunt*, declares unions and strikes legal

1844 Samuel F. B. Morse sends first telegraph message

1845 Irish potato famine begins, spurring major emigration to America

Native American Party formed to combat immigration

Female Labor Reform Association established at Lowell

1846 Rotary press invented, making possible rapid printing of newspapers

Associated Press organized

1847 John Deere begins manufacturing steel plows

1848 Failed revolution in Germany spurs emigration to America

Wisconsin enters Union

1850 Nativists form Supreme Order of the Star-Spangled Banner to oppose immigration

1852 American Party (Know-Nothings) formed

chinery, or relied on agricultural products (as in flour milling, meatpacking, whiskey distilling, and the making of leather goods). As this suggests, industry was on the whole much less important in the Northwest than farming.

Some areas of the Northwest were not yet dominated by whites. Indians remained the most numerous inhabitants of large portions of most of the upper third of the Great Lakes states until after the Civil War. In those areas, hunting and fishing, along with some sedentary agriculture, remained the principal economic activities. But the tribes did not become integrated into the new commercialized economy that was emerging elsewhere in the Northwest.

For the white (and occasionally black) settlers who populated the lands farther south that they had by now largely wrested from the natives, the Northwest was primarily an agricultural region. Its rich and plentiful lands made farming a lucrative and expanding activity there, in contrast to the declining agrarian Northeast. Thus the typical citizen of the Northwest was not the industrial worker or poor, marginal farmer, but the owner of a reasonably prosperous family farm. The average size of western farms was 200 acres, the great majority of them owned by the people who worked them.

Rising farm prices around the world provided a strong incentive for these western farmers to engage in commercial agriculture: to concentrate on growing a single crop for market (corn, wheat, cattle, sheep, hogs, and others). In the early years of white settlement in the Northwest, farm prices rose because of the debilitation of European agriculture in the aftermath of the Napoleonic Wars and the growing urban population (and hence the growing demand for food) of industrializing areas of Europe. Europe found it necessary to import American products to feed its people. The Northwest, with good water routes on the Mississippi for getting its crops to oceangoing vessels, profited from this international trade.

But industrialization, in both the United States and Europe, provided the greatest boost to agriculture. With the growth of factories and cities in the Northeast, the domestic market for farm goods increased dramatically. The growing national and worldwide demand for farm products resulted in steadily rising farm prices. For most farmers, the 1840s and early 1850s were years of increasing prosperity.

The expansion of agricultural markets had profound effects on sectional alignments in the United States. The Northwest sold most of its products to the residents of the Northeast and was thus dependent on eastern purchasing power. Eastern industry, in turn, found an important market for its products in the prospering West. Between the two sections a strong economic relationship was emerging that was profitable to both—and that was increasing the isolation of the South within the Union.

To meet the increasing demand for its farm products, residents of the Northwest worked strenuously, and often frantically, to increase their productive capacities. Many tried to take advantage of the large areas of still uncultivated land and to enlarge the area of white settlement during the 1840s. By 1850, the growing western population was moving into the prairie regions both east and west of the Mississippi: into areas of Indiana, Michigan, Illinois, Missouri, Iowa, and Minnesota. They cleared forest lands or made use of fields the Indians had cleared many years earlier. And they began to develop a timber industry to make use of the forests that remained. Wheat was the staple crop of the region, but other crops—corn, potatoes, and oats—and livestock were also important.

The Northwest increased production not only by expanding the area of settlement, but also by adopting new agricultural techniques that greatly reduced the labor necessary for producing a crop. The new methods were also less destructive than earlier ones and slowed the exhaustion of the region's rich soil. Farmers began to cultivate new varieties of seed, notably Mediterranean wheat, which was hardier than the native type; and they imported better breeds of animals, such as hogs and sheep from England and Spain,

to take the place of native stock. Most important were improved tools and farm machines, which American inventors and manufacturers produced in rapidly increasing numbers. During the 1840s, more efficient grain drills, harrows, mowers, and hay rakes came into wide use. The cast-iron plow, an earlier innovation, remained popular because its parts could be replaced when broken. An even better tool appeared in 1847, when John Deere established at Moline, Illinois, a factory to manufacture plows with steel moldboards, which were more durable than those made of iron.

Two new machines heralded a coming revolution in grain production. The most important was the automatic reaper, the invention of Cyrus H. McCormick of Virginia. The reaper took the place of sickle, cradle, and hand labor and enabled a crew of six or seven men to harvest in a day as much wheat (or any other small grain) as fifteen men could harvest using the older methods. McCormick, who had patented his device in 1834, established a factory at Chicago, in the heart of the grain belt, in 1847. By 1860, more than 100,000 reapers were in use on western farms. Almost as important to the grain grower was the thresher—a machine that separated the grain from the wheat stalks. Threshers appeared in large numbers after 1840. Before that, farmers generally flailed grain by hand (seven bushels a day was a good average for a farm) or used farm animals to tread it (twenty bushels a day on the average). A threshing machine could thresh twenty-five bushels or more in an hour. The Jerome I. Case factory in Racine, Wisconsin manufactured most of the threshers.

The Northwest was the most self-consciously democratic section of the country. But its democracy was of a relatively conservative type—capitalistic, property-conscious, middle-class. Abraham Lincoln, an Illinois Whig, voiced the economic opinions of many of the people of his section. "I take it that it is best for all to leave each man free to acquire property as fast as he can," said Lincoln. "Some will get wealthy. I don't believe in a law to prevent a man from getting rich; it would do more harm than good. . . . When one starts poor, as most do in the race of life, free society is such that he knows he can better his condition; he knows that there is no fixed condition of labor for his whole life."

SUGGESTED READINGS

The Market Revolution.   W. Elliot Brownlee, *Dynamics of Ascent* (1974). Stuart Bruchey, *The Growth of the Modern American Economy* (1975). Christopher Clark, *The Roots of Rural Capitalism: Western Massachusetts, 1780–1860* (1990). Thomas C. Cochran, *Frontiers of Change: Early Industrialization in America* (1981). Paul W. Gates, *The Farmer's Age* (1960). Douglass North, *The Economic Growth of the United States, 1790–1860* (1961). Charles G. Sellers, *The Market Revolution: Jacksonian America, 1815–1846* (1991). Peter Temin, *The Jacksonian Economy* (1969).

Immigration.   Rowland T. Berthoff, *British Immigrants in Industrial America, 1790–1950* (1953). Ray Billington, *The Protestant Crusade, 1800–1860* (1938). Theodore C. Blegen, *Norwegian Migration to America*, 2 vols. (1931–1940). John Bodnar, *The Transplanted: A History of Immigrants in America* (1985). Kathleen N. Conzen, *Immigrant Milwaukee: 1836–1860* (1976). Thomas J. Curran, *Xenophobia and Immigration, 1820–1930* (1975). Hasia Diner, *Erin's Daughters in America* (1983). Jay P. Dolan, *The Immigrant Church: New York's Irish and German Catholics* (1975). Charlotte Erickson, *Invisible Immigrants* (1972). Robert Ernst, *Immigrant Life in New York City, 1825–1863* (1949). Oscar Handlin, *The Uprooted* (1951, rev. 1973); *Boston's Immigrants* (1941). Marcus L. Hansen, *The Immigrant in American History* (1940); *The Atlantic Migration, 1607–1860* (1940). Maldwyn A. Jones, *American Immigration* (1960). I. M. Leonard and R. D. Parmet, *American Nativism, 1830–1860* (1971). Stuart C. Miller, *The Unwelcome Immigrant* (1969). Allan Nevins, *The Ordeal of the Union*, 2 vols. (1947). Harold Runblom and Hans Norman, *From Sweden to America* (1976). Philip Taylor, *The Distant Magnet: European Emigration to the United States of America* (1971). Carl Wittke, *We Who Built America*, rev. ed. (1964); *Refugees of Revolution: The German Forty-Eighters in America* (1952); *The Irish in America* (1956).

Transportation and Communications.   Albert Fishlow, *American Railroads and the Transformation of the Ante-Bellum Economy* (1965). Robert W. Fogel, *Railroads and American Economic Growth* (1964). Carter Goodrich, *Government Promotion of American Canals and Railroads, 1800–1890* (1960). Eric K. Haites, James Mak, and Gary M. Walton, *Western River Transportation: The Era of Early Internal Development, 1800–1860* (1975). Nathan Miller, *The Enterprise of a Free People* (1962). Frank Luther Mott, *American Journalism* (1950). Robert J. Parks, *Democracy's Railroads: Public Enterprise in Michigan* (1972). Harry N. Scheiber, *Ohio Canal Era* (1969). Ronald E. Shaw, *Erie Water West: A History of the Erie Canal* (1966). John F. Stover, *American Railroads* (1961); *The Life and Decline of the American Railroad* (1970); *Iron Road to the West: American Railroads in the 1850s* (1978). George R. Taylor, *The Transportation Revolution* (1951). R. L. Thompson, *Writing a Continent* (1947).

Business and Technology.   Richard D. Brown, *Modernization: The Tranformation of American Life, 1600–1865* (1976). Alfred D. Chandler, Jr., *The Visible Hand: The Managerial Revolution in American Business* (1977). Thomas C. Cochran, *Business in American Life* (1972). Thomas C. Cochran and William Miller, *The Age of Enterprise* (1942). E. P. Douglas, *The Coming of Age of American Business* (1971). Siegfried Giedion, *Mechanization Takes Command* (1948). H. J. Habbakuk, *American and British Technology in the Nineteenth Century* (1962). David J. Jeremy, *Transatlantic Industrial Revolution: The Diffusion of Textile Technologies Between Britain and America, 1780–1830* (1981). John F. Kasson, *Civilizing the Machine: Technology and Republican Values in America, 1776–1900* (1976). Diane Lindstrom, *Economic Development in the Philadelphia Region, 1810–1850* (1978). Otto Mayr and Robert C. Post, eds., *Yankee Enterprise: The Rise of the American System of Manufactures* (1981). Judith A. McGaw, *Most Wonderful Machine: Mechanization and Social Change in Berkshire Paper Making, 1815–1885* (1987). James Norris, *R. G. Dun & Co., 1841–1900* (1978). Nathan Rosenberg, *Technology and American Economic Growth* (1972). Merritt Roe Smith, *Harpers Ferry Armory and the New Technology* (1977). Peter Temin, *Iron and Steel in Nineteenth-Century America* (1964).

Factories and the Working Class.   Mary H. Blewett, *Men, Women, and Work* (1988); *We Will Rise in Our Might: Workingwomen's Voices from Nineteenth-Century New England* (1991). Arthur H. Cole, *The American Wool Manufacture*, 2 vols. (1926). Alan Dawley, *Class and Community: The Industrial Revolution in Lynn* (1976). Thomas Dublin, *Women at Work* (1979). Susan E. Hirsch, *Roots of the American Working Class: The Industrialization of Crafts in Newark, 1800–1860* (1978). David A. Hounshell, *From the American System to Mass Production, 1800–1932: The Development of Manufacturing Technology in the United States* (1985). Alice Kessler-Harris, *Out to Work: A History of Wage-Earning Women in the United States* (1982). Bruce Laurie, *Working People of Philadelphia* (1980). Bruce Levine, *The Spirit of 1848: German Immigrants, Labor Conflict, and the Coming of the Civil War* (1992). Henry Pelling, *American Labor* (1960). David R. Roediger, *The Wages of Whiteness: Race and the Making of the American Working Class* (1991). W. J. Rorabaugh, *The Craft Apprentice: From Franklin to the Machine Age* (1986). Steven J. Ross, *Workers on the Edge: Work, Leisure, and Politics in Industrializing Cincinnati, 1788–1890* (1985). Christine Stansell, *City of Women: Sex and Class in New York, 1789–1860* (1986). Barbara M. Tucker, *Samuel Slater and the Origins of the American Textile Industry, 1790–1860* (1985). Joseph E. Walker, *Hopewell: A Social and Economic History of an Ironmaking Community* (1966). Caroline Ware, *The Early New England Cotton Manufacture* (1931). Norman Ware, *The Industrial Worker, 1840–1860* (1924). Sean Wilentz, *Chants Democratic: New York City and the Rise of the American Working Class, 1788–1850* (1984). David A. Zonderman, *Aspirations and Anxieties: New England Workers and the Mechanized Factory System, 1815–1850* (1992).

Society and Culture.   Rowland T. Berthoff, *An Unsettled People: Social Order and Disorder in American History* (1971). Stuart Blumin, *The Urban Threshold: Growth and Change in a*

Nineteenth-Century Community (1976). Daniel Boorstin, *The Americans: The National Experience* (1965). John L. Brooke, *The Heart of the Commonwealth: Society and Political Culture in Worcester County, Massachusetts, 1713–1861* (1989). Leonard P. Curry, *The Free Black in Urban America, 1800–1850* (1981). Don Doyle, *The Social Order of a Frontier Community: Jacksonville, Illinois, 1825–1870* (1978). Michael Frisch, *Town into City: Springfield, Massachusetts, and the Meaning of Community, 1840–1880* (1972). Paul A. Gilje, *The Road to Mobocracy: Popular Disorder in New York City, 1763–1834* (1987). Jonathan A. Glickstein, *Concepts of Free Labor in Antebellum America* (1991). Clyde Griffen and Sally Griffen, *Natives and Newcomers: The Ordering of Opportunity in Mid-Nineteenth-Century Poughkeepsie* (1978). Paul Johnson, *A Shopkeeper's Milennium: Society and Revivals in Rochester, New York, 1815–1837* (1978). Hannah Josephson, *The Golden Threads* (1949). Peter Knights, *The Plain People of Boston, 1830–1860* (1971). Raymond A. Mohl, *Poverty in New York, 1783–1825* (1971). Edward Pessen, *Riches, Classes, and Power Before the Civil War* (1973). David Thelen, *Paths of Resistance: Tradition and Dignity in Industrializing Missouri* (1986). Stephan Thernstrom, *Poverty and Progress* (1964). Glyndon Van Deusen, *Horace Greeley* (1953). Richard C. Wade, *The Urban Frontier, 1790–1830* (1957). Anthony F. C. Wallace, *Rockdale: The Growth of an American Village in the Early Industrial Revolution* (1977). Sam Bass Warner, Jr., *The Urban Wilderness* (1972).

Women and Family. Jeanne Boydston, *Home and Work* (1990). Nancy F. Cott, *The Bonds of Womanhood: "Woman's Sphere" in New England, 1780–1835* (1977). Ruth Schwartz Cowan, *More Work for Mother: The Ironies of Household Technology from the Open Hearth to the Microwave* (1983). Carl Degler, *At Odds: Women and the Family in America from the Revolution to the Present* (1980). Dolores Hayden, *The Grand Domestic Revolution: A History of Feminist Designs for American Homes, Neighborhoods, and Cities* (1981). Ellen K. Rothman, *Hands and Heart: A History of Courtship in America* (1987). Mary Ryan, *Cradle of the Middle Class: The Family in Oneida County, New York, 1790–1865* (1981). Kathryn K. Sklar, *Catherine Beecher: A Study in American Domesticity* (1973). Carroll Smith-Rosenberg, *Disorderly Conduct: Visions of Gender in Victorian America* (1985). Christine Stansell, *City of Women: Sex and Class in New York, 1789–1860* (1986). Susan Strasser, *Never Done: A History of American Housework* (1983). Gwendolyn Wright, *Building the Dream: A Social History of Housing in America* (1981).

THE AMERICAN ENVIRONMENT

THE FLOW OF WATER

No ELEMENT OF THE North American landscape was more basic to the development of the young republic than water. The earliest settlements on the eastern seaboard were all at the ocean's edge, where they had ready access to transatlantic trade. Each major city in the new nation—Boston, New York, Philadelphia, Baltimore, Charleston, New Orleans—began life as a port. The interior trade of the continent concentrated almost entirely along natural watercourses. Water was the catalyst that made trade and settlement possible.

Thus it is not surprising that some of the earliest large-scale manipulations of the American landscape had to do with redirecting the flow of water. Until the 1820s, most crops raised west of the Appalachians traveled to market by floating downstream toward New Orleans on the Ohio, the Mississippi, or the Missouri River. The great wave of canal building that swept the nation in the 1820s and 1830s was designed to divert that southward flow of commerce north toward the Great Lakes and east to the port towns on the Atlantic coast. The most dramatic success was of course the Erie Canal, which enabled New York City to capture the trade of the Great Lakes and Ohio Valley. The emergence of New York as the greatest metropolis on the continent occurred at the same time that settlement exploded on the shores of the Great Lakes, and both were encouraged by the canal. The canal also contributed to the decline of agriculture in New England, as farmers on marginal land found themselves unable to compete with abundant grain crops from the western prairies.

In addition, to rearranging the American agricultural landscape, canals had unexpected ecological consequences. The Erie Canal introduced to Lake Ontario the sea lamprey, a parasitic fish that attaches itself to other fish and weakens or kills them by sucking their blood. It had never before inhabited the Great Lakes, but it began to put pressure on the lake's native whitefish, trout, and salmon. A complex redistribution of the lake's fish population was the long-term result, with many species declining and even disappearing. When Canada's Welland Canal finally opened water access around Niagara Falls, the lamprey moved into the upper Great Lakes, and the same story repeated itself there.

If canals created an artificial system of waterways, dams created an equally artificial system of power that altered traditional ways of consuming energy in the American economy. The industrial revolution came to the United States not with the steam engine but with the waterwheel. Falling water had been used since earliest colonial times to grind flour and saw lumber. Mills were some of the earliest town sites in the interior countryside. But large-scale exploitation of water power did not occur until New England capitalists used British technology to mechanize the production of textiles. The best known of the New England textile towns is probably Lowell, Massachusetts, which is justly renowned in American history for the new labor system it introduced in its factories. But Lowell's success would have been impossible had the city not harnessed the potential energy of the Merrimack River to drive its factories.

The implications of this new use of water were dramatic. Formerly, the energy that had driven the American economy had been biologically limited by the strength of

THE AMERICAN ENVIRONMENT

WATER-POWERED FACTORY ON THE GREEN RIVER, MASSACHUSETTS
American factories in the early nineteenth century depended much more on water than on
steam. They were typically located near major falls or rapids on large rivers, so that canals
could divert water through wheels and turbines beneath the factory, supplying power to
the machinery within. *(Bettmann)*

horses and human workers. Now an even larger share of the energy came from inani-
mate sources—first rivers, and later coal-powered steam. Power could be concentrated
into an ever-expanding network of tools and machines, with dramatic implications for
technological change and industrial productivity. At the same time, the natural flow of
rivers was brought under human control, with diastrous results for certain fish species,
like the salmon, which had formerly swum upstrean to spawn. As dams blocked major rivers of the East Coast, salmon disappeared from most of their former homes.

The typical industrial town of the water power era had certain features that are evident even today. It was always located beside a natural waterfall or rapids where a
river dropped quickly from a higher to a lower elevation. A dam upstream from the
town diverted water into a complicated network of canals and underground conduits.
These diverted it to the factories, which straddled the natural drop in elevation. As the
water flowed beneath the buildings, it turned large waterwheels and turbines. Long
leather belts transmitted the resulting energy to driveshafts running the length of the
factory. Unlike modern factories, which have horizontal one-story layouts because they
use smaller and more flexible electric motors, water power factories had vertical plans,
rising several stories to prevent friction from dissipating the power in their driveshafts.
Energy was transmitted from the central shafts to individual machines by hundreds of

THE AMERICAN ENVIRONMENT

THE GREAT NEW YORK FIRE OF DECEMBER 16, 1835
One of the most devastating fires in New York City's history destroyed hundreds of buildings on December 16, 1835. Without an effective municipal water supply, firefighters had
to bring water to the scene in tank carts and hand-pump it onto the flames. The fire encouraged New York citizens to support construction of the Croton Aqueduct. *(Bettmann)*

long leather belts spinning at high speeds. There were no guards to protect workers
from these exposed belts, and so injuries—lost fingers, broken bones, amputated limbs,
and even deaths—were an almost daily occurrence.

Water power towns lived and died with water. In winter, when rivers froze with ice,
factories sometimes had to shut down for lack of power. (The same was true of canals:
the canal economy regularly went into hibernation during the winter months, with trade
coming nearly to a standstill between December and April.) Worse, water power towns
were regularly subject to flooding during storms and spring runoffs, and could suffer
devastating destruction from the very source that ordinarily sustained them. This was
one reason why the housing in such towns was often arranged so that the workers lived

THE AMERICAN ENVIRONMENT

THE CROTON AQUEDUCT BRINGS WATER TO NEW YORK CITY, 1842
When the Croton Aqueduct was completed, bringing water from the upper Hudson Valley to the southern tip of Manhattan, the residents of New York City staged an immense celebration. A new fountain was built in honor of the event. The aqueduct continues to supply the city with water today. *(The Research Library, The New York Public Library)*

nearest the factories, in flimsy structures erected on the floodplain, while managers and owners lived on the hillsides in more expensive houses that were less exposed to flooding.

The final elements of the new water landscape of nineteenth-century America were in the cities. Although rarely located at water power sites like the factory towns, the great port cities of the East Coast were no less eager to manipulate the water around them. To increase their supply of drinking water and to protect themselves from frequent fires, they constructed great reservoir systems like New York's Croton Aqueduct, completed in 1842, which brought water from dozens of miles away. A little later, they introduced sewers to dispose of dangerous urban wastes downstream from drinking supplies. As a result, the water-borne epidemics of cholera that had devastated the United States in 1832, 1849, and 1866 had nearly vanished by the end of the century.

Ports, canals, dams, factories, reservoirs, sewers: today these are such familiar features of the American landscape that we scarcely even notice them. At the time they were constructed, however, they constituted a revolution in the way Americans traveled, worked, drank, bathed, and protected themselves from disease. Controlling the flow of water was among the greatest environmental and technological changes of the nineteenth century.

"HAULING THE WHOLE WEEK'S PICKING"
The artist William Henry Brown created this illustration of slaves carrying the week's cotton
to the cotton gin in 1842.   *(Historic New Orleans Collection)*

CHAPTER ELEVEN

COTTON, SLAVERY, AND THE OLD SOUTH

T HE SOUTH, LIKE THE North, experienced dramatic growth in the middle years of the nineteenth century. Southerners fanned out into the new territories of the Southwest and established new communities, new states, and new markets. The southern agricultural economy grew increasingly productive and increasingly prosperous. Trade in such staples as sugar, rice, tobacco, and above all cotton made the South a major force in international commerce and created substantial wealth within the region. It also tied the South securely to the emerging capitalist world of the United States and its European trading partners. Southern society, southern culture, southern politics—all changed in response to these important demographic and economic changes. The South in the 1850s was a very different place from the South of the first years of the century.

Yet for all the expansion and all the changes, the South experienced a much less fundamental transformation in these years than did the North. It had begun the nineteenth century a primarily agricultural region; it remained overwhelmingly agrarian in 1860. It had begun the century with few important cities and little industry; and so it remained sixty years later. In 1800, a plantation system dependent on slave labor had dominated the southern economy; by 1860, that system had only strengthened its grip on the region. As one historian has written, "The South grew, but it did not develop." And as a result, it became increasingly unlike the North and increasingly sensitive to what it considered to be threats to its distinctive way of life.

THE COTTON ECONOMY

The most important economic development in the mid-nineteenth-century South was the shift of economic power from the "upper South," the original southern states along the Atlantic coast, to the "lower South," the expanding agricultural regions in the new states of the Southwest. That shift reflected above all the growing dominance of cotton in the southern economy.

The Rise of King Cotton

Much of the upper South continued in the nineteenth century to rely, as it always had, on the cultivation of tobacco. But the market for that crop was notoriously unstable, subject to recurrent depressions, including a prolonged one that began in the 1820s and extended into the 1850s. And tobacco rapidly exhausted the land on which it grew; it was difficult for most growers to remain in business in the same place for very long. By the 1830s, therefore, many farmers in the old tobacco-growing regions of Virginia, Maryland, and North Carolina were shifting to other crops—notably wheat—while the center of tobacco cultivation was moving westward, into the Piedmont area.

The southern regions of the coastal South—South Carolina, Georgia, and parts of Florida—continued to rely on the cultivation of rice, a more stable and lu-

THE NEW ORLEANS COTTON EXCHANGE
Edgar Degas, the great French artist, painted this scene of cotton traders examining samples in the New Orleans cotton exchange in 1873. By this time the cotton trade was producing less impressive profits than those that had made it the driving force of the booming southern economy of the 1850s. Degas's mother came from a Creole family of cotton brokers in New Orleans, and two of the artist's brothers (depicted here reading a newspaper and leaning against a window) joined the business in America. *(Giraudon/Art Resource)*

• *LONG STAPLE COTTON* •

crative crop. But rice demanded substantial irrigation and needed an exceptionally long growing season (nine months), so cultivation of that staple remained restricted to a relatively small area. Sugar growers along the Gulf Coast, similarly, enjoyed a reasonably profitable market for their crop. Sugar cultivation required intensive (and debilitating) labor and a long growing time; only relatively wealthy planters could afford to engage in it. And producers faced major competition from the great sugar plantations of the Caribbean. Sugar cultivation, therefore, did not spread much beyond a small area in southern Louisiana and eastern Texas. Long-staple (Sea Island) cotton was another lucrative crop, but like rice and sugar, it could grow only in a limited area—the coastal regions of the Southeast.

The decline of the tobacco economy in the upper South, and the inherent limits of the sugar, rice, and long-staple cotton economies farther south, might have forced the region to shift its attention in the nineteenth century to other, nonagricultural pursuits, had it not been for the growing importance of a new product

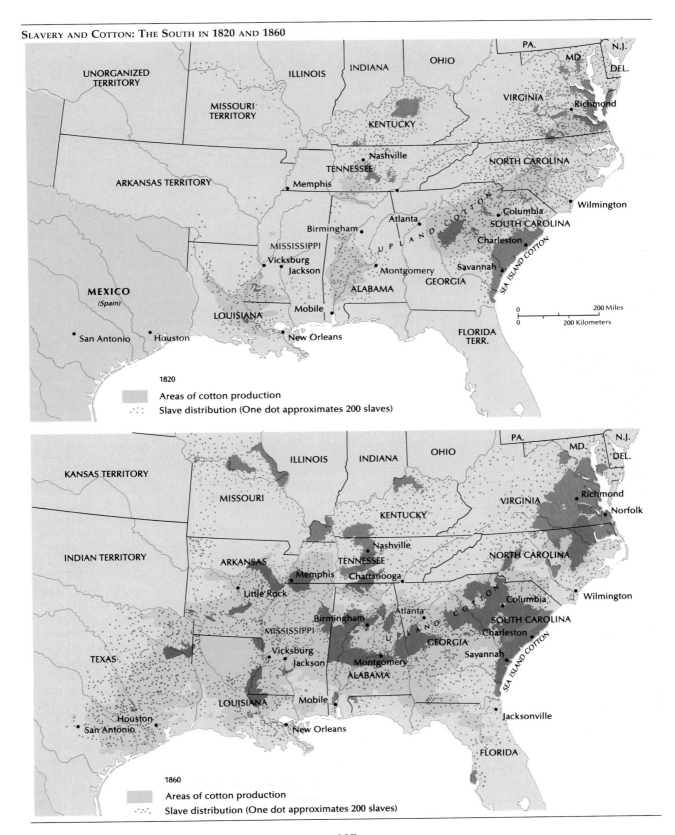

SHORT STAPLE

which soon overshadowed all else: short-staple cotton. This was a hardier and coarser strain of cotton which could grow successfully in a variety of climates and in a variety of soils. It was harder to process than the long-staple variety; its seeds were more difficult to remove from the fiber. But the invention of the cotton gin (see p. 192) had largely solved that problem.

Demand for cotton was growing rapidly. The growth of the textile industry in Britain in the 1820s and 1830s, and in New England in the 1840s and 1850s, created an enormous demand for the crop. Existing cotton lands could not satisfy the demand, and ambitious men and women rapidly moved into new lands—many of them newly open to planter settlement after the relocation of the tribes in the 1820s and 1830s—to establish new cotton-growing regions.

Beginning in the 1820s, therefore, cotton production spread rapidly. From the western areas of South Carolina and Georgia, production moved steadily—first into Alabama and Mississippi, then into northern Louisiana, Texas, and Arkansas. By the 1850s, cotton had become the linchpin of the southern economy. In 1820, the South had produced only about 500,000 bales of cotton. By 1850 it was producing nearly 3 million bales a year, and by 1860 nearly 5 million. There were periodic fluctuations in cotton prices, resulting generally from overproduction; periods of boom frequently gave way to abrupt busts. But the cotton economy continued to grow, even if in fits and starts. By the time of the Civil War, cotton constituted nearly two-thirds of the total export trade of the United States and was bringing in nearly $200 million a year. The annual value of the rice crop, in contrast, was $2 million. It was little wonder that southern politicians now proclaimed: "Cotton is king!"

Cotton production dominated the relatively recently settled areas of what came to be known as the "lower South" (or, in a later era, the "Deep South"). Some began to call it the "Cotton Kingdom." And settlement of the region bore some resemblance to the rush of gold seekers to a new frontier. The prospect of tremendous profits drew settlers to the lower South by the thousands. Some were wealthy planters from the older states who transferred their assets and slaves to a cotton plantation. Most were small slaveholders or slaveless farmers who hoped to move into the planter class.

A similar shift, if involuntary, occurred in the slave population. In the period 1820–1860, the number of slaves in Alabama leaped from 41,000 to 435,000, and in Mississippi from 32,000 to 436,000. In the same period, the increase in Virginia was only from 425,000 to 490,000. Between 1840 and 1860, according to some estimates, 410,000 slaves moved from the upper South to the cotton states—either accompanying masters who were themselves migrating to the Southwest, or (more often) sold to planters already there. Indeed, the sale of slaves to the Southwest became an important economic activity in the upper South and helped the troubled planters of that region compensate for the declining value of their crops.

Southern Trade and Industry

In the face of this booming agricultural expansion, other forms of economic activity developed slowly in the South. The business classes of the region—the manufacturers and merchants—were not unimportant. There was growing activity in flour milling and in textile and iron manufacturing, particularly in the upper South. The Tredegar Iron Works in Richmond, for example, compared favorably with the best iron mills in the Northeast. But industry remained an insignificant force in comparison with the agricultural economy. The total value of southern textile manufactures in 1860 was $4.5 million—a threefold increase over the value of those goods twenty years before, but only about 2 percent of the value of the cotton exported that year.

To the degree that the South developed a nonfarm commercial sector, it was largely to serve the needs of the plantation economy. Particularly important were the brokers, or "factors," who marketed the planters' crops. These merchants tended to live in such towns as New Orleans, Charleston, Mobile, and Savannah, where they worked to find buyers for cotton and other crops and where they purchased goods for the planters they served. The South had only a very rudimentary financial system, and the factors often also served the planters as bankers, providing them with credit. Planters frequently accumulated substantial debts, particularly during periods when cotton prices were in decline; and the southern merchant-bankers thus became figures of considerable influence and importance in the region. There were also substantial groups of professional people in the South—lawyers, editors, doctors, and others. In most parts of the region, however, they too were closely tied to and dependent on the plantation economy.

The rudimentary character of the region's financial system matched a lack of development in other basic services and structures necessary for industrial development. Perhaps most notable was the South's inadequate transportation system. In the North in the antebellum period, enormous sums were invested in roads,

rudimentary

professionals

canals, and above all railroads to knit the region together into an integrated market. In the South there were no such investments. Canals were almost nonexistent; most roads were crude and unsuitable for heavy transport; and railroads, although they expanded substantially in the 1840s and 1850s, failed to tie the region together effectively. Such towns as Charleston, Atlanta, Savannah, and Norfolk had direct connections with Memphis, and thus with the Northwest; and Richmond was connected, via the Virginia Central, with the Memphis and Charleston Railroad. In addition, several independent lines furnished a continuous connection between the Ohio River and New Orleans. Most of the South, however, remained unconnected to the national railroad system. Most lines in the region were short and local. The principal means of transportation was water. Planters generally shipped their crops to market along rivers or by sea; most manufacturing was in or near port towns.

However important manufacturers, merchants, and professionals might have been to southern society, they were relatively unimportant in comparison with the manufacturers, merchants, and professionals of the North, on whom southerners were coming more and more (and increasingly unhappily) to depend. Perceptive southerners recognized the economic subordination of their region. "From the rattle with which the nurse tickles the ear of the child born in the South to the shroud that covers the cold form of the dead, everything comes to us from the North," the Arkansas journalist Albert Pike lamented.

Perhaps the most prominent advocate of southern economic independence was James B. D. De Bow, a resident of New Orleans. He published a magazine advocating southern commercial and agricultural expansion, *De Bow's Review,* which survived from its founding in 1846 until 1880. De Bow made his journal into a tireless advocate of southern economic independence from the North, warning constantly of the dangers of the "colonial" relationship between the sections. One writer noted in the pages of his magazine: "I think it would be safe to estimate the amount which is lost to us annually by our vassalage to the North at $100,000,000. Great God!" Yet *De Bow's Review* was itself evidence of the dependency of the South on the North. It was printed in New York, because no New Orleans printer had facilities adequate to the task; it was filled with advertisements from northern manufacturing firms; and its circulation was always modest in comparison with those of northern publications. In Charleston, for example, it sold an average of 173 copies per issue; *Harper's Magazine* of New York regularly sold 1,500 copies to South Carolinians.

Sources of Southern Difference

Despite this growing concern about the region's "colonial dependency," the South made few serious efforts to build an economy that might challenge that dependency. An important question about antebellum southern history, therefore, is why the region did so little to develop a larger industrial and commercial economy of its own. Why did it remain so different from the North?

Part of the reason was the great profitability of the region's agricultural system, and particularly of cotton production. In the Northeast, many people had turned to manufacturing as the agricultural economy of the region declined. In the South, the agricultural economy was booming, and ambitious people eager to profit from the emerging capitalist economy had little incentive to look elsewhere. Another reason was that wealthy southerners had so much capital invested in their land and their slaves that they had little left for other investments. Some historians have suggested that the southern climate—with its long, hot, steamy summers—was less suitable for industrial development than the climate of the North. Still others have gone so far as to claim that southern work habits (perhaps a reflection of the debilitating effects of the climate) impeded industrialization; some white southerners appeared—at least to many northern observers—not to work very hard, to lack the strong work ethic that fueled northern economic development.

But the southern failure to create a flourishing commercial or industrial economy was also in part the result of a set of values distinctive to the South that discouraged the growth of cities and industry. Many white southerners liked to think of themselves as representatives of a special way of life: one based on traditional values of chivalry, leisure, and elegance. Southerners were, they argued, "cavaliers"—people happily free from the base, acquisitive instincts of northerners, people more concerned with a refined and gracious way of life than with rapid growth and development. But appealing as the "cavalier" image was to southern whites, it conformed to the reality of southern society in very limited ways.

SOUTHERN SOCIETY

Only a small minority of southern whites owned slaves. In 1850, when the total white population of the South was over 6 million, the number of slaveholders was only 347,525. In 1860, when the white population was

FRENCH LONG LOT LANDSCAPE IN IBERVILLE PARISH, LOUISIANA, 1858

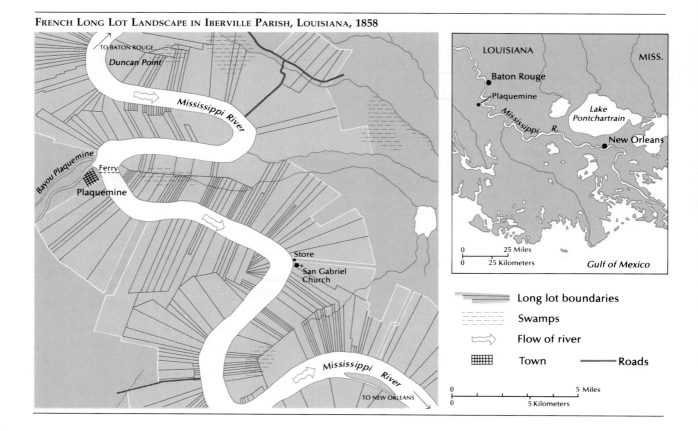

just above 8 million, the number of slaveholders had risen to only 383,637. These figures are somewhat misleading, since each slaveholder was normally the head of a family averaging five members. But even with all members of slave-owning families included in the figures, those owning slaves still amounted to perhaps no more than one quarter of the white population. And of the minority of whites holding slaves, only a small proportion owned them in substantial numbers.

The Planter Class

How, then, did the South come to be seen—both by the outside world and by many southerners themselves—as a society dominated by great plantations and wealthy landowning planters? In large part, it was because the planter aristocracy—the cotton magnates, the sugar, rice, and tobacco nabobs, the whites who owned at least forty or fifty slaves and 800 or more acres—exercised power and influence far in excess of their numbers. They stood at the apex of society, de-

termining the political, economic, and even social life of their region. Enriched by vast annual incomes, dwelling in palatial homes, surrounded by broad acres and many black servants, they became a class to which all others deferred. The wealthiest of them maintained homes in towns or cities and spent several months of the year there, engaged in a glittering social life. Others traveled widely, especially to Europe, as an antidote to the isolation of plantation life. And many used their plantations to host opulent social events.

White southerners liked to compare their planter class to the old upper classes of England and Europe: true aristocracies, long entrenched. In fact, however, the southern upper class was in most cases not at all similar to the landed aristocracies of the Old World. In some areas of the upper South—the tidewater region of Virginia, for example—many of the great aristocrats were indeed people whose families had occupied positions of wealth and power for generations. In most of the South, however, a longstanding landed aristocracy, though central to the "cavalier" image, was largely a myth. Even the most important planters in

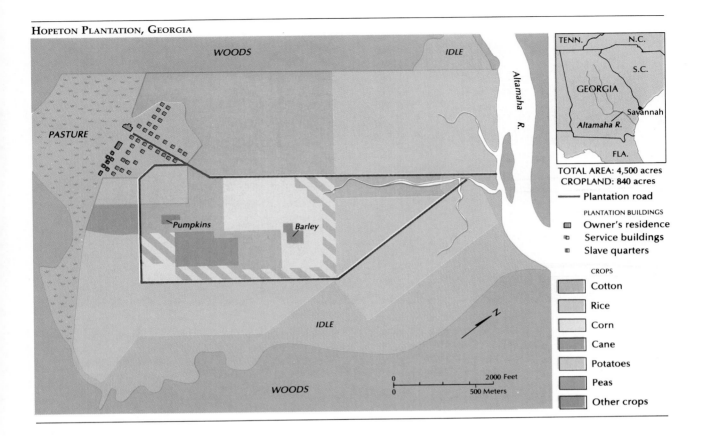

HOPETON PLANTATION, GEORGIA

WOODS

IDLE

PASTURE

Pumpkins

Barley

IDLE

WOODS

Altamaha R.

TENN. N.C.

S.C.

GEORGIA

Savannah

Altamaha R.

FLA.

TOTAL AREA: 4,500 acres
CROPLAND: 840 acres

—— Plantation road

PLANTATION BUILDINGS

▫ Owner's residence
▫ Service buildings
▫ Slave quarters

CROPS

Cotton
Rice
Corn
Cane
Potatoes
Peas
Other crops

0   2000 Feet
0   500 Meters

the cotton-growing areas of the region were, typically, new to their wealth and power. As late as the 1850s, many of the great landowners in the lower South were still first-generation settlers, who had arrived with only modest resources, struggled for many years to clear land and develop a plantation in what was at first a rugged wilderness, and only relatively recently started to live in the comfort and luxury for which they became famous. Large areas of the "Old South" (as Americans later called the South of the pre–Civil War era) had been settled and cultivated for less than two decades at the time of the Civil War.

Nor was the world of the planter nearly as leisured and genteel as the "cavalier" myth would suggest. Growing staple crops was a business—often a big and highly profitable business—which was in its own way just as competitive and just as risky as the industrial enterprises of the North. Planters had to supervise their operations carefully if they hoped to make a profit. They were, in many respects, just as much competitive capitalists as the industrialists of the North whose lifestyles they claimed to hold in contempt.

Even many affluent planters lived rather modestly, their wealth so heavily invested in land and slaves that there was little left for personal comfort. And white planters, even some substantial ones, tended to move frequently as new and presumably more productive areas opened up to cultivation.

Indeed, it may have been the newness and precariousness of the plantation way of life, and the differences between the reality of that life and the image of it, that made many southern planters determined to portray themselves as genteel aristocrats. Having struggled so hard to reach and maintain their position, they were all the more determined to defend it. Perhaps that was why the defense of slavery and of the South's "rights" was stronger in the new, booming regions of the lower South and weaker in the more established and less flourishing areas of the Tidewater.

Wealthy southern whites sustained their image of themselves as aristocrats in many ways. They adopted an elaborate code of "chivalry," which obligated white men to defend their "honor," often through dueling—which survived in the South long after it had largely

code of chivalry

ST. JOHN PLANTATION, LOUISIANA
This Greek Revival "big house" of the St. John Plantation in St. Martin Parish, Louisiana, still stands today. In 1861, when the artist Adrien Persac painted this view of it, it stood at the center of a 5,000-acre sugar plantation and was the setting of the self-consciously elegant life of the planter and his family. To the right is a brick sugar factory and the cabins of the plantation's slaves, who performed the arduous work of sugar harvesting and production. *(Louisiana State University Museum of Art)*

vanished in the North. They avoided such "coarse" occupations as trade and commerce; those who did not become planters often gravitated toward the military, a "suitable" career for men raised in a culture in which medieval knights (as portrayed in the novels of Walter Scott) were a powerful and popular image. The aristocratic ideal also found reflection in the definition of a special role for southern white women.

The "Southern Lady"

In some respects, affluent white women in the South occupied roles very similar to those of middle-class white women in the North. Their lives generally centered in the home, where (according to the South's social ideal) they served as companions to and hostesses for their husbands and as nurturing mothers for their children. Even less frequently than in the North did "genteel" southern white women engage in public activities or find income-producing employment.

But the life of the "Southern lady" was also in many

ways very different from that of her northern counterpart. For one thing, the cult of honor in the region meant that southern white men gave particular importance to the "defense" of women. In practice, this generally meant that white men were even more dominant and white women even more subordinate in southern culture than they were in the North. George Fitzhugh, one of the South's most important social theorists, wrote in the 1850s: "Women, like children, have but one right, and that is the right to protection. The right to protection involves the obligation to obey."

More important in determining the role of southern white women, however, were the social and economic realities in which they lived. The vast majority of females in the region lived on farms, relatively isolated from people outside their own families, with virtually no access to the "public world" and thus few opportunities to look beyond their roles as wives and mothers. And because the family was the principal economic unit on most farms, the dominance of husbands and fathers over wives and children was even greater than in those northern families in which income-producing activities had moved out of the home and into the factory or office. For many white women, living on farms of modest size meant a fuller engagement in the economic life of the family than was becoming typical for middle-class women in the North. These women engaged in spinning, weaving, and other production; they participated in agricultural tasks; they helped supervise the slave work force. On the larger plantations, however, even these limited roles were often considered unsuitable for white women; and the "plantation mistress" became, in some cases, more an ornament for her husband than an active part of the economy or the society.

Southern white women also had less access to education than their northern counterparts. Nearly a quarter of all white women over twenty were completely illiterate; relatively few women had more than a rudimentary exposure to schooling. Even wealthy planters were not much interested in extensive schooling for their daughters. The few female "academies" in the South trained women primarily to be suitable wives.

Southern white women had other special burdens as well. The southern white birth rate remained nearly 20 percent higher than that of the nation as a whole, and infant mortality in the region remained higher than elsewhere; nearly half the children born in the South in 1860 died before they reached five years of age. And the slave labor system had a mixed impact on white women. It helped spare many of them from certain kinds of arduous labor, but it also threatened their relationships with their husbands. Male slaveowners had frequent sexual relationships with the female slaves on their plantations; the children of those unions became part of the plantation labor force and served as a constant reminder to white women of their husbands' infidelity. Black women (and men) were obviously the most important victims of such practices. But white women suffered too.

A few southern white women rebelled against their roles and against the prevailing assumptions of their region. Some became outspoken abolitionists and joined northerners in the crusade to abolish slavery. Some agitated for other reforms within the South itself. Most white women, however, found few outlets for whatever discontent they felt with their lives. Instead, they generally convinced themselves of the benefits of their position and—often even more fervently than southern white men—defended the special virtues of the Southern way of life. Upper-class white women in the South were particularly energetic in defending the class lines that separated them from poorer whites.

The Plain Folk

The typical white southerner was not a great planter and slaveholder, but a modest yeoman farmer. Some of these "plain folk," as they have become known, owned a few slaves, with whom they worked and lived far more closely than did the larger planters. Most (in fact, three-quarters of all white families) owned no slaves at all. Some plain folk, most of whom owned their own land, devoted themselves largely to subsistence farming; others grew cotton or other crops for the market, but usually could not produce enough to allow them to expand their operations or even get out of debt. During the 1850s, the number of nonslaveholding landowners increased much faster than the number of slaveholding landowners. While there were occasional examples of poor farmers moving into the ranks of the planter class, such cases were rare. Most yeomen knew that they had little prospect of substantially bettering their lot.

One reason was the southern educational system, which provided poor whites with few opportunities to learn and thus limited their chances of advancement. For the sons of wealthy planters, the region provided ample opportunities to gain an education. In 1860 there were 260 southern colleges and universities, public and private, with 25,000 students enrolled in them, or more than half the total number of students in the United States. But universities were only within the reach of the upper class. The elementary and secondary schools of the South were not only fewer but also inferior to those of the Northeast (although not much worse than the crude schools of the Northwest). The South had more than 500,000 illiterate whites, or over half the country's total.

That a majority of the South's white population consisted of modest farmers largely excluded from the dominant plantation society raises important questions about the antebellum South. Why did the plain folk have so little power in the public world of the Old South? Why did they not oppose the aristocratic social system in which they shared so little? Why did they not resent the system of slavery, from which they generally did not benefit?

Some nonslaveowning whites did oppose the planter elite, but for the most part in limited ways and in a relatively few, isolated areas. These were the southern highlanders, the "hill people," who lived in the Appalachian ranges east of the Mississippi, in the Ozarks to the west of the river, and in other "hill country" or "backcountry" areas cut off from the more commercial world of the plantation system. Of all southern whites, they were the most isolated from the mainstream of the region's life. They practiced a simple form of subsistence agri-culture, owned practically no slaves, and had a proud sense of seclusion. They were, in most respects, un-connected to the new commercial economy that dom-inated the great cotton-planting region of the South. They produced almost no surplus for the market, had little access to money, and often bartered for the goods they could not grow themselves.

To such men and women, slavery was unattractive for many of the same reasons it was unappealing to work-ers and small farmers in the North: because it threat-ened their sense of their own independence. Upcoun-try farmers lived in a society of unusual individual freedom and unusual isolation from modern notions of property. They also held to older political ideals, which for many included the ideal of loyalty to the na-tion as a whole.

Such whites frequently expressed animosity toward the planter aristocracy of the other regions of the South. The mountain region was the only part of the South to defy the trend toward sectional conformity, and it was the only part to resist the movement toward secession when it finally developed. Even during the Civil War itself, many refused to support the Confed-eracy; some went so far as to fight for the Union.

Far greater in number, however, were the non-slaveowning whites who lived in the midst of the plan-tation system. Many, perhaps most of them, accepted that system because they were tied to it in important ways. Small farmers depended on the local plantation aristocracy for many things: access to cotton gins, mar-kets for their modest crops and their livestock, credit or other financial assistance in time of need. In many areas, there were also extensive kinship networks link-ing lower- and upper-class whites. The poorest resi-dent of a county might easily be a cousin of the rich-est aristocrat. Taken together, these mutual ties—a system of vaguely paternal relationships—helped mute what might otherwise have been pronounced class ten-sions.

Small farmers felt tied to the plantation society in other ways as well. For white men, at least, the South was an unusually democratic society, in the sense that participation in politics—both through voting and through attending campaign meetings and barbe-cues—was even more widespread than in the North, where participation was also high. Just as political par-ticipation gave workers in the North a sense of con-nection to the social order, so it did for farmers in the South—even though officeholders in the South, even more than in the North, were almost always members of the region's elites. In the 1850s, moreover, the boom in the cotton economy allowed many small farmers to improve their economic fortunes. Some bought more land, became slaveowners, and moved into at least the fringes of plantations society. Others simply felt more secure now in their positions as independent yeomen and hence more likely to embrace the fierce regional loyalty that was spreading throughout the white South in these years.

Small farmers, even more than great planters, were also committed to a traditional patriarchal family structure. Their household-centered economies re-quired the participation of all family members and, they believed, a stable system of gender relations to ensure order and stability. Men were the unquestioned masters of their homes; women and children, who were both family and work force, were firmly under the master's control. As the northern attack on slavery increased in the 1840s and 1850s, it was easy for such farmers to believe—and easy for ministers, politicians, and other propagandists for slavery to persuade them—that an assault on one hierarchical system (slavery) would open the way to an assault on another such sys-tem (patriarchy).

There were other white southerners, however, who did not share in the plantation economy in even lim-ited ways and yet continued to accept its premises. These were the members of that degraded class—num-bering perhaps a half-million in 1850—known vari-ously as "crackers," "sand hillers," or "poor white trash." Occupying the infertile lands of the pine bar-rens, the red hills, and the swamps, they lived in mis-erable cabins amid genuine squalor. Many owned no land (or owned land on which virtually nothing could be grown) and supported themselves by foraging or hunting. Others worked at times as common laborers for their neighbors, although the slave system limited their opportunities to do that. Their degradation re-sulted partly from dietary deficiencies and disease. They resorted at times to eating clay (hence the ten-dency of more affluent whites to refer to them dis-paragingly as "clay eaters"); and they suffered from pellagra, hookworm, and malaria. Planters and small farmers alike held them in contempt. They formed a true underclass. In some material respects, their plight was worse than that of the black slaves (who them-selves often looked down on the poor whites).

Even among these southerners—the true outcasts of white society in the region—there was no real oppo-sition to the plantation system or slavery. In part, un-doubtedly, this was because these men and women were so benumbed by poverty that they had little strength to protest. But it resulted also from perhaps the single greatest unifying factor among the southern white population, the one force that was most responsible for reducing tensions among the various classes. That force was their perception of race. However poor and miserable white southerners might be, they could still consider themselves members of a ruling race; they could still look down on the black population of the region and feel a bond with their fellow whites born of a determination to maintain their racial supremacy. As Frederick Law Olmsted, a northerner who visited the South and chronicled southern society in the 1850s, wrote: "From childhood, the one thing in their condition which has made life valuable to the mass of whites has been that the niggers are yet their inferiors."

THE "PECULIAR INSTITUTION"

White southerners often referred to slavery as the "peculiar institution." By that they meant not that the institution was odd, but that it was distinctive, special. The description was apt, for American slavery was indeed distinctive. The South in the mid-nineteenth century was the only area in the Western world—except for Brazil and Cuba—where slavery still existed. Slavery, more than any other single factor, isolated the South from the rest of American society. And as that isolation increased, so did the commitment of southerners to defend the institution. William Harper, a prominent South Carolina politician in the 1840s, wrote: "The judgment is made up. We can have no hearing before the tribunal of the civilized world. Yet, on this very account, it is more important that we, the inhabitants of the slave-holding States, insulated as we are by this institution, and cut off, in some degree, from the communion and sympathies of the world by which we are surrounded, . . . and exposed continually to their animadversions and attacks, should thoroughly understand this subject, and our strength and weakness in relation to it."

Within the South itself, the institution of slavery had paradoxical results. On the one hand, it isolated blacks from whites, drawing a sharp and inviolable racial line dividing one group of southerners from another. As a result, African Americans under slavery began to develop a society and culture of their own, one in many ways unrelated to the white civilization around them. On the other hand, slavery created a unique bond between blacks and whites—masters and slaves—in the South. The two groups may have maintained separate spheres, but each sphere was deeply influenced by, indeed dependent on, the other.

Varieties of Slavery

Slavery was an institution established and regulated in detail by law. The slave codes of the southern states forbade slaves to hold property, to leave their masters'

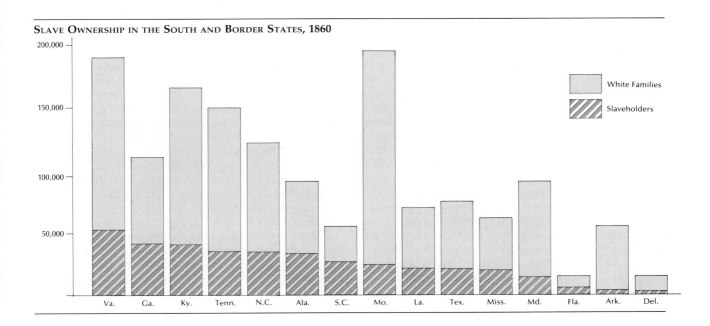

SLAVE OWNERSHIP IN THE SOUTH AND BORDER STATES, 1860

White Families

Slaveholders

Va. Ga. Ky. Tenn. N.C. Ala. S.C. Mo. La. Tex. Miss. Md. Fla. Ark. Del.

RETURNING FROM THE COTTON FIELD
In this photograph, South Carolina field workers return after a day of picking cotton, some of their harvest carried in bundles on their heads. A black slave driver leads the way. *(New-York Historical Society)*

premises without permission, to be out after dark, to congregate with other slaves except at church, to carry firearms, or to strike a white person even in self-defense. The codes prohibited whites from teaching slaves to read or write and denied to slaves the right to testify in court against white people. The laws contained no provisions to legalize slave marriages or divorces. If an owner killed a slave while punishing him, the act was generally not considered a crime. Slaves, however, faced the death penalty for killing or even resisting a white person and for inciting to revolt. The codes also contained extraordinarily rigid provisions for defining a person's race. Anyone with even a trace of African ancestry was defined as black. And anyone even rumored to possess any such trace was presumed to be black unless he or she could prove otherwise—which was, of course, difficult to do.

These and dozens of other restrictions might seem to suggest that slaves lived under a uniformly harsh and dismal regime. Had the laws been rigidly en-

forced, that might have been the case. In fact, however, enforcement was spotty and uneven. Some slaves did acquire property, did learn to read and write, and did assemble with other slaves, in spite of laws to the contrary. Although the major slave offenses generally fell under the jurisdiction of the courts (and thus of the slave codes), white owners handled most transgressions and inflicted widely varying punishments. In other words, despite the rigid provisions of law, there was in reality considerable variety within the slave system. Some blacks lived in almost prisonlike conditions, rigidly and harshly controlled by their masters. Many (probably most) others enjoyed some flexibility and (at least in comparison to the regimen prescribed by law) a striking degree of autonomy.

The nature of the relationship between masters and slaves depended in part on the size of the plantation. The typical master had a different image of slavery from that of the typical slave. Most masters possessed very few slaves, and their experience with (and image

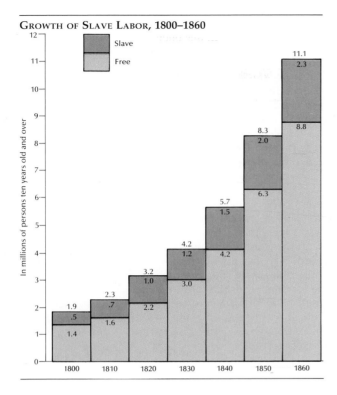

GROWTH OF SLAVE LABOR, 1800–1860

common in rice culture, under which slaves were assigned a particular task in the morning, for example, hoeing one acre; after completing the job, they were free for the rest of the day. The other, far more common, was the gang system, employed on the cotton, sugar, and tobacco plantations, under which slaves were simply divided into groups, each of them directed by a driver, and compelled to work for as many hours as the overseer considered a reasonable workday.

Life Under Slavery

Slaves generally received at least enough necessities to enable them to live and work. Their masters usually furnished them with an adequate if rough diet, consisting mainly of cornmeal, salt pork, molasses, and on special occasions fresh meat or poultry. Many slaves cultivated gardens for their own use. They received cheap clothing and shoes. They lived in rude cabins, called slave quarters, usually clustered together in a complex near the master's house. The plantation mistress or a doctor retained by the owner provided some medical care; but slave women themselves—as "healers" and midwives, or simply as mothers—were the more important source.

Slaves worked hard, beginning with light tasks as children; and their workdays were longest at harvest time. Slave women worked particularly hard. They generally labored in the fields with the men, and they assumed as well the crucial chores traditionally reserved for women—cooking, cleaning, and child rearing. Because slave families were often divided, with husbands and fathers frequently living on neighboring plantations (or, at times, sold to plantation owners far away), black women often found themselves acting in effect as single parents. Within the slave family, therefore, women had special burdens but also a special authority.

Slaves were, as a group, much less healthy than southern whites. After 1808, when the importation of slaves became illegal, the proportion of blacks to whites in the nation as a whole steadily declined. In 1820, there was one African American to every four whites; in 1840, one to every five. The slower increase of the black population was a result of its comparatively high death rate. Slave mothers had large families, but the enforced poverty in which virtually all African Americans lived ensured that fewer of their children would survive to adulthood than the children of white parents. Even those who did survive typically died at a younger age than the average white person.

Even so, according to some historians, the material conditions of slavery may, in fact, have been better

of) slavery was a reflection of the special nature of slavery on the small farm. White farmers with few slaves generally supervised their workers directly and often worked closely alongside them. On such farms, blacks and whites developed a form of intimacy unknown on larger plantations. The paternal relationship between such masters and their slaves could, like relationships between fathers and children, be warm and in many ways benevolent. It could also be tyrannical and cruel. In general, the evidence suggests, African Americans themselves preferred to live on larger plantations, where they had more privacy and a chance for a social world of their own.

Although the majority of slaveowners were small farmers, the majority of slaves lived on plantations of medium or large size, with sizable slave work forces. Thus the relationship between master and slave was much less intimate for the typical slave than for the typical slaveowner. Substantial planters often hired overseers and even assistant overseers to represent them. "Head drivers," trusted and responsible slaves often assisted by several subdrivers, acted under the overseer as foremen.

Larger planters generally used one of two methods of assigning slave labor. One was the task system, most

than those of many northern factory workers and considerably better than those of both peasants and industrial workers in nineteenth-century Europe. The conditions of American slaves were certainly less severe than those of slaves in the Caribbean and much of South America. That was in part because plantations in other parts of the Americas tended to grow crops that required more arduous labor; sugar production in the Caribbean islands, in particular, involved extraordinarily backbreaking work. In addition, Caribbean and South American planters continued to use the African slave trade well into the nineteenth century to replenish their labor supply, so they had less incentive than American planters (who no longer had much access to that trade) to protect their existing laborers. Working and living conditions in these other slave societies were arduous, and masters at times literally worked their slaves to death. Growing cotton, the activity for most slaves in the United States, was much less debilitating than growing sugar; and planters had strong economic incentives to maintain a healthy slave population. One result of this was that America became the only country where a slave population actually increased through natural reproduction (although it grew much more slowly than the white population).

Most masters did make some effort to preserve the health—and thus the usefulness—of their slaves. One example was the frequent practice of protecting slave children from hard work until early adolescence. Masters believed that doing so would make young slaves more loyal and would also ensure better health as adults. Another example was the use of hired labor, when available, for the most unhealthy or dangerous tasks. A traveler in Louisiana noted, for example, that Irishmen were employed to clear malarial swamps and to handle cotton bales at the bottom of chutes extending from the river bluff down to a boat landing. If an Irish worker died of disease or in an accident, a master could hire another for a dollar a day or less. But a master would lose an investment of perhaps $1,000 or more if a prime field hand died. Still, cruel masters might forget their pocketbooks in the heat of anger. And slaves were often left to the discipline of overseers, who had less of an economic stake in their well-being; overseers were paid in proportion to the amount of work they could get out of the slaves they supervised.

Household servants had a somewhat easier life—physically at least—than did field hands. On a small plantation, the same slaves might do both field work and housework. But on a large estate, there would generally be a separate domestic staff: nursemaids, housemaids, cooks, butlers, coachmen. These people lived close to the master and his family, eating the leftovers from the family table and in some cases even sleeping in the "big house." Between the blacks and whites of such households affectionate, almost familial relationships might develop. More often, however, house servants resented their isolation from their fellow slaves and the lack of privacy that came with living in such close proximity to the master's family. Among other things, that proximity meant that their transgressions were more visible than those of field hands, and so they received punishments more often than did other slaves. When emancipation came after the Civil War, it was often the house servants who were the first to leave the plantations of their former owners.

Female household servants were especially vulnerable to sexual abuse by their masters and white overseers, who sometimes pressured them into ostensibly consensual sexual relationships and sometimes literally raped them. In addition to unwanted sexual attentions from white men, female slaves often received vindictive treatment from white women. Plantation mistresses naturally resented the sexual liaisons between their husbands and female slaves. Punishing their husbands was not usually possible, so they often punished the slaves instead—with arbitrary beatings, increased workloads, and various forms of psychological torment.

Slavery in the Cities

The conditions of slavery in the cities differed significantly from those in the countryside. On the relatively isolated plantations, slaves had little contact with free blacks and lower-class whites, and masters maintained a fairly direct and effective control; a deep and seemingly unbridgeable chasm yawned between slavery and freedom. In the city, however, a master often could not supervise his slaves closely and at the same time use them profitably. Even if they slept at night in carefully watched backyard barracks, they moved about during the day alone, performing errands of various kinds.

There was a considerable market in the South for common laborers, particularly since, unlike in the North, there were few European immigrants to perform menial chores. Even the poorest whites tended to prefer working on farms to doing ordinary labor, and so masters often hired out slaves for such tasks. Slaves on contract worked in mining and lumbering (often far from cities); but others worked on the docks and on construction sites, drove wagons, and performed other unskilled jobs in cities and towns. Slave women and children worked in the region's few textile mills. Particularly skilled workers such as blacksmiths or carpenters were also often hired out. After regular working hours, many of them fended for themselves; neither their owners nor their employers both-ered to supervise them. Thus urban slaves gained numerous opportunities to mingle with free blacks and with whites. In the cities, the line between slavery and freedom became increasingly indistinct.

Indeed, white southerners generally considered slavery to be incompatible with city life, and as southern cities grew the number of slaves in them declined, relatively if not absolutely. The reasons were social rather than economic. Fearing conspiracies and insurrections, urban slaveowners sold off much of their male property to the countryside. Remaining behind in the cities was a slave population in which black women outnumbered black men. The same cities also had more white men than women—a situation that helped account for the birth of many mulattoes. Even while slavery in the cities was declining, forced segregation of urban blacks, both free and slave, from white society increased. Segregation was a means of social control intended to make up for the loosening of the discipline of slavery itself in urban areas.

Free Blacks

There were about 250,000 free blacks in the slaveholding states by the start of the Civil War, more than half of them in Virginia and Maryland. In some cases, they were slaves who had somehow earned money with which they managed to buy their own and their families' freedom, usually by developing a skill they could market independently of their masters. It was usually urban blacks, with their greater freedom of movement and activity, who could take that route. One example was Elizabeth Keckley, a slave woman who bought freedom for herself and her son with proceeds from sewing. She later became a seamstress, personal servant, and companion to Mary Todd Lincoln in the White House. But few masters had any incentive, or inclination, to give up their slaves, so this route was open to relatively few people.

Some slaves were set free by a master who had moral qualms about slavery, or by a master's will after his death—for example, the more than 400 slaves belonging to John Randolph of Roanoke, freed in 1833. From the 1830s on, however, state laws governing slavery became more rigid. That was in part a response to the fears Nat Turner's revolt (see p. 322) created among white southerners: free blacks, removed from close supervision by whites, might generate more violence and rebellion than slaves. It was also in part because the community of free blacks in southern cities was becoming larger and, to whites, more threatening—a dangerous example to blacks still in slavery. The rise of abolitionist agitation in the North—and the fear that it would inspire slaves to rebel—also persuaded southern whites to tighten their system. The new laws made it more and more difficult, and in some cases practically impossible, for owners to set free (or "manumit") their slaves; all forbade free blacks from entering the state. Arkansas even forced the freed slaves living there to leave.

A few free blacks (generally those on the northern fringes of the slaveholding regions) attained wealth and prominence. Some owned slaves themselves, usually relatives whom they had bought in order to ensure their ultimate emancipation. In a few cities—New Orleans, Natchez, Charleston—free black communities managed to flourish relatively unmolested by whites and with some economic stability. Most free blacks, however, lived in abject poverty, under conditions worse than those of blacks in the North. Law or custom closed many occupations to them, forbade them to assemble without white supervision, and placed numerous other restraints on them. They were only quasi-free, and yet they had all the burdens of freedom: the necessity to support themselves, to find housing, to pay taxes. Yet great as were the hardships of freedom, blacks usually preferred them to slavery.

The Slave Trade

The transfer of slaves from one part of the South to another was one of the most important consequences of the development of the Southwest. Sometimes slaves moved to the new cotton lands in the company of their original owners, who were migrating themselves. More often, however, the transfer occurred through the medium of professional slave traders. Traders transported slaves over long distances on trains or on river or ocean steamers. On shorter journeys, the slaves moved on foot, trudging in coffles of hundreds along dusty highways—just as their ancestors had marched to the ports in Africa from which they had embarked to America. Eventually they arrived at some central market such as Natchez, New Orleans, Mobile, or Galveston, where purchasers gathered to bid for them. At the auction, the bidders checked the slaves like livestock, watching them as they were made to walk or trot, inspecting their teeth, feeling their arms and legs, looking for signs of infirmity or age. Some traders tried to deceive buyers by blacking gray hair, oiling withered skin, and concealing physical defects in other ways. A sound young field hand would fetch a price that, during the 1840s and 1850s, varied from $500 to $1,700, depending mainly on fluctuations in the price of cotton. An attractive, sexually desirable woman might bring much more.

The domestic slave trade was essential to the growth and prosperity of the whole system. It was also

"THE OLD PLANTATION"
This painting, by an unidentified folk artist of the early nineteenth century, suggests the importance of music in the lives of plantation slaves in America. The banjo, which the black musician at right is playing, was originally an African instrument. *(Abby Aldrich Rockefeller Folk Art Center)*

one of its most horrible aspects. The trade dehumanized all who were involved in it. It separated children from parents, and parents from each other. Even families kept together by scrupulous masters might be broken up in the division of the estate after the master's death. Planters might deplore the trade, but they eased their consciences by holding the traders in contempt and assigning them a low social position.

The foreign slave trade was as bad or worse. Although federal law had prohibited the importation of slaves from 1808 on, some continued to be smuggled into the United States as late as the 1850s. The numbers can only be estimated. There were not enough such imports to satisfy all planters, and the southern commercial conventions, which met annually to consider means of making the South economically independent, began to discuss the legal reopening of the trade. "If it is right to buy slaves in Virginia and carry

them to New Orleans," William L. Yancey of Alabama asked his fellow delegates at the 1858 meeting, "why is it not right to buy them in Cuba, Brazil, or Africa and carry them there?" The convention that year voted to recommend the repeal of all laws against slave imports. Only the delegates from the states of the upper South, which profited from the domestic trade, opposed the foreign competition.

Slave Resistance

Few issues have sparked as much debate among historians as the effects of slavery on the blacks themselves. (See "Where Historians Disagree," pp. 322–323.) Slaveowners, and many white Americans after emancipation, liked to argue that the slaves were generally content, "happy with their lot." That may well have

HARRIET TUBMAN WITH ESCAPED SLAVES
Harriet Tubman (c. 1820–1913) was born into slavery in Maryland. In 1849, when her master died, she escaped to Philadelphia to avoid being sold out of state. Over the next ten years, she assisted first members of her own family and then up to 300 other slaves to escape from Maryland to freedom. During the Civil War, she served alternately as a nurse and as a spy for Union forces in South Carolina. She is shown here, on the left, with some of the slaves she had helped to free. *(Smith College)*

been true in some cases. But it is clear that the vast majority of southern blacks were not content with being slaves, that they yearned for freedom even though most realized there was little they could do to secure it. Evidence for that conclusion can be found, if nowhere else, from the reaction of slaves when emancipation finally came. Virtually all reacted to freedom with joy and celebration; relatively few chose to remain in the service of the whites who had owned them before the Civil War (although most blacks, of course, remained for many years subservient to whites in one way or another).

Rather than contented acceptance, the dominant response of blacks to slavery was a complex one: a combination of adaptation and resistance. At the extremes, slavery could produce two very different reactions, each of which served as the basis for a powerful stereotype in white society. One extreme was what became known as the "Sambo"—the shuffling, grinning, head-scratching, deferential slave who acted out the role that he recognized the white world expected of him. More often than not, the "Sambo" pattern of behavior was a charade, a facade assumed in the presence of whites. The other extreme was the slave rebel—the African American who could not bring himself or herself to either acceptance or accommodation but remained forever rebellious.

Actual slave revolts were extremely rare, but the knowledge that they were possible struck terror into the hearts of white southerners everywhere. In 1800,

THE CHARACTER OF PLANTATION SLAVERY

NO ISSUE IN AMERICAN history has produced a richer literature or a more spirited debate than the nature of American slavery. The debate began even before the Civil War, when abolitionists strove to expose slavery to the world as a brutal, dehumanizing institution, while southern defenders of slavery tried to depict it as a benevolent, paternalistic system. That same debate continued for a time after the Civil War; but by the late nineteenth century, with white Americans eager for sectional conciliation, both northern and southern chroniclers of slavery began to accept a romanticized and unthreatening picture of the Old South and its "peculiar institution."

The first major scholarly examination of slavery was fully within this romantic tradition. Ulrich B. Phillips's *American Negro Slavery* (1918) portrayed slavery as an essentially benign institution in which kindly masters looked after submissive, childlike, and generally contented African Americans. Phillips's apologia for slavery remained the authoritative work on the subject for nearly thirty years.

In the 1940s, as concern about racial injustice increasingly engaged the attention of white Americans, challenges to Phillips began to emerge. In 1941, Melville J. Herskovits challenged Phillips's contention that black Americans retained little of their African cultural inheritance. In 1943, Herbert Aptheker published a chronicle of slave revolts as a way of challenging Phillips's claim that blacks were submissive and content.

A somewhat different challenge to Phillips emerged in the 1950s from historians who emphasized the brutality of the institution. Kenneth Stampp's *The Peculiar Institution* (1956) and, even more powerfully, Stanley Elkins's *Slavery* (1959) described a labor system that did serious physical and psychological damage to its victims. Stampp and Elkins portrayed slavery as something like a prison, in which men and women had virtually no space in which to develop their own social and cultural lives. Elkins compared the system to Nazi concentration camps during World War II and likened the childlike "Sambo" personality of slavery to the tragic distortions of character produced by the Holocaust.

In the early 1970s, an explosion of new scholarship on slavery shifted the emphasis away from the damage the system inflicted on African

---

Gabriel Prosser gathered 1,000 rebellious slaves outside Richmond; but two Africans gave the plot away, and the Virginia militia stymied the uprising before it could begin. Prosser and thirty-five others were executed. In 1822, the Charleston free black Denmark Vesey and his followers—rumored to total 9,000—made preparations for revolt; but again word leaked out, and suppression and retribution followed. In 1831, Nat Turner, a slave preacher, led a band of African Americans who armed themselves with guns and axes and, on a summer night, went from house to house in Southampton County, Virginia. They killed sixty white men, women, and children before being overpowered by state and federal troops. More than a hundred blacks were executed in the aftermath. Nat Turner's was the only actual slave insurrection in the nineteenth-century South, but fear of slave conspiracies

and renewed violence pervaded the section as long as slavery lasted.

For the most part, however, resistance to slavery took other, less drastic forms. Some blacks attempted to resist by running away. A small number managed to escape to the North or to Canada, especially after sympathetic whites began organizing the so-called underground railroad to assist them in flight. But the odds against a successful escape, particularly from the Deep South, were almost impossibly high. The hazards of distance and the slaves' ignorance of geography were serious obstacles. So were the white "slave patrols," which stopped wandering blacks on sight throughout the South demanding to see travel permits. Without such a permit, slaves were presumed to be runaways and were taken captive. For blacks who attempted to escape through the woods, slave patrols of-

WHERE HISTORIANS DISAGREE

Americans and toward the striking success of the slaves in building a culture of their own despite their enslavement. John Blassingame in 1973, echoing Herskovitz's claims of thirty years earlier, argued that "the most remarkable aspect of the whole process of enslavement is the extent to which the American-born slaves were able to retain their ancestors' culture." Herbert Gutman, in *The Black Family in Slavery and Freedom* (1976), challenged the prevailing belief that slavery had weakened and even destroyed the African-American family. On the contrary, he argued, the black family survived slavery with impressive strength, although with some significant differences from the prevailing form of the white family. Eugene Genovese's *Roll, Jordan, Roll* (1974) revealed how African Americans manipulated the paternalist assumptions at the heart of slavery to build a large cultural space of their own within the system where they could develop their own family life, social traditions, and religious patterns. That same year, Robert Fogel and Stanley Engerman published their controversial *Time on the Cross*, a highly quantitative study that sup-

ported some of the claims of Gutman and Genovese about black achievement but that went much further in portraying slavery as a successful and reasonably humane (if ultimately immoral) system. Slave workers, they argued, were better treated and lived in greater comfort than most northern industrial workers of the same era. Their conclusions produced a storm of criticism.

Some of the most important recent scholarship on slavery has focused on the role of women within it. Elizabeth Fox-Genovese's *Within the Plantation Household* (1988) examined the lives of both white and black women on the plantation. Rejecting the claims of some feminist historians that black and white women shared a common female identity born of their shared subordination to men, she portrayed slave women as defined by their dual roles as members of the plantation work force and anchors of the black family. Slave women, she argued, professed loyalty to their mistresses when forced to serve them as domestics; but their real loyalty remained to their own communities and families.

ten employed bloodhounds. Despite all the obstacles to success, however, blacks continued to run away from their masters in large numbers. Some did so repeatedly, undeterred by the whippings and other penalties inflicted on them when captured.

But perhaps the most important method of resistance was simply a pattern of everyday behavior by which blacks defied their masters. That whites so often considered blacks to be lazy and shiftless suggests one means of resistance: refusal to work hard. Some slaves stole from their masters or from neighboring whites. Some performed isolated acts of sabotage: losing or breaking tools (southern planters gradually began to buy unusually heavy hoes because so many of the lighter ones got broken) or performing tasks improperly. In extreme cases, blacks might make themselves useless by cutting off their fingers or even com-

mitting suicide. Or, despite the terrible consequences, a few turned on their masters and killed them. The extremes, however, were very rare. For the most part, blacks resisted by building into their normal patterns of behavior subtle methods of rebellion.

THE CULTURE OF SLAVERY

Resistance was only part of the slave response to slavery. Another was an elaborate process of adaptation— a process that did not imply contentment with bondage but a recognition that there was no realistic alternative. One of the ways blacks adapted was by developing their own, separate culture, one that enabled them to sustain a sense of racial pride and unity.

Language and Music

In many areas, slaves retained a language of their own, sometimes incorporating African speech patterns into English. Having arrived in America speaking many different African languages, the first generations of slaves had as much difficulty communicating with one another as they did with white people. To overcome these barriers, they learned a simple, common language (known to linguists as "pidgin"). It retained some African words, but it drew primarily, if selectively, from English. And while slave language grew more sophisticated as blacks spent more time in America—and as new generations grew up never having known African tongues—some features of this early pidgin survived in black speech for many generations.

Music was especially important in slave society—much more important than in most white cultures. In some ways, it was as important to African Americans as language. Again, the African heritage was an important influence. African music relied heavily on rhythm, and so did black music in America. Africans thought of music as an accompaniment to dance, and so did blacks in America. The banjo, an instrument original to Africa, became important to slave music. But most important were voices and song.

Field workers often used songs to pass the time in the fields; since they sang them in the presence of the whites, they usually attached relatively innocuous words to them. But African Americans also created more emotionally rich and politically challenging music in the relative privacy of their religious services. It was there that the tradition of the spiritual emerged in the early nineteenth century. And through the spiritual, Africans in America not only expressed their Christian faith, but also lamented their bondage and expressed continuing hope for freedom. Similar sentiments surfaced throughout slave religion.

African-American Religion

A separate slave religion was not supposed to exist. Almost all African Americans were Christians by the early nineteenth century. Some had converted voluntarily and some after coercion from their masters and Protestant missionaries who evangelized among them. Masters expected their slaves to worship under the supervision of white ministers. Indeed, autonomous black churches were banned by law; and many slaves became members of the same denominations as their owners—usually Baptist or Methodist. In the 1840s and 1850s, as slavery expanded in the South, missionary efforts increased. Vast numbers of blacks became members of Protestant churches in those years.

Nevertheless, blacks throughout the South developed their own version of Christianity, at times incorporating into it such practices as voodoo or other polytheistic religious traditions of Africa. Or they simply bent religion to the special circumstances of bondage. Natural leaders emerging within the slave community rose to the rank of preacher.

African-American religion was more emotional than its white counterparts and reflected the influence of African customs and practices. Slave prayer meetings routinely involved fervent chanting, spontaneous exclamations from the congregation, and ecstatic conversion experiences. Black religion was also more joyful and affirming than that of many white denominations. And above all, black religion emphasized the dream of freedom and deliverance. In their prayers and songs and sermons, black Christians talked and sang of the day when the Lord would "call us home," "deliver us to freedom," "take us to the Promised Land." And while their white masters generally chose to interpret such language merely as the expression of hopes for life after death, many blacks themselves used the images of Christian salvation to express their own dream of freedom in the present world. Christian images, and biblical injunctions, were central to Gabriel Prosser, Denmark Vesey, Nat Turner, and others who planned or engaged in open resistance to slavery.

PLANTATION RELIGION
A black preacher leads his fellow slaves, as well as the family of the master, in a Sunday service in the modest plantation chapel. African-American religious services were considerably less restrained when white people were not present—one reason why blacks withdrew so quickly from white churches after the Civil War and formed their own. *(Bettmann)*

SIGNIFICANT EVENTS

1800 Gabriel Prosser organizes unsuccessful slave revolt in Virginia

1808 Importation of slaves to United States banned

1820s Prolonged depression in tobacco prices begins

English market for cotton textiles boosts prices and causes explosion in cotton production in Southwest

1822 Denmark Vesey thwarted in plans for slave rebellion in Charleston

1831 Nat Turner slave rebellion breaks out in Virginia

1833 John Randolph of Roanoke frees 400 slaves

1837 Cotton prices plummet

1846 *De Bow's Review* founded in New Orleans

1849 Rise in cotton prices spurs production boom

In cities and towns in the South, some African Americans had their own churches, where free blacks occasionally worshiped alongside slaves. In the countryside, however, slaves usually attended the same churches as their masters—sometimes a chapel on the plantation itself, sometimes a church serving a larger farm community. Seating in such churches was usually segregated. Blacks sat in the rear or in balconies. They held their own services later, often in secret, usually at night.

The Slave Family

The slave family was the other crucial institution of black culture in the South. Like religion, it suffered from certain legal restrictions—most notably the lack of legal marriage. Nevertheless, what we now call the "nuclear family" consistently emerged as the dominant kinship model among African Americans.

Such families did not always operate according to white customs. Black women generally began bearing children at younger ages than most whites, often as early as age fourteen or fifteen. Slave communities did not condemn premarital pregnancy in the way white society did, and black couples would often begin living together before marrying. It was customary, however, for couples to marry—in a ceremony involving formal vows—soon after conceiving a child. Often, marriages occurred between slaves living on neighboring plantations. Husbands and wives sometimes visited each other with the permission of their masters, but often such visits had to be in secret, at night. Family ties were no less strong than those of whites,

and many slave marriages lasted throughout the course of long lifetimes.

When marriages did not survive, it was often because of circumstances over which blacks had no control. Up to a third of all black families were broken apart by the slave trade; an average slave might expect during a lifetime to see ten or more relatives sold. And that accounted for some of the other distinctive characteristics of the black family, which adapted itself to the cruel realities of its own uncertain future. Extended kinship networks—which grew to include not only spouses and their children, but aunts, uncles, grandparents, even distant cousins—were strong and important and often helped compensate for the breakup of nuclear families. A slave forced suddenly to move to a new area, far from his or her family, might create fictional kinship ties and become "adopted" by a family in the new community. Even so, the impulse to maintain contact with a spouse and children remained strong long after the breakup of a family. One of the most frequent causes of flight from the plantation was a slave's desire to find a husband, wife, or child who had been sent elsewhere.

It was not only by breaking up families through sale that whites intruded on black family life. Black women, usually powerless to resist the sexual advances of their masters, often bore the children of whites—children whom the whites almost never recognized as their own and who were consigned to slavery from birth.

In addition to establishing social and cultural institutions of their own, slaves adapted themselves to slavery by forming complex relationships with their masters. However much blacks resented their lack of freedom, they often found it difficult to maintain an entirely hostile attitude toward their owners. Not only were they dependent on whites for the material means of existence—food, clothing, and shelter; they also often derived from their masters a sense of security and protection. There was, in short, a paternal relationship between slave and master—sometimes harsh, sometimes kindly, but almost invariably important. That paternalism, in fact, became (even if not always consciously) a vital instrument of white control. By creating a sense of mutual dependence, whites helped reduce resistance to an institution that, in essence, served only the interests of the ruling race.

Suggested Readings

Culture and Society in the White South. Edward L. Ayers, *Vengeance and Justice: Crime and Punishment in the Nineteenth-Century American South* (1984). David T. Bailey, *Shadow on the Church: Southwestern Evangelical Religion and the Issue of Slavery, 1783–1860* (1985). Fred Bateman, *A Deplorable Scarcity: The Failure of Industrialism in the Slave Economy* (1981). Dickson D. Bruce, *Violence and Culture in the Antebellum South* (1979). Orville Vernon Burton, *In My Father's House Are Many Mansions: Family and Community in Edgefield, South Carolina* (1985). W. J. Cash, *The Mind of the South* (1941). Bruce Collins, *White Society in the Antebellum South* (1985). Avery Craven, *The Growth of Southern Nationalism* (1953). Clement Eaton, *Freedom of Thought in the Old South* (1940); *The Growth of Southern Nationalism, 1848–1861* (1961). Drew Gilpin Faust, *A Sacred Circle: The Dilemma of the Intellectual in the Old South* (1977); *James Henry Hammond and the Old South: A Design for Mastery* (1982). John Hope Franklin, *The Militant South* (1956). Frank Freidel, *Francis Lieber* (1947). Steven Hahn, *The Roots of Southern Populism: Yeomen Farmers and the Transformation of the Georgia Upcountry, 1850–1890* (1983). Ann C. Loveland, *Southern Evangelicals and the Social Order, 1800–1860* (1980). Donald G. Mathews, *Religion in the Old South* (1977). John McCardell, *The Idea of a Southern Nation* (1979). Rollin G. Osterweis, *Romanticism and Nationalism in the Old South* (1949). Charles S. Sydnor, *The Development of Southern Sectionalism, 1819–1848* (1948). William R. Taylor, *Cavalier and Yankee: The Old South and American National Character* (1961). Bertram Wyatt-Brown, *Southern Honor: Ethics and Behavior in the Old South* (1982); *Yankee Saints and Southern Sinners* (1985).

The Plantation Economy. Eugene Genovese, *The Political Economy of Slavery* (1965). Lewis C. Gray, *History of Agriculture in the Southern United States to 1860*, 2 vols. (1933). J. William Harris, *Plain Folk and Gentry in a Slave Society* (1985). Peter Kolchin, *Unfree Labor: American Slavery and Russian Serfdom* (1987). Frank L. Owsley, *Plain Folk of the Old South* (1949). Ulrich B. Phillips, *Life and Labor in the Old South* (1929). R. R. Russel, *Economic Aspects of Southern Sectionalism, 1840–1861* (1924). Ralph A. Wooster, *Politicians, Planters, and Plain Folk* (1975). Gavin Wright, *The Political Economy of the Cotton South: Households, Markets, and Wealth in the Nineteenth Century* (1978).

The Planters. Carol Blesser, *The Hammonds of Redcliffe* (1981). Elizabeth Fox-Genovese, *Within the Plantation Household: Black and White Women of the Old South* (1988). Eugene Genovese, *The World the Slaveholders Made* (1969). Kenneth S. Greenberg, *Masters and Statesmen: The Political Culture of American Slavery* (1985). Frances Ann Kemble, *Journal of a Residence on a Georgian Plantation in 1838–1839* (1863). Robert Manson Myers, ed., *The Children of Pride* (1972). James Oakes, *The Ruling Race: A History of American Slaveholders* (1982); *Slavery and Freedom: An Interpretation of the Old South* (1990). Mary D. Robertson ed., *Lucy Breckinridge of Grove Hill* (1979).

Southern White Women. Victoria E. Bynum, *Unruly Women: The Politics of Social and Sexual Control in the Old South* (1992). Jane Turner Censer, *North Carolina Planters and Their Children, 1800–1860* (1984). Mary Boykin Chesnut, *A Diary from Dixie* (1981, ed. by C. Vann Woodward). Catherine Clinton, *The Plantation Mistress: Woman's World in the Old South* (1982). Elizabeth Fox-Genovese, *Within the Plantation Household* (1988). Suzanne Lebsock, *The Free Women of Petersburg: Status and Culture in a Southern Town* (1984). Anne Firor Scott, *The Southern Lady* (1970).

Society, Culture, and Slavery in the Black South. Herbert Aptheker, *American Negro Slave Revolts* (1943). Ira Berlin, *Slaves Without Masters* (1974). John Blassingame, *The Slave Community* (1973). John B. Boles, *Black Southerners, 1619–1869* (1983). Judith Chase, *Afro-American Art and Craft* (1971). Leonard P. Curry, *The Free Black in Urban America: The Shadow of the Dream* (1981). P. A. David et al., *Reckoning with Slavery* (1976). David Brion Davis, *Slavery and Human Progress* (1984). Carl Degler, *Neither Black nor White* (1971). Stanley Elkins, *Slavery* (1959). Dena J. Epstein, *Sinful Tunes and Spirituals: Black Folk Music to the Civil War* (1977). Barbara Jean Fields, *Slavery and Freedom on the Middle Ground* (1985). Robert Fogel, *Without Consent or Contract: The Rise and Fall of American Slavery* (1989). Robert Fogel and Stanley Engerman, *Time on the Cross*, 2 vols. (1974). Eugene Genovese, *Roll, Jordan, Roll: The World the Slaves Made* (1974). Claudia D. Goldin, *Urban Slavery in the American South, 1820–1860* (1876). Herbert Gutman, *Slavery and the Numbers Game* (1975); *The Black Family in Slavery and Freedom* (1976). Melville J. Herskovits, *The Myth of the Negro Past* (1941). Michael P. Johnson and James L. Roark, *Black Masters* (1984). Jacqueline Jones, *Labor of Love, Labor of Sorrow: Black Women, Work and the Family from Slavery to the Present* (1985). Lawrence W. Levine, *Black Culture and Black Consciousness: Afro-American Folk Thought from Slavery to Freedom* (1977). Leon Litwack, *North of Slavery* (1961). Stephen B.

Oates, *The Fires of Jubilee* (1974). Leslie Howard Owens, *This Species of Property: Slave Life and Slave Culture in the Old South* (1976). Orlando Patterson, *Slavery and Social Death: A Comparative Study* (1982). Ulrich B. Phillips, *American Negro Slavery* (1981); *Life and Labor in the Old South* (1929). Albert J. Raboteau, *Slave Religion* (1978). George P. Rawick, *From Sundown to Sunup: The Making of the Black Community* (1973). Kenneth Stampp, *The Peculiar Institution* (1955). Robert Starobin, *Denmark Vesey* (1970); *Industrial Slavery in the Old South* (1970). Richard C. Wade, *Slavery in the Cities* (1964). Thomas L. Weber, *Deep Like Rivers: Education in the Slave Quarters, 1831–1865* (1978). Deborah G. White, *Ar'n't I a Woman?* (1985). Joel Williamson, *New People: Miscegenation and Mulattoes in the United States* (1980).

135,000 SETS, 270,000 VOLUMES SOLD.

UNCLE TOM'S CABIN

FOR SALE HERE.

AN EDITION FOR THE MILLION, COMPLETE IN 1 Vol., PRICE 37 1-2 CENTS.
" " IN GERMAN, IN 1 Vol., PRICE 50 CENTS.
" " IN 2 Vols., CLOTH, 6 PLATES, PRICE $1.50.
SUPERB ILLUSTRATED EDITION, IN 1 Vol., WITH 153 ENGRAVINGS,
PRICES FROM $2.50 TO $5.00.

The Greatest Book of the Age.

Uncle Tom's Cabin
Of all the many reform movements that flourished in antebellum America, none became more powerful than abolitionism. Drawing from ideas about individual freedom and fulfillment that had informed earlier reform movements, the abolitionists built a movement that helped reshape American politics. Perhaps its most influential document was Harriet Beecher Stowe's abolitionist novel, *Uncle Tom's Cabin*, which did much to inflame public opinion in both the North and the South in the last years before the Civil War. When Abraham Lincoln was introduced to Stowe once in the White House, he reportedly said to her: "So you are the little lady that has brought this great war." *(Bettmann)*

CHAPTER TWELVE

AN AGE OF REFORMS

T HE UNITED STATES IN the mid-nineteenth century was a society in transition. The nation was growing rapidly in geographical extent, in the size and diversity of its population, and in the dimensions and complexity of its economy. And like any people faced with such rapid and fundamental alterations in their surroundings, Americans reacted with ambiguity. On the one hand, they were excited by the new possibilities that economic growth was providing. On the other hand, they were painfully aware of the dislocations that it was creating: the challenges to traditional values and institutions, the social instability, the increasing inequality, the uncertainty about the future.

One result of these conflicting attitudes was the emergence of a broad array of movements intended to adapt society to its new realities, to "reform" the nation. These reform efforts took many different shapes, but in general they reflected one of two basic impulses, and at times elements of both. Many of these movements rested on an optimistic faith in human nature, a belief that within every individual resided a spirit that was basically good and that society should attempt to unleash. This assumption—which spawned in both Europe and America a movement known, in its artistic aspects at least, as romanticism—stood in marked contrast to traditional Protestant assumptions of original sin, which humans needed to overcome through a disciplined, virtuous life. Instead, reformers now argued, individuals should strive to give full expression to the inner spirit, should work to unleash their innate capacity to experience joy and to do good.

A second impulse, which appeared directly to contradict the first but in practice often existed alongside it, was a desire for order and control. With society changing so rapidly, with traditional values and institutions under assault and often eroding, many Americans yearned above all for a restoration of stability and discipline to their nation. Often, this impulse embodied a conservative nostalgia for better, simpler times. But it also inspired forward-looking efforts to create new institutions of social control, suited to the realities of the new age.

The reforms that flowed from these two impulses came in many guises and mobilized many different groups. Reformers were far more numerous and influential in the North and Northwest than in the South, but reform activity could be found in all areas of the nation. In the course of the 1840s, however, one issue—slavery—came to overshadow all others. And one group of reformers—the abolitionists—became the most visible of all. At that point, the reform impulse, which at first had been a force that tended to unify the sections, became another wedge between the North and the South.

THE ROMANTIC IMPULSE

"In the four quarters of the globe," wrote the English wit Sydney Smith in 1820, "who reads an American book? or goes to an American play? or looks at an

American picture or statue?" The answer, he assumed, was obvious: no one. American intellectuals were painfully aware of the low regard in which Europeans held their artistic and intellectual life, and in the middle decades of the nineteenth century they continued to work for a liberation of their nation's culture—for the creation of an American artistic world independent of Europe, one that would express their nation's special virtues.

At the same time, however, some of the nation's cultural leaders were beginning to strive for another kind of liberation, one that would gradually come almost to overshadow their self-conscious nationalism. That impulse—which was, ironically, largely an import from Europe—was the spirit of romanticism. In literature, in philosophy, in art, even in politics and economics, American intellectuals were committing themselves to the liberation of the human spirit.

Literature and the Quest for Liberation

The effort to create a distinctively American literature, which Washington Irving and others had advanced in the first decades of the century, made considerable progress in the 1820s with the emergence of the first great American novelist: James Fenimore Cooper. The author of over thirty novels in the space of three decades, Cooper was known to his contemporaries as a master of adventure and suspense. What most distinguished his work, however, was its evocation of the American wilderness. Cooper had grown up in central New York, at a time when the edge of white settlement was not far away; and he retained throughout his life a fascination with man's relationship to nature and with the challenges (and dangers) of America's expansion westward. His most important novels—the "Leatherstocking Tales," among them *The Last of the Mohicans* (1826) and *The Deerslayer* (1841)—explored the American frontiersman's experience with Indians, pioneers, violence, and the law.

Cooper's novels were a continuation, in many ways a culmination, of the early nineteenth-century effort to produce a truly American literature. But they also served as a link to the concerns of later intellectuals. For in the "Leatherstocking Tales" could be seen not only a celebration of the American spirit and landscape but an evocation, through the character of Natty Bumppo, of the ideal of the independent individual, with a natural inner goodness. There was also evidence of another impulse that would motivate American reform: the fear of disorder. In portraying other characters, who exemplified the vicious, grasping nature of some of the nation's western settlers, Cooper was sug-

gesting a need for social discipline even in the wilderness.

Another group of important American writers emerged on the heels of Cooper. They displayed even more clearly the grip of romanticism on the nation's intellectual life. Walt Whitman, the self-proclaimed poet of American democracy, was the son of a Long Island carpenter and lived for many years roaming from place to place, doing odd jobs. Finally, in 1855, he hired a printer and published a first, thin volume of work: *Leaves of Grass*. His poems were an unrestrained celebration of democracy, of the liberation of the individual, and of the pleasures of the flesh as well as of the spirit. In these poems, as well as in a large body of other work spanning nearly forty more years until his death in 1892, Whitman not only helped liberate verse from traditional, restrictive conventions but helped express the soaring spirit of individualism that characterized his age.

The new literary concern with the unleashing of human emotions did not always produce such optimistic works, as the work of Herman Melville suggests. Born in New York in 1819, Melville ran away to sea as a youth and spent years sailing the world (including the South Seas) before returning home to become the greatest American writer of his era. The most important of his novels was *Moby Dick*, published in 1851. His portrayal of Ahab, the powerful, driven captain of a whaling vessel, was a story of courage and of the strength of individual will; but it was also a tragedy of pride and revenge. Ahab's maniacal search for Moby Dick, a great white whale that had maimed him, suggested how the search for personal fulfillment and triumph could not only liberate but destroy. The result of Ahab's great quest was the annihilation of Ahab himself, reflecting Melville's conviction that the human spirit was a troubled, often self-destructive force.

Similarly bleak were the works of one of the few southern writers of the time to embrace the search for the essence of the human spirit: Edgar Allan Poe. In the course of his short and unhappy life (he died in 1849 at the age of forty), Poe produced stories and poems that were primarily sad and macabre. His first book, *Tamerlane and Other Poems* (1827), received little recognition. But later works, including his most famous poem, "The Raven" (1845), established him as a major, if controversial, literary figure. Poe evoked images of individuals rising above the narrow confines of intellect and exploring the deeper world of the spirit and the emotions. Yet that world, he seemed to say, contained much pain and horror. Other American writers were contemptuous of Poe's work and his message, but he was ultimately to have a profound effect on European poets such as Baudelaire.

Literature in the Antebellum South

Poe, however, was something of an exception in the world of southern literature. The South experienced a literary flowering of its own in the mid-nineteenth century, and it produced writers and artists who were, like their northern counterparts, concerned with defining the nature of American society and of the American nation. But white southerners tended to produce very different images of what that society was and should be.

Southern novelists of the 1830s (among them Beverly Tucker, William Alexander Caruthers, and John Pendleton Kennedy), some of them writers of great talent, many of them residents of Richmond, produced historical romances or romantic eulogies of the plantation system of the upper South. In the 1840s, the southern literary capital moved to Charleston, home of the most distinguished of the region's men of letters: William Gilmore Simms. For a time, his work expressed a broad nationalism that transcended his regional background; but by the 1840s he too had become a strong defender of southern institutions—especially slavery—against the encroachments of the North. There was, he believed, a unique quality to southern life that it was the duty of intellectuals to defend.

One group of southern writers, however, produced works that were more distinctively American and less committed to a glorification of the peculiarities of southern life. These were writers from the fringes of plantation society, who depicted the world of the backwoods rural areas. Augustus B. Longstreet, Joseph G. Baldwin, Johnson J. Hooper, and others focused not on aristocratic "cavaliers," but on ordinary people and poor whites. Instead of romanticizing their subjects, they were deliberately and sometimes painfully realistic. And they seasoned their sketches with a robust, vulgar humor that was new to American literature. These southern realists established a tradition of American regional humor that was ultimately to find a supreme exponent in Mark Twain.

The Transcendentalists

One of the outstanding expressions of the romantic impulse in America came from a group of New England writers and philosophers known as the transcendentalists. Borrowing heavily from German philosophers such as Kant, Hegel, and Schelling, and from the English writers Coleridge and Carlyle, the transcendentalists embraced a theory of the individual that rested on a distinction (first suggested by Kant) between what they called "reason" and "understanding." Reason, as

RALPH WALDO EMERSON
Along with Margaret Fuller and Henry David Thoreau, Emerson helped make Concord, Massachusetts, the center of American transcendentalism. He derived many of his ideas about the mystical union between human beings and nature from the works of the English poets Thomas Carlyle, Samuel Taylor Coleridge, and William Wordsworth. *(Bettmann)*

they defined it, was the highest human faculty; it was the individual's innate capacity to grasp beauty and truth through giving full expression to the instincts and emotions. Understanding, by contrast, was the use of intellect in the narrow, artificial ways imposed by society; it involved the repression of instinct and the victory of externally imposed learning. Every person's goal, therefore, should be liberation from the confines of "understanding" and the cultivation of "reason." Each individual should strive to "transcend" the limits of the intellect and allow the emotions, the "soul," to create an "original relation to the Universe."

Transcendentalist philosophy emerged first among a small group of intellectuals centered in Concord, Massachusetts. Their leader and most eloquent voice was Ralph Waldo Emerson. A Unitarian minister in his

Emerson—transcendentalist

youth, Emerson left the church in 1832 to devote himself entirely to writing and teaching the elements of transcendentalism. He produced a significant body of poetry, but he was most renowned for his essays and lectures. In "Nature" (1836), one of his best-known essays, Emerson wrote that in the quest for self-fulfillment, individuals should work for a communion with the natural world: "in the woods, we return to reason and faith. . . . Standing on the bare ground—my head bathed by the blithe air, and uplifted into infinite space,—all mean egotism vanishes. . . . I am part and particle of God." In other essays, he was even more explicit in advocating a commitment of the individual to the full exploration of inner capacities. "Nothing is at last sacred," he wrote in "Self-Reliance" (1841), perhaps his most famous essay, "but the integrity of your own mind." The quest for self-reliance, he explained, was really a search for communion with the unity of the universe, the wholeness of God, the great spiritual force that he described as the "Oversoul." Each person's innate capacity to become, through his or her private efforts, a part of this essence was perhaps the classic expression of the romantic belief in the "divinity" of the individual. Emerson was also a committed nationalist, an ardent proponent of American cultural independence. His belief that truth and beauty could be derived as much from instinct as from learning suggested that Americans, lacking the rich cultural heritage of European nations, could still aspire to artistic and literary greatness.

Almost as influential as Emerson was another leading Concord transcendentalist, Henry David Thoreau. Thoreau went even further than his friend Emerson in repudiating the repressive forces of society, which produced, he said, "lives of quiet desperation." Individuals should work for self-realization by resisting pressures to conform to society's expectations and responding instead to their own instincts. Thoreau's own effort to free himself—immortalized in his most famous book, *Walden* (1854)—led him to build a small cabin in the Concord woods on the edge of Walden Pond, where he lived alone for two years as simply as he could. "I went to the woods," he explained, "because I wished to live deliberately, to front only the essential facts of life, and see if I could not learn what it had to teach, and not, when I came to die, discover that I had not lived."

Thoreau's rejection of what he considered the artificial constraints of society extended as well to his relationship with government. In 1846, he went to jail (briefly) rather than agree to pay a poll tax. He would not, he insisted, give financial support to a government that permitted the existence of slavery. In his 1849 essay "Resistance to Civil Government," he explained his refusal by claiming that the individual's personal morality had the first claim on his or her actions, that a government which required violation of that morality had no legitimate authority. The proper response was "civil disobedience," or "passive resistance"—a public refusal to obey unjust laws.

Visions of Utopia

Although transcendentalism was above all an individualistic philosophy, it helped spawn the most famous of all nineteenth-century experiments in communal living: Brook Farm, which the Boston transcendentalist George Ripley established as an experimental community in West Roxbury, Massachusetts, in 1841. There, according to Ripley, individuals would gather to create a new form of social organization, one that would permit every member of the community full opportunity for self-realization. All residents would share equally in the labor of the community so that all could share too in the leisure, for it was leisure that was the first necessity for cultivation of the self. (Ripley was one of the first Americans to attribute positive connotations to the idea of leisure; most of his contemporaries equated it with laziness and sloth.) Participation in manual labor served another purpose as well: it helped individuals bridge the gap between the world of the intellect and the world of the body, thus aiding them to become whole people.

The obvious tension between the ideal of individual freedom and the demands of a communal society took their toll on Brook Farm. Increasingly, individualism gave way to a form of socialism. Many residents became disenchanted and left; when a fire destroyed the central building of the community in 1847, the experiment dissolved.

Among the original residents of Brook Farm was the writer Nathaniel Hawthorne, who expressed his disillusionment with the experiment and, to some extent, with transcendentalism in a series of notable novels. In *The Blithedale Romance* (1852), he wrote scathingly of Brook Farm itself, portraying the disastrous consequences of the experiment on the individuals who submitted to it. In other novels—most notably *The Scarlet Letter* (1850) and *The House of Seven Gables* (1851)—he wrote equally passionately about the price individuals pay for cutting themselves off from society. Egotism, he claimed (in an indirect challenge to the transcendentalist faith in the self), was the "serpent" that lay at the heart of human misery.

The failure of Brook Farm did not, however, prevent the formation of other experimental communities. Some borrowed, as Ripley had done, from the ideas of the French philosopher Charles Fourier, whose ideas of socialist communities organized as cooperative "phalanxes" received wide attention in America. Others drew from the ideas of the Scottish industrialist and philanthropist Robert Owen. Owen himself founded an experimental community in Indiana in 1825, which he named New Harmony. It was to be a "Village of Cooperation," in which every resident worked and lived in total equality. The community was an economic failure, but the vision that had inspired it continued to enchant Americans. Dozens of other "Owenite" experiments began in other locations in the following years.

Redefining Gender Roles

One of the principal concerns of many of the new utopian communities (and of the new social philosophies on which they rested) was the relationship between men and women. In transcendentalism and other movements of this period can be seen expressions of a kind of feminism that would not gain a secure foothold in American society until the late twentieth century. Margaret Fuller, a leading transcendentalist, suggested the important relationship between the discovery of the "self" that was so central to antebellum reform and the questioning of gender roles: "Many women are considering within themselves what they need and what they have not," she wrote in 1845. "I would have Woman lay aside all thought, such as she habitually cherishes, of being taught and led by men."

A redefinition of gender roles was crucial to one of the most enduring of the utopian colonies of the nineteenth century: the Oneida Community, established in 1848 in upstate New York by John Humphrey Noyes. The Oneida "Perfectionists," as residents of the community called themselves, rejected traditional notions of family and marriage. All residents, Noyes declared, were "married" to all other residents; there were to be no permanent conjugal ties. But Oneida was not, as its horrified critics often claimed, an experiment in unrestrained "free love." It was a place where the community carefully monitored sexual behavior; where women were to be protected from unwanted childbearing; in which children were raised communally, often seeing little of their own parents. The Oneidans took special pride in what they considered the liberation of their women from the demands of male "lust" and from the traditional bonds of family.

The Shakers, even more than the Oneidans, made a redefinition of traditional sexuality and gender roles central to their society. Founded by "Mother" Ann Lee in the 1770s, the society of the Shakers survived throughout the nineteenth century and into the twentieth. (A tiny remnant survives today.) But the Shakers attracted a particularly large following in the an-

tebellum period and established more than twenty communities throughout the Northeast and Northwest in the 1840s. They derived their name from a unique religious ritual, a sort of ecstatic dance, in which members of a congregation would "shake" themselves free of sin while performing a loud chant.

The most distinctive feature of Shakerism, however, was its commitment to complete celibacy—which meant, of course, that no one could be born to Shakerism; all Shakers had to choose the faith voluntarily. Shaker communities attracted about 6,000 members in the 1840s, more women than men; and members lived in conditions in which contacts between men and women were very limited. Shakers openly endorsed the idea of sexual equality; they even embraced the idea of a God who was not clearly male or female. Indeed, within the Shaker society as a whole, it was women who exercised the most power. Mother Ann Lee was succeeded as leader of the movement by Mother Lucy Wright. Shakerism, one observer wrote in the 1840s, was a refuge from the "perversions of marriage" and "the gross abuses which drag it down."

The Shakers were not, however, motivated only by a desire to escape the burdens of traditional gender roles. They were trying as well to create a society separated and protected from the chaos and disorder that they believed had come to characterize American life as a whole. They were less interested in personal freedom than in social discipline. And in that, they were like some other dissenting religious sects and utopian communities of their time. Another example was the Amana Community, founded by German immigrants in 1843; its members settled in Iowa in 1855. The Amanas attempted to realize Christian ideals by creating an ordered, socialist society.

The Mormons

Among the most important efforts to create a new and more ordered society within the old was that of the Church of Jesus Christ of Latter Day Saints—the Mormons. Mormonism began in upstate New York as a result of the efforts of Joseph Smith, a young, energetic, but economically unsuccessful man, who had spent most of his twenty-four years moving restlessly through New England and the Northeast. Then, in 1830, he published a remarkable document—the Book of Mormon, named for the ancient prophet who he claimed had written it. It was, he said, a translation of a set of golden tablets he had found in the hills of New York, revealed to him by an angel of God. The Book of Mormon told the story of an ancient civilization in America, whose now vanished kingdom could become a model for a new holy community in the United States.

THE MORMONS IN UTAH
The great Mormon migration to Utah was the biggest single movement of people to the West in American history. Mormons had experienced years of hostility and violence from other communities further east, and they moved to what became Salt Lake City to create an isolated sanctuary for their new religion. *(Brigham Young University Museum of Art)*

Gathering a small group of believers around him, Smith began in 1831 trying to find a sanctuary for his new community of "saints," an effort that would continue unhappily for more than twenty years. Time and again, the Mormons attempted to establish their "New Jerusalem." Time and again, they met with persecution from surrounding communities suspicious of their radical religious doctrines—which included polygamy (the right of men to take several wives), a rigid form of social organization, and particularly damaging to their image, an intense secrecy, which gave rise to wild rumors among their critics of conspiracy and depravity.

Driven from their original settlements in Independence, Missouri, and Kirtland, Ohio, the Mormons moved on to the new town of Nauvoo, Illinois, which in the early 1840s became an imposing and economi-

cally successful community. In 1844, however, Joseph Smith was arrested, charged with treason (for conspiring against the government to win foreign support for a new Mormon colony in the Southwest), and imprisoned in Carthage, Illinois. There an angry mob attacked the jail, forced Smith from his cell, and shot and killed him. The Mormons now abandoned Nauvoo and, under the leadership of Smith's successor, Brigham Young, traveled across the desert—a society of 12,000 people, in one of the largest single group migrations in American history—and established a new community in Utah, the present Salt Lake City. There, at last, the Mormons were able to create a permanent settlement. And although they were not long to remain as isolated from the rest of American society as they were at the beginning, never again were they to be dislodged.

Like other experiments in social organization of the era, Mormonism reflected a belief in human perfectibility. God had once been a man, the church taught, and thus every man or woman could aspire to become—as Joseph Smith had done—a god. But unlike other new communities, the Mormons did not embrace the doctrine of individual liberty. Instead, they created a highly organized, centrally directed, almost militarized social structure, a refuge against the disorder and uncertainty of the secular world. They placed particular emphasis on the structure of the family. Mormon religious rituals even included a process by which men and women went through a baptism ceremony in the name of a deceased ancestor; as a result, they believed, they would be reunited with those ancestors in heaven. The intense Mormon interest in genealogy, which continues today, is a reflection of this belief in the possibility of reuniting present generations with those of the past.

The original Mormons were, for the most part, men and women who felt displaced in their rapidly changing society—economically marginal people left behind by the material growth and social progress of their era. In the new religion, they found genuine faith. In the society it created, they found security and order.

REMAKING SOCIETY

The simultaneous efforts to liberate the individual and impose order on a changing world also helped create a wide range of new movements to remake society— movements in which, to a striking degree, women formed the real rank and file and often the leadership as well. By the 1830s, such movements had taken the form of organized reform societies. "In no country in the world," Tocqueville had observed, "has the principle of association been more successfully used, or more unsparingly applied to a multitude of different objects, than in America. . . . for there is no end which the human will, seconded by the collective exertions of individuals, despairs of attaining."

The new organizations did indeed work on behalf of a wide range of goals: temperance; education; peace; the care of the poor, the handicapped, and the mentally ill; the treatment of criminals; the rights of women; and many more. Few eras in American history have witnessed as wide a range of reform efforts. And few eras have exposed more clearly the simultaneous attraction of Americans to the ideas of personal liberty and social order.

Revivalism, Morality, and Order

The philosophy of reform arose from two distinct sources. One was the optimistic vision of those who, like the transcendentalists, rejected Calvinist doctrines and preached the divinity of the individual. These included not only Emerson, Thoreau, and their followers, but a much larger group of Americans who embraced the doctrines of Unitarianism and Universalism and absorbed European romanticism.

The second, and in many respects more important, source was Protestant revivalism—the movement that had begun with the Second Great Awakening early in the century and had, by the 1820s, evolved into a powerful force for social reform. Although the New Light revivalists were theologically far removed from the transcendentalists and Unitarians, they had come to share the optimistic belief that every individual was capable of salvation. According to Charles Grandison Finney, a Presbyterian minister who became the most influential revival evangelist of the 1820s and 1830s, traditional Calvinist doctrines of predestination and individual human helplessness were both obsolete and destructive. Each person, he preached, contained within himself or herself the capacity to experience spiritual rebirth and achieve salvation. A revival need not depend on a miracle from God; it could be created by individual effort.

Finney enjoyed particular success in upstate New York, where he helped launch a series of passionate revivals in towns along the Erie Canal—a region so prone to religious awakenings that it was known as the "burned-over district." It was no coincidence that the new revivalism should prove so powerful there, for this region of New York was experiencing—largely as a result of the construction of the canal—a major economic transformation. And with that transformation had come changes in the social fabric so profound that many men and women felt baffled and disoriented. (It was in roughly this same area of New York that Joseph Smith first organized the Mormon church.)

Finney's doctrine of personal regeneration appealed strongly to those who felt threatened by change. In Rochester, New York, the site of his greatest success, he staged a series of emotionally wrenching religious meetings that aroused a large segment of the community. He had particular success in mobilizing women, on whom he tended to concentrate his efforts—both because women found the liberating message of revivalism particularly appealing and because, Finney discovered, they provided him with access to their male relatives. Gradually, he developed a large following among the relatively prosperous citizens of the region, who were enjoying the economic benefits of the new commercial growth but who were also uneasy about some of the social changes accompanying it (among them the introduction into their community of a new, undisciplined pool of transient laborers). For them, revivalism became not only a means of personal salvation but a mandate for the reform (and control) of the larger society. Finney's revivalism became a call for a crusade against personal immorality. "The church," he maintained, "must take right ground on the subject of Temperance, the Moral Reform, and all the subjects of practical morality which come up for decision from time to time."

The Temperance Crusade *against drinking*

Evangelical Protestantism added major strength to one of the most influential reform movements of the era: the crusade against drunkenness. No social vice, argued some reformers (including, for example, many of Finney's converts in cities such as Rochester), was more responsible for crime, disorder, and poverty than the excessive use of alcohol. Women, who were particularly active in the temperance movement, claimed that alcoholism placed a special burden on them: men spent money on alcohol that their families needed for basic necessities; and drunken husbands often abused their wives and children.

In fact, alcoholism was an even more serious problem in antebellum America than it has been in the twentieth century. The supply of alcohol was growing rapidly, particularly in the West; farmers there grew more grain than they could sell in the still-limited markets in this pre-railroad era, so they distilled much of it into whiskey. But in the East, too, commercial distilleries and private stills were widespread. The appetite for alcohol was growing as well: in isolated western settlements, where drinking provided a social pastime in towns and helped ease the loneliness and

THE DRUNKARD'S PROGRESS

This 1846 lithograph by Nathaniel Currier shows what temperance advocates argued was the inevitable consequence of alcohol consumption. Beginning with an apparently innocent "glass with a friend," the young man rises step by step to the summit of drunken revelry, then declines to desperation and suicide while his abandoned wife and child grieve. *(Library of Congress)*

isolation on farms; in pubs and saloons in eastern cities, where drinking was the principal leisure activity for many workers. The average male in the 1830s drank nearly three times as much alcohol as the average person does today. And as that figure suggests, many people drank habitually and excessively, with bitter consequences for themselves and others. Among the many supporters of the temperance movement were people who saw it as a way to overcome their own problems with alcoholism.

Although advocates of temperance had been active since the late eighteenth century, the new reformers gave the movement an energy and influence it had never previously known. In 1826, the American Society for the Promotion of Temperance emerged as a co-ordinating agency among various groups; it attempted to use many of the techniques of revivalism in preaching abstinence. Then, in 1840, six reformed alcoholics in Baltimore organized the Washington Temperance Society and began to draw large crowds to hear their

impassioned and intriguing confessions of past sins. By then, temperance advocates had grown dramatically in numbers; more than a million people had signed a formal pledge to forgo hard liquor.

As the movement gained in strength, it also became divided in purpose. Some temperance advocates now urged that abstinence include not only liquor but beer and wine; not everyone agreed. Some began to demand state legislation to restrict the sale and consumption of alcohol (Maine passed such a law in 1851); others insisted that temperance must rely on the conscience of the individual. Whatever their disagreements, however, most temperance advocates shared similar motives. By promoting abstinence, reformers were attempting to promote the moral self-improvement of individuals. They were also trying to impose discipline on society.

The latter impulse was particularly clear in the battle over prohibition laws, which pitted established Protestants against new Catholic immigrants, to many of whom drinking was an important social ritual and an integral part of the life of their community. The arrival of the immigrants was profoundly disturbing to established residents of many communities, and the restriction of alcohol seemed to them a way to curb the disorder they believed the new population was creating.

Trends in Health and Science

For some Americans, the search for individual and social perfection led to an interest in new theories of health and knowledge. Threats to public health were critical to the sense of insecurity that underlay many reform movements, especially after the terrible cholera epidemics of the 1830s and 1840s. Cholera is a severe bacterial infection of the intestines, usually a result of consuming contaminated food or water. In the nineteenth century, long before the discovery of antibiotics, fewer than half of those who contracted the disease normally survived. Thousands of people died of the disease during its occasional outbreaks, and in certain cities—New Orleans in 1833 and St. Louis in 1849—the effects were truly catastrophic. Nearly a quarter of the population of New Orleans died in the 1833 epidemic. Many municipalities, pressured by reformers, established city health boards to try to find solutions to the problems of epidemics. But the medical profession of the time, unaware of the nature of bacterial infections, had no answers; and the boards therefore found little to do.

Instead, many Americans turned to nonscientific theories for improving health. Affluent men and, especially, women flocked to health spas for the celebrated "water cure" (known to scientists as hydrotherapy), which purported to improve health through immersing people in hot or cold baths or wrapping them in wet sheets. Although the water cure in fact delivered few of the benefits its promoters promised, it did have some therapeutic value; some forms of hydrotherapy are still in use today. Other people adopted new dietary theories. Sylvester Graham, a Connecticut-born Presbyterian minister and committed reformer, won many followers with his prescriptions for eating fruits, vegetables, and bread made from coarsely ground flour—a prescription not unlike some dietary theories today—instead of meat. (The "Graham cracker" is made from a kind of flour named for him.) Graham accompanied his dietary prescriptions with moral warnings about the evils of excess and luxury.

Perhaps strangest of all to modern sensibilities was the widespread belief in the new "science" of phrenology, which appeared first in Germany and became popular in the United States beginning in the 1830s through the efforts of Orson and Lorenzo Fowler, publishers of the *Phrenology Almanac*. Phrenologists argued that the shape of an individual's skull was an important indicator of his or her character and intelligence. They made elaborate measurements of bumps and indentations to calculate the size (and, they claimed, the strength) of different areas of the brain. For a time, phrenology seemed to many Americans an important vehicle for improving society. It provided a way of measuring an individual's fitness for various positions in life and seemed to promise an end to the arbitrary process by which people matched their talents to occupations and responsibilities. The theory is now universally believed to have no scientific value at all.

Education

One of the outstanding reform movements of the mid-nineteenth century was the effort to produce a system of universal public education. As of 1830, no state could yet boast such a system, although some states—such as Massachusetts—had supported a limited version for many years. Now, however, interest in public education grew rapidly. It was a reflection of the new belief in the innate capacity of every person and of society's obligation to tap that capacity; but it was a reflection, too, of the desire to expose students to stable social values as a way to resist instability.

The greatest of the educational reformers was Horace Mann, the first secretary of the Massachusetts Board of Education, which was established in 1837. To Mann and his followers, education was the only way to "counterwork this tendency to the domination of capital and the servility of labor." It was also the only way to protect democracy, for an educated electorate was essential to the workings of a free political system. Mann reorganized the Massachusetts school system, lengthened the academic year (to six months), doubled teachers' salaries (although he did nothing to eliminate the large disparities between the salaries of male and female teachers), enriched the curriculum, and introduced new methods of professional training for teachers.

Other states experienced similar expansion and development. They built new schools, created teachers' colleges, and offered vast new groups of children access to education. Henry Barnard helped produce a new educational system in Connecticut and Rhode Island. Pennsylvania passed a law in 1835 appropriating state funds for the support of universal education. Governor William Seward of New York extended public support of schools throughout the state in the early 1840s. By the 1850s, the principle of tax-supported el-

GIRLS' EVENING SCHOOL (C. 1840), ANONYMOUS
Schooling for women, which expanded significantly in the
mid-nineteenth century, included training in domestic arts
(as indicated by the sewing table at right), as well as in
reading, writing, and other basic skills. *(Museum of Fine
Arts, Boston)*

ementary schools had been accepted in all the states;
and all, despite continuing opposition from certain
groups, were making at least a start toward putting
the principle into practice.

Yet the quality of the new education continued to
vary widely. In some places—Massachusetts, for example, where Mann established the first American
state-supported teachers' college in 1839 and where the
first professional association of teachers was created in
1845—educators were usually capable men and
women, often highly trained, and with an emerging
sense of themselves as career professionals. In other
areas, however, teachers were often barely literate, and
funding for education was so limited as to restrict opportunities severely. In the newly settled regions of the
West, where the white population was highly dispersed, many children had no access to schools at all.
In the South, the entire black population had no access
to education (although approximately 10 percent of the

slaves managed to achieve literacy anyway), and only
about a third of all white children of school age actually enrolled in schools in 1860. In the North the percentage was 72 percent, but even there, many students
attended classes only briefly and casually.

The interest in education (and, implicitly, in the unleashing of individual talents that could result from it)
was visible too in the growing movement to educate
American Indians in the antebellum period. Some reformers held racist assumptions about the unre-
deemability of nonwhite peoples; but even many who
accepted that idea about African Americans continued
to believe that Indians could be "civilized" if only they
could be taught the ways of the white world. Efforts
by missionaries and others to educate Indians and encourage them to assimilate were particularly prominent in such areas of the Far West as Oregon, where
substantial numbers of whites were beginning to settle in the 1840s but where conflicts with the natives
had not yet become acute. Nevertheless, the great majority of Native Americans remained outside the reach
of educational reform, either by choice or by circumstance or both.

Despite limitations and inequities, the achievements of the school reformers were impressive by any
standard. By the beginning of the Civil War, the United
States had one of the highest literacy rates of any nation of the world: 94 percent of the population of the
North and 83 percent of the white population of the
South (58 percent of the total population).

The conflicting impulses that underlay the movement for school reform were visible in some of the different educational institutions that emerged. In New
England, for example, the transcendentalist Bronson
Alcott established an experimental school in Concord
that reflected his strong belief in the importance of
complete self-realization. He urged children to learn
from their own inner wisdom, not from the imposition
of values by the larger society. Children were to teach
themselves, rather than rely on teachers.

A similar emphasis on the potential of the individual sparked the creation of new institutions to help the
handicapped, institutions that formed part of a great
network of charitable activities known as the Benevolent Empire. Among them was the Perkins School for
the Blind in Boston, the first such school in America.
Nothing better exemplified the romantic impulse of
the era than the belief of those who founded Perkins
that even society's supposedly least-favored members—the blind and otherwise handicapped—could be
helped to discover inner strength and wisdom. One
teacher at the school expressed such attitudes when he
described to the visiting English writer Charles Dick-

ens the case of a blind, deaf, and speechless young woman who had been taught to communicate with the world. Although the "darkness and the silence of the tomb were around her," the teacher explained, "the immortal spirit which had been implanted within her could not die, nor be maimed nor mutilated." Gradually, she had learned to deal with the world around her, even to sew and knit, and most importantly, to speak through sign language. No longer was she a "dog or parrot." She was "an immortal spirit, eagerly seizing upon a new link of union with other spirits!"

More typical of educational reform, however, were efforts to use schools to impose a set of social values on children—the values that reformers believed were appropriate for their new, industrializing society. These values included thrift, order, discipline, punctuality, and respect for authority. Horace Mann, for example, spoke frequently of the role of public schools in extending democracy and expanding individual opportunity. But he spoke, too, of their role in creating social order. "The unrestrained passions of men are not only homicidal, but suicidal," he said in words that directly contradicted the emphasis of Alcott and other transcendentalists on instinct and emotion. "Train up a child in the way he should go, and when he is old he will not depart from it."

Rehabilitation

Similar impulses helped create another powerful movement of reform: the creation of "asylums," as they were now called for the first time, for criminals and for the mentally ill. On the one hand, in advocating prison and hospital reform, Americans were reacting against one of society's most glaring ills. Criminals of all kinds, debtors unable to pay their debts, the mentally ill, even senile paupers—all were crowded together indiscriminately into prisons and jails, which in some cases were literally holes; one jail in Connecticut was an abandoned mine shaft. Beginning in the 1820s, numerous states replaced these antiquated facilities with new "penitentiaries" and mental institutions designed to provide a proper environment for inmates. New York built the first penitentiary at Auburn in 1821. In Massachusetts, the reformer Dorothea Dix began a national movement for new methods of treating the mentally ill. Imprisonment of debtors and paupers gradually disappeared, as did such traditional practices as public hangings.

But the creation of "asylums" for social deviants was not simply an effort to curb the abuses of the old system. It was also an attempt to reform and rehabilitate the inmates. New forms of rigid prison discipline were designed to rid criminals of the "laxness" that had presumably led them astray. Solitary confinement and the imposition of silence on work crews (both adopted in Pennsylvania and New York in the 1820s) were meant to give prisoners opportunities to meditate on their wrongdoings. (Hence the term "penitentiary": a place for individuals to cultivate penitence.) Some reformers argued that the discipline of the asylum could serve as a model for other potentially disordered environments—for example, factories and schools. But penitentiaries and many mental hospitals soon fell victim to overcrowding, and the original reform ideal gradually faded. Most prisons ultimately degenerated into little more than warehouses for criminals, with scant emphasis on rehabilitation. The idea, in its early stages, had envisioned far more.

The "asylum" movement was not, however, restricted only to criminals and people otherwise considered "unfit." The idea that a properly structured institution could prevent moral failure or rescue individuals from failure and despair helped spawn the creation of new orphanages designed as educational institutions. Such institutions, reformers believed, would provide an environment in which children who might otherwise be drawn into criminality could be trained to become useful citizens. Similar institutions emerged to provide homes for "friendless" women—women without families or homes, but otherwise respectable, for whom the institutions might provide an opportunity to build a new life. (Such homes were in part an effort to prevent such women from turning to prostitution.)

Some of these same impulses underlay the emergence in the 1840s and 1850s of a new "reform" approach to the problems of Native Americans: the idea of the reservation. For several decades, the dominant thrust of U.S. policy toward the Indians in areas of white settlement had been relocation. The principal motive behind relocation had always been a simple one: getting the tribes out of the way of white civilization. But among some whites there had also been another, if secondary, intent: to move the Indians to a place where they would be protected from whites and allowed to develop to a point where assimilation might be possible. Even Andrew Jackson, whose animus toward Indians was legendary, once described the removals as part of the nation's "moral duty . . . to protect and if possible to preserve and perpetuate the scattered remnants of the Indian race." It was a small step from the idea of relocation to the idea of the reservation: the idea of creating an enclosed region in which Indians would live in isolation from white society. Again, the reservations served white economic pur-

A Pennsylvania Asylum
In 1843 the United States had only thirteen mental hospitals. Most communities locked the mentally ill in jails with common criminals and often confined them to the worst quarters. By the 1880s, largely as a result of the work of the Massachusetts reformer Dorothea Dix, who worked tirelessly prodding states to build new facilities, there were more than 120 asylums for the insane—including this one in Berks County, Pennsylvania, which also served as an almshouse for the poor. *(Historical Society of Berks County, Reading, Pennsylvania)*

poses above all—moving Native Americans out of good lands that white settlers wanted. But they were also supposed to serve a reform purpose. Just as prisons, asylums, and orphanages would provide society with an opportunity to train and uplift misfits and unfortunates within white society, so the reservations might provide a way to undertake what one official called "the great work of regenerating the Indian race." Indians on reservations, reformers argued, would learn the ways of civilization in a protected setting and would progress toward (in the words of an Indian commissioner of the time) "a point at which they will be able to compete with a white population, and to sustain themselves under any probable circumstances of contact or connexion with it."

The Rise of Feminism

The reform ferment of the antebellum period had a particular meaning for American women. They played central roles in a wide range of reform movements and a particularly important role in the movement on behalf of the abolition of slavery. In the process, they expressed their awareness of the problems that women themselves faced in a male-dominated society. The result was the creation of the first important American feminist movement, one that laid the groundwork for more than a century of agitation for women's rights.

Women in the 1830s and 1840s suffered not only all the traditional restrictions imposed on members of their sex by society, but a new set of barriers that had emerged from the transformation of the family. Many women who began to involve themselves in reform movements in the 1820s and 1830s came to look on such restrictions with rising resentment. Some began to defy them. Sarah and Angelina Grimké, sisters born in South Carolina who had become active and outspoken abolitionists, ignored attacks by men who claimed that their activities were inappropriate for their sex. "Men and women were CREATED EQUAL," they argued. "They are both moral and accountable beings, and whatever is right for man to do, is right for women to do." Other reformers—Catharine Beecher, Harriet Beecher Stowe (her sister), Lucretia Mott, Elizabeth Cady Stanton, and Dorothea Dix—also chafing at the restrictions placed on them by men, similarly pressed at the boundaries of "acceptable" female behavior.

Finally, in 1840, the patience of several women snapped. A group of American female delegates arrived at a world antislavery convention in London, only to be turned away by the men who controlled the proceedings. Angered at the rejection, several of the delegates—notably Lucretia Mott and Elizabeth Cady Stanton—became convinced that their first duty as reformers should now be to elevate the status of women. Over the next several years, Mott, Stanton, and others began drawing pointed parallels between the plight of women and the plight of slaves; and in 1848, they organized a convention in Seneca Falls, New York, to discuss the question of women's rights. Out of the meeting emerged a "Declaration of Sentiments and Resolutions" (patterned on the Declaration of Independence), which stated that "all men and women are created equal," that women no less than men have certain inalienable rights. Their most prominent demand was for the right to vote, thus launching a movement for woman suffrage that would continue until 1920. But the document was in many ways more important for its rejection of the whole notion that men and women should be assigned separate "spheres" in society.

It should not be surprising, perhaps, that many of the women involved in these feminist efforts were Quakers. Quakerism had long embraced the ideal of sexual equality and had tolerated, indeed encouraged, the emergence of women as preachers and community leaders. Women taught to expect the absence of gender-based restrictions in their own communities naturally resented the restrictions they encountered when they moved outside them. Quakers had also been among the leaders of the antislavery movement, and Quaker women had played a leading role within those efforts.

Not all Quakers went so far as to advocate full sexual equality in American society; but enough Quaker women coalesced around such demands to cause a schism in the yearly meeting of Friends in Genesee, New York, in 1848. That dissident faction formed the core of the group that organized the Seneca Falls convention. Of the women who drafted the Declaration of Sentiments there, all but Elizabeth Cady Stanton were Quakers.

Progress toward feminist goals was limited in the antebellum years, but certain individual women did manage to break the social barriers to advancement. Elizabeth Blackwell, born in England, gained acceptance and fame as a physician. Her sister-in-law Antoinette Brown Blackwell became the first ordained woman minister in the United States; and another sister-in-law, Lucy Stone, took the revolutionary step of retaining her maiden name after marriage (as did the abolitionist Angelina Grimké). Stone became a successful and influential lecturer on women's rights. Emma Willard, founder of the Troy Female Seminary in 1821, and Catharine Beecher, who founded the Hartford Female Seminary in 1823, worked on behalf of women's education. Some women expressed their feminist sentiments even in their choice of costume—by wearing a distinctive style of dress (introduced in the 1850s) that combined a short skirt with full length pantalettes—an outfit that allowed freedom of movement without loss of modesty. Introduced by the famous actress Fanny Kemble, it came to be called the "bloomer" costume, after one of its advocates, Amelia Bloomer. (It provoked so much controversy that feminists finally abandoned it, convinced that the furor was drawing attention away from their more important demands.)

Yet there was an irony in this rise of interest in the rights of women. Feminists benefited greatly from their association with other reform movements, most notably abolitionism; but they also suffered from them. For the demands of women were usually assigned—even by some women themselves—a secondary position to what many considered the far greater issue of the rights of slaves.

THE CRUSADE AGAINST SLAVERY

The antislavery movement was not new to the mid-nineteenth century. There had been efforts even before the Revolution to limit, and even eliminate, the institution, efforts that had helped remove slavery from most of the North by the end of the eighteenth century. There were powerful antislavery movements in England and Europe that cried out forcefully against human bondage. But American antislavery sentiment remained relatively muted in the first decades after independence. Not until 1830 did it begin to gather the force that would ultimately enable it to overshadow virtually all other efforts at social reform.

Early Opposition to Slavery

In the early years of the nineteenth century, those who opposed slavery were, for the most part, a calm and genteel lot, expressing moral disapproval but engaging in few overt activities. To the extent that there was an organized antislavery movement, it centered on the concept of colonization—the effort to encourage the resettlement of American blacks in Africa or the Caribbean. In 1817, a group of prominent white Virginians organized the American Colonization Society (ACS), which worked carefully to challenge slavery without challenging property rights or southern sensibilities. The ACS proposed a gradual manumission (or freeing) of slaves, with masters receiving compensation through funds raised by private charity or appropriated by state legislatures. The Society would then transport liberated blacks out of the country and help them to establish a new society of their own elsewhere.

The ACS was not without impact. It received some funding from private donors, some from Congress, some from the legislatures of Virginia and Maryland. And it arranged the shipment of several groups of blacks out of the country, some of them to the west

coast of Africa where in 1830 they established the nation of Liberia (which became an independent black republic in 1846—its capital, Monrovia, named for the American president who had presided over the initial settlement).

But the ACS was in the end a negligible force. Neither private nor public funding was nearly enough to carry out the vast projects its supporters envisioned. In the space of a decade, they managed to "colonize" fewer slaves than were born in the United States in a month. Nothing, in fact, would have been enough; there were far too many blacks in America in the nineteenth century to be transported to Africa by any conceivable program. And in any case, the ACS met resistance from African Americans themselves, many of whom were now three or more generations removed from Africa and had no wish to move to a land of which they knew almost nothing. (The Massachusetts free black Paul Cuffe had met similar resistance from members of his race in the early 1800s when he proposed a colonization scheme of his own.)

By 1830, in other words, the early antislavery movement was rapidly losing strength. Colonization was proving not to be a viable method of attacking the institution, particularly since the cotton boom in the Deep South was increasing the commitment of planters to their "peculiar" labor system. Those opposed to slavery had reached what appeared to be a dead end.

Garrison and Abolitionism

It was at this crucial juncture, with the antislavery movement seemingly on the verge of collapse, that a new figure emerged to transform it into a dramatically different phenomenon. He was William Lloyd Garrison. Born in Massachusetts in 1805, Garrison was an assistant in the 1820s to the New Jersey Quaker Benjamin Lundy, who published the leading antislavery newspaper of the time—the *Genius of Universal Emancipation*—in Baltimore. Garrison shared Lundy's abhorrence of slavery, but he soon grew impatient with his employer's moderate tone and mild proposals for reform. In 1831, therefore, he returned to Boston to found his own weekly newspaper, the *Liberator*.

Garrison's philosophy was so simple as to be genuinely revolutionary. Opponents of slavery, he said, should view the institution from the point of view of the black man, not the white slaveowner. They should not, as earlier reformers had done, talk about the evil influence of slavery on white society; they should talk about the damage the system did to blacks. And they should, therefore, reject "gradualism" and demand the immediate, unconditional, universal abolition of slav-

WILLIAM LLOYD GARRISON
Garrison was the first member of the antislavery movement to call publicly for "immediate and complete emancipation" of blacks. That was in 1831, and for the next three decades he remained a stern and uncompromising enemy of slavery. After the Civil War, however, Garrison displayed little interest in the plight of the blacks he had tried to emancipate. In the last years before his death in 1879, he worked on behalf of woman suffrage, Indian rights, and the prohibition of alcohol. *(Wichita State University Library, Wichita, Kansas)*

ery. Garrison spoke with particular scorn about the advocates of colonization. They were not emancipationists, he argued; on the contrary, their real aim was to strengthen slavery by ridding the country of those blacks who were already free. The true aim of foes of slavery, he insisted, must be to extend to blacks all the rights of American citizenship. As startling as the drastic nature of his proposals was the relentless, uncompromising tone with which he promoted them. "I am aware," he wrote in the very first issue of the *Liberator*, "that many object to the severity of my language; but is there not cause for severity? I will be as harsh as truth, and as uncompromising as justice. . . . I am in earnest—I will not equivocate—I will not excuse—I will not retreat a single inch—AND I WILL BE HEARD."

Garrison soon attracted a large group of followers throughout the North, enough to enable him to found the New England Antislavery Society in 1832 and a year later, after a convention in Philadelphia, the American Antislavery Society. Membership in the new organizations mushroomed. By 1835, there were more than 400 chapters of the societies; by 1838, there were 1,350, with more than 250,000 members. Antislavery sentiment was developing a strength and assertiveness greater than at any point in the nation's history.

This success was in part a result of the similarity between abolitionism and other reform movements of the era. Like reformers committed to other causes, abolitionists were calling for an unleashing of the individual human spirit, the elimination of artificial social barriers to fulfillment. Who, after all, was more in need of assistance in realizing individual potential than enslaved men and women? Theodore Dwight Weld, a prominent New England abolitionist (and husband of Angelina Grimké), expressed this belief in an 1833 letter to Garrison. Slavery was a sin, Weld wrote, because "no condition of birth, no shade of color, no mere misfortune of circumstances can annul the birthright charter, which God has bequeathed to every being upon whom he has stamped his own image, by making him a free moral agent."

Black Abolitionists

Abolitionism had a particular appeal to the free blacks of the North, who in 1850 numbered about 250,000, mostly concentrated in cities. They lived in conditions of poverty and oppression often worse than those of their slave counterparts in the South. An English traveler who had visited both sections of the country wrote in 1854 that he was "utterly at a loss to imagine the source of that prejudice which subsists against [the black man] in the Northern states, a prejudice unknown in the South, where the relations between the Africans and the European [white American] are so much more intimate." This confirmed an earlier observation by Tocqueville that "the prejudice which repels the Negroes seems to increase in proportion as they are emancipated." Northern blacks were often victimized by mob violence; they had virtually no access to education; they could vote in only a few states; and they were barred from all but the most menial of occupations. Most worked either as domestic servants or as sailors in the American merchant marine, and their wages were such that they lived, for the most part, in squalor. Some were kidnapped by whites and forced back into slavery.

For all their problems, however, northern blacks were aware of, and fiercely proud of, their freedom. And they remained acutely sensitive to the plight of those members of their race who remained in bondage, aware that their own position in society would remain precarious as long as slavery existed. Many in the 1830s came to support Garrison. But there were also important black leaders who expressed the aspirations of their race. One of the most militant was David Walker, a free black from Boston, who in 1829 published a harsh pamphlet: *Walker's Appeal . . . to the Colored Citizens.* In it he declared: "America is more our country than it is the whites'—we have enriched it with our blood and tears." He warned: "The whites want slaves, and want us for their slaves, but some of them will curse the day they ever saw us." Slaves should, he declared, cut their masters' throats, should "kill, or be killed!"

Most black critics of slavery, however, were less violent in their rhetoric. The greatest of them all—one of the most electrifying orators of his time, black or white—was Frederick Douglass. Born a slave in Maryland, Douglass escaped to Massachusetts in 1838, became an outspoken leader of antislavery sentiment, and spent two years lecturing in England, where members of that country's vigorous antislavery movement lionized him. On his return to the United States in 1847, Douglass purchased his freedom from his Maryland owner and founded an antislavery newspaper, the *North Star,* in Rochester, New York. He achieved wide renown as well for his autobiography, *Narrative of the Life of Frederick Douglass* (1845), in which he presented a damning picture of slavery. Douglass demanded for African Americans not only freedom but full social and economic equality. Black abolitionists had been active for years; they had held their first national convention in 1830. But with Douglass's leadership, they became a more influential force; and they began, too, to forge alliances with white antislavery leaders such as Garrison.

Anti-Abolitionism

The rise of abolitionism was a powerful force, but it provoked a powerful opposition as well. Almost all white southerners, of course, looked on the movement with fear and contempt. But so too did many northern whites. Indeed, even in the North, abolitionists were never more than a small, dissenting minority.

To its critics, the abolitionist crusade was a dangerous and frightening threat to the existing social system. Some whites (including many substantial businessmen) warned that it would produce a destructive war between the sections. Others feared that it might lead to a great influx of free blacks into the North. The strident, outspoken movement seemed to many northern whites a sign of the disorienting social changes their society was experiencing, yet another threat to stability and order.

The result was an escalating wave of violence directed against abolitionists in the 1830s. When Prudence Crandall attempted to admit several African-American girls to her private school in Connecticut, local citizens had her arrested, threw filth into her well, and forced her to close down the school. A mob in Philadelphia attacked the abolitionist headquarters, the "Temple of Liberty," in 1834, burned it to the ground, and began a bloody race riot. Another mob seized Garrison on the streets of Boston in 1835 and threatened to hang him. Authorities saved him from death only by locking him in jail. Elijah Lovejoy, the editor of an abolitionist newspaper in Alton, Illinois, was a repeated victim of mob violence. Three times angry whites invaded his offices and smashed his presses. Three times Lovejoy installed new machines and began publishing again. When a mob attacked his office a fourth time, late in 1837, he tried to defend his press. The attackers set fire to the building and, as Lovejoy fled, shot and killed him.

That so many men and women continued to embrace abolitionism in the face of such vicious opposition from within their own communities suggests much about the nature of the movement. Abolitionists were not people who made their political commitments lightly or casually. They were strong-willed, passionate crusaders, displaying enormous courage and moral strength, and displaying too at times a level of fervency that many of their contemporaries (and some later historians) found disturbing. Abolitionists were widely denounced, even by some who shared their aversion to slavery, as wild-eyed fanatics bent on social revolution. The anti-abolitionist mobs, in other words, were only the most violent expression of a sentiment that many other white Americans shared.

Abolitionism Divided

By the mid-1830s, the abolitionist crusade had become impossible to ignore. It had also begun to experience serious internal strains and divisions. One reason was the violence of the anti-abolitionists, which persuaded some members of the movement that a more moderate approach was necessary. Another reason was the growing radicalism of William Lloyd Garrison, who shocked even many of his own allies (including Frederick Douglass) by attacking not only slavery but the

FREDERICK DOUGLASS

Frederick Douglass, an escaped slave and active abolitionist, was one of the great orators of his age, widely admired among antislavery groups in the United States and Great Britain. So central did he become in the imagination of antislavery men and women that he inspired tributes such as this "Fugitive's Song," published in Boston in 1845. *(Bettmann)*

government itself. The Constitution, he said, was "a covenant with death and an agreement with hell." The nation's churches, he claimed, were bulwarks of slavery. In 1840, finally, Garrison precipitated a formal division within the American Antislavery Society by insisting that women, who had always been central to the organization's work, be permitted to participate in the movement on terms of full equality. He continued after 1840 to arouse controversy with new and even more radical stands: an extreme pacifism that rejected

even defensive wars; opposition to all forms of coercion—not just slavery but prisons and asylums; and finally, in 1843, a call for northern disunion from the South. The nation could, he suggested, purge itself of the sin of slavery by expelling the slave states from the Union.

From 1840 on, therefore, abolitionism moved in many channels and spoke with many different voices. The Garrisonians remained influential, with their uncompromising moral stance. Others operated in

SIGNIFICANT EVENTS

1817 American Colonization Society founded

1821 New York constructs first penitentiary

1823 Catharine Beecher founds Hartford Female Seminary

1825 Robert Owen founds New Harmony community in Indiana

1826 James Fenimore Cooper publishes *The Last of the Mohicans*

American Society for the Promotion of Temperance founded

1829 David Walker published *Appeal . . . to the Colored Citizens*

1830 Joseph Smith publishes the Book of Mormon

American Colonization Society helps create Liberia for emigrating American slaves

1831 William Lloyd Garrison begins publishing *The Liberator*

1833 American Antislavery Society founded

1834 Anti-abolitionist mob burns abolitionist headquarters in Philadelphia

1837 Horace Mann becomes first secretary of Massachusetts Board of Education

Elijah Lovejoy killed by anti-abolitionist mob in Illinois

1840 Garrison demands admission of women into American Antislavery Society, precipitating schism

Liberty Party formed

1841 Brook Farm founded in Roxbury, Massachusetts

1842 Supreme Court, in *Prigg* v. *Pennsylvania*, rules states do not have to enforce return of fugitive slaves

1843 Amana Community founded

1844 Joseph Smith killed

1845 Frederick Douglass publishes autobiography

Edgar Allan Poe publishes "The Raven"

First professional teachers' association formed in Massachusetts

1847 Brook Farm dissolved

Mormons found Salt Lake City

1848 Women's rights convention held at Seneca Falls, New York

Oneida Community founded in New York

Debate over women's rights causes schism in Society of Friends (Quakers)

1850 Nathaniel Hawthorne publishes *The Scarlet Letter*

1851 Herman Melville publishes *Moby Dick*

1852 Harriet Beecher Stowe publishes *Uncle Tom's Cabin*

1854 Henry David Thoreau publishes *Walden*

1855 Walt Whitman publishes *Leaves of Grass*

more moderate ways, arguing that abolition could be accomplished only as the result of a long, patient, peaceful struggle—"immediate abolition gradually accomplished," as they called it. At first, such moderates depended on "moral suasion." They would appeal to the conscience of the slaveholders and convince them that their institution was sinful. When that produced no results, they turned to political action, seeking to induce the northern states and the federal government to aid the cause wherever possible. They joined the Garrisonians in helping runaway slaves find refuge in the North or in Canada through the so-called underground railroad (although their efforts were never as highly organized as the term suggests). After the

Supreme Court (in *Prigg* v. *Pennsylvania,* 1842) ruled that states need not aid in enforcing the 1793 law requiring the return of fugitive slaves to their owners, abolitionists secured the passage of "personal liberty laws" in several northern states. These laws forbade state officials to assist in the capture and return of runaways. Above all, the antislavery societies petitioned Congress to abolish slavery in places where the federal government had jurisdiction—in the territories and in the District of Columbia—and to prohibit the interstate slave trade. But political abolitionism had severe limits. Few members of the movement believed that Congress could constitutionally interfere with a "domestic" institution such as slavery within the individual states themselves.

While the abolitionists engaged in pressure politics, they never actually formed a political party with an abolition platform. Antislavery sentiment underlay the formation in 1840 of the Liberty Party, which offered the Kentucky antislavery leader James G. Birney as its presidential candidate. But this party, and its successors, never campaigned for outright abolition (an illustration of the important fact that "antislavery" and "abolitionism" were not always the same thing). They stood instead for "free soil," for keeping slavery out of the territories. Some free-soilers were concerned about the welfare of blacks; others cared nothing about slavery but simply wanted to keep the West a country for whites. Garrison dismissed free-soilism as "whitemanism." But the free-soil position would ultimately do what abolitionism never could accomplish: attract the support of large numbers, even a majority, of the white population of the North. (See pp. 371–372.)

The frustrations of political abolitionism drove some critics of slavery to embrace more drastic measures. A few began to advocate violence; it was a group of prominent abolitionists in New England, for example, who funneled money and arms to John Brown for his bloody uprisings in Kansas and Virginia. (See pp. 371, 376–377.) Others attempted to arouse widespread public anger through propaganda. Abolitionist descriptions of slavery—for example, Theodore Dwight Weld and Angelina Grimké's *American Slavery as It Is: Testimony of a Thousand Witnesses* (1839)—presented what the authors claimed were careful, factual pictures of slavery but what were in fact highly polemical, often wildly distorted images.

The most powerful document of abolitionist propaganda, however, was a work of fiction: Harriet Beecher Stowe's *Uncle Tom's Cabin.* It appeared first, in 1851–1852, as a serial in an antislavery weekly. Then, in 1852, it was published as a book. It rocked the nation. It sold more than 300,000 copies within a year of publication and was later issued again and again to become one of the most remarkable best-sellers in American history. And it succeeded, as a result, in bringing the message of abolitionism to an enormous new audience—not only those who read the book but those who watched dramatizations of its story by countless theater companies throughout the nation. The novel's emotional portrayal of good, kindly blacks victimized by a cruel system; of the loyal, trusting Uncle Tom; of the vicious overseer Simon Legree (described as a New Englander so as to prevent the book from seeming to be an attack on southern whites); of the escape of the beautiful Eliza; of the heart-rending death of Little Eva—all became a part of American popular legend. Reviled throughout the South, Stowe became a hero to many in the North. And in both regions, her novel helped to inflame sectional tensions to a new level of passion. Few books in American history have had so great an impact on the course of public events.

Even divided, therefore, abolitionism remained a powerful influence on the life of the nation. Only a relatively small number of people before the Civil War ever accepted the abolitionist position that slavery must be entirely eliminated in a single stroke. But the crusade that Garrison had launched, and that thousands of committed men and women kept alive for three decades, was a constant, visible reminder of how deeply the institution of slavery was dividing America.

Suggested Readings

Antebellum Literature and Popular Culture. Nina Baym, *Woman's Fiction: A Guide to Novels by and About Women in America, 1820–1870* (1978). Carl Bode, *The American Lyceum: Town Meeting of the Mind* (1968). Van Wyck Brooks, *The Flowering of New England, 1815–1865* (1936). Vincent Buranelli, *Edgar Allan Poe* (1977). Ann Douglas, *The Feminization of American Culture* (1977). David Grimsted, *Melodrama Unveiled: American Theater and Culture, 1800–1850* (1968). Neil Harris, *Humbug: The Art of P. T. Barnum* (1973). Mary Kelley, *The Limits of Sisterhood* (1988). Mary Kupiec Cayton, *Emerson's Emergence: Self and Society in the Transformation of New England, 1800–1845* (1989). David Levin, *History as Romantic Art: Bancroft, Prescott, Motley, and Parkman* (1963). Kenneth S. Lynn, *Mark Twain and Southwestern Humor* (1972). Leo Marx, *The Machine and the Garden* (1964). F. O. Matthiessen, *American Renaissance* (1941). Henry F. May, *The Enlightenment in America* (1976). James Meellow, *Nathaniel Hawthorne in His Time* (1980). Vernon L. Parrington, *The Romantic Revolution in America, 1800–1860* (1927). David Reynolds, *Beneath the American Renaissance: The Subversive Imagination in the Age of Emerson and Melville* (1988). Henry Nash Smith, *Democracy and the Novel: Popular Resistance to Classic American Writers* (1978). Robert C. Toll, *Blacking Up: The Minstrel Show in Nineteenth-Century America* (1974). Larzer Ziff, *Literary Democracy: The Declaration of Cultural Independence in America* (1981).

Social Philosophies and Utopias. Gay Wilson Allen, *Waldo Emerson* (1981). Arthur Bestor, *Backwoods Utopias: The Sectarian and Owenite Phases of Communitarian Socialism in America, 1663–1829* (1950). P. F. Boller, Jr., *American Transcendentalism, 1830–1860: An Intellectual Inquiry* (1974). Priscilla Brewer, *Shaker Communities and Shaker Lives* (1986). Fawn Brodie, *No Man Knows My Name: The Life of Joseph Smith* (1945). Maren L. Carden, *Oneida: Utopian Community to Modern Corporation* (1971). Henry Steele Commager, *Theodore Parker* (1936). Michael Fellman, *The Unbounded Frame: Freedom and Community in Nineteenth-Century America* (1973). Lawrence Foster, *Religion and Sexuality: The Shakers, the Mormons, and the Oneida Community* (1984); *Women, Family, and Utopia: Communal Experiments of the Shakers, the Oneida Community, and the Mormons* (1991). Klaus J. Hansen, *Quest for Empire* (1967). J. F. C. Harrison, *Quest for the New Moral World: Robert Owen and the Owenites in Britain and America* (1969). Carol Kolmerten, *Women in Utopia* (1990). Richard Lebeaux, *Young Man Thoreau* (1977). Perry Miller, *The Transcendentalists* (1950); and *The Life of the Mind in America: From the Revolution to the Civil War* (1966). Raymond Muncy, *Sex and Marriage in Utopian Communities* (1973). Ann Rose, *Transcendentalism as a Social Movement* (1981). Arthur M. Schlesinger, Jr., *Orestes A. Brownson: A Pilgrim's Progress* (1939). Wallace Stegner, *The Gathering of Zion* (1964). R. D. Thomas, *The Man Who Would Be Perfect: John Humphrey Noyes and the Utopian Impulse* (1977).

Antebellum Reforms. C. C. Cole, Jr., *The Social Ideas of the Northern Evangelists, 1826–1860* (1954). Whitney R. Cross, *The Burned-Over District* (1950). James D. Davies, *Phrenology: Fad and Science* (1955). Estelle Freedman, *Their Sister's Keepers: Women's Prison Reform in America, 1830–1930* (1981). Gerald W. Grob, *Mental Institutions in America: Social Policy to 1875* (1973). Charles A. Johnson, *The Frontier Camp Meeting* (1955). Paul Johnson, *A Shopkeeper's Millennium* (1978). W. David Lewis, *From Newgate to Dannemora: The Rise of the Penitentiary* (1965). Robert Mennel, *Thorns and Thistles* (1973). William G. McLoughlin, *Revivals, Awakenings, and Reform* (1978). Stephen L. Nissenbaum, *Sex, Diet, and Debility in Jacksonian America: Sylvester Graham and Health Reform* (1980). W. J. Rorabaugh, *The Alcoholic Republic* (1979). Charles Rosenberg, *The Cholera Years: The United States in 1832, 1849, and 1866* (1962). David Rothman, *The Discovery of the Asylum* (1971). Timothy L. Smith, *Revivalism and Social Reform in Mid-Nineteenth Century America* (1957). William W. Sweet, *Revivalism in America* (1949). Alice Felt Tyler, *Freedom's Ferment* (1944). Ian R. Tyrrell, *Sobering Up: From Temperance to Prohibition in Antebellum America, 1800–1860* (1979). Ronald G. Walters, *American Reformers, 1815–1860* (1978).

Education. Carl Bode, *The American Lyceum* (1956). Lawrence A. Cremin, *American Education: The National Experience* (1980). Michael Katz, *The Irony of Early School Reform* (1968). Jonathan Messerli, *Horace Mann* (1972). Paul Monroe, *The Founding of the American Public School System* (1949). Stanley K. Schultz, *The Culture Factory: Boston's Public Schools, 1789–1860* (1973). Robert Trennert, *Alternatives to Extinction: Federal Indian Policy and the Beginning of the Reservation System* (1975).

Feminism. Margaret H. Bacon, *Mothers of Feminism: The Story of Quaker Women in America* (1986). Lois Banner, *Elizabeth Cady Stanton* (1980). Kathleen Barry, *Susan B. Anthony* (1988). Barbara J. Berg, *The Remembered Gate: Origins of American Feminism: The Woman and the City* (1977). Nancy Cott, *The Bonds of Womanhood: "Woman's Sphere" in New England, 1780–1835* (1977). Carl Degler, *At Odds, Women and the Family in America from the Revolution to the Present* (1980). Ellen C. Du Bois, *Feminism and Suffrage: The Emergence of an Independent Woman's Movement in America, 1848–1860* (1978). Barbara Leslie Epstein, *The Politics of Domesticity: Women, Evangelism, and Temperance in Nineteenth-Century America* (1981). Eleanor Flexner, *Century of Struggle*, rev. ed. (1975). Lori D. Ginzberg, *Women and the Work of Benevolence: Morality, Politics, and Class in the Nineteenth-Century United States* (1990). Elisabeth Griffith, *In Her Own Right: The Life of Elizabeth Cady Stanton* (1984). Nancy A. Hewitt, *Women's Activism and Social Change: Rochester, New York, 1822–1872* (1988). William L. O'Neill, *Everyone Was Brave: The Rise and Fall of Feminism in the United States* (1970). Kathryn K. Sklar, *Catharine Beecher: A Study in American Domesticity* (1973).

Antislavery and Abolitionism. Richard H. Abbott, *Cotton and Capital: Boston Businessmen and Antislavery Reform, 1854–1868* (1991). Robert Abzug, *Theodore Dwight Weld* (1980). G. H. Barnes, *The Antislavery Impulse* (1933). Irving Bartlett, *Wendell Phillips* (1962). Arna Bontemps, *Free at Last: The Life* of Frederick Douglass (1971). David Brion Davis, *The Problem of Slavery in the Age of Revolution, 1770–1823* (1975). M. L. Dillon, *The Abolitionists* (1974). Martin Duberman, ed., *The Anti-Slavery Vanguard* (1965). Louis Filler, *The Crusade Against Slavery* (1960). Betty Fladeland, *James Gillespie Birney* (1955). George Frederickson, *The Black Image in the White Mind: The Debate on Afro-American Character and Destiny, 1817–1914* (1971). Lawrence J. Friedman, *Gregarious Saints: Self and Community in American Abolitionism* (1982). Blanche G. Hersh, *Slavery of Sex: Feminist Abolitionists in America* (1978). Nathan Huggins, *Slave and Citizen* (1980). Aileen Kraditor, *Means and Ends in American Abolitionism: Garrison and His Critics on Strategy and Tactics, 1834–1850* (1967). Alan Kraut, ed., *Crusaders and Compromisers* (1983). Gerda Lerner, *The Grimké Sisters of South Carolina: Rebels Against Slavery* (1967). William S. McFeely, *Frederick Douglass* (1991). John McKivigan, *The War Against Proslavery Religion* (1984). William H. Pease and Jane H. Pease, *They Would Be Free* (1974). Lewis Perry, *Radical Abolitionism: Anarchy and the Government of God in Antislavery Thought* (1973). Lewis Perry and Michael Fellman, eds., *Antislavery Reconsidered: New Perspectives on the Abolitionists* (1979). Benjamin Quarles, *Black Abolitionists* (1969). Leonard L. Richards, *"Gentlemen of Property and Standing": Anti-Abolition Mobs in Jacksonian America* (1970). Gerald Sorin, *Abolitionism* (1972). James Brewer Stewart, *Holy Warriors* (1976); *Wendell Phillips* (1987). John L. Thomas, *The Liberator* (1963). Peter F. Walker, *Moral Choices: Memory, Desire, and Imagination in Nineteenth Century Abolition* (1978). Ronald G. Walters, *The Antislavery Appeal: American Abolitionists After 1830* (1976). Bertram Wyatt-Brown, *Lewis Tappan and the Evangelical War Against Slavery* (1969). Jean Fagan Yellin, *The Antislavery Feminists in American Culture* (1989).

"BLEEDING KANSAS"
The battle over the fate of slavery in Kansas was one of the most turbulent events of the 1850s. This 1855 poster invites antislavery forces to a meeting to protest the actions of the "bogus" pro-slavery territorial legislature, which had passed laws that, among other things, made it illegal to speak or write against slavery. "Squatter sovereignty" was another term for "popular sovereignty," the doctrine that gave residents of a prospective state the power to decide the fate of slavery there. *(Bettmann)*

CHAPTER THIRTEEN

THE IMPENDING CRISIS

UNTIL THE 1840s, THE tensions between the North and the South remained relatively contained. Had no new sectional controversies arisen, the United States might have avoided a civil war and the two sections might have resolved their differences peaceably over time. But new controversies did arise, all of them centered on slavery. From the North came the strident and increasingly powerful abolitionist movement, which kept the issue alive in the public mind and increased sectional animosities. From the South came an increasingly belligerent defense of slavery and a rising insistence on its expansion.

But the West brought these differences to a head most forcefully. Ironically, the vigorous nationalism that was in some ways helping to keep the United States together was also producing a desire for territorial expansion that would tear the nation apart. As the nation annexed extensive new lands—Texas, the Southwest territories, California, Oregon country, and others—the question began to arise: What would be the status of slavery in the territories? By the late 1840s, differences over this question had created a dangerous and persistent crisis. And by the end of the 1850s, that crisis had produced such bitterness, such anger, and such despair on both sides that it could no longer be contained.

LOOKING WESTWARD

The United States acquired more than a million square miles of new territory in the 1840s—the greatest wave of expansion since the Louisiana Purchase nearly forty years before. By the end of the decade, the nation possessed all the territory of the present-day United States except Alaska, Hawaii, and a few relatively small areas acquired later through border adjustments. Many factors accounted for this great new wave of expansion, the most important of which were the hopes and ambitions of the many thousands of Americans who moved into or invested in these new territories. Advocates of expansion justified their goals with a carefully articulated set of ideas—an ideology known as "Manifest Destiny," which itself became one of the factors driving white Americans to look to the West.

Manifest Destiny

Manifest Destiny reflected both the burgeoning pride that characterized American nationalism in the midnineteenth century and the idealistic vision of social perfection that fueled so much of the reform energy of the time. It rested on the idea that America was des-

EXPANDING SETTLEMENT, 1810–1850

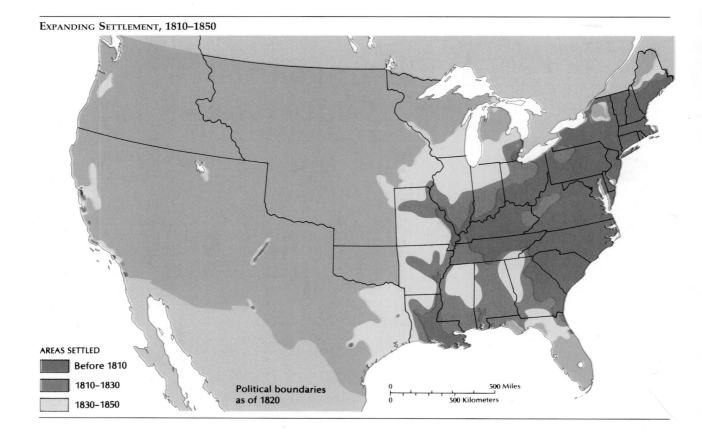

AREAS SETTLED

- Before 1810
- 1810–1830
- 1830–1850

Political boundaries
as of 1820

0   500 Miles
0   500 Kilometers

tined—by God and by history—to expand its boundaries over a vast area, an area that included, but was not necessarily restricted to, the continent of North America. American expansion was not selfish, its advocates insisted; it was an altruistic attempt to extend American liberty to new realms. John L. O'Sullivan, the influential Democratic editor who gave the movement its name, wrote in 1845 that the American claim to new territory

> . . . is by the right of our manifest destiny to overspread and to possess the whole of the continent which Providence has given us for the development of the great experiment of liberty and federative self government entrusted to us. It is a right such as that of the tree to the space of air and earth suitable for the full expansion of its principle and destiny of growth.

By the 1840s, the idea of Manifest Destiny had spread throughout the nation, publicized by the new "penny press" (inexpensive newspapers aimed at a mass audience), and fanned by the rhetoric of nationalist politicians. Advocates of Manifest Destiny disagreed, however, about how far and by what means

the nation should expand. Some had relatively limited territorial goals; others envisioned a vast new "empire of liberty" that would include Canada, Mexico, Caribbean and Pacific islands, and ultimately, a few dreamed, much of the rest of the world. Some believed America should use force to achieve its expansionist goals, others that the nation should expand peacefully or not at all.

Not everyone embraced the idea of Manifest Destiny. Henry Clay and other prominent politicians feared, correctly as it turned out, that territorial expansion would reopen the painful controversy over slavery and threaten the stability of the Union. But their voices were barely audible over the clamor of enthusiasm for expansion in the 1840s, which began with the issues of Texas and Oregon.

Texas

The United States had once claimed Texas—which until the 1830s was part of the Republic of Mexico—as a part of the Louisiana Purchase, but it had renounced

THE LONE STAR FLAG
Almost from the moment Texas won its independence from Mexico in 1836, it sought admission to the United States as a state. Controversies over the status of slavery in the territories prevented its admission until 1845, and so for nine years it was an independent republic. The tattered banner pictured here was one of the republic's original flags. *(Frank Lerner, from Showers-Brown Collection, Star of the Republic Museum)*

the claim in 1819. Twice thereafter the United States had offered to buy Texas, only to meet with indignant Mexican refusals.

But in the early 1820s, the Mexican government launched an ill-advised experiment that would eventually cause it to lose its great northern province: it encouraged American immigration into Texas. The Mexicans hoped to strengthen the economy of the territory and increase their own tax revenues. They also liked the idea of the Americans sitting between Mexican settlement and the large and sometimes militant Indian tribes to the north. They convinced themselves, too, that settlers in Texas would serve as an effective buffer against United States expansion into the region; the Americans, they thought, would soon become loyal to the Mexican government. An 1824 colonization law designed to attract American settlers promised the newcomers cheap land and a four-year exemption from taxes.

Thousands of Americans, attracted by the rich soil in Texas, took advantage of Mexico's welcome. Since much of the available land was suitable for growing cotton, the great majority of the immigrants were southerners, many of whom brought slaves with them. By 1830, there were about 7,000 Americans living in Texas, more than twice the number of Mexicans there.

The Mexican government offered land directly to immigrants, but most of the settlers came to Texas through the efforts of American intermediaries (known to the Mexicans as *empresarios*), who received sizable land grants from Mexico in return for promising to bring settlers into the region. The most successful of these *empresarios* was Stephen F. Austin, a young immigrant from Missouri who had established the first legal American settlement in Texas in 1822. Austin and other intermediaries were effective in recruiting American immigrants to Texas, but they also created centers of power in the region that competed with the Mexican government. In 1826, one *empresario* led a revolt to establish Texas as an independent nation (which he proposed calling Fredonia.) The Mexicans quickly crushed it and, four years later, passed new laws barring any further American immigration into the region. They were too late. Americans kept flowing into the territory, and in 1833 Mexico dropped the futile immigration ban. By 1835 over 30,000 Americans, white and black, had settled in Texas.

Friction between the American settlers and the Mexican government continued to grow. It arose, in part, from the continuing cultural and economic ties of the immigrants to the United States and their desire to create stronger bonds with their former home. It arose, too, from their desire to legalize slavery, which the Mexican government had made illegal in Texas (as it was in Mexico) in 1830. But the Americans were divided over how to address their unhappiness with Mexican rule. Austin and his followers wanted to reach a peaceful settlement that would give Texas more autonomy within the Mexican republic. Others wanted to fight for independence.

In the mid-1830s, instability in Mexico itself drove General Antonio Lopez de Santa Ana to seize power as a dictator and impose a new, more conservative and autocratic regime on the nation and its territories. A new law increased the powers of the national government of Mexico at the expense of the state governments, a measure that Texans from the United States assumed Santa Ana was aiming specifically at them. The Mexicans even imprisoned Stephen Austin in Mexico City for a time, claiming that he was encouraging revolts among his fellow Americans in Texas. Sporadic fighting between Americans and Mexicans in Texas began in 1835 and escalated as the Mexican government sent more troops into the territory. In 1836, the American settlers defiantly proclaimed their independence from Mexico.

Santa Ana led a large army into Texas, where the American settlers were having enormous difficulties organizing an effective defense of their new "nation." Several different factions claimed to be the legitimate government of Texas, and American soldiers could not even agree on who their commanders were. Mexican forces annihilated an American garrison at the Alamo mission in San Antonio after a famous, if futile, defense by a group of Texas "patriots," a group that included, among others, the renowned frontiersman and former Tennessee congressman Davy Crockett. Another garrison at Goliad suffered substantially the same fate when the Mexicans executed most of the force after it had surrendered. By the end of 1836, the rebellion appeared to have collapsed. Americans were fleeing east toward Louisiana to escape Santa Ana's army.

But General Sam Houston managed to keep a small force together. And on April 23, 1836, at the Battle of San Jacinto (near the present-day city of Houston), he defeated the Mexican army and took Santa Ana prisoner. American troops then killed many of the Mexican soldiers in retribution for the executions at Goliad. Santa Ana, under pressure from his captors, signed a treaty giving Texas independence. And while the Mexican government repudiated the treaty, there were no further military efforts to win Texas back.

A number of Mexican residents of Texas (*Tejanos*) had fought with the Americans in the revolution. But soon after Texas won its independence, their positions grew difficult. The Americans did not trust them, feared that they were agents of the Mexican government, and in effect drove many of them out of the new republic. Most of those who stayed had to settle for a politically and economically subordinate status within the fledgling nation.

Above all, American Texans hoped for annexation by the United States. One of the first acts of the new president of Texas, Sam Houston, was to send a delegation to Washington with an offer to join the Union. There were supporters of expansion in the United States who welcomed these overtures; indeed, expansionists in the United States had been supporting and encouraging the revolt against Mexico for years. But there was also opposition. Many American northerners opposed acquiring a large new slave territory, and others opposed increasing the southern votes in Congress and in the electoral college. Unfortunately for the Texans, one of the opponents was President Jackson, who feared annexation might cause a dangerous sectional controversy and even a war with Mexico. He therefore did not support annexation and even delayed recognizing the new republic until 1837. Presidents Martin Van Buren and William Henry Harrison also refrained from pressing the issue during their terms of office.

Spurned by the United States, Texas cast out on its own. Its leaders sought money and support from Europe. Some of them dreamed of creating a vast southwestern nation, stretching to the Pacific, that would rival the United States—a dream that appealed to European nations eager to counter the growing power of America. England and France quickly recognized and concluded trade treaties with Texas. In response, President Tyler persuaded Texas to apply for statehood again in 1844. But when Secretary of State Calhoun presented an annexation treaty to Congress as if its only purpose were to extend slavery, northern senators rebelled and defeated it. Rejection of the treaty only spurred advocates of Manifest Destiny to greater efforts toward their goal. The Texas question quickly became the central issue in the election of 1844.

Oregon

Control of what was known as Oregon country, in the Pacific Northwest, was another major political issue in the 1840s. Its half-million square miles included the present states of Oregon, Washington, and Idaho, parts of Montana and Wyoming, and half of British Columbia. Both Britain and the United States claimed sovereignty in the region—the British on the basis of explorations in the 1790s by George Vancouver, a naval officer; the Americans on the basis of simultaneous claims by Robert Gray, a fur trader. Unable to resolve their conflicting claims diplomatically, they agreed in an 1818 treaty to allow citizens of each country equal access to the territory. This arrangement, known as "joint occupation," continued for twenty years.

In fact, by the time of the treaty neither Britain nor the United States had established much of a presence in Oregon country. White settlement in the region consisted largely of American and Canadian fur traders; and the most significant white settlements were the fur trading post established by John Jacob Astor's com-

joint occupation

WESTERN TRAILS TO 1860

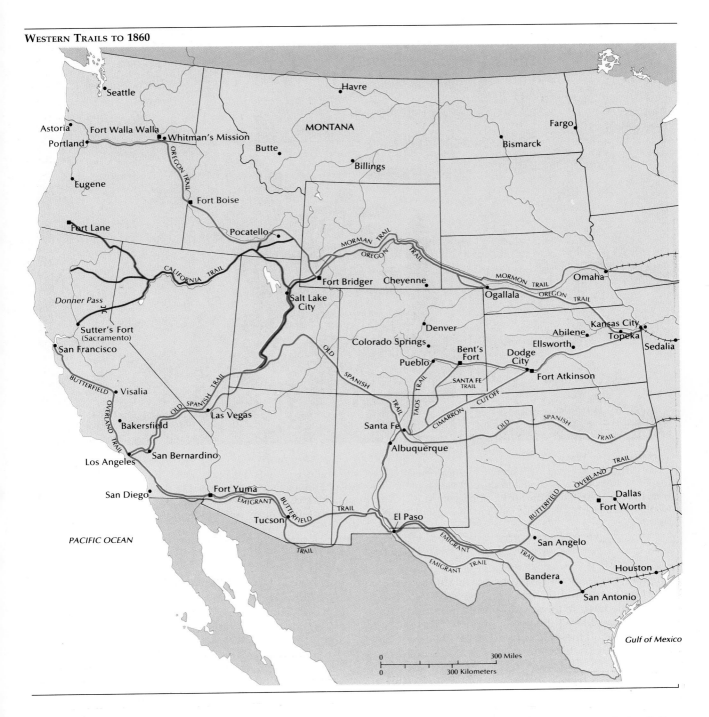

pany at Astoria and other posts built by the British Hudson Bay Company north of the Columbia River— where residents combined fur trading with farming and recruited Indian labor to compensate for their small numbers.

But American interest in Oregon grew substantially in the 1820s and 1830s. Missionaries considered the territory an attractive target for evangelical efforts, especially after the strange appearance of four Nez Percé and Flathead Indians in St. Louis in 1831. White Amer-

Promoting the West
Cyrus McCormick was one of many American businessmen with an interest in the peopling of the American West. The reaper he invented was crucial to the cultivation of the new agricultural regions, and the rapid settlement of those regions was, in turn, essential to the health of his company. In this poster, the McCormick Reaper Company presents a romantic, idealized image of vast, fertile lands awaiting settlement, an image that drew many settlers westward. *(Chicago Historical Society)*

icans never discovered what had brought the Indians (who spoke no English) from Oregon to Missouri, and all four died before they could find out. But some missionaries considered the visit a divinely inspired invitation to extend their efforts westward. They were also motivated by a desire to counter the Catholic missionaries from Canada, whose presence in Oregon many believed threatened American hopes for annexation. The missionaries had little success with the tribes they attempted to convert, and some—embittered by Indian resistance to their efforts—began encouraging white immigration into the region, arguing that by repudiating Christianity the Indians had abdicated their right to the land. "When a people refuse or neglect to fill the designs of Providence, they ought not

to complain of the results," said the missionary Marcus Whitman who, with his wife Narcissa, had established an important, if largely unsuccessful, mission among the Cayuse Indians east of the Cascade Mountains.

Significant numbers of white Americans began emigrating to Oregon in the early 1840s, and they soon substantially outnumbered the British settlers there. They also devastated much of the Indian population, in part through a measles epidemic that spread through the Cayuse. The tribe blamed the Whitman mission for the plague, and in 1847 they attacked it and killed thirteen whites, including Marcus and Narcissa. But such resistance did little to stem the white immigration. By the mid-1840s, American settlements had spread up and down the Pacific Coast; and the new settlers (along with advocates of Manifest Destiny in the East) were urging the United States government to take possession of the disputed Oregon territory.

The Westward Migration

The migrations into Texas and Oregon were part of a larger movement that took hundreds of thousands of white and black Americans into the far western regions of the continent between 1840 and 1860. Southerners flocked mainly to Texas. But the largest number of migrants came from the Old Northwest (today's Midwest)—white men and women, and a few blacks, who undertook arduous journeys in search of new opportunities. Most traveled in family groups, until the early 1850s, when the great gold rush attracted many single men. (See pp. 364–366.) Most were relatively young people. Most had undertaken earlier, if usually shorter, migrations in the past. Few were wealthy, but many were relatively prosperous. Poor people could not afford the expensive trip and the cost of new land. Those without money who wished to migrate usually had to do so by joining more established families or groups as laborers—men as farm or ranch hands, women as domestic servants, teachers, or, in some cases, prostitutes. The character of the migrations varied according to the destination of the migrants. Groups headed for areas where mining or lumbering was the principal economic activity consisted mostly of men. Those heading for farming regions traveled mainly as families.

All the migrants were in search of a new life, but they harbored many different visions of what the new life would bring. Some—particularly after the discovery of gold in California in 1849—hoped for quick riches. Others planned to take advantage of the vast public lands the federal government was selling at modest prices to acquire property for farming or speculation. Still others hoped to establish themselves as merchants and serve the new white communities developing in the West. Some (among them the Mormons) were on religious missions or were attempting to escape the epidemic diseases that were plaguing many cities in the East. But the vast majority of migrants were looking for economic opportunities. They formed a vanguard for the expanding capitalist economy of the United States. Perhaps not surprisingly, migrations were largest during boom times in the United States and dwindled during recessions.

Most migrants—about 300,000 between 1840 and 1860—traveled west along the great overland trails. They generally gathered in one of several major depots in Iowa and Missouri (Independence, St. Joseph, or Council Bluffs), joined a wagon train led by hired guides, and set off with their belongings piled in covered wagons, livestock trailing behind. The major route west was the 2,000-mile Oregon Trail, which stretched from Independence across the Great Plains and through the South Pass of the Rocky Mountains. From there, migrants moved north into Oregon or south (along the California trail) to the northern California coast. Other migrations moved along the Santa Fe Trail, southwest from Independence into New Mexico.

However they traveled, overland migrants faced considerable hardships—although the death rate for travelers was only slightly higher than the rate for the American population as a whole. The mountain and desert terrain in the later portions of the trip were particularly difficult. Most journeys lasted five or six months (from May to November), and there was always pressure to get through the Rockies before the snows began, not always an easy task given the very slow pace of most wagon trains (about fifteen miles a day). And although some migrants were moving west at least in part to escape the epidemic diseases of eastern cities, they were not immune from plagues. Thousands of people died on the trail of cholera during the great epidemic of the early 1850s.

Only a very small number of expeditions encountered Indian attacks. Indeed, in the twenty years before the Civil War, fewer than 400 migrants (about one-tenth of 1 percent) died in conflicts with the tribes. In fact, Indians were usually more helpful than dangerous to the white migrants. They often served as guides through difficult terrain or aided travelers in crossing streams or herding livestock. They maintained an extensive trade with the white travelers in horses, clothing, and fresh food. But stories of the occasional conflicts between migrants and Indians on the trail created widespread fear among white travelers, even though more Indians than white people (and relatively few of either) died in those conflicts.

Life on the trail was obviously very different from life on a farm or in a town. But the society of the trail re-created many of the patterns of conventional American society. Families divided tasks along gender lines: the men driving and, when necessary, repairing the wagons or hunting game; the women cooking, washing clothes, and caring for children. Almost everyone, male or female, walked the great majority of the time, to lighten the load for the horses drawing the wagons; and so the women, many of whose chores came at the end of the day, generally worked much harder than the men, who usually rested when the caravan halted.

Despite the traditional image of westward migrants as rugged individualists, most travelers found the journey a highly collective experience. That was partly because many expeditions consisted of groups of friends, neighbors, or relatives who had decided to pull up stakes and move west together. And it was partly because of the intensity of the experience: many weeks of difficult travel with no other human contacts except, occasionally, with Indians. Indeed, one of the most frequent causes of disaster for travelers was the breakdown of the necessarily communal character of the migratory companies. Even so, it was a rare expedition in which there were not some internal conflicts before the trip was over.

EXPANSION AND WAR

The increasing numbers of white Americans in the lands west of the Mississippi put great pressure on the government in Washington. Advocates of Manifest Destiny were propagandizing on behalf of annexing Texas, Oregon, and other lands. The settlers themselves—and their friends, relatives, and business partners in the East—were lobbying for expansion as well. Others, however, feared annexation would cause sectional conflicts, and they sought to avoid or at least defer action. Their efforts were in vain, for in the 1840s the expansionists helped push the United States into a war that—however dubious its origins—became a triumph for Manifest Destiny.

The Democrats and Expansion

Most Americans had expected the election of 1844 to be a contest between two old foes: the Whig Henry Clay and the Democratic former president Martin Van Buren. In preparing for the race, both men tried to avoid taking a stand on the controversial issue of the annexation of Texas. Their separate statements on the question were so similar that many suspected they had collaborated in preparing them. Both favored annexation, but only with the consent of Mexico. Since such consent was unlikely, the statements meant virtually nothing.

Because sentiment for expansion was mild within the Whig Party, Clay had no difficulty securing the nomination despite his noncommittal position. Among the Democrats, however, there were many supporters of annexation, particularly in the South, and they resented Van Buren's equivocal stand. The expansionists took control of the Democratic convention and nominated a strong supporter of annexation, James K. Polk—the first "dark horse" to win the presidential nomination of his party.

Polk was not as obscure as his Whig critics claimed, but neither was he a genuinely major figure within his party. For fourteen years, beginning in 1825, he had represented Tennessee in the U.S. House of Representatives, four of them as Speaker. Most recently, he had been governor of Tennessee. But in 1844 he had been out of public office—and for the most part out of the public mind—for three years. What made his victory possible was the belief, expressed in the Democratic platform, "that the re-occupation of Oregon and the re-annexation of Texas at the earliest practicable period are great American measures." By combining the Oregon and Texas questions, the Democrats hoped to appeal to both northern and southern expansionists.

In a belated effort to catch up with public sentiment in midcampaign, Clay announced support for annexing Texas. But his tardy and apparently cynical straddling probably cost him more votes than it gained. Polk carried the election by 170 electoral votes to 105, although his popular majority was less than 40,000. The Liberty party, running James G. Birney a second time, polled 62,000 votes (as compared with 7,000 in 1840), mainly from antislavery Whigs who had turned against Clay.

Polk may have been obscure, but he was intelligent and energetic. He entered office with a clear set of goals and with plans for attaining them. John Tyler accomplished the first of Polk's goals for him in the last days of his presidency. Interpreting the election returns as a mandate for accepting Texas into the union, the outgoing president persuaded Congress to approve an annexation treaty in February 1845. That December, Texas became a state.

Polk himself resolved the Oregon question, although not without difficulty and not without disappointing some expansionist Democrats. Publicly, Polk seemed to support American title to all of the Oregon territory, but privately he was willing to compromise—to set the boundary at the 49th parallel. When the British minister in Washington rejected Polk's offer without even referring it to London, Polk toughened his stance and reasserted the American claim to all of Oregon. There was loose talk of war on both sides of the Atlantic—talk that in the United States often took the form of the bellicose slogan "Fifty-four forty or fight!" (a reference to the latitude where some Americans hoped to draw the northern boundary of Oregon). But neither country really wanted to fight. Finally, the British government offered to accept Polk's original proposal and divide the territory at the 49th parallel. The president, reluctant to alienate nationalists who wanted more, submitted the British proposal to the Senate without supporting it. No doubt to his relief, the Senate accepted the agreement; and on June

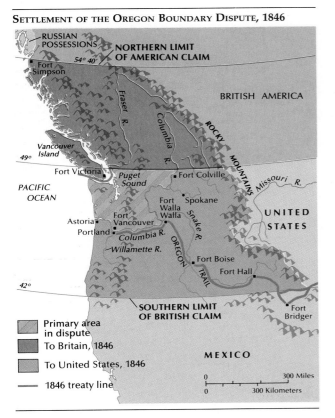

SETTLEMENT OF THE OREGON BOUNDARY DISPUTE, 1846

RUSSIAN POSSESSIONS
NORTHERN LIMIT OF AMERICAN CLAIM
54° 40′
Fort Simpson
Fraser R.
BRITISH AMERICA
Columbia R.
ROCKY MOUNTAINS
Vancouver Island
49°
Fort Victoria
Puget Sound
Fort Colville
PACIFIC OCEAN
Fort Walla Walla
Spokane
Snake R.
Missouri R.
UNITED STATES
Astoria
Portland
Fort Vancouver
Columbia R.
Willamette R.
OREGON TRAIL
Fort Boise
Fort Hall
42°
SOUTHERN LIMIT OF BRITISH CLAIM
Fort Bridger

Primary area in dispute
To Britain, 1846
To United States, 1846
1846 treaty line

MEXICO

0   300 Miles
0   300 Kilometers

15, 1846, a treaty fixed the boundary between the United States and Canada at the 49th parallel, where it remains today.

The Southwest and California

One of the reasons why the Senate and the president had agreed so readily to the British proposal for settling the Oregon question was that new tensions were emerging in the Southwest—tensions that ultimately led to a war with Mexico. As soon as the United States admitted Texas to statehood in 1845, the Mexican government broke diplomatic relations with Washington. To make matters worse, a dispute then developed over the boundary between Texas and Mexico. Texans claimed the Rio Grande as both their western and southern border, a claim that would have added much of what is now New Mexico to Texas. Mexico still refused formally to concede the loss of Texas but argued nevertheless that the border had always been the Nueces River, to the north of the Rio Grande. Polk recognized the Texas claim, and in the summer of 1845 he

sent a small army under General Zachary Taylor to the Nueces line—to protect Texas, he claimed, against a possible Mexican invasion.

Part of the area in dispute was New Mexico, which remained one of the northernmost outposts of Mexican civilization. Its trading center was the town of Santa Fe, 300 miles from the nearest settlements to the south and more than 1,000 miles from Mexico City and Vera Cruz; and its Spanish and Indian residents lived in a multiracial society that had by the 1840s lasted for nearly a century and a half.

In the 1820s, the Mexican government had invited American traders into the region (just as it was inviting American settlers into Texas), hoping to speed development of the province. And New Mexico, like Texas, soon began to become more American than Mexican. A flourishing commerce soon developed between Santa Fe and Independence, Missouri, with long caravans moving back and forth along the Santa Fe Trail, carrying manufactured goods west and bringing gold, silver, furs, and mules east in return. The Santa Fe trade, as it was called, further increased the American presence in New Mexico and signaled to advocates of expansion another direction for their efforts.

Americans were also increasing their interest in an even more distant province of Mexico: California. In this vast region lived members of several western Indian tribes and perhaps 7,000 Mexicans, mostly descendants of Spanish colonists. Gradually, however, white Americans began to arrive: first maritime traders and captains of Pacific whaling ships, who stopped to barter goods or buy supplies; then merchants, who established stores, imported merchandise, and developed a profitable trade with the Mexicans and Indians; and finally pioneering farmers, who entered California from the east by land and settled in the Sacramento Valley. By 1845, there were 700 Americans in California, most of them concentrated in the valley of the Sacramento River, and their numbers were increasing rapidly. The overlord of this region was John A. Sutter, who had lived in Germany and Switzerland before moving to America and who had migrated to California in 1839 and become a Mexican citizen. His headquarters at Sutter's Fort was the center of a magnificent domain where he ranched thousands of cattle and horses and maintained a network of small manufacturing shops to supply his armed retainers.

Some of these new settlers began to dream of bringing California into the United States. Thomas O. Larkin, for example, set up a business in Monterey in 1832, established himself as a leading citizen of the region, and in 1844 accepted appointment as American consul, with quiet instructions from Washington to arouse sentiment among Californians for annexation.

Sacramento in the 1850s
The busy river port of Sacramento served the growing agricultural and mining economies of north central California in the 1850s—years in which the new state began the dramatic population growth that a century later would make it the nation's largest. *(California State Library, Sacramento)*

President Polk soon came to share their dream and committed himself to acquiring both New Mexico and California for the United States. At the same time that he dispatched the troops under Taylor to the Nueces in Texas, he sent secret instructions to the commander of the Pacific naval squadron to seize the California ports if Mexico declared war on the United States. Representatives of the president quietly informed Americans in California that the United States would respond sympathetically to a revolt against Mexican authority there.

The Mexican War

Having appeared to prepare for war, Polk turned once more to diplomacy and dispatched a special minister, John Slidell, to try to buy off the Mexicans. But Mexican leaders rejected Slidell's offer to purchase the disputed territories. On January 13, 1846, as soon as he heard the news, Polk ordered Taylor's army in Texas to move across the Nueces to the Rio Grande. For months, the Mexicans refused to fight. But finally, according to the accounts of American commanders, some Mexican troops crossed the Rio Grande and attacked a unit of American soldiers. Polk, who had been

planning to request a declaration of war even without a military encounter, now told Congress: "War exists by the act of Mexico herself." On May 13, 1846, Congress declared war by votes of 40 to 2 in the Senate and 174 to 14 in the House.

The war had many opponents in the United States. Whig critics charged from the beginning (perhaps correctly) that the Polk administration had deliberately maneuvered the country into the conflict and had staged the border incident that had precipitated the declaration of war. Many argued that the hostilities with Mexico were draining resources and attention away from the more important issue of the Pacific Northwest; and when the United States finally reached its agreement with Britain on the Oregon question, opponents claimed that Polk had settled for less than he should have because he was preoccupied with Mexico. Opposition intensified as the war continued and as the public became aware of the casualties and expense.

Although American forces were generally successful in their campaigns against the Mexicans, final victory did not come nearly as quickly as Polk had hoped. Through most of the war, the president himself planned the military strategy. He ordered Taylor to cross the Rio Grande and seize parts of northeastern

THE MEXICAN WAR, 1846–1848

Mexico, beginning with the city of Monterrey, before marching south to Mexico City itself. Taylor attacked Monterrey in September 1846 and, after a hard fight, captured it. But he let the Mexican garrison evacuate without pursuit. Polk now began to doubt the feasibility of the advance on Mexico City. Among other things, he came to believe that Taylor lacked the tactical skill for the campaign, and he became convinced

that an advance south through the mountains would involve impossible supply problems. He also feared that, if successful, Taylor would become a powerful political rival (as, in fact, he did).

In the meantime, Polk ordered other offensives against New Mexico and California. In the summer of 1846, a small army under Colonel Stephen W. Kearny made the long march to Santa Fe and occupied the

SCOTT'S ARMY IN MEXICO CITY
General Winfield Scott leads an American army into the capital of Mexico in September 1847, the culminating triumph of the Mexican War. George W. Kendall of the New Orleans *Picayune* was one of the first war correspondents to accompany an army on its campaigns and was with Scott throughout the assault on the city. This print appeared in a history of the war that Kendall published several years later. *(Library of Congress)*

Trist had violated his instructions, but he soon realized that he had no choice but to accept the treaty. Some ardent expansionists were demanding that he hold out for annexation of—in a phrase widely bandied about at the time—"All Mexico!" Antislavery leaders, in the meantime, were charging that the idea of acquiring Mexico was part of a southern scheme to extend slavery to new realms. To silence this bitter and potentially destructive debate, Polk submitted the Trist treaty to the Senate, which approved it by a vote of 38 to 14. The war was over, and America had gained a vast new territory in the West. But it had also acquired a new set of troubling and divisive issues.

THE SECTIONAL DEBATE

James Polk tried to be a president whose policies transcended sectional issues. But conciliating the sections was becoming an ever more difficult task, and Polk gradually earned the enmity of both northerners and westerners, many of whom believed his policies (and particularly his enthusiasm for territorial expansion in the Southwest) favored the South at their expense. In this tense political climate, an exceptionally dangerous issue emerged.

Slavery and the Territories

In August 1846, while the Mexican War was still in progress, Polk asked Congress to appropriate $2 million for purchasing peace with Mexico. Representative David Wilmot of Pennsylvania, an antislavery Democrat, introduced an amendment to the appropriation bill that would have prohibited slavery in any territory acquired from Mexico. The so-called Wilmot Proviso passed the House but failed in the Senate. It would resurface in congressional debates for years.

Southern militants, in the meantime, had a plan of their own. They claimed that since the territories belonged to the entire nation, all Americans had equal rights in them, including the right to move their slaves (which they considered property) there. Neither Congress nor a territorial legislature (which was a creation of Congress) had the authority to prohibit or even regulate slavery in any territories.

As the sectional debate intensified, moderates attempted to craft a new compromise. President Polk supported a proposal to extend the Missouri Compromise line through the new territories to the Pacific coast, banning slavery north of the line and permitting it south of the line. Others supported a plan, originally known as "squatter sovereignty" and later by the more dignified title of "popular sovereignty," which would allow the people of each territory (acting through their legislature) to decide the status of slavery there. The debate over these various proposals dragged on for many months, and they remained unresolved when Polk left office in 1849. There was still no territorial government for California or the New Mexico territory (which included most of present New Mexico and Arizona, all of Utah and Nevada, and parts of Colorado and Wyoming).

The presidential campaign of 1848 dampened the controversy for a time as both Democrats and Whigs

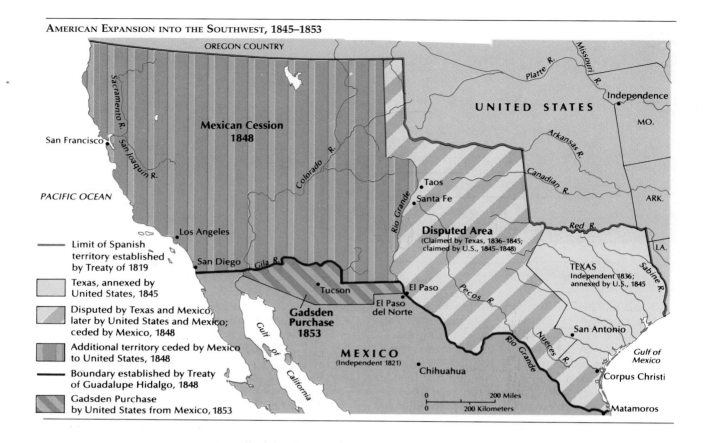

AMERICAN EXPANSION INTO THE SOUTHWEST, 1845–1853

Legend:
- Limit of Spanish territory established by Treaty of 1819
- Texas, annexed by United States, 1845
- Disputed by Texas and Mexico, later by United States and Mexico; ceded by Mexico, 1848
- Additional territory ceded by Mexico to United States, 1848
- Boundary established by Treaty of Guadalupe Hidalgo, 1848
- Gadsden Purchase by United States from Mexico, 1853

tried to avoid the slavery question. Polk, damaged politically by the sectional animosities his policies had helped arouse, and in declining health (he would die in 1849), refused to run again. The Democrats nominated Lewis Cass of Michigan, a dull, aging party regular. The Whigs nominated a military hero of the Mexican War with no political record, General Zachary Taylor of Louisiana. Opponents of slavery found the choice of candidates unsatisfying, and out of their discontent emerged the Free-Soil Party, which drew from the existing Liberty Party and the antislavery wings of the Whig and Democratic Parties and which endorsed the Wilmot Proviso. Its candidate was former president Martin Van Buren.

Taylor won a narrow victory. But while Van Buren failed to carry a single state, he polled an impressive 291,000 votes (10 percent of the total), and the Free-Soilers elected ten members to Congress. Van Buren probably drew enough Democratic votes away from Cass, particularly in New York, to throw the election to Taylor. The emergence of the Free-Soil Party as an important political force, like the emergence of the Know Nothing and Liberty Parties before it, signaled the inability of the existing parties to contain the po-

litical passions slavery was creating, and was an important step toward the collapse of the second party system in the 1850s.

The California Gold Rush

By the time Taylor took office, the pressure to resolve the question of slavery in the far western territories had become more urgent as a result of dramatic events in California. In January 1848, James Marshall, a carpenter working on one of John Sutter's sawmills, found traces of gold in the foothills of the Sierra Nevada mountains. Sutter tried to suppress the news, fearing a gold rush would destroy his own substantial empire in the region. But by May, word of the discovery had reached San Francisco; by late summer, it had reached the East Coast of the United States and much of the rest of the world. Almost immediately, hundreds of thousands of people from around the world began flocking to California in a frantic search for gold. The non–Indian population increased nearly twentyfold in four years: from 14,000 in 1848 to over 220,000 in 1852.

GOLD MINING IN CALIFORNIA IN THE 1850S
This photograph shows a sluice, used in placer mining. A "placer" was a deposit of sand, dirt, or clay—often in the bed of a stream—that contained fine particles of gold, which could be mined by washing. The "sluice" was a wooden trough into which miners shoveled the earth and then ran a steady stream of water over it. Heavy particles (such as gold) would sink to the bottom, where they were caught by cleats (known as "riffles"). Placer mining was one of the simplest and cheapest methods of extracting gold from the land, but it seldom produced large strikes. *(Bettmann)*

The atmosphere in California at the peak of the gold rush was one of almost crazed excitement and greed. For a short time San Francisco was almost completely depopulated as residents raced to the mountains to search for gold; the city's principal newspaper (which had been criticizing the gold mania) had to stop publication because it could no longer find either staff or readers. "Nothing but the introduction of insane asylums can effect a cure," one visitor remarked of the gold mania.

Most migrants to the Far West prepared carefully before making the journey. But the California migrants (known as "Forty-niners") threw caution to the winds. They abandoned farms, jobs, homes, families; they piled onto ships and flooded the overland trails—many carrying only what they could pack on their backs. The overwhelming majority of the Forty-niners (perhaps 95 percent) were men, and the society they created on their arrival in California was unusually fluid and volatile because of the almost total absence of women, children, or families.

The gold rush also attracted some of the first Chinese migrants to the western United States. News of the discoveries created great excitement in China, particularly in impoverished areas, where letters from Chinese already in California and reports from Americans visiting in China spread the word. It was, of course, extremely difficult for a poor Chinese peasant to get to America; but many young, adventurous people (mostly men) decided to go anyway—in the belief that they could quickly become rich and then return to China. Emigration brokers loaned many migrants money for passage to California, which the migrants paid off out of their earnings there. The migration was almost entirely voluntary (unlike the forced movement of kidnapped "coolies" to such places as Peru and Cuba at about the same time). The Chinese in California were, therefore, free laborers and merchants, looking for gold or, more often, hoping to profit from other economic opportunities the gold boom was creating.

The gold rush created a serious labor shortage in California, as many male workers left their jobs and flocked to the gold fields. That created opportunities for many people who needed work (including Chinese immigrants). It also led to an overt exploitation of Indians that resembled slavery in all but name. At the same time that white vigilantes, who called themselves "Indian hunters," were hunting down and killing thousands of Indians (contributing to the process by which the native population of California declined from 150,000 to 30,000 between the 1850s and 1870), a state law permitted the arrest of "loitering" or orphaned Indians and their assignment to a term of "indentured" labor.

The gold rush was of critical importance to the growth of California, but not for the reasons most of the migrants hoped. There was substantial gold in the hills of the Sierra Nevada, and many people got rich from it. But only a tiny fraction of the Forty-niners ever found gold, or even managed to stake a claim to land on which they could look for gold. Some disappointed migrants returned home after a while. But many stayed in California and swelled both the agricultural and urban populations of the territory. By 1856, for example, San Francisco—whose population had been 1,000 before the gold rush (and at one point declined to about 100 as people left for the mines)—was the home of over 50,000 people. By the early 1850s, California, which had always had a diverse population, had become remarkably heterogeneous. The gold rush had attracted not just white Americans, but Europeans, Chinese, South Americans, Mexicans, free blacks, and slaves who accompanied southern migrants. Conflicts over gold intersected with racial and ethnic tensions to make the territory an unusually turbulent place. As a result, pressure grew to create a more stable and effective government. The gold rush, therefore, became another factor putting pressure on the United States to resolve the status of the territories—and of slavery within them.

Rising Sectional Tensions

Zachary Taylor was a southerner and a slaveholder, but from his long years in the army he had acquired a national outlook. He recognized at once the importance of dealing with the problems of the newly acquired territories, which—in the absence of territorial governments—were still under the control of the military. There was particular pressure to establish a new government in California, after the enormous boom following the gold rush that had begun in 1848.

Taylor believed statehood could become the solution to the issue of slavery in the territories. As long as the new lands were territories, the federal government was responsible for deciding the fate of slavery within them. But once they became states, their own governments would be able to settle the slavery question. Taylor ordered military officials in California and New Mexico to speed up the statehood movements. California promptly adopted a constitution that prohibited slavery, and in December 1849 Taylor asked Congress to admit California as a free state. New Mexico, he added, should be granted statehood as soon as it was ready and should, like California, be permitted to decide for itself what it wanted to do about slavery.

Congress balked, in part because of several other controversies involving slavery that were complicating the debate over the territories. One was the effort of antislavery forces to abolish slavery in the District of Columbia, a movement white southerners bitterly resisted. Another was the emergence of the "personal liberty laws" in northern states, which barred courts and police officers from helping to return runaway slaves to their owners. In response, southerners in Congress demanded a stringent national law to require northern states to return fugitive slaves to their owners. Still another controversy involved a border dispute between Texas and New Mexico, and the Texans' resentment at the failure of the federal government to take over the debts they had accumulated during their brief independence. But the biggest obstacle to the president's program was the white South's fear that two new free states would tip the balance of national

politics further against them. The number of free and slave states in 1849 was equal—fifteen of each. But the admission of California would upset the balance; and New Mexico, Oregon, and Utah—all of which seemed likely to become free states—might upset it further, leaving the South with a minority in the Senate as it already had in the House.

Tempers were now rising to dangerous levels. Even many otherwise moderate southern leaders were beginning to talk about secession from the Union, while all but one northern state legislature adopted a resolution demanding the prohibition of slavery in the territories.

The Compromise of 1850

Clay's Bill

Faced with this mounting crisis, moderates and Unionists spent the winter of 1849–1850 trying to frame a great compromise. The aging Henry Clay, who was spearheading the effort, believed that no compromise could work unless it settled all the issues in dispute between the sections. As a result, he took several originally separate measures and combined them into a single piece of legislation, which he presented to the Senate on January 29, 1850. The bill had five provisions: (1) that California be admitted as a free state; (2) that in the rest of the lands acquired from Mexico, territorial governments be formed without restrictions on slavery; (3) that Texas yield in its boundary dispute with New Mexico and that the federal government compensate it by taking over its public debt; (4) that the slave trade, but not slavery itself, be abolished in the District of Columbia; and (5) that a new and more effective fugitive slave law be passed. These resolutions launched a debate that raged for seven months—both in Congress and throughout the nation. The debate occurred in two phases, and the differences between them revealed much about how American politics was changing in the 1850s.

In the first phase of the debate, the dominant voices in Congress were those of older men—national leaders who still remembered Jefferson, Adams, and other founders—who argued for or against the compromise on the basis of broad ideals. Clay himself, seventy-three years old in 1850, was the most prominent of these spokesmen. He made a broad plea for sectional conciliation and appealed to shared sentiments of nationalism.

Early in March, another of the older leaders—John C. Calhoun, sixty-eight years old and so ill that he had to sit grimly in his seat while a colleague read his speech for him—joined the debate. Calhoun insisted

SLAVE AND FREE TERRITORIES ACCORDING TO THE COMPROMISE OF 1850

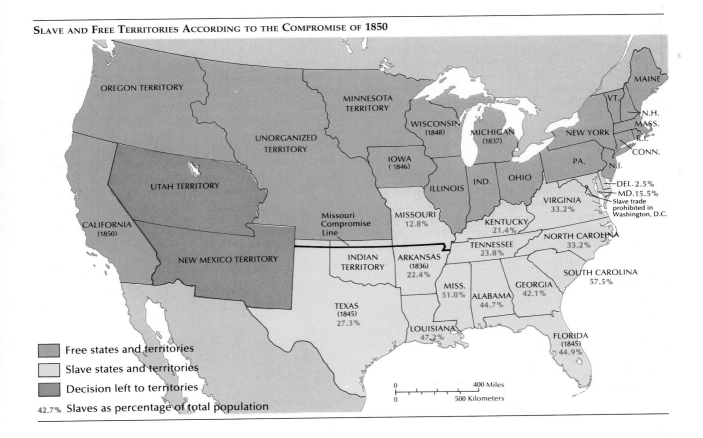

Free states and territories

Slave states and territories

Decision left to territories

42.7% Slaves as percentage of total population

that the North grant the South equal rights in the territories, that it agree to observe the laws concerning fugitive slaves, that it cease attacking slavery, and that it accept an amendment to the Constitution guaranteeing a balance of power between the sections. The amendment would provide for the election of dual presidents, one from the North and one from the South, each possessing a veto power. Calhoun was making radical demands that had no chance of passage. But he was expressing his belief in the importance of saving the Union; and like Clay, he was offering what he considered a comprehensive, permanent solution to the sectional problem—even if one that would have required an abject surrender by the North.

After Calhoun came the third of the elder statesmen, the sixty-eight-year-old Daniel Webster. His "Seventh of March Address" was probably the greatest oratorical effort of his long career. Still nourishing presidential ambitions, he sought to calm angry passions and to rally northern moderates to support Clay's compromise.

After six months of debate, however—a debate dominated by ringing appeals to the memory of the founders, to nationalism, to idealism—the effort to win approval of the compromise failed. In July, Congress defeated the Clay proposal; and with that the controversy moved into its second phase, in which a very different cast of characters predominated. Clay, ill and tired, left Washington to spend the summer resting in the mountains. He would return, but never with his old vigor; he died in 1852. Calhoun had died even before the vote in July. And Webster in the course of the summer accepted a new appointment as secretary of state, thus removing himself from the Senate and from the debate.

In place of these leaders, a new, younger group now emerged as the dominant voices. There was William H. Seward of New York, forty-nine years old, a wily political operator who staunchly opposed the proposed compromise. The ideals of Union were less important to him than the issue of eliminating slavery. The new voice of the South was Jefferson Davis of Mississippi, forty-two years old, a representative not of the old aristocratic South of Calhoun but of the new, cotton South—a hard, newly settled, and rapidly growing region. To him, the slavery issue was one not only of principles and ideals but also of economic self-interest.

Most important of all, there was Stephen A. Douglas, a thirty-seven-year-old Democratic senator from Illinois. A westerner from a rapidly growing state, he was an open spokesman for the economic needs of his section—and especially for the construction of railroads. His was a career devoted not to broad national goals, as Clay's, Webster's, and even Calhoun's had often been, but one frankly committed to sectional gain and personal self-promotion.

The new leaders of the Senate were able, where the old leaders were not, to produce a compromise in 1850. In part they benefited from the great prosperity of the early 1850s, which was a result of expanding foreign trade, the flow of gold from California, and a boom in railroad construction. Conservative economic interests everywhere wanted to end the sectional dispute and concentrate on economic growth. Progress toward the compromise was also helped by the disappearance of its most powerful opponent: the president. President Taylor had been adamant that only after the admission of California and possibly New Mexico as states could other measures be discussed. He had threatened not only to veto any measure that diverged from this proposal but to use force against the southern states, even to lead the troops in person if they attempted to secede. But on July 9, 1850, Taylor suddenly died. He had attended a Fourth of July celebration in a blazing sun, eaten too much, and succumbed to heat prostration and a violent stomach disorder. His successor was Millard Fillmore of New York—a handsome, dignified, lightly regarded man who understood the political importance of flexibility. He supported the compromise and used his powers of persuasion to swing northern Whigs into line.

The new leaders also benefited from their own pragmatic tactics. Douglas's first step, after Clay's departure, was to break up the "omnibus bill" that Clay had envisioned as a great comprehensive solution to the sectional crisis and to introduce instead a series of separate measures to be voted on individually. Thus representatives of different sections could support those elements of the compromise favorable to them and abstain from voting on or vote against those they opposed. Douglas also gained support by avoiding the grand appeals to patriotism Clay and Webster had made and resorting instead to complicated backroom deals—linking the compromise to such non-ideological matters as the sale of government bonds and the

construction of railroads. As a result of his efforts, by mid-September Congress had passed all the components of the compromise and the president had signed them.

The outcome was a great if clouded victory for Douglas and the forces of conciliation. The Compromise of 1850, unlike the Missouri Compromise thirty years before, was not a product of widespread agreement on common national ideals. It was, rather, a triumph of self-interest that did not resolve the underlying problems. Still, members of Congress hailed the measure as a triumph of statesmanship; and Millard Fillmore, approving it, called it a just settlement of the sectional problem, "in its character final and irrevocable."

THE CRISES OF THE 1850S

For a few years after the Compromise of 1850, sectional conflict seemed to subside amid booming prosperity and growth. But tensions between North and South remained. And in 1854, they burst into the open once more.

The Uneasy Truce

Both major parties endorsed the Compromise of 1850 in their platforms in 1852, and both parties nominated presidential candidates unlikely to arouse passionate opposition in either North or South. The Democrats chose the obscure New Hampshire politician Franklin Pierce. The Whigs selected the military hero General Winfield Scott, a man whose political views were so undefined that no one knew what he thought about the Compromise.

The gingerly way in which party leaders dealt with the sectional question could not prevent its divisive influence from intruding on the election. The Whigs were the principal victims. Already plagued by the continuing defections of antislavery northerners into the Free-Soil Party (which had repudiated the Compromise of 1850), they alienated still more party members—the "Conscience" Whigs—by straddling the slavery issue and refusing openly to condemn it. The divisions among the Whigs helped produce a victory for the Democrats in 1852.

Franklin Pierce, a charming, amiable man of no great distinction, attempted to maintain party—and national—harmony by avoiding divisive issues, and particularly by avoiding the issue of slavery. But those issues arose despite him. They arose, in particular, because of northern opposition to the Fugitive Slave Act. Under the law, blacks accused of having escaped from slavery had no right to a trial by jury and could not testify on their own behalf; a federal judge or commissioner could turn alleged runaways over to slaveowners simply on the basis of affidavits from slaveowners. Northern hostility to these provisions intensified after 1850 when southerners began appearing occasionally in northern states to pursue fugitives or to claim as slaves blacks who had been living in northern communities for years. Several northern states passed new personal liberty laws, which attempted to use state authority to interfere with the deportation of fugitive slaves. The supreme court of Wisconsin, in *Ableman v. Booth* (1857), even declared the federal Fugitive Slave Act void and ignored the U.S. Supreme Court when it overruled the Wisconsin ruling.

So fervent was the resentment of many opponents of slavery that mobs formed in several cities to prevent enforcement of the law. In 1854, for example, a Boston mob stormed a courthouse and killed a guard in an effort to rescue a fugitive slave who was about to be returned to the South. President Pierce sent troops to Boston to ensure enforcement of the law; tens of thousands of Bostonians lined the streets in protest as the soldiers marched the fugitive to the ship that would return him to slavery.

White southerners watched with growing anger and alarm as the one element of the Compromise of 1850 they had considered a victory became, as they saw it, virtually meaningless because of mob action and unconstitutional legalisms in the North.

"Young America"

One of the ways Franklin Pierce tried to dampen sectional controversy was through his support of a movement in the Democratic Party known as "Young America." Those who joined the movement hoped the expansion of American democracy throughout the world could become a diversion from what they considered the transitory issue of slavery. The great liberal and nationalist revolutions of 1848 in Europe stirred them to dream of a republican Europe with governments based on the model of the United States. They dreamed as well of expanding American commerce in the Pacific and acquiring new territories in the Western Hemisphere.

Few Americans in North or South objected to displays of nationalism. But efforts to extend the nation's domain could not avoid becoming entangled with the sectional crisis. Pierce had been unsuccessfully attempting through diplomacy to buy Cuba from the Spanish Empire (efforts begun in 1848 by Polk), when a group of his envoys sent him a private document from Ostend, Belgium, making the case for seizing Cuba by force. When the Ostend Manifesto, as it became known, leaked to the public, it enraged many antislavery northerners, who charged the administration with conspiring to bring a new slave state into the Union.

The South, for its part, opposed all efforts to acquire new territory that would not support a slave system. The kingdom of Hawaii—which had a substantial population of American planters—agreed to join the United States in 1854; but the treaty died in the Senate because it contained a clause prohibiting slavery in the islands. A powerful movement to annex Canada to the United States—a movement that had the support of many Canadians eager for access to American markets—similarly foundered, at least in part because of slavery.

Slavery, Railroads, and the West

What fully revived the sectional crisis, however, was the same issue that had produced it in the first place: slavery in the territories. By the 1850s, the line of white settlement had moved west to the great bend of the Missouri River. Beyond the boundaries of what is now Minnesota, Iowa, and Missouri stretched a great expanse of plains, which many white Americans had long believed was unfit for cultivation. (Some called it the Great American Desert.) The government had assigned much of this territory to the Indian tribes it had dislodged from the more fertile lands to the east. Now it was becoming apparent that large sections of this region were, in fact, suitable for farming. In the states of the Old Northwest, prospective settlers urged the government to open the area to them, provide territorial governments, and—despite its previous solemn assurances to the Indians of the sanctity of their lands—dislodge the tribes so as to make room for white settlers. There was relatively little opposition from any segment of white society to the violation of Indian rights proposed by these demands. But the interest in further settlement raised two issues that did prove highly divisive and that gradually became intertwined: railroads and slavery.

As the nation expanded westward and as the problem of communication between the older states and the so-called trans-Mississippi West (the areas west of the Mississippi River) became more and more

370 THE IMPENDING CRISIS

critical, broad support began to emerge for building a transcontinental railroad. The problem was where to place it—and in particular, where to locate the railroad's eastern terminus. Northerners favored Chicago, the rapidly growing capital of the free states of the Northwest. Southerners supported St. Louis, Memphis, or New Orleans—all located in slave states.

Pierce's secretary of war, Jefferson Davis of Mississippi, tried to enhance the chances of a southern route, by removing a territorial obstacle. After surveys indicated that a road with a southern terminus would have to pass through an area in Mexican territory, Davis dispatched James Gadsden, a southern railroad builder, to buy the region in question from Mexico. In 1853 Gadsden persuaded the Mexican government to accept $10 million in exchange for a strip of land that today comprises part of Arizona and New Mexico, the so-called Gadsden Purchase. The acquisition intensified the sectional debate.

The Kansas-Nebraska Controversy

As a senator from Illinois, a resident of Chicago, and the acknowledged leader of northwestern Democrats, Stephen Douglas naturally wanted the transcontinental railroad for his own city and section. He also realized the strength of the principal argument against the northern route: that west of the Mississippi it would run largely through country with a substantial Indian population. Like Jefferson Davis, therefore, he attempted to improve his region's chances by removing the obstacle. In the process, he made a fateful proposal that finally destroyed the Compromise of 1850. In 1854 he introduced a bill to organize (and thus open to white settlement) a huge new territory west of Iowa and Missouri. It would be known as Nebraska.

Douglas knew the South would oppose his bill because it would prepare the way for a new free state: the proposed territory was in the area of the Louisiana Purchase north of the Missouri Compromise line and hence closed to slavery. In an effort to make the measure acceptable to southerners, Douglas inserted a provision that the status of slavery in the new territory would be determined by the territorial legislature—that is, according to popular sovereignty. In theory, the region could choose to open itself to slavery (although few believed it actually would). When southern Democrats demanded more, Douglas agreed to two changes in the bill: a clause specifically repealing the antislavery provision of the Missouri Compromise (which the popular sovereignty provision of his original bill had done implicitly); and the division of the area into two territories, Nebraska and Kansas, instead of one. The new second territory (Kansas) was more likely to become a slave state. In its final form the measure was known as the Kansas-Nebraska Act. President Pierce supported the bill; and after a strenuous debate, it became law in May 1854 with the unanimous support of the South and the partial support of northern Democrats.

No other piece of legislation in American history produced so many immediate, sweeping, and ominous changes as the Kansas-Nebraska Act. It destroyed the Whig Party, which virtually disappeared by 1856, and along with it a conservative, nationalistic influence in American politics. It divided the northern Democrats (many of whom were appalled at the repeal of the Missouri Compromise, which they considered an almost sacred part of the fabric of Union) and drove many of them from the party.

Most important of all, it spurred the creation of a new party that was frankly sectional in composition and creed. In 1854, Whigs, Democrats, and Free-Soilers opposed to the Kansas-Nebraska Act formed the Republican Party. Instantly, it became a major force in American politics. In the elections of that year, the Republicans won enough seats in Congress to permit them, in combination with allies among the Know Nothings, to organize the House of Representatives.

"Bleeding Kansas"

Events in Kansas itself in the next two years increased the popular excitement in the North. White settlers from both the North and the South began moving into the territory almost immediately after the passage of the Kansas-Nebraska Act. In the spring of 1855, there were elections for a territorial legislature. Only about 1,500 legal voters lived in Kansas by then, but more than 6,000 people actually voted. That was because thousands of Missourians, some traveling in armed bands, crossed into Kansas to vote. As a result, proslavery forces elected a majority to the legislature, which proceeded immediately to enact a series of laws legalizing slavery. Outraged free-staters defied the legislature and in a separate election chose delegates to a constitutional convention, which met at Topeka and adopted a constitution excluding slavery. The free-staters then chose their own governor and legislature and petitioned Congress for statehood. President Pierce denounced the free-staters as traitors and threw the full support of the federal government behind the pro-slavery territorial legislature.

A few months later a pro-slavery federal marshal assembled a large posse, consisting mostly of Missourians, to arrest the free-state leaders, who had set up their headquarters in Lawrence. The posse sacked the town, burned the "governor's" house, and destroyed several printing presses. Retribution came quickly.

Among the most fervent opponents of slavery in Kansas was John Brown, a fiercely committed abolitionist originally from Ohio, who considered himself an instrument of God's will to destroy slavery. He had moved to Kansas with his sons so they could fight to make it a free state. After the events in Lawrence, he gathered six followers (including four of his sons) and in one night murdered five pro-slavery settlers, leaving their mutilated bodies to discourage other supporters of slavery from entering Kansas. The episode, known as the Pottawatomie Massacre, led to more civil strife in Kansas—irregular, guerrilla warfare conducted by armed bands, some of them more interested in land claims or loot than in ideologies. Northerners and southerners alike came to believe the events in Kansas illustrated (and were a result of) the aggressive designs of the other section. "Bleeding Kansas" became a powerful symbol of the sectional hostility.

Another symbol soon appeared, in the United States Senate. In May 1856, Charles Sumner of Massachusetts rose to give a speech entitled "The Crime Against Kansas." Handsome, eloquent, humorless, and passionately doctrinaire, Sumner was a militant opponent of slavery. And in his speech, he gave particular attention to his colleague, Senator Andrew P. Butler of South Carolina, an outspoken defender of slavery. The South Carolinian was, Sumner claimed, the "Don Quixote" of slavery, having "chosen a mistress . . . who, though ugly to others, is always lovely to him, though polluted in the sight of the world, is chaste in his sight . . . the harlot slavery."

The pointedly sexual references and the general viciousness of the speech enraged Butler's nephew, Preston Brooks, a member of the U.S. House of Representatives from South Carolina, who decided to punish Sumner publicly. Several days after the speech, Brooks approached Sumner at his desk in the Senate chamber during a recess, raised a heavy cane, and began beating him repeatedly on the head and shoulders. Sumner, trapped behind his desk, rose in agony with such strength that he tore the desk from the bolts holding it to the floor; he then collapsed, bleeding and unconscious. So severe were his injuries that he was unable to return to the Senate for four years, during which time his state refused to replace him. He became a symbol throughout the North—a martyr to the barbarism of the South.

Preston Brooks became a symbol too. Censured by the House, he resigned his seat, returned to South Carolina, and stood successfully for reelection. He had become a southern hero. Like Sumner, he served as evidence of how deep the antagonism between North and South had become.

The Free-Soil Ideology

What had happened to produce such deep hostility between the two sections? In part, the tensions were a reflection of the two sections' differing economic and territorial interests. But they were also a reflection of a hardening of ideas in both North and South. As the nation expanded and political power grew more dispersed, each section became concerned with ensuring that its vision of America's future would be the dominant one. And those visions were becoming—partly as a result of internal developments within the sections themselves, partly because of each region's conceptions (and misconceptions) of what was happening outside it—increasingly distinct and increasingly rigid.

In the North, assumptions about the proper structure of society came to center on the belief in "free soil" and "free labor." The abolitionists generated some support for their argument that slavery was a moral evil and must be eliminated. But theirs was never the dominant voice of the North. Instead, an increasing number of northerners, gradually becoming a majority, came to believe that the existence of slavery was dangerous not because of what it did to blacks but because of what it threatened to do to whites. At the heart of American democracy, they believed, was the right of all citizens to own property, to control their own labor, and to have access to opportunities for advancement. The ideal society, in other words, was one of small-scale capitalism, in which everyone could aspire to a stake and to upward mobility.

According to this vision, the South was the antithesis of democracy. It was a closed, static society, in which the slave system preserved an entrenched aristocracy and where common whites had no opportunity to improve themselves. More than that, the South was a backward society—decadent, lazy, dilapidated. While the North was growing and prospering, displaying thrift, industry, and a commitment to progress, the South was stagnating, rejecting the northern values of individualism and progress. The South was, northern free-laborites further maintained, engaged in a conspiracy to extend slavery throughout the nation and thus to destroy the openness of northern capitalism and replace it with the closed, aristocratic system of the South. This "slave power conspiracy," as it came to be known, threatened the future of every white laborer and property owner in the North. The only solution was to fight the spread of slavery and work for the day when the nation's democratic (i.e., free-labor) ideals extended to all sections of the country—the day of the victory of what northerners called "Freedom National."

This ideology lay at the heart of the new Republican Party. There were abolitionists and others in the party who sincerely believed in the rights of African Americans to freedom and citizenship. More important, however, were those who cared principally about the threat they believed slavery posed to white labor and to individual opportunity. This ideology also strengthened the commitment of Republicans to the Union. Since the idea of continued growth and progress was central to the free-labor vision, the prospect of dismemberment of the nation—a diminution of America's size and economic power—was unthinkable.

The Pro-Slavery Argument

In the South, in the meantime, a very different ideology was emerging—one that was entirely incompatible with the free-labor ideology developing in the North. It emerged out of a rapid hardening of position among southern whites on the issue of slavery.

As late as the early 1830s, a substantial number of southern whites had harbored reservations about slavery. Between 1829 and 1832, for example, a Virginia constitutional convention, and then the state legislature—under pressure from non-slaveholders in the western part of the state—had seriously considered ending slavery through compensated emancipation. The effort failed in large part because of the tremendous expense it would have entailed. There had been many antislavery societies in the South—more there in 1827 than there were in the North, most of them in the border states. And there were prominent southern politicians who spoke openly in opposition to slavery—among them Cassius M. Clay of Kentucky, who edited an abolitionist newspaper for a time in Lexington.

By the mid-1830s, however, a militant defensiveness regarding the system was beginning to replace this ambivalence. In part, the change was a result of events in the South. The Nat Turner uprising in 1831 (see p. 322) terrified whites throughout the region, and reinforced their determination to make slavery secure. There was also an economic incentive to defend the system. With the expansion of the cotton economy into the Deep South, slavery—which had begun to seem unprofitable in many areas of the upper South—now became lucrative once again.

But the change was also a result of events in the North, and particularly of the growth of the Garrisonian abolitionist movement, with its strident attacks on southern society. The popularity of Harriet Beecher Stowe's *Uncle Tom's Cabin* (see p. 347) was perhaps the most glaring evidence of the success of those attacks; but other abolitionist writings had been antagonizing white southerners for years. Abolitionists were a minority in the North, mistrusted and even despised by many people who were much less opposed to slavery (and much more concerned about avoiding sectional conflict) than they were. But an increasing number of white southerners came to believe that the abolitionists represented the opinion of the North as a whole.

ANTI-ABOLITIONIST VIOLENCE
This 1838 woodcut depicts the anti-abolitionist riot in Alton, Illinois, in which Elijah P. Lovejoy, publisher of an abolitionist newspaper, was slain on November 7, 1837. The death of Lovejoy aroused the antislavery movement throughout the United States. *(Library of Congress)*

In response to these pressures, a growing number of white southerners began to elaborate an intellectual defense of slavery. It began as early as 1832, when Professor Thomas R. Dew of the College of William and Mary outlined the case for slavery. It matured in 1852, when apologists for slavery summarized their views in an anthology that gave their ideology its name: *The Pro-Slavery Argument.* John C. Calhoun stated the essence of the case in 1837: Southerners should stop apologizing for slavery as a necessary evil and defend it as "a good—a positive good." It was good for the slaves, pro-slavery southerners argued, because, blacks needed the guidance of white masters. Indeed, they claimed, the slaves were better off—better fed, better clothed, better housed, more secure—than northern factory workers. Slavery was also good for southern society as a whole because it was the only way the two races could live together in peace. It was good for the entire country because the southern economy, based on slavery, was the key to the prosperity of the nation.

Racist assumptions about the inferiority of blacks—sustained by elaborate philosophical and even "scientific" arguments—underlay the pro-slavery rationale. No group was more effective in using such assumptions to promote the argument than the southern Protestant clergy. Many southern ministers had opposed slavery as late as the 1820s; but by the end of the 1830s, the great majority of the clergy was defending the institution in simultaneously racist and Christian terms. Because African Americans were inferior, they argued, it was the responsibility of the white race to nurture them, teach them morality and efficiency, and protect them from the evils of the world; it was necessary, in other words, to maintain slavery, not just because of the economic needs of slaveowners, but also because of the physical and spiritual needs of the slaves themselves. Since many northern clergy were, at the same time, making powerful religious arguments against slavery, serious tensions arose within some denominations. Both the Baptist and Methodist churches divided into northern and southern branches in the 1840s.

The pro-slavery argument became an essential part of a larger project: a defense of the southern way of life. It was, many white southerners argued, a way of life superior to any other in the United States, perhaps in the world. White southerners looking at the North saw a society they believed was abandoning traditional American values and replacing them with a spirit of greed, debauchery, and destructiveness. "The masses of the North are venal, corrupt, covetous, mean and selfish," wrote one southerner. Others wrote with horror of the factory system and the crowded, pestilential cities filled with unruly immigrants. The South, in contrast, was a stable, orderly society, operating at a slow and human pace. Its labor system avoided the feuds between capital and labor plaguing the North, protected the welfare of its workers, and allowed the aristocracy to enjoy a refined and accomplished cultural life. It was, in short, as nearly perfect as any human civilization could become, an ideal social order in which all elements of the population were secure and content.

Some pro-slavery propagandists even argued that slavery was such a valuable institution that it should extend to the North and include white workers there. George Fitzhugh of Virginia—in *Sociology for the South, or the Failure of Free Society* (1854), *Cannibals All* (1857), and other writings—claimed that all society lived on forced labor, that some of the greatest civilizations (ancient Greece, ancient Rome) had thrived because of it. In the South, they claimed, masters at least acknowledged responsibility for those whose labor they were exploiting. In the North, employers felt no obligation to care for their workers. Such arguments fueled the fears of those northern advocates of free labor who argued that the South was plotting to extend slavery everywhere, even into the factory system.

By the 1850s, some southern leaders had not only committed themselves to a militant pro-slavery ideology, they had also become convinced that they must silence their opponents. Some southern critics of slavery found it advisable to leave the region. Beginning in 1835 (when a Charleston mob destroyed sacks containing abolitionist literature in the city post office), southern postmasters generally refused to deliver antislavery mail. Southern state legislatures passed resolutions demanding that northern states suppress the "incendiary" agitation of the abolitionists. Southern representatives even managed for a time to impose a "gag rule" (adopted in 1836, repealed in 1844) on Congress, according to which all antislavery petitions would be tabled without being read. This growing intolerance of criticism further encouraged those northerners who warned of the "slave power conspiracy" against their liberties.

Buchanan and Depression

In this unpromising climate—with much of the nation passionately aroused by the Brooks assault on Sumner and the continuing violence in Kansas; with citizens of each section becoming increasingly militant in support of their own ideology—the presidential campaign of 1856 began. Democratic Party leaders wanted a candidate who had not made many enemies and who was not closely associated with the explosive question of

"Bleeding Kansas." They chose James Buchanan of Pennsylvania, a reliable party stalwart who as minister to England had been conveniently out of the country during the recent troubles. The Republicans, participating in their first presidential contest, denounced the Kansas-Nebraska Act and the expansion of slavery but also endorsed a program of internal improvements, thus combining the idealism of antislavery with the North's economic aspirations. They were as eager as the Democrats to present a safe candidate. They nominated John C. Fremont, who had made a national reputation as an explorer of the Far West and who had no political record. In the meantime, the Native American, or Know-Nothing, Party was beginning to break apart. At its convention, many northern delegates withdrew because the platform was not sufficiently firm in opposing the expansion of slavery. The remaining delegates nominated former president Millard Fillmore. The remnant of the Whig Party, those who could not bring themselves to support either Buchanan or Fremont, endorsed Fillmore as well.

After a heated, even frenzied campaign, Buchanan won a narrow victory. He polled a plurality but not a majority of the popular votes: 1,833,000 to 1,340,000 for Fremont and 872,000 for Fillmore. A slight shift of votes in Pennsylvania and Illinois would have thrown those states into the Republican column and elected Fremont. More significant, perhaps, was that Fremont, who attracted virtually no votes at all in the South, received a third of all votes cast. In the North, he outpolled all other candidates.

At the time of his inauguration Buchanan had been in public life for more than forty years, and at age sixty-five he was the oldest president, except for William Henry Harrison, ever to have taken office. Whether because of his age and physical infirmities or because of a more fundamental weakness of character, he became a painfully timid and indecisive president at a time when the nation cried out for strong, effective leadership.

In the year Buchanan took over, a financial panic struck the country, followed by a depression that lasted several years. European demand for American food had risen during the Crimean War of 1854–1856. When the war ended and that demand fell off, agricultural prices declined. In the North, the depression strengthened the Republican Party. Distressed manufacturers and farmers came to believe that the hard times were the result of the unsound policies of southern-controlled Democratic administrations. They advocated a high protective tariff (Congress had lowered the tariff again in 1857), a homestead act, and internal improvements—all measures the South opposed. The frustrated economic interests of the North were moving into an alliance with antislavery elements and thus into the Republican party.

The Dred Scott Decision

The Supreme Court of the United States now thrust itself into the sectional controversy with one of the most controversial decisions in its history: its ruling in the case of *Dred Scott* v. *Sanford*, handed down two days after Buchanan was inaugurated. Dred Scott had been a Missouri slave. His owner, an army surgeon, had taken Scott with him to Illinois, a free state, and to the Wisconsin Territory, where slavery was forbidden by the Missouri Compromise. Some abolitionists persuaded Scott to sue for his freedom in the Missouri courts on the grounds that residence in a free territory had made him a free man. The state supreme court decided against him. By then, the surgeon had died and Scott had become the legal property of his widow's brother, J. F. A. Sanford, an abolitionist who lived in New York. The shift of ownership from Missouri to New York allowed Scott's lawyers to move the case into the federal courts on the grounds that the suit lay between citizens of different states. There was no longer any doubt about Scott's eventual freedom; Sanford was determined to liberate him. The case was designed not to resolve Scott's future, but to affect the future of slavery in the territories.

The Supreme Court was so divided that it was unable to issue a single ruling on the case and released separate decisions on each of several major issues. Moreover, each of the justices wrote a separate opinion. The thrust of the rulings, however, was a major defeat for the antislavery movement and an affirmation of the South's argument that the Constitution guaranteed the existence of slavery. Chief Justice Roger Taney, who wrote one of the majority opinions, declared that Scott was not a citizen of Missouri or of the United States and hence could not bring a suit in the federal courts. According to Taney, no person of African descent could qualify as a citizen; indeed, blacks had virtually no rights at all under the Constitution. He went on to argue that Scott's sojourn in the North had not affected his status as a slave. Slaves were property, said Taney, and the Fifth Amendment prohibited Congress from taking property without "due process of law." Consequently, Congress possessed no authority to pass a law depriving persons of their slave property in the territories. The Missouri Compromise, therefore, had always been unconstitutional.

The ruling did nothing to challenge the right of an individual state to prohibit slavery within its borders, but the statement that the federal government was powerless to act on the issue was a drastic and startling one. Few judicial opinions have stirred as much popular anger and elation. Southern whites were ecstatic. The highest tribunal in the land had sanctioned parts of the most extreme southern argument. In the North, the decision produced widespread dismay. Republicans claimed that the decision deserved as much respect as a pronouncement by a group of political hacks "in any Washington bar room." When they secured control of the national government, they threatened, they would reverse the decision — by "packing" the Court with new members. Frederick Douglass, however, most accurately predicted the impact of *Dred Scott* when he said: "This very attempt to blot out forever the hopes of an enslaved people may be one necessary link in the chain of events preparatory to the complete overthrow of the whole slave system."

Deadlock over Kansas

President Buchanan endorsed the *Dred Scott* decision. At the same time, he sought to resolve the controversy over Kansas by supporting its admission to the Union as a slave state. In response, the pro-slavery territorial legislature called an election for delegates to a constitutional convention. The free-state residents refused to participate, claiming that the legislature had discriminated against them in drawing district lines. As a result, the pro-slavery forces won control of the convention in an election in which fewer than 10 percent of the eligible voters participated. The convention met in 1857 at Lecompton, framed a constitution legalizing slavery, and scheduled a referendum not on the constitution itself, but on the narrower question of whether to allow more slaves to enter Kansas. At the next election for the territorial legislature, antislavery groups turned out in force and won a majority. The new legislature promptly submitted the whole Lecompton constitution to the voters, who rejected it by more than 10,000 votes.

Both sides had resorted to fraud and violence, but it was clear nevertheless that a majority of the people of Kansas opposed slavery. Buchanan, however, ignored the evidence and urged Congress to admit Kansas under the Lecompton constitution. Stephen A. Douglas and other western Democrats refused to support the president's position, on the grounds that it violated the principle of popular sovereignty. "I care not whether [slavery] is voted down or voted up," Dou-

glas explained. But in Kansas, he said, the "fair expression of the will of the people" had clearly opposed slavery; only through "trickery and jugglery" had pro-slavery forces prevailed. Buchanan's proposal passed the Senate, but western Democrats helped block it in the House.

Finally, in April 1858, Congress approved a compromise: The Lecompton constitution would be resubmitted to the voters of Kansas. If the document won approval, Kansas would be admitted to the Union; if it was rejected, statehood would be postponed until the population of the territory reached the 93,600 level required for a representative in Congress. Again, Kansas voters decisively rejected the Lecompton constitution. Not until the closing months of Buchanan's administration in 1861, when a number of southern states had withdrawn from the Union, did Kansas finally enter the Union—as a free state.

The Emergence of Lincoln

Given the gravity of the sectional crisis, the congressional elections of 1858 took on a special importance. Of particular note was the U. S. Senate election in Illinois, which pitted Stephen A. Douglas, the most prominent northern Democrat, against Abraham Lincoln, the most skillful politician in the Republican Party.

Lincoln had been the leading Whig and was now the leading Republican in Illinois. But since he was not a national figure comparable to Douglas, he sought to increase his visibility by engaging Douglas in a series of debates. The Lincoln-Douglas debates attracted enormous crowds and received wide national attention. By the time they ended, Lincoln had become nationally prominent.

The content of the debates revealed the deep disagreements between the two parties in the North. Douglas, defending popular sovereignty, accused the Republicans of promoting a war of sections, of wishing to interfere with slavery in the South, and of advocating social equality of the races. Lincoln denied these charges (properly, since neither he nor his party had ever advocated any of these things). He, in turn, accused the Democrats of conspiring to extend slavery into the territories and possibly into the free states as well (a charge that was equally unfounded).

At the heart of the debate, however, was a basic difference on the issue of slavery. Douglas appeared to have no moral position on the issue; as evidence for that, Lincoln cited Douglas's statement that he did not care whether slavery was "voted up, or voted down"

in Kansas. Lincoln's opposition to slavery was more fundamental. If the nation could accept that African Americans were not entitled to basic human rights, he argued, then it could accept that other groups—immigrant laborers, for example—could be deprived of rights too. And if slavery were to extend into the western territories, he argued, opportunities for poor white laborers to better their lots there might be lost. The nation's future, he argued (reflecting the central idea of the Republican Party), rested on the spread of free labor.

Lincoln believed slavery was morally wrong, but he was not an abolitionist. That was in large part because he could not envision an alternative to it in the areas where it already existed. He shared the prevailing view among northern whites that the black race was not prepared (and perhaps never would be) to live on equal terms with whites. "We have a due regard to the actual presence of [slavery] amongst us and the difficul-

ties of getting rid of it in any satisfactory way and all the constitutional obligations thrown about it," he once said. He and his party would "arrest the further spread" of slavery, that is, prevent its expansion into the territories; they would not directly challenge it where it already existed.

Yet the implications of Lincoln's argument were more sweeping than this relatively moderate formula suggests, for both he and other Republicans believed that by restricting slavery to the South, they would be consigning the institution to its "ultimate extinction," that the institution would ultimately wither away. As he said in the most famous speech of the campaign:

> A house divided against itself cannot stand. I believe this government cannot endure permanently half slave and half free. I do not expect the Union to be dissolved—I do not expect the house to fall—but I do expect it will cease to be divided. It will become all one thing, or all the other.

In the debate at Freeport, Lincoln asked Douglas if the people of a territory could exclude slavery prior to the formation of a state constitution. Or, in other words, was popular sovereignty still workable despite the *Dred Scott* decision? Douglas replied that the people of a territory could legally exclude slavery before forming a state constitution simply by refusing to pass laws recognizing the right of slave ownership. Without such laws, he claimed, slavery could not exist. Douglas's reply became known as the Freeport Doctrine or, in the South, the Freeport Heresy. It satisfied his antislavery followers sufficiently to win him reelection to the Senate, but it destroyed his hopes of attracting support in the South and damaged his national political ambitions.

Outside Illinois, the elections went heavily against the Democrats, who lost ground in almost every northern state. The party retained control of the Senate but lost its majority in the House, with the result that the congressional sessions of 1858 and 1859 were bitterly deadlocked.

John Brown's Raid

The battles in Congress, however, were almost entirely overshadowed by a spectacular event that enraged and horrified the entire South and greatly hastened the rush toward disunion. In the fall of 1859, John Brown, the antislavery zealot whose bloody actions in Kansas had inflamed the crisis there, staged an even more dramatic episode, this time in the South itself. With encouragement and financial aid from some eastern abolitionists (later known as the "Secret Six"), he had been

JOHN BROWN
Even in this formal photographic portrait (taken in 1859, the last year of his life), John Brown conveys the fierce sense of righteousness that fueled his extraordinary activities in the fight against slavery. *(Library of Congress)*

making elaborate plans for over a year to seize a mountain fortress in Virginia to which slaves and free blacks might flee. From there, he believed, he could foment a slave insurrection in the South. On October 16, he and a group of eighteen followers attacked and seized control of a United States arsenal in Harpers Ferry, Virginia. But the slave uprising Brown hoped to inspire did not occur, and he quickly found himself besieged in the arsenal by citizens, local militia companies, and before long United States troops under the command of Robert E. Lee. After ten of his men were killed, Brown surrendered. He was promptly tried in a Virginia court for treason against the state, found guilty, and sentenced to death. On December 2, 1859, he was hanged. Six of his followers met a similar fate.

Probably no other single event had as much influence as the Harpers Ferry raid in convincing white southerners that they could not live safely in the Union. Despite their militant defense of slavery, many were consumed with one great, if often secret, fear: the possibility of a general slave insurrection. And John Brown's raid suggested to them that the North was now committed to producing just such an insurrection. Southern whites were wrong in believing that the raid had the support of the North generally or of the Republican Party; most northerners and most Republicans condemned Brown's actions. But correspondence seized when Brown was arrested made clear the extent of his broad ties to northern abolitionists. The southern fear of a northern conspiracy against slavery grew stronger when abolitionists such as Wendell Phillips and Ralph Waldo Emerson began to glorify Brown as a new saint and when his execution made him a martyr to thousands of northerners.

The Election of Lincoln

The presidential election of 1860 had the most momentous consequences of any in American history. It was also among the most complicated.

Battles between southerners, who demanded a strong endorsement of slavery, and westerners, who supported popular sovereignty, had torn apart the Democratic Party. The party convention met in April in Charleston, South Carolina—an inopportune location, given that South Carolina was the center of pro-slavery extremism. When the convention endorsed popular sovereignty, delegates from eight states in the lower South walked out. The remaining delegates could not agree on a presidential candidate and finally adjourned the convention to meet again in Baltimore in June. The decimated convention at Baltimore nominated Stephen Douglas for president. In the meantime,

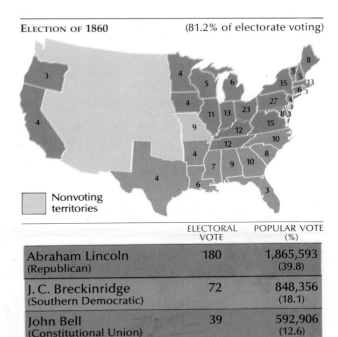

some disenchanted southern Democrats met in Richmond and nominated John C. Breckinridge of Kentucky.

The leaders of the Republican Party, in the meantime, were working to broaden the base of their party. No longer content to present themselves just as opponents of slavery, they now tried to appeal to every major interest group in the North that feared the South was blocking its economic aspirations. Their platform endorsed such traditional Whig positions as a high tariff, internal improvements, a homestead bill, and a railroad to the Pacific to be built with federal financial assistance. They supported the right of each state to decide the status of slavery within its borders. But they also insisted that neither Congress nor territorial legislatures could legalize slavery in the territories. Passing over more prominent candidates (among them William H. Seward of New York, the most prominent Republican in the country), the convention chose Abraham Lincoln as the party's presidential nominee. Lincoln was eminent enough to be respectable but (unlike Seward) obscure enough to have made few enemies. He was radical enough to please the antislavery faction in the party but conservative enough to satisfy many ex-Whigs.

ELECTION OF 1860   (81.2% of electorate voting)

Nonvoting territories

	ELECTORAL VOTE	POPULAR VOTE (%)
Abraham Lincoln (Republican)	180	1,865,593 (39.8)
J. C. Breckinridge (Southern Democratic)	72	848,356 (18.1)
John Bell (Constitutional Union)	39	592,906 (12.6)
Stephen A. Douglas (Northern Democratic)	12	1,382,713 (29.5)

SIGNIFICANT EVENTS

1818 U.S. and Great Britain sign treaty sharing rights to Oregon Country

1822 Mexico wins independence from Spain

Stephen F. Austin establishes first legal American settlement in Texas

1824 Mexico passes colonization law to attract American settlers to Texas

1826 American settlers in Texas revolt unsuccessfully against Mexican rule

1830 Mexican Government bars further American immigration into Texas

1833 Mexico drops Texas immigration ban

1836 Texas declares independence from Mexico

Battle of San Jacinto in Texas Revolution

1844 James K. Polk elected president

1845 Texas admitted to Union

1846 Oregon boundary dispute settled

United States declares war on Mexico

Congress approves tariff reduction

Wilmot Proviso introduced in Congress

Antislavery Free Soil Party formed

1848 Treaty of Guadalupe Hidalgo settles Mexican War

Zachary Taylor elected president

Gold discovered in Sacramento Valley, California, sparking gold rush

1850 Compromise of 1850 enacted

Taylor dies

Millard Fillmore succeeds him

California admitted to Union

1852 Franklin Pierce elected president

The Pro-Slavery Argument published

Harriet Beecher Stowe publishes *Uncle Tom's Cabin*

1853 Gadsden Purchase

1854 Kansas-Nebraska Act passed

Republican Party formed

Commodore Matthew Perry opens Japan to American trade

1855–1856 Violence breaks out in "Bleeding Kansas"

1856 Preston Brooks canes Charles Sumner

James Buchanan elected president

1857 George Fitzhugh publishes *Cannibals All*

Hinton Rowan Helper publishes *Impending Crisis of the South*

Supreme Court hands down *Dred Scott* decision

1858 Pro-slavery Lecompton constitution defeated by popular referendum in Kansas

Lincoln and Douglas debate

1859 John Brown raids Harpers Ferry

1860 Democratic Party splits

Lincoln elected president

Process of secession begins

But the Republicans were not yet conservative enough to satisfy all the former Whigs. In May, a group of them—mostly moderates from the North and the South, many of them conservative elder statesmen—met in Baltimore and formed the Constitutional Union Party in an effort to transcend sectional passions and create a truly national political movement. They nom-inated John Bell of Tennessee for president and Edward Everett of Massachusetts for vice president. They endorsed the Constitution and the Union and avoided taking a clear stand on the issue of slavery.

In the November election, Lincoln won the presidency with a majority of the electoral votes but only about two-fifths of the fragmented popular votes.

Moreover, the Republicans failed to win a majority in Congress; and, of course, they did not control the Supreme Court. Even so, the election of Lincoln became the final signal to many white southerners that their position in the Union was hopeless. And within a few weeks of Lincoln's victory, the process of dis-

union began—a process that would quickly lead to a prolonged and bloody war between two groups of Americans, each heir to more than a century of struggling toward nationhood, each now convinced that it shared no common ground with the other.

SUGGESTED READINGS

Westward Expansion. E. C. Barker, *Mexico and Texas, 1821–1835* (1928). Ray Allen Billington, *Westward Expansion,* rev. ed. (1974); *The Far Western Frontier, 1830–1860* (1956). William C. Brinkley, *The Texas Revolution* (1952). R. G. Cleland, *From Wilderness to Empire: A History of California, 1542–1900* (1944). R. L. Duffus, *The Santa Fe Trail* (1930). John M. Faragher, *Women and Men on the Overland Trail* (1979). T. R. Fehrenbach, *Lone Star: A History of Texas and the Texans* (1968). William H. Goetzmann, *Exploration and Empire* (1966). Norman A. Graebner, *Empire of the Pacific* (1955). J. S. Holiday, *The World Rushed In* (1981). Frederick Merk, *History of the Westward Movement* (1978); *Manifest Destiny and Mission in American History* (1963); *Fruits of Propaganda in the Tyler Administration* (1971); *Slavery and the Annexation of Texas* (1972); *The Oregon Question* (1967); *The Monroe Doctrine and American Expansionism, 1843–1849* (1966); Francis Parkman, *The Oregon Trail* (1849). R. W. Paul, *California Gold* (1947). Henry Nash Smith, *Virgin Land* (1950). John D. Unruh, *The Plains Across: The Overland Emigrants and the Trans-Mississippi West, 1840–1860* (1979). Albert K. Weinberg, *Manifest Destiny* (1935). O. O. Winther, *The Great Northwest,* rev. ed. (1950).

Expansion and the Mexican War. K. Jack Bauer, *The Mexican-American War, 1846–1848* (1974). Samuel F. Bemis, ed., *American Secretaries of State,* vols. 5 and 6 (1928). G. M. Brack, *Mexico Views Manifest Destiny, 1821–1846* (1975). S. V. Conner and O. B. Faulk, *North America Divided* (1971). C. W. Elliott, *Winfield Scott* (1937). Holman Hamilton, *Zachary Taylor, Soldier of the Republic* (1941). Robert W. Johnson, *To the Halls of Montezuma: The Mexican War in the American Imagination* (1985). Robert E. May, *The Southern Dream of a Caribbean Empire, 1854–1861* (1973). David M. Pletcher, *The Diplomacy of Annexation: Texas, Oregon, and the Mexican War* (1973). Basil Rauch, *American Interest in Cuba, 1848–1855* (1948). J. S. Reeves, *American Diplomacy Under Tyler and Polk* (1907). John H. Schroeder, *Mr. Polk's War: American Opposition and Dissent* (1973). Charles G. Sellers, *James K. Polk: Continentalist, 1843–1846* (1966). Otis A. Singletary, *The Mexican War* (1960). David J. Weber, *The Mexican Frontier, 1821–1846: The American Southwest Under Mexico* (1982).

The Sectional Crisis: General Studies. William J. Cooper, *The South and the Politics of Slavery, 1828–1856* (1978); *Liberty and Slavery* (1983). Avery Craven, *The Coming of the Civil War* (1942). William W. Freehling, *The Road to Disunion. Vol. 1: Secessionists at Bay, 1776–1854* (1990). Michael Holt, *The Political Crisis of the 1850s* (1978). James M. McPherson, *Ordeal by* *Fire* (1981); *Battle Cry of Freedom* (1988). Allan Nevins, *The Ordeal of the Union,* 2 vols. (1947); and *The Emergence of Lincoln,* 2 vols. (1950). Roy F. Nichols, *The Disruption of American Democracy* (1948). David Potter, *The Impending Crisis, 1848–1861* (1976). James G. Randall and David Donald, *The Civil War and Reconstruction,* rev. ed. (1969). Richard H. Sewell, *A House Divided: Sectionalism and the Civil War, 1848–1865* (1988).

The Compromise of 1850. Kinley J. Bauer, *Cotton Versus Conscience: Massachusetts Whig Politics and Southern Expansion, 1843–1858* (1967). Richard N. Current, *Daniel Webster and the Rise of National Conservatism* (1955). Robert F. Dalzell, Jr., *Daniel Webster and the Trial of American Nationalism, 1843–1852* (1973). Holman Hamilton, *Prologue to Conflict: The Crisis and Compromise of 1850* (1964); *Zachary Taylor: Soldier in the White House* (1951). Thelma Jennings, *The Nashville Convention* (1980). Robert W. Johannsen, *Stephen A. Douglas* (1973). Chaplain W. Morrison, *Democratic Politics and Sectionalism: The Wilmot Proviso Controversy* (1973). Robert V. Remini, *Henry Clay: Statesman for the Union* (1991). Charles M. Wiltse, *John C. Calhoun: Sectionalist, 1840–1850* (1951).

Sectional Crises in the 1850s. Dale Baum, *The Civil War Party System: The Case of Massachusetts 1848–1876* (1984). R. O. Boyer, *The Legend of John Brown* (1973). David Donald, *Charles Sumner and the Coming of the Civil War* (1960). Don E. Fehrenbacher, *The Dred Scott Case* (1978). Eric Foner, *Free Soil, Free Labor, Free Men* (1970); *Politics and Ideology in the Age of the Civil War* (1980). J. C. Furnas, *The Road to Harpers Ferry* (1959). Paul W. Gates, *Fifty Million Acres: Conflict over Kansas Land Policy, 1854–1890* (1954). William E. Gienapp, *The Origins of the Republican Party, 1852–1856* (1987). William Jenkins, *Pro-Slavery Thought in the Old South* (1935). James C. Malin, *The Nebraska Question* (1953). Truman Nelson, *The Old Man: John Brown at Harpers Ferry* (1973). Stephen Oates, *To Purge This Land with Blood: A Biography of John Brown* (1970). Benjamin Quarles, *Allies for Freedom* (1974). Kenneth M. Stampp, *America in 1857; A Nation on the Brink* (1990). Harvey Wish, *George Fitzhugh: Propagandist of the Old South* (1943). Gerald Wolff, *The Kansas-Nebraska Bill* (1977).

The Emergence of Lincoln. Richard N. Current, *The Lincoln Nobody Knows* (1958). David Donald, *Lincoln Reconsidered* (1956). Don E. Fehrenbacher, *Prelude to Greatness: Lincoln in the 1850's* (1962). George B. Forgie, *Patricide in the House Divided* (1979). Henry V. Jaffa, *Crisis of the House Divided: An Interpretation of the Lincoln-Douglas Debates* (1959).

PICKETT'S CHARGE

Union soldiers fight off a wave of Confederate troops, who had climbed the heavily defended Seminary Ridge in what became known as Pickett's Charge. Only a third of the 15,000 Confederate soldiers made it to the top of the ridge, and they were eventually forced to retreat. The bold if futile charge soon became an important part of the Southern legend of the "Lost Cause," which survived for many decades after the war ended. *(Bettmann)*

CHAPTER FOURTEEN

THE CIVIL WAR

B Y THE END OF 1860, the cords that had once bound the Union together seemed to have snapped. The almost mystical veneration of the Constitution and its framers was no longer working to unite the nation; most residents of the North and South—particularly after the controversial Dred Scott decision—now differed fundamentally over what the Constitution said and what the framers had meant. The romantic vision of America's great national destiny had ceased to be a unifying force; the two sections now defined that destiny in different and apparently irreconcilable terms. The stable two-party system could not dampen sectional conflict any longer; that system had collapsed in the 1850s, to be replaced by a new one that accentuated rather than muted regional controversy. Above all, the federal government was no longer the remote, unthreatening presence it once had been; the need to resolve the status of the territories had made it necessary for Washington to deal with sectional issues in a direct and forceful way. And thus, beginning in 1860, the divisive forces that had always existed within the United States were no longer counterbalanced by unifying forces. As a result, the Union began to dissolve.

THE SECESSION CRISIS

Almost as soon as the news of Abraham Lincoln's election reached the South, the militant leaders of the re-gion—the champions of the new concept of "Southern nationalism," men known both to their contemporaries and to history as the "fire-eaters"—began to demand an end to the Union.

The Withdrawal of the South

South Carolina, long the hotbed of Southern separatism, went first. It called a special convention, which voted unanimously on December 20, 1860, to withdraw the state from the Union. By the time Lincoln took office, six other states—Mississippi (January 9, 1861), Florida (January 10), Alabama (January 11), Georgia (January 19), Louisiana (January 26), and Texas (February 1)—had seceded. In February 1861, representatives of the seven seceded states met at Montgomery, Alabama, and formed a new nation: the Confederate States of America. The response from the North was confused and indecisive. President James Buchanan told Congress in December 1860 that no state had the right to secede from the Union but suggested that the federal government had no authority to stop a state if it did.

The seceding states immediately seized the federal property—forts, arsenals, government offices—within their boundaries. But at first they did not have sufficient military power to seize two fortified offshore military installations: Fort Sumter, on an island in the harbor of Charleston, South Carolina, garrisoned by a small force under Major Robert Anderson; and Fort Pickens in the harbor of Pensacola, Florida. South Car-

THE PROCESS OF SECESSION

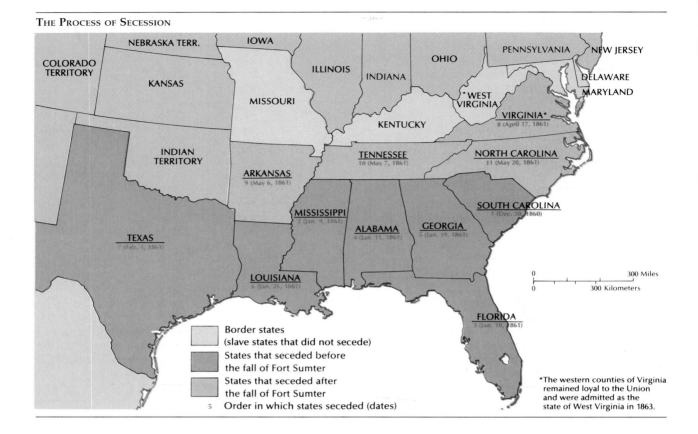

COLORADO TERRITORY

NEBRASKA TERR.

KANSAS

IOWA

ILLINOIS

INDIANA

OHIO

PENNSYLVANIA

NEW JERSEY

DELAWARE

MARYLAND

MISSOURI

*WEST VIRGINIA

VIRGINIA*
8 (April 17, 1861)

KENTUCKY

INDIAN TERRITORY

ARKANSAS
9 (May 6, 1861)

TENNESSEE
10 (May 7, 1861)

NORTH CAROLINA
11 (May 20, 1861)

MISSISSIPPI
2 (Jan. 9, 1861)

ALABAMA
4 (Jan. 11, 1861)

GEORGIA
5 (Jan. 19, 1861)

SOUTH CAROLINA
1 (Dec. 20, 1860)

TEXAS
7 (Feb. 1, 1861)

LOUISIANA
6 (Jan. 26, 1861)

FLORIDA
3 (Jan. 10, 1861)

0   300 Miles
0   300 Kilometers

Border states
(slave states that did not secede)

States that seceded before
the fall of Fort Sumter

States that seceded after
the fall of Fort Sumter

5   Order in which states seceded (dates)

*The western counties of Virginia
remained loyal to the Union
and were admitted as the
state of West Virginia in 1863.

olina sent commissioners to Washington to ask for the surrender of Sumter; but Buchanan, timid though he was, refused to yield it. Indeed, in January 1861 he ordered an unarmed merchant ship to proceed to Fort Sumter with additional troops and supplies. Confederate guns on shore fired at the vessel—the first shots between North and South—and turned it back. Still, neither section was yet ready to concede that war had begun. And in Washington, efforts began once more to forge a compromise.

The Failure of Compromise

Gradually, the compromise forces gathered behind a proposal first submitted by Senator John J. Crittenden of Kentucky and known as the Crittenden Compromise. It called for several constitutional amendments, which would guarantee the permanent existence of slavery in the slave states and would satisfy southern demands on such issues as fugitive slaves and slavery in the District of Columbia. But the heart of Critten-

den's plan was a proposal to reestablish the Missouri Compromise line in all present and future territory of the United States: Slavery would be prohibited north of the line and permitted south of it. Southerners in the Senate seemed willing to accept the plan, but the Republicans were not. The compromise would have required the Republicans to abandon their most fundamental position: that slavery not be allowed to expand.

And so nothing had been resolved when Abraham Lincoln arrived in Washington for his inauguration—sneaking into the city in disguise on a night train to avoid assassination as he passed through the slave state of Maryland. In his eloquent inaugural address, Lincoln laid down several basic principles. Since the Union was older than the Constitution, no state could leave it. Acts of force or violence to support secession were insurrectionary. And the government would "hold, occupy, and possess" federal property in the seceded states—a clear reference to Fort Sumter.

Conditions at Fort Sumter were deteriorating quickly. Union forces were running short of supplies; unless they received fresh provisions the fort would have to be evacuated. Lincoln believed that if he surrendered Sumter, his commitment to maintaining the Union would no longer be credible. So he sent a relief expedition to the fort, carefully informing the South Carolina authorities that there would be no attempt to send troops or munitions unless the supply ships met with resistance.

The new Confederate government now faced a dilemma. Permitting the expedition to land would seem to be a tame submission to federal authority. Firing on the ships or the fort would seem (to the North at least) to be aggression. But Confederate leaders finally decided that to appear cowardly would be worse than to appear belligerent, and they ordered General P. G. T. Beauregard, commander of Confederate forces at Charleston, to take the island, by force if necessary. When Anderson refused to surrender the fort, the Confederates bombarded it for two days, April 12–13, 1861. On April 14, Anderson surrendered. The Civil War had begun.

Almost immediately, Lincoln began mobilizing the North for war. And equally promptly, four more slave states seceded from the Union and joined the Confederacy: Virginia (April 17, 1861), Arkansas (May 6), Tennessee (June 8), and North Carolina (May 20). The four remaining slave states—Maryland, Delaware, Kentucky, and Missouri—cast their lot with the Union (under heavy political and even military pressure from Washington).

Was the outbreak of war inevitable? Was there anything that Lincoln (or those before him) could have done to settle the sectional conflict peaceably? Those questions have preoccupied historians for more than a century without resolution. (See "Where Historians Disagree," pp. 384–385.)

In one sense, the war was not inevitable. If the nation had not acquired new western territories in the 1840s, if the Supreme Court had ruled differently (or not at all) in the *Dred Scott* case, if Lincoln had not rejected the Crittenden Compromise, or if the North had agreed (as some urged) to let the South secede in peace—if any number of things had happened differently, there might have been no war. The real question, however, is not what hypothetical situations might have reversed the trend toward war but whether the preponderance of forces in the nation were acting to hold the nation together or to drive it apart. And by 1861, it seems clear that in both the North and the South, sectional antagonisms—whether justified or not—had risen to such a point that the existing terms of union had become untenable. People in both regions had come to believe that two distinct and incompatible civilizations had developed in the United States and that those civilizations were incapable of living together in peace. Ralph Waldo Emerson, speaking for much of the North, said at the time: "I do not see how a barbarous community and a civilized community can constitute one state." And a slaveowner, expressing the sentiments of much of the South, said shortly after the election of Lincoln: "These [Northern] people hate us, annoy us, and would have us assassinated by our slaves if they dared. They are a different people from us, whether better or worse, and there is no love between us. Why then continue together?"

That the North and the South had come to believe these things helped lead to secession and war. Whether these things were actually true—whether the North and the South were really as different and incompatible as they thought—is another question, one that the preparations for and conduct of the war help to answer.

The Opposing Sides

As the war began, only one thing was clear: all the important material advantages lay with the North. Its population was more than twice as large as that of the South (and nearly four times as large as the nonslave population of the South), so the Union had a much greater manpower reserve both for its armies and its work force. The North had an advanced industrial system and was able by 1862 to manufacture almost all its own war materials. The South had almost no industry at all and, despite impressive efforts to increase its manufacturing capacity, had to rely on imports from Europe throughout the war.

In addition, the North had a much better transportation system than did the South, and in particular more and better railroads: twice as much trackage as the Confederacy, and a much better integrated system of lines. During the war, moreover, the already inferior Confederate railroad system steadily deteriorated and by the beginning of 1864 had almost collapsed.

But in the beginning the North's material advantages were not as decisive as they appear in retrospect. The South was, for the most part, fighting a defensive war on its own land and thus had the advantage of local support and familiarity with the territory. The Northern armies, on the other hand, were fighting mostly within the South, with long lines of communications, amid hostile local populations, and with access only to the South's own inadequate transportation system. The commitment of the white population of the South to the war was, with limited exceptions, clear and firm. In the North, opinion about the war was more divided and support for it remained shaky until very near the end. A major Southern victory at any one

THE CAUSES OF THE CIVIL WAR

DEBATE OVER THE CAUSES of the Civil War began even before the war itself. In 1858, Senator William H. Seward of New York took note of the two competing explanations of the sectional tensions that were then inflaming the nation. On one side, he claimed, stood those who believed the sectional hostility to be "accidental, unnecessary, the work of interested or fanatical agitators." Opposing them stood those (like Seward himself) who believed there to be "an irrepressible conflict between opposing and enduring forces." Although he did not realize it at the time, Seward was drawing the outlines of a debate that would survive among historians for more than a century.

The "irrepressible conflict" argument was the first to dominate historical discussion. In the first decades after the fighting, histories of the Civil War generally reflected the views of Northerners who had themselves participated in the conflict. To them, the war appeared to be a stark moral conflict in which the South was clearly to blame, a conflict that arose inevitably as a result of the militant immorality of slave society. Henry Wilson's *History of the Rise and Fall of the Slave Power* (1872–1877) was a particularly vivid version of this moral interpretation of the war, which argued that Northerners had fought to preserve the Union and a system of free labor against the aggressive designs of the South.

A more temperate interpretation, but one that reached generally the same conclusions, emerged in the 1890s, when the first serious histories of the war began to appear. Preeminent among them was the seven-volume *History of the United States from the Compromise of 1850 . . .* (1893–1900) by James Ford Rhodes. Like Wilson and others, Rhodes identified slavery as the central, indeed virtually the only, cause of the war. "If the Negro had not been brought to America," he wrote, "the Civil War could not have occurred." And because the North and South had reached positions on the issue of slavery that were both irreconcilable and unalterable, the conflict had become "inevitable."

Although Rhodes placed his greatest emphasis on the moral conflict over slavery, he suggested that the struggle also reflected fundamental differences between the Northern and Southern economic systems. Not until the 1920s, however, did the idea of the war as an irrepressible *economic* rather than *moral* conflict receive full expression, from Charles and Mary Beard in *The Rise of American Civilization* (2 vols., 1927). Slavery, the Beards claimed, was not so much a social or cultural institution as an economic one, a labor system. There were, they insisted, "inherent antagonisms" between Northern industrialists and Southern planters. Each group sought to control the federal government so as to protect its own economic interests. Both groups used arguments over slavery and states' rights only as smoke screens.

The economic determinism of the Beards influenced a generation of historians in important ways, but ultimately most of those who believed the Civil War to have been "irrepressible" returned to an emphasis on social and cultural factors. Allan Nevins argued as much in his great work, *The Ordeal of the Union* (8 vols., 1947–1971). The North and the South, he wrote, "were rapidly becoming separate peoples." At the root of these cultural differences was the "problem of slavery," but the "fundamental assumptions, tastes, and cultural aims" of the two regions were diverging in other ways as well.

More recent proponents of the "irrepressible conflict" argument have taken different views of the Northern and Southern positions on the conflict but have been equally insistent on the role of culture and ideology in creating them. Eric Foner, in *Free Soil, Free Labor, Free Men* (1970) and other writings, emphasized the importance of the "free-labor ideology" to Northern opponents of slavery. The moral concerns of the abolitionists were not the dominant sentiments in the North,

WHERE HISTORIANS DISAGREE

he claimed. Instead, most Northerners (including Abraham Lincoln) opposed slavery largely because they feared it might spread to the North and threaten the position of free white laborers. Convinced that Northern society was superior to that of the South, increasingly persuaded of the South's intentions to extend the "slave power" beyond its existing borders, Northerners were embracing a viewpoint that made conflict almost inevitable. Eugene Genovese, writing of Southern slaveholders in *The Political Economy of Slavery* (1965), emphasized their conviction that the slave system provided a far more humane society than industrial labor, that the South had constructed "a special civilization built on the relation of master to slave." Just as Northerners were becoming convinced of a Southern threat to their economic system, so Southerners believed that the North had aggressive and hostile designs on the Southern way of life. Like Foner, therefore, Genovese saw in the cultural outlook of the section the source of an all but inevitable conflict.

Historians who argue that the conflict emerged naturally, even inevitably, out of a fundamental divergence between the sections have therefore disagreed markedly over whether moral, cultural, social, ideological, or economic issues were the primary causes of the Civil War. But they have been in general accord that the conflict between North and South was deeply embedded in the nature of the two societies, that the crisis that ultimately emerged was irrepressible. Other historians, however, have questioned that assumption and have argued that the Civil War could have been avoided, that the differences between North and South were not important enough to have necessitated war. Like proponents of the "irrepressible conflict" school, advocates of the war as a "repressible conflict" emerged first in the nineteenth century. President James Buchanan, for example, believed that extremist agitators were to blame for the conflict, and many Southerners writing of the war in the late nineteenth century claimed that only the fanaticism of the Republican Party could account for the conflict.

The idea of the war as avoidable did not gain wide recognition among historians until the 1920s and 1930s, when a group known as the "revisionists" began to offer new accounts of the origins of the conflict. One of the leading revisionists was James G. Randall, who saw in the social and economic systems of the North and the South no differences so fundamental as to require a war. Slavery, he suggested, was an essentially benign institution; it was in any case already "crumbling in the presence of nineteenth century tendencies." Only the political ineptitude of a "blundering generation" of leaders could account for the Civil War, he claimed. Avery Craven, another leading revisionist, placed more emphasis on the issue of slavery than had Randall. But in *The Coming of the Civil War* (1942) he too argued that slave laborers were not much worse off than Northern industrial workers, that the institution was already on the road to "ultimate extinction," and that war could therefore have been averted had skillful and responsible leaders worked to produce compromise.

More recent students of the war have kept elements of the revisionist interpretation alive by emphasizing the role of political agitation in the coming of the war. In 1960, for example, David Herbert Donald argued that the politicians of the 1850s were not unusually inept, but that they were operating in a society in which traditional restraints were being eroded in the face of the rapid extension of democracy. Thus the sober, statesmanlike solution of differences was particularly difficult. Michael Holt, in *The Political Crisis of the 1850s* (1978), emphasized the role of parties and especially the collapse of the second party system, rather than the irreconcilable differences between sections, in explaining the conflict, although he avoided placing blame on any one group. "Much of the story of the coming of the Civil War," he wrote, "is the story of the successful efforts of Democratic politicians in the South and Republican politicians in the North to keep the sectional conflict at the center of the political debate."

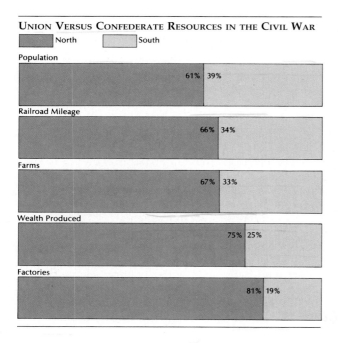

Union Versus Confederate Resources in the Civil War

North ▪ South ▫

Population
61% | 39%

Railroad Mileage
66% | 34%

Farms
67% | 33%

Wealth Produced
75% | 25%

Factories
81% | 19%

of several crucial moments might have proved decisive by breaking the North's will to continue the struggle. Finally, many Southerners believed that the dependence of the English and French textile industries on American cotton would require them to intervene on the side of the Confederacy.

THE MOBILIZATION OF THE NORTH

In the North, the war produced considerable discord, frustration, and suffering. But it also produced prosperity and economic growth by giving a major stimulus to both industry and agriculture.

Economic Measures

With Southern forces now gone from Congress, the Republican Party could exercise virtually unchallenged authority. During the war, it enacted an aggressively nationalistic program to promote economic development, particularly in the West. The Homestead Act of 1862 permitted any citizen or prospective citizen to claim 160 acres of public land and to purchase it for a small fee after living on it for five years. The Morrill

Act of the same year transferred substantial public acreage to the state governments, which were to sell the land and use the proceeds to finance public education. This act led to the creation of many new state colleges and universities, the so-called land-grant institutions. Congress also passed a series of tariff bills that by the end of the war had raised duties to the highest level in the nation's history—a great boon to domestic industries eager for protection from foreign competition.

Congress also moved to complete the dream of a transcontinental railroad. It created two new federally chartered corporations: the Union Pacific Railroad Company, which was to build westward from Omaha, and the Central Pacific, which was to build eastward from California. The two projects were to meet in the middle and complete the link. The government provided free public lands and generous loans to the companies.

The National Bank Acts of 1863–1864 created a new national banking system. Existing or newly formed banks could join the system if they had enough capital and were willing to invest one-third of it in government securities. In return, they could issue U.S. Treasury notes as currency. The new system eliminated much of the chaos and uncertainty in the nation's currency and created a uniform system of national bank notes.

More difficult than promoting economic growth was financing the war itself. The government tried to do so in three ways: by levying taxes, issuing paper currency, and borrowing. Congress levied new taxes on almost all goods and services; and in 1861 the government levied an income tax for the first time, with rates that eventually rose to 10 percent on incomes above $5,000. But taxation raised only a small proportion of the funds necessary for financing the war, and strong popular resistance prevented the government from raising the rates.

At least equally controversial was the printing of paper currency, or "greenbacks." The new currency was backed not by gold or silver, but simply by the good faith and credit of the government (much like today's currency). The value of the greenbacks fluctuated according to the fortunes of the Northern armies. Early in 1864, with the war effort bogged down, a greenback dollar was worth only 39 percent of a gold dollar. Even at the close of the war, it was worth only 67 percent of a gold dollar. Because of the difficulty of making purchases with this uncertain currency, the government used greenbacks sparingly. The Treasury issued only $450 million worth of paper currency—a small proportion of the cost of the war but enough to produce significant inflation.

WAR BY RAILROAD
Union soldiers pose beside a mortar mounted on a railroad car in July 1864, during the siege of Petersburg, Virginia. Six days after this photograph was taken, Union forces exploded a huge mine in a futile effort to take the city. After that, Grant dug in for a nine-month siege. Petersburg did not fall until April 2, 1865, only a week before the end of the war. *(National Archives)*

By far the largest source of financing for the war was loans from the American people. In previous wars, the government had sold bonds only to banks and to a few wealthy investors. Now, however, the Treasury persuaded ordinary citizens to buy over $400 million worth of bonds—the first example of mass financing of a war in American history. Still, bond purchases by individuals constituted only a small part of the government's borrowing, which in the end totaled $2.6 billion. Most of the loans came from banks and large financial interests.

Raising the Union Armies

Over 2 million men served in the Union armed forces during the course of the Civil War. But at the begin-ning of 1861, the regular army of the United States consisted of only 16,000 troops, many of them stationed in the West to protect white settlers from Indians. So the Union, like the Confederacy, had to raise its army mostly from scratch. Lincoln called for an increase of 23,000 in the regular army, but the bulk of the fighting, he knew, would have to be done by volunteers in state militias. When Congress convened in July 1861, it authorized enlisting 500,000 volunteers for three-year terms (as opposed to the customary three-month terms).

This voluntary system of recruitment produced adequate forces only briefly. After the first flush of enthusiasm for the war, enlistments declined. By March 1863, Congress was forced to pass a national draft law. Virtually all young adult males were eligible to be drafted; but a man could escape service by hiring some-

one to go in his place or by paying the government a fee of $300. Only about 46,000 men were ever actually conscripted, but the draft greatly increased voluntary enlistments.

To a people accustomed to a remote and inactive national government, conscription was strange and ominous. Opposition to the law was widespread, particularly among laborers, immigrants, and Democrats opposed to the war (known as "Peace Democrats"). Occasionally it erupted into violence. Demonstrators against the draft rioted in New York City for four days in July 1863, after the first names were selected for conscription. Over 100 people died, mostly blacks. Irish workers were at the center of the violence. They were angry because black strikebreakers had been used against them in a recent longshoremen's strike; and they blamed African Americans generally for the war, which they thought was being fought for the benefit of slaves who would soon be competing with white workers for jobs. The rioters lynched a dozen African Americans, burned down homes and businesses, mostly those of free blacks, and even destroyed an orphanage for African-American children. Only the arrival of federal troops subdued the rioters.

Wartime Politics

When Abraham Lincoln arrived in Washington early in 1861, many politicians—noting his lack of national experience and his folksy, unpretentious manner—considered him a minor politician from the prairies, a man whom the real leaders of his party would easily control. But the new president moved quickly to establish his own authority. He assembled a cabinet representing every faction of the Republican Party and every segment of Northern opinion—men of exceptional prestige and influence and in some cases arrogance, several of whom believed that they, not Lincoln, should be president. Lincoln moved boldly as well to use the war powers of the presidency, ignoring inconvenient parts of the Constitution because, he said, it would be foolish to lose the whole by being afraid to disregard a part. He sent troops into battle without asking Congress for a declaration of war. (Lincoln insisted on calling the conflict a domestic insurrection, which required no formal declaration of war; to ask for a declaration would, he believed, constitute implicit recognition of the Confederacy as an independent nation.) He increased the size of the regular army without receiving legislative authority to do so. He unilaterally proclaimed a naval blockade of the South.

Lincoln's greatest political problem was the widespread popular opposition to the war, mobilized by factions in the Democratic Party. The Peace Democrats (or, as their enemies called them, "Copperheads") feared that agriculture and the Northwest were losing influence to industry and the East and that Republican nationalism was eroding states' rights. Lincoln used extraordinary methods to suppress them. He ordered military arrests of civilian dissenters and suspended the right of habeas corpus (the right of an ar-

HANGING A NEGRO IN CLARKSON STREET.

THE NEW YORK CITY DRAFT RIOT, 1863
Opposition to the Civil War draft was widespread in the
North and in July 1863 produced a violent four-day uprising in New York City in which as many as 100 people
died. The riot began on July 13 with a march by 4,000 men,
mostly poor Irish laborers, who were protesting the provisions by which some wealthy people could be exempted
from conscription. "Rich man's war, poor man's fight," the
demonstrators cried. Many New Yorkers also feared that
the war would drive black workers north to compete for
their jobs. The demonstration turned violent when officials
began drawing names for the draft. The crowd burned the
draft building and then split into factions. Some rioters attacked symbols of wealth: exclusive shops and mansions.
Others terrorized black neighborhoods and lynched scores
of residents. This contemporary engraving depicts one
such lynching. Only by transferring five regiments to the
city from Gettysburg (less than two weeks after the great
battle there) was the government able to restore order.
(The Granger Collection)

rested person to a speedy trial). At first, Lincoln used
these methods only in sensitive areas such as the border states; but in 1862, he proclaimed that all persons
who discouraged enlistments or engaged in disloyal
practices were subject to martial law. In all, more than
13,000 persons were arrested and imprisoned for varying periods. The most prominent Copperhead in the
country—Clement L. Vallandigham, a member of Congress from Ohio—was seized by military authorities
and exiled to the Confederacy after he made a speech

claiming that the purpose of the war was to free the
blacks and enslave the whites. Lincoln defied all efforts to curb his authority to suppress opposition. He
even defied the Supreme Court. When Chief Justice
Taney issued a writ (*Ex parte Merryman*) requiring him
to release an imprisoned Maryland secessionist leader,
Lincoln simply ignored it. (After the war, in 1866, the
Supreme Court held, in *Ex parte Milligan,* that military
trials in areas where the civil courts existed were unconstitutional.)

The presidential election of 1864 occurred, therefore, in the midst of considerable political dissension.
The Republicans had suffered heavy losses in 1862,
and in response leaders of the party tried to create a
broad coalition of all the groups that supported the
war. They called the new organization the Union
Party, but in reality it was little more than the Republican Party and a small faction of War Democrats. The
Union Party nominated Lincoln for another term as
president and Andrew Johnson of Tennessee, a War
Democrat who had opposed his state's decision to secede, for the vice presidency.

The Democrats nominated George B. McClellan, a
celebrated former Union general who had been relieved of his command by Lincoln, and adopted a platform denouncing the war and calling for a truce. Mc-
Clellan repudiated that demand, but the Democrats
were clearly the peace party in the campaign, trying
to profit from growing war weariness and from the
Union's discouraging military position in the summer
of 1864.

At this crucial moment, however, several Northern
military victories, particularly the capture of Atlanta,
Georgia, early in September, rejuvenated Northern
morale and boosted Republican prospects. Lincoln
won reelection comfortably, with 212 electoral votes to
McClellan's 21; the president carried every state except
Kentucky, New Jersey, and Delaware. But Lincoln's
lead in the popular vote was a more modest 10 percent. Had Union victories not occurred when they did,
and had Lincoln not made special arrangements to allow Union troops to vote, the Democrats might have
won.

The Politics of Emancipation

Despite their surface unity in 1864 and their general
agreement on most economic matters, the Republicans
disagreed sharply on the issue of slavery. Radicals—
led in Congress by such men as Representative
Thaddeus Stevens of Pennsylvania and Senators
Charles Sumner of Massachusetts and Benjamin Wade
of Ohio—wanted to use the war to abolish slavery im-

mediately and completely. Conservatives favored a slower, more gradual, and, they believed, less disruptive process for ending slavery; in the beginning, at least, they had the support of the president.

Despite Lincoln's cautious view of emancipation, momentum began to gather behind it early in the war. In 1861, Congress passed the Confiscation Act, which declared that all slaves used for "insurrectionary" purposes (that is, in support of the Confederate military effort) would be considered freed. Subsequent laws in the spring of 1862 abolished slavery in the District of Columbia and in the western territories, and compensated owners. In July 1862, the Radicals pushed through Congress the second Confiscation Act, which declared free the slaves of persons aiding and supporting the insurrection (whether or not the slaves themselves were doing so) and authorized the president to employ African Americans, including freed slaves, as soldiers.

As the war progressed, much of the North seemed slowly to accept emancipation as a central war aim; nothing less, many believed, would justify the enormous sacrifices of the struggle. As a result, the Radicals increased their influence within the Republican Party—a development that did not go unnoticed by the president, who decided to seize the leadership of the rising antislavery sentiment himself.

On September 22, 1862, after the Union victory at the Battle of Antietam, the president announced his intention to use his war powers to issue an executive order freeing all slaves in the Confederacy. And on January 1, 1863, he formally signed the Emancipation Proclamation, which declared forever free slaves in all areas of the Confederacy except those already under Union control: Tennessee, western Virginia, and southern Louisiana. The proclamation did not apply to the border slave states, which had never seceded from the Union and which were not therefore subject to the president's war powers.

The immediate effect of the proclamation was limited, since it applied only to slaves still under Confederate control. But the document was of great importance nevertheless, because it clearly and irrevocably established that the war was being fought not only to preserve the Union but also to eliminate slavery. Eventually, as federal armies occupied much of the South, the proclamation became a practical reality and led directly to the freeing of thousands of slaves. About 186,000 of these emancipated blacks served as soldiers, sailors, and laborers for the Union forces (alongside free blacks from the North, who had served in the Union army almost from the start of the war). Even in areas not directly affected by the proclamation, the antislavery impulse gained strength. By the end of the war, slavery had been abolished in two Union slave states, Maryland and Missouri, and in three Confederate states occupied by Union forces: Tennessee, Arkansas, and Louisiana. The final step came in 1865, when Congress approved and the necessary states ratified the Thirteenth Amendment, abolishing slavery as an institution in all parts of the United States. After more than two centuries, legalized slavery finally ceased to exist in the United States.

The War and Economic Development

The Civil War did not, as some historians used to claim, transform the North from an agrarian to an industrial society. Industrialization was already far advanced when the war began, and in some areas, the war actually retarded growth—by cutting manufacturers off from their Southern markets and sources of raw material, and by diverting labor and resources to military purposes.

On the whole, however, the war sped the economic development of the North. That was in part a result of the political dominance of the Republican Party and its promotion of nationalistic economic legislation. But it was also because the war itself required the expansion of certain sectors of the economy. Coal production increased by nearly 20 percent during the war. Railroad facilities improved—mainly through the adoption of a standard gauge (track width) on new lines. The loss of farm labor to the military forced many farmers to increase the mechanization of agriculture.

The war was a difficult experience for many American workers. Industrial laborers experienced a substantial loss of purchasing power, as prices in the North rose by more than 70 percent during the war while wages rose only about 40 percent. That was partly because liberalized immigration laws permitted a flood of new workers into the labor market and helped keep wages low. It was also because the increasing mechanization of production eliminated the jobs of many skilled workers. One result of these hardships was a substantial increase in union membership in many industries and the creation of several national unions, for coal miners, railroad engineers, and others—organizations bitterly opposed and rigorously suppressed by employers.

Women, Nursing, and the War

Women found themselves, either by choice or by necessity, thrust into new and often unfamiliar roles during the war. They took over positions vacated by men

THE U.S. SANITARY COMMISSION
Mathew Brady took this photograph of female nurses and Union soldiers standing before an infirmary at Brandy Station, Virginia, near Petersburg, in 1864. The infirmary was run by the U.S. Sanitary Commission, the government-supported nursing corps that became indispensable to the medical care of wounded soldiers during the Civil War. *(Bettmann)*

and worked as teachers, retail sales clerks, office workers, and mill and factory hands. They were responding not only to the needs of employers for additional labor, but to their own, often desperate, need for money. With husbands and fathers away in the army, many women were left destitute—particularly since military pay was low and erratic.

Above all, women entered nursing, a field previously dominated by men. The U.S. Sanitary Commission, an organization of civilian volunteers led by Dorothea Dix, mobilized large numbers of female nurses to serve in field hospitals. By the end of the war, women were the dominant force in nursing; by the end of the century, nursing had become an almost entirely female profession. Female nurses not only cared for patients but performed other tasks considered appropriate for women: cooking, cleaning, and laundering.

Female nurses encountered considerable resistance from male doctors, many of whom considered women too weak for medical work and who, in any case, found the sight of women taking care of strange men inappropriate. The Sanitary Commission tried to counter such arguments by attributing to nursing many of the domestic ideals that American society attributed to women's work in the home. Women as nurses were to play the same maternal, nurturing, instructive role they played as wives and mothers. The commission was, according to its own literature, "a great artery that bears the people's love to the army." Just as women cared for sick people at home, so they could—and must—do so in the military hospitals. "The right of

woman to her sphere, which includes housekeeping, cooking, and nursing, has never been disputed," one Sanitary Commission official insisted. But not all women who worked for the commission were content with a purely maternal role; some challenged the dominance of men in the organization and even stood up against doctors whom they considered incompetent, increasing the resentment felt toward them by many men. In the end, though, the work of female nurses was so indispensable to the military that the complaints of male doctors were irrelevant.

Nurses, and many others, found the war a liberating experience, in which (as one Sanitary Commission nurse later wrote) the American woman "had developed potencies and possibilities of which she had been unaware and which surprised her, as it did those who witnessed her marvelous achievement." Some women, especially those who had been committed to feminist causes earlier, came to see the war as an opportunity to win support for their own goals. Elizabeth Cady Stanton and Susan B. Anthony, who together founded the National Woman's Loyal League in 1863, worked simultaneously for the abolition of slavery and the awarding of suffrage to women. Clara Barton, who was active during the war in collecting and distributing medical supplies and who later became an important figure in the nursing profession (and a founder of the American Red Cross), said in 1888: "At the war's end, woman was at least fifty years in advance of the normal position which continued peace would have assigned her." That may have been a considerable exaggeration; but it captured the degree to which many women looked back on the war as a crucial moment in the redefinition of female roles and in the awakening of a sense of independence and new possibilities.

Whatever nursing may have done for the status of women, it had an enormous impact on the medical profession and on the treatment of wounded soldiers during the war. The U.S. Sanitary Commission not only organized women to serve at the front, it also funneled medicine and supplies to badly overtaxed field hospitals. The commission also (as its name suggests) helped spread ideas about the importance of sanitary conditions in hospitals and clinics and probably contributed to the relative decline of death by disease in the Civil War. Nevertheless twice as many soldiers died of diseases—malaria, dysentery, typhoid, gangrene, and others—as died in combat during the war. Even minor injuries could lead to fatal infections.

THE MOBILIZATION OF THE SOUTH

Early in February 1861, representatives of the seven states that had seceded from the Union met at Montgomery, Alabama, to create a new Southern nation. When Virginia seceded several months later, the government of the Confederacy moved to Richmond—one of the few Southern cities large enough to house a national government.

Many Southerners boasted loudly of the differences between their new nation and the nation they had left. Those differences were real. But there were also important similarities between the Union and the Confederacy, which became particularly clear as the two sides mobilized for war: similarities in their political systems, in the methods they used for financing the war and conscripting troops, and in the way they fought.

The Confederate Government

The Confederate constitution was almost identical to the Constitution of the United States, with several significant exceptions: It explicitly acknowledged the sovereignty of the individual states (although not the right of secession); and it specifically sanctioned slavery and made its abolition (even by one of the states) practically impossible.

The constitutional convention at Montgomery named a provisional president and vice president: Jefferson Davis of Mississippi and Alexander H. Stephens of Georgia, who were later chosen by the general elec-

torate, without opposition, for six-year terms. Davis had been a moderate, but not an extreme, secessionist before the war. Stephens had argued against secession. The Confederate government, like the Union government, was dominated throughout the war by men of the center. Also like the Union, it was dominated less by the old aristocracy of the East than by the newer aristocrats of the West, of whom Davis was the most prominent example.

Davis was, in the end, an unsuccessful president. He was a reasonably able administrator and the dominating figure in his government, encountering little interference from the generally tame members of his unstable cabinet and serving as his own secretary of war. But he rarely provided genuinely national leadership. He spent too much time on routine items; and unlike Lincoln, he displayed a punctiliousness about legal and constitutional niceties inappropriate to the needs of a new nation at war. One shrewd Confederate official wrote: "All the revolutionary vigor is with the enemy. . . . With us timidity—hair splitting."

There were no formal political parties in the Confederacy, but its congressional and popular politics were rife with dissension nevertheless. Some white Southerners (and of course most African Americans who were aware of the course of events) opposed secession and war altogether. Many white people in poorer "backcountry" and "upcountry" regions, where slavery was limited, refused to recognize the new Confederate government or to serve in the Southern army; some worked or even fought for the Union. Most white Southerners supported the war, but as in the North many were openly critical of the government and the military, particularly as the tide of battle turned against the South and the Confederate economy decayed.

Money and Manpower

Financing the Confederate war effort was a monumental and ultimately impossible task. It involved creating a national revenue system in a society unaccustomed to significant tax burdens. It depended on a small and unstable banking system that had little capital to lend. Because most wealth in the South was invested in slaves and land, liquid assets were scarce; and the Confederacy's only specie—seized from U.S. mints located in the South -- was worth only about $1 million.

The Confederate Congress tried at first not to tax the people directly but to requisition funds from the individual states. But most of the states were also unwilling to tax their citizens and paid their shares, when they paid them at all, with bonds or notes of dubious worth. In 1863, therefore, the congress enacted an in-

CONFEDERATE VOLUNTEERS
Young Southern soldiers posed for this photograph in 1861, shortly before the first Battle of Bull Run. The Civil War was the first major military conflict in the age of photography, and it launched the careers of many of America's early photographers. *(Cook Collection, Valentine Museum)*

come tax—which planters could pay "in kind" (as a percentage of their produce). But taxation never provided the Confederacy with very much revenue; it produced only about 1 percent of the government's total income. Borrowing was not much more successful. The Confederate government issued bonds in such vast amounts that the public lost faith in them and stopped buying them, and efforts to borrow money in Europe using cotton as collateral fared no better.

As a result the Confederacy had to pay for the war through the least stable, most destructive form of financing: paper currency, which it began issuing in 1861. By 1864, the Confederacy had issued the staggering total of $1.5 billion in paper money, more than twice what the Union had produced. And unlike the Union, the Confederacy did not establish a uniform currency system; the national government, states, cities, and private banks all issued their own notes, producing widespread chaos and confusion. The result was a disastrous inflation, far worse than anything the North experienced. Prices in the North rose 80 per-

cent in the course of the war; in the South they rose 9,000 percent, with devastating effects on the new nation's morale.

Like the United States, the Confederacy first raised a military by calling for volunteers. And as in the North, by the end of 1861 voluntary enlistments were declining. In April 1862, therefore, the congress enacted a Conscription Act, which subjected all white males between the ages of eighteen and thirty-five to military service for three years. As in the North, a draftee could avoid service if he furnished a substitute. But since the price of substitutes was high, the provision aroused such opposition from poorer whites that it was repealed in 1863. Even more controversial was the exemption from the draft of one white man on each plantation with twenty or more slaves, a provision that caused smaller farmers to complain: "It's a rich man's war but a poor man's fight." Many more white Southerners were exempted from military service than Northerners.

Even so, conscription worked for a time. At the end of 1862, about 500,000 men were in the Confederate military. (A total of approximately 900,000 served in the course of the entire war.) That number did not include the many slave men and women recruited by the military to perform such services as cooking, laundry, and manual labor, hence freeing additional white manpower for fighting. (Only late in the war, when the military situation was becoming desperate, was there any effort to involve slaves in combat.) After 1862, however, conscription began producing fewer men. That was in part because the Union had by then begun to seize large areas of the Confederacy and thus had cut off much of the population from conscription or recruitment. The armed forces steadily decreased in size.

As 1864 opened, the government faced a critical manpower shortage. In a desperate move, the Confederate Congress began trying to draft men as young as seventeen and as old as fifty. But in a nation suffering from intense war weariness, where many had concluded that defeat was inevitable, nothing could attract or retain an adequate army any longer. In 1864–1865 there were 100,000 desertions. In a frantic final attempt to raise men, the congress authorized the conscription of 300,000 slaves, but the war ended before the government could attempt this incongruous experiment.

States' Rights Versus Centralization

The greatest source of division in the South, however, was not differences of opinion over the war, but the doctrine of states' rights. States' rights had become such a cult among many white Southerners that they resisted virtually all efforts to exert national authority, even those necessary to win the war. States' rights enthusiasts obstructed the conduct of the war in many ways. They restricted Davis's ability to impose martial law and suspend habeas corpus. They obstructed conscription. Recalcitrant governors such as Joseph Brown of Georgia and Zebulon M. Vance of North Carolina tried at times to keep their own troops apart from the Confederate forces and insisted on hoarding surplus supplies for their own states' militias.

But the Confederate government did make substantial strides in centralizing power in the South. By the end of the war, the Confederate bureaucracy was larger than its counterpart in Washington. The national government experimented, successfully for a time, with a "food draft"—which permitted soldiers to feed themselves by seizing crops from farms in their path. The government impressed slaves, often over the objections of their owners, to work as laborers on military projects. The Confederacy seized control of the railroads and shipping; it imposed regulations on industry; it limited corporate profits. States' rights sentiment was a significant handicap, but the South nevertheless took dramatic steps in the direction of centralization—becoming in the process increasingly like the region whose institutions it was fighting to escape.

Economic and Social Effects of the War

The war had a devastating effect on the economy of the South. It cut off Southern planters and producers from the markets in the North on which they had depended; it made the sale of cotton overseas much more difficult; it robbed farms and industries that did not have large slave populations of a male work force, leaving some of them unable to function effectively. While in the North production of all goods, agricultural and industrial, increased somewhat during the war, in the South it declined by more than a third.

Most of all, perhaps, the fighting itself wreaked havoc on the Southern economy. Almost all the major battles of the war occurred within the Confederacy; both armies spent most of their time on Southern soil. As a result of the savage fighting, the South's already inadequate railroad system was nearly destroyed; much of its most valuable farmland, and many of its most successful plantations, were ruined by Union troops (especially in the last year of the war).

Once the Northern naval blockade became effective, the South experienced massive shortages of almost everything. The region was overwhelmingly agricultural, but since it had concentrated so single-mindedly on producing cotton and other export crops, it did not grow enough food to meet its own needs. And despite the efforts of women and slaves to keep farms functioning, the departure of white male workers seriously diminished the region's ability to keep up what food production there had been. Large numbers of doctors were conscripted to serve the needs of the military, leaving many communities without any medical care. Blacksmiths, carpenters, and other craftsmen were similarly in short supply.

As the war continued, the shortages, the inflation, and the suffering created increasing instability in Southern society. There were major food riots, some led by women, in Georgia, North Carolina, and Alabama in 1863, as well as a large demonstration in Richmond that quickly turned violent. Resistance to conscription, food impressment, and taxation increased throughout the Confederacy, as did hoarding and black-market commerce.

In economic terms, in other words, the war affected the South very differently from the way it affected the North. In other respects, however, the war transformed Confederate society in many of the same ways that it was changing the society of the Union. It was particularly significant for Southern women. Because so many men left the farms and plantations to fight, the task of keeping families together and maintaining agricultural production fell increasingly to women. Slaveowners' wives often became responsible for managing large slave work forces; the wives of more modest farmers learned to plow fields and harvest crops. Substantial numbers of females worked in government agencies in Richmond. Even larger numbers chose nursing, both in hospitals and in temporary facilities set up to care for wounded soldiers. Others became schoolteachers.

The long-range results of the war for Southern women are more difficult to measure but equally profound. The experience of the 1860s almost certainly forced many women to question the prevailing Southern assumption that females were unsuited for certain activities, that they were not fit to participate actively in the public sphere. A more concrete legacy was the decimation of the male population and the creation of a major gender imbalance in the region. After the war, there were many thousands more women in the South than men. In Georgia, for example, women outnumbered men by 36,000 in 1870; in North Carolina by 25,000. The result, of course, was a large number of unmarried or widowed women who, both during and after the war, had no choice but to find employment—thus, by necessity rather than choice, expanding the number of acceptable roles for women in Southern society.

Even before emancipation, the war had far-reaching effects on the lives of slaves. Confederate leaders were even more terrified of slave revolts during the war than they had been in peacetime, and they enforced slave codes and other regulations with particular severity. Even so, many slaves—especially those near the front—found ways to escape their masters and cross behind Union lines in search of freedom. Those who had no realistic avenue for escape seemed, to their owners at least, to be particularly resistant to authority during the war. That was in part because on many plantations, the masters and overseers for whom they were accustomed to working were away at war; they found it easier to resist the authority of the women and boys left behind to manage the farms.

STRATEGY AND DIPLOMACY

Militarily, the initiative in the Civil War lay mainly with the North, since it needed to defeat the Confederacy while the South needed only to avoid defeat. Diplomatically, however, the initiative lay with the South. It needed to enlist the recognition and support of foreign governments; the Union wanted only to preserve the status quo.

The Commanders

The most important Union military commander was Abraham Lincoln, whose previous military experience consisted only of brief service in his state militia during the Black Hawk War. Lincoln was a successful commander in chief because he realized that numbers and resources were on his side, and because he took advantage of the North's material advantages. He realized, too, that the proper objective of his armies was the destruction of the Confederate armies and not the occupation of Southern territory. It was well that Lincoln had a good grasp of strategy, because many of his generals did not. The problem of finding adequate commanders for the troops in the field plagued him throughout the first three years of the war.

From 1861 to 1864, Lincoln tried time and again to find a chief of staff capable of orchestrating the Union war effort. He turned first to General Winfield Scott, the aging hero of the Mexican War. But Scott was unprepared for the magnitude of the new conflict and retired on November 1, 1861. Lincoln replaced him with the young George B. McClellan, commander of the Union armies in the east, the Army of the Potomac; but the proud, arrogant McClellan had a wholly inadequate grasp of strategy and in any case returned to the field in March 1862. For most of the rest of the year,

Lincoln had no chief of staff at all. And when he finally appointed General Henry W. Halleck to the post, he found him an ineffectual strategist who left all substantive decision making to the president. Not until March 1864 did Lincoln finally find a general he trusted to command the war effort: Ulysses S. Grant, who shared Lincoln's belief in making enemy armies and resources, not enemy territory, the target of military efforts. Lincoln gave Grant a relatively free hand, but the general always submitted at least the broad outlines of his plans to the president for advance approval.

Lincoln's (and later Grant's) handling of the war effort faced constant scrutiny from the Committee on the Conduct of the War, a joint investigative committee of the two houses of Congress and the most powerful voice the legislative branch has ever had in formulating war policies. Established in December 1861 and chaired by Senator Benjamin F. Wade of Ohio, it complained constantly of the insufficient ruthlessness of Northern generals, which Radicals on the committee attributed (largely inaccurately) to a secret sympathy among the officers for slavery. The committee's efforts often seriously interfered with the conduct of the war.

Southern command arrangements centered on President Davis, who unlike Lincoln was a trained professional soldier but who, also unlike Lincoln, failed ever to create an effective command system. Early in 1862, Davis named General Robert E. Lee as his principal military adviser. But in fact, Davis had no intention of sharing control of strategy with anyone. After a few months, Lee left Richmond to command forces in the field, and for the next two years Davis planned strategy alone. In February 1864, he named General Braxton Bragg as a military adviser; but Bragg never provided much more than technical advice. Not until February 1865 did the Confederate Congress create the formal position of general in chief. Davis named Lee to the post but made clear that he expected to continue to make all basic decisions. In any case, the war ended before this last command structure had time to take shape.

At lower levels of command, men of markedly similar backgrounds controlled the war in both the North and the South. Many of the professional officers on both sides were graduates of the United States Military Academy at West Point and the United States Naval Academy at Annapolis and thus had been trained in similar ways. Many were closely acquainted, even friendly, with their counterparts on the other side. And all were imbued with the classic, eighteenth-century models of warfare that the service academies still taught. The most successful officers were those who, like Grant and Sherman, were able to see beyond their academic training and envision a new kind of

ULYSSES S. GRANT
One observer said of Grant (seen here posing for a photograph during the Wilderness campaign of 1864): "He habitually wears an expression as if he had determined to drive his head through a brick wall, and was about to do it." It was an apt metaphor for Grant's military philosophy, which relied on constant, unrelenting assault. One result was that Grant was willing to fight when other Northern generals held back. Another was that Grant presided over some of the worst carnage of the Civil War. *(Library of Congress)*

warfare in which destruction of resources was as important as battlefield tactics.

Amateur officers played an important role in both armies as commanders of volunteer regiments. In both North and South, such men were usually economic or social leaders in their communities who appointed themselves officers and rounded up troops to lead. The system was responsible for recruiting considerable numbers of men into the armies of the two nations. Only occasionally, however, did it produce officers of real ability.

The Role of Sea Power

The Union had an overwhelming advantage in naval power, and it gave its navy two important roles in the war. One was enforcing a blockade of the Southern coast, which the president ordered on April 19, 1861. The other was assisting the Union armies in field operations.

The blockade of the South was never fully effective, but it had a major impact on the Confederacy nevertheless. The U.S. Navy could generally keep oceangoing ships out of Confederate ports. For a time, small blockade runners continued to slip through. But gradually, federal forces tightened the blockade by seizing the ports themselves. The last important port in Confederate hands—Wilmington, North Carolina—fell to the Union early in 1865.

The Confederates made bold attempts to break the blockade with new weapons. Foremost among them was an ironclad warship, constructed by plating with iron a former United States frigate, the *Merrimac*, which the Yankees had scuttled in Norfolk harbor when Virginia seceded. On March 8, 1862, the refitted *Merrimac*, renamed the *Virginia*, left Norfolk to attack a blockading squadron of wooden ships at nearby Hampton Roads. It destroyed two of the ships and scattered the rest. But the Union government had already built ironclads of its own. And one of them, the *Monitor*, arrived off the coast of Virginia only a few hours after the *Virginia*'s dramatic foray. The next day, it met the *Virginia* in the first battle between ironclad ships. Neither vessel was able to sink the other, but the *Monitor* put an end to the *Virginia*'s raids and preserved the blockade. The Confederacy experimented as well with other naval innovations, such as small torpedo boats and hand-powered submarines. But despite occasional small successes with these new weapons, the South never managed to overcome the Union's naval advantages.

As a supporter of land operations, the Union navy was particularly important in the western theater of war—the vast region between the Appalachian Mountains and the Mississippi River—where the major rivers were navigable by large vessels. The navy transported supplies and troops and joined in attacking Confederate strong points. With no significant navy of its own, the South could defend only with fixed land fortifications, which proved no match for the mobile land-and-water forces of the Union.

Europe and the Disunited States

Judah P. Benjamin, the Confederate secretary of state for most of the war, was a clever and intelligent man, but he lacked strong convictions and confined most of

ROBERT E. LEE
Lee was a moderate by the standards of Southern politics in the 1850s. He opposed secession and was ambivalent about slavery. But he could not bring himself to break with his region, and he left the U.S. army to lead Confederate forces beginning in 1861. He was (and remains) the most revered of all the white Southern leaders of the Civil War. For decades after his surrender at Appomattox, he was a symbol to white Southerners of the "Lost Cause." (*Bettmann*)

States, an increasingly powerful commercial rival; and some admired the supposedly aristocratic social order of the South, which they believed resembled the hierarchical structures of their own societies. But France was unwilling to take sides in the conflict unless England did so first. And in England, the government was reluctant to act because there was powerful popular support for the Union. Important English liberals such as John Bright and Richard Cobden considered the war a struggle between free and slave labor and urged their followers to support the Union cause. The politically conscious but largely unenfranchised workers in Britain expressed their sympathy for the North frequently and unmistakably—in mass meetings, in resolutions, and through their champions in Parliament. After Lincoln issued the Emancipation Proclamation, these groups worked particularly avidly for the Union.

Southern leaders hoped to counter the strength of the British antislavery forces by arguing that access to Southern cotton was vital to the English and French textile industries. But this "King Cotton diplomacy," on which the Confederacy had staked so many of its hopes, was a failure. English manufacturers had a surplus of both raw cotton and finished goods on hand in 1861 and could withstand a temporary loss of access to American cotton. Later, as the supply of cotton began to diminish, both England and France managed to keep at least some of their mills open by importing cotton from Egypt, India, and other sources. Equally important, English workers, the people most seriously threatened by the cotton shortage, did not clamor to have the blockade broken. Even the 500,000 English textile workers thrown out of jobs as a result of mill closings continued to support the North. In the end, therefore, no European nation offered diplomatic recognition to the Confederacy or intervened in the war. No nation wanted to antagonize the United States unless the Confederacy seemed likely to win, and the South never came close enough to victory to convince its potential allies to support it.

Even so, there was considerable tension, and on occasion near hostilities, between the United States and Britain, beginning in the first days of the war. Great Britain declared itself neutral as soon as the fighting began, followed by France and other nations. The Union government was furious. Neutrality implied that the two sides to the conflict had equal stature, but Washington was insisting that the conflict was simply a domestic insurrection, not a war between two legitimate governments.

A more serious crisis, the so-called *Trent* affair, began in late 1861. Two Confederate diplomats, James M. Mason and John Slidell, had slipped through the then-ineffective Union blockade to Havana, Cuba, where they boarded an English steamer, the *Trent*, for Eng-

his energy to routine administrative tasks. William Seward, his counterpart in Washington, gradually became one of the great American secretaries of state. He had invaluable assistance from Charles Francis Adams, the American minister to London, who had inherited the considerable diplomatic talents of his father, John Quincy Adams, and his grandfather, John Adams.

At the beginning of the war, the ruling classes of England and France, the two nations whose support was most crucial to both sides, were generally sympathetic to the Confederacy, for several reasons. The two nations imported much Southern cotton for their textile industries; they were eager to weaken the United

land. Waiting in Cuban waters was the American frigate *San Jacinto,* commanded by the impetuous Charles Wilkes. Acting without authorization, Wilkes stopped the British vessel, arrested the diplomats, and carried them in triumph to Boston. The British government demanded the release of the prisoners, reparations, and an apology. Lincoln and Seward, aware that Wilkes had violated maritime law and unwilling to risk war with England, spun out the negotiations until American public opinion had cooled off, then released the diplomats with an indirect apology.

A second diplomatic crisis produced problems that lasted for years. Unable to construct large vessels itself, the Confederacy bought six ships, known as commerce destroyers, from British shipyards. The best known of them were the *Alabama,* the *Florida,* and the *Shenandoah.* The United States protested that this sale of military equipment to a belligerent violated the laws of neutrality, and the protests became the basis, after the war, of damage claims by the United States against Great Britain. (See p. 429.)

The American West and the War

Most of the states and territories of the American West, about which there had been so much controversy in the years leading up to the Civil War, were far removed from the major fighting. But they played a continuing political, diplomatic, and military part in the conflict nevertheless.

Except for Texas, which joined the Confederacy, all the western states and territories remained officially loyal to the Union—but not without controversy and conflict. Southerners and Southern sympathizers were active throughout the West encouraging secession and attempting to enlist both white settlers and Indians to support the Confederacy. And in some places, there was actual combat between Unionists and secessionists.

There was particularly vicious fighting in Kansas and Missouri, the scene of so much bitterness before the war. The same pro-slavery and free-state forces who had fought one another in the 1850s continued to do so, with even more deadly results. William C. Quantrill, an Ohio native who had spent much of his youth in the West, became a captain in the Confederate army after he organized a band of guerrilla fighters (mostly teenage boys) with which he terrorized areas around the Kansas-Missouri border. Quantrill and his band were an exceptionally murderous group, notorious for killing almost everyone in their path. Their most infamous act was a siege of Lawrence, Kansas, during which they slaughtered 150 civilians, adults and children alike. Quantrill finally died at the hands of Union troops shortly after the end of the war.

Union sympathizers in Kansas, organized in bands known as the Jayhawkers, were only marginally less savage, as they moved across western Missouri exacting reprisals for the actions of Quantrill and other Confederate guerrillas. One Jayhawk unit was commanded by the son of John Brown and the brother of Susan B. Anthony, men who brought the fervor of abolitionists to their work. Even without a major battle, the border areas of Kansas and Missouri were among the bloodiest and most terrorized places in the United States during the Civil War.

Not long after the war began, Confederate agents tried to negotiate alliances with the Five Civilized Tribes living in Indian Territory (later Oklahoma), in hopes of recruiting their support against Union forces in the West. The Indians themselves were divided. Some wanted to support the South, both because they resented the way the United States government had treated them and because some tribal leaders were themselves slaveholders. But other Indians supported the North out of a general hostility to slavery (both in the South and in their own nation).

One result of these divisions was something of a civil war within Indian territory itself. Another was that Indian regiments fought for both the Union and the Confederacy during the war. But the tribes themselves never formally allied themselves with either side.

CAMPAIGNS AND BATTLES

In the absence of direct intervention by the European powers, the two contestants in America were left to resolve the conflict between themselves. They did so in four long years of bloody combat that produced more carnage than any war in American history, before or since. More than 618,000 Americans died in the Civil War, far more than the 115,000 who perished in World War I or the 318,000 who died in World War II, more, indeed, than died in all other American wars prior to Vietnam combined. There were nearly 2,000 deaths for every 100,000 of population during the Civil War. In World War I, the comparable figure was 109; in World War II, 241.

Despite the gruesome cost, the Civil War has become the most romanticized and the most intently studied of all American wars. In part, that is because the conflict produced—in addition to terrible fatalities—a series of military campaigns of classic strategic interest and a series of military leaders who displayed unusual brilliance and daring.

? carnage?

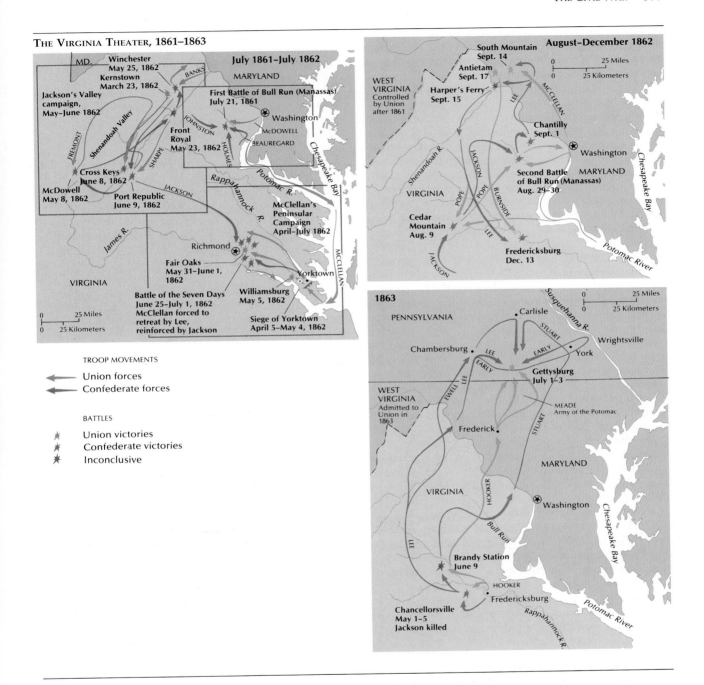

THE VIRGINIA THEATER, 1861–1863

TROOP MOVEMENTS

← Union forces

← Confederate forces

BATTLES

✱ Union victories

✱ Confederate victories

✱ Inconclusive

The Opening Clashes, 1861

The Union and the Confederacy fought their first major battle of the war in northern Virginia. A Union army of over 30,000 men under the command of General Irvin McDowell was stationed just outside Washing-

ton. About thirty miles away, at the town of Manassas, was a slightly smaller Confederate army under P. G. T. Beauregard. If the Northern army could destroy the Southern one, Union leaders believed, the war might end at once. In mid-July, McDowell marched his inexperienced troops toward Manassas. Beauregard moved his troops behind Bull Run, a small stream north of Manassas, and called for reinforcements, which reached him the day before the battle. The two armies were now approximately the same size.

On July 21, in the First Battle of Bull Run, or First Battle of Manassas, McDowell almost succeeded in dispersing the Confederate forces. But the Southerners stopped a last strong Union assault and then began a savage counterattack. The Union troops, exhausted after hours of hot, hard fighting, suddenly panicked. They broke ranks and retreated chaotically. McDowell was unable to reorganize them, and he had to order a retreat to Washington—a disorderly withdrawal complicated by the presence along the route of many civilians who had ridden down from the capital, picnic baskets in hand, to watch the battle from nearby hills. The Confederates, as disorganized by victory as the Union forces were by defeat, and short of supplies and transportation, did not pursue. The battle was a severe blow to Union morale and to the president's confidence in his officers. It also dispelled the illusion that the war would be a quick one.

Elsewhere in 1861, Union forces were achieving some small but significant victories. In Missouri, rebel forces gathered behind Governor Claiborne Jackson and other state officials who wanted to take the state out of the Union. Nathaniel Lyon, who commanded a small regular army force in St. Louis, moved his troops into southern Missouri to face the secessionists. On August 10, at the Battle of Wilson's Creek, he was defeated and killed—but not before he had seriously weakened the striking power of the Confederates. Union forces were subsequently able to hold most of the state.

Meanwhile, a Union force under George B. McClellan moved east from Ohio into western Virginia. By the end of 1861, it had "liberated" the anti-secession mountain people of the region. They created their own state government loyal to the Union and were admitted to the Union as West Virginia in 1863. The occupation of western Virginia was of limited military value, since the mountains cut the area off from the rest of Virginia. It was, however, an important symbolic victory for the North.

The Western Theater

After the battle at Bull Run, military operations in the east settled into a long and frustrating stalemate. The first decisive operations in 1862 occurred, therefore, in the western theater. Union forces were trying to seize control of the southern part of the Mississippi River, which would divide the Confederacy and give the North easy transportation into the heart of the South. Northern soldiers advanced on the southern Mississippi from both the north and south, moving down river from Kentucky and up from the Gulf of Mexico toward New Orleans.

In April, a Union squadron of ironclads and wooden vessels commanded by David G. Farragut gathered in the Gulf of Mexico, then smashed past weak Confederate forts near the mouth of the Mississippi, and from there sailed up to New Orleans, which was virtually defenseless because the Confederate high command had expected the attack to come from the north. The city surrendered on April 25—the first major Union victory and an important turning point in the war. From then on, the mouth of the Mississippi was closed to Confederate trade; and the South's largest city and most important banking center was in Union hands.

Farther north in the western theater, Confederate troops under the command of Albert Sidney Johnston were stretched out in a long defensive line whose center was at two forts in Tennessee, Fort Henry and Fort Donelson, on the Tennessee and Cumberland Rivers respectively. But the forts were located well behind the main Southern flanks, a fatal weakness that Union commanders recognized and exploited. Early in 1862, Ulysses S. Grant attacked Fort Henry, whose defenders, awed by the ironclad river boats accompanying the Union army, surrendered with almost no resistance on February 6. Grant then moved both his naval and ground forces to Fort Donelson, where the Confederates put up a stronger fight but finally, on February 16, had to surrender. By cracking the Confederate center, Grant had gained control of river communications and forced Confederate forces out of Kentucky and half of Tennessee.

With about 40,000 men, Grant now advanced south along the Tennessee River to seize control of railroad lines vital to the Confederacy. From Pittsburg Landing, he marched to nearby Shiloh, Tennessee, where a force almost equal to his own and commanded by Albert Sidney Johnston and P. G. T. Beauregard caught him by surprise. The result was the Battle of Shiloh, April 6–7. In the first day's fighting (during which Johnston was killed), the Southerners drove Grant back to the river. But the next day, reinforced by 25,000 fresh troops, Grant recovered the lost ground and forced Beauregard to withdraw. After the narrow Union victory at Shiloh, Northern forces occupied Corinth, Mississippi, the hub of several important railroads, and established control of the Mississippi River as far south as Memphis.

Braxton Bragg, now in command of the Confederate army in the west, gathered his forces at Chat-

THE WAR IN THE WEST, 1861–1863

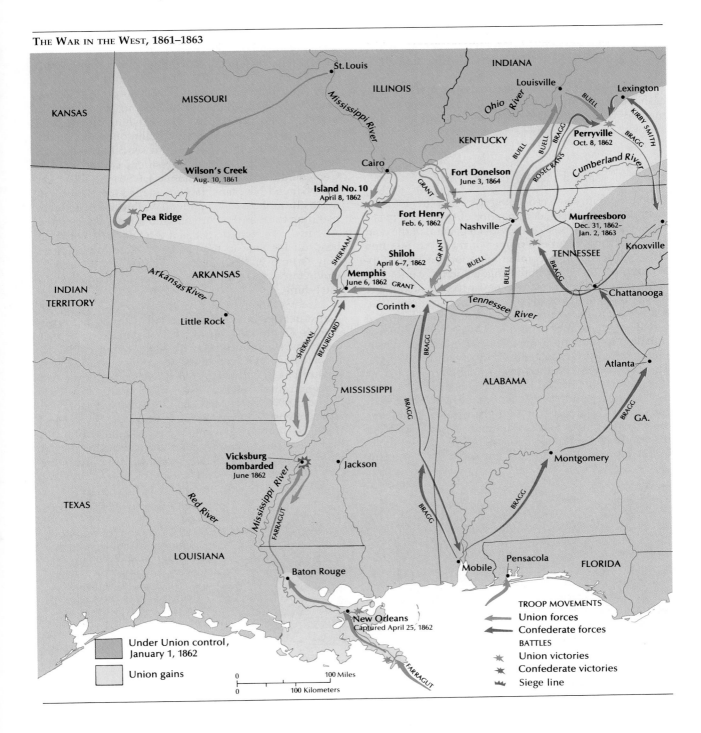

Under Union control, January 1, 1862

Union gains

TROOP MOVEMENTS
Union forces
Confederate forces
BATTLES
Union victories
Confederate victories
Siege line

tanooga, in eastern Tennessee, which the Confederacy still controlled. He hoped to win back the rest of the state and then move north into Kentucky. But first he had to face a Union army (commanded by Don Car-

los Buell and later by William S. Rosecrans), whose assignment was to capture Chattanooga. The two armies maneuvered for advantage inconclusively in northern Tennessee and southern Kentucky for several months until they finally met, December 31–January 2, in the Battle of Murfreesboro, or Stone's River. Bragg was forced to withdraw to the south, his campaign a failure.

By the end of 1862, Union forces had made considerable progress in the west. But the major conflict remained in the east, where they were having much less success.

The Virginia Front, 1862

Union operations were being directed in 1862 by George B. McClellan, commander of the Army of the Potomac and the most controversial general of the war. McClellan was a superb trainer of men, but he often appeared reluctant to commit his troops to battle. Opportunities for important engagements came and went, and McClellan seemed never to take advantage of them—claiming always that his preparations were not yet complete or that the moment was not right.

During the winter of 1861–1862, McClellan concentrated on training his army of 150,000 men near Washington. Finally, he designed a spring campaign whose purpose was to capture the Confederate capital at Richmond. But instead of heading overland directly toward Richmond, McClellan chose a complicated, roundabout route that he thought would circumvent the Confederate defenses. The navy would carry his troops down the Potomac to a peninsula east of Richmond, between the York and James Rivers. The army would approach the city from there. It became known as the Peninsular Campaign.

McClellan began the campaign with only part of his army. Approximately 100,000 men accompanied him down the Potomac. Another 30,000—under General Irvin McDowell—remained behind to protect Washington. McClellan insisted that Washington was safe as long as he was threatening Richmond, and finally persuaded Lincoln to promise to send him the additional men. But before the president could do so, a Confederate army under Thomas J. ("Stonewall") Jackson changed his plans. Jackson staged a rapid march north through the Shenandoah Valley, as if he were planning to cross the Potomac and attack Washington. Alarmed, Lincoln dispatched McDowell's corps to head off Jackson. In the brilliant Valley campaign of May 4–June 9, 1862, Jackson defeated two separate Union forces and slipped away before McDowell could catch him.

Meanwhile, Confederate troops under Joseph E. Johnston were attacking McClellan's advancing army outside Richmond. But in the two-day Battle of Fair Oaks, or Seven Pines (May 31–June 1), they could not repel the Union forces. Johnston, badly wounded, was replaced by Robert E. Lee, who then recalled Stonewall Jackson from the Shenandoah Valley. With a combined force of 85,000 to face McClellan's 100,000, Lee launched a new offensive, known as the Battle of the Seven Days (June 25—July 1). Lee wanted to cut McClellan off from his base on the York River and then destroy the isolated Union army. But McClellan fought his way across the

ANTIETAM
The Civil War was one of the bloodiest military conflicts in the history of warfare to that point. Even now, it remains the costliest war in American history. Antietam (September 1862) produced the worst single-day casualties of the war, as this photograph of carnage on the battlefield after a day's fighting suggests. *(Bettmann)*

peninsula and set up a new base on the James. There, with naval support, the Army of the Potomac was safe.

McClellan was now only twenty-five miles from Richmond, with a secure line of water communications, and thus in a good position to renew the campaign. Time and again, however, he found reasons for delay. Instead of replacing McClellan with a more aggressive commander, Lincoln finally ordered the army to move to northern Virginia and join a smaller force under John Pope. The president hoped to begin a new offensive against Richmond on the direct overland route that he himself had always preferred.

As the Army of the Potomac left the peninsula by water, Lee moved north with the Army of Northern Virginia to strike Pope before McClellan could join him. Pope was as rash as McClellan was cautious, and he attacked the approaching Confederates without waiting for the arrival of all of McClellan's troops. In the ensuing Second Battle of Bull Run, or Second Battle of Manassas (August 29–30), Lee threw back the assault and routed Pope's army, which fled to Washington. With hopes for an overland campaign against Richmond now in disarray, Lincoln removed Pope from command and put McClellan in charge of all the Union forces in the region.

Lee soon went on the offensive again, heading north through western Maryland, and McClellan moved out to meet him. McClellan had the good luck to get a copy of Lee's orders, which revealed that a part of the Confederate army, under Stonewall Jackson, had separated from the rest to attack Harpers Ferry. But instead of attacking quickly before the Confederates could recombine, McClellan stalled and gave Lee time to pull most of his forces together behind Antietam Creek, near the town of Sharpsburg. There, on September 17, in the bloodiest single-day engagement of the war, McClellan's 87,000-man army repeatedly attacked Lee's force of 50,000, with enormous casualties on both sides. Six thousand soldiers died, and 17,000 sustained injuries. Late in the day, just as the Confederate line seemed ready to break, the last of Jackson's troops arrived from Harpers Ferry to reinforce it. McClellan might have broken through with one more assault. Instead, he allowed Lee to retreat into Virginia. Technically, Antietam was a Union victory, but in reality, it was an opportunity squandered. In November, Lincoln finally removed McClellan from command for good.

McClellan's replacement, Ambrose E. Burnside, was a short-lived mediocrity. He tried to move toward Richmond by crossing the Rappahannock at Fredericksburg, the strongest defensive point on the river. There, on December 13, he launched a series of attacks against Lee, all of them bloody, all of them hopeless. After losing a

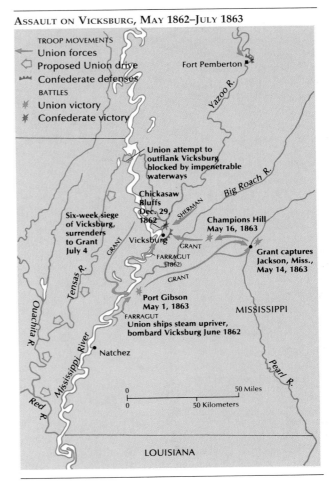

ASSAULT ON VICKSBURG, MAY 1862–JULY 1863

TROOP MOVEMENTS
→ Union forces
⬡ Proposed Union drive
⌒ Confederate defenses
BATTLES
✷ Union victory
✷ Confederate victory

Fort Pemberton

Yazoo R.

Union attempt to outflank Vicksburg blocked by impenetrable waterways

Chickasaw Bluffs Dec. 29, 1862

Big Roach R.

SHERMAN

Champions Hill May 16, 1863

Six-week siege of Vicksburg, surrenders to Grant July 4

GRANT

Vicksburg

GRANT

FARRAGUT (1862)

GRANT

Grant captures Jackson, Miss., May 14, 1863

Tensas R.

Ouachita R.

Port Gibson May 1, 1863

FARRAGUT
Union ships steam upriver, bombard Vicksburg June 1862

MISSISSIPPI

Natchez

Pearl R.

0   50 Miles
0   50 Kilometers

Mississippi River

Red R.

LOUISIANA

large part of his army, he withdrew to the north bank of the Rappahannock. He was relieved at his own request.

1863: Year of Decision

At the beginning of 1863, General Joseph Hooker was in command of the still-formidable Army of the Potomac, whose 120,000 troops remained north of the Rappahannock, opposite Fredericksburg. But despite his reputation as a fighter (his popular nickname was "Fighting Joe"), Hooker showed little resolve as he launched his own campaign in the spring. Taking part of his army, Hooker crossed the river above Fredericksburg and moved toward the town and Lee's army. But at the last minute, he apparently lost his nerve and drew back to a defensive position in a desolate area of brush and scrub trees known as the Wilderness. Lee had only half as many men as Hooker did, but he boldly

THE BATTLE OF GETTYSBURG, JULY 1–3, 1863

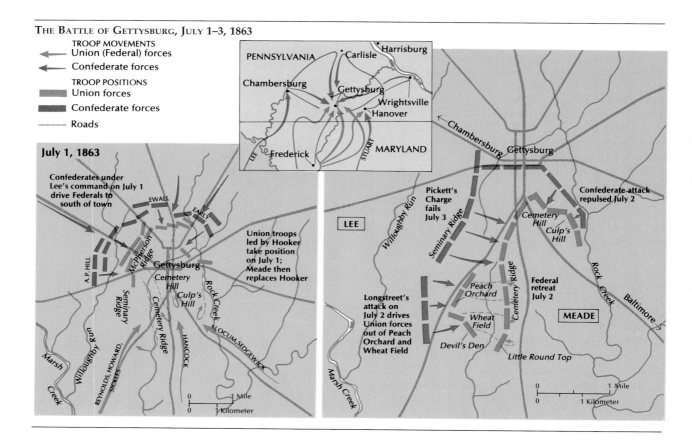

divided his forces for a dual assault on the Union army. In the Battle of Chancellorsville, May 1–5, Stonewall Jackson attacked the Union right and Lee himself charged the front. Hooker barely managed to escape with his army. Lee had defeated the Union objectives, but he had not destroyed the Union army. And his ablest officer, Jackson, was fatally wounded during the battle.

While the Union forces were suffering repeated frustrations in the east, they were continuing to win important victories in the west. In the spring of 1863, Ulysses S. Grant was driving at Vicksburg, Mississippi, one of the Confederacy's two remaining strongholds on the southern Mississippi River. Vicksburg was well protected, surrounded by rough country on the north and low, marshy ground on the west, and with good artillery coverage of the river itself. But in May, Grant boldly moved men and supplies—overland and by water—to an area south of the city, where the terrain was better. He then attacked Vicksburg from the rear. Six weeks later, on July 4, Vicksburg—whose residents were by then literally starving as a result of a prolonged siege—surrendered. At almost the same time, the other Confederate strong point on the river, Port Hudson,

Louisiana, also surrendered—to a Union force that had moved north from New Orleans. The Union had achieved one of its basic military aims: control of the whole length of the Mississippi. The Confederacy was split in two, with Louisiana, Arkansas, and Texas cut off from the other seceded states. The victories on the Mississippi were one of the great turning points of the war.

Early in the siege of Vicksburg, Lee proposed an invasion of Pennsylvania, which would, he argued, divert Union troops north and remove the pressure on the lower Mississippi. Further, he argued, if he could win a major victory on Northern soil, England and France might come to the Confederacy's aid. The war-weary North might even quit the war before Vicksburg fell.

In June 1863, Lee moved up the Shenandoah Valley into Maryland and then entered Pennsylvania. The Union Army of the Potomac, commanded first by Hooker and then by George C. Meade, also moved north, parallel with the Confederates' movement, staying between Lee and Washington. The two armies finally encountered one another at the small town of Gettysburg, Pennsylvania. There, on July 1–3, 1863,

VIRGINIA CAMPAIGNS, 1864–1865

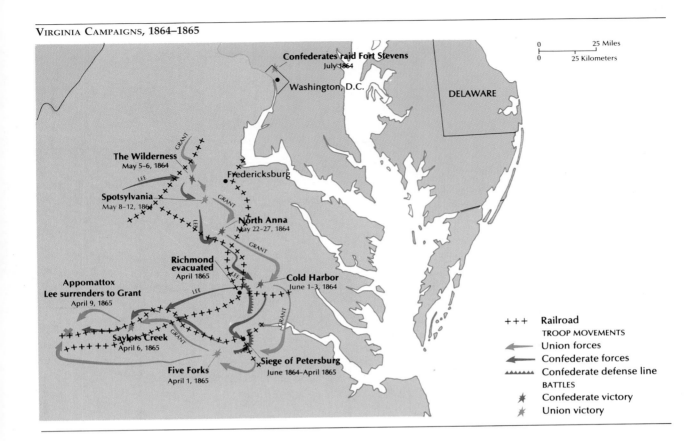

they fought the most celebrated battle of the war.

Meade's army established a strong, well-protected position on the hills south of the town. The confident and combative Lee attacked, even though his army was outnumbered 75,000 to 90,000. His first assault on the Union forces on Cemetery Ridge failed. A day later he ordered a second, larger effort. In what is remembered as Pickett's Charge, a force of 15,000 Confederate soldiers advanced for almost a mile across open country while being swept by Union fire. Only about 5,000 made it up the ridge, and this remnant finally had to surrender or retreat. By now Lee had lost nearly a third of his army. On July 4, the same day as the surrender of Vicksburg, he withdrew from Gettysburg—another major turning point in the war. Never again were the weakened Confederate forces able to seriously threaten Northern territory.

Before the end of the year, there was a third important turning point, this one in Tennessee. After occupying Chattanooga on September 9, Union forces under William Rosecrans began an unwise pursuit of Bragg's retreating Confederate forces. Bragg was waiting for them just across the Georgia line, with reinforcements from Lee's army. The two armies engaged in the Battle of Chickamauga (September 19–20), one of the few battles in which the Confederates enjoyed a numerical superiority (70,000 to 56,000). Union forces could not break the Confederate lines and retreated back to Chattanooga.

Bragg now began a siege of Chattanooga itself, seizing the heights nearby and cutting off fresh supplies to the Union forces. Grant came to the rescue. In the Battle of Chattanooga (November 23–25), the reinforced Union army drove the Confederates back into Georgia. Northern troops then occupied most of eastern Tennessee. Union forces had now achieved a second important objective: control of the Tennessee River. Four of the eleven Confederate states were now effectively cut off from the Southern nation. No longer could the Confederacy hope to win independence through a decisive military victory. They could hope to win only by holding on and exhausting the Northern will to fight.

The Last Stage, 1864–1865

By the beginning of 1864, Ulysses S. Grant had become general in chief of all the Union armies. At long last,

SIGNIFICANT EVENTS

1860   South Carolina secedes from Union

1861   Ten more Southern states secede

Confederate States of America formed

Jefferson Davis named president of Confederacy

Conflict at Fort Sumter, South Carolina (April 12–14), begins Civil War

George B. McClellan appointed commander of Army of the Potomac

Union blockades Confederate coast

Trent affair imperils U.S. relations with Britain

First Battle of Bull Run

1862   Battle of Shiloh (April 6–7)

Union forces capture New Orleans (May 1)

Second Battle of Bull Run (August 29–30)

Battle of Antietam (September 17)

Battle of Fredericksburg (December 13)

McClellan removed from command

Robert E. Lee named commander of Confederate armies

Homestead Act and Morrill Land Grant Act passed

Union Pacific Railroad chartered

Confederacy enacts military draft

Republicans experience heavy losses in congressional elections

1863   Lincoln issues Emancipation Proclamation (January 1)

Battle of Chancellorsville (May 1–5)

Battle of Gettysburg (July 1–3)

Vicksburg surrenders (July 4)

Battle of Chattanooga (November 23–25)

Union enacts military draft

Antidraft riots break out in New York City

South experiences food riots

West Virginia admitted to Union

1864   Battle of the Wilderness (May 5–7)

Petersburg, Virginia, besieged

Sherman captures Atlanta (September 2)

Sherman's "March to the Sea" begins

Lincoln reelected president

Central Pacific Railroad chartered

1865   Lee surrenders to Grant at Appomattox (April 9)

Thirteenth Amendment, abolishing slavery, ratified

---

the president had found a commander whom he could rely on to pursue the war doggedly and tenaciously. Grant was not a subtle strategic or tactical general; he believed in using the North's overwhelming advantage in troops and material resources to overwhelm the South. He was not afraid to absorb massive casualties as long as he was inflicting similar casualties on his opponents.

Grant planned two great offensives for 1864. In Virginia, the Army of the Potomac (technically under Meade's command, but really now under Grant's) would advance toward Richmond and force Lee into a decisive battle. In Georgia, the western army, under William T. Sherman, would advance east toward Atlanta and destroy the remaining Confederate force further south, which was now under the command of Joseph E. Johnston.

The northern campaign began when the Army of the Potomac, 115,000 strong, plunged into the rough, wooded Wilderness area of northwestern Virginia in pursuit of Lee's 75,000-man army. After avoiding an engagement for several weeks, Lee turned Grant back in the Battle of the Wilderness (May 5–7). But Grant was undeterred. Without stopping to rest or reorga-

SHERMAN'S MARCH TO THE SEA, 1863–1865

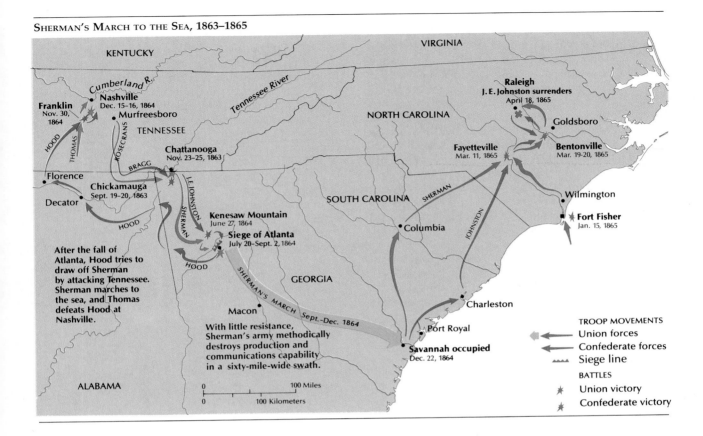

After the fall of Atlanta, Hood tries to draw off Sherman by attacking Tennessee. Sherman marches to the sea, and Thomas defeats Hood at Nashville.

With little resistance, Sherman's army methodically destroys production and communications capability in a sixty-mile-wide swath.

TROOP MOVEMENTS
Union forces
Confederate forces
Siege line

BATTLES
Union victory
Confederate victory

nize, he resumed his march toward Richmond. He met Lee again in the bloody, five-day Battle of Spotsylvania Court House, in which 12,000 Union troops and a large but unknown number of Confederates died or were wounded. Despite the enormous losses, Grant kept moving. But victory continued to elude him. Lee kept his army between Grant and the Confederate capital and on June 1–3 repulsed the Union forces again, just northeast of Richmond, at Cold Harbor. The monthlong Wilderness campaign had cost Grant 55,000 men (killed, wounded, and captured) to Lee's 31,000. And Richmond still had not fallen.

Grant now changed his strategy. He moved his army east of Richmond, bypassing the capital altogether, and headed south toward the railroad center at Petersburg. If he could seize Petersburg, he could cut off the capital's communications with the rest of the Confederacy. But Petersburg had strong defenses; and once Lee came to the city's relief, the assault became a prolonged siege, which lasted nine months.

In Georgia, meanwhile, Sherman was facing a less ferocious resistance. With 90,000 men, he confronted Confederate forces of 60,000 under Johnston, who was

unwilling to risk a direct engagement. As Sherman advanced, Johnston tried to delay him by maneuvering. The two armies fought only one real battle—at Kennesaw Mountain, northwest of Atlanta, on June 27—where Johnston scored an impressive victory. Even so, he was unable to stop the Union advance toward Atlanta. Davis replaced Johnston with the combative John B. Hood, who twice daringly attacked Sherman's army but accomplished nothing except seriously weakening his own forces. Sherman took Atlanta on September 2. News of the victory electrified the North and helped unite the previously divided Republican Party behind President Lincoln.

Hood now tried unsuccessfully to draw Sherman out of Atlanta by moving back up through Tennessee and threatening an invasion of the North. Sherman did not take the bait. But he did send Union troops to reinforce Nashville. In the Battle of Nashville on December 15–16, 1864, Northern forces practically destroyed what was left of Hood's army.

Meanwhile, Sherman had left Atlanta to begin his soon-to-be-famous March to the Sea. Living off the land, destroying supplies it could not use, his army cut a sixty-mile-wide swath of desolation across Georgia. "War is all hell," Sherman had once said. By that he meant not that war is a terrible thing to be avoided, but that it should be made as horrible and costly as possible for the opponent. He sought not only to deprive the Confederate army of war materials and railroad communications but also to break the will of the Southern people, by burning towns and plantations along his route. By December 20, he had reached Savannah, which surrendered two days later. Sherman offered it to President Lincoln as a Christmas gift. Early in 1865, having left Savannah largely undamaged, Sherman continued his destructive march northward through South Carolina. He was virtually unopposed until he was well inside North Carolina, where a small force under Johnston could do no more than cause a brief delay.

In April 1865, Grant's Army of the Potomac—still engaged in the prolonged siege at Petersburg—finally captured a vital railroad junction southwest of the town. Without rail access to the South, cut off from other Confederate forces, Lee could no longer hope to defend Richmond. With the remnant of his army, now about 25,000 men, Lee began moving west in the forlorn hope of finding a way around the Union forces so he could head south and link up with Johnston in North Carolina. But the Union army pursued him and blocked his escape route. Finally recognizing that further bloodshed was futile, Lee arranged to meet Grant at a private home in the small town of Appomattox Courthouse, Virginia. There, on April 9, he surrendered what was left of his forces. Nine days later, near Durham, North Carolina, Johnston surrendered to Sherman.

In military terms, at least, the long war was now effectively over, even though Jefferson Davis refused to accept defeat. He fled south from Richmond and was finally captured in Georgia. A few Southern diehards continued to fight, but even their resistance collapsed before long. Well before the last shot was fired, the difficult process of reuniting the shattered nation had begun.

SUGGESTED READINGS

General Studies. Bruce Catton, *This Hallowed Ground* (1956). Shelby Foote, *The Civil War: A Narrative*, 3 vols. (1958–1974). James M. McPherson, *Battle Cry of Freedom* (1988); *Ordeal by Fire*, rev. ed. (1985). Allan Nevins, *The War for the Union*, 4 vols. (1959–1971). James G. Randall and David Donald, *The Civil War and Reconstruction*, rev. ed. (1969).

The Secession Crisis. William L. Barney, *The Road to Secession* (1972); *The Secessionist Impulse: Alabama and Mississippi in 1860* (1974). Steven A. Channing, *Crisis of Fear* (1970). Daniel W. Crofts, *Reluctant Confederates: Upper South Unionists in the Secession Crisis* (1989). Richard N. Current, *Lincoln and the First Shot* (1963). Michael P. Johnson, *Toward a Patriarchal Republic* (1977). David Potter, *Lincoln and His Party in the Secession Crisis* (1942). Kenneth M. Stampp, *And the War Came* (1950). Ralph A. Wooster, *The Secession Conventions of the South* (1962).

Lincoln. Robert V. Bruce, *Lincoln and the Tools of War* (1956). Harry J. Carman and Reinhard Luthin, *Lincoln and the Patronage* (1943). LaWanda Cox, *Lincoln and Black Freedom* (1981). David Donald, *Lincoln Reconsidered: Essays on the Civil War Era* (2nd ed., 1956). William B. Hesseltine, *Lincoln and the War Governors* (1948). James M. McPherson, *Abraham Lincoln and the Second American Revolution* (1990). Mark E. Neely, *The Fate of Liberty: Abraham Lincoln and Civil Liberties* (1991); *The Last Best Hope of Earth: Abraham Lincoln and the Promise of America* (1993). Stephen B. Oates, *With Malice Toward None: The Life of Abraham Lincoln* (1979). James G. Randall, *Lincoln the President*, 4 vols. (1945–1955), the final volume completed by Richard N. Current. Carl Sandburg, *Abraham Lincoln*, 6 vols. (1929–1939). Benjamin Thomas, *Abraham Lincoln* (1952). T. Harry Williams, *Lincoln and the Radicals* (1941); and *Lincoln and His Generals* (1952).

Politics and Society in the North. Daniel Aaron, *The Unwritten War* (1973). Iver Bernstein, *The New York City Draft Riots* (1990). John P. Bugardt, ed., *Civil War Nurse* (1980). Adrian Cook, *The Armies of the Streets: The New York City Draft Riots of 1863* (1974). David Donald, *Charles Sumner and the Rights of Man* (1970). Martin Duberman, *Charles Francis Adams* (1961). Eric Foner, *Politics and Ideology in the Age of the Civil War* (1980). George Fredrickson, *The Inner Civil War: Northern Intellectuals and the Crisis of the Union* (1965). Paul G. Gates, *Agriculture and the Civil War* (1965). Wood Gray, *The Hidden Civil War* (1942). Alvin M. Josephy, Jr., *The Civil War in the American West* (1991). Frank L. Klement, *The Copperheads in the Middle West* (1960); *Dark Lanterns: Secret Political Societies, Conspiracies, and Treason Trials in the Civil War* (1984). Mary E. Massey, *Bonnet Brigades: American Women and the Civil War* (1966). William Q. Maxwell, *Lincoln's Fifth Wheel: The Political History of the United States Sanitary Commission* (1956).

James H. Moorhead, *American Apocalypse: Yankee Protestants and the Civil War* (1978). Grace Palladino, *Another Civil War: Labor, Capital, and the State in Anthracite Regions of Pennsylvania, 1840–1868* (1990). Philip Shaw Paludan, *"A People's Contest": The Union and the Civil War, 1861–1868* (1988). James G. Randall, *Constitutional Problems Under Lincoln* (1926). Susan M. Reverby, *Ordered to Care: The Dilemma of American Nursing, 1850–1945* (1987). Robert P. Sharkey, *Money, Class, and Party* (1959). Benjamin P. Thomas and Harold M. Hyman, *Stanton* (1962). Glyndon Van Deusen, *William Henry Seward* (1967). Wendy Hamand Venet, *Neither Ballots nor Bullets: Women Abolitionists and the Civil War* (1991). Edmund Wilson, *Patriotic Gore* (1962).

African Americans and Emancipation. Ira Berlin, Leslie Rowland, et al., eds., *Freedom: A Documentary History of Emancipation, 1861–1867*, Series II: *The Black Military Experience* (1982). John W. Blassingame, *Black New Orleans* (1973). Dudley T. Cornish, *The Sable Arm: Negro Troops in the Union Army* (1966). Joseph T. Glatthaar, *Forged in Battle: The Civil War Alliance of Black Soldiers and White Officers* (1990). Peter Kolchin, *First Freedom* (1972). Leon Litwack, *Been in the Storm So Long: The Aftermath of Slavery* (1979). James M. McPherson, *The Struggle for Equality* (1964); *The Negro's Civil War* (1965). Clarence L. Mohr, *On the Threshold of Freedom: Masters and Slaves in Civil War Georgia* (1986). Benjamin Quarles, *Lincoln and the Negro* (1962); *The Negro in the Civil War* (1953).

The Confederacy. Thomas B. Alexander and Richard E. Beringer, *The Anatomy of the Confederate Congress* (1972). E. Merton Coulter, *The Confederate States of America* (1950). Clement Eaton, *A History of the Southern Confederacy* (1954); *Jefferson Davis* (1978). Paul D. Escott, *After Secession* (1978); *Slavery Remembered (1979); Many Excellent People* (1985). Drew Gilpin Faust, *The Creation of Confederate Nationalism* (1988). Ella Lonn, *Desertion During the Civil War* (1928). Frank L. Owsley, *State Rights in the Confederacy* (1952). James L. Roark, *Masters Without Slaves: Southern Planters in the Civil War and Reconstruction* (1978). Charles P. Roland, *The Confederacy* (1960). Hudson Strode, *Jefferson Davis*, 3 vols. (1955–1964). Georgia Lee Tatum, *Disloyalty in the Confederacy* (1934). Emory Thomas, *The Confederacy as a Revolutionary Experience* (1971); *The Confederate Nation* (1979); *The Confederate State of Richmond* (1971). Bell I. Wiley, *The Life of Johnny Reb* (1943); *The Plain People of the Confederacy* (1943). C. Vann Woodward, ed., *Mary Chesnut's Civil War* (1982). W. Buck Yearns, *The Confederate Congress* (1960).

Diplomacy. Stuart L. Bernath, *Squall Across the Atlantic: American Civil War Prize Cases and Diplomacy* (1970). David P. Crook, *Diplomacy During the American Civil War* (1975); *The North, the South, and the Powers, 1861–1865* (1974). Frank L.

Owsley and Harriet Owsley, *King Cotton Diplomacy*, rev. ed. (1959). Gordon H. Warren, *Fountain of Discontent: The Trent Affair and Freedom of the Seas* (1981).

Military Histories.   Richard E. Beringer et al., *Why the South Lost the Civil War* (1986). John Carpenter, *Ulysses S. Grant* (1976). Bruce Catton, *Mr. Lincoln's Army* (1951); *Glory Road* (1952); *A Stillness at Appomattox* (1954); *America Goes to War* (1958); *Banners at Shenandoah* (1956); *Grant Moves South* (1960). Thomas L. Connelly, *The Marble Man* (1977). Burke Davis, *Sherman's March* (1980). David Donald, ed., *Why the North Won the Civil War* (1960). Shelby Foote, *The Civil War: A Narrative*, 3 vols. (1958–1974). Douglas Southall Freeman, *Robert E. Lee*, 4 vols. (1934–1935). Herman Hattaway and Archer Jones, *How the North Won* (1983). Archer Jones et al., *Why the South Lost the Civil War* (1986). Gerald F. Linderman, *Embat-tled Courage: The Experience of Combat in the American Civil War* (1987). Thomas L. Livermore, *Numbers and Losses in the Civil War in America* (1957). C. E. MacCartney, *Mr. Lincoln's Admirals* (1956). Wiliam McFeely, *Grant* (1981). John Niven, *Gideon Welles, Lincoln's Secretary of the Navy* (1973). Charles Royster, *The Destructive War: William Tecumseh Sherman, Stonewall Jackson, and the Americans* (1991). Stephen W. Sears, *George B. McClellan: The Young Napoleon* (1988); *Landscape Turned Red: The Battle of Antietam* (1983). William N. Still, Jr., *Iron Afloat: The Story of the Confederate Armorclads* (1971); *Confederate Shipbuilding* (1969). Richard S. West, Jr., *Mr. Lincoln's Navy* (1957). Bell Wiley, *The Life of Billy Yank* (1952). Kenneth P. Williams, *Lincoln Finds a General*, 4 vols. (1949–1952). T. Harry Williams, *McClellan, Sherman, and Grant* (1962); *P. G. T. Beauregard, Napoleon in Gray* (1955).

A RECONSTRUCTION-ERA TRIBUTE TO THE ELECTION OF AFRICAN AMERICANS TO CONGRESS
From left to right: Sen. Hiram R. Revels, Rep. Benjamin S. Turner, the Reverend Richard Allen, Frederick Douglass, Representative Josiah T. Walls, Representative Joseph H. Rainy, and writer William Wells Brown. *(Library of Congress)*

CHAPTER FIFTEEN

RECONSTRUCTION AND THE NEW SOUTH

EW PERIODS IN THE history of the United States have produced as much bitterness or created such enduring controversy as the era of Reconstruction—the years following the Civil War when Americans attempted to reunite their shattered nation. Those who lived through Reconstruction viewed it in sharply different ways. To many white Southerners, it was a vicious and destructive experience—a time when vindictive Northerners inflicted humiliation and revenge on the prostrate South and unnecessarily delayed a genuine reunion of the sections. Northern defenders of Reconstruction, in contrast, argued that their policies were the only way to keep unrepentant Confederates from restoring Southern society as it had been before the war; without forceful federal intervention, it would be impossible to stop the reemergence of a backward aristocracy and the continued subjugation of former slaves—no way, in other words, to prevent the same sectional problems that had produced the Civil War in the first place.

To most African Americans at the time, and to many people of all races since, Reconstruction was notable for other reasons. Neither a vicious tyranny, as white Southerners charged, nor a thoroughgoing reform, as many Northerners claimed, it was, rather, a small but important first step in the effort by former slaves to secure civil rights and economic power. Reconstruction did not provide African Americans with either the legal protections or the material resources to assure them anything like real equality. And when it came to an end, finally, in the late 1870s—as a result of an economic crisis, a lack of political will in the North, and organized, at times violent, resistance by white Southerners—the freed slaves found themselves abandoned by the federal government to face a system of economic peonage and legal subordination alone. For the remainder of the nineteenth century, those blacks who continued to live in what came to be known as the New South were unable effectively to resist oppression. And yet for all its shortcomings, Reconstruction did help African Americans create institutions and legal precedents that they carried with them into the twentieth century and that became the basis for later efforts to win freedom and equality.

THE PROBLEMS OF PEACEMAKING

In 1865, as it became clear that the war was almost over, no one in Washington knew quite what to do. Abraham Lincoln could not negotiate a treaty with the defeated government; he continued to insist that the Confederate government had no legal right to exist. Yet neither could he simply readmit the Southern states into the Union as if nothing had happened.

The Aftermath of War and Emancipation

The South after the Civil War was a desolate place. Towns had been gutted, plantations burned, fields neglected, bridges and railroads destroyed. Many white

413

Southerners, stripped of their slaves through emancipation and stripped of the capital they had invested in now worthless Confederate bonds and currency, had almost no personal property. More than 258,000 Confederate soldiers had died in the war; thousands more returned home wounded or sick. Many families had to rebuild their fortunes without the help of adult males. Some white Southerners faced starvation and homelessness.

If conditions were bad for many Southern whites, they were far worse for most Southern blacks—the 4 million men and women emerging from bondage. Some of them had also seen service during the war—as servants to Confederate officers or as teamsters and laborers for the Southern armies. Nearly 200,000 had fought for the Union, and 38,000 had died. Others had worked as spies or scouts for Union forces in the South. Many more had flocked to the Union lines to escape slavery. As soon as the war ended, hundreds of thousands of other former slaves—young and old, healthy and sick—left their plantations in search of a new life in freedom. But most had nowhere to go. Many of them trudged to the nearest town or city, roamed the countryside camping at night on the bare ground, or gathered around Union occupation forces, hoping for assistance. Few had any possessions except the clothes they wore.

In 1865, in short, Southern society was in disarray. Blacks and whites, men and women faced a future of great uncertainty, for which traditional institutions and assumptions were no longer adequate. Yet people of both races faced this future with some very clear aspirations. For both blacks and whites, Reconstruction became a struggle to define the meaning of freedom. But the former slaves and the defeated whites had very different conceptions of what freedom meant.

For African Americans, freedom meant above all an end to slavery and to all its injustices and humiliations. But it also meant the acquisition of rights and protections that would allow them to live as free men and women in the same way white people did. "If I cannot do like a white man," one African-American man told his former master, "I am not free."

Blacks differed with one another on how to achieve that freedom. Some demanded a redistribution of economic resources, especially land, because, as a convention of Alabama freedmen put it in a formal resolution, "The property which they hold was nearly all earned by the sweat of *our* brows." Others asked simply for legal equality, confident that given the same opportunities as white citizens they could advance successfully in American society.

But whatever their particular demands, virtually all former slaves were united in their desire for independence from white control. Freed from slavery, blacks throughout the South began almost immediately to create autonomous African-American communities. They pulled out of white-controlled churches and established their own. They created fraternal, benevolent, and mutual aid societies. When they could, they began their own schools.

For most white Southerners, freedom meant something very different. It meant the ability to control their own destinies without interference from the North or the federal government. And in the immediate aftermath of the war, they attempted to exercise this version of freedom by trying to restore their society to its antebellum form. Slavery had been abolished in the former Confederacy by the Emancipation Proclamation, and everywhere (as of December 1865) by the Thirteenth Amendment. But many white planters wanted to continue slavery in an altered form by keeping black workers legally tied to the plantations. When these white Southerners fought for what they considered freedom, they were fighting above all to preserve local and regional autonomy and white supremacy.

The federal government kept troops in the South after the war to preserve order and protect the freedmen. In March 1865, Congress established the Freedmen's Bureau, an agency of the army directed by General Oliver O. Howard. The Freedmen's Bureau distributed food to millions of former slaves. It established schools staffed by missionaries and teachers who had been sent to the South by Freedmen's Aid Societies and other private and church groups in the North. It made modest efforts to settle blacks on lands of their own. (The Bureau also offered considerable assistance to poor whites, many of whom were similarly destitute and homeless after the war.) But the Freedmen's Bureau was not a permanent solution. It had authority to operate for only one year; and in any case it was far too small to deal effectively with the enormous problems facing Southern society. By the time the war ended, other proposals for reconstructing the defeated South were emerging.

Issues of Reconstruction

The terms by which the Southern states rejoined the Union had important implications for both major political parties. The Republican victories in 1860 and 1864 had been a result in large part of the division of the Democratic Party and, later, the removal of the South from the electorate. Readmitting the South, leaders of both parties believed, would reunite the Democrats and weaken the Republicans. In addition, the Republican Party had taken advantage of the South's absence from Congress to pass a program of nationalistic economic legislation—railroad subsidies, protective tariffs, banking and currency reforms, and other measures to benefit Northern business leaders and industrialists. Should the Democratic Party regain power with heavy Southern support, these programs would be in jeopardy. Complicating these practical questions were emotional concerns. Many Northerners believed the South should be punished in some way for the suffering and sacrifice its rebellion had caused. Many Northerners believed, too, that the South should be transformed, made over in the North's urbanized image—its supposedly backward, feudal, undemocratic society civilized and modernized.

Even among the Republicans in Congress, there was considerable disagreement about the proper approach to Reconstruction—disagreement that reflected the same factional division (between the party's Conservatives and Radicals) that had created disputes over emancipation during the war. Conservatives insisted that the South accept the abolition of slavery, but proposed few other conditions for the readmission of the seceded states. The Radicals, led by Representative Thaddeus Stevens of Pennsylvania and Senator Charles Sumner of Massachusetts, urged that the civil and military leaders of the Confederacy be punished, that large numbers of Southern whites be disenfranchised, that the legal rights of blacks be protected, and that the property of wealthy white Southerners who had aided the Confederacy be confiscated and distributed among the freedmen. Some Radicals favored granting suffrage to the former slaves. Others hesitated, since few Northern states permitted blacks to vote. Between the Radicals and the Conservatives stood a faction of uncommitted Republicans, the Moderates, who rejected the punitive goals of the Radicals but supported extracting at least some concessions from the South on black rights.

Plans for Reconstruction

President Lincoln's sympathies lay with the Moderates and Conservatives of his party. He believed that a lenient Reconstruction policy would encourage Southern Unionists and other former Whigs to join the Republican Party and would thus prevent the readmission of the South from strengthening the Democrats. More immediately, the Southern Unionists could become the nucleus of new, loyal state governments in the South. Lincoln was not uninterested in the fate of the freedmen, but he was willing to defer questions about their future for the sake of rapid reunification.

Lincoln's Reconstruction plan, which he announced in December 1863, offered a general amnesty to white Southerners—other than high officials of the Confederacy—who would pledge loyalty to the government and accept the elimination of slavery. Whenever 10 percent of the number of voters in 1860 took the oath in any state, those loyal voters could set up a state government. Lincoln also hoped to extend suffrage to those blacks who were educated, owned property, and had served in the Union army. Three Southern states—Louisiana, Arkansas, and Tennessee, all under Union occupation—reestablished loyal governments under the Lincoln formula in 1864.

The Radical Republicans were astonished at the mildness of Lincoln's program. They persuaded Congress to deny seats to representatives from the three "reconstructed" states and refused to count the electoral vote of those states in the election of 1864. But for the moment, the Radicals were uncertain about what form their own Reconstruction plan should take.

Their first effort to resolve that question was the Wade-Davis bill, passed by Congress in July 1864. It authorized the president to appoint a provisional governor for each conquered state. When a majority (not Lincoln's 10 percent) of the white males of the state pledged their allegiance to the Union, the governor could summon a state constitutional convention, whose delegates were to be elected by those who would swear (through the so-called Ironclad Oath) that they had never borne arms against the United States—another departure from Lincoln's plan. The new state constitutions would have to abolish slavery, disfranchise Confederate civil and military leaders, and repudiate debts accumulated by the state governments during the war. After a state had met these conditions, Congress would readmit it to the Union. Like the president's proposal, the Wade-Davis bill left up to the states the question of political rights for blacks.

Congress passed the bill a few days before it adjourned in 1864, and Lincoln disposed of it with a pocket veto. His action enraged the Radical leaders, and the pragmatic Lincoln became convinced he would have to accept at least some of the Radical demands. He began to move toward a new approach to Reconstruction.

The Death of Lincoln

What plan he might have produced no one can say. On the night of April 14, 1865, Lincoln and his wife at-

ABRAHAM LINCOLN AND HIS SON TAD
During the last difficult months of the Civil War, Lincoln often found relief from the strains of his office in the company of his young son, Thomas (known as "Tad"), shown here with his father in an 1864 photograph by Mathew Brady. Much has been written about Lincoln's turbulent family life. His wife, Mary Todd Lincoln, was apparently a moody and difficult woman, but the marriage seems generally to have been a happy one. The Lincolns did, however, experience a series of heartbreaking bereavements as three of their four sons died in childhood. Their second child, Edward, died in 1850 at the age of three; their third, "Willie," died of fever in 1862 at the age of eleven; Tad outlived his father by only a few years and died in 1871 at the age of eighteen. Robert Todd Lincoln, the president's eldest son, lived a long, successful, but not very happy life, during which he served as secretary of war, American minister to England, and president of the Pullman Railroad Car Company. *(Library of Congress)*

tended a play at Ford's Theater in Washington. As they sat in the presidential box, John Wilkes Booth, an unsuccessful actor obsessed with aiding the Southern cause, entered the box from the rear and shot Lincoln in the head. The president was carried unconscious to a house across the street, where early the next morning, surrounded by family, friends, and political associates (among them a tearful Charles Sumner), he died.

The circumstances of Lincoln's death earned him immediate martyrdom. It also produced something close to hysteria throughout the North. There were accusations that Booth had acted as part of a great conspiracy—accusations that contained some truth. Booth did indeed have associates, one of whom shot and wounded Secretary of State Seward the night of the assassination, another of whom abandoned at the last moment a scheme to murder Vice President Johnson. Booth himself escaped on horseback into the Virginia countryside, where, on April 26, he was cornered by Union troops and shot to death in a blazing barn. A military tribunal convicted eight other people of participating in the conspiracy (at least two of them on the basis of virtually no evidence). Four were hanged.

To many Northerners, however, the murder of the president seemed evidence of an even greater conspiracy—one masterminded and directed by the unrepentant leaders of the defeated South. Militant Republicans exploited such suspicions relentlessly for months, ensuring that Lincoln's death would help doom his plans for a relatively easy peace.

Johnson and "Restoration"

Leadership of the Moderates and Conservatives fell to Lincoln's successor, Andrew Johnson, who was not well suited, either by circumstance or personality, for the task. A Democrat until he had joined the Union ticket with Lincoln in 1864, he became a Republican president at a moment when partisan passions were growing. Johnson himself was an intemperate and tactless man, filled with resentments and insecurities. He was also openly hostile to the freed slaves and unwilling to support any plans that guaranteed them civil equality or enfranchisement. He once declared, "White men alone must manage the South."

Johnson revealed his plan for Reconstruction—or "Restoration," as he preferred to call it—soon after he took office, and implemented it during the summer of 1865 when Congress was in recess. Like Lincoln, he offered amnesty to those Southerners who would take an oath of allegiance. (High-ranking Confederate officials and any white Southerner with land worth $20,000 or more would have to apply to the president for individual pardons. Johnson, a self-made man, liked the thought of the great planter aristocrats humbling themselves before him.) In most other respects, however, his plan resembled that of the Wade-Davis bill. For each state, the president appointed a provisional governor, who was to invite qualified voters to elect delegates to a constitutional convention. Johnson did not specify how many qualified voters were necessary, but he implied that he would require a majority (as

had the Wade-Davis bill). In order to win readmission to Congress, a state had to revoke its ordinance of secession, abolish slavery and ratify the Thirteenth Amendment, and repudiate the Confederate and state war debts. The final procedure before restoration was for a state to elect a state government and send representatives to Congress.

By the end of 1865, all the seceded states had formed new governments—some under Lincoln's plan, some under Johnson's—and were prepared to rejoin the Union as soon as Congress recognized them. But Radical Republicans vowed not to recognize the Johnson governments, just as they had previously refused to recognize the Lincoln regimes; for by now, Northern opinion had become more hostile toward the South than it had been a year earlier when Congress passed the Wade-Davis bill. Many Northerners were disturbed by the apparent reluctance of some delegates to the Southern conventions to abolish slavery, and by the refusal of all the conventions to grant suffrage to any blacks. They were astounded that states claiming to be "loyal" should elect as state officials and representatives to Congress prominent leaders of the recent Confederacy. Particularly hard to accept was Georgia's choice of Alexander H. Stephens, former Confederate vice president, as a United States senator.

RADICAL RECONSTRUCTION

Reconstruction under Johnson's plan—often known as "presidential Reconstruction"—continued only until Congress reconvened in December 1865. At that point, Congress refused to seat the senators and representatives of the states the president had "restored." Instead, it set up a new Joint Committee on Reconstruction to investigate conditions in the South and to help Congress create a Reconstruction policy of its own. The period of "congressional" or "Radical" Reconstruction had begun.

The Black Codes

Meanwhile, events in the South were driving Northern opinion even more toward the Radicals. Throughout the South in 1865 and early 1866, state legislatures were enacting sets of laws known as the Black Codes, modeled in many ways on the codes that had regulated free blacks in the prewar South. The laws were designed to reestablish planter control over black workers. Although there were variations from state to state, all the codes authorized local officials to appre-

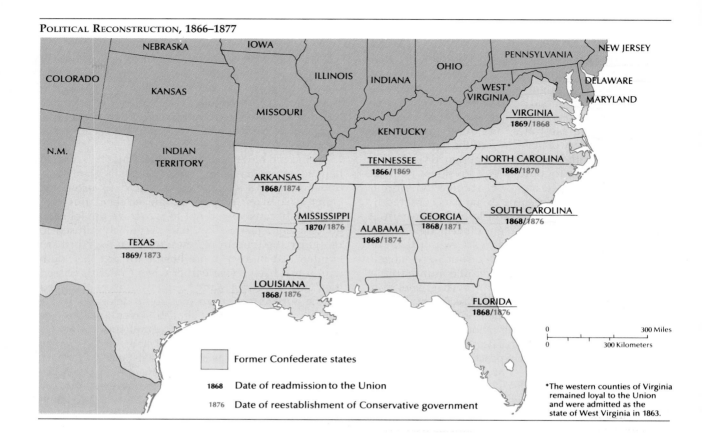

NEBRASKA
IOWA
COLORADO
KANSAS
MISSOURI
N.M.
INDIAN TERRITORY
ARKANSAS
1868/1874
TEXAS
1869/1873
LOUISIANA
1868/1876
ILLINOIS
INDIANA
OHIO
PENNSYLVANIA
NEW JERSEY
DELAWARE
MARYLAND
WEST* VIRGINIA
VIRGINIA
1869/1868
KENTUCKY
TENNESSEE
1866/1869
NORTH CAROLINA
1868/1870
MISSISSIPPI
1870/1876
ALABAMA
1868/1874
GEORGIA
1868/1871
SOUTH CAROLINA
1868/1876
FLORIDA
1868/1876

0   300 Miles
0   300 Kilometers

Former Confederate states

1868 Date of readmission to the Union

1876 Date of reestablishment of Conservative government

*The western counties of Virginia remained loyal to the Union and were admitted as the state of West Virginia in 1863.

hend unemployed blacks, fine them for vagrancy, and hire them out to private employers to satisfy the fine. Some of the codes forbade blacks to own or lease farms or to take any jobs other than as plantation workers or domestic servants. To much of the white South, the Black Codes were a realistic approach to a great social problem. To most of the North, and to most African Americans, they represented a return to slavery in all but name.

Congress's first response to the Black Codes was to extend the life of the Freedmen's Bureau and to widen its powers. It could now establish special courts for settling labor disputes, which could nullify work agreements forced on freedmen under the Black Codes. In April, Congress struck again at the Black Codes by passing the First Civil Rights Act, which declared blacks to be citizens of the United States and empowered the federal government to intervene in state affairs when necessary to protect the rights of citizens. Johnson vetoed both the Freedmen's Bureau and Civil Rights bills, but Congress eventually overrode him.

✳The Fourteenth Amendment ✳

In April 1866, the Radicals acted again. The Joint Committee on Reconstruction submitted a proposed Fourteenth Amendment to the Constitution, which Congress approved in early summer and sent to the states for ratification. Eventually, it became one of the most important of all the provisions in the Constitution.

The amendment offered the first constitutional definition of American citizenship. Everyone born in the United States, and everyone naturalized, was automatically a citizen and entitled to equal protection of the laws by both state and national governments. There could be no other citizenship requirements. The amendment also imposed penalties—reduction of representation in Congress and on the electoral college—on states that denied suffrage to any adult male inhabitants. (This was the first time the Constitution made reference to gender, and the wording clearly reflected the prevailing view in Congress and elsewhere that the franchise was properly restricted to men.) Finally, it prohibited those who had taken an oath to support the Constitution (that is, members of Congress and other federal officials) and later had aided the Confederacy from holding any state or federal office unless two-thirds of Congress voted to pardon them.

Congressional Radicals made it clear that if Southern legislatures ratified the Fourteenth Amendment, their states would be readmitted to the Union. But only Tennessee did so. The refusal of the former Confederate states to ratify, along with the refusal of Kentucky

THE MEMPHIS RACE RIOT, 1866
Angry whites (shown here shooting down blacks) rampaged through the black neighborhoods of Memphis, Tennessee, during the first three days of May 1866, burning homes, schools, and churches and leaving forty-six people dead. Some claimed the riot was a response to strict new regulations protecting blacks that had been imposed on Tennessee by General George Stoneman, the military commander of the district; others argued that it was an attempt by whites to intimidate and control a black population that was trying to exercise its new freedom. Such riots were among the events that persuaded Radical Republicans in Congress to press for a harsher policy of Reconstruction. *(The Granger Collection)*

and Delaware, denied the amendment the necessary approval of three-fourths of the states and temporarily derailed it.

In the meantime, however, the Radicals were growing stronger, in part because of Northern anger at the South's and Johnson's recalcitrance. Bloody race riots broke out in 1866 in New Orleans, Memphis, and other Southern cities in which angry whites rampaged through black neighborhoods, burning homes, schools, and churches. In Memphis, 46 people, almost all blacks, died. Radicals cited the riots as evidence of the inadequacy of Johnson's policy.

In the 1866 congressional elections, Johnson campaigned actively for Conservative candidates, but he did his own cause more harm than good with his intemperate speeches. The voters returned an overwhelming majority of Republicans, most of them Radicals, to Congress. In the Senate, there were now 42 Republicans to 11 Democrats; in the House, 143 Republicans to 49 Democrats. (The South remained largely unrepresented in both chambers.) Nothing now prevented the Republicans in Congress from devising a Reconstruction plan of their own.

The Congressional Plan

The Radicals passed three Reconstruction bills early in 1867. Johnson vetoed them all, and Congress overrode him each time. Finally, nearly two years after the end of the war, the federal government had established a coherent plan for Reconstruction.

That two-year delay significantly affected the South's reaction to the program. In 1865, with the South reeling from its defeat and nearly prostrate, the federal government could probably have imposed almost any plan on the region without much resistance. But by 1867, the South had already begun to reconstruct itself under the reasonably generous terms Lincoln and Johnson had extended. Measures that might once have seemed moderate to most white Southerners now seemed radical and tyrannical, and the congressional Reconstruction plan created deep resentments and continuing resistance.

Under the congressional plan, Tennessee, which had ratified the Fourteenth Amendment, was promptly readmitted. But the Lincoln-Johnson governments of the other ten Confederate states were rejected. Those states were now combined into five military districts, each under a military commander who—in preparation for the readmission of the states—was to register qualified voters, defined as all adult black males and those white males who had not participated in the rebellion. After the completion of registration, voters would elect a convention to prepare a new state constitution, which had to include provisions for black suffrage. Once voters ratified the new constitution, states could hold elections for a government. Finally, if Congress approved the state's new constitution, if the state legislature ratified the Fourteenth Amendment, and if enough other states ratified it to make the amendment part of the Constitution, then the state was to be restored to the Union.

By 1868, seven more of the former Confederate states (Arkansas, North Carolina, South Carolina, Louisiana, Alabama, Georgia, and Florida) had fulfilled these conditions (including ratification of the Fourteenth Amendment, which now became part of the Constitution) and were readmitted to the Union. Conservative whites held up the return of Virginia and Texas until 1869 and of Mississippi until 1870. By then, Congress had added an additional requirement for readmission: ratification of another constitutional amendment.

The Fifteenth Amendment

This was the Fifteenth Amendment, which forbade the states and the federal government to deny suffrage to any citizen on account of "race, color, or previous condition of servitude." Several Northern and border states refused to approve it, and it was adopted only with the support of the four Southern states that had to ratify it in order to be readmitted to the Union.

The Fifteenth Amendment was important in theory, but in practice it had little effect on black suffrage for many years. It was, the historian Henry Adams once wrote, "more remarkable for what it does not than for what it does contain." The amendment guaranteed African Americans the right to vote, but not the right to hold public office. It did nothing to prohibit the literacy, property, and educational tests and the poll taxes that would be used by generations of white Southern leaders to prevent most blacks (and many poor whites) from voting.

Nor did the amendment make any reference to women. That was a particularly bitter blow to some feminists, because they had worked since the Civil War to ensure that any efforts to extend suffrage would link the black vote with the female vote. In 1866, Elizabeth Cady Stanton, Susan B. Anthony, Lucy Stone, and others had joined together in the Equal Rights Association, which worked to incorporate woman suffrage in state constitutions. In 1868, they created the Working Women's Association, which embraced a broad agenda of feminist and labor causes, including woman suffrage. And in 1869, Stanton and Anthony (now leading the National Woman Suffrage Association) opposed the Fifteenth Amendment because of its failure to include women in its provisions and because, some said, it elevated black men over white women. Without woman suffrage, Stanton argued, political power would flow to "the lower orders of Chinese, Africans, Germans, and Irish, with their low ideals of womanhood." By opposing the Fifteenth Amendment, Stanton and Anthony alienated many more moderate feminists (among them Lucy Stone) and caused a final breakdown of the alliance between feminists and abolitionists, who had worked together so closely since the 1840s.

The limits of the Fifteenth Amendment reflected the politics of its principal sponsors. Southern Republicans and Northern Radicals did not want to guarantee universal suffrage, because they feared that in doing so they would assure former Confederates the right to vote. Many Northern politicians, moreover, wanted to preserve voting restrictions in their own states. Some western states, for example, prohibited Chinese from voting, and several New England states retained property and literacy requirements. Republicans, in other words, wanted to expand their own electoral strength in the South (by enfranchising former slaves while disenfranchising former Confederates) without upsetting existing voting restrictions in the North, some of which also helped the Republicans.

Impeaching the President, Assaulting the Courts

To stop the president from interfering with their designs, Radicals in Congress passed two remarkable laws in 1867. One, the Tenure of Office Act, forbade the president to remove civil officials, including members of his cabinet, without the consent of the Senate. The principal purpose of the law was to protect the job of Secretary of War Edwin M. Stanton, the only Lincoln appointee still in the Cabinet, who was cooperating with the Radicals. The other law, the Command of the Army Act, prohibited the president from issuing military orders except through the commanding general of the army (General Grant), whose headquarters were to be in Washington and who could not be relieved or assigned elsewhere without the consent of the Senate.

President Johnson had long since ceased to be a serious obstacle to the passage of Radical legislation. But he was still the official charged with administering the Reconstruction programs, and as such, the Radicals believed, he was a serious impediment to their plans. Early in 1867 they began looking for a way to remove him. The only constitutional grounds for impeachment were "high crimes or misdemeanors." Republicans could find nothing on which to base such charges until Johnson gave them what they considered a plausible reason for action. He deliberately violated the Tenure of Office Act—in hopes of bringing a test case of the law before the courts. He dismissed Secretary of War Stanton even after Congress had refused to agree.

In the House of Representatives, elated Radicals impeached the president on eleven charges and sent them

THADDEUS STEVENS
Stern, uncompromising, and severe, Thaddeus Stevens of Pennsylvania was the incarnation of the North's vindictive designs, according to many Southerners during (and long after) Reconstruction. Others admired him as one of the few white leaders who remained firmly committed to racial equality. He served in the House of Representatives from 1849 to 1853 and again, more prominently, from 1859 until his death in 1868. He spent much of the last year of his life organizing and managing the impeachment trial of Andrew Johnson. *(Library of Congress)*

to the Senate for trial. The first nine counts dealt with the violation of the Tenure of Office Act. The tenth and eleventh charged Johnson with slandering Congress and with not enforcing the Reconstruction Acts.

The trial before the Senate lasted through April and May 1868. The president's accusers argued that Johnson had defied Congress and was indeed guilty of high crimes and misdemeanors. His defenders claimed that he had acted properly in challenging what he considered an unconstitutional law. Radicals put heavy pressure on all the Republican senators, but the Moderates (who were losing faith in the Radical program) vacil-

lated. On the first three charges to come to a vote, seven Republicans joined the twelve Democrats to support acquittal. The vote was 35 to 19, one short of the constitutionally required two-thirds majority. After that, the Radicals dropped the impeachment campaign.

The congressional Radicals also took action to stop the Supreme Court from interfering with their plans. In 1866, the Court had declared in *Ex parte Milligan* that military tribunals were unconstitutional in places where civil courts were functioning, a decision that seemed to threaten the system of military government the Congress was establishing in the South. Radicals immediately proposed legislation to require a two-thirds majority of the justices to overrule a law of Congress, to deny the Court jurisdiction in Reconstruction cases, to reduce its membership to three, and even to abolish it. The justices apparently took note. Over the next two years, the Court refused to accept jurisdiction in any cases involving Reconstruction. The bills affecting the Court never passed.

THE SOUTH IN RECONSTRUCTION

When white Southerners spoke bitterly in later years of the effects of Reconstruction, they referred most frequently to the governments Congress helped impose on them—governments they claimed were both incompetent and corrupt, that saddled the region with enormous debts, and that trampled on the rights of citizens. When black Southerners and their defenders condemned Reconstruction, in contrast, they spoke of the failure of the national and state governments to go far enough to guarantee freedmen even the most elemental rights of citizenship—a failure that resulted in a harsh new system of economic subordination. (See "Where Historians Disagree," pp. 432–433.)

The Reconstruction Governments

In the ten states of the South that were reorganized under the congressional plan, approximately one-fourth of the white males were at first excluded from voting or holding office. That produced black majorities among voters in South Carolina, Mississippi, and Louisiana (states where blacks were also a majority of the population), and in Alabama and Florida (where they were not). But the government soon lifted most suffrage restrictions so that nearly all white males could soon vote. After that, Republicans maintained control only with the support of many Southern whites.

THE BURDENED SOUTH

This Reconstruction-era cartoon expresses the South's sense of its oppression at the hands of Northern Republicans. President Grant (whose hat bears Abraham Lincoln's initials) rides in comfort in a giant carpetbag, guarded by bayonet-wielding soldiers, as the South staggers under the burden in chains. More evidence of destruction and military occupation is visible in the background. *(Culver)*

Critics called these Southern white Republicans "scalawags." Many were former Whigs who had never felt comfortable in the Democratic Party—some of them wealthy (or once wealthy) planters or businessmen interested in the economic development of the region. Others were farmers who lived in remote areas where there had been little or no slavery and who hoped the Republican program of internal improvements would help end their economic isolation. Despite their diverse social positions, scalawags shared a belief that the Republican Party would serve their economic interests better than the Democrats.

White men from the North also served as Republican leaders in the South. Critics of Reconstruction referred to them pejoratively as "carpetbaggers," which conveyed an image of penniless adventurers who arrived with all their possessions in a carpetbag (a common kind of cheap suitcase covered with carpeting material). In fact, most of the so-called carpetbaggers were well-educated people of middle-class origin, many of them doctors, lawyers, and teachers. Most were veterans of the Union army who looked on the South as a new frontier, more promising than the West. They had settled there at war's end as hopeful planters, or as business and professional people.

But the most numerous Republicans in the South were the black freedmen, most of whom had no previous experience in politics and who tried, therefore, to build institutions through which they could learn to exercise their power. In several states, African-American voters held their own conventions to chart their future course. One such "colored convention," as Southern whites called them, assembled in Alabama in 1867 and announced: "We claim exactly the same rights, privileges and immunities as are enjoyed by white men—we ask nothing more and will be content with nothing less." The black churches freedmen created after emancipation, when they withdrew from the white-dominated churches they had been compelled to attend under slavery, also helped give unity and political self-confidence to the former slaves.

African Americans played a significant role in the politics of the Reconstruction South. They served as delegates to the constitutional conventions. They held public offices of practically every kind. Between 1869 and 1901, twenty blacks served in the U.S. House of Representatives, two in the Senate (Hiram Revels of Mississippi and Blanche K. Bruce of Virginia). African Americans served, too, in state legislatures and in various other state offices. Southern whites complained loudly (both at the time and for generations to come) about "Negro rule" during Reconstruction, but no such thing ever actually existed in any of the states. No black man was ever elected governor of a Southern state (although Lieutenant Governor P. B. S. Pinchback briefly performed gubernatorial duties in Louisiana). Blacks never controlled any of the state legislatures, although they held a majority in the lower house in South Carolina for a time. In the South as a whole, the percentage of black officeholders was always far lower than the percentage of blacks in the population.

The record of the Reconstruction governments is mixed. Critics at the time and since denounced them for corruption and financial extravagance, and there is some truth to both charges. Officeholders in many states enriched themselves through graft and other illicit activities. State budgets expanded to hitherto unknown totals, and state debts soared to previously un-

SENATOR HIRAM REVELS
White Southerners complained bitterly of "Negro rule" during Reconstruction. In fact, African Americans never occupied more than a small minority of elected positions in the Reconstruction South. One of the most prominent was Hiram R. Revels, who served as a United States Senator from Mississippi in the 1870s. *(United States Senate)*

dreamed-of heights. In South Carolina, for example, the public debt increased from $7 million to $29 million in eight years.

But the corruption in the South, real as it was, was hardly unique to the Reconstruction governments. Corruption was at least as rampant in the Northern states. And in both North and South, it was a result of the same thing: a rapid economic expansion of government services (and revenues) that put new strains on (and new temptations before) elected officials everywhere. The end of Reconstruction did not end corruption in Southern state governments. In many states, in fact, corruption increased.

And the state expenditures of the Reconstruction years were huge only in comparison with the meager budgets of the antebellum era. They represented an effort to provide the South with desperately needed services that antebellum governments had never offered:

public education, public works programs, poor relief, and other costly new commitments. There were, to be sure, graft and extravagance in Reconstruction governments; there were also positive and permanent accomplishments.

Education

Perhaps the most important of those accomplishments was a dramatic improvement in Southern education—an improvement that benefited both whites and blacks. In the first years of Reconstruction, much of the impetus for educational reform in the South came from outside groups—from the Freedmen's Bureau, from Northern private philanthropic organizations, from many Northern women, black and white, who traveled to the South to teach in freedmen's schools—and from Southern blacks themselves. Over the opposition of many Southern whites, who feared that education would give blacks "false notions of equality," these reformers established a large network of schools for former slaves—4,000 schools by 1870, staffed by 9,000 teachers (half of them black), teaching 200,000 students (about 12 percent of the total school-age population of the freedmen). In the 1870s, Reconstruction governments began to build a comprehensive public school system in the South. By 1876, more than half of all white children and about 40 percent of all black children were attending schools in the South. Several black "academies," offering more advanced education, also began operating. Gradually, these academies grew into an important network of black colleges and universities, which included such distinguished schools as Fisk and Atlanta Universities and Morehouse College.

Already, however, Southern education was becoming divided into two separate systems, one black and one white. Early efforts to integrate the schools of the region were a dismal failure. The Freedmen's Bureau schools, for example, were open to students of all races, but almost no whites attended them. New Orleans set up an integrated school system under the Reconstruction government; again, whites almost universally stayed away. The one federal effort to mandate school integration—the Civil Rights Act of 1875—had its provisions for educational desegregation removed before it was passed. As soon as the Republican governments of Reconstruction were replaced, the new Southern Democratic regimes quickly abandoned all efforts to promote integration.

Landownership and Tenancy

The most ambitious goal of the Freedmen's Bureau, and of some Republican Radicals in Congress, was to

The Southern Plantation Before and After Emancipation: Barrow Plantation, Oglethorpe County, Georgia

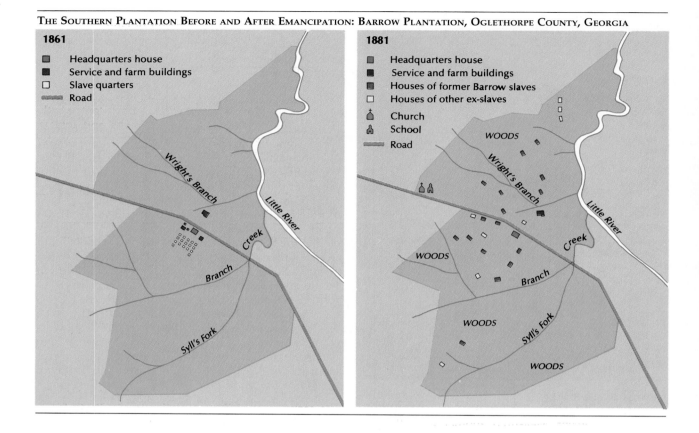

make Reconstruction the vehicle for a fundamental reform of landownership in the South. The effort failed. In the last years of the war and the first years of Reconstruction, the Freedmen's Bureau did oversee the redistribution of substantial amounts of land to freedmen in a few areas—notably the Sea Islands of South Carolina and Georgia, and areas of Mississippi that had once belonged to the family of Jefferson Davis. By June 1865, the Bureau had settled nearly 10,000 black families on their own land—most of it drawn from abandoned plantations—arousing dreams among former slaves throughout the South of "forty acres and a mule."

By the end of that year, however, the experiment was already collapsing. Southern plantation owners were returning and demanding the restoration of their property, and President Johnson was supporting their demands. Despite the resistance of the Freedmen's Bureau, the government eventually returned most of the confiscated land to the original white owners. Congress, moreover, never had much stomach for the idea of land redistribution. Very few Northern Republicans

believed that the federal government had the right to confiscate property.

Even so, distribution of landownership in the South changed considerably in the postwar years. Among whites, there was a striking decline in landownership, from 80 percent before the war to 67 percent by the end of Reconstruction. Some whites lost their land because of unpaid debt or increased taxes; some left the marginal lands they had owned to move to more fertile areas, where they rented. Among blacks, during the same period, the proportion who owned land rose from virtually none to more than 20 percent. Many black landowners acquired their property through hard work or luck or both. But some relied on assistance from white-dominated financial or philanthropic institutions. One of them was the Freedman's Bank, established in 1865 by antislavery whites in an effort to promote landownership among blacks. They persuaded thousands of freedmen to deposit their modest savings in the bank, but then invested heavily in unsuccessful enterprises. It was ill prepared, therefore, for the national depression of the 1870s and it failed in 1874.

Still, most blacks, and a growing minority of whites, did not own their own land during Reconstruction; and some who acquired land in the 1860s had lost it by the 1890s. These people worked for others in one form or another. Many black agricultural laborers—perhaps 25 percent of the total—simply worked for wages. Most, however, became tenants of white landowners—working their own plots of land and paying their landlords either a fixed rent or a share of their crop. (See pp. 437–440.)

The new system represented a repudiation by blacks of the gang-labor system of the antebellum plantation, in which slaves had lived and worked together under the direction of a master. As tenants and share-croppers, blacks enjoyed at least a physical independence from their landlords and had the sense of working their own land, even if in most cases they could never hope to buy it. But tenantry also benefited landlords in some ways, relieving them of any responsibility for the physical well-being of their workers.

Incomes and Credit

In some respects, the postwar years were a period of remarkable economic progress for blacks. If the material benefits they had received under slavery are calculated as income, then prewar blacks had earned about a 22 percent share of the profits of the plantation system. By the end of Reconstruction, they were earning 56 percent. Measured another way, the per capita income of blacks rose 46 percent between 1857 and 1879, while the per capita income of whites declined 35 percent. This represented one of the most significant redistributions of income in American history.

But these figures are somewhat misleading. For one thing, while the black share of profits was increasing, the total profits of Southern agriculture were declining—a result of the dislocations of the war and a reduction in the world market for cotton. For another thing, while blacks were earning a greater return on each hour of labor than they had under slavery, they were working fewer hours. Women and children were less likely to labor in the fields than in the past. Adult men tended to work shorter days. In all, the black labor force worked about one-third fewer hours during Reconstruction than it had been compelled to do under slavery—a reduction that brought the working schedule of blacks roughly into line with that of white farm laborers. Nor did the income redistribution of the post-war years lift many blacks out of poverty. Black per capita income rose from about one quarter of white per capita income to about one-half in the first few years after the war. And after this initial increase, it rose hardly at all.

For blacks and poor whites alike, whatever gains there might have been as a result of land and income redistribution were often overshadowed by the ravages of the crop lien system. Few of the traditional institutions of credit in the South—the "factors" and banks—returned after the war. In their stead emerged a new system of credit, centered in large part on local country stores, some of them owned by planters, others by independent merchants. Blacks and whites, landowners and tenants—all depended on these stores for such necessities as food, clothing, seed, and farm implements. And since farmers did not have the same steady cash flow as other workers, customers usually had to rely on credit from these merchants in order to purchase what they needed. Most local stores had no competition (and went to great lengths to ensure that things stayed that way). As a result, they were able to set interest rates as high as 50 or 60 percent. Farmers had to give the merchants a lien (or claim) on their crops as collateral for the loans (thus the term "crop lien system," generally used to describe Southern farming in this period). Farmers who suffered a few bad years in a row, as often happened, could become trapped in a cycle of debt from which they could never escape.

This burdensome credit system had a number of effects on the region, almost all of them unhealthy. One was that some blacks who had acquired land during the early years of Reconstruction gradually lost it as they fell into debt. So, to a lesser extent, did white small landowners. Another was that Southern farmers became almost wholly dependent on cash crops—and most of all on cotton—because only such marketable commodities seemed to offer any possibility of escape from debt. Thus Southern agriculture, never sufficiently diversified even in the best of times, became more one-dimensional than ever. The relentless planting of cotton, moreover, was contributing to an exhaustion of the soil. The crop lien system, in other words, was not only helping to impoverish small farmers; it was also contributing to a general decline in the Southern agricultural economy.

The African-American Family in Freedom

One of the most striking features of the black response to Reconstruction was the effort to build or rebuild family structures and to protect them from the interference they had experienced under slavery. A major reason for the rapid departure of so many blacks from plantations was the desire to find lost relatives and reunite families. Thousands of African Americans wandered through the South looking for husbands, wives, children, or other relatives from whom they had been

AFRICAN-AMERICAN WORK AFTER SLAVERY
Black men and women engaged in a wide range of economic activities in the aftermath of slavery. But discrimination by white Southerners and the former slaves' own lack of education limited most of them to relatively menial jobs. Many black women (including this former slave) earned money for their families by working as "washer women," doing laundry for white people. *(Historic New Orleans Collection)*

separated. Former slaves rushed to have marriages, previously without legal standing, sanctified by church and law. Black families resisted living in the former slave quarters and moved instead to small cabins scattered widely across the countryside, where they could enjoy at least some privacy.

Within the black family, the definition of male and female roles quickly came to resemble that within white families. Many women and children ceased working in the fields. Such work, they believed, was a badge of slavery. Instead, many women restricted themselves largely to domestic tasks—cooking, cleaning, gardening, raising children, attending to the needs of their husbands. Some black husbands refused to allow their wives to work as servants in white homes. "When I married my wife I married her to wait on me," one freedman told a former master who was attempting to hire his wife as a servant. "She got all she can do right here for me and the children."

Still, middle-class notions of domesticity were often difficult to sustain in the impoverished circumstances of most former slaves. Economic necessity required many black women to engage in income-producing activities, including activities that they and their husbands resisted because it reminded them of slavery: working as domestic servants, taking in laundry, or helping in the field. By the end of Reconstruction, half of all black women over the age of sixteen were working for wages. And unlike white working women, most black female income-earners were married.

THE GRANT ADMINISTRATION

Exhausted by the political turmoil of the Johnson administration, American voters in 1868 yearned for a strong, stable figure to guide them through the troubled years of Reconstruction. They did not find one. Instead, they turned trustingly to General Ulysses S. Grant, the hero of the war and, by 1868, a revered national idol. Grant was a failure as president. During his two terms in office, he faced problems that would have taxed the abilities of a master of statecraft. Grant, however, was a dull and unimaginative man with few political skills and little vision.

The Soldier President

Grant could have had the nomination of either party in 1868. But believing that Republican Reconstruction policies were more attuned to public opinion than the Democratic alternatives, he accepted the Republican nomination. The Democrats nominated former governor Horatio Seymour of New York. The campaign was an exceptionally bitter one, in large part because the Democrats, desperate to revive their party's declining fortunes, chose to make opposition to Reconstruction and an open defense of white supremacy the basis of their appeal. The Ku Klux Klan (see p. 430), in the meantime, terrorized Southern Republicans, both black and white, in an effort to discourage them from voting. One member of Congress from Arkansas and three members of the South Carolina legislature were assassinated in the violence and terror that accompanied the campaign in the South.

The 1868 election was also the first in which Northern capitalists united behind the Republicans, making the party the principal defender of industrial growth in American politics, as it would remain for several generations. It was also in 1868 that the so-called Stalwarts established their dominance within the party. Fervently committed to the economic interests of Northern capitalists, they worked from within to shift the party's concerns away from issues related to the South and the freedmen and toward industrialization.

Grant's triumph in the end was surprisingly narrow, an indication, perhaps of how unpopular Reconstruction was already becoming. He carried twenty-six states to Seymour's eight. But Grant's popular majority was a scant 310,000 votes, a result of 500,000 black votes in the reconstructed states of the South.

Grant entered the White House with no political experience of any kind, and his performance in office was clumsy and ineffectual from the start. Except for Hamilton Fish, whom Grant appointed secretary of state and who served for eight years with great distinction, most members of the cabinet were as dull and inept as the president. Grant relied chiefly, and increasingly, on the machine leaders in the party—the group most ardently devoted to the spoils system.

Grant used the spoils system even more blatantly than most of his predecessors. And in doing so, he provoked the opposition of Senator Charles Sumner and other Republican leaders, who joined with reformers to agitate for a new civil service system to limit the president's appointive powers. Nothing came of their efforts. Grant soon attracted the hostility of other Republicans as well. Many Northerners were growing disillusioned with Reconstruction, disgusted by stories of corruption, extravagance, and incompetence in the South. They opposed Grant's continuing support of radical programs there. Some Republicans suspected (correctly) that there was corruption in the Grant administration itself. Still others criticized Grant because he did not support a tariff reduction.

The Liberal Republicans

By the end of Grant's first term, therefore, a substantial faction of the party—those who called themselves Liberal Republicans—had come to oppose what they called "Grantism." They had many disagreements with the president, but among the most important was their distaste for the way he used the patronage system to reward political cronies. They agitated, therefore, for a civil service system, which would limit the president's powers of appointment and, presumably, raise the quality of those working in government. Such scholarly journalists as E. L. Godkin of *The Nation* and

George William Curtis of *Harper's Weekly* argued that the government should base its appointments not on services to the party but on fitness for office as determined by competitive examinations, as the British government already was doing. Grant reluctantly agreed to establish a civil service commission, which Congress authorized in 1871, to devise a system of hiring based on merit. It proposed a set of rules that Grant seemed to approve; but the president was not really much interested in reform, and even if he had been he could not have persuaded his followers to accept a new system that would undermine the very basis of party loyalty—patronage. Nothing came of the commission's work.

Debate over civil service reform remained one of the leading political issues of the next three decades. The debate involved more than simply an argument over patronage and corruption. It also reflected basic differences of opinion over who was fit to serve in public life. Middle-class reformers were saying, implicitly, that only educated, middle-class people (the "best men") should be permitted access to government office. Their concerns grew in large part out of their alarm over the character of those who served in the Reconstruction governments and their fear that the growing immigrant population of the North would produce similarly unfit leaders there. As Charles Francis Adams, Jr., one of the leaders of the Liberal Republicans, once said: "Universal suffrage can only mean in plain English the government of ignorance and vice:—it means a European, and especially Celtic proletariat on the Atlantic coast, an African proletariat on the shores of the Gulf, and a Chinese proletariat on the Pacific." Civil service reform would, in short, help limit the power of democracy to debase public life.

Those opposing civil service reform included not just party leaders but immigrants, workers, some farmers, and others. They argued that the establishment of an elite corps of civil servants would be undemocratic. It would exclude them from participation in government and restrict power to the upper classes. That was precisely what the reformers hoped to do.

In 1872, hoping to prevent Grant's reelection, the Liberal Republicans deserted the party and nominated their own presidential candidate: Horace Greeley, veteran editor and publisher of the *New York Tribune*. The Democrats, somewhat reluctantly, named Greeley their candidate as well, hoping that the alliance with the Liberals would enable them to defeat Grant. But the effort was in vain. Grant won a substantial victory, polling 286 electoral votes and 3,597,000 popular votes to Greeley's 66 and 2,834,000. Greeley had carried only two Southern and four border states. Three weeks later, apparently crushed by his defeat, Greeley died.

Le voleur de « troisième mandat. » — Dessin de Houssot, d'après une gravure originale.

THE GRANT SCANDALS
This hostile cartoon suggests the growing popular discontent at the many scandals plaguing the Grant administration in its last years. Although the president himself was never proved to have been involved in any illegality, the scandals damaged his reputation nevertheless and helped thwart his hope of winning a third term as president. *(Bettmann)*

The Grant Scandals

During the 1872 campaign, the first of a series of political scandals came to light that would plague Grant and the Republicans for the next eight years. It involved the Crédit Mobilier, a French-owned construction company that had helped build the Union Pacific Railroad. The heads of Crédit Mobilier had used their positions as Union Pacific stockholders to steer large and fraudulent contracts to their construction company, in the process bilking the Union Pacific (and the federal government, which provided large subsidies to the railroad) of millions. To prevent investigations, the directors had transferred some Crédit Mobilier stock to key members of Congress. But in 1872, Congress did

investigate and revealed that some highly placed Republicans—including Schuyler Colfax, now Grant's vice president—had accepted stock.

One dreary episode followed another in Grant's second term. Benjamin H. Bristow, Grant's third Treasury secretary, discovered that some of his officials and a group of distillers operating as a "Whiskey ring" were cheating the government out of taxes by filing false reports. Among those involved was the president's private secretary, Orville E. Babcock. Then a House investigation revealed that William W. Belknap, secretary of war, had accepted bribes to retain an Indian-post trader in office; it became known as the "Indian ring." Other, lesser scandals added to the growing impression that "Grantism" had brought rampant corruption to government.

The Greenback Question

Compounding Grant's, and the nation's, problems was the financial crisis known as the Panic of 1873. It began with the failure of a leading investment banking firm, Jay Cooke and Company, which had invested too heavily in postwar railroad building. There had been panics before—in 1819, 1837, and 1857—but this was the worst one yet. The depression it produced lasted four years.

Debtors now pressured the government to inflate the currency, which would have made it easier for them to pay their debts. More specifically, they urged the government to redeem its war bonds with "greenbacks"—paper currency of the sort issued during the Civil War—which would increase the amount of money in circulation, lower the value of the dollar, and hence reduce the value of their debts. But Grant and most Republicans favored a "sound" currency—based solidly on gold reserves—which would favor the interests of banks and other creditors by keeping the dollar, and hence the value of the debts owed to them, high.

The greenback question would not go away. For one thing, there was the approximately $356 million in paper currency issued during the Civil War that was still in circulation. And in 1873, when the Supreme Court ruled in *Knox* v. *Lee* that greenbacks were legal, the Treasury issued more in response to the panic. The following year, Congress voted to raise the total further. But Grant, under pressure from eastern financial interests, vetoed the measure—over the loud objections of many Republicans.

In 1875, Republican leaders in Congress, in an effort to crush the greenback movement for good, passed the Specie Resumption Act. This law provided that after January 1, 1879, the greenback dollars, whose value constantly fluctuated, would be redeemed by the government and replaced with new certificates, firmly pegged to the price of gold. The law satisfied creditors, who had worried that debts would be repaid in debased paper currency. But "resumption" did nothing for debtors, because the gold-based money supply was not able to expand enough to help them.

In 1875, the greenbackers, as the inflationists were called, formed their own political organization: the National Greenback Party. It was active in the next three presidential elections, but it failed to gain widespread support. It did, however, keep the money issue alive. And in the 1880s, the greenback forces began to merge with another, more powerful group of currency reformers—those who favored silver as the basis of currency—to help produce a political movement that would ultimately attain enormous strength. The question of the proper composition of the currency was to remain one of the most controversial and enduring issues in late-nineteenth-century American politics.

Republican Diplomacy

The Johnson and Grant administrations achieved their greatest successes in foreign affairs. The accomplishments were the work not of the presidents themselves, who displayed little aptitude for diplomacy, but of two talented secretaries of state: William H. Seward, who had served Lincoln and who served throughout the two terms of the Grant administration.

An ardent expansionist and advocate of a vigorous foreign policy, Seward acted with as much daring as the demands of Reconstruction politics and the Republican Party's hatred of President Johnson would permit. Seward agreed to a Russian offer to sell Alaska to the United States for $7.2 million. Only with great difficulty was he able to persuade Congress to authorize the purchase, and he faced criticism from many who considered Alaska a useless frozen wasteland and called it "Seward's Folly." But Seward knew that Alaska was an important fishing center and a potential source of valuable resources such as gold. In 1867, Seward also engineered the American annexation of the tiny Midway Islands west of Hawaii.

In contrast with its sometimes shambling course in domestic politics, the diplomatic performance of the Grant administration under Hamilton Fish was generally decisive and firm. Fish was in many ways the personification of northeastern conservatism and, while officially a Republican, had opposed virtually all the party's Reconstruction policies. But he was a skilled and effective diplomat. His first major challenge was resolving a burning controversy with England. Many Americans believed that the British government had violated the neutrality laws during the Civil War by permitting English shipyards to build ships (among them the *Alabama*) for the Confederacy. American demands that England pay for the damage these vessels had caused became known as the "Alabama claims."

Seward had tried to settle the Alabama claims through the Johnson-Clarendon Convention of 1869, which would have submitted the matter to arbitration. But the Senate rejected it because it contained no British apology. In 1871, Fish succeeded in forging a new agreement: the Treaty of Washington, which provided for international arbitration of the claims and in which Britain expressed regret for the escape of the *Alabama* from England.

THE ABANDONMENT OF RECONSTRUCTION

As the North grew increasingly preoccupied with its own political and economic problems, interest in Reconstruction began to wane. The Grant administration continued to protect Republican governments in the South, but less because of any interest in ensuring the position of freedmen than because of a desire to prevent the reemergence of a strong Democratic Party in the region. But even the presence of federal troops was not enough to prevent white Southerners from overturning the Reconstruction regimes. By the time Grant left office, Democrats had taken back (or, as white Southerners liked to put it, "redeemed") the governments of seven of the eleven former Confederate states.

For three other states—South Carolina, Louisiana, and Florida—the end of Reconstruction had to wait for the withdrawal of the last federal troops in 1876, a withdrawal that was the result of a long process of political bargaining and compromise at the national level. (One former Confederate state, Tennessee, had never been part of the Reconstruction process.)

The Southern States "Redeemed"

In the states where whites constituted a majority—the states of the upper South—overthrowing Republican control was relatively simple. By 1872, all but a handful of Southern whites had regained suffrage. Now a clear majority of the electorate, they needed only to organize and vote for their candidates.

In other states, where blacks were a majority or the populations of the two races were almost equal, whites used intimidation and violence to undermine the Reconstruction regimes. Secret societies—the Ku Klux Klan, the Knights of the White Camellia, and others—used terrorism to frighten or physically bar blacks from voting or otherwise exercising citizenship. Paramilitary organizations—the Red Shirts and White Leagues—armed themselves to "police" elections and worked to force all white males to join the Democratic Party and to exclude all blacks from meaningful political activity.

The Ku Klux Klan was the largest and most effective of these organizations. Organized in 1866 and led by former Confederate General Nathan Bedford Forrest, it gradually absorbed many of the smaller terrorist organizations. Its leaders devised rituals, costumes, secret languages, and other airs of mystery to create a bond among its members and make it seem even more terrifying to those it was attempting to intimidate. The Klan's "midnight rides"—bands of men clad in white sheets and masks, their horses covered with white robes and with hooves muffled—created terror in black communities throughout the South.

Many white Southerners considered the Klan and the other secret societies and paramilitary groups proud, patriotic societies. Together such groups served, in effect, as a military force (even if a decentralized and poorly organized one) continuing the battle against Northern rule. They worked in particular to advance the interests of those with the most to gain from a restoration of white supremacy—above all the planter class and the Southern Democratic Party.

Even stronger than the Klan in discouraging black political power, however, was the simple weapon of economic pressure. Some planters refused to rent land to Republican blacks; storekeepers refused to extend them credit; employers refused to give them work.

In the meantime, Southern blacks were losing the support of many of their former supporters in the North. After the adoption of the Fifteenth Amendment in 1870, some reformers convinced themselves that their long campaign in behalf of black people was now over; that with the vote, blacks ought to be able to take care of themselves. Former Radical leaders such as Charles Sumner and Horace Greeley now began calling themselves Liberals, cooperating with Democrats, and at times outdoing even the Democrats in denouncing what they viewed as black and carpetbag misgovernment. Within the South itself, many white Republicans joined the Liberals and eventually moved into the Democratic Party.

The Panic of 1873 further undermined support for Reconstruction. In the congressional elections of 1874, the Democrats won control of the House of Representatives for the first time since 1861. Grant took note of the changing temper of the North and made use of military force to prop up the Republican regimes that were still standing in the South.

By the end of 1876, only three states were left in the hands of the Republicans—South Carolina, Louisiana, and Florida. In state elections that year, Democrats (after using terrorist tactics) claimed victory in all three. But the Republicans challenged the results and claimed victory as well, and they were able to remain in office because of the presence of federal troops. Without federal troops, it was now clear, the last of the Republican regimes would quickly fall.

The Compromise of 1877

Grant had hoped to run for another term in 1876, but most Republican leaders—shaken by recent Democrat successes, afraid of the scandals with which Grant was associated, and concerned about the president's failing health—resisted. Instead, they sought a candidate not associated with the problems of the Grant years, one who might entice Liberals back and unite the party again. They settled on Rutherford B. Hayes, a former Union army officer, governor, and congressman, champion of civil service reform. The Democrats united behind Samuel J. Tilden, the reform governor of New York who had been instrumental in overthrowing the corrupt Tweed Ring of New York City's Tammany Hall.

Although the campaign was a bitter one, there were few differences of principle between the candidates, both of whom were conservatives committed to moderate reform. The November election produced an apparent Democratic victory. Tilden carried the South and several large Northern states, and his popular margin over Hayes was nearly 300,000 votes. But disputed returns from Louisiana, South Carolina, Florida, and Oregon, whose total electoral vote was 20, threw the election in doubt. Tilden had undisputed claim to 184 electoral votes, only one short of a majority. But Hayes could still win if he managed to receive all 20 disputed votes.

The Constitution had established no method to determine the validity of disputed returns. It was clear that the decision lay with Congress, but it was not clear with which house or through what method. (The Senate was Republican, the House Democratic.) Members of each party naturally supported a solution that would yield them the victory.

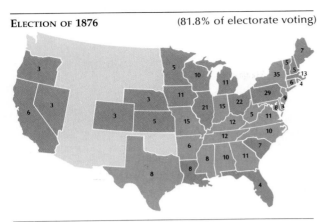

ELECTION OF 1876 (81.8% of electorate voting)

	ELECTORAL VOTE	POPULAR VOTE (%)
Rutherford B. Hayes (Republican)	185	4,036,298 (48)
Samuel J. Tilden (Democratic)	184	4,300,590 (51)

Finally, late in January 1877, Congress tried to break the deadlock by creating a special electoral commission to judge the disputed votes. The commission was to be composed of five senators, five representatives, and five justices of the Supreme Court. The congressional delegation would consist of five Republicans and five Democrats. The Court delegation would include two Republicans, two Democrats, and an independent. But the independent seat ultimately went to a justice whose real sympathies were with the Republicans. The commission voted along straight party lines, 8 to 7, awarding every disputed vote to Hayes. Congress accepted their verdict on March 2. Two days later, Hayes was inaugurated.

Behind the resolution of the deadlock however, lay a series of elaborate compromises among leaders of both parties. When a Democratic filibuster threatened to derail the commission's report, Republican Senate leaders met secretly with Southern Democratic leaders to work out terms by which the Democrats would allow the election of Hayes. According to traditional accounts, Republicans and Southern Democrats met at Washington's Wormley Hotel. In return for a Republican pledge that Hayes would withdraw the last federal troops from the South, thus permitting the overthrow of the last Republican governments there, the Southerners agreed to abandon the filibuster.

Actually, the story behind the "Compromise of 1877" is somewhat more complex. Hayes was already

on record favoring withdrawal of the troops, so Republicans needed to offer more than that if they hoped for Democratic support. The real agreement, the one that won over the Southern Democrats, was reached well before the Wormley meeting. As the price of their cooperation, the Southern Democrats (among them some former Whigs) exacted several pledges from the Republicans in addition to withdrawal of the troops: the appointment of at least one Southerner to the Hayes cabinet, control of federal patronage in their areas, generous internal improvements, and federal aid for the Texas and Pacific Railroad. Many powerful Southern Democrats supported industrializing their region. They believed Republican programs of federal support for business would aid the South more than the states' rights policies of the Democrats.

In his inaugural address, Hayes announced that the South's most pressing need was the restoration of "wise, honest, and peaceful local self-government"— a signal that he planned to withdraw federal troops and let white Democrats take over the state governments. That statement, and Hayes's subsequent actions, supported the widespread charges that he was paying off the South for acquiescing in his election and strengthened those who referred to him as "his Fraudulency." Hayes tried to counter such charges by projecting an image of stern public (and private) rectitude. But the election had already created such bitterness that even Hayes's promise to serve only one term could not mollify his critics.

The president and his party had hoped to build up a "new Republican" organization in the South drawn from Whiggish conservative white groups and committed to some modest acceptance of African-American rights. But all such efforts failed. Although many white Southern leaders sympathized with Republican economic policies, popular resentment of Reconstruction was so deep that supporting the party was politically impossible. At the same time, the withdrawal of federal troops was a signal that the national government was giving up its attempt to control Southern politics and to improve the lot of blacks in Southern society.

The Legacy of Reconstruction

Reconstruction made some important contributions to the efforts of former slaves to achieve dignity and equality in American life. There was a significant redistribution of income, from which blacks benefited. There was a more limited but not unimportant redistribution of landownership, which enabled some former slaves to acquire property. There was both a relative and an absolute improvement in the economic

RECONSTRUCTION

DEBATE OVER THE NATURE of Reconstruction—not only among historians, but among the public at large—has created so much controversy over the decades that one scholar, writing in 1959, described the issue as a "dark and bloody ground." Among historians, the passions of the debate have to some extent subsided since then; but in the popular mind, Reconstruction continues to raise "dark and bloody" images.

For many years, a relatively uniform and highly critical view of Reconstruction prevailed among historians, a reflection of broad currents in popular thought. By the late nineteenth century, most white Americans in both the North and the South had come to believe that few real differences any longer divided the sections, that the nation should strive for a genuine reconciliation. And most white Americans believed as well in the superiority of their race, in the inherent unfitness of blacks for political or social equality. Out of this mentality was born the first major historical interpretation of Reconstruction, through the work of William A. Dunning. In *Reconstruction, Political and Economic* (1907), Dunning portrayed Reconstruction as a corrupt outrage perpetrated on the prostrate South by a vicious and vindictive cabal of Northern Republican Radicals. Reconstruction governments were based on "bayonet rule." Unscrupulous and self-aggrandizing carpetbaggers flooded the South to profit from the misery of the defeated region. Ignorant, illiterate blacks were thrust into positions of power for which they were entirely unfit. The Reconstruction experiment, a moral abomination from its first moments, survived only because of the determination of the Republican Party to keep itself in power. (Some later writers, notably Howard K. Beale, added an economic motive—to protect Northern business interests.) Dunning and his many students (who together formed what became known as the "Dunning school") compiled state-by-state evidence to show that the legacy of Reconstruction was corruption, ruinous taxation, and astronomical increases in the public debt.

The Dunning school not only shaped the views of several generations of historians. It also reflected and helped to shape the views of much of the public. Popular depictions of Reconstruction for years to come (as the book and movie *Gone with the Wind* suggested) portrayed the era as one of tragic exploitation of the South by the North. Even today, many white southerners and many others continue to accept the basic premises of the Dunning interpretation. Among historians, however, the old view of Reconstruction has gradually lost all credibility.

The great black scholar W. E. B. Du Bois was among the first to challenge the Dunning view in a 1910 article and, later, in a 1935 book, *Black Reconstruction*. To him, Reconstruction politics in the Southern states had been an effort on the part of the masses, black and white, to create a more democratic society. The misdeeds of the Reconstruction governments, he claimed, had been greatly exaggerated, and their achievements overlooked. The governments had been expensive, he insisted, because they had tried to provide public education and other public services on a scale never before attempted in the South. But Du Bois's use of Marxist theory in his work caused many historians who did not share his philosophy to dismiss his argument; and it remained for a group of less radical, white historians to shatter the Dunning image of Reconstruction.

In the 1940s, historians such as C. Vann Woodward, David Herbert Donald, Thomas B. Alexander, and others began to reexamine the record of the Reconstruction governments in the South and to suggest that their record was not nearly as bad as most historians had previously assumed. They also looked at the Radical Republicans in Congress and suggested that they had not been motivated by vindictiveness and

WHERE HISTORIANS DISAGREE

partisanship alone. By the early 1960s, a new view of Reconstruction as emerging from these efforts, a view whose appeal to historians grew stronger with the emergence of the "Second Reconstruction," the civil rights movement. The revisionist approach was summarized by John Hope Franklin in *Reconstruction After the Civil War* (1961) and Kenneth Stampp in *The Era of Reconstruction* (1965), which claimed that the postwar Republicans had been engaged in a genuine, if flawed, effort to solve the problem of race in the South by providing much-needed protection to the freedmen. The Reconstruction governments, for all their faults, had been bold experiments in interracial politics. The congressional Radicals were not saints, but they had displayed a genuine concern for the rights of slaves. And Andrew Johnson was not a martyred defender of the Constitution, but an inept, racist politician who resisted reasonable compromise and brought the government to a crisis. There had been no such thing as "bayonet rule" or "Negro rule" in the South. Blacks had played only a small part in Reconstruction governments and had generally acquitted themselves well. The Reconstruction regimes had, in fact, brought important progress to the South, establishing the region's first public school system and other important social changes. Corruption in the South had been no worse than corruption in the North at that time. What was tragic about Reconstruction, the revisionist view claimed, was not what it did to Southern whites but what it did not do for Southern blacks. By stopping short of the reforms necessary to ensure blacks genuine equality, Reconstruction had consigned them to more than a century of injustice and discrimination.

By the 1970s, then, the Dunning view of Reconstruction had all but disappeared from serious scholarly discussion. Instead, historians seemed to agree that Reconstruction had in fact changed the South relatively little; and they began to debate why Reconstruction fell as far short as it did of guaranteeing racial justice. Some

scholars have claimed that conservative obstacles to change were so great that the Radicals, despite their good intentions, simply could not overcome them. Others have argued that the Radicals themselves were not sufficiently committed to the principle of racial justice, that they abandoned the cause quickly when it became clear to them that the battle would not easily be won.

In recent years scholars have begun to question the revisionist view—not in an effort to revive the old Dunning interpretation, but in an attempt to draw attention to those things Reconstruction in fact achieved. Leon Litwack's *Been in the Storm So Long* (1979) reveals that former slaves used the relative latitude they enjoyed under Reconstruction to build a certain independence for themselves within Southern society. They strengthened their churches; they reunited their families; they refused to work in the "gang labor" system of the plantations and forced the creation of a new labor system in which they had more control over their own lives. Eric Foner, in *Nothing but Freedom* (1983) and *Reconstruction: America's Unfinished Revolution* (1988), compared the aftermath of slavery in the United States with similar experiences in the Caribbean and concluded that what is striking about the American experience in this context is not how little was accomplished, but how far the former slaves moved toward freedom and independence in a short time, and how large a role African Americans themselves played in shaping Reconstruction. During Reconstruction, blacks won a certain amount of legal and political power in the South; and even though they held that power only temporarily, they used it for a time to strengthen their economic and social positions and to win a position of limited but genuine independence. Through Reconstruction they won, if not equality, a measure of individual and community autonomy, building blocks of the freedom that emancipation alone had not guaranteed.

circumstances of most blacks. Perhaps most of all, there was a large, and largely successful, effort by blacks themselves to carve out a society and culture of their own within the American South, to create or strengthen their own institutions, and to convince themselves that they were, indeed, no longer slaves.

Reconstruction was not as disastrous an experience for Southern whites as most believed at the time. The region had emerged from a prolonged and bloody war defeated and devastated, and yet within little more than a decade, the white South had regained control of its own institutions and, to a great extent, restored its traditional ruling class to power. Former Confederate leaders received no severe punishments. The federal government imposed no drastic economic reforms on the region, and indeed few lasting political changes of any kind other than the abolition of slavery. Not many conquered peoples have fared as well.

But Reconstruction was as notable for its limitations as it was for its achievements. For in those years the United States failed in its first serious effort to resolve its oldest and deepest social problem—the problem of race. What was more, the experience so disappointed, disillusioned, and embittered white Americans that it would be nearly a century before they would try again in any serious way.

Why did this great assault on racial injustice not achieve more? In part, it was because of the weaknesses and errors of the people who directed it. But in greater part, it was because attempts to produce solutions ran up against conservative obstacles so deeply embedded in the nation's life that they could not be dislodged. Veneration of the Constitution sharply limited the willingness of national leaders to infringe on the rights of states and individuals. A profound respect for private property and free enterprise prevented any real assault on economic privilege in the South. Above all, perhaps, a pervasive belief among many of even the most liberal whites that African Americans were inherently inferior served as an obstacle to equality. Given the context within which Americans of the 1860s and 1870s were working, what is surprising, perhaps, is not that Reconstruction did so little, but that it did even as much as it did.

Considering the odds confronting them, therefore, African Americans had reason for pride in the gains they were able to make during Reconstruction. And future generations had reason for gratitude for two great charters of freedom—the Fourteenth and Fifteenth Amendments to the Constitution—which, although largely ignored at the time, would one day serve as the basis for a "Second Reconstruction" that would renew the drive to bring freedom and equality to all Americans.

The New South

The agreement between southern Democrats and northern Republicans that helped settle the disputed election of 1876 was supposed to be the first step toward developing a stable, permanent Republican Party in the South. In that respect, at least, it failed. In the years following the end of Reconstruction, white southerners established the Democratic Party as the only viable political organization for the region's whites. Even so, the South did change in the years after Reconstruction in some of the ways the framers of the Compromise of 1877 had hoped.

The "Redeemers"

By the end of 1877—after the last withdrawal of federal troops—every southern state government had been "redeemed." That is, political power had been restored to white Democrats. Many white southerners rejoiced at the restoration of what they liked to call "home rule." But in reality, political power in the region was soon more restricted than at any time since the Civil War. Once again, the South fell under the control of a powerful, conservative oligarchy, whose members were known variously as the "Redeemers" (to themselves and their supporters) or the "Bourbons" (a term for aristocrats used by some of their critics).

In a few places, this post-Reconstruction ruling class was much the same as the ruling class of the antebellum period. In Alabama, for example, the old planter elite—despite challenges from new merchant and industrial forces—retained much of its former power and continued largely to dominate the state for decades. In most areas, however, the Redeemers constituted a genuinely new ruling class. They were merchants, industrialists, railroad developers, and financiers. Some of them were former planters, some of them northern immigrants who had become absorbed into the region's life, some of them ambitious, upwardly mobile white southerners from the region's lower social tiers. They combined a commitment to "home rule" and social conservatism with a commitment to economic development.

The various Bourbon governments of the New South behaved in many respects quite similarly. Conservatives had complained that the Reconstruction governments fostered widespread corruption, but the Redeemer regimes were, if anything, even more awash in waste and fraud. (In this, they were little different from governments in every region of the country.) At the same time, virtually all the new Democratic regimes lowered taxes, reduced spending, and drastically diminished state services—including many of the most important accomplishments of Reconstruction. In one state after another, for example, state support for public school systems was reduced or eliminated. "Schools are not a necessity," an economy-conscious governor of Virginia commented.

By the late 1870s, significant dissenting groups were challenging the Bourbons: protesting the cuts in services and denouncing the commitment of the Redeemer governments to paying off the prewar and Reconstruction debts in full, at the original (usually high) rates of interest. In Virginia, for example, a vigorous "Readjuster" movement emerged, demanding that the state revise its debt payment procedures so as to make more money available for state services. In 1879, the Readjusters won control of the legislature, and in the next few years they captured the governorship and a U.S. Senate seat. Other states produced similar movements, some of them adding demands as well for greenbacks, debt relief, and other economic reforms. (A few such independent movements included significant numbers of blacks in their ranks, but all consisted primarily of lower-income whites.) By the mid-1880s, however, conservative southerners—largely by exploiting racial prejudice—had effectively destroyed most of the dissenting movements.

Industrialization and the "New South"

Many white southern leaders in the post-Reconstruction era hoped to see their region become the home of a vigorous industrial economy. The South had lost the war, many argued, because its economy had been unable to compete with the modernized manufacturing capacity of the North. Now the region must "out-Yankee the Yankees" and build a "New South." Henry Grady, editor of the *Atlanta Constitution,* and other prominent spokesmen for a New South seldom challenged white supremacy, but they did advocate other important changes in southern values. Above all, they promoted the virtues of thrift, industry, and progress—qualities that prewar southerners had often denounced in northern society. "We have sown towns and cities in the place of theories," Grady boasted to a New England audience in the 1880s, "and put business above politics. . . . We have fallen in love with work."

But even the most fervent advocates of the New South creed were generally unwilling to break entirely with the Southern past. That was evident in, among other things, the popular literature of the region. At the same time that white southern writers were ex-

tolling the virtues of industrialization in newspaper editorials and speeches, they were painting nostalgic portraits of the Old South in their literature. Few southerners advocated a literal return to the old ways, but most whites eagerly embraced romantic talk of the "Lost Cause." And they responded warmly to the local-color fiction of such writers as Joel Chandler Harris, whose folk tales—the most famous being *Uncle Remus* (1880)—portrayed the slave society of the antebellum years as a harmonious world marked by engaging dialect and close emotional bonds between the races. Thomas Nelson Page similarly extolled the old Virginia aristocracy. The white leaders of the New South, in short, faced their future with one foot still in the past.

Even so, New South enthusiasts did help southern industry expand dramatically in the years after Reconstruction and become a more important part of the region's economy than ever before. Most visible was the growth in textile manufacturing, which increased ninefold in the last twenty years of the century. In the past, southern planters had usually shipped their cotton out of the region to manufacturers in the North or in Europe. Now textile factories appeared in the South itself—many of them drawn to the region from New England by the abundance of water power, the ready supply of cheap labor, the low taxes, and the accommodating conservative governments. The tobacco-processing industry, similarly, established an important foothold in the region, largely through the work of James B. Duke of North Carolina, whose American Tobacco Company established for a time a virtual monopoly over the processing of raw tobacco into marketable materials. In the lower South, and particularly in Birmingham, Alabama, the iron (and, later, steel) industry grew rapidly. By 1890, the southern iron and steel industry represented nearly a fifth of the nation's total capacity.

Railroad development increased substantially in the post-Reconstruction years—at a rate far greater than that of the nation at large. Between 1880 and 1890, trackage in the South more than doubled. And the South took a major step toward integrating its transportation system with that of the rest of the country when, in 1886, it changed the gauge (width) of its trackage to correspond with the standards of the North. No longer would it be necessary for cargoes heading into the South to be transferred from one train to another at the borders of the region.

Yet southern industry developed within strict limits, and its effects on the region were never even remotely comparable to the effects of industrialization on the North. The southern share of national manufacturing doubled in the last twenty years of the cen-

THE CROP-LIEN SYSTEM: THE SOUTH IN 1880

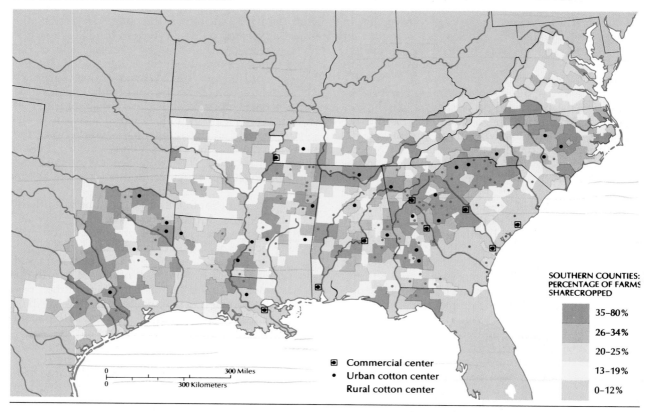

SOUTHERN COUNTIES:
PERCENTAGE OF FARMS
SHARECROPPED

- 35–80%
- 26–34%
- 20–25%
- 13–19%
- 0–12%

◙ Commercial center
• Urban cotton center
  Rural cotton center

0   300 Miles
0   300 Kilometers

tury, to 10 percent of the total. But that percentage was the same the South had claimed in 1860; the region, in other words, had done no more than regain what it had lost during the war and its aftermath. The region's per capita income increased 21 percent in the same period. But at the end of the century, average income in the South was only 40 percent of that in the North; in 1860 it had been more than 60 percent. And even in those areas where development had been most rapid—textiles, iron, railroads—much of the capital had come from the North. In effect, the South was developing a colonial economy.

The growth of industry in the South required the region to recruit a substantial industrial work force for the first time. From the beginning, a high percentage of the factory workers (and an especially high percentage of textile workers) were women. Heavy male casualties in the Civil War had helped create a large population of unmarried women who desperately needed employment. Factories also hired entire families, many of whom were moving into towns from failed farms. Hours were long (often as much as twelve

hours a day) and wages were far below the northern equivalent; indeed one of the greatest attractions of the South to industrialists was that employers were able to pay workers there as little as one-half what northern workers received. Life in most mill towns was rigidly controlled by the owners and managers of the factories. They rigorously suppressed attempts at protest or union organization. Company stores sold goods to workers at inflated prices and issued credit at exorbitant rates (much like country stores in agrarian areas), and mill owners ensured that no competitors were able to establish themselves in the community. At the same time, however, the conditions of the mill town helped create a strong sense of community and solidarity among workers (even if they seldom translated such feelings into militancy).

Some industries, textiles for example, offered virtually no opportunities to African American workers. Others—tobacco, iron, and lumber, among others—did provide some employment for blacks, usually the most menial and lowest-paid positions. Some mill towns, therefore, were places where black and white

TUSKEGEE INSTITUTE, 1881
From these modest beginnings, Booker T. Washington's Tuskegee Institute in Alabama became the preeminent academy offering technical and industrial training to black men. It deliberately deemphasized the traditional liberal arts curricula of most colleges. Washington considered such training an unnecessary frill and encouraged his students to work on developing practical skills. *(Bettmann)*

culture came into close contact. That proximity contributed less to the growth of racial harmony than to the determination of white leaders to take additional measures to protect white supremacy.

At times, industrialization proceeded on the basis of no wage-paying employment at all. Through the "convict-lease" system, southern states leased gangs of convicted criminals to private interests as a cheap labor supply. The system exposed the convicts to brutal and at times fatal mistreatment. It paid them nothing (the leasing fees went to the states, not the workers).

And it denied employment in railroad construction and other projects to the free labor force.

Tenants and Sharecroppers

Despite significant growth in southern industry, the region remained primarily agrarian. The most important economic reality in the post-Reconstruction South, therefore, was the impoverished state of agriculture. The 1870s and 1880s saw an acceleration of the process that had begun in the immediate postwar years: the

THE ORIGINS OF SEGREGATION

NOT UNTIL AFTER WORLD War II, when the emergence of the civil rights movement forced white Americans to confront the issue of racial segregation, did historians pay much attention to the origins of the institution. Most had assumed that the separation of the races had emerged naturally and even inevitably out of the abolition of slavery. It had been a response to the failure of Reconstruction, the weakness and poverty of the black community, and the pervasiveness of white racism. It was, in effect, the way things had always been.

The first major challenge to these assumptions, indeed the first serious scholarly effort to explain the origins of segregation, was C. Vann Woodward's *The Strange Career of Jim Crow* published in 1956. Not only was it important in reshaping scholarship. It had a significant political impact as well. As a southern liberal, Woodward was eager to refute assumptions that segregation was part of an unchanging and unchangeable southern tradition. He wanted to convince scholars that the history of the South had been one of sharp discontinuities; and he wanted to convince a larger public that the racial institutions they considered part of a long, unbroken tradition were in fact the product of a particular set of historical circumstances.

In the aftermath of emancipation, and indeed for two decades after Reconstruction, Woodward argued, race relations in the South had remained relatively fluid. Blacks and whites did not often interact as equals, certainly, but black Southerners enjoyed a degree of latitude in social and even political affairs that they would subsequently lose. Blacks and whites often rode together in the same railroad cars, ate in the same restaurants, used the same public facilities. Blacks voted in significant numbers. Blacks and whites considered a number of different visions of how the races should live together, and as late as 1890 it was not at all clear which of those visions would prevail. By the end of the nineteenth century, however, a great wave of racist legislation—the Jim Crow laws, which established the basis of segregation—had hardened race relations and destroyed the gentler alternatives that many whites and blacks had considered viable only a few years before. The principal reason, Woodward argued, was the populist political insurgency of the 1890s, which mobilized blacks and whites alike and which frightened many white southerners into thinking that blacks might soon be a major political power in the region. Southern conservatives, in particular, used the issue of white supremacy to attack the populists and to prevent blacks from forming an alliance with them. The result was disenfranchisement and segregation.

Woodward's argument suggested that laws were important in shaping social behavior—that laws had made segregation and, by implication, other laws could unmake it. Not all historians agreed. A more pessimistic picture of segregation emerged in 1965 from Joel Williamson's study of South Carolina, *After Slavery.* Williamson argued that the laws of the 1890s did not mean very much, that they simply ratified a set of conditions that had been firmly established by the end of Reconstruction. As early as the mid-1870s,

imposition of systems of tenantry and debt peonage on much of the region; the reliance on a few cash crops rather than on a diversified agricultural system; and increasing absentee ownership of valuable farmlands (many of them purchased by merchants and industrialists who paid little attention to whether the land was being properly used). During Reconstruction, perhaps a third or more of the farmers in the South were tenants; by 1900 the figure had increased to 70 percent. That was in large part the result of the crop-lien system that had emerged in the aftermath of the Civil War. Farmers who owned their own land often lost it

WHERE HISTORIANS DISAGREE

Williamson claimed, the races had already begun to live in two separate societies. Blacks had constructed their own churches, schools, businesses, and neighborhoods; whites had begun to exclude blacks from white institutions. The separation was partly a result of pressure and coercion from whites, partly a result of the desire of blacks to develop their own, independent culture. Whatever the reasons, however, segregation was largely in place by the end of the 1870s, continuing in a different form a pattern of racial separation established under slavery. The laws of the 1890s did little more than codify an already established system.

More recently, scholars have revised or challenged both these interpretations by attempting to link the rise of legal segregation to changing social and economic circumstances in the South. Howard Rabinowitz's *Race Relations in the Urban South* (1978) links the rise of segregation to the new challenge of devising a form of race relations suitable to life in the growing southern cities, into which rural blacks were moving in substantial numbers. The creation of separate public facilities—schools, parks, waiting rooms, etc.—was not so much an effort to drive blacks out of white facilities; they had never had access to those facilities, and few whites had ever been willing to consider granting them access. It was, rather, an attempt to create for a black community that virtually all whites agreed must remain essentially separate a set of facilities where none had previously existed. Without segregation, in other words, urban blacks would have had no schools or parks at all. The alternative to segregation, Rabinowitz suggests, was not integration, but exclusion.

In the early 1980s, a number of scholars began examining segregation anew in light of the rising American interest in South Africa, whose system of *apartheid* seemed to them to be similar in many ways to the by-then largely dismantled Jim Crow system in the South. John Cell's *The Highest Stage of White Supremacy* (1982) used the comparison to construct a revised explanation of how segregation emerged in the American South. Like Rabinowitz, he considered the increasing urbanization of the region the principal factor. But he ascribed different motives to those whites who promoted the rise of Jim Crow. The segregation laws, Cell argues, were a continuation of an unchanging determination by southern whites to retain control over the black population. What had shifted was not their commitment to white supremacy but the things necessary to preserve it. The emergence of large black communities in urban areas and of a significant black labor force in factories presented a new challenge to white southerners. They could not control these new communities in the same informal ways they had been able to control rural blacks, who were more directly dependent on white landowners and merchants than their urban counterparts. In the city, blacks and whites were in more direct competition than they had been in the countryside. There was more danger of social mixing. The city therefore required different, and more rigidly institutionalized, systems of control. The Jim Crow laws were a response not just to an enduring commitment to white supremacy, but to a new reality that required white supremacy to move to its "highest stage," where it would have a rigid legal and institutional basis.

as merchants seized it for payment of liens. Farmers who rented could never accumulate enough capital to buy land.

Tenantry took several forms. Farmers who owned tools, equipment, and farm animals—or who had the money to buy them—usually paid an annual cash rent

for their land. But many farmers (including most black ones) had no money or equipment at all. Landlords would supply them with land, a crude house, a few tools, seed, and sometimes a mule. In return, farmers would promise the landlord a large share of the annual crop—hence the term "sharecropping." After paying their landlords and their local furnishing merchants (who were often the same people), sharecroppers seldom had anything left to sell on their own.

The crop-lien system was one of several factors contributing to a particularly harsh social and economic transformation of the southern backcountry, the piney woods and mountain regions where cotton and slavery had always been rare and where farmers lived ruggedly independent lives. Subsistence agriculture had long been the norm in these areas; but as indebtedness grew, many farmers now had to grow cash crops such as cotton instead of the food crops they had traditionally cultivated in order to make enough money to pay off their loans.

But the transformation of the backcountry was a result of other factors as well. Many backcountry residents had traditionally subsisted by raising livestock, which had roamed freely across the landscape. In the 1870s, as commercial agriculture began to intrude into these regions, many communities began to pass "fence laws," which required farmers to fence in their animals (as opposed to fencing off their crops, as had once been the custom). There were widespread protests against the new laws, and at times violent efforts to resist them. But the existence of the open range (which had once been as much a part of life in the backcountry South as it was in the American West) could not survive the spread of commercial agriculture. Increasingly, therefore, opportunities for families to live largely self-sufficiently were declining. At the same time, opportunities for profiting within the market remained slim. The people of the backcountry, perhaps even more than other groups for whom agriculture had always been a business, felt the pain of losing their economic independence. They would be among the most important constituents for the populist protests of the 1880s and 1890s.

The crop-lien system was particularly devastating to southern blacks, few of whom owned their own land to begin with. These economic difficulties were compounded by social and legal discrimination, which in the post-Reconstruction era began to take new forms and to inspire new responses.

African Americans and the New South

The "New South creed" was not the property of whites alone. Many African Americans were attracted to the vision of progress and self-improvement as well. Some blacks succeeded in elevating themselves into a distinct middle class—economically inferior to the white middle class, but nevertheless significant. These were former slaves (and, as the decades passed, their offspring) who managed to acquire property, establish small businesses, or enter professions. A few blacks accumulated substantial fortunes by establishing banks and insurance companies for their race. One of those was Maggie Lena, a black woman who became the first female bank president in the United States when she founded the St. Luke Penny Savings Bank in Richmond in 1903. Most middle-class blacks experienced more modest gains by becoming doctors, lawyers, nurses, or teachers serving members of their own race.

A cardinal tenet of this rising group of blacks was that education was vital to the future of their race. With the support of northern missionary societies and, to a far lesser extent, a few southern state governments, they expanded the network of black colleges and institutes that had taken root during Reconstruction into an important educational system.

The chief spokesman for this commitment to education, and for a time the major spokesman for his race as a whole, was Booker T. Washington, founder and president of the Tuskegee Institute in Alabama. Born into slavery, Washington had worked his way out of poverty after acquiring an education (at Virginia's famous Hampton Institute). He urged other blacks to follow the same road to self-improvement.

Washington's message was both cautious and hopeful. African Americans should attend school, learn skills, and establish a solid footing in agriculture and the trades. Industrial, not classical, education should be their goal. Blacks should, moreover, refine their speech, improve their dress, and adopt habits of thrift and personal cleanliness; they should, in short, adopt the standards of the white middle class. Only thus, he claimed, could they win the respect of the white population, the prerequisite for any larger social gains. Blacks should forgo agitating for political rights, he said, and concentrate on self-improvement and preparation for equality.

In a famous speech in Georgia in 1895, Washington outlined a philosophy of race relations that became widely known as the Atlanta Compromise. "The wisest among my race understand," he said, "that the agitation of questions of social equality is the extremest folly." Rather, blacks should engage in "severe and constant struggle" for economic gains; for, as he explained, "no race that has anything to contribute to the markets of the world is long in any degree ostracized." If blacks were ever to win the rights and privileges of citizenship, they must first show that they were "prepared for the exercise of these privileges."

Washington offered a powerful challenge to those whites who wanted to discourage African Americans from acquiring an education or winning any economic gains. He helped awaken the interest of a new gener-

JIM CROW AT WORK
The formal separation (or "segregation") of the races spread through the South in the 1890s and early twentieth century, producing signs such as these—many of which survived into the 1960s. *(Library of Congress)*

ation to the possibilities for self-advancement through self-improvement. But his message was also an implicit promise that blacks would not challenge the system of segregation that whites were then in the process of erecting.

The Birth of Jim Crow

Few white Southerners had ever accepted the idea of racial equality. That the former slaves acquired any legal and political rights at all after emancipation was in large part the result of federal support. That support all but vanished after 1877. Federal troops withdrew. Congress lost interest. And the Supreme Court effectively stripped the Fourteenth and Fifteenth Amendments of much of their significance. In the so-called civil rights cases of 1883, the Court ruled that the Fourteenth Amendment prohibited state governments from discriminating against people because of race but did not restrict private organizations or individuals from doing so. Thus railroads, hotels, theaters, and the like could legally practice segregation.

Eventually, the Court also validated state legislation that institutionalized the separation of the races. In *Plessy v. Ferguson* (1896), a case involving a Louisiana law that required separate seating arrangements for the races on railroads, the Court held that separate accommodations did not deprive blacks of equal rights if the accommodations were equal, a decision that survived for years as part of the legal basis of segregated schools. In *Cumming v. County Board of Education* (1899), the Court ruled that laws establishing separate schools for whites were valid even if there were no schools for blacks comparable to the white schools from which they were excluded.

Even before these decisions, white southerners were working to strengthen white supremacy and to separate the races to the greatest extent possible. One illustration of this movement from subordination to segregation was black voting rights. In some states, disfranchisement had begun almost as soon as Reconstruction ended. But in other areas, black voting continued for some time after Reconstruction—largely because conservative whites believed they could control the black electorate and use it to beat back the attempts of poor white farmers to take control of the Democratic Party.

In the 1890s, however, franchise restrictions became much more rigid. During those years, some small white farmers began to demand complete black disfranchisement—both because of racial prejudice and because they objected to the black vote being used against them by the Bourbons. At the same time, many

A LYNCH MOB, 1893
A large, almost festive crowd gathers to watch the lynching of a black man accused of the murder of a three-year-old white girl. Lynchings remained frequent in the South until as late as the 1930s, but they reached their peak in the 1890s and the first years of the twentieth century. Lynchings such as this one—publicized well in advance and attracting whole families who traveled great distances to see them—were relatively infrequent. Most lynchings were the work of smaller groups, operating with less visibility. *(Library of Congress)*

members of the conservative elite began to fear that poor whites might unite politically with poor blacks to challenge them. They too began to support further franchise restrictions.

In devising laws to disfranchise black males (black females, like white women, had never voted), the southern states had to find ways to evade the Fifteenth Amendment, which prohibited states from denying anyone the right to vote because of race. Two devices emerged before 1900 to accomplish this goal. One was the poll tax or some form of property qualification; few blacks were prosperous enough to meet such requirements. Another was the "literacy" or "understanding" test, which required voters to demonstrate an ability to read and to interpret the Constitution. Even those

African Americans who could read had difficulty passing the difficult test white officials gave them.

Such restrictions were often applied unequally. Literacy tests for whites, for example, were sometimes much easier than those for blacks. Even so, the laws affected poor white voters as well as blacks. By the late 1890s, the black vote had decreased by 62 percent, the white vote by 26 percent. One result was that some states passed so-called grandfather laws, permitting men who could not meet the literacy and property qualification to be enfranchised if their ancestors had voted before Reconstruction began, thus barring the descendants of slaves from the polls while allowing poor whites access to them. In many areas, however, ruling elites were quite content to see poor whites, a potential source of opposition to their power, barred from voting.

The Supreme Court proved as compliant in ruling on the disfranchising laws as it was in dealing with the civil rights cases. The Court eventually voided the grandfather laws, but it validated the literacy test (in the 1898 case of *Williams* v. *Mississippi*) and displayed a general willingness to let the southern states define their own suffrage standards as long as evasions of the Fifteenth Amendment were not too glaring.

Laws restricting the franchise and segregating schools were only part of a network of state statutes—known as the Jim Crow laws—that by the first years of the twentieth century had institutionalized an elaborate system of segregation reaching into almost every area of southern life. Blacks and whites could not ride together in the same railroad cars, sit in the same waiting rooms, use the same washrooms, eat in the same restaurants, or sit in the same theaters. Blacks had no access to many public parks, beaches, picnic areas; they could not be patients in many hospitals. Much of the new legal structure did no more than confirm what had already been widespread social practice in the South since well before the end of Reconstruction. But the Jim Crow laws also stripped blacks of many of the modest social, economic, and political gains they had made in the more fluid atmosphere of the late nineteenth century. They served, too, as a means for whites to retain control of social relations between the races in the newly growing cities and towns of the South, where traditional patterns of deference and subjugation were more difficult to preserve than in the countryside. What had been maintained by custom in the rural South was to be maintained by law in the urban South.

More than legal efforts were involved in this process. The 1890s witnessed a dramatic increase in white violence against blacks, which, along with the Jim Crow laws, served to inhibit black agitation for equal rights. The worst such violence—lynching of blacks by white mobs, either because the victims were accused of crimes or because they had seemed somehow to violate their proper station—reached appalling levels. In the nation as a whole in the 1890s, there was an average of 187 lynchings each year, more than 80 percent of them in the South. The vast majority of victims were black.

The most celebrated lynchings occurred in cities and towns, where large, well-organized mobs—occasionally with the tacit cooperation of local authorities—seized black prisoners from the jails and hanged them in great public rituals. Such public lynchings were often planned well in advance and elaborately organized. They attracted large audiences from surrounding regions. Entire families traveled many miles to witness the spectacles. But such great public lynchings were relatively rare. Much more frequent, and more dangerous to blacks because less visible or predictable, were lynchings performed by small vigilante mobs, often composed of friends or relatives of the victim (or supposed victim) of a crime. Those involved in lynchings often saw their actions as a legitimate form of law enforcement; and indeed, some victims of lynchings had in fact committed crimes. But lynchings were also a means by which whites controlled the black population through terror and intimidation. Thus, some lynch mobs killed blacks whose only "crime" had been presumptuousness. Others chose as victims outsiders in the community, whose presence threatened to disturb the normal pattern of race relations. Black men who had made any sexual advances toward white women (or who white men thought had done so) were particularly vulnerable to lynchings; the fear of black sexuality, and the unspoken fear among many men that white women might be attracted to that sexuality, was always an important part of the belief system that supported segregation. Whatever the reasons or circumstances, the victims of lynch mobs were denied the protection of the laws and the opportunity to prove their innocence.

The rise of lynchings shocked the conscience of many white Americans in a way that other forms of racial injustice did not. Almost from the start there was a substantial anti-lynching movement. In 1892 Ida B. Wells, a committed black journalist, launched what became an international anti-lynching movement with a series of impassioned articles after the lynching of three of her friends in Memphis, Tennessee, her home. The movement gradually gathered strength in the first years of the twentieth century, attracting substantial support from whites in both the North and South (particularly from white women). Its goal was a federal anti-lynching law, which would allow the national government to do what state and local governments in the South were generally unwilling to do: punish those responsible for lynchings.

But the substantial white opposition to lynchings in the South stood as an exception to the general white support for suppression of African Americans. Indeed, just as in the antebellum period, the shared commitment to white supremacy helped dilute class animosities between poorer whites and the Bourbon oligarchies. Economic issues tended to play a secondary role to race in southern politics, distracting people from the glaring social inequalities that afflicted blacks and whites alike. The commitment to white supremacy, in short, was a burden for poor whites as well as for blacks.

SIGNIFICANT EVENTS

1863 Lincoln announces preliminary Reconstruction plan

1864 Louisiana, Arkansas, and Tennessee readmitted to Union under Lincoln plan

Wade-Davis bill passed

1865 Lincoln assassinated; Andrew Johnson becomes president (April 14)

Johnson readmits rest of Confederate states to Union under Lincoln plan

Black Codes enacted in South

Freedmen's Bureau established

Congress reconvenes (December) and refuses to admit Southern representatives; creates Joint Committee on Reconstruction

1866 Freedmen's Bureau Act renewed

Congress approves Fourteenth Amendment; most Southern states reject it

Republicans gain in congressional elections

Ex parte Milligan challenges Radicals' Reconstruction plans

Ku Klux Klan formed in South

1867 Military Reconstruction Act (and two supplementary acts) outlines congressional plan of Reconstruction

Tenure of Office Act and Command of the Army Act restrict presidential power

Southern states establish Reconstruction governments under congressional plan

U.S. purchases Alaska

1868 Most Southern states readmitted to Congress under congressional plan

Andrew Johnson impeached but not convicted

Fourteenth Amendment ratified

Ulysses S. Grant elected president

SUGGESTED READINGS

Reconstruction: General Studies. E. Merton Coulter, *The South During Reconstruction* (1947). W. E. B. Du Bois, *Black Reconstruction* (1935). William A. Dunning, *Reconstruction, Political and Economic, 1865–1877* (1907). Eric Foner, *Reconstruction: America's Unfinished Revolution, 1863–1877* (1988). John Hope Franklin, *Reconstruction After the Civil War* (1961). Rembert Patrick, *The Reconstruction of the Nation* (1967). Kenneth M. Stampp, *The Era of Reconstruction, 1865–1877* (1965).

Early Reconstruction. Richard H. Abbott, *The First Southern Strategy: The Republican Party and the South, 1855–1877* (1986). Herman Belz, *Reconstructing the Union* (1969). Louis S. Gerteis, *From Contraband to Freedman* (1973). William B. Hesseltine, *Lincoln's Plan of Reconstruction* (1960). Willie Lee Rose, *Rehearsal for Reconstruction: The Port Royal Experiment* (1964). Brooks D. Simpson, *Let Us Have Peace: Ulysses S. Grant and the Politics of War and Reconstruction, 1861–1868* (1991).

Congressional Reconstruction. Howard K. Beale, *The Critical Year: A Study of Andrew Johnson and Reconstruction* (1930). Herman Belz, *A New Birth of Freedom* (1976); *Emancipation and*

Equal Rights (1978). Michael Les Benedict, *A Compromise of Principle: Congressional Republicans and Reconstruction, 1863–1869* (1974); *The Impeachment and Trial of Andrew Johnson* (1973). Richard Franklin Bensel, *Yankee Leviathan: The Origins of Central State Authority in America, 1859–1877* (1990). William R. Brock, *An American Crisis* (1963). Fawn Brodie, *Thaddeus Stevens* (1959). La Wanda Cox and John H. Cox, *Politics, Principles, and Prejudice, 1865–1867* (1963). Richard N. Current, *Old Thad Stevens* (1942). David Donald, *Charles Sumner and the Rights of Man* (1970); *The Politics of Reconstruction* (1965). Charles Fairman, *Reconstruction and Reunion* (1971). William Gillette, *The Right to Vote* (1965). Harold Hyman, *A More Perfect Union* (1973). Stanley Kutler, *The Judicial Power and Reconstruction Politics* (1968). Eric McKitrick, *Andrew Johnson and Reconstruction* (1960). Mark W. Summers, *Railroads, Reconstruction, and the Gospel of Prosperity* (1984). Hans L. Trefousse, *The Radical Republicans* (1963); *The Impeachment of a President* (1975); *Andrew Johnson: A Biography* (1989).

The South in Reconstruction. Roberta Alexander, *North Carolina Faces the Freedmen: Race Relations During Presidential*

SIGNIFICANT EVENTS

1869	Congress passes Fifteenth Amendment		Last federal troops withdrawn from South after Compromise of 1877
	First "redeemer" governments elected in South		Last Southern states "redeemed"
1870	Last Southern states readmitted to Congress	**1879**	Readjusters win control of Virginia legislature
	"Force acts" passed	**1880**	Joel Chandler Harris publishes *Uncle Remus*
1871	Alabama claims settled	**1883**	Supreme Court upholds segregation in private institutions
1872	Liberal Republicans defect		
	Grant reelected president	**1890s**	"Jim Crow" laws passed throughout South
1873	Commercial and financial panic disrupts economy		Lynchings increase in South
1875	Specie Resumption Act passed	**1895**	Booker T. Washington outlines Atlanta Compromise
	"Whiskey ring" scandal discredits Grant administration	**1896**	*Plessy* v. *Ferguson* upholds "separate but equal" racial facilities
1877	Rutherford B. Hayes elected president after disputed election	**1898**	*Williams* v. *Mississippi* validates literacy tests for voting

Reconstruction, 1865–1867 (1985). James D. Anderson, *The Education of Blacks in the South* (1989). George Bentley, *A History of the Freedmen's Bureau* (1955). Dan Carter, *When the War Was Over: The Failure of Self-Reconstruction in the South, 1865–1867* (1985). Richard N. Current, *Those Terrible Carpetbaggers* (1988). Barbara Fields, *Slavery and Freedom on the Middle Ground* (1985). Eric Foner, *Nothing but Freedom: Emancipation and Its Legacy* (1983). William Gillette, *Retreat from Reconstruction, 1869–1879* (1980); *The Right to Vote: Politics and Passage of the Fifteenth Amendment* (1969). William C. Harris, *The Day of the Carpetbagger: Republican Reconstruction in Mississippi, 1867–1875* (1979). Robert Higgs, *Competition and Coercion: Blacks in the American Economy, 1865–1914* (1977). Thomas Holt, *Black over White: Negro Political Leadership in South Carolina During Reconstruction* (1977). Elizabeth Jacoway, *Yankee Missionaries in the South* (1979). Jacqueline Jones, *Soldiers of Light and Love: Northern Teachers and Georgia Blacks, 1865–1873* (1980); *Labor of Love, Labor of Sorrow: Black Women, Work, and the Family from Slavery to the Present* (1985). Peter Kolchin, *First Freedom: The Responses of Alabama's Blacks to Emancipation* (1972). Leon Litwack, *Been in the Storm So Long: The Aftermath of Slavery* (1979). Richard Lowe, *Republicans and Reconstruction in Virginia, 1865–1870* (1991). Peyton McCrary, *Abraham Lincoln and Reconstruction* (1978). William S. McFeely, *Yankee Stepfather: General O. O. Howard and the Freedmen* (1968). Otto Olsen, *Carpetbagger's Crusade: Albion Winegar Tourgé* (1965). Michael Perman, *Reunion Without Compromise* (1973); *The Road to Redemption: Southern Politics, 1869–1979* (1984). L. N. Powell, *New Masters: Northern Planters During the Civil War and Reconstruction* (1980). Roger L. Ransom and Richard Sutch, *One Kind of Freedom: The Economic Consequences of Emancipation* (1977). C. Peter Ripley, *Slaves and Freedmen in Civil War Louisiana* (1976). James Sefton, *The United States Army and Reconstruction* (1967). Crandall A. Shifflett, *Patronage and Poverty in the Tobacco South: Louisa County, Virginia, 1860–1900* (1982). Joel G. Taylor, *Louisiana Reconstructed* (1974). Allen Trelease, *White Terror: The Ku Klux Klan Conspiracy and Southern Reconstruction* (1967). Michael Wayne, *The Reshaping of Plantation Society: The Natchez District* (1983). Vernon Wharton, *The Negro in Mississippi, 1865–1890* (1965). Sarah Wiggins, *The Scalawag in Alabama Politics, 1865–1881* (1977). Joel Williamson, *After Slavery: The Negro in South Carolina During Reconstruction* (1965).

The Grant Administration. William B. Hesseltine, *U. S. Grant, Politician* (1935). Ari Hoogenboom, *Outlawing the Spoils* (1961). David Loth, *Public Plunder* (1938). William McFeely, *Grant* (1981). Allan Nevins, *Hamilton Fish* (1936). K. I. Polakoff, *The Politics of Inertia* (1973). John G. Sproat, *"The Best Men"* (1968). Margaret S. Thompson, *The "Spider Web": Con-*

gress and Lobbying in the Age of Grant (1985). Irwin Unger, *The Greenback Era* (1964). C Vann Woodward, *Reunion and Reaction* (1951).

The New South.   Edward L. Ayers, *The Promise of the New South: Life After Reconstruction* (1992). Paul Buck, *The Road to Reunion* (1937). Orville Vernon Burton, *In My Father's House* (1985). Orville Vernon Burton and Robert C. McMath, Jr., eds., *Toward a New South?* (1982). W. J. Cash, *The Mind of the South* (1941). Paul Gaston, *The New South Creed* (1970). J. Morgan Kousser and James M. McPherson, eds., *Region, Race, and Reconstruction (1982).* Jonathan Wiener, *Social Origins of the New South: Alabama, 1860–1885* (1978). C. Vann Woodward, *Origins of the New South* (1951); *The Burden of Southern History* (rev., 1968); *American Counterpoint* (1971); *Thinking Back* (1986); *The Future of the Past* (1989).

Politics in the New South.   Kenneth E. Davison, *The Presidency of Rutherford B. Hayes* (1972). Carl Degler, *The Other South: Southern Dissenters in the Nineteenth Century* (1974). Vincent P. DeSantis, *Republicans Face the Southern Question: The New Departure Years, 1877–1897* (1959). Sheldon Hackney, *Populism to Progressivism in Alabama* (1959). Stanley P. Hirshson, *Farewell to the Bloody Shirt: Northern Republicans and the Southern Negro* (1962). V. O. Key, Jr., *Southern Politics and the Nation* (1949). J. Morgan Kousser, *The Shaping of Southern Politics: Suffrage Restriction and the Establishment of the One-Party South, 1880–1910* (1974). Paul Lewinson, *Race, Class, and Party* (1932). David Potter, *The South and the Concurrent Majority* (1972). Francis B. Simkins, *Pitchfork Ben Tillman* (1944). Joseph F. Wall, *Henry Watterson: Reconstructed Rebel* (1956). C. Vann Woodward, *Reunion and Reaction* (1951); *Tom Watson: Agrarian Rebel* (1938).

Race, Economics, and Social Structure.   Francis Broderick, *W. E. B. DuBois* (1959). David Carlton, *Mill and Town in South Carolina, 1880–1920* (1982). Melvin Greenhut and W. Tate Whitman, eds., *Essays in Southern Economic Development* (1964). Steven Hahn, *The Roots of Southern Populism: Yeoman Farmers and the Transformation of the Georgia Upcountry* (1983). Steven Hahn and Jonathan Prude, eds., *The Countryside in the Age of Capitalist Transformation* (1985). Jacquelyn Dowd Hall et al., *Like a Family: The Making of a Southern Cotton Mill World* (1987). Louis R. Harlan, *Booker T. Washington: The Making of a Black Leader, 1856–1901* (1972); *Booker T. Washington: The Wizard of Tuskegee: 1901–1915* (1983). Robert Higgs, *Competition and Coercion: Blacks in the American Economy, 1865–1914* (1977). Melton A. McLaurin, *Paternalism and Protest: Southern Cotton Mill Workers and Organized Labor* (1971). James M. McPherson, *The Abolitionist Legacy: From Reconstruction to the NAACP* (1975). August Meier, *Negro Thought in America* (1963). Cynthia Neverdon-Morton, *Afro-American Women of the South and the Advancement of the Race, 1895–1925* (1989). Howard Rabinowitz, *Race Relations in the Urban South, 1865–1890* (1978). Roger Ransom and Richard Sutch, *One Kind of Freedom* (1977). Elliott M. Rudwick, *W. E. B. DuBois: Propagandist of Negro Protest* (rev., 1969). Altina L. Waller, *Feud: Hatfields, McCoys, and Social Changes: Appalachia, 1860–1900* (1988). Joel Williamson, *After Slavery* (1965); *The Crucible of Race: Black-White Relations in the American South Since Emancipation* (1985); *A Rage for Order* (1986), an abridgment of *The Crucible of Race.* C. Vann Woodward, *The Strange Career of Jim Crow* (rev., 1974). Gavin Wright, *Old South, New South: Revolutions in the Southern Economy Since the Civil War* (1986).

***AMERICAN PROGRESS*, 1872**
John Gast, an artist in Brooklyn, New York, painted this tribute to westward expansion—a
picture of hardy pioneers marching toward the frontier, protected by the goddess of
progress—at the request of a publisher of travel guides. Engravings adapted from the painting appeared in one guide book, and color reproductions were offered to customers as a
bonus for subscribing to others. It is an example of the wide-ranging promotional effort—by
railroads, landowners, farm-equipment manufacturers, even guidebook publishers—designed
to persuade Americans to move into the western territories in the late nineteenth century.
(Gene Autry Western Heritage Museum)

CHAPTER SIXTEEN

The Conquest of the Far West

THROUGH MUCH OF THE first half of the nineteenth century, relatively few English-speaking Americans considered moving into the vast lands west of the Mississippi River. For some the obstacle was distance; for others it was lack of money; for many more it was the image of much of the Far West, popularized by some early travelers, as the "Great American Desert," unfit for civilization.

By the mid-1840s, however, enough migrants from the eastern regions of the nation had settled in the West to begin to challenge that image. Some were farmers, who had found fertile land in areas once considered too arid for agriculture. Others were ranchers, who had discovered great open grasslands on which they could raise large herds of cattle or sheep for the market. Many were miners, including some of the hundreds of thousands of people who had flocked to California during the 1848–1849 gold rush. By the end of the Civil War, the West had already become legendary in the eastern states. No longer the Great American Desert, it was now the "frontier": an empty land awaiting settlement and civilization; a place of wealth, adventure, opportunity, and untrammeled individualism; a place of fresh beginnings and bold undertakings.

In fact, the real West of the mid-nineteenth century bore little resemblance to either of these images. It was a diverse land, with many different regions, many different climates, many different stores of natural resources. And it was extensively populated, with a number of well-developed societies and cultures. The English-speaking migrants of the late nineteenth century did not find an empty, desolate land. They found Indians, Mexicans, French and British Canadians, Asians, and others, some of whose families had been living in the West for generations.

The Anglo-American settlers helped create new civilizations in this vast and complicated land, but they did not do so by themselves. Although they tried, with considerable success, to conquer and disperse many of the peoples already living in the region, they were never able to make the West theirs alone. They interacted in countless ways with the existing population. Almost everything the Anglo-Americans did and built reflected the influence of these other cultures.

Most of all, however, English-speaking Americans transformed the West by connecting it with, and making it part of, the growing capitalist economy of the East. And despite their self-image as rugged individualists, they relied heavily on assistance from the federal government—land grants, subsidies, and military protection—as they developed the region.

THE SOCIETIES OF THE FAR WEST

The Far West (or what many called the "Great West")—the region beyond the Mississippi River into which millions of Anglo-Americans moved in the years after the Civil War—was in fact many lands. It contained some of the most arid territory in the United States, and some of the wettest and lushest. It contained the flattest plains and the highest mountains. It contained vast treeless prairies and deserts and great forests. And it contained many peoples.

The Western Tribes

The largest and most important western population group before the great American migration was the Indian tribes. Some were members of eastern tribes— Cherokee, Creek, and others—who had been forcibly resettled west of the Mississippi to "Indian Territory" (later Oklahoma) and elsewhere before the Civil War. But most were members of tribes indigenous to the West.

The western tribes had developed a number of patterns of civilization. More than 300,000 Indians (among them the Serrano, Chumash, Pomo, Maidu, Yurok, and Chinook) had lived on the Pacific Coast before the arrival of Spanish settlers. Disease and dislocation decimated the tribes, but in the mid-nineteenth century 150,000 remained—some living within the Hispanic society the Spanish and Mexican settlers had created, many still living within their own tribal communities.

The Pueblos of the Southwest had long lived largely as farmers and had established permanent settlements there even before the Spanish arrived in the seventeenth century. The Pueblos grew corn; they built towns and cities of adobe houses; they practiced elaborate forms of irrigation; and they participated in trade and commerce. In the eighteenth and nineteenth centuries, their intimate relationship with the Spanish (later Mexicans) produced, in effect, an alliance against the Apaches, Navajos, and Commanches of the region.

The complex interaction between the Pueblos and the Spanish, and between both of them and other tribes, produced an elaborate caste system in the Southwest. At the top were the Spanish or Mexicans, who owned the largest estates and controlled the trading centers at Santa Fe and elsewhere. The Pueblos, subordinate but still largely free, were below them. Apaches, Navajos, and others—some captured in war and enslaved for a fixed time, others men and women and they had left their own tribes—were at the bottom. They were known as *genizaros*, Indians without tribes, and they had become in many ways part of Spanish society. This caste system reflected the preoccupation of the society of the Spanish Empire in America with racial ancestry; almost everyone in the Southwest—not just Spanish and Indians, but several categories of mulattoes and mestizos (people of mixed race) had a clear place in an elaborate social hierarchy.

The most widespread Indian groups in the West were the Plains Indians. They were, in fact, many tribal

BUFFALO CHASE
The painter George Catlin captured this scene of Plains Indians in the 1830s hunting among the great herds of buffalo, which provided the food and materials on which many tribes relied. *(National Museum of American Art/Art Resource)*

and language groups. Some formed alliances with one another; others were in constant conflict. Some lived more or less sedentary lives as farmers; others were highly nomadic hunters. Despite their differences, however, the tribes shared some traits. Their cultures were based on close and extended family networks and on an intimate relationship with nature. Tribes (which sometimes numbered several thousand) were generally subdivided into "bands" of up to 500 men and women, usually made up of highly interrelated people. Each band had its own governing council, but the community had a decision-making process in which most members participated. Within each band, tasks were divided by gender. Women's roles were largely domestic and artistic: raising children, cooking, gathering roots and berries, preparing hides, and creating many of the impressive artworks of tribal culture. They also tended fields and gardens in those places where bands remained settled long enough to raise crops. Men worked as hunters and traders and supervised the religious and military life of the band. Most of the Plains Indians practiced a religion centered on a belief in the spiritual power of the natural world—of plants and animals and the rhythms of the days and the seasons.

Many of the Plains tribes—including some of the most powerful tribes in the Sioux nation—subsisted largely through hunting buffalo. Riding small but powerful horses, descendants of Spanish stock, the tribes moved through the grasslands following the herds. Permanent settlements were rare. When a band halted, it constructed tepees as temporary dwellings; when it departed, it left the landscape almost completely undisturbed, a reflection of the deep reverence for nature that was central to Indian culture and religion.

The magnet that drew the hunters and guided their routes was the buffalo, or bison. This huge grazing animal provided the economic basis for the Plains Indians' way of life. Its flesh was their principal source of food, and its skin supplied materials for clothing, shoes, tepees, blankets, robes, and utensils. "Buffalo chips"—dried manure—provided fuel; buffalo bones became knives and arrow tips; buffalo tendons formed the strings of bows.

THE TRANSCONTINENTAL RAILROAD

This complicated trestle under construction by the Union Pacific was one of many large spans necessary for the completion of the transcontinental railroad. It gives some indication of the enormous engineering challenges the railroad builders had to overcome. *(Union Pacific Museum)*

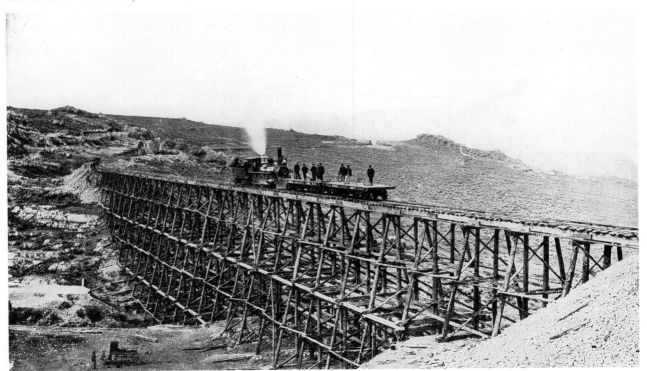

The Plains Indians were proud and aggressive warriors, schooled in warfare from their frequent (and usually brief) skirmishes with rival tribes. The male members of each tribe were, in effect, a warrior class. They competed with one another to develop reputations for fierceness and bravery both as hunters and as soldiers. By the early nineteenth century, the Sioux had become the most powerful tribe in the Missouri River Valley and had begun expanding west and south until they dominated much of the Plains and were the most important military force in the region.

The Plains warriors proved to be the most formidable foes white settlers encountered. But they also suffered from several serious weaknesses that in the end made it impossible for them to prevail. One weakness was the inability of the various tribes (and often even of the bands within tribes) to unite against white aggression. This was a problem that had plagued Native Americans in the East for centuries and had contributed to their ultimate undoing. The western tribes, like the eastern ones, were culturally ill-disposed toward political or military centralization. Not only were they seldom able to draw together a coalition large enough to counter white power, they were also frequently distracted from their battles with whites by conflicts among the tribes themselves. And at times, tribal warriors faced white forces who were being assisted by guides and even fighters from other, usually rival, tribes.

Even so, some tribes were able to overcome their divisions and unite effectively. By the mid-nineteenth century, for example, the Sioux, Arapaho, and Cheyenne had forged a powerful alliance that dominated the northern Plains. The more important weaknesses of the western tribes in their contest with white society were, in fact, ecological and economic. Indians were tragically vulnerable to eastern infectious diseases. Smallpox epidemics, for example, decimated the Pawnees in Nebraska in the 1840s and many of the California tribes in the early 1850s. And the tribes were, of course, at a considerable disadvantage in any long-term battle with an economically and industrially advanced people. They were, in the end, outmanned and outgunned.

Hispanic New Mexico

For centuries, much of the Far West had been part of, first, the Spanish Empire and, later, the Mexican Republic. Although the lands the United States acquired in the 1840s did not include any of Mexico's most populous regions, considerable numbers of Mexicans did live in them and suddenly became residents of American territory. Most of them stayed.

Spanish-speaking communities were scattered throughout the Southwest, from Texas through New Mexico and Arizona, and into California. All of them were transformed in varying degrees by the arrival of Anglo-American migrants and, equally important, by the expansion of the American capitalist economy into the region. For some, the changes created opportunities for greater wealth. But for most it meant an end to the more communal societies and economies they had built over many generations.

In New Mexico, the centers of Spanish-speaking society were the farming and trading communities the Spanish had established in the seventeenth century. (See p. 12.) Descendants of the original Spanish settlers (and more recent migrants from Mexico) lived alongside the Pueblo Indians and some American traders and engaged primarily in cattle and sheep ranching. There was a small aristocracy of great landowners, whose estates radiated out from the major trading center at Santa Fe. And there was a large population of Spanish (later Mexican) peasants, who worked on the great estates, farmed small plots of their own, or otherwise scraped out a subsistence. There were also large groups of Indian laborers, some enslaved or indentured.

When the United States acquired title to New Mexico in the aftermath of the Mexican War, General Stephen Kearney—who had commanded the American troops in the region during the conflict—tried to establish a territorial government that excluded the established Mexican ruling class (the landed aristocrats from around Santa Fe and the most influential priests). He drew most of the officials from among the approximately 1,000 Anglo-Americans in the region, ignoring the over 50,000 Hispanics. There were widespread fears among Hispanics and Indians alike that the new American rulers of the region would confiscate their lands and otherwise threaten their societies. In 1847, Taos Indians rebelled; they killed the new governor and other Anglo-American officials before being subdued by United States army forces. New Mexico remained under military rule for three years, until the United States finally organized a territorial government there in 1850.

By the 1870s, the government of New Mexico was dominated by one of the most notorious of the many "territorial rings" that sprang up in the West in the years before statehood. These were circles of local businesspeople and ambitious politicians with access to federal money who worked together to make the territorial government mutually profitable. In Santa Fe, the ring used its influence to gain control of over 2 million acres of land, much of which had long been in the possession of the original Mexican residents of the territory. The old Hispanic elite in New Mexico had lost much of its political and economic authority.

Even without its former power, Hispanic society in New Mexico survived and even grew in the face of the expansion of Anglo-American settlement in the Southwest. The U.S. Army finally did what the Hispanic residents had been unable to accomplish for 200 years: it broke the power of the Navajo, Apache, and other tribes that had so often harassed the residents of New Mexico and prevented them from expanding their society and commerce. The defeat of the tribes led to substantial Hispanic migration into other areas of the Southwest and as far north as Colorado. Most of the expansion involved peasants and small tradespeople who were looking for land or new opportunities for commerce. The pattern of large estates and a self-conscious aristocracy did not repeat itself in the newer Hispanic settlements.

Hispanic societies survived in the Southwest in part because they were so far from the centers of English-speaking society that Anglo-American migrants (and the railroads that carried them) were slow to get there. But Mexican Americans in the region also fought at times to preserve control of their societies. In the late 1880s, for example, Mexican peasants in an area of what is now Nevada harassed English-speaking cattle ranchers who were attempting to move into the region and successfully fended off their encroachments.

But by then, such successes were already the exception. The Anglo-American presence in the Southwest grew rapidly once the railroads established lines into the region in the 1880s and early 1890s. With the railroads came extensive new ranching, farming, and mining. The expansion of economic activity in the region attracted a new wave of Mexican immigrants—perhaps as many as 100,000 by 1900—who moved across the border (which was unregulated until World War I) in search of work. But the new immigrants, unlike the earlier Hispanic residents of the Southwest, were coming to a society in which they were from the beginning subordinate to Anglo-Americans. The English-speaking proprietors of the new enterprises restricted most Mexicans to the lowest-paying and least stable jobs.

Hispanic California and Texas

In California, Spanish settlement began in the eighteenth century with a string of Christian missions along the Pacific coast. The missionaries and the soldiers who accompanied them gathered most of the coastal Indians into their communities, some forcibly

THE *CALIFORNIOS*
Before the arrival of large waves of immigrants from the United States, California was the home of a flourishing Mexican ranching and mission culture, with a wealthy aristocracy—as this 1850 painting of the Don Manuel family suggests. *(Courtesy W. Graham Arader, III, San Francisco)*

and some by persuasion. The Indians were targets of the evangelizing efforts of the missionaries, who baptized over 50,000 of them. But they were also a labor force for the flourishing and largely self-sufficient economies the missionaries created; the Spanish forced most of these laborers into a state of servitude little different from slavery. The missions had enormous herds of cattle, horses, sheep, and goats, most of them tended by Indian workers; they had brickmakers, blacksmiths, weavers, and farmers, most of them Indians as well. Few of the profits of the mission economy flowed to the workers.

In the 1830s, after the new Mexican government began reducing the power of the church, the mission society largely collapsed, despite strenuous resistance from the missionaries themselves. In its place emerged a secular Mexican aristocracy, which controlled a chain of large estates (some of them former missions) in the fertile lands west of the Sierra mountains. For them, the arrival of Anglo-Americans before and after the Civil War was disastrous. So vast were the numbers of English-speaking immigrants that the *californios* (as the Hispanic residents of the state were known) had little power to resist the onslaught. In the central and northern parts of the state, where the Anglo population growth was greatest, the *californios* experienced a series of defeats. English-speaking prospectors organized to exclude them, sometimes violently, from the mines during the gold rush. Many *californios* also lost their lands—either through corrupt business deals or through outright seizure (sometimes with the help of the courts and often through simple occupation by squatters). Years of litigation by the displaced Hispanics had very little effect on the changing distribution of landownership.

In the southern areas of California, where there were at first fewer migrants, some Mexican landowners managed to hang on for a time. The booming Anglo communities in the north of the state created a large market for the cattle that southern *rancheros* were raising. But a combination of reckless expansion, growing indebtedness, and a severe drought in the 1860s devastated the Mexican ranching culture. By the 1880s, the Hispanic aristocracy in California had largely ceased to exist.

Increasingly, Mexicans and Mexican Americans became part of the lower end of the state's working class, clustered in *barrios* in Los Angeles or elsewhere, or becoming migrant farmworkers. Even small landowners who managed to hang on to their farms found themselves unable to raise livestock, as the once communal grazing lands fell under the control of powerful Anglo ranchers. The absence of herding destroyed many family economies and, by forcing farmers into migrant work, displaced much of the peasantry.

A similar pattern of dispossession and exploitation occurred in Texas, where many Mexican landowners lost their land after the territory joined the United States. (See pp. 352–354.) This occurred as a result of fraud, coercion, and the inability of even the most substantial Mexican ranchers to compete with the enormous Anglo-American ranching kingdoms that were emerging. In 1859, Mexican resentments erupted in an armed challenge to American power: a raid on a jail in Brownsville, led by the rancher Juan Cortina, who freed all the Mexican prisoners inside. But such resistance had little long-term effect. Cortina continued to harass Anglo communities in Texas until 1875, but the Mexican government finally captured and imprisoned him. As in California, Mexicans in southern Texas (who constituted nearly three quarters of the population there) became an increasingly impoverished working class relegated largely to unskilled farm or industrial labor.

On the whole, the great Anglo-American migration was less catastrophic for the Hispanic population of the West than it was for the Indian tribes. Indeed, for some Hispanics, it created new opportunities for wealth and station. For the most part, however, the late nineteenth century saw the destruction of Mexican Americans' authority in a region they had long considered their home; and it saw the movement of large numbers of Hispanics—both longtime residents of the West and more recent immigrants—into an impoverished working class serving the expanding capitalist economy of the United States.

The Chinese Migration

At the same time that ambitious or impoverished Europeans were crossing the Atlantic in search of opportunities in the new world, many Chinese crossed the Pacific in hopes of better lives than they could expect in their own poverty-stricken land. Not all came to the United States. Many Chinese moved to Hawaii, Australia, Latin America, South Africa, and even the Caribbean—some as "coolies" (indentured servants whose condition was close to slavery).

A few Chinese had come to California even before the gold rush (see pp. 364–366), but after 1848 the flow increased dramatically. By 1880, more than 200,000 Chinese had settled in the United States, mostly in California, where they constituted nearly a tenth of the population. Almost all came as free laborers. For a time, white Americans welcomed the Chinese as a conscientious, hardworking people. In 1852, the governor of California called them "one of the most worthy classes of our newly adopted citizens" and called for more Chinese immigration to swell the territory's inadequate labor force. Very quickly, however, white opinion turned hostile—in part because the Chinese were so industrious and successful that some white Americans began considering them rivals, even threats. The experience of Chinese immigrants in the West became, therefore, a struggle to advance economically in the face of racism and discrimination.

In the early 1850s, large numbers of Chinese immigrants worked in the gold mines. Many of them were well-organized, hardworking prospectors, and for a time some of them enjoyed considerable success. But opportunities for Chinese to prosper in the mines were fleeting. In 1852, the California legislature began trying to exclude the Chinese from gold mining by enacting a "foreign miners" tax (which also helped exclude Mexicans). A series of other laws in the 1850s were designed to discourage Chinese immigration into the territory. Gradually, the effect of the discriminatory laws, the hostility of white miners, and the declining profitability of the surface mines drove most Chinese out of prospecting. Those who remained in the mountains became primarily hired workers in the mines built by corporations with financing from the East. These newer mines—which extended much deeper into the mountains than individual prospectors or small, self-financed groups had been able to go—replaced the early, smaller operations.

As mining declined as a source of wealth and jobs for the Chinese, railroad employment grew. Beginning in 1865, over 12,000 Chinese found work building the transcontinental railroad. In fact, Chinese workers formed 90 percent of the labor force of the Central Pacific and were mainly responsible for construction of the western part of the new road. The company preferred them to white workers because they worked hard, made few demands, and accepted relatively low wages. Many of the workers were recruited for the railroad in China by agents for the Central Pacific. Once employed, they were organized into work gangs under Chinese supervisors.

Work on the Central Pacific was arduous and often dangerous. As the railroad moved through the mountains, the company made few concessions to the difficult conditions and provided their workers with little protection from the elements. Work continued through the winter, and many Chinese tunneled into snow banks at night to create warm sleeping areas for themselves. The tunnels frequently collapsed, suffocating those inside; but the company allowed nothing to disrupt construction.

But the Chinese laborers were not always as docile as their employers imagined them to be. In the spring of 1866, 5,000 Chinese railroad workers went on strike demanding higher wages and a shorter workday. The company isolated them, surrounded them with strikebreakers, and starved them into submission. The strike failed, and most of the workers returned to their jobs.

In 1869 the transcontinental railroad was completed. Thousands of Chinese were now out of work. Some

AN ANTI-CHINESE RIOT
White citizens of Denver attacked the Chinese community of the city in 1880, beating many of its residents and vandalizing their homes and businesses. It was one of a number of anti-Chinese riots in the cities of the West. They were a result of a combination of racism and resentment by white workers at what they considered unfair competition from Chinese laborers who were willing to work for very low wages. *(Bettmann)*

hired themselves out on vast drainage and irrigation projects in the agricultural valleys of central California. Some became common agricultural laborers, picking fruit for low wages. Some became tenant farmers, often on marginal lands that white owners saw no profit in working themselves. Some managed to acquire land of their own and established themselves as modestly successful truck farmers.

Increasingly, however, Chinese immigrants flocked to cities. By 1900, nearly half the Chinese population of California lived in urban areas. By far the largest single Chinese community was in San Francisco. Much of community life there, and in other "Chinatowns" throughout the West, revolved around organizations—usually formed by people from the same clan or community in China—that functioned as something like benevolent societies and filled many of the roles that political machines often served in immigrant communities in eastern cities. They were often led by prominent merchants. (In San Francisco, the leading merchants—known as the "Six Companies"—often worked together to advance their interests in the larger community of the city and state.) These organizations became, in effect, employment brokers, unions, arbitrators of disputes, defenders of the community against outside persecution, and dispensers of social services. They also organized the elaborate festivals and celebrations that were such a conspicuous and important part of life in Chinatowns.

Other Chinese organizations were secret societies, known as "tongs." And some of the tongs were violent criminal organizations, involved in the opium trade and prostitution. Few people outside the Chinese communities were aware of their existence, except when rival tongs engaged in violent conflict (or "tong wars"), as occurred frequently in San Francisco in the 1880s.

Life was hard for most urban Chinese, in San Francisco and elsewhere. The Chinese usually occupied the lower rungs of the employment ladder in the western cities in which most lived. Many worked as common laborers, servants, and unskilled factory hands. Some established their own small businesses, especially laundries. They moved into this business not because of experience—there were few commercial laundries in China—but because they were excluded from so many other areas of employment. Laundries could be started with very little capital, and required only limited command of English. By the 1890s, Chinese constituted over two-thirds of all the laundry workers in California, many of them in shops they themselves owned and ran.

The relatively small number of Chinese women fared even worse. During the earliest Chinese migra-

tions to California, virtually all the women who made the journey did so because they had been sold into prostitution in China. As late as 1880, nearly half the Chinese women in California were prostitutes. Both Anglo and Chinese reformers tried to stamp out the prostitution in Chinatowns in the 1890s, but more effective than their efforts was the growing number of Chinese women in America. Once the sex ratio became more balanced, Chinese men were more likely to seek companionship in families.

Anti-Chinese Sentiments

As Chinese communities grew larger and more conspicuous in western cities, anti-Chinese sentiment among white residents became increasingly virulent. In fact, next to the Indians, the Chinese probably suffered the most intense persecution from white Americans in the West. Anti-coolie clubs emerged in the 1860s and 1870s seeking a ban on employing Chinese and organizing boycotts of products made with Chinese labor. Some of these clubs attacked Chinese workers in the streets and were suspected of setting fire to factories in which Chinese worked. These activities reflected the resentment of many white workers toward Chinese laborers for accepting low wages and thus undercutting union members. As the political value of attacking the Chinese grew in California, the Democratic Party took up the call. So did the Workingmen's Party of California—created in 1878 by Denis Kearney, an Irish immigrant—which gained significant political power in the state in large part on the basis of its hostility to the Chinese. By the mid 1880s, anti-Chinese agitation and violence had spread up and down the Pacific Coast and into other areas of the West.

But the denunciations of the Chinese did not rest on economic grounds alone. They rested on cultural and racial arguments as well. For example, the reformer Henry George, a critic of capitalism and a champion of the rights of labor (see p. 490), described the Chinese as products of a civilization that had failed to progress, that remained mired in barbarism and savagery. They were, therefore, "unassimilable" and should be excluded.

In 1882, Congress responded to the political pressure and the growing violence by passing the Chinese Exclusion Act, which banned Chinese immigration into the United States for ten years and barred Chinese already in the country from becoming naturalized citizens. Support for the act came from representatives from all regions of the country. It reflected the growing fear of unemployment and labor unrest throughout the nation and the belief that excluding "an industrial army of Asiatic laborers" would protect

"American" workers and help reduce class conflict. Congress renewed the law for another ten years in 1892 and made it permanent in 1902. It had a dramatic effect on the Chinese population, which declined by more than 40 percent in the forty years after its passage.

The Chinese in America did not accept the new laws quietly. They were shocked by the anti-Chinese rhetoric that lumped them together with African Americans and Indians. They were, they insisted, descendants of a great and enlightened civilization. How could they be compared to people who knew "nothing about the relations of society"? White Americans, they said, did not protest the great waves of immigration by Italians ("the most dangerous of men," one Chinese American said) or Irish or Jews. "They are all let in, while Chinese, who are sober, are duly law abiding, clean, educated and industrious, are shut out." The Six Companies in San Francisco organized strenuous letter-writing campaigns, petitioned the president, and even filed suit in federal court. Their efforts had no significant effect.

Migration from the East

The great wave of new settlers in the West from the eastern United States came on the heels of important earlier migrations. California and Oregon had substantial Anglo-American settlements and were both already states of the Union by 1860. There were large and growing Anglo- and African-American communities in Texas, which had entered the Union in 1845 and had been part of the Confederacy during the war. And from Texas and elsewhere, traders, farmers, and ranchers had begun to establish Anglo-American outposts in parts of New Mexico, Arizona, and other areas of the Southwest.

But the scale of the postwar migration dwarfed everything that had preceded it. In previous decades, the settlers had come in thousands. Now they came in millions, spreading throughout the vast western territories—into empty and inhabited lands alike. Most of the new settlers were from the established Anglo-American societies of the eastern United States, but substantial numbers—over 2 million between 1870 and 1900—were foreign-born immigrants from Europe: Scandinavians, Germans, Irish, Russians, Czechs, and others.

They came for many reasons. Settlers were attracted by gold and silver deposits, by the shortgrass pasture for cattle and sheep, and ultimately by the sod of the Plains and the meadowlands of the mountains, which they discovered were suitable for farming or ranching. The completion of the great transcontinental railroad line in 1869, and the construction of the many subsidiary lines that spread out from it, also encouraged settlement.

The land policies of the federal government also worked to encourage settlement. The Homestead Act of 1862 permitted settlers to buy plots of 160 acres for a small fee if they occupied the land they purchased for five years and improved it. The Homestead Act was intended as a progressive measure. It would give a free farm to any American who needed one. It would be a form of government relief to people who otherwise might have no prospects. And it would help create new markets and new outposts of commercial agriculture for the nation's growing economy.

But the Homestead Act rested on a number of misperceptions. The framers of the law had assumed that mere possession of land would be enough to sustain a farm family. They had not recognized the effects of the increasing mechanization of agriculture and the rising costs of running a farm. Moreover, they had made many of their calculations on the basis of eastern agricultural experiences that were inappropriate for the region west of the Mississippi. A unit of 160 acres was too small for the grazing and grain farming of much of the Great Plains. Although over 400,000 homesteaders stayed on Homestead Act claims long enough to gain title to their land, a much larger number abandoned the region before the end of the necessary five years, unable to cope with the bleak life on the windswept plains and the economic realities that were making it difficult for families without considerable resources to thrive.

Not for the last time, beleaguered westerners looked to the federal government for solutions to their problems. In response to their demands, Congress increased the homestead allotments. The Timber Culture Act (1873) permitted homesteaders to receive grants of 160 additional acres if they planted 40 acres of trees on them. The Desert Land Act (1877) provided that claimants could buy 640 acres at $1.25 an acre provided they irrigated part of their holdings within three years. The Timber and Stone Act (1878), which presumably applied to nonarable land, authorized sales at $2.50 an acre. These laws ultimately made it possible for individuals to acquire as much as 1,280 acres of land at little cost. Some enterprising settlers got much more. Fraud ran rampant in the administration of the acts. Lumber, mining, and cattle companies, by employing "dummy" registrants and using other illegal devices, seized millions of acres of the public domain.

Political organization followed on the heels of settlement. After the admission of Kansas as a state in 1861, the remaining territories of Washington, New Mexico, Utah, and Nebraska were divided into smaller

SODBUSTERS
As farmers moved onto the Great Plains in Nebraska and other states on the agrarian frontier, their first task was to cut through the sod that covered the land to get to soil in which they could plant crops. The sod itself was so thick and solid that some settlers (including the Summers family of West Custer County, Nebraska, pictured here in 1888) used it to build their houses. The removal of the sod made cultivation of the plains possible; it also removed the soil's protective covering and contributed to the great dust storms that plagued the region in times of drought.   *(Nebraska State Historical Society)*

units that would presumably be easier to organize. By the close of the 1860s, territorial governments were in operation in the new provinces of Nevada, Colorado, Dakota, Arizona, Idaho, Montana, and Wyoming. Statehood rapidly followed. Nevada became a state in 1864, Nebraska in 1867, and Colorado in 1876. In 1889, North and South Dakota, Montana, and Washington won admission; Wyoming and Idaho entered the next year. Congress denied Utah statehood until its Mormon leaders convinced the government in 1896 that polygamy (the practice of men taking several wives) had been abandoned. At the turn of the century, only three territories remained outside the union. Arizona and New Mexico were excluded because their scanty white populations remained minorities in the territories, because their politics was predominantly Democratic in a Republican era, and because they were un-

willing to accept admission as a single state. Oklahoma (formerly Indian Territory) was opened to white settlement and granted territorial status in 1889–1890.

THE CHANGING WESTERN ECONOMY

Among the many effects on the Far West of the new wave of Anglo-American settlement was a transformation of the region's economy. The new American settlers tied the West firmly to the growing industrial economy of the East (and of much of the rest of the world). Mining, timbering, ranching, commercial farming, and many other economic activities relied on the

East for markets and for capital. Some of the most powerful economic institutions in the West were great eastern corporations that controlled mines, ranches, and farms.

Labor in the West

As commercial activity increased, many farmers, ranchers, and miners found it necessary to recruit a paid labor force—not an easy task for those far away from major population centers and unable or unwilling to hire Indian workers. The labor shortage of the region led to higher wages for workers than were typical in most areas of the East. But working conditions were often arduous, and job security was almost nonexistent. Once a railroad was built, a crop harvested, a herd sent to market, a mine played out, hundreds and even thousands of workers could find themselves suddenly unemployed. Competition from Chinese immigrants, whom employers could usually hire for considerably lower wages than they had to pay whites, also forced some Anglo-Americans out of work. Communities of the jobless gathered in the region's few cities, in mining camps, and elsewhere; other unemployed people moved restlessly from place to place in search of work.

Those who owned no land were highly mobile, mostly male, and seldom married. Indeed, the West had the highest percentage of single people (10 percent) of any region in the country—one reason why single women found working in dance halls and as prostitutes among the most readily available forms of employment.

Despite the enormous geographical mobility in western society, actual social mobility was limited. Many Americans thought of the West as a land of limitless opportunity, but as in the rest of the country, advancement was easiest and most rapid for those who were economically advantaged to begin with. Studies of western communities suggest that social mobility in most of them was no greater than it was in the East. And the distribution of wealth in the region was little different from that in the older states as well.

Even more than in many parts of the East, the western working class was highly multiracial. English-speaking whites worked alongside African Americans and immigrants from southern and eastern Europe, as they did in the East. Even more, they worked with Chinese, Filipinos, Mexicans, and Indians. But the work force was highly stratified along racial lines. In almost every area of the western economy, white workers (whatever their ethnicity) occupied the upper tiers of employment: management and skilled labor. The lower tiers—unskilled and often arduous work in the mines, on the railroads, or in agriculture—consisted overwhelmingly of nonwhites.

Reinforcing this dual labor system was a set of racial assumptions developed and sustained largely by white employers. Chinese, Mexicans, and Filipinos, they argued, were genetically or culturally suited to manual labor. Because they were small, those who promoted these racist stereotypes argued, they could

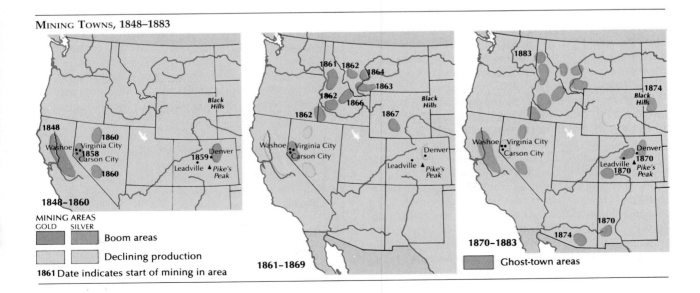

MINING TOWNS, 1848–1883

1848–1860

1861–1869

1870–1883

MINING AREAS
GOLD   SILVER
Boom areas
Declining production
1861 Date indicates start of mining in area
Ghost-town areas

COLORADO BOOM TOWN
After a prospector discovered silver nearby in 1890, miners flocked to the town of Creede, Colorado. For a time in the early 1890s, 150 to 300 people arrived there daily. Although the town was located in a canyon so narrow that there was room for only one street, buildings sprouted rapidly to serve the growing community. Like other such boom towns, however, Creede's prosperity was short-lived. In 1893 the price of silver collapsed, and by the end of the century, Creede was almost deserted. *(Henry Ford Museum)*

work better in deep mines than whites. Because they were accustomed to heat, they could withstand arduous work in the fields better than whites. Because they were unambitious and unconcerned about material comfort, they would accept low wages and live in conditions that white people would not tolerate.

These racial myths served the interests of employers above all, but white workers tended to embrace them too. That was in part because the myths supported a system that reserved whatever mobility there was largely for whites. An Irish common laborer might hope in the course of a lifetime to move several rungs up the occupational ladder. A Chinese or Mexican worker in the same job had no realistic prospects of doing the same. Poor whites in the American South often believed they had more in common with wealthy planters than they did with black workers. Similarly in the West, white laborers—when forced to choose sides—often supported white bosses over nonwhite fellow workers. That was one reason why workers in

the West, like those in the South, often had difficulty organizing effectively to challenge their employers.

The western economy was, however, no more a single entity than the economy of the East. In the late nineteenth century, the region produced three major industries, each with a distinctive history and distinctive characteristics: mining, ranching, and commercial farming.

The Arrival of the Miners

The first economic boom in the Far West came in mining, and the first part of the area to be extensively settled by migrants was the mineral-rich region of mountains and plateaus, where settlers hoped to make quick fortunes by finding precious metals. The life span of the mining boom was relatively brief. It began in earnest around 1860 (although there had, of course, been some earlier booms, most notably in California), and flourished until the 1890s. And then it abruptly declined.

News of a gold or silver strike in an area would start a stampede reminiscent of the California gold rush of 1849, followed by several stages of settlement. Individual prospectors would exploit the first shallow deposits of ore largely by hand, with pan and placer mining. After these surface deposits dwindled, corporations moved in to engage in lode or quartz mining, which dug deeper beneath the surface. Then, as those deposits dwindled, commercial mining either disappeared or continued on a restricted basis, and ranchers and farmers moved in and established a more permanent economy.

The first great mineral strikes (other than the California gold rush) occurred just before the Civil War. In 1858, gold was discovered in the Pike's Peak district of what would soon be the territory of Colorado; the following year, 50,000 prospectors stormed in from California, the Mississippi Valley, and the East. Denver and other mining camps blossomed into "cities" overnight. Almost as rapidly as it had developed, the boom ended. Eventually, corporations, notably the Guggenheim interests, revived some of the profits of the gold boom, and the discovery of silver near Leadville supplied a new source of mineral wealth.

While the Colorado rush of 1859 was still in progress, news of another strike drew miners to Nevada. Gold had been found in the Washoe district, but the most valuable ore in the great Comstock Lode (first discovered in 1858 by Henry Comstock) and other veins was silver. The first prospectors to reach the Washoe fields came from California; and from the beginning, Californians dominated the settlement and development of Nevada. In a remote desert without railroad transportation, the territory produced no supplies of its own, and everything—from food and machinery to whiskey and prostitutes—had to be shipped from California to Virginia City, Carson City, and other roaring camp towns. When the first placer (or surface) deposits ran out, California and eastern capitalists bought the claims of the pioneer prospectors and began to use the more difficult process of quartz mining, which enabled them to retrieve silver from deeper veins. For a few years these outside owners reaped tremendous profits; from 1860 to 1880 the Nevada lodes yielded bullion worth $306 million. After that, the mines quickly played out.

The next important mineral discoveries came in 1874, when gold was found in the Black Hills of southwestern Dakota Territory. Prospectors swarmed into the area, then (and for years to come) accessible only by stagecoach. Like the others, the boom flared for a time, until surface resources faded and corporations took over from the miners. One enormous company, the Homestake, came to dominate the fields. Popula-

tion declined, and the Dakotas, like other boom areas of the mineral empire, ultimately developed a largely agricultural economy.

Although the gold and silver discoveries generated the most popular excitement, in the long run other, less glamorous natural resources proved more important to the development of the West. The great Anaconda copper mine launched by William Clark in 1881 marked the beginning of an industry that would remain important to Montana for many decades. In other areas, mining operations had significant success with lead, tin, quartz, and zinc. Such efforts generally proved more profitable in the long run than the usually short-lived gold and silver extraction.

Life in the boomtowns had a hectic tempo and a gaudy flavor unknown in any other part of the Far West. A speculative spirit, a mood of heady optimism, gripped almost everyone and dominated every phase of community activity. And while relatively few of the prospectors and miners who flocked to the bonanzas ever "struck it rich," there was at least some truth to the popular belief that mining provided opportunities for sudden wealth. The "bonanza kings"—the miners who did become enormously wealthy off a strike—were much more likely to have come from modest or impoverished backgrounds than the industrial tycoons of the East.

The conditions of mine life in the boom period—the presence of precious minerals, the vagueness of claim boundaries, the cargoes of gold being shipped out—attracted to the camps outlaws and "bad men," operating as individuals or gangs. When the situation became intolerable in a community, those members interested in order began enforcing their own laws through vigilance committees, an unofficial system of social control used earlier in California. Vigilantes were unconstrained by the legal system, and they often imposed their notion of justice arbitrarily and without regard for any form of due process. Sometimes criminals themselves secured control of the committees. Some vigilantes continued to operate as private "law" enforcers after the creation of regular governments.

Men greatly outnumbered women in the mining towns, and younger men in particular had difficulty finding female companions of comparable age. Those women who did gravitate to the new communities often came with their husbands, and their activities were generally (although not always) confined to the same kinds of domestic tasks that eastern women performed. Single women, or women whose husbands were earning no money, did choose (or find it necessary) to work for wages at times, as cooks, laundresses, and tavern keepers. And in the sexually imbalanced mining communities, there was always a ready market for prostitutes.

The thousands of people who flocked to the mining towns in search of quick wealth and who failed to find it often remained as wage laborers in corporate mines after the boom period. Working conditions were almost uniformly terrible. The corporate mines were deep and extremely hot, with temperatures often exceeding 100 degrees Fahrenheit. Some workers died of heatstroke (or of pneumonia, a result of experiencing sudden changes of temperature when emerging from the mines.) Poor ventilation meant large accumulations of poisonous carbon dioxide, which caused dizziness, nausea, and headaches. Lethal dusts stayed in the stagnant air to be inhaled over and over by the miners, many of whom developed silicosis (a disabling disease of the lungs) as a result. There were frequent explosions, cave-ins, and fires, and there were many accidents with the heavy machinery they used to bore into the earth. In the 1870s, before technological advances eliminated some of the dangers, one worker in every thirty was disabled in the mines, and one in every eighty was killed. That rate fell later in the nineteenth century, but mining remained one of the most dangerous and arduous working environments in the United States.

The Cattle Kingdom

A second important element of the changing economy of the Far West was cattle ranching. The open range—the vast grasslands of the public domain—provided a huge area on the Great Plains where cattle raisers could graze their herds free of charge and unrestricted by the boundaries of private farms. The railroads gave birth to the range-cattle industry by giving it access to markets. Eventually, the same railroads ended it by bringing farmers to the plains and thus destroying the open range.

The western cattle industry was Mexican and Texan by ancestry. Long before citizens of the United States invaded the Southwest, Mexican ranchers had developed the techniques and equipment that the cattlemen and cowboys of the Great Plains later employed: branding (a device known in all frontier areas where stock was common), roundups, roping, and the gear of the herders—their lariats, saddles, leather chaps, and spurs. Americans in Texas adopted these methods and carried them to the northernmost ranges of the cattle kingdom. Texas also had the largest herds of cattle in the country; the animals were descended from imported Spanish stock—wiry, hardy longhorns—and allowed to run wild or semiwild. From Texas, too, came the horses that enabled the caretakers of the herds, the

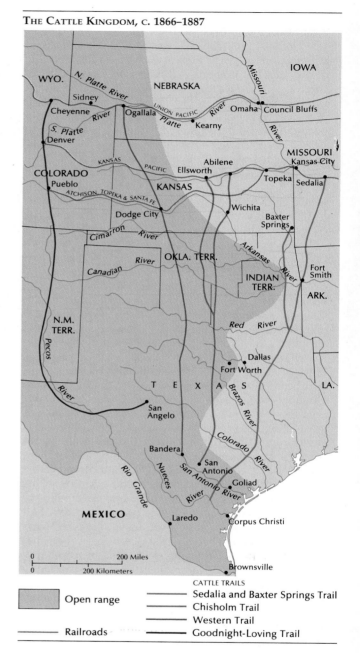

THE CATTLE KINGDOM, C. 1866–1887

CATTLE TRAILS

Open range

Railroads

—— Sedalia and Baxter Springs Trail
—— Chisholm Trail
—— Western Trail
—— Goodnight-Loving Trail

cowboys, to control them—small, muscular broncos or mustangs well suited to the requirements of cattle country.

At the end of the Civil War, an estimated 5 million cattle roamed the Texas ranges. Eastern markets were offering fat prices for steers in any condition, and the

THE CATTLE DRIVE
Cowboys round up a herd near Cheyenne, Wyoming, during one of the great cattle drives that briefly characterized the ranching economy of the West. *(American Heritage Center, University of Wyoming)*

challenge facing the cattle industry was getting the animals from the range to the railroad centers. Early in 1866, some Texas cattle ranchers began driving their combined herds, some 260,000 head, north to Sedalia, Missouri, on the Missouri Pacific Railroad. Traveling over rough country and beset by outlaws, Indians, and property-conscious farmers, the caravan suffered heavy losses, and only a fraction of the animals arrived in Sedalia. But the drive was an important experiment. It proved that cattle could be driven to distant markets and pastured along the trail, and that they would even gain weight during the journey. This earliest of the "long drives," in other words, established the first, tentative link between the isolated cattle breeders of west Texas and the booming urban markets of the East. The drive laid the groundwork for the explosion of the industry—for the creation of the "cattle kingdom."

With the precedent of the long drive established, the next step was to find an easier route through more accessible country. Market facilities grew up at Abilene, Kansas, on the Kansas Pacific Railroad, and for years the town reigned as the railhead of the cattle kingdom. Between 1867 and 1871, cattlemen drove nearly 1.5 million head up the Chisholm Trail to Abilene—a town that, when filled with rampaging cowboys at the end of a drive, rivaled the mining towns in rowdiness. But by the mid-1870s, agricultural development in western Kansas was eating away at the open range land at the same time that the supply of animals was increasing. Cattlemen therefore had to develop other trails and other market outlets. As the railroads began to reach farther west, Dodge City and Wichita in Kansas, Ogallala and Sidney in Nebraska, Cheyenne and Laramie in Wyoming, and Miles City and Glendive in Montana all began to rival Abilene as major centers of stock herding.

A long drive was a spectacular sight, and it is perhaps unsurprising that it became the most romanticized and mythologized aspect of life in the West. It began with the spring, or calf, roundup. The cattlemen of a district met with their cowboys at a specified place to round up stock from the open range; these herds contained the stock of many different owners, with only their brands to distinguish them from one another. As the cattle were driven in, the calves were branded with the marks of their mothers. Stray calves with no identifying symbols, "mavericks," were divided on a pro-rata basis. Then the cows and calves were turned loose to pasture, while the yearling steers (year-old males) were readied for the drive to the north. The combined herds, usually numbering from 2,000 to 5,000 head, moved out. Cowboys representing each of the major ranchers accompanied them. Most of the cowboys in the early years were veterans of the Confederate army. The next largest group consisted of African Americans—over half a million of them. They were more numerous than white northerners or Mexicans and other foreigners. They were usually assigned such jobs as wrangler (herdsman) or cook.

Every cattleman had to have a permanent base from which to operate, and so the ranch emerged. A ranch consisted of the employer's dwelling, quarters for employees, and a tract of grazing land. In the early years of the cattle kingdom, most ranches were relatively small, since so much of the grazing occurred in the vast, open areas that cattlemen shared. But as farmers and sheep breeders began to compete for the open plains, ranches became larger and more clearly defined; cattlemen gradually had to learn to raise their stock on their own fenced land.

There had always been an element of risk and speculation in the open-range cattle business. At any time, "Texas fever"—a disease transmitted to cattle by parasite-carrying ticks—might decimate a herd. Rustlers and Indians frequently seized large numbers of animals. But as settlement of the plains increased, new forms of competition joined these traditional risks. Sheep breeders from California and Oregon brought their flocks onto the range to compete for grass. Farmers ("nesters") from the East threw fences around their claims, blocking trails and breaking up the open range. A series of "range wars"—between sheepmen and cattlemen, between ranchers and farmers—erupted out of the tensions between these competing groups. Some of the wars resulted in significant loss of life and extensive property damage.

Accounts of the lofty profits to be made in the cattle business—it was said that an investment of $5,000 would return $45,000 in four years—tempted eastern, English, and Scottish capital to the plains. Increasingly, the structure of the cattle economy became corporate; in one year, twenty corporations with a combined capital of $12 million were chartered in Wyoming. The inevitable result of this frenzied, speculative expansion was that the ranges, already severed and shrunk by the railroads and the farmers, became overstocked. There was not enough grass to support the crowding herds or sustain the long drives. Finally nature intervened with a destructive finishing blow. Two severe winters, in 1885–1886 and 1886–1887, with a searing summer between them, stung and scorched the plains.

Hundreds of thousands of cattle died, streams and grass dried up, princely ranches and costly investments disappeared in a season.

The open-range industry never recovered; the long drive disappeared for good. Railroads displaced the trail as the route to market for livestock. But the established cattle ranches—with fenced-in grazing land and stocks of hay for winter feed—survived, grew, and prospered, eventually producing more beef than ever.

Although the cattle industry was overwhelmingly male in its early years, there were always a few women involved in ranching and driving. As ranching became more sedentary, the presence of women greatly increased. By 1890, more than 250,000 women owned ranches or farms in the western states (many of them as proxies for their husbands or fathers, but some in their own right). Indeed, the region provided women with many opportunities that were closed to them in the East—including the opportunity to participate in politics. Wyoming was the first state in the Union to guarantee woman suffrage; and throughout the West, women established themselves as an important political presence (and occasionally as significant officeholders).

The Romance of the West

The supposedly unsettled West had always occupied a special place in the Anglo-American imagination, beginning in the seventeenth century when the first white settlers along the Atlantic coast began to look to the interior for new opportunities and for refuge from the civilized world. But the vast regions of this "last frontier" had a particularly strong romantic appeal to many whites. Some of the reasons were obvious. The Great Plains, the Rocky Mountains, the basin and plateau region beyond the Rockies, and the Sierra Nevada–Cascade ranges beyond that—all constituted a landscape of brilliant diversity and spectacular grandeur, different from anything white Americans had encountered before. It was little wonder that newcomers looked on it with reverence and wonder. Painters of the new "Rocky Mountain School"—of whom the best known was Albert Bierstadt—celebrated the new West in grandiose canvases, some of which were taken on tours around the eastern and midwestern states and attracted enormous crowds, eager for a vision of the Great West. Such paintings emphasized the ruggedness and dramatic variety of the region, and reflected the same awe toward the land that earlier regional painters had displayed toward the Hudson River Valley and other areas.

Even more appealing than the landscape, perhaps, was the rugged, free-spirited lifestyle that many Americans associated with the West—a lifestyle that supposedly stood in sharp contrast to the increasingly stable and ordered world of the East. Many nineteenth-century Americans came to romanticize, especially, the figure of the cowboy and transformed him remarkably quickly from the low-paid worker he actually was into a powerful and enduring figure of myth. Admiring Americans seldom thought about the many dismal aspects of the cowboy's life: the tedium, the loneliness, the physical discomforts, the relatively few opportunities for advancement. Instead, in western novels such as Owen Wister's *The Virginian* (1902), they romanticized his freedom from traditional social constraints, his affinity with nature, even his supposed propensity for violence. The cowboy became a powerful and enduring symbol of what had long been an important ideal in the American mind: the ideal of the natural man (the same idea that had shaped such earlier novels as James Fenimore Cooper's *The Deerslayer* and *The Last of the Mohicans*). That symbol has survived into the late twentieth century—in popular literature, in song, in film, and on television.

Yet it was not simply the particular character of the new West that made it so important to the nation's imagination. It was also the fact that many Americans considered it the last frontier. Since the earliest moments of European settlement in America, the image of uncharted territory to the west had always comforted and inspired those who dreamed of starting life anew. Now, with the last of that unsettled land being slowly absorbed into the nation's civilization, that image exercised a stronger pull than ever. Mark Twain, one of the great American writers of the nineteenth century, gave voice to this romantic vision of the frontier in a series of brilliant novels and memoirs. In some of his writings—notably *Roughing It* (1872)—he wrote of the Far West, and of his own experience as a newspaper reporter in Nevada during the mining boom. His greatest works, however, dealt with life on an earlier frontier: the Mississippi Valley of his boyhood. In *The Adventures of Tom Sawyer* (1876) and *The Adventures of Huckleberry Finn* (1885), he produced characters who repudiated the constraints of organized society and attempted to escape into a more natural world. For Huck Finn, the vehicle of escape might be a small raft on the Mississippi, but the yearning for freedom reflected a larger vision of the West as the last refuge from the constraints of civilization.

One of the clearest and most influential statements of this romantic vision of the frontier came not from an artist but from the historian Frederick Jackson Turner, of the University of Wisconsin. In 1893, the thirty-three-year-old Turner delivered a memorable paper to a meeting of the American Historical Association in Chicago entitled "The Significance of the Frontier in American History." In it, he cited the findings of the 1890 census that the unsettled area of the West had been "so broken into by isolated bodies of settlement" that a continuous frontier line could no longer be drawn. The passing of that line, he argued, ended an era in the nation's history. For, as Turner stated, "the existence of an area of free land, its continuous recession, and the advance of settlement westward, explain American development." This experience of expansion into the frontier had stimulated individualism, nationalism, and democracy. It had kept opportunities for advancement alive. It had made Americans the distinctive people that they were. "Now," Turner concluded portentously, "four centuries from the discovery of America, at the end of a hundred years of life under the Constitution, the frontier has gone and with its going has closed the first period of American history."

In fact, Turner's assessments were both inaccurate and premature. The West had never been a "frontier" in the sense he meant the term: an empty, uncivilized land awaiting settlement. White migrants into the region had joined (or displaced) already established societies and cultures. At the same time, considerable unoccupied land remained in the West for many years to come. A vast public domain still existed in the 1890s, and during the forty years thereafter the government was to give away many more acres than it had granted as homesteads in the past. But Turner did express a growing and generally accurate sense that much of the best farming and grazing land was now taken, that in the future it would be more difficult for individuals to acquire valuable land for little or nothing.

In accepting the idea of the "passing of the frontier," many Americans were acknowledging the end of one of their most cherished myths. As long as it had been possible for them to consider the West an empty, open land, it was possible to believe that there were constantly revitalizing opportunities in American life. Now there was a vague and ominous sense of opportunities foreclosed, of individuals losing their ability to control their own destinies. The psychological loss was all the greater because of what historian Henry Nash Smith would later call, in *Virgin Land* (1950), the "myth of the garden": the once widely shared belief that the West had the potential to be a virtual Garden of Eden, where a person could begin life anew and where the ideals of democracy could be restored. That, too, was a theme in late-nineteenth-century fiction. For

THE FRONTIER AND THE WEST

THE AMERICAN WEST, AND the process by which people of European descent settled there, has been central to the national imagination for at least two centuries. It has also, at times, been central to American historical scholarship.

Through most of the nineteenth century, the history of the West reflected the romantic and optimistic view of the region beloved by many Americans. The lands west of the Mississippi River were places of adventure and opportunity. The West was a region where life could start anew, where brave and enterprising people endured great hardships to begin building a new civilization. Francis Parkman's *The Oregon Trail* (1849), a classic of American literature, expressed many of these assumptions and in the process shaped the way in which later generations of Americans would view the West and its past. But the emergence of western history as an important field of scholarship can best be traced to the famous paper Frederick Jackson Turner delivered at a meeting of the American Historical Association in 1893. It was entitled "The Significance of the Frontier in American History." The "Turner thesis" or "frontier thesis," as his argument quickly became known, shaped both popular and scholarly views of the West (and of much else) for two generations.

Turner stated his thesis simply. The settlement of the West by white people—"the existence of an area of free land, its continuous recession, and the advance of American settlement westward"—was the central story of American history. The process of westward expansion had transformed a desolate and savage land into modern civilization. It had also continually renewed American ideas of democracy and individualism and had, therefore, shaped not just the

West but the nation as a whole. "What the Mediterranean Sea was to the Greeks, breaking the bonds of custom, offering new experiences, calling out new institutions and activities, that, and more, the ever retreating frontier has been to the United States."

The Turner thesis shaped the writing of American history for a generation, and it shaped the writing of western American history for even longer. In the first half of the twentieth century, virtually all the major figures in the field echoed and elaborated at least part of Turner's argument. Ray Allen Billington's *Westward Expansion* (1949) was for decades the standard textbook in the field; his skillful revision of the Turner thesis kept the idea of what he called the "westward course of empire" (the movement of Europeans into an unsettled land) at the center of scholarship. In *The Great Plains* (1931) and *The Great Frontier* (1952), Walter Prescott Webb similarly emphasized the bravery and ingenuity of white settlers in Texas and the Southwest in overcoming obstacles (most notably, in Webb's part of the West, aridity) to create a great new civilization.

The Turner thesis was never without its critics. But serious efforts to displace it as the explanation of western American history did not begin in earnest until after World War II. In *Virgin Land* (1950), Henry Nash Smith examined many of the same heroic images of the West that Turner and his disciples had presented; but he treated those images less as descriptions of reality than as myths, which many Americans had used to sustain an image of themselves that the actual character of the modern world contradicted. Earl Pomeroy, in an influential 1955 essay and in many other works, challenged Turner's notion of the West as a place of individualism, innovation, and democratic renewal. "Conservatism, inheritance, and continuity bulked at least as large," he claimed. "The westerner has been fundamentally imitator rather than innovator. . . . He was often the most ardent

WHERE HISTORIANS DISAGREE

of conformists." Howard Lamar, in *Dakota Territory, 1861–1889* (1956) and *The Far Southwest* (1966), emphasized the highly diverse experiences of different areas of the West and thus challenged the emphasis of the Turnerians on a distinctive western environment as the crucial determinant of western experience.

The generation of western historians who began to emerge in the late 1970s launched an even more emphatic attack on the Turner thesis and the idea of the "frontier." Echoing the interest of historians in other fields in issues of race, gender, ethnicity, and culture, "new" western historians such as Richard White, Patricia Nelson Limerick, William Cronon, Donald Worster, Peggy Pascoe, and many others challenged the Turnerians on a number of points.

Turner saw the nineteenth-century West as "free land" awaiting the expansion of Anglo-American settlement and American democracy. Pioneers settled the region by conquering the "obstacles" in the way of civilization—the "vast forests," the "mountainous ramparts," the "desolate, grass-clad prairies, barren oceans of rolling plains, arid deserts, and a fierce race of savages." The "new western historians" have rejected the concept of a "frontier" and emphasize, instead, the elaborate and highly developed civilizations (Native American, Hispanic, mixed-blood, and others) that already existed in the region. White, English-speaking Americans, they have argued, did not so much settle the West as conquer it. And that conquest was never complete. Anglo-Americans in the West continue to share the region not only with the Indians and Hispanics who preceded them there, but also with African Americans, Asians, Latin Americans, and others who flowed into the West at the same time they did. Western history, these recent scholars have claimed, is a process of cultural "convergence," a constant competition and interaction—economic, political, cultural, and linguistic—among diverse peoples.

The Turnerian West was a place of heroism, triumph, and above all progress, dominated by the feats of brave white men. The West the new historians describe is a less triumphant (and less masculine) place in which bravery and success coexist with oppression, greed, and failure; in which decaying ghost towns, bleak Indian reservations, impoverished barrios, and ecologically devastated landscapes are as characteristic of western development as great ranches, rich farms, and prosperous cities; and in which women are as important as men in shaping the societies that emerged. This aspect of the "new western history" has attracted particular criticism from those attached to more traditional accounts. The novelist Larry McMurtry, for example, has denounced the new scholarship as "Failure Studies." He has insisted that in rejecting the romantic image westerners had of themselves, the revisionists omit an important part of the western experience.

To Turner and his disciples, the nineteenth-century West was a place where rugged individualism flourished and replenished American democracy. To the new scholars, western individualism is a self-serving myth. The region was inextricably tied to a national and international capitalist economy; indeed, the only thing that sustained Anglo-American settlement of the West was the demand in other places for its natural resources. Western "pioneers" were never self-sufficient. They depended on government-subsidized railroads for access to markets, federal troops for protection from Indians, and (later) government-funded dams and canals for irrigating their fields and sustaining their towns.

And while Turner defined the West as a process—a process of settlement that came to an end with the "closing of the frontier" in the late nineteenth century—the new historians see the West as a region. Its history does not end in 1890. It continues into our own time.

example, In *Ramona* (1884), the novelist Helen Hunt Jackson wrote of California before American settlement as an agrarian paradise of rugged Hispanic pioneers and saintly missionaries. The setting for utopia, once the New World as a whole, had shrunk to the West of the United States. And now even that West seemed to be vanishing.

THE DISPERSAL OF THE TRIBES

Having imagined the West as a "virgin land" awaiting civilization by white people, many Americans tried to force the region to match their image of it. That meant, above all, ensuring that the Indian tribes would not remain obstacles to the spread of white society.

White Tribal Policies

The traditional policy of the federal government was to regard the tribes simultaneously as independent nations and as wards of the president, and to negotiate treaties with them that were solemnly ratified by the Senate. This limited concept of Indian sovereignty had been responsible for the government's attempt before 1860 to erect a permanent frontier between whites and Indians, to reserve the region west of the bend of the Missouri River as permanent Indian country. However, treaties or agreements with the tribes seldom survived the pressure of white settlers eager for access to Indian lands. The history of relations between the United States and the Native Americans was, therefore, one of nearly endless broken promises.

By the early 1850s, the idea of establishing one great enclave in which many tribes could live gave way, in the face of white demands for access to lands in Indian Territory, to a new reservations policy, known as "concentration." In 1851, each tribe was assigned its own defined reservation, confirmed by separate treaties—treaties often illegitimately negotiated with unauthorized "representatives" chosen by whites, people known sarcastically as "treaty chiefs". The new arrangement had many benefits for whites and few for the Indians. It divided the tribes from one another and made them easier to control. It allowed the government to force tribes into scattered locations and to take over the most desirable lands for white settlement. But it did not survive as the basis of Indian policy for long.

In 1867, in the aftermath of a series of bloody conflicts, Congress established an Indian Peace Commission, composed of soldiers and civilians, to recommend a new and presumably permanent Indian policy.

The commission recommended replacing the "concentration" policy with a new one. The government would move all the Plains tribes into two large reservations—one in Indian Territory (Oklahoma), the other in the Dakotas. At a series of meetings with the tribes, government agents cajoled, bribed, and tricked representatives of the Arapaho, Cheyenne, Sioux, and other tribes into agreeing to treaties establishing the new reservations.

But this "solution" worked little better than previous ones. Part of the problem was the way in which the government administered the reservations it had established. White management of Indian matters was entrusted to the Bureau of Indian Affairs, located in the Department of the Interior. The bureau was responsible for distributing land, making payments, and supervising the shipment of supplies. Its record was appalling. The bureau's agents in the West, products of political patronage, were often men of extraordinary incompetence and dishonesty. But even the most honest and diligent agents were generally ill-prepared for their jobs, had no understanding of tribal ways, and had little chance of success. The poor and usually corrupt administration of the reservations was one reason for the constant conflicts between the tribes and the whites who were surrounding them.

But the problem was also a result of what was, in effect, economic warfare by whites: the relentless slaughtering of the buffalo herds that supported the tribes' way of life. Even in the 1850s, whites had been killing buffalo at a rapid rate to provide food and supplies for the large bands of migrants traveling to the gold rush in California. After the Civil War the white demand for buffalo hides became a national phenomenon—partly for economic reasons and partly as a fad. (Everyone east of the Missouri seemed to want a buffalo robe from the romantic West, and there was a strong demand for buffalo leather, which was used to make machine belts in eastern factories.) Gangs of professional hunters swarmed over the Plains to shoot the huge animals. Some hunters killed merely for the sport of the chase, although the lumbering victims did not present much of a challenge. Railroad companies hired riflemen (such as Buffalo Bill Cody) and arranged large shooting expeditions to kill large numbers of buffalo, hoping to thin the herds, which were obstructions to railroad traffic. Some Indian tribes (notably the Blackfeet) also began killing large numbers of buffalo to sell in the booming new market.

But it was not just the hunting that threatened the buffalo. It was the ecological changes that white settlement brought to the region—the reduction and in some areas virtual disappearance of the open plains on which the buffalo depended. The southern herd was virtually exterminated by 1875, and within a few years the smaller northern herd had met the same fate. In 1865, there had been at least 15 million buffalo; a decade later, fewer than a thousand of the great beasts survived. The army and the agents of the Bureau of Indian Affairs condoned and even encouraged the killing. By destroying the buffalo herds, whites were destroying the Indians' source of food and supplies and their ability to resist the white advance. They were also contributing to a climate in which Indian warriors felt the need to fight to preserve their way of life.

The Indian Wars

There was almost incessant fighting between whites and Indians from the 1850s to the 1880s, as Indians struggled against the growing threats to their civilizations. Indian warriors, usually traveling in raiding parties of thirty to forty men, attacked wagon trains, stagecoaches, and isolated ranches, often in retaliation for earlier attacks on them by whites. As the United States Army became more deeply involved in the fighting, the tribes began to focus more of their attacks on white soldiers.

At times, this small-scale fighting escalated into something close to a war. During the Civil War, the eastern Sioux in Minnesota, cramped on an inadequate reservation and exploited by corrupt white agents, suddenly rebelled against the restrictions imposed on them by the government's policies. Led by Little Crow, they killed more than 700 whites before being subdued by a force of regulars and militiamen. Thirty-eight of the Indians were hanged, and the tribe was exiled to the Dakotas.

At the same time, fighting flared up in eastern Colorado, where the Arapaho and Cheyenne were coming into conflict with white miners settling in the region. Bands of Indians attacked stagecoach lines and settlements in an effort to regain territory they had lost. In response to these incidents, whites called up a large territorial militia, and the army issued dire threats of retribution. The governor urged all friendly Indians to congregate at army posts for protection before the army began its campaign. One Arapaho and Cheyenne band under Black Kettle, apparently in response to the invitation, camped near Fort Lyon on Sand Creek in November 1864. Some members of the party were warriors, but Black Kettle believed he was under official protection and exhibited no hostile intention. Nevertheless, Colonel J. M. Chivington, apparently encouraged by the army commander of the district, led a volunteer militia force—largely consisting of unemployed miners, many of whom were apparently drunk—to the

unsuspecting camp and massacred 133 people, 105 of them women and children. Black Kettle himself escaped the Sand Creek massacre. Four years later, in 1868, he and his Cheyennes, some of whom were now at war with the whites, were caught on the Washita River, near the Texas border, by Colonel George A. Custer. White troops killed the chief and slaughtered his people.

At the end of the Civil War, white troops stepped up their wars against the western Indians on several fronts. The most serious and sustained conflict was in Montana, where the army was attempting to build a road, the Bozeman Trail, to connect Fort Laramie, Wyoming, to the new mining centers. The western Sioux resented this intrusion into the heart of their buffalo range. Led by one of their great chiefs, Red Cloud, they so harried the soldiers and the construction party—among other things, burning the forts that were supposed to guard the route—that the road could not be used.

But it was not only the United States military that harried the tribes. It was also unofficial violence by white vigilantes who engaged in what became known as "Indian hunting." In California, in particular, tracking down and killing Indians became for some whites a kind of sport. Some who did not engage in killing offered rewards (or bounties) to those who did; these bounty hunters brought back scalps and skulls as proof of their deeds. Sometimes the killing was in response to Indian raids on white communities. But often it was in service to a more basic and terrible purpose. Considerable numbers of whites were committed to the goal of literal "elimination" of the tribes, a goal that rested on the belief in the essential inhumanity of Indians and the impossibility of white society's coexisting with them. In Oregon in 1853, for example, whites who had hanged a seven-year-old Indian boy explained themselves by saying simply "nits breed lice." In California, civilians killed close to 5,000 Indians between 1850 and 1880—one of many factors (disease and poverty being the more important) that reduced the Indian population of the state from 150,000 before the Civil War to 30,000 in 1870.

The treaties negotiated in 1867 brought a temporary lull to many of the conflicts. But new forces soon shattered the peace again. In the early 1870s, more waves of white settlers, mostly miners, began to penetrate some of the lands in Dakota territory supposedly guaranteed to the tribes in 1867. At the same time, the federal government, responding to the recommendations of a commission, decided that it would no longer recognize the tribes as independent entities and would no longer negotiate with tribal chiefs. This step was intended to undermine the collective nature of Indian

THE BATTLE OF THE LITTLE BIG HORN: AN INDIAN VIEW
This 1898 watercolor by one of the Indian participants portrays the aftermath of the Battle of the Little Big Horn, June 25–26, 1876, in which an army unit under the command of General George Armstrong Custer was surrounded and wiped out by Sioux and Cheyenne warriors. This grisly painting shows Indians on horseback riding over the corpses of Custer and his men. Custer can be seen lying at left center, dressed in yellow buckskin with his hat beside him. The four standing men at center are Sitting Bull, Rain-in-the-Face, Crazy Horse, and Kicking Bear (the artist). At lower right, Indian women begin preparations for a ceremony to honor the returning warriors. *(Southwest Museum, Pasadena, California)*

life and to force the Indians to assimilate into white culture—a goal cherished by many white reformers, who believed that only through assimilation could the Indians achieve genuine "civilization."

Indian resistance flared anew, this time with even greater strength. In the northern plains, the Sioux, in response to the entrance of miners into the Black Hills and in anger at the corrupt behavior of white agents, rose up in 1875 and left their reservation. When white officials ordered them to return, bands of warriors gathered in Montana and united under two great leaders: Crazy Horse and Sitting Bull.

Three army columns set out to round them up and force them back onto the reservation. With the expedition, as colonel of the famous Seventh Cavalry, was the colorful and controversial George A. Custer, golden-haired romantic and glory seeker. At the Battle of the Little Bighorn in southern Montana in 1876—perhaps the most famous of all conflicts between whites and Indians—the tribal warriors surprised Custer and part

of his regiment, surrounded them, and killed every man. Custer has been accused of rashness, but he seems to have encountered something that no white man would likely have predicted. The chiefs had gathered together between 2,500 and 4,000 warriors, one of the largest Indian armies ever assembled at one time in the United States.

But the Indians did not have the political organization or the supplies to keep their troops united. Soon the warriors drifted off in bands to elude pursuit or search for food, and the army ran them down singly and returned them to Dakota. The power of the Sioux was soon broken. The proud leaders, Crazy Horse and Sitting Bull, accepted defeat and the monotony of life on reservations. Both were later killed by reservation police after being tricked or taunted into a last pathetic show of resistance.

One of the most dramatic episodes in Indian history occurred in Idaho in 1877. The Nez Percé were a small and relatively peaceful tribe, some of whose members had managed to live unmolested in Oregon into the 1870s without ever signing a treaty with the United States. But under pressure from white settlers, the government forced them to move into a reservation that another branch of the tribe had accepted by treaty in the 1850s. With no realistic prospect of resisting, the Indians began the journey to the reservation; but on the way, several younger Indians, drunk and angry, killed four white settlers.

The leader of the band, Chief Joseph, persuaded his followers to flee from the expected retribution. American troops pursued and attacked them, only to be driven off in a battle at White Bird Canyon. After that, the Nez Percé scattered in several directions and became part of a remarkable chase. Joseph moved with 200 men and 350 women, children, and old people in an effort to reach Canada and take refuge with the Sioux there. Pursued by four columns of American soldiers smarting from their defeat at White Bird Canyon, the Indians covered 1,321 miles in seventy-five days, repelling or evading the army time and again. They were finally caught just short of the Canadian boundary. Some escaped and slipped across the border; but Joseph and most of his followers, weary and discouraged, finally gave up. "Hear me, my chiefs," Joseph said after meeting with the American general Nelson Miles. "I am tired. My heart is sick and sad. From where the sun now stands, I will fight no more forever." He surrendered to Miles in exchange for a promise that his band could return to the Nez Percé reservation in Idaho. But the government refused to honor Miles's promise, and the Nez Percé were shipped from one place to another for several years; in the process, many of them died of disease and malnutrition (although Joseph himself lived until 1908).

The last Indians to maintain organized resistance against the whites were the Chiricahua Apaches, who fought intermittently from the 1860s to the late 1880s. The two ablest chiefs of this fierce tribe were Mangas Colorados and Cochise. Mangas was murdered during the Civil War by white soldiers who tricked him into surrendering, and in 1872 Cochise agreed to peace in exchange for a reservation that included some of the tribe's traditional land. But Cochise died in 1874, and his successor, Geronimo—unwilling to bow to white pressures to assimilate—fought on for more than a decade longer, establishing bases in the mountains of Arizona and Mexico and leading warriors in intermittent raids against white outposts. With each raid, however, the number of warring Apaches dwindled, as some warriors died and others drifted away to the reservation. By 1886, Geronimo's plight was hopeless. His band consisted of only about thirty people, including women and children, while his white pursuers numbered perhaps ten thousand. Geronimo recognized the odds and surrendered, an event that marked the end of formal warfare between Indians and whites.

The Apache wars were the most violent of all the Indian conflicts, perhaps because the tribes were now the most desperate. But it was the whites who committed the most flagrant and vicious atrocities. In 1871, for example, a mob of white miners invaded an Apache camp, slaughtered over a hundred Indians, and captured children, whom they sold as slaves to rival tribes. On other occasions, white troops murdered Indians who responded to invitations to peace conferences, once killing them with poisoned food.

Nor did the atrocities end with the conclusion of the Apache wars. Another tragic encounter occurred in 1890 as a result of a religious revival among the Sioux—a revival that itself symbolized the catastrophic effects of the white assaults on Indian civilization. The Sioux were by now aware that their culture and their glories were irrevocably fading; some were also near starvation because corrupt government agents had reduced their food rations. As other tribes had done in trying times in the past, many of these Indians turned to a prophet who led them into a religious revival.

This time the prophet was Wovoka, a Paiute who inspired an ecstatic spiritual awakening that began in Nevada and spread quickly to the plains. The new revival emphasized the coming of a messiah, but its most conspicuous feature was a mass, emotional "Ghost Dance," which inspired ecstatic visions that many participants believed were genuinely mystical. Among these visions were images of a retreat of white people from the plains and a restoration of the great buffalo herds. White agents on the Sioux reservation watched the dances in bewilderment and fear; some believed they might be the preliminary to hostilities.

On December 29, 1890, the Seventh Cavalry (which had once been Custer's regiment) tried to round up a group of about 350 cold and starving Sioux at Wounded Knee, South Dakota. Fighting broke out in which about 40 white soldiers and more than 300 of the Indians, including women and children, died. What precipitated the conflict is a matter of dispute. An Indian may well have fired the first shot, but the battle soon turned into a one-sided massacre, as the white soldiers turned their new machine guns on the Indians and mowed them down in the snow.

The Dawes Act

Even before the Ghost Dance and the Wounded Knee tragedy, the federal government had moved to destroy forever the tribal structure that had always been the cornerstone of Indian culture. Reversing its policy of

nearly fifty years of creating reservations in which the
tribes would be isolated from white society, Congress
abolished the practice by which tribes owned reservation lands communally. Some supporters of the new
policy believed they were acting for the good of the
Indians, whom they considered a "vanishing race" in
need of rescue by white society. But the action was
frankly designed to force Indians to become landowners and farmers, to abandon their collective society and
culture and become part of white civilization.

The Dawes Severalty Act of 1887 (usually known
simply as the Dawes Act) provided for the gradual
elimination of tribal ownership of land and the allotment of tracts to individual owners: 160 acres to the
head of a family, 80 acres to a single adult or orphan,
40 acres to each dependent child. Adult owners were
given United States citizenship, but unlike other citizens, they could not gain full title to their property for
twenty-five years (supposedly to prevent them from
selling the land to speculators). The act applied to most
of the western tribes. The Pueblo, who continued to
occupy lands long ago guaranteed them, were excluded from its provisions.

In applying the Dawes Act, the Bureau of Indian
Affairs relentlessly promoted the idea of assimilation
that lay behind it. Not only did they try to move Indian families onto their own plots of land; they also
took Indian children away from their families and sent
them to boarding schools run by whites, where they
believed the young people could be educated to abandon tribal ways. They also moved to stop Indian religious rituals and encouraged the spread of Christianity and the creation of Christian churches on the reservations.

Few Indians were prepared for this wrenching
change from their traditional collective society to capitalist individualism. In any case, white administration
of the program was so corrupt and inept that ultimately
the government simply abandoned it. Much of the
reservation land, therefore, was never distributed to
individual owners. Congress attempted to speed the
transition with the Burke Act of 1906, but Indians continued to resist forced assimilation.

Neither then nor later could legislation provide a
satisfactory solution to the problem of the Indians, largely because there was no entirely happy solution to be
had. The interests of the Indians were not compatible
with those of the expanding white civilization. Whites
successfully settled the American West only at the expense of the region's indigenous people.

THE RISE AND DECLINE OF THE WESTERN FARMER

The arrival of the miners, the empire building of the
cattle ranchers, the dispersal of the Indian tribes—all
served as a prelude to the decisive phase of white settlement of the Far West. Even before the Civil War,
farmers had begun moving into the plains region, challenging the dominance of the ranchers and the Indians and occasionally coming into conflict with both.

By the 1870s, what was once a trickle had become a deluge. Farmers poured into the plains and beyond, enclosed land that had once been hunting territory for Indians and grazing territory for cattle, and established a new agricultural region.

For a time in the late 1870s and early 1880s, the new western farmers flourished, enjoying the fruits of an agricultural economic boom comparable in many ways to the booms that eastern industry periodically enjoyed. Beginning in the mid-1880s, however, the boom turned to bust. American agriculture—not only in the new West but in the older Middle West and the South as well—was producing more than it ever had, too much for the market to absorb. For that and other reasons, prices for agricultural goods declined. Both economically and psychologically, the agricultural economy began a long, steady decline.

Farming on the Plains

Many factors combined to produce this surge of western settlement, but the most important was the railroads. Before the Civil War, the Great Plains had been accessible only through a difficult journey by wagon. But beginning in the 1860s, a great new network of railroad lines developed, spearheaded by the transcontinental routes Congress had authorized and subsidized in 1862. They made huge new areas of settlement accessible.

The building of the transcontinental line was a dramatic and monumental achievement. Thousands of immigrant workers—mostly Irish on the eastern route, Chinese on the western—labored in what were at times unimaginably difficult conditions to penetrate mountain ranges, cross deserts, protect themselves against Indians, and—finally—connect the two lines at Promontory Point in northern Utah in the spring of 1869.

But while this first transcontinental line captured the public imagination, the construction of subsidiary lines in the following years proved of greater importance to the West. State governments, imitating Washington, encouraged railroad development by offering direct financial aid, favorable loans, and more than 50 million acres of land (on top of the 130 million acres the federal government had already provided). Although operated by private corporations, the railroads were essentially public projects.

It was not only by making access to the Great Plains easier that the railroads helped spur agricultural settlement there. The railroad companies themselves actively promoted settlement, both to provide themselves with customers for their services and to increase the value of their vast landholdings. In addition, the companies set rates so low for settlers that almost anyone could afford the trip west. And they sold much of their land at very low prices and provided liberal credit to prospective settlers.

Contributing further to the great surge of white agricultural expansion was a temporary change in the climate of the Great Plains. For several years in succession, beginning in the 1870s, rainfall in the plains states was well above average. White Americans now rejected the old idea that the region was the Great American Desert. Some even claimed that cultivation of the plains actually encouraged rainfall.

Even under the most favorable conditions, farming on the plains presented special problems. First was the problem of fencing. Farmers had to enclose their land,

Held Up by Buffalo
Once among the most numerous creatures in North America, the buffalo became almost extinct as a result of their indiscriminate slaughter by white settlers and travelers, who often fired at herds from moving trains simply for the sport of it. This scene was painted around 1880 by N. H. Trotter. *(Smithsonian Institution)*

SIGNIFICANT EVENTS

1847 Taos Indians rebel in New Mexico, killing American governor and precipitating military rule

1848–1849 California gold rush begins

1851 "Concentration" policy devised for western tribes

1852 California legislature passes "foreign miners' tax" to exclude Chinese from gold mining

1858 Comstock Lode silver deposits discovered in Nevada

1859 Colorado gold rush launches western mining bonanza

Mexicans in Texas raid Brownsville jail

1861 Kansas admitted to Union

1862 Homestead Act passed

1864 Nevada admitted to Union

1865 U.S. troops massacre Arapaho and Cheyenne at Sand Creek

1865–1867 Sioux War

1866 "Long drives" launch western cattle bonanza

Chinese workers strike against Union Pacific

1867 Nebraska admitted to Union

Indian Peace Commission establishes "Indian Territory" (later Oklahoma)

1868 Black Kettle and his Cheyenne warriors captured and killed by U.S. forces

1869 Union Pacific, first transcontinental railroad, completed

1872 Cochise, chief of Chiricahua Apaches, agrees to treaty with U.S.

1873 Barbed wire invented

Timber Culture Act passed

1874 Gold rush begins in Black Hills, Dakota Territory

1875 Sioux uprising begins

Southern buffalo herd virtually extinguished

1876 Battle of Little Bighorn

Colorado admitted to Union

---

if for no other reason than to protect it from the herds of the open-range cattlemen. But traditional wood or stone fences were too expensive and were ineffective as barriers to cattle. In the mid-1870s, however, two Illinois farmers, Joseph H. Glidden and I. L. Ellwood, solved this problem by developing and marketing barbed wire, which became standard equipment on the plains and revolutionized fencing practices all over the country.

The second problem was water. Water was scarce even when rainfall was above average. After 1887, a series of dry seasons began, and lands that had been fertile now returned to semi-desert. Some farmers dealt with the problem by using deep wells pumped by steel windmills, or by turning to what was called dryland farming (a system of tillage designed to conserve moisture in the soil by covering it with a dust blanket), or by planting drought-resistant crops. In many areas of the plains, however, only large-scale irrigation could save the endangered farms. But irrigation projects of the necessary magnitude required government assistance, and neither the state nor federal governments were prepared to fund the projects.

Most of the people who moved into the region had previously been farmers in the Middle West, the East, or Europe. In the booming years of the early 1880s, with land values rising, the new farmers had no problem obtaining extensive and easy credit and had every reason to believe they would soon be able to retire their debts. But the arid years of the late 1880s—during which crop prices were falling while production was becoming more expensive—changed that prospect. Tens of thousands of farmers could not pay their debts and were forced to abandon their farms. There was, in effect, a reverse migration: white settlers moving back east, sometimes turning once-flourishing communities

SIGNIFICANT EVENTS

1877 Desert Land Act passed

Nez Percé Indians resist relocation

1878 California Workingmen's Party founded and attacks Chinese immigration

Timber and Stone Act passed

1881 Anaconda copper mine begins operations in Montana

1882 Congress passes Chinese Exclusion Act

1884 Helen Hunt Jackson publishes *Ramona*

1885–1887 Harsh winters help destroy open-range cattle raising

1885 Mark Twain publishes *Huckleberry Finn*

1886 Geronimo surrenders, ending Apache resistance

1887 Dawes Act passed

Prolonged drought in Great Plains begins

1889 North Dakota, South Dakota, Montana, and Washington admitted to Union

Oklahoma (formerly "Indian Territory") opened to white settlement

1890 Indian "Ghost Dance" revival

Battle of Wounded Knee

Wyoming and Idaho admitted to Union

1891 Hamlin Garland publishes *Main-Traveled Roads*

1892 Congress renews Chinese Exclusion Act

1893 Frederick Jackson Turner proposes "Turner thesis"

1896 Utah admitted to Union

1902 Congress makes Chinese Exclusion Act permanent

Owen Wister publishes *The Virginian*

1906 Congress passes Burke Act to speed assimilation of tribes

into desolate ghost towns. Those who remained continued to suffer from falling prices (for example, wheat, which had sold for $1.60 a bushel at the end of the Civil War, dropped to 49 cents in the 1890s) and persistent indebtedness.

Commercial Agriculture

American farming by the late nineteenth century no longer bore very much relation to the comforting image many Americans continued to cherish. The sturdy, independent farmer of popular myth was being replaced by the commercial farmer—attempting to do in the agricultural economy what industrialists were doing in the manufacturing economy.

Commercial farmers were not self-sufficient and made no effort to become so. They specialized in cash crops which they sold in national or world markets. They did not make their own household supplies or grow their own food but bought them instead at town or village stores. This kind of farming, when it was successful, raised the farmers' living standards. But it also made them dependent on bankers and interest rates, railroads and freight rates, national and European markets, world supply and demand. And unlike the capitalists of the industrial order, they could not regulate their production or influence the prices of what they sold.

Between 1865 and 1900, agriculture became an international business. Farm output increased dramatically, not only in the United States but in Brazil, Argentina, Canada, Australia, New Zealand, Russia, and elsewhere. At the same time, modern forms of communication and transportation—the telephone, telegraph, steam navigation, railroads—were creating new markets around the world for agricultural goods. American commercial farmers, constantly opening new lands, produced much more than the domestic market could absorb; they relied on the world market to absorb their surplus, but in that market they faced major competition. Cotton farmers depended on export sales for 70 percent of their annual income, wheat farmers for 30 to 40 percent; but the volatility of the international market put them at great risk.

Beginning in the 1880s, worldwide overproduction led to a drop in prices for most agricultural goods and hence to great economic distress for many of the more than 6 million American farm families. By the 1890s, 27 percent of the farms in the country were mortgaged; by 1910, 33 percent. In 1880, 25 percent of all farms had been operated by tenants; by 1910, the proportion had grown to 37 percent. Commercial farming made some people fabulously wealthy. But the farm economy as a whole was suffering a significant decline relative to the rest of the nation.

The Farmers' Grievances

American farmers were painfully aware that something was wrong. But few yet understood the implications of national and world overproduction. Instead, they concentrated their attention and anger on more immediate, more comprehensible—and no less real—problems: inequitable freight rates, high interest charges, and an inadequate currency.

The farmers' first and most burning grievance was against the railroads. In many cases, the railroads charged higher rates for farm goods than for other goods, and higher rates in the South and West than in the Northeast. Railroads also controlled elevator and warehouse facilities in buying centers and charged arbitrary storage rates.

Farmers also resented the institutions controlling credit—banks, loan companies, insurance corporations. Since sources of credit in the West and South were few, farmers had to take loans on whatever terms they could get, often at interest rates of from 10 to 25 percent. Many farmers had to pay these loans back in years when prices were dropping and currency was becoming scarce. Increasing the volume of currency eventually became an important agrarian demand.

A third grievance concerned prices—both the prices farmers received for their products and the prices they paid for goods they bought. Farmers sold their products in a competitive world market over which they had no control and of which they had no advance knowledge. A farmer could plant a large crop at a moment when prices were high and find that by the time of the harvest the price had declined. Farmers' fortunes rose and fell in response to unpredictable forces. But many farmers became convinced (often with some rea-

son) that "middlemen"—speculators, bankers, regional and local agents—were combining to fix prices so as to benefit themselves at the growers' expense. Many farmers also came to believe (again, not entirely without reason) that manufacturers in the East were conspiring to keep the prices of farm goods low and the prices of industrial goods high. Although farmers sold their crops in a competitive world market, they bought manufactured goods in a domestic market protected by tariffs and dominated by trusts and corporations.

The Agrarian Malaise

These economic difficulties produced a series of social and cultural resentments. In part, this was a result of the isolation of farm life. Farm families in some parts of the country—particularly in the prairie and plains regions, where large farms were scattered over vast areas—were virtually cut off from the outside world and human companionship. During the winter months and spells of bad weather, the loneliness and boredom could become nearly unbearable. Many farmers lacked access to adequate education for their children, to proper medical facilities, to recreational or cultural activities, to virtually anything that might give them a sense of being members of a community. Older farmers felt the sting of watching their children leave the farm for the city. They felt the humiliation of being ridiculed as "hayseeds" by the new urban culture that was coming to dominate American life.

The result of this sense of isolation and obsolescence was a growing malaise among many farmers, a discontent that would help create a great national political movement in the 1890s. It found reflection, too, in the literature that emerged from rural America. Writers in the late nineteenth century might romanticize the rugged life of the cowboy and the western miner. For the farmer, however, the image was often different. Hamlin Garland, for example, reflected the growing disillusionment in a series of novels and short stories. In the past, Garland wrote in the introduction to his novel *Jason Edwards* (1891), the agrarian frontier had seemed to be "the Golden West, the land of wealth and freedom and happiness. All of the associations called up by the spoken word, the West, were fabulous, mythic, hopeful." Now, however, the bright promise had faded. The trials of rural life were crushing the human spirit. "So this is the reality of the dream!" a character in *Jason Edwards* exclaims. "A shanty on a barren plain, hot and lone as a desert. My God!" Once, sturdy yeoman farmers had viewed themselves as the backbone of American life. Now they were becoming painfully aware that their position was declining in relation to the rising urban-industrial society to the east.

SUGGESTED READINGS

General Works. Ray A. Billington and Martin Ridge, *Westward Expansion*, 5th ed. (1982). Thomas D. Clark, *Frontier America* (rev. 1969). William Cronon et al., eds., *Under An Open Sky: Rethinking America's Western Past* (1992). Robert V. Hine, *The American West*, 2nd ed. (1984). Patricia Nelson Limerick, *The Legacy of Conquest: The Unbroken Past of the American West* (1987). Patricia Nelson Limerick et al., eds., *Trails: Toward a New Western History* (1992). Frederick Merk, *History of the Westward Movement* (1978). Rodman W. Paul, *The Far West and the Great Plains in Transition, 1859–1900* (1988). Rodman W. Paul and Richard W. Etulain, *The Frontier and the American West* (1977). Richard White, *"It's Your Misfortune and None of My Own": A History of the American West* (1991).

Migrations and Communities. Gunther Barth, *Bitter Strength: A History of the Chinese in the United States, 1850–1870* (1964). Albert Camarillo, *Chicanos in a Changing Society: From Mexican Pueblos to American Barrios in Santa Barbara and Southern California* (1979). Sucheng Chan, *This Bittersweet Soil: The Chinese in California Agriculture, 1860–1910* (1986). Richard Griswold del Castillo, *La Familia: Chicano Families in the Urban Southwest, 1848 to the Present* (1984); *The Los Angeles Barrio, 1850–1890* (1979). Arnold De Leon, *They Called Them Greasers: Anglo Attitudes Toward Mexicans in Texas, 1821–1900* (1983). Sarah Deutsch, *No Separate Refuge: Culture, Class, and Gender on the Anglo-Hispanic Frontier in the Early Southwest, 1880–1940* (1987). Mario T. Garcia, *Desert Immigrants: The Mexicans of El Paso, 1880–1920* (1981). Robert V. Hine, *Community on the American Frontier* (1980). Richard Hogan, *Class and Community in Frontier Colorado* (1979). Howard R. Lamar, *Dakota Territory, 1861–1889* (1956); *The Far Southwest, 1846–1912* (1966); *Texas Crossings: The Lone Star State and the American Far West, 1836–1986* (1991). Timothy R. Mahoney, *River Towns in the Great West* (1990). Leonard Pitt, *The Decline of the Californios: A Social History of the Spanish-Speaking Californians, 1846–1890* (1960). Earl Pomeroy, *The Pacific Slope: A History of California, Oregon, Washington, Idaho, Utah, and Nevada* (1965). Andrew F. Rolle, *California: A History* (2nd ed., 1969). Robert J. Rosebaum, *Mexicano Resistance in the Southwest* (1981). Alexander Saxton, *The Indispensable Enemy: Labor and the Anti-Chinese Movement in California* (1971). Lillian Schlissel, *Women's Diaries of the Westward Journey* (1982). Thomas Sheridan, *Los Tucsonenses: The Mexican Community in Tucson, 1854–1941* (1986). Ronald Takaki, *Strangers from a Different Shore: A History of Asian Americans* (1989). Shih-shan Henry Tsai, *The Chinese Experience in America* (1986). Oscar O. Winther, *The Transportation Frontier: The Trans-Mississippi West, 1865–1890* (1964).

Miners and Cattlemen. Andy Adams, *The Log of a Cowboy* (1927). Lewis Atherton, *The Cattle Kings* (1961). Gunther Barth, *Instant Cities* (1975). Edward E. Dale, *The Range Cattle Industry*, rev. ed. (1969). Philip Durham and Everett L. Jones, *The Negro Cowboys* (1965). Robert K. Dykstra, *The Cattle Towns* (1968). Odie B. Faulk, *Tombstone: Myth and Reality* (1972). Joe B. Frantz and Julian Choate, *The American Cowboy: The Myth and the Reality* (1955). Marion S. Goldman, *Gold Diggers & Silver Miners: Prostitution and Social Life on the Comstock* (1981). William S. Greever, *Bonanza West: Western Mining Rushes* (1963). Ralph Mann, *After the Gold Rush: Society in Grass Valley and Nevada City, California, 1849–1870* (1982). Ernest E. Osgood, *The Day of the Cattleman* (1929). Rodman W. Paul, *Mining Frontiers of the Far West, 1848–1880* (1963); *The Far West and the Great Plains in Transition, 1859–1900* (1988). Wilson P. Rodman, *Mining Frontiers of the Far West* (1963). J. M. Skaggs, *The Cattle Trailing Industry* (1973). Richard W. Slatta, *Cowboys of the Americas* (1990). Duane A. Smith, *Rocky Mountain Mining Camps* (1967); *Mining America: The Industry and the Environment, 1800–1980* (1987). L. Steckmesser, *The Western Hero in History and Legend* (1965). Donald E. Worcester, *The Chisholm Trail* (1980).

Indians. Ralph K. Andrist, *The Long Death: The Last Days of the Plains Indians* (1964). Robert F. Berkhofer, Jr., *The White Man's Indian* (1978). Donald J. Berthrong, *The Southern Cheyennes* (1963). Dee Brown, *Bury My Heart at Wounded Knee: An Indian History of the American West* (1970). Margret Coel, *Chief Left Hand: Southern Arapaho* (1981). Angie Debo, *Geronimo* (1976). Richard Drinnon, *Facing West: The Metaphysics of Indian-Hating and Empire-Building* (1980). Thomas W. Dunlay, *Wolves for the Blue Soldiers* (1982). Loretta Fowler, *Arapahoe Politics, 1851–1978: Symbols in Crisis of Authority* (1982). William T. Hagan, *The Indian Rights Association: The Herbert Welsh Years, 1882–1904* (1985); *American Indians* (1961). Howard L. Harrod, *Renewing the World: Plains Indians Religion and Morality* (1987). Dwight L. Hoover, *The Red and the Black* (1976). Frederick E. Hoxie, *A Final Promise: The Campaign to Assimilate the Indians, 1880–1920* (1984); *The Crow* (1989). Peter Inverson, *The Navajos* (1990). Robert Mardock, *Reformers and the American Indian* (1971). Janet A. McDonnell, *The Dispossession of the American Indian, 1887–1934* (1991). John G. Neihardt, *Black Elk Speaks* (1932). James C. Olson, *Red Cloud and the Sioux Problem* (1965). Theda Perdue, *The Cherokee* (1989). John Powell, *People of the Sacred Mountain: A History of the Northern Cheyenne Chiefs and Warrior Societies, 1830–1879*, 2 vols. (1981). Francis P. Prucha, *American Indian Policy in Crisis* (1976); *The Great White Father: The United States Government and the American Indians* (1984). Willard H. Rollings, *The Comanche* (1989). Mari Sandoz, *Crazy Horse* (1961). Edwin R. Sweeney, *Cochise: Chiricahua Apache Chief* (1991). Robert M. Utley, *Last Days of the Sioux Nation* (1963); *Frontiersmen in Blue: The United States Army and the Indian, 1848–1865* (1967); *Frontier Regulars: The United States Army and the Indian* (1973); *The Indian Frontier of the American West, 1846–1890* (1984). Wilcomb E. Washburn, *The Indian in America* (1975); *Red Man's Land/White Man's Law* (1971). Richard White, *The Roots of Dependency: Subsistence, Environment, and Social Change Among the Choctaws, Pawnees, and Navajos* (1983). Charles F. Wilkinson, *American Indians, Time, and the Law: Native Societies in a Modern Constitutional Democracy* (1987).

Western Women. Susan Armitage and Elizabeth Jameson, eds., *The Women's West* (1987). John Mack Faragher, *Women and Men on the Overland Trail* (1979). Elizabeth Hampsten,

Read This Only to Yourself: The Private Writings of Midwestern Women, 1880–1910 (1982). Dolores Janiewski, *Sisterhood Denied* (1985). Julie Jeffrey, *Frontier Women: The Trans-Mississippi West, 1840–1880* (1979). Polly Welts Kaufman, *Women Teachers on the Frontier* (1984). Ruth Moynihan, *Rebel for Rights: Abigail Scott Dunaway* (1983). Sandra L. Myres, *Westering Women and the Frontier Experience, 1880–1915* (1982); *Westering Women and the Frontier Experience, 1800–1915* (1982). Peggy Pascoe, *Relations of Rescue: The Search for Female Moral Authority in the American West, 1874–1939* (1990). Glenda Riley, *Women and Indians on the Frontier, 1825–1915* (1984); *A Place to Grow* (1992). Joanna L. Stratton, *Pioneer Women: Voices from the Kansas Frontier* (1981).

Western Agriculture.   Allan Bogue, *From Prairie to Corn Belt* (1963). Everett Dick, *The Sod-House Frontier* (1937). John Mack Faragher, *Sugar Creek: Life on the Illinois Prairie* (1986). Gilbert Fite, *The Farmer's Frontier, 1865–1900* (1966). Paul W. Gates, *History of Public Land Development* (1968). Norris Hundley, Jr., *The Great Thirst: Californians and Water, 1770s–1990s* (1992).

D. Aidan McQuillen, *Prevailing over Time: Ethnic Adjustment on the Kansas Prairies, 1875–1925* (1990). Nell Irvin Painter, *Exodusters: Black Migration to Kansas After Reconstruction* (1976). Fred A. Shannon, *The Farmer's Last Frontier, 1860–1897* (1945). Walter Prescott Webb, *The Great Plains* (1931). Thomas A. Woods, *Knights of the Plow: Oliver H. Kelley and the Origins of the Grange in Republican Ideology* (1991). (See also bibliography for Chapter 19.)

The Idea of the West and the Western Environment.   Ray A. Billington, *Frederick Jackson Turner* (1973). William Cronon, *Nature's Metropolis: Chicago and the Great West* (1991). John Mack Faragher, *Daniel Boone: The Life and Legend of an American Pioneer* (1992). Richard Slotkin, *The Fatal Environment: The Myth of the Frontier in the Age of Industrialization* (1985); *Gunfighter Nation* (1992). Henry Nash Smith, *Virgin Land* (1950). Frederick Jackson Turner, *The Frontier in American History* (1920). Donald Worster, *Under Western Skies: Nature and History in the American West* (1992); *Rivers of Empire* (1985).

THE STEEL MILL

This 1895 painting of a Bethlehem Steel Company mill shows workers preparing to pour (or "teem") a ladle of molten steel, the product of a Bessemer converter, into cast iron molds to form steel ingots. The ingots will later be rolled into various shapes. Bessemer was one of the two leading processes for converting iron into steel; the other was the open-hearth method. Together, these processes propelled the American steel industry—and through it the industrial economy as a whole—into a period of dramatic growth. *(Bethlehem Steel)*

CHAPTER SEVENTEEN

INDUSTRIAL SUPREMACY

ITH A STRIDE THAT astonished statisticians, the conquering hosts of business enterprise swept over the continent; twenty-five years after the death of Lincoln, America had become, in the quantity and value of her products, the first manufacturing nation of the world. What England had accomplished in a hundred years, the United States had achieved in half the time." So wrote the historians Charles and Mary Beard in the 1920s, expressing the amazement many Americans felt when they considered the remarkable expansion of their industrial economy in the late nineteenth and early twentieth centuries.

In fact, America's rise to industrial supremacy was not as sudden as such observers suggested. The nation had been building a manufacturing economy since early in the nineteenth century, and industry was well established before the Civil War. But Americans were clearly correct in observing that the accomplishments of the last three decades of the nineteenth century overshadowed all that had come earlier. Those years witnessed nothing less than the transformation of the national economy.

The remarkable growth did much to increase the wealth and improve the lives of many Americans. But the benefits were not universal. While industrial titans and a growing middle class were enjoying a prosperity without precedent in the nation's history, workers, farmers, and others were experiencing a disorienting and often painful transition that slowly edged the United States toward a great economic and political crisis.

SOURCES OF INDUSTRIAL GROWTH

Many factors contributed to the growth of American industry: abundant raw materials; a large and growing labor supply; a surge in technological innovation; the emergence of a talented, ambitious, and often ruthless group of entrepreneurs; a federal government eager to assist the growth of business; and a great and expanding domestic market for the products of manufacturing.

New Technologies and New Industries

The rapid emergence of new technologies and the discovery of new materials and productive processes were prerequisites to late-nineteenth-century industrial growth. In the entire history of the United States up to 1860, the government had granted only 36,000 patents. For the period from 1860 to 1890, the figure was 440,000. Americans also benefited from comparable technological advances in Europe.

Some of the most important innovations were in communications. In 1866, Cyrus W. Field laid a transatlantic telegraph cable to Europe. During the next decade, Alexander Graham Bell developed the first commercially useful telephone; and by the 1890s, the American Telephone and Telegraph Company, which handled his interests, had installed nearly half a million telephones in American cities. Other inventions that speeded the pace of business organization were the typewriter (by Christopher L. Sholes in 1868), the cash register (by James Ritty in 1879), and the calculating or adding machine (by William S. Burroughs in 1891).

Among the most revolutionary innovations was the introduction in the 1870s of electricity as a source of light and power. Two pioneers of electrical lighting were Charles F. Brush, who devised the arc lamp for street illumination, and Thomas A. Edison, who invented the incandescent lamp (or light bulb), which could be used for both street and home lighting. Edison and others designed improved generators and built large power plants to furnish electricity to whole cities. By the turn of the century, electric power was becoming commonplace in street railway systems, in the elevators of urban skyscrapers, in factories, and increasingly in offices and homes.

A process by which iron could be transformed into steel—a much more durable and versatile material— had been discovered in the 1850s almost simultaneously by an Englishman, Henry Bessemer, and by an American, William Kelly. The process consisted of blowing air through molten iron to burn out the impurities and became known as the Bessemer process, and after the Civil War it transformed the metal industry. In 1868, the New Jersey ironmaster Abram C. Hewitt introduced from Europe another method of making steel—the open-hearth process. These techniques made possible the production of steel in great quantities and in large dimensions, for use in the manufacture of locomotives, steel train tracks, and girders for the construction of tall buildings.

The steel industry emerged first in western Pennsylvania and eastern Ohio, a region where iron ore and coal were abundant and where there was already a flourishing iron industry. Pittsburgh quickly became the center of the steel world. But the industry was growing so fast that new sources of ore were soon necessary. The upper peninsula of Michigan, the Mesabi range in Minnesota, and the area around Birmingham, Alabama, became important ore-producing centers by the end of the century, and new centers of production emerged in cities that were at once near the mines and close to waterways: Cleveland, Detroit, Chicago, and Birmingham, among others.

The oil industry emerged in the late nineteenth century largely in response to the steel industry's need for lubrication for its machines. (Not until later did oil become important primarily for its potential as a fuel.) The existence of petroleum reserves in western Pennsylvania, where oil often seeped to the surface of streams and springs, had been common knowledge for some time. At first, however, no one was sure what it was or what

to do with it. Then, in the 1850s, experiments commissioned by the Pennsylvania businessman George Bissell showed that the substance could be burned in lamps and that it could also yield such products as paraffin, naphtha, and lubricating oil. Bissell then raised money to begin drilling; and in 1859, Edwin L. Drake, one of his employees, established the first oil well near Titusville, Pennsylvania. It was soon producing 500 barrels of oil a month. Demand for petroleum grew quickly, and promoters soon developed other fields in Pennsylvania, Ohio, and West Virginia. By the 1870s, oil had advanced to fourth place among the nation's exports.

Thirty years later, the demand for oil had expanded dramatically, as its value as a fuel became apparent. But the available reserves in the East had begun to run out. A search began in other parts of the country for new oil deposits, much of it spearheaded by ambitious independent explorers (known as "wildcatters") whose search for the "black gold" resembled the search for actual gold in California and elsewhere decades before. In 1901, explorers discovered the Spindletop oil field in Texas, one of the greatest oil deposits in the world, and Standard Oil (the dominant firm in the industry) quickly established facilities there. A few years later, more discoveries followed in other parts of Texas and in Oklahoma. Those states became the leading oil producers in the nation and remained so for decades. Other important oil fields were discovered in California at about the same time. The emergence of these great new oil fields soon broke Standard Oil's monopoly of the industry. It was unable to dominate the vast new producing regions in the way it had dominated the fields in Pennsylvania and Ohio.

By the beginning of the twentieth century, other great innovations were emerging. In the 1890s, the Italian inventor Guglielmo Marconi was taking the first steps toward the development of radio. The Wright brothers launched the first airplane flight at Kitty Hawk, North Carolina, in 1903. Perhaps most important, the automobile was in development. In the 1870s, designers in France, Germany, and Austria—inspired by the success of railroad engines—were already beginning to develop motors that might drive independently controlled vehicles. They achieved early successes with an "internal combustion engine," which used the expanding power of burning gas to drive pistons; and with this new engine they created the first automobiles.

Charles and Frank Duryea built the first gasoline-driven motor vehicle in America in 1893. Three years later, Henry Ford produced the first of the famous cars that would bear his name. By 1910, the industry had become a major force in the economy, and the automobile had begun to reshape the American landscape.

THE ASSEMBLY LINE
Workers in the Ford Motor Company's plant in Highland Park, Michigan, guide auto bodies down a ramp onto chassis that have moved into position from below. This was the final stage of the assembly line, which Henry Ford pioneered and which by 1914 (when this photograph was taken) had become common in other industries as well. *(Henry Ford Museum & Greenfield Village)*

In 1895, there had been only four automobiles on the American highways. By 1917, there were nearly 5 million.

The Science of Production

Central to the growth of the automobile and other industries were changes in the techniques of production. By the turn of the century, many industrialists were turning to the new principles of "scientific management." Those principles were often known as "Taylorism," after their leading theoretician, Frederick Winslow Taylor. Taylor's ideas were controversial during his lifetime and have remained controversial since. Taylor himself, and his many admirers, argued that scientific management was a way to manage human labor to make it compatible with the demands of the machine age. But scientific management was also a way to increase the employer's control of the workplace, to make working people less independent.

Taylor urged employers to reorganize the production process by subdividing tasks. This would speed up production; it would also make workers more interchangeable and thus diminish a manager's dependence on any particular employee. And it would reduce the need for highly trained skilled workers. If properly managed by trained experts, Taylor claimed,

workers using modern machines could perform simple tasks at much greater speed, significantly increasing productive efficiency.

Manufacturers also began placing greater emphasis on industrial research. In part because of the phenomenal success of Thomas Edison's famous industrial laboratory in Menlo Park, New Jersey, dozens of corporations were, by the early years of the twentieth century, establishing laboratories of their own. By 1913, Bell Telephone, Du Pont, General Electric, Eastman Kodak, and about fifty other companies were budgeting hundreds of thousands of dollars each year for research by their own engineers and scientists.

The most important change in production technology in the industrial era was the emergence of mass production and, above all, the moving assembly line, which Henry Ford introduced in his automobile plants in 1914. This revolutionary technique cut the time for assembling a chassis from twelve and a half to one and a half hours. It enabled Ford to raise the wages and reduce the hours of his workers while cutting the base price of his Model T from $950 in 1914 to $290 in 1929. Ford's assembly line became a standard for many other industries.

Railroad Expansion

The principal agent of industrial development in the late nineteenth century was the expansion of the railroads. Railroads promoted economic growth in many ways. They were the nation's main method of transportation and gave industrialists access to distant markets and distant sources of raw materials. They were the nation's largest businesses and created new forms of corporate organization that served as models for other industries. And they were America's biggest investors, stimulating economic growth through their own enormous expenditures on construction and equipment.

Every decade in the late nineteenth century, total railroad trackage increased dramatically: from 30,000 miles in 1860 to 52,000 miles in 1870, to 93,000 in 1880, to 163,000 in 1890, and to 193,000 by 1900. Subsidies from federal, state, and local governments—as well as investments from abroad—were vital to these vast undertakings, which required far more capital than private entrepreneurs in America could raise by themselves. Equally important was the emergence of great railroad combinations that brought most of the nation's rails under the control of a very few men. Many railroad combinations continued to be dominated by individuals. The achievements (and excesses) of these tycoons—Cornelius Vanderbilt, James J. Hill, Collis P. Huntington, and others—became symbols to much of the nation of great economic power concentrated in in-

RAILROADS, 1870–1890

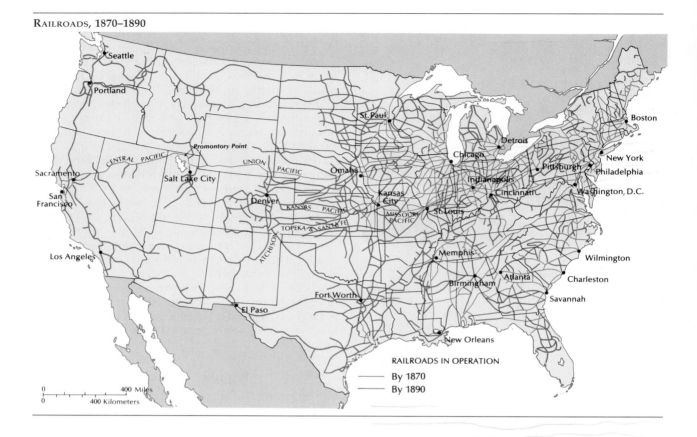

dividual hands. But railroad development was less significant for the individual barons it created than for its contribution to the growth of a new institution: the modern corporation.

The Corporation

There had been various forms of corporations in America since colonial times, but the modern corporation emerged as a major force only after the Civil War, when railroad magnates and other industrialists realized that no single person or group of limited partners, no matter how wealthy, could finance their great ventures.

Under the laws of incorporation passed in many states in the 1830s and 1840s, business organizations could raise money by selling stock to members of the public; after the Civil War, one industry after another began doing so. At the same time, affluent Americans began to consider the purchase of stock a good investment even if they were not themselves involved in

the business whose stock they were purchasing. What made the practice appealing was that investors had only "limited liability"—that is, they risked only the amount of their investments; they were not liable for any debts the corporation might accumulate beyond that. The ability to sell stock to a broad public made it possible for entrepreneurs to gather vast sums of capital and undertake great projects.

The Pennsylvania Railroad and others were among the first to adopt the new corporate form of organization. But it quickly spread beyond the railroad industry. In steel, the central figure was Andrew Carnegie, a Scottish immigrant who had worked his way up from modest beginnings and in 1873 opened his own steelworks in Pittsburgh. Soon he dominated the industry. His methods were much like those of other industrial titans. He cut costs and prices by striking deals with the railroads and then bought out rivals who could not compete with him. With his associate Henry Clay Frick, he bought up coal mines and leased part of the Mesabi iron range in Minnesota, operated a fleet of ore ships on the Great Lakes, and acquired railroads. Ul-

ANDREW CARNEGIE
Carnegie was one of a relatively small number of great industrialists of the late nineteenth century who genuinely rose "from rags to riches." Born in Scotland, he came to the United States in 1848, at the age of thirteen, and soon found work as a messenger in a Pittsburgh telegraph office. His skill in learning to transcribe telegraphic messages (he became one of the first telegraphers in the country able to take messages by sound) brought him to the attention of a Pennsylvania Railroad official, and before he was twenty, he had begun his ascent to the highest ranks of industry. After the Civil War, he shifted his attention to the growing iron industry; in 1873 he invested all his assets in the development of the first American steel mills. Two decades later he was one of the wealthiest men in the world. In 1901 he abruptly resigned from his businesses and spent the remaining years of his life as a philanthropist. By the time of his death in 1919, he had given away some $350 million. *(Culver)*

timately, he controlled the processing of his steel from mine to market. He financed his undertakings not only out of his own profits but out of the sale of stock. Then, in 1901, he sold out for $450 million to the banker J. Pierpont Morgan, who merged the Carnegie interests with others to create the giant United States Steel Corporation—a $1.4 billion enterprise that controlled almost two-thirds of the nation's steel production.

There were similar developments in other industries. Gustavus Swift developed a relatively small Chicago meatpacking company into a great national corporation, in part because of profits he earned selling to the military in the Civil War. Isaac Singer patented a sewing machine in 1851 and created I. M. Singer and Company, one of the first modern manufacturing corporations.

Many of the corporate organizations developed a new approach to management. Large, national business enterprises needed more systematic administrative structures than the limited, local ventures of the past. As a result, corporate leaders introduced a set of managerial techniques—the genesis of modern business administration—that relied on the division of responsibilities, a carefully designed hierarchy of control, modern cost-accounting procedures, and perhaps above all a new breed of business executive: the "middle manager," who formed a layer of command between workers and owners. Beginning in the railroad corporations, these new management techniques moved quickly into virtually every area of large-scale industry. Efficient administrative capabilities helped make possible another major feature of the modern corporation: consolidation.

Consolidating Corporate America

Businessmen created large, consolidated organizations primarily through two methods. One was "horizontal integration"—the combining of a number of firms engaged in the same enterprise into a single corporation. The consolidation of many different railroad lines into one company was an example. Another method, which became popular in the 1890s, was "vertical integration"—the taking over of all the different businesses on which a company relied for its primary function. Carnegie Steel, which came to control not only steel mills, but mines, railroads, and other enterprises, was an example of vertical integration.

The most celebrated corporate empire of the late nineteenth century was John D. Rockefeller's Standard Oil, a great combination created through both horizontal and vertical integration. Shortly after the Civil

War, Rockefeller launched a refining company in Cleveland and immediately began trying to eliminate his competition. Allying himself with other wealthy capitalists, he proceeded methodically to buy out competing refineries. In 1870, he formed the Standard Oil Company of Ohio; within a few years it had acquired twenty of the twenty-five refineries in Cleveland, as well as plants in Pittsburgh, Philadelphia, New York, and Baltimore.

So far, Rockefeller had expanded only horizontally. But soon he began expanding vertically as well. He built his own barrel factories, terminal warehouses, and pipelines. Standard Oil owned its own freight cars and developed its own marketing organization. By the 1880s, Rockefeller had established such dominance within the petroleum industry that to much of the nation he served as the leading symbol of monopoly. He controlled access to 90 percent of the refined oil in the United States.

Rockefeller and other industrialists saw consolidation as a way to cope with what they believed was the greatest curse of the modern economy: "cutthroat competition." Most businessmen claimed to believe in free enterprise and a competitive marketplace, but in fact they feared the existence of too many competing firms, convinced that substantial competition could spell instability and ruin for all. A successful enterprise, many capitalists believed (but did not say publicly), was one that could eliminate or absorb its competitors.

As the movement toward combination accelerated, new vehicles emerged to facilitate it. The railroads began with so-called pool arrangements—informal agreements among various companies to stabilize rates and divide markets (arrangements that would in later years be known as cartels). But the pools did not work very well. If even a few firms in an industry were unwilling to cooperate (as was almost always the case), the pool arrangements collapsed.

The failure of the pools led to new techniques of consolidation resting less on cooperation than on centralized control. At first, the most successful such technique was the creation of the "trust"—pioneered by Standard Oil in the early 1880s and perfected by the banker J. P. Morgan. Over time, the word "trust" became a term for any great economic combination. But the trust was in fact a particular kind of organization. Under a trust agreement, stockholders in individual corporations transferred their stocks to a small group of trustees in exchange for shares in the trust itself. Owners of trust certificates often had no direct control over the decisions of the trustees; they simply received a share of the profits of the combination. The trustees themselves, on the other hand, might literally own

only a few companies but could exercise effective control over many.

In 1889, the state of New Jersey helped produce a third form of consolidation by changing its laws of incorporation to permit companies actually to buy up other companies. Other states soon followed. That made the trust unnecessary and permitted actual corporate mergers. Rockefeller, for example, quickly relocated Standard Oil in New Jersey and created there what became known as a "holding company"—a central corporate body that would buy up the stock of various members of the Standard Oil trust and establish direct, formal ownership of the corporations in the trust.

By the end of the nineteenth century, as a result of corporate consolidation, 1 percent of the corporations in America were able to control more than 33 percent of the manufacturing. A system of economic organization was emerging that lodged enormous power in the hands of a very few men: the great bankers of New York such as J. P. Morgan, industrial titans such as Rockefeller (who himself gained control of a major bank), and others.

Whether or not this relentless concentration of economic power was the only way or the best way to promote industrial expansion became a major source of debate in America in the late nineteenth century and beyond. But it is clear that, whatever else they may have done, the industrial giants of the era were responsible for substantial economic growth. They were integrating operations, cutting costs, creating a great industrial infrastructure, stimulating new markets, creating jobs for a vast new pool of unskilled workers, and opening the way to large-scale mass production. They were also creating the basis for some of the greatest public controversies of their era.

CAPITALISM AND ITS CRITICS

The rise of big business was not without its critics. Farmers and workers saw in the growth of the new corporate power centers a threat to notions of a republican society in which wealth and authority were widely distributed. Middle-class critics pointed to the corruption that the new industrial titans seemed to produce in their own enterprises and in local, state, and national politics. The growing criticisms challenged the captains of industry to create a defense of the new corporate economy, to convince the public (and themselves) that it was compatible with the ideology of individualism and equal opportunity that had long been central to the American self-image.

"MODERN COLOSSUS OF (RAIL) ROADS"
Cornelius Vanderbilt, known as the "Commodore," accumulated one of America's great fortunes by consolidating several large railroad companies under his control in the 1860s. His name became a synonym not only for enormous wealth, but also (in the eyes of many Americans) for excessive corporate power—as suggested in this cartoon, showing him standing astride his empire and manipulating its parts. *(Culver)*

The "Self-Made Man"

The rationale for modern capitalism rested squarely on the older ideology of individualism. The new industrial economy, its defenders argued, was not reducing opportunities for individual advancement, it was expanding them. It was providing every individual with a chance to succeed and attain great wealth.

There was an element of truth in such claims, but only a small one. Before the Civil War there had been few millionaires in America; by 1892 there were more than 4,000. Some were in fact what almost all millionaires claimed to be: "self-made men." Carnegie had worked as a bobbin boy in a Pittsburgh cotton mill; John D. Rockefeller had begun as a clerk in a Cleveland commission house; E. H. Harriman, a great railroad tycoon, had begun as a broker's office boy. But most of the new business tycoons had begun their careers from positions of wealth and privilege.

Nor was their rise to power and prominence always a result simply of hard work and ingenuity, as they liked to claim. It was also a result of ruthlessness, arrogance, and, at times, rampant corruption. The railroad magnate Cornelius Vanderbilt expressed the attitude of many corporate tycoons with his belligerent question: "Can't I do what I want with my own?" So did his son William, with his oft-quoted statement: "The public be damned." Once, when the elder Vanderbilt's lawyers warned him that a move he contemplated was illegal, he bellowed: "What do I care about the law? H'aint I got the power?"

Industrialists made large financial contributions to politicians, political parties, and government officials in exchange for assistance and support. And more often than not, politicians responded as they hoped. Cynics said that Standard Oil did everything to the Ohio legislature except refine it. A member of the Pennsylvania legislature once reportedly said: "Mr. Speaker, I move we adjourn unless the Pennsylvania Railroad has more business for us to transact." During the notorious "Erie War" of 1868, in which Cornelius Vanderbilt did battle against Jay Gould and Jim Fisk for control of the Erie Railroad, both sides in the dispute offered lavish bribes to members of the New York State legislature to support measures favorable to their cause. The market price of legislators during the fight was $15,000 a head. One enterprising politician collected $75,000 from Vanderbilt and $100,000 from Gould. Politicians were not innocent victims of this corruption. Many of them openly demanded bribes and in effect blackmailed businessmen.

The average industrialist of the late nineteenth century was not, however, a Rockefeller or a Vanderbilt, but a more modest entrepreneur engaged in highly risky ventures in an unstable economy. For every successful millionaire, there were dozens of aspiring businessmen whose efforts failed. Some industries fell under the monopolistic control of a single firm or a small group of large firms. But many more industries remained fragmented, with many small companies struggling to carve out a stable position for themselves in an uncertain, highly competitive environment. The annals of business did indeed include real stories of individuals rising from rags to riches. They also included stories of people moving from riches back to rags.

Survival of the Fittest

Most tycoons liked to claim that they had attained their wealth and power through hard work, acquisitiveness, and thrift—the traditional virtues of Protestant America. Those who succeeded, they argued, deserved their success. "God gave me my money," explained John D. Rockefeller, expressing the assumption that riches were a reward for worthiness. Those who failed had earned their failure—through their own laziness, stupidity, or carelessness. "Let us remember," said a prominent Protestant minister, "that there is not a poor person in the United States who was not made poor by his own shortcomings."

Such assumptions became the basis of a popular social theory of the late nineteenth century: Social Darwinism, the application to human society of Charles Darwin's laws of evolution and natural selection among species. Just as only the fittest survived in the process of evolution, so in human society only the fittest individuals survived and flourished in the marketplace.

The English philosopher Herbert Spencer was the first and most important proponent of this theory. Society, he argued, benefited from the elimination of the unfit and the survival of the strong and talented. Spencer's books were popular in America in the 1870s and 1880s. And his teachings found prominent supporters among American intellectuals, most notably William Graham Sumner of Yale, who promoted similar ideas in lectures, articles, and a famous 1906 book, *Folkways.* Sumner did not agree with everything Spencer wrote, but he did share Spencer's belief that individuals must have absolute freedom to struggle, to compete, to succeed, or to fail.

Many industrialists seized on the theories of Spencer and Sumner to justify their own power. "The growth of a large business is merely the survival of the fittest," Rockefeller proclaimed. "This is not an evil tendency in business. It is merely the working out of the law of nature and a law of God." Carnegie, who became the leading exponent of Social Darwinism among American industrialists, later described his reaction on first reading Spencer: "I remember that light came as in a flood and all was clear."

Social Darwinism appealed to businessmen because it seemed to legitimize their success and confirm their virtues. It appealed to them because it placed their activities within the context of traditional American ideas of freedom and individualism. Above all, it appealed to them because it justified their tactics. Social Darwinists insisted that all attempts by labor to raise wages by forming unions and all endeavors by government to regulate economic activities would fail, because economic life was controlled by a natural law, the law of competition. And Social Darwinism coincided with another "law" that seemed to justify business practices and business dominance: the law of supply and demand as defined by Adam Smith and the classical economists. The economic system, they argued, was like a great and delicate machine functioning by natural and automatic rules, by the "invisible hand" of market forces. The greatest among these rules, the law of supply and demand, determined all economic values—prices, wages, rents, interest rates—at a level that was just to all concerned. Supply and demand worked because human beings were essentially economic creatures who understood and pursued their own interests, and because they operated in a free market regulated only by competition.

But Social Darwinism and the ideas of classical economics did not have very much to do with the realities of the corporate economy. At the same time that businessmen were celebrating the virtues of competition and the free market, they were actively seeking to protect themselves from competition and to replace the natural workings of the marketplace with control by great combinations. Rockefeller's great Standard Oil monopoly was the clearest example of the effort to free an enterprise from competition. But many businessmen made similar attempts on a smaller scale. Vicious competitive battle—something Spencer and Sumner celebrated and called a source of healthy progress—was in fact the very thing that American businessmen most feared and tried to eliminate.

The Gospel of Wealth

Some businessmen attempted to temper the harsh philosophy of Social Darwinism with a more gentle, if in some ways equally self-serving idea: the "gospel of wealth." People of great wealth, advocates of this idea argued, had not only great power but great responsibilities. It was their duty to use their riches to advance social progress. Andrew Carnegie elaborated on the creed in his 1901 book *The Gospel of Wealth,* in which he wrote that the wealthy should consider all revenues in excess of their own needs as "trust funds" to be used for the good of the community; the person of wealth, he said, was "the mere trustee and agent for his poorer brethren." Carnegie was only one of many great industrialists who devoted large parts of their fortunes to philanthropic works—much of it to libraries and

schools, institutions he believed would help the poor to help themselves.

The notion of private wealth as a public blessing existed alongside another popular concept: the notion of great wealth as something available to all. Russell H. Conwell, a Baptist minister, became the most prominent spokesman for the idea by delivering one lecture, "Acres of Diamonds," more than 6,000 times between 1880 and 1900. Conwell told a series of stories, which he claimed were true, of individuals who had found opportunities for extraordinary wealth in their own backyards. (One such story involved a modest farmer who discovered a vast diamond mine in his own fields in the course of working his land.) "I say to you," he told his rapt audiences, "that you have 'acres of diamonds' beneath you right here . . . that the men and women sitting here have within their reach opportunities to get largely wealthy. . . . I say that you ought to get rich, and that it is your duty to get rich." Most of the millionaires in the country, Conwell claimed (inaccurately), had begun on the lowest rung of the economic ladder and had worked their way to success. Every industrious individual had the chance to do likewise.

Horatio Alger was the most famous promoter of the success story. Alger was originally a minister in a small town in Massachusetts but was driven from his pulpit as a result of a sexual scandal. He moved to New York, where he wrote his celebrated novels—more than 100

in all, which together sold more than 20 million copies. The titles varied: *Andy Grant's Pluck, Ragged Dick, Tom the Bootblack, Sink or Swim.* But the story and message were invariably the same: A poor boy from a small town went to the big city to seek his fortune. By work, perseverance, and luck, he became rich.

Alternative Visions

Alongside the celebrations of competition, the justifications for great wealth, and the legitimization of the existing order stood a group of alternative philosophies, challenging the corporate ethos and at times capitalism itself.

One such philosophy emerged in the work of the sociologist Lester Frank Ward. Ward was a Darwinist, but he rejected the application of Darwinian laws to human society. In *Dynamic Sociology* (1883) and other books, he argued that civilization was not governed by natural selection but by human intelligence, which was capable of shaping society as it wished. Unlike Sumner, who believed that state intervention to remodel the environment was futile, Ward thought that an active government engaged in positive planning was society's best hope. The people, through their government, could intervene in the economy and adjust it to serve their needs.

Other Americans skeptical of the laissez-faire ideas of the Social Darwinists adopted more drastic approaches to reform. Some dissenters found a home in the Socialist Labor Party, founded in the 1870s and led for many years by Daniel De Leon, an immigrant from the West Indies. De Leon attracted a modest following in the industrial cities, but the party failed to become a major political force. It never polled more than 82,000 votes. De Leon's theoretical and dogmatic approach appealed to intellectuals more than to workers. A dissident faction of his party, eager to forge ties with organized labor, broke away and in 1901 formed the more enduring American Socialist Party.

Other radicals gained a wider following. One of the most influential was Henry George of California. His angrily eloquent *Progress and Poverty*, published in 1879, became one of the best-selling nonfiction works in American publishing history. George tried to explain why poverty existed amidst the wealth created by modern industry. "This association of poverty with progress is the great enigma of our times," he wrote. "So long as all the increased wealth which modern progress brings goes but to build up great fortunes, to increase luxury and make sharper the contrast between the House of Have and the House of Want, progress is not real and cannot be permanent."

George blamed social problems on the ability of a few monopolists to grow wealthy as a result of rising land values. An increase in the value of land, he claimed, was a result not of any effort by the owner, but of the growth of society around the land. It was an "unearned increment," and it was rightfully the property of the community. And so George proposed a "single tax," to replace all other taxes, which would return the increment to the people. The tax, he argued, would destroy monopolies, distribute wealth more equally, and eliminate poverty. Single-tax societies sprang up in many cities. George himself moved east to New York; and in 1886, with the support of labor and the socialists, he narrowly missed being elected mayor.

Rivaling George in popularity was Edward Bellamy, whose Utopian novel *Looking Backward*, published in 1888, sold more than 1 million copies. It described the experiences of a young Bostonian who went into a hypnotic sleep in 1887 and awoke in the year 2000 to find a new social order where want, politics, and vice were unknown. The new society had emerged from a peaceful, evolutionary process. The large trusts of the late nineteenth century had continued to grow in size and to combine with one another until ultimately they formed a single great trust, controlled by the government, which absorbed all the businesses of all the citizens and distributed the abundance of the industrial economy equally among all the people. Society had become a great machine, "so logical in its principles and direct and simple in its work-

ings" that it almost ran itself. "Fraternal cooperation" had replaced competition. Class divisions had disappeared. Bellamy labeled the philosophy behind this vision "nationalism," and his work inspired the formation of more than 160 Nationalist Clubs to propagate his ideas.

The Problems of Monopoly

Relatively few Americans shared the views of those who questioned capitalism itself. But by the end of the century a growing number of people were becoming deeply concerned about a particular, glaring aspect of capitalism: the growth of monopoly (control of the market by large corporate combinations).

By the end of the century, a wide range of groups had begun to assail monopoly and economic concentration. Laborers, farmers, consumers, small manufacturers, conservative bankers and financiers, advocates of radical change—all joined the attack. They blamed monopoly for creating artificially high prices and for producing a highly unstable economy. Beginning in 1873, the economy fluctuated erratically, with severe recessions creating havoc every five or six years, each recession worse than the previous one, until finally, in 1893, the system seemed on the verge of total collapse.

Adding to the resentment of monopoly was the emergence of a new class of enormously and conspicuously wealthy people, whose lifestyles became an affront to those struggling to stay afloat in the erratic economy. According to one estimate early in the century, 1 percent of the families in America controlled nearly 88 percent of the nation's assets. Some of the wealthy—Andrew Carnegie, for example—lived relatively modestly and donated large sums to charities. Others, however, lived in almost grotesque luxury. Like a clan of feudal barons, the Vanderbilts maintained, in addition to many country estates, seven opulent mansions on seven blocks of New York City's Fifth Avenue. Other wealthy New Yorkers lavished vast sums on parties. The most notorious, a ball on which Mrs. Bradley Martin spent $368,000, created such a furor that she and her husband fled to England to escape public abuse.

Observing their flagrant displays of wealth were the four-fifths of the American people who lived modestly, and at least 10 million people who lived below the commonly accepted poverty line. The standard of living was rising for everyone, but the gap between rich and poor was increasing. To those in difficult economic circumstances, the sense of relative deprivation could be almost as frustrating and embittering as poverty itself.

INDUSTRIAL WORKERS IN THE NEW ECONOMY

The American working class was both a beneficiary and a victim of the growth of industrial capitalism. Many workers in the late nineteenth century experienced a real rise in their standard of living. But they did so at the cost of arduous and often dangerous working conditions, diminishing control over their own work, and a growing sense of powerlessness.

The Immigrant Work Force

The industrial work force expanded dramatically in the late nineteenth century as demand for factory labor grew. The source of that expansion was a massive migration into industrial cities—migration of two sorts. The first was the continuing flow of rural Americans into factory towns and cities—people disillusioned with or bankrupted by life on the farm and eager for new economic and social opportunities. The second was the great wave of immigration from Mexico, Asia, Canada, and above all Europe in the decades following the Civil War—an influx greater than that of any previous era. The 25 million immigrants who arrived in the United States between 1865 and 1915 were more than four times the number who had arrived in the fifty years before.

In the 1870s and 1880s, most of the immigrants to eastern industrial cities came from the nation's traditional sources: England, Ireland, and northern Europe. By the end of the century, however, the major sources of immigration had shifted, with large numbers of southern and eastern Europeans (Italians, Poles, Russians, Greeks, Slavs, and others) moving to America and into the industrial work force. In the West, the major sources of immigration were Mexico and, until the Chinese Exclusion Act of 1882, Asia. No reliable figures are available for either group, but an estimated 1 million Mexicans entered the United States in the first three decades of the twentieth century, many of them swelling the industrial work force of western cities.

The new immigrants were coming to America in part to escape poverty and oppression in their homelands. But they were also lured to the United States by expectations of new opportunities. Sometimes such expectations were realistic, but often they were the result of false promises. Railroads tried to lure immigrants into their western landholdings by distributing misleading advertisements overseas. Industrial employers actively recruited immigrant workers under the Labor Contract Law, which—until its repeal in 1885—permitted them to pay for the passage of workers in advance and deduct the amount later from their wages. Even after the repeal of the law, employers continued to encourage the immigration of unskilled laborers, often with the assistance of foreign-born labor brokers, such as the Greek and Italian *padrones* who recruited work gangs of their fellow nationals.

The arrival of these new groups introduced heightened ethnic tensions into the dynamic of the working class. Low-paid Poles, Greeks, and French Canadians began to displace higher-paid British and Irish workers in the textile factories of New England. Italians, Slavs, and Poles emerged as a major source of labor for the mining industry in the East, traditionally dominated by

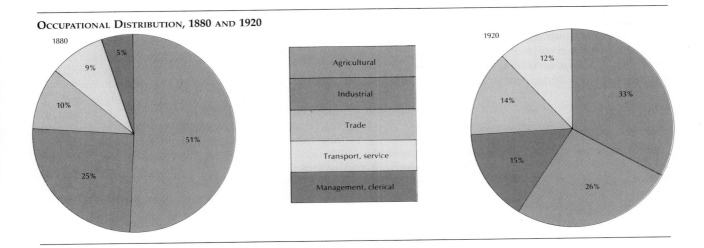

OCCUPATIONAL DISTRIBUTION, 1880 AND 1920

ELLIS ISLAND
The great photographer Lewis Hine took this picture of an Italian mother with her three children arriving on Ellis Island, the processing center for the millions of immigrants who entered the United States through New York City. *(Bettmann)*

native workers or northern European immigrants. Chinese and Mexicans competed with Anglo-Americans and African Americans in mining, farmwork, and factory labor in California, Colorado, and Texas. Even within industries, moreover, workers tended to cluster in particular occupations (and thus, often, at particular income levels) by ethnic group.

Wages and Working Conditions

The average standard of living for workers rose in the years after the Civil War, but for many laborers, the return for their labor remained very small. At the turn of the century, the average income of the American worker was $400 to $500 a year—below the $600 figure widely considered the minimum for a reasonable level of comfort. Nor did workers have much job security. All workers were vulnerable to the boom-and-

bust cycle of the industrial economy, and some lost their jobs because of technological advances or because of the cyclical or seasonal nature of their work. Even those who kept their jobs could find their wages suddenly and substantially cut in hard times. Few workers, in other words, were ever very far from poverty.

American laborers faced other hardships as well. For first-generation workers accustomed to the patterns of agrarian life, there was a difficult adjustment to the nature of modern industrial labor: the performance of routine, repetitive tasks, often requiring little skill, on a strict and monotonous schedule. To skilled artisans whose once-valued tasks were now performed by machines, the new system was impersonal and demeaning. Factory laborers worked ten-hour days, six days a week; in the steel industry they worked twelve hours a day. Many worked in appallingly unsafe or unhealthy factories. Industrial accidents were frequent and severe. Compensation to the victims, either from their employers or from the government, was often limited, until many states began passing workmen's compensation laws in the early twentieth century.

For many workers, the most disturbing aspect of factory labor in the new industrial system was their loss of control over the conditions of their work. Skilled workers had been accustomed to running their own shops. Even semiskilled workers and common laborers had managed to maintain some control over their labor in the relatively informal working conditions of the early and mid-nineteenth century. As the corporate form of organization spread, employers set out to make the factory more efficient (often in response to the principles of scientific management). That meant, they believed, centralizing control of the workplace in the hands of managers, ensuring that workers had no authority or control that might disrupt the flow of production. This loss of control, as much as the low wages and long hours, lay behind the substantial working-class militancy in the late nineteenth century.

Women and Children at Work

The decreasing need for skilled work in factories induced many employers to increase the use of women and children, whom they could hire for lower wages than adult males. By 1900, women made up 17 percent of the industrial work force, a fourfold increase since 1870; and 20 percent of all women (well over 5 million) were wage earners. Some of these working women were single and took jobs to support themselves or their parents or siblings. Many others were married and had to work to supplement the inadequate earnings of their husbands; for many working-

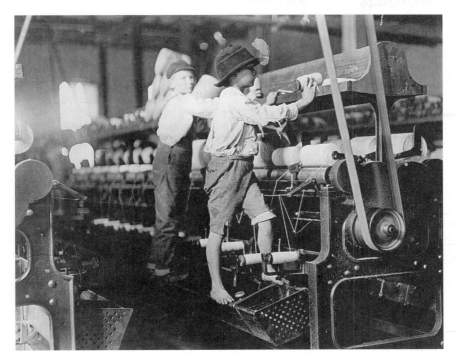

CHILDREN OF WEALTH
The children of the wealthy railroad executive George Jay Gould (son of the notorious financier Jay Gould) ride through a Paris park in "voiturettes," miniature automobiles manufactured in France. *(Culver)*

class families, two incomes were required to support even a minimal standard of living. Even so, in some communities the aversion to seeing married women work was so strong—among both men and women—that families struggled on inadequate wages rather than see a wife and mother take a job.

Women industrial workers were overwhelmingly white and mostly young, 75 percent of them under twenty-five. The vast majority were immigrants or the daughters of immigrants. There were some women in all areas of industry, even in some of the most arduous jobs. Most women, however, worked in a few industries where unskilled and semiskilled machine labor (as opposed to heavy manual labor) prevailed. The textile industry remained the largest single industrial employer of women. (Domestic service remained the most common female occupation overall.) Women worked for wages as low as $6 to $8 a week, well below the minimum necessary for survival (and well below the wages paid to men working the same jobs). At the turn of the century, the average annual wage for a male industrial worker was $597; for a woman, it was $314. Even highly skilled women workers made about half what men doing the same job earned. Advocates of a minimum wage law for women created a sensation when they brought several women to a hearing in Chicago to testify that low wages and desperate poverty had driven them to prostitution. (The testimony was not, however, sensational enough for the Illinois legislature, which promptly defeated the bill.)

At least 1.7 million children under sixteen years of age were employed in factories and fields, more than twice the number of thirty years before. Ten percent of all girls aged ten to fifteen, and 20 percent of all boys, held jobs. Under the pressure of outraged public opinion, thirty-eight state legislatures passed child labor laws in the late nineteenth century; but these laws were of limited impact. Sixty percent of child workers were employed in agriculture, which was typically exempt from the laws; such children often worked twelve-hour days picking or hoeing in the fields. And even for children employed in factories, the laws merely set a minimum age of twelve years and a maximum workday of ten hours, standards that employers often ignored in any case. In the cotton mills of the South, children working at the looms all night were kept awake by having cold water thrown in their faces. In canneries, little girls cut fruits and vegetables sixteen hours a day. Exhausted children were particularly susceptible to injury while working at dangerous machines, and they were maimed and even killed in industrial accidents at an alarming rate.

As much as the appalling conditions of woman and child workers troubled the national conscience, condi-

tions for many men were at least equally dangerous. In mills and mines, and on the railroads, the American accident rate was higher than that of any industrial nation in the world. As late as 1907, an average of twelve railroad men a week died on the job. In factories, thousands of workers faced such occupational diseases as lead or phosphorus poisoning, against which few employers took precautions.

The Struggle to Unionize

Labor attempted to fight back against such conditions by adopting some of the same tactics their employers had used so effectively: creating large combinations, or unions. But by the end of the century their efforts had met with little success.

There had been craft unions in America, representing small groups of skilled workers, since well before the Civil War. Alone, however, individual unions could not hope to exert significant power in the new corporate economy, and in the 1860s some labor leaders began to search for ways to combine the energies of the various labor organizations. The first attempt to federate separate unions into a single national organization came in 1866, when William H. Sylvis founded the National Labor Union—a polyglot association, claiming 640,000 members, that included a variety of reform groups having little direct relationship with labor. After the Panic of 1873 the National Labor Union disintegrated and disappeared.

The National Labor Union, like most of the individual unions that joined it, excluded women workers. Male workers argued (not entirely incorrectly) that women were used to drive down their wages; and they justified their hostility by invoking the ideal of domesticity. "Woman was created to be man's companion," a National Labor Union official said, "to be the presiding deity of the home circle." Most women workers agreed that "man should be the breadwinner," as one female union organizer said. But many argued that as long as conditions made it impossible for men to support their families, women should have full and equal opportunities in the workplace.

Unions faced special difficulties during the recession years of the 1870s. Not only was there widespread unemployment, which depression conditions created; there was also widespread middle-class hostility toward the unions. When labor disputes with employers turned bitter and violent, as they occasionally did, much of the public instinctively blamed the workers (or the "radicals" and "anarchists" they believed were influencing the workers) for the trouble, rarely the employers. Particularly alarming to middle-class Americans was the emergence of the "Molly Maguires," a militant labor organization in the anthracite coal region of Pennsylvania. The Mollies operated within the Ancient Order of Hibernians, an Irish fraternal society, and sometimes used terrorist tactics. They attempted to intimidate the coal operators through violence and occasionally murder, and they added to the growing perception that labor activism was motivated by dangerous radicals. Much of the violence attributed to the Molly Maguires, however, was instigated or performed by informers and agents employed by the mine owners, who wanted a pretext for ruthless measures to suppress unionization.

Excitement over the Molly Maguires paled beside the near hysteria that gripped the country during the railroad strike of 1877, which began when the eastern railroads announced a 10 percent wage cut and which soon expanded into something approaching a class war. Strikers disrupted rail service from Baltimore to St. Louis, destroyed equipment, and rioted in the streets of Pittsburgh and other cities. State militias were called out, and in July President Hayes ordered federal troops to suppress the disorders in West Virginia. In Baltimore, eleven demonstrators died and forty were wounded in a conflict between workers and militiamen. In Philadelphia, state militia opened fire on thousands of workers and their families who were attempting to block the railroad crossings and killed twenty people. In all, over 100 people died before the strike finally collapsed several weeks after it had begun.

The great railroad strike was America's first major, national labor conflict, and it illustrated how disputes between workers and employers could no longer be localized in the increasingly national economy. It illustrated as well the depth of resentment among many American workers toward their employers (and toward the governments allied with them) and the lengths to which they were prepared to go to express that resentment. And finally, it was an indication of the frailty of the labor movement. The failure of the strike seriously weakened the railroad unions and damaged the reputation of labor organizations in other industries as well.

The Knights of Labor

The first major effort to create a genuinely national labor organization was the founding in 1869 of the Noble Order of the Knights of Labor, under the leadership of Uriah S. Stephens. Membership was open to all who "toiled," a definition that included all workers and most business and professional people. The only excluded groups were lawyers, bankers, liquor dealers, and professional gamblers. Unlike most labor organizations of the time, the Knights welcomed women members—not just female factory workers, but domestic servants and women who worked in their own homes. Leonora Barry, an Irish immigrant who had worked in a New York hosiery factory, ran the Woman's Bureau of the Knights. Under her effective leadership, the Knights enlisted 50,000 women members (both black and white) and created over a hundred all-female locals.

The Knights were loosely organized, without much central direction. Members met in local "assemblies," which took many different forms. They were loosely affiliated with a national "general assembly." Their program was similarly vague. Although they championed an eight-hour day and the abolition of child labor, the leaders were more interested in long-range reform of the economy. Leaders of the Knights hoped to replace the "wage system" with a new "cooperative system," in which workers would themselves control a large part of the economy.

For several years, the Knights remained a secret fraternal organization. But in the late 1870s, under the leadership of Terence V. Powderly, the order moved into the open and entered a spectacular period of expansion. By 1886, it claimed a total membership of over 700,000, including some militant elements that the moderate leadership could not always control. Local unions or assemblies associated with the Knights launched a series of strikes in the 1880s in defiance of Powderly's wishes. In 1885, striking railway workers forced the Missouri Pacific, a link in the Gould system, to restore wage cuts and recognize their union. But the victory was temporary. In the following year, a strike on another Gould road, the Texas and Pacific, was crushed, and the power of the unions in the Gould system was broken. Their failure helped discredit the organization. By 1890, the membership of the Knights had shrunk to 100,000. A few years later, the organization disappeared altogether.

The AFL

Even before the Knights began to decline, a rival organization based on a very different organizational concept appeared. In 1881, representatives of a number of existing craft unions formed the Federation of Organized Trade and Labor Unions of the United States and Canada. Five years later, it changed its name to the American Federation of Labor (AFL), and it soon became the most important and enduring labor group in the country. Rejecting the Knights' idea of one big union for everybody, the Federation was an association of essentially autonomous craft unions and represented mainly skilled workers. It was generally hostile to organizing unskilled workers, who did not fit comfortably within the craft–based structure of existing organizations.

Toward women, the AFL adopted an apparently contradictory policy. On the one hand, the male leaders of the AFL were essentially hostile to the idea of women entering the paid work force. Because women were weak, they believed, employers could easily take advantage of them by paying them less than men. As a result, women workers drove down wages for everyone. "It is the so-called competition of the unorganized, defenceless woman worker, the girl and the wife, that often tends to reduce the wages of the father and husband," Samuel Gompers, the powerful leader of the AFL, once said. He talked often about the importance of women remaining in the home, and argued, incorrectly, that "There is no necessity of the wife contributing to the support of the family by working." More than that, female labor was, the AFL newspaper wrote, "the knife of the assassin, aimed at the family circle."

Though hostile to the idea of women workers, the AFL nevertheless sought equal pay for those women who did work and even hired some female organizers to encourage unionization in industries dominated by women. These positions were, in fact, less contradictory than they seem. By raising the pay of women, the AFL could make them less attractive to employers and, in effect, drive them out of the work force.

Gompers accepted the basic premises of capitalism; his goal was simply to secure for the workers he represented a greater share of capitalism's material rewards. Gompers rejected the idea of fundamental economic reform; he opposed the creation of a worker's party; he was generally hostile to any government efforts to protect labor or improve working conditions, convinced that what government could give it could also take away. The AFL concentrated instead on the relationship between labor and management. It supported the immediate objectives of most workers: better wages, hours, and working conditions. And while it hoped to attain its goals by collective bargaining, it was ready to use strikes if necessary.

As one of its first objectives, the AFL demanded a national eight-hour day and called for a general strike if workers did not achieve the goal by May 1, 1886. On that day, strikes and demonstrations for a shorter workday took place all over the country, most of them staged by AFL unions but a few by more radical groups.

In Chicago, a center of labor and radical strength, a strike was already in progress at the McCormick Harvester Company when the general strike began. City

SAMUEL GOMPERS
Gompers migrated to the United States from England as a boy and began work at the age of thirteen as a cigar maker, rising to become head of his local union. When the American Federation of Labor was organized in 1886, Gompers became its first president, a position he held (with only a single, one-year interruption) until 1924. Gompers helped the AFL to become the premier labor organization in the United States; he also helped commit the organization to a narrow, craft-oriented view of unionism that excluded an increasing proportion of workers as mass-production industries rose to prominence. He is shown here during a union-organizing drive in West Virginia. *(George Meany Memorial Archives)*

police had been harassing the strikers, and labor and radical leaders called a protest meeting at Haymarket Square. When the police ordered the crowd to disperse, someone threw a bomb that killed seven officers and injured sixty-seven other people. The police, who had killed four strikers the day before, fired into the crowd and killed four more people. Conservative, property-conscious Americans, frightened and outraged, demanded retribution, even though no one knew who had thrown the bomb. Chicago officials finally rounded up eight anarchists and charged them with murder, on the grounds that their statements had incited whoever had hurled the bomb. All eight scapegoats were found guilty after a remarkably injudicious trial. Seven were sentenced to death. One of the condemned committed suicide, four were executed, and two had their sentences commuted to life imprisonment.

To most middle-class Americans, the Haymarket bombing was an alarming symbol of social chaos and radicalism. "Anarchism" now became a code word in the public mind for terrorism and violence, even though most anarchists were relatively peaceful visionaries dreaming of a new social order. For the next thirty years, the specter of anarchism remained one of the most frightening concepts in the American middle-class imagination. It also became a constant obstacle to the goals of the AFL and other labor organizations, and it was particularly devastating to the Knights of Labor, which, as the most radical of the major labor organizations, never recovered from the post-Haymarket hysteria. However much they tried to distance themselves from radicals, unions were always vulnerable to accusations of anarchism, as the violent strikes of the 1890s occasionally illustrated.

The Homestead Strike

The Amalgamated Association of Iron and Steel Workers, which was affiliated with the American Federation of Labor, was the most powerful trade union in the country. Its members were skilled workers, in great demand by employers and thus able to exercise significant power in the workplace. Employers sometimes called such workers "little shopfloor autocrats," and they resented the substantial control over working conditions these skilled laborers often had. The union had a rulebook with fifty-six pages of what workers called "legislation" limiting the power of employers. In the emerging corporate world of the late nineteenth century, such challenges to management control were beginning to seem intolerable to many employers.

By the mid-1880s, the steel industry had introduced new production methods and new patterns of organization that were streamlining the steelmaking process and, in the process, reducing the companies' dependence on skilled labor. In the Carnegie system, which was coming to dominate the steel industry, the union had a foothold in only one of the corporation's three major factories—the Homestead plant near Pittsburgh.

By 1890, Carnegie and his chief lieutenant, Henry Clay Frick, had decided that the Amalgamated "had to go," even at Homestead. Over the next two years, they repeatedly cut wages at Homestead. At first, the union acquiesced, aware that it was not strong enough to wage a successful strike.

In 1892, the company stopped even discussing its decisions with the Amalgamated, in effect denying the union's right to negotiate at all. Finally, when Frick announced another wage cut at Homestead and gave the union two days to accept it, the Amalgamated called for a strike. Frick abruptly shut down the plant and called in 300 guards from the Pinkerton Detective Agency to enable the company to hire non-union workers. The hated Pinkertons were well-known strikebreakers, and their mere presence was often enough to incite workers to violence.

The Pinkertons approached the plant by river on barges on July 6, 1892. The strikers prepared for them by pouring oil on the water and setting it on fire, and they met the guards at the docks with guns and dynamite. After several hours of pitched battle, which brought death to three guards and ten strikers and injuries to many others, the Pinkertons surrendered and were escorted roughly out of town.

But the workers' victory was temporary. The governor of Pennsylvania, at the company's request, sent the state's entire National Guard contingent, some 8,000 troops, to Homestead. Production resumed, with strikebreakers now protected by troops. And public opinion turned against the strikers when a radical made an attempt to assassinate Frick. Slowly workers drifted back to their jobs; and finally—four months after the strike began—the Amalgamated surrendered. By 1900, every major steel plant in the Northeast had broken with the Amalgamated, which now had virtually no power to resist. Its membership shrank from a high of 24,000 in 1891 (two-thirds of all eligible steelworkers) to fewer than 7,000 a decade later. Its decline was symbolic of the general erosion of union strength in the late nineteenth century, as factory labor became increasingly unskilled and workers thus became easier to replace. The AFL unions were often powerless in the face of these changes.

The Pullman Strike

A dispute of greater magnitude and equal bitterness, if less violence, was the Pullman strike in 1894. The Pullman Palace Car Company manufactured sleeping and parlor cars for railroads, which it built and repaired at a plant near Chicago. There the company built the 600-acre town of Pullman and rented its trim, orderly houses to the employees. George M. Pullman, owner of the company, considered the town a model solution to the industrial problem; he referred to the workers as his "children." But many residents chafed at the regimentation and the high rents.

In the winter of 1893–1894, the Pullman Company slashed wages by about 25 percent, citing the declining revenues the depression was causing. At the same time, Pullman refused to reduce rents in its model town, which were 20 to 25 percent higher than for comparable accommodations in surrounding areas. Workers went on strike and persuaded the militant American Railway Union, led by Eugene V. Debs, to support them by refusing to handle Pullman cars and equipment. Opposing the strikers was the General Managers' Association, a consortium of twenty-four Chicago railroads. It persuaded its member companies to discharge switchmen who refused to handle Pullman cars. Every time this happened, Debs's union instructed its members who worked for the offending companies to walk off their jobs. Within a few days thousands of railroad workers in twenty-seven states and territories were on strike, and transportation from Chicago to the Pacific Coast was paralyzed.

Most state governors responded readily to appeals from strike-threatened businesses; but the governor of Illinois, John Peter Altgeld, was a man with demonstrated sympathies for workers and their grievances. Altgeld had criticized the trials of the Haymarket anarchists and had pardoned the convicted men who were still in prison when he took office. He refused to call out the militia to protect employers now. Bypassing Altgeld, railroad operators asked the federal government to send regular army troops to Illinois, on the pretext that the strike was preventing the movement of mail on the trains. President Grover Cleveland and Attorney General Richard Olney, a former railroad lawyer and a bitter foe of unions, complied. In July 1894, over Altgeld's objections, the president ordered 2,000 troops to the Chicago area. A federal court issued an injunction forbidding the union to continue the strike. When Debs and his associates defied it, they were arrested and imprisoned. With federal troops protecting the hiring of new workers and with the union leaders in a federal jail, the strike quickly collapsed.

Sources of Labor Weakness

The last decades of the nineteenth century were years in which labor, despite its organizing efforts, made few real gains and suffered many important losses. In a rapidly expanding industrial economy, wages for

THE PULLMAN STRIKE
Railroad workers, striking in sympathy with the employees of the Pullman Palace Car Company, burned 600 freight cars in the Chicago railroad yards in July 1894. *(Bettmann)*

workers rose hardly at all, and not nearly enough to keep up with the rising cost of living. Labor leaders won a few legislative victories: the abolition by Congress in 1885 of the Contract Labor Law; the establishment by Congress in 1868 of an eight-hour day on public works projects and in 1892 of an eight-hour day for government employees; state laws governing hours of labor and safety standards; and gradually some guaranteed compensation for workers injured on the job. But many of these laws were not enforced, and neither strikes nor protests seemed to have much effect. The end of the century found most workers with less political power and considerably less control of the workplace than they had had forty years before.

Workers failed to make greater gains for many reasons. The principal labor organizations represented only a small percentage of the industrial work force. Four percent of all workers (fewer than 1 million people) belonged to unions in 1900. The AFL, the most important, excluded unskilled workers, who were emerging as the core of the industrial work force, and along with them most women, blacks, and recent immigrants. Women responded to this exclusion in 1903 by forming their own organization, the Women's Trade Union League. But the WTUL was mostly interested in securing protective legislation for women workers, not in a general organization and mobilization of labor; and the WTUL would have found little support within the AFL or other male-dominated organizations even if its goals had been more expansive. Other divisions within the work force contributed fur-

SIGNIFICANT EVENTS

1851 I. M. Singer and Company, one of first modern corporations, founded

1859 First oil well drilled in Pennsylvania

1866 William H. Sylvis founds National Labor Union

First transatlantic cable laid

1868 Open-hearth steelmaking begins in America

1869 Knights of Labor founded

1870 John D. Rockefeller founds Standard Oil

1873 Carnegie Steel founded

Commercial and financial panic disrupts economy

1876 Alexander Graham Bell invents telephone

1877 Railroad workers strike nationwide

1879 Thomas A. Edison invents electric light bulb

Henry George publishes *Progress and Poverty*

1881 American Federation of Labor founded

1882 Rockefeller creates first trust

1886 Haymarket bombing blamed on anarchists

1888 Edward Bellamy publishes *Looking Backward*

1892 Workers strike Homestead plant

1893 Depression begins

1894 Workers strike Pullman Company

1901 J. P. Morgan creates United States Steel Corporation

American Socialist Party founded

Spindletop oil field discovered in Texas

1903 Women's Trade Union League founded

Wright brothers make first successful flight at Kitty Hawk, North Carolina

1906 Henry Ford produces his first automobiles

William Graham Sumner publishes *Folkways*

1914 Ford introduces assembly line in his factories

---

ther to union weakness. Tensions between different ethnic and racial groups kept laborers divided.

Another source of labor weakness was the shifting nature of the work force. Many immigrant workers came to America intending to remain only briefly, to earn some money and return home. The assumption that they had no long-range future in the country (even though it was often a mistaken one) eroded their willingness to organize. Other workers—natives and immigrants alike—were in constant motion, moving from one job to another, one town to another, seldom in one place long enough to establish any sort of institutional ties or exert any real power. A study of Newburyport, Massachusetts over a thirty-year period shows that 90 percent of the workers there vanished from the town records in those years, many of them because they moved elsewhere.

Even workers who stayed put often did not remain in the same job for long. The rags-to-riches stories of the Horatio Alger novels had few counterparts in reality. But some real social mobility did exist. Workers might move from unskilled to semiskilled or skilled jobs during their lifetimes; their children might become foremen or managers. The gains were small, but they were enough to inspire considerable (and often unrealistic) hopes and to persuade some workers that they were not part of a permanent working class.

Above all, workers made few gains in the late nineteenth century because of the strength of the forces arrayed against them. They faced corporate organizations of vast wealth and power, which were generally determined to crush any efforts by workers to challenge their prerogatives—not just through brute force, but also through infiltration of unions, espionage within working-class communities, and sabotage of organizational efforts. And as the Homestead and Pullman strikes suggest, the corporations had the support of local, state, and federal authorities, who were willing to send in troops to "preserve order" and crush labor uprisings on demand.

Despite the creation of new labor unions, despite a wave of strikes and protests that in the 1880s and 1890s reached startling proportions, workers in the late nineteenth century failed on the whole to create successful organizations or to protect their interests in the way the large corporations managed to do. In the battle for power within the emerging industrial economy, almost all the advantages seemed to lie with capital.

SUGGESTED READINGS

General Histories.   Daniel Boorstin, *The Americans: The Democratic Experience* (1973). Thomas C. Cochran and William Miller, *The Age of Enterprise* (1942). Carl Degler, *The Age of the Economic Revolution* (1977). John A. Garraty, *The New Commonwealth* (1968). Ray Ginger, *The Age of Excess* (1963). Samuel P. Hays, *The Response to Industrialism, 1885–1914* (1957). Robert L. Heilbroner, *The Economic Transformation of America* (1977). Robert Higgs, *The Transformation of the American Economy, 1865–1914* (1971). Edward C. Kirkland, *Industry Comes of Age: Business, Labor, and Public Policy, 1860–1897* (1961). Alan Trachtenberg, *The Incorporation of America: Culture and Society in the Gilded Age* (1982). Robert Wiebe, *The Search for Order, 1877–1920* (1968).

Technology.   Robert W. Bruce, *Bell* (1973). Roger Burlingame, *Engines of Democracy: Inventions and Society in Mature America* (1940); *Henry Ford* (1957). Robert Conot, *A Streak of Luck* (1979). Richard N. Current, *The Typewriter and the Men Who Made It* (1954). George Daniels, *Science and Society in America* (1971). Frank E. Hill, *Ford* (1954). Thomas P. Hughes, *Networks of Power: Electrification in Western Society, 1880–1930* (1983). Judith McGaw, *Most Wonderful Machine: Mechanization and Social Change in Berkshire Paper Making, 1801–1885* (1988). Martin V. Melosi, *Coping with Abundance: Energy and Environment in Industrial America* (1985). Elting E. Morison, *Men, Machines, and Modern Times* (1966). Lewis Mumford, *Technics and Civilization* (1934). Allan Nevins, *Ford*, 3 vols. (1954–1962). David F. Noble, *America by Design: Science, Technology, and the Rise of Corporate Capitalism* (1977). Leonard S. Reich, *The Making of American Industrial Research: Science and Business at GE and Bell, 1876–1926* (1985). Nathan Rosenberg, *Technology and American Economic Growth* (1972). Peter Temin, *Steel in Nineteenth Century America* (1964). Wyn Wachhorst, *Thomas Alva Edison: An American Myth* (1981). Frederick A. White, *American Industrial Research Laboratories* (1961).

Railroads.   Lee Benson, *Merchants, Farmers, and Railroads* (1955). Edward G. Campbell, *The Reorganization of the American Railroad System* (1938). Thomas C. Cochran, *Railroad Leaders* (1953). Robert Fogel, *Railroads and American Economic Growth* (1964). Edward C. Kirkland, *Men, Cities, and Transportation*, 2 vols. (1948). Gabriel Kolko, *Railroads and Regulation, 1877–1916* (1965). George H. Miller, *Railroads and the Granger Laws* (1971). Richard C. Overton, *Burlington West* (1941); *Gulf to Rockies* (1953). John F. Stover, *The Life and Decline of the American Railroad* (1970); *The Railroads of the South, 1865–1900* (1955). George R. Taylor and I. D. Neu, *The American Railroad Network, 1861–1890* (1956). Anthony F. C. Wallace, *St. Clair: A Nineteenth-Century Coal Town's Experience with a Disaster-Prone Industry* (1987).

The Corporation.   Alfred D. Chandler, Jr., *Strategy and Structure: Chapters in the History of the American Industrial Enterprise* (1962); *Pierre S. DuPont and the Making of the Modern Corporation* (1971); *The Visible Hand: The Managerial Revolution in American Business* (1977); *Scale and Scope: The Dynamics of Industrial Capitalism* (1990). David F. Hawkes, *John D.: The Founding Father of the Rockefellers* (1980). Matthew Josephson, *The Robber Barons* (1934). Maury Klein, *The Life and Legend of Jay Gould* (1986). Norma R. Lamoreaux, *The Great Merger Movement in American Business, 1895–1904* (1985). Harold C. Livesay, *Andrew Carnegie and the Rise of Big Business* (1975). Allan Nevins, *Study in Power: John D. Rockefeller*, 2 vols. (1953). Glenn Porter and Harold C. Livesay, *Merchants and Manufacturers* (1971). Joseph Wall, *Andrew Carnegie* (1970). Bernard Weisberger, *The Dream Maker* (1979). Olivier Zunz, *Making America Corporate, 1870–1920* (1990).

Ideologies.   Charles A. Baker, *Henry George* (1955). Robert C. Bannister, *Social Darwinism: Science and Myth in Anglo-American Social Thought* (1967). Samuel Chugerman, *Lester F. Ward: The American Aristotle* (1939). Sidney Fine, *Laissez Faire and the General Welfare State: A Study of Conflict in American Thought, 1865–1901* (1956). Louis Galambos, *The Public Image of Big Business in America, 1880–1940* (1975). Richard Hofstadter, *Social Darwinism in American Thought* (rev. ed., 1955). Edward C. Kirkland, *Dream and Thought in the Business Community, 1860–1900* (1956). T. J. Jackson Lears, *No Place of Grace: Antimodernism and the Transformation of American Culture, 1880–1920* (1981). Robert G. McCloskey, *American Conservatism in the Age of Enterprise* (1951). Arthur E. Morgan, *Edward Bellamy* (1944). Daniel T. Rodgers, *The Work Ethic in Industrial America, 1850–1920* (1978). David Thelen, *Paths of Resistance: Tradition and Dignity in Industrializing Missouri* (1986). John L. Thomas, *Alternative America: Henry George, Edward Bellamy, Henry Demarest Lloyd, and the Adversary Tradition* (1983). Irvin G. Wylie, *The Self-Made Man in America* (1954).

Labor.   Paul Avrich, *The Haymarket Tragedy* (1984). John Bodnar, *Immigration and Industrialization: Ethnicity in an American Mill Town* (1977). Stanley Buder, *Pullman* (1967). John T. Cumbler, *Working-Class Community in Industrial America* (1979). Henry David, *The Haymarket Affair* (1936). Ileen A. De-

Vault, *Sons and Daughters of Labor: Class and Clerical Work in Turn-of-the-Century Pittsburgh* (1990). Melvyn Dubofsky, *Industrialism and the American Worker, 1865–1920* (1975). Melvyn Dubofsky and Warren Van Tine, eds., *Labor Leaders in America* (1987). P. K. Edwards, *Strikes in the United States, 1881–1974* (1981). Leon Fink, *Workingmen's Democracy: The Knights of Labor and American Politics* (1983). Samuel Gompers, *Seventy Years of Life and Labor*, 2 vols. (1975). David M. Gordon, Richard Edwards, and Michael Reich, *Segmented Work, Divided Workers: The Historical Transformation of Labor in the United States* (1982). Brian Greenberg, *Worker and Community: Response to Industrialization in a Nineteenth-Century American City, Albany, New York, 1850–1884* (1985). Herbert G. Gutman, *Work, Culture, and Society in Industrializing America* (1976). Willam F. Hartford, *Working People of Holyoke: Class and Ethnicity in a Massachusetts Mill Town, 1850–1960* (1990). Stuart Kaufman, *Samuel Gompers and the Origins of the American Federation of Labor* (1978). Alexander Keyssar, *Out of Work: The First Century of Unemployment in Massachusetts* (1986). S. J. Kleinberg, *The Shadow of the Mills: Working-Class Families in Pittsburgh, 1870–1907* (1989). David Montgomery, *Beyond Equality* (1975); *Workers' Control in America: Studies in the History of Work, Technology, and Labor Struggles* (1979); *The Fall of the House of Labor: The Workplace, the State, and American Labor Activism, 1865–1925* (1987). Daniel Nelson, *Managers and Workers: Origins of the New Factory System in the United States, 1880–1920* (1975). Richard J. Oestreicher, *Solidarity and Fragmentation: Working People and Class Consciousness: Detroit, 1875–1900* (1986). Henry Pelling, *American Labor* (1960). Peter Rachleff, *Black Labor In Richmond, 1865–1890* (1984). Roy Rosenzweig, *"Eight Hours for What We Will": Workers and Leisure in an Industrial City, 1870–1920* (1983). Steven J. Ross, *Workers on the Edge: Work, Leisure, and Politics in Industrializing Cincinnati, 1788–1890* (1985). Peter R. Shergold, *Working Class Life* (1982). Sheldon Stromquist, *A Generation of Boomers: The Pattern of Railroad Labor Conflict in Nineteenth-Century America* (1987). Philip Taft, *The A. F. of L. in the Time of Gompers*, 2 vols. (1957–1959). Daniel J. Walkowitz, *Worker City, Company Town: Iron and Cotton Workers Protest in Troy and Cohoes, New York, 1855–1884* (1978). Leon Wolff, *Lockout: The Story of the Homestead Strike of 1892* (1965).

Women. Mary Blewett, *Men, Women, and Work Culture: Class, Gender, and Protest in the New England Shoe Industry* (1988). Patricia Cooper, *Once a Cigar Maker: Men, Women, and Work Culture in American Cigar Factories, 1900–1919* (1987). Tamara Hareven, *Family Time and Industrial Time: The Relationship Between the Family and Work in a New England Industrial Community* (1982). Paula Hyman, Charlotte Baum, Sonya Michel, *The Jewish Woman in America* (1975). Susan E. Kennedy, *If All We Did Was to Weep at Home: A History of White Working-Class Women in America* (1979). Alice Kessler-Harris, *Out to Work: A History of Wage-Earning Women in the United States* (1982). Susan Levine, *Labor's True Women: Carpet Weavers, Industrialization, and Labor Reform in the Gilded Age* (1984). Elizabeth Anne Payne, *Reform, Labor, and Feminism* (1988). Barbara Wertheimer, *We Were There: The Story of Working Women in America* (1977).

The Left. Mari Jo Buhle, *Women and American Socialism, 1870–1920* (1981). Melvyn Dubofsky, *We Shall Be All: A History of the Industrial Workers of the World* (1969). Gerald N. Grob, *Workers and Utopia* (1961). J. H. M. Laslett, *Labor and the Left* (1970). Margaret M. Marsh, *Anarchist Women: 1870–1920* (1981). Nick Salvatore, *Eugene V. Debs: Citizen and Socialist* (1982).

THE AMERICAN ENVIRONMENT

THE LOCOMOTIVE'S MAGIC WAND

THE RAILROAD WORKED A revolution in the nineteenth-century American landscape. The story of the railroad's construction is among the most familiar narratives of American history. For contemporary observers, the locomotive was the great icon of the age, a "magic wand" that transformed city and country alike. Most saw in it the central symbol of American progress. The writer Caroline Kirkland was typical in describing the railroad as "the resistless chariot of civilization with scythed axles mowing down ignorance and prejudice as it whirls along," driving "the shadows of the past . . . into the dim woods." Among the "shadows" that fled before it were some of the most familiar features of American ecosystems.

The basic achievement of the railroad, in the most abstract economic terms, was to reduce the cost of space by accelerating the speed at which one could move across it. In the 1830s, traveling from New York to Chicago by lake and canal took roughly three weeks. By railroad in the 1850s, it took less than two days. The difference was even more impressive for roads. Whereas a team of horses was doing well to haul a wagonload of grain a dozen miles in a day, a railroad could transport the same grain *hundreds* of miles in the same time. No less important, the railroad liberated America's rural economy from the forced hibernation of winter. While roads and canals sat idle under winter ice, locomotives kept hauling goods to market no matter how cold the weather. As a result, the entire economy became more productive.

This was why the railroad seemed such a symbol of progress. Wherever it went, farms and towns sprang up in response to the new opportunities it brought. The pace of western development increased dramatically as settlers followed the railroads out onto the midwestern prairies in increasing numbers. As they plowed up the sod to raise grain, they dismantled the tallgrass prairie, so much so that it had almost disappeared by the end of the century. The same fate befell the white pine forests of northern Michigan, Wisconsin, and Minnesota. Sawed into lumber and shipped south on Lake Michigan or the Mississippi River, pine trees were delivered by rail to prairie farmers who used them for fences and houses. By 1900, the pines had nearly vanished from their former homes, and midwestern lumber companies were moving their operations elsewhere.

Farther west, an equally dramatic fate befell the great bison herds which had been the mainstay of Great Plains Indian life for generations. With the coming of the Union Pacific in the north and the Kansas Pacific in the south, bison were slaughtered at an almost unimaginable rate. A single hunting party could gun down hundreds in a day for their skins, while tourists could shoot from the windows of their trains without even stopping to inspect their kills. Within half a decade of the arrival of the railroads, over 4 million bison died on the southern plains alone. By 1883, the last major herd had vanished from the plains. An animal that had numbered in the tens of millions less than a quarter-century before now teetered on the brink of extinction. It was no accident that the last major battles between Plains Indians and the U.S. Army took place at exactly the same time. In addition to facili-

THE AMERICAN ENVIRONMENT

tating the movement of soldiers in such conflicts, the railroad had helped destroy the ecological foundation of the Indian economy.

The railroad also introduced the herds of livestock that soon replaced the bison. The drives that brought longhorn steers from Texas to the Kansas cattle towns did so for only one reason: to reach the railroad. As livestock expanded into the grasslands where bison had once grazed, it was the railroad that permitted them to be shipped to market. The result was a newly integrated regional economy that fundamentally altered the environments that sustained it. By the late nineteenth century, the old shortgrass prairies of the high plains were raising range-fed cattle, their native bison having almost entirely disappeared. The tallgrass prairies of Iowa and Illinois had been converted to corn production. Their native bluestem grasses had been plowed under, and much of the grain they now raised was used in feedlots where western cattle were fattened for final sale. Whether raised in Texas, Mon-

EARLY RAILROAD CONSTRUCTION CREW
For many nineteenth-century Americans, the appearance of railroad surveyors and construction crews seemed to herald a new era. The locomotive symbolized progress, bringing in its wake a sudden growth of farms, factories, and towns. *(Bettmann)*

THE AMERICAN ENVIRONMENT

tana, or Illinois, cattle eventually made their way to Chicago's great Union Stock-yard. There they were slaughtered and shipped to the eastern markets, where they were finally eaten.

Without the railroad, none of this would have occurred when and how it did. By the end of the century, the new technology had linked together the different regional environments of the continent with great urban markets. No matter where they lived, no matter what the time of year, Americans relied on the railroad to satisfy their basic needs with products from distant places: Minnesota flour, Texas beef, and Washington lumber all reached their customers via the iron horse. The widespread availability of such products liberated Americans from the constraints of local resources and created a truly national market. These benefits had been earned at the cost of immense ecological changes, but those changes were rarely evident to customers living hundreds of miles from landscapes they never saw. Had they seen the ties between their own lives and the slaughtered bison herds, vanished prairies, and disappearing forests, they would almost certainly have joined Caroline Kirkland in regarding them as reasonable costs of civilized progress.

Just how thoroughly the railroads altered the landscape of the United States can be suggested by one further change. Until the 1880s, every community in America had its own "local" time. People set their clocks according to the rules of astronomy: noon was the moment when the sun stood highest in the midday sky. When it was noon in Chicago, it was 11:50 A.M. in St. Louis, 11:27 A.M. in Omaha, and 12:18 P.M. in Detroit, with every possible variation in between. For the railroad companies, trying to keep track of hundreds of different times was a nightmare, since a train leaving a station at one local time arrived at its destination at an entirely different local time. Such scheduling problems could even cause train wrecks. And so, on November 18, 1883, the major railroad companies carved up the continent into four uniform time zones and declared that they intended to ignore all local times. Henceforth, for railroad purposes, every community in a time zone would have the same time. The U.S. government did not finally ratify this change until 1918, but most communities adopted railroad "standard" time very quickly. The magic wand of the locomotive had managed to change not just the many natural environments of North America, but time itself.

THE BOWERY AT NIGHT, 1895
This painting by Louis Sontag of lower Manhattan portrays many of the new technologies
that were transforming American cities in the late nineteenth century. The elevated railroad
and electric streetcars move alongside older, horse-drawn vehicles. Shops are illuminated
by new electric lights. *(Mueseum of the City of New York)*

CHAPTER EIGHTEEN

THE AGE OF THE CITY

HE INDUSTRIALIZATION AND COMMERCIALIZA-
TION of America changed the face of society
in countless ways. Nowhere were those
changes more profound than in the growth
of cities and the creation of an urban society and culture. Having begun its life as a primarily agrarian republic, the United States in the late nineteenth century was becoming an urban nation.

The change did not come easily. Cities grew so rapidly that their facilities and institutions could not keep pace. Housing, transportation, sewers, social services, governments—all lagged far behind the enormous demands the new urban population was placing on them. American sensibilities lagged behind as well. Many people rebelled at the new and intimidating pace of urban life and at the dazzling and at times uncomfortable diversity of the urban population. "Our cities," wrote the sociologist Charles Horton Cooley, "are full of the disintegrated materials of the old order looking for a place in the new."

THE URBANIZATION OF AMERICA

The great migration from the countryside to the city was not unique to the United States. It was occurring simultaneously throughout much of the Western world in response to industrialization and the factory system.

But America, a society with little experience of great cities, found urbanization particularly jarring—but also particularly alluring.

The Lure of the City

"We cannot all live in cities," Horace Greeley wrote shortly after the Civil War, "yet nearly all seem determined to do so." The urban population of America increased sevenfold in the half-century after the Civil War. And in 1920, the census revealed that for the first time, a majority of the American people lived in "urban" areas—defined as communities of 2,500 people or more. New York and its environs grew from 1 million in 1860 to over 3 million in 1900. Chicago had 100,000 residents in 1860 and more than a million in 1900. Cities were experiencing similar growth in all areas of the country.

Natural increase accounted for only a small part of the urban growth. In fact, urban families experienced a high rate of infant mortality, a declining fertility rate, and a high death rate from disease. Without immigration, cities would have grown relatively slowly, if at all. The city attracted people from the countryside because it offered conveniences, entertainments, and cultural experiences unavailable in rural communities. But it attracted people most of all because it offered more and better-paying jobs than were available in rural America or in the foreign economies many immigrants were fleeing.

AMERICA IN 1900

People moved to cities, too, because new forms of transportation made it easier for them to get there. Railroads made simple, quick, and relatively inexpensive what once might have seemed a daunting journey from parts of the American countryside to nearby cities. The development of large, steam-powered ocean liners created a highly competitive shipping industry in which Europeans and Asians could cross the oceans to America much more cheaply and quickly than they had in the past.

Migrations

As a result, the late nineteenth century was an age of unprecedented geographical mobility, as Americans left the declining agricultural regions of the East at a dramatic rate. Some who left were moving to the newly developing farmlands of the West. But almost as many were moving to the cities of the East and the Midwest.

Among those leaving rural America for industrial cities in the late nineteenth century were young rural women, for whom opportunities in the farm economy were limited. As farms grew larger, more commercial, and more mechanized, they became increasingly male preserves; and since much of the work force on many farms consisted of unskilled and often transient workers, there were fewer family units than before. Farm women had once been essential for making clothes and other household goods, but those goods were now available in stores or through catalogs. Hundreds of thousands of women moved to the cities, therefore, in search of work and community.

Southern blacks were also beginning what would be a nearly century-long exodus from the countryside into the city. That was a testament to the poverty, debt, violence, and oppression African Americans encountered in the late-nineteenth-century rural South, because the opportunities they found in cities were limited. Factory jobs for blacks were rare and professional opportunities almost nonexistent. Urban blacks tended to work as cooks, janitors, domestic servants, and in other low-paying service occupations. Since many such jobs were considered women's work, black women often out-

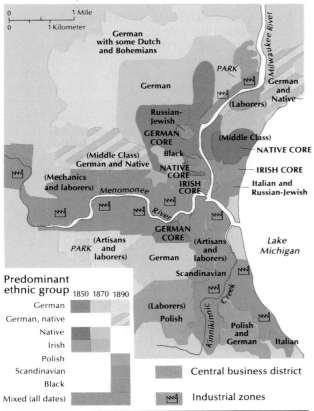

EVOLVING ETHNIC AND CLASS SEGREGATION IN MILWAUKEE, 1850–1890

German with some Dutch and Bohemians

Milwaukee River

PARK

German

German and Native

(Laborers)

Russian-Jewish

GERMAN CORE

(Middle Class)

(Middle Class) German and Native

Black

NATIVE CORE

NATIVE CORE

(Mechanics and laborers)

Menomonee

IRISH CORE

IRISH CORE

Italian and Russian-Jewish

River

GERMAN CORE

(Artisans and laborers)

PARK

(Artisans and laborers)

German

Lake Michigan

Scandinavian

Kinnikinnic Creek

(Laborers)

Polish

Polish and German

Italian

Predominant ethnic group   1850 1870 1890

German

German, native

Native

Irish

Polish

Scandinavian

Black

Mixed (all dates)

☐ Central business district

Industrial zones

---

numbered black men in the cities. By the end of the nineteenth century, there were substantial African-American communities (10,000 people or more) in over thirty cities—many of them in the South, but some (New York, Chicago, Washington, Baltimore) in the North or in border states. Much more substantial African-American migration was to come during World War I and after; but the black communities established in the late nineteenth century paved the way for the great population movements of the future.

The most important source of urban population growth in the late nineteenth century, however, was the arrival of great numbers of new <u>immigrants</u> from abroad: 10 million between 1860 and 1890, 18 million more in the three decades after that. Some came from Canada, Mexico, Latin America, and—particularly on the West Coast—China and Japan. But by far the greatest number came from Europe. After 1880, the flow of new arrivals began for the first time to include large numbers of people from southern and eastern Europe:

Italians, Greeks, Slavs, Slovaks, Russians, Jews, Armenians, and others. By the 1890s, more than half of all immigrants came from these new regions, as opposed to fewer than 2 percent in the 1860s.

In earlier stages of immigration, most new immigrants from Europe (with the exception of the Irish) were at least modestly prosperous and educated. Germans and Scandinavians in particular had headed west on their arrival, either to farm or to work as businessmen, merchants, professionals, or skilled laborers in midwestern cities such as St. Louis, Cincinnati, and Milwaukee. Most of the new immigrants of the late nineteenth century lacked the capital to buy farmland and lacked the education to establish themselves in professions. So, like the poor Irish immigrants before the Civil War, they settled overwhelmingly in industrial cities, where most of them took unskilled jobs.

The Ethnic City

By 1890, most of the population of some major urban areas consisted of foreign-born immigrants and their children: 87 percent of the population of Chicago, 80 percent in New York, 84 percent in Milwaukee and Detroit. (London, the largest industrial city in Europe, by contrast had a population that was 94 percent native.) New York had more Irish than Dublin and more Germans than Hamburg. Chicago eventually had more Poles than Warsaw.

Equally striking was the diversity of the new immigrant populations. In other countries experiencing

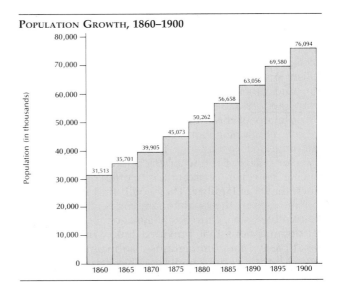

POPULATION GROWTH, 1860–1900

Population (in thousands)

1860	31,513
1865	35,701
1870	39,905
1875	45,073
1880	50,262
1885	56,658
1890	63,056
1895	69,580
1900	76,094

IMMIGRATION'S CONTRIBUTION TO
POPULATION GROWTH, 1860–1920

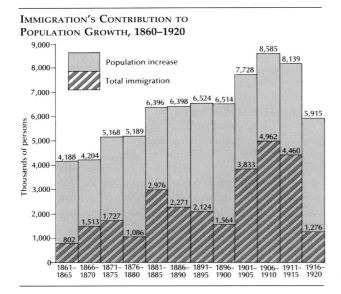

heavy immigration in this period, most of the new arrivals were coming from one or two sources: Argentina, for example, was experiencing great migrations too, but almost everyone was coming from Italy and Spain. In the United States, however, no single national group dominated. In the last four decades of the nineteenth century, substantial groups arrived from Italy, Germany, Scandinavia, Austria, Hungary, Russia, Great Britain, Ireland, Poland, Greece, Canada, Japan, China, Holland, Mexico, and many other nations. In some towns, a dozen different ethnic groups might find themselves living in close proximity.

Most of the new immigrants were rural people, and their adjustment to city life was often a painful one. To help ease the transition, many national groups formed close-knit ethnic communities within the cities: Italian, Polish, Jewish, Slavic, Chinese, French-Canadian, Mexican and other neighborhoods (often called "immigrant ghettoes") that attempted to re-create in the New World many of the features of the Old.

Some ethnic neighborhoods consisted of people who had migrated to America from the same province, town, or village. Even when the population was more diverse, however, the community offered newcomers much that was familiar. They could find newspapers and theaters in their native languages, stores selling their native foods, churches or synagogues, and fraternal organizations that provided links with their national pasts. Many immigrants also maintained close ties with their native countries. They stayed in touch with relatives who had remained behind. Some (per-

haps as many as a third in the early years) returned to Europe or Asia or Mexico after a relatively short time; others helped bring the rest of their families to America.

The cultural cohesiveness of the ethnic communities clearly eased the pain of separation from the immigrants' native lands. What role it played in helping immigrants become absorbed into the economic life of America is a more difficult question to answer. It is clear that some ethnic groups (Jews and Germans in particular) advanced economically more rapidly than others (for example, the Irish). One explanation is that, by huddling together in ethnic neighborhoods, immigrant groups tended to reinforce the cultural values of their previous societies. When those values were particularly well suited to economic advancement in an industrial society—as was, for example, the high value Jews placed on education—ethnic identification may have helped members of a group to improve their lots. When other values predominated—maintaining community solidarity, sustaining family ties, preserving order—progress could be less rapid.

But other factors were at least as important in determining how well immigrants fared in the New World. Immigrants who aroused strong racial prejudice among native-born whites—most notably African Americans, Asians, and Mexicans—found it very difficult to advance whatever their talents. Among others, however, those who arrived with a valuable skill did better than those who did not. Those who arrived with at least some capital had an enormous advantage over those who were penniless. And over time, those

TOTAL IMMIGRATION, 1860–1900

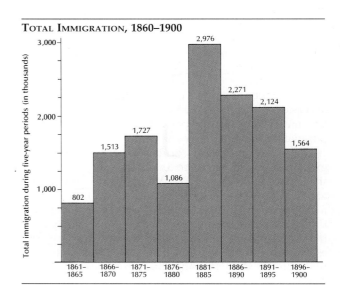

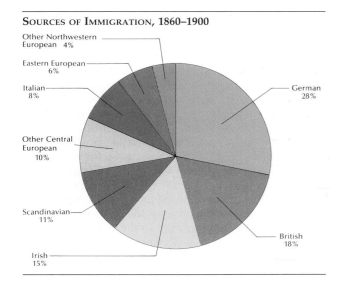

SOURCES OF IMMIGRATION, 1860–1900

Other Northwestern European 4%

Eastern European 6%

Italian 8%

Other Central European 10%

Scandinavian 11%

Irish 15%

German 28%

British 18%

who lived in cities where people of their own nationality came to predominate—for example, the Irish in New York and Boston, or the Germans in Milwaukee—gained a tremendous advantage as they learned to exert their political power.

Assimilation

Despite the substantial differences among the various immigrant communities, virtually all groups of the foreign-born had certain things in common. Most immigrants, of course, shared the experience of living in cities (and of adapting from a rural past to an urban present). Most were young; the majority of newcomers were between fifteen and forty-five years old. And in virtually all communities of foreign-born immigrants, the strength of ethnic ties had to compete against another powerful force: the desire for assimilation.

Many of the new arrivals from abroad had come to America with romantic visions of the New World. And however disillusioning they might find their first contact with the United States, they usually retained the dream of becoming true "Americans." Even some first-generation immigrants worked hard to rid themselves of all vestiges of their old cultures, to become thoroughly Americanized. Second-generation immigrants were even more likely to attempt to break with the old ways, to try to assimilate completely into what they considered the real American culture. Some even looked with contempt on parents and grandparents who continued to preserve traditional ethnic habits and values.

The urge to assimilate put a particular strain on relations between men and women in immigrant communities. Many of the foreign-born came from cultures in which women were even more subordinate to men, and even more fully lodged within the family, than women in the United States. In some immigrant cultures, parents expected to arrange their children's marriages and to control almost every moment of their daughters' lives until marriage. But either out of choice or out of economic necessity, many immigrant women (and even more of the American-born daughters of immigrants) began working outside the home and developing friendships, interests, and attachments outside the family. The result was not the collapse of the family-centered cultures of immigrant communities; those cultures proved remarkably durable. But there were important adjustments to the new and more fluid life of the American city, and often considerable tension in the process.

Assimilation was not, of course, entirely a matter of choice. Native-born Americans encouraged it, both deliberately and inadvertently, in countless ways. Public schools taught children in English, and employers often insisted that workers speak English on the job. Although there were merchants in immigrant communities who sold ethnically distinctive foods and clothing, most stores by necessity sold mainly American products, forcing immigrants to adapt their diets, wardrobe, and lifestyles to American norms. Church leaders were often native-born Americans or more assimilated immigrants who encouraged their parishioners to adopt American ways. Some even reformed their theology and liturgy to make it more compatible with the norms of the new country. Reform Judaism, imported from Germany to the United States in the mid-nineteenth century, was an effort by American Jewish leaders (as it had been among German ones) to make their faith less "foreign" to the dominant culture of a largely Christian nation.

Exclusion

The arrival of so many new immigrants, and the way many of them clung to old ways and created culturally distinctive communities, provoked fear and resentment among some native-born Americans, just as earlier arrivals had done. Some people reacted against the immigrants out of generalized fears and prejudices, seeing in their "foreignness" the source of all the disorder and corruption of the urban world. "These people," a Chicago newspaper wrote shortly after the Haymarket bombing, referring to striking immigrant workers, "are not American, but the very scum and offal of Europe . . . Europe's human and inhuman rubbish." Native-born Americans on the West Coast had a similar cultural aversion to Mexican, Chinese, and Japanese immigrants. Others had economic concerns. Native laborers were often incensed by the willingness of the immigrants to accept lower wages and to take over the jobs of strikers.

The rising nativism provoked political responses. In 1887, Henry Bowers, a self-educated lawyer obsessed with a hatred of Catholics and foreigners, founded the American Protective Association, a group committed to stopping the immigrant tide. By 1894, membership in the organization had reportedly reached 500,000, with chapters throughout the Northeast and Midwest. That same year a more genteel organization, the Immigration Restriction League, was founded in Boston by five Harvard alumni. It was dedicated to the belief that immigrants should be screened, through literacy tests and other standards designed to separate the desirable from the undesirable. The league avoided the crude conspiracy theories and the rabid xenophobia of the American Protective Association, and its more sophisticated nativism made it possible for many educated, middle-class people to support the restrictionist cause.

Even before the rise of these new organizations, politicians were struggling to find answers to the "immigration question." In 1882 Congress had responded to strong anti-Asian sentiment in California and elsewhere and excluded the Chinese, even though they made up only 1.2 percent of the population of the West Coast. (See pp. 456–457.) In the same year, Congress denied entry to "undesirables"—convicts, paupers, the mentally incompetent—and placed a tax of 50 cents on each person admitted. Later legislation of the 1890s enlarged the list of those barred from immigrating and increased the tax.

But these laws kept out only a small number of aliens, and more ambitious restriction proposals made little progress. Congress passed a literacy requirement for immigrants in 1897, but President Grover Cleveland vetoed it. The restrictions had limited success because many native-born Americans, far from fearing immigration, welcomed it and exerted strong political pressure against the restrictionists. Immigration was providing a rapidly growing economy with a cheap and plentiful labor supply; many argued that America's industrial (and indeed agricultural) development would be impossible without it.

The Urban Landscape

The city was a place of remarkable contrasts. It had homes of almost unimaginable size and grandeur, and hovels of indescribable squalor. It had conveniences unknown to earlier generations, and problems that seemed beyond society's capacity to solve. Both the attractions and the problems were a result of the stunning pace at which cities were growing. The expansion of the urban population helped spur important new technological and industrial developments. But the rapid growth also produced misgovernment, poverty, congestion, filth, epidemics, and great fires. Planning and building simply could not match the pace of growth. "The problem in America," a municipal reformer wrote, "has been to make a great city in a few years out of nothing."

One of the greatest problems of this precipitous growth was finding housing for the thousands of new residents who were pouring into the cities every day. For the prosperous, housing was seldom a worry. The availability of cheap labor and the increasing accessibility of tools and materials reduced the cost of building in the late nineteenth century and let anyone with even a moderate income afford a house. Many of the richest urban residents lived in palatial mansions in the heart of the city and created lavish "fashionable districts." These wealthy residents were the principal force behind the creation of the great art museums, concert halls, opera houses, and parks that cities began to build in the late nineteenth century.

The moderately well-to-do (and as time went on, increasing numbers of wealthy people as well) took advantage of the less expensive land on the edges of the city and settled in new suburbs, linked to the downtowns by trains or streetcars or improved roads. Chicago in the 1870s, for example, boasted nearly one hundred residential suburbs connected with the city by railroad and offering the joys of "pure air, peacefulness, quietude, and natural scenery." Boston, too, saw the development of some of the earliest "streetcar suburbs"—Dorchester, Brookline, and others—which catered to both the wealthy and the middle class. New Yorkers of moderate means settled in new suburbs on the northern fringes of Manhattan and commuted downtown by trolley or riverboat. Real estate developers worked to create and promote suburban communities that would appeal to the nostalgia for the countryside that many city dwellers felt. Affluent suburbs, in particular, were notable for lawns, trees, and houses designed to look manorial. Even more modest communities strove to emphasize the opportunities suburbs provided for owning land.

Most urban residents, however, could not afford either to own a house in the city or to move to the suburbs. Instead, they stayed in the city centers and rented. And because demand was so high and space so scarce, they had little bargaining power in the process. Land-

STREETCAR SUBURBS IN NINETEENTH-CENTURY NEW ORLEANS

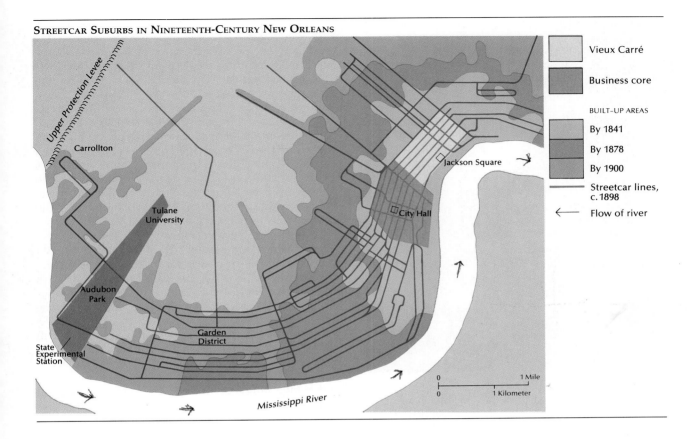

Vieux Carré

Business core

BUILT-UP AREAS

By 1841

By 1878

By 1900

Streetcar lines, c. 1898

Flow of river

lords tried to squeeze as many rent-paying residents as possible into the smallest available space. In Manhattan, for example, the average population density in 1894 was 143 people per acre—a higher rate than that of the most crowded cities of Europe (Paris had 127 per acre, Berlin 101) and far higher than in any other American city then or since. In some neighborhoods—the lower East Side, for example—density was more than 700 people per acre, among the highest levels in the world.

Landlords were reluctant to invest much in immigrant housing, confident they could rent dwellings for a profit regardless of their conditions. In the cities of the South—Charleston, New Orleans, Richmond—poor blacks lived in crumbling former slave quarters. In Boston, they moved into cheap three-story wooden houses ("triple deckers"), many of them decaying fire hazards. In Baltimore and Philadelphia, they crowded into narrow brick row houses. And in New York and many other cities, more than a million people lived in tenements.

The word "tenement" had originally referred simply to a multiple-family rental building, but by the late nineteenth century it was being used to describe slum dwellings only. The first tenements, built in 1850, had been hailed as a great improvement in housing for the poor. "It is built with the design of supplying the laboring people with cheap lodgings," a local newspaper commented, "and will have many advantages over the cellars and other miserable abodes which too many are forced to inhabit." But tenements themselves soon became "miserable abodes," with many windowless rooms, little or no plumbing or central heating, and perhaps a row of privies in the basement. A New York state law of 1870 required a window in every bedroom of tenements built after that date; developers complied by adding small, sunless air shafts to their buildings. Most of all, tenements were impossibly crowded, with three, four, and sometimes many more people crammed into each small room.

Jacob Riis, a Danish immigrant and New York newspaper reporter and photographer, shocked many

A NEW YORK TENEMENT, 1910
This photograph of a woman and her children in a rear
tenement bedroom was meant to illustrate the crowding
and squalor of urban immigrant life. The photographer
was Lewis Hine, who from 1907 to 1914 worked for a government committee investigating child labor and whose
efforts to expose social conditions helped spur legislative
action. He was also a pioneer in industrial photography
and created some of the classic early images of factory
production. *(George Eastman House)*

middle-class Americans with his sensational (and
some would say sensationalized) descriptions and pictures of tenement life in his 1890 book *How the Other
Half Lives.* Slum dwellings, he said, were almost universally sunless, practically airless, and "poisoned" by
"summer stenches." "The hall is dark and you might
stumble over the children pitching pennies back
there." But the solution many reformers (including
Riis) favored, and that governments sometimes
adopted, was to raze slum dwellings without building
any new housing to replace them.

Urban growth posed monumental transportation
challenges. Old downtown streets were often too narrow for the heavy traffic that was beginning to move
over them. Most were without a hard, paved surface
and resembled either a sea of mud or a cloud of dust,
depending on the weather. In the last decades of the

century, more and more streets were paved, usually
with wooden blocks, bricks, or asphalt; but paving
could not keep up with the number of new thorough-
fares the expanding cities were creating. By 1890,
Chicago had paved only about 600 of its more than
2,000 miles of streets.

But it was not simply the conditions of the streets
that impeded urban transportation. It was the numbers of people who needed to move every day from
one part of the city to another, numbers that mandated
the development of mass transportation. Streetcars
drawn on tracks by horses had been introduced into
some cities even before the Civil War. But the horse-
cars were not fast enough, so many communities developed new forms of mass transit. In 1870, New York
opened its first elevated railway, whose noisy, filthy
steam-powered trains moved rapidly above the city
streets on massive iron structures. New York, Chicago,
San Francisco, and other cities also experimented with
cable cars, towed by continuously moving underground cables. Richmond, Virginia, introduced the
first electric trolley line in 1888, and by 1895 such systems were operating in 850 towns and cities. Boston in
1897 opened the first American subway when it put
some of its trolley lines underground. At the same
time, cities were developing new techniques of road
and bridge building. One of the great technological
marvels of the 1880s was the completion of the Brooklyn Bridge in New York, a dramatic steel-cable suspension span designed by John A. Roebling.

Cities were growing upward as well as outward.
The first modern "skyscraper"—by later standards
a relatively modest building, ten stories high, constructed in Chicago in 1884—launched a new era in urban architecture. Once builders perfected the technique of constructing tall buildings with cast iron and
then steel beams, and once other inventors produced
the electric elevator, no obstacle remained to even
higher buildings. The greatest figure in the early development of the skyscraper was the Chicago architect Louis Sullivan, who introduced many of the modern, functional elements to the genre—large windows,
sheer lines, limited ornamentation—in an attempt to
emphasize the soaring height of the building as its
most distinctive feature. Sullivan's students, among
them Frank Lloyd Wright, expanded the influence of
these innovations still further and applied them to low
buildings as well as tall ones.

Strains of Urban Life

The increasing congestion of the cities and the absence
of adequate public services produced serious hazards.
One was fires. In one major city after another, fires destroyed large downtown areas, where many buildings

CHICAGO IN FLAMES
The great Chicago fire of 1871 (which legend attributes to a kerosene lantern kicked over by "Mrs. O'Leary's cow") devastated much of the central part of the city, just as great fires destroyed parts of other large cities (among them San Francisco and Boston) in the late nineteenth century. The fires were tragedies for those who lost their property or their lives; but they were opportunities for speculators and developers, who used the destruction as an opportunity to build new, "modern" city centers. *(Chicago Historical Society)*

were still constructed of wood. Chicago and Boston suffered "great fires" in 1871. Other cities—among them Baltimore and San Francisco, where a tremendous earthquake produced a catastrophic fire in 1906—experienced similar disasters. The great fires were terrible and deadly experiences, but they were also important events in the development of the cities involved. They encouraged the construction of fireproof buildings and the development of professional fire departments. They also forced cities to rebuild at a time when new technological and architectural innovations were available. Some of the modern, high-rise downtowns of American cities arose out of the rubble of great fires.

An even greater hazard than fire was disease, especially in poor neighborhoods with inadequate sanitation facilities. But an epidemic that began in a poor neighborhood could (and often did) spread easily into other neighborhoods as well. Few municipal officials recognized the relationship of improper sewage disposal and water contamination to such epidemic diseases as typhoid fever and cholera; and many cities lacked adequate systems for disposing of human waste until well into the twentieth century. Flush toilets and sewer systems began to appear in the 1870s, but they could not solve the problem as long as sewage continued to flow into open ditches or streams, polluting cities' water supplies.

Above all, perhaps, the expansion of the cities spawned widespread and often desperate poverty. Despite the rapid growth of urban economies, the sheer number of new residents ensured that many people would be unable to earn enough for a decent subsistence. Public agencies and private philanthropic or-

CITY STREETS
The unpaved streets of many major cities became almost impassable seas of mud after rain storms. The garbage and horse manure that accumulated with the mud also made them major health hazards. Some of the terrible epidemics of the late nineteenth century were a direct result of the unsanitary conditions in city streets. *(Library of Congress)*

ganizations offered very limited relief, and even they were generally dominated by middle-class people, who tended to believe that too much assistance would breed dependency and that poverty was the fault of the poor themselves—a result of laziness or alcoholism or other kinds of irresponsibility. Most tried to restrict aid to the "deserving poor"—those who truly could not help themselves (at least according to the standards of the organizations themselves, which conducted elaborate "investigations" to separate the "deserving" from the "undeserving"). Other charitable societies—for example, the Salvation Army, which began operating in America in 1879, one year after it was founded in London—concentrated more on religious revivalism than on the relief of the homeless and hungry. Tensions often arose between native Protestant philanthropists and Catholic immigrants over religious doctrine and standards of morality. Middle-class faith in the idea of self-improvement led to a widespread inattention to the structural roots of urban poverty. Middle-class people grew particularly alarmed over the rising number of poor children in the cities, some of them orphans or runaways, living alone or in small groups scrounging for food. These "street arabs," as they were often called, attracted more attention from reformers than

any other group—although that attention produced no lasting solutions to their problems.

Poverty and crowding naturally bred crime and violence. Much of it was relatively minor, the work of pickpockets, con artists, swindlers, and petty thieves. But some was more dangerous. The American murder rate rose rapidly in the late nineteenth century (even as such rates were declining in Europe), from 25 murders for every million people in 1880 to over 100 by the end of the century. That reflected in part a very high level of violence in some nonurban areas: the American South, where lynching and homicide were particularly high; and the West, where the rootlessness and instability of new communities (cow towns, mining camps, and the like) created much violence. But the cities contributed their share to the increase in crime as well. Native-born Americans liked to believe that crime was a result of the violent proclivities of immigrant groups, and they cited the rise of gangs and criminal organizations in various ethnic communities. But even in the cities, native-born Americans were as likely to commit crimes as immigrants. The rising crime rates encouraged many cities to develop larger and more professional police forces. But police forces themselves could spawn corruption and brutality, particularly since jobs on them were often filled through political patronage. Some members of the middle class, fearful of urban insurrections, felt the need for even more substantial forms of protection. Urban national guard groups (many of them created and manned by middle-class elites) built imposing armories on the outskirts of affluent neighborhoods and stored large supplies of weapons and ammunition in preparation for uprisings that, in fact, virtually never occurred.

Americans and Europeans alike reacted to life in the city with marked ambivalence. It was a place of strong allure and great excitement. Yet it was also a place of alienating impersonality, of a new feeling of anonymity, of a different kind of work with which the individual could feel only limited identification. To some, it was also a place of degradation and exploitation. Theodore Dreiser's novel *Sister Carrie* (1900) exposed one troubling aspect of urban life: the plight of single women (like Dreiser's heroine, Carrie) who moved from the countryside into the city and found themselves without any means of support. Carrie first took an exhausting and ill-paying job in a Chicago shoe factory, then drifted into a life of "sin," exploited by predatory men. Many women were experiencing in reality the dilemmas Carrie experienced in fiction. Living in conditions of extreme poverty and hardship, some moved into prostitution—which, degrading and dangerous as it was, also produced a livelihood and a sense of community for desperate people.

The Machine and the Boss

Newly arrived immigrants, many of whom could not speak English, needed help in adjusting to American urban life: its laws, its customs, usually its language. Some ethnic communities created their own self-help organizations. But for many residents of the inner cities, the principal source of assistance was the political machine.

The urban machine was one of America's most distinctive political institutions. It owed its existence to the power vacuum that the chaotic growth of cities (and the very limited growth of governments) had created. It was also a product of the potential voting power of large immigrant communities. Any politician who could mobilize that power stood to gain enormous influence, if not public office. And so there emerged a group of urban "bosses," themselves often of foreign birth or parentage. Many were Irish, because they spoke English and because some had acquired previous political experience from the long Irish struggle against the English at home. All were men (unsurprisingly, since in most states women could not yet vote).

The principal function of the political boss was simple: to win votes for his organization. That meant winning the loyalty of his constituents. To do so, a boss might provide them with occasional relief—baskets of groceries, bags of coal. He might step in to save those arrested for petty crimes from jail. When he could, he found jobs for the unemployed. Above all, he rewarded many of his followers with patronage: with jobs in city government or in such city agencies as the police (which the machine's elected officials often controlled); with jobs building or operating the new transit systems; and with opportunities to rise in the political organization itself.

Machines were also vehicles for making money. Politicians enriched themselves and their allies through various forms of graft and corruption. Some of it might be fairly open—what George Washington Plunkitt of New York's Tammany Hall called "honest graft." For example, a politician might discover in advance where a new road or streetcar line was to be built, buy an interest in the land near it, and profit when the city had to buy the land from him or when property values rose as a result of the construction. But there was also covert graft: kickbacks from contractors in exchange for contracts to build streets, sewers, public buildings, and other projects; the sale of franchises for the operation of such public utilities as street railways, waterworks, and electric light and power systems. The most famously corrupt city boss was William M. Tweed, boss of New York City's Tammany Hall in the 1860s and 1870s, whose excesses finally landed him in jail in 1872.

"KEEPING TAMMANY'S BOOTS SHINED," C. 1887
This lithograph by cartoonist Joseph Keppler shows the heavy foot of New York City's Tammany Hall sitting atop City Hall, while Hugh Grant, a Tammany sheriff later elected mayor, applies the patronage polish that was the organization's lifeblood. The strap dangling from the boot bears the name of Richard Croker, who emerged as one of Tammany's principal leaders after the fall of Boss Tweed and who served as the undisputed chief of the organization from 1886 until 1901. *(Bettmann)*

Middle-class critics saw the corrupt machines as blights on the cities and obstacles to progress. In fact, political organizations were responsible not just for corruption, but also for modernizing city infrastructures, for expanding the role of government, and for creating stability in a political and social climate that otherwise would have lacked a center. The motives of the bosses may have been largely venal, but their achievements were often greater than those of the more scrupulous reformers who challenged them.

Several factors made boss rule possible. One was the power of immigrant voters, who were less concerned with middle-class ideas of political morality than with obtaining the services that machines provided and reformers did not. Another was the link between the political organizations and wealthy, prominent citizens who profited from their dealings with bosses and resisted efforts to overthrow them. Still another was the structural weakness of city governments. Within the municipal government, no single official usually had decisive power or responsibility. Instead, authority was generally divided among many officeholders and was limited by the state legislature. The boss, by virtue of his control over his machine, formed an "invisible government" that provided an alternative to the inadequacy of the regular government. Through his organization, he might control a majority of those who were in office even if (as was usually the case) he did not hold public office himself.

The urban machine was not without competition. Reform groups frequently mobilized public outrage at the corruption of the bosses and often succeeded in driving machine politicians from office. Tammany, for example, saw its candidates for mayor and other high city offices lose almost as often as they won in the last decades of the nineteenth century. But the reform organizations typically lacked the permanence of the machine, and more often than not, their power faded after a few years. Thus, many critics of machines began to argue for more basic reforms: for structural changes in the nature of city government.

SOCIETY AND CULTURE IN URBANIZING AMERICA

For urban middle-class Americans, the last decades of the nineteenth century were a time of dramatic advances. Indeed, it was in those years that a distinctive middle-class culture began to exert a powerful influence over the whole of American life. Much of the rest of American society—the majority of the population, which was neither urban nor middle class—advanced less rapidly or not at all; but almost no one was unaffected by the rise of the new urban, consumer culture.

The Rise of Mass Consumption

The growth of American industry could not have occurred without the expansion of markets for the goods being produced. Much of the emerging mass market for industrial goods consisted of the increasingly wealthy middle class. But much of it consisted of less affluent people, who consumed more because their incomes were increasing too, even if modestly, and because mass production and mass distribution were making consumer goods less expensive.

Incomes in the industrial era were rising for almost everyone, although at highly uneven rates. While the most conspicuous result of the new economy was the creation of vast fortunes, more important for society as a whole was the growth and increasing prosperity of the middle class. The salaries of clerks, accountants, middle managers, and other "white collar" workers rose on average by a third between 1890 and 1910—and in some parts of the middle class salaries rose by much more. Doctors, lawyers, and other professionals, for example, experienced a particularly dramatic increase in both the prestige and the profitability of their professions. Working-class incomes rose too in those years, although from a much lower base and considerably more slowly. Iron and steel workers, despite the setbacks their unions suffered, saw their hourly wages increase by a third between 1890 and 1910; but industries with large female, African-American, or Mexican work forces—shoes, textiles, paper, laundries, many areas of commercial agriculture—saw very small increases, as did almost all industries in the South. Still, even some workers in these industries experienced a rise in family income because women and children often worked to supplement the husband's and father's earnings, or because families took in boarders or laundry or otherwise supplemented their incomes.

Also important to the new mass market was the development of affordable products and the creation of new merchandising techniques, which made many consumer goods available to a broad market for the first time. A good example of such changes was the emergence of ready-made clothing. In the early nineteenth century, most Americans had made their own clothing—usually from cloth they bought from merchants, at times from fabrics they spun and wove themselves. More affluent people contracted with private tailors to make their clothes. But the invention of the sewing machine and the spur that the Civil War (and its demand for uniforms) gave to the manufacture of clothing created an enormous industry devoted to producing ready-made garments. By the end of the century, virtually all Americans bought their clothing from stores. Partly as a result, much larger numbers of people became concerned with personal style. Interest in women's fashion, for example, had once been a luxury reserved for the relatively affluent. Now middle-class and even working-class women could strive to develop a distinctive style of dress.

Another example of the rise of the mass market was the way Americans bought and prepared food. The development and mass production of tin cans in the 1880s created a large new industry devoted to packaging and selling canned food and (as a result of the techniques Gail Borden discovered in the 1850s) condensed milk. Refrigerated railroad cars made it possible for perishables—meats, vegetables, dairy products, and other foodstuffs—to travel over long distances without spoiling. The development of artificially frozen ice made it possible for many more households to afford iceboxes. Among other things, the changes

THE DEPARTMENT STORE, C. 1892
This detail from an advertisement shows an interior cross section of the Abraham and Straus department store in Brooklyn, New York. Early department stores boasted not just of the amount and variety of their merchandise but also of the magical qualities of the consumer world they created. *(New-York Historical Society)*

meant improved diets and better health; life expectancy rose six years in the first two decades of the twentieth century.

Changes in marketing also altered the way Americans bought goods. Small local stores faced competition from new "chain stores." The Great Atlantic & Pacific Tea Company (the A & P) began creating a national network of grocery stores in the 1870s. F. W. Woolworth built a chain of dry goods stores. Sears Roebuck established a large market for its mail-order merchandise by distributing an enormous catalog each year. Even people in remote rural areas could order its products.

In larger cities, the emergence of great department stores (which had appeared earlier in Europe) helped transform buying habits and turn shopping into a more alluring and glamorous activity. Marshall Field in Chicago created one of the first American department stores—a place deliberately designed to create a sense of wonder and excitement. Similar stores emerged elsewhere: Macy's in New York, Abraham and Straus in Brooklyn, Jordan Marsh and Filene's in Boston, Wanamaker's in Philadelphia.

The rise of mass consumption had particularly dramatic effects on American women, who were generally the primary consumers within families. Women's clothing styles changed much more rapidly and dra-

matically than men's, which encouraged more frequent purchases. Women generally bought and prepared food for their families, so the availability of new food products changed not only the way everyone ate, but also the way women shopped and cooked. Canning and refrigeration meant greater variety in the diet. It also meant that food did not always have to be purchased on the day it was eaten. The consumer economy produced new employment opportunities for women as sales clerks in department stores and as waitresses in the rapidly proliferating restaurants. And it spawned the creation of a new movement in which women were to play a vital role: the consumer protection movement. The National Consumers League, formed in the 1890s under the leadership of Florence Kelley, attempted to mobilize the power of women as consumers to force retailers and manufacturers to improve wages and working conditions.

Leisure and Sport

Closely related to the growth of consumption was an increasing interest in leisure time, which for many people was expanding rapidly. Members of the urban middle and professional classes had large blocks of time in which they were not at work—evenings, weekends, even vacations (previously almost unknown

THE AMERICAN NATIONAL GAME
Long before the modern major leagues began, local baseball clubs were active throughout much of the United States establishing the game as the "national pastime." This print of a "grand match for the championship" depicts an 1866 game at Elysian Fields, a popular park just across the river from New York City in Hoboken, New Jersey. (*National Baseball Library, Cooperstown, N.Y.*)

among salaried workers). Working hours in many factories declined, from an average of nearly seventy hours a week in 1860 to under sixty in 1900. Even farmers found that the mechanization of agriculture gave them more free time. The lives of many Americans were becoming compartmentalized, with clear distinctions between work and leisure that had not existed in the past. The change produced a search for new forms of recreation and entertainment.

Among the responses to this search was the rise of organized spectator sports, and especially baseball, which by the end of the century was well on its way to becoming the "national pastime." A game much like baseball, known as "rounders" and derived from cricket, had enjoyed limited popularity in Great Britain in the early nineteenth century. Versions of the game began to appear in America in the early 1830s, well before Abner Doubleday supposedly "invented" baseball. (Doubleday, in fact, had almost nothing to do with the creation of baseball and actually cared little for sports. Alexander Cartwright, a member of a New York City baseball club, defined many of the rules and features of the game as we know it today in the 1840s.)

By the end of the Civil War, interest in baseball had grown rapidly. More than 200 amateur or semiprofessional teams or clubs existed, many of which joined a national association and agreed on standard rules. As the game grew in popularity, it became a source of profit. The first salaried team, the Cincinnati Red Stockings, was formed in 1869. Other cities soon fielded professional teams, and in 1876, at the urging of Albert Spalding, they banded together in the National League. A rival league, the American Association, soon appeared. It eventually collapsed, but in 1901 the American League emerged to replace it. In 1903, the first modern World Series was played, in which the American League Boston Red Sox beat the National League Pittsburgh Pirates. By then, baseball had become an important business and a great national preoccupation (at least among men), attracting paying crowds at times as large as 50,000.

Baseball had great appeal to working-class males. Baseball players tended to be men from modest backgrounds, and in the beginning at least, baseball crowds were made up largely of male urban laborers. The second most popular game, football, appealed at first to a more elite segment of the male population, in part because it originated in colleges and universities. The first intercollegiate football game in America occurred between Princeton and Rutgers in 1869, and soon the game began to become entrenched as part of collegiate life. Early intercollegiate football bore only an indirect relation to the modern game; it was more similar to what is now known as rugby. By the late 1870s, however, the game was becoming standardized and was taking on the outlines of its modern form.

As college football grew in popularity, it spread to other sections of the country, notably to the midwestern state universities, which were destined soon to replace the eastern schools as the great powers of the game. It also began to exhibit the taints of professionalism that have marked it ever since. Some schools used "ringers," tramp athletes who were not even registered as students. In an effort to eliminate such abuses, Amos Alonzo Stagg, athletic director and coach at the University of Chicago, led in forming the Western Conference, or Big Ten, in 1896, which established rules governing eligibility. Football also became known for a high level of violence on the field; eighteen college students died of football-related injuries and over a hundred were seriously hurt in 1905. The carnage prompted a White House conference on organized sports convened by President Theodore Roosevelt. As a result of its deliberations, a new intercollegiate association (which in 1910 became known as the National College Athletic Association, the NCAA) revised the rules of the game in an effort to make it safer and more honest.

Other popular spectator sports were emerging at about the same time. Basketball was invented in 1891 at Springfield, Massachusetts, by Dr. James A. Naismith, a Canadian working as athletic director for a local college. Boxing, which had long been a disreputable activity concentrated primarily among the urban lower classes, became by the 1880s a more popular and in some places more reputable sport, particularly after the adoption of the Marquis of Queensberry rules (by which fighters wore padded gloves and fought in three-minute rounds). The first modern boxing hero, John L. Sullivan, became heavyweight champion of the world in 1882. Even so, boxing remained illegal in some states until after World War I.

The major spectator sports of the era were activities open almost exclusively to men. But a number of other sports were emerging in which women became important participants. Golf and tennis seldom attracted crowds in the late nineteenth century, but both experienced a rapid increase in participation among relatively wealthy men and women. Bicycling and croquet also enjoyed widespread popularity in the 1890s among women as well as men. Women's colleges were beginning to introduce their students to more strenuous sports as well—track, crew, swimming, and (beginning in the late 1890s) basketball—challenging the once prevalent notion that vigorous exercise was dangerous to women.

Leisure and Popular Culture

Other forms of popular entertainment developed in the cities in response to the large potential markets there.

Many ethnic communities maintained their own theaters, in which immigrants listened to the music of their homelands and heard comedians making light of their experiences in the New World. Urban theaters also introduced one of the most distinctively American entertainment forms: the musical comedy, which evolved gradually from the comic operettas of European theater. George M. Cohan, an Irish vaudeville entertainer, became the first great creator of musical comedies in the early twentieth century; in the process of creating his many shows, he wrote a series of patriotic songs—"Yankee Doodle Dandy," "Over There," and "You're a Grand Old Flag"—that remained popular many decades later.

Vaudeville, a form of theater adapted from French models, was the most popular urban entertainment in the first decades of the twentieth century. Even saloons and small community theaters could afford to offer their customers vaudeville, which consisted of a variety of acts (musicians, comedians, magicians, jugglers, and others) and was, at least in the beginning, inexpensive to produce. As the economic potential of vaudeville grew, some promoters—most prominently Florenz Ziegfeld of New York—staged much more elaborate spectacles.

Vaudeville was also one of the few entertainment media open to black performers. They brought to it elements of the minstrel shows they had earlier developed for black audiences in the late nineteenth century. Some minstrel singers (including the most famous, Al Jolson) were whites wearing heavy makeup (or "blackface"). But most were black. Performers of both races performed music based on the gospel and folk tunes of the plantation and on the jazz and ragtime of black urban communities. Performers of both races also tailored their acts to prevailing white prejudices, ridiculing blacks by acting out demeaning stereotypes.

The most important form of mass entertainment (until the invention of radio and television), and the one that reached most widely across the nation, was the movies. Thomas Edison and others had created the technology of the motion picture in the 1880s. Not long after, short films became available to individual viewers through "peep shows" in pool halls, penny arcades, and amusement parks. Soon larger projectors made it possible to project the images onto big screens, which permitted substantial audiences to see films in theaters. By 1900, Americans were becoming attracted in large numbers to these early movies—usually plotless films of trains or waterfalls or other spectacles designed mainly to show off the technology. D. W. Griffith carried the motion picture into a new era with his silent epics—*The Birth of a Nation* (1915), *Intolerance* (1916), and others—which introduced serious plots and elaborate productions to filmmaking. Some of them also contained notoriously racist messages, an indication, among other things, that the audiences for these early films were overwhelmingly white. Motion pictures were the first truly mass entertainment medium, reaching all areas of the country and almost all groups in the population.

Particularly striking about popular entertainment in the late nineteenth and early twentieth centuries was its public quality. Americans of diverse classes and backgrounds spent their leisure time in places where they would find not only entertainment, but also other people. Thousands of working-class New Yorkers flocked to the amusement park at Coney Island, for example, not just for the rides and shows, but for the excitement of the crowds, as did the thousands who spent evenings in dance halls, vaudeville houses, and concert halls. More affluent New Yorkers enjoyed afternoons in Central Park, where a principal attraction was seeing other people (and being seen by them). Moviegoers were attracted not just by the movies themselves, but by the energy of the audiences at the lavish "movie palaces" that began to appear in cities in the early twentieth century, just as sports fans were drawn by the crowds as well as by the games.

Mass entertainment did not always bridge differences of class or race; there were relatively few places where people of widely diverse backgrounds gathered together. When the classes did meet in public spaces—as they did, for example, in city parks—there was often considerable conflict over what constituted appropriate public behavior. Elites in New York City, for example, tried to prohibit anything but quiet, "genteel" activities in Central Park, while working-class people wanted to use the public spaces for sports and entertainments. But even divided by class, leisure and popular entertainment did help sustain a vigorous public culture.

Not all popular entertainment, however, involved public events. Many Americans amused themselves privately by reading novels and poetry. The so-called dime novels, cheaply bound and widely circulated, became popular after the Civil War, with tales of the Wild West, detective stories, sagas of scientific adventure (such as the Tom Swift stories), and novels of "moral uplift" (among them those of Horatio Alger). Publishers also distributed sentimental novels of romance, which developed a large audience among women, as did books about animals and about young children growing up. Louisa May Alcott's *Little Women,* most of whose readers were women, sold more than 2 million copies.

Mass Communications

Urban industrial society created a vast market for new vehicles for transmitting news and information. And so American publishing and journalism experienced an important change in the decades following the Civil War. Between 1870 and 1910, the circulation of daily newspapers increased nearly ninefold (from under 3 million to more than 24 million), a rate three times as great as the rate of population increase. And while standards varied widely from one paper to another, American journalism began to develop the beginnings of a professional identity. Salaries of reporters increased; many newspapers began separating the reporting of news from the expression of opinion; and newspapers themselves became important businesses.

One striking change was the emergence of national press services, which made use of the telegraph to supply news and features to papers throughout the country and which contributed as a result to the standardization of the product. By the turn of the century important newspaper chains had emerged as well. The most powerful was William Randolph Hearst's, which by 1914 controlled nine newspapers and two magazines. Hearst and rival publisher Joseph Pulitzer helped popularize what became known as "yellow journalism"—a deliberately sensational, often lurid style of reporting presented in bold graphics, designed to reach a mass audience. Another major change occurred in the nature of American magazines. Beginning in the 1880s, a new kind of magazine appeared, also designed for a mass audience. One of the pioneers was Edward W. Bok, who took over the *Ladies' Home Journal* in 1899 and, by targeting a mass female audience, built its circulation to over 700,000.

HIGH CULTURE IN THE AGE OF THE CITY

In addition to the important changes in popular culture that accompanied the rise of cities and industry, there were profound changes in the realm of "high culture"—in the ideas and activities of intellectuals and elites. Even the notion of a distinction between "highbrow" and "lowbrow" culture was relatively new to the industrial era. In the early nineteenth century, most cultural activities attracted people of widely varying backgrounds and targeted people of all classes. By the late nineteenth century, however, elites were developing a cultural and intellectual life quite separate from the popular amusements of the urban masses.

The Literature of Urban America

Many foreign observers and even some Americans in the late nineteenth century viewed the culture of the United States with contempt. Critics claimed that American life, despite its glittering surface, was essentially acquisitive and corrupt, with little cultural depth. But whatever the quality of culture and society in late-nineteenth-century America, the growth of industry and the rise of the city were having profound effects on them. Some writers and artists—the local-color writers of the South, for example, and Mark Twain, in such novels as *Huckleberry Finn* and *Tom Sawyer*—responded to the new civilization by evoking an older, more natural world. But others grappled directly with the modern order.

One of the strongest impulses in late-nineteenth- and early-twentieth-century American literature was the effort to re-create urban social reality. This trend toward realism found an early voice in Stephen Crane, who—although best known for his novel of the Civil War, *The Red Badge of Courage* (1895)—was the author of an earlier, powerful indictment of the plight of the working class. Crane created a sensation in 1893 when he published *Maggie: A Girl of the Streets*, a grim picture of urban poverty and slum life. Theodore Dreiser was even more influential in encouraging writers to abandon the genteel traditions of earlier times and turn to the social dislocations and injustices of the present. He did so both in *Sister Carrie* and in other, later novels (including *An American Tragedy*, perhaps his greatest work, published in 1925).

Many of Dreiser's contemporaries followed him in chronicling the oppression of America's poor. In 1901 Frank Norris published *The Octopus*, an account of a struggle between oppressed wheat ranchers and powerful railroad interests in California. Upton Sinclair's *The Jungle* (1906) exposed abuses in the American meat-packing industry and helped inspire legislative action to deal with the problem. Kate Chopin, a southern writer who explored the oppressive features of traditional marriage, encountered widespread public abuse after publication of her shocking novel *The Awakening* in 1899. It described a young wife and mother who abandoned her family in search of personal fulfillment. It was formally banned in some communities. William Dean Howells, in *The Rise of Silas Lapham* (1884) and other works, described what he considered the shallowness and corruption in ordinary American lifestyles.

Other critics of American society responded to the new civilization not by attacking it but by withdrawing from it. The historian Henry Adams published an autobiography in 1906, *The Education of Henry Adams*, in which he portrayed himself as a man disillusioned with and unable to relate to his society, even though he continued to live in it. The novelist Henry James lived the major part of his adult life in England and Europe and produced a series of coldly realistic novels—*The American* (1877), *Portrait of a Lady* (1881), *The Ambassadors* (1903), and others—that showed his ambivalence about the merits of both American and European civilization.

Art in the Age of the City

American art through most of the nineteenth century had been overshadowed by the art of Europe. By 1900, however, a number of American artists, although some continued to study and even live in Europe, broke from the Old World traditions and experimented with new styles. Winslow Homer was vigorously American in his paintings of New England maritime life and other native subjects. James McNeil Whistler was one of the first Western artists to appreciate the beauty of Japanese color prints and to introduce Oriental concepts into American and European art.

By the first years of the new century, some American artists were turning decisively away from the traditional academic style, a style perhaps best exemplified in America by the brilliant portraitist John Singer Sargent. Instead, many younger painters were exploring the same grim aspects of modern life that were becoming the subject of American literature. Members of the so-called Ashcan School produced work startling in its naturalism and stark in its portrayal of the social realities of the era. John Sloan portrayed the dreariness of American urban slums; George Bellows caught the vigor and violence of his time in paintings and drawings of prize fights; Edward Hopper explored the starkness and loneliness of the modern city. The Ashcan artists were also among the first Americans to appreciate expressionism and abstraction; and they showed their interest in new forms in 1913 when they helped stage the famous and controversial "Armory Show" in New York City, which displayed works of the French post-impressionists and of some American moderns.

The work of these and other artists marked the beginning in America of an artistic movement known as modernism, a movement that had counterparts in many other areas of cultural and intellectual life as well. Rejecting the heavy reliance on established forms that characterized the "genteel tradition" of the nineteenth-century art world, modernists rejected the past and embraced new subjects and new forms. Where the genteel tradition emphasized the "dignified" and

HAIRDRESSER'S WINDOW
This 1907 painting is by John Sloan, an American artist who belonged to the so-called Ashcan School. Sloan and others were in revolt against what they considered the sterile formalism of academic painting and chose instead to portray realistic scenes of ordinary life. In 1913 they stirred the art world with a startling exhibition in New York, known as the Armory Show. In it they displayed not only their own work (which was relatively conventional in technique, even if sometimes daring in its choice of subjects) but also the work of innovative European artists, who were already beginning to explore wholly new artistic forms. *(Wadsworth Atheneum, Hartford)*

"elevated" aspects of civilization (and glorified the achievements of gifted elites), modernism gloried in the ordinary, even the coarse. Where the genteel tradition placed great importance on respect for the past and the maintenance of "standards," modernism looked to the future and gloried in the new. Eventually, modernism developed strict orthodoxies of its own. But in its early stages, it seemed to promise an escape from rigid, formal traditions and an unleashing of individual creativity.

The Impact of Darwinism

The single most profound intellectual development in the late nineteenth century was the widespread acceptance of the theory of evolution, associated most prominently with the English naturalist Charles Darwin. Darwinism argued that the human species had evolved from earlier forms of life (and most recently from simian creatures similar to apes) through a process of "natural selection." It challenged the biblical story of the Creation and almost every other tenet of traditional American religious faith. History, Darwinism suggested, was not the working out of a divine plan, as most Americans had always believed. It was a random process dominated by the fiercest or luckiest competitors.

The theory of evolution met widespread resistance at first from educators, theologians, and even many scientists. By the end of the century, however, the evolutionists had converted most members of the urban professional and educated classes. Even many middle-

DEMPSEY AND FIRPO
The artist George Bellows began paint-ing fight scenes in the first years of the twentieth century, when boxing appealed primarily to working-class urban communities. By 1924, when he painted this view of the Dempsey-Firpo fight, prizefighting had become one of the most popular sports in America. *(Whitney Museum of American Art, New York; gift of Gertrude Vanderbilt Whitney)*

class Protestant religious leaders had accepted the doc-trine, making significant alterations in theology to ac-commodate it. Evolution had become enshrined in schools and universities; virtually no serious scientist any longer questioned its basic validity.

Unseen by most urban Americans at the time, how-ever, the rise of Darwinism was contributing to a deep schism between the new, cosmopolitan culture of the city—which was receptive to new ideas such as evo-lution—and a more traditional, provincial culture located mainly (although not wholly) in rural areas—which remained wedded to more fundamentalist reli-gious beliefs and older values. Thus the late nineteenth century saw not only the rise of a liberal Protestantism in tune with new scientific discoveries. It also saw the beginning of an organized Protestant fundamentalism, which would make its presence felt politically in the 1920s and again in the 1980s.

Darwinism helped spawn other new intellectual currents. There was the Social Darwinism of William Graham Sumner and others, which industrialists used so enthusiastically to justify their favored position in American life. But there were also more sophisticated philosophies, among them a doctrine that became known as "pragmatism," which seemed peculiarly a product of America's changing material civilization. William James, a Harvard psychologist and brother of the novelist Henry James, was the most prominent publicist of the new theory, although earlier intellec-tuals such as Charles S. Peirce and later ones such as John Dewey were also important to its development and dissemination. According to the pragmatists, mod-ern society should rely for guidance not on inherited ideals and moral principles but on the test of scientific inquiry. No idea or institution (not even religious faith) was valid, they claimed, unless it worked and unless

CHARLES DARWIN
Darwin's theories of natural selection, or evolution, revolutionized biological science. They also had a stunning impact on religious and even social thought. By challenging large parts of traditional religion and by suspecting that species were changeable, Darwinism opened the way for decades of theological controversy and for a series of spurious applications of his ideas to contemporary social problems. *(Bettmann)*

it stood the test of experience. "The ultimate test for us of what a truth means," James wrote, "is the conduct it dictates or inspires."

A similar concern for scientific inquiry was intruding into the social sciences and challenging traditional orthodoxies. Economists such as Richard T. Ely and Simon Patten argued for a more active and pragmatic use of scientific discipline. Sociologists such as Edward A. Ross and Lester Frank Ward urged applying the scientific method to the solution of social and political problems. Historians such as Frederick Jackson Turner and Charles Beard argued that economic factors more than spiritual ideals had been the governing force in historical development. John Dewey proposed a new approach to education that placed less emphasis on the rote learning of traditional knowledge and more on a flexible, democratic approach to schooling, one that enabled students to acquire knowledge that would help them deal with the realities of their society.

The relativistic implications of Darwinism also promoted the growth of anthropology and encouraged some scholars to begin examining other cultures— most significantly, perhaps, the culture of American Indians—in new ways. A few white Americans began to look at Indian society as a coherent culture with its own norms and values that were worthy of respect and preservation, even though different from those of white society. But such ideas about native Americans found very little support outside a few corners of the intellectual world until much later in the twentieth century.

Toward Universal Schooling

A society that was coming to depend increasingly on specialized skills and scientific knowledge was, of course, a society with a high demand for education. The late nineteenth century, therefore, was a time of rapid expansion and reform of American schools and universities.

One example was the spread of free public primary and secondary education. In 1860, there were only 100 public high schools in the entire United States. By 1900, the number had reached 6,000 and by 1914 over 12,000. By 1900, compulsory school attendance laws were in effect in thirty-one states and territories. But education was still far from universal. Rural areas lagged far behind urban-industrial ones in funding public education. And in the South, many blacks had access to no schools at all.

Educational reformers, few of whom shared the more relativistic views of anthropologists, sought to provide educational opportunities for the Indian tribes as well, in an effort to "civilize" them and help them adapt to white society. In the 1870s, reformers recruited small groups of Indians to attend Hampton Institute, a primarily black college. In 1879, Richard Henry Pratt, a former army officer, organized the Carlisle Indian Industrial School in Pennsylvania. Like many black colleges, Carlisle emphasized the kind of practical "industrial" education that Booker T. Washington had urged on blacks. Equally important, it isolated Indians from their tribes and tried to force them to assimilate to white norms. The purpose, Pratt said, was to "kill the Indian and save the man." Carlisle spawned other, similar schools in the West. The tribes themselves resisted this new approach to Indian education, both because of the hostility of the white educators to tribal culture and because the schools were often dreary and dangerous places. Ultimately, the reform efforts failed, although less because of Indian resistance than because of inadequate funding, incompetent administration, and poor teaching.

Colleges and universities were also proliferating rapidly in the late nineteenth century. They benefited particularly from the Morrill Land Grant Act of the

SIGNIFICANT EVENTS

1836 Mount Holyoke College founded as seminary for women

1839 Abner Doubleday establishes rules for baseball

1865 Vassar College founded

1869 Princeton and Rutgers play first intercollegiate football game

1870 New York City opens elevated railroads

Wellesley College founded

1871 Great fires destroy much of Chicago and Boston

Smith College founded

1872 Tammy's Boss Tweed convicted of corruption

1876 Baseball's National League founded

Johns Hopkins University creates first modern graduate school

1879 Carlisle Indian Industrial School founded in Pennsylvania

1882 Congress restricts Chinese Immigration

1884 First "skyscraper" built in Chicago

William Dean Howells publishes *The Rise of Silas Lapham*

1887 American Protective Association founded

1890 Jacob Riis publishes *How the Other Half Lives*

1891 James Naismith invents basketball

1894 Immigration Restriction League founded

1895 Stephen Crane publishes *The Red Badge of Courage*

1897 Boston opens first subway in America

1899 Kate Chopin publishes *The Awakening*

1900 Theodore Dreiser publishes *Sister Carrie*

1901 Baseball's American League founded

1903 Boston Red Sox win first World Series

Henry James publishes *The Ambassadors*

1906 Earthquake and fire destroy much of San Francisco

Upton Sinclair publishes *The Jungle*

1910 National College Athletic Association founded to regulate collegiate football

1913 Ashcan School artists stage Armory Show in New York City

---

Civil War era, by which the federal government had donated land to states for the establishment of colleges. After 1865, states in the South and West took particular advantage of the law. In all, sixty-nine "land-grant" institutions were established in the last decades of the century—among them the state university systems of California, Illinois, Minnesota, and Wisconsin. Other universities benefited from millions of dollars contributed by business and financial tycoons. Rockefeller, Carnegie, and others gave generously to such schools as Columbia, Chicago, Harvard, Northwestern, Princeton, Syracuse, and Yale. Other philanthropists founded new universities or reorganized and renamed older ones to perpetuate their family names—Vanderbilt, Johns Hopkins, Cornell, Duke, Tulane, and Stanford.

Education for Women

The post-Civil War era saw, too, an important expansion of educational opportunities for women, although such opportunities continued to lag far behind those available to men and were almost always denied to black women.

Most public high schools accepted women readily, but opportunities for higher education were few. At the end of the Civil War, only three American colleges were coeducational. In the years after the war, many of the land-grant colleges and universities in the Middle West and such private universities as Cornell and Wesleyan began to admit women along with men. But coeducation played a less crucial role in the education of women in this period than the creation of a network of women's colleges. Mount Holyoke, which had begun its life in 1836 as a "seminary" for women, became a full-fledged college in the 1880s. At about the same time, entirely new female institutions were emerging: Vassar, Wellesley, Smith, Bryn Mawr, Wells, and Goucher. A few of the larger private universities created separate colleges for women on their campuses (Barnard at Columbia and Radcliffe at Harvard, for example). Proponents of women's colleges saw the institutions as places where female students would not be treated as "second-class citizens" by predominantly male student bodies and faculties.

The female college was part of an important phenomenon in the history of modern American women: the emergence of a distinctive women's community. Most faculty members and many administrators were women (usually unmarried). And the life of the college produced a spirit of sorority and commitment among educated women that had important effects in later years, as women became the leaders of many reform activities. Most female college graduates ultimately married, but they married at a later age than their non-college-educated counterparts and in some cases continued to pursue careers after marriage and motherhood. A significant minority, perhaps over 25 percent, did not marry at all, but devoted themselves exclusively to careers. A leader at Bryn Mawr remarked, "Our failures marry." That was surely hyperbole. But the growth of female higher education clearly became for some women a liberating experience, persuading them that they had roles to perform in society in addition to those of wives and mothers.

SUGGESTED READINGS

General Histories. Howard Chudacoff, *The Evolution of American Urban Society*, rev. ed. (1981). Charles N. Glaab and Andrew T. Brown, *A History of Urban America* (1967). Constance M. Green, *The Rise of Urban America* (1965). Blake McKelvey, *The Urbanization of America* (1963). Lewis Mumford, *The Culture of the Cities* (1938); *The City in History* (1961). Arthur M. Schlesinger, *The Rise of the City, 1878–1898* (1933). Jon C. Teaford, *City and Suburb: The Political Fragmentation of Urban America* (1979); *The Twentieth-Century American City: Problem, Promise, and Reality* (1986). Sam Bass Warner, Jr., *The Urban Wilderness* (1972); *Streetcar Suburbs* (1962).

Mobility and Race. Howard Chudacoff, *Mobile Americans: Residential and Social Mobility in Omaha, 1880–1920* (1972). Michael Frisch, *Town into City* (1972). Clyde Griffen and Sally Griffen, *Natives and Newcomers* (1977). Gerald D. Jaynes, *Branches Without Roots: Genesis of the Black Working Class in the American South, 1862–1882* (1986). David M. Katzman, *Before the Ghetto* (1966). Kenneth L. Kusmer, *A Ghetto Takes Shape* (1976). Roger Lane, *The Roots of Black Violence in Philadelphia, 1860–1900* (1986). Gilbert Osofsky, *Harlem: The Making of a Ghetto* (1966). Richard Sennett, *Families Against the City* (1970). Allan H. Spear, *Black Chicago (1967)*. Stephan Thernstrom, *Poverty and Progress* (1964); *The Other Bostonians* (1973). Stephan Thernstrom and Richard Sennett, eds., *Nineteenth Century Cities* (1969). Olivier Zunz, *The Changing Face of Inequality: Urbanization, Industrial Development, and Immigrants in Detroit, 1880–1920* (1982).

Immigration. Thomas J. Archdeacon, *Becoming American: An Ethnic History* (1983). Josef Barton, *Peasants and Strangers: Italians, Rumanians, and Slovaks in an American City* (1975). John Bodnar, *The Transplanted: A History of Immigrants in America* (1985); *Immigration and Industrialization* (1977). John W. Briggs, *An Italian Passage* (1978). Jack Chen, *The Chinese of America* (1980). Robert D. Cross, *The Church and the City* (1967). Leonard Dinnerstein and David Reimers, *Ethnic Americans: A History of Immigration and Assimilation* (1975). John B. Duff, *The Irish in the United States* (1971). Elizabeth Ewen, *Immigrant Women in the Land of Dollars: Life and Culture on the Lower East Side, 1890–1925* (1985). Lawrence H. Fuchs, *The American Kaleidoscope: Race, Ethnicity, and the Civic Culture* (1990). Mario T. Garcia, *Desert Immigrants: The Mexicans of El Paso, 1880–1920* (1981). Nathan Glazer and Daniel P. Moynihan, *Beyond the Melting Pot* (1963). Susan A. Glenn, *Daughters of the Shtetl: Life and Labor in the Immigrant Generation* (1990). Milton M. Gordon, *Assimilation in American Life* (1964). Victor Greene, *For God and Country: The Rise of Polish and Lithuanian Ethic Consciousness in America* (1975). Oscar Handlin, *The Uprooted*, rev. ed. (1973). Marcus Hansen, *The Immigrant in American History* (1940). John Higham, *Strangers in the Land* (1955); *Send These To Me: Jews and Other Immigrants in Urban America* (1975). John Higham, ed., *Ethnic Leadership in America* (1978). Francis L. K. Hsu, *The Challenge of the American Dream: The Chinese in the United States* (1971). Maldwyn A. Jones, *American Immigration* (1960). Edward R. Kantowicz, *Polish-American Politics in Chicago* (1975). Thomas Kessner, *The Golden Door: Italian and Jewish Immigrant Mobility* (1977). Harry Kitano, *Japanese-Americans: The Evolution of a Subculture* (1969). Alan M. Kraut, *The Huddled Masses: The Immigrant in American Society, 1880–1921* (1982). Matt S. Maier and Feliciano Rivera, *The Chicanos: A History of Mexican-Americans* (1972). Gwendolyn Mink, *Old Labor and New Immigrants in American Political Development: Union, Party, and State, 1875–1920* (1986). Ewa Morawska, *For Bread and Butter: The Life-Worlds of East Central Europeans in Johnstown, Pennsylvania, 1890–1940* (1985). Stanley Nadel, *Ethnicity, Religion, and Class in New York City, 1845–1880* (1990). Humbert S. Nelli, *The Italians of Chicago* (1970). Moses Rischin, *The Promised City: New York's Jews* (1962). Barbara Solomon, *Ancestors and Im-*

migrants (1965). Thomas Sowell, *Ethnic America* (1981). Philip Taylor, *The Distant Magnet: European Emigration to the U.S.A.* (1971). David Ward, *Cities and Immigrants* (1965). Virginia Yans-McLaughlin, *Family and Community: Italian Immigrants in Buffalo, 1880–1930* (1977).

Urban Poverty and Reform. Robert H. Bremner, *From the Depths* (1956). Stephan F. Brumberg, *Going to America, Going to School* (1986). James H. Cassedy, *Charles V. Chapin and the Public Health Movement* (1962). Allen F. Davis, *Spearheads for Reform* (1967). Barbara Gutmann Rosencrantz, *Public Health and the State* (1972). Marvin Lazerson, *Origins of the Urban School* (1971). James T. Patterson, *America's Struggle Against Poverty* (1981). Thomas L. Philpott, *The Slum and the Ghetto* (1978). James F. Richardson, *The New York Police* (1970). Jacob Riis, *How the Other Half Lives* (1890); *Children of the Poor* (1892); *The Battle with the Slum* (1902). Selwyn K. Troen, *The Public and the Schools* (1975). David B. Tyack, *The One Best System: A History of American Urban Education* (1974).

Urban Politics. John M. Allswang, *Bosses, Machines and Urban Voters* (1977). Alexander B. Callow, *The Tweed Ring* (1966). Brian J. Cudahy, *Cash, Tokens, and Transfers: A History of Urban Mass Transit in North America* (1990). Lyle Dorsett, *The Pendergast Machine* (1968). Lori Ginzberg, *Women and the Work of Benevolence: Morality, Politics, and Class in the Nineteenth-Century United States* (1990). Roger Lane, *Policing the City: Boston, 1822–1885* (1967). Seymour Mandelbaum, *Boss Tweed's New York* (1965). Christine M. Rosen, *The Limits of Power: Great Fires and the Process of City Growth in America* (1986). John Sproat, *The Best Men* (1968). Zane L. Miller, *Boss Cox's Cincinnati: Urban Politics in the Progressive Era* (1968).

Social Thought and Urban Culture. Martha Banta, *Imaging American Women: Idea and Ideals in Cultural History* (1987). Stuart Blumin, *The Emergence of the Middle Class: Social Experience in the American City, 1760–1900* (1989). Gunther Barth, *City People: The Rise of Modern City Culture in Nineteenth-Century America* (1980); *Instant Cities: Urbanization and the Rise of San Francisco and Denver* (1975). Susan Porter Benson, *Counter Cultures: Saleswomen, Managers, and Customers in American Department Stores, 1890–1940* (1986). Henry C. Binford, *The First Suburbs: Residential Communities on the Boston Periphery, 1815–1860* (1985). Paul Boyer, *Urban Masses and Moral Order in America, 1820–1920* (1978). Marc Carnes, *Secret Ritual and Manhood in Victorian America* (1989). Clifford E. Clark, *The American Family Home, 1800–1960* (1986). Lawrence Cremin, *The Transformation of the School* (1961). Perry Duis, *The Saloon: Public Drinking in Chicago and Boston, 1880–1920* (1983). Lewis A. Erenberg, *Steppin' Out: New York Nightlife and the*

Transformation of American Culture, 1890–1930 (1981). Charles V. Forcey, *The Crossroads of Liberalism* (1961). Timothy J. Gilfoyle, *City of Eros: New York City, Prostitution, and the Commercialization of Sex, 1790–1920* (1992). Eliot Gorn, *The Manly Art: Bare-Knuckle Prize Fighting in America* (1986). Harvey Green, *Fit for America: Fitness, Sport, and American Society* (1986). Allen Guttmann, *A Whole New Ball Game: An Interpretation of American Sports* (1988). Karen Halttunen, *Confidence Men and Painted Women: A Study of Middle-Class Culture in America, 1830–1870* (1982). Neil Harris, *Cultural Excursions: Marketing Appetites and Cultural Tastes in Modern America* (1990). Daniel Horowitz, *The Morality of Spending: Attitudes Toward the Consumer Society in America, 1875–1940* (1985). Kenneth T. Jackson, *The Crabgrass Frontier: The Suburbanization of the United States* (1985). John F. Kasson, *Amusing the Million: Coney Island at the Turn of the Century* (1978); *Rudeness and Civility: Manners in Nineteenth-Century Urban America* (1990). William Leach, *True Love and Perfect Union: The Feminist Reform of Sex and Society* (1980); *Land of Desire: Merchants, Power, and the Rise of a New American Culture* (1993). T. J. Jackson Lears, *No Place of Grace: Antimodernism and the Transformation of American Culture, 1880–1920* (1981). T. J. Jackson Lears and Richard Wightman Fox, eds., *The Culture of Consumption* (1983). Godfrey M. Lebhar, *Chain Stores in America* (1962). Lawrence Levine, *Highbrow/Lowbrow: The Emergence of a Cultural Hierarchy in America* (1988). John A. Lucas and Ronald Smith, *Saga of American Sport* (1978). D. W. Marcell, *Progress and Pragmatism* (1974). Jay Martin, *Harvests of Change* (1967). Martin V. Melosi, ed., *Pollution and Reform in American Cities* (1980). Steven Mintz and Susan Kellogg, *Domestic Revolutions: A Social History of American Family Life* (1988). Frank Luther Mott, *American Journalism*, rev. ed. (1962). Donald R. Mrozek, *Sport and American Mentality, 1880–1910* (1983). Lewis Mumford, *The Brown Decades* (1931). David Nasaw, *Going Out: The Rise and Fall of Public Amusements* (1993); *Schooled to Order: A Social History of Public Schooling in the United States* (1979). James D. Norris, *Advertising and the Transformation of American Society, 1865–1920* (1990). Kathy Peiss, *Cheap Amusements: Working Women and Leisure in Turn-of-the-Century New York* (1986). Alexander Saxton, *The Rise and Fall of the White Republic: Class Politics and Mass Culture in Nineteenth-Century America* (1990). Robert W. Snyder, *The Voice of the City: Vaudeville and Popular Culture in New York* (1989). Dale Somers, *The Rise of Sports in New Orleans* (1972). Susan Strasser, *Satisfaction Guaranteed: The Making of the American Mass Market* (1989). Christopher Tunnard and H. H. Reed, *American Skyline* (1955). Morton White, *Social Thought in America* (1949). Larzer Ziff, *The American 1890s: Life and Times of a Lost Generation* (1966).

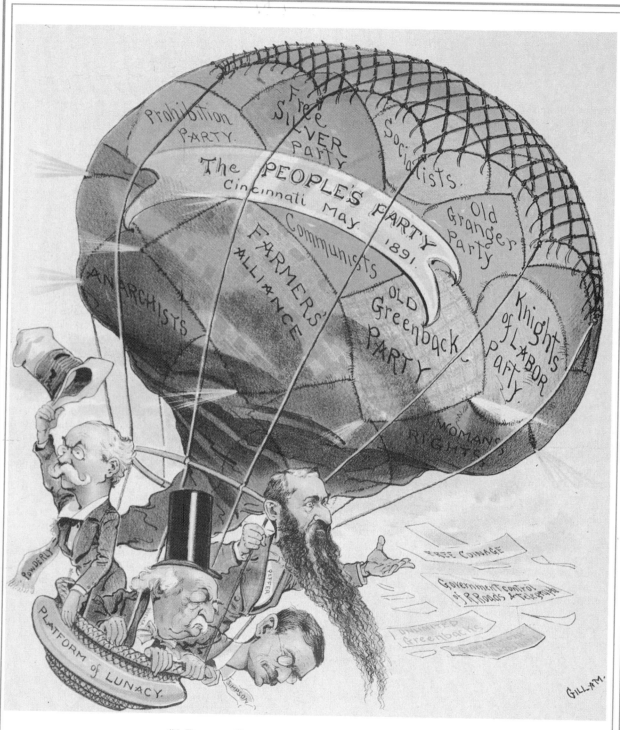

"A Party of Patches," *Judge* **Magazine, June 6, 1891**
This political cartoon suggests the contempt and fear with which many easterners, in
particular, viewed the emergence of the People's Party in 1891. *(Kansas State Historical Society)*

CHAPTER NINETEEN

FROM STALEMATE TO CRISIS

paradox

T HE ENORMOUS CHANGES AMERICA was experiencing in the late nineteenth century strained not only the nation's traditional social arrangements but its political institutions as well. Economic growth brought both progress and disorder. And it was to government, gradually, that Americans began to look for leadership in their search for stability.

Yet American government during much of this period was ill equipped to deal with the new challenges confronting it. In the face of unprecedented dilemmas, it responded with apparent passivity and confusion. Its leaders, for the most part, seemed political mediocrities. The issues with which it was concerned were often irrelevant to the nation's most serious problems. Rather than taking active leadership of the nation's dramatic transformation, the American political system for nearly two decades after the end of Reconstruction was locked in a rigid stalemate—watching the remarkable changes that were occurring in the nation and doing little to affect them. The result was a set of problems and grievances that festered and grew without any natural outlet. And it was not surprising, under the circumstances, that in the 1890s the United States entered a period of national crisis.

THE POLITICS OF EQUILIBRIUM

To modern eyes, the nature of the American political system in the late nineteenth century appears in many ways paradoxical. The two political parties enjoyed a strength and stability during those years that neither was ever to know again. And yet the federal government, which the two parties were struggling to control, was doing relatively little of importance. In fact, most Americans in those years engaged in political activity less because of their interest in national issues than because of broad regional, ethnic, or religious sentiments. Party loyalty had less to do with positions on public policy than with the way Americans defined themselves culturally.

The Party System

The most striking feature of the late-nineteenth-century party system was its remarkable stability. From the end of Reconstruction until the late 1890s, the electorate was divided almost precisely evenly between the Republicans and the Democrats. Loyalties fluctuated almost not at all. Sixteen states were solidly and consistently Republican, and fourteen states (most of them in the South) were solidly and consistently Democratic. Only five states were usually in doubt, and it was there that national elections were commonly decided, often on the basis of voter turnout. The Republican Party captured the presidency in all but two of the elections of the era, but the party was not really as dominant as that suggests. In the five presidential elections beginning in 1876, the average popular-vote margin separating the Democratic and Republican candidates was 1.5 percent. The congressional balance was

531

temperance legislation

similarly stable. Between 1875 and 1895, the Republicans generally controlled the Senate and the Democrats generally controlled the House; in any given election, the number of seats that shifted from one party to the other was very small.

As striking as the balance between the parties was the intensity of public loyalty to them. In most of the country, Americans adhered to their party affiliations with a passion and enthusiasm that are difficult for later generations to understand. Voter turnout in presidential elections between 1860 and 1900 averaged over 78 percent of all eligible voters. Even in nonpresidential years, from 60 to 80 percent of the voters turned out to cast ballots for congressional and local candidates. Large groups of potential voters were disfranchised in these years: women in most states; almost all blacks and many poor whites in the South. But for adult white males outside the South, there were few franchise restrictions. The remarkable turnout represented a genuinely mass-based politics.

Party politics in the late nineteenth century occupied a central position in American culture, comparable in some ways to the role that spectator sports and mass popular entertainment play today. Political campaigns were often the most important public events in the lives of communities. Political organizations served important social and cultural functions. Political identification was almost as important to most individuals as identification with a church or an ethnic group. Partisanship was an intense, emotional force, widely admired and often identified with patriotism.

What explains this remarkable loyalty to the two political parties? It was not, certainly, that the parties took distinct positions on important public issues. Both parties were solidly committed to the growth of the corporate industrial economy. Both were hostile to all forms of economic and social radicalism. Both were committed (at least until the 1890s) to a "sound currency" and to the existing structure of the financial system.

What determined party loyalties was less concrete issues than other factors. Region was perhaps the most important. To white southerners, loyalty to the Democratic Party was a matter of unquestioned faith. It was the vehicle by which they had triumphed over Reconstruction, the vehicle for the preservation of white supremacy. To many old-stock northerners, white and black, Republican loyalties were equally intense for the opposite reason. The party of Lincoln had freed the slaves and preserved the Union; it was a bulwark against slavery and treason.

Religious and ethnic differences also shaped party loyalties. The Democratic Party attracted most Catholic voters, most recent immigrants, and most of the poorer workers; those three groups, of course, often overlapped. The Republican Party appealed to northern Protestants and citizens of old stock. Among the few substantive issues on which the parties took clearly different stands were matters concerning immigrants. The Republicans tended to be more nativist and to support measures restricting immigration. They also tended to favor temperance legislation. Catholics and immigrants viewed such proposals as an assault on their culture and lifestyle and opposed them, and the Democratic Party followed their lead.

For many Americans, in other words, party identification was usually more a reflection of vague cultural inclinations than a calculation of economic interest. Individuals might affiliate with a party because their parents had done so, or because it was the party of their region, their church, or their ethnic group. Most clung to their party loyalties with great persistence and passion.

The National Government

One reason the two parties managed to avoid substantive issues was that the federal government (and for the most part state and local governments as well) did relatively little. The government in Washington was responsible for delivering the mails, for maintaining a national military, for conducting foreign policy, and for collecting tariffs and taxes. It had few other responsibilities. And it had few institutions with which to engage in additional responsibilities even if it chose to do so.

There was one significant exception. From the end of the Civil War to the early twentieth century, the federal government administered a system of annual pensions for Civil War veterans who had retired from work, and for their widows. At its peak, this pension system was making payments to a majority of the male citizens (black and white) of the North, and to many women as well. Some activists hoped to see it made permanent and universal; they pressured the government to create a system of old-age pensions for all Americans. But their efforts failed. That was in part because the Civil War pension system was awash in party patronage and was widely viewed as corrupt. Other reformers—believers in "good government"—saw elimination of the pension system as a way to fight graft, corruption, and party rule. When the Civil War generation died out, the pension system died with it.

In most other respects, the United States in the late nineteenth century was a society without a modern, national state. The most powerful national political institutions were the two political parties and the federal courts (a fact that has led one scholar to refer to the American government of that era as a "state of courts and parties"). The national leaders of both parties were primarily concerned not with policy but with office—with winning elections and controlling patronage.

Both parties were dominated by powerful bosses and machines chiefly concerned with controlling and dispensing jobs. The Democrats relied on the big city organizations (such as New York's Tammany Hall), which enabled them to mobilize the voting power of immigrants. The Republicans tended to depend on strong statewide organizations such as those of Roscoe Conkling in New York and Matt Quay of Pennsylvania.

Presidents and Patronage

The power of party bosses had a significant effect on the power of the presidency. The office had great symbolic importance, but its occupants were unable to do very much except distribute government appointments. A new president had to make almost 100,000 appointments (most of them in the post office, the only really large government agency); and to do that, he had to rely on a tiny staff working in a few rooms in the White House. James Garfield, who became president in 1881, once complained, "I have heretofore been treating of the fundamental principles of government, and here I am considering all day whether A or B should be appointed to this or that office." Even in making appointments, presidents had limited latitude, since they had to avoid offending the various factions within their own parties.

Sometimes that proved impossible, as the presidency of Rutherford B. Hayes demonstrated. The victor of the disputed election of 1876, Hayes was harried by angry Democrats (who called him "His Fraudulency") from the moment he entered office to the moment he left. But he was crippled as well by his own party. By the end of his term, two groups—the Stalwarts, led by Roscoe Conkling of New York, and the Half-Breeds, captained by James G. Blaine of Maine—were competing for control of the Republican Party and threatening to split it. The dispute between the Stalwarts and the Half-Breeds was characteristic of the political battles of the era. It had virtually no substantive foundation. Rhetorically, the Stalwarts favored traditional, professional machine politics while the Half-Breeds favored reform. In fact, neither group was much interested in political change; each simply wanted a larger share of the patronage pie. Hayes tried to satisfy both and ended up satisfying neither.

The battle over patronage overshadowed all else during Hayes's unhappy presidency. His one impor-

President and Mrs. Rutherford B. Hayes
Hayes was one of a series of generally undistinguished late-nineteenth-century presidents whose subordination to the fiercely competitive party system left them with little room for independent leadership. This photograph captures the dignity and sobriety that Hayes and his wife sought to convey to the public. His wife was a temperance advocate and refused to serve alcoholic beverages in the White House, thereby earning the nickname "Lemonade Lucy." Hayes attracted less whimsical labels. Because of the disputed 1876 election that had elevated him to the presidency, critics referred to him throughout his term as "His Fraudulency." *(Library of Congress)*

tant substantive initiative—an effort to create a civil service system—attracted no support from either party. And his early announcement that he would not seek re-election only weakened him further. He had virtually no power in Congress. The Democrats controlled the House throughout his presidency, and the Senate during the last two years of his term. And Senate Republicans, led by Roscoe Conkling, opposed his efforts to defy the machines in making appointments. Hayes's presidency was a study in frustration.

The Republicans managed to retain the presidency in 1880, in part because they managed to agree on a ticket that made it possible for the Stalwarts and the Half-Breeds briefly to paper over their differences. After a long convention deadlock, they nominated a "dark horse," James A. Garfield, a veteran congressman from Ohio and a Half-Breed; to conciliate the Stalwarts, the convention gave the vice presidential nomination to Chester A. Arthur, a Conkling henchman. To oppose Garfield, the Democrats nominated General Winfield Scott Hancock, a minor Civil War commander with no national following. Garfield won a decisive electoral victory, but his popular vote margin was very thin. The Republicans also captured both houses of Congress.

Garfield began his presidency by trying to defy Conkling and the Stalwarts in his appointments and by showing support for civil service reform. He soon found himself embroiled in an ugly public quarrel with both Conkling and Thomas Platt, the other senator from New York and another important Stalwart leader. But before it could be resolved, Garfield was victimized by the spoils system in a more terrible sense. On July 2, 1881, only four months after his inauguration, Garfield was shot twice while standing in the Washington railroad station by an apparently deranged gunman (and unsuccessful office seeker) who shouted, "I am a Stalwart and Arthur is president now!" Garfield lingered for nearly three months and finally died, a victim as much of bungled medical treatment as of the wounds themselves.

Chester A. Arthur, who succeeded Garfield, had spent a political lifetime as a devoted, skilled, and open spoilsman and a close ally of Roscoe Conkling. But on becoming president, he tried—like Hayes and Garfield before him—to follow an independent course and even to promote reform. The terrible circumstances that had brought him to the presidency undoubtedly shaped his behavior. He realized that the Garfield assassination had to some degree discredited the traditional spoils system.

The "new" Arthur dismayed the party bosses. He kept most of Garfield's appointees in office. He also supported civil service reform, aware that the legislation was likely to pass whether he supported it or not. In 1883, finally, Congress passed the first national civil service measure, the Pendleton Act, which identified a limited number of federal jobs to be filled by competitive written examinations rather than by patronage. Relatively few offices fell under civil service at first, but its reach extended steadily so that by the mid-

twentieth century most federal employees were civil servants.

The Return of the Democrats

The unsavory election of 1884 was typical of national political contests in the late nineteenth century in its emphasis on personalities rather than policies. The Republicans repudiated Arthur (who was in any case already suffering from an illness that would kill him two years later) and chose instead their most popular and controversial figure, Senator James G. Blaine of Maine—known to his adoring admirers as "the plumed knight" but to thousands of other Americans as a symbol of seamy party politics. An independent reform faction, known derisively by their critics as the "mugwumps," announced they would bolt the party and support an honest Democrat. Rising to the bait, the Democrats nominated Grover Cleveland, the "reform" governor of New York. He differed from Blaine on no substantive issues but had acquired a reputation as an enemy of corruption.

In a campaign filled with personal invective, what may have decided the election was the last-minute introduction of a religious controversy. Shortly before the election, a delegation of Protestant ministers called on Blaine in New York City; their spokesman, Dr. Samuel Burchard, referred to the Democrats as the party of "rum, Romanism, and rebellion." Blaine was slow to repudiate Blanchard's indiscretion, and Democrats quickly spread the news that Blaine had tolerated a slander on the Catholic church. Cleveland's narrow victory may well have been a result of a heavy Catholic vote for the Democrats in New York. Cleveland won 219 electoral votes to Blaine's 182; his popular margin was only 23,000.

Grover Cleveland was respected, if not often liked, for his stern and righteous opposition to politicians, grafters, pressure groups, and Tammany Hall. He had become famous as the "veto governor," as an official who was not afraid to say no. He was the embodiment of an era in which few Americans believed the federal government could, or should, do very much. His administration was characterized from beginning to end by an unwavering commitment to economy in government. No one should forget, he explained, that "though the people support the Government, the Government should not support the people."

Cleveland did grapple with one major economic issue. He had always doubted the wisdom of protective tariffs. And he concluded finally that the existing high rates were responsible for the annual surplus in federal revenues, which was tempting Congress to pass

THE STATE, WAR, AND NAVY BUILDING
This sprawling Victorian office building was one of the largest in Washington when it was constructed shortly after the Civil War. It housed the State, War, and Navy Departments until not long before World War II. It suggests both the degree to which the federal government was growing in the late nineteenth century and, more importantly, the degree to which it remained a tiny entity compared to what it would later become. This building, which stands directly next door to the White House, today houses a part (but only a part) of the president's staff. *(Library of Congress)*

the "reckless" and "extravagant" legislation he so frequently vetoed. In December 1887, therefore, he asked Congress to reduce the tariff rates. Democrats in the House approved a tariff reduction, but Senate Republicans defiantly passed a bill of their own actually raising rates. The resulting deadlock made the tariff an issue in the election of 1888.

The Democrats renominated Cleveland and supported tariff reductions. The Republicans settled on former Senator Benjamin Harrison of Indiana, who was obscure but respectable (and the grandson of President William Henry Harrison); and they endorsed protection. The campaign was the first since the Civil War to involve a clear question of economic difference between the parties. It was also one of the most corrupt (and one of the closest) elections in American history. Harrison won an electoral majority of 233 to 168, but Cleveland's popular vote exceeded Harrison's by 100,000—making this one of only two presidential elections in American history (the other was 1876) in which the loser in the popular vote was the victor in the electoral college.

Tariffs, Trusts, and Railroads

Benjamin Harrison's record as president was little more substantial than that of his grandfather, who had died a month after taking office. One reason for Harrison's failure was the intellectual drabness of the members of his administration—beginning with the president himself and extending through his cabinet. Another was Harrison's unwillingness to make any effort to influence Congress. And yet during Harrison's dreary administration, public opinion was beginning to force the government to confront some of the pressing social and economic issues of the day. Most notably, perhaps, sentiment was rising in favor of legislation to curb the power of trusts.

By the mid-1880s, fifteen western and southern states had adopted laws prohibiting combinations that restrained competition. But corporations found it easy to escape limitations by incorporating in states such as New Jersey and Delaware that offered them special privileges. If antitrust legislation was to be effective, it would have to come from the national government.

THE TOURNAMENT OF TO-DAY.—A SET-TO BETWEEN LABOR AND MONOPOLY.

LABOR AND MONOPOLY

This 1883 cartoon appeared in *Puck,* a magazine popular for its satirical treatment of American politics. It expresses a common sentiment of the Populists and many others: that ordinary men and women (portrayed here by the pathetic figure of "labor" and by the grim members of the audience) were almost hopelessly overmatched by the power of corporate monopolies. The knight's shield, labeled "corruption of the legislature," and his spear, labeled "subsidized press," make clear that—in the view of the cartoonist at least—corporations had many allies in their effort to oppress workers. *(Culver)*

Responding to growing popular demands, both houses of Congress passed the Sherman Antitrust Act in July 1890, almost without dissent. Most members of Congress saw it as a largely symbolic measure to help deflect public criticism, not likely to have any real effect on corporate power.

For over a decade after its passage, the Sherman Act had virtually no impact. As of 1901, the Justice Department had instituted only fourteen suits under the law against business combinations and had obtained few convictions. It had used the law much more frequently against labor unions. The courts, meanwhile, weakened the bill considerably. In *United States* v. *E. C. Knight Co.* (1895), in which the government charged that a single trust controlled 98 percent of refined sugar manufacturing in the country, the Supreme Court rejected the government's case. The sugar trust was engaged in manufacturing, not in interstate commerce, the Court declared; and since Congress's authority to control interstate commerce was its only authority for regulating corporations, the trust, despite its obviously monopolistic characteristics, was not illegal.

SHACKLED BY THE TARIFF
This 1894 cartoon by the political satirist Louis Dalrymple portrays an unhappy Uncle Sam bound hands and feet by the McKinley Tariff and by what tariff opponents considered a closely related evil—monopoly. Members of the Senate are portrayed as tools of the various industries and special interests protected by the tariff. The caption, "A Senate for Revenue Only," is a parody of the anti-tariff rallying cry, "A tariff for revenue only," meaning that duties should be designed only to raise money for the government, not to stop imports of particular goods to protect domestic industries. *(The Granger Collection)*

The Republicans were more interested, however, in the issue they believed had won them the 1888 election: the tariff. Representative William McKinley of Ohio and Senator Nelson W. Aldrich of Rhode Island drafted the highest protective measure ever proposed to Congress. Known as the McKinley Act, it became law in October 1890. But Republican leaders apparently misinterpreted public sentiment, for the party suffered a stunning reversal in the 1890 congressional election. Their substantial Senate majority in the Senate was slashed to 8; in the House, they retained only 88 of the 323 seats. McKinley himself was among those who went down to defeat. Nor were the Republicans able to recover in the course of the next two years. In the presidential election of 1892, Benjamin Harrison once again supported protection and Grover Cleveland, renominated by the Democrats, once again opposed it. Only a new third party, the People's Party, with James B. Weaver as its candidate, advocated any serious economic reform. (See p. 540.) Cleveland won 277 electoral votes to Harrison's 145 and had a popular margin of 380,000. Weaver ran far behind. For the first time since 1878, the Democrats won a majority of both houses of Congress.

The policies of Cleveland's second term were much like those of his first—devoted to minimal government and hostile to active state measures to deal with social or economic problems. But this time, a major economic crisis (see p. 545) created popular demands for a more active government. For the most part, Cleveland resisted those pressures.

Again, he supported a tariff reduction, which the House approved but the Senate gutted. Cleveland denounced the result but allowed it to become law as the Wilson-Gorman Tariff. The bill threw one small crumb to agrarian interests: a small federal income tax (2 percent of incomes over $4,000). But the Supreme Court declared it unconstitutional. Only after approval of the Sixteenth Amendment in 1913 was the federal government able to tax incomes. Public pressure was also growing in the 1880s for regulation of the railroads. Farm organizations in the Midwest (most notably the Grangers—see pp. 538–539) had persuaded several state legislatures to pass regulatory legislation in the early 1870s. But in 1886, the Supreme Court—in *Wabash, St. Louis, and Pacific Railway Co.* v. *Illinois,* known as the *Wabash* case)—ruled one of the Granger laws in Illinois unconstitutional, calling it an attempt to control interstate commerce that infringed on the exclusive power of Congress. Later, the Courts limited the powers of the states to regulate commerce even within their own boundaries.

Railroad regulation, it was now clear, could only come from the federal government. Congress grudgingly responded to public pressure in 1887 with the Interstate Commerce Act, which banned discrimination in rates between long and short hauls, required railroads to publish their rate schedules and file them with the government, and declared that all interstate rail rates must be "reasonable and just"—although the bill did not define what that meant. A five-person agency, the Interstate Commerce Commission (ICC), was to administer the act. But it had to rely on the courts to enforce its rulings. For almost twenty years after its passage, the Interstate Commerce Act—haphazardly enforced and narrowly interpreted by the courts—was without practical effect.

The controversies over the tariff, the trusts, and the railroads were signs that the dramatic changes in the American economy were creating problems that much of the public considered too important and dangerous to ignore. But the federal government's response to that agitation reflected the continuing weakness of the American state. The government still lacked institutions adequate to perform any significant role in American economic life. And not enough Americans had yet embraced a political ideology that would justify any major expansion of government responsibilities. The effort to create such institutions and to promote such an ideology would occupy much of American public life in the coming decades. Among the first signs of that effort was a dramatic dissident movement that shattered the political equilibrium the nation had experienced for the previous twenty years.

THE AGRARIAN REVOLT

No group watched the performance of the federal government in the 1880s with more dismay than American farmers. Isolated from the urban-industrial society that was beginning to dominate national life, suffering from a long economic decline, afflicted with a painful sense of obsolescence, rural Americans were keenly aware of the problems of the modern economy and particularly eager for government assistance in dealing with them. The result of their frustrations was the emergence of one of the most powerful movements of political protest in American history: what became known as Populism.

The Grangers

According to popular myth, American farmers were the most individualistic of citizens, the least likely to join together in a cooperative economic or political movement. In reality, however, farmers had been making efforts to organize for many decades. There had been occasional cooperative movements in the first decades of the nineteenth century, but the first major farm organization appeared in the 1860s: the Grange. It was less a movement of protest than a social and self-help association. The depression of 1873 turned it into an agency of political change.

"THE GRANGE AWAKENING THE SLEEPERS"
This 1873 cartoon suggests the way the Grange embraced many of the same concerns that the Farmers' Alliances and their People's Party later expressed. A farmer is attempting to arouse passive citizens (lying in place of the "sleepers," or cross ties on railroad tracks), who are about to be crushed by a train. The cars bear the names of the costs of the railroads' domination of the agrarian economy. *(Culver)*

The Grange had its origins shortly after the Civil War in a tour through the South by a minor Agriculture Department official, Oliver H. Kelley. Kelley was appalled by what he considered the isolation and drabness of rural life, and in 1867 he left the government and, with other department employees, founded the National Grange of the Patrons of Husbandry, to which he devoted years of labor as secretary and from which emerged a network of local organizations. At first, the Granges defined their purposes modestly. They attempted to bring farmers together to learn new scientific agricultural techniques—to keep farming "in step with the music of the age." The Granges also hoped to create a feeling of community, to relieve the loneliness of rural life. An elaborate system of initiation and ritual and a strict code of secrecy lent to the organization many of the trappings of urban fraternal organizations.

At first the Grange grew slowly. But when the depression of 1873 caused a major decline in farm prices, membership rapidly increased. By 1875, the Grange claimed over 800,000 members and 20,000 local lodges; it had chapters in almost every state but was strongest, naturally, in the great staple-producing regions of the South and the Midwest.

As membership grew, the lodges in the Midwest began to focus less on the social benefits of organization and more on the economic possibilities. They attempted to organize marketing cooperatives to allow farmers to circumvent the hated middlemen. And they urged cooperative political action to curb the monopolistic practices of the railroads and warehouses. Throughout the Midwest on Independence Day 1873, embittered farmers assembled to hear Granger orators read "The Farmers' Declaration of Independence," which proclaimed that the time had come for farmers, "suffering from long continued systems of oppression and abuse, to rouse themselves from an apathetic indifference to their own interests." The declaration also vowed that farmers would use "all lawful and peaceful means to free [themselves] from the tyranny of monopoly."

The Grangers set up cooperative stores, creameries, elevators, warehouses, insurance companies, and factories that produced machines, stoves, and other items. Some 400 enterprises were in operation at the height of the movement, and some of them forged lucrative relationships with existing businesses. One corporation emerged specifically to meet the needs of the Grangers: the first mail-order business, Montgomery Ward and Company, founded in 1872. Eventually, however, most of the Grange enterprises failed, both because of the inexperience of their operators and because of the opposition of the middlemen whose businesses they were challenging.

The Grangers also worked to elect state legislators pledged to their program. Usually they operated through the existing parties, although occasionally they ran candidates under such independent party labels as "Antimonopoly" and "Reform." At their peak, they managed to gain control of the legislatures in most of the midwestern states. Their purpose, openly and angrily announced, was to subject the railroads to government controls. The Granger laws of the early 1870s, by which many states imposed strict regulations on railroad rates and practices, seemed for a time to vindicate the predictions of those farmers who claimed that their new organization foretold a permanent change in the political status of agriculture. But the new regulations were soon destroyed by the courts. That defeat, combined with the political inexperience of many Grange leaders and above all the temporary return of agricultural prosperity in the late 1870s, produced a dramatic decline in the power of the association. Some of the Granger cooperatives survived as effective economic vehicles for many years, but the movement as a whole dwindled rapidly. By 1880, its membership had shrunk to 100,000.

The Alliances

The successor to the Granges as the leading vehicle of agrarian protest began to emerge even before the Granger movement had faded. As early as 1875, farmers in parts of the South (most notably in Texas) were banding together in so-called Farmers' Alliances. By 1880, the Southern Alliance had more than 4 million members; and a comparable Northwestern Alliance was taking root in the plains states and the Midwest and developing ties with its southern counterpart.

Like the Granges, the Alliances were principally concerned with local problems. They formed cooperatives and other marketing mechanisms. They established stores, banks, processing plants, and other facilities for their members—to free them from dependence on the hated "furnishing merchants" who kept so many farmers in debt. Some Alliance leaders, however, also saw the movement in larger terms: as an effort to build a society in which economic competition might give way to cooperation. They did not advocate rigid collectivism; instead, they argued for a sense of mutual, neighborly responsibility that would enable farmers to resist oppressive outside forces. Alliance lecturers traveled throughout rural areas lambasting the concentration of power in great corporations and financial institutions and promoting cooperation as an alternative economic system.

The Alliances were notable, too, for the prominent role women played within them. From the beginning, women were full voting members in most local Alliances. Many held offices and served as lecturers. A few, most notably Mary E. Lease, went on to become fiery populist orators. (Lease was famous for urging farmers to "raise less corn and more hell.") Most others emphasized issues of particular concern to women, especially temperance. Like women in urban areas concerned about the impact of drinking on family life, agrarian women argued that sobriety was a key to stability in rural society.

Although the Alliances quickly became far more widespread than the Granges had ever been, they suffered from similar problems. Their cooperatives did not always work well, partly because the market forces operating against them were sometimes too strong to be overcome, partly because the cooperatives themselves were often mismanaged. These economic frustrations helped push the movement into a new phase at the end of the 1880s: the creation of a national political organization.

A POPULIST GATHERING
Populism was a response to real economic and political grievances. But like most political movements of its time, it was also important as a cultural experience. For farmers in sparsely settled regions in particular, it provided an antidote to isolation and loneliness. This gathering of Populist farmers in Dickinson County, Kansas, suggests how the political purposes of the movement were tightly bound up with its social purposes. *(Kansas State Historical Society)*

In 1889, the Southern and Northwestern Alliances, despite continuing differences between them, agreed to a loose merger. The next year the Alliances held a national convention at Ocala, Florida, and issued the so-called Ocala Demands, which were, in effect, a party platform. In the 1890 off-year elections, candidates supported by the Alliances won partial or complete control of the legislatures in twelve states. They also won six governorships, three seats in the U.S. Senate, and approximately fifty in the U.S. House of Representatives. Many of the successful Alliance candidates were simply Democrats who had benefited—often passively—from Alliance endorsements. But dissident farmers drew enough encouragement from the results to contemplate further political action, including forming a party of their own.

Sentiment for a third party was strongest among the members of the Northwestern Alliance. But several southern leaders supported the ideas as well—among them Tom Watson of Georgia, the only Southern congressman elected in 1890 openly to identify with the Alliance, and Leonidas L. Polk of North Carolina, per-

haps the ablest mind in the movement. Alliance leaders discussed plans for a third party at meetings in Cincinnati in May 1891 and St. Louis in February 1892—meetings attended by many Northern Alliance members, a smaller but still significant number of Southern Alliance leaders, and representatives of the fading Knights of Labor, whom some farm leaders hoped to bring into the coalition. Then, in July 1892, 1,300 exultant delegates poured into Omaha, Nebraska, to proclaim the creation of the new party, approve an official set of principles, and nominate candidates for the presidency and vice presidency. The new organization's official name was the People's Party, but the movement was more commonly referred to as Populism.

The election of 1892 demonstrated the potential power of the new movement. The Populist presidential candidate—James B. Weaver of Iowa, a former Greenbacker who received the nomination after the death of Leonidas Polk, the early favorite—polled more than 1 million votes, 8.5 percent of the total, and carried six mountain and plains states for 22 electoral votes. Nearly

POPULISM AND THE NEW DAWN
In 1892, when the People's Party ran its first candidate for president, many reformers throughout the United States welcomed it as a healthy challenge to the stale thinking within the two major parties. Later, as conservative opponents began portraying the Populists as ignorant "hayseeds" or dangerous revolutionaries, optimistic images like these became increasingly rare. James B. Weaver, portrayed here standing beside a lion, received 8 percent of the vote in 1892 and 22 electoral votes. *(Kansas State Historical Society)*

1,500 Populist candidates won election to seats in state legislatures. The party elected three governors, five senators, and ten congressmen. It could also claim the support of many Republicans and Democrats in Congress who had been elected by appealing to populist sentiment.

The Populist Constituency

The Populists dreamed of creating a broad political coalition that included many groups. But Populism always appealed principally to farmers, and particularly to small farmers with little long-range economic security—people whose operations were only minimally mechanized, if at all, who relied on one crop, and who had access only to limited and unsatisfactory mechanisms of credit. In the Midwest, the Populists were usually family farmers struggling to hold on to their land (or to get it back if they had lost it). In the South, there were many modest landowners too, but in addition there were significant numbers of sharecroppers and tenant farmers. Whatever their differences, however, most Populists had at least one thing in common: they were engaged in a type of farming that was becoming less viable in the face of new, mechanized, diversified, and consolidated commercial agriculture.

There is evidence, too, that Populists tended to be not only economically but culturally marginal, that the movement appealed above all to geographically isolated farmers who felt cut off from the mainstream of national life and resented their isolation. Populism gave such people an outlet for their grievances; it also provided them with a social experience, a sense of belonging to a community that they had previously lacked.

But the Populists were also notable for the groups they failed to attract. There were energetic efforts to include labor within the coalition. Representatives of the Knights of Labor attended early organizational meetings; the new party added a labor plank to its platform—calling for shorter hours for workers and restrictions on immigration, and denouncing the use of private detective agencies as strikebreakers in labor disputes. On the whole, however, Populism never attracted significant labor support in part because the economic interests of labor and the interests of farmers were often at odds.

One exception was the Rocky Mountain states, where the Populists did have some significant success in attracting miners to their cause. They did so partly because local Populist leaders supported a broader platform than the national party embraced. In particular, they endorsed a demand that the national party only later accepted: "free silver," the idea of permitting silver to become, along with gold, the basis of the currency so as to expand the money supply. In Colorado, Idaho, Nevada, and other areas of the Far West where silver mining was an important activity, the Populist constituency contained more working-class people and more immigrants than it did elsewhere; and the People's Party enjoyed substantial, if temporary, success there.

In the South (and to a lesser degree elsewhere), white Populists struggled with the question of accepting African Americans into the party. Their numbers and poverty made black farmers possibly valuable allies. And indeed there was an important black component to the movement—a network of "Colored Alliances" that by 1890 numbered over one and a quarter million members. But most white Populists were willing to accept the assistance of African Americans only as long as it was clear that whites would remain indisputably in control. When southern conservatives began to attack the Populists for undermining white supremacy, the interracial character of the movement quickly faded.

Most of the Populist leaders were members of the rural middle class: professional people, editors and lawyers, or longtime politicians and agitators. Few were

WHERE HISTORIANS DISAGREE

POPULISM

AMERICAN HISTORY OFFERS FEW examples of successful popular movements operating outside the two major parties. Perhaps that is why Populism, which in its brief, meteoric life became one of the few such phenomena to gain real national influence, has attracted particular attention from historians. It has also produced deep disagreements among them. Scholars have differed in many ways in their interpretations of Populism, but at the heart of most such disagreements have been disparate views of the value of popular, insurgent politics. Some historians have harbored a basic mistrust of such mass uprisings and have therefore viewed the Populists with suspicion and hostility. Others have viewed such insurgency approvingly, as evidence of a healthy resistance to oppression and exploitation; and to them, the Populists have appeared as essentially admirable, democratic activists.

This latter view was the basis of the first, and for many years the only, general history of Populism: John D. Hicks's *The Populist Revolt* (1931). Rejecting the then-prevailing view of the Populists as misguided and unruly radicals, Hicks described them as people reacting rationally and progressively to economic misfortune. Hicks was writing in an era in which the ideas of Frederick Jackson Turner were dominating historical studies, and he brought to his analysis of Populism a strong emphasis on regionalism. Populists, he argued, were part of the democratic West, resisting the pressures from the more aristocratic East. (He explained southern Populism by describing the South as an "economic frontier" region—not newly settled like the West, but prey to many of the same pressures and misfortunes.) The Populists, Hicks suggested, were aware of the harsh, even brutal, impact of eastern industrial growth on rural society. They were proposing reforms that would limit the oppressive power of the new financial titans and restore a measure of control to the farmers. Populism was, he wrote, "the last phase of a long and perhaps a losing struggle—the struggle to save agricultural America from the devouring jaws of industrial America." A losing struggle, perhaps, but not a vain one; for many of the reforms the Populists advocated, Hicks implied, became the basis of later progressive legislation.

This generally approving view of Populism prevailed among historians for more than two decades. But in the early 1950s—when the memory of European fascism and uneasiness about contemporary communism combined to create a general hostility among scholars toward mass popular politics—a harsh new view of the Populist movement appeared in a work by one of the nation's leading historians. Richard Hofstadter, in *The Age of Reform* (1955), admitted that Populism embraced some progressive ideas and advocated some sensible reforms. But the bulk of his effort was devoted to exposing both the "soft" and the "dark" sides of the movement. Populism was "soft," he claimed, because it rested on a nostalgic and unrealistic myth, because it romanticized the nation's agrarian past and refused to confront the realities of modern life. Farmers were, he argued, themselves fully committed to the values of the capitalist system they claimed to abhor. And Populism was "dark," he argued, because it was permeated with bigotry and ignorance. Populists, he claimed, revealed anti-Semitic tendencies, and they displayed animosity toward intellectuals, easterns, and urbanites as well.

Almost immediately, historians more favorably disposed toward mass politics in general,

themselves marginal farmers. Almost all leaders were, like most of their constituents, Protestants. But beyond these basic characteristics there were wide variations. Some Populist leaders were somber, serious theoreticians; others were semihysterical rabble-rousers. In the South, in particular, Populism produced the first generation of what was to become a distinctive and enduring political breed—the "southern demagogue." Tom Watson in Georgia, Jeff Davis in Arkansas, and others attracted widespread popular support by arousing the resentment of poor southerners against the entrenched Bourbon aristocracy.

WHERE HISTORIANS DISAGREE

and Populism in particular, began to challenge what became known as the "Hofstadter thesis." Norman Pollack argued in a 1962 study, *The Populist Response to Industrial America,* and in a number of articles that the agrarian revolt had rested not on nostalgic, romantic concepts but on a sophisticated, farsighted, and even radical vision of reform—one that recognized, and even welcomed, the realities of an industrial economy, but that sought to make that economy more equitable and democratic by challenging many of the premises of capitalism. Walter T. K. Nugent, in *Tolerant Populists* (1963), argued—as his title implies—that the Populists in Kansas were far from bigoted, that they not only tolerated but welcomed Jews and other minorities into their party, and that they offered a practical, sensible program.

Not until 1976, however, did a comprehensive study of Populism emerge that could rival Hicks and Hofstadter in influence. Lawrence Goodwyn, in *Democratic Promise* (and in an abridged version of the same work, *The Populist Moment,* published in 1978), described the Populists as members of a "cooperative crusade," battling against the "coercive potential of the emerging corporate state." Populists were more than the nostalgic bigots Hofstadter described, more even than the progressive reformers portrayed by Hicks. They offered a vision of truly radical change, widely disseminated through what Goodwyn called a "movement culture." They advocated an intelligent, and above all a democratic, alternative to the inequities of modern capitalism.

At the same time that historians were debating the question of what Populism meant, they were also arguing over who the Populists were. Hicks, Hofstadter, and Goodwyn disagreed on many things, but they shared a general view of the Populists as victims of economic distress—usually one-crop farmers in economically marginal agricultural regions victimized by drought and debt. Other scholars, however, have suggested that the problem of identifying the Populists is more complex. Sheldon Hackney, in *Populism to Progressivism in Alabama* (1969), argued that the Populists were not only economically troubled but socially rootless, "only tenuously connected to society by economic function, by personal relationships, by stable community membership, by political participation, or by psychological identification with the South's distinctive myths." Peter Argersinger, Stanley Parsons, James Turner, and others have similarly suggested that Populists were characterized by a form of social and even geographical isolation. Steven Hahn's 1983 study *The Roots of Southern Populism* identifies poor white farmers in the "upcountry" as the core of Populist activity in Georgia; and he argues that they were reacting not simply to the psychic distress of being "left behind," but also to a real economic threat to their way of life—to the encroachments of a new commercial order of which they had never been and could never be a part.

Finally, there has been continuing debate over the legacy of Populism. Historians and politicians alike have argued repeatedly that a populist tradition has survived throughout the twentieth century, influencing movements as disparate as those led by Huey Long in the 1930s, George Wallace in the 1960s, and Ross Perot in the 1990s. Others have maintained that the term "populism" has been used (and misused) so widely as to have become virtually meaningless, that its only real value is in reference to the agrarian insurgents of the 1890s, who first gave meaning to the word.

There were similarly flamboyant leaders in the Midwest: "Sockless" Jerry Simpson of Kansas, for example, and Ignatius Donnelly of Minnesota. Donnelly, in particular, seemed to exemplify the divided character of the movement: sincere idealism combined with crassness and opportunism. A committed, principled man who spoke eloquently on behalf of populist ideals and appeared sincerely to believe in them, Donnelly was also at times something of a charlatan. As a member of Congress, he compiled a shabby legislative record marked, among other things, by a series of seamy, secret deals with railroad companies.

TAKING ARMS AGAINST THE POPULISTS
Kansas was a Populist stronghold in the 1890s, but the new party faced powerful challenges. In 1893 state Republicans disputed an election that the Populists believed had given them control of the legislature. When the Populists occupied the statehouse, Republicans armed themselves, drove out the Populists, and seized control of the state government. Republican members of the legislature pose here with their weapons in a photograph perhaps intended as a warning to any Populists inclined to challenge them. *(Kansas State Historical Society)*

Populist Ideas

The reform program of the Populists was spelled out first in the Ocala Demands of 1890 and then, even more clearly, in the Omaha platform of 1892. It proposed a system of "subtreasuries," which would replace and strengthen the cooperatives with which both the Grangers and Alliances had been experimenting for years. The government would establish a network of warehouses, where farmers could deposit their crops. Using those crops as collateral, growers could then borrow money from the government at low rates of interest and wait for the price of their goods to go up before selling them. In addition, the Populists called for the abolition of national banks, which they believed were dangerous institutions of concentrated power; the end of absentee ownership of land; the direct election of United States senators (which would weaken the power of conservative state legislatures); and

other devices to improve the ability of the people to influence the political process. They called as well for regulation and (after 1892) government ownership of railroads, telephones, and telegraphs. And they demanded a system of government-operated postal savings banks, a graduated income tax, and the inflation of the currency. Eventually, the party as a whole embraced (with varying degrees of enthusiasm) the demand of its western members for the remonetization of silver.

Some Populists were openly anti-Semitic, pointing to the Jews as leaders of the obscure financial forces attempting to enslave them. Others were anti-intellectual, anti-eastern, and anti-urban. A few of the leading Populists gave an impression of personal failure, brilliant instability, and brooding communion with mystic forces. Ignatius Donnelly, for example, wrote one book locating the lost isle of Atlantis, another claiming that Bacon had written Shakespeare's plays, and still another—*Caesar's Column* (1891)—embodying an almost lunatic vision of bloody revolution and the creation of a populist utopia. Tom Watson, once a champion of interracial harmony, ended his career baiting blacks and Jews.

Yet the occasional bigotry of some Populists should not be allowed to dominate the image of Populism as a whole, which was a serious and usually responsible effort to find solutions to real problems. Populists emphatically rejected the laissez-faire orthodoxies of their time, the idea that the rights of ownership are absolute. They raised one of the most overt and powerful challenges of the era to the direction in which American industrial capitalism was moving. Populism was not a challenge to industrialization or to capitalism itself, but a response to what the Populists considered the brutal and chaotic way in which the economy was developing. Progress and growth should continue, they urged, but it should be more strictly defined by the needs of individuals and communities.

THE CRISIS OF THE 1890S

The agrarian protest was only one of many indications of the national political crisis emerging in the 1890s. There was a severe depression, which began in 1893. There was widespread labor unrest and violence, culminating in the tumultuous strikes of 1894. There was the continuing failure of either major party to respond to the growing distress. And there was the rigid conservatism of Grover Cleveland, who took office for the second time just at the moment that the economy collapsed. Out of this growing sense of crisis came some of the most heated political battles in American history, culminating in the dramatic campaign of 1896, on which, many Americans came to believe, the future of the nation hung.

The Panic of 1893

The Panic of 1893 precipitated the most severe depression the nation had yet experienced. It began in March 1893, when the Philadelphia and Reading Railroad, unable to meet payments on loans it had secured from British banks, declared bankruptcy. Two months later, the National Cordage Company (a new corporation that was trying unsuccessfully to establish itself as the dominant force in its industry) failed as well. Together, the two corporate failures triggered a collapse of the stock market. And since many of the major New York banks were heavy investors in the market, a wave of

THE PANIC OF 1893
The floor of the New York stock exchange was a scene of pandemonium on May 5, 1893, when a collapse in stock prices helped usher in the devastating depression of the 1890s. The artist Charles Broughton made sketches of the scene on the spot and later used them as the basis of this drawing. *(Bettmann)*

bank failures soon began. That caused a contraction of credit, which meant that many of the new, aggressive businesses that had recently begun operations soon went bankrupt because they were unable to secure the loans they needed.

There were other, longer-range causes of the financial collapse. Depressed prices in agriculture since 1887 had weakened the purchasing power of farmers, the largest group in the population. Depression conditions that had begun earlier in Europe were resulting in a loss of American markets abroad and a withdrawal by foreign investors of gold invested in the United States. Railroads and other major industries had expanded too rapidly, well beyond market demand. The depression reflected, too, the degree to which the American economy was now interconnected, the degree to which failures in one area affected all other areas. And the depression showed how dependent the economy was on the health of the railroads, which remained the nation's most powerful corporate and financial institutions. When the railroads suffered, as they did beginning in 1893, everything suffered.

Once the panic began, its effects spread with startling speed. Within six months, more than 8,000 businesses, 156 railroads, and 400 banks failed. Already-low agricultural prices tumbled further. Up to 1 million workers, 20 percent of the labor force, lost their jobs—the highest level of unemployment in American history to that point, a level comparable to that of the Great Depression of the 1930s. The leading financial newspaper of the time declared in the summer of 1893: "The month of August will long remain memorable in our industrial history. Never before has there been such a sudden and striking cessation of industrial activity. Nor is any section of the country exempt from the paralysis." The depression was unprecedented not only in its severity but also in its persistence. Although there was slight improvement beginning in 1895, prosperity did not fully return until 1901.

The suffering the depression caused naturally produced social unrest, not least among the enormous numbers of unemployed workers. In 1894, Jacob S. Coxey, an Ohio businessman and Populist, began advocating a massive public works program to create jobs for the unemployed and an inflation of the currency. When it became clear that his proposals were making no progress in Congress, Coxey announced that he would "send a petition to Washington with boots on"—a march of the unemployed to the capital to present their demands to the government. "Coxey's Army," as it was known, numbered only about 500 when it reached Washington, after having marched on foot from Masillon, Ohio. Armed police barred them from the Capitol and arrested Coxey (who was later convicted—of walking on the grass). He and his followers were herded into camps because their presence supposedly endangered public health. Congress took no action on their demands.

There were many signs of union unrest as well during the decade—the Homestead and Pullman strikes, for example. (See above, pp. 497–498.) To many middle-class Americans, the labor turmoil was a sign of a dangerous instability, even perhaps a revolution. Labor radicalism—some of it real, much of it imagined by the frightened middle class—was of persistent concern to much of the public, heightening the general sense of crisis.

The Silver Question

The financial panic weakened the government's monetary system. President Cleveland was one of many people who believed that the instability of the currency was the primary cause of the depression. The "money question," therefore, became the basis for some of the most dramatic political conflicts of the era.

The currency issue is a complicated and confusing one, and later generations have often had difficulty understanding the enormous passions the controversy aroused. The heart of the debate was over what would form the basis of the dollar, what would lie behind it and give it value. Today, the value of the dollar rests on little more than public confidence in the government. But in the nineteenth century, currency was assumed to be worthless if there was not something concrete behind it—precious metal (specie), which holders of paper money could collect if they presented their currency to a bank or to the Treasury.

During most of its existence as a nation, the United States had recognized two metals—gold and silver—as a basis for the dollar, a situation known as "bimetallism." In the 1870s, however, that had changed. The official ratio of the value of silver to the value of gold for purposes of creating currency (the "mint ratio") was 16 to 1: sixteen ounces of silver equaled one ounce of gold. But the actual commercial value of silver (the "market ratio") was much higher than that. Owners of silver could get more by selling it for manufacture into jewelry and other objects than they could by taking it to the mint for conversion to coins. So they stopped taking it to the mint, and the mint stopped coining silver.

In 1873, Congress passed a law that seemed simply to recognize the existing situation by officially discontinuing silver coinage. Few objected at the time. But in the course of the 1870s, the market value of silver fell well below the official mint ratio of 16 to 1. (Sixteen ounces of silver, in other words, were now worth *less*, not more, than one ounce of gold.) Silver was available for coinage again. Congress had foreclosed a potential method of expanding the currency. Before long, many Americans concluded that a conspiracy of big bankers had been responsible for the "demonetization" of silver and referred to the law as the "Crime of '73."

Two groups of Americans were especially determined to undo the "Crime of '73." One consisted of the silver-mine owners, now understandably eager to have the government take their surplus silver and pay them much more than the market price. The other group consisted of discontented farmers, who wanted an increase in the quantity of money—an inflation of the currency—as a means of raising the prices of farm products and easing payment of the farmers' debts. The inflationists demanded that the government return at once to "free silver"—that is, to the "free and unlimited coinage of silver" at the old ratio of 16 to 1. But by the time the depression began in 1893, Congress had made no more than a token response to their demands.

At the same time, the nation's gold reserves were steadily dropping. And the panic of 1893 intensified the demands on those reserves. President Cleveland believed that the chief cause of the weakening gold reserves was the Sherman Silver Purchase Act of 1893, which had required the government to purchase (but not to coin) silver, and to pay for it in gold. Early in his second administration, therefore, a special session responded to his request and repealed the Sherman Act—although only after a bitter and divisive battle that helped create a permanent split in the Democratic Party. The president's gold policy had aligned the southern and western Democrats in a solid phalanx against him and his eastern followers.

By now, both sides had invested the currency question with great symbolic and emotional importance. Indeed, the issue aroused passions rarely seen in American politics, culminating in the tumultuous presidential election of 1896. Supporters of the gold standard considered its survival essential to the honor and stability of the nation. Supporters of free silver considered the gold standard an instrument of tyranny. "Free silver" became to them a symbol of liberation. Silver would be a "people's money," as opposed to gold, the money of oppression and exploitation. It would eliminate the indebtedness of farmers and of whole regions of the country. A graphic illustration of the popularity of the silver issue was the enormous success of William H. Harvey's *Coin's Financial School*, published in 1894, which became one of the great best sellers of its age. The fictional Professor Coin ran an imaginary school specializing in finance, and the book consisted of his lectures and his dialogues with his students. The professor's brilliant discourses left even his most vehement opponents dazzled as he persuaded his listeners, with simple logic, of the almost miraculous restorative qualities of free silver: "It means the reopening of closed factories, the relighting of fires in darkened furnaces; it means hope instead of despair; comfort in place of suffering; life instead of death."

"A Cross of Gold"

Most Populists did not pay much attention to the silver issue at first. But as the party developed strength, the money question became more important to its leaders. The Populists desperately needed funds to finance their campaigns. Silver-mine owners were willing to provide them but insisted on an elevation of the currency plank. And the Populists needed to form alliances with other political groups. The "money question" seemed a way to win the support of many people not engaged in farming but nevertheless starved for currency.

As the election of 1896 approached, Republicans, watching the failure of Cleveland and the Democrats to deal effectively with the depression, were confident of success. Party leaders, led by the Ohio boss Marcus A. Hanna, settled on Governor William McKinley of Ohio, author of the 1890 tariff act, as the party's presidential candidate. The Republican platform opposed the free coinage of silver except by agreement with the leading commercial nations (which everyone realized was unlikely). Thirty-four delegates from the mountain and plains states walked out in protest and joined the Democratic Party.

The Democratic convention of 1896 was the scene of unusual drama. Southern and western delegates, eager to fight off the challenge of the People's Party, were determined to seize control of the party from conservative easterners and incorporate some Populist demands—among them free silver—into the Democratic platform. They wanted as well to nominate a pro-silver candidate. The divided platform committee presented two reports to the convention. The majority report, the work of westerners and southerners, called for tariff reduction, an income tax, "stricter control" of trusts and railroads, and—most prominently—free silver. The minority report, the product of the party's eastern wing, echoed the Republican platform by opposing the free coinage of silver except by international agreement. The debate over the two competing platforms dominated the convention.

Defenders of the gold standard seemed to dominate the debate, until the final speech. Then William Jennings Bryan, a handsome, thirty-six-year-old congressman from Nebraska already well known as an effective orator, mounted the podium to address the convention. His great voice echoed through the hall as

WILLIAM JENNINGS BRYAN
Bryan addresses a crowd late in his career, displaying the flamboyant oratorical style that characterized his public life from the beginning. The poster at the lower left of the platform shows him as he appeared in the 1890s, when, as a young congressman from Nebraska, he became known as the "Boy Orator of the Platte" and the leader of the national free-silver movement. *(Library of Congress)*

he delivered what became one of the most famous political speeches in American history in support of free silver. The closing passage sent his audience into something close to a frenzy: "If they dare to come out in the open and defend the gold standard as a good thing, we will fight them to the uttermost. Having behind us the producing masses of this nation and the world, supported by the commercial interests, the laboring interests and the toilers everywhere, we will answer their demand for a gold standard by saying to them: 'You shall not press down upon the brow of labor this crown of thorns; you shall not crucify mankind upon a cross of gold.'" It became known as the "Cross of Gold" speech.

The convention voted to adopt the pro-silver platform. Perhaps more important, the agrarians had found a leader. And the following day, Bryan (as he had eagerly and not entirely secretly hoped) was nominated for president on the fifth ballot. He was, and remains, the youngest person ever nominated for president by a major party. Republican and conservative Democrats attacked Bryan as a dangerous demagogue. But his many admirers hailed him as the Great Com-

moner. Born in Illinois of typical middle-class stock, he had attended a small sectarian college, had practiced law with only average success, and then, repeating a normal American pattern, had moved to Nebraska, a frontier area, in search of opportunity. He served as a potent symbol of rural, Protestant, middle-class America.

The choice of Bryan and the nature of the Democratic platform created a quandary for the Populists. They had expected both major parties to adopt conservative programs and nominate conservative candidates, leaving the Populists to represent the growing forces of protest. But now the Democrats had stolen much of their thunder. The Populists faced the choice of naming their own candidate and splitting the protest vote or endorsing Bryan and losing their identity as a party. By now, the Populists had embraced the free-silver cause, but somewhat reluctantly. Most Populists still believed that other issues were more important. Many argued that "fusion" with the Democrats—who had endorsed free silver but ignored most of the other Populist demands—would destroy their party. But the majority concluded that there was no viable alternative. Amid considerable acrimony, the convention voted to support Bryan.

The Conservative Victory

The campaign of 1896 produced desperation among conservatives. The business and financial community, frightened beyond reason at the prospect of a Bryan victory, contributed lavishly to the Republican campaign, which may have spent as much as $7 million, as compared to the Democrats' $300,000. From his home at Canton, Ohio, McKinley conducted a dignified "front-porch" campaign before pilgrimages of the Republican faithful, organized and paid for by Hanna.

Bryan showed no such restraint. He became the first presidential candidate in American history to stump every section of the country systematically, to appear in villages and hamlets, indeed the first to say frankly to the voters that he wanted to be president. He traveled 18,000 miles and addressed an estimated 5 million people. But Bryan may have done himself more harm than good. His revivalistic, camp-meeting style pleased old-stock Protestants, but it antagonized many of the immigrant Catholics and other ethnics who normally voted Democratic. By violating a longstanding tradition by which presidential candidates remained aloof from their own campaigns (the tradition by which they "stood" for office rather than "running" for it), Bryan helped establish the modern form of presidential politics. But he also antagonized many voters, who considered his campaign undignified.

On election day, McKinley polled 271 electoral votes to Bryan's 176 and received 51.1 percent of the popular vote to Bryan's 47.7. Bryan carried only those areas of the South and West where miners or struggling staple farmers predominated. The Democratic program, like that of the Populists, had been too narrow to win a national election.

For the Populists and their allies, the election results were a disaster. They had gambled everything on their "fusion" with the Democratic Party and lost. Within months of the election, the People's Party began to dissolve. Never again would American farmers unite so militantly to demand economic reform. And never again would so large a group of Americans raise so forceful a protest against the nature of the industrial economy.

McKinley and Recovery

The administration of William McKinley, which began in the aftermath of turmoil, saw a return to relative calm. One reason was the exhaustion of dissent. By

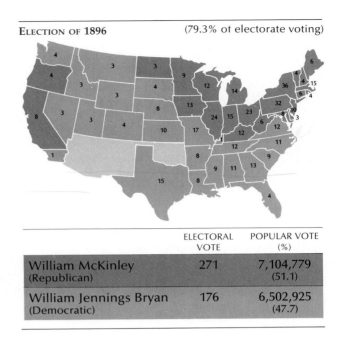

ELECTION OF **1896** (79.3% of electorate voting)

	ELECTORAL VOTE	POPULAR VOTE (%)
William McKinley (Republican)	271	7,104,779 (51.1)
William Jennings Bryan (Democratic)	176	6,502,925 (47.7)

1897, when McKinley took office, the labor unrest that had so frightened many middle-class Americans and so excited working-class people had subsided. With the simultaneous decline of agrarian protest, the greatest destabilizing forces in the nation's politics were—temporarily at least—in retreat. Another reason was the character of the McKinley administration itself, which was politically shrewd and committed to a reassuring stability. Most important, however, was the gradual easing of the economic crisis, a change that undercut many of those who were agitating for change.

McKinley and his allies committed themselves fully to only one issue, one on which they knew virtually all Republicans agreed: the need for higher tariff rates. Within weeks of his inauguration, the administration won approval of the Dingley Tariff, raising the duties to the highest point in American history. The administration dealt more gingerly with the explosive silver question (an issue that McKinley himself had never considered very important in any case). McKinley sent a commission to Europe to explore the possibility of a silver agreement with Great Britain and France. As he and everyone else anticipated, the effort produced no agreement. The Republicans then enacted the Currency, or Gold Standard, Act of 1900, which confirmed the nation's commitment to the gold standard.

And so the "battle of the standards" ended in victory for the forces of conservatism. Economic developments at the time seemed to vindicate the Republi-

SIGNIFICANT EVENTS

1867 National Grange founded	McKinley Tariff enacted
1873 Congress discontinues coinage of silver	Southern and Northwestern Alliances hold national convention at Ocala, Florida
1875 First Farmers' Alliances form in Texas	**1892** Cleveland elected president again
1877 *Munn* v. *Illinois* upholds Granger Laws regulating railroads	People's Party formed in Omaha
1880 James A. Garfield elected president	**1893** Commercial and financial panic launches severe and prolonged depression
1881 Garfield assassinated	Congress repeals Sherman Silver Purchase Act
Chester A. Arthur succeeds him	**1894** Wilson-Gorman Tariff enacted
1883 Congress passes Pendleton Act, first national civil service law	Coxey's Army marches on Washington
1884 Grover Cleveland elected president	William Harvey publishes *Coin's Financial School*
1886 Supreme Court in *Wabash* case restricts state regulation of commerce	**1895** *United States* v. *E. C. Knight Co.* weakens Sherman Antitrust Act
1887 Interstate Commerce Act passed	**1896** William Jennings Bryan wins Democratic nomination after "Cross of Gold" speech at convention
Farm prices collapse	Populists endorse Bryan for president
1888 Benjamin Harrison elected president	William McKinley elected president
1890 Sherman Antitrust Act passed	**1898** Economy begins to revive
Sherman Silver Purchase Act passed	**1900** Gold Standard Act passed

cans. Prosperity began to return in 1898. Foreign crop failures sent farm prices surging upward, and American business entered another cycle of expansion. Prosperity and the gold standard, it seemed, were closely allied.

But while the free-silver movement had failed, it had raised an important question for the American economy. In the quarter century before 1900, the countries of the Western world had experienced a spectacular growth in productive facilities and population. Yet the supply of money had not kept pace with economic progress, because the supply was tied to gold and the amount of gold had remained practically constant. Had it not been for a dramatic increase in the gold supply in the late 1890s (a result of new techniques for extracting gold from low-content ores and the discovery of huge new gold deposits in Alaska, South Africa, and Australia), populist predictions of financial disaster might in fact have proved correct. In 1898, two and a half times as much gold was produced as in 1890, and the currency supply was soon inflated far beyond anything Bryan and the free-silver forces had anticipated.

By then, however, Bryan—like many other Americans—was becoming engaged with another major issue: a growing United States presence in world affairs and the possibility of America becoming an imperialist nation.

SUGGESTED READINGS

General Histories. Sean Dennis Cashman, *America and the Gilded Age* (1984). Carl N. Degler, *The Age of the Economic Revolution, 1876–1900*, 2nd. ed. (1977). John H. Dobson, *Politics in the Gilded Age* (1972). Harold U. Faulkner, *Politics, Reform, and Expansion* (1959). John A. Garraty, *The New Commonwealth* (1969). Samuel P. Hays, *The Response to Industrialism, 1885–1914* (1957). Nell Irvin Painter, *Standing at Armageddon: The United States, 1877–1919* (1987). Alan Trachtenberg, *The Intercorporation of America: Culture and Society in the Gilded Age* (1982). Robert Wiebe, *The Search for Order, 1877–1920* (1967). R. Hal Williams, *Years of Decision: American Politics in the 1890s* (1978).

Politics, Reform, and the States. Geoffrey Blodgett, *The Gentle Reformers* (1966). Ruth Bourdin, *Women and Temperance: The Quest for Power and Liberty, 1873–1900* (1980). James Bryce, *The American Commonwealth*, 2 vols. (1888). Ari Hoogenboom, *Outlawing the Spoils: The Civil Service Movement* (1961). Richard Jensen, *The Winning of the Midwest: Social and Political Conflict, 1888–1896* (1971). Matthew Josephson, *The Politicos* (1963). Morton Keller, *Affairs of State* (1977). Paul Kleppner, *The Cross of Culture: A Social Analysis of Midwestern Politics, 1850–1900* (1970); *The Third Electoral System, 1853–1892* (1979). J. Morgan Kousser, *The Shaping of Southern Politics: Suffrage Restriction and the Establishment of the One-Party South, 1880–1910* (1974). Michael P. Malone, *The Battle for Butte: Mining and Politics on the Northern Frontier, 1864–1906* (1981). Robert D. Marcus, *Grand Old Party* (1971). Gerald W. McFarland, *Mugwumps, Morals, and Politics, 1884–1920* (1975). Michael E. McGerr, *The Decline of Popular Politics* (1986). H. Wayne Morgan, *From Hayes to McKinley* (1969). Walter T. K. Nugent, *Money and American Society, 1865–1880* (1968). David J. Rothman, *Politics and Power: The United States Senate, 1869–1901* (1966). Martin J. Sklar, *The Corporate Reconstruction of American Capitalism, 1890–1916* (1988). Stephen Skowronek, *Building a New American State: The Expansion of National Administrative Capacities, 1877–1920* (1982). John Sproat, "The Best Men": Liberal Reformers in the Gilded Age* (1968). Tom E. Terrill, *The Tariff, Politics, and American Foreign Policy, 1874–1901* (1973). Irwin Unger, *The Greenback Era* (1964). Leonard D. White, *The Republican Era* (1958).

Party Leaders. Harry Barnard, *Rutherford B. Hayes and His America* (1954). Herbert Croly, *Marcus Alonzo Hanna* (1912). Kenneth Davison, *The Presidency of Rutherford B. Hayes* (1972). Lewis L. Gould, *The Presidency of William McKinley* (1981). David Jordan, *Roscoe Conkling of New York* (1971). Margaret Leech, *In the Days of McKinley* (1959). Margaret Leech and Harry J. Brown, *The Garfield Orbit* (1978). Horace Samuel Merrill, *Bourbon Leader: Grover Cleveland and the Democratic Party*

(1957). H. Wayne Morgan, *William McKinley and His America* (1963). Allan Nevins, *Grover Cleveland: A Study in Courage* (1933). Allan Peskin, *Garfield* (1978). Thomas C. Reeves, *Gentleman Boss: The Life of Chester Alan Arthur* (1975). Nick Salvatore, *Eugene V. Debs: Citizen and Socialist* (1982). Harry J. Sievers, *Benjamin Harrison*, 3 vols. (1952-1968).

The Depression. Ray Ginger, *Altgeld's America* (1958); *The Bending Cross* (1949). Almot Lindsey, *The Pullman Strike* (1942). Donald McMurray, *Coxey's Army* (1929). Samuel McSeveney, *The Politics of Depression* (1972). Carlos A. Schwantes, *Coxey's Army* (1955).

Populism. Peter Argersinger, *Populism and Politics: William Alfred Peffer and the People's Party* (1974). O. Gene Clanton, *Populism: The Humane Preference in America, 1890–1900* (1991); *Kansas Populism: Ideas and Men* (1969). Robert F. Durden, *The Climax of Populism: The Election of 1896* (1965). Lawrence Goodwyn, *Democratic Promise* (1976); *The Populist Moment* (1978), an abridgement of *Democratic Promise*. Sheldon Hackney, *Populism to Progressivism in Alabama* (1969). Steven Hahn, *The Roots of Southern Populism: Yeoman Farmers and the Transformation of the Georgia Upcountry, 1850–1890* (1983). John D. Hicks, *The Populist Revolt* (1931). Richard Hofstadter, *The Age of Reform* (1954). Robert McMath, *Populist Vanguard* (1975). Theodore R. Mitchell, *Political Education in the Southern Farmers Alliance, 1887–1900* (1987). Walter T. K. Nugent, *The Tolerant Populists* (1960). Bruce Palmer, *Man over Money* (1980). Stanley Parsons, *The Populist Context: Rural Versus Urban Power on a Great Plains Frontier* (1973). Norman Pollack, *The Populist Response to Industrial America* (1962); *The Just Polity: Populism, Law, and Human Welfare* (1987). Martin Ridge, *Ignatius Donnelly: Portrait of a Politician* (1962). Theodore Saloutos, *Farmer Movements in the South, 1865–1933* (1960). Fred Shannon, *The Farmer's Last Frontier* (1945). Barton C. Shaw, *The Wool-Hat Boys: Georgia's Populist Party* (1984). Francis B. Simkins, *Pitchfork Ben Tillman* (1944). Allan Weinstein, *Prelude of Populism: Origins of the Silver Issue* (1970). C. Vann Woodward, *Origins of the New South* (1972); *Tom Watson, Agrarian Rebel* (1938). James E. Wright, *The Politics of Populism: Dissent in Colorado* (1974).

The "Battle of the Standards" and the Election of 1896. Paolo Coletta, *William Jennings Bryan*, 3 vols., (1964–1969). Milton Friedman and Anna J. Schwartz, *A Monetary History of the United States* (1963). Paul Glad, *McKinley, Bryan, and the People* (1964); *The Trumpet Soundeth* (1960). J. Rogers Hollingsworth, *The Whirligig of Politics: The Democracy of Cleveland and Bryan* (1963). Stanley Jones, *The Presidential Election of 1896* (1964).

"MEASURING UNCLE SAM FOR A NEW SUIT," BY J. S. PUGHE, IN _PUCK_ MAGAZINE, 1900
President William McKinley is favorably depicted here as a tailor, measuring his client for a
suit large enough to accommodate the new possessions the United States obtained in the
aftermath of the Spanish-American War. The cartoon tries to link this expansion with
earlier, less controversial ones such as the Louisiana Purchase. *(Culver)*

CHAPTER TWENTY

THE IMPERIAL REPUBLIC

HE AMERICAN REPUBLIC HAD been an expansionist nation since the earliest days of its existence. Throughout the first half of the nineteenth century, as the population of the United States grew and pressed westward, the government had continually acquired new territory: the trans-Appalachian West, the Louisiana Territory, Florida, Texas, Oregon, California, New Mexico, Alaska. It was the nation's "Manifest Destiny," many Americans believed, to expand into new realms.

In the last years of the nineteenth century, with little potential left for territorial growth on the North American continent, U.S. expansionism moved into a new phase. In the past, the nation had generally annexed land adjacent to its existing boundaries into which American citizens could move relatively easily and which could ultimately become states of the Union. But the expansionism of the 1890s, the new Manifest Destiny, involved acquiring possessions separate from the continental United States: island territories, many thickly populated, most of which would not attract massive settlement from America, and few of which were likely to become states. The United States was joining England, France, Germany, and others in the great imperial drive that by the end of the century was to bring much of the underdeveloped world under the control of the industrial powers of the West.

STIRRINGS OF IMPERIALISM

For over two decades after the Civil War, the United States expanded hardly at all. By the 1890s, however, some Americans were ready—indeed, eager—to resume the course of Manifest Destiny that had inspired their ancestors to wrest an empire from Mexico in the expansionist 1840s.

The New Manifest Destiny

Several developments helped shift American attention to lands across the seas. The experience of subjugating the Indian tribes had established a precedent for exerting colonial control over dependent peoples. The concept of the "closing of the frontier," widely heralded by Frederick Jackson Turner and many others in the 1890s, produced fears that natural resources would soon dwindle and that alternative sources must be found abroad. The depression that began in 1893 encouraged some businessmen to look overseas for new markets. The bitter social protests of the time—the Populist movement, the free-silver crusade, the bloody labor disputes—led some politicians to urge a more aggressive foreign policy as an outlet for frustrations that would otherwise destabilize domestic life.

IMPERIALISM AT HIGH TIDE: THE WORLD IN 1900

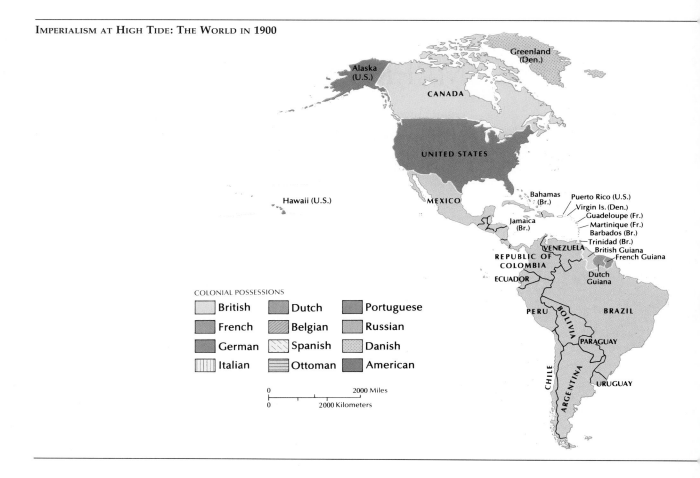

COLONIAL POSSESSIONS

British Dutch Portuguese
French Belgian Russian
German Spanish Danish
Italian Ottoman American

0   2000 Miles
0   2000 Kilometers

Foreign trade was becoming increasingly important to the American economy in the late nineteenth century. The nation's exports had totaled about $392 million goods in 1870; by 1890, the figure was $857 million; and by 1900, $1.4 billion. Many Americans began to consider the possibility of acquiring colonies that might expand such markets further. "Today," Senator Albert J. Beveridge of Indiana cried in 1899, "we are raising more than we can consume. Today, we are making more than we can use. Therefore, we must find new markets for our produce, new occupation for our capital, new work for our labor."

Americans were, moreover, well aware of the imperialist fever that was raging through Europe and leading the major powers to partition most of Africa among themselves and to turn eager eyes on the Far East and the feeble Chinese Empire. Some Americans feared that their nation would soon be left out, that no territory would remain to be acquired. Senator Henry Cabot Lodge of Massachusetts, a leading imperialist, warned that the United States "must not fall out of the line of march."

Scholars and others found a philosophic justification for expansionism in Charles Darwin's theories. They contended that nations or "races," like biological species, struggled constantly for existence and that only the fittest could survive. For strong nations to dominate weak ones was, therefore, in accordance with the laws of nature. (This was an application to world affairs of the same distortion of Darwinism that industrialists and others had long been applying to domestic economic affairs in the form of Social Darwinism.)

One of the first to advance this argument was the popular writer John Fiske, who predicted in an 1885 article in *Harper's Magazine* that the English-speaking peoples would eventually control every land that was not already the seat of an "established civilization." The experience of white Americans in subjugating the native population of their own continent, Fiske argued,

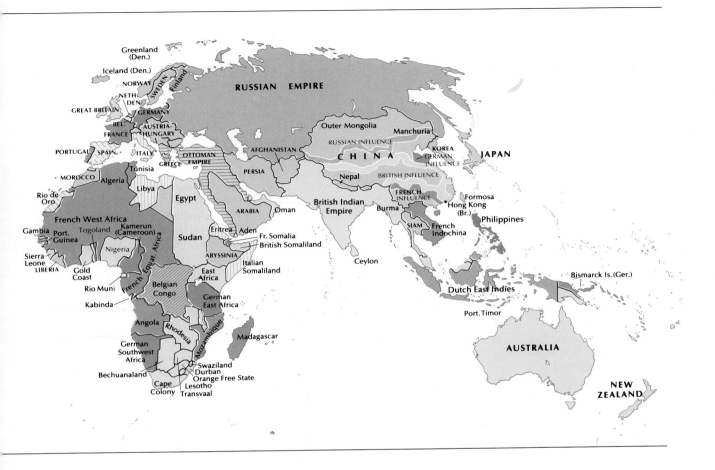

was "destined to go on" in other parts of the world. Support for Fiske's position came the same year from Josiah Strong, a Congregational clergyman and champion of overseas missionary work. In a book entitled *Our Country: Its Possible Future and Its Present Crisis* (1885), Strong declared that the Anglo-Saxon "race," and especially its American branch, represented the great ideas of civil liberty and pure Christianity and was "divinely commissioned" to spread its institutions over the earth. John W. Burgess, founder of Columbia University's School of Political Science, gave a stamp of scholarly approval to imperialism. In his 1890 study *Political Science and Comparative Law*, he flatly stated that the Anglo-Saxon and Teutonic nations possessed the highest political talents. It was their duty, therefore, to uplift less fortunate peoples, even to force superior institutions on them if necessary. "There is," he wrote, "no human right to the status of barbarism."

The ablest and most effective apostle of imperialism was Alfred Thayer Mahan, a captain and later ad-miral in the United States Navy. Mahan's thesis, presented in *The Influence of Sea Power upon History* (1890) and other works, was simple: Countries with sea power were the great nations of history; the greatness of the United States, bounded by two oceans, would rest on its sea power. The prerequisites for sea power were a productive domestic economy, foreign commerce, a strong merchant marine, a navy to defend trade routes—and colonies, which would provide raw materials and markets and could serve as bases for the navy. Specifically, Mahan advocated that the United States construct a canal across the isthmus of Central America to join the oceans, acquire defensive bases on both sides of the canal in the Caribbean and the Pacific, and take possession of Hawaii and other Pacific islands. "Whether they will or no," he proclaimed, "Americans must now begin to look outward."

Mahan feared the United States did not have a large enough navy to play the great role he envisioned. But during the 1870s and 1880s, the government launched a shipbuilding program that by 1898 had moved the United States to fifth place among the world's naval powers, and by 1900 to third.

Hemispheric Hegemony

James G. Blaine, who served as secretary of state in two Republican administrations in the 1880s, led early efforts to expand American influence into Latin America, where, he believed, the United States must look for markets for its surplus goods. In October 1889, Blaine helped organize the first Pan-American Congress, which attracted delegates from nineteen nations. The delegates agreed to create the Pan-American Union, a weak international organization located in Washington which served as a clearinghouse for distributing information to the member nations. But they rejected Blaine's more substantive proposals: for an inter-American customs union and arbitration procedures for hemispheric disputes.

The Cleveland administration took a similarly active interest in Latin America. In 1895, it supported Venezuela in a dispute with Great Britain over the boundary between Venezuela and British Guiana. When the British ignored American demands that the matter be submitted to arbitration, Secretary of State Richard Olney charged that Britain was violating the Monroe Doctrine. When Britain still did not act, Cleveland created a special commission to determine the boundary line; if Britain resisted the commission's decision, he insisted, the United States should be willing to go to war to enforce it. As war talk raged throughout the country, the British government finally realized that it had stumbled into a genuine diplomatic crisis and agreed to arbitration.

Hawaii and Samoa

The islands of Hawaii in the mid-Pacific had been an important way station for American ships in the China trade since the early nineteenth century. By the 1880s, officers of the expanding American navy were looking covetously at Pearl Harbor on the island of Oahu as a possible permanent base for United States ships. Pressure for an increased American presence in Hawaii was emerging from another source as well: the growing number of Americans who had settled on the islands and who had gradually come to dominate their economic and political life.

In doing so, the Americans were wresting authority away from the leaders of an ancient civilization. Settled by Polynesian people beginning in about 1500 B.C., Hawaii had developed an agricultural and fishing society in which different islands (and different communities on the same islands), each with its own chieftain, lived more or less self-sufficiently. When the first Americans arrived in Hawaii in the 1790s on merchant ships from New England, there were perhaps a half million people living there.

Battles among rival communities were frequent, as ambitious chieftains tried to consolidate power over their neighbors. In 1810, after a series of such battles, King Kamehameha I established his dominance over the other chieftains on Hawaii. He welcomed American traders and helped them develop a thriving trade between Hawaii and China, from which the natives profited along with the merchants. But Americans soon wanted more than trade. Missionaries began settling there in the early nineteenth century; and in the 1830s, William Hooper, a Boston trader, became the first of many Americans to buy land and establish a sugar plantation on the islands.

The arrival of these merchants, missionaries, and planters was devastating to Hawaiian society. The newcomers inadvertently brought infectious diseases to which the Hawaiians, like the American Indians before them, were tragically vulnerable. By the mid-nineteenth century, more than half the native population had died. By the turn of the century, disease had cut the population by more than half again. But the Americans brought other incursions as well. Missionaries worked to undermine native religion. Other white settlers introduced liquor, firearms, and a commercial economy, all of which eroded the traditional character of Hawaiian society. By the 1840s, American planters had spread throughout the islands; and an American settler, G. P. Judd, had become prime minister of Hawaii under King Kamehameha III, who had agreed to establish a constitutional monarchy. Judd governed Hawaii for over a decade.

In 1887, the United States negotiated a treaty with Hawaii that permitted it to open a naval base at Pearl Harbor. By then, growing sugar for export to America had become the basis of the Hawaiian economy—as a result of an 1875 agreement allowing Hawaiian sugar to enter the United States duty-free. The American-dominated sugar plantation system not only displaced native Hawaiians from their lands but relied heavily for workers on Asian immigrants, whom the Americans considered more reliable and more docile than the natives. Indeed, finding adequate labor, and keeping it under control, was the principal concern of many planters. Some deliberately sought to create a mixed-race work force (Chinese, Japanese, native Hawaiian, Filipinos, Portuguese, and others) as a way to keep the workers divided and unlikely to challenge them.

Native Hawaiians did not accept their subordination without protest. In 1891, they elevated a power-

ful nationalist to the throne: Queen Liliuokalani, who set out to challenge the growing American control of the islands. But she remained in power only two years. In 1890, the United States had eliminated the privileged position of Hawaiian sugar in international trade. The result was devastating to the economy of the islands, and American planters concluded that the only way for them to recover was to become part of the United States (and hence exempt from its tariffs). In 1893 they staged a revolution and called on the United States for protection. After the American minister ordered marines from a warship in Honolulu harbor to go ashore to aid the rebels, the queen yielded her authority.

A provisional government, dominated by Americans (who constituted less than 5 percent of the population of the islands), immediately sent a delegation to Washington to negotiate a treaty of annexation. President Harrison signed an annexation agreement in February 1893, just before leaving office. But the Senate, controlled by Democrats after the 1892 election, refused to ratify the treaty, and Grover Cleveland, the new president, refused to support it. Debate over the annexation of Hawaii continued until 1898, when the Republicans returned to power and approved the agreement.

Three thousand miles south of Hawaii, the Samoan islands, had also long served as a way station for American ships in the Pacific trade. As American commerce with Asia increased, business groups in the United States regarded Samoa with new interest, and the American navy began eyeing the Samoan harbor at Pago Pago. In 1878, the Hayes administration extracted a treaty from Samoan leaders for an American naval station at Pago Pago. It bound the United States to arbitrate any differences between Samoa and other nations. Clearly, the United States now expected to have a voice in Samoan affairs.

But Great Britain and Germany were also interested in the islands, and they too secured treaty rights from the native princes. For the next ten years the three powers jockeyed for dominance in Samoa, playing off one native ruler against another and coming dangerously close to war. Finally, the three powers agreed to create a tripartite protectorate over Samoa, with the native chiefs exercising only nominal authority. The three-way arrangement failed to halt the intrigues and rivalries of its members; and in 1899, the United States and Germany divided the islands between them, compensating Britain with territories elsewhere in the Pacific. The United States retained the harbor at Pago Pago.

WAR WITH SPAIN

Imperial ambitions had thus begun to stir within the United States well before the late 1890s. But a war with Spain in 1898 turned those stirrings into overt expansionism. The war transformed America's relationship to the rest of the world, and left the nation with a far-flung overseas empire.

THE DUTY OF THE HOUR:—TO SAVE HER NOT ONLY FROM SPAIN BUT FROM A WORSE FATE.

"THE DUTY OF THE HOUR"
This 1892 lithograph was no doubt inspired by the saying "Out of the frying pan and into the fire." A despairing Cuba, struggling to escape from the frying pan of Spanish misrule, contemplates an even more dangerous alternative: "anarchy" (or home rule). Cartoonist Louis Dalrymple here suggests that the only real solution to Cuba's problems is control by the United States, whose "duty" to Cuba is "To Save Her Not Only from Spain but from a Worse Fate."   *(The Granger Collection)*

Controversy over Cuba

The Spanish-American War emerged out of events in Cuba, which along with Puerto Rico represented virtually all that remained of Spain's once extensive American empire. Cubans had been resisting Spanish rule since at least 1868, when they began a long but ultimately unsuccessful fight for independence. Many Americans had sympathized with the Cubans during that ten-year struggle, but the United States did not intervene.

In 1895, the Cubans rose up again. (Although their goal was an end to Spanish misrule, the island's problems were now in part a result of the Wilson-Gorman Tariff of 1894, whose high duties on sugar had prostrated Cuba's important sugar economy by cutting off exports to the United States, the island's principal market.) This rebellion produced a ferocity on both sides that horrified Americans. The Cubans deliberately devastated the island to force the Spaniards to

leave. The Spanish, commanded by General Valeriano Weyler (known in the American press as "Butcher" Weyler), confined civilians in some areas to hastily prepared concentration camps, where they died by the thousands, victims of disease and malnutrition.

The Spanish had used some of these same savage methods during the earlier struggle in Cuba without shocking American sensibilities. But the revolt of 1895 was reported more fully and floridly by the American press, which helped create the impression that the Spaniards were committing all the atrocities, when in fact there was considerable brutality on both sides.

The conflict in Cuba came at a particularly opportune moment for the publishers of some American newspapers. Joseph Pulitzer with his New York *World* and William Randolph Hearst with his New York *Journal* were revolutionizing American journalism in the late nineteenth century by creating a new "penny press," which catered openly to a broad popular au-

863,956
WORLDS CIRCULATED YESTERDAY

The World

863,956
WORLDS CIRCULATED YESTERDAY

MAINE EXPLOSION CAUSED BY BOMB OR TORPEDO

Capt. Sigsbee and Consul-General Lee Are in Doubt---The World Has Sent Special Tug, With Submarine Divers, to Havana to Find Out---Lee Asks for an Immediate Court of Inquiry---Capt. Sigsbee's Suspicions.

CAPT. SIGSBEE, IN A SUPPRESSED DESPATCH TO THE STATE DEPARTMENT, SAYS THE ACCIDENT WAS MADE POSSIBLE BY AN ENEMY

Dr. E. C. Pendleton, Just Arrived from Havana, Says He Overheard Talk There of a Plot to Blow Up the Ship---Capt. Zalinski, the Dynamite Expert, and Other Experts Report to The World that the Wreck Was Not Accidental---Washington Officials Ready for Vigorous Action if Spanish Responsibility Can Be Shown---Divers to Be Sent Down to Make Careful Examinations.

THE YELLOW PRESS AND THE WRECK OF THE *MAINE*

No evidence was ever found tying the Spanish to the explosion in Havana harbor that destroyed the American battleship *Maine* in February 1898. Indeed, most evidence indicated that the blast came from inside the ship, a fact that suggests an accident rather than sabotage. Nevertheless, the newspapers of Joseph Pulitzer and William Randolph Hearst ran sensational stories about the incident that were designed to arouse public sentiment in support of a war against the Spanish. This front page from Pulitzer's *New York World* is an example of the lurid coverage the event received. Circulation figures at the top of the page suggest, too, how successful the coverage was in selling newspapers. (*The Granger Collection*)

dience, lower in economic status than the traditional press. Their papers specialized in lurid and sensational news; when such news did not exist, editors were not above creating it. More traditional journalists referred to the new form as "yellow journalism." In the 1890s, Hearst and Pulitzer were engaged in a ruthless circulation war, and they saw the struggle in Cuba as a great opportunity. Both sent batteries of reporters and illustrators to the island with orders to provide accounts of Spanish atrocities. "You furnish the pictures," Hearst supposedly told an overly scrupulous artist, "and I'll furnish the war."

A growing population of Cuban émigrés in the United States—centered in Florida, New York, Philadelphia, and Trenton, New Jersey—gave extensive support to the Cuban Revolutionary Party (whose headquarters was in New York) and helped publicize its leader, José Martí, who was killed in Cuba in 1895. Later, Cuban Americans formed other clubs and associations to support the cause of *Cuba Libre*. In some areas of the country, their efforts were as important as those of the yel-

low journalists in generating popular support for the revolution.

The mounting storm of indignation against Spain did not persuade President Cleveland, who proclaimed American neutrality and tried to stop the agitation by Cuban refugees in New York City. But when McKinley became president in 1897, he took a stronger stand. He formally protested Spain's "uncivilized and inhuman" conduct, causing the Spanish government (fearful of American intervention) to recall Weyler, modify the concentration policy, and grant the island a qualified autonomy. At the end of 1897, with the insurrection losing ground, it seemed that American involvement in the war might be averted.

But whatever chances there were for a peaceful settlement vanished as a result of two dramatic incidents in February 1898. The first occurred when a Cuban agent in Havana stole a private letter written by Dupuy de Lôme, the Spanish minister in Washington, and turned it over to the American press. The letter described McKinley as a weak man and "a bidder for the

THE SPANISH-AMERICAN WAR IN CUBA, 1898

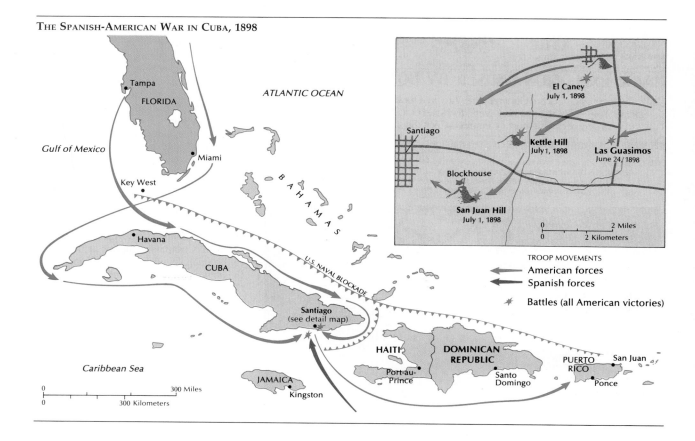

admiration of the crowd." This was no more than many Americans, including some Republicans, were saying about their president. (Theodore Roosevelt described McKinley as having "no more backbone than a chocolate eclair.") But coming from a foreigner, it created intense popular anger. Dupuy de Lôme promptly resigned.

While excitement over the de Lôme letter was still high, the American battleship *Maine* blew up in Havana harbor with a loss of more than 260 people. The ship had been ordered to Cuba in January to protect American lives and property against possible attacks by Spanish loyalists. Many Americans assumed that the Spanish had sunk the ship, particularly when a naval court of inquiry hastily and inaccurately reported that an external explosion by a submarine mine had caused the disaster. (Later evidence suggested that the disaster was actually the result of an accidental explosion inside one of the engine rooms.) War hysteria swept the country, and Congress unanimously appropriated $50 million for military preparations. "Remember the Maine!" became a national chant for revenge.

McKinley still hoped to avoid a conflict. But others in his administration (including Assistant Secretary of the Navy Theodore Roosevelt) were clamoring for war. In March 1898, the president asked Spain to agree to an armistice, negotiations for a permanent peace, and end to the concentration camps. Spain agreed to stop the fighting and eliminate the concentration camps but refused to negotiate with the rebels and reserved the right to resume hostilities at its discretion. That satisfied neither public opinion nor the Congress; and a few days later McKinley asked for and, on April 25, received a congressional declaration of war.

"A Splendid Little War"

Secretary of State John Hay called the Spanish-American conflict "a splendid little war," an opinion that most Americans—with the exception of many of the enlisted men who fought in it—seemed to share. Declared in April, it was over in August. That was in part because Cuban rebels had already greatly weakened the Spanish resistance, which made the American intervention in many respects little more than a "mopping up" exercise. Only 460 Americans were killed in battle or died of wounds, although some 5,200 others perished of disease: malaria, dysentery, and typhoid, among others. Casualties among Cuban insurgents, who continued to bear the brunt of the fighting, were much higher.

And yet the American war effort was not without difficulties. United States soldiers faced serious supply problems: a shortage of modern rifles and ammunition, uniforms too heavy for the warm Caribbean weather, inadequate medical services, and skimpy, almost indigestible food. The regular army numbered only 28,000 troops and officers, most of whom had experience in quelling Indian outbreaks but none in larger-scale warfare. That meant that, as in the Civil War, the United States had to rely heavily on National Guard units, organized by local communities and commanded for the most part by local leaders without military experience. The entire mobilization process was conducted with remarkable inefficiency.

There were also racial conflicts. A significant proportion of the American invasion force consisted of black soldiers. Some were volunteer troops put together by African-American communities (although some governors refused to allow the formation of such units). Others were members of the four black regiments in the regular army, who had been stationed on the frontier to defend white settlements against Indians and were now transferred east to fight in Cuba. As the black soldiers traveled through the South toward the training camps, they chafed at the rigid segregation to which they were subjected and occasionally resisted the restrictions openly. Black soldiers in Georgia deliberately made use of a "whites only" park; in Florida, they beat a soda-fountain operator for refusing to serve them; in Tampa, white provocations and black retaliation led to a nightlong riot that left thirty wounded.

Racial tensions continued in Cuba itself, where American blacks played crucial roles in some of the important battles of the war (including the famous charge at San Juan Hill) and won many medals. Nearly half the Cuban insurgents fighting with the Americans were black, and unlike their American counterparts they were fully integrated into the rebel army. (Indeed, one of the leading insurgent generals, Antonio Maceo, was a black man.) The sight of black Cuban soldiers fighting alongside whites as equals gave American blacks a stronger sense of the injustice of their own position.

Seizing the Philippines

No agency in the American military had clear authority over strategic planning. Only the navy had worked out an objective, and its objective had little to do with freeing Cuba. Assistant Secretary of the Navy Theodore Roosevelt was an ardent imperialist, active proponent of war, and a man uninhibited by the knowledge that he was a relatively minor figure in the military hierarchy. Roosevelt strengthened the navy's Pacific squadron and instructed its commander, Commodore George Dewey, to attack Spanish naval forces in the Philippines, a colony of Spain, in the event of war.

Immediately after war was declared, Dewey sailed for Manila. On May 1, 1898, he steamed into Manila Bay and completely destroyed the aging Spanish fleet stationed there. Only one American sailor died in the battle (of heatstroke), and George Dewey, immediately promoted to admiral, had become the first hero of the war. Several months later, after the arrival of an American expeditionary force, the Spanish surrendered the city of Manila itself. In the rejoicing over Dewey's victory, few Americans paused to note that the character of the war was changing. What had begun as a war to free Cuba was becoming a war to strip Spain of its colonies.

The Battle for Cuba

But Cuba remained the principal focus of American military efforts. At first, the American commanders planned a long period of training before actually sending troops into combat. But when a Spanish fleet under Admiral Pascual Cervera slipped past the American navy into Santiago harbor on the southern coast of Cuba, plans changed quickly. The American Atlantic fleet quickly bottled Cervera up in the harbor. And the U.S. Army's commanding general, Nelson A. Miles, hastily altered his strategy and left Tampa in June with a force of 17,000 to attack Santiago. Both the departure from Florida and the landing in Cuba were scenes of fantastic incompetence. It took five days for this relatively small army to be put ashore, and that with the enemy offering no opposition.

General William R. Shafter, the American commander, moved toward Santiago, which he planned to surround and capture. On the way he met and defeated Spanish forces at Las Guasimas and, a week later, in two simultaneous battles, El Caney and San Juan Hill. At the center of the fighting (and on the front pages of the newspapers) during most of these engagements was a cavalry unit known as the Rough Riders. Nominally commanded by General Leonard Wood, its real leader was Colonel Theodore Roosevelt, who had resigned from the Navy Department to get into the war and who had struggled with an almost desperate fury to ensure that his regiment made it to the front before the fighting ended. Roosevelt rapidly emerged as a hero of the conflict. His fame rested in large part on his role in leading a bold, if perhaps reck-

THE ROUGH RIDERS
Theodore Roosevelt resigned as assistant secretary of the navy to lead a volunteer regiment in the Spanish-American War. They were known as the Rough Riders, and their bold charge during the battle of San Juan Hill made Roosevelt a national hero. Roosevelt is shown here (at center with hat and glasses) posing with the other members of the regiment. *(Bettmann)*

less, charge up Kettle Hill (a charge that was a minor part of the larger battle for the adjacent San Juan Hill) directly into the face of Spanish guns. Roosevelt himself emerged unscathed, but nearly a hundred of his soldiers were killed or wounded. To the end of his life, he remembered the battle as "the great day of my life."

Although Shafter was now in position to assault Santiago, his army was so weakened by sickness that he feared he might have to abandon his position, particularly once the commander of the American naval force blockading Santiago refused to enter the harbor because of mines. Disaster seemed imminent. But unknown to the Americans, the Spanish government had by now decided that Santiago was lost and had ordered Cervera to evacuate. On July 3, believing the effort to defend the port was hopeless, Cervera tried to escape the harbor. The waiting American squadron destroyed his entire fleet. On July 16, the commander of Spanish ground forces in Santiago surrendered. At about the same time, an American army landed in Puerto Rico and occupied it against virtually no opposition. On August 12, an armistice ended the war.

Under the terms of the armistice, Spain recognized the independence of Cuba. It ceded Puerto Rico (now occupied by American troops) and the Pacific island of Guam to the United States. And it accepted contin-

"SMOKED YANKEES"
Nearly one-fourth of the American invasion force in Cuba consisted of African-American soldiers, many of whom had already served with distinction in campaigns against Indians in the West. Spanish troops called them "smoked Yankees" and often looked on them with more respect than did their American commanders, who kept black troops in rigidly segregated units. In this painting members of the all-black Tenth Cavalry support a charge by the Rough Riders. Members of the Twenty-fourth and Twenty-fifth Negro Infantry Divisions played a crucial role at the Battle of San Juan Hill.
(Library of Congress)

ued American occupation of Manila pending the final disposition of the Philippines.

Puerto Rico and the United States

The annexation of Puerto Rico produced relatively little controversy in the United States—ironically, since of all the territory America acquired as a result of the Spanish-American war, Puerto Rico would be the most important to the nation's future.

The island of Puerto Rico had been a part of the Spanish Empire since Ponce de León arrived there in 1508, and it had contained Spanish settlements since the founding of San Juan in 1521. The native people of the island, the Arawaks, disappeared almost entirely as a result of infectious diseases, Spanish brutality, and poverty. Puerto Rican society developed, therefore, with a Spanish ruling class and a large African work force for the coffee and sugar plantations that came to dominate its economy.

As Puerto Rican society became increasingly distinctive, resistance to Spanish rule began to emerge, just as it had emerged in Cuba. Uprisings occurred intermittently beginning in the 1820s; the most important of them—the so-called Lares Rebellion—was, like the others, effectively crushed by the Spanish in 1868. But the growing resistance did prompt some reforms: the abolition of slavery in 1873, representation in the Spanish parliament, and other changes. Demands for independence continued to grow, and in 1898, in response to political pressure organized by Luis Muñoz Rivera, Spain granted the island a degree of independence. But before the changes had any chance to take effect, control of Puerto Rico shifted to the United States.

American military forces occupied the island during the war. They remained in control until 1900, when the Foraker Act ended military rule and established a formal colonial government: an American governor, a two-chamber legislature (the members of the upper chamber appointed by the United States, the members of the lower elected by the Puerto Rican people). The United States could amend or veto any legislation the Puerto Ricans passed. Agitation for independence continued. And in 1917, under pressure to clarify the relationship between Puerto Rico and America, Congress passed the Jones Act, which declared Puerto Rico to be United States territory and made all Puerto Ricans American citizens.

The Puerto Rican sugar industry flourished as it took advantage of the American market that was now open to it without tariffs. As in Hawaii, Americans began establishing large sugar plantations on the island and hired natives to work them; many of the planters did not even live in Puerto Rico. The growing emphasis on sugar as a cash crop, and the transformation of many Puerto Rican farmers into paid laborers led to a reduction in the growing of food for the island. Puerto Ricans became increasingly dependent on imported food and hence increasingly a part of the international commercial economy. When international sugar prices were high, Puerto Rico did well. When they dropped, the island's economy sagged, pushing the many plantation workers—already desperately poor—into destitution. Unhappy with the instability, the poverty among natives, and the American threat to Hispanic culture, many Puerto Ricans continued to agitate for independence. Others, however, began to envision closer relations with the United States, even statehood.

The Debate over the Philippines

If the annexation of Puerto Rico produced relatively little controversy, the annexation of the Philippines occasioned a long and impassioned debate. Controlling a nearby Caribbean island fit reasonably comfortably into America's sense of itself as the dominant power in the Western Hemisphere. Controlling a large and densely populated territory thousands of miles away seemed different, and to many Americans more ominous.

McKinley claimed to be reluctant to support annexation. But, according to his own accounts, he came to believe there were no acceptable alternatives. Emerging from what he described as an "agonizing night of prayer," he claimed divine guidance for his decision to accept responsibility for the islands. Returning them to Spain would be "cowardly and dishonorable," he claimed. Turning them over to another imperialist power (France, Germany, or Britain) would be "bad business and discreditable." Granting the islands independence would be irresponsible; the Filipinos were "unfit for self government." The only solution was "to take them all and to educate the Filipinos, and uplift and Christianize them, and by God's grace do the very best we could by them." Growing popular support for annexation and the pressure of the imperialist leaders of his party undoubtedly helped him reach this decision of conscience.

The Treaty of Paris, signed in December 1898, brought a formal end to the war. It confirmed the terms of the armistice concerning Cuba, Puerto Rico, and Guam. But American negotiators startled the Spanish by demanding that they cede the Philippines to the United States, something the original armistice had not included. The Spanish objected briefly, but an American offer of $20 million for the islands softened their resistance. They accepted all the American terms.

In the United States Senate, however, resistance was fierce. During debate over ratification of the treaty, a powerful anti-imperialist movement arose around the country to oppose acquisition of the Philippines. The anti-imperialists included some of the nation's wealthiest and most powerful figures: Andrew Carnegie, Mark Twain, Samuel Gompers, Senator John Sherman, and others. Their motives were various. Some believed simply that imperialism was immoral, a repudiation of America's commitment to human freedom. Some feared "polluting" the American population by introducing "inferior" Asian races into it. Industrial workers feared being undercut by a flood of cheap laborers from the new colonies. Conservatives feared the large standing army and entangling foreign alliances that they believed imperialism would require and that they feared would threaten American liberties. Sugar growers and others feared unwelcome competition from the new territories. The Anti-Imperialist League, established by upper-class Bostonians, New Yorkers, and others late in 1898 to fight against annexation, attracted a widespread following in the Northeast and waged a vigorous campaign against ratification of the Paris treaty.

Favoring ratification was an equally varied group. There were the exuberant imperialists such as Theodore Roosevelt, who saw the acquisition of empire as a way to reinvigorate the nation, and keep alive what they considered the healthy, restorative influence of the war. Some businessmen saw opportunities to profit in the Philippines and believed annexation would position the United States to dominate the Oriental trade. And most Republicans saw partisan advantages in acquiring valuable new territories through a war fought and won by a Republican administration. Perhaps the strongest argument in favor of annexation, however, was the apparent ease with which it could be accomplished. After all, the United States already possessed the islands.

When anti-imperialists warned of the danger of acquiring territories with large populations who might have to become citizens, the imperialists had a ready answer. The nation's longstanding policies toward Indians—treating them as dependents rather than as citizens—had created a precedent for annexing land without absorbing people. Senator Henry Cabot Lodge of Massachusetts, one of the leading imperialists in Congress, made the point explicitly:

> The other day . . . a great Democratic thinker announced that a Republic can have no subjects. He seems to have forgotten that this Republic not only has held subjects from the beginning, . . . but [that we have] acquired them by purchase. . . . [We] denied to the Indian tribes even the right to choose their allegiance, or to become citizens.

Other supporters of annexation argued that the "uncivilized" Filipinos "would occupy the same status precisely as our Indians. . . . They are, in fact, 'Indians'—and the Fourteenth Amendment does not make citizens of Indians."

The fate of the treaty remained in doubts for weeks, until it received the unexpected support of William Jennings Bryan, a fervent anti-imperialist. He backed ratification not because he approved of annexation but because he hoped to move the issue out of the Senate and make it the subject of a national referendum in 1900, when he expected to be the Democratic presidential candidate again. Bryan persuaded a number of anti-imperialist Democrats to support the treaty so as to set up the 1900 debate. The Senate ratified it finally on February 6, 1899.

But Bryan miscalculated. If the election of 1900 was in fact a referendum on the Philippines, as Bryan tried to make it, it proved beyond doubt that the nation had decided in favor of imperialism. Once again Bryan ran against McKinley; and once again McKinley won—even more decisively than in 1896. It was not only the issue of the colonies, however, that ensured McKinley's victory. The Republicans were the beneficiaries of growing national prosperity—and also of the colorful personality of their vice presidential candidate, Colonel Theodore Roosevelt, the hero of San Juan Hill.

THE REPUBLIC AS EMPIRE

The new American empire was small by the standards of the great imperial powers of Europe. But it created large challenges. It embroiled the United States in the politics of both Europe and the Far East in ways the nation had always tried to avoid in the past. It also drew Americans into a brutal war in the Philippines.

Governing the Colonies

Three of the new American dependencies—Hawaii, Alaska, and Puerto Rico—presented relatively few problems. They received territorial status (and their residents American citizenship) relatively quickly: Hawaii in 1900, Alaska in 1912, and Puerto Rico by 1917. The navy took control of Guam and Tutuila. And some of the smallest, least populated Pacific islands now under American control the United States simply left alone.

Cuba was a thornier problem. American military forces, commanded by General Leonard Wood, remained there until 1902 to prepare the island for independence. They built roads, schools, and hospitals, reorganized the legal, financial, and administrative systems, and introduced medical and sanitation reforms. But the United States also laid the basis for years of American economic domination of the island.

When Cuba drew up a constitution that made no reference to the United States, Congress responded by passing the Platt Amendment in 1901 and pressuring Cuba into incorporating its terms into its constitution. The Platt Amendment barred Cuba from making treaties with other nations (thus, in effect, giving the United States control of Cuban foreign policy); gave the United States the right to intervene in Cuba to preserve independence, life, and property; and required Cuba to permit American naval stations on its territory. The amendment left Cuba only nominally independent politically. And American capital, which quickly took over the island's economy, made the new nation an American economic appendage as well. American investors poured into Cuba, buying up plantations, factories, railroads, and refineries. Absentee American ownership of many of the island's most important resources was the source of resentment and agitation for decades. Resistance to "Yankee imperialism" produced intermittent revolts against the Cuban government—revolts that at times prompted U.S. military intervention. American troops occupied the island from 1906 to 1909 after one such rebellion; they returned again in 1912, to suppress a revolt by black plantation workers. As in Puerto Rico and Hawaii,

FILIPINO PRISONERS
American troops guard captured Filipino guerrillas in Manila. The suppression of the Filipino insurrection was a much longer and costlier military undertaking than the Spanish-American War, by which the United States first gained possession of the islands. By mid-1900 there were 70,000 American troops in the Philippines, under the command of General Arthur MacArthur (whose son, Douglas, won fame in the Philippines during World War II). *(Library of Congress)*

sugar production—spurred by access to the American market—increasingly dominated the island's economy and subjected it to the same cycle of booms and busts that so plagued other sugar-producing appendages of the United States economy.

The Philippine War

Americans did not like to think of themselves as imperial rulers in the European mold. Yet like other imperial powers, the United States soon discovered—as it had discovered at home in its relations with the Indians—that subjugating another people required more than ideals; it also required strength and brutality. That, at least, was the lesson of the American experience in the Philippines, where American forces soon became engaged in a long and bloody war with insurgent forces fighting for independence.

The conflict in the Philippines is the least remembered of all American wars. It was also one of the long-

est (it lasted from 1898 to 1902) and one of the most vicious. It involved 200,000 American troops and resulted in 4,300 American deaths, nearly ten times the number who had died in combat in the Spanish-American War. The number of Filipinos killed in the conflict is still in dispute, but it seems likely that at least 50,000 natives (and perhaps many more) died. The American occupiers faced guerrilla tactics in the Philippines very similar to those the Spanish occupiers had faced prior to 1898 in Cuba. And they soon found themselves drawn into the same pattern of brutality that had outraged so many Americans when Weyler had used them in the Caribbean.

The Filipinos had been rebelling against Spanish rule even before 1898. And as soon as they realized the Americans had come to stay, they rebelled against them as well. Ably led by Emilio Aguinaldo, who claimed to head the legitimate government of the nation, Filipinos harried the American army of occupation from island to island for more than three years. At first,

THE AMERICAN SOUTH PACIFIC EMPIRE, 1900

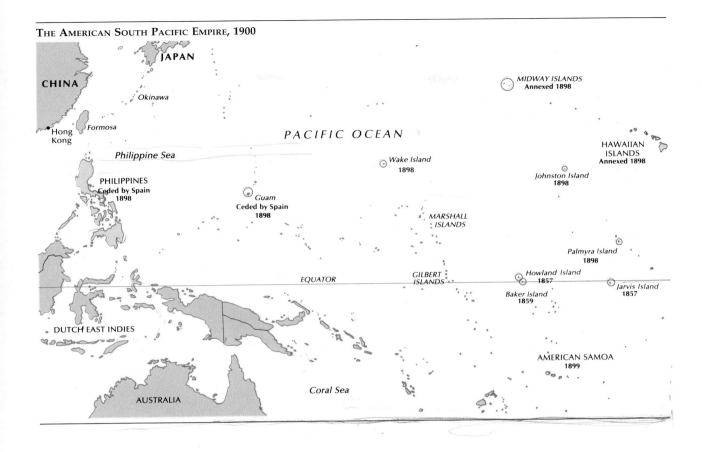

American commanders believed the rebels had only a small popular following. But by early 1900, General Arthur MacArthur (father of General Douglas MacArthur), an American commander in the islands, was writing: "I have been reluctantly compelled to believe that the Filipino masses are loyal to Aguinaldo and the government which he heads."

To MacArthur and others, that realization was not a reason to moderate American tactics or conciliate the rebels. It was a reason to adopt more severe measures. Gradually, the American military effort became more systematically vicious and brutal. Captured Filipino guerrillas were treated not as prisoners of war, but as murderers. Most were summarily executed. On some islands, entire communities were evacuated—the residents forced into concentration camps while American troops destroyed their villages, farms, crops, and livestock. A spirit of savagery grew among some American soldiers, who came to view the Filipinos as almost subhuman and at times seemed to take pleasure in killing almost arbitrarily. One American commander ordered his troops "to kill and burn, the more

you kill and burn the better it will please me. . . . Shoot everyone over the age of 10." Over fifteen Filipinos were killed for every one wounded; in the American Civil War—the bloodiest conflict in U.S. history to that point—one person had died for every five wounded.

By 1902, reports of the brutality and of the American casualties had soured the American public on the war. But by then, the rebellion had largely exhausted itself and the occupiers had established control over most of the islands. The key to their victory was the March 1901 capture of Aguinaldo, who later signed a document urging his followers to stop fighting and declaring his own allegiance to the United States. (Aguinaldo then retired from public life and lived quietly until 1964.) Fighting continued in some places for another year, and the war revived intermittently until as late as 1906; but American possession of the Philippines was now secure.

In the summer of 1901, the military transferred authority over the islands to William Howard Taft, who became their first civilian governor. Taft announced that the American mission in the Philippines was to

SIGNIFICANT EVENTS

1868–1878 Cubans revolt against Spanish rule in Ten Years' War

1875 U.S. agrees to allow Hawaii to export sugar to America duty-free

1878 U.S. gains treaty rights for base at Pago Pago in Samoa

1887 U.S. gains treaty rights for base at Pearl Harbor in Hawaii

1889 First Pan-American Congress meets

1890 Alfred Thayer Mahan publishes *The Influence of Sea Power upon History*

U.S. ends favored status of Hawaii in sugar trade, damaging Hawaiian economy

1893 American planters in Hawaii stage revolution

Harrison signs annexation agreement with Hawaii, but Cleveland rejects it

1894 Wilson-Gorman Tariff on sugar ravages Cuban economy

1895 United States and Britain dispute Venezuelan boundary

Insurrection against Spanish begins in Cuba

1896 Alaska gold rush begins

1897 McKinley offers to mediate Cuban conflict, Spain refuses

1898 William Randolph Hearst publishes de Lôme letter

U.S. battleship *Maine* explodes in Havana harbor

Congress declares war on Spain (April 25), Spanish army in Cuba retreats

Dewey captures Philippines

United States and Spain sign armistice (August 12)

Treaty of Paris cedes Puerto Rico, Philippines, and other Spanish possessions to United States and recognizes Cuban independence

United States formally annexes Hawaii

Anti-Imperialist League formed

1898–1902 Philippines revolt against American rule

1899 Senate ratifies Treaty of Paris

Hay releases "Open Door notes"

1900 Foraker Act establishes civil government in Puerto Rico

Hawaii granted territorial status

Boxer Rebellion breaks out in China

McKinley reelected president

1901 Americans capture Emilio Aguinaldo in Philippines

U.S. establishes civil government in Philippines

Congress passes Platt Amendment

1912 Alaska given territorial status

1917 Puerto Ricans granted U.S. citizenship

1946 United States grants Philippines independence

prepare the islands for independence, and he gave the Filipinos broad local autonomy. The Americans also built roads, schools, bridges, and sewers; instituted major administrative and financial reforms; and established a public health system. The Philippine economy—dominated by fishing, agriculture, timber, and mining—also became increasingly linked to the economy of the United States. Americans did not make many investments in the Philippines, and few Americans moved there. But trade with the United States grew to the point that the islands were almost completely dependent on American markets.

In the meantime, a succession of American governors gradually increased Filipino political autonomy.

"PLAYING THE WAR GAME"
Students at the U.S. Army Officer Training School at Fort Leavenworth, Kansas, engage in simulated planning for battle. The school of Fort Leavenworth and other facilities were part of the American effort in the early twentieth century to create a modern command structure for the nation's military. *(Arms Research Library, U. S. Army Command and General Staff College, Fort Leavenworth, Kansas)*

But not until July 4, 1946, did the islands finally gain their independence.

The Open Door

The acquisition of the Philippines greatly increased the already strong American interest in Asia. Americans were particularly concerned about the future of China, with which the United States already had an important trade and which was now so enfeebled that it provided a tempting target for exploitation by stronger countries. By 1900, England, France, Germany, Russia, and Japan were beginning to carve up China among themselves. They pressured the Chinese government for "concessions," which gave them effective control over various regions of China. In some cases, they simply seized Chinese territory and claimed it as their own. Many Americans feared the process would soon cut them out of the China trade altogether.

Eager for a way to protect American interests in China without risking war, McKinley issued a statement in September 1898 saying the United States wanted access to China, but no special advantages there. "Asking only the open door for ourselves, we are ready to accord the open door to others." Later, Secretary of State John Hay translated those words into policy when he addressed identical messages—which became known as the "Open Door notes"—to England, Germany, Russia, France, Japan, and Italy. He asked them to approve three principles: Each nation with a sphere of influence in China was to respect the rights and privileges of other nations in its sphere; Chinese officials were to continue to collect tariff duties in all spheres (the existing tariff favored the United States);

and nations were not to discriminate against other nations in levying port dues and railroad rates within their own spheres. Together, these principles would allow the United States to trade freely with the Chinese without fear of interference and without having to become militarily involved in the region. They would also retain the illusion of Chinese sovereignty and thus prevent formal colonial dismemberment of China, which might also create obstacles to American trade.

But Europe and Japan received the Open Door proposals coolly. Russia openly rejected them; the other powers claimed to accept them in principle but to be unable to act unless all the other powers agreed. Hay refused to consider this a rebuff. He boldly announced that all the powers had accepted the principles of the Open Door in "final and definitive" form and that the United States expected them to observe those principles. But unless the United States was willing to go to war, it could not prevent any nation that wanted to violate the Open Door from doing so.

No sooner had the diplomatic maneuvering over the Open Door ended than the Boxers, a secret Chinese martial-arts society with highly nationalist convictions, launched a revolt against foreigners in China. The climax of the Boxer Rebellion was a siege of the entire foreign diplomatic corps, which took refuge in the British embassy in Peking. The imperial powers (including the United States) sent an international expeditionary force into China to rescue the diplomats. In August 1900, it fought its way into Peking and broke the siege.

McKinley and Hay had agreed to American participation in quelling the Boxer Rebellion so as to secure a voice in the settlement of the uprising and to prevent the partition of China by the European powers. Hay now won support for his Open Door approach from England and Germany and induced the other participating powers to accept compensation from the Chinese for the damages the Boxer Rebellion had caused. Chinese territorial integrity survived at least in name, and the United States retained access to its lucrative trade.

A Modern Military System

The war with Spain had revealed glaring deficiencies in the American military system. The army had exhibited the greatest weaknesses, but the entire military organization had demonstrated problems of supply, training, and coordination. Had the United States been fighting a more powerful nation, disaster might have resulted. After the war, McKinley appointed Elihu Root, an able corporate lawyer in New York, as secretary of war to supervise a major overhaul of the armed forces. (Root was one of the first of several generations of attorney-statesmen who moved easily between public and private roles and constituted much of what has often been called the American "foreign policy establishment.") Between 1900 and 1903, Root created a new military system.

The Root reforms enlarged the regular army from 25,000 to a maximum of 100,000. They established federal command of the National Guard, ensuring that never again would the nation fight a war with volunteer regiments over which the federal government had limited control. They sparked the creation of a system of officer training schools, including the Army Staff College (later the Command and General Staff School) at Fort Leavenworth, Kansas, and the Army War College at Washington. And in 1903, they established a general staff (which they named the Joint Chiefs of Staff) to act as military advisers to the secretary of war. It was this last reform that Root considered most important: the creation of a central planning agency modeled on the example of European general staffs. The Joint Chiefs were charged with many functions. They were to "supervise" and "coordinate" the entire army establishment, and they were to establish an office that would plan for possible wars. An Army and Navy Board, on which both services were represented, was to foster interservice cooperation. As a result of the new reforms, the United States entered the twentieth century with something resembling a modern military system. The country would make substantial use of it in the turbulent century to come.

SUGGESTED READINGS

General Histories. Robert L. Beisner, *From the Old Diplomacy to the New, 1865–1900*, 2nd ed. (1986). Charles S. Campbell, *The Transformation of American Foreign Relations, 1865–1900* (1976). John Dobson, *America's Ascent: The United States Becomes a Great Power, 1880–1914* (1978). Foster Rhea Dulles, *Prelude to World Power, 1865–1900* (1965). J. A. S. Grenville and George Berkeley Young, *Politics, Strategy and American Diplomacy: Studies in Foreign Policy, 1873–1917* (1966). David F. Healy, *U.S. Expansionism: Imperialist Urge in the 1890s* (1970). Walter LeFeber, *The New Empire* (1963). Ernest May, *Imperial Democracy* (1961); *American Imperialism: A Speculative Essay* (1968). H. Wayne Morgan, *America's Road to Empire* (1965). Milton Plesur, *America's Outward Thrust: Approaches to Foreign Affairs, 1865–1890* (1971). David M. Pletcher, *The Awkward Years: American Foreign Relations under Garfield and Arthur* (1962). Julius W. Pratt, *Expansionists of 1898* (1936). Emily S. Rosenberg, *Spreading the American Dream: American Economic and Cultural Expansion, 1890–1945* (1982). Albert K. Weinberg, *Manifest Destiny: A Study in Nationalist Expansion in American History* (1935). William Appleman Williams, *The Tragedy of American Diplomacy* (rev. ed., 1972).

The Spanish-American War. Richard Challener, *Admirals, Generals, and American Foreign Policy, 1889–1914* (1973). Graham A. Cosmas, *An Army for Empire: The United States Army in the Spanish-American War* (1971). Philip S. Foner, *The Spanish-Cuban-American War and the Birth of American Imperialism*, 2 vols. (1972). Frank Freidel, *The Splendid Little War* (1958). Willard B. Gatewood, Jr., *Black Americans and the White Man's Burden, 1898–1903* (1975); *"Smoked Yankees": Letters from Negro Soldiers, 1898–1902* (1971). Gerald F. Linderman, *The Mirror of War: American Society and the Spanish-American War* (1974). Walter Millis, *The Martial Spirit* (1931). Joyce Milton, *The Yellow Journalists* (1989). Edmund Morris, *The Rise of Theodore Roosevelt* (1979). John L. Offner, *An Unwanted War: The Diplomacy of the United States and Spain over Cuba, 1895–1898* (1992). Louis A. Perez, Jr., *Cuba Between Empires, 1868–1902* (1983). Hyman Rickover, *How the Battleship Maine Was Destroyed* (1976). David F. Trask, *The War with Spain in 1898* (1981). Richard S. West, Jr., *Admirals of the American Empire* (1948).

Imperialism and Anti-Imperialism. Robert L. Beisner, *Twelve Against Empire* (1968). Kendrick A. Clements, *William Jennings Bryan* (1983). James H. Hitchman, *Leonard Wood and Cuban Independence, 1898–1902* (1971). Frederick Merk, *Manifest Destiny and Mission in American History* (1963). Thomas J. Osborne, *"Empire Can Wait": American Opposition to Hawaiian Annexation, 1893–1898* (1891). William J. Pomeroy, *American Neo-Colonialism: Its Emergence in the Philippines and Asia* (1970). Julius W. Pratt, *America's Colonial Empire* (1950). Robert Seager II, *Alfred Thayer Mahan* (1977). E. Berkeley Tompkins, *Anti-Imperialism in the United States, 1890–1920: The Great Debate* (1970).

The Pacific Empire. John Morgan Gates, *Schoolbooks and Krags: The United States Army in the Philippines, 1898–1902* (1971). Stanley Karnow, *In Our Image: America's Empire in the Philippines* (1989). Paul M. Kennedy, *The Samoan Tangle* (1974). Glenn A. May, *Social Engineering in the Philippines* (1980). Stuart Creighton Miller, *"Benevolent Assimilation": The American Conquest of the Philippines, 1899–1903* (1982). Daniel B. Schirmer, *Republic or Empire? American Resistance to the Philippine War* (1972). Peter Stanley, *A Nation in the Making: The Philippines and the United States* (1974). Merze Tate, *The United States and the Hawaiian Kingdom* (1965). Richard E. Welch, Jr., *Response to Imperialism: The United States and the Philippine-American War, 1899–1902* (1979). Leon Wolff, *Little Brown Brother* (1961).

America and Asia. Warren Cohen, *America's Response to China* (rev. ed., 1980). Kenton Clymer, *John Hay: Gentleman as Diplomat* (1975). Patricia Hill, *The World Their Household: The American Women's Foreign Mission Movement and Cultural Transformation* (1985). Michael Hunt, *The Making of a Special Relationship: The United States and China to 1914* (1983). Jane Hunter, *The Gospel of Gentility: American Women Missionaries in Turn-of-the-Century China* (1984). Akira Iriye, *Across the Pacific* (1967); *Pacific Estrangement: Japanese and American Expansion* (1972). Robert McClellan, *The Heathen Chinese: A Study of American Attitudes Toward China* (1971). Thomas J. McCormick, *China Market: America's Quest for Informal Empire, 1893–1901* (1967). Charles Neu, *The Troubled Encounter* (1975). James C. Thomsen, Jr., *Peter W. Stanley, and John Curtis Perry, Sentimental Imperialists: The American Experience in East Asia* (1981). Paul Varg, *The Making of a Myth: The United States and China, 1897–1912* (1968); *Missionaries, Chinese and Diplomats* (1958). Marilyn B. Young, *The Rhetoric of Empire: American China Policy, 1895–1901* (1968).

McCLURE'S MAGAZINE

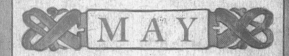

MAY

LINCOLN STEFFENS'S exposure of another type of municipal grafting; how Pittsburg differs from St. Louis and Minneapolis.

THE END OF THE WORLD, by Professor Newcomb. A powerful story, yet a scientific prediction; pictures by the famous French artist, Henri Lanos.

IDA M. TARBELL on the Standard tactics which brought on the famous oil crisis of 1878.

SIX SHORT STORIES

McCLURE'S MAGAZINE, MAY 1903
McClure's was the leading outlet for a form of journalism known as "muckraking," which attempted to expose social and economic scandals in the hope of promoting reform. This issue contains articles by two of the leading muckrakers, Lincoln Steffens and Ida Tarbell.
(Culver)

CHAPTER TWENTY-ONE

THE RISE OF PROGRESSIVISM

ELL BEFORE THE TURN of the century, many Americans had become convinced that the rapid industrialization and urbanization of their society had created intolerable problems, that the nation's most pressing need was to impose order on the growing chaos and to curb industrial society's most glaring injustices. In the early years of the new century, that outlook acquired a name: progressivism.

Not even the progressives themselves could always agree on what the word really meant. Indeed, more than one historian has suggested that the word "progressive" ultimately came to mean so many different things to so many different people that it ceased to mean anything at all. (See "Where Historians Disagree," pp. 574–577.) Yet if progressivism was a phenomenon of great scope and diversity, it was also one that rested on an identifiable set of central assumptions.

THE PROGRESSIVE IMPULSE

Progressivism was, first, an optimistic vision. Progressives believed, as their name implies, in the idea of progress. They believed that society was capable of improvement and that continued growth and advancement were the nation's destiny.

But progressives believed, too, that growth and progress could not continue to occur recklessly, as they had in the late nineteenth century. The "natural laws" of the marketplace, and the doctrines of laissez-faire and Social Darwinism that celebrated those laws, were not sufficient to create the order, stability, and justice their growing society required. Direct, purposeful human intervention in social and economic affairs was essential to ordering and bettering society.

Varieties of Progressivism

Progressives did not always agree on the form their intervention should take, and the result was a variety of reform impulses that sometimes seemed to have little in common.

One powerful impulse was the spirit of "antimonopoly," the fear of concentrated power and the urge to limit and disperse authority and wealth. This impulse, which had much in common with populism, appealed not only to many workers and farmers but to some middle-class Americans as well. And it helped empower government to regulate or break up trusts at both the state and national level.

Another progressive impulse was a belief in the importance of social cohesion: the belief that individuals are not autonomous but part of a great web of social relationships, that the welfare of any single person is dependent on the welfare of society as a whole. That assumption produced a concern about the "victims" of industrialization. A large number of progressive initiatives and reforms involved efforts to help women, children, industrial workers, immigrants, and—to a lesser extent—African Americans.

WHERE HISTORIANS DISAGREE

PROGRESSIVISM

Few issues in the history of twentieth-century America have inspired more disagreement, even confusion, than the nature of progressivism. Until about 1950, most historians were in general accord about the nature of the progressive "movement." It was, they generally agreed, just what it purported to be: a movement by the "people" to curb the power of the "special interests." In particular, it was a protest by an aroused citizenry against the excessive power of urban bosses, corporate moguls, and corrupt elected officials.

In the early 1950s, however, a new interpretation emerged to challenge the traditional view. Without abandoning the earlier view of progressivism as a largely political movement, it offered a new explanation of who the progressives were and what they were trying to do. George Mowry, in *The California Progressives* (1951), described the reform movement in the state not as a protest by the mass of the people, but as an effort by a relatively small and privileged group of business and professional men to limit the over-bearing power of large corporations and labor unions. Viewing themselves as natural social leaders, they resented their loss of political power to these new economic forces and envisioned reform as a way to restore both their economic fortunes and their social importance and self-esteem. Richard Hofstadter expanded on this idea in *The Age of Reform* (1955), in which he described progressives throughout the country as people suffering from "status anxiety"—old, formerly influential, upper-middle-class families seeking to restore their fading prestige by challenging the powerful new institutions that had begun to displace them. Like the Populists, Hofstadter suggested, the progressives were suffering from psychological, not economic, discontent.

The Mowry-Hofstadter thesis was never without its critics. In particular, it received strong challenges from historians who disagreed with two of the basic assumptions of the interpretation. First, these scholars maintained, Mowry and Hofstadter were mistaken in examining progressivism purely in terms of its visible political leaders. It was a movement with a far broader

---

Still another impulse was a deep faith in knowledge—in the possibilities of applying to society the principles of natural and social sciences. To some, those principles seemed a route to organization and efficiency. Many reformers believed that social order was a result of intelligent social organization and rational procedures for guiding social and economic life. To others, knowledge was more important as a vehicle for making society more equitable and humane.

Most progressives believed, too, that a modernized government could—and must—play an important role in the process of improving and stabilizing society. Modern life was too complex to be left in the hands of party bosses, untrained amateurs, and antiquated institutions. It required new and enhanced institutions of government, and a new breed of leaders and experts.

These varied reform impulses were not always as mutually incompatible as they seemed. Many progressives made use of all these ideas (and others), separately or in combination, as they tried to bring order and progress to their turbulent society.

The Muckrakers

Among the first people to articulate the new spirit of reform were crusading journalists who began in the late nineteenth and early twentieth centuries to direct public attention toward social, economic, and political injustices. They became known as the "muckrakers," after Theodore Roosevelt accused one of them of raking up muck through his writings. They were committed to exposing scandal, corruption, and injustice to public view.

social and economic base. Second, they claimed, progressive reformers were not expressing a vague psychological malaise, but a clear recognition of their own self-interest. Beyond that, the new historians of progressivism often disagreed with one another as much as they disagreed with Mowry and Hofstadter.

Perhaps the harshest challenge to earlier interpretations came from Gabriel Kolko, whose influential 1963 study *The Triumph of Conservatism* dismissed the supposedly "democratic" features of progressivism as meaningless rhetoric and examined instead the actual impact of progressive economic reforms. Progressivism was, he agreed, an effort to regulate business. But it was not the "people" who were responsible for this regulation. It was the businessmen who saw in government supervision a way to protect themselves from competition. Regulation, Kolko claimed, was "invariably controlled by the leaders of the regulated industry and directed towards ends they deemed acceptable or desirable."

A somewhat more moderate challenge to the "psychological" interpretation of progressivism came from historians embracing a new "organizational" view of history. Samuel P. Hays was among the first to suggest this approach in *The Response to Industrialism, 1885–1914* (1957) and other writings. Hays argued that progressives were indeed businessmen, as Kolko had suggested. But their impulse was not so much narrow self-interest as a broad desire to bring order and efficiency to political and, hence, economic life. The most important progressives, he claimed, were members of the upper class, who viewed a restoration of stability as essential to the preservation of their privileged position.

Even more influential was a 1967 study by Robert Wiebe, *The Search for Order, 1877–1920.* Wiebe saw progressivism as a response to dislocations in American life that had resulted from rapid changes in the nature of the economy unaccompanied by corresponding changes in social and political institutions. Economic power had moved to large, national organizations, while social and political life remained centered primarily in local communities. The result was widespread disorder and unrest, culminating in the turbulent 1890s. Progressivism, Wiebe argued, was the effort of a "new middle class"—a class

At first, their major targets were the trusts and particularly the railroads, which the muckrakers considered dangerously powerful and deeply corrupt. Exposés of the great corporate organizations began to appear as early as the 1860s, when Charles Francis Adams, Jr., and others uncovered corruption among the railroad barons. Such inquiries continued into the twentieth century. The most notable of them was Ida Tarbell's enormous and influential study of the Standard Oil trust (published first in magazines and then as a two-volume book in 1904).

By the turn of the century, many muckrakers were turning their attention to government and particularly to the urban political machines. The most influential, perhaps, was Lincoln Steffens, a reporter for *McClure's* magazine. His portraits of "machine government" and "boss rule," his exposure of "boodlers" in cities as diverse as St. Louis, Minneapolis, Cleveland, Cincinnati, Chicago, Philadelphia, and New York; his tone of studied moral outrage (as reflected in the title of his series and of the book that emerged from it, *The Shame of the Cities*)—all helped arouse sentiment for urban political reform. The alternative to leaving government in the hands of corrupt party leaders, the muckrakers argued, was for the people themselves to take a greater interest in public life. Indeed, some journalists seemed less outraged at the bosses themselves than at the apathetic public that seemed not to care about the corruption occurring in their midst.

The muckrakers reached the peak of their influence in the first decade of the twentieth century. They investigated governments, labor unions, and corporations. They explored the problems of child labor, immigrant ghettoes, prostitution, and family disorgan-

tied to the emerging national economy—to stabilize and enhance their position in society.

Yet despite all the challenges to the original view of progressivism as a popular democratic movement, some historians continued to produce evidence that the reform phenomenon was indeed a movement of the people against the special interests, although some identified the "people" somewhat differently from earlier such interpretations. J. Joseph Huthmacher argued in 1962 that much of the force behind progressivism came from members of the working class, especially immigrants, who pressed for such reforms as workmen's compensation and wage and hour laws. John Buenker strengthened this argument in *Urban Liberalism and Progressive Reform* (1973), claiming that political machines and urban "bosses" were important sources of reform energy and helped create twentieth-century liberalism.

David P. Thelen, in a 1972 study of progressivism in Wisconsin, *The New Citizenship,* offered an even broader challenge to both the "status anxiety" and the "conservatism-organizational" views. Thelen found a real clash between the "public interest" and "corporate privilege" in Wisconsin. The depression of the 1890s had mobilized a broad coalition of citizens of highly diverse backgrounds behind efforts to make both business and government responsible to the popular will. It marked the emergence of a new "consumer" consciousness that crossed boundaries of class and community, religion and ethnicity.

Other historians writing in the 1970s and 1980s tackled the question of the nature of progressivism less by looking at particular reformers or particular reforms than by trying to identify some of the broad processes of political change that had created the public battles of the era. Richard L. McCormick's *From Realignment to Reform* (1981), for example, studied political change in New York state and argued that the crucial change in this era was the decline of the political parties as the vital players in public life and the rise of interest groups working for particular social and economic goals. Progressivism, he suggested, was not so much a coherent "movement" as part of a broader process of political adaptation to the realities of modern industrial society. At the same time, many histori-

ization. They denounced the waste and destruction of natural resources, the subjugation of women, even occasionally the oppression of blacks. By presenting social problems to the public with indignation and moral fervor, they helped inspire other Americans to take action. In the process they expressed some of the most basic progressive impulses: the opposition to monopoly, the belief in the need for social unity in the face of corruption and injustice, even at times the cry for efficiency and organization.

The Social Gospel

The moralistic tone of the muckrakers' exposés reflected one important aspect of emerging progressive sentiment: a sense of outrage at social and economic injustice. That outrage, combined with a humanitarian sense of social responsibility, helped produce many reformers committed to the pursuit of social justice. A clear expression of that concern was the rise of what became known as the "Social Gospel." By the early twentieth century, it had become a powerful movement within American Protestantism (and, to a lesser extent, within American Catholicism and Judaism). It was chiefly concerned with redeeming the nation's cities.

The Salvation Army, which began in England but soon spread to the United States, was one example of the fusion of religion with reform. A Christian social welfare organization with a vaguely military structure, by 1900 it had recruited 3,000 "officers" and 20,000 "privates" and was offering both material aid and spiritual service to the urban poor. In addition, many ministers, priests, and rabbis left traditional parish work to serve in the troubled cities. Charles Sheldon's *In His*

WHERE HISTORIANS DISAGREE

ans were focusing on the role of women (and the vast network of voluntary associations they created) in shaping and promoting progressive reform and were seeing in these efforts concerns rooted in the female experience. Some progressive battles, these historians argued, were part of an effort by women to protect their interests within the domestic sphere in the face of jarring challenges to that sphere from the new industrial world. That drew them to such issues as temperance, divorce, and prostitution. Many women mobilized behind protective legislation for female and children workers. Other women worked to expand their own roles in the public world. Progressivism cannot be understood, historians of women contend, without understanding the role of women and the importance of issues involving the family and the private world within it.

Given the range of disagreement over the nature of the progressive movement, it is hardly surprising that some historians have despaired of finding any coherent definition for the term at all. Peter Filene, for one, suggested in 1970 that the concept of progressivism as a "movement" had outlived its usefulness. "It is time," he sug-

gested, "to tear off the familiar label and, thus liberated from its prejudice, see the history between 1890 and 1920 for what it was—ambiguous, inconsistent, moved by agents and forces more complex than a [single, uniform] progressive movement." Critics said that Filene's view was an argument for abandoning the search for any historical meaning in the politics of the early twentieth century. But Daniel Rodgers, in an important 1982 article, "In Search of Progressivism," disagreed. His review of the new scholarship on the progressive era concluded:

> Whether historians of the 1980s will call off the search for that great, overarching thing called "progressivism" is hard to predict. Certainly historians in the 1970s manifestly failed to find it. In recompense they found out a vast amount about the world in which the progressives lived and the structures of social and political power shifting so rapidly around them. To acknowledge that these are the questions that matter and to abandon the hunt for the *essence* of the noise and tumult of that era may not be, as Filene's first critics feared, to lose the whole enterprise of historical comprehension. It may be to find it.

Steps (1898), the story of a young minister who abandoned a comfortable post to work among the needy, sold more than 15 million copies and established itself as the most successful novel of the era.

Walter Rauschenbusch, a Protestant theologian with socialist inclinations from Rochester, New York, published a series of influential discourses on the possibilities for human salvation through Christian reform. To him, the message of Darwinism was not that the individual was engaged in a brutal struggle for survival of the fittest, but that all individuals should work to ensure a humanitarian evolution of the social fabric. "Translate the evolutionary themes into religious faith," he wrote, "and you have the doctrine of the Kingdom of God." Some American Catholics seized on the 1893 publication of Pope Leo XIII's encyclical *Rerum Novarum* ("New Things") as justification for their own crusade for social justice. Catholic liberals such as

Father John A. Ryan took to heart the pope's warning that "a small number of very rich men have been able to lay upon the masses of the poor a yoke little better than slavery itself. . . . No practical solution of this question will ever be found without the assistance of religion and the church." For decades, he worked to expand the scope of Catholic social welfare organizations.

The Social Gospel was never the dominant element in the movement for urban reform. Some progressives dismissed it as irrelevant moralization; others viewed it as little more than a useful complement to their own work. But the engagement of religion with reform helped bring to progressivism a powerful moral component and a commitment to redeem the lives of even the least favored citizens. Walter Rauschenbusch captured some of both the optimism and the spirituality of the Social Gospel with his proud comment, after a

"THE BOSSES OF THE SENATE" (1889), BY JOSEPH KEPPLER
Keppler was a popular political cartoonist of the late nineteenth century who shared the growing concern about the power of the trusts—portrayed here as bloated, almost reptilian figures standing menacingly over the members of the U.S. Senate, to whose chamber the "people's entrance" is "closed." *(The Granger Collection)*

visit to a New York slum known as Hell's Kitchen, where Christian reformers were hard at work: "One could hear human virtue cracking and crashing all around."

The Settlement House Movement

One of the strongest elements of much progressive thought was the belief in the influence of the environment on individual development. Social Darwinists such as William Graham Sumner had argued that people's fortunes reflected their inherent "fitness" for survival. Many progressive theorists disagreed. Ignorance, poverty, even criminality, they argued, were not the result of inherent moral or genetic failings or of the workings of providence; they were, rather, the effects of an unhealthy environment. To elevate the distressed, therefore, required an improvement of the conditions in which they lived.

Nothing produced more distress, many reformers believed, than the crowded immigrant neighborhoods of American cities, which publicists such as Jacob Riis were exposing through vivid photographs and lurid descriptions. (See pp. 512–514.) One response to the problems of such communities, borrowed from England, was the settlement house. The most famous, and one of the first, was Hull House, which opened in 1889 in Chicago as a result of the efforts of Jane Addams. It became a model for more than 400 similar institutions throughout the nation. Staffed by members of the educated middle class, imbued with ideas derived from the social sciences, settlement houses sought to help immigrant families adapt to the language and customs of their new country. Settlement houses avoided the condescension and moral disapproval of earlier philanthropic efforts. But they generally embraced a belief that middle-class Americans had a responsibility to impart their own values to immigrants and to teach

The settlement houses also helped spawn another important institution of reform: the profession of social work—a profession in which women were also to play a vital role. Workers at Hull House, for example, maintained a close relationship with the University of Chicago's pioneering work in the field of sociology. A growing number of programs for the professional training of social workers began to appear in the nation's leading universities, partly in response to the activities of the settlements. The professional social worker combined a compassion for the poor with a commitment to the values of bureaucratic progressivism: scientific study, efficient organization, reliance on experts. The new profession produced elaborate surveys and reports, collected statistics, and published scholarly tracts on the need for urban reform.

The Allure of Expertise

As the emergence of the social work profession suggests, progressives involved in humanitarian efforts placed a high value on knowledge and expertise. Even nonscientific problems, they believed, could be analyzed and solved scientifically. Many reformers came to believe that only enlightened experts and well-designed bureaucracies could create the stability and order America needed.

This belief found expression in many ways, among them in the writings of a new group of scholars and intellectuals. Unlike the social Darwinists of the nineteenth century, these theorists were no longer content with merely justifying the existing industrial system. They spoke instead of the creation of a new civilization, in which the expertise of scientists and engineers could be brought to bear on the problems of the economy and society. Among the most influential was the social scientist Thorstein Veblen. Harshly critical of the industrial tycoons of the late nineteenth century—the "leisure class" as he satirically described them in his first major work, *A Theory of the Leisure Class* (1899)—Veblen proposed instead a new economic system in which power would reside in the hands of highly trained engineers. Only they, he argued, could fully understand the "machine process" by which modern society must be governed.

In practical terms, the impulse toward expertise and organization helped produce the idea of scientific management, or "Taylorism." (See p. 483.) It encouraged the development of modern mass-production techniques and, above all, the assembly line. But it also inspired a revolution in American education and the creation of a new area of inquiry: social science, the use of scientific techniques in the study of society and its

BAXTER STREET, NEW YORK
The Danish immigrant Jacob Riis rose from modest beginnings to become a successful journalist and a prominent crusader against the miserable living conditions in urban immigrant neighborhoods. He wrote powerfully of those conditions in his famous book *How the Other Half Lives* (1890); equally powerful were the many photographs he took during his investigations. This picture shows conditions in a crowded tenement neighborhood in lower Manhattan. *(Museum of the City of New York)*

them how to create middle-class lifestyles. Even the word "settlement" suggested as much: middle-class people "settling" in the inner city and bringing civilization to the urban frontier.

Central to the settlement houses were the efforts of college women. Indeed, the movement became a training ground for many important female leaders of the twentieth century, including Eleanor Roosevelt. The settlement houses provided these women with an environment and a role that society considered "appropriate" for unmarried women: urban "homes" where settlement workers helped immigrants to become better members of society. (The settlement house was "home" only to some of the reformers; their immigrant constituents did not live there.)

TENEMENT CIGARMAKERS
Among the social problems Jacob Riis attempted to illuminate were those of working conditions in immigrant communities. In this photograph from *How the Other Half Lives*, a cigarmaker works in his already crowded home surrounded by his children. Such home workers—many, perhaps most, of whom were women—were normally paid by the "piece," that is, by the amount of work they performed rather than the number of hours; the result was very long hours of labor (often with the help of the young children in the home) and very low pay. *(Museum of the City of New York)*

institutions. It produced a generation of bureaucratic reformers concerned with the structure of organizations and committed to building new political and economic institutions capable of managing a modern society. It also helped create a movement toward organization among the expanding new group of middle-class professionals.

The Professions

The late nineteenth century saw a dramatic expansion in the number of Americans engaged in administrative and professional tasks. Industries needed managers, technicians, and accountants as well as workers. Cities required commercial, medical, legal, and educational services. New technology required scientists and engineers who, in turn, required institutions and instructors to train them. By the turn of the century, those performing these services had come to constitute a distinct social group—what some have called a new middle class.

The new middle class placed a high value on education and individual accomplishment. By the early twentieth century, its millions of members were building organizations and establishing standards to secure their position in society. As their principal vehicle, they created the modern, organized professions. The idea of professionalism had been a frail one in America even as late as 1880. When every patent-medicine salesman could claim to be a doctor, when every frustrated politician could set up shop as a lawyer, when anyone who could read and write could pose as a teacher, a professional label by itself carried little weight. There were, of course, skilled and responsible doctors, lawyers, teachers, and others; but they had no way of controlling or distinguishing themselves clearly from the amateurs, charlatans, and incompetents who presumed to practice their trades. As the demand for professional services increased, so did the pressures for reform.

Among the first to respond was the medical profession. Throughout the 1890s, doctors who considered themselves trained professionals began forming local associations and societies. In 1901, they reorganized the American Medical Association into a national professional society. By 1920, nearly two-thirds of all American doctors were members. The AMA quickly called for strict, scientific standards for admission to the practice of medicine, with doctors themselves serving as protectors of the standards. State and local governments responded by passing new laws requiring the licensing of all physicians and restricting licenses to those practitioners approved by the profession.

Accompanying the emphasis on strict regulation of the profession came a concern for rigorous scientific training and research. By 1900, medical education at a few medical schools—notably Johns Hopkins in Baltimore (founded in 1893)—compared favorably with that in the leading institutions of Europe. Doctors such as William H. Welch at Hopkins revolutionized the teaching of medicine by moving students out of the classrooms and into laboratories and clinics. Rigorous new standards forced many inadequate medical schools out of existence, and those that remained were obliged to adopt a strict scientific approach.

There was similar movement in other professions. By 1916, lawyers in all forty-eight states had established professional bar associations; and virtually all of them had succeeded in creating central examining boards, composed of lawyers, to regulate admission to the profession. Increasingly, aspiring lawyers found it necessary to enroll in graduate programs, and the nation's law schools accordingly expanded greatly, both in numbers and in the rigor of their curricula. Businessmen supported the creation of schools of business administration and created their own national organizations: the National Association of Manufacturers in 1895 and the United States Chamber of Commerce in 1912. Even farmers, long the symbol of the romantic spirit of individualism, responded to the new order by forming, through the National Farm Bureau Federation, a network of agricultural organizations designed to spread scientific farming methods, teach sound marketing techniques, and lobby for the interests of their members.

Among the purposes of the new professionalism was guarding entry into the professions. This was only partly an effort to defend the professions from the untrained and incompetent. The admission requirements also protected those already in the professions from excessive competition and lent prestige and status to the professional level. Some professionals used their entrance requirements to exclude blacks, women, immigrants, and other "undesirables" from their ranks. Others used them simply to keep the numbers down, to ensure that demand for the services of existing members would remain high.

Women and the Professions

Both by custom and by active barriers of law and prejudice, American women found themselves excluded from most of the emerging professions. But a substantial number of middle-class women—particularly those emerging from the new women's colleges and from the coeducational state universities—entered professional careers nevertheless.

A few women managed to establish themselves as physicians, lawyers, engineers, scientists, and corporate managers. Several leading medical schools admitted women, and in 1900 about 5 percent of all American physicians were female (a proportion that remained unchanged until the 1960s). Most, however, turned by necessity to those professions that society considered suitable for women. Settlement houses and social work provided two "appropriate" professional outlets for women. The most important, however, was teaching. Indeed, in the late nineteenth century, more than two-thirds of all grammar school teachers were women, and perhaps 90 percent of all professional women were teachers. For educated black women, in particular, teaching was often the only professional opportunity they could hope to find. The existence of segregated black schools in the South created a substantial market for African-American teachers.

Women also dominated other professional activities. Nursing had become primarily a women's field during and after the Civil War, when it was still considered a menial occupation, akin to domestic service. But by the early twentieth century, it was adopting professional standards. Prospective nurses generally needed certification from schools of nursing and could not simply learn on the job. Women also found opportunities as librarians, another field beginning to define itself in professional terms. And many women entered academia—often receiving advanced degrees at such predominantly male institutions as the University of Chicago, MIT, or Columbia, and finding professional opportunities in the new and expanding women's colleges.

The "women's professions" had much in common with other professions: the value they placed on training and expertise, the creation of professional organizations and a professional "identity," the monitoring of admission to professional work. But they also had distinctive qualities. Teaching, nursing, library work, and others were "helping" professions. They usually involved working primarily with other women or with children. Their activities occurred in places that seemed different from the offices that dominated the predominantly male business and professional worlds; such places as schools, hospitals, and libraries had a vaguely "domestic" image.

WOMEN AND REFORM

The prominence of women in reform movements is one of the most striking features of progressivism. In most states in the early twentieth century, women could not vote. They almost never held public office. They had footholds in only a few (and usually primarily female) professions. They lived in a culture in which most people, male and female, believed that women were not suited for the male-dominated public world, that they did, and should, inhabit their own sphere. What, then, explains the prominent role so many women played in the reform activities of the period? In fact, female activism in the progressive era represented both an expansion of women's separate sphere and a confirmation of it.

The "New Woman"

The phenomenon of the "new woman," widely remarked upon at the time, was a product of social and economic changes that affected the private world as much as the public one. By the end of the nineteenth century, almost all income-producing activity had moved out of the home and into the factory or the office. At the same time, children were beginning school at earlier ages and spending more time there. For wives and mothers who did not work for wages, the home was a less all-consuming place. Most women still oversaw the domestic functions of the home. Technological innovations such as running water, electricity, and eventually household appliances made housework less onerous (even if higher standards of cleanliness counterbalanced many of these gains); and for middle-class women with domestic help, housework occupied only a small part of the day. It was not surprising, perhaps, that more and more women were looking for activities outside the home.

Declining family size also changed the lives of many women. Middle-class white women in the late nineteenth century had fewer children than their mothers and grandmothers had borne. They also lived longer than previous generations. Many women thus now spent fewer years with young children in the home

and lived more years after their children were grown.

There were also many more women who lived outside traditional families altogether. Some educated women shunned marriage entirely, believing that only by remaining single could they play the roles they envisioned in the public world; approximately 10 percent of all American women in the last decades of the nineteenth century never married—a high proportion of them middle-class women. Single women were among the most prominent female reformers of the time: Jane Addams and Lillian Wald in the settlement house movement; Frances Willard in the temperance movement; Anna Howard Shaw in the suffrage movement; and many others. Some of these women lived alone. Others lived with other women, often in long-term relationships—some of them secretly romantic—that were known at the time as "Boston marriages." The divorce rate also rose rapidly in the late nineteenth century, from one divorce for every twenty-one marriages in 1880 to one in nine by 1916; women initiated the great majority of them.

Higher levels of education also contributed to the prominence of women in reform activities. The proliferation of women's colleges and of coeducational public universities in the late nineteenth-century produced the first generation of women in which significant numbers had education above the high-school level. (See pp. 527–528.) The new colleges also helped create female communities, within which women could find support for their ambitions and companionship for their activities.

There was, in the end, no single profile for the "new woman." But a growing number of American women at the beginning of the twentieth century were defining their lives in ways that included a substantial amount of activity outside the home, and they were deriving from their identity as women a set of distinctive concerns that defined—and limited—their public activities.

The Clubwomen

Among the most visible signs of the increasing public roles of women in the late nineteenth and early twentieth centuries were the women's clubs—a large network of women's associations that proliferated rapidly beginning in the 1880s and 1890s and that became the vanguard of many important reforms.

The women's clubs began largely as cultural organizations to provide middle- and upper-class women with an outlet for their intellectual energies. In 1892, when women formed the General Federation of Wom-

THE SHIRTWAIST STRIKE, 1909
More than 30,000 workers in shirtwaist factories in New
York went on strike in November 1909—one of the largest
labor actions in American history involving mostly women
workers. Members of Local 25 of the International Ladies
Garment Workers Union organized the strike. When the
ILGWU hesitated to support them, the local turned to the
new Women's Trade Union League for help. The strike attracted substantial public support (including support from
some of New York's wealthiest women) and soon spread
to other cities as well. It ultimately failed to achieve most
of its goals, but it did lead to the organization of many garment workers and greatly strengthened both the ILGWU
and the WTUL. *(Brown Brothers, courtesy ILGWU)*

en's Clubs to coordinate the activities of local organizations, there were more than 100,000 members in
nearly 500 clubs. Eight years later, there were 160,000
members; and by 1917, over 1 million.

By the early twentieth century, the clubs were becoming less concerned with cultural activities and
more concerned with contributing to social betterment.
Because many club members were from wealthy families, some organizations had substantial funds at their
disposal to make their influence felt. And ironically,
because women could not vote, the clubs had a nonpartisan image that made them more difficult for
politicians to dismiss.

Black women occasionally joined clubs dominated
by whites. But most such clubs excluded blacks, and
so African Americans formed clubs of their own, some
of which affiliated with the General Federation, but
more of which became part of the independent National Association of Colored Women. They modeled
themselves primarily on their white counterparts, but
some black clubs also took positions on issues of particular concern to blacks. Some crusaded against lynching and called for congressional legislation to make
lynching a federal crime. Others protested aspects of
segregation.

The women's club movement raised few overt challenges to prevailing assumptions about the proper role
of women in society. But it did represent an important
effort by women to extend their influence beyond the
traditional female sphere within the home and the
family. Few clubwomen were willing to accept the
arguments of such committed feminists as Charlotte
Perkins Gilman, who in her 1898 book *Women and Economics* argued that the traditional definition of gender
roles was exploitive and obsolete. The club movement,
rather, allowed women to define a space for themselves in the public world without openly challenging
the existing, male-dominated order. And it gave many
women access to a female community in which they
were able to act and express themselves in ways usually impossible in male-dominated institutions. As one
Boston clubwoman said, "We need to feel the cheer
and inspiration of meeting each other, we gain the
courage and fresh life that comes from the mingling of
congenial souls, of those working for the same ends."

But the importance of the club movement did not
lie simply in what it did for middle-class women. It
lay also in what those women accomplished for the
working-class people they attempted to help. Much of
what the clubs did was uncontroversial: planting trees;
supporting schools, libraries, and settlement houses;
building hospitals and parks. But clubwomen also
supported measures that attracted significant opposition. They were an important force in winning passage
of state (and ultimately federal) laws that regulated the
conditions of woman and child labor, that established
government inspection of workplaces, that regulated
the food and drug industries, that reformed policies
toward the Indian tribes, and that applied new standards to urban housing. They were instrumental in
pressuring state legislatures in most states to provide
pensions to widowed or abandoned mothers with
small children—a system known as "mother's pensions," which ultimately became absorbed into the Social Security system. In 1912, they pressured Congress
into establishing the Children's Bureau in the Labor
Department, an agency directed to develop policies to
protect children.

In many of these efforts, the clubwomen formed alliances with other women's groups, such as the Wom-
en's Trade Union League, founded in 1903 by female
union members and upper-class reformers and committed to persuading women to join unions. In addition to working on behalf of protective legislation for
women, WTUL members held public meetings on be-

half of female workers, raised money to support strikes, marched on picket lines, and bailed striking women out of jail.

Women reformers often worked closely with men; and of course the success of most of their efforts depended on the support of male voters, legislators, and public officials. What made their crusades palatable to men was also what made them appealing to many women: their self-consciously "maternal" character. In campaigning for measures to protect women and children workers and to assist the most powerless members of society, women's clubs emphasized the "nurturing" and "protective" features of their work and fought for "moral uplift." In doing so, they were reflecting contemporary ideas about the natural inclinations of women.

Woman Suffrage

Perhaps the largest single reform movement of the progressive era, indeed one of the largest in American history, was the fight for woman suffrage—a movement that attracted support from both women and men but whose most important leaders were women.

It is sometimes difficult for today's Americans to understand why the suffrage issue could have become the source of such enormous controversy. But at the time, suffrage seemed to many of its critics a very radical demand, in part because of the rationale some of its early supporters used to advance it. Throughout the late nineteenth century, many suffrage advocates presented their views in terms of "natural rights," arguing that women deserved the same rights as men—including, first and foremost, the right to vote. Elizabeth Cady Stanton, for example, wrote in 1892 of woman as "the arbiter of her own destiny. . . . if we are to consider her as a citizen, as a member of a great nation, she must have the same rights as all other members." A woman's role as "mother, wife, sister, daughter" was "incidental" to her larger role as a part of society.

This was an argument that boldly challenged the views of the many men (and even many women) who believed that society required a distinctive female "sphere" in which women would serve first and foremost as wives and mothers. And so a powerful antisuffrage movement emerged, dominated by men but with the active support of many women, which challenged this apparent threat to the existing social order. There were antisuffrage organizations, some with substantial memberships; antisuffrage newspapers; rallies; petitions to legislatures; and widely circulated tracts. Opponents railed against the threat suffrage posed to the "natural order" of civilization. Woman, said one opponent, "was made man's helper, was

SUFFRAGISTS
Suffrage activists hang posters along the boardwalk in the beachfront town of Long Branch, New Jersey. Twenty-nine states had permitted women at least some access to the ballot before ratification of the Nineteenth Amendment in 1920. New Jersey was not one of them. *(Culver)*

given a servient place (not necessarily inferior) and man the dominant place (not necessarily superior) in the division of labor." Antisuffragists associated suffrage with divorce (not without some reason, since many suffrage advocates also supported revising the laws to make it easier for women to obtain a divorce). They linked suffrage with promiscuity, looseness, and neglect of children.

In the first years of the twentieth century, the suffrage movement began to overcome this opposition and win some substantial victories. In part that was because suffragists were becoming better organized and more politically sophisticated than their opponents. Under the leadership of Anna Howard Shaw, a Boston social worker, and Carrie Chapman Catt, a journalist from Iowa, membership in the National American Woman Suffrage Association grew from about 13,000 in 1893 to over 2 million in 1917. The involvement of such well-known and widely admired women as Jane Addams gave added respectability to the cause.

But the movement also gained strength because many of its most prominent leaders began to justify suffrage in "safer," less threatening ways. Suffrage, some supporters began to argue, would not challenge the "separate sphere" in which women resided. It would allow women to bring their special and distinct virtues more widely to bear on society's problems. It was, they claimed, precisely because women occupied a distinct sphere—because as mothers and wives and homemakers they had special experiences and special sensitivities to bring to public life—that woman suffrage could make such an important contribution to politics. Jane Addams expressed this more maternalist justification for suffrage in a 1909 article: "If women would effectively continue their old avocations, they must take part in the slow upbuilding of that code of legislation which is alone sufficient to protect the home from its dangers incident to modern life."

In particular, many suffragists argued that enfranchising women would help the temperance movement, by giving its largest group of supporters a political voice. Some suffrage advocates claimed that once women had the vote, war would become a thing of the past, since women would—by their calming, maternal influence—help curb the belligerence of men. That was one reason why World War I gave a final, decisive push to the movement for suffrage.

Suffrage also attracted support for other, less optimistic reasons. Many middle-class people found persuasive the argument that if blacks, immigrants, and other "base" groups had access to the franchise, then it was not only a matter of justice but of common sense to allow educated, "well-born" women to vote. Some people, in fact, supported woman suffrage because they believed that it would add to the constituency that supported immigration restriction and racial disfranchisement. Florence Kelley, a prominent social reformer who was later to help organize the NAACP, remarked unhappily in 1906 on this aspect of the suffrage movement: "I have rarely heard a ringing suffrage speech which did not refer to the 'ignorant and degraded' men, or the 'ignorant immigrants' as our masters. This is habitually spoken with more or less bitterness."

Not all suffragists abandoned the more radical rationales. Among working-class, immigrant, and black women in particular, suffrage continued to generate substantial support precisely because it seemed so radical, because it promised to reshape the role of women and reform the social order. But among members of the middle class, the separation of the suffrage movement from more radical feminist goals, and its association with other reform causes of concern to many Americans, helped it gain widespread support.

The principal triumphs of the suffrage movement began in 1910. That year, Washington became the first state in fourteen years to extend suffrage to women. California followed a year later, and four other western states in 1912. This impressive early strength of the suffrage movement in the western states was a result, in part, of the absence of large Catholic communities in the region. In the East, battles over suffrage seemed inevitably to become linked to ethnic battles over cultural issues—most notably temperance—that divided Catholics and Protestants. In the West, the suffrage fight only rarely intersected with other, more divisive issues.

In 1913, Illinois became the first state east of the Mississippi to embrace woman suffrage. And in 1917 and 1918, New York and Michigan—two of the most populous states in the Union—gave women the vote. By 1919, thirty-nine states had granted women the right to vote in at least some elections; fifteen had allowed them full participation. In 1920, finally, suffragists won ratification of the Nineteenth Amendment, which guaranteed political rights to women throughout the nation.

To some feminists, however, the victory seemed less than complete. Alice Paul, head of the militant National Woman's Party (founded in 1916), never accepted the relatively conservative "separate sphere" justification for suffrage. She argued that the Nineteenth Amendment alone would not be sufficient to protect women's rights. Women needed more: a constitutional amendment that would provide clear, legal protection for their rights and would prohibit all discrimination on the basis of sex. But Alice Paul's argument found limited favor even among many of the most important leaders of the recently triumphant suffrage crusade. Jane Addams, Florence Kelley, Carrie Chapman Catt, and others showed no interest in the Equal Rights Amendment. Some, such as Addams, denounced it bitterly, fearing it would invalidate the special protective legislation for women that they had fought so hard to have enacted. It would be many years before the divisions between these two wings of American feminism were healed.

As the controversy over the Equal Rights Amendment suggests, the suffrage movement did not, in the end, produce a coherent movement behind any issue other than securing women the vote. On most other questions, in fact, women were generally no more in agreement than men. Once enfranchised, the new voters did little to support the arguments of those suffragists who had claimed that women would operate in politics as a coherent force for reform.

THE ASSAULT ON THE PARTIES

Sooner or later, most progressive goals required the involvement of government. Only government, reformers agreed, could effectively counter the many powerful private interests that threatened the nation. But American government at the dawn of the new century was, progressives believed, poorly adapted to perform their ambitious tasks. At every level political institutions were outmoded, inefficient, and corrupt. Before they could reform society effectively, they would have to reform government itself. In the beginning, at least, many reformers believed the first step must be an assault on the dominant role the political parties played in the life of the state. They considered the parties corrupt, undemocratic, and reactionary.

Early Attacks

Attacks on party dominance had been frequent in the late nineteenth century. Greenbackism and Populism, for example, had been efforts to break the hammerlock with which the Republicans and Democrats controlled public life. The Independent Republicans (or mugwumps) had attempted to challenge the grip of partisanship; and former mugwumps became important supporters of progressive political reform activity in the 1890s and later.

The early assaults enjoyed some success. In the 1880s and 1890s, for example, most states adopted the secret ballot. Prior to that, the political parties themselves had printed ballots (or "tickets"), with the names of the party's candidates, and no others. They distributed the tickets to their supporters, who then simply went to the polls to deposit them in the ballot box. The old system had made it possible for bosses to monitor the voting behavior of their constituents; it had also made it difficult for voters to "split" their tickets—to vote for candidates of different parties for different offices. The new secret ballot—printed by the government and distributed at the polls to be filled out and deposited in secret—helped chip away at the power of the parties over the voters.

By the late 1890s, critics of the parties were expanding their goals. Party rule could be broken, they believed, in one of two ways. It could be broken by increasing the power of the people, by permitting them to circumvent partisan institutions and express their will directly at the polls. Or it could be broken by placing more power in the hands of nonpartisan, nonelective officials, insulated from political life. Reformers promoted measures that moved along both those paths.

Municipal Reform

Many progressives believed the impact of party rule was most damaging in the cities. Municipal government therefore became the first target of those working for political reform. Muckraking journalists such as Lincoln Steffens were especially successful in arousing public outrage at corruption and incompetence in city politics.

The muckrakers struck a responsive chord among a powerful group of urban middle-class progressives. For several decades after the Civil War, "respectable" citizens of the nation's large cities had avoided participation in municipal government. Viewing politics as a debased and demeaning activity, they shrank from contact with the "vulgar" elements who were coming to dominate public life. By the end of the century, however, a new generation of activists—some of them members of old aristocratic families, others a part of the new middle class—were taking a growing interest in government.

They faced a formidable array of opponents. In addition to challenging the powerful city bosses and their entrenched political organizations, they were attacking a large group of special interests: saloon owners, brothel keepers, and perhaps most significantly, those businessmen who had established lucrative relationships with the urban machines and who viewed reform as a threat to their profits. Allied with these in-

terests were many influential newspapers, which ridiculed the reformers as naive do-gooders. Finally, there was the great constituency of urban working people, many of them recent immigrants, to whom the machines were a source of needed jobs and services. Gradually, however, the reformers gained in political strength—in part because of their own growing numbers, in part because of the failures of the existing political leadership. And in the first years of the twentieth century, they began to score some important victories.

One of the first major successes came in Galveston, Texas, where the old city government proved completely unable to deal with the effects of a destructive tidal wave in 1900. Capitalizing on public dismay, reformers, many of them local businessmen, won approval of a new city charter. The mayor and council were replaced by an elected, nonpartisan commission. In 1907, Des Moines, Iowa, adopted its own version of the commission plan, and other cities soon followed.

Another approach to municipal reform, similarly motivated by the desire to remove city government from the hands of the parties, was the city-manager plan, by which elected officials hired an outside expert—often a professionally trained business manager or engineer—to take charge of the government. The city manager would presumably remain untainted by the corrupting influence of politics. By the end of the progressive era, almost 400 cities were operating under commissions, and another 45 employed city managers.

In most urban areas, and in the larger cities in particular, the enemies of party had to settle for less absolute victories. Some cities made the election of mayors nonpartisan (so that the parties could not choose the candidates) or moved them to years when no presidential or congressional races were in progress (to reduce the influence of the large turnouts that party organizations produced on such occasions). Reformers tried to make city councilors run at large, to limit the influence of ward leaders and district bosses. They tried to strengthen the power of the mayor at the expense of the city council, on the assumption that reformers were more likely to succeed in getting a sympathetic mayor elected than they were to win control of the entire council.

Indeed, some of the most successful reformers emerged not from the new commission and city-manager systems but from conventional political structures that progressives came to control. Tom Johnson, the celebrated reform mayor of Cleveland, waged a long and difficult war against the powerful streetcar interests in his city, fighting to raise the ridiculously low assessments on railroad and utilities properties, to lower streetcar fares to 3 cents, and ultimately to impose municipal ownership on certain basic utilities. After Johnson's defeat and death, his talented aide Newton D. Baker won election as mayor and helped maintain Cleveland's reputation as the best-governed city in America. Hazen Pingree of Detroit, Samuel "Golden Rule" Jones of Toledo, and other mayors effectively challenged local party bosses to bring the spirit of reform into city government.

Statehouse Progressivism

The assault on boss rule in the cities did not, however, always produce results satisfying to reformers. As a result, many progressives turned to state government as an agent for reform. These state-level progressives, like their municipal counterparts, considered existing state governments unfit to answer society's needs. They looked with particular scorn on state legislatures, whose ill-paid, relatively undistinguished members they believed were generally incompetent, often corrupt, and totally controlled by party bosses. Many reformers began looking for ways to circumvent the legislatures (and the party bosses that controlled them) by increasing the power of the electorate.

Two of the most important changes were innovations first proposed by Populists in the 1890s: the initiative and the referendum. The initiative allowed reformers to circumvent state legislatures altogether by submitting new legislation directly to the voters in general elections. The referendum provided a method by which actions of the legislature could be returned to the electorate for approval. By 1918, more than twenty states had enacted one or both of these reforms.

Similarly, the direct primary and the recall were efforts to limit the power of party and improve the quality of elected officials. The primary election was an attempt to take the selection of candidates away from the bosses and give it to the people. In the South, it was also an effort to limit black voting—since primary voting, many white southerners believed, would be easier to control than general elections. The recall gave voters the right to remove a public official from office at a special election, which could be called after a sufficient number of citizens had signed a petition. By 1915 every state in the nation had instituted primary elections for at least some offices. The recall encountered more strenuous opposition, but a few states adopted it as well.

Other reform measures attempted to clean up the legislatures themselves by limiting the influence of corporations on their activities and on the behavior of the parties. Between 1903 and 1908, twelve states passed laws restricting lobbying by business interests in state legislatures. In those same years, twenty-two states banned campaign contributions by corporations, and twenty-four states forbade public officials from accepting free passes from railroads.

ROBERT LA FOLLETTE CAMPAIGNING IN WISCONSIN
After three terms as governor of Wisconsin, La Follette began a long career in the United States Senate in 1906 during which he worked uncompromisingly for advanced progressive reforms—so uncompromisingly, in fact, that he was often almost completely isolated. He entitled a chapter of his autobiography "Alone in the Senate." La Follette had a greater impact on his own state, whose politics he and his sons dominated for nearly forty years and where he was able to win passage of many reforms that the federal government resisted. *(State Historical Society of Wisconsin)*

Reform efforts proved most effective in states that elevated vigorous and committed politicians to positions of leadership. In New York, Governor Charles Evans Hughes exploited progressive sentiment to create a commission to regulate public utilities. In California, Governor Hiram Johnson used the new reforms to limit the political power of the Southern Pacific Railroad. In New Jersey, Woodrow Wilson, the Princeton University president elected governor in 1910, used executive leadership to win reforms designed to end New Jersey's widely denounced position as the "mother of trusts."

But the most celebrated state-level reformer was Robert M. La Follette of Wisconsin. Elected governor in 1900, he helped turn his state into what reformers across the nation described as a "laboratory of progressivism." Under his leadership the Wisconsin progressives won approval of direct primaries, initiatives, and referendums. They regulated railroads and utilities. They passed laws to regulate the workplace and provide compensation for laborers injured on the job. They instituted graduated taxes on inherited fortunes, and they nearly doubled state levies on railroads and other corporate interests.

La Follette brought to progressivism his own fervent, almost evangelical, commitment to reform; and he used his personal magnetism to widen public awareness of progressive goals and to mobilize the energies of many previously passive groups. Reform was not simply the responsibility of politicians, he argued, but of newspapers, citizens' groups, educational institutions, and business and professional organizations. Ultimately, La Follette would be overshadowed by other national progressive leaders. In the early years of the century, however, few men were as effective in publicizing the message of reform. None was as successful in bending state government to that goal.

Parties and Interest Groups

The reformers did not, of course, eliminate parties from American political life. But they did contribute to a decline in party influence. Evidence of that came from, among other things, the decline in voter turnout. In the late nineteenth century, up to 81 percent of eligible voters routinely turned out for national elections. In the early twentieth century, while turnout remained very high by today's standards, the figure declined markedly. In the presidential election of 1900, 73 percent of the electorate voted. By 1912, it had declined to about 59 percent. Never again did voter turnout reach as high as 70 percent.

At the same time that parties were declining, other power centers were beginning to replace them: what

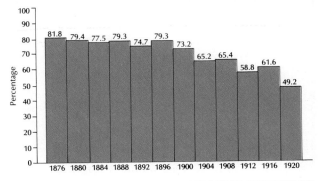

VOTER PARTICIPATION IN PRESIDENTIAL ELECTIONS, 1876–1920

have become known as "interest groups." Beginning late in the nineteenth century and accelerating rapidly in the twentieth, new organizations emerged outside the party system, designed to pressure government to do their members' bidding: professional organizations, trade associations representing particular businesses and industries, labor organizations, farm lobbies, and many others. Social workers, the settlement house movement, women's clubs, and others learned to operate as interest groups to advance their demands. A new pattern of politics, in which many individual interests organized to influence government directly rather than through party structures, was emerging. It would become the characteristic form of American politics in the twentieth century.

SOURCES OF PROGRESSIVE REFORM

Middle-class reformers, most of them from the East, dominated the public image and much of the substance of progressivism in the late nineteenth and early twentieth centuries. But they were not alone in seeking to improve social conditions. Working-class Americans, African Americans, westerners, even party bosses also played crucial roles in advancing some of the important reforms of the era.

Labor, the Machine, and Reform

Although the American Federation of Labor, and its leader Samuel Gompers, remained largely aloof from many of the reform efforts of the time (reflecting Gom-

THE TRIANGLE SHIRTWAIST FIRE
Policemen and investigators stand amid the coffins of victims of the 1911 fire in the Triangle Shirtwaist Factory in New York City, in which 146 workers (almost all of them women) died. Although the proprietors of the factory, who had locked the emergency exits, were acquitted of criminal charges in the deaths, the fire spurred reform and labor groups—most notably the International Ladies Garment Workers Union—to agitate for government action to improve conditions in the sweatshops. *(Culver)*

pers's firm belief that workers should not rely on government to improve their lot), some unions nevertheless played important roles in reform battles. In San Francisco, for example, workers in the Building Trades Council spearheaded the formation of the new Union Labor Party, committed to a program of reform almost indistinguishable from that of middle-class and elite progressives in the city. Corruption and ineptitude within the new party's leadership limited its effectiveness, but the party did manage to elect two of its candidates mayor. Although the workers never controlled enough votes in the state legislature to have much direct influence, other Bay Area politicians supported pro-labor legislation in an effort to appeal to the party's constituency. Between 1911 and 1913, California passed a child labor law, a workmen's compensation law, and a limitation on working hours for women. Union pressures contributed to the passage of similar laws in many other states as well.

One result of the assault on the parties was a change in the party organizations themselves, which attempted to adapt to the new realities so as to preserve their influence. Some party machines emerged from the progressive era almost as powerful as they had entered it. In large part, this was because bosses themselves recognized that they must change in order to survive. Thus they sometimes allowed their machines to become vehicles of social reform. One example was New York's Tammany Hall, the nation's oldest and most notorious city machine. Its astute leader, Charles Francis Murphy, began in the early years of the century to fuse the techniques of boss rule with some of the concerns of social reformers. Murphy did nothing to challenge the fundamental workings of Tammany Hall. But Tammany began to take an increased interest in state and national politics, which it had traditionally scorned; and it used its political power on behalf of legislation to improve working conditions, protect child laborers, and eliminate the worst abuses of the industrial economy.

In 1911, a terrible fire swept through the factory of the Triangle Shirtwaist Company in New York; 146 workers, most of them women, died. Many of them had been trapped inside the burning building because management had locked the emergency exits to prevent malingering. For the next three years, a state commission studied not only the background of the fire but the general condition of the industrial workplace. It was responding to intense public pressure from women's groups and New York City labor unions—and to less-public pressure from Tammany Hall. By 1914, the commission had issued a series of reports calling for major reforms in the conditions of modern labor.

The report itself was a classic progressive document, based on the testimony of experts, filled with statistics and technical data. Yet when its recommendations reached the New York Legislature, its most effective supporters were not middle-class progressives but two Tammany Democrats from working-class backgrounds: Senator Robert F. Wagner and Assemblyman Alfred E. Smith. With the support of Murphy and the backing of other Tammany legislators, they steered through a series of pioneering labor laws that imposed strict regulations on factory owners and established effective mechanisms for enforcement.

Western Progressives

The American West produced some of the most notable progressive leaders of the time: Hiram Johnson of California, George Norris of Nebraska, William Borah of Idaho, and others—almost all of whom spent at least some of their political careers in the United States Senate. That was because for western states, the most important target of reform energies was not state or local governments, which had relatively little power, but the federal government, which exercised a kind of authority in the West that it had never possessed in the East.

That was in part because some of the most important issues to the future of the West required action above the state level. Disputes over water, for example, almost always involved rivers and streams that crossed state lines. The question of who had the rights to the waters of the Colorado River created a political battle that no state government could resolve; the federal government had to arbitrate. More significant, perhaps, the federal government exercised enormous power over the lands and resources of the western states and provided substantial subsidies to the region in the form of land grants and support for railroad and water projects. Huge areas of the West remained (and still remain) public lands, controlled by Washington—a far greater proportion than in any states east of the Mississippi; and much of the growth of the West was (and continues to be) a result of federally funded dams and water projects.

Because so much authority in the region rested in federal bureaucracies which state and local governments could not control, political parties in most of the West were relatively weak. That was one reason why western states could move so quickly and decisively to embrace reforms that parties did not like: the initiative, the referendum, the recall, direct primaries. It is also why aspiring politicians were much quicker to look to Washington as a place from which they could influence the future of their region.

African Americans and Reform

One social question that received relatively little attention from white progressives was race. But among African Americans themselves, the progressive era produced some significant challenges to existing racial norms.

African Americans faced greater obstacles—legal, economic, social, and political—than any other group

W. E. B. DU BOIS
Although Du Bois, unlike Booker T. Washington, never developed a large popular following, he was the acknowledged leader of the black elite in the late nineteenth and early twentieth centuries. He was the first African American ever to earn a doctorate at Harvard University, and he published a number of distinguished works of history and sociology during his long career. He also served for more than twenty years as editor of *The Crisis*, the newspaper of the NAACP. He died in 1963, at the age of ninety-five, having lived long enough to see the emergence of a powerful civil rights movement dedicated to achieving many of the goals for which he had fought throughout his life. This pastel portrait was drawn around 1925 by Winhold Reiss. *(National Portrait Gallery)*

in challenging their own oppressed status and seeking reform. Thus it was not surprising, perhaps, that so many embraced the message of Booker T. Washington in the late nineteenth century, to "put down your bucket where you are," to work for immediate self-improvement rather than long-range social change. Not all blacks, however, were content with this approach. And by the turn of the century a powerful challenge was emerging—to the philosophy of Washington and, more important, to the entire structure of race relations. The chief spokesman for this new approach was W. E. B. Du Bois.

Du Bois, unlike Washington, had never known slavery. Born in Massachusetts, educated at Fisk University in Nashville and at Harvard, he grew to maturity with a more expansive view than Washington of the goals of his race and the responsibilities of white society to eliminate prejudice and injustice. In *The Souls of Black Folk* (1903), he launched an open attack on the philosophy of the Atlanta Compromise, accusing Washington of encouraging white efforts to impose segregation and of unnecessarily limiting the aspirations of his race. "Is it possible and probable," he asked, "that nine millions of men can make effective progress in economic lines if they are deprived of political rights, made a servile caste, and allowed only the most meager chance for developing their exceptional men? If history and reason give any distinct answer to these questions, it is an emphatic No."

Rather than content themselves with education at the trade and agricultural schools, Du Bois advocated, talented blacks should accept nothing less than a full university education. They should aspire to the professions. They should, above all, fight for the immediate restoration of their civil rights, not simply wait for them to be granted as a reward for patient striving. In 1905, Du Bois and a group of his supporters met at Niagara Falls—on the Canadian side of the border because no hotel on the American side of the Falls would have them—and launched what became known as the Niagara Movement. Four years later, after a race riot in Springfield, Illinois, they joined with white progressives sympathetic to their cause to form the National Association for the Advancement of Colored People (NAACP). Whites held most of the offices at first, but Du Bois, its director of publicity and research, was the guiding spirit. In the ensuing years, the new organization led the drive for equal rights, using as its principal weapon lawsuits in the federal courts.

Within less than a decade, the NAACP had begun to win some important victories. In *Guinn* v. *United States* (1915), the Supreme Court supported their position that the grandfather clause in an Oklahoma law was unconstitutional. (The statute denied the vote to any citizen whose ancestors had not been enfranchised in 1860.) In *Buchanan* v. *Worley* (1917), the Court struck down a Louisville, Kentucky, law requiring residential segregation. Disfranchisement and segregation would survive through other methods for many decades to come, but the NAACP had established a pattern of black resistance that would ultimately bear important fruits. It had also established itself, particularly after Booker T. Washington's death in 1915, as

one of the nation's leading black organizations, a position it would maintain for many years.

The NAACP was not a radical, or even an egalitarian, organization. It relied, rather, on the efforts of the most intelligent and educated members of the black race, the "talented tenth" as Du Bois called them. And it stressed not so much the elevation of all blacks from poverty and oppression as the opportunity for exceptional blacks to gain positions of full equality. Ultimately, its members believed, such efforts would benefit all blacks. By creating a trained elite, blacks would in effect be creating a leadership group capable of fighting for the rights of the race as a whole.

CRUSADES FOR ORDER AND REFORM

Reformers directed many of their energies at the political process. But they also crusaded on behalf of what they considered moral issues. There were campaigns to eliminate alcohol from national life, to curb prostitution, and to limit divorce. And there were efforts to restrict immigration or curb the power of monopoly in the industrial economy. Proponents of each of those reforms believed that success would help regenerate society as a whole.

The Temperance Crusade

Many progressives considered the elimination of alcohol from American life a necessary step in restoring order to society. Workers in settlement houses and social agencies abhorred the effects of drinking on working-class families: scarce wages vanished as workers spent hours in the saloons. Drunkenness spawned violence, and occasionally murder, within urban families. Women, in particular, saw alcohol as a source of some of the greatest problems of working-class wives and mothers, and hoped through temperance to reform male behavior and thus improve women's lives. Employers, too, regarded alcohol as an impediment to industrial efficiency; workers often missed time on the job because of drunkenness or, worse, came to the factory intoxicated and performed their tasks sloppily and dangerously. Critics of economic privilege denounced the liquor industry as one of the nation's most sinister trusts. And political reformers, who (correctly) looked on the saloon as one of the central institutions of the urban machine, saw an attack on drinking as part of an attack on the bosses. Out of such sentiments emerged the temperance movement.

CRUSADING FOR TEMPERANCE
This unflattering painting by Ben Shahn portrays late-nineteenth-century women demonstrating grimly in front of a saloon. It suggests the degree to which temperance and prohibition had fallen out of favor with liberals and progressives by the 1930s, when Shahn was working. In earlier years, however, temperance attracted the support of some of the most advanced American reformers. *(Museum of the City of New York)*

Temperance had been a major reform movement before the Civil War, mobilizing large numbers of people (and particularly large numbers of women) in a crusade with strong evangelical overtones. Beginning in the 1870s, it experienced a major resurgence. As in the antebellum years, the movement was led and supported primarily by women. In 1873, temperance advocates formed the Women's Christian Temperance Union (WCTU), led after 1879 by Frances Willard. By 1911, it had 245,000 members and had become the single largest women's organization in American history to that point. The WCTU publicized the evils of alcohol and the connection between drunkenness and family violence, unemployment, poverty, and disease. In 1893, the Anti-Saloon League joined the temperance movement and, along with the WCTU, began to press for a specific legislative solution: the legal abolition of saloons. Gradually, that demand grew to include the complete prohibition of the sale and manufacture of alcoholic beverages.

Despite substantial opposition from immigrant and working-class voters, pressure for prohibition grew steadily through the first decades of the new century. By 1916, nineteen states had passed prohibition laws. But since the consumption of alcohol was actually increasing in many unregulated areas, temperance advocates were beginning to advocate a national prohibition law. America's entry into World War I, and the moral fervor it unleashed, provided the last push to the advocates of prohibition. In 1917, with the support of rural fundamentalists who opposed alcohol on moral and religious grounds, progressive advocates of prohibition steered through Congress a constitutional amendment embodying their demands. Two years later, after ratification by every state in the nation except Connecticut and Rhode Island (bastions of Catholic immigrants), the Eighteenth Amendment became law, to take effect in January 1920.

Immigration Restriction

Virtually all reformers agreed that the growing immigrant population had created social problems, but there was wide disagreement on how to best respond.

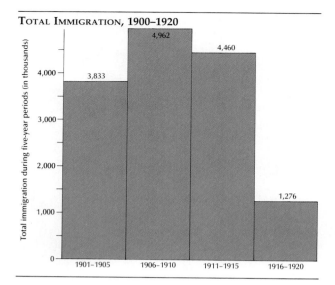

TOTAL IMMIGRATION, 1900–1920

Total immigration during five-year periods (in thousands)

- 1901–1905: 3,833
- 1906–1910: 4,962
- 1911–1915: 4,460
- 1916–1920: 1,276

Some progressives believed that the proper approach was to help the new residents adapt to American society. Others argued that efforts at assimilation had failed and that the only solution was to limit the flow of new arrivals.

In the first decades of the century, therefore, pressure grew to close the nation's gates. New scholarly theories, appealing to the progressive respect for expertise, argued that the introduction of immigrants into American society was polluting the nation's racial stock. The spurious "science" of eugenics spread the belief that human inequalities were hereditary and that immigration was contributing to the multiplication of the unfit. Skillful publicists such as Madison Grant, whose *The Passing of the Great Race* (1916) established him as the nation's most effective nativist, warned of the dangers of racial "mongrelization" and of the importance of protecting the purity of Anglo-Saxon and other Nordic stock from pollution by eastern Europeans, Hispanics, and Asians.

A special federal commission of "experts," chaired by Senator William P. Dillingham of Vermont, issued an elaborate study filled with statistics and scholarly testimony. The Dillingham Report argued that the newer immigrant groups—largely southern and eastern Europeans—had proven themselves less assimilable than earlier immigrants. Immigration, the report implied, should be restricted by nationality. But even many people who rejected these racial arguments supported limiting immigration as a way to solve such urban problems as overcrowding, unemployment, strained social services, and social unrest.

The combination of these concerns gradually won for the nativists the support of some of the nation's leading progressives: Theodore Roosevelt, Henry Cabot Lodge, and others. Powerful opponents—employers who saw immigration as a source of cheap labor, immigrants themselves and their political representatives—managed to block the restriction movement for a time. But by the beginning of World War I (which itself effectively blocked immigration temporarily), the nativist tide was clearly gaining strength.

The Dream of Socialism

At no time in the history of the United States to that point, and seldom after, did radical critiques of the capitalist system attract more support than in the period between 1900 and 1914. Although never a force to rival or even seriously threaten the two major parties, the Socialist Party of America grew during the progressive era into a force of considerable strength. In the election of 1900, it had attracted the support of fewer than 100,000 voters; in 1912, its durable leader and perennial presidential candidate, Eugene V. Debs, received nearly 1 million ballots. Strongest in urban immigrant communities, particularly among Germans and Jews, it also attracted the loyalties of a substantial number of Protestant farmers in the South and Midwest. Socialists won election to over 1,000 state and local offices. And they had the support at times of such intellectuals as Lincoln Steffens, the crusader against municipal corruption, and Walter Lippmann, the brilliant young journalist and social critic. Florence Kel-

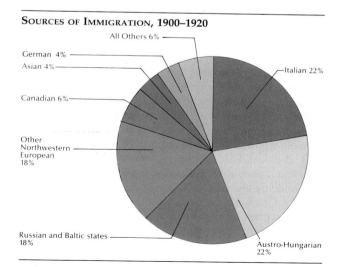

SOURCES OF IMMIGRATION, 1900–1920

- Italian 22%
- Austro-Hungarian 22%
- Russian and Baltic states 18%
- Other Northwestern European 18%
- Canadian 6%
- All Others 6%
- German 4%
- Asian 4%

SIGNIFICANT EVENTS

1873   Women's Christian Temperance Union (WCTU) founded

1889   Jane Addams opens Hull House in Chicago

1892   General Federation of Women's Clubs founded

1893   Johns Hopkins Medical School established

Anti-Saloon League founded

1895   National Association of Manufacturers founded

1898   Charles Sheldon publishes *In His Steps*

Charlotte Perkins Gilman publishes *Women and Economics*

1899   Thorstein Veblen publishes *A Theory of the Leisure Class*

1900   Galveston, Texas, establishes commission government

Robert La Follette elected governor of Wisconsin

1901   American Medical Association reorganized

1902   Oregon adopts initiative and referendum

Mississippi adopts direct primary

1903   Women's Trade Union League founded

1904   Ida Tarbell publishes exposé of Standard Oil

1905   National Education Association founded

1909   Herbert Croly publishes *The Promise of American Life*

1911   Fire kills 146 workers at Triangle Shirtwaist Company in New York City

1912   United States Chamber of Commerce founded

1913   Dayton, Ohio, establishes city-manager government

Louis D. Brandeis publishes *Other People's Money*

1914   Walter Lippmann publishes *Drift and Mastery*

1916   Madison Grant publishes *The Passing of the Great Race*

1919   Eighteenth Amendment (prohibition) ratified

1920   Nineteenth Amendment (woman suffrage) ratified

ley, Frances Willard, and other women reformers were attracted to socialism too, in part because of its support for pacifism and labor militancy.

Virtually all socialists agreed on the need for basic structural changes in the economy, but they differed widely on the extent of those changes and the tactics necessary to achieve them. Some endorsed the radical goals of European Marxists; others envisioned a more moderate reform that would allow small-scale private enterprise to survive but would nationalize major industries. Some believed in working for reform through electoral politics; others favored militant direct action.

Most conspicuous among the militants was the radical labor union the Industrial Workers of the World (IWW), known to opponents as the "Wobblies." Under the leadership of William ("Big Bill") Haywood, the IWW advocated a single union for all workers and abolition of the "wage slave" system; it rejected political action in favor of strikes—especially the general strike. The Wobblies were widely believed to have been responsible for the dynamiting of railroad lines and power stations and other acts of terror, although evidence of their actually engaging in such activities was slim.

The IWW was one of the few labor organizations of the time to champion the cause of unskilled workers, and it had particular strength in the West—where a large group of migratory laborers (miners, timbermen, and others) found it very difficult to organize or sustain conventional unions. The Wobblies created not just a union, but a far-flung social network that became something of a home to workers who were otherwise largely rootless.

In 1917, a strike by IWW timber workers in Washington and Idaho virtually shut down production in the industry. That brought down upon the union the wrath of the federal government, which had just begun mobilizing for war and needed timber for war production. Federal authorities imprisoned the leaders of the union, and state governments between 1917 and 1919 passed a series of laws that effectively outlawed the IWW. The organization survived for a time, but never fully recovered.

More moderate socialists who advocated peaceful change through political struggle dominated the party. They emphasized a gradual education of the public to the need for change and patient efforts within the system to enact it. But by the end of World War I, because the party had refused to support the war effort and because of a growing wave of antiradicalism that subjected the socialists to enormous harassment and persecution, socialism was in decline as a significant political force.

Decentralization and Regulation

Many reformers agreed with the socialists that the greatest threat to the nation's economy was excessive corporate centralization and consolidation, but most progressives retained a faith in the possibilities of reform within a capitalist system. Rather than nationalize basic industries, many reformers hoped to restore the economy to a more human scale. Few envisioned a return to a society of small, local enterprises; some consolidation, they recognized, was inevitable. They did, however, argue that the federal government should work to break up the largest combinations and enforce a balance between the need for bigness and the need for competition. This viewpoint came to be identified particularly closely with Louis D. Brandeis, a brilliant lawyer and later justice of the Supreme Court, who spoke and wrote widely (most notably in his 1913 book *Other People's Money*) about the "curse of bigness." "If the Lord had intended things to be big," Brandeis once wrote, "he would have made man bigger—in brains and character."

Brandeis and his supporters opposed bigness in part because they considered it inefficient. But their opposition had a moral basis as well. Bigness was a threat not just to efficiency but to freedom. It limited the ability of individuals to control their own destinies. It encouraged abuses of power. Government must, Brandeis insisted, regulate competition in such a way as to ensure that large combinations did not emerge.

Other progressives were less enthusiastic about the virtues of competition. More important to them was efficiency, which they believed economic concentration usually encouraged. What government should do, they argued, was not to fight "bigness," but to guard against abuses of power by large institutions. It should distinguish between "good trusts" and "bad trusts," encouraging the good while disciplining the bad. Since economic consolidation was destined to remain a permanent feature of American society, continuing oversight by a strong, modernized government was essential. One of the most influential spokesmen for this emerging "nationalist" position was Herbert Croly, whose 1909 book *The Promise of American Life* became one of the most influential progressive documents.

Increasingly, the attention of nationalists such as Croly focused on some form of coordination of the industrial economy. Society must act, Walter Lippmann wrote in a notable 1914 book, *Drift and Mastery,* "to introduce plan where there has been clash, and purpose into the jungles of disordered growth." To some, that meant businesses themselves learning new ways of cooperation and self-regulation; some of the most energetic "progressive" reformers of the period, in fact, were businessmen searching for ways to bring order to their own troubled world. To others, the solution was for government to play a more active role in regulating and planning economic life. One of those who came to endorse that position (although not fully until after 1910) was Theodore Roosevelt, who once said: "We should enter upon a course of supervision, control, and regulation of those great corporations—a regulation which we should not fear, if necessary, to bring to the point of control of monopoly prices." Roosevelt became for a time the most powerful symbol of the reform impulse at the national level.

SUGGESTED READINGS

Progressivism: Overviews. John D. Buenker, John C. Burnham, and Robert M. Crunden, *Progressivism* (1977). John W. Chambers II, *The Tyranny of Change: America in the Progressive Era, 1900–1917* (1980). John Milton Cooper, *The Pivotal Decades: The United States, 1900–1920* (1990). Alan Dawley, *Struggles for Justice: Social Responsibility and the Liberal State* (1991). Richard Hofstadter, *The Age of Reform: From Bryan to FDR* (1955). Gabriel Kolko, *The Triumph of Conservatism: A Reinterpretation of American History* (1963). Arthur S. Link and Richard L. McCormick, *Progressivism* (1983). Nell Irvin Painter, *Standing at Armageddon: The United States, 1877–1919* (1987). James Weinstein, *The Corporate Ideal in the Liberal State, 1900–1918* (1969). Robert Wiebe, *The Search for Order, 1877–1920* (1967).

The Muckrakers. David Chalmers, *The Social and Political Ideas of the Muckrakers* (1964). Louis Filler, *The Muckrakers*, rev. ed. (1980). Leon Harris, *Upton Sinclair* (1975). Justin Kaplan, *Lincoln Steffens* (1974). C. C. Regier, *The Era of the Muckrakers* (1932). Harold S. Wilson, *McClure's Magazine and the Muckrakers* (1970).

Progressive Thought. Richard Abrams, *The Burdens of Progress* (1978). Carl N. Degler, *In Search of Human Nature: The Decline and Revival of Darwinism in American Social Thought* (1991). Arthur Ekirch, *Progressivism in America* (1974). Charles V. Forcey, *The Crossroads of Liberalism: Croly, Weyl, Lippmann* (1961). Sudhir Kakar, *Frederick Taylor* (1970). D. W. Marcell, *Progress and Pragmatism: James, Dewey, Beard and the American Idea of Progress* (1974). David W. Noble, ed., *The Progressive Mind*, rev. ed. (1981). Jean B. Quandt, *From the Small Town to the Great Community: The Social Thought of Progressive Intellectuals* (1970). Robert Westbrook, *John Dewey and American Democracy* (1991). Morton White, *Social Thought in America* (1949).

Social Work and the Social Gospel. Jane Addams, *Twenty Years at Hull House* (1910). Paul Boyer, *Urban Masses and Moral Order, 1820–1920* (1978). Mina Carson, *Settlement Folk: Social Thought and the American Settlement Movement, 1885–1930* (1990). Robert M. Crunden, *Ministers of Reform: The Progressives' Achievement in American Civilization, 1889–1920* (1982). Susan Curtis, *A Consuming Faith: The Social Gospel and Modern American Culture* (1991). Allen F. Davis, *Spearheads of Reform: The Social Settlements and the Progressive Movement, 1890–1914* (1968); *American Heroine: The Life and Legend of Jane Addams* (1973). C. H. Hopkins, *The Rise of the Social Gospel in American Protestantism* (1940). William R. Hutchinson, *The Modernist Impulse in American Protestantism* (1982). Rivka Shpak Lissak, *Pluralism and Progressives: Hull House and the New Immigrants, 1890–1919* (1989). Roy Lubove, *The Progressives and the Slums: Tenement House Reform in New York City* (1962). Henry May, *Protestant Churches and Industrial America* (1949). Timothy Miller, *Following in His Steps: A Biography of Charles M. Sheldon* (1987).

Education and the Professions. Clyde W. Barrow, *Universities and the Capitalist State: Corporate Liberalism and the Reconstruction of American Higher Education, 1894–1928* (1990). Burton Bledstein, *The Culture of Professionalism* (1976). Lawrence A. Cremin, *The Transformation of the Schools: Progressivism in American Education, 1876–1957* (1971). Lynn D. Gordon, *Gender and Higher Education in the Progressive Era* (1990). Samuel Haber, *The Quest for Authority and Honor in the American Professions, 1750–1900* (1991). Barbara Harris, *Beyond Her Sphere: Women and the Professions in American History* (1978). Thomas L. Haskell, *The Emergence of Professional Social Science* (1977). Morton J. Horwitz, *The Transformation of American Law, 1870–1960: The Crisis of Legal Orthodoxy* (1992). Kenneth M. Ludmerer, *Learning to Heal: The Development of American Medical Education* (1985). Regina Markell Morantz-Sanchez, *Sympathy and Science: Women Physicians in American Medicine* (1985). Barbara Miller Solomon, *In the Company of Educated Women: A History of Women in Higher Education in America* (1985). Paul Starr, *The Social Transformation of American Medicine* (1982). David Tyack and Elizabeth Hansot, *Managers of Virtue: Public School Leadership in America, 1820–1980* (1982). Lawrence Veysey, *The Emergence of the American University* (1970).

Municipal Reform. John D. Buenker, *Urban Liberalism and Progressive Reform* (1973). James B. Crooks, *Politics and Progress: The Rise of Urban Progressivism in Baltimore* (1968). Oscar Handlin, *Al Smith and His America* (1958). Melvin G. Holli, *Reform in Detroit: Hazen S. Pingree and Urban Politics* (1969). J. Joseph Huthmacher, *Senator Robert F. Wagner and the Rise of Urban Liberalism* (1971). Michael Kazin, *Barons of Labor: The San Francisco Building Trades and Union Power in the Progressive Era* (1981). Zane Miller, *Boss Cox's Cincinnati* (1968). Martin J. Schiesl, *The Politics of Efficiency: Municipal Administration and Reform in America, 1880–1920* (1977).

Women, Reform, and Suffrage. Paula Baker, *The Moral Frameworks of Public Life: Gender, Politics, and the State in Rural New York, 1870–1930* (1991). Karen Blair, *The Clubwoman as Feminist* (1980). Mari Jo Buhle, *Women and American Socialism* (1983). Norman H. Clark, *Deliver Us From Evil: An Interpretation of American Prohibition* (1976). Mark T. Connelly, *The Response to Prohibition in the Progressive Era* (1980). Nancy Cott, *The Grounding of Modern Feminism* (1987). Ellen C. DuBois, *Feminism and Suffrage: The Emergence of an Independent Women's Movement in America, 1848–1869* (1978). Nancy Shrom Dye, *As Equal as Sisters: Feminism, The Labor Movement, and the Women's Trade Union League of New York* (1981). Eleanor Flexner, *Century of Struggle* (1959). Linda Gordon, *Woman's Body, Woman's Right: A Social History of Birth Control* (1976). Alan P. Grimes, *The Puritan Ethic and Woman Suffrage* (1967). Jacquelyn Dowd Hall, *The Revolt Against Chivalry* (1979). David M. Kennedy, *Birth Control in America: The Career of Margaret Sanger* (1970). Aileen S. Kraditor, *Ideas of the*

Woman Suffrage Movement (1965). Ellen C. Lagemann, *A Generation of Women: Education in the Lives of Progressive Reformers* (1979). Elaine Tyler May, *Great Expectations: Marriage and Divorce in Post-Victorian America* (1980). David Morgan, *Suffragists and Democrats: The Politics of Woman Suffrage in America* (1972). Robyn Muncy, *Creating a Female Dominion in American Reform, 1890–1935* (1991). William O'Neill, *Divorce in the Progressive Era* (1967); *Everyone Was Brave: The Rise and Fall of Feminism in America* (1969). Ruth Rosen, *The Lost Sisterhood: Prostitutes in America, 1900–1918* (1982). Rosalind Rosenberg, *Beyond Separate Spheres: Intellectual Roots of Modern Feminism* (1982). Elyce J. Rotella, *From Home to Office: U.S. Women and Work, 1870–1930* (1981). Sheila M. Rothman, *Woman's Proper Place* (1978). Anne F. Scott, *Making the Invisible Woman Visible* (1984).

Racial Issues. John Dittmer, *Black Georgia in the Progressive Era, 1900–1920* (1977). George Fredrickson, *The Black Image in the White Mind* (1968). Paula Giddings, *When and Where I Enter: The Impact of Black Women on Race and Sex in America* (1984). Louis Harlan, *Booker T. Washington: The Making of a Black Leader* (1856); *Booker T. Washington: The Wizard of Tuskegee, 1901–1915* (1983). Charles F. Kellogg, *NAACP* (1970). Jack Temple Kirby, *Darkness at Dawning: Race and Reform in the Progressive South* (1972). Ralph E. Luker, *The Social Gospel in Black and White: American Racial Reform, 1885–1912* (1991). James M. McPherson, *The Abolitionist Legacy: From Reconstruction to the NAACP* (1975). August Meier, *Negro Thought in America, 1880–1915* (1963). Cynthia Neverdon-Morton, *Afro-American Women of the South and the Advancement of the Race, 1885–1925* (1989). Elliott Rudwick, *W. E. B. Du Bois* (1969). Donald Spivey, *Schooling for the New Slavery: Black Industrial Education* (1978). Joel Williamson, *The Crucible of Race: Black-White Relations in the American South Since Emancipation* (1985).

State-Level Reform. Richard M. Abrams, *Conservatism in a Progressive Era: Massachusetts* (1964). Dewey Grantham, *Southern Progressivism: The Reconciliation of Progress and Tradition* (1983). Sheldon Hackney, *Populism to Progressivism in Alabama* (1969). Robert S. Maxwell, *La Follette and the Rise of Progressivism in Wisconsin* (1944). Richard L. McCormick, *From Realignment to Reform: Political Change in New York State, 1893–1910* (1981). George E. Mowry, *California Progressives* (1951). Russel B. Nye, *Midwestern Progressive Politics* (1951). David P. Thelen, *The New Citizenship: Origins of Progressivism in Wisconsin* (1972); *Robert M. La Follette and the Insurgent Spirit* (1976); *Paths of Resistance: Tradition and Dignity in Industrializing Missouri* (1986). Robert F. Wesser, *Charles Evans Hughes: Politics and Reform in New York State, 1905–1910* (1967). C. Vann Woodward, *Origins of the New South* (1951). Irwin Yellowitz, *Labor and the Progressive Movement in New York State* (1965).

National Issues. Ruth Bourdin, *Women and Temperance: The Quest for Power and Liberty, 1873–1900* (1980). Melvyn Dubofsky, *We Shall Be All* (1969). Sidney Fine, *Laissez Faire and the General Welfare State* (1956). Joseph Gusfield, *Symbolic Crusade: Status Politics and the Temperance Movement* (1963). John Higham, *Strangers in the Land* (1955). Michael E. McGerr, *The Decline of Popular Politics: The American North, 1865–1928* (1986). Bruno Ramirez, *When Workers Organize: The Politics of Industrial Relations in the Progressive Era, 1898–1916* (1978). James T. Timberlake, *Prohibition and the Progressive Movement* (1963). James Weinstein, *The Decline of Socialism in America* (1967). Robert Wiebe, *Businessmen and Reform: A Study of the Progressive Movement* (1962). Olivier Zunz, *Making America Corporate, 1870–1920* (1990).

" 'Terrible Teddy' Waits for 'The Unknown,' " by Joseph Keppler, Jr.
This cartoon conveys the widespread (and in the end correct) belief that Theodore Roosevelt
was an unbeatable candidate for election to the presidency in 1904. To oppose him, the
Democrats nominated Alton B. Parker, a New York appeals court judge who was indeed
virtually "unknown" to most of the public. *(The Granger Collection)*

CHAPTER TWENTY-TWO

THE BATTLE FOR NATIONAL REFORM

FFORTS TO REFORM THE industrial economy encountered repeated frustrations at the state and local levels. The great combinations were national in scope, and reformers gradually concluded that only national action could effectively control their power. Beginning early in the twentieth century, they began to look to the federal government.

But like state and local government, the national government—bureaucratically weak and mired in partisan politics—seemed poorly suited to serve as an agent of reform. Progressives attempted to make it more responsive to their demands. Some reformers, for example, urged an end to the system by which United States senators were elected by the members of their state legislatures; they proposed instead a direct popular election, which they believed would force the Senate to react to public demands. The Seventeenth Amendment, passed by Congress in 1912 and ratified by the states in 1913, brought about that change.

Even a reformed Congress, however, could not provide the kind of coherent leadership the progressive agenda required. If the federal government was truly to fulfill its mission, most reformers agreed, it would require leadership from the one office capable of providing it: the presidency.

THEODORE ROOSEVELT AND THE MODERN PRESIDENCY

"Presidents in general are not lovable," the writer Walter Lippmann, who had known many, said near the end of his life. "They've had to do too much to get where they are. But there was one President who was lovable—Teddy Roosevelt—and I loved him."

Lippmann was not alone. To a generation of progressive reformers, Theodore Roosevelt was more than an admired public figure; he was an idol. No president before, and few since, attracted such attention and devotion. Yet for all his popularity among reformers, Roosevelt was in many respects decidedly conservative. He earned his extraordinary popularity less because of the extent of the reforms he championed than because he brought to his office a broad conception of its powers and invested the presidency with something of its modern status as the center of national political life.

The Accidental President

When President William McKinley suddenly died in September 1901, the victim of an assassination, Roosevelt (who had been elected vice president less than a year before) was only forty-two years old, the youngest man ever to assume the presidency. Already, however, he had achieved a considerable reputation within the Republican Party as something of a wild man. Party leaders sensed his independence and despaired of controlling him. "I told William McKinley that it was a mistake to nominate that wild man at Philadelphia," party boss Mark Hanna was reported to have exclaimed. "I asked him if he realized what would happen if he should die. Now look, that damned cowboy is President of the United States!"

Roosevelt's reputation as a wild man was a result less of the substance of his early political career than of its style. As a young member of the New York legislature, he had displayed an energy seldom seen in that lethargic body. As a rancher in the Dakota Badlands (where he retired briefly after the sudden death of his first wife), he had helped capture outlaws. As New York City police commissioner, he had been a flamboyant battler against crime and vice. As assistant secretary of the navy, he had been a bold proponent of American expansion. As commander of the Rough Riders, he had led a heroic, if militarily useless, charge in the battle of San Juan Hill in Cuba during the Spanish-American War.

But Roosevelt as president never openly rebelled against the leaders of his party. He became, rather, a champion of cautious, moderate change. Reform, he believed, was less a vehicle for remaking American society than for protecting it against more radical challenges.

Government, Capital, and Labor

Roosevelt envisioned the federal government not as the agent of any particular interest but as a mediator of the public good, with the president at its center. These attitudes found expression in Roosevelt's poli-

MAKING SAUSAGES
Upton Sinclair's 1906 novel *The Jungle* contained, among other things, nauseating descriptions of the process by which meat factories (such as the one shown here) made sausages. Partly in response to the success of his book, Congress passed the Meat Inspection Act the same year, establishing federal standards for the industry. *(Bettmann)*

ESTABLISHMENT OF NATIONAL PARKS AND FORESTS

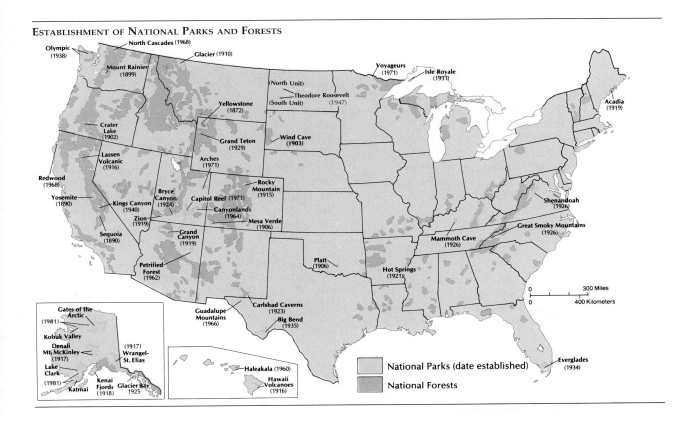

cies toward the great industrial combinations. He was not opposed to the principle of economic concentration, but he acknowledged that consolidation produced dangerous abuses of power. He allied himself, therefore, with those progressives who urged regulation (but not destruction) of the trusts.

At the heart of Roosevelt's policy was his desire to win for government the power to investigate the activities of corporations and publicize the results. The pressure of educated public opinion, he believed, would alone eliminate most corporate abuses. Government could legislate solutions for those that remained. The new Department of Commerce and Labor, established in 1903 (later to be divided into two separate departments), was to assist in this task through its investigatory arm, the Bureau of Corporations..

Although Roosevelt was not a trust buster at heart, he made a few highly publicized efforts to break up combinations. In 1902, he ordered the Justice Department to invoke the Sherman Antitrust Act against a great new railroad monopoly in the Northwest, the Northern Securities Company, a $400 million enterprise pieced together by J. P. Morgan, E. H. Harriman,

and James J. Hill. To Morgan, accustomed to a warm, supportive relationship with Republican administrations, the action was baffling. Hurrying to the White House with two conservative senators in tow, he told the president, "If we have done anything wrong, send your man to my man and they can fix it up." Roosevelt proceeded with the case nonetheless, and in 1904 the Supreme Court ruled that the Northern Securities Company must be dissolved. At the same time, however, he assured Morgan and others that the suit did not signal a general campaign to dissolve trusts. Although he filed more than forty additional antitrust suits during the remainder of his presidency, Roosevelt had no serious commitment to reverse the prevailing trend toward economic concentration.

A similar commitment to establishing the government as an impartial regulatory mechanism shaped Roosevelt's policy toward labor. In the past, federal intervention in industrial disputes had almost always meant action on behalf of employers. Roosevelt was willing to consider labor's position as well. When a bitter 1902 strike by the United Mine Workers against the anthracite coal industry dragged on long enough to endanger coal supplies for the coming winter,

Roosevelt asked both the operators and the miners to accept impartial federal arbitration. When the mine owners balked, Roosevelt threatened to send federal troops to seize the mines and resume coal production. The operators finally relented. Arbitrators awarded the strikers a 10 percent wage increase and a nine-hour day, although no recognition of their union—less than they had wanted but more than they would likely have won without Roosevelt's intervention. Despite such episodes, Roosevelt viewed himself as no more the champion of labor than of management. On several occasions, he ordered federal troops to intervene in strikes on behalf of employers.

The Square Deal

Reform was not Roosevelt's top priority during his first years as president. He was principally concerned with winning reelection, which required that he not antagonize the conservative Republican Old Guard. By skillfully dispensing patronage to conservatives and progressives alike, by reshuffling the leadership of unstable Republican organizations in the South, by winning the support of northern businessmen while making adroit gestures to reformers, Roosevelt had all but neutralized his opposition within the party by early 1904. He won its presidential nomination with ease. And in the general election, where he faced a pallid conservative Democrat, Alton B. Parker, he captured over 57 percent of the popular vote and lost no states outside the South. Now, relieved of immediate political concerns, he was free to display the extent—and the limits—of his commitment to reform.

During the 1904 campaign, Roosevelt boasted that he had worked in the anthracite coal strike to provide everyone with a "square deal." In his second term, he tried to extend his square deal further. One of his first targets was the powerful railroad industry. The Interstate Commerce Act of 1887, establishing the Interstate Commerce Commission (ICC), had been an early effort to regulate the industry; but over the years, the courts had sharply limited its influence. Roosevelt asked Congress for legislation to increase the government's power to oversee railroad rates. The Hepburn Railroad Regulation Act of 1906 sought to restore some regulatory authority to the government, although the bill was so cautious that it satisfied few progressives. Some reformers were enraged. Robert La Follette, now a U.S. Senator, never forgave Roosevelt for the concessions he made.

Roosevelt also pressured Congress to enact the Pure Food and Drug Act, which, despite weaknesses in its enforcement mechanisms, restricted the sale of dangerous or ineffective medicines. When Upton Sinclair's powerful novel *The Jungle* appeared in 1906, featuring appalling descriptions of conditions in the meatpacking industry, Roosevelt pushed for passage of the Meat Inspection Act, which ultimately helped eliminate many diseases once transmitted in impure meat. Starting in 1907, he proposed even more stringent measures: an eight-hour day for workers, broader compensation for victims of industrial accidents, inheritance and income taxes, regulation of the stock market, and others. He also started openly to criticize conservatives in Congress and the judiciary who were obstructing these programs. The result was not only a general stalemate in Roosevelt's reform agenda, but a widening gulf between the president and the conservative wing of his party.

ROOSEVELT AND MUIR IN YOSEMITE
John Muir, founder and leader of the Sierra Club, considered Theodore Roosevelt a friend and ally—a relationship cemented by a four-day camping trip the two men took together in Yosemite National Park in 1903. Roosevelt was indeed a friend to the national park and national forest systems and added considerable acreage to both. Among other things, he expanded Yosemite (at Muir's request). But unlike Muir, Roosevelt was also committed to economic development. As a result, he was not always a reliable ally of the most committed preservationists. *(Bettmann)*

Conservation

Roosevelt's aggressive policies on behalf of conservation contributed to that gulf. An ardent sportsman and naturalist, he had long been concerned about the unregulated exploitation of America's natural resources and its remaining wilderness. Using executive powers, he restricted private development on millions of acres of undeveloped government land—most of it in the West—by adding them to the previously modest national forest system. When conservatives in Congress restricted his authority over public lands in 1907, Roosevelt and his chief forester, Gifford Pinchot, worked furiously to seize all the forests and many of the water power sites still in the public domain before the bill became law.

Roosevelt was the first president to take an active interest in the new and struggling American conservation movement, and his policies had a lasting effect on national environmental policies. More than most public figures, he was sympathetic to the concerns of the naturalists—those within the movement committed to protecting the natural beauty of the land and the health of its wildlife from human intrusion. Early in his presidency, Roosevelt even spent four days camping in the Sierras with John Muir, the nation's leading preservationist and the founder of the Sierra Club. But Roosevelt's actual policies tended to favor another faction within the conservation movement: those who believed in carefully managed development. That was in part a result of the influence of Pinchot, the first director of the National Forest Service (which he had helped create), who supported rational and efficient human use of the wilderness. The Sierra Club might argue for the "aesthetic" value of the forests; Pinchot insisted, in contrast, that "the whole question is a practical one." He and Roosevelt both believed that trained experts in forestry and resource management, such men as Pinchot himself, should apply to the landscape the same scientific standards that others were applying to the management of cities and industries. The president did side with the preservationists on certain issues, but the more important legacy of his conservation policy was to establish the government's role as manager of the continuing development of the wilderness.

The Old Guard may have opposed Roosevelt's efforts to extend government control over vast new lands. But they eagerly supported another important aspect of Roosevelt's natural resource policy: public reclamation and irrigation projects. In 1902, the president backed the National Reclamation Act, better known as the Newlands Act (named for its sponsor, Nebraska congressman Francis Newlands). It was the culmination of years of lobbying by businessmen and others from the West (through the National Irrigation Association). Frustrated by the failure of private capital and state governments to develop their water resources, they wanted the federal government to take over such projects. The Newlands Act provided federal funds for the construction of dams, reservoirs, and canals in the West—projects that would open new lands for cultivation and (years later) provide cheap electric power. It was the beginning of many years of critical federal aid for irrigation and power development in the western states, even though the Newlands Act (and the Bureau of Reclamation it created) had relatively little impact for more than twenty years after passage.

The Panic of 1907

Despite the flurry of reforms Roosevelt was able to enact, the government still had relatively little control over the industrial economy. That became clear in 1907, when a serious panic and recession began. As in 1893, American industrial production had outrun the capacity of either domestic or foreign markets to absorb it. Once again, the banking system and the stock market had displayed pathetic inadequacies. Once again, irresponsible speculation and rampant financial mismanagement had helped shatter a prosperity that many had come to believe was now permanent.

Conservatives blamed Roosevelt's "mad" economic policies for the disaster. And while the president, naturally (and correctly), disagreed, he nevertheless acted quickly to reassure business leaders that he would not interfere with their recovery efforts. J. P. Morgan, in a spectacular display of his financial power, helped construct a pool of the assets of several important New York banks to prop up shaky financial institutions. The key to the arrangement, Morgan told the president, was the purchase by U.S. Steel of the shares of the Tennessee Coal and Iron Company, currently held by a threatened New York bank. He would, he insisted, need assurances that the purchase would not prompt antitrust action. Roosevelt tacitly agreed, and the Morgan plan proceeded. Whether or not as a result, the panic soon subsided.

Roosevelt loved being president. He had made that plain during his first moments in office, when, torn between his excitement at his new position and his distress at McKinley's death, he had written, "It is a dreadful thing to come into the Presidency in this way; but it would be a far worse thing to be morbid about it." As his years in office produced increasing political successes, as his public popularity continued to rise, more and more observers began to assume that he would run for reelection in 1908, despite the long-standing tradition of presidents serving no more than two terms.

But the panic of 1907, combined with Roosevelt's growing "radicalism" during his second term, so alienated conservatives in his own party that he might have had difficulty winning the Republican nomination for another term. In 1904, moreover, he had made a public promise to step down four years later. And so, after nearly eight energetic years in the White House, during which he had transformed the role of the presidency in American government, Theodore Roosevelt, fifty years old, retired from public life—briefly.

THE TROUBLED SUCCESSION

William Howard Taft, who assumed the presidency in 1909, had been Theodore Roosevelt's most trusted lieutenant and his hand-picked successor; progressive reformers believed him to be one of their own. But Taft had also been a restrained and moderate jurist, a man with a punctilious regard for legal process; conservatives expected him to abandon Roosevelt's aggressive use of presidential powers. By seeming acceptable to almost everyone, Taft won election to the White House in 1908 with almost ridiculous ease. He received his party's nomination virtually uncontested. His victory in the general election in November—over William Jennings Bryan, running forlornly for the Democrats for the third time—was a foregone conclusion. Taft entered the White House on a wave of good feeling.

Four years later, however, Taft would leave office the most decisively defeated president of the twentieth century, with his party deeply divided and the government in the hands of a Democratic administration for the first time in twenty years.

It had been obvious from the start that Taft and Roosevelt were not at all alike, but not until Taft took office did the real extent of the differences become clear. Roosevelt had been the most dynamic public figure of his age; Taft was stolid and respectable and little more. Roosevelt was an ardent sportsman and athlete; Taft was sedentary and obese—he weighed over 300 pounds and required a special, oversized bathtub to be installed in the White House. Most of all, Roosevelt had taken an expansive view of the powers of his office; Taft, in contrast, was slow, cautious, even lethargic, insistent that the president take pains to observe the strict letter of the law.

Yet even had Taft been the most dynamic of political figures, he would still have had difficulties as president. Having come into office as the darling of pro-

WILLIAM HOWARD TAFT
Taft could be a jovial companion in small groups, but his public image was of a dull, stolid man who stood in sharp and unfortunate contrast to his dynamic predecessor, Theodore Roosevelt. Taft also suffered public ridicule for his enormous size. He weighed as much as 350 pounds at times, and wide publicity accompanied his installation of a special oversized bathtub in the White House. *(UPI/Bettmann)*

gressives and conservatives alike, he soon found that he could not please them both. Gradually he found himself, without really intending it, pleasing the conservatives and alienating the progressives.

Taft and the Progressives

Taft's first problem arose in the opening months of the new administration, when he called Congress into special session to lower protective tariff rates, an old progressive demand. But having proposed the legislation, the president made no effort to overcome the opposition to it of the congressional Old Guard, arguing that to do so would violate the constitutional doctrine of separation of powers. The result was the feeble Payne-Aldrich Tariff, which reduced tariff rates scarcely at all and in some areas actually raised them. Progressives resented the president's passivity and were suspicious of his motives.

With Taft's standing among Republican progressives deteriorating and with the party growing more and more deeply divided, a sensational controversy broke out late in 1909 that helped destroy Taft's popularity with reformers for good. Many progressives had been unhappy when Taft replaced Roosevelt's secretary of the interior, James R. Garfield, an aggressive conservationist, with Richard A. Ballinger, a more conservative corporate lawyer. Suspicion of Ballinger grew when he attempted to invalidate Roosevelt's actions in removing nearly 1 million acres of forests and mineral reserves from the public lands available for private development.

In the midst of this mounting concern, Louis Glavis, an Interior Department investigator, charged the new secretary with having once connived to turn over valuable public coal lands in Alaska to a private syndicate for personal profit. Glavis took the evidence to Gifford Pinchot, still head of the Forest Service and a critic of Ballinger's policies, and Pinchot took the charges to the president. Taft ordered his attorney general to investigate them and eventually decided they were groundless.

But Pinchot was not satisfied, particularly after Taft fired Glavis for his part in the episode. He leaked the story to the press and asked Congress to investigate the scandal. The president discharged him for insubordination, and the congressional committee appointed to study the controversy, dominated by the Old Guard, exonerated Ballinger. But progressives throughout the country supported Pinchot. The controversy aroused as much public passion as any dispute of its time; and when it was over, Taft had alienated the supporters of Roosevelt completely and, it seemed, irrevocably.

To many reformers at the time, the Pinchot-Ballinger controversy was a simple morality tale. In reality, it represented a clash between two competing visions of economic development. Pinchot represented those who wanted carefully supervised economic growth in the American West. Ballinger (himself a westerner) represented many western entrepreneurs who saw federal regulations as an impediment to their own economic ambitions. Progressives portrayed Ballinger as the defender of corporate power; in fact, Pinchot was the more popular among leaders of large corporations, who generally supported his conservation policies, while Ballinger had the support of small businessmen, who had always opposed such policies.

The Return of Roosevelt

During most of these controversies, Theodore Roosevelt was far away: on a long hunting safari in Africa and an extended tour of Europe. To the American public, however, Roosevelt remained a formidable presence. His return to New York in the spring of 1910 was a major public event; and progressives noted that, although he turned down an invitation from Taft to visit the White House, he met at once with Gifford Pinchot (who had already traveled to England to see him several months before).

Roosevelt insisted that he had no plans to return to active politics, but his resolve lasted less than a week. Politicians began flocking immediately to his home at Oyster Bay, Long Island, for conferences. Roosevelt took an active role in several New York political controversies; and within a month, he announced that he would embark on a national speaking tour before the end of the summer. Furious with Taft, who had, he believed, "completely twisted around the policies I advocated and acted upon," he was becoming convinced that he alone was capable of reuniting the Republican Party.

The real signal of Roosevelt's decision to assume leadership of Republican reformers was a speech on September 1, 1910, in Osawatomie, Kansas, where he outlined a set of principles that he labeled the "New Nationalism" and that made clear he had moved a considerable way from the cautious conservatism of the first years of his presidency. Social justice, he argued, was possible only through the vigorous efforts of a strong federal government whose executive acted as the "steward of the public welfare." Those who thought primarily of property rights and personal profit "must now give way to the advocate of human welfare, who rightly maintains that every man holds his property subject to the general right of the community to regulate its use to whatever degree the public welfare may require it." He supported graduated income and inheritance taxes, workers' compensation for industrial accidents, regulation of the labor of women and children, tariff revision, and firmer regulation of corporations.

Spreading Insurgency

The congressional elections of 1910 provided further evidence of how far the progressive revolt had spread. In primary elections, conservative Republicans suffered defeat after defeat while almost all the progres-

ROOSEVELT AT OSAWATOMIE
Roosevelt's famous speech at Osawatomie, Kansas, in 1910 was the most radical of his career and openly marked his break with the Taft administration and the Republican leadership. "The essence of any struggle for liberty," he told his largely conservative audience, "has always been, and must always be to take from some one man or class of men the right to enjoy power, or wealth, or position or immunity, which has not been earned by service to his or their fellows." *(Brown Brothers)*

sive incumbents were reelected. In the general election, the Democrats, who were now offering progressive candidates of their own, won control of the House of Representatives for the first time in sixteen years and gained strength in the Senate. Reform sentiment seemed clearly on the rise. But Roosevelt still denied any presidential ambitions and claimed that his real purpose was to pressure Taft to return to progressive policies. Two events, however, changed his mind.

The first was a 1911 antitrust decision by the Taft administration. Taft had been more active than Roosevelt in enforcing the provisions of the Sherman Antitrust Act and had launched dozens of suits against corporate combinations. And on October 27, 1911, the administration announced a suit against U.S. Steel,

charging, among other things, that the 1907 acquisition of the Tennessee Coal and Iron Company had been illegal. Roosevelt had approved that acquisition in the midst of the 1907 panic, and he was enraged by the implication that he had acted improperly.

But Roosevelt was still reluctant to become a candidate for president, largely because Senator Robert La Follette had been working since 1911 to secure the presidential nomination for himself. La Follette's candidacy stumbled, however, in February 1912, when, exhausted and distraught about his daughter's illness, he appeared to suffer a breakdown during a speech in Philadelphia. With almost indecent haste, many of his supporters abandoned him and turned to Roosevelt, who announced his candidacy on February 22.

The Republican Schism

La Follette retained some diehard support. But for all practical purposes, the campaign for the Republican nomination had now become a battle between Roosevelt, the champion of the progressives, and Taft, the candidate of the conservatives. Roosevelt scored overwhelming victories in all thirteen presidential primaries and arrived at the convention convinced that he was the choice of the party rank and file. Taft, however, remained the choice of most party leaders, whose preference was decisive.

The battle for the nomination at the Chicago convention revolved around an unusually large number of contested delegates: 254 in all. Roosevelt needed fewer than half the disputed seats to clinch the nomination. But the Republican National Committee, controlled by the Old Guard, awarded all but 19 of them to Taft. At a rally the night before the convention opened, Roosevelt addressed 5,000 cheering supporters and announced that if the party refused to seat his delegates, he would continue his own candidacy outside the party. "We stand at Armageddon," he told the roaring crowd, "and we battle for the Lord." The next day, he led his supporters out of the convention, and out of the party. The remaining delegates then quietly nominated Taft on the first ballot.

With financial support from newspaper magnate Frank Munsey and industrialist George W. Perkins, Roosevelt summoned his supporters back to Chicago in August for another convention, to launch the new Progressive Party and nominate him as its presidential candidate. Jane Addams was one of those who placed his name in nomination, and a large number of prominent women reformers played an active role in the new party. Roosevelt approached the battle feeling, as he put it, "fit as a bull moose" (thus giving his new party an enduring nickname). But by then, he was aware that his cause was virtually hopeless. That was partly because many of the insurgents who had supported him during the primaries refused to follow him out of the Republican Party. It was also because of the man the Democrats had nominated for president.

WOODROW WILSON AND THE NEW FREEDOM

The 1912 presidential contest was not simply one between conservatives and reformers. It was also one between two brands of progressivism, expressing two different views of America's future. And it matched

WILSON IN PHILADELPHIA
Wilson spent most of his life as a scholar and university president, but he was a remarkably effective politician once he entered the public world. He is shown here in 1914, speaking to a Fourth of July rally at Independence Hall in Philadelphia. *(UPI/Bettmann)*

the two most important national leaders of the early twentieth century in unequal contest.

The Rise of Wilson

Reform sentiment had been gaining strength within the Democratic as well as the Republican Party in the first years of the century. At the 1912 Democratic convention in Baltimore in June, Champ Clark, the conservative Speaker of the House, was unable to assemble the two-thirds majority necessary to win because of progressive opposition. Finally, on the forty-sixth ballot, Woodrow Wilson, the governor of New Jersey and the only genuinely progressive candidate in the race, emerged as the party's nominee.

Born in Virginia and raised in Confederate Georgia and Reconstruction South Carolina, Wilson had risen to political prominence by an unusual path. An 1879 graduate of Princeton University, he attended law school and for a time engaged unhappily in practice in Atlanta. But he was really more interested in politics and government, and after a few years he enrolled at Johns Hopkins University, where he earned a doctorate in political science. By virtue of his effective teaching and his lucid if unprofound books on the American political system, he rose steadily through the academic ranks until in 1902 he was promoted from the faculty to the presidency of Princeton.

There he displayed some of the strengths and weaknesses that would characterize his later political career. A champion of academic reform, he acted firmly and energetically to place Princeton on the road to becoming a great national university. At the same time, however, he displayed during controversies a self-righteous morality that at times made it nearly impossible for him to compromise.

A series of such stalemates helped propel him out of academia and into politics. Elected governor of New Jersey in 1910, he brought to his new office a commitment to reform that he had already displayed as a university president; and during his two years in the statehouse, he earned a national reputation for winning passage of progressive legislation.

As a presidential candidate in 1912, Wilson presented a brand of progressivism different from Theodore Roosevelt's New Nationalism, a program that came to be called the "New Freedom." The New Freedom differed most clearly from the New Nationalism in its approach to economic policy and the trusts. Roosevelt believed in accepting economic concentration and using government to regulate and control it. Wilson seemed to side with those who (like Brandeis) believed that bigness was both unjust and inefficient, that the proper response to monopoly was not to regulate it but to destroy it.

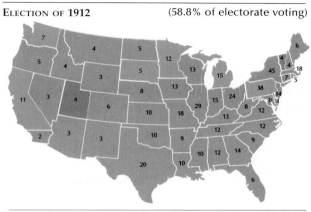

ELECTION OF 1912 (58.8% of electorate voting)

	ELECTORAL VOTE	POPULAR VOTE (%)
Woodrow Wilson (Democratic)	435	6,293,454 (41.9)
Theodore Roosevelt (Progressive/Bull Moose)	88	4,119,538 (27.4)
William H. Taft (Republican)	8	3,484,980 (23.2)
Eugene V. Debs (Socialist)	—	900,672 (6.0)
Other parties (Prohibition; Socialist Labor)	—	235,025

The presidential campaign was something of an anticlimax. William Howard Taft, resigned to defeat, delivered a few desultory conservative speeches and then lapsed into silence. Roosevelt campaigned energetically (until a gunshot wound from a would-be assassin forced him to the sidelines during the last weeks before the election), but he failed to draw any significant numbers of Democratic progressives away from Wilson. In November, Roosevelt and Taft split the Republican vote; Wilson held on to most of the Democrats and won. He polled only a plurality of the popular vote: 42 percent, to 27 percent for Roosevelt, 23 percent for Taft, and 6 percent for the socialist Eugene Debs. But in the electoral college, Wilson won 435 of the 531 votes. Roosevelt had carried only six states, Taft two, Debs none.

The Scholar as President

Wilson was a bold and forceful president. More than William Howard Taft, more even than Theodore Roosevelt, he concentrated the powers of the executive branch in his own hands. He exerted firm control over his cabinet, and he delegated real authority only to those whose loyalty to him was beyond question. Perhaps the clearest indication of his style of leadership was the identity of the most powerful figure in his administration: Colonel Edward M. House, a man who held no office and whose only claim to authority was his personal intimacy with the president.

In legislative matters, Wilson skillfully used his position as party leader and his appointive powers to weld together a coalition of conservatives and progressives who would, he believed, support his program. Democratic majorities in both houses of Congress made his task easier, as did the realization of many Democrats that the party must enact a progressive program in order to maintain those majorities.

Wilson's first triumph as president was a substantial lowering of the protective tariff. The Underwood-Simmons Tariff, passed in a special session of Congress Wilson summoned shortly after his inauguration, provided cuts substantial enough, progressives believed, to introduce real competition into American markets and thus to help break the power of trusts. It passed easily in the House, and despite Senate efforts to weaken its provisions, the bill survived more or less intact. Wilson had succeeded where Roosevelt and Taft had not. To make up for the loss of revenue under the new tariff, Congress approved a graduated income tax, which the recently adopted Sixteenth Amendment to the Constitution now permitted. This first modern income tax imposed a 1 percent tax on individuals and corporations earning over $4,000, with rates ranging up to 6 percent on incomes over $500,000.

Wilson held Congress in session through the summer to work on a major reform of the American banking system. Few doubted the necessity of change, but there were many different opinions about how best to attack the problem. Some legislators, among them Representative Carter Glass of Virginia, wanted to decentralize control of the banking system so as to limit the power of the great Wall Street financiers without substantially increasing the power of government. Others, including William Jennings Bryan and fellow agrarians who had long detested the "money trust," wanted firm government control. Wilson endorsed a plan that divided power in the system. The government would have substantial control at the national level; the bankers would retain control at the local level. The Federal Reserve Act passed both houses of Congress and was signed by the president on December 23, 1913. It was the most important piece of domestic legislation of Wilson's administration.

The Federal Reserve Act created twelve regional banks, each to be owned and controlled by the individual banks of its district. The regional Federal Reserve banks would hold a certain percentage of the assets of their member banks in reserve; they would use those reserves to support loans to private banks at an interest (or "discount") rate that the Federal Reserve system would set; they would issue a new type of paper currency—Federal Reserve notes—which would become the nation's basic medium of trade and would be backed by the government. Most important, perhaps, they would serve as central institutions able to shift funds quickly to troubled areas—to meet increased demands for credit or to protect imperiled banks. Supervising and regulating the entire system was a national Federal Reserve Board, whose members were appointed by the president. All "national" banks were required to join the system; smaller banks were encouraged to do so. Nearly half the nation's banking resources were represented in the system within a year, and 80 percent by the late 1920s.

The Problem of the Trusts

The cornerstone of Wilson's campaign for the presidency had been his promise to attack economic concentration, most notably to destroy monopolistic trusts. By the beginning of his second year in office, however, his approach to the trusts appeared to have changed. He was moving away from his earlier insistence that government dismantle the combinations and toward a commitment to regulating them. On this issue, at least, the New Freedom was beginning to resemble the New Nationalism.

In 1914, he proposed two measures to deal with the problem of monopoly. There was a proposal to create a federal agency through which the government would help business police itself—in other words, a regulatory commission of the type Roosevelt had advocated in 1912. There were, in addition, proposals to strengthen the government's power to prosecute and dismantle the trusts—a decentralizing approach more characteristic of Wilson's campaign. The two measures took shape, ultimately, as the Federal Trade Commission Act and the Clayton Antitrust Act.

The Federal Trade Commission Act created a regulatory agency of the same name that would help businesses determine in advance whether their actions would be acceptable to the government. It would also have authority to launch prosecutions against "unfair trade practices," which the law did not define, and it would have wide power to investigate corporate behavior. The act, in short, increased the government's regulatory authority significantly. Wilson signed it happily. But he seemed to lose interest in the Clayton Antitrust bill and did little to protect it from conservative assaults, which greatly weakened it. The vigorous legal pursuit of monopoly that Wilson had promised in 1912 never materialized. The future, he

had apparently decided, lay with government supervision.

Retreat and Advance

By the fall of 1914, Wilson believed that the program
of the New Freedom was essentially complete and that
agitation for reform should (and would) now subside.
As a result, he himself began a conspicuous retreat
from activism. Citing the doctrine of states' rights, he
refused to support the movement for national woman
suffrage. Bowing to the inclinations of the many southerners in his cabinet (and perhaps also to his own
southern heritage), he condoned the reimposition of
segregation in the agencies of the federal government
(in contrast to Theodore Roosevelt, who had ordered
the elimination of many such barriers and had even
taken the unprecedented step of inviting a black man—
Booker T. Washington—to the White House). When
congressional progressives attempted to enlist his support for new reform legislation, he dismissed their proposals as unconstitutional or unnecessary.

The congressional elections of 1914, however, shattered the president's complacency. Democrats suffered
major losses in the House of Representatives, and voters who in 1912 had supported the Progressive Party
began returning to the Republicans. Wilson would not
be able to rely on a divided opposition when he ran
for reelection in 1916. By the end of 1915, Wilson had
begun to support a second flurry of reforms. In January 1916, he appointed Louis Brandeis to the Supreme
Court, making him not only the first Jew but the most
advanced progressive to serve there. Later, he supported a measure to make it easier for farmers to receive credit and one creating a system of workers' compensation for federal employees.

Much of this renewed effort at reform revealed that
Wilson had moved even closer to the New Nationalism. He was sponsoring measures that expanded the
role of the national government in important ways,
giving it new instruments by which it could regulate
the economy and help shape the economic and social
structure. In 1916, for example, Wilson supported the
Keating-Owen Act, the first federal law regulating
child labor. The measure prohibited the shipment,
across state lines, of goods produced by underage children, thus giving an expanded importance to the constitutional clause assigning Congress the task of regulating interstate commerce. (It would be some years
before the Supreme Court would uphold this interpretation of the clause; the Court invalidated the Keating-Owen Act in 1918.) The president similarly supported measures that used federal taxing authority as
a vehicle for legislating social change. When the Court
struck down Keating-Owen, a new bill attempted to

LOUIS BRANDEIS
Brandeis graduated from Harvard Law School in 1877 with
the best academic record of any student in the school's previous or subsequent history. His success in his Boston law
practice was such that by the early twentieth century he
was able to spend much of his time in unpaid work for
public causes. His investigations of monopoly power soon
made him a major figure in the emerging progressive
movement. Woodrow Wilson nominated him for the
United States Supreme Court in January 1916. He was one
of the few nominees in the Court's history never to have
held prior public office, and he was the first Jew ever to
have been nominated. The appointment aroused five
months of bitter controversy in the Senate before Brandeis
was finally confirmed. For the next twenty years, he was
one of the Court's most powerful members—all the while
lobbying behind the scenes on behalf of the many political
causes (preeminent among them Zionism, the founding of
a Jewish state) to which he remained committed.
(UPI/Bettmann)

achieve the same goal by imposing a heavy tax on the products of child labor. (The Court later struck it down too.) The Smith-Lever Act of 1914 had used federal spending to change public behavior by offering matching federal grants to states that agreed to support agricultural extension education.

"THE BIG STICK": AMERICA AND THE WORLD, 1901–1917

American foreign policy during the progressive years reflected many of the same impulses that were motivating domestic reform. But more than that, it reflected the nation's new sense of itself as a world power with far-flung economic and political interests. To the general public, foreign affairs remained largely remote. Walter Lippmann once wrote: "I cannot remember taking any interest whatsoever in foreign affairs until after the outbreak of the First World War." But to Theodore Roosevelt and later presidents, that made foreign affairs even more appealing. There the president could act with less regard for the Congress or the courts. There he could free himself from concerns about public opinion. Overseas, the president could exercise power unfettered and alone.

Roosevelt and "Civilization"

Theodore Roosevelt was well suited, by both temperament and conviction, for an activist foreign policy. He believed in the value and importance of using

American power in the world (a conviction he once described by citing the proverb, "Speak softly, but carry a big stick"). And he believed that an important distinction existed between the "civilized" and "uncivilized" nations of the world. "Civilized" nations, as he defined them, were predominantly white and Anglo-Saxon or Teutonic; "uncivilized" nations were generally nonwhite, Latin, or Slavic. But racism was only partly the basis of the distinction. At least as important was economic development. He believed, therefore, that Japan, a rapidly industrializing society, had earned admission to the ranks of the civilized.

Civilized nations were, by Roosevelt's definition, producers of industrial goods; uncivilized nations were sources of raw materials and markets. There was, he believed, an economic relationship between the two parts that was vital to both of them. A civilized society, therefore, had the right and duty to intervene in the affairs of a "backward" nation to preserve order and stability—for the sake of both nations. Accordingly, Roosevelt became an early champion of the development of American sea power, which he considered vital to the nation's ability to exert influence beyond its borders. By 1906, his support had enabled the American navy to attain a size and strength surpassed only by that of Great Britain (although Germany was fast gaining ground).

Protecting the Open Door in Asia

Roosevelt considered the "Open Door" vital for maintaining American trade in the Pacific and for preventing any single nation from establishing dominance there. (See above, pp. 569–570.) He looked with alarm, therefore, at the military rivalries involving Japan, Russia, Germany, and France in Asia.

In 1904 the Japanese attacked the Russian fleet at Port Arthur in southern Manchuria, a province of China that both Russia and Japan hoped to control. Roosevelt, hoping to prevent either nation from becoming dominant there, agreed in 1905 to a Japanese request to mediate an end to the conflict. Russia, faring badly in the war and already plagued by the domestic instability that twelve years later would lead to revolution, had no choice but to agree. At a peace conference in Portsmouth, New Hampshire, Roosevelt extracted from the embattled Russians a recognition of Japan's territorial gains and from the Japanese an agreement to cease the fighting and expand no further. At the same time, he negotiated a secret agreement with the Japanese to ensure that the United States could continue to trade freely in the region.

Roosevelt won the Nobel Peace Prize in 1906 for his work in ending the Russo-Japanese War. But in the years that followed, relations between the United States and Japan steadily deteriorated. Having destroyed the Russian fleet at Port Arthur, Japan now emerged as the preeminent naval power in the Pacific and soon began to exclude American trade from many of the territories it controlled.

A domestic controversy in California soon threatened Japanese-American relations again. In the process of agitating for an extension of the Chinese Exclusion Act, white workers in San Francisco added a demand for the legal exclusion of Japanese immigrants. At first nothing came of these efforts. But in 1906, the school board of San Francisco voted to require all Asian schoolchildren in the city to attend a separate "Oriental School." Anti-Asian riots in California and inflammatory stories in the Hearst papers about the "Yellow Peril" further fanned resentment in Japan.

The president persuaded the San Francisco school board to rescind its edict in return for a Japanese agreement to stop the flow of agricultural immigrants into California. Then, lest the Japanese government interpret his actions as a sign of weakness, he sent sixteen battleships of the new American navy (known as the "Great White Fleet") on an unprecedented voyage around the world that included a call on Japan—to remind the Japanese of the potential might of the United States.

The Iron-Fisted Neighbor

Theodore Roosevelt took a special interest in events in what he (and most other Americans) considered the nation's principal sphere of interest: Latin America. Unwilling to share United States trading rights, let alone military control, with any other nation, Roosevelt embarked on a series of ventures in the Caribbean and South America that established a pattern of American intervention in the region that would long survive his presidency.

Crucial to Roosevelt's thinking was an incident early in his administration. When the government of Venezuela began in 1902 to renege on debts to European bankers, naval forces of Britain, Italy, and Germany blockaded the Venezuelan coast. Then German ships began to bombard a Venezuelan port amid rumors that Germany planned to establish a permanent base in the region. Roosevelt used the threat of American naval power to pressure the German navy to withdraw.

The incident helped persuade Roosevelt that European intrusions into Latin America could result not only from aggression but from instability or irresponsibility (such as defaulting on debts) within the Latin American nations themselves. As a result, in 1904 he

THE UNITED STATES IN LATIN AMERICA, 1895–1941

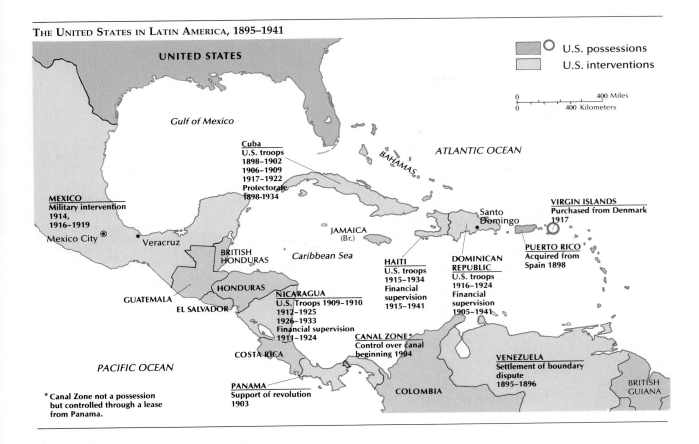

added a new "Roosevelt corollary" to the Monroe Doctrine. The United States, he claimed, had the right not only to oppose European intervention in the Western Hemisphere but to intervene itself in the domestic affairs of its neighbors if they proved unable to maintain order on their own.

The immediate motivation for the Roosevelt corollary, and the first opportunity for using it, was a crisis in the Dominican Republic. A revolution had toppled its corrupt and bankrupt government in 1903, but the new regime proved no better able than the old to make good on the country's $22 million in debts to European nations. Using the "Roosevelt corollary" as a rationale, Roosevelt established, in effect, an American receivership, assuming control of Dominican customs and distributing 45 percent of the revenues to the Dominicans and the rest to foreign creditors. This arrangement lasted, in one form or another, for more than three decades.

In 1902, the United States had granted political independence to Cuba, but only after the new government had agreed to the so-called Platt Amendment to its constitution, giving the United States the right to prevent any foreign power from intruding in the new nation. (See p. 565.) In 1906, when domestic uprisings seemed to threaten the internal stability of the island, Roosevelt reasoned that America must intervene to "protect" Cuba from disorder. American troops landed in Cuba, quelled the fighting, and remained there for three years.

The Panama Canal

The most celebrated accomplishment of Roosevelt's presidency was the construction of the Panama Canal. Creating a channel through Central America linking the Atlantic and the Pacific had been an unfulfilled dream of many nations since the mid-nineteenth century. Roosevelt was determined to achieve it.

The first step was the 1901 Hay-Pauncefote Treaty between America and Britain, canceling an 1850 pact by which the two nations had agreed to construct any canal together. The United States was now free to act alone. The next step was to choose a site for the canal.

OPENING THE PANAMA CANAL
The great Miraflores locks of the Panama Canal open in October 1913 to admit the first ship to pass through the channel. The construction of the canal was one of the great engineering feats of the early twentieth century. But the heavy-handed political efforts of Theodore Roosevelt were at least equally important to its completion. *(UPI/Bettmann)*

At first, Roosevelt and many others favored a route across Nicaragua, which would permit a sea-level canal requiring no locks. But they soon turned instead to the narrow Isthmus of Panama in Colombia, the site of an earlier, failed effort by a French company to construct a channel. Although the Panama route was not at sea level (and would thus require locks), it was shorter than the one in Nicaragua. And construction was already about 40 percent complete. When the French company lowered the price for its holdings from $109 million to $40 million, the United States chose Panama.

Roosevelt dispatched John Hay, his secretary of state, to negotiate an agreement with Colombian diplomats in Washington that would allow construction to begin without delay. Under heavy American pressure, the Colombian chargé d'affaires, Tomás Herrán, unwisely signed an agreement giving the United States

perpetual rights to a six-mile-wide "canal zone" across Colombia; in return, it would pay Colombia $10 million and an annual rental of $250,000. The treaty produced outrage in the Colombian Senate, which refused to ratify it. Colombia then sent a new representative to Washington with instructions to demand at least $20 million from the Americans plus a share of the payment to the French.

Roosevelt was furious. The Colombians, he charged, were "inefficient bandits" and "blackmailers." He began to look for ways to circumvent the Colombian government. Philippe Bunau-Varilla, chief engineer of the French canal project, was ready to help. In November 1903, he helped organize and finance a revolution in Panama. There had been many previous revolts, all of them failures. But this one had the support of the United States. Roosevelt landed troops from the *U.S.S. Nashville* in Panama to "maintain order." Their presence prevented Colombian forces from suppressing the rebellion, and three days later Roosevelt recognized Panama as an independent nation. The new Panamanian government quickly agreed to a new treaty. It granted America a canal zone ten miles wide; the United States would pay Panama the $10 million fee and the $250,000 annual rental that the Colombian Senate had rejected. Work on the canal proceeded rapidly, despite the enormous cuts and elaborate locks the construction required. It opened in 1914, three years after Roosevelt had proudly boasted to a university audience: "I took the Canal Zone and let Congress debate!"

Taft and "Dollar Diplomacy"

Like his predecessor, William Howard Taft worked to advance the nation's economic interests overseas. But he showed little interest in Roosevelt's larger vision of world stability. Taft's secretary of state, the corporate attorney Philander C. Knox, worked aggressively to extend American investments into less-developed regions. Critics called his policies "Dollar Diplomacy."

The Taft-Knox foreign policy faced its severest test, and encountered its greatest failure, in the Far East. Ignoring Roosevelt's tacit 1905 agreement with Japan to limit American involvement in Manchuria, the new administration responded to pressure from American bankers and moved aggressively to increase America's economic influence in the region. In particular, Knox worked to include the United States in a consortium of Western powers formed to build railroads in China; and when the Europeans agreed, he went further and tried to exclude the Japanese from any role in Manchuria's railroads. When Japan responded by forming a loose alliance with Russia, the entire railroad project quickly collapsed.

In the Caribbean, the new administration continued and even expanded upon Roosevelt's policies of limiting European and expanding American influence. That meant, Taft and Knox believed, not only preventing disorder but also establishing a significant American economic presence there: replacing the investments of European nations with investments from the United States. But Dollar Diplomacy also had a more violent side. When a revolution broke out in Nicaragua in 1909, the administration quickly sided with the insurgents (who had been inspired to revolt by an American mining company) and sent American troops into the country to seize the customs houses. As soon as peace was restored, Knox encouraged American bankers to offer substantial loans to the new government, thus increasing Washington's financial leverage over the country. When the new pro-American government faced an insurrection less than two years later, Taft again landed American troops in Nicaragua, this time to protect the existing regime. The troops remained there for more than a decade.

Diplomacy and Morality

Woodrow Wilson entered office with little experience or interest in diplomacy. "It would be the irony of fate," he remarked shortly before assuming the presidency, "if my administration had to deal chiefly with foreign affairs." Ironic or not, Wilson faced international challenges of a scope and gravity unmatched by any president before him. Although the greatest test of Wilsonian diplomacy did not occur until after World War I, many of the qualities that he would bring to that ordeal were evident in his foreign policy from his first moments in office, and particularly in his dealings with Latin America—where he continued the interventionist policies of his predecessors.

Having already seized control of the finances of the Dominican Republic in 1905, the United States established a military government there in 1916, when the Dominicans refused to accept a treaty that would have made the country a virtual American protectorate. The military occupation lasted eight years. In Haiti, which shares the island of Hispaniola with the Dominican Republic, Wilson landed the marines in 1915 to quell a revolution in the course of which a mob had murdered an unpopular president. American officers drafted the new Haitian constitution adopted in 1918, and American military forces remained in the country until 1934. When Wilson began to fear that the Danish West Indies might be about to fall into the hands of Germany, he bought the colony from Denmark and renamed it the Virgin Islands. Concerned about the possibility of European influence in Nicaragua, he signed a treaty with that country's government ensuring that no other nation would build a canal there and winning for the United States the right to intervene in Nicaragua's internal affairs to protect American interests.

But Wilson's view of America's role in the Western Hemisphere became clearest in his dealings with Mexico. For many years, under the friendly auspices of the corrupt dictator Porfirio Díaz, American businessmen had been establishing an enormous economic presence in Mexico. In 1910, however, Díaz had been overthrown by the popular leader Francisco Madero, who promised democratic reform but who also seemed hostile to American businesses in Mexico. With American approval, Madero was himself deposed early in 1913 by a reactionary general, Victoriano Huerta.

The Taft administration, in its last weeks in office, prepared to recognize the new Huerta regime and wel-

SIGNIFICANT EVENTS

1898 Theodore Roosevelt elected governor of New York

1900 Roosevelt elected vice president

1901 McKinley assassinated, Roosevelt becomes president

Hay-Pauncefote Treaty ratified

1902 Northern Securities antitrust case filed

Roosevelt intervenes in anthracite coal strike

Newlands Reclamation Act passed

1903 Department of Commerce and Labor created

1904 Roosevelt mediates settlement of Russo-Japanese War

"Roosevelt Corollary" announced

United States orchestrates Panamanian independence; new government signs treaty allowing United States to build Panama Canal

Roosevelt elected president

1906 Hepburn Railroad Regulation Act passed

Upton Sinclair publishes *The Jungle*

Meat Inspection Act passed

American troops intervene in Cuba

1907 Financial panic and recession

1908 William Howard Taft elected president

1909 Payne-Aldrich Tariff passed

Pinchot-Ballinger dispute begins

U.S. troops intervene in Nicaragua

1910 Roosevelt's Osawatomie speech outlines "New Nationalism"

Woodrow Wilson elected governor of New Jersey

Porfirio Díaz overthrown by Francisco Madero in Mexico

1911 Taft administration files antitrust suit against U.S. Steel

1912 Roosevelt challenges Taft for Republican nomination, wins all party primaries

Taft receives Republican nomination, Roosevelt and followers walk out

Roosevelt forms Progressive Party

Woodrow Wilson elected president

1913 Thirteenth Amendment, establishing direct popular election of U.S. senators, ratified

Federal Reserve Act passed

Victoriano Huerta overthrows Madero in Mexico

1914 Federal Trade Commission Act passed

Clayton Antitrust Act passed

Panama Canal opens

U.S. troops intervene in Haiti

Tampico incident strains U.S. relations with Mexico

Venustiano Carranza deposes Huerta in Mexico

1916 Wilson appoints Louis Brandeis to Supreme Court

United States establishes military government in Dominican Republic

U.S. troops pursue Pancho Villa into Mexico

1917 United States recognizes Carranza government

come back a receptive environment for American investments in Mexico. Two things happened before it could do so: agents of the new government murdered Madero, and Woodrow Wilson took office in Washington. The new president instantly announced that

he would never recognize Huerta's "government of butchers."

The problem dragged on for years. At first, Wilson hoped that simply by refusing to recognize Huerta he could help topple the regime and bring to power the opposing Constitutionalists, led by Venustiano Carranza. But when Huerta (supported by American business interests in Mexico) established a full military dictatorship in October 1913, the president became more assertive. He pressured the British to stop supporting Huerta. Then he offered to send American troops to assist Carranza. Carranza, aware that such an open alliance with the United States would undermine his popular support in Mexico, declined the offer, but he did secure the right to buy arms in the United States.

In April 1914, a minor naval incident provided the president with an excuse for more open intervention. An officer in Huerta's army briefly arrested several American sailors from the U.S.S. *Dolphin* who had gone ashore in Tampico. The men were immediately released, but the American admiral—unsatisfied with the apology he received—demanded that the Huerta forces fire a twenty-one-gun salute to the American flag as a public display of penance. The Mexicans refused. Wilson seized on the trivial incident as a pretext for seizing the Mexican port of Veracruz.

Wilson had envisioned a bloodless action, but in a clash with Mexican troops in Veracruz, the Americans killed 126 of the defenders and suffered 19 casualties of their own. Now at the brink of war, Wilson began to look for a way out. His show of force, however, had helped strengthen the position of the Carranza faction, which captured Mexico City in August and forced Huerta to flee the country. At last, it seemed, the crisis might be over.

But Wilson was not yet satisfied. He reacted angrily when Carranza refused to accept American guidelines for the creation of a new government, and he briefly considered throwing his support to still another aspirant to leadership: Carranza's erstwhile lieutenant Pancho Villa, who was now leading a rebel army of his own. When Villa's military position deteriorated, however, Wilson abandoned him; finally, in October 1915, he granted preliminary recognition to the Carranza government.

By now, however, he had created yet another crisis. Villa, angry at what he considered an American betrayal, retaliated in January 1916 by taking sixteen Americans from a train in northern Mexico and shooting them. Two months later, he led his soldiers (or bandits, as the United States government called them) across the border into Columbus, New Mexico, where they killed seventeen more Americans. His goal, apparently, was to destabilize relations between Wilson and Carranza and to provoke a war between them, which might provide him with an opportunity to improve his own declining fortunes.

Wilson ordered General John J. Pershing to lead an American expeditionary force across the Mexican border in pursuit of Villa. The American troops never found Villa, but they did engage in two ugly skirmishes with Carranza's army, in which forty Mexicans and twelve Americans died. Again the United States and Mexico stood at the brink of war. But at the last minute, Wilson drew back. He quietly withdrew American troops from Mexico; and in March 1917, having spent four years of effort and gained nothing for it but a lasting Mexican hostility toward the United States, he at last granted formal recognition to the Carranza regime.

By now, however, Wilson's attention was turning elsewhere: to the far greater international crisis engulfing the European continent and ultimately much of the world.

SUGGESTED READINGS

General Histories. John Milton Cooper, Jr., *The Warrior and the Priest: Woodrow Wilson and Theodore Roosevelt* (1983). Arthur Link, *Woodrow Wilson and the Progressive Era, 1910–1917* (1954). George E. Mowry, *The Era of Theodore Roosevelt* (1958). (See also Suggested Readings for Chapter 21.)

Theodore Roosevelt. John Morton Blum, *The Republican Roosevelt* (1954). G. Wallace Chessman, *Theodore Roosevelt and the Politics of Power* (1969). John A. Garraty, *The Life of George W. Perkins* (1960). Lewis L. Gould, *The Presidency of Theodore Roosevelt* (1991). William H. Harbaugh, *Power and Responsibility* (1961); published in paperback as *The Life and Times of Theodore Roosevelt*. Horace S. Merrill and Marion G. Merrill, *The Republican High Command* (1971). Edmund Morris, *The Rise of Theodore Roosevelt* (1979). Henry F. Pringle, *Theodore Roosevelt* (1931).

William Howard Taft. Donald E. Anderson, *William Howard Taft* (1973). Paolo E. Coletta, *The Presidency of William Howard Taft* (1973). George Mowry, *Theodore Roosevelt and the Progressive Movement* (1946). Henry F. Pringle, *The Life and Times of William Howard Taft*, 2 vols. (1939). Norman Wilensky, *Conservatives in the Progressive Era: The Taft Republicans of 1912* (1965).

Woodrow Wilson. John Morton Blum, *Joseph Tumulty and the Wilson Era* (1951); *Woodrow Wilson and the Politics of Morality* (1956). Alexander George and Juliette George, *Woodrow*

Wilson and Colonel House (1956). L. J. Holt, *Congressional Insurgents and the Party System, 1909–1916* (1967). Arthur S. Link, *Woodrow Wilson*, 5 vols. (1947–1965). Edwin A. Weinstein, *Woodrow Wilson: A Medical and Psychological Biography* (1981).

National Issues. O. E. Anderson, *The Health of a Nation* (1958). Stephen R. Fox, *The American Conservation Movement: John Muir and His Legacy* (1981). Samuel P. Hays, *The Gospel of Efficiency: The Progressive Conservation Movement, 1890–1920* (1962). James Holt, *Congressional Insurgents and the Party System* (1969). Susan Kleinberg, *The Shadow of the Mills: Working Class Families in Pittsburgh, 1870–1907* (1989). Naomi Lamoreaux, *The Great Merger Movement in American Business, 1895–1904* (1985). Albro Martin, *Enterprise Denied: Origins of the Decline of the American Railroads, 1897–1917* (1971). Thomas K. McCraw, ed., *Regulation in Perspective* (1981). Roderick Nash, *Wilderness and the American Mind* (1967). James Penick, Jr., *Progressive Politics and Conservation: The Ballinger-Pinchot Affair* (1968). Harold T. Pinkett, *Gifford Pinchot: Private and Public Forester* (1970). Elmo P. Richardson, *The Politics of Conservation* (1962). David Sarasohn, *The Party of Reform: The Democrats in the Progressive Era* (1989). Martin J. Sklar, *The Corporate Reconstruction of American Capitalism, 1890–1916: The Market, the Law, and Politics* (1988). Peter Temin, *Taking Your Medicine: Drug Regulation in the U.S.* (1980). Melvin I. Urofsky, *Louis D. Brandeis and the Progressive Tradition* (1981). Craig West, *Banking Reform and the Federal Reserve, 1863–1923* (1977). Robert Wiebe, *Businessmen and Reform: A Study of the Progressive Movement* (1962).

Roosevelt's Foreign Policy. Howard K. Beale, *Theodore Roosevelt and the Rise of America to World Power* (1956). David H. Burton, *Theodore Roosevelt: Confident Imperialist* (1969). Richard Challener, *Admirals, Generals, and American Foreign Policy, 1898–1914* (1973). Raymond A. Esthus, *Theodore Roose-velt and International Rivalries* (1970). Michael H. Hunt, *The Making of a Special Relationship: The United States and China to 1914* (1983). Akira Iriye, *Pacific Estrangement: Japanese and American Expansion, 1897–1911* (1972). Richard Leopold, *Elihu Root and the Conservative Tradition* (1954). Charles E. Neu, *An Uncertain Friendship: Roosevelt and Japan, 1906–1909* (1967). Bradford Perkins, *The Great Rapprochement: England and the United States, 1895–1914* (1968). Julius W. Pratt, *Challenge and Rejection: The United States and World Leadership, 1900–1921* (1967). Charles Vevier, *United States and China* (1955).

America and the Caribbean. P. Edward Haley, *Revolution and Intervention: The Diplomacy of Taft and Wilson with Mexico, 1910–1917* (1975). David Healy, *The United States in Cuba, 1898–1902* (1963). Walter LaFeber, *The Panama Canal* (1978). Lester E. Langley, *The Banana Wars: An Inner History of American Empire, 1900–1934* (1983). David McCullough, *The Path Between the Seas* (1977). Dwight C. Miner, *Fight for the Panama Route* (1966). Dana G. Munro, *Intervention and Dollar Diplomacy in the Caribbean, 1900–1921* (1964). Louis A. Perez, Jr., *Cuba Under the Platt Amendment* (1988). Walter Scholes and Marie Scholes, *The Foreign Policies of the Taft Administration* (1970). John Womack, *Zapata and the Mexican Revolution* (1968).

Wilson's Foreign Policy. Kenneth Grieb, *The United States and Huerta* (1969). David Healy, *Gunboat Diplomacy in the Wilson Era: The U.S. Navy in Haiti, 1915–1916* (1976). Arthur Link, *Wilson the Diplomatist* (1957); *Woodrow Wilson: Revolution, War, and Peace* (1979). Dana Munro, *Intervention and Dollar Diplomacy in the Caribbean, 1900–1914* (1964). Robert Quirk, *An Affair of Honor: Woodrow Wilson and the Occupation of Veracruz* (1962); *The Mexican Revolution, 1914–1915* (1960). James Reed, *The Missionary Mind and America's East Asian Policy, 1911–1915* (1983). Robert Freeman Smith, *The United States and Revolutionary Nationalism in Mexico, 1916–1932* (1972).

THE AMERICAN ENVIRONMENT

SAVING THE FORESTS

FROM THE EARLIEST DAYS of European settlement in North America, people depended for their very survival on forests. Lumber was essential not just for houses and farm buildings, but for fences and vehicles as well. Most Americans heated their homes with firewood until late in the nineteenth century, when coal finally gained ascendancy. The nation's early steam engines, including railroad locomotives and steamboats, were fueled mainly with wood, and iron was forged with charcoal. Tree bark was the major source of tannin, which was used in curing leather. When trees were burned to clear land, their ashes were turned into potash, which was used in making soap. Next to food, wood was the most basic resource in the American economy.

It was also the most wasted. The paradox of the American forest was that although its trees were essential to frontier settlements, they were also the chief obstacle to those settlements. East of the Mississippi River, creating new farming communities usually meant cutting down forests. Although trees were cut for lumber and fuel, the main reason for their removal was simply clearing. To prepare land for crops, farmers "girdled" trees by removing a ring of bark from their base, stopping nutrients from reaching leaves and quickly killing them. With the leaves gone, sunlight reached the forest floor and corn could be planted amid the stumps. In time, the dead trees could be cut and burned to fertilize the soil in preparation for plowing. Within a decade or two, few signs would remain that the new cornfield or pasture had ever been a forest at all.

The American forest seemed so endless that few worried about conserving it. As a result, the nineteenth-century inhabitants of the United States destroyed trees at an astonishing rate. By 1850, over 100 million acres of land—an area roughly the size of modern California—had been cleared since the time of the first colonists. Moreover, the rate of forest destruction was increasing, so that over the next ten years another 40 million acres were cleared—as if the entire state of Georgia had been deforested in a single decade. The 1850s saw fully one-third as many trees cut down as had been cleared during the preceding two centuries.

Although most Americans still regarded their forests as limitless, a few began to voice concern about what might happen if deforestation continued at this rapid pace. The most influential of these was a remarkable Vermonter named George Perkins Marsh. A scholar who read a dozen or more European languages, Marsh served as the U.S. ambassador to Turkey from 1849 to 1854, and to Italy from 1860 until his death in 1882. During his many years living on the shores of the Mediterranean, Marsh became interested in the environmental effects of classical civilizations. He gathered evidence from his travels and readings to demonstrate that deforestation had wreaked havoc with the earth.

The result was one of the most important books in the history of American conservation. Published in 1864, Marsh's *Man and Nature* warned of the dangerous consequences that might result if the United States did not stop destroying its forests. Losing access to lumber and fuel was the least of the problems he named. Much more

THE AMERICAN ENVIRONMENT

A NEWLY CLEARED FARM, 1790S
Clearing forests was the essential first step toward establishing a new farm and thereby "improving" land. Farmers killed trees by stripping their bark and then planted crops amid the remaining stumps. Settlers used lumber to build houses and barns, erect fences, and supply fireplaces with fuel. *(Bettmann)*

important, he said, was the forest's role in stabilizing the natural environment. According to Marsh's theories, trees slowed the rate at which water drained from the soil. They prevented erosion, maintained soil fertility, and stabilized the flow of natural springs and streams. Removing them laid the groundwork for environmental disaster. In addition to promoting erosion, drying up rivers, and causing floods, forest destruction decreased the amount of water evaporating into the air and so reduced the total amount of rain that fell in an area. In the end, it would turn the landscape into a desert.

For proof of his claims, Marsh offered evidence from around the world. He described springs he had known as a child in Vermont that had since dried up as the trees around them were cleared. He listed floods that had become more frequent in lumbered areas of the northeastern United States. As evidence that cutting down forests could lead to desertification, he pointed to North Africa and the Middle East, holding them up as examples of what America might become if its citizens refused to heed his warnings. Only

THE AMERICAN ENVIRONMENT

a strong commitment to conserving the forest and other natural resources could save the nation from its folly. "Man has too long forgotten," he wrote, "that the earth was given to him for usufruct alone, not for consumption, still less for profligate waste."

Marsh's book drew wide attention from scientists and politicians all over the United States. From the 1870s forward, increasing numbers of Americans began to express concern about the future of the nation's forests, and laws started to be passed for their protection and restoration. Although many of Marsh's theories about the climatic influence of forests would eventually prove to be overstated or wrong, they became the basis for laws in the 1870s that offered free land on the Great Plains to settlers who planted trees there. Such stands of trees did not increase rainfall as the authors of the laws had hoped, but other early efforts at conserving forests were more effective.

The most important of these occurred in the state of New York. There, people worried that falling water levels in the Erie Canal might threaten the very lifeblood of the state's economy and might foreshadow problems for New York City's water supply as well. Following Marsh's theories, they attributed the problem to deforestation in the state's heavily lumbered Adirondack Mountains. Various citizens began to lobby for

---

Early Lumbering in Michigan

As pioneer farmers moved west, a parallel migration of woodcutters took place. By the second half of the nineteenth century, pine lumber was being shipped by rail out of the north woods of Maine, New York, Michigan, and Minnesota to supply farmers on the treeless prairies with the construction materials and fuel that were essential to an agricultural economy. *(Bettmann)*

THE AMERICAN ENVIRONMENT

THE ADIRONDACK FOREST: "FOREVER WILD"
By the closing decades of the nineteenth century, Americans had become so worried about
the destruction of eastern forests that they increased their efforts to protect them. One important consequence was the creation of the Adirondack Forest Preserve in northern New
York. A unique provision of the 1894 state constitution mandated that the Adirondacks
were to be left "forever wild." *(The Adirondack Museum, Blue Mountain Lake, N.Y.)*

protection of the Adirondack forests, and the result was a law in 1885 creating a huge
"forest reserve" there. To guarantee that the Adirondacks would remain "forever wild,"
defenders saw that a clause to this effect was inserted into the new state constitution in
1894.

THE AMERICAN ENVIRONMENT

The Adirondack Forest Reserve was a model for the nation as a whole. In 1891, seeking specifically to protect watersheds, Congress passed the Forest Reserve Act, empowering the president to set aside any "public lands wholly or in part covered with timber or undergrowth." The act became the basis for the National Forest system of the United States. Conservation of the forest reserves soon emerged as a chief political objective of Theodore Roosevelt's presidency. Saving the forests had become national policy, in no small measure because of the book Marsh had published four decades earlier.

HALT the HUN!

BUY U.S. GOVERNMENT BONDS

WORLD WAR I LIBERTY LOAN POSTER

In this 1918 propaganda poster issued by the U. S. government, an American soldier prevents a "Hun" from ravaging a young woman and her baby—a reference to the widespread and largely erroneous belief that German troops had massacred women and children in Belgium early in the war. *(The Granger Collection)*

CHAPTER TWENTY-THREE

AMERICA AND THE GREAT WAR

HE GREAT WAR, as it was known to a generation unaware that another, greater war would soon follow, began relatively inconspicuously in August 1914 when forces of the Austro-Hungarian empire invaded the tiny Balkan nation of Serbia. Within weeks, however, it had grown into a widespread conflagration, engaging the armies of almost all the major nations of Europe and shattering forever the delicate balance of power that had maintained a general peace on the Continent since the early nineteenth century. Most Americans looked on with horror as the war became the most savage in history, but also at first with a conviction that the conflict had little to do with them.

After nearly three years of attempting to affect the outcome of the conflict without becoming embroiled in it, the United States formally entered the war in April 1917. In doing so, it joined the most savage conflict in history. The fighting had already dragged on for two and a half years, inconclusive, almost inconceivably murderous, engaging not only the armies of the contending nations but their civilian populations as well. Although the American Civil War had greatly increased the ferocity and extent of combat, World War I was the first truly "total" war. It pitted entire societies against one another, and by 1917 it had left Europe exhausted and on the brink of utter collapse. By the time it ended late in 1918, Germany had lost nearly

2 million soldiers in battle, Russia 1.7 million, France 1.4 million, Great Britain 900,000. A generation of European youth was decimated; centuries of political, social, and economic traditions were damaged and all but destroyed.

For America, however, the war was the source of a very different experience. As a military struggle, it was brief, decisive, and—in relative terms—without great cost. Only 112,000 American soldiers died in the conflict, half of them from influenza and other diseases rather than in combat. Economically, it was the source of a great industrial boom, which helped spark the years of prosperity that would follow. And the war propelled the United States into a position of international preeminence.

In other respects, World War I was a painful, even traumatic experience for the American people. At home, the nation became obsessed with a search not just for victory but also for social unity—a search that continued and even intensified in the troubled years following the armistice, and that helped shatter many of the progressive ideals of the first years of the century. And abroad, once the conflict ended, the United States encountered frustration and disillusionment. The "war to end wars," the war "to make the world safe for democracy," became neither. Instead, it led directly to twenty years of international instability that would ultimately generate another great conflict.

THE ROAD TO WAR

The causes of the war in Europe—indeed the question of whether there were any significant causes at all, or whether the entire conflict was the result of a tragic series of blunders—have been the subject of continued debate for nearly eighty years. What is clear is that the European nations had by 1914 created an unusually precarious international system that careened into war very quickly on the basis of what most historians agree was a minor series of provocations.

The Collapse of the European Peace

The major powers of Europe were organized by 1914 in two great, competing alliances. The "Triple Entente" linked Britain, France, and Russia. The "Triple Alliance" united Germany, the Austro-Hungarian Empire, and Italy. The chief rivalry, however, was not between the two alliances, but between the great powers that dominated them: Great Britain and Germany—the former long established as the world's most powerful colonial and commercial nation, the latter ambitious to expand its own empire and become at least Britain's equal.

The Anglo-German rivalry may have been the most important underlying source of the tensions that led to World War I, but it was not the immediate cause of its outbreak. The conflict emerged most directly out of a controversy involving nationalist movements within the Austro-Hungarian Empire. On June 28, 1914, the Archduke Franz Ferdinand, heir to the throne of the tottering empire, was assassinated while paying a state visit to Sarajevo. Sarajevo was the capital of Bosnia, a province of Austria-Hungary that Slavic nationalists wished to annex to neighboring Serbia; the Archduke's assassin was a Serbian nationalist.

This local controversy quickly escalated through the workings of the system of alliances that the great powers had constructed. With support from Germany, Austria-Hungary launched a punitive assault on Serbia. The Serbians called on Russia to help with their defense. The Russians began mobilizing their army on July 30. Things quickly careened out of control. By August 3, Germany had declared war on both Russia and France and had invaded Belgium in preparation for a thrust across the French border. On August 4, Great Britain—ostensibly to honor its alliance with France, but more importantly to blunt the advance of its principal rival—declared war on Germany. Russia and the Austro-Hungarian Empire formally began hostilities on August 6. Italy, although an ally of Germany in 1914, remained neutral at first and later entered the war on the side of the British and French. The Ottoman Empire (Turkey) and other, smaller nations all joined the fighting later in 1914 or in 1915. Within less than a year, virtually the entire European continent and part of Asia were embroiled in a major war.

Wilson's Neutrality

Wilson called on his fellow citizens in 1914 to remain "impartial in thought as well as deed." But that was impossible, for several reasons. For one thing, many Americans were not, in fact, genuinely impartial. Some

THE SINKING OF THE *LUSITANIA*
On the afternoon of May 7, 1915, the British passenger liner *Lusitania* sank after having been attacked by German torpedoes. Among those who perished were 150 American passengers. The event was one of many that pushed the United States toward intervention in World War I. *(Bettmann)*

sympathized with the German cause (German Americans because of affection for Germany, Irish Americans because of hatred of Britain). Many more (including Wilson himself) sympathized with Britain. Wilson himself was only one of many Americans who fervently admired England—its traditions, its culture, its political system; almost instinctively, these Americans attributed to the cause of the Allies (Britain, France, Italy, Russia) a moral quality that they denied to the Central Powers (Germany, the Austro-Hungarian Empire, and the Ottoman Empire). Lurid reports of German atrocities in Belgium and France, skillfully exaggerated by British propagandists, strengthened the hostility of many Americans toward Germany.

Economic realities also made it impossible for the United States to deal with the belligerents on equal terms. The British had imposed a naval blockade on Germany to prevent munitions and supplies from reaching the enemy. As a neutral, the United States had the right, in theory, to trade with Germany. A truly neutral response to the blockade would have been to stop trading with Britain as well. But while the United States could survive an interruption of its relatively modest trade with the Central Powers, it could not easily weather an embargo on its much more extensive trade with the Allies, particularly when war orders from Britain and France soared after 1914, helping to produce one of the greatest economic booms in the nation's history. So America tacitly ignored the blockade of Germany and continued trading with Britain. By 1915, the United States had gradually transformed itself from a neutral power into the arsenal of the Allies.

The Germans, in the meantime, were resorting to a new and, in American eyes, barbaric tactic: submarine warfare. Unable to challenge British domination on the ocean's surface, Germany began early in 1915 to use the newly improved submarine to try to stem the flow of supplies to England. Enemy vessels, the Germans announced, would be sunk on sight. Months later, on May 7, 1915, a German submarine sank the British passenger liner *Lusitania* without warning, causing the deaths of 1,198 people, 128 of them Americans. The ship was, it later became clear, carrying not only passengers but munitions; but most Americans considered the attack what Theodore Roosevelt called it: "an act of piracy."

Wilson angrily demanded that Germany promise not to repeat such outrages and that the Central Powers affirm their commitment to neutral rights (among which, he implausibly insisted, was the right of American citizens to travel on the nonmilitary vessels of belligerents). The Germans finally agreed to Wilson's demands, but tensions between the nations continued to

grow. Early in 1916, in response to an announcement that the Allies were now arming merchant ships to sink submarines, Germany proclaimed that it would fire on such vessels without warning. A few weeks later it attacked the unarmed French steamer *Sussex*, injuring several American passengers. Again Wilson demanded that Germany abandon its "unlawful" tactics; again the German government relented. Lacking sufficient naval power to enforce an effective blockade against Britain, the Germans decided that the marginal advantages of unrestricted submarine warfare did not yet justify the possibility of drawing America into the war.

Preparedness Versus Pacifism

Despite the president's increasing bellicosity in 1916, he was still far from ready to commit the United States to war. One obstacle was American domestic politics. Facing a difficult battle for reelection, Wilson could not ignore the powerful factions that continued to oppose intervention. His policies, therefore, represented an effort to balance the demands of those who, like Theodore Roosevelt, insisted that the nation defend its "honor" and economic interests against the demands

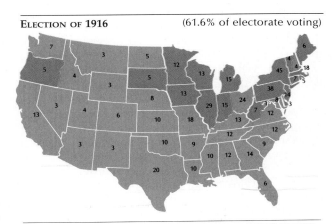

ELECTION OF 1916   (61.6% of electorate voting)

	ELECTORAL VOTE	POPULAR VOTE (%)
Woodrow Wilson (Democratic)	277	9,129,606 (49.4)
Charles E. Hughes (Republican)	254	8,538,221 (46.2)
A. L. Benson (Socialist)	—	585,113 (3.2)
Other parties (Prohibition; Socialist Labor)	—	233,909

of those who, like Bryan, La Follette, and others (including many German Americans and Irish Americans hostile to Britain), denounced any action that seemed to increase the chance of war.

The question of whether America should make military and economic preparations for war provided the first issue over which pacifists and interventionists could openly debate. Wilson at first sided with the anti-preparedness forces, denouncing the idea of an American military buildup as needless and provocative. As tensions between the United States and Germany grew, however, he changed his mind. In the fall of 1915, he endorsed an ambitious proposal by American military leaders for a large and rapid increase in the nation's armed forces. Amid expressions of outrage from pacifists in Congress and elsewhere, he worked hard to win approval of it. He even embarked on a national speaking tour early in 1916 to arouse support for the proposal. By midsummer 1916, armament for a possible conflict was well under way.

Still, the peace faction wielded considerable political strength, as became clear at the Democratic Convention in the summer of 1916. The convention became almost hysterically enthusiastic when the keynote speaker, enumerating Wilson's accomplishments, punctuated his list of the president's diplomatic achievements with the chant, "What did we do? What did we do? . . . We didn't go to war! We didn't go to war!" That speech helped produce one of the most prominent slogans of Wilson's reelection campaign (although one the president himself never used or entirely approved): "He kept us out of war." During the campaign, Wilson did nothing to discourage those who argued that the Republican candidate, the progressive New York governor Charles Evans Hughes (supported by the bellicose Theodore Roosevelt), was more likely than he to lead the nation into war. And when pro-war rhetoric became particularly heated, Wilson spoke defiantly of the nation being "too proud to fight." He ultimately won reelection by one of the smallest margins for an incumbent in American history: fewer than 600,000 popular votes and only 23 electoral votes. The Democrats retained a precarious control over Congress.

A War for Democracy

The election was behind him, and tensions between the United States and Germany were unabated. But Wilson still required a justification for American intervention that would unite public opinion and satisfy his own sense of morality. In the end, he created that rationale himself. The United States, Wilson insisted,

had no material aims in the conflict. Rather, the nation was committed to using the war as a vehicle for constructing a new world order, one based on the same progressive ideals that had motivated reform in America. In a speech before Congress in January 1917, he presented a plan for a postwar order in which the United States would help maintain peace through a permanent league of nations—a peace that would ensure self-determination for all nations, a "peace without victory." These were, Wilson believed, goals worth fighting for if there was sufficient provocation. Provocation came quickly.

In January, after months of inconclusive warfare in the trenches of France, the military leaders of Germany decided on one last dramatic gamble to achieve victory. They would launch a series of major assaults on the enemy's lines in France. At the same time, they would begin unrestricted submarine warfare (against American as well as Allied ships) to cut Britain off from vital supplies. The Allied defenses would collapse, they hoped, before the United States could intervene.

The new German policy made American entry into the war virtually inevitable. Two additional events helped clear the way. On February 25, the British gave Wilson a telegram they had intercepted from the German foreign minister, Arthur Zimmermann, to the government of Mexico. It proposed that in the event of war between Germany and the United States, the Mexicans should join with Germany against the Americans. In return, they would regain their "lost provinces" (Texas and much of the rest of the American Southwest) to the north when the war was over. (The Germans understood that anti-American sentiment was still high in Mexico after the interventions of the previous few years.) Widely publicized by British propagandists and in the American press, the Zimmermann telegram inflamed public opinion and helped build popular sentiment for war. A few weeks later, in March 1917, a revolution in Russia toppled the reactionary czarist regime and replaced it with a new, republican government. The United States would now be spared the embarrassment of allying itself with a despotic monarchy. The war for a progressive world order could proceed untainted.

On the rainy evening of April 2, two weeks after German submarines had torpedoed three American ships, Wilson appeared before a joint session of Congress and asked for a declaration of war:

> It is a fearful thing to lead this great peaceful people into war, into the most terrible and disastrous of all wars, civilization itself seeming to be in the balance. But the right is more precious than peace, and we shall fight for the things which we have always carried nearest our hearts—

for democracy, for the right of those who submit to authority to have a voice in their own Governments, for the rights and liberties of small nations, for a universal dominion of right by such a concert of free peoples as shall bring peace and safety to all nations and make the world itself at last free.

Even then, opposition remained. For four days, pacifists in Congress carried on their futile struggle. When the declaration of war finally passed on April 6, fifty representatives and six senators voted against it.

"WAR WITHOUT STINT"

Armies on both sides in Europe were decimated and exhausted by the time of Woodrow Wilson's declaration of war. The German offensives of early 1917 had failed to produce an end to the struggle, and French and British counteroffensives had accomplished little beyond adding to the appalling number of casualties. The Allies looked desperately to the United States for help. Wilson, who had called on the nation to wage war "without stint or limit," was eager to oblige.

Entering the War

American intervention had its most immediate effect on the conflict at sea. By the spring of 1917, Great Britain was suffering such vast losses from attacks by German submarines—one of every four ships setting sail from British ports never returned—that its ability to continue receiving vital supplies from across the Atlantic was in question. Within weeks of joining the war, the United States had begun to alter the balance. A fleet of American destroyers aided the British navy in its assault on the U-boats. Other American warships escorted merchant vessels across the Atlantic. Americans also helped sow antisubmarine mines in the North Sea. The results were dramatic. Sinkings of Allied ships had totaled nearly 900,000 tons in the month of April 1917; by December, the figure had dropped to 350,000; by October 1918, it had declined to 112,000.

Many Americans had hoped that providing naval assistance alone would be enough to turn the tide in the war, but it quickly became clear that a major commitment of American ground forces would also be necessary to shore up the tottering Allies. Britain and France had few remaining reserves. By early 1918, Russia had withdrawn from the war altogether. After the Bolshevik Revolution in November 1917, the new government, led by V. I. Lenin, negotiated a hasty and costly peace with the Central Powers, thus freeing additional German troops to fight on the western front.

The American Expeditionary Force

But the United States did not have a large enough standing army to provide the necessary ground forces in 1917. There were only about 120,000 soldiers in the army and perhaps 80,000 more in the National Guard. Neither group had any combat experience; and except for the small number of officers who had participated in the Spanish American war two decades before and the Mexican intervention of 1916, few commanders had any experience in battle either.

Some urged a voluntary recruitment process to raise the needed additional forces. Among the advocates of this approach was Theodore Roosevelt, now old and ill, who swallowed his hatred of Wilson and called on him at the White House with an offer to raise a regiment to fight in Europe. But the president and his secretary of war, Newton D. Baker, decided that only a national draft could provide the needed men; and despite the protests of those who agreed with House Speaker Champ Clark that "there is precious little difference between a conscript and a convict," he won passage of the Selective Service Act in mid-May. The draft brought nearly 3 million men into the army; another 2 million joined various branches of the armed services voluntarily. Together, they formed what became known as the American Expeditionary Force (AEF).

In some respects, it was the most diverse fighting force the United States had ever assembled. For the first time, women were permitted to enlist in the military—over ten thousand in the navy and a few hundred in the marines. They were not permitted in combat, but they served crucial auxiliary roles in hospitals and offices.

Over 300,000 black soldiers enlisted in or were drafted into the army and navy as well. The marines would not accept them. And while most of them performed relatively menial tasks on military bases in the United States, more than 50,000 went to France. African-American soldiers served in segregated, all-black units under white commanders; and even in Europe, most of them were assigned to non-combat duty. But some black units fought valiantly in the great offensives of 1918.

Most African-American soldiers learned to live with the racism they encountered—in part because they hoped their military service would ultimately improve their status. But a few responded to provocations violently. In August 1917, a group of black soldiers in Houston, subjected to continuing abuse by people in

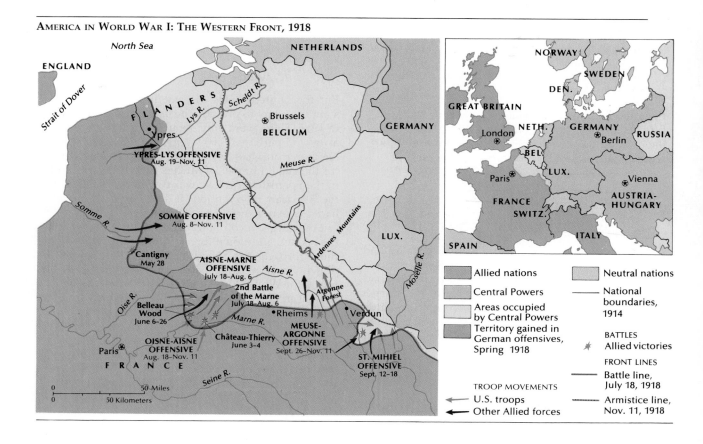

America in World War I: The Western Front, 1918

---

the community, used military weapons to kill seventeen whites. Retribution was quick. Thirteen black soldiers were hanged, and another forty were sentenced to life terms in military jails.

Having assembled this first genuinely national army, the War Department permitted the American Psychological Association to study it. The psychologists gave thousands of them a new test designed to measure intelligence: the "Intelligence Quotient" or "IQ" test. In fact, the tests were less effective in measuring intelligence than in measuring education; and they reflected the educational expectations of the white middle class people who had devised them. It is not surprising, therefore, that the largely working-class and racially mixed group of soldiers the psychologists examined performed poorly. Half the whites and the vast majority of the African Americans taking the test scored at levels that classified them as "morons." In reality, most of them were simply people who had not had very much access to education.

The Military Struggle

The engagement of these forces in combat was intense but brief. Not until the spring of 1918 were significant numbers of American troops available for battle. Eight months later, the war was over. Under the command of General John J. Pershing, the American troops joined the existing Allied forces in turning back a series of new German assaults. In early June, they assisted the French in repelling a bitter German offensive at Château-Thierry, near Paris. Six weeks later, the Americans helped turn away another assault, at Rheims, farther south. By July 18, the Allies had halted the German advance and were beginning a successful offensive of their own.

On September 26, an American fighting force of over 1 million soldiers advanced against the Germans in the Argonne Forest as part of a 200-mile attack (the Meuse-Argonne offensives) that lasted nearly seven weeks. By the end of October, they had helped push

AMERICANS IN FRANCE, 1918
Members of the U.S. Twenty-third Infantry fire at German positions in France in 1918. The scarred landscape reflects the cost of four years of inconclusive trench warfare on the western front. *(U.S. Signal Corps)*

the Germans back toward their own border and had cut the enemy's major supply lines to the front.

Faced with an invasion of their own country, German military leaders now began to seek an armistice—an immediate cease-fire that would, they hoped, serve as a prelude to negotiations among the belligerents. Pershing wanted to drive on into Germany itself; but other Allied leaders, after first insisting on terms that made the agreement little different from a surrender, accepted the German proposal. On November 11, 1918, the Great War shuddered to a close.

THE WAR AND
AMERICAN SOCIETY

The American experience in World War I was brief, but it had profound effects on the government, on the economy, and on society. Mobilizing an industrial economy for total war required an unprecedented degree of government involvement in industry, agriculture, and other areas. It also required, many believed, a strenuous effort to ensure the loyalty and commitment of the people.

Organizing the Economy for War

By the time the war ended, the United States government had appropriated $32 billion for expenses directly related to the conflict. This was a staggering sum by the standards of the time. The entire federal budget had seldom exceeded $1 billion before 1915, and as recently as 1910 the nation's entire gross national product had been only $35 billion. To raise the money, the government relied on two devices. First, it launched a major drive to solicit loans from the American people by selling "Liberty Bonds" to the public. By 1920, the sale of bonds, accompanied by elaborate patriotic appeals, had produced $23 billion. At the same time, new taxes were bringing in an additional sum of nearly $10 billion—some from levies on the "excess profits" of corporations, much from new, steeply graduated income and inheritance taxes that ultimately rose as high as 70 percent in some brackets.

An even greater challenge was organizing the economy to meet war needs. The administration tried two very different approaches. In 1916, Wilson established a Council of National Defense, composed of members of his cabinet, and a Civilian Advisory Commission, which set up local defense councils in every state and locality. Economic mobilization, according to this first plan, was to rest on a large-scale dispersal of power to local communities.

But this early administrative structure soon proved completely unworkable. Some members of the Council of National Defense, many of them disciples of the social engineering gospel of Thorstein Veblen and the "scientific management" principles of Frederick Winslow Taylor, urged a more centralized approach. Instead of dividing the economy geographically, they proposed dividing it functionally by organizing a series of planning bodies, each to supervise a specific sector of the economy. Thus one agency would control transportation, another agriculture, another manufacturing. The administrative structure that slowly emerged from such proposals was dominated by a series of "war boards," one to oversee the railroads, one to supervise fuel supplies (largely coal), another to handle food (a board that helped elevate to prominence the brilliant young engineer and business executive Herbert Hoover). The boards were not without weaknesses, but they generally succeeded in meeting essential war needs without paralyzing the domestic economy.

At the center of the effort to rationalize the economy was the War Industries Board, an agency created in July 1917 to coordinate government purchases of military supplies. Casually organized at first, it stumbled badly until March 1918, when Wilson restruc-

FINANCING THE WAR
The Liberty Loan bond-selling drives, heavily promoted by the government in posters such as this one, raised $23 billion for the war effort, an almost unimaginable sum to Americans at the time. Prior to World War I, the total federal budget had seldom exceeded $1 billion. *(Culver)*

tured it and placed it under the control of the Wall Street financier Bernard Baruch. From then on, the board wielded powers greater (in theory at least) than any government agency had ever possessed. Baruch decided which factories would convert to the production of which war materials and set prices for the goods they produced. When materials were scarce, Baruch decided to whom they should go. When corporations were competing for government contracts, he chose among them. He was, it seemed, providing the centralized regulation of the economy that some progressives had long urged.

In reality, the vaunted efficiency of the WIB was something of a myth. The agency was, in fact, plagued by mismanagement and inefficiency. It was less important to the nation's ability to meet its war needs than the sheer extent of American resources and productive capacities. Nor was the WIB in any real sense an example of state control of the economy. Baruch viewed himself, openly and explicitly, as the partner of business; and within the WIB, businessmen themselves—the so-called dollar-a-year men, who took paid

leave from their corporate jobs and worked for the government for a token salary—supervised the affairs of the private economy. Baruch ensured that manufacturers who coordinated their efforts in accord with his goals would be exempt from antitrust laws. He helped major industries earn enormous profits from their efforts. Rather than working to restrict private power and limit corporate profits, as many progressives had urged, the government was working to enhance the private sector through a mutually beneficial alliance.

The effort to organize the economy for war produced some spectacular accomplishments: Hoover's efficient organization of domestic food supplies, William McAdoo's success in untangling the railroads, and others. In some areas, however, progress was so slow that the war was over before many of the supplies ordered for it were ready. Even so, many leaders of both government and industry emerged from the experience convinced of the advantages of a close, cooperative relationship between the public and private sectors. Some hoped to continue and extend the wartime experiments in peacetime.

Labor and the War

This growing link between the public and private sectors extended, although in greatly different form, to labor. The National War Labor Board, established in April 1918 to resolve labor disputes, pressured industry to grant important concessions to workers: an eight-hour day, the maintenance of minimal living standards, equal pay for women doing equal work, recognition of the right of unions to organize and bargain collectively. In return, it insisted that workers forgo all strikes and that employers not engage in lockouts. Membership in labor unions increased by more than 1.5 million between 1917 and 1919.

The war provided workers with important, if usually temporary, gains. But it did not stop labor militancy. That was particularly clear in the West, where the Western Federation of Miners staged a series of strikes to improve the terrible conditions in the underground mines. In Ludlow, Colorado, in 1917, workers (mostly Italians, Greeks, and Slavs) walked out of coal mines owned by John D. Rockefeller. Joined by their wives and daughters, they continued the strike even after they had been evicted from company housing and had moved into hastily erected tents. The state militia was called into the town to protect the mines, but in fact (as was often the case in labor actions), it actually worked to help employers defeat the strikers. Joined by strikebreakers and others, the militia attacked the workers' tent colony; and in the battle that followed, 39 people died, among them eleven children. The episode became known as the Ludlow Massacre.

Economic and Social Results of the War

Whatever its other effects, the war helped produce a remarkable period of economic growth in the United States—a boom that began in 1914 (when European demands for American products began to increase) and accelerated after 1917 (when demand from the United States war effort fueled production). Industrial production soared, and manufacturing activity expanded in regions that had previously had relatively little of it. The shipbuilding industry, for example, grew rapidly on the West Coast. Employment increased dramatically; and because so many men were away at war, new opportunities for female, African American, Mexican, and Asian workers appeared. Inflation cut into the wage increases American workers won from employers, but most workers nevertheless experienced a significant growth in income. The agricultural economy profited from the war as well. Farm prices rose to their highest levels in decades, and agricultural production increased dramatically as a result.

One of the most important social changes of the war years was the migration of hundreds of thousands of African Americans from the rural South into northern industrial cities. It became known as the "Great Migration." Like most migrations, it was a result of both a "push" and a "pull." The push was the poverty, indebtedness, racism, and violence most blacks experienced in the South. The pull was the prospect of factory jobs in the urban North and the opportunity to live in communities where blacks could enjoy more freedom and autonomy. In the labor-scarce economy of the war years, northern factory owners dispatched agents to the South to recruit African-American workers. Black newspapers advertised the prospects for employment in the North. And perhaps most important, those who migrated first sent word back to friends and families of the opportunities they encountered—one reason for the heavy concentration of migrants from a single area of the South in certain cities in the North. In Chicago, for example, the more than 70,000 new black residents came disproportionately from a few areas of Alabama and Mississippi.

The result was a dramatic growth in black communities in northern industrial cities such as New York, Chicago, Cleveland, and Detroit. Older, more established black residents of these cities were unsettled by these new arrivals, with their country ways and their revivalistic religion; the existing African-American communities considered the newcomers coarse and feared that their presence would increase their own vulnerability to white racism. But the movement could not be stopped. New churches sprang up in black neighborhoods (many of them simple storefronts, from which self-proclaimed preachers searched for congregations). Low-paid black workers crowded into inadequate housing—small apartments known as kitchenettes, in which several families sometimes lived together. As the black communities expanded, they inevitably began to rub up against white neighborhoods, with occasionally violent results. In East St. Louis, Illinois, a white mob attacked a black neighborhood on July 2, 1917, burned down many houses, and shot the residents of some of them as they fled. As many as forty black people died.

For American women, black and white, the war meant new opportunities for employment. A million or more women worked in a wide range of industrial jobs that, in peacetime, were considered male preserves: steel, munitions, trucking, public transportation. Most of them had been working in other, less well-paying jobs earlier. Among some feminists, the war inspired hopes of a lasting change in the role of women in the economy and the society. Margaret Dreier Robins, an official of the Women's Trade Union

League, said in 1918: "The war has created new values. Men and women are conscious that as citizens they must . . . share in the management of industry and the administration of government." But whatever changes the war brought were temporary ones. As soon as the war was over, almost all of the women working in previously male industrial jobs quit or were fired; in fact, the percentage of women working for wages actually declined between 1910 and 1920.

The Search for Social Unity

The idea of unity—not only in the direction of the economy but in the nation's social purpose—had been the dream of many progressives for decades. To them, the war seemed to offer an unmatched opportunity for America to close ranks behind a great common cause. In the process, they hoped, society could achieve a lasting sense of collective purpose. In fact, however, the search for unity produced considerable repression.

The Peace Movement

Government leaders, and many others, realized that public sentiment about American involvement in the war had been deeply divided before April 1917 and remained so even after the declaration of war.

The peace movement in the United States before 1917 had many constituencies: German Americans, who opposed American intervention against Germany; Irish Americans, who opposed any support for the British; religious pacifists (Quakers, Mennonites, and others); intellectuals such as Randolph Bourne and groups on the left such as the Socialist Party and the Industrial Workers of the World, all of whom considered the war a meaningless battle among capitalist nations for commercial supremacy—an opinion many others, in America and Europe, later came to share. But the most active and widespread peace activism came from the women's movement. In 1915, Carrie Chapman Catt, a leader of the fight for woman suffrage, helped create the Woman's Peace Party, with a small but active membership. As the war in Europe intensified, the party's efforts to keep the United States from intervening grew.

Women peace activists were sharply divided once America entered the war in 1917. The National American Woman Suffrage Association, the single largest women's organization, supported the war and, more

Women War Workers
With much of the male work force fighting overseas, women moved into occupations that in other times would have been considered unsuitable for them. One such occupation, pictured here, was delivering huge blocks of ice daily to households to be used (in this age before electric refrigeration) in wooden iceboxes. *(National Archives)*

than that, presented itself as a patriotic organization dedicated to advancing the war effort. Its membership grew dramatically as a result. Catt, who was among those who abandoned the peace cause, now began calling for woman suffrage as a "war measure," to ensure that women (whose work was essential to the war effort) would feel fully a part of the nation. But many other women refused to support the war even after April 1917. Among them were Jane Addams, who was widely reviled as a result, and Charlotte Perkins Gilman, a leading feminist activist.

Women peace activists shared many of the political and economic objections to the war of the Socialist Party (to which some of them belonged). But some criticized the war on other grounds as well, arguing that as wives and mothers they had a special moral basis for their pacifism. The Woman's Peace Party had claimed to represent the "mother half of humanity," and a similarly maternal opposition to war shaped the position of the many women who remained in opposition after 1917.

Selling the War and Suppressing Dissent

Government leaders were painfully aware of the continuing opposition to the war. Many believed that a crucial prerequisite for victory was to unite public opinion behind the military effort.

The most conspicuous government effort to do that was a vast propaganda campaign to drum up enthusiasm for the conflict. It was orchestrated by the Committee on Public Information (CPI), under the direction of the Denver journalist George Creel, who spoke openly of the importance of achieving social unity:

> When I think of the many voices that were heard before the war and are still heard, interpreting America from a class or sectional or selfish standpoint, I am not sure that, if the war had to come, it did not come at the right time for the preservation and reinterpretation of American ideals.

The CPI supervised the distribution of innumerable tons of pro-war literature (75 million pieces of printed material in all). War posters plastered the walls of offices, shops, theaters, schools, churches, and homes. Newspapers dutifully printed official government accounts of the reasons for the war and the prospects for quick victory. Creel encouraged reporters to exercise "self-censorship" when reporting news about the struggle, and although many people in the press resented the suggestion, the veiled threats that accompanied it persuaded most of them to comply.

The CPI attempted at first to distribute only the "facts," believing that the truth would speak for itself. As the war continued, however, their tactics became increasingly crude. Government-promoted posters and films, at first relatively mild in tone, were by 1918 becoming lurid portrayals of the savagery of the Germans, bearing such titles as *The Prussian Cur* and *The Kaiser: Beast of Berlin*, encouraging Americans to think of the German people as something close to savages.

The government soon began more coercive efforts to suppress dissent. The CPI ran full-page advertisements in popular magazines like the *Saturday Evening Post* urging citizens to notify the Justice Department when they encountered "the man who spreads the pessimistic stories . . . , cries for peace, or belittles our efforts to win the war." The Espionage Act of 1917 gave the government new tools with which to respond to such reports. It created stiff penalties for spying, sabotage, or obstruction of the war effort (crimes that were often broadly defined); and it empowered the post office to ban "seditious" material from the mails, a responsibility Postmaster General Albert Sidney Burleson accepted with great relish. Sedition, he said, included statements that might "impugn the motives of the government and thus encourage insubordination," anything that suggested "that the government is controlled by Wall Street or munitions manufacturers, or any other special interests." He included in that category all publications of the Socialist Party.

More repressive were two measures of 1918: the Sabotage Act of April 20 and the Sedition Act of May 16. These bills expanded the meaning of the Espionage Act to make illegal any public expression of opposition to the war; in practice, it allowed officials to prosecute anyone who criticized the president or the government. Senator Hiram Johnson of California offered a bitter description of the provisions of the law. He said: "You shall not criticize anything or anybody in the Government any longer or you shall go to jail."

The most frequent targets of the new legislation (and one of the reasons for its enactment in the first place) were such anticapitalist groups (and now antiwar) groups as the Socialist Party and the Industrial Workers of the World. Many Americans had favored the repression of socialists and radicals even before the war; the wartime policies now made it possible to move against them with full legal sanction. Eugene V. Debs, the humane leader of the party and an opponent of the war, was sentenced to ten years in prison in 1918. Only a pardon by President Warren G. Harding ultimately won his release in 1921. Big Bill Haywood and members of the IWW were especially energetically prosecuted. Only by fleeing to the Soviet Union did Haywood avoid long imprisonment. In all, more than 1,500 people were arrested in 1918 for the crime of criticizing the government.

State and local governments, corporations, universities, and private citizens contributed as well to the climate of repression. Vigilante mobs sprang up to "discipline" those who dared challenge the war. A dissident Protestant clergyman in Cincinnati was pulled from his bed one night by a mob, dragged to a nearby hillside, and whipped "in the name of the women and children of Belgium." An IWW organizer in Montana was seized by a mob and hanged from a railroad bridge.

A cluster of citizens' groups emerged to mobilize "respectable" members of their communities to root out disloyalty. The American Protective League, probably the largest of such groups, enlisted the services of 250,000 people, who served as "agents"—prying into the activities and thoughts of their neighbors, opening mail, tapping telephones, and in general attempting to impose unity of opinion on their communities. It received government funds to support its work. Attorney General Thomas W. Gregory, a particularly avid supporter of repressing dissent, described them approvingly as "patriotic organizations." Other vigilante organizations—the National Security League, the Boy Spies of America, the American Defense Society—performed much the same function.

There were many victims of such activities: socialists, labor activists, female pacifists (some of whom were arrested and imprisoned simply for criticizing the government or capitalism). But the most frequent targets of repression were immigrants: Irish Americans because of their historic animosity toward the British and because some had, before 1917, expressed hopes for a German victory; Jews because many had expressed opposition to the anti-Semitic policies of the Russian government, until 1917 one of the Allies; and others. "Loyalist" citizens' groups policed immigrant neighborhoods. They monitored meetings and even conversations for signs of disloyalty. Even some settlement house workers, many of whom had once championed ethnic diversity, contributed to such efforts. The director of the National Security League described the origins of the anti-immigrant sentiment, which was producing growing support for what many were now calling "100 percent Americanism":

> . . . the melting pot has not melted. . . . there are vast communities in the nation thinking today not in terms of America, but in terms of Old World prejudices, theories, and animosities. . . . In the bottom of the melting pot there lie heaps of unfused metal.

The greatest target of abuse was the German-American community. Its members had unwittingly contributed to their plight. In the first years of the war in Europe, some had openly advocated American assistance to the Central Powers, and many had opposed United States intervention on behalf of the Allies. But while most German Americans supported the American war effort once it began, public opinion turned bitterly hostile. A campaign to purge society of all things German quickly gathered speed, at times assuming ludicrous forms. Sauerkraut was renamed "liberty cabbage." Hamburger became "liberty sausage." Performances of German music were frequently banned. German books were removed from the shelves of libraries. Courses in the German language were removed from school curricula; the California Board of Education called it "a language that disseminates the

ideals of autocracy, brutality, and hatred." Germans were routinely fired from jobs in war industries, lest they "sabotage" important tasks. Some were fired from positions entirely unrelated to the war—for example Karl Muck, the German-born conductor of the Boston Symphony Orchestra. Vigilante groups routinely subjected Germans to harassment and beatings, including a lynching in southern Illinois in 1918. Relatively few Americans favored such extremes, but many came to agree with the belief of the eminent psychologist G. Stanley Hall that "there is something fundamentally wrong with the Teutonic soul."

THE SEARCH FOR A NEW WORLD ORDER

Woodrow Wilson had led the nation into war promising a more just and stable peace at its conclusion. Well before the armistice, he was preparing to lead the fight for what he considered a democratic postwar settlement. That settlement, he believed, must rest on a set of war aims reflecting a philosophy of internationalist relations that became known as Wilsonianism.

The Fourteen Points

On January 8, 1918, Wilson appeared before Congress to present the principles for which he claimed the nation was fighting. The war aims had fourteen distinct provisions, widely known as the Fourteen Points; but they fell into three broad categories. First, Wilson's proposals contained eight specific recommendations for adjusting postwar boundaries and for establishing new nations to replace the defunct Austro-Hungarian and Ottoman Empires. Those recommendations reflected his belief in the right of all peoples to self-determination. Second, there were five general principles to govern international conduct in the future: freedom of the seas, open covenants instead of secret treaties, reductions in armaments, free trade, and impartial mediation of colonial claims. Finally, there was a proposal for a league of nations that would help implement these new principles and territorial adjustments and resolve future controversies.

There were serious flaws in Wilson's proposals. He provided no formula for deciding how to implement the "national self-determination" he promised for subjugated peoples. He said little about economic rivalries and their effect on international relations, even though such economic tensions had been in large part responsible for the war. Nevertheless, Wilson's international vision quickly came to enchant not only much of his own generation (in both America and Europe), but members of generations to come. It reflected his belief, strongly rooted in the ideas of progressivism, that the world was as capable of just and efficient government as were individual nations; that once the international community accepted certain basic principles of conduct, and once it constructed modern institutions to implement them, the human race could live in peace.

The Fourteen Points were also an answer to the new Bolshevik government in Russia. In December 1917, Lenin issued his own statement of war aims strikingly similar to Wilson's own. Wilson's announcement, which came just three weeks later, was, among other things, a last-minute (and unsuccessful) effort to persuade the Bolshevik regime to keep Russia in the war. But Wilson also realized that Lenin was now a competitor in the effort to lead the postwar order. And he announced the Fourteen Points in part to ensure that the world looked to the United States, and not Russia, for guidance. "Liberalism," he said, referring to his own ideals, "is the only thing that can save civilization from chaos—from a flood of ultra-radicalism that will swamp the world . . . Liberalism must be more liberal than ever before, it must even be radical, if civilization is to escape the typhoon."

Early Obstacles

Wilson was confident, as the war neared its end, that popular support would enable him to win Allied approval of his peace plan. But there were ominous signs both at home and abroad that his path might be more difficult than he expected. In Europe, leaders of the Allied powers were preparing to resist him even before the armistice was signed. Most of them resented what they considered Wilson's tone of moral superiority. They had reacted unhappily when Wilson refused to make the United States their "ally" but had kept his distance as an "associate" of his European partners. They had been offended by his insistence on keeping American military forces separate from the Allied armies they were joining. Most of all, however, Britain and France, having suffered incalculable losses in their long years of war, and having stored up an enormous reserve of bitterness toward Germany as a result, were in no mood for a benign and generous peace. The British prime minister, David Lloyd George, insisted for a time that the German Kaiser be captured and executed. He and Georges Clemenceau, president of France, remained determined to the end to gain something from the struggle to compensate them for the catastrophe they had suffered.

At the same time, Wilson was encountering problems at home. In 1918, with the war almost over, Wilson unwisely appealed to the American voters to support his peace plans by electing Democrats to Congress in the November elections. A Republican victory, he declared, would be "interpreted on the other side of the water as a repudiation of my leadership." Days later, the Republicans captured majorities in both houses. Domestic economic troubles, more than international issues, had been the most important factor in the voting; but because of the president's ill-timed appeal, the results damaged his ability to claim broad popular support for his peace plans.

The leaders of the Republican Party, in the meantime, were developing their own reasons for opposing Wilson. Some were angry that he had tried to make the 1918 balloting a referendum on his war aims, especially since many Republicans had been supporting the Fourteen Points. Wilson further antagonized them when he refused to appoint any important Republicans to the negotiating team that would represent the United States at the peace conference in Paris.

But the president considered such matters unimportant. Only one member of the American negotiating party would have any real authority: Wilson himself. And once he had produced a just and moral treaty, he believed, the weight of world and American opinion would compel his enemies to support him. As he sailed for Paris late in 1918, he said:

> In the name of the people of the United States, I have uttered as the objects of this great war ideals and nothing but ideals, and the war has been won by that inspiration. . . . There is a great wind of moral force moving through the world, and every man who opposes that wind will go down in disgrace.

The Paris Peace Conference

Wilson arrived in Europe to a welcome such as few men in history have experienced. To the war-weary people of the Continent, he was nothing less than a savior, the man who would create a new and better world. When he entered Paris on December 13, 1918, he was greeted, some claimed, by the largest crowd in the history of France. The negotiations themselves, however, proved less satisfying.

The principal figures in the negotiations were the leaders of the victorious allied nations: Lloyd George representing Great Britain; Clemenceau representing France; Vittorio Orlando, the prime minister of Italy;

and Wilson, who hoped to dominate them all. Some of Wilson's advisers had warned him that if agreement could not be reached at the "summit," there would be nowhere else to go, and that it would therefore be better to begin negotiations at a lower level. Wilson, however, was adamant; he alone would represent the United States.

From the beginning, the atmosphere of idealism Wilson had sought to create was competing with a spirit of national aggrandizement. There was, moreover, a pervasive sense of unease about the unstable situation in eastern Europe and the threat of communism. Russia, whose new Bolshevik government was still fighting "White" counterrevolutionaries, was unrepresented in Paris; but the radical threat it seemed to pose to Western governments was never far from the minds of any of the delegates, least of all Wilson himself. Indeed, not long before he came to Paris, Wilson ordered the landing of American troops in the Soviet Union. They were there, he claimed, to help a group of 60,000 Czech soldiers trapped in Russia to escape. But the Americans soon became involved, both directly and indirectly, in assisting the White Russians (the anti-Bolsheviks) in their fight against the new regime. Some American troops remained as late as April 1920. Lenin's regime survived these challenges, but Wilson refused to recognize his new government nevertheless. Diplomatic relations between the United States and the Soviet Union were not restored until 1933.

In the tense and often vindictive atmosphere these competing concerns produced in Paris, Wilson was un-able to win approval of many of the broad principles he had espoused: freedom of the seas, which the British refused even to discuss; free trade; "open covenants openly arrived at" (the Paris negotiations themselves were often conducted in secret). Despite his support for "impartial mediation" of colonial claims, he was forced to accept a transfer of German colonies in the Pacific to Japan, to whom the British had promised them in exchange for Japanese assistance in the war. His pledge of "national self-determination" for all peoples suffered numerous assaults. Economic and strategic demands were constantly coming into conflict with the principle of cultural nationalism.

Where the treaty departed most conspicuously from Wilson's ideals was on the question of reparations. As the conference began, the president opposed demanding compensation from the defeated Central Powers. The other Allied leaders, however, were intransigent, and slowly Wilson gave way and accepted the principle of reparations, the specific sum to be set later by a commission. That figure, established in 1921, was $56 billion, supposedly to pay for damages to civilians and for military pensions. There were continued negotiations for a decade, which scaled the sum back considerably. In the end, Germany paid only $9 billion, which was still more than its crippled economy could afford. The reparations, combined with other territorial and economic penalties, constituted an effort to keep Germany not only weak but prostrate for the indefinite future. Never again, the Allied leaders believed, should the Germans be allowed to become powerful enough to threaten the peace of Europe.

Wilson did manage to win some important victories in Paris in setting boundaries and dealing with former colonies. He secured approval of a plan to place many former colonies and imperial possessions (among them Palestine) in "trusteeship" under the League of Nations—the so-called mandate system. He blocked a French proposal to break up western Germany into a group of smaller states. He helped design the creation of two new nations: Yugoslavia and Czechoslovakia, which were welded together out of, among other territories, pieces of the former Austro–Hungarian Empire. Each contained an uneasy collection of ethnic groups that had frequently battled one another in the past.

But Wilson's most visible triumph, and the one most important to him, was the creation of a permanent international organization to oversee world affairs and prevent future wars. On January 25, 1919, the Allies voted to accept the "covenant" of the League of Nations; and with that, Wilson believed, the peace treaty was transformed from a disappointment into a success. Whatever mistakes and inequities had emerged from the peace conference, he was convinced, could be corrected later by the League.

The covenant provided for an assembly of nations that would meet regularly to debate means of resolving disputes and protecting the peace. Authority to implement League decisions would rest with a nine-member Executive Council; the United States would be one of five permanent members of the council, along with Britain, France, Italy, and Japan. The covenant left many questions unanswered, most notably how the League would enforce its decisions. Wilson, however, was confident that once established, the new organization would find suitable answers.

The Ratification Battle

Wilson was well aware of the political obstacles awaiting him at home. Many Americans, accustomed to their nation's isolation from Europe, questioned the wisdom of this major new commitment to internationalism. Others had serious reservations about the specific features of the treaty and the covenant. After a brief trip to Washington in February 1919, during which he listened to harsh objections to the treaty from members of the Senate and others, he returned to Europe and insisted on several modifications in the covenant to satisfy his critics. The revisions limited America's obligations to the League by ensuring that the United States would not be obliged to accept a League mandate to oversee a territory and that the League would not challenge the Monroe Doctrine. But

the changes were not enough to mollify his opponents, and Wilson refused to go further. When Colonel House, his close friend and trusted adviser, told him he must be prepared to compromise more, the president retorted sharply: "I have found that you get nothing in this world that is worth-while without fighting for it." His long friendship with House ended abruptly.

Wilson presented the Treaty of Versailles (which took its name from the palace outside Paris where the final negotiating sessions had taken place) to the Senate on July 10, 1919, asking, "Dare we reject it and break the heart of the world?" In the weeks that followed, he refused to consider even the most innocuous compromise. His deteriorating physical condition—he was suffering from hardening of the arteries and had apparently experienced something like a mild stroke in Paris—may have contributed to his intransigence.

The Senate, in the meantime, was raising many objections. Some senators—the fourteen so-called "irreconcilables," many of them western isolationists—opposed the agreement on principle. But other opponents, with less fervent convictions, were principally concerned with constructing a winning issue for the Republicans in 1920 and with weakening a president whom they had come to despise. Most notable of these was Senator Henry Cabot Lodge of Massachusetts, the powerful chairman of the Foreign Relations Committee. A man of stunning arrogance and a close friend of Theodore Roosevelt (who had died early in 1919, spouting hatred of Wilson to the end), Lodge loathed the president with genuine passion. "I never thought I could hate a man as I hate Wilson," he once admitted. He used every possible tactic to obstruct, delay, and amend the treaty. Wilson, for his part, despised Lodge as much as Lodge despised him. He made his feelings clear when he described his opponents in the Senate (obviously thinking primarily of Lodge) as "contemptible, narrow, selfish, poor little minds that never get anywhere."

Public sentiment clearly favored ratification, so at first Lodge could do little more than play for time. When the document reached his committee, he spent two weeks slowly reading aloud each word of its 300 pages; then he held six weeks of public hearings to air the complaints of every disgruntled minority (Irish Americans, for example, angry that the settlement made no provision for an independent Ireland). Gradually, Lodge's general opposition to the treaty crystallized into a series of "reservations"—amendments to the League covenant limiting American obligations to the organization.

At this point Wilson might still have won approval if he had agreed to some relatively minor changes in the language of the treaty. But the president refused to yield. The United States had a moral obligation, he claimed, to respect the terms of the agreement precisely as they stood. When he realized the Senate would not budge, he decided to appeal to the public.

Wilson's Ordeal

What followed was a political disaster and a personal tragedy. Wilson embarked on a grueling, cross-country speaking tour to arouse public support for the treaty. In a little more than three weeks, he traveled over 8,000 miles by train, speaking as often as four times a day, resting hardly at all. Finally, he reached the end of his strength. After speaking at Pueblo, Colorado, on September 25, he collapsed with severe headaches. Canceling the rest of his itinerary, he rushed back to Washington, where, a few days later, he suffered a major stroke. For two weeks he was close to death; for six weeks more, he was so seriously ill that he could conduct virtually no public business. His wife and his doctor formed an almost impenetrable barrier around him, shielding him from any official pressures that might impede his recovery, preventing the public from receiving any accurate information about the gravity of his condition.

Wilson ultimately recovered enough to resume a limited official schedule, but he was essentially an invalid for the remaining eighteen months of his presidency. His left side was partially paralyzed; more important, like many stroke victims, he had only partial control of his mental and emotional state. His condition only intensified what had already been his strong tendency to view public issues in moral terms and to resist any attempts at compromise. When the Senate Foreign Relations Committee finally sent the treaty to the full Senate for ratification, recommending nearly fifty amendments and reservations, Wilson refused to consider any of them. When the full Senate voted in November to accept fourteen of the reservations, Wilson gave stern directions to his Democratic allies: They must vote only for a treaty with no changes whatsoever; any other version must be defeated. On November 19, 1919, forty-two Democrats, following the president's instructions, joined with the thirteen Republican "irreconcilables" to reject the amended treaty. When the Senate voted on the original version without any reservations, thirty-eight senators, all but one a Democrat, voted to approve it; fifty-five voted no.

There were sporadic efforts to revive the treaty over the next few months. But Wilson's opposition to anything but the precise settlement he had negotiated in Paris remained too formidable an obstacle to surmount. He was, moreover, becoming convinced that the 1920 national election would serve as a "solemn referendum" on the League. By now, however, public interest in the peace process had begun to fade—partly as a reaction against the tragic bitterness of the ratification fight, but more in response to a series of other crises.

A SOCIETY IN TURMOIL

Even during the Paris Peace Conference, many Americans were less concerned about international matters than about turbulent events at home. In the aftermath of the war, various groups of Americans set out to claim the social advances that the idealistic justifications of the conflict seemed to have promised them. But the social environment after 1918 was no longer receptive to progressive reform. The American economy experienced a severe postwar recession. And much of middle-class America responded to demands for change with a fearful, conservative hostility. The aftermath of war brought not the age of liberal reform that progressives had predicted, but a period of repression and reaction.

Industry and Labor

Citizens of Washington, on the day after the armistice, found it impossible to place long-distance telephone calls: the lines were jammed with officials of the war agencies canceling government contracts. The fighting had ended sooner than anyone had anticipated, and without warning, without planning, the nation was launched into the difficult task of economic reconversion.

At first, the wartime boom continued. But the postwar prosperity rested largely on the lingering effects of the war (government deficit spending continued for some months after the armistice) and on sudden, temporary demands (a booming market for scarce consumer goods at home and a strong market for American products in the war-ravaged nations of Europe). The postwar boom was accompanied, moreover, by raging inflation, a result in part of the precipitous abandonment of wartime price controls. Through most of 1919 and 1920, prices rose at an average of more than 15 percent a year.

Finally, late in 1920, the economic bubble burst, as many of the temporary forces that had created it disappeared and as inflation began killing the market for consumer goods. Between 1920 and 1921, the gross na-

UNION MEMBERSHIP, 1900–1920

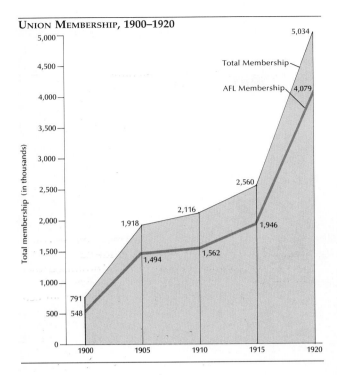

radicals, made the Seattle incident reverberate loudly throughout the country.

In September, there was a strike by the Boston police force, which was responding to layoffs and wage cuts by demanding recognition of its union. Seattle had remained generally calm; but with its police off the job, Boston erupted in violence and looting. Efforts by local businessmen, veterans, and college students to patrol the streets proved ineffective; and finally Governor Calvin Coolidge called in the National Guard to restore order. (His public statement that "there is no right to strike against the public safety by anybody, anywhere, any time" attracted national acclaim.) Eventually, Boston officials dismissed the entire police force and hired a new one.

In September 1919, the greatest strike in American history began, when 350,000 steelworkers in several eastern and midwestern cities walked off the job, demanding an eight-hour day and recognition of their union. The steel strike was long, bitter, and violent—most of the violence coming from employers, who hired armed guards to disperse picket lines and escort strikebreakers into factories. It climaxed in a riot in Gary, Indiana, in which eighteen strikers were killed. Steel executives managed to keep most plants running with non-union labor, and public opinion was so hostile to the strikers that the AFL—having at first endorsed the strike—soon timidly repudiated it. By January, the strike had collapsed. It was a setback from which organized labor would not recover for more than a decade.

The wave of strikes was a reflection of the high expectations workers had in the aftermath of a war they believed had been fought, in part, to secure their rights. It was also a reflection of the power of the forces arrayed against them. An official of the War Labor Board, observing the dismal postwar experience of unions, said in 1919: "The workers of the Allied world have been told that they were engaged in a democracy. . . . They are asking now, 'Where is that democracy for which we fought?'"

The Demands of African Americans

The black men who had served in the armed forces during the war (367,000 of them) came home in 1919 and marched down the main streets of the industrial cities with other returning troops. And then (in New York and other cities), they marched again through the streets of black neighborhoods such as Harlem, led by jazz bands, cheered by thousands of African Americans, worshiped as heroes. The black soldiers were an inspiration to thousands of urban African Americans, a sign, they thought, that a new age had come, that the

tional product (GNP) declined nearly 10 percent; 100,000 businesses went bankrupt; 453,000 farmers lost their land; nearly 5 million Americans lost their jobs.

In this unpromising economic environment, leaders of organized labor set out to consolidate the advances they had made in the war, which now seemed in danger of being lost. The raging inflation of 1919 wiped out the modest wage gains workers had achieved during the war; many laborers worried about job security as hundreds of thousands of veterans returned to the work force; arduous working conditions—such as the twelve-hour day in the steel industry—continued to be a source of discontent. Employers aggravated the resentment by using the end of the war (and the end of government controls) to rescind benefits they had been forced to concede to workers in 1917 and 1918—most notably recognition of unions.

The year 1919, therefore, saw an unprecedented wave of strikes—more than 3,600 in all, involving over 4 million workers. In January, a walkout by shipyard workers in Seattle, Washington, evolved into a general strike that brought the entire city to a virtual standstill. The mayor requested and received the assistance of U.S. Marines to keep the city running, and eventually the strike failed. But the brief success of a general strike, something Americans associated with European

THE GREAT STEEL STRIKE
Mounted police charge a group of striking steelworkers in Philadelphia during the steel strike of 1919. The strike lasted three and a half months and was the greatest single labor action in American history to that point. The strike centered around five demands: recognition of the steelworkers' union, the right of workers to bargain collectively with management through the union, abolition of the twelve-hour day, abolition of company unions, and wage increases. It finally dissolved in failure in early January 1920. *(Culver)*

glory of black heroism in the war would make it impossible for white society ever again to treat African Americans as less than equal citizens.

In fact, that black soldiers had fought in the war had almost no impact at all on white attitudes. But it did have a profound effect on black attitudes: it accentuated African-American bitterness—and increased black determination to fight for their rights. For soldiers, there was an expectation of some social reward for their service. For many other American blacks, the war had raised economic expectations, as they moved into industrial and other jobs vacated by white workers, jobs to which they had previously had no access. Just as black soldiers expected their military service to enhance their social status, so black factory workers regarded their move north as an escape from racial prejudice and an opportunity for economic gain.

By 1919, however, the racial climate had become savage and murderous. In the South, there was a sudden increase in lynchings: more than seventy blacks, some of them war veterans, died at the hands of white mobs in 1919 alone. In the North, black factory workers faced widespread layoffs as returning white veterans displaced them from their jobs. Black veterans found no significant new opportunities for advancement. Rural black migrants to northern cities encountered white communities unfamiliar with and generally hostile to them; and as whites became convinced that black workers with lower wage demands were hurting them economically, animosity grew rapidly.

The wartime riots in East St. Louis and elsewhere were a prelude to a summer of much worse racial violence in 1919. In Chicago, a black teenager swimming in Lake Michigan on a hot July day happened to drift

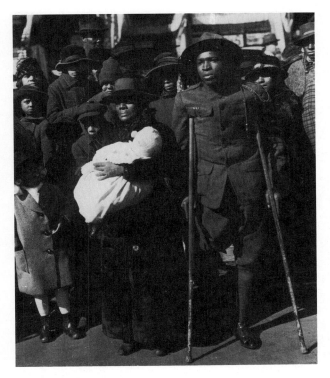

A BLACK VETERAN
Residents of Harlem watch the 309th Colored Infantry parading through New York on the occasion of their return from Europe in March 1919. One little girl stares intently at a disabled veteran still in uniform, who is standing somberly among the crowd—as if already aware of the disappointments awaiting other black veterans as they reentered civilian life. *(UPI/Bettmann)*

toward a white beach. Whites on shore allegedly stoned him unconscious; he sank and drowned. Angry blacks gathered in crowds and marched into white neighborhoods to retaliate; whites formed even larger crowds and roamed into black neighborhoods shooting, stabbing and beating passersby, destroying homes and properties. For more than a week, Chicago was virtually at war. In the end, 38 people died—15 whites and 23 blacks—and 537 were injured; over 1,000 people were left homeless. The Chicago riot was the worst but not the only racial violence during the so-called red summer of 1919; in all, 120 people died in such racial outbreaks in the space of little more than three months.

Racial violence, and even racially motivated urban riots, were not new. The deadliest race riot in American history had occurred in New York during the Civil War. But the 1919 riots were different in one respect: they did not just involve white people attacking blacks; they also involved blacks fighting back. The NAACP signaled this change by urging blacks not just to demand government protection, but also to retaliate, to defend themselves. The poet Claude McKay, one of the major figures of what would shortly be known as the Harlem Renaissance, wrote a poem after the Chicago riot called "If We Must Die":

Like men we'll face the murderous cowardly pack.
Pressed to the wall, dying, but fighting back.

At the same time, a black Jamaican, Marcus Garvey, began to attract a wide American following, mostly among poor urban blacks, with an ideology of black nationalism. Garvey encouraged African Americans to

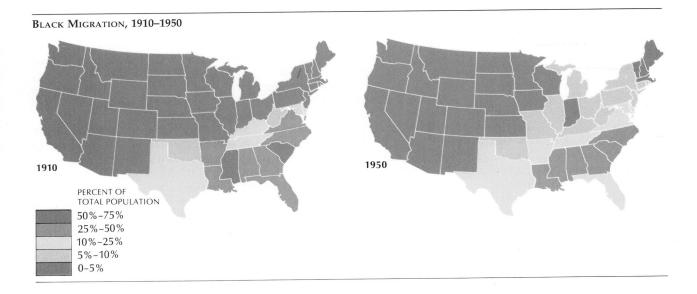

BLACK MIGRATION, 1910–1950

1910

1950

PERCENT OF
TOTAL POPULATION

50%–75%
25%–50%
10%–25%
5%–10%
0–5%

take pride in their own achievements and to develop an awareness of their African heritage—to reject assimilation into white society and develop pride in their own race and culture (which was, he claimed, superior to that of white society). His United Negro Improvement Association (UNIA) launched a chain of black-owned grocery stores and pressed for the creation of other black businesses. Eventually, Garvey began urging his supporters to leave America and return to Africa, where they could create a new society of their own. In the 1920s, the Garvey movement experienced explosive growth for a time; and the UNIA became notable for its mass rallies and parades, for the opulent uniforms of its members, and for the growth of its enterprises. It began to decline, however, after Garvey was indicted in 1923 on charges of business fraud. He was deported to Jamaica two years later. But the allure of black nationalism, which he helped make visible to millions of African Americans, survived in black culture long after Garvey himself was gone.

The Red Scare

To much of the white middle class at the time, the industrial warfare, the racial violence, the demands of feminists all appeared to be frightening omens of instability and radicalism. This was in part because other evidence emerging at the same time seemed likewise to suggest the existence of a radical menace. The Russian Revolution of November 1917 made it clear that communism was no longer simply a theory, but now an important regime. Concerns about the communist threat grew in 1919 when the Soviet government announced the formation of the Communist International (or Comintern), whose purpose was to export revolution around the world. And in America itself, there were, in addition to the great number of imagined radicals, a modest number of real ones. The American Communist Party began its life in 1919, and there were other radical groups (many of them dominated by immigrants from Europe who had been involved in radical politics before coming to America). Some of these radicals were presumably responsible for a series of bombings in the spring of 1919 that produced great national alarm. In April, the post office intercepted several dozen parcels addressed to leading businessmen and politicians that were triggered to explode when opened. Several of them reached their destinations, and one of them exploded, severely injuring a domestic servant of a public official in Georgia. Two months later, eight bombs exploded in eight cities within minutes of one another, suggesting a nation-

COLLECTING "SUBVERSIVE" LITERATURE, 1919
Even before the Palmer Raids of 1919–1920 put the federal government behind the effort to suppress radical groups, state and local governments were taking heavy-handed action. Here a group of local law enforcement officials display a stash of "Red" literature they had seized on November 11, 1919, from a Communist Party headquarters in Cambridge, Massachusetts, near Harvard University. *(UPI/Bettmann)*

wide conspiracy. One of them damaged the facade of Attorney General A. Mitchell Palmer's home in Washington. In 1920, there was a terrible explosion in front of the Morgan bank on Wall Street, which killed thirty people (although only one person in the bank itself—a clerk).

The bombings crystallized what was already a growing determination among many middle-class Americans (and some government officials) to fight back against radicalism—a determination steeled by the repressive atmosphere of the war years. This antiradicalism accompanied, and reinforced, the already strong commitment among old-stock Protestants to the idea of "100 Percent Americanism." And it produced what became known as the Red Scare.

Antiradical newspapers and politicians now began to portray almost every form of instability or protest as signs of a radical threat. Race riots, one newspaper claimed, were the work of "armed revolutionaries running rampant through our cities." The steel strike, the *Philadelphia Inquirer* claimed, was "penetrated with the Bolshevik idea . . . steeped in the doctrines of the class struggle and social overthrow." Nearly thirty states enacted new peacetime sedition laws imposing harsh

SIGNIFICANT EVENTS

1914 Austria invades Serbia

World War I begins

Wilson declares American neutrality

1915 Wartime economic boom begins

Great Migration of blacks to the North begins

Woman's Peace Party founded

Germany begins submarine warfare

Lusitania torpedoed

Wilson launches preparedness program

1916 *Sussex* attacked

Wilson reelected president

1917 Germany announces unrestricted submarine warfare

Germans launch major offensive in France

Zimmermann telegram disclosed

Russian czar overthrown

United States declares war on Central Powers

Selective Service Act passed

War Industries Board created

Espionage Act passed

Race riot in East St. Louis, Illinois

Racial tensions lead to violence among soldiers based in Houston

Coal miners' strike in Ludlow, Colorado, ends in massacre of 39 people

1918 Russia signs a separate peace with Central Powers

Sedition Act passed

U.S. troops repel Germans at Château Thierry and Rheims

U.S. troops launch offensive in Argonne Forest

Bernard Baruch takes over War Industries Board

Wilson announces Fourteen Points

American troops land in Soviet Union

Republicans gain control of Congress

Armistice ends war (November 11)

Paris Peace Conference convenes

1919 Treaty of Versailles signed

Senate proposes modifications to treaty

Wilson suffers stroke

Senate rejects treaty

Economy experiences postwar inflation

Race riots break out in Chicago and other cities

Workers stage steel strike and other actions

Soviet Union creates Comintern

Theodore Roosevelt dies

1920 Nineteenth Amendment gives suffrage to women

Economic recession disrupts economy

United States reacts to "radicalism" with Palmer Raids and Red Scare

Sacco and Vanzetti charged with murder

Warren G. Harding elected president

1924 Woodrow Wilson dies

1927 Sacco and Vanzetti executed

penalties on those who promoted revolution; some 300 people went to jail as a result—many of them people whose "crime" had been nothing more than opposition to the war. There were spontaneous acts of violence against supposed radicals in some communities. A mob of off-duty soldiers in New York City ransacked the offices of a socialist newspaper and beat up its staff. Another mob, in Centralia, Washington, dragged an IWW agitator from jail and castrated him before hanging him from a bridge. Citizens in many communities removed "subversive" books from the shelves of libraries; administrators in some universities dismissed "radical" members from their faculties. Women's groups such as the National Consumers' League came under attack by antiradicals because so many feminists had opposed American intervention in the fighting in Europe.

Perhaps the greatest contribution to the Red Scare came from the federal government. On New Year's Day, 1920, Attorney General A. Mitchell Palmer and his ambitious assistant, J. Edgar Hoover, orchestrated a series of raids on alleged radical centers throughout the country and arrested more than 6,000 people. The Palmer Raids had been intended to uncover huge caches of weapons and explosives; they netted a total of three pistols and no dynamite. Most of those arrested were ultimately released, but about 500 who were not American citizens were summarily deported.

The ferocity of the Red Scare soon abated, but its effects lingered well into the 1920s, most notably in the celebrated case of Sacco and Vanzetti. In May of 1920, two Italian immigrants, Nicola Sacco and Bartolomeo Vanzetti, were charged with the murder of a paymaster in Braintree, Massachusetts. The evidence against them was questionable; but because both men were confessed anarchists, they faced a widespread public presumption of guilt. They were convicted in a trial of extraordinary injudiciousness, before an openly bigoted judge, Webster Thayer, and were sentenced to death. Over the next several years, public support for Sacco and Vanzetti grew to formidable proportions. But all requests for a new trial or a pardon were denied. On August 23, 1927, amid widespread protests around the world, Sacco and Vanzetti, still proclaiming their innocence, died in the electric chair. Theirs was a cause that a generation of Americans never forgot. Fifty years later, the writer Katherine Anne Porter, who had demonstrated on their behalf, described the case as the "Never-Ending Wrong." It kept the bitter legacy of the Red Scare alive for many years.

The Retreat from Idealism

On August 26, 1920, the Nineteenth Amendment, guaranteeing women the right to vote, became part of the Constitution. To the woman suffrage movement, this was the culmination of nearly a century of struggle. To many progressives, who had seen the inclusion of women in the electorate as a way of bolstering their political strength, it seemed to promise new support for reform. Yet the passage of the Nineteenth Amendment marked not the beginning of an era of reform, but the end of one.

Economic problems, feminist demands, labor unrest, racial tensions, and the intensity of the antiradicalism they helped create—all combined in the years immediately following the war to produce a general sense of disillusionment. That became particularly apparent in the election of 1920. Woodrow Wilson wanted the campaign to be a referendum on the League of Nations, and the Democratic candidates, Ohio Governor James M. Cox and Assistant Secretary of the Navy Franklin D. Roosevelt, tried to keep Wilson's ideals alive. The Republican presidential nominee, however, offered a different vision. He was Warren Gamaliel Harding, an obscure Ohio senator whom party leaders had chosen as their nominee confident that he would do their bidding once in office. Harding offered no ideals, only a vague promise of a return, as he later phrased it, to "normalcy." He won in a landslide. The Republican ticket received 61 percent of the popular vote and carried every state outside the South. The party made major gains in Congress as well.

Woodrow Wilson, who had tried and failed to create a postwar order based on democratic ideals, stood repudiated. Early in 1921, he retired to a house on S Street in Washington, where he lived quietly until his death in 1924. In the meantime, for most Americans, a new era had begun.

SUGGESTED READINGS

The Road to War.   Thomas A. Bailey and Paul B. Ryan, *The Lusitania Disaster* (1975). John Coogan, *The End to Neutrality* (1981). John Milton Cooper, Jr., *The Vanity of Power: American Isolation and the First World War* (1969). Patrick Devlin, *Too Proud to Fight: Woodrow Wilson's Neutrality* (1974). Ross Gregory, *The Origins of American Intervention in the First World War* (1971). Manfred Jonas, *The United States and Germany* (1984). C. Roland Marchand, *The American Peace Movement and Social Reform* (1973). Ernest R. May, *The World War and American Isolation* (1959). Emily Rosenberg, *Spreading the American Dream* (1982). Jeffrey J. Sanford, *Wilsonian Maritime Diplomacy* (1978). Daniel Smith, *Robert Lansing and American Neutrality* (1958); *The Great Departure: The United States and World War I, 1914–1920,* (1965). Barbara Tuchman, *The Zimmermann Telegram* (1958); *The Guns of August* (1962).

Military Histories.   A. E. Barbeau and Florette Henri, *The Unknown Soldiers: Black American Troops in World War I* (1974). Christopher Campbell, *Aces and Aircraft of World War I* (1981). John Whiteclay Chambers, *To Raise an Army* (1987). J. Garry Clifford, *The Citizen Soldiers* (1972). Edward M. Coffman, *The War to End All Wars* (1969). Harvey A. DeWeerd, *President Wilson Fights His War* (1968). Frank Freidel, *Over There: The Story of America's First Great Overseas Crusade* (1964). Robert Jackson, *Fighter Pilots in World War I* (1977). Herbert M. Mason, Jr., *The Lafayette Escadrille* (1964). Donald Smythe, *Pershing* (1986). Lawrence Stallings, *The Doughboys: The Story of the AEF, 1917–1918* (1963). David Trask, *The United States in the Supreme War Council* (1961). Frank E. Vandiver, *Black Jack: The Life and Times of John J. Pershing* (1977). Russell Weigley, *The American Way of War* (1973).

Wartime Diplomacy.   Kathleen Burk, *Britain, America, and the Sinews of War* (1985). W. B. Fowler, *British-American Relations, 1917–1918* (1969). John Lewis Gaddis, *Russia, the Soviet Union and the United States* (1978). George F. Kennan, *Russia Leaves the War* (1956); *Russia and the West Under Lenin and Stalin* (1961). Carl Parrini, *Heir to Empire: United States Economic Diplomacy, 1916–1923* (1969).

Politics and Government in Wartime.   Ray H. Abrams, *Preachers Present Arms: The Role of the American Churches and Clergy in World Wars I and II* (1969). Daniel R. Beaver, *Newton D. Baker and the American War Effort, 1917–1919* (1966). George T. Blakey, *Historians on the Homefront* (1970). William J. Breen, *Uncle Sam at Home* (1984). Zechariah Chaffee, Jr., *Free Speech in the United States* (1941). Charles Chatfield, *For Peace and Justice: Pacifism in America, 1914–1941* (1971). Edward M. Coffman, *The Hilt of the Sword: The Career of Peyton C. Marsh* (1966). Valerie Jean Conner, *The National War Labor Board* (1983). Alfred E. Conrebise, *War as Advertised: The Four Minute Men and America's Crusade, 1917–1918* (1984). Wayne Cornelius, *Building the Cactus Curtain: Mexican Migration and U.S. Responses from Wilson to Carter* (1980). Robert D. Cuff, *The War Industries Board: Business-Government Relations During World War I* (1973). Charles DeBenedettis, *Origins of the Modern Peace Movement* (1978). Harvey A. DeWeerd, *President Wilson Fights His War* (1968). Charles V. Forcey, *The Crossroads of Liberalism* (1961). Charles Gilbert, *American Financing of World War I* (1970). Otis L. Graham, Jr., *The Great Campaigns* (1971). Ellis W. Hawley, *The Great War and the Search for a Modern Order* (1979). Sondra Herman, *Eleven Against War* (1969). Donald Johnson, *The Challenge to America's Freedoms* (1963). David M. Kennedy, *Over Here* (1980). Seward Livermore, *Politics Is Adjourned* (1966). J. R. Mock and Cedric Larson, *Words That Won the War* (1939). Paul L. Murphy, *World War I and the Origins of Civil Liberties* (1984). George Nash, *The Life of Herbert Hoover: The Humanitarian, 1914–1917* (1990). Harold C. Peterson, *Propaganda for War: The Campaign Against American Neutrality, 1914–1917* (1968). Harold C. Peterson and Gilbert Fite, *Opponents of War, 1917–1918* (1957). Richard Polenberg, *Fighting Faiths: The Abrams Case, the Supreme Court, and Free Speech* (1987). William Preston, Jr., *Aliens and Dissenters: Federal Suppression of Radicals, 1903–1933* (1963). Ronald Schaffer, *America in the Great War: The Rise of the War Welfare State* (1991). Harry N. Scheiber, *The Wilson Administration and Civil Liberties, 1917–1921* (1960). Jordan Schwarz, *The Speculator: Bernard M. Baruch in Washington, 1917–1965* (1981). John A. Thomas, *Reformers and War* (1987). Stephen Vaughn, *Holding Fast the Inner Lines: Democracy, Nationalism, and the Committee on Public Information* (1979). Neil A. Wynn, *From Progressivism to Prosperity: World War I and American Society* (1986).

Wartime Society and Culture.   Allan M. Brandt, *No Magic Bullet: A Social History of Venereal Disease in the United States* (1985). Paul Chapman, *Schools as Sorters* (1988). Stanley Cooperman, *World War I and the American Novel* (1970). Alfred W. Crosby, Jr., *Epidemic and Peace, 1918* (1976). Maurine W. Greenwald, *Women, War, and Work* (1980). Carol S. Gruber, *Mars and Minerva* (1975). John Higham, *Strangers in the Land: Patterns of American Nativism* (1955). Michael T. Isenberg, *War on Film* (1981). Frederick C. Luebke, *Bonds of Loyalty: German-Americans and World War I* (1974). Elizabeth Payne, *Reform, Labor, and Feminism: Margaret Dreier Robins and the Women's Trade Union League* (1988). Michael Pearlman, *To Make Democracy Safe for America: Patricians and Preparedness in the Progressive Era* (1984). Barbara J. Steinson, *American Women's Activism in World War I* (1982).

Wilson and the Peace.   Lloyd Ambrosius, *Woodrow Wilson and the American Diplomatic Tradition* (1987). John Morton Blum, *Woodrow Wilson and the Politics of Morality* (1956). Robert H. Ferrell, *Woodrow Wilson and World War I* (1985). Peter Filene, *Americans and the Soviet Experiment* (1967). Denna Fleming, *The United States and the League of Nations* (1932). Inga Floto, *Colonel House at Paris* (1980). John L. Gaddis, *Russia, the Soviet Union, and the United States* (1978). Lloyd C. Gardner, *Safe for Democracy: The Anglo-American Response to Revolution, 1913–1923* (1984). John A. Garraty, *Henry Cabot Lodge* (1953). Robert Jackson, *At War with the Bolsheviks: The*

Allied Intervention into Russia, 1917–1920 (1972). George Kennan, *Decision to Intervene* (1958). Thomas Knock, *To End All Wars: Woodrow Wilson and the Quest for a New World Order* (1992). Warren F. Kuehl, *Seeking World Order* (1969). Christopher Lasch, *The American Liberals and the Russian Revolution* (1962). N. Gordon Levin, Jr., *Woodrow Wilson and World Politics* (1968). Arthur S. Link, *Woodrow Wilson*, 5 vols. (1947–1965); *Wilson the Diplomatist* (1957); *Woodrow Wilson: War, Revolution, and Peace* (1979). Arno Mayer, *Political Origins of the New Diplomacy, 1917–1918* (1963); *Wilson vs. Lenin* (1959); *Politics and Diplomacy of Peacemaking: Containment and Counterrevolution* (1965). Charles L. Mee, Jr., *The End of Order: Versailles 1919* (1980). Robert E. Osgood, *Ideals and Self-Interest in American Foreign Relations* (1953). Klaus Schwabe, *Woodrow Wilson, Revolutionary Germany, and Peacemaking, 1918–1919* (1985). Gene Smith, *When the Cheering Stopped* (1964). Ronald Steel, *Walter Lippmann and the American Century* (1980). Ralph Stone, *The Irreconcilables: The Fight Against the League of Nations* (1970). Arthur Walworth, *Wilson and the Peacemakers* (1986). William C. Widenor, *Henry Cabot Lodge and the Search for an American Foreign Policy* (1980).

Postwar America. Wesley M. Bagby, Jr., *The Road to Normalcy* (1962). David Brody, *Steelworkers in America* (1960); *Labor in Crisis: The Steel Strike of 1919* (1965). Stanley Coben, *A. Mitchell Palmer* (1963). David Cronon, *Black Moses* (1955). Roberta Strauss Feuerlicht, *Justice Crucified: The Story of Sacco and Vanzetti* (1977). Robert L. Friedheim, *The Seattle General Strike* (1965). Amy J. Garvey, *Garvey and Garveyism* (1963). Robert V. Haynes, *A Night of Violence: The Houston Riot of 1917* (1976). Florette Henri, *Black Migration: Movement Northward, 1900–1920* (1975). Kenneth Kusmer, *A Ghetto Takes Shape* (1976). David Montgomery, *The Fall of the House of Labor: The Workplace, the State, and American Labor Activism, 1865–1921* (1987). Robert K. Murray, *The Red Scare: A Study in National Hysteria, 1919–1920* (1955). Burl Noggle, *Into the Twenties* (1974). Stuart I. Rochester, *American Liberal Disillusionment in the Wake of World War I* (1977). Elliot Rudwick, *Race Riot at East St. Louis* (1964). Francis Russell, *A City in Terror* (1975). Alan Spear, *Black Chicago* (1967). Judith Stein, *The World of Marcus Garvey* (1986). William M. Tuttle, Jr., *Race Riot: Chicago in the Red Summer of 1919* (1970). Theodore Vincent, *Black Power and the Garvey Movement* (1971).

The "Jazz Age"

One of the most popular images of the 1920s, captured here by the magazine illustrator John Held Jr., was of a new, exuberant youth culture in which women—liberated from Victorian constraints—were free to smoke cigarettes, drink alcohol, and socialize with men in ways that had seldom been possible before. The rapid proliferation of the automobile was among many sources of the new freedoms some young people enjoyed. The image of the "Jazz Age," however, reflected mainly the experiences of a small part of the middle-class elite. Most Americans in the 1920s continued to live in ways bound by tradition and economic limits. *(Culver)*

CHAPTER TWENTY-FOUR

THE NEW ERA

HE IMAGE OF THE 1920s in the American popular imagination is of an era of affluence, conservatism, and cultural frivolity: the Roaring Twenties; what Warren G. Harding once called the age of "normalcy." In reality, the decade was a time of significant, even dramatic social, economic, and political change. It was an era in which the American economy not only enjoyed spectacular growth but developed new forms of organization. It was a time in which American popular culture reshaped itself to reflect the urban, industrial, consumer-oriented society America was becoming. And it was a decade in which American government, for all its conservatism, experimented with new approaches to public policy that helped pave the way for the important period of reform that was to follow. Contemporaries liked to refer to the 1920s as the "New Era"—an age in which America was becoming a modern nation.

At the same time, however, the decade saw the rise of a series of spirited and at times effective rebellions against the modern developments that were transforming American life. The intense cultural conflicts that characterized the 1920s were evidence of how many Americans remained outside the reach of the new, affluent consumer culture; and evidence, too, of how some of those inside it remained unreconciled to the modernizing currents of the New Era.

THE NEW ECONOMY

After the recession of 1921–1922, the United States began a long period of almost uninterrupted prosperity and economic expansion. Less visible at the time, but equally significant, was the survival (and even the growth) of serious inequalities and imbalances.

Economic Growth and Organization

No one could deny the remarkable, some believed miraculous, feats of the American economy in the 1920s. The nation's manufacturing output rose by more than 60 percent during the decade. Per capita income grew by a third. Inflation was negligible. A mild recession in 1923 interrupted the pattern of growth, but when it subsided early in 1924, the economy expanded with even greater vigor than before.

The economic boom was a result of many things. An immediate cause was the debilitation of European industry in the aftermath of World War I, which left the United States for a short time the only truly healthy industrial power in the world. More important in the long run was technology, and the great industrial expansion it made possible. The automobile industry, as a result of the development of the assembly line and other innovations, now became one of the most important industries in the nation. It stimulated growth in many related industries as well. Auto manufacturers purchased the products of steel, rubber, glass, and tool companies. Auto owners bought gasoline from the oil corporations. Road construction in response to the proliferation of motor vehicles became an important industry. The increased mobility that the automobile made possible increased the demand for suburban housing, fueling a boom in the construction industry.

Other new industries benefiting from technological innovations contributed as well to the economic growth. Radio expanded rapidly within a few years of its commercial debut in 1920. The motion picture industry grew dramatically, especially after the introduction of sound in 1927. Aviation, electronics, home appliances, plastics, synthetic fibers, aluminum, magnesium, oil, electric power, and other industries fueled by technological advances—all grew impressively and spurred the economic boom. Cheap, readily available energy—from newly discovered oil reserves, from the expanded network of electric power, and from the nation's abundant coal fields—further enhanced the ability of industry to produce.

Large sectors of American business were also accelerating their drive toward national organization and consolidation. Certain industries—notably those, such as steel, dependent on large-scale mass production—seemed naturally to move toward concentrating production in a few large firms; U.S. Steel, the nation's largest corporation, was so dominant that almost everyone used the term "Little Steel" to refer to all of its competitors. Other industries, such as textiles, that were less dependent on technology and less susceptible to great economies of scale, proved more resistant to consolidation, despite the efforts of many businessmen to promote it.

In those areas where industry did consolidate, new forms of corporate organization emerged to advance the trend. General Motors, which by 1920 was not only the largest automobile manufacturer but the fifth largest American corporation, was a classic example. GM's founder, William Durant, had expanded the company dramatically but had never replaced the informal, personal management style with which he began. When GM foundered in the 1920 recession, leadership of the company fell to Alfred P. Sloan, who created a modern administrative system with an efficient divisional organization. The new system not only made it easier for GM to control its many subsidiaries; it also made it simpler for it—and for the many other corporations that adopted similar administrative systems—to expand further.

Some industries less susceptible to domination by a few great corporations attempted to stabilize themselves not through consolidation but through cooperation. An important vehicle was the trade association—a national organization created by various members of an industry to encourage coordination in production and marketing techniques. Trade associations worked reasonably well in the mass-production industries that had already succeeded in limiting competition through consolidation. But in more decentralized industries, such as cotton textiles, their effectiveness was limited.

The strenuous efforts by industrialists throughout the economy to find ways to curb competition through consolidation or cooperation reflected a strong fear of overproduction. Even in the booming 1920s, industrialists remembered how too-rapid expansion had helped produce recessions in 1893, 1907, and 1920. The great, unrealized dream of the New Era was to find a way to stabilize the economy so that such collapses would never occur again.

Labor in the New Era

The remarkable economic growth was accompanied by a continuing, and in some areas even increasing, maldistribution of wealth and purchasing power. More than two-thirds of the American people in 1929 lived at no better than what one major study described as the "minimum comfort level." Half of those languished at or below the level of "subsistence and poverty." Large segments of society, unable to organize, were without power to protect their economic interests.

American industrial workers experienced both the successes and the failures of the 1920s as much as any other group. On the one hand, most workers saw their standard of living rise during the decade; many enjoyed greatly improved working conditions and other benefits. Some employers in the 1920s, eager to avoid disruptive labor unrest and forestall the growth of independent trade unions, adopted paternalistic techniques that came to be known as "welfare capitalism." Henry Ford, for example, shortened the workweek, raised wages, and instituted paid vacations. U.S. Steel made conspicuous efforts to improve safety and sanitation in its factories. For the first time, some workers became eligible for pensions on retirement—nearly 3 million by 1926. When labor grievances surfaced despite these efforts, workers could voice them through the so-called company unions that were emerging in many industries—workers' councils and shop committees, organized by the corporations themselves.

THE STEAMFITTER
Lewis Hine was among the first American photographers to recognize his craft as an art. In this photograph from the mid-1920s, Hine made a point that many other artists were making in other media: The rise of the machine could serve human beings, but might also bend them to its own needs. The steamfitter (carefully posed by the photographer) is forced to shape his body to the contours of his machine in order to complete his task. (*International Museum of Photography at George Eastman House*)

Welfare capitalism brought many workers important economic benefits, but it did not help them gain any real control over their own fates. Company unions were feeble vehicles, forbidden in most industries from raising the issues most important to workers. And welfare capitalism survived only as long as industry prospered. After 1929, with the economy in crisis, the entire system quickly collapsed.

Welfare capitalism affected only a relatively small number of workers, in any case. Most laborers worked for employers interested primarily in keeping their labor costs to a minimum. Workers as a whole, therefore, received wage increases that were proportionately far below increases in production and profits.

Unskilled workers, in particular, saw their wages increase almost imperceptibly—by only a little over 2 percent between 1920 and 1926. In the end, American workers in the 1920s remained a relatively impoverished and powerless group. Their wages rose; but the average annual income of a worker remained below $1,500 a year when $1,800 was considered necessary to maintain a minimally decent standard of living. Only by relying on the earnings of several family members at once could many working-class families make ends meet. And almost all such families had to live with the very real possibility of one or more members' losing their jobs. Unemployment was lower in the 1920s than it had been in the previous two decades, and much lower than it would be in the 1930s. But a large proportion of the work force was out of work for at least some period during the decade—in part because the rapid growth of industrial technology made many jobs obsolete. The unemployment rate for the 1920s is difficult to calculate, but scholars estimate that an average of 5 to 7 percent of the work force was without a job at any given time.

Many laborers continued to regard an effective, independent union movement as their best hope. But the New Era was a bleak time for labor organization, in part because the unions themselves were generally conservative and failed to adapt to the realities of the modern economy. The American Federation of Labor remained wedded to the concept of the craft union, in which workers were organized on the basis of particular skills. It continued to make no provision for the fastest-growing area of the work force: unskilled industrial workers, many of them immigrants from southern or eastern Europe. Ignored by the craft unions, they had few organizations of their own. William Green, who became president of the AFL in 1924, was committed to peaceful cooperation with employers and to strident opposition to communism and socialism. He frowned on strikes.

Women and Minorities in the Work Force

A growing proportion of the work force consisted of women, who were concentrated in what have since become known as "pink-collar" jobs—low-paying service occupations with many of the same problems as manufacturing employment. Large numbers of women worked as secretaries, salesclerks, telephone operators, and other, similarly underpaid jobs. Because technically such positions were not industrial jobs, the AFL and other labor organizations were generally uninterested in organizing these workers.

Similarly, the half-million African Americans who had migrated from the rural South into the cities during the Great Migration after 1914 had few opportunities for union representation. The skilled crafts represented in the AFL often worked actively to exclude blacks from their trades and organizations. Most blacks worked in jobs in which the AFL took no interest at all—as janitors, dishwashers, garbage collectors, commercial laundry attendants, domestics, and in other types of service jobs. The Brotherhood of Sleeping Car Porters, founded in 1925 and led for years by A. Philip Randolph, was a notable exception: a vigorous union, led by an African American, and representing a virtually all-black work force. Over time, Randolph won some significant gains for his members—increased wages, shorter working hours, and other benefits. He also enlisted the union in battles for civil rights for African Americans.

In the West and the Southwest, the ranks of the unskilled included considerable numbers of Asians and Hispanics, few of them organized, most actively excluded from white-dominated unions. In the wake of the Chinese Exclusion Acts, Japanese immigrants increasingly took the place of the Chinese in menial jobs in California, despite the continuing hostility of the white population. They worked on railroads, construction sites, farms, and in many other low-paying workplaces. Some Japanese managed to escape the ranks of the unskilled by forming their own small businesses or setting themselves up as truck farmers; and many of the Issei (Japanese immigrants) and Nisei (their American-born children) enjoyed significant economic success—so much so that California passed laws in 1913 and 1920 to make it more difficult for them to buy land. Other Asians—most notably Filipinos—also swelled the unskilled work force and generated considerable hostility. Anti-Filipino riots in California beginning in 1929 helped produce legislation in 1934 virtually eliminating immigration from the Philippines.

Mexican immigrants formed a major part of the unskilled work force throughout the Southwest and California. Nearly half a million Mexicans entered the United States in the 1920s, more than any other national group, increasing the total Mexican population to over a million. Most lived in California, Texas, Arizona, and New Mexico; and by 1930, most lived in cities. Large Mexican barrios—usually raw urban communities, often without even such basic services as plumbing and sewage—grew up in Los Angeles, El Paso, San Antonio, Denver, and many other cities and towns. Some of the residents found work locally in factories and shops; others traveled to mines or did migratory labor on farms, but returned to the cities between jobs. Mexican workers, too, faced hostility and discrimination from the Anglo population of the region; but there were few efforts actually to exclude

them. Employers in the relatively underpopulated West needed this ready pool of low-paid, unskilled, and unorganized workers.

The "American Plan"

Whatever the weaknesses of the unions and of unorganized, unskilled workers, the strength of the corporations was the principal reason for the absence of effective labor organization. After the turmoil of 1919, corporate leaders worked hard to spread the doctrine that unionism was somehow subversive, that a crucial element of democratic capitalism was the protection of the open shop (a shop in which no worker could be required to join a union). The crusade for the open shop, euphemistically titled the "American Plan," received the endorsement of the National Association of Manufacturers in 1920 and became a pretext for a harsh campaign of union busting across the country.

When such tactics proved insufficient to counter union power, government assistance often made the difference. In 1921, the Supreme Court upheld a lower-court ruling that declared picketing illegal and supported the right of courts to issue injunctions against strikers. In 1922, the Justice Department intervened to quell a strike by 400,000 railroad workers. In 1924, the courts refused protection to members of the United Mine Workers Union when mine owners launched a violent campaign in western Pennsylvania to drive the union from the coal fields. As a result of these developments, union membership fell from more than 5 million in 1920 to under 3 million in 1929.

The Plight of the Farmer

Like industry, American agriculture in the 1920s was embracing new technologies for increasing production. The number of tractors on American farms, for example, quadrupled during the 1920s, helping to open 35 million new acres to cultivation. At the same time, agricultural production was increasing rapidly in other parts of the world as well. Unlike increased industrial production, increased agricultural production did not stimulate consumer demand. The result was overproduction, a disastrous decline in food prices, and a severe drop in income for farmers beginning early in the 1920s. In 1920, farm income had been 15 percent of the national total; by 1929, it was 9 percent. The average farmer made only about a quarter as much money each year in the 1920s as the average nonfarmer. More than 3 million people left agriculture altogether in the course of the decade. Of those who remained, many were forced into tenancy—los-

FARM TENANCY, 1910 AND 1930

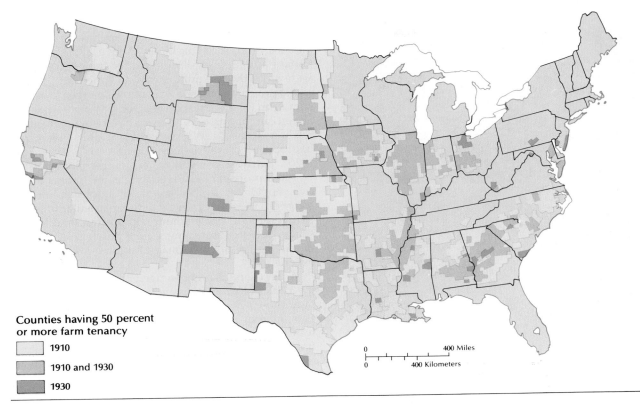

Counties having 50 percent or more farm tenancy

- 1910
- 1910 and 1930
- 1930

0 — 400 Miles
0 — 400 Kilometers

ing ownership of their lands and having to rent instead from banks or other landlords.

In response, some farmers began to demand relief in the form of government price supports. A few gravitated to such vaguely radical organizations as the Nonpartisan League of North Dakota or its successor, the Farmer-Labor Party, which established a foothold as well in Minnesota and other Midwestern states. Most farmers, however, were more moderate. Through such organizations as the American Farm Bureau Federation, they put increasing pressure on Congress (where farmers continued to enjoy disproportionately high representation). And while reform sentiment generally made little headway in the 1920s, farmers' organizational strength boosted the cause of agrarian reform.

One price-raising scheme in particular came to dominate agrarian demands: the idea of parity. "Parity" referred to a formula for guaranteeing farmers a fair price for their crops regardless of how national or international agricultural markets might fluctuate. In the 1920s, the formula was based on the average price of the crop during the half-decade preceding World War I (a good time for farmers) as compared with the general average of all prices during the same period. Champions of parity urged high tariffs against foreign agricultural goods and a government commitment to buy surplus domestic crops at parity and sell them abroad at whatever the market would bring.

The legislative expression of the demand for parity was the McNary-Haugen bill, named after its two principal sponsors in Congress and introduced repeatedly between 1924 and 1928. In 1926, Congress approved a bill requiring parity for grain, cotton, tobacco, and rice, but President Coolidge vetoed it. In 1928, it won congressional approval again, only to succumb to another presidential veto.

THE NEW CULTURE

The increasingly urban and consumer-oriented culture of the 1920s helped many Americans in all regions live their lives and perceive their world in increasingly similar ways. That same culture exposed them to a new

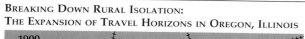

BREAKING DOWN RURAL ISOLATION:
THE EXPANSION OF TRAVEL HORIZONS IN OREGON, ILLINOIS

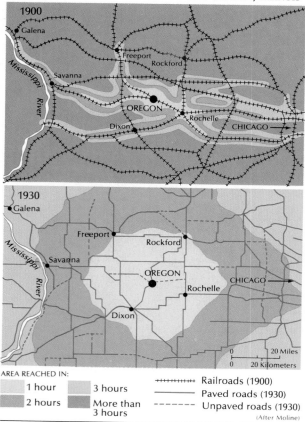

AREA REACHED IN:
1 hour
2 hours
3 hours
More than 3 hours

+++++++++ Railroads (1900)
————— Paved roads (1930)
- - - - - Unpaved roads (1930)

(After Moline)

set of values that reflected the prosperity and complexity of the modern economy. But the new culture could not, of course, erase the continuing, and indeed increasing, diversity of the United States. The relatively uniform mass culture reached Americans divided by region, race, religion, gender, and class, and those characteristics shaped the way individuals responded to national cultural messages.

Consumerism and Communications

Among the many changes industrialization produced in the United States was the creation of a mass consumer culture. By the 1920s, America was a society in which many men and women (although not, of course, all) could afford not merely the means of subsistence, but a considerable measure of additional, discretionary goods and services; a society in which people could buy items not just because of need but for pleasure. Middle-class families purchased such new appliances as electric refrigerators, washing machines, and vacuum cleaners. Men and women wore wristwatches and smoked cigarettes. Women purchased cosmetics and mass-produced fashions. Above all, Americans bought automobiles. By the end of the decade, there were more than 30 million cars on American roads.

No group was more aware of the emergence of consumerism (or more responsible for creating it) than the advertising industry. The first advertising and public relations firms (N. W. Ayer and J. Walter Thompson) had appeared well before World War I; but in the 1920s, partly as a result of techniques pioneered by wartime propaganda, advertising came of age. Publicists no longer simply conveyed information; they sought to identify products with a particular lifestyle, to invest them with glamour and prestige, and to persuade potential consumers that purchasing a commodity could be a personally fulfilling and enriching experience.

Advertisers also encouraged the public to absorb the values of promotion and salesmanship and to admire those who were effective "boosters" and publicists. One of the most successful books of the 1920s was *The Man Nobody Knows*, by advertising executive Bruce Barton. It portrayed Jesus Christ as not only a religious prophet but also a "super salesman," who "picked up twelve men from the bottom ranks of business and forged them into an organization that conquered the world." The parables, Barton claimed, were "the most powerful advertisements of all time." Barton's message was fully in tune with the new spirit of the consumer culture. Jesus had been a man concerned with living a full and rewarding life in this world; twentieth-century men and women should do the same. ("Life is meant to live and enjoy as you go along," Barton once wrote.) Jesus had succeeded because he knew how to make friends, to become popular, to please others; that talent was a prescription for success in the modern era as well.

The advertising industry could never have had the impact it did without the emergence of new vehicles of communication that made it possible to reach large audiences quickly and easily. Newspapers were being absorbed into national chains. New or expanded mass-circulation magazines—*Time, Reader's Digest,* the *Saturday Evening Post,* and others—attracted broad, national, audiences.

At the same time, movies were becoming an ever more popular and powerful form of mass communication. Over 100 million people saw films in 1930, as compared to 40 million in 1922. The addition of sound to motion pictures—beginning in 1927 with the first

THE NEW KITCHEN AND THE NEW WOMAN
Manufacturers attempted to associate their new consumer appliances with the elegant lifestyle of the affluent middle class. Advertisers tried to suggest that modern conveniences could liberate the "new woman" from the drudgery of housework and enable her to enter the glamorous world of society. *(Culver)*

feature-length "talkie," *The Jazz Singer*, with Al Jolson—created nationwide excitement. An embarrassing scandal in 1921 involving the popular comedian Fatty Arbuckle produced public outrage and political pressure to "clean up" Hollywood. In response, the film industry introduced "standards" to its films. Studio owners created the Motion Picture Association, a new trade association, and hired former postmaster general Will Hays to head it. More important, they gave Hays broad powers to review films and to ban anything likely to offend viewers (or politicians). Hays exercised his powers broadly and imposed on the film industry a safe, sanctimonious conformity for many years.

The most important communications vehicle was the only one truly new to the 1920s: radio. The first commercial radio station in America, KDKA in Pittsburgh, began broadcasting in 1920; and the first national radio network, the National Broadcasting Company, was formed in 1927. By 1923, there were more than 500 radio stations, covering virtually every area of the country; by 1929, more than 12 million families owned radio sets. The radio industry, too, feared government regulation and control; the national networks, and most radio stations, monitored program content carefully and excluded controversial or provocative material. But radio was much less centralized than filmmaking. Individual stations had considerable autonomy, and even carefully monitored stations and networks could not control the countless hours of programming as effectively as the Hays office could control films. Radio programming, therefore, was more diverse—and at times more controversial and even subversive—than film.

The influence of the consumer culture, and its increasing emphasis on immediate, personal fulfillment, was visible even in religion. Theological modernists—among them Harry Emerson Fosdick and A. C. McGiffert—taught their followers to abandon some of the traditional tenets of evangelical Christianity (literal interpretation of the Bible, belief in the Trinity, attribution of human traits to the deity) and to accept a faith that would help individuals to live more fulfilling lives in the present world.

Women and the New Culture

In the 1920s college-educated women were no longer pioneers. There were now two and even three generations of graduates of women's or coeducational colleges and universities; and some were making their presence felt in professional areas that in the past they had rarely penetrated. A substantial group of women now combined marriage and careers; 25 percent of all women workers in the 1920s were married. In the progressive era, middle-class women had usually had to choose between work and family. Still, professional opportunities for women remained limited by society's assumptions (assumptions prevalent among many women as well as among most men) about what were suitable female occupations. Although there were notable success stories about female business executives, journalists, doctors, and lawyers, most professional women remained confined to such traditionally "feminine" fields as fashion, education, social work, and nursing, or to the lower levels of business management. The "new professional woman" was a vivid and widely publicized image in the 1920s. In reality, however, most employed women were nonprofessional, lower-class workers. Middle-class married women, in the meantime, remained largely in the home.

Yet the 1920s constituted a new era for middle-class women nonetheless. In particular, the decade saw a redefinition of the idea of motherhood. Shortly after World War I, an influential group of psychologists—the "behaviorists," led by John B. Watson—began to challenge the long-held assumption that women had an instinctive capacity for motherhood. Maternal affection was not, they claimed, sufficient preparation for child rearing. Instead, mothers should rely on the

advice and assistance of experts and professionals: doctors, nurses, and trained educators in nursery schools and kindergartens.

For many middle-class women, these changes helped redefine what had been an all-consuming activity. Motherhood was no less important in behaviorist theory than it had been before; if anything it was more so. But for many women it was less emotionally fulfilling, less connected to their instinctive lives, more dependent on (and tied to) people and institutions outside the family. Many attempted to compensate by devoting new attention to their roles as wives and companions, to developing what became known as the "companionate marriage." The middle-class wife shared increasingly in her husband's social life; she devoted more attention to cosmetics and clothing; she was less willing to allow children to interfere with the development of the marital relationship. Most of all, many women now found support for thinking of their sexual relationships with their husbands not simply as a means of procreation, as earlier generations had been taught to do, but as an important and pleasurable experience in its own right, as the culmination of romantic love.

Progress in the development of birth control was both a cause and a result of this change. The pioneer of the American birth-control movement was Margaret Sanger, who had become committed to the cause in part because of the influence of Emma Goldman—a Russian immigrant and political radical who had agitated for birth control before World War I. Sanger began her career promoting the diaphragm and other birth-control devices out of a concern for working-class women, believing that large families were among the major causes of poverty and distress in poor communities. By the 1920s, partly because she had limited success in persuading working-class women to accept her teachings, she was becoming more concerned with persuading middle-class women of the benefits of birth control. Women, she argued, should be free to enjoy the pleasures of sexual activity without any connection to procreation. Birth-control devices began to find a large market among middle-class women, even though some techniques remained illegal in many states (and abortion remained illegal nearly everywhere).

The new, more secular view of womanhood had effects on women beyond the middle class as well. Some women concluded that in the "New Era" it was no longer necessary to maintain a rigid, Victorian female "respectability." They could smoke, drink, dance, wear seductive clothes and makeup, and attend lively parties. They could strive for physical and emotional fulfillment, for release from repression and inhibition.

ALICE PAUL
Alice Paul's National Woman's Party campaigned for, among other things, an Equal Rights Amendment to the Constitution. It provided a strong feminist voice during the years after the victory of the suffrage movement, when many women activists withdrew from politics, believing they had achieved their most important goals. Alice Paul is shown here, in April 1922, speaking to a radio audience about plans for the dedication of the new national headquarters of her party in Washington, D.C. *(UPI/Bettmann)*

(The wide popularity of Freudian ideas in the 1920s—often simplified and distorted for mass consumption—contributed to the growth of these impulses.)

Such assumptions became the basis of the "flapper"—the modern woman whose liberated lifestyle found expression in dress, hairstyle, speech, and behavior. The "flapper" lifestyle had a particular impact on lower-middle-class and working-class single women, who were flocking to new jobs in industry and the service sector. (The young "Bohemian" women most often associated with the "flapper" image were, in fact, imitating a style that emerged among this larger group.) At night, such women flocked to clubs and dance halls in search of excitement and companionship.

Despite all the changes, most women remained highly dependent on men—both in the workplace, where they were usually poorly paid, and in the home—and relatively powerless when men exploited that dependence. The realization that the "new woman" was as much myth as reality inspired some American feminists to continue their crusade for reform. The National Woman's Party, under the leadership of Alice Paul, pressed on with its campaign for the Equal Rights Amendment, although it found little support in Congress (and met continued resistance from other feminist groups). Nevertheless, women's organizations and female political activities grew in many ways in the 1920s. Responding to the suffrage victory, women organized the League of Women Voters and the women's auxiliaries of both the Democratic and Republican Parties. Female-dominated consumer groups grew rapidly and increased the range and energy of their efforts.

Women activists won a significant triumph in 1921, when they helped secure passage in Congress of a measure in keeping with the traditional feminist goal of securing "protective" legislation for women: the Sheppard-Towner Act. It provided federal funds to states to establish prenatal and child healthcare programs. From the start, however, the bill produced controversy. Alice Paul and her supporters opposed the measure, complaining that it classified all women as mothers. Margaret Sanger complained that the new programs would discourage birth-control efforts. More important, the American Medical Association fought Sheppard-Towner, warning that it would introduce untrained outsiders into the health-care field. In 1929, Congress terminated the program.

The demise of Sheppard-Towner illustrated the power of the medical profession. It also revealed how little woman suffrage had done to support the hopes of many of its supporters (and the fears of many of its foes). When Congress passed Sheppard-Towner in 1921, its members did so in part because they assumed the new female electorate would become a potent political force, generating substantial pressure on behalf of "female" issues. By 1929, it was clear that women voters changed electoral outcomes hardly at all; the female vote distributed itself almost precisely the same as the male vote. As a result, male politicians, in Congress and elsewhere, felt less concern about the consequences of opposing the demands of female reformers.

Education and Youth

The growing secularism of American culture and its expanding emphasis on training and expertise found reflection in the increasingly important role of education in the lives of American youth. The changes were evident in numerous ways. First, more people were going to school in the 1920s than ever before. High-school attendance more than doubled during the decade: from 2.2 million to over 5 million. Enrollment in colleges and universities increased threefold between 1900 and 1930, with much of that increase occurring after World War I. In 1918, there had been 600,000 college students; in 1930, there were 1.2 million, nearly 20 percent of the college-age population. Attendance was increasing as well at trade and vocational schools and in other institutions providing the specialized training that the modern economy demanded. Schools were also beginning to perform new and more varied functions. Instead of offering instruction only in the traditional disciplines, they were providing training in modern technical skills: engineering, management, economics.

The growing importance of education contributed to the emergence of a separate youth culture. The idea of adolescence as a distinct period in the life of an individual was for the most part new to the twentieth century. In some measure it was a result of the influence of Freudian psychology. But it was a result, too, of society's recognition that a more extended period of training and preparation was necessary before a young person was ready to move into the workplace. Schools and colleges provided adolescents with a setting in which they could develop their own social patterns, their own hobbies, their own interests and activities. An increasing number of students saw school as a place not just for academic training but for organized athletics, other extracurricular activities, clubs, and fraternities and sororities—that is, as an institution that allowed them to define themselves less in terms of their families and more in terms of their peer group.

The Decline of the "Self-Made Man"

The increasing importance of education and the changing nature of adolescence underscored one of the most important changes in American society: the gradual disappearance of the reality, and to some degree even of the ideal, of the "self-made man." The belief that any person could, simply through hard work and innate talent, achieve wealth and renown had always been largely a myth; but it had had enough basis in reality to remain a convincing myth for generations. The ideal of sturdy independence had long been central to the identities of many men, in particular.

Beginning in the late nineteenth century and accelerating in the early twentieth, it became more difficult to believe any longer that success was possible without education and training. "The self-made manager in business," wrote *Century Magazine* in 1925, "is nearing the end of his road. He cannot escape the relentless pursuit of the same forces that have eliminated self-made lawyers and doctors and admirals."

That sense of losing control, of becoming ever more dependent on rules and norms established by large, impersonal bureaucracies, created a crisis of self-identification among many American men. Robbed of the independence and control that had once defined "masculinity," many men looked for other means to do so. Theodore Roosevelt, for example, had glorified warfare and the "strenuous life" as a route to "manhood." Other men turned to fraternal societies, to athletics, and to other settings where they found confirmation of their masculinity.

The "Doom of the Self-Made Man," as *Century* described it, produced marked ambivalence. These mixed feelings were reflected in the identity of three men who became the most widely admired heroes of the New Era: Thomas Edison, the inventor of the electric light bulb and many other technological marvels; Henry Ford, the creator of the assembly line and one of the founders of the automobile industry; and Charles Lindbergh, the first aviator to make a solo flight across the Atlantic Ocean. All received the adulation of much of the American public. Lindbergh, in particular, became a national hero the like of which the country had never seen before.

The reasons for their popularity indicated much about how Americans viewed the new epoch in which they were living. On the one hand, all three men represented the triumphs of the modern technological and industrial society. On the other hand, all three had risen to success without the benefit of formal education and at least in part through their own efforts. They were, their admirers liked to believe, genuinely self-made men. Even many Americans who were happily embracing a new society and a new culture were doing so without entirely diverting their gaze from a simpler past.

The Disenchanted

The generation of artists and intellectuals coming of age in the 1920s found the new society in which they lived especially disturbing. Many were experiencing a disenchantment with modern America so fundamental that they were often able to view it only with contempt. As a result, they adopted a role sharply different from that of most intellectuals of most earlier eras. Rather than trying to influence and reform their society, they isolated themselves from it and embarked on a restless search for personal fulfillment. Gertrude Stein once referred to the young Americans emerging from World War I as a "Lost Generation." For some writers and intellectuals, at least, it was an apt description.

At the heart of the Lost Generation's critique of modern society was a sense of personal alienation, a belief that contemporary America no longer provided individuals with avenues by which they could achieve personal fulfillment. This disillusionment had its roots in many things, but in nothing so deeply as the experience of World War I. To those who had fought in the conflict, and even to many who had not, the aftermath of the war was shattering. The repudiation of Wilsonian idealism, the restoration of "business as usual," the growing emphasis on materialism and consumerism suggested that nothing had been gained. The war had been a fraud; the suffering and the dying had been in vain. Ernest Hemingway, one of the most celebrated (and most commercially successful) of the new breed of writers, expressed the generation's contempt for the war in his novel *A Farewell to Arms* (1929). Its protagonist, an American officer fighting in Europe, decides that there is no justification for his participation in the conflict and deserts the army with a nurse with whom he has fallen in love. Hemingway made it clear that the officer was to be admired for doing so.

But however disillusioning intellectuals found the war, they were equally disturbed by the character of American society in peacetime. To many, it was a society and culture utterly devoid of idealism or vision, steeped in outmoded and priggish morality, obsessed with materialism and consumerism, alienating and dehumanizing.

One result of this alienation was a series of savage critiques of modern society by a wide range of writers, some of whom were known as the "debunkers." Among them was the Baltimore journalist H. L. Mencken. His magazines—first the *Smart Set* and later the *American Mercury*—delighted in ridiculing everything most middle-class Americans held dear: religion, politics, the arts, even democracy itself. Mencken could not believe, he claimed, that "civilized life was possible under a democracy," because it was a form of government that placed power in the hands of the common people, whom he ridiculed as the "booboisie." When someone asked Mencken why he continued to live in a society he found so loathsome, he replied: "Why do people go to the zoo?" Echoing Mencken's contempt was the novelist Sinclair Lewis, the first American to win a Nobel Prize in literature. In a series of savage novels—*Main Street* (1920), *Babbitt* (1922), *Arrowsmith* (1925), and others—he lashed out at one aspect of modern society after another: the small town, the modern city, the medical profession, popular religion.

Intellectuals of the 1920s claimed to reject the "success ethic" that they believed dominated American life (even though many of them hoped for—and a few achieved—commercial and critical success). The novelist F. Scott Fitzgerald, for example, ridiculed the American obsession with material success in *The Great Gatsby* (1925). The novel's title character, Jay Gatsby, spends his life accumulating wealth and social prestige in order to win the woman he loves. The world to which he has aspired, however, turns out to be one of pretension, fraud, and cruelty, and it ultimately destroys him.

Some artists and intellectuals responded to their disillusionment by leaving America to live in France, making Paris for a time a center of American artistic life. Others moved to supposedly more isolated and "natural" communities in the American West; colonies of artists and writers settled in Taos and Santa Fe, New Mexico. Some adopted hedonistic lifestyles, involving drinking, drugs, casual sex, and wild parties. For most of these young men and women, however, the only real refuge from the travails of modern society was art. Only art, they argued, could allow them full individual expression; only the act of creation could offer them fulfillment.

The result of this quest for fulfillment through art was not, for the most part, personal satisfaction for the writers and artists involved. They did, however, produce a body of work that made the decade one of the great eras of American literature. The roster of important American writers who did significant work in the 1920s may have no equal in any other period: Hemingway, Fitzgerald, Lewis, Thomas Wolfe, John Dos Passos, Ezra Pound, T. S. Eliot, Gertrude Stein, Edna Ferber, Willa Cather, William Faulkner, Eugene O'Neill.

Not all intellectuals of the 1920s expressed alienation and despair. Some expressed reservations about their society not by withdrawing from it but by advocating reform. John Dewey, for example, kept alive the philosophical tradition of pragmatism and appealed for "practical" education and experimentation in social policy. Charles and Mary Beard, perhaps the most influential historians of their day, stressed economic factors in tracing the development of modern society and, like other progressive reformers, emphasized the clash of economic interests as central to American history.

To another group of intellectuals, the solution to contemporary problems lay neither in escapism nor in progressivism, but in an exploration of their own cultural or regional origins. In New York City, a new generation of black intellectuals created a flourishing African-American culture widely described as the "Harlem Renaissance." The Harlem poets, novelists, and artists drew heavily from their African roots in an effort to prove the richness of their own racial heritage (and not incidentally, to prove to whites that their race was worthy of respect). The poet Langston Hughes captured much of the spirit of the movement in a single sentence: "I am a Negro—and beautiful." Other black writers in Harlem and elsewhere—James Weldon Johnson, Countee Cullen, Zora Neale Hurston, Claude McKay, Alain Locke—as well as black artists and musicians helped establish a thriving culture rooted in the historical legacy of their people.

A strangely similar effort was under way among an influential group of white southern intellectuals. Known first as the "Fugitives" and later as the "Agrarians," these young poets, novelists, and critics sought to counter the depersonalization of industrial society by evoking the strong rural traditions of their own region. In their controversial manifesto *I'll Take My Stand* (1930), a collection of essays by twelve southern intellectuals, they issued a simultaneously radical and conservative appeal for a rejection of the doctrine of "economic progress" and the spiritual debilitation that had accompanied it. The supposedly "backward" South, they argued, could serve as a model for a nation drunk with visions of limitless growth and modernization.

A CONFLICT OF CULTURES

The modern, secular culture of the 1920s was not unchallenged. It grew up alongside older, more traditional cultures, with which it continually and often bitterly competed. The older cultures expressed the outlook of generally less affluent, less urban, more provincial Americans—men and women who continued to revere traditional values and customs and who feared and resented the modernist threats to their way of life. Their convictions and their fears resulted in a series of harsh cultural controversies.

Prohibition

When the prohibition of the sale and manufacture of alcohol went into effect in January 1920, it had the support of most members of the middle class and most of those who considered themselves progressives. Within a year, however, it had become clear that the "noble experiment," as its defenders called it, was not working well. Prohibition did substantially reduce drinking, at least in some regions of the country. But it also produced conspicuous and growing violations that made the law an almost immediate source of disillusionment and controversy.

The federal government hired only 1,500 agents to enforce the prohibition laws, and in many places they received little help from local police. Before long, it was almost as easy to acquire illegal alcohol in much of the country as it had once been to acquire legal alcohol. And since an enormous, lucrative industry was now barred to legitimate businessmen, organized crime figures took it over. In Chicago, Al Capone built a crimi-

nal empire based largely on illegal alcohol. He guarded it against interlopers with an army of as many as 1,000 gunmen, whose zealousness contributed to the violent deaths of more than 250 people in the city between 1920 and 1927. Other regions produced gangsters and gang wars of their own.

Many middle-class progressives who had originally supported prohibition soon soured on the experiment. But an enormous constituency of provincial, largely rural, Protestant Americans continued vehemently to defend it. To them, prohibition had always carried implications far beyond the issue of drinking itself. It represented the effort of an older America to maintain its dominance in a society in which they were becoming relatively less powerful. Drinking, which they associated with the modern city and with Catholic immigrants, became a symbol of the new culture they believed was displacing them.

As the decade proceeded, opponents of prohibition (or "wets," as they came to be known) gained steadily in influence. Not until 1933, however, when the Great Depression added weight to their appeals, were they finally able effectively to challenge the "drys" and win repeal of the Eighteenth Amendment.

Nativism and the Klan

Like prohibition (which was itself in part a result of old-stock Americans trying to discipline the new immigrant population), agitation for a curb on foreign immigration to the United States had begun in the nineteenth century; and like prohibition, it had gathered strength in the years before the war largely because of the support of middle-class progressives. Such concerns had not been sufficient in the first years of the century to win passage of curbs on immigration; but in the troubled and repressive years immediately following the war, many old-stock Americans began to associate immigration with radicalism. Sentiment on behalf of restriction grew rapidly as a result.

In 1921, Congress passed an emergency immigration act, establishing a quota system by which annual immigration from any country could not exceed 3 percent of the number of persons of that nationality who had been in the United States in 1910. The new law cut immigration from 800,000 to 300,000 in any single year, but the nativists remained unsatisfied and pushed for a harsher law. The National Origins Act of 1924 banned immigration from east Asia entirely. That provision deeply angered Japan, which understood that the Japanese were the principal target; Chinese immigration had been illegal since 1892. The law also reduced the quota for Europeans from 3 to 2 percent. The quota would be based, moreover, not on the 1910 census, but on the census of 1890, a year in which there had been many fewer southern and eastern Europeans in the country. What immigration there was, in other words, would heavily favor northwestern Europeans—people of "Nordic" or "Teutonic" stock. Five years later, a further restriction set a rigid limit of 150,000 immigrants a year. In the years that followed, immigration officials seldom permitted even half that number actually to enter the country.

TOTAL IMMIGRATION, 1920–1960

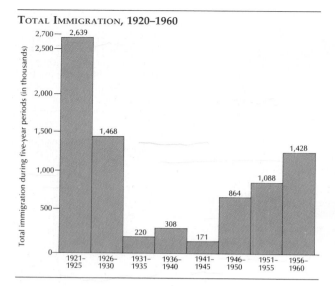

But the nativism of the 1920s extended well beyond restricting immigration. To defenders of an older, more homogeneous America, the growth of large communities of foreign peoples, alien in their speech, their habits, and their values, came to seem a direct threat to their own embattled way of life. Among other things, this provincial nativism helped instigate the rebirth of the Ku Klux Klan as a major force in American society.

The first Klan, founded during Reconstruction, had died in the 1870s. But in 1915, another group of white southerners met on Stone Mountain near Atlanta and established a modern version of the society. Nativist passions had swelled in Georgia and elsewhere in response to the case of Leo Frank, a Jewish factory manager in Atlanta convicted in 1914 (on very flimsy evidence) of murdering a female employee; a mob stormed Frank's jail and lynched him. The premiere (also in Atlanta) of D. W. Griffith's film *The Birth of a Nation*, which glorified the early Klan, also helped inspire white southerners to join a new one.

At first the new Klan, like the old, was largely concerned with intimidating blacks, who according to Klan leader William J. Simmons were becoming insubordinate. And at first it remained small, obscure, and almost entirely southern. After World War I, however, concern about blacks became secondary to concern about Catholics, Jews, and foreigners. The Klan, its organizers proclaimed, would devote itself to purging American life of impure, alien influences. At that point, membership in the Klan expanded rapidly and dramatically, not just in the small towns and rural ar-

eas of the South, but in industrial cities in the North and Midwest. Indiana had the largest membership of any state, and there were substantial Klans in Chicago, Detroit, and other northern industrial cities as well. The Klan was also strong in the West, with particularly large and active chapters in Oregon and Colorado. By 1923, there were reportedly 3 million members; by 1924, 4 million.

In some communities, where Klan leaders came from the most "respectable" segments of society, the organization operated much like a fraternal society, engaging in nothing more dangerous than occasional political pronouncements. Many Klan units (or "klaverns") tried to present themselves as patriots and defenders of morality. Many established women's and even children's auxiliaries to demonstrate their commitment to the family. Often, however, the Klan also operated as a brutal, even violent, opponent of "alien" groups and as a defender of traditional, fundamentalist morality. Some Klansmen systematically terrorized blacks, Jews, Catholics, and foreigners: boycotting their businesses, threatening their families, and attempting to drive them out of their communities. Occasionally, they resorted to violence: public whipping, tarring and feathering, arson, and lynching.

What the Klan feared, it soon became clear, was not simply "foreign" or "racially impure" groups; it was anyone who posed a challenge to "traditional values," as the Klan defined them. Klansmen persecuted not only immigrants and blacks but those white Protestants they considered guilty of irreligion, sexual promiscuity, or drunkenness. The Klan worked to en-

SOURCES OF IMMIGRATION, 1920–1960

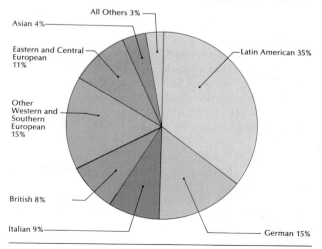

THE KU KLUX KLAN IN WASHINGTON, 1926
So powerful was the Ku Klux Klan in the mid-1920s that its members felt emboldened to march openly and defiantly down the streets of major cities—even down Pennsylvania Avenue in Washington, in the shadow of the Capitol of the United States. *(Culver)*

force prohibition; it attempted to institute compulsory Bible reading in schools; it worked to punish divorce. The Ku Klux Klan, in short, was fighting not just to preserve racial homogeneity but to defend its definition of a traditional culture against the values and morals of modernity.

It also provided its members, many of them people of modest means with little real power in society, with a sense of community and seeming authority. Its bizarre costumes, its elaborate rituals, its "secret" language, its burning crosses—all helped produce a sense of excitement and cohesion. For the many women who joined Klan auxiliaries, the organization served important social functions. The Klan was as committed to defending traditional gender roles as it was to defending white supremacy and Protestant morality, but women found in the Klan opportunities for activism and involvement within the confines of conventional female "spheres."

The organization itself declined quickly after 1925, when a series of internal power struggles and several sordid scandals discredited some of its most important leaders. The most damaging episode involved David

Stephenson, head of the Indiana Klan, who raped a young secretary, kidnapped her, and watched her die rather than call a doctor after she swallowed poison. The Klan staggered on in some areas into the 1930s, but by World War II it was effectively dead. (The postwar Ku Klux Klan, which still survives, is modeled on but has no direct connection to the Klan of the 1920s and 1930s.)

Religious Fundamentalism

Another cultural controversy of the 1920s was the result of a bitter conflict over the place of religion in contemporary society. By 1921, American Protestantism was already divided into two warring camps. On one side stood the modernists: mostly urban, middle-class people who had attempted to adapt religion to the teachings of modern science and to the realities of their modern, secular society. On the other side stood the defenders of traditional faith: provincial, largely (although not exclusively) rural men and women, fighting to maintain the centrality of religion in American life. They became known as "fundamentalists," a term

BRYAN AND DARROW IN DAYTON
Clarence Darrow (left) and William Jennings Bryan pose for photographers during the 1925 Scopes trial in Dayton, Tennessee. Both men are in shirtsleeves; Bryan is tieless and holding a fan—testimony to the intense heat that plagued the large crowd throughout the trial. *(Brown Brothers)*

derived from an influential set of pamphlets, *The Fundamentals*, published just before World War I. The fundamentalists were outraged at the abandonment of traditional beliefs in the face of scientific discoveries. They insisted the Bible was to be interpreted literally. Above all, they opposed the teachings of Charles Darwin, who had openly challenged the biblical story of the Creation. Human beings had not evolved from lower orders of animals, the fundamentalists insisted; they had been created by God, as described in *Genesis*.

Fundamentalism was a highly evangelical movement, interested in spreading the doctrine to new groups. Evangelists, among them the celebrated Billy Sunday, a former professional baseball player, traveled from state to state (particularly in the South and parts of the West) attracting huge crowds to their revival meetings. Protestant modernists looked on much of this activity with condescension and amusement. But by the mid-1920s, to their great alarm, evangelical fundamentalism was gaining political strength in some states with its demands for legislation to forbid the teaching of evolution in the public schools. In Tennessee in March 1925, the legislature actually adopted a measure making it illegal for any public school teacher "to teach any theory that denies the story of the divine creation of man as taught in the Bible."

The Tennessee law attracted the attention of the fledgling American Civil Liberties Union, which had been founded in 1920 by Jane Addams, Norman Thomas, Helen Keller, and others alarmed by the repressive legal and social climate of the war and its aftermath; they had felt the need for an organization to defend (among other things) freedom of speech and belief. The ACLU offered free counsel to any Tennessee educator willing to defy the law and become the defendant in a test case. A twenty-four-year-old biology teacher in the town of Dayton, John T. Scopes, agreed to have himself arrested. And when the ACLU decided to send the famous attorney Clarence Darrow to defend Scopes, the aging William Jennings Bryan (now an important fundamentalist spokesman) announced that he would travel to Dayton to assist the prosecution. Journalists from across the country, among them H. L. Mencken, flocked to Tennessee to cover the trial, which opened in an almost circuslike atmosphere. Scopes had, of course, clearly violated the law; and a verdict of guilty was a foregone conclusion, especially when the judge refused to permit "expert" testimony by evolution scholars. Scopes was fined $100, and the case was ultimately dismissed in a higher court because of a technicality. Nevertheless, Darrow scored an important victory for the modernists by calling Bryan himself to the stand to testify as an "expert on the Bible." In the course of the cross-examination, which was broadcast by radio to much of the nation, Darrow made Bryan's stubborn defense of biblical truths appear foolish and finally tricked him into admitting the possibility that not all religious dogma was subject to only one interpretation.

The Scopes trial was a traumatic experience for many fundamentalists. It isolated and ultimately excluded them from many mainstream Protestant denominations. It helped put an end to much of their political activism. But it did not, of course, change their religious convictions. Even without connection to traditional denominations, fundamentalists continued to congregate in independent churches or new denominations of their own.

The Democrats' Ordeal

The anguish of provincial Americans attempting to defend an embattled way of life proved particularly troubling to the Democratic Party, which suffered during the 1920s as a result of tensions between its urban and rural factions. More than the Republicans, the Democrats were a diverse coalition of interest groups, linked to the party more by local tradition than common commitment. Among those interest groups were prohibitionists, Klansmen, and fundamentalists on one side and Catholics, urban workers, and immigrants on the other.

In 1924, the tensions between them proved devastating. At the Democratic National Convention in New York that summer, bitter conflict broke out over the platform when the party's urban wing attempted to win approval of planks calling for the repeal of prohibition and a denunciation of the Klan. Both planks narrowly failed. More damaging to the party was a deadlock in the balloting for a presidential candidate. Urban Democrats supported Alfred E. Smith, the Irish Catholic Tammanyite who had risen to become a progressive governor of New York. Rural Democrats backed William McAdoo, Woodrow Wilson's Treasury secretary (and son-in-law), later to become a senator from California; he had skillfully positioned himself to win the support of southern and western delegates suspicious of Tammany Hall and modern urban life. The convention dragged on for 103 ballots, until finally, after both Smith and McAdoo withdrew, the party settled on a compromise: the bland corporate lawyer John W. Davis, who had served as solicitor general and ambassador to Britain under Wilson.

A similar schism plagued the Democrats again in 1928, when Al Smith finally secured his party's nomination for president after a much shorter and less acrimonious battle. Smith was not, however, able to unite his divided party—largely because of widespread anti-Catholic sentiment, especially in the South. He was the first Democrat since the Civil War not to carry the entire South. Elsewhere, although he did well in the large

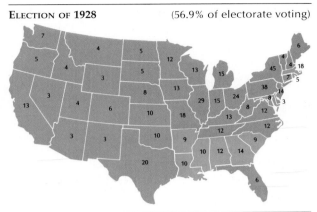

ELECTION OF **1928**   (56.9% of electorate voting)

	ELECTORAL VOTE	POPULAR VOTE (%)
Herbert Hoover (Republican)	444	21,391,381 (58.2)
Alfred E. Smith (Democratic)	87	15,016,443 (40.9)
Norman Thomas (Socialist)	—	267,835 (0.7)
Other parties (Socialist Workers, Prohibition)	—	62,890

cities, he carried no states at all except Massachusetts and Rhode Island. Smith's opponent, and the victor in the presidential election, was a man who perhaps more than any other contemporary politician seemed to personify the modern, prosperous, middle-class society of the New Era: Herbert Hoover. The business civilization of the 1920s, with its new institutions, fashions, and values, continued to arouse the animosity of large portions of the population; but the majority of the American people appeared to have accepted and approved it.

REPUBLICAN GOVERNMENT

For twelve years, beginning in 1921, both the presidency and the Congress rested securely in the hands of the Republican Party—a party in which the power of reformers had greatly dwindled since the heyday of progressivism before the war. For most of those years, the federal government enjoyed a warm and supportive relationship with the American business community. Yet the government of the New Era was more than the passive, pliant instrument that critics often described. It also attempted to serve as an active agent of economic change.

Harding and Coolidge

Nothing seemed more clearly to illustrate the unadventurous character of 1920s politics than the characters of the two men who served as president during most of the decade: Warren G. Harding and Calvin Coolidge.

Harding was elected to the presidency in 1920, having spent many years in public life doing little of note. An undistinguished senator from Ohio, he had received the Republican presidential nomination as a result of an agreement among leaders of his party who considered him, as one noted, a "good second-rater." Harding wanted to be a responsible president. He appointed capable men to the most important cabinet offices; he attempted to stabilize the nation's troubled foreign policy; and he displayed on occasion a vigorous humanity, as when he pardoned Socialist Eugene V. Debs in 1921. But even as he attempted to rise to his office, he seemed baffled by his responsibilities, as if he recognized his own unfitness. "I am a man of limited talents from a small town," he reportedly told friends on one occasion. "I don't seem to grasp that I am President." Unsurprisingly, perhaps, Harding soon found himself delegating much of his authority to oth-

ers: to members of his cabinet, to political cronies, to Congress, to party leaders.

Although Harding appointed several men of real distinction to his cabinet, he lacked the strength to abandon the party hacks who had helped create his political success. One of them, Harry Daugherty, the Ohio party boss principally responsible for his meteoric political ascent, he appointed attorney general. Another, New Mexico Senator Albert B. Fall, he made secretary of the interior. Members of the so-called Ohio Gang filled important offices throughout the administration. Unknown to the public (and perhaps also to Harding), Daugherty, Fall, and others were engaged in fraud and corruption, at least some of which gradually came to light.

The most spectacular scandal involved the rich naval oil reserves at Teapot Dome, Wyoming, and Elk Hills, California. At the urging of Albert Fall, Harding transferred control of those reserves from the Navy Department to the Interior Department. Fall then secretly leased them to two wealthy businessmen and received in return nearly half a million dollars in "loans" to ease his private financial troubles. Fall was ultimately convicted of bribery and sentenced to a year in prison; Harry Daugherty barely avoided a similar fate for his part in another scandal.

In the summer of 1923, only months before Senate investigations and press revelations brought the scandals to light, a tired and depressed Harding left Washington for a speaking tour in the West and a visit to

HARDING AND FRIENDS
President Warren G. Harding (center left, holding a rod) poses with companions during a fishing trip to Miami in 1921. He enjoyed these social and sporting events with wealthy friends and political cronies. Two of his companions here, Attorney General Harry Daugherty (to the left of Harding) and Interior Secretary Albert Fall (at far right) were later principal figures in the scandals that rocked the administration before and after Harding's death. *(UPI/Bettmann)*

Alaska. In Seattle late in July, he suffered severe pain, which his doctors wrongly diagnosed as food poisoning. A few days later, in San Francisco, he died: he had suffered two major heart attacks.

In many ways, Calvin Coolidge, who succeeded Harding in the presidency, was utterly different from his predecessor. Where Harding was genial, garrulous, and debauched, Coolidge was dour, silent, even puritanical. And while Harding was if not personally corrupt then at least tolerant of corruption in others, Coolidge seemed honest beyond reproach. In other ways, however, Harding and Coolidge were similar figures. Both took an essentially passive approach to the presidency.

Like Harding, Coolidge had risen to the presidency on the basis of few substantive accomplishments. Elected governor of Massachusetts in 1919, he had won national attention with his forceful, if laconic, response to the Boston police strike that year. That was enough to make him his party's vice presidential nominee in 1920. Three years later, after news of Harding's death reached him in Vermont, he took the oath of office from his father, a justice of the peace, by the light of a kerosene lamp on the kitchen table. It was the beginning of a skillful reinvention of Coolidge by party leaders and advisers from the advertising industry (among them Bruce Barton). For the next five years, Coolidge built a reputation as a simple man defending country virtues, even though in reality he was a thoroughly urban man of modern sensibilities.

If anything, Coolidge was an even less active president than Harding, partly as a result of his conviction that government should interfere as little as possible in the life of the nation (and, most importantly, in the life of its economy) and partly as a result of his own personal lassitude. He took long naps every afternoon. He kept official appointments to a minimum and engaged in little conversation with those who did manage to see him. He proposed no significant legislation and took little part in the running of the nation's foreign policy. "He aspired," wrote one of his contemporaries, "to become the least President the country ever had. He attained his desire."

In 1924, he received his party's presidential nomination virtually unopposed. Running against John W. Davis, the 1924 Democratic candidate, he won a com-

SIGNIFICANT EVENTS

1914–1920 Great Migration of black southerners into northern cities

1920 First commercial radio station, KDKA in Pittsburgh, begins broadcasting

Prohibition begins

Warren G. Harding elected president

1921 Sheppard-Towner Act funds maternity assistance

Nation experiences economic recession

1922 Sinclair Lewis publishes *Babbitt*

Motion Picture Association, under Will Hays, founded to regulate film industry

1923 Nation experiences mild recession

Harding dies; Calvin Coolidge becomes president

Teapot Dome and other scandals revealed

Ku Klux Klan reaches peak membership

1924 National Origins Act passed

Coolidge elected president

1925 Congress passes McNary-Haugen bill; Coolidge vetoes it

F. Scott Fitzgerald publishes *The Great Gatsby*

Scopes trial in Dayton, Tennessee

A. Philip Randolph founds Brotherhood of Sleeping Car Porters

1927 First feature-length sound motion picture, *The Jazz Singer*, released

Charles Lindbergh makes solo transatlantic flight

1928 Congress passes, and Coolidge vetoes, McNary-Haugen bill again

Herbert Hoover elected president

1929 Sheppard-Towner program terminated

Anti-Filipino riots in California

William Faulkner publishes *The Sound and the Fury*

fortable victory: 54 percent of the popular vote and 382 of the 531 electoral votes. Robert La Follette, the candidate of the reincarnated Progressive Party, received 16.8 percent of the popular vote but carried only his home state of Wisconsin. Coolidge probably could have won renomination and reelection in 1928. Instead, in characteristically laconic fashion, he walked into a press room one day and handed each reporter a slip of paper containing a single sentence: "I do not choose to run for president in 1928."

Government and Business

The story of Harding and Coolidge themselves, however, is only a part—and by no means the most important part—of the story of their administrations. However inept or inert the New Era presidents may have been, much of the federal government was working effectively and efficiently during the 1920s to adapt public policy to the widely accepted goal of the time: helping business and industry operate with maximum efficiency and productivity. The close relationship between the private sector and the federal government that had been forged during World War I continued, although in much altered form.

Secretary of the Treasury Andrew Mellon, the wealthy steel and aluminum tycoon, devoted himself to working for substantial reductions in taxes on corporate profits and personal incomes and inheritances. Largely because of his efforts, Congress cut them all by more than half. Mellon also worked closely with President Coolidge after 1924 on a series of measures to dramatically trim the already modest federal budget. The administration even managed to retire half the nation's World War I debt.

The most prominent member of the cabinet was Commerce Secretary Herbert Hoover, who considered himself, and was considered by others, a notable progressive. During his eight years in the Commerce Department, Hoover constantly encouraged voluntary cooperation in the private sector as the best avenue to stability. But the idea of voluntarism did not require the government to remain passive; on the contrary, Hoover believed public institutions had a duty to play an active role in creating the new, cooperative order. Above all, Hoover championed the concept of business associationalism, the creation of national organizations of businessmen in particular industries. Through these trade associations, Hoover believed, private entrepreneurs could stabilize their industries and promote efficiency in production and marketing. Hoover strongly resisted those who urged that the government sanction collusion among manufacturers to fix prices. But he did believe that shared information and limited cooperation would keep competition from becoming destructive and thus improve the strength of the economy as a whole.

The Supreme Court in the 1920s further confirmed the business orientation of the federal government, particularly after the appointment of William Howard Taft as chief justice in 1921. In one of the most important decisions in its history, *Lochner* v. *New York* (1905), the Court had struck down a New York law limiting the number of hours bakers in New York could be required to work. That law, the justices argued, was an abrogation of the freedom of workers and employers to form contracts; and with that decision, the Court set a nearly impossible standard against which all future economic regulations would have to be measured.

In the 1920s, continuing along the lines the *Lochner* decision had laid out, the Court struck down federal legislation regulating child labor (*Bailey* v. *Drexel Furniture Company*, 1922); nullified a minimum wage law for women in the District of Columbia (*Adkins* v. *Children's Hospital*, 1923); and sanctioned the creation of trade associations, ruling in *United States* v. *Maple Flooring Association* (1925) that such organizations did not violate antitrust statutes as long as some competition survived within an industry. Five years earlier, in *United States* v. *U.S. Steel*, the Court had applied the same doctrine to the monopolistic United States Steel Corporation; there was no illegal "restraint of trade," it ruled, as long as U.S. Steel continued to face any competition, no matter how slight.

The pro-business policies of the Republican administrations were not without their critics. In Congress, progressive reformers of the old school continued to criticize the monopolistic practices of big business, to attack government's alliance with the corporate community, and to decry social injustices. Occasionally, they were able to mobilize enough support to win congressional approval of progressive legislation, most notably the McNary-Haugen plan for farmers and an ambitious proposal to use federal funds to develop public electric power projects on the Tennessee River at Muscle Shoals. But the progressive reformers lacked the power to override the presidential vetoes that their bills almost always received.

Some progressives derived encouragement from the election of Herbert Hoover—widely regarded as the most progressive member of the Harding and Coolidge administrations—to the presidency in 1928. Hoover had easily defeated Alfred Smith, the Democratic candidate. And he entered office promising bold new efforts to solve the nation's remaining economic problems. But Hoover had few opportunities to prove himself. Less than a year after his inauguration, the nation plunged into the severest and most prolonged economic crisis in its history—a crisis that brought many of the optimistic assumptions of the New Era crashing down and launched the nation into a period of unprecedented social innovation and reform.

SUGGESTED READINGS

General Studies. Frederick Lewis Allen, *Only Yesterday* (1931). John Braeman, Robert Bremner, and David Brody, eds., *Change and Continuity in Twentieth Century America: The 1920s* (1968). Ellis Hawley, *The Great War and the Search for a Modern Order* (1979). John D. Hicks, *Republican Ascendancy* (1960). Isabel Leighton, ed., *The Aspirin Age* (1949). William E. Leuchtenburg, *The Perils of Prosperity* (rev. ed. 1994). Donald R. McCoy, *Coming of Age* (1973). Geoffrey Perrett, *America in the Twenties* (1982). Arthur M. Schlesinger, Jr., *The Crisis of the Old Order* (1957). George Soule, *Prosperity Decade: From War to Depression* (1947).

Labor, Agriculture, and Economic Growth. Guy Alchon, *The Invisible Hand of Planning: Capitalism, Social Science, and the State in the 1920s* (1985). Irving Bernstein, *The Lean Years: A History of the American Worker, 1920–1933* (1960). David Brody, *Steelworkers in America* (1960); *Workers in Industrial America* (1980). Alfred Chandler, *Strategy and Structure* (1962). Lisabeth Cohen, *Making a New Deal: Industrial Workers in Chicago, 1919–1939* (1990). Gilbert C. Fite, *George Peek and the Fight for Farm Parity* (1954); *American Farmers: The New Minority* (1981). Louis Galambos, *Competition and Cooperation* (1966). Louis Galambos and Joseph Pratt, *The Rise of the Cor-*

porate *Commonwealth: U.S. Business and Public Policy in the Twentieth Century* (1988). Peter Gottlieb, *Making Their Own Way: Southern Blacks' Migration to Pittsburgh, 1916–1930* (1987). Jim Potter, *The American Economy Between the Wars* (1974). Theodore Saloutos and John D. Hicks, *Twentieth Century Populism* (1951). George Soule, *Prosperity Decade* (1947). Mira Wilkins, *The Maturing of Multinational Enterprise: American Business Abroad from 1914 to 1970* (1974). Leslie Woodcock, *Wage-Earning Women* (1979). Gerald Zahavi, *Workers, Managers, and Welfare Capitalism* (1988). Robert Zieger, *Republicans and Labor* (1969).

The New Culture. Erik Barnouw, *A Tower in Babel: A History of American Radio to 1933* (1966). Daniel Boorstin, *The Americans: The Democratic Experience* (1973). Paul Carter, *The Twenties in America* (1968); *Another Part of the Twenties* (1977). Stanley Coben, *Rebellion Against Victorianism: The Impetus for Cultural Change in 1920s America* (1991). Ed Cray, *Chrome Colossus* (1980). Robert Creamer, *Babe* (1974). Kenneth S. Davis, *The Hero: Charles A. Lindbergh* (1959). Susan J. Douglas, *Inventing American Broadcasting* (1987). Ronald Edsforth, *Class Conflict and Cultural Consensus: The Making of a Mass Consumer Society: Flint, Michigan* (1987). Melvin Patrick Ely, *The Adventures of Amos 'n Andy: A Social History of an American Phenomenon* (1991). Stewart Ewen, *Captains of Consciousness* (1976). James J. Flink, *The Car Culture* (1975); *The Automobile Age* (1988). Stephen Fox, *The Mirror Makers: A History of American Advertising and Its Creators* (1984). Neal Gabler, *An Empire of Their Own: How the Jews Invented Hollywood* (1988). Harvey Green, *Fit for America* (1986). Allen Guttmann, *A Whole New Ball Game* (1988). Sumiko Higashi, *Virgins, Vamps, and Flappers: The American Silent Movie Heroine* (1978). Daniel Horowitz, *The Morality of Spending: Attitudes Toward the Consumer Society in America, 1875–1940* (1985). Robert Lynd and Helen Lynd, *Middletown* (1929). Roland Marchand, *Advertising the American Dream* (1985). Lary May, *Screening Out the Past* (1980). Fred J. McDonald, *Don't Touch That Dial* (1979). Zane Miller, *The Urbanization of America* (1973). Kathy H. Ogren, *The Jazz Revolution: Twenties America and the Meaning of Jazz* (1989). Kathy Peiss, *Cheap Amusements* (1986). Daniel Pope, *The Making of Modern Advertising* (1983). Randy Roberts, *Jack Dempsey, The Manassa Mauler* (1979). Philip T. Rosen, *The Modern Stentors: Radio Broadcasting and the Federal Government, 1920–1933* (1980). Joan Shelley Rubin, *The Making of Middlebrow Culture* (1992). Robert Sklar, *Movie-Made America* (1975). Susan Strasser, *Satisfaction Guaranteed: The Making of the American Mass Market* (1989). Bernard A. Weisberger, *The Dream Maker* (1979).

Women, Family, and Youth. W. Andrew Achenbaum, *Shades of Gray: Old Age, American Values, and Federal Policies Since 1920* (1983). Beth L. Bailey, *From Back Porch to Front Seat* (1988). Lois Banner, *American Beauty* (1983). Susan Porter Benson, *Counter Cultures* (1986). William H. Chafe, *The American Woman: Her Changing Social and Political Roles* (1972). Ellen Chesler, *Woman of Valor: Margaret Sanger and the Birth Control Movement in America* (1992). Howard P. Chudacoff, *How Old Are You? Age in American Culture* (1989). Nancy Cott, *The Grounding of American Feminism* (1987). Ruth Schwarz Cowan, *More Work for Mother* (1983). John D'Emilio and Estelle B. Friedman, *Intimate Matters: A History of Sexuality in America* (1988). Paula Fass, *The Damned and Beautiful* (1977). David H. Fischer, *Growing Old in America* (1977). Linda Gordon, *Woman's Body, Woman's Right* (1976). Helen Lefkowitz Horowitz, *Campus Life: Undergraduate Cultures from the End of the Eighteenth Century to the Present* (1987). Alice Kessler-Harris, *Out to Work: A History of Wage-Earning Women in America* (1982). J. Stanley Lemons, *The Woman Citizen: Social Feminism in the 1920s* (1973). Sheila Rothman, *Woman's Proper Place* (1978). Lois Scharf, *To Work and to Wed* (1980). Virginia Scharff, *Taking the Wheel* (1991). Susan Strasser, *Never Done: A History of American Housework* (1982). Winifred Wandersee, *Women's Work and Family Values, 1920–1940* (1981). Renold Wilk, *Henry Ford and Grass Roots America* (1972).

Intellectuals and the Arts. Charles C. Alexander, *Here the Country Lies: Nationalism and the Arts in Twentieth Century America* (1980). Houston Baker, Jr., *Modernism and the Harlem Renaissance* (1987). Loren Baritz, ed. , *The Culture of the Twenties* (1970). Cleanth Brooks, *William Faulkner: The Yoknapatawpha Country* (1963). Paul Conkin, *The Southern Agrarians* (1988). Malcolm Cowley, *Exiles Return* (1934). Robert Crunden, *From Self to Society: Transition in American Thought, 1919–1941* (1972). George H. Douglas, *H. L. Mencken* (1978). Frederick J. Hoffman, *The Twenties* (1949). Nathan I. Huggins, *Harlem Renaissance* (1971). Gloria T. Hull, *Color, Sex, and Poetry: Three Women Writers of the Harlem Renaissance* (1987). David L. Lewis, *When Harlem Was in Vogue* (1981). Roderick Nash, *The Nervous Generation: American Thought, 1917–1930* (1969). John Stewart, *The Burden of Time* (1965). Kenneth M. Wheeler and Virginia L. Lussier, eds., *Women, the Arts, and the 1920s in Paris and New York* (1982). Edmund Wilson, *The Twenties* (1975).

Cultural Conflicts. Charles C. Alexander, *The Ku Klux Klan in the Southwest* (1965). Paul Avrich, *Sacco and Vanzetti: The Anarchist Background* (1991). Herbert Asbury, *The Great Illusion* (1950). Kathleen M. Blee, *Women of the Klan: Racism and Gender in the 1920s* (1991). David Chalmers, *Hooded Americanism* (1965). Norman Clark, *Deliver Us from Evil* (1976). Elton C. Fax, *Garvey* (1972). Norman Furniss, *The Fundamentalist Controversy* (1954). Ray Ginger, *Six Days or Forever?* (1958). Joseph Gusfeld, *Symbolic Crusade* (1963). John Higham, *Strangers in the Land* (1963). Kenneth Jackson, *The Ku Klux Klan in the City* (1965). K. Austin Kerr, *Organized for Prohibition: A New History of the Anti-Saloon League* (1985). Don Kirschner, *City and Country: Rural Responses to Urbanization in the 1920s* (1970). Lawrence Levine, *Defender of the Faith, William Jennings Bryan: The Last Decade, 1915–1925* (1965). George M. Marsden, *Fundamentalism and American Culture* (1980). William G. McLoughlin, *Modern Revivalism* (1959). Leonard Moore, *Citizen Klansmen: The Ku Klux Klan in Indiana, 1921-1928* (1991). Andrew Sinclair, *The Era of Excess* (1962). Richard K. Tucker, *The Dragon and the Cross: The Rise and Fall of the Ku Klux Klan in Middle America* (1991). Theodore Vincent, *Black Power and the Garvey Movement* (1971).

Politics and Government. Kristi Andersen, *The Creation of a Democratic Majority, 1928–1936* (1979). LeRoy Ashby, *Spearless Leader* (1972). Christine Bolt, *American Indian Policy and American Reform* (1987). David Burner, *The Politics of Provincialism* (1967). David Burner, *Herbert Hoover* (1979). E. Paula Elder, *Governor Alfred E. Smith: The Politician as Reformer* (1983). Frank Freidel, *Franklin D. Roosevelt: The Ordeal* (1954); *Franklin D. Roosevelt: The Triumph* (1956). James N. Giglio, *H. M. Daugherty and the Politics of Expediency* (1978). James Gilbert, *Designing the Industrial State* (1972). Oscar Handlin, *Al Smith and His America* (1958). William Harbaugh, *Lawyer's Lawyer* (1973). Ellis Hawley, *Herbert Hoover as Secretary of Commerce: Studies in New Era Thought and Practice* (1974). Robert F. Himmelberg, *The Origins of the National Recovery Administration: Business, Government, and the Trade Association Issue, 1921–1933* (1976). Alan Lichtman, *Prejudice and the Old Politics* (1979). Richard Lowitt, *George W. Norris*, vol. 2 (1971). Donald R. McCoy, *Calvin Coolidge* (1967). Robert K. Murray, *The Politics of Normalcy* (1973); *The Harding Era* (1969). Burl Noggle, *Teapot Dome* (1962). Elisabeth Israels Perry, *Belle Moskowitz: Feminine Politics and the Exercise of Power in the Age of Alfred E. Smith* (1987). Francis Russell, *The Shadow of Blooming Grove* (1968). Andrew Sinclair, *The Available Man* (1965). David P. Thelen, *Robert M. La Follette and the Insurgent Spirit* (1978). George B. Tindall, *The Emergence of the New South* (1967). Eugene Trani and David Wilson, *The Presidency of Warren G. Harding* (1977). William Allen White, *A Puritan in Babylon* (1940). John Hoff Wilson, *Herbert Hoover: Forgotten Progressive* (1975).

DETAIL FROM *PRIVATE CAR* (1932), BY LECONTE STEWART
Thousands of men left their homes during the Great Depression and traveled from city to city
looking for work, often hopping freight trains for a free, if illegal, ride. *(Museum of Church
History & Art, Salt Lake City, Utah)*

CHAPTER TWENTY-FIVE

THE GREAT DEPRESSION

W E IN AMERICA TODAY," Herbert Hoover proclaimed in August 1928, not long before his election to the presidency, "are nearer to the final triumph over poverty than ever before in the history of any land. The poorhouse is vanishing from among us." Only fifteen months later those words would return to haunt him, as the nation plunged into the severest and most prolonged economic depression in its history—a depression that continued in one form or another for a full decade, not only in the United States but throughout much of the rest of the world. The Depression was a traumatic experience for individual Americans, who faced unemployment, the loss of land and other property, and in some cases homelessness and starvation. It also placed great strains on the political and social fabric of the nation.

THE COMING OF THE GREAT DEPRESSION

The sudden economic decline that began in 1929 came as an especially severe shock because it followed so closely a period in which the New Era seemed to be performing another series of economic miracles.

The Great Crash

In February 1928, stock prices began a steady rise that continued, with only a few temporary lapses, for a year and a half. Between May 1928 and September 1929, the average price of stocks increased over 40 percent. The stocks of the major industrials—the stocks that are used to determine the Dow Jones Industrial Average—doubled in value in that same period. Trading mushroomed from 2 or 3 million shares a day to over 5 million, and at times to as many as 10 or 12 million. There was, in short, a widespread speculative fever that grew steadily more intense, particularly once brokerage firms began encouraging the mania by recklessly offering easy credit to those buying stocks.

In the autumn of 1929, the market began to fall apart. On October 21 and again on October 23, there were alarming declines in stock prices, in both cases followed by temporary recoveries (the second of them engineered by J. P. Morgan and Company and other big bankers, who conspicuously bought up stocks to restore public confidence). But on October 29, "Black Tuesday," all efforts to save the market failed. Sixteen million shares of stock were traded; the industrial index dropped 43 points; stocks in many companies became virtually worthless. In the months that followed, the market continued to decline. It remained deeply depressed for more than four years and did not fully recover for over a decade.

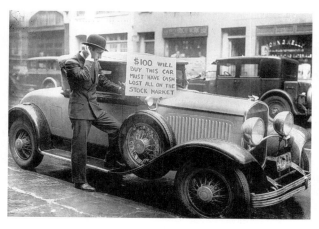

AFTERMATH OF THE CRASH
Walter Thornton, shown here in October 1929 next to an expensive roadster he had bought not long before, was one of many relatively affluent Americans who suffered substantial losses in the crash of the stock market in the fall of 1929. In popular mythology, many such people committed suicide in despair. In reality, almost no one did. Much more common were efforts such as this to sell off assets to make up for the losses. Thornton was more fortunate than many victims of the Depression. Most had few assets to sell. *(UPI/Bettmann)*

Popular folklore has established the stock market crash as the beginning, and even the cause, of the Great Depression. But although October 1929 might have been the first visible sign of the crisis, the Depression had earlier beginnings and more important causes.

Causes of the Depression

Economists, historians, and others have argued for decades about the causes of the Great Depression. But most agree on several things. They agree, first, that what is remarkable about the crisis is not that it occurred; periodic recessions are a normal feature of capitalist economies. What is remarkable is that it was so severe and that it lasted so long. The important question, therefore, is not so much why there was a depression, but why it was such a bad one. Most observers agree, too, that a number of different factors account for the severity of the crisis, even if there is considerable disagreement about which was the most important.

One of those factors was a lack of diversification in the American economy in the 1920s. Prosperity had depended excessively on a few basic industries, no-

tably construction and automobiles. In the late 1920s, those industries began to decline. Expenditures on construction fell from $11 billion to under $9 billion between 1926 and 1929. Automobile sales fell by more than a third in the first nine months of 1929. Newer industries were emerging to take up the slack—among them petroleum, chemicals, plastics, and others oriented toward the expanding market for consumer goods—but had not yet developed enough strength to compensate for the decline in other sectors.

A second important factor was the maldistribution of purchasing power and, as a result, a weakness in consumer demand. As industrial and agricultural production increased, the proportion of the profits going to farmers, workers, and other potential consumers was too small to create an adequate market for the goods the economy was producing. Demand was not keeping up with supply. Even in 1929, after nearly a decade of economic growth, more than half the families in America lived on the edge of or below the minimum subsistence level—too poor to buy the goods the industrial economy was producing.

As long as corporations had continued to expand their capital facilities (factories, warehouses, heavy equipment, and other investments), the economy had flourished. By 1929, however, capital investment had created more plant space than could profitably be used, and factories were producing more goods than consumers could purchase. Industries that were experiencing declining demand (construction, autos, coal, and others) began laying off workers, depleting mass purchasing power further. Even expanding industries often reduced their work forces because of new, less labor-intensive technologies; and in the sluggish economic atmosphere of 1929 and beyond, such workers had difficulty finding employment elsewhere.

A third major problem was the credit structure of the economy. Farmers were deeply in debt—their land mortgaged, crop prices too low to allow them to pay off what they owed. Small banks, especially those tied to the agricultural economy, were in constant trouble in the 1920s as their customers defaulted on loans; many of them failed. Large banks were in trouble too. Although most American bankers were very conservative, some of the nation's biggest banks were investing recklessly in the stock market or making unwise loans. When the stock market crashed, many of these banks suffered losses greater than they could absorb.

A fourth factor contributing to the coming of the Depression was America's position in international trade. Late in the 1920s, European demand for American goods began to decline. That was partly because European industry and agriculture were becoming more productive, and partly because some European

SELLING APPLES, NEW YORK CITY
In the fall of 1931 and again in the fall of 1932, large numbers of the unemployed took to selling apples on the streets of major cities and became in the process a popular symbol of the economic despair of those years. Herbert Hoover later wrote bitterly of the phenomenon: "One incident of these times has persisted as the eternal damnation of Hoover. Some Oregon or Washington growers' association shrewdly appraised the sympathy of the public for the unemployed. They set up a system of selling apples on the street corners in many cities, thus selling their crop and raising their prices. Many persons left their jobs for the more profitable one of selling apples. When any leftwinger wishes to indulge in scathing oratory, he demands, 'Do you want to return to selling apples?' " *(Culver)*

nations (most notably Germany, under the Weimar Republic) were having financial difficulties and could not afford to buy goods from overseas. But it was also because the European economy was being destabilized by the international debt structure that had emerged in the aftermath of World War I.

The international debt structure, therefore, was a fifth factor contributing to the Depression. When the war came to an end in 1918, all the European nations that had been allied with the United States owed large sums of money to American banks, sums much too large to be repaid out of their shattered economies. That was one reason why the Allies had insisted (over Woodrow Wilson's objections) on reparation payments from Germany and Austria. Reparations, they believed, would provide them with a way to pay off their own debts. But Germany and Austria were themselves in economic trouble after the war; they were no more able to pay the reparations than the Allies were able to pay their debts.

The American government refused to forgive or reduce the debts. Instead, American banks began making large loans to European governments, with which they paid off their earlier loans. Thus debts (and reparations) were being paid only by piling up new and greater debts. In the late 1920s, and particularly after the American economy began to weaken in 1929, the European nations found it much more difficult to borrow money from the United States. At the same time, high American protective tariffs were making it difficult for them to sell their goods in American markets. Without any source of foreign exchange with which to repay their loans, they began to default. The collapse of the international credit structure was one of the reasons the Depression spread to Europe (and grew much worse in America) after 1931.

Progress of the Depression

The stock market crash of 1929 did not so much cause the Depression, then, as help trigger a chain of events that exposed longstanding weaknesses in the American economy. During the next three years, the crisis steadily worsened.

A collapse of much of the banking system followed the stock market crash. Over 9,000 American banks either went bankrupt or closed their doors to avoid bankruptcy between 1930 and 1933. Depositors lost over $2.5 billion in deposits. Partly as a result of these banking closures, the nation's money supply greatly decreased. The total money supply, according to some measurements, fell by more than a third between 1930 and 1933. The declining money supply meant a decline in purchasing power, and thus deflation. Manufacturers and merchants began reducing prices, cutting back on production, and laying off workers.

Some economists argue that a severe depression could have been avoided if the Federal Reserve system had acted more responsibly. But the members of the Federal Reserve Board, concerned about protecting its own solvency in a dangerous economic environment, raised interest rates in 1931, which contracted the money supply even further.

The collapse was so rapid and so devastating that at the time it created only bewilderment among many of those who attempted to explain it. The American gross national product plummeted from over $104 billion in 1929 to $76.4 billion in 1932—a 25 percent decline in three years. In 1929, Americans had spent $16.2 billion in capital investment; in 1933, they invested only a third of a billion. The consumer price index declined 25 percent between 1929 and 1933, the wholesale price index 32 percent. Gross farm income dropped from $12 billion to $5 billion in four years. By 1932, according to the relatively crude estimates of the time, 25 percent of the American work force was unemployed (some believe the figure was even higher); another third of the work force experienced cuts in wages or hours or both. For the rest of the decade, unemployment averaged nearly 20 percent, never dropping below 15 percent.

THE AMERICAN PEOPLE IN HARD TIMES

Someone asked the British economist John Maynard Keynes in the 1930s whether he was aware of any historical era comparable to the Great Depression. "Yes," Keynes replied. "It was called the Dark Ages, and it lasted 400 years." The Depression did not last 400 years, but it did bring unprecedented despair to the economies of the United States and much of the Western world. And it had far-reaching effects on American society and culture.

Unemployment and Relief

The suffering extended into every area of society. In the industrial Northeast and Midwest, cities were becoming virtually paralyzed by unemployment. For example, Cleveland, Ohio, in 1932 had an unemployment rate of 50 percent; Akron, 60 percent; Toledo, 80 percent. Many industrial workers were accustomed to periods of unemployment, but no one was prepared for the scale and duration of the joblessness of the 1930s. Most Americans had been taught to believe that every individual was responsible for his or her own fate, that unemployment and poverty were signs of personal failure; and even in the face of national distress, many continued to believe it. Many adult men, in particular, felt deeply ashamed of their joblessness; the helplessness of unemployment was a challenge to traditional notions of masculinity. Unemployed workers walked through the streets day after day looking for jobs that did not exist. An increasing number of families were turning to state and local public relief systems, just to be able to eat. But that system, which in the 1920s had served only a small number of indigents, was totally unequipped to handle the new demands being placed on it. In many places, relief simply collapsed. Private charities attempted to supplement the public relief efforts, but the problem was far beyond their capabilities as well. State governments felt pressure to expand their own assistance to the unemployed; but tax revenues were declining along with everything else, and state leaders balked at placing additional strains on already tight budgets. Moreover, many public officials believed that an extensive welfare system would undermine the moral fiber of its clients.

As a result, American cities experienced scenes that a few years earlier would have seemed almost inconceivable. Bread lines stretched for blocks outside Red Cross and Salvation Army kitchens. Thousands of people sifted through garbage cans for scraps of food or waited outside restaurant kitchens in hopes of receiving plate scrapings. Nearly 2 million men, most of them young (and a much smaller number of women), simply took to the roads, riding freight trains from city to city, living as nomads.

In rural areas conditions were in many ways worse. Farm income declined by 60 percent between 1929 and 1932. A third of all American farmers lost their land.

SOUP KITCHEN IN CHICAGO
This soup kitchen offered free food and coffee to about 3,500 unemployed people a day in Chicago, one of many local efforts to deal with the ravages of the Depression. Unlike some such efforts, however, this one had substantial resources behind it. It was run by the famous Chicago gangster Al Capone. *(UPI/Bettmann)*

In addition, a large area of agricultural settlement in the Great Plains of the South and West was suffering from a catastrophic natural disaster: one of the worst droughts in the history of the nation. Beginning in 1930, a large area of the nation, which came to be known as the "Dust Bowl," stretching north from Texas into the Dakotas, began to experience a steady decline in rainfall and an accompanying increase in heat. The drought continued for a decade, turning what had once been fertile farm regions into virtual deserts. In Kansas, the soil in some places was completely without moisture as far as three feet below the surface. In Nebraska, Iowa, and other states, summer temperatures were averaging over 100 degrees. Swarms of grasshoppers were moving from region to region, devouring what meager crops farmers were able to raise, often even devouring fenceposts or clothes hanging out to dry. Great dust storms—"black blizzards," as they were called— swept across the plains, blotting out the sun and suffocating livestock as well as any people unfortunate or foolish enough to stay outside. (See "The American Environment," pp. 696–698.)

It is a measure of how productive American farmers were and how depressed the market for agricultural goods had become that even with these disastrous conditions, the farm economy continued through the 1930s to produce far more than American consumers could afford to buy. Farm prices fell so low that few growers any longer made any profit at all on their crops. As a result, many farmers, like many urban unemployed, left their homes in search of work. In the South, in particular, many dispossessed farmers—black and white—wandered from town to town, hoping to find jobs or handouts. Hundreds of thousands of families from the Dust Bowl (often known as "Okies," since many came from Oklahoma) traveled to California and other states, where they found conditions little better than those they had left. Owning no land of their own, many worked as agricultural migrants, traveling from farm to farm picking fruit and other crops at starvation wages.

Throughout the nation, problems of malnutrition and homelessness grew at an alarming rate. Hospitals pointed to a striking increase in deaths from starvation. On the outskirts of cities, large shantytowns sprang up in which families lived in makeshift shacks constructed of flattened tin cans, scraps of wood, abandoned crates, and other debris. Many homeless Americans simply kept moving—sleeping in freight cars, in city parks, in subways, or in unused sewer ducts.

African Americans and the Depression

African Americans for the most part had not shared very much in the prosperity of the previous decade. But the Depression was devastating for them nevertheless. They experienced more unemployment, home-

BLACK MIGRANTS
The Great Migration of blacks from the rural South into the cities had begun before World War I. But in the 1930s and 1940s the movement accelerated. Jacob Lawrence, an eminent black artist, created a series of paintings entitled, collectively, *The Migration of the Negro*, to illustrate this major event in the history of American blacks. *(Phillips Collection, Washington, D.C.)*

lessness, malnutrition, and disease than they had in the past, and considerably more than most whites.

As the Depression began, over half of all black Americans still lived in the South. Most were farmers. The collapse of prices for cotton and other staple crops left some with no income at all. Many left the land altogether—either by choice or forced by landlords who no longer found the sharecropping system profitable. Some migrated to southern cities. But unemployed whites in the urban South believed they had first claim to all work. Some of them now began to take positions as janitors, street cleaners, and domestic servants, displacing the blacks who formerly had occupied such jobs.

As the Depression deepened, whites in many southern cities began to demand that all blacks be dismissed from their jobs. In Atlanta in 1930, an organization calling itself the Black Shirts organized a campaign with the slogan "No Jobs for Niggers Until Every White Man Has a Job!" In other areas, whites used intimidation and violence to drive blacks from jobs. By 1932, over half the blacks in the South were without employment. And what limited relief there was went almost invariably to whites first.

Unsurprisingly, therefore, many black southerners—perhaps 400,000 in all—left the South in the 1930s and journeyed to the cities of the North. There they generally found less blatant discrimination. But conditions were in most respects little better than in the South. In New York, black unemployment was nearly 50 percent. In other cities, it was higher. Two million African Americans were on some form of relief by 1932.

Traditional patterns of segregation and disfranchisement in the South survived the Depression largely unchallenged. But a few particularly notorious examples of racism did attract national attention. The most celebrated was the Scottsboro case. In March 1931, nine black teenagers were taken off a freight train in Alabama (in a small town near Scottsboro) and arrested for vagrancy and disorder. Later, two white women who had also been riding the train accused them of rape. In fact, there was overwhelming evidence, medical and otherwise, that the women had not been raped at all; they may have made their accusations out of fear of being arrested themselves. Nevertheless, an all-white jury in Alabama quickly convicted all nine of the "Scottsboro boys" (as they were known to both friends and foes) and sentenced eight of them to death.

The Supreme Court overturned the convictions in 1932, and a series of new trials began that attracted increasing national attention. The International Labor Defense, an organization associated with the Communist Party, came to the aid of the accused youths and began to publicize the case. Later, the NAACP provided assistance as well. The trials continued throughout the 1930s. Although the white southern juries who sat on the case never acquitted any of the defendants, all of them eventually gained their freedom—four because the charges were dropped, four because of early paroles, and one because he escaped. But the last of the Scottsboro defendants did not leave prison until 1950.

The Depression was a time of important changes in the role and behavior of leading black organizations. The NAACP, for example, began to work diligently to win a position for blacks within the emerging labor movement, supporting the formation of the Congress of Industrial Organizations and helping to break down racial barriers within labor unions. Walter White, secretary of the NAACP, once even made a personal appearance at an auto plant to implore blacks not to work as strikebreakers. Partly as a result of such efforts, more than half a million blacks were able to join the labor movement. In the Steelworkers Union, for example, African Americans constituted about 20 percent of the membership.

Hispanics and Asians in Depression America

Similar patterns of discrimination confronted Mexicans and Mexican Americans. The Hispanic population of the United States had been growing steadily since early in the century, largely in California and other areas of the Southwest through massive immigration from Mexico (which was specifically excluded from the immigration restriction laws of the 1920s). In the 1930s, there were approximately 2 million Hispanics in the United States. Chicanos (as Mexican Americans are known) filled many of the same menial jobs in the West and elsewhere that blacks filled in other regions. Some farmed small, marginal tracts. Some became agricultural migrants, traveling from region to region harvesting fruit, lettuce, and other crops. But most lived in urban areas—in California, New Mexico, and Arizona, but also in Detroit, Chicago, New York, and other eastern industrial cities— and occupied the lower ranks of the unskilled labor force in such industries as steel, automobiles, and meatpacking. Even during the prosperous 1920s, theirs had been a precarious existence. The Depression made things significantly worse. As in the South, unemployed white Anglos in the Southwest demanded jobs held by Hispanics, jobs that the Anglos had previously considered beneath them. Thus Mexican unemployment rose quickly to levels far higher than those for Anglos. Some Mexicans were, in effect, forced to leave the country by officials who arbitrarily removed them from relief rolls or simply rounded them up and transported them across the border. Perhaps half a million Chicanos left the United States for Mexico in the first years of the Depression.

Those who remained faced persistent discrimination. Most relief programs excluded Mexicans from their rolls or offered them benefits far below those available to whites. Hispanics generally had no access to American schools. Many hospitals refused them admission. American blacks had established educational and social facilities of their own in response to discrimination, but Hispanics generally had fewer institutional supports. Some joined the American Communist Party. Some turned to the Mexican consulates or to the social and economic leaders of Mexican-American communities, but with little effect. Even many who possessed American citizenship found themselves treated like foreigners.

Occasionally, there were signs of organized resistance by Mexican Americans themselves, most notably in California, where some formed a union of migrant farmworkers. But harsh repression by local growers and the public authorities allied with them prevented such organizations from having much impact. Like African-American farm workers, many Hispanics began as a result to migrate to cities such as Los Angeles, where they lived in a poverty comparable to that of urban blacks in the South and Northeast.

For Asian Americans, too, the Depression reinforced longstanding patterns of discrimination and economic marginalization. In California, where the largest Japanese-American and Chinese-American populations were, even educated Asians had always found it difficult, if not impossible, to move into mainstream professions. Japanese-American college graduates often found themselves working in family fruit stands; 20 percent of all Nisei in Los Angeles worked at such stands at the end of the 1930s. For those who found jobs (usually poorly paid) in the industrial or service economy, employment was precarious; like blacks and Hispanics, they often lost jobs to white Americans desperate for work that a few years earlier they would not have considered. Japanese farmworkers, like Chicano farmworkers, suffered from the increasing competition for even these low-paying jobs from white migrants from the Great Plains.

In California, younger Nisei tried to challenge the obstacles facing them through politics. They organized Japanese American Democratic Clubs in several cities, which worked for, among other things, laws protecting racial and ethnic minorities from discrimination. At the same time, some Japanese-American businessmen and professionals tried to overcome obstacles by changing the Nisei themselves, by encouraging them to become more assimilated, more "American." They formed the Japanese American Citizens League in 1930 to promote their goals. By 1940, it had nearly 6,000 members.

Chinese Americans fared no better. The overwhelming majority continued to work in Chinese-owned laundries and restaurants. Those who moved outside the Asian community could rarely find jobs above the entry level. Chinese women, for example, might find work as stock girls in department stores, but almost never as salesclerks. Educated Chinese men and women could hope for virtually no professional opportunities outside the world of the Chinatowns.

Women and Families in the Great Depression

The economic crisis served in many ways to strengthen the widespread belief that a woman's proper place was in the home. Most men and many women believed that with employment so scarce, what work there was should go to men. There was a particularly strong belief that no woman whose husband was employed should accept a job. Indeed, from 1932 until 1937, it was illegal for more than one member of a family to hold a federal civil service job.

But the widespread assumption that married women, at least, should not work outside the home did not stop them from doing so. Both single and married women worked in the 1930s, despite public condemnation of the practice, because they or their families needed the money. In fact, the largest new group of female workers consisted of precisely those people who, according to popular attitudes, were supposed to be leaving the labor market: wives and mothers. By the end of the Depression, 25 percent more women were working than had been doing so at the beginning.

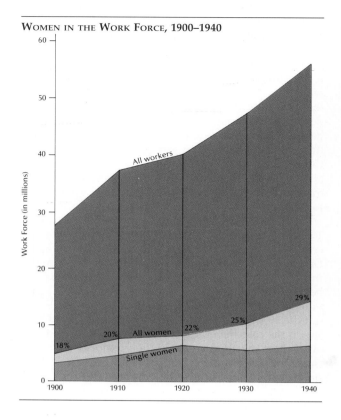

WOMEN IN THE WORK FORCE, 1900–1940

The increase occurred despite considerable obstacles. Professional opportunities for women declined because unemployed men began moving into professions such as teaching and social work that had previously been considered women's fields. Female industrial workers were more likely to be laid off or to experience wage reductions than their male counterparts. But white women also had certain advantages in the workplace. The nonprofessional jobs that women traditionally held—as salesclerks and stenographers, and in other service positions—were less likely to disappear than the predominantly male jobs in heavy industry. Nor were many men, even unemployed men, likely to ask for such jobs.

Black women, however, enjoyed few such advantages. Particularly in the South, they suffered massive unemployment because of a great reduction of domestic service jobs. As many as half of all black working women lost their jobs in the 1930s. Even so, at the end of the 1930s, 38 percent of black women were employed, as compared to 24 percent of white women. That was because black women—both married and unmarried—had always been more likely to work than white women, less out of preference than out of economic necessity.

For American feminists, the Depression years were, on the whole, a time of frustration. Although economic pressures pushed more women into the work force, those same pressures helped to erode the frail support that feminists had won in the 1920s for the idea of women becoming economically and professionally independent. In the difficult years of the 1930s, such aspirations seemed to many to be less important than dealing with economic hardship. The Depression saw the virtual extinction of the National Woman's Party, which had fought throughout the 1920s for the Equal Rights Amendment and other egalitarian goals. Even more moderate feminists, committed to "protective" legislation for women, saw their influence decline—although they did achieve some significant gains in the early years of the New Deal. (See pp. 721–722.) By the end of the 1930s, American feminism had reached its lowest ebb in nearly a century.

The economic hardships of the Depression years placed great strains on American families. Middle-class families that had become accustomed in the 1920s to a steadily rising standard of living now found themselves plunged suddenly into uncertainty, because of unemployment or the reduction of incomes among those who remained employed. Some working-class families, too, had achieved a precarious prosperity in the 1920s and saw their gains disappear in the 1930s.

Such circumstances forced many families to retreat from the consumer patterns they had developed in the 1920s. Women often returned to sewing clothes for themselves and their families and to preserving their own food rather than buying such products in stores. Others engaged in home businesses—taking in laundry, selling baked goods, accepting boarders. Many households expanded to include more distant relatives. Parents often moved in with their children and grandparents with their grandchildren, or vice versa.

But the Depression also eroded the strength of many family units. There was a decline in the divorce rate, but largely because divorce was now too expensive for some. More common was the informal breakup of families, particularly the desertion of families by unemployed men bent on escaping the humiliation of being unable to earn a living. The marriage and birth rates declined simultaneously for the first time since the early nineteenth century.

The Depression and Values

Prosperity and industrial growth had done much to shape American values in the 1920s. Mainstream culture, at least, had celebrated affluence and consumerism and had stressed the importance of personal gratification through both. Many Americans assumed, there-fore, that the experience of hard times would have profound effects on the nation's social values.

In general, however, American social values seemed to change relatively little in response to the Depression. Rather, many people responded to hard times by redoubling their commitment to familiar ideas and goals. The sociologists Robert and Helen Merrell Lynd, who had published a celebrated study of Muncie, Indiana, in 1929 (*Middletown*) returned there in the mid-1930s to see how the city had changed. They described their findings in their 1937 book, *Middletown in Transition,* and they concluded that in most respects "the texture of Middletown's culture has not changed. . . . Middletown is overwhelmingly living by the values by which it lived in 1925." Above all, the men and women of "Middletown"—and by implication many other Americans—remained committed to the traditional American emphasis on the individual.

No assumption would seem to have been more vulnerable to erosion during the Depression than the belief that the individual was in control of his or her own fate, that anyone displaying sufficient talent and industry could become a success. And in some respects, the economic crisis did work to undermine the traditional "success ethic" in America. Many people began to look to government for assistance; many blamed corporate moguls, international bankers, "economic royalists," and others for their distress. Yet the Depression did not, in the end, seriously erode the success ethic.

The survival of the ideals of work and individual advancement was evident in many ways, not least in the reactions of those most traumatized by the Depression: conscientious working people who suddenly found themselves without employment. Some expressed anger and struck out at the economic system. Many, however, seemed to blame themselves. Nothing so surprised foreign observers of America in the 1930s as the apparent passivity of the unemployed, many of whom were so ashamed of their joblessness that they refused to leave their homes. Perhaps that was why people who continued in the 1930s to work and to live more or less as they always had sometimes found it easy to forget that there was an economic crisis. The Depression was sometimes hard to see, because the unemployed tended to hide themselves, unwilling to display to the world what many of them considered their own personal failure.

At the same time, millions responded eagerly to reassurances that they could, through their own efforts, restore themselves to prosperity and success. Dale Carnegie's *How to Win Friends and Influence People* (1936), a self-help manual preaching individual initiative, was one of the best-selling books of the decade. Carnegie's message was not only that personal initiative was the route to success; it was also that the best way for people to make something of themselves was to adapt to the world in which they lived, to understand the values and expectations of others and mold themselves accordingly. The way to get ahead, Carnegie taught, was to fit in and make other people feel important. Similarly, Harry Emerson Fosdick, a Protestant theologian who preached the virtues of positive thinking and individual initiative, attracted large audiences with his radio addresses.

Not all Americans, of course, responded to the crisis of the Depression so self-reflectively. Many men and women believed that the economic problems of their time were the fault of society, not of individuals, and that some collective social response was necessary. Such beliefs found expression in, among other places, American artistic and intellectual life.

The Depression and the Arts

Just as many progressives had become alarmed when, early in the twentieth century, they "discovered" the existence of widespread poverty in the cities, so many Americans were shocked during the 1930s at their discovery of debilitating rural poverty. Perhaps most effective in conveying the dimensions of this poverty was a group of documentary photographers, many of them employed by the federal Farm Security Administration in the late 1930s, who traveled through the South recording the nature of agricultural life. Men such as Roy Stryker, Walker Evans, Arthur Rothstein, and Ben Shahn and women such as Margaret Bourke-White and Dorothea Lange produced memorable studies of farm families and their surroundings, studies designed to reveal the savage impact of a hostile environment on its victims.

Many writers, similarly, turned away from the personal concerns of the 1920s and devoted themselves to exposés of social injustice. Erskine Caldwell's *Tobacco Road* (1932), which later became a long-running play, was an exposé of poverty in the rural South. James Agee's *Let Us Now Praise Famous Men* (1941), with photographs by Walker Evans, was a careful, nonjudgmental description of the lives of three poor rural families in the South. Richard Wright, a major African American novelist, exposed the plight of residents of the urban ghetto in *Native Son* (1940). John Steinbeck's *The Grapes of Wrath* (1939) portrayed the trials of a migrant family in California, concluding with an open call for collective social action against injustice. John Dos Passos's trilogy *U.S.A.* (1930) attacked modern capitalism outright. Playwright Clifford Odets provided an explicit demonstration of the appeal of political radicalism in *Waiting for Lefty* (1935).

But the cultural products of the 1930s that attracted the widest popular audiences were those that diverted attention away from the Depression. The two most powerful instruments of popular culture in the 1930s—radio and the movies—provided mostly light and diverting entertainment. Although radio stations occasionally carried socially and politically provocative programs, the staple of broadcasting was escapism: comedies such as *Amos 'n Andy* (with its humorous but demeaning picture of urban blacks); adventures such as *Superman*, *Dick Tracy*, and *The Lone Ranger*; and other entertainment programs. Hollywood continued to exercise tight control over its products through its resilient censor Will Hays, who ensured that most movies carried only safe, conventional messages.

A few films, such as King Vidor's *Our Daily Bread* (1932) and John Ford's adaptation of *The Grapes of Wrath* (1940), did explore political themes. The director Frank Capra provided a muted social message in several of his comedies—*Mr. Deeds Goes to Town* (1936), *Mr. Smith Goes to Washington* (1939), and *Meet John Doe* (1941)—which celebrated the virtues of the small town and the decency of the common people in contrast to the selfish, corrupt values of the city and the urban rich. Gangster movies portrayed a dark, gritty, violent world with which few Americans were familiar; but their desperate stories were popular nevertheless with those engaged in their own difficult struggles. More often, however, the commercial films of the 1930s were deliberately and explicitly escapist: lavish musicals such as *Gold Diggers of 1933* (whose theme song was "We're in the Money"), "screwball" comedies such as Capra's *It Happened One Night* or the many films of the Marx Brothers—films designed to divert audiences from their troubles and, often, indulge their fantasies about quick and easy wealth.

Popular literature, similarly, offered Americans an escape from the Depression. Two of the best-selling novels of the decade were romantic sagas set in earlier eras: Margaret Mitchell's *Gone with the Wind* (1936) and Hervey Allen's *Anthony Adverse* (1933). Leading magazines, and particularly such popular new photographic journals as *Life*, focused mainly on fashions, stunts, and eye-catching scenery. Even the newsreels distributed to movie theaters across the country tended to give more attention to beauty contests and ship launchings than to the Depression itself.

The Allure of the Left

For a relatively small but important group of Americans—among them some intellectuals, artists, workers, African Americans, Mexican Americans, and others who became disenchanted for various reasons with the

THE JOAD FAMILY
John Steinbeck's 1939 novel *The Grapes of Wrath* was a notable exception to the generally escapist character of popular fiction in the 1930s. It portrayed the travails of the Joad family, who lost their farm in Oklahoma and traveled to California in search of opportunity. In 1940, director John Ford adapted the novel to film. In this still, the Joads sit around a table in their farmhouse shortly before leaving it for California. Tom Joad, played by Henry Fonda, sits to the left of the window, looking at his mother (standing), played by Jane Darwell.   *(Twentieth Century Fox)*

structure and values of the dominant culture—the Depression produced a commitment, for a time at least, to radical politics. Some became members of the American Communist Party, which achieved a size, visibility, and influence in the 1930s that it had never attained before and would never attain again. Others expressed sympathy for communist ideas without joining the party. By the standards of the rest of the world, radicalism in the United States remained relatively limited. By America's own modest standards, however, the 1930s to some degree deserved the label some commentators gave it: the "Red Decade."

For intellectuals, in particular, the left offered an escape from the lonely and difficult stance of detachment and alienation many had embraced in the 1920s. It combined a harsh critique of mainstream American society with an intense commitment to a political movement. The importance of the Spanish Civil War to many American intellectuals was a good example of how the left helped give meaning and purpose to individual lives. The battle against the Spanish fascists of Francisco Franco (who was receiving support from Hitler and Mussolini) attracted a substantial group of young Americans—more than 3,000 in all—who formed the Abraham Lincoln brigade and traveled to Spain to join in the fight. About a third of its members died in combat; but those who survived remembered the experience with pride, as one of the great moments of their lives. Ernest Hemingway, who spent time as a correspondent in Spain during the conflict, wrote in his novel *For Whom the Bell Tolls* (1940) of how the war provided those Americans who fought in it with "a part in something which you could believe in wholly and completely and in which you felt an absolute brotherhood with others who were engaged in it."

Instrumental in creating the Lincoln brigade, and directing many of its activities, was the American Communist Party. The party's membership peaked at perhaps 100,000 during its heyday in the mid-1930s; and for a time it presented itself as a genuinely American organization, no more threatening or alien than any other political organization. For several years beginning in 1935, the party dropped its insistence on working completely apart from other organizations and began to advocate a democratic alliance of all antifascist groups in the United States, a "Popular Front." It began to praise Franklin Roosevelt and John L. Lewis, a powerful (and strongly anticommunist) labor leader, and it adopted the slogan "Communism is twentieth-century Americanism."

The party was active in organizing the unemployed in the early 1930s and staged a hunger march in Washington, D.C., in 1931. Party members were among the most effective union organizers in some industries. And the party was virtually alone among political organizations in taking a firm stand in favor of racial justice; its active defense of the Scottsboro defendants was but one example of its efforts to ally itself with the aspirations of African Americans. It also helped organize a union of black sharecroppers in Alabama, which resisted—in several instances violently—efforts of white landowners and authorities to displace them from their farms.

But despite its efforts to appear a patriotic organization, the American Communist Party was always under the close and rigid supervision of the Soviet Union. Its leaders took their orders from the Comintern in Moscow. Most members obediently followed the "party line" (although there were many areas in which Communists were active for which there was no party line, areas in which members acted independently). The subordination of the party leadership to the Soviet Union was most clearly demonstrated in 1939, when Stalin signed a nonaggression pact with Nazi Germany. Moscow then sent orders to the American Communist Party to abandon the Popular Front and return to its old stance of harsh criticism of American liberals; and the leaders in the United States immediately obeyed—although thousands of disillusioned members left the party as a result.

The Socialist Party of America, now under the leadership of Norman Thomas, also cited the economic crisis as evidence of the failure of capitalism and sought vigorously to win public support for its own political program. Among other things, it attempted to mobilize support among the rural poor. The Southern Tenant Farmers Union, supported by the party and organized by a young socialist, H. L. Mitchell, attempted to create a biracial coalition of sharecroppers, tenant farmers, and others to demand economic reform. Neither the STFU nor the party itself, however, made any real progress toward establishing socialism as a major

force in American politics. By 1936, in fact, membership in the Socialist Party had fallen below 20,000.

At few times before (and few since) in American history did being part of the left seem so respectable and even conventional among workers, intellectuals, and others. Thus the 1930s witnessed an impressive, if temporary, widening of the ideological range of mainstream politics. But antiradicalism remained a powerful force in the 1930s, just as it had been during and after World War I and would be again in the 1940s and 1950s. Hostility toward the Communist Party, in particular, was intense at many levels of government. Congressional committees chaired by Hamilton Fish of New York and Martin Dies of Texas investigated communist influence wherever they could find it (or imagine it). State and local governments harried and sometimes imprisoned communist organizers. White southerners tried to drive communist organizers out of the countryside, just as growers in California and elsewhere tried (unsuccessfully) to keep communists from organizing Mexican-American and other workers. However strong the radical sentiments of the era, antiradical sentiments were stronger.

THE ORDEAL OF HERBERT HOOVER

Herbert Hoover entered the presidency in March 1929 believing, like most Americans, that the nation faced a bright and prosperous future. For the first six months of his administration, he attempted to expand the policies he had advocated during his eight years as secretary of commerce, policies that he believed would complete a stable system of cooperative individualism and sustain a successful economy. The economic crisis that began before the year was out forced the president to deal with a new set of problems; but for most of the rest of his term, he continued to rely on the principles that had always governed his public life.

The Hoover Program

Hoover's first response to the Depression was to attempt to restore public confidence in the economy. "The fundamental business of this country, that is, production and distribution of commodities," he said in 1930, "is on a sound and prosperous basis." Subsequently, he summoned leaders of business, labor, and agriculture to the White House and urged upon them a program of voluntary cooperation for recovery. He

HERBERT HOOVER RECEIVING A LOAD OF POTATOES
The Maine Potato Growers Association sent a team of oxen to Washington with a load of Maine potatoes in 1931. They presented them as a gift to President Hoover on the White House lawn on November 23, reminding him of the difficulties that faced the agricultural economy as the Great Depression worsened.   *(UPI/Bettmann)*

implored businessmen not to cut production or lay off workers; he talked labor leaders into forgoing demands for higher wages or better hours. But by mid-1931, economic conditions had deteriorated so much that this structure of voluntary cooperation collapsed. Frightened industrialists soon began cutting production, laying off workers, and slashing wages. Hoover was powerless to stop them.

Hoover also attempted to use government spending as a tool for fighting the Depression. Rejecting the demands of fiscal conservatives that the government balance its own budget whatever the cost, the president proposed to Congress an increase of $423 million —then a substantial sum—in federal public works programs, and he exhorted state and local governments to engage in the "energetic yet prudent pursuit" of public construction. But Hoover was not willing to spend enough money, or to spend it for a long enough time, to do any good; and while he was not as committed to a balanced budget as some of his advisers, he was not willing to tolerate deficits indefinitely. When economic conditions worsened, he became less willing to increase government spending, worrying instead about maintaining federal solvency. In 1932, at the depth of the Depression, he proposed a tax increase to help the government avoid a deficit.

Even before the stock market crash, Hoover had begun to construct a program to assist the troubled agri-cultural economy. In April 1929, he proposed the Agricultural Marketing Act, which established for the first time a government bureaucracy to help farmers maintain prices. A federally sponsored Farm Board would administer a budget of $500 million, from which it could make loans to national marketing cooperatives or establish corporations to buy surpluses and thus raise prices. At the same time, Hoover attempted to protect American farmers from international competition by raising agricultural tariffs. The Hawley-Smoot Tariff of 1930 contained protective increases on seventy-five farm products and raised rates to the highest point in American history—to an average of 50 percent on protected commodities.

Neither the Agricultural Marketing Act nor the Hawley-Smoot Tariff ultimately helped American farmers significantly. The Marketing Act relied on voluntary cooperation among farmers and gave the government no authority to do what the agricultural economy most badly needed: limit production. Hoover's call for a reduction of the wheat crop, for example, resulted in a drop in acreage of only 1 percent in Kansas. The Farm Board lacked sufficient funds to deal effectively with the crisis. Prices continued to fall despite its efforts. The Hawley-Smoot Tariff was an unqualified disaster—as 1,000 members of the American Economics Association had warned the president it would be even before he signed it. It provoked foreign governments to enact trade restrictions of their own in reprisal, further diminishing the market for American agricultural goods. And it raised rates on 925 manufactured goods, making industrial products more expensive for farmers to buy.

A Deepening Crisis

By the spring of 1931, Herbert Hoover's political position had deteriorated considerably. In the 1930 congressional elections, Democrats won control of the House and made substantial gains in the Senate. Many Americans held the president personally to blame for the crisis. Shantytowns established on the outskirts of cities were labeled "Hoovervilles," and the president became the target of cruel jokes and vicious attacks. Progressive reformers urged the president to support more vigorous programs of relief and public spending. Instead, Hoover seized on a slight improvement in economic conditions early in 1931 as proof that his policies were working.

The international financial panic of the spring of 1931 destroyed the illusion that the economic crisis was coming to an end. Throughout the 1920s, European nations had depended on loans from American banks to allow them to make payments on their debts. After 1929, when they could no longer get such loans, the financial fabric of several European nations began to unravel. In May 1931, the largest bank in Austria collapsed. Over the next several months, panic gripped the financial institutions of neighboring countries. European governments, desperate for sound assets, withdrew their gold reserves from American banks. European investors, in need of dollars to pay off their loans and protect their solvency, dumped their shares of American stocks onto the market, further depressing prices. Some European nations abandoned the gold standard and devalued their currencies, leaving the United States, which remained tied to gold, at a disadvantage in international trade. The American economy rapidly declined to new lows.

Hoover argued that the economic crisis in the United States was not the result of problems in the American economy but of the collapse of the European financial system. He proposed a moratorium on payment of war debts and reparations, and later on the payment of private debts as well. It was a sound proposal, but it was not enough to stop the downward slide.

By the time Congress convened in December 1931, conditions had grown so desperate that Hoover decided to support a series of measures to keep endangered banks afloat and protect homeowners from fore-closure on their mortgages. More important was a bill passed in January 1932 establishing the Reconstruction Finance Corporation (RFC), a government agency whose purpose was to provide federal loans to troubled banks, railroads, and other businesses. It even made funds available to local governments to support public works projects and assist relief efforts. Unlike some earlier Hoover programs, it operated on a large scale: in 1932, the RFC had a budget of $1.5 billion for public works alone.

Nevertheless, the new agency failed to deal directly or forcefully enough with the real problems of the economy to produce any significant recovery. Because the RFC was permitted to lend funds only to those financial institutions with sufficient collateral, much of its money went to large banks and corporations, prompting some critics to call it a "bread line for big business." And at Hoover's insistence, it helped finance only those public works projects that promised ultimately to pay for themselves (toll bridges, public housing, and others). Its chairman, the conservative Texas banker Jesse Jones, prided himself on the solvency of his agency and followed sound, prudent banking practices. This meant that the RFC itself remained healthy by refusing to make loans to those institutions that most desperately needed them. Above all, the RFC did not have enough money to make any real impact on the Depression; and it did not even spend all the money it had. Of the $300 million available to support local relief efforts, the RFC lent out only $30 million in 1932. Of its $1.5 billion public works budget, it released only about 20 percent.

Popular Protest

For the first several years of the Depression, most Americans were either too stunned or too confused to raise many effective protests. By the middle of 1932, however, radical and dissident voices were becoming loud and pervasive.

In the Midwest, farmers called for legislation similar to the McNary-Haugen bill of the 1920s by which the government would guarantee them a return on their crops at least equal to the cost of production. Lobbyists from the larger farm organizations pressured members of Congress to act, and some disgruntled farmers staged public protests in the capital. But neither the president nor Congress showed any signs of movement.

In the summer of 1932, a group of unhappy farm owners gathered in Des Moines, Iowa, to establish a new organization: the Farmers' Holiday Association, which endorsed the withholding of farm products

CLEARING OUT THE BONUS MARCHERS
In July 1932, President Hoover ordered the Washington, D.C., police to evict the Bonus Marchers from some of the public buildings and land they had been occupying. The result was a series of pitched battles (one of them visible here), in which both veterans and police sustained injuries. Such skirmishes persuaded Hoover to call out the army to finish the job. *(UPI/Bettmann)*

from the market—in effect a farmers' strike. The strike began in August in western Iowa, spread briefly to a few neighboring areas, and succeeded in blockading several markets; but in the end it dissolved in failure. The scope of the effort was too modest to affect farm prices, and in any case many farmers in the region refused to cooperate. After several violent clashes between strikers and local authorities, the organization's leader, Milo Reno, called off the strike. Nevertheless, the uprising created considerable consternation in state governments in the farm belt and even more in Washington, where the president and much of Congress were facing a national election.

A more celebrated protest movement emerged from a less likely quarter: American veterans. In 1924, Congress had approved the payment of a $1,000 bonus to all those who had served in World War I, the money to be distributed beginning in 1945. By 1932, however, many veterans were demanding that the bonus be paid immediately. Hoover, concerned about balancing the budget, refused to comply. In June, more than 20,000 veterans, members of the self-proclaimed "Bonus Expeditionary Force" (after the "American Expeditionary Force" of World War I, in which the veterans had served) marched into Washington, built crude camps around the city, and promised to stay until Congress approved legislation to pay the bonus. A few of the veterans departed in July, after Congress had voted down their proposal. Most, however, remained where they were.

Their continued presence in Washington was an embarrassment to Herbert Hoover. Finally, in mid-July, he ordered police to clear the marchers out of several abandoned federal buildings in which they had been staying. A few marchers threw rocks at the police, and someone opened fire; two veterans fell dead.

Hoover considered the incident evidence of dangerous radicalism, and ordered the U.S. Army to assist the police in clearing out the buildings.

General Douglas MacArthur, the army chief of staff, carried out the mission himself and greatly exceeded the president's orders. He led the Third Cavalry (under the command of George S. Patton), two infantry regiments, a machine-gun detachment, and six tanks down Pennsylvania Avenue in pursuit of the Bonus Army. By his side was his deputy, Dwight D. Eisenhower. The veterans fled in terror as the troops hurled tear gas canisters and flailed at them with their bayonets. MacArthur followed them across the Anacostia River, where he ordered the soldiers to burn their tent city to the ground. More than 100 marchers were injured. One baby died.

The incident served as perhaps the final blow to Hoover's already battered political standing. Many American newspapers (owned by conservative publishers) applauded the use of troops; but to much of the public, he now stood confirmed as an aloof and insensitive figure, locked in the White House, uncomprehending of the distress around him. Hoover's own cold and gloomy personality did nothing to change the public image, and some of his embattled statements at the time made his plight worse. "Nobody is actually starving," he assured reporters (inaccurately) in 1932. "The hoboes, for example, are better fed than they have ever been." The Great Engineer, the personification of the optimistic days of the 1920s, had become a symbol of the nation's failure to deal effectively with its startling reversal of fortune.

The Election of 1932

As the 1932 presidential election approached, few people doubted the outcome. The Republican Party dutifully renominated Herbert Hoover for a second term in office, but the lugubrious atmosphere of their convention made it clear that few delegates believed he could win. The Democrats, in the meantime, gathered jubilantly in Chicago to nominate the governor of New York, Franklin Delano Roosevelt.

Roosevelt had already been a well-known figure in the party for many years. A Hudson Valley aristocrat, a distant cousin of Theodore Roosevelt (a connection strengthened by his marriage in 1904 to the then-president's niece, Eleanor), and a handsome, charming young man, he had progressed rapidly: from a seat in the New York state legislature, to a position as assistant secretary of the navy under Woodrow Wilson during World War I, to his party's vice presidential nomination in 1920 on the ill-fated ticket with James M.

THE CHANGING OF THE GUARD
Long before the event actually occurred, Peter Arno of the *New Yorker* magazine drew this image of Franklin D. Roosevelt and Herbert Hoover traveling together to the Capitol for Roosevelt's inauguration. It predicted with remarkable accuracy the mood of the uncomfortable ride—Hoover glum and uncommunicative, Roosevelt buoyant and smiling. This was to have been the magazine's cover for the week of the inauguration, but after an attempted assassination of the president-elect several weeks earlier in Florida (in which the mayor of Chicago was killed), the editors decided to substitute a more subdued drawing. *(©1933, 1961 Peter Arno/Franklin D. Roosevelt Library)*

Cox. Less than a year later, he was stricken with polio. And while he was never again able to walk without the use of crutches and braces, he built up sufficient physical strength to return to politics in 1928. When Al Smith received the Democratic nomination for president that year, Roosevelt was elected to succeed him as governor. In 1930, he easily won reelection.

S I G N I F I C A N T   E V E N T S

1929 Stock market crash signals onset of Great Depression

Agricultural Marketing Act passed

1930 Hawley-Smoot Tariff enacted

Ten-year drought begins in South and Midwest (the Dust Bowl)

White workers in Atlanta organize Black Shirts to fight African-American competition for jobs

Nisei form Japanese-American Citizens' League

John Dos Passos publishes *U.S.A.* trilogy

1931 Federal Reserve raises interest rates

Depression spreads to Europe and deepens in United States

Scottsboro defendants arrested

Communist Party stages hunger march in Washington

1932 Erskine Caldwell publishes *Tobacco Road*

Glass-Steagall Banking Act passed

Reconstruction Finance Corporation established

Farm Holiday Association formed in Iowa

Bonus Marchers come to Washington, D.C.

Banking crisis

Franklin D. Roosevelt elected president

1934 Southern Tenant Farmers Union organized

1935 American Communist Party proclaims Popular Front

Race riot in Harlem

1936 Dale Carnegie publishes *How to Win Friends and Influence People*

Margaret Mitchell publishes *Gone with the Wind*

1939 John Steinbeck publishes *The Grapes of Wrath*

Nazi-Soviet pact weakens American Communist Party

1940 Richard Wright publishes *Native Son*

Ernest Hemingway publishes *For Whom the Bell Tolls*

1941 James Agee and Walker Evans publish *Let Us Now Praise Famous Men*

Roosevelt worked no miracles in New York, but he did initiate enough positive programs of government assistance to be able to present himself as a more energetic and imaginative leader than Hoover. Equally important, he avoided the inflammatory cultural issues (religion, race, prohibition) that had so divided the party in the 1920s. By emphasizing the economic grievances that most Democrats shared, he assembled a coalition within the party that enabled him to win his party's nomination. In a dramatic break with tradition, he flew to Chicago to address the convention in person and accept the nomination.

In the course of his acceptance speech, Roosevelt roused the delegates with his ringing promise: "I pledge you, I pledge myself, to a new deal for the American people," giving his program a name that would long endure. Neither then nor in the subsequent campaign, however, did Roosevelt give much indica-

tion of what that program would be. But Herbert Hoover's unpopularity virtually ensured Roosevelt's election; his main concern was to avoid offending voters unnecessarily.

There was, however, evidence of important differences between Roosevelt and Hoover. Drawing from the ideas of a talented team of university professors (whom the press quickly dubbed the "Brains Trust"), Roosevelt espoused an amalgam of ideas that combined old progressive reform principles with some of the newer ideas of associationalism that had gained currency in the 1920s. (He also called for a balanced budget and attacked Hoover for his failure to provide one.) Hoover liked to insist that the Depression was international in origin and that any attempt to combat it must be international as well. Roosevelt, in contrast, portrayed the crisis as a domestic (and Republican) problem and argued that the most important solutions

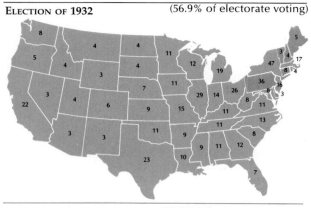

ELECTION OF 1932   (56.9% of electorate voting)

	ELECTORAL VOTE	POPULAR VOTE (%)
Franklin D. Roosevelt (Democratic)	472	22,821,857 (57.4)
Herbert Hoover (Republican)	59	15,761,841 (39.7)
Norman Thomas (Socialist)	—	881,951 (1.2)
Other candidates (Communist, Prohibition, Socialist Labor, Liberty)	—	271,355

could be found at home. Above all, perhaps, Roosevelt's style—his dazzling smile, his floppy broad-brimmed hat, his cigarette holder poised at a jaunty angle between his teeth, his skillful oratory, his lively wit—all combined to win him a wide personal popularity only vaguely related to the specifics of his programs.

In November, to the surprise of no one, Roosevelt won by a landslide. He received 57.4 percent of the popular vote to Hoover's 39.7. In the electoral college, the result was even more overwhelming. Hoover carried Pennsylvania, Connecticut, Vermont, New Hampshire, and Maine. Roosevelt won everything else. Democrats won majorities in both houses of Congress.

It was a broad and convincing mandate, but it was not yet clear what Roosevelt intended to do with it.

The Interregnum

The period between the election and the inauguration (which until the passage of the Twentieth Amendment to the Constitution in 1933 lasted more than four months) was a season of growing economic crisis. Presidents-elect traditionally do not involve themselves directly in government. But in a series of brittle exchanges with Roosevelt in the months following the election, Hoover tried to exact from the president-elect a pledge to maintain policies of economic orthodoxy. Roosevelt genially refused.

In February, only a month before the inauguration, a new crisis developed when the American banking system began to collapse. Public confidence in the banks was ebbing; depositors were withdrawing their money in panic; and one bank after another was closing its doors and declaring bankruptcy. In mid-February, the governor of Michigan, one of the states hardest hit by the panic, ordered all banks temporarily closed. Other states soon followed, and by the end of the month banking activity was restricted drastically in every state but one. Hoover again asked Roosevelt to give prompt public assurances that there would be no tinkering with the currency, no heavy borrowing, no unbalancing of the budget. "I realize," he wrote a Republican senator at the time, "that if these declarations be made by the president-elect, he will have ratified the whole major program of the Republican Administration." Roosevelt realized the same thing and again refused.

March 4, 1933, was, therefore, a day of both economic crisis and considerable personal bitterness. On that morning, Herbert Hoover, convinced that the United States was headed for disaster, rode glumly down Pennsylvania Avenue with a beaming, buoyant Franklin Roosevelt, who would shortly be sworn in as the thirty-second president of the United States.

SUGGESTED READINGS

The Coming of the Depression. Michael Bernstein, *The Great Depression: Delayed Recovery and Economic Change in America, 1929–1939* (1987). Lester V. Chandler, *America's Greatest Depression* (1970). Milton Friedman and Anna Schwartz, *The Great Contraction* (1965); or Chapter 7 of *A Monetary History of the United States* (1963). John Kenneth Galbraith, *The Great Crash* (1954). Susan E. Kennedy, *The Banking Crisis of 1933* (1973). Charles Kindelberger, *The World in Depression* (1973). Broadus Mitchell, *Depression Decade* (1947). Robert Sobel, *The Great Bull Market* (1968). Peter Temin, *Did Monetary Forces Cause the Great Depression?* (1976).

The Impact of the Depression.   Francisco Balerman, *In Defense of La Raza: The Los Angeles Mexican Consulate and the Mexican Community, 1929–1936* (1982). Ann Banks, ed., *First-Person America* (1980). Irving Bernstein, *The Lean Years* (1960). Caroline Bird, *The Invisible Scar* (1966). Glen H. Elder, Jr., *Children of the Great Depression* (1974). Federal Writers' Project, *These Are Our Lives* (1939). James N. Gregory, *American Exodus: The Dust Bowl Migration and Okie Culture in California* (1989). Abraham Hoffman, *Unwanted Mexican-Americans in the Great Depression* (1974). Richard Lowitt and Maurine Beasley, eds., *One-Third of a Nation: Lorena Hickock Reports the Great Depression* (1981). Robert S. McElvaine, ed., *Down and Out in the Great Depression: Letters from the Forgotten Man* (1983). William Mullins, *The Depression and the Urban West Coast, 1929–1933* (1991). Janet Poppendieck, *Breadlines Knee-Deep in Wheat: Food Assistance in the Great Depression* (1986). Arthur M. Schlesinger, Jr., *The Crisis of the Old Order* (1957). Walter Stein, *California and the Dust Bowl Migration* (1973). Bernard Sternsher, *Hitting Home: The Great Depression in Town and Country* (1970). Studs Terkel, *Hard Times* (1970). Tom Terrill and Jerrold Hirsch, *Such as Us: Southern Voices of the Thirties* (1978). Donald Worster, *Dust Bowl: The Southern Plains in the 1930s* (1979).

Depression-Era Culture and Society.   Charles C. Alexander, *Nationalism in American Thought, 1930–1945* (1969). Frederick Lewis Allen, *Since Yesterday* (1940). Andrew Bergman, *We're in the Money: Depression America and Its Films* (1971). Anthony Heilbut, *Exiled in Paradise: German Refugee Artists and Intellectuals in America from the 1930s to the Present* (1938). Richard Krickus, *Pursuing the American Dream* (1976). Robert Lynd and Helen Merrell Lynd, *Middletown in Transition* (1935). Alice Goldfarb Marquis, *Hopes and Ashes: The Birth of Modern Times, 1929–1939* (1986). Jeffrey Meikle, *Twentieth Century Limited: Industrial Design in America, 1925–1939* (1979). Gilbert Osofsky, *Harlem: The Making of a Ghetto* (1966). Gilman Ostrander, *American Civilization in the First Machine Age* (1970). David P. Peeler, *Hope Among Us Yet: Social Criticism and Social Thought in the Depression Years* (1987). Richard Pells, *Radical Visions and American Dreams: Culture and Social Thought in the Depression Years* (1973). Thomas Schatz, *The Genius of the System: Hollywood Film Making in the Studio Era* (1988). Ed Sikov, *Screwball: Hollywood's Madcap Romantic Comedies* (1989). Warren Susman, *Culture as History* (1984). (See Suggested Readings at the end of Chapter 26 for more literature on African Americans, Hispanic Americans, Asian Americans, Indians, and labor during the Depression.)

Women and the Depression.   Julia K. Blackwelder, *Women of the Depression: Caste and Culture in San Antonio, 1919–1939* (1984). William Chafe, *The American Woman* (1972). Joan Jensen and Lois Scharf, eds., *Decades of Discontent: The Women's Movement, 1920–1940* (1983). Marjorie Rosen, *Popcorn Venus: Women, Movies, and the American Dream* (1971). Vicki Ruiz, *Cannery Women, Cannery Lives: Mexican Women, Unionization, and the California Food Processing Industry, 1930–1950* (1987). Lois Scharf, *To Work and to Wed: Female Employment, Feminism, and the Great Depression* (1980). Susan Ware, *Holding Their Own: American Women in the 1930s* (1982). Jeane Westin, *Making Do: How Women Survived the '30s* (1976). Patricia Zavella, *Women's Work and Chicano Families* (1987).

The Hoover Presidency.   William J. Barber, *From New Era to New Deal: Herbert Hoover, The Economists, and American Economic Policy, 1921–1933* (1985). David Burner, *Herbert Hoover* (1978). Martin Fausold, *The Presidency of Herbert C. Hoover* (1985). Martin Fausold and George Mazuzun, eds., *The Hoover Presidency* (1974). Herbert Hoover, *The Great Depression* (1952). James S. Olsen, *Herbert Hoover and the Reconstruction Finance Corporation* (1977); *Saving Capitalism: The Reconstruction Finance Corporation and the New Deal, 1933–1940* (1988). Albert U. Romasco, *The Poverty of Abundance* (1965). Jordan Schwarz, *The Interregnum of Despair* (1970). Harris Warren, *Herbert Hoover and the Great Depression* (1959). Joan Hoff Wilson, *Herbert Hoover: Forgotten Progressive* (1975).

Politics and Protest.   David Burner, *The Politics of Provincialism* (1967). Roger Daniels, *The Bonus March* (1971). Frank Freidel, *The Triumph* (1956); *Launching the New Deal* (1973). Donald Grubbs, *Cry from the Cotton* (1971). Dorothy Healey and Maurice Isserman, *Dorothy Healey Remembers: A Life in the American Communist Party* (1990). Irving Howe and Lewis Coser, *The American Communist Party: A Critical History* (1957). Robin D. G. Kelley, *Hammer and Hoe: Alabama Communists During the Great Depression* (1990). Thomas Kessner, *Fiorello H. La Guardia and the Making of Modern New York* (1989). Harvey Klehr, *The Heyday of American Communism: The Depression Decade* (1984). Donald Lisio, *The President and Protest: Hoover, Conspiracy, and the Bonus Riot* (1974). Mark Naison, *Communistis in Harlem During the Depression* (1983). Eliot Rosen, *Hoover, Roosevelt, and the Brains Trust* (1977). Arthur M. Schlesinger, Jr., *The Crisis of the Old Order* (1957). John Shover, *Cornbelt Rebellion* (1965). Rexford G. Tugwell, *The Brains Trust* (1968).

THE AMERICAN ENVIRONMENT

DUST BOWL

THE DUST BOWL OF the 1930s was one of the great environmental disasters of American history. Although historians have often attributed it solely to an especially severe natural drought, it was in fact a much more complicated event that had as much to do with people as with nature.

The origins of the Dust Bowl stretched back more than half a century. As American settlers moved out onto the western plains after the Civil War, they encountered a more arid climate than any they had known in the East. Farming techniques that had been successful elsewhere failed as rain became scarcer. The biggest problem with the plains was the unreliability of rainfall from year to year: years of above-average rainfall alternated at unpredictable intervals with years of drought. The prosperity farmers enjoyed during good years encouraged them to hang on even if they might face economic ruin when the rains failed.

To deal with the problems of too little rain, farmers experimented with new ways of farming. By plowing the soil deeply, stirring up a fine layer of dust on the surface, and leaving fields bare to gather moisture when not being cropped, they sought to conserve water as best they could. At the same time, they grew less corn and introduced winter wheats from central Europe that were especially well adapted to dry conditions. These techniques worked well enough to encourage farmers to expand into new areas.

DUST STORM, SOUTHWEST PLAINS, 1937
The dust storms of the 1930s were a terrifying experience for all who lived through them. Appearing as a black wall sweeping in from the western horizon, such a storm engulfed farms and towns alike, blotting out the light of the sun and covering everything with fine dirt. *(UPI/Bettmann)*

THE AMERICAN ENVIRONMENT

The great period of expansion for plains farmers came during World War I. European demand and government subsidies sent the price of wheat soaring past $2 per bushel, and other grains rose as well. Farmers responded by planting as never before. By 1919, Colorado, Nebraska, Kansas, Oklahoma, and Texas had expanded their wheat acreage by 13.5 million acres—11 million of which had been covered with native grasses. To handle this vast new cropland, farmers invested in new mechanical equipment: disk plows, combines , and tractors. Tractors quickly replaced horses as the universal power source on Great Plains farms, and their total numbers grew accordingly. In 1915, there had been approximately 3,000 tractors in all of Kansas. Five years later, there were over 17,000, and by 1930 the number had risen to more than 66,000. More and more of the basic work of the farm was performed by internal combustion engines burning gasoline.

The new machinery enabled farm families to produce more grain per capita than ever before, but also exposed them to new risks. Equipment was expensive: a typical tractor in the 1920s cost several hundred dollars, and a typical combine two or three thousand. Most farmers financed such purchases with loans. They also planted larger acreages to take advantage of the new equipment, and incurred additional debts for their new land. Paying off debts was no problem during good years, but could become a nightmare if economic or climatic conditions became unfavorable. Unfortunately, both went bad at once during the 1920s.

By 1930, the world wheat market was in deep trouble, and farmers had no choice but to plant as many acres as possible in a desperate effort to earn enough to pay their debts. At the same time, rain failed up and down the plains. Starting in 1931, areas in the southern plains that ordinarily received eighteen inches of rain each year—the bare minimum for many types of farming—had annual deficits of three to seven inches. Crops died. The parched soil baked and cracked in the sun as thermometers rose above 100 degrees each day for weeks on end. Even many native grasses eventually succumbed. The region was entering its worst drought in recorded history, and it would be a decade before rainfall became abundant once again.

The drought of the 1930s was unprecedented not just in its severity, but also in its human costs. Never before had so many farmers carried so high a burden of debt. The collapse of crop prices meant that thousands of acres, now uncultivated, stood naked in the sun. The native grasses of the plains had once formed a tight natural sod that could withstand a drought even if many individual plants died. Now the sod was gone and nothing remained to protect soil from the wind.

Dust storms had been part of life on the plains for centuries, especially in western Kansas, Oklahoma, and the Texas panhandle, where the soil was sandy and especially susceptible to blowing. Now, however, they fueled themselves in a vicious cycle of ecological and economic disaster. A single famous storm in May 1934 carried 300 million tons of Great Plains soil all the way to the Atlantic Ocean, dropping dust in New York and Washington and even on ships 300 miles at sea. On the southern plains, such storms became a regular occurrence for the better part of the 1930s. They darkened the sky at midday, seeped dust into houses, blew drifts along fencerows, even killed animals and people who were unlucky enough to be caught in their midst. "Three little words," wrote a reporter for the Associated Press in 1935, "achingly familiar on a Western farmer's tongue—rule life today in the dust bowl of the continent. . . . If it rains." And so the southern plains gained a new name: Dust Bowl.

THE AMERICAN ENVIRONMENT

CONTOUR PLOWING
Farmers responded to the dust storms by adopting new cultivation practices designed to prevent soil from blowing away in the wind. Among the most important techniques was contour plowing, which raised furrows in the soil to break the wind's velocity as it moved across the surface. Contour plowing also discouraged water erosion. *(Bettmann)*

There were 22 dust storms in 1934, 40 in 1935, 68 in 1936, 72 in 1937, 61 in 1938, 30 in 1939, and 17 each in 1940 and 1941. Unplanted soil made conditions perfect for dust storms when the drought finally hit, and the combined force of economic depression and too little rain left farmers with few defenses once the cycle got going. Many families eventually abandoned their farms and took to the road, becoming the "Okies" who migrated to California in search of a better life. A number of New Deal agencies stepped in to try to help with a variety of programs. The Resettlement Administration sought to buy up farms on soils that were too marginal for safe agricultural production. The Forest Service planted over 200 million trees as "shelter belts" designed to slow the dusty winds. And the Soil Conservation Service promoted new forms of tillage that held the soil better.

All these things helped, but it was not until 1941, when the rains returned in earnest and World War II began to generate massive new demand for crops, that the Dust Bowl came to an end. New farming techniques, including irrigation systems that tapped underground water supplies, have prevented the return of dust storms on anything like the scale of the 1930s, though lesser storms have from time to time blown through the region. Whether they return in the future depends on whether farmers remember the lessons of the Dust Bowl and adapt their methods to the special needs of their land.

WPA Poster, 1930s

The Works Progress Administration, which this striking poster celebrates, was the New Deal's most prominent experiment in work relief. In addition to providing jobs for unemployed farmers and industrial workers (as depicted here), it created programs to assist writers, artists, actors, and others. *(Library of Congress)*

CHAPTER TWENTY-SIX

THE NEW DEAL

F RANKLIN ROOSEVELT SERVED LONGER as president than anyone else before or since, and during his twelve years in office he became more central to the life of the nation than any chief executive before him. Most important, his administration constructed a series of programs that permanently altered the federal government and its relationship to society.

By the end of the 1930s, the New Deal (as the Roosevelt program was called) had created many of the broad outlines of the political world we know today. It had constructed the foundations of the federal welfare system. It had extended national regulation over new areas of the economy. It had presided over the birth of the modern labor movement. It had made the government a major force in the agricultural economy. It had created a powerful coalition within the Democratic Party that would dominate American politics for most of the next thirty years. And it had produced the beginnings of a new liberal ideology that would govern reform efforts for several decades after the war.

One thing the New Deal had not done, however, was end the Great Depression. It had helped stop the disastrous downward spiral in 1933, and there had been a limited, if erratic, recovery in some areas after that. But by the end of 1939, many of the basic problems of the Depression remained unsolved. An estimated 15 percent of the work force remained unemployed. The gross national product was no larger than it had been ten years before.

LAUNCHING THE NEW DEAL

Roosevelt's first task upon taking office was to alleviate the panic that was threatening to create chaos in the financial system. He did so in part by force of personality and in part by constructing very rapidly an ambitious and diverse program of legislation.

Restoring Confidence

Much of Roosevelt's success was a result of his ebullient personality. Beginning with his inaugural address—in which he assured the American people that "the only thing we have to fear is fear itself"—he projected an infectious optimism that helped alleviate the growing despair. He was the first president to make regular use of the radio, and his friendly "fireside chats," during which he explained his programs and plans to the people, helped build public confidence in the administration. Roosevelt held frequent informal press conferences and won the respect and the friendship of most reporters. Their regard for him was such that by unwritten agreement, no journalist ever photographed the president getting into or out of his car or being wheeled in his wheelchair. Much of the American public remained unaware throughout the Roosevelt years that the president's legs were completely paralyzed.

THE RADIO PRESIDENT
Franklin D. Roosevelt was the first American president to master the use of radio. Beginning in his first days in office, he regularly bypassed the newspapers (many of which were hostile to him) and communicated directly with the people through his famous "Fireside Chats." He is shown here speaking in 1938, urging communities to continue to provide relief work for the unemployed. *(Franklin D. Roosevelt Library)*

But Roosevelt could not rely on image alone. On March 6, two days after taking office, he issued a proclamation closing all American banks for four days until Congress could meet in special session to consider banking-reform legislation. So great was the panic about bank failures that the "bank holiday," as the president euphemistically described it, created a general sense of relief. Three days later, Roosevelt sent to Congress the Emergency Banking Act, a generally conservative bill (much of it drafted by holdovers from the Hoover administration) designed primarily to protect the larger banks from being dragged down by the weakness of smaller ones. The bill provided for Treasury Department inspection of all banks before they would be allowed to reopen, for federal assistance to some troubled institutions, and for a thorough reorganization of those in the greatest difficulty. A confused and frightened Congress passed the bill within four hours of its introduction. "I can assure you," Roosevelt told the public on March 12, in his first fireside chat, "that it is safer to keep your money in a reopened bank than under the mattress." Whatever else the new law accomplished, it helped dispel the panic. Three quarters of the banks in the Federal Reserve system reopened within the next three days, and $1 billion in hoarded currency and gold flowed back into them within a month. The immediate banking crisis was over.

On the morning after passage of the Emergency Banking Act, Roosevelt sent to Congress another measure—the Economy Act—designed to convince fiscally conservative Americans (and especially the business community) that the federal government was in safe, responsible hands. The act proposed to balance the federal budget by cutting the salaries of government employees and reducing pensions to veterans by as much as 15 percent. Otherwise, the president warned, the nation faced a $1 billion deficit. Like the banking bill, this one passed through Congress almost instantly—despite heated protests from some congressional progressives.

Roosevelt also moved in his first days in office to put to rest one of the divisive issues of the 1920s. He supported and then signed a bill to legalize the manufacture and sale of beer with a 3.2 percent alcohol content—an interim measure pending the repeal of prohibition, for which a constitutional amendment (the Twenty-first) was already in process. The amendment was ratified later in 1933.

Agricultural Adjustment

These initial actions were largely stopgaps, to buy time for more comprehensive measures. The first such program was the Agricultural Adjustment Act, which Congress passed in May 1933. It reflected the demands of various farm organizations and the ideas of Henry A. Wallace, Roosevelt's secretary of agriculture, and it included scraps and reworkings of many long-cherished agricultural schemes (including McNary-Haugen). But its most important feature was its provision for reducing crop production to end agricultural surpluses and halt the downward spiral of farm prices.

Under the "domestic allotment" system of the act, producers of seven basic commodities (wheat, cotton, corn, hogs, rice, tobacco, and dairy products) would decide on production limits for their crops. The government, through the Agricultural Adjustment Administration (AAA), would then tell individual farmers how much they should plant and pay them subsidies for leaving some of their land idle. A tax on food processing (for example, the milling of wheat) would provide the funds for the new payments. Farm prices were to be subsidized up to the point of parity.

Because the 1933 agricultural season was already under way by the time the AAA began operations, the agency oversaw a large-scale destruction of existing crops and livestock to reduce surpluses. Six million pigs and 220,000 sows were slaughtered. Cotton farmers plowed under a quarter of their crop. In a society plagued by want, in which many families were suffering from malnutrition and starvation, it was difficult for the government to explain the need for destroying surpluses, and the crop and livestock destruction remained controversial for many years. Beginning in 1934, however, the government used less provocative methods for limiting crop and livestock production.

The results of the AAA efforts were in many ways heartening. Prices for farm commodities did indeed rise in the years after 1933, and gross farm income increased by half in the first three years of the New Deal. The agricultural economy as a whole emerged from the 1930s stabler and more prosperous than it had been in many years. The AAA did, however, tend to favor larger farmers over smaller ones, particularly since local administration of its programs often fell into the hands of the most powerful producers in a community. New Deal farm programs actually dispossessed some struggling farmers, even if unintentionally. In the cotton belt, for example, planters who were reducing their acreage evicted tenants and sharecroppers and fired many field hands.

In January 1936, the Supreme Court struck down the crucial provisions of the Agricultural Adjustment Act, arguing that the government had no constitutional authority to require farmers to limit production. But within a few weeks the administration had secured passage of new legislation (the Soil Conservation and Domestic Allotment Act), which survived judicial scrutiny. It permitted the government to pay farmers to reduce production so as to "conserve soil," prevent erosion, and accomplish other secondary goals. It also attempted to correct one of the injustices of the original act: its failure to protect sharecroppers and tenant farmers. Now landlords were required to share the payments they received for cutting back production with those who worked their land. The new requirements were, however, largely evaded.

The administration launched other efforts to assist poor farmers as well. The Resettlement Administration, established in 1935, and its successor, the Farm Security Administration, created in 1937, provided loans to help farmers cultivating submarginal soil to relocate on better lands. But the programs never moved more than a few thousand farmers. More effective was the Rural Electrification Administration, created in 1935, which worked to make electric power available for the first time to thousands of farmers through utility cooperatives.

Industrial Recovery

The challenge of rescuing the industrial economy from the spiraling deflation of the early 1930s was even more important to the administration. Ever since 1931, leaders of the U.S. Chamber of Commerce and many others had been urging the government to adopt an anti-deflation scheme that would permit trade associations to cooperate in stabilizing prices within their industries. Existing antitrust laws clearly forbade such practices, but businesspeople argued that the economic emergency justified a suspension of the restrictions. Herbert Hoover had refused to endorse suspension of the antitrust laws. But the Roosevelt administration was more receptive.

SALUTING THE BLUE EAGLE
Eight thousand San Francisco schoolchildren assembled on a baseball field in 1933 to form the symbol of the National Recovery Administration: an eagle clutching a cogwheel (to symbolize industry) and a thunderbolt (to symbolize energy). They are evidence of the widespread (if brief) popular enthusiasm the NRA produced. NRA administrators drew from their memories of World War I Liberty Loan drives and tried to establish the Blue Eagle as a symbol of patriotic commitment to recovery. *(UPI/Bettmann)*

In exchange for relaxing antitrust provisions, however, New Dealers insisted on additional provisions that would deal with other economic problems. Businesspeople would have to make important concessions to labor—recognize their right to organize and bargain collectively through unions—to ensure that the incomes of workers would rise along with prices. And to ensure that consumer buying power would not lag behind, the administration added a major program of public works spending designed to pump needed funds into the economy. The result of these and many other impulses was the National Industrial Recovery Act, one of the most complicated pieces of legislation in American history to that point. Congress passed it in June 1933. Roosevelt, signing the bill, called it "the most important and far-reaching legislation ever en-

acted by the American Congress." Businesspeople hailed it as the beginning of a new era of cooperation between government and industry. Labor leaders praised it as a "Magna Carta" for trade unions.

At first the new program appeared to work miracles. At its center was a new federal agency, the National Recovery Administration (NRA). Its director was the flamboyant and energetic Hugh S. Johnson, a retired general and successful businessman. Johnson envisioned himself as a kind of evangelist, whose major mission was to generate public enthusiasm and corporate support for the NRA. He approached his task in two ways.

First, he called on every business establishment in the nation to accept a temporary "blanket code": a minimum wage of between 30 and 40 cents an hour, a max-

WPA WORKERS ON THE JOB
The Works Progress Administration funded an enormous variety of work projects to provide jobs for the unemployed. But most WPA employees worked on construction sites of one kind or another. Here, WPA workers labor on a bridge project in the Bronx, in New York City. *(UPI/Bettmann)*

imum workweek of 35 to 40 hours, and the abolition of child labor. The result, he claimed, would be to raise consumer purchasing power, increase employment, and eliminate the sweatshop. To generate enthusiasm for the blanket code, Johnson devised a symbol—the famous NRA Blue Eagle—which employers who accepted the provisions could display in their windows. Soon Blue Eagle flags, posters, and stickers, carrying the NRA slogan "We Do Our Part," were decorating commercial establishments in every part of the country—just as parents of soldiers or purchasers of war bonds had decorated their homes and offices with patriotic reminders during World War I.

At the same time, Johnson was busy negotiating another, more specific set of codes with leaders of the nation's major industries. These industrial codes set floors below which no company would lower prices or wages in its search for a competitive advantage, and they included agreements on maintaining employment and production. He quickly won agreements from almost every major industry in the country.

From the beginning, however, the NRA encountered serious difficulties, and the entire effort ultimately dissolved in failure. The codes themselves were hastily and often poorly written. Administering them was far beyond the capacities of federal officials with no prior experience in running so vast a program. Large producers consistently dominated the code-writing process and ensured that the new regulations would work to their advantage and to the disadvantage of smaller firms. And the codes at times did more than simply set floors under prices; they actively and artificially raised them—at times to levels higher than was necessary to ensure a profit and far higher than market forces would have dictated.

Attempts to increase consumer purchasing power did not progress as quickly as the efforts to raise prices. Section 7(a) of the National Industrial Recovery Act promised workers the right to form unions and engage in collective bargaining and encouraged many workers to join unions for the first time. But Section 7(a) contained no enforcement mechanisms. Hence recognition of unions by employers (and thus the significant wage increases the unions were committed to winning) did not follow. The Public Works Administration (PWA), established by the bill to administer spending programs and directed by Secretary of the Interior Harold Ickes, only gradually allowed the $3.3 billion in public works funds to trickle out. Not until 1938 was the PWA budget pumping an appreciable amount of money into the economy.

Perhaps the clearest evidence of the NRA's failure was that industrial production actually declined in the months after its establishment—from an index of 101

in July 1933 to 71 in November—despite (some argued because of) the rise in prices that the codes had helped to create. By the spring of 1934, therefore, the NRA was besieged by criticism. Businessmen were flouting its provisions, cutting wages and prices or violating agreements on levels of production—claiming as they did so that the wage requirements of the codes (which many of them were ignoring anyway) were making it impossible to earn adequate profits. Employers were also openly ignoring the provisions requiring them to bargain with unions, and so organized labor grew increasingly hostile toward the NRA. Economists were charging that the price fixing permitted by the codes was undermining efforts to raise purchasing power. Reformers were complaining that the NRA was encouraging economic concentration and monopoly. A national Recovery Review Board, chaired by the famous criminal lawyer Clarence Darrow, reported in the spring of 1934 that the NRA was excessively dominated by big business and unduly encouraging monopoly; and Hugh Johnson's angry, vituperative response served only to undermine the agency's prestige even further. That fall, Roosevelt pressured Johnson to resign and established a new board of directors to oversee the NRA. Then in 1935, the Supreme Court intervened.

The constitutional basis for the NRA had been Congress's power to regulate commerce among the states, a power the administration had interpreted very broadly but that the Court continued to interpret narrowly. The case before the Court involved alleged NRA code violations by the Schechter brothers, who operated a wholesale poultry business confined to Brooklyn, New York. The Court ruled unanimously that the Schechters were not engaged in interstate commerce and, further, that Congress had unconstitutionally delegated legislative power to the president to draft the NRA codes. It nullified the legislation establishing the agency.

Roosevelt denounced the justices for their "horse-and-buggy" interpretation of the interstate commerce clause. He was rightly concerned, for the reasoning in the *Schechter* case threatened many other New Deal programs as well. But the destruction of the NRA itself may have been a blessing for the New Deal, providing it with a face-saving way to abolish the failed experiment.

Regional Planning

The AAA and the NRA reflected the beliefs of New Dealers who favored economic planning but wanted private interests (farmers or business leaders) to dom-

THE TENNESSEE VALLEY AUTHORITY

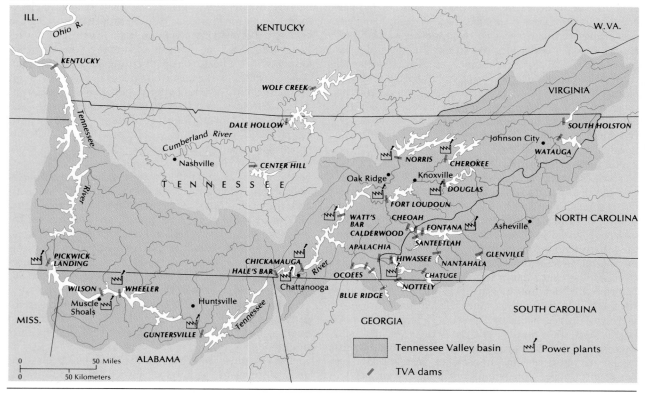

inate the planning process. In some areas, however, other reformers—those who believed that the government itself should be the chief planning agent in the economy—managed to establish dominance. Their most conspicuous success, and one of the most celebrated accomplishments of the New Deal, was an unprecedented experiment in regional planning: the Tennessee Valley Authority (TVA).

The TVA had its roots in a political controversy of the 1920s. Progressive reformers had agitated for years for public development of the nation's water resources as a source of cheap electric power. In particular, they had urged completion of a great dam at Muscle Shoals on the Tennessee River in Alabama—a dam begun during World War I but left unfinished when the war ended. Opposition from utilities companies, however, had been too powerful to overcome.

But in 1932, one of the great utility empires—that of the electricity magnate Samuel Insull—had collapsed spectacularly, amid widely publicized exposés of corruption. Hostility to the utilities soon grew so intense that the companies were no longer able to block the public-power movement. The result was legislation supported by the president and enacted by Congress in May 1933 creating the Tennessee Valley Authority. The TVA was intended not only to complete the dam at Muscle Shoals and build others in the region, and not only to generate and sell electricity from them to the public at reasonable rates. It was also to be the agent for a comprehensive redevelopment of the entire region: for stopping the disastrous flooding that had plagued the Tennessee Valley for centuries, for encouraging the development of local industries, for supervising a substantial program of reforestation, and for helping farmers improve productivity.

Opposition by conservatives within the administration ultimately blocked some of the most ambitious social planning projects proposed by the more visionary TVA administrators, but the project revitalized the region in numerous ways. It built dams and waterways. It virtually eliminated flooding in the region. It provided electricity to thousands who had never before had it. Throughout the country, largely because of the "yardstick" provided by the TVA's cheap production of electricity, private power rates declined. Still, the Authority worked no miracles. The Tennessee Valley remained a generally impoverished region despite its efforts. And like many other New Deal programs, it made no serious effort to challenge local customs and racial prejudices.

Financial Reforms

Roosevelt was not an inflationist at heart, but he soon came to consider the gold standard a major obstacle to the restoration of adequate prices. On April 18, 1933, the president made the shift off the gold standard official with an executive order. A few weeks later, Congress passed legislation confirming his decision. By itself, the repudiation of the gold standard meant relatively little. But both before and after the April decision, the administration experimented in various ways with manipulating the value of the dollar—by making substantial purchases of gold and silver and later by establishing a new, fixed standard for the dollar (reducing its gold content substantially from the 1932 amount). The resort to government-managed currency—that is, to a dollar whose value could be raised or lowered by government policy according to economic circumstances—created an important precedent for future federal policies and permanently altered the relationship between the public and private sectors. It did not, however, have any immediate impact on the depressed American economy.

Through other legislation, the early New Deal increased federal authority over previously unregulated or weakly regulated areas of the economy. The Glass-Steagall Act of June 1933 gave the government authority to curb irresponsible speculation by banks. More important, perhaps, it established the Federal Deposit Insurance Corporation, which guaranteed all bank deposits up to $2,500. In other words, even should a bank fail, small depositors would be able to recover their money. Finally, in 1935, Congress passed a major banking act that transferred much of the authority once wielded by the regional Federal Reserve banks to the Federal Reserve Board in Washington.

To protect investors in the stock market, Congress passed the so-called Truth in Securities Act of 1933, requiring corporations issuing new securities to provide full and accurate information about them to the public. Another act of June 1934 established the Securities and Exchange Commission (SEC) to police the stock market. Among other things, the establishment of the SEC was an indication of how far the financial establishment had fallen in public estimation. In earlier years, J. P. Morgan and other important financiers could have wielded enough influence to stop such government interference in the financial world. Now Morgan could not even get a respectful hearing on Capitol Hill. The criminal trials of a number of once-respected Wall Street figures for grand larceny and fraud (including the conviction and imprisonment of Richard Whitney, onetime head of the New York Stock Exchange and a close Morgan associate) eroded the public stature of the financial community still further.

The Growth of Federal Relief

Millions of Americans were unemployed and in desperate need of assistance in 1933, and the relief efforts of private organizations and state and local governments were unable to meet the demand. Although the Roosevelt administration did not consider relief its most important task, it recognized the necessity of doing something to help impoverished Americans survive until the New Deal could revive the economy to the point where relief might not be necessary.

Among Roosevelt's first acts as president was the establishment of the Federal Emergency Relief Administration (FERA), which provided cash grants to states to prop up bankrupt relief agencies. To administer the program, he chose the director of the New York State relief agency, Harry Hopkins. Hopkins disbursed the FERA grants widely and rapidly. But both Hopkins and Roosevelt had misgivings about establishing a government dole. "It is probably going to undermine the independence of hundreds of thousands of families," he once lamented.

They felt somewhat more comfortable with another form of government assistance: work relief. Unlike the dole, Hopkins believed, work relief "preserves a man's morale. It saves his skill. It gives him a chance to do something socially useful." Thus when it became clear that the FERA grants would not be sufficient to pull the country through the winter, the administration established a second program: the Civil Works Administration (CWA). Between November and April, it put more than 4 million people to work on temporary projects. Some of them were of lasting value, such as the construction of roads, schools, and parks; others were little more than make-work. To Hopkins, however, the important thing was pumping money into an economy badly in need of it and providing assistance to people with nowhere else to turn. This use of government spending to stimulate the economy—known at the time as "pump priming" and later as Keynesianism—was one of the New Deal's most important contributions to public policy. But in 1933, at least, members of the administration were only vaguely aware of the broad effects of this spending on the economy as a whole.

Evidence of this limited view of the value of government spending was that most of these early relief programs had short lives. Like the FERA, the CWA was intended to be only a temporary expedient. In the spring of 1934, the president began to dismantle the agency, and ultimately he disbanded it altogether. Most economists now agree that massive and sustained government spending would have been the quickest and most effective way to end the Depression. But few policymakers in the 1930s shared that belief.

Roosevelt's favorite relief project was the Civilian Conservation Corps. Established in the first weeks of the new administration, the CCC was designed to provide employment to the millions of urban young men who could find no jobs in the cities and who, unemployed and restless, were raising fears of urban violence. At the same time, it was intended to advance the work of conservation and reforestation—goals Roosevelt had long cherished. The CCC created a series of camps in national parks and forests and in other rural and wilderness settings. There young men (women were excluded from the program) worked in a semimilitary environment on such projects as planting trees, building reservoirs, developing or maintaining parks, and improving agricultural irrigation. CCC camps were segregated by race—the vast majority reserved for whites, a few open to blacks.

Mortgage relief was a pressing need of millions of farm owners and homeowners. The Farm Credit Administration, which within two years refinanced one-fifth of all farm mortgages in the United States, was one response to that problem. The Frazier-Lemke Farm Bankruptcy Act of 1933 was another. It enabled some farmers to regain their land even after foreclosure on their mortgages. Despite such efforts, however, by 1934 25 percent of all American farm owners had lost their land. Homeowners were similarly troubled, and in June 1933 the administration established the Home Owners' Loan Corporation, which by 1936 had refinanced the mortgages of more than 1 million householders. A year later, Congress established the Federal Housing Administration to insure mortgages for new construction and home repairs—a measure that combined an effort to provide relief with a program to stimulate lasting recovery of the construction industry.

The relief efforts of the first two years of the New Deal were intended to be limited and temporary. But they helped establish the basis of other forms of social protection. Ultimately, the creation of a permanent welfare system would be one of the New Deal's most important and lasting accomplishments.

THE NEW DEAL IN TRANSITION

Seldom has an American president enjoyed such remarkable popularity as Franklin Roosevelt during his first two years in office. But by early 1935, with no end to the Depression yet in sight, the New Deal was beginning to find itself the target of fierce public criticism. In the spring of 1935, partly in response to these growing attacks, Roosevelt launched an ambitious new program of legislation that has often been called the "Second New Deal."

Attacks from Right and Left

Some of the most strident attacks on the New Deal came from critics on the right. Roosevelt had tried for a time to conciliate conservatives and business leaders. By the end of 1934, however, it was clear that the American right in general, and much of the corporate world in particular, had become irreconcilably hostile to the New Deal. So intense was conservative animosity toward the New Deal's "reckless spending," "economic crackpots," and "socialist" reforms that some of Roosevelt's critics could not even bear to say the president's name. They called him, simply and bitterly, "that man in the White House." In August 1934, a group of the most fervent (and wealthiest) Roosevelt opponents, led by members of the Du Pont family, formed the American Liberty League, designed specifically to arouse public opposition to the New Deal's "dictatorial" policies and its supposed attacks on free enterprise. The new organization generated wide publicity and caused some concern within the administration. In fact, however, it was never able to expand its constituency very much beyond the northern industrialists who had founded it. At its peak, membership in the organization numbered only about 125,000.

In 1936, at least, the real impact of the Liberty League and other conservative attacks on Roosevelt was not to undermine the president's political strength, but to convince Roosevelt that there was no longer any point in trying to conciliate the business community. The forces of "organized money," he said near the end of his campaign for reelection, "are unanimous in their hate for me—and I welcome their hatred."

Roosevelt's critics on the left also managed to produce alarm among some supporters of the administration; but like the conservatives, they proved to have only limited strength. The Communist Party, the Socialist Party, and other radical and semiradical organizations were at times harshly critical of Roosevelt.

But they were also sympathetic to some New Deal initiatives. And they were at times uncertain about how best to combine their commitment to radical change with their fervent opposition to the growth of fascism elsewhere in the world. The Communist Party, in particular, spent much of the 1930s tacitly and at times openly supporting the Roosevelt programs.

Popular Protest

More menacing to the New Deal than either the far right or the far left was a group of dissident political movements that defied easy ideological classification. Some were marginal "crackpot" organizations with little popular following. Others gained substantial public support within particular states and regions. Three men, however, succeeded in mobilizing genuinely national followings.

Dr. Francis E. Townsend, an elderly California physician, rose from obscurity to lead a movement of more than 5 million members with his plan for federal pensions for the elderly. According to the Townsend plan, all Americans over the age of sixty would receive monthly government pensions of $200, provided they retired (thus freeing jobs for younger, unemployed Americans) and spent the money in full each month (which would pump needed funds into the economy). By 1935, the Townsend Plan had attracted the support of many older men and women. And while the plan itself made little progress in Congress, the public sentiment behind it helped build support for the Social Security system, which Congress did approve in 1935.

Even greater renown (and eventually great notoriety) came to Father Charles E. Coughlin, a Catholic priest in the Detroit suburb of Royal Oak, Michigan, through his weekly sermons broadcast nationally over the radio. He criticized "rapacious capitalists" for their abdication of social responsibility; and he proposed a series of monetary reforms—remonetization of silver, issuing of greenbacks, and nationalization of the banking system—that he insisted would restore prosperity and ensure economic justice. At first a warm supporter of Franklin Roosevelt, by 1934 he had become disheartened by what he claimed was the president's failure to deal harshly enough with the "money powers." In the spring of 1935, he established his own political organization, the National Union for Social Justice, which some believed was a first step toward forming a new political party. He was also displaying an apparently remarkable influence in Congress. (An avalanche of telegrams inspired by a Coughlin radio sermon was generally believed to have been responsible for the defeat in the Senate of a treaty admitting the United States to the World Court.) And he was attracting public support throughout much of the nation—primarily from Catholics, but from others as well. Father Coughlin was widely believed to have one of the largest regular radio audiences of anyone in America.

Most alarming of all to the administration was the growing national popularity of Senator Huey P. Long of Louisiana. Long had risen to power in his home state through his strident attacks on the banks, oil companies, and utilities, and on the conservative political oligarchy allied with them. Elected governor in 1928, he

HUEY LONG
Few public speakers could arouse a crowd more effectively than Huey Long of Louisiana, known to many as "the Kingfish" (a nickname borrowed from the popular radio show *Amos 'n Andy*). It was Long's effective use of radio, however, that contributed most directly to his spreading national popularity in the early 1930s. *(Culver)*

launched an assault on his opposition so thorough and forceful that soon they were left with virtually no political power at all. Long dominated the legislature, the courts, and the executive departments, and he brooked no interference. When opponents accused him of violating the Louisiana constitution, he brazenly replied, "I'm the Constitution here now." Many claimed that he had, in effect, become a dictator. But he also maintained the overwhelming support of the Louisiana electorate, in part because of his flamboyant personality and in part because of his solid record of conventional progressive accomplishment: building roads, schools, and hospitals; revising the tax codes; distributing free textbooks; lowering utility rates. Barred by law from succeeding himself as governor, he ran in 1930 for a seat in the U.S. Senate, won easily, and left the state government in the hands of loyal, docile allies.

Long, like Coughlin, supported Franklin Roosevelt in 1932. But within six months of Roosevelt's inauguration he had broken with the president. As an alternative to the New Deal, he advocated a drastic program of wealth redistribution, a program he ultimately named the Share-Our-Wealth Plan. The government, he claimed, could end the Depression easily by using the tax system to confiscate the surplus riches of the wealthiest men and women in America, whose fortunes were, he claimed, so bloated that not enough wealth remained to satisfy the needs of the great mass of citizens. That surplus wealth would allow the government to guarantee every family a minimum "homestead" of $5,000 and an annual wage of $2,500.

Long made little effort to disguise his interest in running for president. In 1934, he established his own national organization: the Share-Our-Wealth Society, which soon attracted a large following—not only in Long's native South but in New York, Pennsylvania, parts of the Midwest, and above all California. A poll by the Democratic National Committee in the spring of 1935 disclosed that Long might attract more than 10 percent of the vote if he ran as a third-party candidate, enough to tip a close election to the Republicans.

Long, Coughlin, Townsend, and other dissidents had certain concerns in common. They spoke harshly of the "plutocrats," "international bankers," and other remote financial powers who were, they claimed, not only impoverishing the nation but exercising tyrannical power over individuals and communities. They spoke equally harshly, however, of the dangers of excessive government bureaucracy, attacking the New Deal for establishing a menacing, "dictatorial" state. They envisioned a society in which government would, through a series of simple economic reforms, guarantee prosperity to every American without exercising intrusive control over individuals and communities.

To members of the Roosevelt administration, the dissident politics appeared in 1935 to have become a genuine threat to the president. An increasing number of advisers were warning Roosevelt that he would have to do something dramatic to counter their strength.

The "Second New Deal"

In the spring of 1935, Roosevelt launched a series of important new programs—often called the "Second New Deal"—in response both to the growing political pressures and to the continuing economic crisis. They represented, if not a new direction, at least a change in the emphasis of New Deal policy.

Perhaps the most conspicuous change was in the administration's attitude toward big business. Symbolically at least, the president was now willing openly to attack corporate interests. In March, for example, he asked Congress for a law to break up the great utility holding companies and justified it by speaking harshly of the injustices inherent in their monopolistic position. Congress did indeed pass the Holding Company Act of 1935 (often known as the "death sentence" bill), but furious lobbying by the utilities resulted in amendments that sharply limited its effects.

Equally alarming to affluent Americans was a series of tax reforms proposed by the president in 1935, a program conservatives quickly labeled a "soak the rich" scheme. Apparently designed to undercut the appeal of Huey Long's Share-Our-Wealth Plan, the Roosevelt proposals called for establishing the highest and most progressive peacetime tax rates in history. Rates in the highest brackets reached 75 percent on income, 70 percent on inheritances, and 15 percent on corporate incomes. In fact, the actual impact of these taxes was far less radical than the president liked to claim (as Huey Long quickly pointed out); few people made enough money to qualify for the upper brackets, and most of them were able to find ways to avoid the full tax burden in any case. The next tax laws were more important symbolically than they were economically.

The Supreme Court decision in 1935 to invalidate the National Industrial Recovery Act solved some problems for the administration, but it also created others. Section 7(a) of the now defunct act had guaranteed workers the right to organize and bargain collectively. Supporters of labor, both in the administration and in Congress, advocated quick action to restore that protection. With the president himself slow to respond, a group of progressives in Congress led by Senator Robert F. Wagner of New York introduced what became the National Labor Relations Act of 1935. The new law, popularly known as the Wagner Act, provided workers with more federal protection than Section 7(a) of the National Industrial Recovery Act had offered; it provided a crucial enforcement mechanism, the National Labor Relations Board (NLRB), which would have power to compel employers to recognize and bargain with legitimate unions. The president was not entirely happy with the bill, but he signed it. That was in large part because American workers themselves had become so important and vigorous a force by 1935 that Roosevelt realized his own political future would depend in part on responding to their demands.

Labor Militancy

The emergence of a powerful American trade union movement in the 1930s was one of the most important social and political developments of the decade. It occurred partly in response to government efforts to enhance the power of unions; but it was also a result of the increased militancy of American workers and their leaders.

During the 1920s, most workers had displayed relatively little militancy in challenging employers or demanding recognition of their unions. In the 1930s, however, many of the factors that had impeded militancy vanished or grew weaker. Business leaders and industrialists lost (at least temporarily) the ability to control government policies. Congress passed both Section 7(a) of the National Industrial Recovery Act of 1933 and the Wagner Act of 1935 over the strong objections of most (although not all) corporate leaders. Equally important, new and more militant labor organizations emerged to challenge the established, conservative unions.

The growing militancy first became obvious in 1934, when newly organized workers (many of them inspired by the collective bargaining provisions of the National Industrial Recovery Act) demonstrated a determination and radicalism not seen since 1919 and became involved in militant, occasionally violent, confrontations with employers and local authorities. Industrial workers were, it was clear, becoming too militant to ignore any longer. But it was equally clear that without stronger legal protection, their organizing drives would end in frustration. Once the Wagner Act became law, the search for more effective forms of organization rapidly gained strength in labor ranks.

The American Federation of Labor, now under the leadership of William Green, remained committed to the idea of the craft union: the idea of organizing workers on the basis of their skills. It had little to offer unskilled laborers, who now constituted the bulk of the industrial work force. During the 1930s, therefore, another concept of labor organization challenged the craft union ideal: industrial unionism. Advocates of this approach argued that all the workers in a particular industry should be organized in a single union, regardless of what functions they performed. All auto workers should be in a single automobile union; all steel workers should be in a single steel union. United in this way, workers would greatly increase their power.

Leaders of the AFL craft unions for the most part opposed the new concept. But industrial unionism found a number of important advocates, most prominent among them John L. Lewis, the talented, flamboyant, and eloquent leader of the United Mine Workers—the oldest major union in the country. At first, Lewis and his allies attempted to work within the AFL, but friction between the new industrial organizations Lewis was promoting and the older craft unions grew rapidly.

At the 1935 AFL convention, Lewis became embroiled in a series of angry confrontations (and one celebrated fistfight) with craft union leaders before finally walking out. A few weeks later, he created the Committee on Industrial Organization—a body officially within the AFL but unsanctioned by its leadership. After a series of bitter jurisdictional conflicts, the AFL finally expelled the new committee from its ranks, and along with it all the industrial unions it represented. In response, Lewis renamed the committee the Congress of Industrial Organizations (CIO), established it in 1936 as an organization directly rivaling the AFL, and became its first president. The schism clearly weakened the labor movement in many ways. But by freeing the advocates of industrial unionism from the restrictive rules of the AFL, it gave impetus to the creation of powerful new organizations.

The CIO expanded the constituency of the labor movement. It was more receptive to women and to blacks than the AFL had been, in part because women and blacks were more likely to be relegated to unskilled jobs, in part because CIO organizing drives targeted previously unorganized industries (textiles, laundries, tobacco factories, and others) where women and minorities constituted much of the work force. The CIO was also a more militant organization than the AFL. And by the time of the 1936 schism, it was already engaged in major organizing battles in the automobile and steel industries.

Organizing Battles

The new organizations had been struggling for recognition even before the schism of 1936. Major battles were under way, in particular, in the automobile and steel industries.

Out of several competing auto unions, the United Auto Workers (UAW) was gradually emerging preeminent in the early and mid-1930s. But although it was gaining recruits, it was making little progress in winning recognition from the corporations. Then, in December 1936, auto workers employed a controversial and effective new technique for challenging corporate opposition: the sit-down strike. Employees in several General Motors plants in Detroit simply sat down inside the plants, refusing either to work or to leave, thus preventing the company from using strikebreakers. The tactic spread to other locations, and by February 1937 strikers had occupied seventeen GM plants.

The strikers ignored court orders and local police efforts to force them to vacate the buildings. When Michigan's governor, Frank Murphy, a liberal Democrat, refused to call up the National Guard to clear out the strikers, and when the federal government also refused to intervene on behalf of employers, General Motors relented. In February 1937, GM became the first major manufacturer to recognize the UAW; other automobile companies followed. The sit-down strike proved effective for rubber workers and others as well, but it survived only briefly as a labor technique. Its apparent illegality aroused so much public opposition that labor leaders soon abandoned it.

In the steel industry, the battle for unionization was more difficult. In 1936, the Steel Workers' Organizing Committee (later United Steelworkers of America) began a major organizing drive involving thousands of workers and frequent, often bitter strikes. These conflicts were notable not only for the militancy of the (predominantly male) steelworkers themselves, but for the involvement of thousands of women (many of them wives or relatives of workers), who provided important logistical support for the strikers and who at times took direct action by creating a buffer between strikers and the police.

In March 1937, to the surprise of almost everyone, United States Steel, the giant of the industry, recognized the union rather than risk a costly strike at a time when it sensed itself on the verge of recovery from the Depression. But the smaller companies (known collectively as "Little Steel") remained unyielding in their opposition. On Memorial Day 1937, a group of striking workers from Republic Steel gathered with their families for a picnic and demonstration in South Chicago. When they attempted to march peacefully (and legally) toward the steel plant, police opened fire on them. Ten demonstrators were killed; another ninety were wounded. Despite a public outcry against the "Memorial Day Massacre," the harsh tactics of "Little Steel" were successful. The 1937 strike failed.

But the victory of Little Steel was one of the last gasps of the kind of brutal strikebreaking that had proved so effective in the past. In 1937 alone, there

THE LITTLE STEEL STRIKE, 1937
Al Balant, a leader of the Steel Workers Organizing Committee in Ohio, addresses a rally he has organized at city hall in Cleveland to protest the importation of strikebreakers by Republic Steel. The march to city hall occurred between outbreaks of violence at the Cleveland plants. Similar, and worse, violence was occurring in other cities during the bitter and ultimately unsuccessful strike against the "Little Steel" companies. *(UPI/Bettmann)*

were 4,720 strikes—over 80 percent of them settled in favor of the unions. By the end of the year, more than 8 million workers were members of unions recognized as official bargaining units by employers—as compared with 3 million in 1932. By 1941, that number had expanded to 10 million and included the workers of Little Steel, where employers had finally recognized the SWOC.

Social Security

From the first moments of the New Deal, important members of the administration, most notably Secretary of Labor Frances Perkins, had been lobbying for a system of federally sponsored social insurance for the elderly and the unemployed. In 1935, Roosevelt gave public support to what became the Social Security Act, which Congress passed the same year. It established several distinct programs.

For the elderly, there were two types of assistance. Those who were destitute at the time the bill passed could begin receiving up to $15 a month in federal assistance. More important for the future, many Americans presently working were incorporated into a pension system, to which they and their employers would contribute by paying a payroll tax and which would provide them with an income on retirement. Pension payments would not begin until 1940, and even then would provide recipients only $10 to $85 a month. And broad categories of workers (including domestic servants and agricultural laborers, many of whom were blacks and women) were excluded from the program. But the act was a crucial first step in creating the nation's most important social program for the elderly.

In addition, the Social Security Act created a system of unemployment insurance, to which employers alone would contribute and which made it possible for workers laid off from their jobs to receive government assistance for a limited period of time. It also provided aid to blind and otherwise handicapped people and to dependent children.

The framers of the Social Security Act wanted to create a system of "insurance," not "welfare." And the largest programs (old-age pensions and unemployment insurance) were in many ways similar to private insurance programs, with contributions from participants and benefits available to all. But the act also provided considerable direct assistance based on need—to the elderly poor, to the disabled, to dependent children and their mothers. In 1935, these groups were widely perceived to be small and genuinely unable to support themselves, but in the years to come the programs would expand and assume dimensions that the planners of Social Security neither foresaw nor desired. Aid to Dependent Children, envisioned as a relatively modest program to aid a small number of needy people, would in the 1950s (renamed Aid to Families with Dependent Children) expand to become one of the cornerstones of the modern welfare system.

The distinction built into the Social Security Act between "insurance" and "public assistance" institutionalized a set of cultural biases that would continue to influence the politics of welfare for the rest of the twentieth century. New Dealers, like most other Americans, believed that some people had "earned" social protection—either because they (or their employers) had contributed to the programs from which they drew, as was the case with old-age pensions and unemployment compensation; or because they had performed some special service to the nation, as had been the case

in the past for Civil War and World War I veterans. Other people (many of them women) "needed" benefits because they were incapable of supporting themselves; and while New Dealers (and progressive reformers before them) were willing to provide such benefits, they did so less generously and much more demeaningly (because of elaborate eligibility requirements) than they did for those they believed had earned them. Whatever its limits, however, it is clear that the 1935 act was the most important single piece of social welfare legislation in American history.

New Directions in Relief

Social Security was designed primarily to fulfill long-range goals. But millions of unemployed Americans had immediate needs. To help meet those needs, the administration established in 1935 the Works Progress Administration (WPA). Like the Civil Works Administration and other earlier efforts, the WPA established a system of work relief for the unemployed. But it was much bigger than the earlier agencies, both in the size of its budget ($5 billion at first) and in the energy and imagination of its operations.

Under the direction of Harry Hopkins, the WPA kept an average of 2.1 million workers employed between 1935 and 1941. The agency was responsible ultimately for building or renovating 110,000 public buildings (schools, post offices, public libraries, government office buildings, and others) and for constructing almost 600 airports, more than 500,000 miles of roads, and over 100,000 bridges. In the process, it provided incomes to unemployed workers and stimulated the economy by increasing the flow of money into it.

The WPA also displayed remarkable flexibility and imagination in offering assistance to those whose occupations did not fit into any traditional category of relief. The Federal Writers Project of the WPA, for example, gave unemployed writers a chance to do their work and receive a government salary. The Federal Arts Project, similarly, helped painters, sculptors, and others to continue their careers. The Federal Music Project and the Federal Theater Project oversaw the production of concerts and plays, creating work for unemployed musicians, actors, directors, and others. Other relief agencies emerged alongside the WPA. The National Youth Administration provided work and scholarship assistance to high-school and college-age men and women. The Emergency Housing Division of the Public Works Administration began federal sponsorship of public housing. It cleared some of the nation's most notorious slums and built instead some fifty new housing developments, containing nearly

WPA MURAL ART
The Federal Arts Project of the Works Progress Administration commissioned an impressive series of public murals from the artists it employed. Many of these murals adorned post offices, libraries, and other public buildings constructed by the WPA. William Gropper's *Construction of a Dam*, a detail of which is seen here, is typical of much of the mural art of the 1930s in its celebration of the workingman. Workers are depicted in heroic poses, laboring in unison to complete a great public project. *(Department of the Interior)*

22,000 units—although most of them were priced too high for those who had been displaced by slum clearance. Not until 1937, when Congress approved Senator Wagner's bill creating the United States Housing Authority, did the government begin to provide a substantial amount of housing for the truly poor.

The hiring practices of the WPA, the NYA, and other work-relief programs—like the character of the Social Security Act—revealed another important, if at the time largely unrecognized, feature of the New Deal welfare system. Men and women alike were in distress in the 1930s (as in all difficult times). But the new welfare system dealt with members of the two sexes in very different ways. For men, the government concentrated mainly on work relief—on such programs as the CCC, the CWA, and the WPA, all of which were overwhelmingly male. The WPA did provide some jobs for women, although usually in such domestic settings as sewing rooms, nursery schools, and handicraft programs. Even these few jobs tended to be quickly eliminated when WPA funds became tight.

The principal government aid to women was not work relief, but cash assistance—most notably through the Aid to Dependent Children program of Social Se-

curity, which was designed largely to assist single mothers. This disparity in treatment reflected a widespread assumption, shared even by some of the many women who helped design the programs, that men were the principal "breadwinners" and the bulk of the paid work force and that women should be treated within the context of the family. In fact, millions of women were already employed by the 1930s, and millions of women lived outside the framework of the conventional family and depended on their own earnings for survival.

The 1936 "Referendum"

The presidential election of 1936, it was clear from the start, was to be a national referendum on Franklin Roosevelt and the New Deal. And while in 1935 there had been reason to question the president's political prospects, by the middle of 1936 his reelection was virtually certain. The Republican Party nominated the moderate governor of Kansas, Alf M. Landon, and produced a program that promised, in effect, to continue the programs of the New Deal—but "constitutionally," and without running a deficit. Republican conservatives seemed impotent even within their own party.

Roosevelt's dissident challengers seemed similarly powerless. One reason was the violent death of their most effective leader, Huey Long, who was assassinated in Louisiana in September 1935. Another reason was the ill-fated alliance among several of the remaining dissident leaders in 1936. Father Coughlin, Dr. Townsend, and Gerald L. K. Smith (a henchman of Huey Long) joined forces that summer to establish a new political movement—the Union Party. But the incessant squabbling among them, combined with the colorlessness of their presidential candidate—an undistinguished North Dakota congressman, William Lemke—doomed the new party to ineffectuality. After its demise, two of its embittered leaders, Coughlin and Smith, moved quickly to the right; they also became notorious for their anti-Semitism and, in Coughlin's case, overt fascist sympathies.

The result was the greatest landslide in American history to that point. Roosevelt polled just under 61 percent of the vote, to Landon's 36 percent. The Republican candidate carried only Maine and Vermont. The Democrats increased their already large majorities in both houses of Congress. The Union Party received fewer than 900,000 votes.

The election displayed the party realignment that the New Deal had produced. The Democrats now controlled a broad coalition of western and southern farmers, the urban working classes, the poor and unemployed, and the black communities of the northern cities, as well as traditional progressives and committed new liberals—a coalition that constituted a substantial majority of the electorate. It would be decades before the Republican Party could again produce a true majority coalition of its own.

THE NEW DEAL IN DISARRAY

Roosevelt emerged from the 1936 election at the zenith of his popularity. Within months, however, the New Deal was mired in serious new difficulties—a result of continuing opposition, the president's own political errors, and major economic setbacks.

The Court Fight and the "Purge"

Frankin Roosevelt had become convinced that no program of reform could long survive the obstructionist justices of the Supreme Court who had already struck down the NRA and the AAA and threatened to in-

validate even more legislation. The 1936 mandate, he believed, made it possible for him to do something about the problem. In February 1937, he offered a solution. Without informing congressional leaders in advance, he sent a surprise message to Capitol Hill proposing a general overhaul of the federal court system and including, among many provisions, one to add up to six new justices to the Supreme Court. The courts were "overworked," he claimed, and needed additional manpower and younger blood to enable them to cope with their increasing burdens. But Roosevelt's real purpose, which almost everyone understood, was to give himself the opportunity to appoint new, liberal justices and change the ideological balance of the Court.

Conservatives were outraged at the "Court-packing plan," and even many Roosevelt supporters were disturbed by what they considered evidence of the president's hunger for power. Still, Roosevelt might well have persuaded Congress to approve at least a compromise measure had not the Supreme Court itself intervened. Even before the Court-packing fight began, the ideological balance of the Court had been precarious. Four justices consistently opposed the New Deal, and three generally supported it. Of the remaining two, Chief Justice Charles Evans Hughes often sided with the progressives and Associate Justice Owen J. Roberts usually voted with the conservatives.

On March 29, 1937, Roberts, Hughes, and the three progressive justices voted together to uphold a state minimum-wage law—in the case of *West Coast Hotel* v. *Parrish*—thus reversing a 5-to-4 decision of the previous year invalidating a similar law (and suggesting the first movement away from the narrow interpretation of contracts and the interstate commerce clause that the 1905 *Lochner* decision had helped establish). Two weeks later, again by a 5-to-4 margin, the Court upheld the Wagner Act; and in May, it validated the Social Security Act. The Court had prudently moderated its position to make the Court-packing bill unnecessary. Congress ultimately defeated it.

On one level, the affair was a significant victory for Franklin Roosevelt. The Court was no longer an obstacle to New Deal reforms, particularly after the older justices began to retire, to be replaced by Roosevelt appointees. But the Court-packing episode did lasting damage to the administration. By giving members of his own party an excuse to oppose him, he had helped destroy his congressional coalition. From 1937 on, southern Democrats and other Democratic conservatives voted against his measures much more often than in the past. In combination with Republicans, they constituted a powerful enough force to block many New Deal measures.

One casualty of this newly powerful conservative coalition was an ambitious plan to reorganize the executive branch of government, which Roosevelt also presented to Congress in 1937. The president promoted the measure by emphasizing its potential contribution to governmental "efficiency"; his opponents characterized it, to some degree correctly, as an effort to increase the power of the president over the federal bureaucracy. Executive reorganization, like Court packing, reinforced conservative arguments that the president was aspiring to become a "dictator." The original bill failed, although a much-reduced reorganization plan passed Congress in 1939.

In the spring of 1938, the president's political situation deteriorated further. Determined to regain the initiative in his legislative battles, Roosevelt openly campaigned in several Democratic primary contests against members of his own party who had opposed his programs. Not only was he unable to unseat any of the five Democratic senators against whom he campaigned, but his "purge" efforts drove an even deeper wedge between the administration and its conservative opponents.

But the greatest blow to the administration as it began its second term was an economic one: a serious new recession that threatened to discredit everything the New Deal had done.

Retrenchment and Recession

By the summer of 1937, the national income, which had dropped from $82 billion in 1929 to $40 billion in 1932, had risen to nearly $72 billion. Other economic indices showed similar improvements. Roosevelt seized on these improvements as an excuse to try to balance the federal budget, convinced by Treasury secretary Henry Morgenthau and many economists that the real danger now was no longer depression but inflation. Between January and August 1937, for example, he cut the WPA in half, laying off 1.5 million relief workers.

A few weeks later, the fragile boom collapsed. The index of industrial production dropped from 117 in August 1937 to 76 in May 1938. Four million additional workers lost their jobs. Economic conditions were soon almost as bad as in the bleak days of 1932–1933.

The recession of 1937 came as a terrible shock to New Dealers, and many others, who had convinced themselves that the Depression was already over. It was a result of many factors. But to many observers at the time (including, apparently, Roosevelt), it seemed to be a direct result of the administration's unwise decision to reduce spending. And so the new crisis forced a reevaluation of policies within the administration.

The advocates of government spending as an antidote to the Depression stood vindicated, it seemed; and the notion of using government deficits to stimulate the economy established a frail foothold in American public policy. In April 1938, the president asked Congress for an emergency appropriation of $5 billion for public works and relief programs, and government funds soon began pouring into the economy once again. Within a few months, another tentative recovery seemed to be under way, and the advocates of spending pointed to it as proof of the validity of their approach.

At the same time, a group of younger liberals in the administration, who saw the recession as the result of excessively concentrated corporate power, were urging the president to launch a new assault on monopoly. In April 1938, Roosevelt sent a stinging message to Congress, vehemently denouncing what he called an unjustifiable concentration of economic power and asking for the creation of a commission to examine the problem, with an eye to major reforms in the antitrust laws. In response, Congress established the Temporary National Economic Committee (TNEC), including representatives of both houses of Congress and of several executive agencies. At about the same time, Roosevelt appointed a new head of the antitrust division of the Justice Department: Thurman Arnold, a Yale Law School professor who soon proved to be the most vigorous (and controversial) director ever to serve in that office.

By the end of 1938, however, it was becoming clear that these ambitious new goals faced an uncertain future. For the New Deal had by then essentially come to an end. Congressional opposition now made it difficult for the president to enact any major new programs. But more important, perhaps, the threat of world crisis hung heavy in the political atmosphere, and Roosevelt was gradually growing more concerned with persuading a reluctant nation to prepare for war than with pursuing new avenues of reform.

LIMITS AND LEGACIES OF THE NEW DEAL

In the 1930s, Roosevelt's principal critics were conservatives, who accused him of abandoning the Constitution and establishing a menacing, even tyrannical state. In more recent years, the New Deal's major critics have attacked it from the left, pointing to the major problems it left unsolved and the important groups it failed to represent. A full understanding of the New

MAJOR LEGISLATION OF THE NEW DEAL

1933 Emergency Banking Act
Economy Act
Civilian Conservation Corps
Agricultural Adjustment Act
Tennessee Valley Authority
National Industrial Recovery Act
Banking Act
Federal Emergency Relief Act
Home Owners' Refinancing Act
Civil Works Administration
Federal Securities Act
1934 National Housing Act
Securities and Exchange Act
Home Owners' Loan Act

1935 Works Progress Administration
National Youth Administration
Social Security Act
National Labor Relations Act
Public Utilities Holding Company Act
Resettlement Administration
Rural Electrification Administration
Revenue Act ("wealth tax")
1936 Soil Conservation and Domestic Allotment Act
1937 Farm Security Administration
National Housing Act
1938 Second Agricultural Adjustment Act
Fair Labor Standards Act
1939 Executive Reorganization Act

Deal requires examining both its achievements and its limits.

The Idea of the "Broker State"

In 1933, many New Dealers dreamed of using their new popularity and authority somehow to remake American capitalism—to produce new forms of cooperation and control that would create a genuinely harmonious, ordered economic world. By 1939, it was clear that what they had created was in fact something quite different. But rather than bemoan the gap between their original intentions and their ultimate achievements, New Deal liberals, both in 1939 and in later years, chose to accept what they had produced and to celebrate it—to use it as a model for future reform efforts.

What they had created was something that in later years would become known as the "broker state." Instead of forging all elements of society into a single, harmonious unit, as some reformers had once hoped to do, the real achievement of the New Deal was to elevate and strengthen new interest groups so as to allow them to compete more effectively in the national marketplace. And it was to make the federal government a mediator in that continuous competition—a force that could intercede when necessary to help some groups and limit the power of others.

In 1933, there had been only one great interest group (albeit a varied and divided one) with genuine power in the national economy: the corporate world. By the end of the 1930s, American business found it-

self competing for influence with an increasingly powerful labor movement, with an organized agricultural economy, and with aroused consumers. In later years, the "broker state" idea would expand to embrace other groups as well: racial, ethnic, and religious minorities, women, and many others. Thus, one of the enduring legacies of the New Deal was to make the federal government a protector of interest groups and a supervisor of the competition among them, rather than an instrument attempting to create a universal harmony of interests.

What determines which interest groups receive government assistance in a "broker state"? The experience of the New Deal suggests that such assistance goes largely to those groups able to exercise enough political or economic power to demand it. Thus in the 1930s, farmers—after decades of organization and agitation—and workers—as the result of militant action and mass mobilization—won from the government new and important protections. Other groups, less well organized perhaps but politically important because so numerous and visible, won more limited assistance as well: imperiled homeowners, the unemployed, the elderly.

By the same token, the interest-group democracy that the New Deal came to represent offered much less to those groups either too weak to demand assistance or not visible enough to arouse widespread public support. And yet those same groups were often the ones most in need of help from their government. One of the important limits of the New Deal, therefore, was its very modest record on behalf of several important social groups.

WHERE HISTORIANS DISAGREE

THE NEW DEAL

For many years, debate among historians over the nature of the New Deal mirrored the debate among Americans in the 1930s over the achievements of the Roosevelt administration. Historians struggled, just as contemporaries had done, to decide whether the New Deal was a good thing or a bad thing. Did it go too far in expanding the size and power of the government? Did it go far enough in helping the dispossessed and reforming capitalism?

The conservative critique of the New Deal has received relatively little scholarly expression. Edgar Robinson, in *The Roosevelt Leadership* (1955), and John T. Flynn, in *The Roosevelt Myth* (1956), attacked Roosevelt as both a radical and a despot; but few historians have ever taken such charges seriously. By far the dominant view of the New Deal among scholars has been an approving, liberal interpretation—one that has appeared in various forms but that rests on several common assumptions. First, liberals maintain, the New Deal was not a radical, socialistic, or communistic program. It was firmly within the mainstream of the American political tradition. Second, they argue, the New Deal represented a powerful (and overdue) response by government to glaring social needs that had long gone unmet. And third, it marked a decisive repudiation of old orthodoxies about the proper relationships among government, business, labor, and other groups in society.

The leading voice in the liberal chorus has long been Arthur M. Schlesinger, Jr. , who argued in the three volumes of *The Age of Roosevelt* (1957–1960) that the New Deal marked a continuation of the long struggle between public power and private interests, but that Roosevelt had moved that struggle to a new level. The unrestrained power of the business community was finally confronted with an effective challenge, and what emerged was a system of reformed capitalism, with far more protection for workers, farmers, consumers, and others than in the past.

Other liberals have gone further. Carl Degler, in *Out of Our Past* (1959), called the Roosevelt years a "Third American Revolution" (the first two being the Revolution of 1776 and the Civil War). It marked, he claimed, "the crossing of a

African Americans and the New Deal

One group the New Deal did relatively little to assist was African Americans. The administration was not hostile to black aspirations. On the contrary, the New Deal was probably more sympathetic to them than any previous government of the twentieth century. Eleanor Roosevelt spoke throughout the 1930s on behalf of racial justice and put continuing pressure on her husband and others in the federal government to ease discrimination against blacks. She was also partially responsibile for what was, symbolically at least, one of the most important events of the decade for African Americans. When the black singer Marian Anderson was refused permission in the spring of 1939 to give a concert in the auditorium of the Daughters of the American Revolution (Washington's only concert hall), Eleanor Roosevelt resigned from the organization and then (along with Interior Secretary Harold

Ickes, another champion of racial equality) helped secure government permission for her to sing on the steps of the Lincoln Memorial. Anderson's Easter Sunday concert attracted 75,000 people and became, in effect, the first modern civil-rights demonstration.

The president himself appointed a number of blacks to significant second-level positions in his administration. Roosevelt appointees such as Robert Weaver, William Hastie, and Mary McLeod Bethune created an informal network of officeholders who consulted frequently with one another and who became known as the "Black Cabinet." Eleanor Roosevelt, Harold Ickes, and Harry Hopkins all made efforts to ensure that New Deal relief programs did not exclude blacks; and by 1935, perhaps a quarter of all African Americans were receiving some form of government assistance. One result was a historic change in black electoral behavior. As late as 1932, most American blacks were voting Republican, as they had since the Civil War. By 1936,

WHERE HISTORIANS DISAGREE

divide from which, it would seem, there could be no turning back." Eric Goldman, in *Rendezvous with Destiny* (1952) and later works, called the New Deal the culmination of a "Half-Century of Revolution." Although Roosevelt drew heavily on the traditions of the progressive past, "there was something more to New Deal liberalism" because it included unprecedented new departures such as Social Security.

Richard Hofstadter offered a more skeptical assessment of the New Deal in the 1950s, but one that fell largely within the liberal framework. In *The Age of Reform* (1955), he emphasized the New Deal's discontinuities with the past. It was, he said, a "drastic new departure . . . different from anything that had yet happened in the United States"—a program that even many old progressives found alarming, and opposed. The New Deal had largely abandoned the progressive concern about reshaping the corporate world, what Hofstadter called "entrepreneurial" reform. Instead, New Deal liberalism took on a "social-democratic tinge that had never before been present in American reform movements" and raised a new set of issues to prominence: "so-

cial security, unemployment insurance, wages and hours, and housing."

Hofstadter not only echoed the view of other liberals that the New Deal marked an important break with the past; he also gave early expression to some of the criticisms that historians in the 1960s would begin to offer. In *The American Political Tradition* (1948) and again in *The Age of Reform*, he complained that the New Deal's fragmented, "pragmatic" aproach had lacked a central, guiding philosophy. James MacGregor Burns, in *Roosevelt: The Lion and the Fox* (1956), raised other objections: that Roosevelt's wily political methods had often led him away from the proper goals to reform; that he had failed to make full use of his potential as a leader but had accommodated himself unnecessarily to existing patterns of political power.

The first systematic "revisionist" interpretation of the New Deal came in 1963, in William Leuchtenburg's *Franklin D. Roosevelt and the New Deal*. Leuchtenburg was a sympathetic critic, arguing that most of the limitations of the New Deal were a result of the restrictons imposed on Roosevelt by the political and ideological realities of

more than 90 percent of them were voting Democratic—the beginnings of a political alliance that would endure for decades.

Blacks supported Franklin Roosevelt because they knew he was not their enemy. But they had few illusions that the New Deal represented a millennium in American race relations. For example, the president was never willing to risk losing the support of southern Democrats by supporting legislation to make lynching a federal crime. Nor would he endorse efforts in Congress to ban the poll tax, one of the most potent tools by which white southerners kept blacks from voting.

New Deal relief agencies did not challenge, and indeed reinforced, existing patterns of discrimination. The Civilian Conservation Corps established separate black camps. The NRA codes tolerated paying blacks less than whites doing the same jobs. Blacks were largely excluded from employment in the TVA. The Federal Housing Administration refused to provide

mortgages to blacks moving into white neighborhoods, and the first public housing projects financed by the federal government were racially segregated. The WPA routinely relegated black, Hispanic, and Asian workers to the least-skilled and lowest-paying jobs, or excluded them altogether; when funding ebbed, nonwhites, like women, were among the first to be dismissed.

The New Deal was not hostile to black Americans, and it did much to help them advance. But it refused to make the issue of race a significant part of its agenda.

The New Deal and the "Indian Problem"

In many respects, government policies toward the Indian tribes in the 1930s were simply a continuation of the long-established effort to encourage Native Americans to assimilate. Senator Burton K. Wheeler of Mon-

his time—that the New Deal probably could not have done much more than it did. Nevertheless, Leuchtenburg openly challenged earlier views of the New Deal as a revolution in social policy. He was able to muster only enough enthusiasm to call it a "halfway revolution," one that enhanced the positions of some previously disadvantaged groups (notably farmers and factory workers) but did little or nothing for many others (including blacks, sharecroppers, and the urban poor). Ellis Hawley augmented these moderate criticisms of the Roosevelt record in *The New Deal and the Problem of Monopoly* (1966). In examining 1930s economic policies, Hawley challenged liberal assumptions that the New Deal acted as the foe of private business interests. On the contrary, he argued, New Deal efforts were in many cases designed to enhance the position of private entrepreneurs—even, at times, at the expense of some of the liberal reform goals that administration officials espoused.

Other historians in the 1960s, writing from the perspective of the New Left, expressed much harsher criticisms of the New Deal. Barton Bernstein, in a 1968 essay, compiled a dreary chroni-

cle of missed opportunites, inadequate responses to problems, and damaging New Deal initiatives. The Roosevelt administration may have saved capitalism, Bernstein charged, but it failed to help—and in many ways actually harmed—those groups most in need of assistance. Paul Conkin, in *The New Deal* (1967), similarly chastised the government of the 1930s for its policies toward marginal farmers, its failure to institute meaningful tax reform, and its excessive generosity toward certain business interests. And Ronald Radosh, in 1968, portrayed the New Deal as an effective agent for the consolidation of modern corporate capitalism. Several essays by Thomas Ferguson in the 1980s and Colin Gordon's 1994 book *New Deals* took such arguments further. They cited the close ties between the New Deal and internationalist financiers and industrialists; the liberalism of the1930s was a product of their shared interest in stabilizing capitalism.

Until the work of Ferguson and Gordon, the New Left attack on the New Deal never developed very far beyond preliminary statements. Instead, by the 1970s and 1980s, most scholars seemed largely to have accepted the revised lib-

tana expressed the sentiments of many members of Congress (and many other white Americans) when he said in 1934, in the midst of a hearing on an Indian reform bill, "What we are trying to do is get rid of the Indian problem rather than add to it." By that he meant that the purpose of reforms should be to reduce the numbers of Native Americans who identified themselves as members of tribes and increase the number of those who attempted to become part of the larger society and culture.

But the principal elements of federal policy in the New Deal years worked to advance a very different goal, largely because of the efforts of the extraordinary commissioner of Indian affairs in those years, John Collier. Collier was a former social worker who had become committed to the cause of the Indians after exposure to tribal cultures in New Mexico in the 1920s. More important, he was greatly influenced by the

work of twentieth-century anthropologists who promoted the idea of cultural relativism—the idea that every culture should be accepted and respected on its own terms and that no culture was inherently superior to another. Cultural relativism was a challenge to the three-centuries-old assumption among white Americans that Indians were "savages" and that white society was inherently superior and more "civilized."

Collier promoted legislation that would, he hoped, reverse the pressures on Native Americans to assimilate and would allow them the right to remain Indians. Not all tribal leaders agreed with Collier; indeed, his belief in the importance of preserving Indian culture would not find its broadest support among the tribes until the 1960s. Nevertheless, Collier effectively promoted legislation—which became the Indian Reorganization Act of 1934—to advance his goals. Among other things it restored to the tribes the right to own

WHERE HISTORIANS DISAGREE

eral view: that the New Deal was a significant (and most agree valuable) chapter in the history of reform, but one that worked within rigid, occasionally crippling limits. Much of the recent work on the New Deal, therefore, has been less interested in the question of whether it was a "conservative" or "revolutionary" phenomenon than in the question of the constraints within which it was operating. The sociologist Theda Skocpol, in an important series of articles, has emphasized (along with others) the issue of "state capacity" as an important New Deal constraint; ambitious reform ideas often foundered, she argued, because of the absence of a government bureaucracy with sufficient strength and expertise to shape or administer them. James T. Patterson, Barry Karl, Mark Leff, and others have emphasized the political constraints the New Deal encountered. Both in Congress and among the public, conservative inhibitions about government remained strong; the New Deal was as much a product of the pressures of its conservative opponents as of its liberal supporters. Frank Freidel, Ellis Hawley, Herbert Stein, and many others point as well to the ideological constraints

affecting Franklin Roosevelt and his supporters. Alan Brinkley, in *The End of Reform* (1995), has described a transition in New Deal thinking from a regulatory view of government to one that envisioned relatively little direct interference by government in the corporate world; a movement toward an essentially "compensatory" state centered on Keynesian welfare state programs.

The phrase "New Deal liberalism" has come in the postwar era to seem synonymous with modern ideas of aggressive federal management of the economy, elaborate welfare systems, a powerful bureaucracy, and large-scale government spending. The "Reagan Revolution" of the 1980s often portrayed itself as a reaction to the "legacy of the New Deal." Many historians of the New Deal, however, would argue that the modern idea of "New Deal liberalism" bears only a limited relationship to the ideas that New Dealers themselves embraced. The liberal accomplishments of the 1930s can only be understood in the context of their own time; later liberal efforts drew from that legacy but also altered it to fit the needs and assumptions of a very different era.

land collectively (reversing the allotment policy adopted in 1887, which encouraged the breaking up of tribal lands into individually owned plots—a policy that had led to the loss of over 90 million acres of tribal land to white speculators and others). In the thirteen years after passage of the 1934 bill, tribal land increased by nearly 4 million acres, and Indian agricultural income increased dramatically (from under $2 million in 1934 to over $49 million in 1947).

Even with the redistribution of lands under the 1934 act, however, Indians continued to possess, for the most part, only territory whites did not want—much of it arid, some of it desert. And as a group, they continued to constitute the poorest segment of the population. The efforts of the 1930s did not solve what some called the "Indian problem." They did, however, provide Indians with some tools for rebuilding the viability of the tribes.

Women and the New Deal

The New Deal was not hostile to feminist aspirations, but neither did it do a great deal to advance them. That was largely because such aspirations did not have sufficiently widespread support (even among women) to make it politically advantageous for the administration to back them.

There were, to be sure, important symbolic gestures on behalf of women. Roosevelt appointed the first female cabinet member in the nation's history, Secretary of Labor Frances Perkins. He also named more than 100 other women to positions at lower levels of the federal bureaucracy. They created an active female network within the government and cooperated with one another in advancing causes of interest to women. Such appointments were in part a response to pressure from Eleanor Roosevelt, who was a committed advo-

ELEANOR ROOSEVELT AND MARY MCLEOD BETHUNE
Mary McLeod Bethune was one of a small but energetic group of African-American officeholders in the Roosevelt administration. Together they formed an informal network known as the "Black Cabinet." Among their most important allies was Eleanor Roosevelt, who is shown here appearing with Bethune at a 1937 "National Conference on Problems of the Negro and Negro Youth," organized by the National Youth Administration. Bethune was the NYA's Director of Negro Activities. *(UPI/Bettmann)*

cate of women's rights and a champion of humanitarian causes. Molly Dewson, head of the Women's Division of the Democratic National Committee, was also influential in securing federal appointments for women as well as in increasing their role within the Democratic Party. Several women received appointments to the federal judiciary. And one, Hattie Caraway of Arkansas, became in 1934 the first woman ever elected to a full term in the U.S. Senate. (She was running to succeed her husband, who had died in office.)

But New Deal support for women operated within limits, partly because New Deal women themselves had limited views of what their aims should be. Frances Perkins and many others in the administration emerged out of the feminist tradition of the progressive era, which emphasized not so much sexual equality as special protections for women. Perkins herself had been instrumental in fighting for passage of various state laws safeguarding female workers. She opposed the National Woman's Party and its goal of securing the Equal Rights Amendment because she feared the amendment would threaten the protective mechanisms that she had helped to establish. Perkins and other women reformers were instrumental in creating support for, and shaping the character of, the Social Security Act of 1935. But they built into that bill their own notion of women's special place in a male-dominated economy. The principal provision of the bill

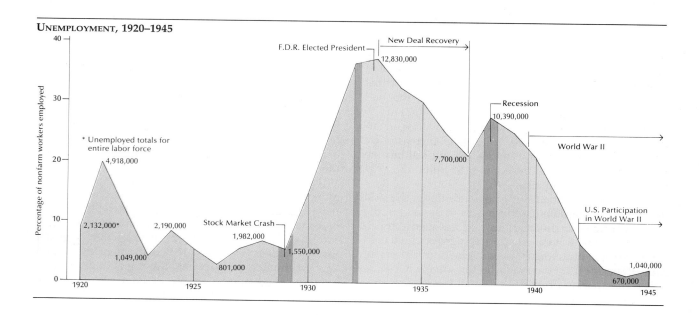

UNEMPLOYMENT, 1920–1945

specifically designed for women—the Aid to Dependent Children program—was modeled on the state-level mothers' pensions that generations of progressive women had worked to pass earlier in the century.

The New Deal generally supported the prevailing belief that in hard times women should withdraw from the workplace to open up more jobs for men. Even Frances Perkins spoke out against what she called the "pin-money worker"—the married woman working to earn extra money for the household. New Deal relief agencies offered relatively little employment for women. The NRA sanctioned sexually discriminatory wage practices. The Social Security program at first excluded domestic servants, waitresses, and other predominantly female occupations.

As with blacks, so also with women: the New Deal was not actively hostile; in many ways, it was unprecedentedly supportive. It did, however, accept prevailing cultural norms. There was not yet sufficient political pressure from women themselves to persuade the administration to do otherwise.

The New Deal and the West

One part of American society that did receive special attention from the New Deal was the American West, which benefited disproportionately from New Deal relief and public works programs. The West received more federal funds per capita through New Deal relief programs than any other region.

Most westerners were eager for the assistance New Deal agencies provided, but their political leaders were not always as supportive. In Colorado, for example, the state legislature refused to provide the required matching funds for FERA relief in 1933. When, in response, Harry Hopkins cut Colorado off from the program, unemployed people rioted in Denver and looted food stores. Only then did the legislature reverse course and provide funding.

Just as in the South locally administered relief programs did not challenge prevailing racial norms, so in the West New Deal programs sustained existing racial and ethnic prejudices. In several states, relief agencies paid different groups at different rates: white Anglos received the most generous aid; blacks, Indians, and Mexican American received lower levels of support. In the CCC camps in New Mexico, Hispanics and Anglos sometimes worked in the same camps, but there were frequent tensions and occasional conflicts between them.

But the main reason for the New Deal's particular impact on the West was that conditions in the region

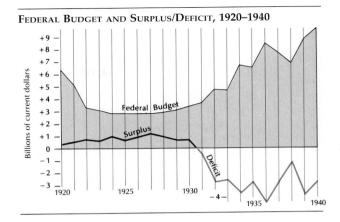

FEDERAL BUDGET AND SURPLUS/DEFICIT, 1920–1940

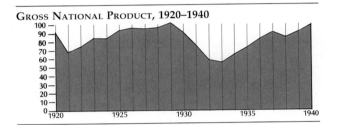

GROSS NATIONAL PRODUCT, 1920–1940

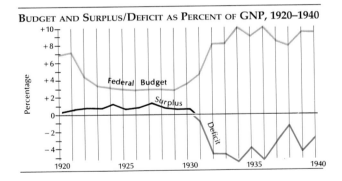

BUDGET AND SURPLUS/DEFICIT AS PERCENT OF GNP, 1920–1940

made the government's programs especially important. Federal agricultural programs had an enormous impact on the West because farming remained so much more central to the economy of the region than it did in much of the East. The largest New Deal public works programs—the great dams and power stations—were mainly in the West, both because the best

SIGNIFICANT EVENTS

1933 Franklin Roosevelt inaugurated

"First New Deal" legislation enacted

United States officially abandons gold standard

Prohibiton ends with repeal of Twenty-first Amendment

Dr. Francis Townsend begins campaign for old-age pensions

1934 Conservatives create American Liberty League

Huey Long establishes Share-Our-Wealth Society

Labor militancy increases

Indian Reorganization Act passed

1935 Supreme Court invalidates NRA

"Second New Deal" legislation passed

Father Charles Coughlin establishes National Union for Social Justice

John L. Lewis and allies break with AFL

Huey Long assassinated

1936 Supreme Court invalidates Agricultural Adjustment Act

CIO established

Sit-down strikes begin

Roosevelt wins reelection by record margin

1937 U.S. Steel recognizes Steel Workers' Organizing Committee

Roosevelt proposes "Court-packing" plan

Supreme Court validates Wagner Act

"Memorial Day Massacre" in Chicago

New Deal spending reduced

Severe recession begins

1938 Roosevelt proposes new spending measures

Temporary National Economic Committee established

Executive reorganization plan proposed

1939 Marian Anderson sings at Lincoln Memorial

---

locations for such facilities were there and because the West had the most need for new sources of water and power. The Grand Coulee dam on the Columbia River was the largest public works project in American history to that point, and it provided cheap electric power for much of the Northwest. Its construction, and the construction of other, smaller dams and water projects in the region, created a basis for economic development in the region.

Without this enormous public investment by the federal government, much of the economic development that transformed the West after World War II would have been much more difficult, if not impossible, to achieve. But the region paid a price for the government's beneficence. For generations after the Great Depression, the federal government maintained a much greater and more visible bureaucratic presence in the West than in any other region.

The New Deal and the National Economy

The most frequent criticisms of the New Deal involve its failure genuinely to revive or reform the American economy. New Dealers never fully recognized the value of government spending as a vehicle for recovery, and their efforts along other lines never succeeded in ending the Depression. The economic boom sparked by World War II, not the New Deal, finally ended the crisis. Nor did the New Deal substantially alter the distribution of power within American capitalism; and it had only a small impact on the distribution of wealth among the American people.

Nevertheless, the New Deal did have a number of important and lasting effects on both the behavior and the structure of the American economy. It helped elevate new groups—workers, farmers, and others—to positions from which they could at times effectively challenge the power of the corporations. It contributed to the economic development of the West and, to a lesser degree, the South. It increased the regulatory functions of the federal government in ways that helped stabilize previously troubled areas of the economy: the stock market, the banking system, and others. And the administration helped establish the basis for new forms of federal fiscal policy, which in the postwar years would give the government tools for promoting and regulating economic growth.

The New Deal also created the basis of the federal welfare state, through its many relief programs and above all through the Social Security system. The conservative inhibitions New Dealers brought to this task ensured that the welfare system that ultimately emerged would be limited in its impact (at least in comparison with those of other industrial nations), would reinforce some traditional patterns of gender and racial discrimination, and would be expensive and cumbersome to administer. But for all its limits, the new system marked a historic break with the federal government's traditional reluctance to offer public assistance to its neediest citizens.

The New Deal and American Politics

Perhaps the most dramatic effect of the New Deal was on the structure and behavior of American government itself and on the character of American politics. Franklin Roosevelt helped enhance the power of the federal government as a whole. By the end of the 1930s, state and local governments were clearly of secondary importance to the government in Washington; in the past, that had not always been clear. Roosevelt also established the presidency as the preeminent center of authority within the federal government. Never again would Congress be able to wield as much independent power as it had in the years before the New Deal. And never again would it have the same control over presidential authority.

Finally, the New Deal had a profound impact on how the American people defined themselves politically. It took a weak, divided Democratic Party, which had been a minority force in American politics for many decades, and turned it into a mighty coalition that would dominate national party competition for more than forty years. It turned the attention of many voters away from some of the cultural issues that had preoccupied them in the 1920s and awakened in them an interest in economic matters of direct importance to their lives. And it created among the American people greatly increased expectations of government—expectations that the New Deal itself did not always fulfill but that survived to become the basis of new liberal crusades in the postwar era.

SUGGESTED READINGS

General and Biographical Studies. Anthony J. Badger, *The New Deal* (1989). John Braeman et al., eds., *The New Deal*, 2 vols. (1975). James MacGregor Burns, *Roosevelt: The Lion and the Fox* (1956). Blanche Wiesen Cooke, *Eleanor Roosevelt* (1992). Paul Conkin, *The New Deal*, 2nd ed. (1975). Kenneth Davis, *FDR: The New York Years: 1928–1933* (1985); *FDR: The New Deal Years, 1933–1937* (1986); *FDR: Into the Storm, 1937-1940* (1993). Peter Fearon, *War, Prosperity, and Depression* (1987). Steve Fraser and Gary Gerstle, eds., *The Rise and Fall of New Deal Liberalism* (1988). Frank Freidel, *Franklin D. Roosevelt*, 4 vols. (1952–1973); *Franklin D. Roosevelt: A Rendezvous with Destiny* (1990). Joseph P. Lash, *Eleanor and Franklin* (1971). William E. Leuchtenburg, *Franklin D. Roosevelt and the New Deal* (1963); *In the Shadow of FDR* (1983). Katie Louchheim, *The Making of the New Deal* (1983). Richard Lowitt, *The New Deal and the West* (1984). Robert S. McElvaine, *The Great Depression* (1984). Gerald Nash, *The Great Depression and World War II* (1979). Edgar Robinson, *The Roosevelt Leadership* (1955). Arthur M. Schlesinger, Jr., *The Age of Roosevelt*, 3 vols. (1957–1960). Harvard Sitkoff, ed., *Fifty Years Later: The New Deal Evaluated* (1985). Geoffrey Ward, *Before the Trumpet: Young Franklin Roosevelt, 1882–1905* (1985); *A First-Class Temperament: The Emergence of Franklin Roosevelt* (1989). J. H. Wilson and Marjorie Lightman, eds., *Without Precedent: The Life and Career of Eleanor Roosevelt* (1984).

New Deal Politics and Programs. Mimi Abramowitz, *Regulating the Lives of Women* (1988). Bernard Bellush, *The Failure of the NRA* (1975). Donald Brand, *Corporatism and the Rule of Law* (1988). William R. Brock, *Welfare, Democracy, and the New Deal* (1987). Searle Charles, *Minister of Relief* (1963). Ralph F. De Bedts, *The New Deal's SEC* (1964). Herbert Feis, *Characters in Crisis* (1966). Sidney Fine, *The Automobile Under the Blue Eagle* (1963). Frank Freidel, *Launching the New Deal* (1973). Gerald H. Gamm, *The Making of New Deal Democrats: Voting Behavior and Realignment in Boston, 1920–1940* (1989). Otis Graham, *Encore for Reform* (1967). Nancy L. Grant, *TVA and Black Americans: Planning for the Status Quo* (1990). Ellis Hawley, *The New Deal and the Problem of Monopoly* (1966). Peter H. Irons, *The New Deal Lawyers* (1982). Mark Leff, *The Limits of Symbolic Reform: The New Deal and Taxation, 1933–1939* (1984). Thomas K. McCraw, *TVA and the Power Fight* (1971). George McJimsey, *Harry Hopkins: Ally of the Poor and Defender of Democracy* (1987). Raymond Moley and Eliot Rosen, *The First New Deal* (1966). Michael Parrish, *Securities Regulation and the New Deal* (1970). James T. Patterson, *America's Struggle Against Poverty, 1900–1980* (1981). Albert U. Romasco, *The Politics of Recovery: Roosevelt's New Deal* (1983). John Salmond, *The Civilian Conservation Corps* (1967). Bonnie Fox Schwartz, *The Civil Works Administration, 1933–1934* (1984). Jordan Schwarz, *The New Dealers* (1993). Susan Ware, *Beyond Suffrage* (1981); *Partner and I: Molly Dewson, Feminism, and New Deal Politics* (1987).

Agriculture. Christina Campbell, *The Farm Bureaus* (1962). David Conrad, *The Forgotten Farmers* (1965). Lowell K. Dyson,

Red Harvest: The Communist Party and American Farmers (1982). Gilbert Fite, *George M. Peek and the Fight for Farm Parity* (1954). David Hamilton, *From New Day to New Deal: American Farm Policy from Hoover to Roosevelt, 1928–1933* (1991). Richard S. Kirkendall, *Social Scientists and Farm Politics in the Age of Roosevelt* (1966). Paul Mertz, *The New Deal and Southern Rural Poverty* (1978). Van L. Perkins, *Crisis in Agriculture* (1969). Bruce Shulman, *From Cotton Belt to Sunbelt* (1991).

Depression Dissidents. David H. Bennett, *Demagogues in the Depression* (1969). Alan Brinkley, *Voices of Protest: Huey Long, Father Coughlin, and the Great Depression* (1982). Donald Grubbs, *Cry from the Cotton* (1971). Glen Jeansonne, *Gerald L. K. Smith: Minister of Hate* (1988). Abraham Holzman, *The Townsend Movement* (1963). R. Alan Lawson, *The Failure of Independent Liberalism* (1971). Donald McCoy, *Angry Voices: Left-of-Center Politics in the New Deal Era* (1958). Leo Ribuffo, *The Old Christian Right: The Protestant Far Right from the Great Depression to the Cold War* (1983). Arthur M. Schlesinger, Jr., *The Politics of Upheaval* (1960). Charles J. Tull, *Father Coughlin and the New Deal* (1965). T. Harry Williams, *Huey Long* (1969). George Wolfskill, *Revolt of the Conservatives* (1962).

The "Second New Deal". Sidney Baldwin, *Poverty and Politics: The Farm Security Administration* (1968). Paul Conkin, *Tomorrow a New World* (1971). J. Joseph Huthmacher, *Senator Robert Wagner and the Rise of Urban Liberalism* (1968). Roy Lubove, *The Struggle for Social Security* (1968). William F. McDonald, *Federal Relief Administration and the Arts* (1968). Jerre Mangione, *The Dream and the Deal* (1972). Jane deHart Matthews, *The Federal Theater* (1967). W. D. Rowley, *M. L. Wilson and the Campaign for Domestic Allotment* (1970).

The Late New Deal. Leonard Baker, *Back to Back* (1967). Alan Brinkley, *The End of Reform: New Deal Liberalism in Recession and War* (1995); Frank Freidel, *FDR and the South* (1965). Barry Karl, *Executive Reorganization and Reform in the New Deal* (1963). William Leuchtenburg, "The Origins of Franklin D. Roosevelt's 'Court-Packing' Plan," in Philip B. Kurland, ed., *The Supreme Court Review* (1966). Dean May, *From New Deal to New Economics* (1981). James T. Patterson, *Congressional Conservatism and the New Deal* (1967); *The New Deal and the States* (1969). Richard Polenberg, *Reorganizing Roosevelt's Government* (1966). Theodore Rosenof, *Dogma and Depression* (1972); *Patterns of Political Economy in America* (1983). Herbert Stein, *The Fiscal Revolution in America* (1969). Charles Trout, *Boston: The Great Depression and the New Deal* (1977). George Wolfskill and John Hudson, *All But the People* (1969).

Blacks, Hispanics, Indians. Rodolfo Acuna, *Occupied America: A History of Chicanos* (rev. ed. 1988). Francisco E. Balerman, *In Defense of La Raza* (1982). Ralph Bunche, *The Political Status of the Negro in the Age of FDR* (1973). Dan T. Carter, *Scottsboro* (1969). Vine DeLoria, Jr., *The Nations Within* (1984). Sarah Deutsch, *No Separate Refuge: Culture, Class, and*

Gender on the Anglo-Hispanic Frontier in the American Southwest, 1880–1940 (1987). John Dollard, *Caste and Class in a Southern Town*, 3rd ed. (1957). Cheryl Lynn Greenberg, *"Or Does It Explode?": Black Harlem in the Great Depression* (1991). Laurence M. Hauptman, *The Iroquois and the New Deal* (1981). Abraham Hoffman, *Unwanted Mexican Americans in the Great Depression* (1974). Laurence C. Kelly, *The Assault on Assimilation: John Collier and the Origins of Indian Policy Reform* (1983). John B. Kirby, *Black Americans in the Roosevelt Era* (1980). Clifford Lytle, *American Indians, American Justice* (1983). Carey McWilliams, *Factories in the Field* (1939). Donald L. Parman, *The Navajos and the New Deal* (1976). Kenneth R. Philp, *John Collier's Crusade for Indian Reform, 1920–1954* (1977). Harvard Sitkoff, *A New Deal for Blacks* (1978). Graham D. Taylor, *The New Deal and American Indian Tribalism* (1980). Nancy Weiss, *Farewell to the Party of Lincoln: Black Politics in the Age of FDR* (1983); *The National Urban League* (1974). Raymond Wolters, *Negroes and the Great Depression* (1970). Robert L. Zangrando, *The NAACP Crusade Against Lynching* (1980).

Labor. Jerold Auerbach, *Labor and Liberty* (1966). John Barnard, *Walter Reuther and the Rise of the Auto Workers* (1983). Irving Bernstein, *Turbulent Years* (1970); *A Caring Society: The New Deal, the Worker, and the Great Depression* (1985). David Brody, *Workers in Industrial America* (1980). Bert Cochran, *Labor and Communism* (1977). Lizabeth Cohen, *Making a New Deal: Industrial Workers in Chicago, 1919–1939* (1990). Melvyn Dubofsky and Warren Van Tine, *John L. Lewis* (1977). Elizabeth Faue, *Community of Suffering and Struggle: Women, Men, and the Labor Movement in Minnesota, 1915–1945* (1991). Sidney Fine, *Sit-Down* (1969). Steve Fraser, *Labor Will Rule: Sidney Hillman and the Rise of American Labor* (1991). Joshua Freeman, *In Transit: The Transport Workers Union in New York City, 1933–1966* (1989). Peter Friedlander, *The Emergence of a UAW Local* (1975). Gary Gerstle, *Working-Class Americanism: The Politics of Labor in a Textile City 1914–1960* (1989). John W. Hevener, *Which Side Are You On? The Harlan County Coal Miners, 1931–1939* (1978). August Meier and Elliott Rudwick, *Black Detroit and the Rise of the UAW* (1979). David Milton, *The Politics of U.S. Labor: From the Great Depression to the New Deal* (1980). Bruce Nelson, *Workers on the Waterfront: Seamen, Longshoremen, and Unionism in the 1930s* (1988). Daniel Nelson, *American Rubber Workers and Organized Labor, 1900–1941* (1988). Paula F. Pfeffer, *A. Philip Randolph, Pioneer of the Civil Rights Movement* (1990). Ronald W. Schatz, *The Electrical Workers* (1983). George G. Suggs, Jr., *Union Busting in the Tristate: The Oklahoma, Kansas, and Missouri Metal Workers Strike of 1935* (1986). Christopher L. Tomlins, *The State and the Unions* (1985). Robert H. Zieger, *John L. Lewis: Labor Leader* (1988); *American Workers, American Unions, 1920–1985* (1986).

EXHORTING HITLER'S LEGIONS
"This hand guides the Reich," this Nazi propaganda poster of the 1930s read. The hand was
Adolf Hitler's, and, the poster continued, "German youth follow it in the ranks of the
Hitler Youth." *(Institute of Contemporary History and Wiener Library, Ltd., London)*

CHAPTER TWENTY-SEVEN

THE GLOBAL CRISIS, 1921–1941

ENRY CABOT LODGE OF Massachusetts, chairman of the Senate Foreign Relations Committee and one of the most powerful figures in the Republican Party, led the fight against ratification of the Treaty of Versailles in 1918 and 1919. In part because of his efforts, the Senate defeated the treaty; the United States failed to join the League of Nations; and American foreign policy embarked on an independent course that for the next two decades would attempt, but ultimately fail, to expand American influence and maintain international stability without committing the United States to any lasting relationships with other nations.

Lodge was not an isolationist. He recognized that America had emerged from World War I the most powerful nation in the world. He believed the United States should use that power and should exert its influence internationally. But he believed, too, that America's expanded role in the world should reflect the nation's own interests and its own special virtues; it should leave the nation unfettered with obligations to anyone else. He said in 1919:

> We are a great moral asset of Christian civilization. . . . How did we get there? By our own efforts. Nobody led us, nobody guided us, nobody controlled us. . . . I would keep America as she has been—not isolated, not prevent her from joining other nations for . . . great purposes—but I wish her to be master of her own fate.

Lodge was not alone in voicing such sentiments. Throughout the 1920s, those controlling American foreign policy attempted to increase America's role in the world while at the same time keeping the nation free of burdensome commitments that might limit its own freedom of action. In 1933, Franklin Roosevelt became president, and brought his own legacy as a leading Wilsonian internationalist and erstwhile supporter of the League of Nations. But for more than six years, Roosevelt also attempted to keep America the "master of her own fate," to avoid important global commitments that might reduce the nation's ability to pursue its own ends.

In the end, the cautious, limited American internationalism of the interwar years proved insufficient to protect the interests of the United States, to create global stability, or to keep the nation from becoming involved in the greatest war in human history.

THE DIPLOMACY OF THE NEW ERA

Critics of American foreign policy in the 1920s often used a single word to describe the cause of their disenchantment: isolationism. Having rejected the Wilsonian vision of a new world order, they claimed, the nation had turned its back on the rest of the globe and repudiated its international responsibilities. In fact, the United States played a more active role in world affairs in the 1920s than it had at almost any previous time in its history—even if not the role the Wilsonians had prescribed.

Replacing the League

It was clear when the Harding administration took office in 1921 that American membership in the League of Nations was no longer a realistic possibility. As if finally to bury the issue, Secretary of State Charles Evans Hughes secured legislation from Congress in 1921 declaring the war with Germany at an end, and then proceeded to negotiate separate peace treaties with the former Central Powers. Through these treaties, American policymakers believed, the United States would receive all the advantages of the Versailles Treaty with none of the burdensome responsibilities. But Hughes was committed to finding something to replace the League as a guarantor of world peace and stability. He therefore, embarked on a series of efforts to build safeguards against future wars—but safeguards that would not hamper American freedom of action in the world.

The most important such effort was the Washington Conference of 1921—an attempt to prevent what was threatening to become a costly and destabilizing naval armaments race between America, Britain, and Japan. In his opening speech Hughes startled the delegates by proposing a plan for dramatic reductions in the fleets of all three nations and a ten-year moratorium on the construction of large warships. He called for the actual scrapping of nearly 2 million tons of existing shipping. Far more surprising than that proposal was the fact that the conference ultimately agreed to accept most of its terms, something that Hughes himself apparently had not anticipated. The Five-Power Pact of February 1922 established both limits for total naval tonnage and a ratio of armaments among the signatories. For every 5 tons of American and British warships, Japan would maintain 3 and France and Italy 1.75 each. (Although the treaty seemed to confirm the military inferiority of Japan, in fact it sanctioned Japanese dominance in East Asia. America and Britain had to spread their fleets across the globe; Japan was concerned only with the Pacific.) The Washington Conference also produced two other, related treaties: the Nine-Power Pact, pledging a continuation of the Open Door policy in China, and the Four-Power Pact, by which the United States, Britain, France, and Japan promised to respect one another's Pacific territories and cooperate to prevent aggression.

The Washington Conference began the New Era effort to protect the peace (and to protect the international economic interests of the United States) without accepting active international duties. The Kellogg-Briand Pact of 1928 concluded it. When the French foreign minister, Aristide Briand, asked the United States in 1927 to join an alliance against Germany, Secretary of State Frank Kellogg (who had replaced Hughes in 1925) instead proposed a multilateral treaty outlawing war as an instrument of national policy. Fourteen nations signed the agreement in Paris on August 27, 1928, amid great solemnity and wide international acclaim. Forty-eight other nations later joined the pact. It contained no instruments of enforcement but rested, as Kellogg put it, on the "moral force" of world opinion.

Debts and Diplomacy

The first responsibility of diplomacy, Hughes, Kellogg, and others agreed, was to ensure that American overseas trade faced no obstacles to expansion and that, once established, it would remain free of interference. Preventing a dangerous armaments race and reducing the possibility of war were steps to that end. So were the new financial arrangements that emerged at the same time. The United States was most concerned about Europe, on whose economic health American prosperity in large part depended. Not only were the major European industrial powers suffering from the devastation World War I had produced; they were also staggering under a heavy burden of debt. The Allied powers were struggling to repay $11 billion in loans they had contracted with the United States during and shortly after the war, loans that the Republican administrations were unwilling to reduce or forgive. "They hired the money, didn't they?" Calvin Coolidge once replied when asked if he favored offering Europe relief from their debts. At the same time, an even more debilitated Germany was attempting to pay the reparations levied against it by the Allies. With the financial structure of Europe on the brink of collapse, the United States stepped in with a solution.

In 1924 Charles G. Dawes, an American banker and diplomat, negotiated an agreement among France, Britain, Germany, and the United States under which American banks would provide enormous loans to the Germans, enabling them to meet their reparations payments; in return, Britain and France would agree to reduce the amount of those payments. Dawes won the Nobel Peace Prize for his efforts, but in fact the Dawes Plan did little to solve the problems it addressed. It was responsible for a growing American economic presence in Germany. It was also the source of a troubling circular pattern in international finance. America would lend money to Germany, which would use that money to pay reparations to France and England, which would in turn use those funds (as well as large loans they themselves were receiving from American banks) to repay war debts to the United States. The flow was able to continue only by virtue of the enormous debts Germany and the other European nations were accumulating to American banks and corporations.

Those banks and corporations were doing more than providing loans. They were becoming a daily presence in the economic life of Europe. American automobile manufacturers were opening European factories, capturing a large share of the overseas market. Other industries in the 1920s were establishing subsidiaries worth more than $10 billion throughout the Continent, taking advantage of the devastation of European industry and the inability of domestic corporations to recover. Some groups within the American government warned that the reckless expansion of overseas loans and investments, many in enterprises of dubious value, threatened disaster; that the United States was becoming too dependent on unstable European economies. The high tariff barriers that the Republican Congress had erected (through the Fordney-McCumber Act of 1922) were creating additional problems, such skeptics warned. European nations, unable to export their goods to the United States, were finding it difficult to earn the money necessary to repay their loans. Such warnings fell for the most part on deaf ears, and American economic expansion in Europe continued until disaster struck in 1931.

The United States government felt even fewer reservations about assisting American economic expansion in Latin America. After all, the United States had long considered that region its exclusive sphere of influence; and its investments there had been large even before World War I. During the 1920s, American military forces maintained a presence in numerous countries in the region. United States investments in Latin America more than doubled between 1924 and 1929; American corporations built roads and other facilities in many areas—partly, they argued, to weaken the appeal of revolutionary forces in the region, but at least equally to increase their own access to Latin America's rich natural resources. American banks were offering large loans to Latin American governments, just as they were in Europe; and just as in Europe, the Latin Americans were having great difficulty earning the money to repay them in the face of the formidable United States tariff barrier. By the end of the 1920s, resentment of "Yankee imperialism" was growing rapidly. The economic troubles after 1929 would only accentuate such problems.

Hoover and the World Crisis

After the relatively placid international climate of the 1920s, the diplomatic challenges facing the Hoover administration must have seemed ominous and bewildering. The world financial crisis that began in 1929 and greatly intensified after 1931 was not only creating economic distress, it was producing a dangerous nationalism that threatened the weak international agreements established during the previous decade. Above all, the Depression was toppling some existing political leaders and replacing them with powerful, belligerent governments bent on expansion as a solution to their economic problems. Hoover was confronted, therefore, with the beginning of a process that would ultimately lead to war. He lacked sufficient tools for dealing with it.

In Latin America, Hoover worked studiously to repair some of the damage created by earlier American policies. He made a ten-week goodwill tour through the region before his inauguration. Once in office, he tried to abstain from intervening in the internal affairs of neighboring nations and moved to withdraw American troops from Haiti. When economic distress led to the collapse of one Latin American regime after another, Hoover announced a new policy: America would grant diplomatic recognition to any sitting government in the region without questioning the means it had used to obtain power. He even repudiated the Roosevelt corollary to the Monroe Doctrine by refusing to permit American intervention when several Latin American countries defaulted on debt obligations to the United States in October 1931.

In Europe, the administration enjoyed few successes in its efforts to promote economic stability. When Hoover's proposed moratorium on debts in 1931 failed to attract broad support or produce financial stability (see p. 690), many economists and political leaders appealed to the president to cancel all war debts to the United States. Like his predecessors, Hoover refused; and several European nations promptly went into default, severely damaging an already tense international climate. American efforts to extend the disarmament agreements of the 1920s met with similar frustration. At a conference in London in January 1930, American negotiators reached agreement with European and Japanese delegates on extending the limits on naval construction established at the Washington Conference of 1921. But France and England, fearful of German resurgence and Japanese expansionism, insisted on so many loopholes as to make the treaty virtually meaningless. The increasing irrelevance of the New Era approach to diplomacy became even clearer at the World Disarmament Conference that opened in Geneva in January 1932. France rejected the idea of disarmament entirely and called for the creation of an international army to counter the growing power of Germany. Hoover continued to urge major reductions in armaments, including an immediate abolition of all

HITLER AND MUSSOLINI IN BERLIN
The German and Italian dictators (shown here reviewing Nazi troops in Berlin in the mid-1930s) acted publicly as if they were equals. Privately, Hitler treated Mussolini with contempt, and Mussolini complained constantly of being a junior partner in the relationship. *(Bettmann)*

"offensive" weapons (tanks, bombers) and a 30 percent reduction in all land and naval forces. The conference ultimately dissolved in failure.

The ineffectiveness of diplomacy in Europe was particularly troubling in view of some of the new governments coming to power on the Continent. Benito Mussolini's Fascist Party had been in control of Italy since the early 1920s; by the 1930s, the regime was growing increasingly nationalistic and militaristic, and Fascist leaders were loudly threatening an active campaign of imperial expansion. Even more ominous was the growing power of the National Socialist (or Nazi) Party in Germany. By the late 1920s, the Weimar Republic, the nation's government since the end of World War I, had lost virtually all popular support, discredited by, among other things, a ruinous inflation. Adolf Hitler, the stridently nationalistic leader of the Nazis, was rapidly growing in popular favor. Although he

lost a 1932 election for chancellor, Hitler would sweep into power less than a year later. His belief in the racial superiority of the Aryan (German) people, his commitment to providing Lebensraum (living space) for his "master race," his pathological anti-Semitism, and his passionate militarism—all posed a threat to European peace.

More immediately alarming to the Hoover administration was a major crisis in Asia—another early step toward World War II. The Japanese, reeling from an economic depression of their own, were concerned about the increasing strength of the Soviet Union and of Chiang Kai-shek's nationalist China. In particular, they were alarmed at Chiang's insistence on expanding his government's power in Manchuria, which remained officially a part of China but over which the Japanese had maintained effective economic control since 1905. When the moderate government of Japan failed to take forceful steps to counter Chiang's ambitions, Japan's military leaders staged what was, in effect, a coup in the autumn of 1931—seizing control of foreign policy from the weakened liberals. Weeks later, they launched a major invasion of northern Manchuria.

The American government had few options. For a while, Secretary of State Henry Stimson (who had served as secretary of war under Taft) continued to hope that Japanese moderates would regain control of the Tokyo government and halt the invasion. The militarists, however, remained in command; and by the beginning of 1932, the conquest of Manchuria was complete. Stimson issued stern (but essentially toothless) warnings to Japan and tried to use moral suasion to end the crisis. But Hoover forbade him to cooperate with the League of Nations in imposing economic sanctions against the Japanese. Stimson's only real tool in dealing with the Manchurian invasion was a refusal to grant diplomatic recognition to the new Japanese territories. Japan was unconcerned and early in 1932 expanded its aggression farther into China, attacking the city of Shanghai and killing thousands of civilians.

By the time Hoover left office early in 1933, it was clear that the international system the United States had attempted to create in the 1920s—a system based on voluntary cooperation among nations and on an American refusal to commit itself to the interests of other countries—had collapsed. The United States faced a choice. It could adopt a more energetic form of internationalism and enter into firmer and more meaningful associations with other nations. Or it could resort to nationalism and rely on its own devices for dealing with its (and the world's) problems. For the next six years, it experimented with elements of both approaches.

ISOLATIONISM AND INTERNATIONALISM

The administration of Franklin Roosevelt faced a dual challenge as it entered office in 1933. It had to deal with the worst economic crisis in the nation's history, and it had to deal with the effects of a decaying international structure. The two problems were not unrelated. It was the worldwide Depression itself that was producing much of the political chaos throughout the globe.

Through most of the 1930s, however, the United States was unwilling to make more than the faintest of gestures toward restoring stability to the world. Like many other peoples suffering economic hardship, most Americans were turning inward. Yet the realities of world affairs were not to allow the nation to remain isolated for very long—as Franklin Roosevelt realized earlier than many other Americans.

Depression Diplomacy

Roosevelt inherited from Herbert Hoover a foreign policy less concerned with issues of war and peace than with matters of economic policy. And although the New Deal rejected some of the initiatives the Republicans had begun, it continued for several years to base its foreign policy almost entirely on the nation's immediate economic needs.

Perhaps Roosevelt's sharpest break with the policies of his predecessor was on the question of American economic relations with Europe. Hoover had argued that only by resolving the question of war debts and reinforcing the gold standard could the American economy hope to recover. He had therefore, agreed to participate in the World Economic Conference, to be held in London in June 1933, to try to resolve these issues. By the time the conference assembled, however, Roosevelt had already decided to allow the gold value of the dollar to fall to enable American goods to compete in world markets. Shortly after the conference convened, Roosevelt released a famous "bombshell" message repudiating the orthodox views of most of the delegates and rejecting any agreement on currency stabilization. The conference quickly dissolved without reaching agreement, and not until 1936 did the administration finally agree to new negotiations to stabilize Western currencies.

At the same time, Roosevelt abandoned the commitments of the Hoover administration to settle the issue of war debts through international agreement. In effect, he simply let the issue die. Not only did he decline to negotiate a solution at the London Conference, but in April 1934 he signed a bill to forbid American banks from making loans to any nation in default on its debts. The result was to stop the old, circular system by which debt payments continued only by virtue of increasing American loans; within months, war-debt payments from every nation except Finland stopped for good.

If the new administration had no interest in international currency stabilization or settlement of war debts, it did have an active interest in improving America's position in world trade. Roosevelt approved the Reciprocal Trade Agreement Act of 1934, authorizing the administration to negotiate treaties lowering tariffs by as much as 50 percent in return for reciprocal reductions by other nations. By 1939, Secretary of State Cordell Hull, a devoted free-trader, had negotiated new treaties with twenty-one countries. The result was an increase in American exports to them of nearly 40 percent. But most of the agreements admitted only products not competitive with American industry and agriculture, so imports into the United States continued to lag. Thus other nations were not obtaining the American currency needed to buy American products or pay off debts to American banks.

America and the Soviet Union

America's hopes of expanding its foreign trade helped produce efforts by the Roosevelt administration to improve relations with the Soviet Union. The United States and Russia had viewed each other with mistrust and even hostility since the Bolshevik Revolution of 1917, and the American government still had not officially recognized the Soviet regime by 1933. But powerful voices within the United States were urging a change in policy—less because the revulsion with which most Americans viewed communism had diminished than because the Soviet Union appeared to be a possible source of trade. The Russians, too, were eager for a new relationship. They were hoping in particular for American cooperation in containing the power of Japan on Russia's southeastern flank. In November 1933, therefore, Soviet Foreign Minister Maxim Litvinov reached an agreement with the president in Washington. The Soviets would cease their propaganda efforts in the United States and protect American citizens in Russia; in return, the United States would recognize the communist regime.

Despite this promising beginning, however, relations with the Soviet Union soon soured once again. American trade failed to establish a foothold in Russia, disappointing hopes in the United States; and the American government did little to reassure the Soviets that it was interested in stopping Japanese expansion in Asia, dousing expectations in Russia. By the end of 1934, the Soviet Union and the United States were once again viewing each other with considerable mistrust. And Stalin, having abandoned whatever hopes he might once have had of cooperation with America, was beginning to consider making agreements of his own with the fascist governments of Japan and Germany.

The Good Neighbor Policy

Somewhat more successful were American efforts to enhance both diplomatic and economic relations with Latin America through what became known as the "Good Neighbor Policy." Latin America was one of the most important targets of the new policy of trade reciprocity. During the 1930s, the United States succeeded in increasing both exports to and imports from the other nations of the Western Hemisphere by over 100 percent. Closely tied to these new economic relationships was a new American attitude toward intervention in Latin America. The Hoover administration had unofficially abandoned the earlier American practice of using military force to compel Latin American governments to repay debts, respect foreign investments, or otherwise behave "responsibly." The Roosevelt administration went further. At the Inter-American Conference in Montevideo in December 1933, Secretary of State Hull signed a formal convention declaring: "No state has the right to intervene in the internal or external affairs of another." Roosevelt respected that pledge throughout his years in office.

The Good Neighbor Policy did not mean, however, that the United States had abandoned its influence in Latin America. On the contrary, it had simply replaced one form of leverage with another. Instead of military force, Americans now tried to use economic influence. The new reliance on economic pressures eased tensions between the United States and its neighbors considerably, eliminating the most abrasive and conspicuous irritants in the relationship. It did nothing to stem the growing American domination of the Latin American economies.

The Rise of Isolationism

The first years of the Roosevelt administration marked not only the death of Hoover's hopes for international economic agreements, but the end of any hopes for world peace through treaties and disarmament as well.

That the international arrangements of the 1920s were no longer suitable for the world of the 1930s became obvious in the first months of the Roosevelt presidency, when the new administration attempted to stimulate movement toward world disarmament. The arms control conference in Geneva had been meeting, without result, since 1932; and in May 1933, Roosevelt attempted to spur it to action by submitting a new American proposal for arms reductions. Negotiations stalled and then broke down on the Roosevelt proposal; and only a few months later, first Hitler and then Mussolini withdrew from the talks altogether. The Geneva Conference, it was clear, was a failure. Two years later, Japan withdrew from the London Naval Conference, which was attempting to draw up an agreement to continue the limitations on naval armaments negotiated at the Washington Conference of 1921.

Faced with a choice between more active efforts to stabilize the world or more energetic attempts to isolate the nation from it, most Americans unhesitatingly chose the latter. Support for isolationism emerged from many quarters. Old Wilsonian internationalists had grown disillusioned with the League of Nations and its inability to stop Japanese aggression in Asia; internationalism, they were beginning to argue, had failed. Other Americans were listening to the argument (popular among populist-minded politicians in the Midwest and West) that powerful business interests—Wall Street, munitions makers, and others—had tricked the United States into participating in World War I. An investigation by a Senate committee chaired by Senator Gerald Nye of North Dakota revealed exorbitant profiteering and blatant tax evasion by many corporations during the war, and it suggested (on the basis of little evidence) that bankers had pressured Wilson to intervene in the war so as to protect their loans abroad.

Roosevelt himself shared some of the suspicions voiced by the isolationists and claimed to be impressed by the findings of the Nye investigation. Nevertheless, he continued to hope for at least a modest American role in maintaining world peace. In 1935, he asked the Senate to ratify a treaty to make the United States a member of the World Court—a treaty that would have expanded America's symbolic commitment to internationalism without increasing its actual responsibilities in any important way. Nevertheless, isolationist opposition (spurred by unrelenting hostility from the Hearst newspapers and a passionate broadcast by Father Charles Coughlin on the eve of the Senate vote) resulted in the defeat of the treaty. It was a devastating political blow to the president, and he would not soon again attempt to challenge the isolationist tide.

That tide seemed to grow stronger in the following months. Through the summer of 1935, it became clear that Mussolini's Italy was preparing to invade Ethiopia in an effort to expand its colonial holdings in Africa. Fearing that a general European war would result, American legislators began to design legal safeguards to prevent the United States from being dragged into the conflict. The result was the Neutrality Act of 1935.

The 1935 act, and the Neutrality Acts of 1936 and 1937 that followed, were designed to prevent a recurrence of the events that many Americans now believed had pressured the United States into World War I. The 1935 law established a mandatory arms embargo against both victim and aggressor in any military conflict and empowered the president to warn American citizens that they might travel on the ships of warring nations only at their own risk. Thus, isolationists believed, the "protection of neutral rights" could not again become an excuse for American intervention in

war. The 1936 Neutrality Act renewed these provisions. And in 1937, with world conditions growing even more precarious, Congress passed a still more stringent measure. The new Neutrality Act established the so-called cash-and-carry policy, by which belligerents could purchase only nonmilitary goods from the United States and had to pay cash and carry the goods away on their own vessels.

The American stance of militant neutrality gained support in October 1935 when Mussolini finally launched his long-anticipated attack on Ethiopia. When the League of Nations protested, Italy simply resigned from the organization, completed its conquest of Ethiopia, and formed an alliance (the "Axis") with Nazi Germany. Most Americans responded to the news with renewed determination to isolate themselves from European instability. Two-thirds of those responding to public opinion polls at the time opposed any American action to deter aggression.

Isolationist sentiment showed its strength once again in 1936–1937 in response to the civil war in Spain. The Falangists of General Francisco Franco, a group much like the Italian fascists, revolted in July 1936 against the existing republican government. Hitler and Mussolini supported Franco, both vocally and with weapons and supplies. Some individual Americans traveled to Spain to assist the republican cause (see p. 687); but the United States government joined with Britain and France in an agreement to offer no assistance to either side—although all three governments were sympathetic to the republicans.

Alarmed by the events of 1935 and 1936, Roosevelt began moving slowly and cautiously to challenge the grip of the isolationists on the nation's foreign policy. For a time, it seemed to be a hopeless cause. The United States was unable to do much more than watch as a series of new dangers emerged that brought the world closer to war.

Particularly disturbing was the deteriorating situation in Asia. Japan's aggressive designs against China had been clear since the invasion of Manchuria in 1931. In the summer of 1937, Tokyo launched an even broader assault, attacking China's five northern provinces. The United States, Roosevelt believed, could not allow the Japanese aggression to go unremarked or unpunished. In a speech in Chicago in October 1937, therefore, the president warned forcefully of the dangers that Japanese aggression posed to world peace. Aggressors, he proclaimed, should be "quarantined" by the international community to prevent the contagion of war from spreading.

The president was deliberately vague about what such a "quarantine" would mean, and there is evidence that he was contemplating nothing more drastic than a break in diplomatic relations with Japan, that he was not considering economic or military sanctions. Nevertheless, public response to the speech was disturbingly hostile. As a result, Roosevelt drew back. Although his strong words encouraged the British government to call a conference in Brussels to discuss the crisis in Asia, the United States refused to make any commitments to collective action, and the conference produced no agreement.

Only months later, another episode gave renewed evidence of how formidable the obstacles to Roosevelt's efforts remained. On December 12, 1937, Japanese aviators bombed and sank the U.S. gunboat *Panay* as it sailed the Yangtze River in China. The attack was almost undoubtedly deliberate. It occurred in broad daylight, with clear visibility, and a large American flag had been painted conspicuously on the *Panay's* deck. Even so, isolationists seized eagerly on Japanese protestations that the bombing had been an accident and pressured the administration into accepting Japan's apologies and overlooking the attack.

The Failure of Munich

In 1936, Hitler had moved the revived German army into the Rhineland, rearming an area that France had, in effect, controlled since World War I. In March 1938, German forces marched into Austria, and Hitler proclaimed a union (or *Anschluss*) between Austria, his native land, and Germany, his adopted one. Neither in America nor in most of Europe was there much more than a murmur of opposition.

The Austrian invasion, however, soon created another crisis; for Hitler had by now occupied territory surrounding three sides of western Czechoslovakia, a region he dreamed of annexing to provide Germany with the Lebensraum he believed it needed. In September 1938, he demanded that Czechoslovakia cede to him part of that region, the Sudetenland, an area on the Austro-German border in which many ethnic Germans lived. Czechoslovakia, which possessed substantial military power of its own, was prepared to fight rather than submit. But it realized it could not hope for success without help from other European nations. It got none. Most Western nations, including the United States, were appalled at the prospect of another war and were willing to pay almost any price to settle the crisis peacefully. On September 29, Hitler met with the leaders of France and Great Britain at Munich in an effort to resolve the crisis. The French and British agreed to accept the German demands in Czechoslovakia in return for Hitler's promise to expand no farther. "This is the last territorial claim I have to make in Europe," the Fuhrer solemnly declared. And Prime Minister Neville Chamberlain returned to England to a hero's welcome, assuring his people that the agree-

The Anschluss
Citizens of Graz in Austria welcome Adolf Hitler shortly after the 1938 *anschluss*, by which Germany annexed Austria (Hitler's native land). *(UPI/Bettmann)*

ment ensured "peace in our time." Among those who had cabled him with encouragement at Munich was Franklin Roosevelt.

The Munich accords were the most prominent element of a policy that came to be known as "appeasement" and that came to be identified (not altogether fairly) almost exclusively with Chamberlain. Whoever was to blame, however, it became clear almost immediately that the policy was a failure. In March 1939, Hitler occupied the remaining areas of Czechoslovakia, violating the Munich agreement unashamedly. And in April, he began issuing threats against Poland. At that point, both Britain and France gave assurances to the Polish government that they would come to its assistance in case of an invasion; they even flirted, too late, with the Stalinist regime in Russia, attempting to draw it into a mutual defense agreement. Stalin, however, had already decided that he could expect no protection from the West; after all, he had not even been invited to attend the Munich Conference. Accordingly, he signed a nonaggression pact with Hitler in August 1939, freeing the Germans for the moment from the danger of a two-front war.

For a few months, Hitler had been trying to frighten the Poles into submitting to German demands. When that failed, he staged an incident on the border to allow him to claim that Germany had been attacked; and on September 1, 1939, he launched a full-scale invasion of Poland. Britain and France, true to their pledges, declared war on Germany two days later. World War II had begun.

FROM NEUTRALITY TO INTERVENTION

"This nation will remain a neutral nation," the president declared shortly after the hostilities began in Europe, "but I cannot ask that every American remain neutral in thought as well." It was a statement that stood in stark and deliberate contrast to Woodrow Wilson's 1914 plea that the nation remain neutral in both deed and thought; and it was clear from the start that among those whose opinions were decidedly unneutral in 1939 was the president himself.

Neutrality Tested

There was never any question that both he and the majority of the American people favored Britain, France, and the other Allied nations in the contest. The ques-

tion was how much the United States was prepared to do to assist them. At the very least, Roosevelt believed, the United States should make armaments available to the Allied armies to help them counter the highly productive German munitions industry. In September 1939, he asked Congress for a revision of the Neutrality Acts. The original measures had forbidden the sale of American weapons to any nation engaged in war; Roosevelt wanted the arms embargo lifted. Powerful isolationist opposition forced him to accept a weaker revision than he would have liked; as passed by Congress, the 1939 measure maintained the prohibition on American ships entering war zones. It did, however, permit belligerents to purchase arms on the same cash-and-carry basis that the earlier Neutrality Acts had established for the sale of nonmilitary materials.

For a time, it was possible to believe that little more would be necessary. After the German armies had quickly subdued Poland, the war in Europe settled into a long, quiet lull that lasted through the winter and spring—a "phony war," some called it. The only real fighting during this period occurred not between the Allies and the Axis, but between Russia and its neighbors. Taking advantage of the situation in the West, the Soviet Union overran and annexed the small Baltic republics of Latvia, Estonia, and Lithuania and then, in late November, invaded Finland. Most Americans were outraged, but neither Congress nor the president was willing to do more than impose an ineffective "moral embargo" on the shipment of armaments to Russia. By March 1940, the Soviet advance was complete.

Whatever illusions anyone may have had about the reality of the war in Western Europe were shattered in the spring of 1940 when Germany launched an invasion to the west—first attacking Denmark and Norway, sweeping next across the Netherlands and Belgium, and driving finally deep into the heart of France. Allied efforts proved futile against the Nazi blitzkrieg. One western European stronghold after another fell into German hands. On June 10, Mussolini brought Italy into the war, invading France from the south as Hitler was attacking from the north. On June 22, finally, France fell to the German onslaught. Nazi troops marched into Paris; a new collaborationist regime assembled in Vichy; and in all Europe, only the shattered remnants of the British army, rescued from the beaches of Dunkirk by a flotilla of military and civilian vessels assembled miraculously quickly, remained to oppose the Axis forces.

Roosevelt had already begun to increase American aid to the Allies. He also began preparations to resist a possible Nazi invasion of the United States. On May 16, he asked Congress for an additional $1 billion for defense (much of it for the construction of an enor-

mous new fleet of warplanes) and received it quickly. With France tottering a few weeks later, he proclaimed that the United States would "extend to the opponents of force the material resources of this nation." And on May 15, Winston Churchill, the new British prime minister, sent Roosevelt the first of many long lists of requests for ships, armaments, and other assistance without which, he insisted, England could not long survive. Many Americans (including the United States ambassador to London, Joseph P. Kennedy) argued that the British plight was already hopeless, that any aid to the English was a wasted effort. The president, however, made the politically dangerous decision to "scrape the bottom of the barrel" to make war materials available to Churchill. He even circumvented the cash-and-carry provisions of the Neutrality Act by trading fifty American destroyers (most of them left over from World War I) to England in return for the right to build American bases on British territory in the Western Hemisphere; and he returned to the factories a number of new airplanes purchased by the American government so that the British could buy them instead.

Roosevelt was able to take such steps in part because of a major shift in American public opinion. Before the invasion of France, most Americans had believed that a German victory in the war would not be a threat to the United States. By July, with France defeated and Britain threatened, more than 66 percent of the public (according to opinion polls) believed that Germany posed a direct threat to the United States. Congress was aware of the change and was becoming more willing to permit expanded American assistance to the Allies. It was also becoming more concerned about the need for internal preparations for war, and in September it approved the Burke-Wadsworth Act, inaugurating the first peacetime military draft in American history.

But while the forces of isolation may have weakened, they were far from dead. On the contrary, a spirited and at times vicious debate began in the summer of 1940 between those who advocated expanded American involvement in the war (who were termed, often inaccurately, "interventionists") and those who continued to insist on neutrality. The celebrated journalist William Allen White served as chairman of a new Committee to Defend America, whose members lobbied actively for increased American assistance to the Allies but opposed actual intervention. Others went so far as to urge an immediate declaration of war (a position that as yet had little public support) and in April created an organization of their own, the Fight for Freedom Committee. Opposing them was a powerful new lobby called the America First Committee, which attracted some of America's most prominent leaders. Its chairman was General Robert E. Wood, until recently the president of Sears Roebuck; and its membership included Charles Lindbergh, General Hugh Johnson, Senator Gerald Nye, and Senator Burton Wheeler. It won the editorial support of the Hearst chain and other influential newspapers, and it had at least the indirect support of a large proportion of the Republican Party. (It also, inevitably, attracted a fringe of Nazi sympathizers and anti-Semites.) The debate between the two sides was loud and bitter. Through the summer and fall of 1940, moreover, it was complicated by a presidential campaign.

The Third-Term Campaign

For many months, the politics of 1940 revolved around the question of Franklin Roosevelt's intentions. Would he break with tradition and run for an unprecedented third term? The president himself was deliberately coy and never publicly revealed his own wishes. But by refusing to withdraw from the contest, he made it virtually impossible for any rival Democrat to establish a foothold within the party. Just before the Democratic Convention in July, he let it be known that he would accept a "draft" from his party. The Democrats quickly renominated him and even reluctantly swallowed his choice for vice president: Agriculture secretary Henry A. Wallace, a man too liberal for the taste of many party leaders.

The Republicans, again, faced a far more difficult task. With Roosevelt effectively straddling the center of the defense debate, favoring neither the extreme iso-

lationists nor the extreme interventionists, the Republicans had few viable alternatives. Their solution was to compete with the president on his own ground. Succumbing to a remarkable popular movement (carefully orchestrated by, among others, Henry Luce, the publisher of *Time* and *Life* magazines), they nominated a dynamic and attractive but politically inexperienced businessman, Wendell Willkie. Both the candidate and the party platform took positions little different from Roosevelt's: they would keep the country out of war but would extend generous assistance to the Allies. Willkie was left, therefore, with the unenviable task of defeating Roosevelt by outmatching him in personal magnetism and by trying to arouse public fears of the dangers of an unprecedented third term. An appealing figure and a vigorous campaigner, he managed to evoke more public enthusiasm than any Republican candidate in decades. In the end, however, he was no match for Franklin Roosevelt. The election was closer than it had been in either 1932 or 1936, but Roosevelt nevertheless won decisively. He received 55 percent of the popular vote to Willkie's 45 percent, and won 449 electoral votes to Willkie's 82.

Neutrality Abandoned

In the last weeks of 1940, with the election behind him, Roosevelt began to make subtle but profound changes in the American role in the war. To the public, he claimed that he was simply continuing the now established policy of providing aid to the embattled Allies. In fact, that aid was taking new and more decisive forms.

In December 1940, Great Britain was virtually bankrupt. No longer could the British meet the cash-and-carry requirements imposed by the Neutrality Acts; yet England's needs, Churchill insisted, were greater than ever. The president therefore suggested a method that would "eliminate the dollar sign" from all arms transactions while still, he hoped, pacifying those who opposed blatant American intervention in the war. The new system was labeled "lend-lease." It would allow the government not only to sell but to lend or lease armaments to any nation deemed "vital to the defense of the United States." In other words, America could funnel weapons to England on the basis of no more than Britain's promise to return or pay for them when the war was over. Isolationists attacked the measure bitterly, arguing (correctly) that it was simply a device to tie the United States more closely to the Allies; but Congress enacted the bill by wide margins.

With lend-lease established, Roosevelt soon faced another serious problem: ensuring that the American supplies would actually reach Great Britain. Shipping

THE QUESTION OF PEARL HARBOR

THE PHRASE "REMEMBER PEARL Harbor!" became a rallying cry during World War II—reminding Americans of the surprise Japanese attack on the American naval base in Hawaii, and arousing the nation to exact revenge. But within a few years of the end of hostilities, some Americans remembered Pearl Harbor for different reasons and began to challenge the official version of the attack on December 7, 1941. Their charges sparked a debate that has never fully subsided. Was the Japanese attack on Pearl Harbor unprovoked, and did it come without warning, as the Roosevelt administration claimed at the time? Or was it part of a deliberate plan by the president to have the Japanese force a reluctant United States into the war? Most controversial of all, did the administration know of the attack in advance? Did Roosevelt deliberately refrain from warning the commanders in Hawaii so that the air raid's effect on the American public would be more profound?

Among the first to challenge the official version of Pearl Harbor was the historian Charles A. Beard, who maintained in *President Roosevelt and the Coming of the War, 1941* (1948) that the United States had deliberately forced the Japanese into a position where they had no choice but

to attack. By cutting off Japan's access to the raw materials it needed for its military adventure in China, by stubbornly refusing to compromise, the United States ensured that the Japanese would stike out into the southwest Pacific to take the needed supplies by force—even at the risk of war with the United States. Not only was American policy provocative in effect, Beard suggested; it was *deliberately* provocative. More than that, the administration, which had some time before cracked the Japanese code, must have known weeks in advance of Japan's plan to attack. Beard supported his argument by citing Secretary of War Henry Stimson's comment in his diary: "The question was how we should maneuver them into the position of firing the first shot."

A partial refutation of the Beard argument appeared in 1950 in Basil Rauch's *Roosevelt from Munich to Pearl Harbor*. The administration did not know in advance of the planned attack on Pearl Harbor, he argued. It did, however, expect an attack somewhere; and it made subtle efforts to "maneuver" Japan into firing the first shot in the conflict. But Richard N. Current, in *Secretary Stimson: A Study in Statecraft* (1954), offered an even stronger challenge to Beard. Stimson did indeed anticipate an attack, Current argued, but not an attack on American territory; rather, he anticipated an assault on British or Dutch possessions in the Pacific. The problem confronting

lanes in the Atlantic had become extremely dangerous; German submarines destroyed as much as a half-million tons of shipping each month. The British navy was losing ships more rapidly than it could replace them and was finding it difficult to transport materials across the Atlantic from America. Secretary of War Henry Stimson (who had been Hoover's secretary of state and who returned to the cabinet at Roosevelt's request in 1940) argued that the United States should itself convoy vessels to England; but Roosevelt decided to rely instead on the concept of "hemispheric defense," by which the United States navy would defend transport ships only in the western Atlantic—which he

argued was a neutral zone and the responsibility of the American nations. By July 1941, American ships were patrolling the ocean as far east as Iceland, escorting convoys of merchant ships, and radioing information to British vessels about the location of Nazi submarines.

At first, Germany did little to challenge these obviously hostile American actions. By the fall of 1941, however, events in Europe changed its position. German forces had invaded the Soviet Union in June of that year, shattering the 1939 Nazi-Soviet pact. The Germans drove quickly and forcefully deep into Russian territory. When the Soviets did not surrender, as many had predicted they would, Roosevelt persuaded

the administration was not how to maneuver the Japanese into attacking the United States, but how to find a way to make a Japanese attack on British or Dutch territory *appear* to be an attack on America. Only thus, Stimson believed, could Congress be persuaded to approve a declaration of war.

Roberta Wohlstetter took a different approach to the question, in *Pearl Harbor: Warning and Decision* (1962), the most thorough scholarly study to appear to that point. De-emphasizing the question of whether the American government *wanted* a Japanese attack, she undertook to answer the question of whether the administration *knew* of the attack in advance. Wohlstetter concluded that the United States had ample warning of Japanese intentions and should have realized that the Pearl Harbor raid was imminent. But government officials failed to interpret the evidence correctly, largely because their preconceptions about Japanese intentions were at odds with the evidence they confronted. Admiral Edwin T. Layton, who had been a staff officer at Pearl Harbor in 1941, also blames political and bureaucratic failures for the absence of advance warning of the attack. In a 1985 memoir, *And I Was There*, he argues that the Japanese attack was not only a result of "audacious planning and skillful execution" by the Japanese, but of "a dramatic breakdown in our intelligence process . . . related directly to feuding among high-level naval officers in Washington."

The most thorough study of Pearl Harbor to date appeared in 1981: Gordon W. Prange's *At Dawn We Slept*. Like Wohlstetter, Prange concluded that the Roosevelt administration was guilty of a series of disastrous blunders in interpreting Japanese strategy; the American government had possession of enough information to predict the attack, but failed to do so. But Prange dismissed the arguments of the "revisionists" (Beard and his successors) that the president had deliberately maneuvered the nation into the war by permitting the Japanese to attack. Instead, he emphasized the enormous daring and great skill with which the Japanese orchestrated an ambitious operation that few Americans believed possible.

But the revisionist claims have not been laid to rest. John Toland revived the charges of a Roosevelt betrayal in 1982, in *Infamy: Pearl Harbor and Its Aftermath*, claiming to have discovered new evidence (the testimony of an unidentified seaman) that proves the navy knew at least five days in advance that Japanese aircraft carriers were heading toward Hawaii. From that, Toland concluded that Roosevelt must have known that an attack was forthcoming and that he allowed it to occur in the belief that a surprise attack would arouse the nation. But like the many previous writers who have made the same argument, Toland was unable to produce any direct evidence of Roosevelt's knowledge of the planned attack.

Congress to extend lend lease privileges to them—the first step toward creating a new relationship with Stalin that would ultimately lead to a formal Soviet-American alliance. Now American industry was providing crucial assistance to Hitler's foes on two fronts, and the navy was playing a more active role than ever in protecting the flow of goods to Europe.

In September, Nazi submarines began a concerted campaign against American vessels. Early that month, a German U-boat fired on the American destroyer *Greer* (which was radioing the U-boat's position to the British at the time). Roosevelt responded by ordering American ships to fire on German submarines "on

sight." In October, Nazi submarines actually hit two American destroyers and sank one of them, the *Reuben James*, killing many American sailors in the process. Enraged members of Congress now voted approval of a measure allowing the United States to arm its merchant vessels and to sail all the way into belligerent ports. The United States had, in effect, launched a naval war against Germany.

At the same time, a series of meetings, some private and one public, were tying the United States and Great Britain more closely together. In April 1941, senior military officers of the two nations met in secret and agreed on the joint strategy they would follow were the United States to enter the war. In August, Roosevelt met with Churchill aboard a British vessel anchored off the coast of Newfoundland. The president made no military commitments, but he did join the prime minister in releasing a document that became known as the Atlantic Charter, in which the two nations set out "certain common principles" on which to base "a better future for the world." It was, in only vaguely disguised form, a statement of war aims that called openly for, among other things, "the final destruction of the Nazi tyranny."

By the fall of 1941, it seemed only a matter of time before the United States became an official belligerent. Roosevelt remained convinced that public opinion would support a declaration of war only in the event of an actual enemy attack. But an attack seemed certain to come, if not in the Atlantic, then in the Pacific.

The Road to Pearl Harbor

In the meantime, Japan was taking advantage of the crisis (which had preoccupied the Soviet Union and the two most powerful colonial powers in Asia, Britain and France) to extend its empire in the Pacific. In September 1940, Japan signed the Tripartite Pact, a loose defensive alliance with Germany and Italy that seemed to extend the Axis into Asia. (In reality, the European Axis powers never developed a very strong relationship with Japan, and the wars in Europe and the Pacific were largely separate conflicts.)

Roosevelt had already displayed his animosity toward Japanese policies by harshly denouncing their continuing assault on China and by terminating a long-standing American commercial treaty with the Tokyo government. Still the Japanese drive continued. In July 1941, imperial troops moved into Indochina and seized the capital of Vietnam, a colony of France (after having demanded and received a base there a year before). The United States, having broken the Japanese codes, knew that their next target would be the Dutch East Indies; and when Tokyo failed to respond to Roosevelt's stern warnings, the president froze all Japanese assets in the United States and established a complete trade embargo, severely limiting Japan's ability to purchase essential supplies (including oil). American public opinion, shaped by strong anti-Japanese prejudices developed over several decades, generally supported these hostile actions.

Tokyo now faced a choice. It would either have to repair relations with the United States to restore the flow of supplies, or it would have to find those supplies elsewhere, most notably by seizing British and Dutch possessions in the Pacific. At first the Tokyo

government seemed willing to compromise. The Japanese prime minister, Prince Konoye, had begun negotiations with the United States even before the freezing of his country's assets, and in August he increased the pace by requesting a personal meeting with President Roosevelt. But the United States rebuffed these overtures. Secretary of State Hull feared that Konoye lacked sufficient power within his own government to be able to enforce any agreement, and he persuaded Roosevelt to say that he would meet with the prime minister only if Japan would give guarantees in advance that it would respect the territorial integrity of China. Konoye could give no such assurances, as Roosevelt and Hull knew, and the negotiations collapsed. In October, militants in Tokyo forced Konoye out of office and replaced him with the leader of the war party, General Hideki Tojo. With Japan's need for new sources of fuel becoming desperate, there now seemed little alternative to war.

For several weeks, the Tojo government kept up a pretense of wanting to continue negotiations. On November 20, 1941, Tokyo proposed a modus vivendi highly favorable to itself and sent its diplomats in Washington to the State Department to discuss it. But Tokyo had already decided that it would not yield on the question of China, and Washington had made clear that it would accept nothing less than a reversal of that policy. Hull rejected the Japanese overtures out of hand; on November 27, he told Secretary of War Henry Stimson, "I have washed my hands of the Japanese situation, and it is now in the hands of you and [Secretary of the Navy Frank] Knox, the Army and Navy." He was not merely speculating. American intelligence had already decoded Japanese messages which made clear that war was imminent, that after November 29 an attack would be only a matter of days.

But Washington did not know where the attack would take place. Most officials were convinced that the Japanese would move first not against American territory but against British or Dutch possessions to the south. American intelligence took note of a Japanese naval task force that began sailing east from the Kurile Islands in the general direction of Hawaii on November 25, and radioed a routine warning to the United States naval facility at Pearl Harbor, near Honolulu. But officials were paying more attention to a large Japanese convoy moving southward through the China Sea. A combination of confusion and miscalculation led the government to overlook indications that Japan intended a direct attack on American forces—partly because Hawaii was so far from Japan that few believed such an attack possible.

At 7:55 A.M. on Sunday, December 7, 1941, a wave of Japanese bombers—taking off from aircraft carriers

SIGNIFICANT EVENTS

1921	Washington Conference leads to reductions in naval armaments
1922	Fordney-McCumber Tariff passed
1924	Dawes Plan renegotiates European debts, reparations
1928	Kellogg-Briand Pact signed
1931	Economic crisis spreads worldwide
	Japan invades Manchuria
1932	World Disarmament Conference held in Geneva
1933	Adolf Hitler becomes chancellor of Germany
	United States scuttles London Economic Conference
	United States establishes diplomatic relations with Soviet Union
	Roosevelt proclaims Good Neighbor Policy
1935	Senate defeats World Court treaty
	Neutrality Act passed
	Italy invades Ethiopia
1936	Spanish Civil War begins
	Germany reoccupies Rhineland
	Second Neutrality Act passed
1937	Japan launches new invasion of China
	Roosevelt gives "quarantine" speech

	Japan attacks U.S. gunboat *Panay*
	Third Neutrality Act passed
1938	Germany annexes Austria (Anschluss)
	Munich Conference
1939	Nazi-Soviet nonaggression pact signed
	Germany invades Czechoslovakia
	Germany invades Poland
	World War II begins
1940	Soviet Union invades Baltic nations, Finland
	German blitzkrieg conquers most of Western Europe
	Germany, Italy, Japan sign Tripartite Pact
	Fight for Freedom Committee founded
	America First Committee founded
	Roosevelt reelected president
	United States makes destroyers-for-bases deal with Britain
1941	Lend-lease plan provides aid to Britain
	American ships confront German submarines in North Atlantic
	Germany invades Soviet Union
	Atlantic Charter signed
	Japan attacks Pearl Harbor
	United States enters war

hundreds of miles away—attacked the United States naval base at Pearl Harbor. A second wave came an hour later. Military commanders in Hawaii had taken no precautions against such an attack and had allowed ships to remain bunched up defenselessly in the harbor and airplanes to remain parked in rows on airstrips. The consequences of the raid were disastrous for America. Within two hours, the United States lost 8 battleships, 3 cruisers, 4 other vessels, 188 airplanes, and several vital shore installations. More than 2,000 soldiers and sailors died, and another 1,000 were injured. The Japanese suffered only light losses.

American forces were now greatly diminished in the Pacific (although by sheer accident, none of the American aircraft carriers—the heart of the Pacific fleet—had been at Pearl Harbor on December 7). Nevertheless, the raid on Pearl Harbor did virtually overnight what more than two years of effort by Roosevelt and others had been unable to do: it unified the American people in a fervent commitment to war. On De-

---

Pearl Harbor, December 7, 1941
The destroyer U.S.S. *Shaw*, immobilized in a floating drydock in Pearl Harbor in December 1941, survived the first wave of Japanese bombers unscathed. But in the second attack, the Japanese scored a direct hit and produced this spectacular explosion, which blew off the ship's bow. Damage to the rest of the ship, however, was slight. Just a few months later the *Shaw* was fitted with a new bow and rejoined the fleet. *(U.S. Navy Photo)*

cember 8, the president traveled to Capitol Hill, where he grimly addressed a joint session of Congress: "Yesterday, December 7, 1941—a date which will live in infamy—the United States of America was suddenly and deliberately attacked by the naval and air forces of the Empire of Japan." Within four hours, the Senate unanimously and the House 388 to 1 (the lone dissenter being Jeanette Rankin of Montana, who had voted

against war in 1917 as well) approved a declaration of war against Japan. Three days later, Germany and Italy, Japan's European allies, declared war on the United States; and on the same day, December 11, Congress reciprocated without a dissenting vote. For the second time in twenty-five years, the United States was engaged in a world war.

Suggested Readings

The 1920s. Thomas Buckley, *The United States and the Washington Conference* (1970). Warren Cohen, *America's Response to China* (1971); *Empire Without Tears* (1987). Frank Costigliola, *Awkward Dominion: American Political, Economic, and Cultural Relations with Europe, 1919–1933* (1984). Roger Dingman, *Power in the Pacific* (1976). L. Ethan Ellis, *Republican Foreign Policy, 1921–1933* (1968). Robert H. Ferrell, *Peace in Their Time* (1952). Michael J. Hogan, *Informal Entente: The Private Struc-* ture of Cooperation in Anglo-American Economic Diplomacy, 1918–1928 (1977). Akira Iriye, *After Imperialism* (1965). William Kamman, *A Search for Stability: United States Diplomacy Toward Nicaragua, 1925-1933* (1968). Melvyn P. Leffler, *The Elusive Quest: America's Pursuit of European Stability and French Security, 1919-1933* (1979). Merlo J. Pusey, *Charles Evans Hughes*, 2 vols. (1963). Joseph Tulchin, *The Aftermath of War* (1971). William Appleman Williams, *The Tragedy of*

American Diplomacy (1962). Joan Hoff Wilson, *American Business and Foreign Policy, 1920–1933* (1968); *Ideology and Economics* (1974).

The Hoover Years.   Alexander DeConde, *Hoover's Latin American Policy* (1951). Robert H. Ferrell, *American Diplomacy in the Great Depression* (1970). Elting Morison, *Turmoil and Tradition* (1960). Raymond O'Connor, *Perilous Equilibrium* (1962). Armin Rappaport, *Stimson and Japan* (1963).

New Deal Diplomacy.   Edward E. Bennett, *Recognition of Russia* (1970). Dorothy Borg, *The United States and the Far Eastern Crisis of 1933–1938* (1964). Robert Browder, *The Origins of Soviet-American Diplomacy* (1953). Bruce J. Calder, *The Impact of Intervention* (1984). Robert Dallek, *Franklin D. Roosevelt and American Foreign Policy, 1932–1945* (1979). Beatrice Farnsworth, *William C. Bullitt and the Soviet Union* (1967). Peter Filene, *Americans and the Soviet Experiment, 1917–1933* (1967). Frank Freidel, *Launching the New Deal* (1973). Lloyd Gardner, *Economic Aspects of New Deal Diplomacy* (1964). Irwin F. Gellman, *Good Neighbor Diplomacy: United States Policies in Latin America, 1933–1945* (1979). David Green, *The Containment of Latin America* (1971). Warren F. Kimball, *The Juggler: Franklin Roosevelt as Wartime Statesman* (1991). Walter LaFeber, *Inevitable Revolutions* (1983). Lorenzo Meyer, *Mexico and the United States in the Oil Controversy* (1977). Bryce Wood, *The Making of the Good Neighbor Policy* (1961).

Isolationism and Pacifism.   Selig Adler, *The Uncertain Giant* (1966); *The Isolationist Impulse* (1957). Charles Chatfield, *For Peace and Justice: Pacifism in America, 1914–1941* (1971). Warren I. Cohen, *The American Revisionists* (1967). Wayne S. Cole, *America First* (1953); *Senator Gerald P. Nye and American Foreign Relations* (1962); *Charles A. Lindbergh and the Battle Against American Intervention in World War II* (1974); *Roosevelt and the Isolationists, 1932–1945* (1983). Charles DeBenedetti, *Origins of the Modern American Peace Movement, 1915–1929* (1978); *The Peace Reform in American History* (1980). Robert Divine, *The Reluctant Belligerent* (1965). Thomas N. Guinsburg, *The Pursuit of Isolation in the United States Senate from Versailles to Pearl Harbor* (1982). Manfred Jonas, *Isolationism in America* (1966). Thomas C. Kennedy, *Charles A. Beard and American Foreign Policy* (1975). William Langer and S. Everett Gleason, *The Challenge to Isolation* (1952); *The Undeclared War* (1953). Richard Lowitt, *George W. Norris*, 3 vols. (1963–1978). John K. Nelson, *The Peace Prophets* (1967). Lawrence Wittner, *Rebels Against War* (1984).

The Coming of World War II.   James MacGregor Burns, *Roosevelt: The Soldier of Freedom* (1970). Garry Clifford and Samuel R. Spencer, Jr., *The First Peacetime Draft* (1986). Roger Dingman, *Power in the Pacific* (1976). Bernard F. Donahoe, *Private Plans and Public Dangers* (1965). Herbert Feis, *The Road to Pearl Harbor* (1950). Waldo H. Heinrichs, Jr., *Threshold of War* (1988). Akira Iriye, *Across the Pacific* (1967); *After Imperialism: The Search for a New Order in the Far East, 1921–1933* (1965); *The Origins of the Second World War in Asia and the Pacific* (1987). Manfred Jonas, *The United States and Germany* (1984). Warren Kimball, *The Most Unsordid Act: Lend-Lease, 1939–1941* (1970). Joseph Lash, *Roosevelt and Churchill* (1976). James Leutze, *Bargaining for Supremacy* (1977). Martin V. Melosi, *The Shadow of Pearl Harbor* (1977). Arnold Offner, *The Origins of the Second World War* (1975). Gordon Prange, *At Dawn We Slept* (1981); *Pearl Harbor* (1986). Michael S. Sherry, *The Rise of American Airpower* (1987). David Reynolds, *The Creation of the Anglo-American Alliance, 1937–1941* (1982). David F. Schmitz, *The United States and Fascist Italy, 1922–1944* (1988). Jonathan Utley, *Going to War with Japan* (1985). Roberta Wohlstetter, *Pearl Harbor: Warning and Decision* (1962). David S. Wyman, *Paper Walls: America and the Refugee Crisis, 1938–1941* (1985).

THE THREE-FRONT WAR
Late in the war, during a meeting with Roosevelt and Churchill, Stalin offered a toast: "To American production, without which the war would have been lost." The American government was well aware of how vital production was to the war effort; it was so important that the American industrial economy in effect constituted a "third front" in the fighting. This propaganda poster was one of many designed to boost morale among (and discourage strikes by) industrial workers in America. *(Bettmann)*

CHAPTER TWENTY-EIGHT

AMERICA IN A WORLD AT WAR

HE ATTACK ON PEARL Harbor thrust the United States into the greatest and most terrible war in the history of humanity. World War I had cost many lives and had destroyed centuries-old European social and political institutions. But World War II created unprecedented carnage and horror in Europe and in much of the rest of the globe. And in the end, it changed the world as profoundly as any event of the twentieth century, perhaps of any century.

Less readily apparent is how profoundly the war changed America—its society, its politics, and its image of itself. Except for the combatants themselves, most Americans experienced the war at a remove of several thousand miles. They endured no bombing, no invasion, no massive dislocations, no serious material shortages. Veterans returning home in 1945 and 1946 found a country that looked very much like the one they had left—something that clearly could not be said of veterans returning home to Britain, France, Germany, Russia, or Japan.

But World War II did transform the United States in profound, if not always in readily visible, ways. As the poet Archibald MacLeish said in 1943: "The great majority of the American people understand very well that this war is not a war only, but an end and a beginning—an end to things known and a beginning of things unknown. We have smelled the wind in the streets that changes weather. We know that whatever the world will be when the war ends, the world will be different." The story of American involvement in the war is not just the story of how the military forces

and the industrial might of the United States helped defeat Germany, Italy, and Japan. It is also the story of the creation of a new world, both abroad and at home.

WAR ON TWO FRONTS

Whatever political disagreements and social tensions may have existed among the American people during World War II, there was striking unity of opinion about the conflict itself—"a unity," as one member of Congress proclaimed shortly after Pearl Harbor, "never before witnessed in this country." America's unity and confidence were severely tested in the first, troubled months of 1942. Despite the impressive display of patriotism and the dramatic flurry of activity, the war was going very badly. Britain appeared ready to collapse. The Soviet Union was staggering. One after another, Allied strongholds in the Pacific were falling to the forces of Japan. The first task facing the United States, therefore, was less to achieve victory than to stave off defeat.

Containing the Japanese

Ten hours after the strike at Pearl Harbor, Japanese airplanes attacked the American airfields at Manila in the Philippines, destroying much of America's remaining air power in the Pacific. Three days later Guam, an American possession, fell to Japan; then Wake Island

World War II in the Pacific

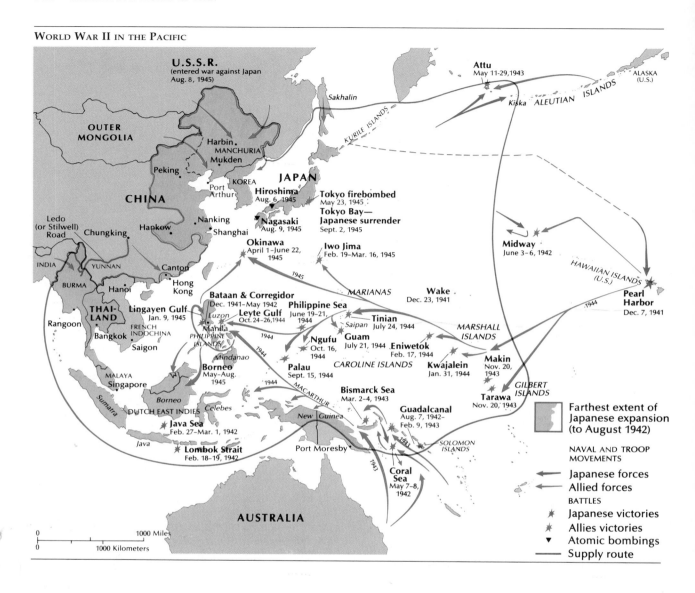

Farthest extent of Japanese expansion (to August 1942)

NAVAL AND TROOP MOVEMENTS
→ Japanese forces
→ Allied forces

BATTLES
✳ Japanese victories
✳ Allies victories
▼ Atomic bombings
— Supply route

and the British colony, Hong Kong. The great British fortress of Singapore in Malaya surrendered in February 1942, the Dutch East Indies in March, Burma in April. In the Philippines, exhausted Filipino and American troops gave up their defense of the islands on May 6.

American strategists planned two broad offensives to turn the tide against the Japanese. One, under the command of General Douglas MacArthur, would move north from Australia, through New Guinea, and eventually back to the Philippines. The other, under Admiral Chester Nimitz, would move west from Hawaii toward major Japanese island outposts in the central Pacific. Ultimately, the two offensives would come together to invade Japan itself.

The Allies achieved their first important victory in the Battle of Coral Sea, just northwest of Australia, on May 7–8, 1942, when American forces turned back the previously unstoppable Japanese fleet. A month later, there was an even more important turning point northwest of Hawaii. An enormous battle raged for four days, June 3–6, 1942, near the small American outpost at Midway Island, at the end of which the United States, despite great losses, was clearly victorious. The

GUADALCANAL
Guadalcanal, in the Solomon Islands, was the scene of some of the bloodiest and most protracted fighting between American and Japanese soldiers in the entire Pacific war. U.S. marines are shown here in a jungle outpost in a part of the island that became known as "Hell's Corner." A Navy bomber flies overhead. *(UPI/Bettmann)*

American navy destroyed four Japanese aircraft carriers while losing only one, and regained control of the central Pacific for the United States.

The Americans took the offensive for the first time several months later in the southern Solomon Islands, to the east of New Guinea. In August 1942, American forces assaulted three of the islands: Gavutu, Tulagi, and Guadalcanal. A struggle of terrible ferocity (and, before it was over, terrible savagery) developed at Guadalcanal and continued for six months, inflicting heavy losses on both sides. In the end, however, the Japanese were forced to abandon the island—and with it their last chance of launching an effective offensive to the south.

Thus in both the southern and central Pacific, the initiative had shifted to the United States by mid-1943. The Japanese advance had come to a stop. With aid from the Australians and the New Zealanders, the Americans now began the slow, arduous process of moving toward the Philippines and Japan itself.

Holding Off the Germans

In the European war, the United States had less control over military operations. It was fighting in cooperation with Britain and with the exiled "Free French" forces in the west; and it was trying also to conciliate its new ally, the Soviet Union, which was fighting Hitler in the east. The army chief of staff, General George C. Marshall, supported a plan for a major Allied invasion of France across the English Channel in the spring of 1943. But the American plan faced challenges from the Allies. The Soviet Union, which was absorbing (as it would throughout the war) the brunt of the German war effort, wanted the Allied invasion to proceed at the earliest possible moment. The British, on the other hand, wanted first to launch a series of Allied offensives around the edges of the Nazi empire—in northern Africa and southern Europe—before undertaking the major invasion of France.

Roosevelt was torn, but ultimately decided to support the British plan—in part because he was eager to get American forces into combat quickly and feared a cross-channel invasion would take a long time to prepare. At the end of October 1942, the British opened a counteroffensive against Nazi forces in North Africa under General Erwin Rommel, who was threatening the Suez Canal at El Alamein, and forced the Germans to retreat from Egypt. On November 8, Anglo-American forces landed at Oran and Algiers in Algeria and at Casablanca in Morocco—areas under the Nazi-controlled French government at Vichy—and began moving east toward Rommel. The Germans threw the full weight of their forces in Africa against the inexperienced Americans and inflicted a serious defeat on them at the Kasserine Pass in Tunisia. General George S. Patton, however, regrouped the American troops and began an effective counteroffensive. With the help of Allied air and naval power and of British forces attacking from the east under Field Marshall Bernard Montgomery (the hero of El Alamein), the American offensive finally drove the last Germans from Africa in May 1943.

The North African campaign had tied up so large a proportion of the Allied resources that the planned May 1943 cross-channel invasion of France had to be postponed, despite angry complaints from the Soviet Union. By now, however, the threat of a Soviet collapse seemed much diminished, for during the winter of 1942–1943 the Red Army had successfully held off

WORLD WAR II IN NORTH AFRICA AND ITALY: THE ALLIED COUNTEROFFENSIVE, 1942–1943

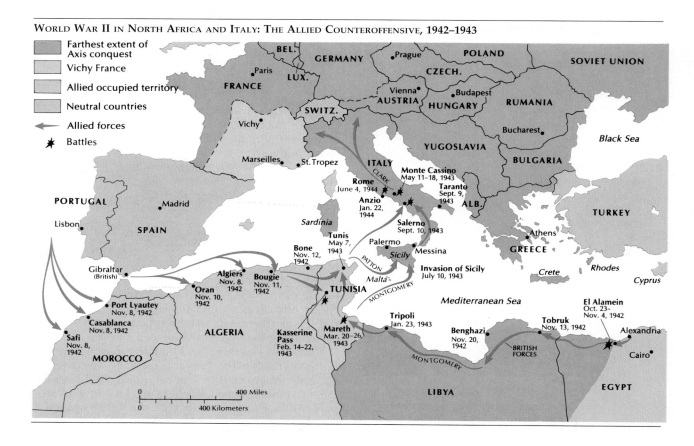

a major German assault at Stalingrad in southern Russia. Hitler had committed such enormous forces to the battle, and had suffered such appalling losses, that he could not continue his eastern offensive.

The Soviet victory had come at a terrible cost. The German siege of Stalingrad had decimated the civilian population of the city and devastated the surrounding countryside. Indeed, throughout the war, the Soviet Union absorbed losses far greater than any other warring nation (up to 20 million casualties)—a fact that continued to haunt the Russian memory and affect Soviet policy generations later. But the Soviet success in beating back the German offensive persuaded Roosevelt to agree, in a January 1943 meeting with Churchill in Casablanca, to a British plan for an Allied invasion of Sicily. General Marshall opposed the plan, arguing that it would further delay the vital invasion of France. But Churchill prevailed with the argument that the operation in Sicily might knock Italy out of the war and tie up German divisions that might otherwise be stationed in France. On the night of July 9, 1943, American and British armies landed in southeast

Sicily; thirty-eight days later they had conquered the island and were moving onto the Italian mainland. In the face of these setbacks, Mussolini's government collapsed and the dictator himself fled north to Germany. But although Mussolini's successor, Pietro Badoglio, quickly committed Italy to the Allies, Germany moved eight divisions into the country and established a powerful defensive line south of Rome. The Allied offensive on the Italian peninsula, which began on September 3, 1943, soon bogged down, especially after a serious setback at Monte Cassino that winter. Not until May 1944 did the Allies resume their northward advance. On June 4, 1944, they captured Rome.

The invasion of Italy contributed to the Allied war effort in several important ways. But it postponed the invasion of France by as much as a year, deeply embittering the Soviet Union, many of whose leaders believed that the United States and Britain were deliberating delaying in order to allow the Russians to absorb the brunt of the fighting. The postponement also gave the Soviets time to begin moving toward the countries of Eastern Europe.

America and the Holocaust

In the midst of this intensive fighting, the leaders of the American government were confronted with one of history's great horrors: the Nazi campaign to exterminate the Jews of Europe—the Holocaust. As early as 1942, high officials in Washington had incontrovertible evidence that Hitler's forces were rounding up Jews and others (including Poles, gypsies, homosexuals, and communists) from all over Europe, transporting them to concentration camps in eastern Germany and Poland, and systematically murdering them. (The death toll would ultimately reach 6 million Jews and approximately 4 million others.) News of the atrocities was reaching the public as well, and public pressure began to build for an Allied effort to end the killing or at least to rescue some of the surviving Jews.

The American government consistently resisted almost all such entreaties. Although Allied bombers were flying missions within a few miles of the most notorious death camp at Auschwitz in Poland, pleas that the planes try to destroy the crematoria at the camp were rejected as militarily unfeasible. So were similar requests that the Allies try to destroy railroad lines leading to the camp. The United States also resisted entreaties that it admit large numbers of the Jewish refugees attempting to escape Europe—a pattern established well before Pearl Harbor. One ship, the St. Louis, had arrived off Miami in 1939 carrying nearly 1,000 escaped German Jews, only to be refused entry and forced to return to Europe. Both before and during the war, the State Department did not even use up the number of visas permitted by law; almost 90 percent of the quota remained untouched. This disgraceful record was not a result of inadvertence. There was, it seems clear, a deliberate effort by officials in the State Department—spearheaded by Assistant Secretary Breckinridge Long, a genteel anti-Semite—to prevent Jews from entering the United States. One opportunity after another to assist the imperiled Jews was either ignored or rejected.

After 1941, there was probably little American leaders could have done, other than defeat Germany, to save most of Hitler's victims. But more forceful action by the United States (and Britain, which was even less amenable to Jewish requests for assistance) might well have saved some lives. That they did not take such action, it seems evident in retrospect, constituted a considerable moral failure. Policymakers at the time, however, justified abandoning the Jews to their fate by concentrating their attention solely on the larger goal of winning the war. Any diversion of energy and attention to other purposes, they claimed, would distract them from the overriding goal of victory.

THE AMERICAN IN WARTIME

"War is no longer simply a battle between armed forces in the field," an American government report of 1939 concluded. "It is a struggle in which each side strives to bring to bear against the enemy the coordinated power of every individual and of every material resource at its command. The conflict extends from the soldier in the front line to the citizen in the remotest hamlet in the rear."

The United States had experienced many wars before. But not since the Civil War had the nation undergone so consuming a military experience as World War II. American armed forces engaged in combat around the globe for nearly four years. American society, in the meantime, underwent changes that reached into virtually every corner of the nation.

Prosperity

World War II had its most profound impact on American domestic life by at last ending the Great Depression. By the middle of 1941, the economic problems of the 1930s—unemployment, deflation, industrial sluggishness—had virtually vanished before the great wave of wartime industrial expansion.

The most important agent of the new prosperity was federal spending, which after 1939 was pumping more money into the economy each year than all the New Deal relief agencies combined had done. In 1939, the federal budget had been $9 billion, the highest level it had ever reached in peacetime; by 1945, it had risen to $100 billion. Largely as a result, the gross national product soared: from $91 billion in 1939 to $166 billion in 1945. Personal incomes in some areas grew by as much as 100 percent or more. The demands of wartime production created a shortage of consumer goods, so many wage earners diverted much of their new affluence into savings, which would later help keep the economic boom alive in the postwar years.

The impact of government spending was perhaps most dramatic in the West, which had long relied on federal largesse more than other regions. The West Coast, naturally, became the launching point for most of the naval war against Japan; and the government created large manufacturing facilities in California and elsewhere to serve the needs of its military. Altogether, the government made almost $40 billion worth of capital investments (factories, military and transportation facilities, highways, power plants) in the West during the war, more than in any other region. Ten percent of all the money the federal government spent between 1940 and 1945 went to California alone. Other western states also shared disproportionately in war contracts and government-funded capital investments.

Henry J. Kaiser, whose construction companies had built some of the great western dams in the 1930s and who in the process had become a great favorite of many members of the Roosevelt administration, singlehandedly steered billions of federal dollars into vast capital projects in the West. He then used the infrastructure he had helped build to create major centers for shipbuilding, steel, magnesium, and aluminum production. By the end of the war, the economy of the Pacific Coast and, to a lesser extent, other areas of the West had been transformed. The Pacific Coast had become the center of the growing American aircraft industry. New yards in southern California, Washington State, and elsewhere made the West a center of the shipbuilding industry. Los Angeles, formerly a medium-sized city notable chiefly for its film industry, now became a major industrial center as well.

Once a lightly industrialized region, parts of the West were now among the most important manufacturing areas in the country. Once a region without adequate facilities to support substantial economic growth, the West now stood poised to become the fastest-growing region in the nation after the war.

Labor and the War

Instead of the prolonged and debilitating unemployment that had been the most troubling feature of the Depression economy, the war created a serious labor shortage. The armed forces took more than 15 million men and women out of the civilian work force at the same time that the demand for labor was rising rapidly. Nevertheless, the civilian work force increased by almost 20 percent during the war. The 7 million who had previously been unemployed accounted for some of the increase; the employment of many people previously considered inappropriate for the work force—the very young, the elderly, and most important, several million women—accounted for the rest.

The war gave an enormous boost to union membership, which rose from about 10.5 million in 1941 to over 13 million in 1945. But it also created important new restrictions on the ability of unions to fight for their members' demands. The government was principally interested in preventing inflation and in keeping production moving without disruption. It managed to win important concessions from union leaders on both scores. One was the so-called Little Steel for-

mula, which set a 15 percent limit on wartime wage increases. Another was the "no-strike" pledge, by which unions agreed not to stop production in wartime. In return, the government provided labor with a "maintenance-of-membership" agreement, which ensured that the thousands of new workers pouring into unionized defense plants would be automatically enrolled in the unions. The agreement ensured the continued health of the union organizations, but in return workers had to give up the right to demand major economic gains during the war.

Many rank-and-file union members, and some local union leaders, resented the restrictions imposed on them by the government and the labor movement hierarchy. Despite the no-strike pledge, there were nearly 15,000 work stoppages during the war, mostly wildcat strikes (strikes unauthorized by the union leadership). When the United Mine Workers defied the government by striking in May 1943, Congress reacted by passing, over Roosevelt's veto, the Smith-Connally Act (War Labor Disputes Act), which required unions to wait thirty days before striking and empowered the president to seize a struck war plant. In the meantime, public animosity toward labor rose rapidly, and many states passed laws to limit union power.

Stabilizing the Boom

The fear of deflation, the central concern of the 1930s, gave way during the war to a fear of inflation, particularly after prices rose 25 percent in the two years before Pearl Harbor. In October 1942, Congress grudgingly responded to the president's request and passed the Anti-Inflation Act, which gave the administration authority to freeze agricultural prices, wages, salaries, and rents throughout the country. Enforcement of these provisions was the task of the Office of Price Administration (OPA), led first by Leon Henderson and then by Chester Bowles. In part because of its success, inflation was a much less serious problem during World War II than it had been during World War I.

Even so, the OPA was never popular. There was widespread resentment of its controls over wages and prices. And there was only grudging acquiescence in its complicated system of rationing scarce consumer goods: coffee, sugar, meat, butter, canned goods, shoes, tires, gasoline, and fuel oil. Black-marketing and overcharging grew to proportions far beyond OPA policing capacity.

From 1941 to 1945, the federal government spent a total of $321 billion—twice as much as it had spent in the entire 150 years of its existence to that point, and ten times as much as the cost of World War I. The national debt rose from $49 billion in 1941 to $259 billion in 1945. The government borrowed about half the revenues it needed by selling $100 billion worth of bonds. Much of the rest it raised by radically increasing income taxes through the Revenue Act of 1942, which established a 94 percent rate for the highest brackets and, for the first time, imposed taxes on the lowest-income families as well. To simplify collection, Congress enacted a withholding system of payroll deductions in 1943.

Mobilizing Production

The search for an effective mechanism to mobilize the economy for war began as early as 1939 and continued for nearly four years. One failed agency after another attempted to bring order to the mobilization effort. Finally, in January 1942, the president responded to widespread criticism by creating the War Production Board (WPB), under the direction of former Sears Roebuck executive Donald Nelson. In theory, the WPB was to be a "superagency," with broad powers over the economy. In fact, it never had as much authority as its World War I equivalent, the War Industries Board. And the genial Donald Nelson never displayed the administrative or political strength of his 1918 counterpart, Bernard Baruch.

Throughout its troubled history, therefore, the WPB found itself constantly outmaneuvered and frustrated. It was never able to win control over military purchases; the army and navy often circumvented the board entirely in negotiating contracts with producers. It was never able to satisfy the complaints of small business, which charged (correctly) that most contracts were going to large corporations. Gradually, the president transferred much of the WPB's authority to a new office located within the White House: the Office of War Mobilization, directed by former Supreme Court justice and South Carolina senator James F. Byrnes. But the OWM was only slightly more successful than the WPB.

Despite the administrative problems, the war economy managed to meet almost all the nation's critical war needs. Enormous new factory complexes sprang up in the space of a few months, many of them funded by the federal government's Defense Plants Corporation. An entire new industry producing synthetic rubber emerged, to make up for the loss of access to natural rubber in the Pacific. By the beginning of 1944, American factories were, in fact, producing more than the government needed. Their output was twice that of all the Axis countries combined. There were even complaints late in the war that military production was

becoming excessive, that a limited resumption of civilian production should begin before the fighting ended. The military staunchly and successfully opposed almost all such demands.

African Americans and the War

During World War I, many African Americans had eagerly seized the chance to serve in the armed forces, believing that their patriotic efforts would win them an enhanced position in postwar society. They had been cruelly disappointed. As World War II approached, blacks were again determined to use the conflict to improve their position in society—this time, however, not by currying favor but by making demands.

In the summer of 1941, A. Philip Randolph, president of the Brotherhood of Sleeping Car Porters (a union with a predominantly black membership), began to insist that the government require companies receiving defense contracts to integrate their work forces. To mobilize support for the demand, Randolph planned a massive march on Washington, which would, he promised, bring over 100,000 demonstrators to the capital. Roosevelt was afraid of both the possibility of violence and the certainty of political embarrassment. He finally persuaded Randolph to cancel the march in return for a promise to establish a Fair Employment Practices Commission to investigate discrimination against blacks in war industries. The FEPC's enforcement powers, and thus its effectiveness, were limited, but its creation was a rare symbolic victory for African-Americans making demands of the government.

The demand for labor in war plants greatly increased the migration of blacks from the rural areas of the South into industrial cities—a migration that continued for more than a decade after the war and brought many more African Americans into northern cities than the first Great Migration of 1914–1919 had done. The migration bettered the economic condition of many African Americans, but it also created urban tensions. On a hot June day in Detroit in 1943, a series of altercations between blacks and whites at a city park led to two days of racial violence in which thirty-four people died, twenty-five of them blacks.

Despite such tensions, the leading black organizations redoubled their efforts during the war to challenge the system of segregation. The Congress of Racial Equality (CORE), organized in 1942, mobilized mass popular resistance to discrimination in a way that the older, more conservative organizations had never done. Randolph, Bayard Rustin, James Farmer,

AFRICAN-AMERICAN TROOPS IN GERMANY, 1945
Many black Americans served in the military during World War II, almost all of them in segregated units. Relatively few black soldiers were sent into combat, but those who were fought with distinction. This platoon of the 104th Division—captured twenty-four SS troops near this spot (Scherfide, Germany) in the last weeks of the war. *(UPI/Bettmann)*

and other, younger black leaders helped organize sit-ins and demonstrations in segregated theaters and restaurants. In 1944, they won a much-publicized victory by forcing a Washington, D.C., restaurant to agree to serve blacks. Their defiant spirit would survive into the 1950s and help produce the civil rights movement.

Pressure for change was also growing within the military. At first, the armed forces maintained their traditional practice of limiting blacks to the most menial assignments, keeping them in segregated training camps and units, and barring them entirely from the Marine Corps and the Army Air Forces. Gradually, however, military leaders were forced to make adjustments—in part because of public and political pressures, but also because they recognized that these forms of segregation were wasting manpower. By the end of the war, the number of black servicemen had increased sevenfold, to 700,000; some training camps were being at least partially integrated; blacks were beginning to serve on ships with white sailors; and more black units were being sent into combat. But tensions remained. In some of the partially integrated army bases—Fort Dix, New Jersey, for example—riots occasionally broke out when African Americans protested having to serve in segregated divisions. Substantial discrimination survived in all the services until well after the war. But within the military, as within the society at large, the traditional pattern of race relations was slowly eroding.

Indians and the War

Approximately 25,000 Indians performed military service during World War II. Many of them served in combat (among them Ira Hayes, one of the men who raised the American flag at Iwo Jima and became part of a legendary photograph and, later, war memorial). Others worked as "code-talkers," working in military communications and speaking their own languages (which enemy forces would be unlikely to understand) over the radio and the telephones.

The war had important effects, too, on those Native Americans who remained civilians. Little war work reached the tribes, and government subsidies dwindled. Many talented young people left the reservations, some to serve in the military, even more (more than 70,000) to work in war plants. This brought many Indians into intimate contact with white society for the first time, and awakened in among some of them a taste for the material benefits of life in capitalist America that they would retain after the war. Some never returned to the reservations, but chose to remain in the non-Indian world and assimilate to its ways. Others found that after the war, employment opportunities that had been available to them during the fighting became unavailable once again, leaving them little alternative but to return to the reservations.

The wartime emphasis on national unity undermined support for the revitalization of tribal autonomy that the Indian Reorganization Act of 1934 had launched.

New pressures emerged to eliminate the reservation system and require the tribes to assimilate into white society—pressures so severe that John Collier, the energetic director of the Bureau of Indian Affairs who had done so much to promote the reinvigoration of the reservations, resigned in 1945.

Mexican-American War Workers

Large numbers of Mexican workers entered the United States during the war in response to labor shortages on the Pacific Coast, the Southwest, and eventually almost all areas of the nation. The American and Mexican government agreed in 1942 to a program by which *braceros* (contract laborers) would be admitted to the United States for a limited time to work at specific jobs, and American employers in some parts of the Southwest began actively recruiting Hispanic workers.

During the Depression, many Mexican farmworkers had been deported to make room for desperate white workers. The wartime labor shortage caused farm owners to begin hiring them again. More important, however, Mexicans were able for the first time to find significant numbers of factory jobs. They formed the second largest group of migrants (after blacks) to American cities in the 1940s. Over 300,000 of them served in the United States military.

The sudden expansion of Mexican-American neighborhoods created tensions and occasionally conflict in some American cities. White residents of Los Angeles became alarmed at the activities of Mexican-American teenagers, many of whom were joining street gangs (*pachucos*). The *pachucos* were particularly distinctive because of their members' style of dress, which whites considered outrageous. They wore long, loose jackets with padded shoulders, baggy pants tied at the ankles, long watch chains, broad-brimmed hats, and greased, ducktail hairstyles. (It was a style borrowed in part from fashions in Harlem.) The outfit was known as a "zoot suit." For those who wore them, as for many adolescents, their style of dress became a symbol of rebellion against and defiance toward conventional white, middle-class society.

In June 1943, animosity toward the zoot-suiters produced a four-day riot in Los Angeles, during which white sailors stationed at a base in Long Beach invaded Mexican-American communities and attacked zoot-suiters (in response to alleged attacks by them on servicemen). The city police did little to restrain the sailors, who grabbed Hispanic teenagers, tore off and burned their clothes, cut off their ducktails, and beat them. But when Hispanics tried to fight back, the police moved in and arrested them. In the aftermath of the "zoot suit riots," Los Angeles passed a law prohibiting the wearing of zoot suits.

Women and Children at War

The war drew increasing numbers of women into roles from which, either by custom or law, they had been largely barred. The number of women in the work force increased by nearly 60 percent, and women accounted for a third of paid workers in 1945 (as opposed to a quarter in 1940). These wage-earning women were more likely to be married and were on the whole older than most of those who had entered the work force in the past.

Many women entered the industrial work force to replace male workers serving in the military. But while economic and military necessity eroded some of the popular objections to women in the workplace, obstacles remained. Many factory owners continued to categorize jobs by gender. (Female work, like male work, was also categorized by race: black women were usually assigned more menial tasks, and paid at a lower rate, than their white counterparts.) Employers also made substantial investments in automated assembly lines to reduce the need for heavy labor. Special recruiting materials presented factory work to women through domestic analogies that male employers assumed females would find easily comprehensible: cutting airplane wings was compared to making a dress pattern, mixing chemicals to making a cake. Many employers treated women in the war plants with a combination of solicitude and patronization, which was also an obstacle to winning genuine equality within the work force. Still, women did make important inroads in industrial employment during the war. Women had been working in industry for over a century, but some began now to take on heavy industrial jobs that had long been considered "men's work." The famous wartime image of "Rosie the Riveter" symbolized the new importance of the female industrial work force. Women workers joined unions in substantial numbers, and they helped erode at least some of the prejudice, including the prejudice against mothers' working, that had previously kept many of them from paid employment.

In the end, however, most women workers during the war were employed not in factories but in service-sector jobs. Above all, they worked for the government, whose bureaucratic needs expanded dramatically alongside its military and industrial needs. Washington, D.C., in particular, was flooded with

SOLDIERS *without guns*

WOMEN AT WAR
Many American women enlisted in the army and navy women's corps during World War II, but an equally important contribution of women to the war effort was their work in factories and offices—often in jobs that would have been considered inappropriate for them in peacetime but that they were able to assume because of the absence of so many men. *(Library of Congress)*

young female clerks, secretaries, and typists—known as "government girls"—most of whom lived in cramped quarters in boardinghouses, private homes, and government dormitories and worked long hours in the war agencies. Public and private clerical employment for women expanded in other urban areas as well, creating high concentrations of young women in places largely depleted of young men. The result was the development of distinctively female communities, in which women, often separated for the first time from home and family, adjusted to life in the work force through their association with other female workers. Even within the military, which enlisted substantial numbers of women as WAACs (army) and WAVEs (navy), most female work was clerical.

The new opportunities produced new problems. Many mothers whose husbands were in the military had to combine working with caring for their children. The scarcity of child-care facilities or other community services meant that some women had no choice but to leave young children—often known as "latchkey children" or "eight-hour orphans"—at home alone (or sometimes locked in cars in factory parking lots) while they worked.

Perhaps in part because of the family dislocations the war produced, juvenile crime rose markedly in the war years. Young boys were arrested at rapidly increasing rates for car theft and other burglary, vandalism, and vagrancy. The arrest rate for prostitutes, many of whom were teenage girls, rose too, as did the incidence of sexually transmitted disease. For many children, however, the distinctive experience of the war years was not crime but work. More than a third of all teenagers between the ages of fourteen and eighteen were employed late in the war, causing some reduction in high-school enrollments.

The return of prosperity during the war helped increase the rate and lower the age of marriage, but many of these young marriages were unable to survive the pressures of wartime separation. The divorce rate rose rapidly. The rise in the birth rate that accompanied the increase in marriages was the first sign of what would become the great postwar "baby boom."

The Internment of the Japanese Americans

World War I had produced a virtual orgy of hatred, vindictiveness, and hysteria in America, as well as widespread and flagrant violations of civil liberties. World War II did not. The government barred from the mails a few papers it considered seditious, among them Father Coughlin's anti-Semitic and pro-fascist *Social Justice*, but there was no general censorship of dissident publications. A few Nazi agents and American fascists were jailed, but there was no major assault on people suspected of sympathizing with the Axis. The most ambitious effort to punish domestic fascists, a sedition trial of twenty-eight people, ended in a mistrial, and the defendants went free. Unlike during World War I, the government generally left socialists and communists (most of whom strongly supported the war effort) alone.

Nor was there much of the ethnic or cultural animosity that had shaped the social climate of the United States during World War I. Americans continued to eat sauerkraut without calling it "liberty cabbage." They displayed little hostility toward German and Italian Americans. Instead, they seemed to share the view of their government's propaganda: that the enemy was less the German and Italian people than the vicious political systems to which they had succumbed.

But there was a glaring exception to the general rule of tolerance: the treatment of the small, politically powerless group of Japanese Americans. From the beginning, Americans adopted a different attitude toward their Asian enemy than they did toward their European foes. They attributed to the Japanese people certain racial and cultural characteristics that made it easier to hold them in contempt. The Japanese, both government and private propaganda encouraged Americans to believe, were a devious, malign, and

cruel people. The infamous attack on Pearl Harbor seemed to many to confirm that assessment.

This racial animosity soon extended to Americans of Japanese descent. There were not many Japanese Americans in the United States—only about 127,000, most of them concentrated in a few areas in California. About a third of them were unnaturalized, first-generation immigrants (Issei); two-thirds were naturalized or native-born citizens of the United States (Nisei). The Japanese in America, like the Chinese, had long been the target of ethnic and racial animosity; and unlike members of European ethnic groups, who had encountered similar resentment, Asians seemed unable to dispel prejudice against them no matter how assimilated they became. Many white Americans continued to consider Asians (even native-born citizens) so "foreign" that they could never become "real" Americans. Partly as a result, much of the Japanese-American population in the West continued to live in close-knit, to some degree even insular, communities, which simply reinforced the belief that they were somehow alien and potentially menacing.

Pearl Harbor inflamed these longstanding suspicions and turned them into active animosity. Wild stories circulated about how the Japanese in Hawaii had helped sabotage Pearl Harbor and how Japanese Americans in California were conspiring to aid an enemy landing on the Pacific coast. There was no evidence to support any of these charges; but according to Earl Warren, then attorney general of California, the apparent passivity of the Japanese Americans was more evidence of the danger they posed. Because they did nothing to allow officials to gauge their intentions, Warren claimed, it was all the more important to take precautions against conspiracies.

Although there was some public pressure in California to remove the Japanese "threat," on the whole popular sentiment was more tolerant of the Nisei and Issei (and more willing to make distinctions between them and the Japanese in Japan) than was official sentiment. The real impetus for taking action came from the government. Secretary of the Navy Frank Knox, for example, said shortly after Pearl Harbor that "the most effective fifth column work of the entire war was done in Hawaii," a statement that later investigations proved to be entirely false. General John L. DeWitt, the senior military commander on the West Coast, claimed to have "no confidence in [Japanese-American] loyalty whatsoever." When asked about the distinction between unnaturalized Japanese immigrants and American citizens, he said, "A Jap is a Jap. It makes no difference whether he is an American citizen or not."

In February 1942, in response to pressure from military officials like DeWitt and Knox and West Coast political leaders like Warren (and over the objections of the attorney general and J. Edgar Hoover, the director of the FBI), the president authorized the army to "intern" the Japanese Americans. He created the War Relocation Authority (WRA) to oversee the project. More than 100,000 people (Issei and Nisei alike) were rounded up, told to dispose of their property however they could (which often meant simply abandoning it), and taken to what the government euphemistically termed "relocation centers" in the "interior." In fact, they were facilities little different from prisons, many of them located in the western mountains and the desert. Conditions in the internment camps were not brutal, but they were harsh and uncomfortable. Government officials talked of them as places where the Japanese could be socialized and "Americanized," much as many officials had at times considered Indian reservations as places for training Native Americans to become more like whites.

But like Indian reservations, the internment camps were more a target of white economic aspirations than of missionary work. The governor of Utah, where many of the internees were located, wanted the federal government to turn over thousands of Japanese Americans to serve as forced laborers. Washington did not comply, but the WRA did hire out many inmates as agricultural laborers.

The internment never produced significant popular opposition. For the most part, once the Japanese were in the camps, other Americans (including their former neighbors on the West Coast) largely forgot about them—except to make strenuous efforts to acquire the property they had abandoned. Even so, beginning in 1943 conditions slowly improved. Some young Japanese Americans left the camps to attend colleges and universities (mostly in the East—the WRA continued to be wary of letting Japanese return to the Pacific Coast). Others were permitted to move to cities to take factory and service jobs (although again, not on the West Coast). Some young men joined and others were drafted into the American military; a Nisei army unit fought with distinction in Europe. In 1944, the Supreme Court ruled in *Korematsu* v. *U.S.* that the relocation was constitutionally permissible. In another case the same year, it barred the internment of "loyal" citizens, but left the interpretation of "loyal" to the discretion of the government. Nevertheless, by the end of 1944 most of the internees had been released; and in early 1945, they were finally permitted to return to the West Coast—where they faced continuing harassment and persecution, and where many found their property and businesses irretrievably lost. Not until 1988

did they win any compensation for their losses, when, after years of agitation by survivors of the camps and their descendants, Congress voted to award them reparations.

Chinese Americans and the War

Just as America's conflict with Japan undermined the position of Japanese Americans, the American alliance with China during World War II significantly enhanced both the legal and social status of Chinese Americans. In 1943, partly to improve relations with the government of China, Congress finally repealed the Chinese Exclusion Acts, which had barred almost all Chinese immigration since 1892. The new quota for Chinese immigrants was miniscule (105 a year), but a substantial number of Chinese women managed to gain entry into the country through other provisions covering war brides and fiancées. Over 4,000 Chinese women entered the United States in the first three years after the war. Permanent residents of the United States of Chinese descent were finally permitted to become citizens.

Racial animosity toward the Chinese did not disappear, but it did decline—in part because government propaganda and popular culture both began presenting positive images of the Chinese (partly to contrast them with the Japanese); in part because Chinese Americans (like African Americans and other previously marginal groups) began taking jobs in war plants and other booming areas suffering from labor shortages and hence moving out of the relatively isolated world of the Chinatowns. A higher proportion of Chinese Americans (22 percent of all adult males) were drafted than of any other national group, and the entire Chinese community in most cities worked hard and conspicuously for the war effort.

The Retreat from Reform

Late in 1943, Franklin Roosevelt publicly suggested that "Dr. New Deal," as he called it, had served its purpose and should now give way to "Dr. Win-the-War." The statement reflected the president's own genuine shift in concern: that victory was now more important than reform. But it also reflected the political reality that had emerged during the first two years of war. Liberals in government were finding themselves unable to enact new programs. They were even finding it difficult to protect existing ones from conservative assault.

Within the administration itself, many liberals found themselves displaced by the new managers of

AMERICANS IN PARIS, 1944
American troop transports roll into Paris in August 1944 to a delirious welcome from French citizens, who had by then lived under Nazi occupation for more than four years. They had given an even warmer greeting to the Free French forces under General Charles De Gaulle, which had arrived in the city a few days earlier. *(UPI/Bettmann)*

the wartime agencies, who came overwhelmingly from large corporations and conservative Wall Street law firms. But the greatest assault on New Deal reforms came from conservatives in Congress, who seized on the war as an excuse to do what many had wanted to do in peacetime: dismantle many of the achievements of the New Deal. They were assisted by the end of mass unemployment, which decreased the need for such relief programs as the Civilian Conservation Corps and the Works Progress Administration (both of which were abolished). They were assisted, too, by their own increasing numbers. In the congressional elections of 1942, Republicans gained 47 seats in the House and 10 in the Senate. Roosevelt continued to talk bravely at times about his commitment to social progress and liberal reform, in part to bolster the flagging spirits of his traditional supporters. But increasingly, the president quietly accepted the defeat or erosion of New Deal measures in order to win support for his war policies

and peace plans. He also accepted the changes because he realized that his chances for reelection in 1944 depended on his ability to identify himself less with domestic issues than with world peace.

Republicans approached the 1944 election determined to exploit what they believed was resentment of wartime regimentation and privation and unhappiness with Democratic reform. They nominated as their candidate the young and vigorous governor of New York, Thomas E. Dewey. Roosevelt was unopposed within his party, but Democratic leaders pressured him to abandon Vice President Henry Wallace, an advanced New Dealer and hero of the CIO, and replace him with a more moderate figure. Roosevelt reluctantly acquiesced in the selection of Senator Harry S. Truman of Missouri. Truman was not a prominent figure in the party, but he had won acclaim as chairman of the Senate War Investigating Committee (known as the Truman Committee), which had compiled an im-

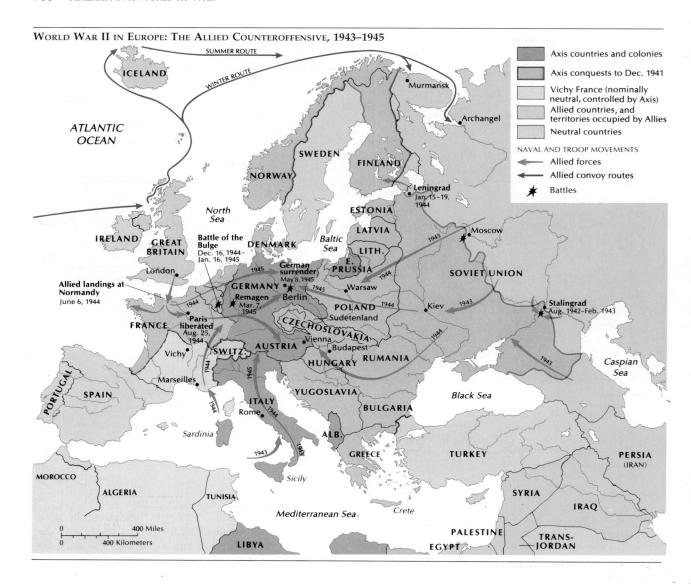

WORLD WAR II IN EUROPE: THE ALLIED COUNTEROFFENSIVE, 1943–1945

pressive record uncovering waste and corruption in wartime production.

The conduct of the war was not an issue in the campaign. Instead, the election revolved around domestic economic issues and, indirectly, the president's health. The president was in fact gravely ill, suffering from, among other things, arteriosclerosis. It may not be too much to say that he was dying. But the campaign seemed momentarily to revive him. He made several strenuous public appearances late in October, which dispelled popular doubts about his health and ensured his reelection. He captured 53.5 percent of the popu-

lar vote to Dewey's 46 percent, and won 432 electoral votes to Dewey's 99. Democrats lost 1 seat in the Senate, gained 20 in the House, and maintained control of both.

THE DEFEAT OF THE AXIS

By the middle of 1943, America and its allies had succeeded in stopping the Axis advance both in Europe and in the Pacific. In the next two years, the Allies themselves seized the offensive and launched a series of powerful drives that rapidly led the way to victory.

The Liberation of France

By early 1944, American and British bombers were attacking German industrial installations and other targets almost round the clock, drastically cutting production and impeding transportation. Especially devastating was the massive bombing of such German cities as Leipzig, Dresden, and Berlin. A February 1945 incendiary raid on Dresden created a great firestorm that destroyed three-fourths of the previously undamaged city and killed approximately 135,000 people, almost all civilians. Military leaders claimed that the bombing destroyed industrial facilities, demoralized the population, and cleared the way for the great Allied invasion of France in the late spring. In fact, the greatest contribution of the bombing to the military struggle was to force the German air force (the *Luftwaffe*) to relocate much of its strength in Germany itself and to engage Allied forces in the air. The air battles over Germany considerably weakened the *Luftwaffe* and made it a less formidable obstacle to the Allied invasion than it might once have been. Preparations for the invasion were also assisted by the success of the Allies in breaking the most secret German codes—a success made possible by the acquisition of an "Ultra" machine, a sophisticated German coding device.

An enormous invasion force had been gathering in England for two years: almost 3 million troops, and perhaps the greatest array of naval vessels and armaments ever assembled in one place. On the morning of June 6, 1944, D-Day, General Dwight D. Eisenhower, the Supreme Commander of the Allied forces, sent this vast armada into action. The landing came not at the narrowest part of the English Channel, where the Germans had expected and prepared for it, but along sixty miles of the Cotentin peninsula on the coast of Normandy. While airplanes and battleships offshore bombarded the Nazi defenses, 4,000 vessels landed troops and supplies on the beaches. (Three divisions of paratroopers had been dropped behind the German lines the night before, amid scenes of great confusion, to seize critical roads and bridges for the push inland.) Fighting was intense along the beach, but the superior manpower and equipment of the Allied forces gradually prevailed. Within a week, the German forces had been dislodged from virtually the entire Normandy coast.

For the next month, further progress remained slow. But in late July in the Battle of Saint-Lô, General Omar Bradley's First Army smashed through the German lines. George S. Patton's Third Army, spearheaded by heavy tank attacks, then moved through the hole Bradley had created and began a drive into the heart of France. On August 25, Free French forces arrived in Paris and liberated the city from four years of German occupation. And by mid-September the Allied armies had driven the Germans almost entirely out of France and Belgium.

The great Allied drive came to a halt, however, at the Rhine River in the face of a firm line of German defenses and a period of cold weather, rain, and floods. In mid-December, German forces struck in desperation along fifty miles of front in the Ardennes Forest. In the Battle of the Bulge (named for a large bulge that appeared in the American lines as the Germans pressed forward), they drove fifty-five miles toward Antwerp before they were finally stopped at Bastogne. The battle ended serious German resistance in the west.

While the Allies were fighting their way through France, Soviet forces were sweeping westward into central Europe and the Balkans. In late January 1945, the Russians launched a great offensive toward the Oder River inside Germany. In early spring, they were ready to launch a final assault against Berlin. By then, Omar Bradley's First Army was pushing into Germany from the west. Early in March, his forces captured the city of Cologne, on the west bank of the Rhine. The next day, in a remarkable stroke of good fortune, he discovered and seized an undamaged bridge over the river at Remagen; Allied troops were soon pouring across the Rhine. In the following weeks the British Field Marshall Bernard Montgomery, commander of Allied ground operations on D-Day and after, pushed into northern Germany with a million troops, while Bradley's army, sweeping through central Germany, completed the encirclement of 300,000 German soldiers in the Ruhr.

The German resistance was now broken on both fronts. American forces were moving eastward faster than they had anticipated and could have beaten the Russians to Berlin and Prague. Instead, the American and British high commands decided to halt the advance along the Elbe River in central Germany to await the Russians. That decision enabled the Soviets to occupy eastern Germany and Czechoslovakia.

On April 30, with Soviet forces on the outskirts of Berlin, Adolf Hitler killed himself in his bunker in the capital. And on May 8, 1945, the remaining German forces surrendered unconditionally. V-E (Victory in Europe) Day prompted great celebrations in Western Europe and in the United States, tempered by the knowledge of the continuing war against Japan.

The Pacific Offensive

In February 1944, American naval forces under Admiral Chester Nimitz won a series of victories in the Marshall Islands and cracked the outer perimeter of the Japanese Empire. Within a month, the navy had destroyed other vital Japanese bastions. American submarines, in the meantime, were decimating Japanese shipping and crippling the nation's domestic economy. By the summer of 1944, the already skimpy food rations for the Japanese people had been reduced by nearly a quarter; there was also a critical gasoline shortage.

Meanwhile, a frustrating struggle was in progress on the Asian mainland. In 1942, the Japanese had forced General Joseph W. Stilwell of the United States out of Burma and had moved their own troops as far west as the mountains bordering India. For a time, Stilwell supplied the isolated Chinese forces continuing to resist Japan with an aerial ferry over the Himalayas. In 1943, finally, he led Chinese, Indian, and a few American troops back through northern Burma, constructing a road and pipeline across the mountains into China (the Burma Road, also known as the Ledo Road or Stilwell Road), which finally opened in the fall of 1944.

By then, however, the Japanese had launched a major counteroffensive and had driven so deep into the Chinese interior that they threatened the terminus of the Burma Road and the center of Chinese government at Chungking. The Japanese offensive precipitated a long-simmering feud between General Stilwell and Premier Chiang Kai-shek of China. Stilwell was indignant because Chiang (whom he called, contemptuously, the "Peanut") was using many of his troops to maintain an armed frontier against the Chinese communists and would not deploy those troops against the Japanese.

The decisive battles of the Pacific War, however, occurred in the Pacific. In mid-June 1944, an enormous American armada struck the heavily fortified Mariana Islands and, after some of the bloodiest operations of the war, captured Tinian, Guam, and Saipan, 1,350 miles from Tokyo. In September, American forces landed on the western Carolines. And on October 20, General MacArthur's troops landed on Leyte Island in the Philippines. The Japanese now used virtually their entire fleet against the Allied invaders in three major encounters—which together constituted the decisive Battle of Leyte Gulf, the largest naval engagement in history. American forces held off the Japanese onslaught and sank four Japanese carriers, all but destroying Japan's capacity to continue a serious naval war.

Nevertheless, as American forces advanced closer to the Japanese mainland early in 1945, the imperial forces seemed only to increase their resistance. In February 1945, American marines seized the tiny volcanic island of Iwo Jima, only 750 miles from Tokyo, but only after the costliest single battle in the history of the Marine Corps. The marines suffered over 20,000 casualties.

The battle for Okinawa, an island only 370 miles south of Japan, was further evidence of the strength of the Japanese resistance in those last desperate months. Week after week, the Japanese sent kamikaze (suicide) planes against American and British ships, sacrificing 3,500 of them while inflicting great damage. Japanese troops on shore launched desperate nighttime attacks on the American lines. The United States and its allies suffered nearly 50,000 casualties before finally capturing Okinawa in late June 1945. Over 100,000 Japanese died in the siege.

The same kind of bitter fighting seemed to await the Americans in Japan itself. But there were signs early in 1945 that such an invasion might not be necessary. The Japanese had almost no ships or planes left with which to fight. In July 1945, for example, American warships stood off the shore of Japan and shelled industrial targets (many already in ruins from aerial bombings) with impunity. A brutal firebombing of Tokyo in March, in which American bombers dropped napalm on the city and created a firestorm in which over 80,000 people died, further weakened the Japanese will to resist. Moderate Japanese leaders, who had long since decided that the war was lost, were gaining power within the government and were looking for ways to bring the war to an end. After the invasion of Okinawa, Emperor Hirohito appointed a new premier and gave him instructions to sue for peace. Although the new leader could not persuade military leaders to give up the fight, he did try, along with the emperor himself, to obtain mediation through the Soviet Union. The Russians showed little interest in playing the role of arbitrator, but other developments made their participation unnecessary. Whether the moderates could ultimately have prevailed is a question about which historians and others continue to disagree. In any case, the question eventually became moot. In mid-July, American scientists conducted a successful test of a new atomic bomb.

The Manhattan Project

In 1939 reports reached the United States through the Italian physicist Enrico Fermi and the German mathematician Albert Einstein (then living in exile in Amer-

THE MANHATTAN PROJECT
J. Robert Oppenheimer, wearing the broad-brimmed hat, was one of the scientific leaders of the Manhattan Project, which developed the atomic bomb during World War II. The military commander of the project was General Leslie Groves. The two men are shown here after the war, examining the charred landscape of the Trinity site in New Mexico, where the first successful detonation of the new weapon occurred in July 1945. *(UPI/Bettman)*

ica) that Nazi scientists had learned how to produce atomic fission in uranium. Acquiring that knowledge, they warned, was the first step toward the creation of an atomic bomb, a weapon more powerful than any ever previously devised. The United States and Britain immediately began a race to develop the weapon before the Germans did.

Over the next three years, the government secretly poured nearly $2 billion into the so-called Manhattan Project—a massive scientific effort conducted at hidden laboratories in Oak Ridge, Tennessee, Los Alamos, New Mexico, Hanford, Washington, and other sites. (It had gotten its name earlier, when many of the atomic physicists had been working at Columbia University in New York.) Hundreds of scientists, many of them not fully aware of what they were working on, labored feverishly to complete two complementary projects. One (at Oak Ridge and Hanford) was the production

of fissionable plutonium, the fuel for an atomic explosion; the other (at Los Alamos, under the supervision of J. Robert Oppenheimer) was the construction of a bomb that could use the fuel.

The scientists pushed ahead much faster than anyone had predicted. Even so, the war in Europe ended before they were ready to test the first bomb. Just before dawn on July 16, 1945, near Alamogordo, New Mexico, the scientists gathered to witness the first atomic explosion in history: a blinding flash of light brighter than any ever seen on earth, and a huge, billowing mushroom cloud. Some were exhilarated by their success. Others, among them J. Robert Oppenheimer, were already troubled by the implications of what they had done. But by then, control of the atomic bomb had already moved into other hands. The bomb was no longer a scientific project; it was a weapon of war.

Atomic Warfare

News of the explosion reached President Harry S. Truman (who had taken office in April on the death of Roosevelt) in Potsdam, Germany, where he was attending a conference of Allied leaders. He issued an ultimatum to the Japanese (signed jointly by the British) demanding that they surrender by August 3 or face complete devastation. The Japanese premier wanted to accept the Allied demand, but by the time the deadline arrived he had not yet been able to persuade the military leaders to agree. There was a possibility that the government might agree to surrender, in return for a promise that the Japanese could retain their emperor. The American government, firmly committed to the idea of "unconditional surrender," disregarded those overtures. When the Japanese failed to meet the deadline, Truman ordered the air force to use the new atomic weapons against Japan.

Controversy has raged for decades over whether Truman's decision to use the bomb was justified and what his motives were. Some have argued that the atomic attack was unnecessary, that had the United States agreed to the survival of the emperor (which it ultimately did agree to in any case), or waited only a few more weeks, the Japanese would have surrendered. Others argue that nothing less than the atomic bombs could have persuaded the Japanese to surrender without a costly American invasion. Some critics of the decision, including some of the scientists involved in the Manhattan Project, have argued that whatever Japanese intentions, the United States, as a matter of morality, should not have used the terrible new weapon. One horrified physicist wrote the president shortly before the attack: "This thing must not be

SIGNIFICANT EVENTS

1941 A. Philip Randolph proposes march on Washington

Roosevelt establishes Fair Employment Practices Commission

1942 Japanese capture Philippines

Battle of Midway

North Africa campaign begins

News of Holocaust reaches United States

War Production Board created

Japanese-Americans interned

Manhattan Project begins

Temporary Mexican workers allowed entry to U.S.

Congress of Racial Equality (CORE) founded

1943 Americans capture Guadalcanal

Soviets defeat Germans at Stalingrad

Allies launch invasion of Italy

Smith-Connally Act passed

Race riot breaks out in Detroit

Sailors battle Mexican-Americans in "zoot suit" riots in Los Angeles

Chinese Exclusion Act repealed

1944 Allies invade Normandy

Roosevelt reelected president

Americans recapture Philippines

Demonstrators force restaurant in Washington, D.C. to desegregate

1945 Roosevelt dies; Truman becomes president

Hitler kills himself

Allies capture Berlin

Germany surrenders

Americans capture Okinawa

Atomic bomb tested in New Mexico

United States drops atomic bombs on Hiroshima and Nagasaki

Japan surrenders

---

permitted to exist on this earth. We must not be the most hated and feared people in the world."

The nation's military and political leaders, however, showed little concern about such matters. Truman, who had not even known of the existence of the Manhattan Project until he became president, was apparently making what he believed to be a simple military decision. A weapon was available that would end the war quickly; he could see no reason not to use it.

Still more controversy has existed over whether there were other motives at work in Truman's decision. With the Soviet Union poised to enter the war in the Pacific, did the United States want to end the conflict quickly to forestall an expanded communist presence in Asia? Did Truman use the bomb as a weapon to intimidate Stalin, with whom he was engaged in difficult negotiations, so the Soviet leader would accept American demands? Little direct evidence is available to support (or definitively refute) either of these accusations.

On August 6, 1945, an American B-29, the *Enola Gay*, dropped an atomic weapon on the Japanese industrial center at Hiroshima. With a single bomb, the United States completely incinerated a four-square-mile area at the center of the previously undamaged city. More than 80,000 civilians died, according to later American estimates. Many more survived to suffer the crippling effects of radioactive fallout or to pass those effects on to their children in the form of birth defects.

The Japanese government, stunned by the attack, was at first unable to agree on a response. Two days later, on August 8, the Soviet Union declared war on Japan. And the following day, the United States sent another American plane to drop another atomic weapon—this time on the city of Nagasaki—inflicting horrible damage and over 100,000 deaths on another unfortunate community. Finally, the emperor intervened to break the stalemate in the cabinet, and on August 14 the government announced that it was ready to give up. On September 2, 1945, on board the American battleship *Missouri*, anchored in Tokyo Bay, Japanese officials signed the articles of surrender.

The greatest war in the history of mankind had come to an end, and the United States had emerged not only victorious but in a position of unprecedented power, influence, and prestige. It was a victory, however, that few could greet with unambiguous joy. Fourteen million combatants had died in the struggle. Many more civilians had perished, from bombings, from disease and starvation, from genocidal cam-

paigns of extermination. The United States had suffered only light casualties in comparison with many other nations, but the cost had still been high: 322,000 dead, another 800,000 injured. And despite the sacrifices, the world continued to face an uncertain future, menaced by the threat of nuclear warfare and by the emerging antagonism between the world's two strongest nations—the United States and the Soviet Union—that would darken the peace for many decades to come.

SUGGESTED READINGS

War and American Society. John Morton Blum, *V Was for Victory* (1976). Mark J. Harris et al., *The Homefront* (1984). Richard R. Lingeman, *Don't You Know There's a War On?* (1970). Gerald D. Nash, *The American West Transformed: The Impact of the Second World War* (1985). Geoffrey Perrett, *Days of Sadness, Years of Triumph: The American People, 1939–1945* (1974). Richard Polenberg, *War and Society* (1972). Studs Terkel, *"The Good War": An Oral History of World War II* (1984).

War Mobilization and Wartime Politics. Oscar E. Anderson, Jr., *The New World* (1962). Ellsworth Barnard, *Wendell Willkie* (1966). Chester Bowles, *Promises to Keep* (1971). Alan Brinkley, *The End of Reform: New Deal Liberalism in Recession and War* (1995). David Brinkley, *Washington Goes to War* (1987). James MacGregor Burns, *Roosevelt: The Soldier of Freedom* (1970). Bruce Catton, *War Lords of Washington* (1946). Lester V. Chandler, *Inflation in the United States, 1940–1948* (1951). Alan Clive, *State of War: Michigan in World War II* (1979). George Q. Flynn, *The Mess in Washington: Manpower Mobilization in World War II* (1979). Leslie R. Groves, *Now It Can Be Told* (1962). Howell John Harris, *The Right to Manage* (1982). Maurice Isserman, *Which Side Were You On? The American Communist Party During World War II* (1982). Eliot Janeway, *Struggle for Survival* (1951). Paul A. C. Koistinen, *The Military-Industrial Complex: A Historical Perspecive* (1980). Philip Knightley, *The First Casualty* (1975). Nelson Lichtenstein, *Labor's War at Home: The CIO in World War II* (1982). Donald Nelson, *Arsenal of Democracy* (1946). Joel Seidman, *American Labor from Defense to Reconversion* (1953). Bradley F. Smith, *The Shadow Warriors: The OSS and the Origins of the CIA* (1983). Richard Steele, *Propaganda in an Open Society* (1985). Patrick S. Washburn, *A Question of Sedition: The Federal Government's Investigation of the Black Press During World War II* (1986). Michi Weglyn, *Years of Infamy: The Untold Story of America's Concentration Camps* (1976). Alan M. Winkler, *The Politics of Propaganda; The Office of War Information, 1942–1945* (1978).

The War and Race. Domenic J. Capeci, Jr., *The Harlem Riot of 1943* (1977); *Race Relations in Wartime Detroit* (1987). Richard M. Dalfiume, *Desegregation of the U.S. Armed Forces* (1969). Roger Daniels, *The Politics of Prejudice* (1962); *Concentration Camps, USA: Japanese Americans and World War II* (1971). John

W. Dower, *War Without Mercy: Race and Power in the Pacific War* (1986). Mario T. Garcia, *Mexican-Americans: Leadership, Ideology, and Identity, 1930–1960* (1989). Herbert Garfinkel, *When Negroes March* (1959). Audrie Girdner and Anne Loftis, *The Great Betrayal* (1969). Bill Hosokawa, *Nisei* (1969). Peter Irons, *Justice at War* (1983). Thomas James, *Exiles Within: The Schooling of Japanese-Americans, 1942–1945* (1987). Philip McGuire, ed., *Taps for a Jim Crow Army: Letters from Black Soldiers in World War II* (1982). Mauricio Mazon, *The Zoot-Suit Riots* (1984). August Meier and Elliott Rudwick, *CORE* (1973). Louis Ruchames, *Race, Jobs, and Politics* (1953). Holly Cowan Shulman, *The Voice of America* (1991). Neil Wynn, *The Afro-American and the Second World War* (1976).

Women and the War. Karen Anderson, *Wartime Women: Sex Roles, Family Relations, and the Status of Women During World War II* (1981). D'Ann Campbell, *Women at War with America* (1984). Sherna B. Gluck, *Rosie the Riveter Revisited* (1987). Susan Hartmann, *The Homefront and Beyond: American Women in the 1940s* (1982). Margaret R. Higgonet et al., *Behind the Lines: Gender and the Two World Wars* (1987). Maureen Honey, *Creating Rosie the Riveter: Class, Gender, and Propaganda During World War II* (1984). Ruth Milkman, *Gender at Work: The Dynamics of Job Segregation by Sex During World War II* (1987). Susan M. Reverby, *Ordered to Care: The Dilemma of American Nursing, 1850–1945* (1987). Leila Rupp, *Mobilizing Women for War* (1978).

Wartime Military and Diplomatic Experiences. Stephen Ambrose, *The Supreme Commander* (1970); *Eisenhower: Soldier, General of the Army, President-Elect* (1983); *D-Day: June 6, 1944* (1994). Albert Russell Buchanan, *The United States and World War II*, 2 vols. (1962). James MacGregor Burns, *Roosevelt: The Soldier of Freedom* (1970). Winston S. Churchill, *The Second World War*, 6 vols. (1948–1953). Robert Divine, *Roosevelt and World War II* (1969); *Second Chance* (1967). Dwight D. Eisenhower, *Crusade in Europe* (1948). John S. D. Eisenhower, *Allies: Pearl Harbor to D-Day* (1982). Kenneth Greenfield, *American Strategy in World War II* (1963). Max Hastings, *Overlord: D-Day and the Battle for Normandy* (1984). Patrick Heardon, *Roosevelt Confronts Hitler: American Entry into World War II* (1987). Godfrey Hodgson, *The Colonel: The Life and Wars of Henry Stimson, 1967–1950* (1990). Michael Howard, *The*

Mediterranean Strategy in World War II (1968). Margaret Hoyle, *A World in Flames* (1970). D. Clayton James, *A Time for Giants: Politics of the American High Command in World War II* (1987). John Keegan, *Six Armies in Normandy: From D-Day to the Liberation of Paris, June 6–August 25, 1944* (1982). Warren Kimball, *The Juggler: Franklin Roosevelt as Wartime Statesman* (1991). E. J. Kind and W. M. Whitehill, *Fleet Admiral King* (1952). Charles B. McDonald, *The Mighty Endeavor* (1969). William Manchester, *American Caesar* (1979). Samuel Eliot Morison, *Strategy and Compromise* (1958); *History of United States Naval Operations in World War II*, 14 vols. (1947–1960); *The Two Ocean War* (1963). Geoffrey Perret, *There's a War to Be Won: The United States Army in World War II* (1991). Forrest Pogue, *George C. Marshall*, 2 vols. (1963–1966). Gordon W. Prange, *At Dawn We Slept: The Untold Story of Pearl Harbor* (1981). Fletcher Pratt, *War for the World* (1951). Cornelius Ryan, *The Longest Day* (1959); *The Last Battle* (1966). Ronald Schaffer, *Wings of Judgment: American Bombing in World War II* (1985). Michael Schaller, *The United States Crusade in China, 1938–1945* (1979). Michael Sherry, *Preparing for the Next War: American Plans for Postwar Defense, 1941–1945* (1977); *The Rise of American Air Power* (1987). Gaddis Smith, *American Diplomacy During the Second World War* (1964). Ronald H. Spector, *Eagle Against the Sun: The American War with Japan* (1985). Mark A. Stoler, *The Politics of the Second Front: Planning and Diplomacy in Coalition Warfare, 1941–1945* (1977). Christopher Thorne, *Allies of a Kind: The United States, Britain and the War Against Japan, 1941–1945* (1978). John Toland, *The Last Hundred Days* (1966); *The Rising Sun* (1970). Barbara Tuchman, *Stilwell and the American Experience in China* (1971). Russell Weigley, *The American Way of War* (1973); *Eisenhower's Lieutenants: The Campaign of France and Germany, 1944–1945* (1981). Chester Wilmot, *The Struggle for Europe* (1952). David S. Wyman, *The Abandonment of the Jews: America and the Holocaust, 1941–1945* (1984).

Atomic Warfare. Gar Alperovitz, *Atomic Diplomacy* (1965). Nuel Davis, *Lawrence and Oppenheimer* (1969). Robert Donovan, *Conflict and Crisis* (1977). Herbert Feis, *The Atomic Bomb and the End of World War II* (1966). Gregg Herken, *The Winning Weapon: The Atomic Bomb in the Cold War* (1980). John Hersey, *Hiroshima* (1946). Robert Jungk, *Brighter Than a Thousand Suns* (1958). Richard Rhodes, *The Making of the Atomic Bomb* (1987). W. S. Schoenberger, *Decision of Destiny* (1969). Martin Sherwin, *A World Destroyed* (1975). Leon V. Sigal, *Fighting to a Finish* (1988).

TRUMAN AND DEWEY, 1948
President Harry S. Truman was once photographed with the actress Lauren Bacall draped across the piano Truman was playing. The artist Ben Shahn satirized that photograph in the unflattering 1948 picture of Truman and his Republican opponent, Governor Thomas E. Dewey of New York. It became a poster for former Vice President Henry A. Wallace, who was running a third-party campaign that year based primarily on opposition to the administration's Cold War foreign policy. *(Harry S. Truman Library)*

CHAPTER TWENTY-NINE

THE COLD WAR

VEN BEFORE THE END of World War II, in which the United States and the Soviet Union had fought together as allies, there were signs of tension between the two nations. Once the hostilities were over, those tensions quickly grew to create what became known as a "Cold War"—a tense and dangerous rivalry that would cast its shadow over international affairs for decades. The Cold War also had profound effects on American domestic life. Among other things, it helped produce the most corrosive outbreak of antiradical hysteria of the century. America in the postwar years was both powerful and prosperous; but it was also for a time troubled and uncertain about the future.

ORIGINS OF THE COLD WAR

No issue in twentieth-century American history has aroused more debate than the question of the origins of the Cold War. Some have claimed that Soviet duplicity and expansionism created the international tensions, others that American provocations and imperial ambitions were at least equally to blame. Most historians agree, however, that wherever the preponderance of blame may lie, both the United States and the Soviet Union contributed to the atmosphere of hostility and suspicion that quickly clouded the peace. (See "Where Historians Disagree," pp. 770–771.)

Soviet-American Tensions

The wartime alliance between the United States and the Soviet Union was an aberration from the normal tenor of Soviet-American relations, for the two nations had long viewed each other with deep mutual mistrust.

The reasons for American hostility toward the Soviet Union were both obvious and many. There was, of course, the fundamental American animosity toward communism, which had strong roots in the nation's past and had been a powerful force in society since well before the Russian Revolution. But there were more specific reasons as well. Almost the first act of the new Soviet regime had been to negotiate a separate peace with Germany in 1917, leaving the West to fight the Central Powers alone. The Soviet Union had called openly and continually for world revolution and the overthrow of capitalist regimes (even if it did little before World War II actively to advance that goal). The Stalinist purges of the 1930s and 1940s—a savage and brutal campaign of extermination against opponents of the regime, real and imagined, that caused the deaths of millions of people—produced understandable revulsion in the West. Stalin, like Hitler, was one of the great tyrants of modern history; and in 1939, these two tyrants had agreed to the short-lived Nazi-Soviet Pact, freeing Germany to launch World War II.

But Soviet hostility toward the United States had deep roots as well. The United States had opposed the revolution in 1917 and had sent troops into Russia at

ORIGINS OF THE COLD WAR

N O ISSUE IN RECENT American history has produced more controversy than that of the origins of the Cold War between the United States and the Soviet Union. Historians have disagreed, often sharply, over the question of who was responsible for the breakdown of American-Soviet relations, and on whether the conflict between the two superpowers was inevitable or could have been avoided.

For more than a decade after the end of World War II, few historians in the United States saw any reason to challenge the official American interpretation of the beginnings of the Cold War. Thomas A. Bailey spoke for most students of the conflict when he argued, in *America Faces Russia* (1950), that the breakdown of relations was a direct result of aggressive Soviet policies of expansion in the immediate postwar years. Stalin's government violated its solemn promises in the Yalta Accords, imposed Soviet-dominated governments on the unwilling nations of Eastern Europe, and schemed to spread communism throughout the world. American policy was the logical and necessary response: a firm commitment to oppose Soviet expansionism and to keep its own armed forces in a continual state of preparedness.

The American involvement in Vietnam disillusioned many historians with the premises of the containment policy and, thus, with the traditional view of the origins of the Cold War. But even before the conflict in Asia had reached major proportions, the first works in what would become known as the "revisionist" interpretation began to appear. William Appleman Williams challenged the accepted wisdom as early as 1952; and in 1959 he published *The Tragedy of American Diplomacy*, which placed the Cold War in the context of American foreign policy throughout the twentieth century. The United States had operated in world affairs, Williams argued, in response to one overriding concern: its commitment to maintaining an "open door" for American trade in world markets. The confrontation with the Soviet Union, therefore, was less a response to Russian aggressive designs than an expression of the American belief in the necessity of capitalist expansion.

Later revisionists modified many of Williams's claims, but most accepted some of the basic outlines of his thesis: that the United States had been primarily to blame for the Cold War; that the Soviet Union had displayed no aggressive designs toward the West (and was too weak and exhausted at the end of World War II to be able to pose a serious threat to America in any case); that the United States had used its nuclear monopoly to attempt to threaten and intimidate Stalin; that Harry Truman had recklessly abandoned the conciliatory policies of Franklin Roosevelt and taken a provocative hard line against the Russians; and that the Soviet response had reflected a legitimate fear of capitalist encirclement. Walter LaFeber, in *America, Russia, and the Cold War, 1945–1967* (1967), maintained that America's supposedly idealistic internationalism at the close of the war—its vision of "One World," with every nation in control of its own destiny—was in reality an effort to ensure a world shaped in the American image, with every nation open to American influence (and American trade).

Crucial to many revisionist arguments was the American decision to use atomic weapons against Japan in the closing days of World War II. As early as 1948, a British physicist, P. M. S. Blackett, wrote in *Fear, War, and the Bomb* that the destruction of Hiroshima and Nagasaki was "not so much the last military act of the second World War as the first major operation of the cold diplomatic war with Russia." Gar Alperovitz expanded that idea in *Atomic Diplomacy* (1965), in

WHERE HISTORIANS DISAGREE

which he claimed that American decision makers used the bombs on an already defeated Japan not to win the war (for the war was already won) but to impress and intimidate the Soviets, to make them more "manageable." In fact, Alperovitz argued, this atomic diplomacy had the opposite effect: it convinced the Soviet Union of America's hostile intentions and helped speed the beginning of the Cold War.

Ultimately, the revisionist interpretation began to produce a reaction of its own, what some have called the "counter-" or "post-revisionist" view of the conflict. Some manifestations of this reaction have consisted of little more than a reaffirmation of the traditional view of the Cold War. Herbert Feis, for example, argued in *The Atomic Bomb and the End of World War II* (1966) that the revisionist claim that the use of nuclear weapons on Japan was a tactic to intimidate the Soviets was unfounded, that Truman had made his decision on purely military grounds—to ensure a speedy American victory and eliminate the need for what was expected to be a long and costly invasion of Japan. Others challenged the revisionists by accepting some of their findings but rejecting their most important claims. Arthur M. Schlesinger, Jr., admitted in a 1967 article that the Soviets may not have been committed to world conquest, as most earlier accounts had claimed. Nevertheless, the Soviets (and Stalin in particular) were motivated by a deep-seated paranoia about the West, which made them insistent on dominating Eastern Europe and rendered any amicable relationship between them and the United States impossible.

But the dominant works of post-revisionist scholarship have attempted to strike a balance between the two camps, to identify areas of blame and misperception on both sides of the conflict. Thomas G. Paterson, in *Soviet-American Confrontation* (1973), viewed Russian hostility and American efforts to dominate the postwar world as equally responsible for the Cold War.

John Lewis Gaddis, in *The United States and the Origins of the Cold War, 1941–1947* (1972), similarly maintained that "neither side can bear sole responsibility for the onset of the Cold War." American policymakers, he argued, had only limited options because of the pressures of domestic politics. And Stalin was immobilized by his obsessive concern with maintaining his own power and ensuring absolute security for the Soviet Union. But if neither side was entirely to blame, Gaddis concluded, the Soviets must be held at least slightly more accountable for the problems, for Stalin was in a much better position to compromise, given his broader power within his own government than the politically hamstrung Truman. Melvyn Leffler's *Preponderance of Power* (1991) argued similarly that American policymakers genuinely believed in the existence of a Soviet threat and were determined to remain consistently stronger than the Soviets in response.

Out of the post-revisionist literature has begun to emerge a new and more complex view of the Cold War, which de-emphasizes the question of who was to blame and adopts a more detached view of the conflict. The Cold War, recent historians suggest, was not so much the fault of one side or the other as it was the natural, perhaps inevitable, result of tensions between the world's two most powerful nations—nations that had been suspicious of, if not hostile toward, one another for nearly a century. As Ernest May wrote in a 1984 essay:

> After the Second World War, the United States and the Soviet Union were doomed to be antagonists. . . . There probably was never any real possibility that the post-1945 relationship could be anything but hostility verging on conflict. . . . Traditions, belief systems, propinquity, and convenience . . . all combined to stimulate antagonism, and almost no factor operated in either country to hold it back.

the end of World War I to work, the Soviets believed, to overthrow their new government. The West had excluded the Soviet Union from the international community throughout the two decades following World War I; Russia had not been invited to participate in either the Versailles Conference in 1919 or the Munich Conference in 1938. The United States had refused to recognize the Soviet government until 1933, sixteen years after the revolution. And just as most Americans viewed communism with foreboding and contempt, so most Russian communists harbored deep suspicions of and a genuine distaste for industrial capitalism. There was, in short, a powerful legacy of mistrust on both sides.

In some respects, the wartime experience helped to abate that mistrust. Both the United States and the Soviet Union tended during the war to focus less on the traditional image of a dangerous potential foe and more on the image of a brave and dauntless ally. Americans expressed open admiration for the courage of Soviet forces in withstanding the Nazi onslaught and began to depict Stalin less as the bloody ogre of the purges than as the wise and persevering "Uncle Joe." The Soviet government, similarly, praised both the American fighting forces and the wisdom and courage of Franklin Roosevelt.

In other respects, however, the war deepened the gulf between the two nations. The Soviet invasion of Finland and the Baltic states late in 1939, once the Allied war with Germany had begun in the west, angered many Americans. So did Soviet wartime brutality— not only toward the fascist enemies but toward supposedly friendly forces such as the Polish resistance fighters. Stalin harbored even greater resentments toward the American approach to the war. Despite repeated assurances from Roosevelt that the United States and Britain would soon open a second front on the European continent, thus drawing German strength away from the assault on Russia, the Allied invasion did not finally occur until June 1944, more than two years after Stalin had first demanded it. In the meantime, the Russians had suffered appalling casualties—some estimates put them as high as 20 million—and it was easy for Stalin to believe that the West had deliberately delayed the invasion to force the Soviets to absorb the brunt of the German strength.

At the heart of the tensions between the Americans and the Soviets in the 1940s, however, was a fundamental difference in the ways the great powers envisioned the postwar world. Many people in the United States embraced a vision first openly outlined in the Atlantic Charter in 1941, and later popularized through a 1943 book by Wendell Willkie, the 1940 Republican presidential candidate, entitled *One World*. In this vision of the world, nations would abandon their traditional belief in military alliances and spheres of influence and govern their relations with one another through democratic processes, with an international organization serving as the arbiter of disputes and the protector of every nation's right of self-determination.

The Soviet Union and to some extent, it gradually became clear, Great Britain held a different vision. Both Stalin and Churchill had signed the Atlantic Charter. But Britain had always been uneasy about the implications of the self-determination ideal for its own enormous empire. And the Soviet Union was determined to create a secure sphere for itself in Eastern Europe as protection against possible future aggression from the West. Both Churchill and Stalin, therefore, tended to envision a postwar structure in which the great powers would control areas of strategic interest to them, in which something vaguely similar to the traditional European balance of power would reemerge.

This difference of opinion was particularly important because the "One World" vision Roosevelt promoted had, by the end of the war, become a fervent commitment among many Americans. Thus when the Soviet Union began to balk at some of the goals the United States was advocating, the debate seemed to become more than a simple difference of opinion; it became an ideological struggle for the future of the world. By the end of the war Roosevelt was able to win at least the partial consent of Winston Churchill to his principles; but although he believed at times that Stalin would similarly relent, he never managed to steer the Soviets from their determination to control Eastern Europe and from their vision of a postwar order in which each of the great powers would dominate its own sphere. Gradually, the differences between these two positions would turn the peacemaking process into a form of warfare.

Wartime Diplomacy

Serious strains began to develop in the alliance with the Soviet Union as early as 1942, a result of Stalin's irritation at delays in opening the second front and his resentment of the Anglo-American decision to invade North Africa before Europe. In this deteriorating atmosphere, Roosevelt and Churchill met in Casablanca, Morocco, in January 1943 to discuss Allied strategy. (Stalin had declined Roosevelt's invitation to attend.) The two leaders could not accept Stalin's most important demand—the immediate opening of a second front. But they tried to reassure him by announcing they would accept nothing less than the unconditional surrender of the Axis powers. It was a signal that the Americans and British would not negotiate a separate peace with Hitler and leave the Soviets to fight on alone.

In November 1943, Roosevelt and Churchill traveled to Teheran, Iran, for their first meeting with Stalin. By now, however, Roosevelt's most effective bargaining tool—Stalin's need for American assistance in his struggle against Germany—was almost gone. The German advance against Russia had failed; Soviet forces were now launching their own westward offensive. Meanwhile, new tensions had emerged in the alliance as a result of the refusal by the British and Americans to allow any Soviet participation in the creation of a new Italian government following the fall of Mussolini. To Stalin, at least, the "One World" doctrine already seemed to be a double standard: America and Britain expected to have a voice in the future of Eastern Europe, but the Soviet Union was to have no voice in the future of the West.

Nevertheless, the Teheran Conference seemed in most respects a success. Roosevelt and Stalin established a cordial personal relationship. Stalin agreed to an American request that the Soviet Union enter the war in the Pacific soon after the end of hostilities in Europe. Roosevelt, in turn, promised that an Anglo-American second front would be established within six months. All three leaders agreed in principle to a postwar international organization and to efforts to prevent a resurgence of German expansionism.

On other matters, however, the origins of future disagreements were already visible. Most important was the question of the future of Poland. Roosevelt and Churchill were willing to agree to a movement of the Soviet border westward, allowing Stalin to annex some historically Polish territory. But on the nature of the postwar government in the portion of Poland that would remain independent, there were sharp differences. Roosevelt and Churchill supported the claims of the Polish government-in-exile that had been functioning in London since 1940; Stalin wished to install another, pro-communist exiled government that had spent the war in Lublin, in the Soviet Union. The three leaders avoided a bitter conclusion to the Teheran Conference only by leaving the issue unresolved.

Yalta

For more than a year after Teheran, the Grand Alliance among the United States, Britain, and the Soviet Union

YALTA

Churchill, Roosevelt, and Stalin (known during the war as the "Big Three") meet at Yalta in the Crimea in February 1945 to try to agree on the outlines of the peace that they knew was soon to come. Instead, they settled on a series of vague compromises that ultimately left all parties feeling betrayed. *(Bettmann)*

alternated between high tension and warm amicability. In the fall of 1944, Churchill flew by himself to Moscow for a meeting with Stalin to resolve issues arising from a civil war in Greece. In return for a Soviet agreement to cease assisting Greek communists, who were challenging the British-supported monarchical government, Churchill consented to a proposal whereby control of Eastern Europe would be divided between Britain and the Soviet Union. "This memorable meeting," Churchill wrote Stalin after its close, "has shown that there are no matters that cannot be adjusted between us when we meet together in frank and intimate discussion." To Roosevelt, however, the Moscow agreement was evidence of how little the Atlantic Charter principles seemed to mean to his two most important allies.

In February 1945, Roosevelt joined Churchill and Stalin for a great peace conference in the Soviet city of Yalta. The meeting began in an atmosphere of some gloom. The American president, his health visibly failing, sensed resistance to his internationalist dreams. The British prime minister was already dismayed by Stalin's unwillingness to make concessions and compromises, warning even before the conference met that "I think the end of this war may well prove to be more disappointing than was the last." Stalin, whose armies were now only miles from Berlin, and aware of how much the United States still wanted his assistance in the Pacific, was confident and determined.

On a number of issues, the Big Three reached mutually satisfactory agreements. In return for Stalin's promise to enter the war against Japan, Roosevelt agreed that the Soviet Union should receive the Kurile Islands north of Japan; that it should regain southern Sakhalin Island and Port Arthur, both of which Russia had lost in the 1904 Russo-Japanese War; and that it could exercise some influence (along with the government of China) in Manchuria. The negotiators also agreed to accept a plan for a new international organization, a plan that had been hammered out the previous summer at a conference in Washington, D.C., at the Dumbarton Oaks estate. The new United Nations would contain a General Assembly, in which every member would be represented. But the most important decision-making body would be a Security Council, with permanent representatives of the five major powers (the United States, Britain, France, the Soviet Union, and China), each of which would have veto power. There would also be temporary delegates from several other nations on the Security Council. These agreements became the basis of the United Nations charter, drafted at a conference of fifty nations beginning April 25, 1945, in San Francisco. The United States Senate ratified the charter in July by a vote of 80 to 2 (a striking contrast to the slow and painful defeat it had administered to the charter of the League of Nations twenty-five years before).

On other issues, however, the Yalta Conference either left fundamental differences unresolved or papered them over with weak and unstable compromises. Fundamental disagreement remained about the postwar Polish government. Stalin, whose armies now occupied Poland, had already installed a government composed of the pro-communist "Lublin" Poles. Roosevelt and Churchill insisted that the pro-Western "London" Poles must be allowed a place in the Warsaw regime. Roosevelt wanted a government based on free, democratic elections—which both he and Stalin recognized the pro-Western forces would win. Stalin agreed to a vague compromise by which he would grant an unspecified number of places in the government to pro-Western Poles, and he reluctantly consented to hold "free and unfettered elections" in Poland. But he made no commitment to a date for them. They did not take place for more than forty years.

Nor was there agreement about the future of Germany. Stalin wanted to impose $20 billion in reparations on the Germans, of which Russia would receive half. Roosevelt and Churchill agreed only to leave final settlement of the issue to a future reparations commission. A more important difference was in the way the leaders envisioned postwar German politics and society. In 1944, Roosevelt and Churchill had met in Quebec and agreed on a plan crafted by the American secretary of the treasury, Henry Morgenthau, for the "pastoralization" of Germany—dismantling its industry and turning it into a largely agricultural society. By the time of the Yalta meeting, however, Roosevelt had changed his mind. He seemed now to want a reconstructed and reunited Germany—one that would be permitted to develop a prosperous, modern economy while remaining under the careful supervision of the Allies. Stalin wanted a permanent dismemberment of Germany.

The final agreement was, like the Polish accord, vague and unstable. The United States, Great Britain, France, and the Soviet Union would each control its own "zone of occupation" in Germany—the zones to be determined by the position of troops at end of the war. Berlin, the German capital, was already well inside the Soviet zone, but because of its symbolic importance it would be divided into four sectors, one for each nation to occupy. At an unspecified date, the nation would be reunited, but there was no agreement on how the reunification would occur. As for the rest of Europe, the conference produced a murky accord on the establishment of interim governments "broadly representative of all democratic elements." They would be replaced ultimately by permanent governments "responsible to the will of the people" and created through free elections. Once again, no specific provisions or timetables accompanied the agreements.

The Yalta accords, in other words, were less a settlement of postwar issues than a set of loose principles that sidestepped the most divisive issues. Roosevelt, Churchill, and Stalin each returned home from the conference apparently convinced that he had signed an important agreement. But the Soviet interpretation of the accords differed so sharply from the Anglo-American interpretation that the illusion endured only briefly. In the weeks following the Yalta Conference, Roosevelt watched with growing alarm as the Soviet Union moved systematically to establish pro-communist governments in one Eastern European nation after another and as Stalin refused to make the changes in Poland that the president believed he had promised.

But Roosevelt did not abandon hope. Still believing the differences could be settled, he left Washington early in the spring for a vacation at his retreat in Warm Springs, Georgia. There, on April 12, 1945, he suffered a sudden, massive stroke and died.

THE SOURING OF THE PEACE

Harry S. Truman, who became president on Roosevelt's death, had almost no familiarity with international issues. Nor did he share Roosevelt's faith in the flexibility of the Soviet Union. Roosevelt had believed that Stalin was, essentially, a reasonable man with whom an ultimate accord could be reached—a belief he was beginning to question at the time of his death, but had not yet abandoned. Truman, in contrast, sided with those in the government (and there were many) who considered the Soviet Union fundamentally untrustworthy and viewed Stalin himself with suspicion and loathing.

The Failure of Potsdam

Truman had been in office only a few days before he decided to "get tough" with the Soviet Union. Stalin had made what the new president considered solemn agreements with the United States at Yalta. The United States would insist that he honor them. Dismissing the advice of Secretary of War Stimson that the Polish question was a lost cause and not worth a world crisis, Truman met on April 23 with Soviet Foreign Minister Molotov and sharply chastised him for violations of the Yalta accords. "I have never been talked to like

that in my life," a shocked Molotov reportedly replied. "Carry out your agreements and you won't get talked to like that," said the president.

In fact, Truman had only limited leverage with which to compel the Soviet Union to carry out its agreements. Russian forces already occupied Poland and much of the rest of Eastern Europe. Germany was already divided among the conquering nations. The United States was still engaged in a war in the Pacific and was neither able nor willing to engage in a new conflict in Europe. Truman insisted that the United States should be able to get "85 percent" of what it wanted, but he was ultimately forced to settle for much less.

He conceded first on Poland. When Stalin made a few minor concessions to the pro-Western exiles, Truman recognized the Warsaw government, hoping that noncommunist forces might gradually expand their influence there. Until the 1980s, they did not. Other questions remained, above all the question of Germany. To settle them, Truman met in July at Potsdam, in Russian-occupied Germany, with Churchill (who was replaced as prime minister by Clement Atlee in the midst of the negotiations) and Stalin. Truman reluctantly accepted adjustments of the Polish-German border that Stalin had long demanded; but he refused to permit the Russians to claim any reparations from the American, French, and British zones of Germany. The result, in effect, was to confirm that Germany would remain divided, with the western zones eventually united into one nation, friendly to the United States, and the Russian zone surviving as another nation, with a pro-Soviet, communist government. Soon, the Soviet Union would be siphoning between $1.5 and $3 billion a year out of its zone of occupation.

The China Problem

Central to American hopes for an open, peaceful world policed by the great powers was a strong, independent China. But even before the war ended, the American government knew that those hopes faced a major, perhaps insurmountable obstacle: the Chinese government of Chiang Kai-shek. Chiang was generally friendly to the United States, but he had few other virtues. His government was corrupt and incompetent. His popular legitimacy was feeble. And Chiang himself lived in a world of almost surreal isolation, unable or unwilling to face the problems that were threatening to engulf him. Ever since 1927, the nationalist government he headed had been engaged in a prolonged and bitter struggle with the communist armies of Mao Zedong. So successful had the communist challenge grown that by 1945 Mao was in control of one-fourth of the population.

At Potsdam, Truman had managed to persuade Stalin to recognize Chiang as the legitimate ruler of China; but Chiang was rapidly losing his grip on his country. Some Americans urged the government to try to find a "third force" to support as an alternative to either Chiang or Mao. A few argued that America should try to reach some accommodation with Mao himself. Truman, however, decided reluctantly that he had no choice but to continue supporting Chiang. That was in part because of the strength in the United States of forces committed to Chiang, including the formidable publisher of *Time* and *Life* magazines, Henry Luce, the son of Chinese missionaries and an inveterate defender of Chiang. The pro-Chiang forces, known as the "China Lobby," would help shape American policy toward Asia for thirty years.

In the last months of the war, American forces diverted attention from the Japanese long enough to assist Chiang against the communists in Manchuria. For the next several years, as the long struggle between the nationalists and the communists erupted into a full-scale civil war, the United States continued to send money and weapons to Chiang, even as it was becoming clear his cause was lost. But Truman was not prepared to intervene militarily to save the nationalist regime.

Instead, the American government was beginning to consider an alternative to China as the strong, pro-Western force in Asia: a revived Japan. Abandoning the restrictive occupation policies of the first years after the war (when General Douglas MacArthur had governed the nation), the United States lifted all limitations on industrial development and encouraged rapid economic growth in Japan. The vision of an open, united Asia had given way, as in Europe, with an acceptance of the necessity of developing a strong, pro-American sphere of influence.

The Containment Doctrine

By the end of 1945, the Grand Alliance of World War II was in a shambles, and with it any realistic hope of a postwar world constructed according to the Atlantic Charter ideals Roosevelt and others had supported. Instead, a new American policy was slowly emerging. Rather than attempting to create a unified, "open" world, the West would work to "contain" the threat of further Soviet expansion. The United States would be the leading force in that effort.

The new doctrine emerged in part as a response to events in Europe in 1946. In Turkey, Stalin was trying

George F. Kennan
Kennan was one of the architects of the policy of containment, which became the basis of foreign policy for over forty years. But almost from the start, he was critical of the United States government's sweeping view of containment. Americans needed, he argued, to define their vital interests more narrowly, to focus their defensive efforts on nations of direct strategic importance to them. That meant, in his view, mainly the industrialized nations of Europe and Japan. In later years, he was outspoken in his attacks on the war in Vietnam. *(Library of Congress)*

to win some control over the vital straits to the Mediterranean. In Greece, communist forces were again threatening the pro-Western government; the British had announced they could no longer provide assistance. Faced with these challenges, Truman decided to enunciate a firm new policy. In doing so, he drew from the ideas of the influential American diplomat George F. Kennan, who warned in a famous telegram from Moscow (and later in an article published under the pseudonym "X") that in the Soviet Union the United States faced "a political force committed fanatically to the belief that with the U.S. there can be no permanent modus vivendi," and that the only answer was "a long-term, patient but firm and vigilant containment of Russian expansive tendencies." On March 12, 1947, Truman appeared before Congress and used Kennan's warnings as the basis of what became known as the Truman Doctrine. "I believe," he argued, "that it must be the policy of the United States to support free peoples who are resisting attempted subjugation by armed minorities or by outside pressures." In the same speech he requested $400 million—part of it to bolster the armed forces of Greece and Turkey, another part to provide economic assistance to Greece. Congress quickly approved the measure.

The American commitment ultimately helped ease Soviet pressure on Turkey and helped the Greek government defeat the communist insurgents. More important, it established a basis for American foreign policy that would survive for over forty years. On the one hand, the Truman Doctrine was a way of accommodating the status quo: it accepted that there was no immediate likelihood of overturning the communist governments Stalin had established in Eastern Europe. On the other hand, it was a strategy for the future: communism was an innately expansionist force, and it must be contained within its present boundaries. Its expansion anywhere could be a threat to democracy everywhere because, as Secretary of State Dean Acheson had argued, the fall of one nation to communism would have a "domino effect" on surrounding nations. It was, therefore, the policy of the United States to assist pro-Western forces in struggles against communism whether those struggles directly involved the Soviet Union or not.

The Marshall Plan

An integral part of the containment policy was a proposal to aid in the economic reconstruction of Western Europe. There were many motives: humanitarian concern for the European people; a fear that Europe would remain an economic drain on the United States if it could not quickly rebuild and begin to feed itself; a desire for a strong European market for American goods. Above all, American policymakers believed that unless something could be done to strengthen the shaky pro-American governments in Western Europe, they might fall under the control of rapidly growing domestic communist parties.

In a June 1947 speech at Harvard, therefore, Secretary of State George C. Marshall announced a plan to provide economic assistance to all European nations (including the Soviet Union) that would join in drafting a program for recovery. Although Russia and its Eastern satellites quickly and predictably rejected the plan, sixteen Western European nations eagerly participated. Whatever domestic opposition there was largely vanished after a coup in Czechoslovakia in February 1948 suddenly established a Soviet-dominated communist government there. In April, Congress approved the creation of the Economic Cooperation Administration, the agency that would administer the Marshall Plan, as it became known. Over the next three years, the Marshall Plan channeled over $12 billion of American aid into Europe, helping to spark a substantial economic revival. By the end of 1950, European industrial production had risen 64 percent, communist strength in the member nations had declined, and opportunities for American trade had revived.

Mobilization at Home

That the United States had fully accepted a continuing commitment to the containment policy became clear in 1947 and 1948 through a series of measures designed to maintain American military power at near-wartime levels. In 1948, at the president's request, Congress approved a new military draft and revived the Selective Service System. In the meantime, the United States, having failed to reach agreement with the Soviet Union on international control of nuclear weapons, redoubled its own efforts in atomic research, elevating nuclear weaponry to a central place in its military arsenal. The Atomic Energy Commission, established in 1946, became the supervisory body charged with overseeing all nuclear research, civilian and military alike.

Particularly important was the National Security Act of 1947, which created several new instruments of foreign policy. A new Department of Defense would oversee all branches of the armed services, combining functions previously performed by the War and Navy Departments. A National Security Council (NSC), operating out of the White House, would advise the president on foreign and military policy. A Central Intelligence Agency (CIA) would be responsible for collecting information through both open and covert methods and, as the Cold War continued, for engaging secretly in political and military operations on behalf of American goals. In other words, the National Security Act gave the government (and particularly the president) expanded powers with which to pursue the nation's international goals. It centralized in the White House control that had once been widely dispersed, enabled the president to take warlike actions without an open declaration of war, and created vehicles by which the government could at times act politically and militarily overseas behind a veil of secrecy.

The Road to NATO

At about the same time, the United States was moving to strengthen the military capabilities of Western Europe. Convinced that a reconstructed Germany was essential to the hopes of the West, Truman reached an

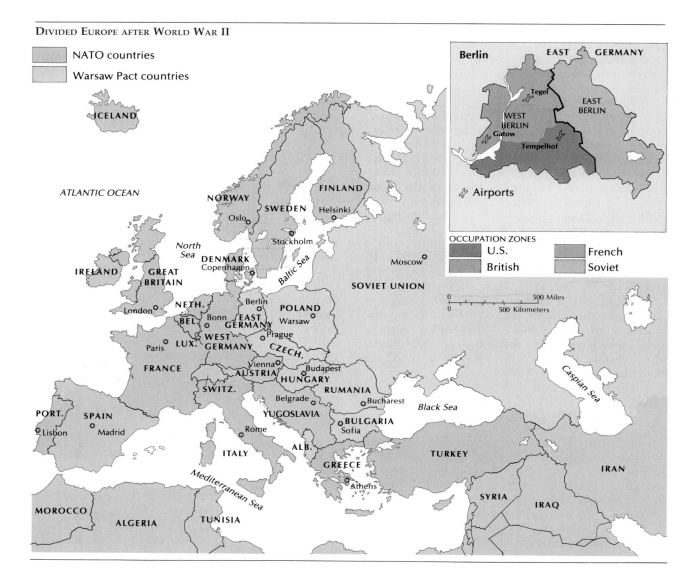

DIVIDED EUROPE AFTER WORLD WAR II

agreement with England and France to merge the three western zones of occupation into a new West German republic (which would include the American, British, and French sectors of Berlin, even though that city lay well within the Soviet zone.) Stalin interpreted the move (correctly) as a direct challenge to his hopes for a subdued Germany and a docile Europe. He was especially alarmed because, at almost the same moment, he was facing a challenge from inside what he considered his own sphere. The government of Yugoslavia, under the leadership of Marshall Josip Broz Tito, broke openly with the Soviet Union and declared the nation an unaligned communist state. The United States offered Tito assistance.

Stalin responded quickly. On June 24, 1948, he imposed a tight blockade around the western sectors of Berlin. If Germany was to be officially divided, he was implying, then the country's Western government would have to abandon its outpost in the heart of the Soviet-controlled eastern zone. Truman refused to comply. Unwilling to risk war through a military response to the blockade, he ordered a massive airlift to supply the city with food, fuel, and supplies. The airlift continued for more than ten months, transporting nearly 2.5 million tons of material, keeping alive a city of 2 million people, and transforming West Berlin into a symbol of the West's resolve to resist communist expansion. In the spring of 1949, Stalin lifted the now in-

effective blockade. And in October, the division of
Germany into two nations—the Federal Republic in
the west and the Democratic Republic in the east—
became official.

The crisis in Berlin accelerated the consolidation of
what was already in effect an alliance among the
United States and the countries of Western Europe. On
April 4, 1949, twelve nations signed an agreement establishing the North Atlantic Treaty Organization
(NATO) and declaring that an armed attack against
one member would be considered an attack against all.
The NATO countries, moreover, agreed to maintain a
standing military force in Europe to defend against
what many believed was the threat of a Soviet invasion. The American Senate quickly ratified the treaty,
which fused European nations that had been fighting
one another for centuries into a strong and enduring
alliance. It also spurred the Soviet Union to create an
alliance of its own with the communist governments
in Eastern Europe—an alliance formalized in 1955 by
the Warsaw Pact.

The Enduring Crisis

For a time, Americans believed that these initial
achievements had turned the tide of the battle against
communism. But a series of events in 1949 eroded that
confidence and launched the Cold War in new directions. An announcement in September that the Soviet
Union had successfully exploded its first atomic

weapon, years earlier than predicted, shocked and
frightened many Americans. So did the collapse of
Chiang Kai-shek's nationalist government in China,
which occurred with startling speed in the last months
of 1949. Chiang fled with his political allies and the
remnants of his army to the offshore island of Formosa
(Taiwan), and the entire Chinese mainland came under the control of a communist government that many
Americans believed to be an extension of the Soviet
Union. Few policymakers shared the belief of the
China Lobby that the United States should now commit itself to the rearming of Chiang Kai-shek. But neither would the United States recognize the new communist regime. The Chinese mainland would remain
almost entirely closed to the West for a generation. The
United States, in the meantime, would devote increased attention to the revitalization of Japan as a
buffer against Asian communism, ending the American occupation in 1952.

In response to these and other setbacks, Truman
called for a thorough review of American foreign policy. The result was a National Security Council report,
commonly known as NSC-68, which outlined a shift
in the American position. The April 1950 document argued that the United States could no longer rely on
other nations to take the initiative in resisting communism. It must itself establish firm and active leadership of the noncommunist world. And it must move
to stop communist expansion anywhere it occurred,
regardless of the intrinsic strategic or economic value

COMMUNIST CHINA
A division of the Red Army marches triumphantly through central China shortly after their 1949 victory in the Chinese civil war. The United States refused to recognize the new government for more than twenty-five years. *(Bettmann)*

of the lands in question. Among other things, the report called for a major expansion of American military power, with a defense budget almost four times the previously projected figure.

AMERICA AFTER THE WAR

The crises overseas were not the only frustrations the American people encountered after the war. The nation also faced serious economic difficulties in adapting to the peace. The resulting instability contributed to an increasingly heated political climate.

The Problems of Reconversion

The bombs that destroyed Hiroshima and Nagasaki ended the war months earlier than almost anyone had predicted and propelled the nation precipitously into a process of reconversion. The lack of planning was soon compounded by a growing popular impatience for a return to normal economic conditions. Under intense public pressure, the Truman administration attempted to hasten that return, despite dire warnings by some planners and economists. The result was a period of economic problems.

They were not, however, the problems that most Americans had feared. There had been many predictions that peace would bring a return of Depression unemployment, as war production ceased and returning soldiers flooded the labor market. But there was no general economic collapse in 1946—for several reasons. Government spending dropped sharply and abruptly, to be sure; $35 billion of war contracts were canceled at a stroke within weeks of the Japanese surrender. But increased consumer demand soon compensated. Consumer goods had been generally unavailable during the war, so many workers had saved a substantial portion of their wages and were now ready to spend. A $6 billion tax cut pumped additional money into general circulation. The Servicemen's Readjustment Act of 1944, better known as the GI Bill of Rights, provided economic and educational assistance to veterans, increasing spending even further.

This flood of consumer demand ensured that there would be no new depression, but it contributed to more than two years of serious inflation, during which prices rose at rates of 14 to 15 percent annually. In the summer of 1946, the president vetoed an extension of the authority of the wartime Office of Price Administration, thus eliminating price controls. (He was not opposed to the controls, but to congressional amendments that had weakened the OPA.) Inflation soared to 25 percent before he relented a month later and signed a bill little different from the one he had rejected.

Compounding the economic difficulties was a sharp rise in labor unrest, driven in part by the impact of inflation. By the end of 1945, there had already been major strikes in the automobile, electrical, and steel industries. In April 1946, John L. Lewis led the United Mine Workers out on strike, shutting down the coal fields for forty days. Fears grew rapidly that without vital coal supplies, the entire nation might virtually grind to a halt. Truman finally forced the miners to return to work by ordering government seizure of the mines. But in the process, he pressured mine owners to grant the union most of its demands, which he had earlier denounced as inflationary. Almost simultaneously, the nation's railroads suffered a total shutdown—the first in the nation's history—as two major unions walked out on strike. By threatening to use the army to run the trains, Truman pressured the workers back to work after only a few days.

Reconversion was particularly difficult for the millions of women and minorities who had entered the work force during the war. With veterans returning home and looking for jobs in the industrial economy, employers tended to push women, blacks, Hispanics, Chinese, and others out of the plants to make room for white males. Some of the war workers, particularly

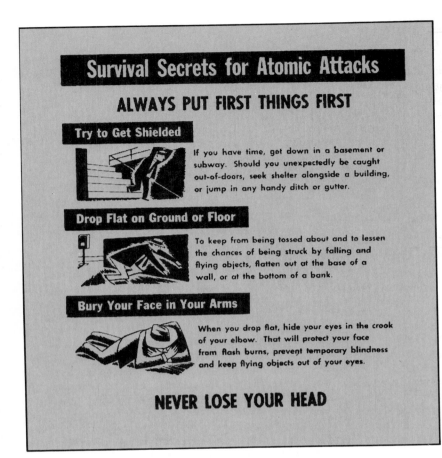

women, left the work force voluntarily, out of a desire to return to their former domestic lives. But as many as 80 percent of women workers, and virtually all black, Hispanic, and Asian males, wanted to continue working. The postwar inflation, the pressure to meet the rising expectations of a high-consumption society, the rising divorce rate, which left many women responsible for their own economic well-being—all combined to create among women a high demand for paid employment. As they found themselves excluded from industrial jobs, therefore, women workers moved increasingly into other areas of the economy (above all, the service sector).

The Fair Deal Rejected

Days after the Japanese surrender, Truman submitted to Congress a twenty-one-point domestic program outlining what he later termed the "Fair Deal." It called for expansion of Social Security benefits; the raising of the legal minimum wage from 40 to 65 cents an hour; a program to ensure full employment through aggressive use of federal spending and investment; a permanent Fair Employment Practices Act; public housing and slum clearance; long-range environmental and public works planning; and government promotion of scientific research. Weeks later he added other proposals: federal aid to funding for the St. Lawrence Seaway, nationalization of atomic energy, and perhaps most important, national health insurance—a dream of welfare-state liberals for decades, but one deferred in 1935 when the Social Security Act was written. The president was declaring an end to the wartime moratorium on liberal reform. He was also symbolizing, as he later wrote, "my assumption of the office of President in my own right."

But the Fair Deal programs fell victim to the same public and congressional conservatism that had crippled the last years of the New Deal. Indeed, that conservatism seemed to be intensifying, as the November 1946 congressional elections suggested. Using the simple but devastating slogan "Had Enough?", the Republican Party won control of both houses of Congress.

The new Republican Congress quickly moved to reduce government spending and chip away at New Deal reforms. The president bowed to what he claimed was the popular mandate to lift most remaining wage and price controls, and Congress moved further to deregulate the economy. Inflation rapidly increased. When a public outcry arose over the soaring prices for meat, Senator Robert Taft, perhaps the most influential Republican conservative in Congress, advised consumers to "Eat less," and added, "We have got to break with the corrupting idea that we can legislate prosperity, legislate equality, legislate opportunity." True to the spirit of Taft's words, the Republican Congress quickly applied what one congressman described as a "meat-axe to government frills." It refused to appropriate funds to aid education, increase Social Security, or support reclamation and power projects in the West. It defeated a proposal to raise the minimum wage. It passed tax measures that cut rates dramatically for high-income families and moderately for those with lower incomes. Only vetoes by the president finally forced a more progressive bill.

The most notable action of the new Congress was its assault on the Wagner Act of 1935. Conservatives had always resented the new powers the legislation had granted unions; and in the light of the labor difficulties during and after the war, such resentments intensified sharply. The result was the Labor-Management Relations Act of 1947, better known as the Taft–Hartley Act. It made illegal the so-called closed shop (a workplace in which no one can be hired without first being a member of a union). And although it continued to permit the creation of so-called union shops (in which workers must join a union after being hired), it permitted states to pass "right-to-work" laws prohibiting even that. Repealing this provision, the controversial Section 14(b), would remain a goal of the labor movement for decades. The Taft–Hartley Act also empowered the president to call for a "cooling-off" period before a strike by issuing an injunction against any work stoppage that endangered national safety or health. Outraged workers and union leaders denounced the measure as a "slave labor bill." Truman vetoed it, but both houses easily overruled him the same day.

The Taft-Hartley Act did not destroy the labor movement, as many union leaders had predicted. But it did damage weaker unions in relatively lightly organized industries such as chemicals and textiles; and it made more difficult the organizing of workers who had never been union members at all, especially women, minorities, and most workers in the South.

The Election of 1948

Truman and his advisers believed the American public was not ready to abandon the achievements of the New Deal, despite the 1946 election results. As they planned strategy for the 1948 campaign, therefore, they placed their hopes in an appeal to enduring Democratic loyalties. Throughout 1948, Truman proposed one reform measure after another (including, on February 2, the first major civil rights bill of the century). Although Congress ignored or defeated them all, the president was building campaign issues for the fall.

There remained, however, the problem of Truman's personal unpopularity—the assumption among much of the electorate that he lacked stature, that his administration was weak and inept—and the deep divisions within the Democratic Party. At the Democratic Convention that summer, two factions abandoned the party altogether. Southern conservatives reacted angrily to Truman's proposed civil rights bill and to the approval at the convention of a civil rights plank in the platform (engineered by Hubert Humphrey, the mayor of Minneapolis). They walked out and formed the States' Rights (or "Dixiecrat") Party, with Governor Strom Thurmond of South Carolina as its presidential nominee. At the same time, the party's left wing formed a new Progressive Party, with Henry A. Wallace as its candidate. Wallace supporters objected to what they considered the slow and ineffective domestic policies of the Truman administration, but they resented even more the president's confrontational stance toward the Soviet Union.

In addition, many Democratic liberals unwilling to leave the party attempted to dump the president in 1948. The Americans for Democratic Action (ADA), a coalition of liberals, tried to entice Dwight D. Eisenhower, the popular war hero, to contest the nomination. Only after Eisenhower had refused did liberals bow to the inevitable and concede the nomination to Truman. The Republicans, in the meantime, had once again nominated Governor Thomas E. Dewey of New York, whose substantial reelection victory in 1946 had made him one of the nation's leading political figures. Austere, dignified, and competent, he seemed to offer an unbeatable alternative to the president. Polls showed Dewey with an apparently insurmountable lead in September, so much so that some opinion analysts stopped taking surveys. Dewey conducted a subdued, statesmanlike campaign and tried to avoid antagonizing anyone.

Only Truman, it seemed, believed he could win. As the campaign gathered momentum, he became ever more aggressive, turning the fire away from himself and toward Dewey and the "do-nothing, good-for-nothing" Republican Congress, which was, he told the

voters, responsible for fueling inflation and abandoning workers and common people. To dramatize his
point, he called Congress into special session in July
to give it a chance, he said, to enact the liberal measures the Republicans had recently written into their
platform. Congress met for two weeks and, predictably, did almost nothing.

The president traveled nearly 32,000 miles and
made 356 speeches, delivering blunt, extemporaneous
attacks. He had told Senator Alben Barkley of Kentucky, his running mate, "I'm going to fight hard. I'm
going to give them hell." He called for repeal of the
Taft-Hartley act, increased price supports for farmers,
and strong civil rights protection for blacks. (He was
the first president to campaign in Harlem.) He sought,
in short, to re-create much of Franklin Roosevelt's New
Deal coalition. To the surprise of virtually everyone,
he succeeded. On election night, he won a narrow but
decisive victory: 49.5 percent of the popular vote to
Dewey's 45.1 percent (with the two splinter parties dividing the small remainder between them), and an
electoral vote margin of 303 to 189. Democrats, in the
meantime, had regained both houses of Congress by
substantial margins. It was the most dramatic upset in
the history of presidential elections.

The Fair Deal Revived

Despite the Democratic victories, the Eighty-first Congress was no more hospitable to Truman's Fair Deal
reform than its Republican predecessor. Truman did

win some important victories, to be sure. Congress
raised the legal minimum wage from 40 cents to 75
cents an hour. It approved an important expansion of
the Social Security system, increasing benefits by 75
percent and extending them to 10 million additional
people. And it passed the National Housing Act of
1949, which provided for the construction of 810,000
units of low-income housing, accompanied by long-
term rent subsidies. (Inadequate funding plagued the
program for years, and it reached its initial goal only
in 1972.)

But on other issues—among them national health
insurance and aid to education—he made no progress.
Nor was he able to persuade Congress to accept the
civil rights legislation he proposed in 1949, which
would have made lynching a federal crime, provided
federal protection of black voting rights, abolished the
poll tax, and established a new Fair Employment Practices Commission to curb discrimination in hiring (to
replace the wartime commission Roosevelt had established in 1940). Southern Democrats filibustered to kill
the bill.

Truman did proceed on his own to battle several
forms of racial discrimination. He ordered an end to
discrimination in the hiring of government employees.
He began to dismantle segregation within the armed
forces. And he allowed the Justice Department to become actively involved in court battles against discriminatory statutes. In the meantime, the Supreme
Court signaled its own growing awareness of the issue by ruling, in *Shelley* v. *Kraemer* (1948), that the

ELECTION OF 1948   (53% of electorate voting)

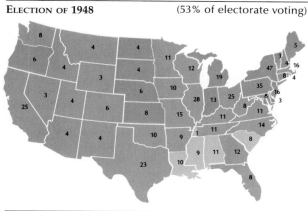

	ELECTORAL VOTE	POPULAR VOTE (%)
Harry S. Truman (Democratic)	303	24,105,695 (49.5)
Thomas E. Dewey (Republican)	189	21,969,170 (45.1)
Strom Thurmond (States' Rights)	39	1,169,021 (2.4)
Henry A. Wallace (Progressive)	—	1,156,103 (2.4)
Other candidates (Socialist, Prohibition, Socialist Labor, Socialist Workers)	—	272,713

courts could not be used to enforce private "covenants" meant to bar blacks from residential neighborhoods. The achievements of the Truman years made only minor dents in the structure of segregation, but they were the tentative beginnings of a federal commitment to confront the problem of race.

THE KOREAN WAR

From the beginning, Truman's domestic policies had had a difficult time competing against the growing national obsession with the Soviet threat in Europe. In 1950, a new and more dangerous element of the Cold War emerged and all but killed hopes for further Fair Deal reform. On June 24, 1950, the armies of communist North Korea swept across their southern border in an invasion of the pro-Western half of the Korean peninsula to the south. Within days, they had occu-

pied much of South Korea, including Seoul, its capital. Almost immediately, the United States committed itself to the conflict. It was the nation's first military engagement of the cold war.

The Divided Peninsula

By the end of 1945, both the United States and the Soviet Union had sent troops into Korea, and neither was willing to leave. Instead, they had divided the nation, supposedly temporarily, along the 38th parallel. The Russians finally departed in 1949, leaving behind a communist government in the north with a strong, Soviet-equipped army. The Americans left a few months later, handing control to the pro-Western government of Syngman Rhee, anticommunist but only nominally democratic. He had a relatively small military, which he used primarily to suppress internal opposition.

The relative weakness of the south offered a strong temptation to nationalists in the North Korean government who wanted to reunite the country. The temptation grew stronger when the American government implied that it did not consider South Korea within its own "defense perimeter." The role of the Soviet Union remains unclear; there is some reason to believe that the North Koreans acted without Stalin's approval. But the Soviets supported the offensive once it began.

The Truman administration responded quickly. On June 27, 1950, the president ordered limited American military assistance to South Korea, and on the same day he appealed to the United Nations to intervene. The Soviet Union was boycotting the Security Council at the time (to protest the council's refusal to recognize the new communist government of China) and thus was unable to exercise its veto power. As a result, American delegates were able to win UN agreement to a resolution calling for international assistance to the Rhee government. On June 30, the United States ordered its own ground forces into Korea, and Truman appointed General Douglas MacArthur to command the UN operations there. (Several other nations provided assistance and troops, but the "UN" armies were, in fact, overwhelmingly American.)

The intervention in Korea was the first expression of the newly expansive American foreign policy outlined in NSC-68. But the administration quickly went beyond NSC–68 and decided that the war would be an effort not simply at containment but also at "liberation." After a surprise American invasion at Inchon in September had routed the North Korean forces from the south and sent them fleeing back across the 38th parallel, Truman gave MacArthur permission to pursue the communists into their own territory. His aim, as an American-sponsored UN resolution proclaimed in October, was to create "a unified, independent and democratic Korea."

From Invasion to Stalemate

For several weeks, MacArthur's invasion of North Korea proceeded smoothly. On October 19, the capital, Pyongyang, fell to the UN forces. Victory seemed near—until the new communist government of China, alarmed by the movement of American forces toward its border, intervened. By November 4, eight divisions

of the Chinese army had entered the war. The UN offensive stalled and then collapsed. Through December 1950, outnumbered American forces fought a bitter, losing battle against the Chinese divisions, retreating at almost every juncture. Within weeks, communist forces had pushed the Americans back below the 38th parallel once again and had captured the South Korean capital of Seoul a second time. By mid-January 1951 the rout had ceased; and by March the UN armies had managed to regain much of the territory they had recently lost, taking back Seoul and pushing the communists north of the 38th parallel once more. But with that, the war degenerated into a protracted stalemate.

THE KOREAN WAR, 1950–1953

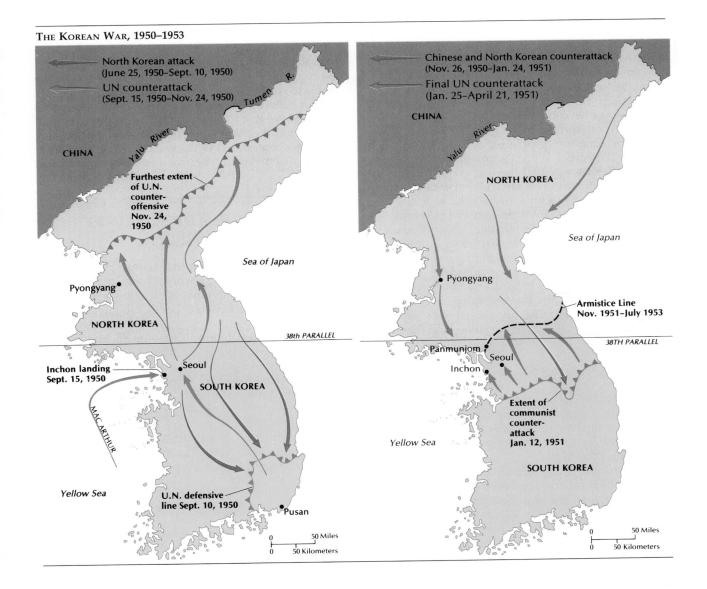

From the start, Truman was determined to avoid a direct conflict with China, which he feared might lead to a new world war. Once China entered the war, he began seeking a negotiated solution to the struggle, and for the next two years he insisted that there be no wider war. But he faced a formidable opponent in General MacArthur, who resisted any limits on his military discretion. The United States was fighting the Chinese, he argued. It should therefore attack China itself, if not through an actual invasion, then at least by bombing communist forces massing north of the Chinese border. In March 1951, he indicated his unhappiness in a public letter to House Republican leader Joseph W. Martin that concluded: "There is no substitute for victory." His position had wide popular support.

The Martin letter came after nine months during which MacArthur had resisted Truman's decisions. More than once, the president had warned the general to keep his objections to himself. The release of the Martin letter, therefore, struck the president as intolerable insubordination. On April 11, 1951, he relieved MacArthur of his command.

There was a storm of public outrage. Sixty-nine percent of the American people supported MacArthur, a Gallup poll reported. When the general returned to the United States later in 1951, he was greeted with wild enthusiasm. His televised farewell appearance before a joint session of Congress—which he concluded by saying "Old soldiers never die, they just fade away"—attracted an audience of millions. Public criticism of Truman finally abated somewhat when a number of prominent military figures, including General Omar Bradley, publicly supported the president's decision. But substantial hostility toward Truman remained.

In the meantime, the Korean stalemate continued. Negotiations between the opposing forces began at Panmunjom in July 1951, but the talks—and the war—dragged on until 1953.

Limited Mobilization

Just as the war in Korea produced only a limited American military commitment abroad, so it created only a limited economic mobilization at home. Still, the government did try to control the wartime economy in several important ways.

First, Truman set up the Office of Defense Mobilization to fight inflation by holding down prices and discouraging high union wage demands. When these cautious regulatory efforts failed, the president took more drastic action. Railroad workers walked off the job in 1951, and Truman ordered the government to seize control of the railroads. That helped keep the trains running, but it had no effect on union demands. Workers ultimately got most of what they had demanded. In 1952, during a nationwide steel strike, Truman seized the steel mills, citing his powers as commander in chief. But in a 6-to-3 decision, the Supreme Court ruled that the president had exceeded his authority, and Truman was forced to relent. A long and costly strike followed, and the president's drastic actions appeared to many to have been both rash and ineffective.

The Korean War gave a significant boost to economic growth by pumping new government funds into the economy at a point when many believed a recession was about to begin. But the war had other, less welcome effects. It came at a time of rising insecurity about America's position in the world and intensified anxiety about communism. As the long stalemate continued, leaving 140,000 Americans dead or wounded, frustration turned to anger. The United States, which had recently won the greatest war in history, seemed unable to conclude what many Americans considered a minor border skirmish in a small country. Many began to believe that something must be deeply wrong—not only in Korea but within the United States as well. Such fears contributed to the rise of the second major campaign of the century against domestic communism.

THE CRUSADE AGAINST SUBVERSION

Why did the American people develop a growing fear of internal communist subversion that by the early 1950s had reached the point of near hysteria? There are many possible answers, but no single definitive explanation.

One factor was obvious. Communism was not an imagined enemy in the 1950s. It had tangible shape, in Joseph Stalin and the Soviet Union. In addition, America had encountered setbacks in its battle against communism: the Korean stalemate, the "loss" of China, the Soviet development of an atomic bomb. Searching for someone to blame, many people were attracted to the idea of a communist conspiracy within American borders. But there were other factors as well, rooted in events in American domestic politics.

HUAC and Alger Hiss

Much of the anticommunist furor emerged out of the Republican Party's search for an issue with which to attack the Democrats, and out of the Democrats' efforts to take that issue away. Beginning in 1947 (with Republicans temporarily in control of Congress), the House Un-American Activities Committee (HUAC) held widely publicized investigations to prove that, under Democratic rule, the government had tolerated (if not actually encouraged) communist subversion. The committee turned first to the movie industry, arguing that communists had infiltrated Hollywood and had tainted America with propaganda. Writers and producers, some of them former communists, were called to testify; and when some of them ("the Hollywood Ten") refused to answer questions about their own political beliefs and those of their colleagues, they were jailed for contempt. Others were barred from employment in the industry when Hollywood, attempting to protect its public image, adopted a blacklist of those of "suspicious loyalty."

More alarming to the public was HUAC's investigation into charges of disloyalty leveled against a former high-ranking member of the State Department: Alger Hiss. In 1948, Whittaker Chambers, a self-avowed former communist agent who had become a conservative editor at *Time* magazine, told the committee that Hiss had passed classified State Department documents through him to the Soviet Union in 1937 and 1938. When Hiss sued him for slander, Chambers produced microfilms of the documents (called the "pumpkin papers," because Chambers had kept them hidden

in a pumpkin in his garden). Hiss could not be tried for espionage because of the statute of limitations (a law that protects individuals from prosecution for most crimes after seven years have passed). But largely because of the relentless efforts of Richard M. Nixon, a freshman Republican congressman from California and a member of HUAC, Hiss was convicted of perjury and served several years in prison. The Hiss case not only discredited a prominent young diplomat; it cast suspicion on a generation of liberal Democrats and made it possible for many Americans to believe that communists had actually infiltrated the government.

The Federal Loyalty Program and the Rosenberg Case

Partly to protect itself against Republican attacks, partly to encourage support for the president's foreign policy initiatives, the Truman administration in 1947 initiated a widely publicized program to review the "loyalty" of federal employees. In August 1950, the president authorized sensitive agencies to fire people deemed no more than "bad security risks." By 1951, more than 2,000 government employees had resigned under pressure and 212 had been dismissed.

The employee loyalty program became a signal throughout the executive branch to launch a major as-

THE ROSENBERGS
Julius and Ethel Rosenberg leave federal court in a police van after being convicted in March 1951 of transmitting atomic secrets to the Soviet Union. A week later, Judge Irving Kaufman sentenced them to death.
(UPI/Bettmann)

sault on subversion. The attorney general established a widely cited list of supposedly subversive organizations. The director of the Federal Bureau of Investigation (FBI), J. Edgar Hoover, investigated and harassed alleged radicals. The anticommunist frenzy quickly grew so intense that even a Democratic Congress felt obliged to bow to it. In 1950, Congress passed the McCarran Internal Security Act, requiring all communist organizations to register with the government and to publish their records and creating other restrictions on "subversive" activity. Truman vetoed the bill. Congress easily overrode his veto.

The successful Soviet detonation of a nuclear weapon in 1949, earlier than generally expected, convinced many people that there had been a conspiracy to pass American atomic secrets to the Russians. In 1950, Klaus Fuchs, a young British scientist, seemed to confirm those fears when he testified that he had delivered to the Russians details of the manufacture of the bomb. The case ultimately settled on an obscure New York couple, Julius and Ethel Rosenberg, members of the Communist Party, whom the government claimed had been the masterminds of the conspiracy. The case against them rested in large part on testimony by Ethel's brother, David Greenglass, a machinist who had worked on the Manhattan Project. Greenglass admitted to channeling secret information to the Soviet Union through other agents (including Fuchs). His sister and brother-in-law had, he claimed, planned and orchestrated the espionage. The Rosenbergs were convicted and, on April 5, 1951, sentenced to death. After two years of appeals and protests by sympathizers, they died in the electric chair on June 19, 1953, proclaiming their innocence to the end.

All these factors—the HUAC investigations, the Hiss trial, the loyalty investigations, the McCarran Act, the Rosenberg case—combined with concern about international events to create a fear of communist subversion that by the early 1950s seemed to have gripped virtually the entire country. State and local governments, the judiciary, schools and universities, labor unions—all sought to purge themselves of real or imagined subversives. A pervasive fear settled on the country—not only the fear of communist infiltration but the fear of being suspected of communism. It was a climate that made possible the rise of an extraordinary public figure, whose behavior at any other time might have been dismissed as preposterous.

McCarthyism

Joseph McCarthy was an undistinguished first-term Republican senator from Wisconsin when, in February 1950, he suddenly burst into national prominence. In the midst of a speech in Wheeling, West Virginia, he raised a sheet of paper and claimed to "hold in my hand" a list of 205 known communists currently working in the American State Department. No person of comparable stature had ever made so bold a charge against the federal government; and in the weeks to come, as McCarthy repeated and expanded on his accusations, he emerged as the nation's most prominent leader of the crusade against domestic subversion.

Within weeks of his charges against the State Department, McCarthy was leveling accusations at other agencies. After 1952, with the Republicans in control of the Senate and McCarthy the chairman of a special subcommittee, he conducted highly publicized investigations of subversion in many areas of the government. His unprincipled assistants, Roy Cohn and David Schine, sauntered arrogantly through federal offices and American embassies overseas looking for evidence of communist influence. One hapless government official after another appeared before McCarthy's subcommittee, where the senator belligerently and often cruelly badgered witnesses and destroyed public careers. McCarthy never produced solid evidence that any federal employee had communist ties. But a growing constituency adored him nevertheless for his coarse, "fearless" assaults on a government establishment that many considered arrogant, effete, even traitorous. Republicans, in particular, rallied to his claims that the Democrats had been responsible for "twenty years of treason," that only a change of parties could rid the country of subversion. McCarthy, in short, provided his followers with an issue into which they could channel a wide range of resentments: fear of communism, animosity toward the country's "eastern establishment," and frustrated partisan ambitions.

For a time, McCarthy intimidated all but a few people from opposing him. Even the highly popular Dwight D. Eisenhower, running for president in 1952, did not speak out against him, even though he disliked McCarthy's tactics and was outraged at, among other things, McCarthy's attacks on General George Marshall.

The Republican Revival

Public frustration over the stalemate in Korea and popular fears of internal subversion combined to make 1952 a bad year for the Democratic Party. Truman, whose own popularity had diminished almost to the vanishing point, wisely withdrew from the presidential contest. The party united instead behind Governor Adlai E. Stevenson of Illinois. Stevenson's dignity, wit, and eloquence made him a beloved figure to many liberals and intellectuals. But those same qualities seemed only to fuel Republican charges that Stevenson lacked

SIGNIFICANT EVENTS

1941 Roosevelt and Churchill draft Atlantic Charter

1943 Wendell Willkie publishes *One World*

Roosevelt, Churchill, and Stalin meet at Teheran

1944 G.I. Bill of Rights enacted

1945 Yalta Conference

Roosevelt dies; Harry S. Truman becomes president

Potsdam Conference

United Nations founded

1946 Atomic Energy Commission established

Postwar inflation

Coal and railroad strikes

Republicans win control of Congress

Crisis in Iran

1947 Truman Doctrine announced

Marshall Plan proposed

National Security Act passed

Taft-Hartley Act passed

HUAC begins investigating Hollywood

Federal employee loyalty program launched

1948 Communists stage coup in Czechoslovakia

Economic Cooperation Administration established

Selective Service System restored

Berlin blockade prompts U.S. airlift

Truman elected president

Hiss case begins

1949 NATO established

Soviet Union explodes atomic bomb

Communists seize power in China

1950 NSC-68 outlines new U.S. policy toward communism

Korean War begins

American troops enter North Korea

Chinese troops enter war

McCarran Act passed

Fuchs-Rosenberg case begins

Joseph McCarthy begins campaign against communists in government

1951 Truman removes MacArthur from command in Korea

Railroad workers strike

Negotiations begin in Korea

1952 American occupation of Japan ends

Steelworkers strike

Dwight D. Eisenhower elected president

---

the strength or the will to combat communism sufficiently. McCarthy described him as "soft" and took delight in deliberately confusing him with Alger Hiss.

Stevenson's greatest problem, however, was the Republican candidate opposing him. Rejecting the efforts of conservatives to nominate Robert Taft or Douglas MacArthur, the Republicans turned to a man who had no previous identification with the party: General Dwight D. Eisenhower, military hero, commander of NATO, president of Columbia University in New York, who won nomination on the first ballot. He chose as his running mate the young California senator who

had gained national prominence through his crusade against Alger Hiss: Richard M. Nixon.

Eisenhower and Nixon were a powerful combination in the autumn campaign. While Eisenhower attracted support through his geniality and his statesmanlike pledges to settle the Korean conflict (at one point dramatically promising to "go to Korea" himself), Nixon effectively exploited the issue of domestic subversion. After surviving early accusations of financial improprieties (which he effectively neutralized in a famous television address, the "Checkers speech"), Nixon went on to launch harsh attacks on Democratic "cowardice," "appeasement," and "treason." He spoke derisively of "Adlai the appeaser" and ridiculed Secretary of State Dean Acheson for running a "cowardly college of communist containment." And he missed no opportunity to publicize Stevenson's early support for Alger Hiss as opposed to Nixon's own role in exposing Hiss. Eisenhower and Nixon both made effective use of allegations of corruption in the Truman administration and pledged repeatedly to "clean up the mess in Washington."

The response at the polls was overwhelming. Eisenhower won both a popular and an electoral landslide: 55 percent of the popular vote to Stevenson's 44 percent, 442 electoral votes to Stevenson's 89. Republicans gained control of both houses of Congress for the first time in two decades. The election of 1952 ended twenty years of Democratic government. And while it might not have seemed so at the time, it also signaled the end of some of the worst turbulence of the postwar era.

SUGGESTED READINGS

Origins of the Cold War. Gar Alperovitz, *Atomic Diplomacy: Hiroshima and Potsdam*, rev. ed. (1985). Stephen Ambrose, *Rise to Globalism*, 5th ed. (1988). Terry H. Anderson, *The United States, Great Britain, and the Cold War, 1944–1947* (1981). H. W. Brands, *Inside the Cold War: Loy Henderson and the Rise of the American Empire, 1918–1961* (1991). Diane Clemens, *Yalta* (1970). Herbert Feis, *Churchill, Roosevelt, and Stalin* (1957); *Between War and Peace: The Potsdam Conference* (1960). John Lewis Gaddis, *Strategies of Containment* (1982); *The United States and the Origins of the Cold War, 1941–1947* (1972); *The Long Peace* (1987). Gregg Herken, *The Winning Weapon: Then Atomic Bomb in the Cold War, 1945–1950* (1980). George C. Herring, Jr., *Aid to Russia* (1973). Timothy P. Ireland, *Creating the Entangling Alliance: The Origins of NATO* (1981). Bruce Kuniholm, *The Origins of the Cold War in the Middle East* (1980). Walter LaFeber, *America, Russia, and the Cold War, 1945–1967* (rev. ed. 1980). Melvyn P. Leffler, *A Preponderance of Power: National Security, the Truman Administration, and the Cold War* (1992). William McNeill, *America, Britain, and Russia* (1953). Wilson D. Miscamble, *George F. Kennan and the Making of American Foreign Policy, 1947–1950* (1992). W. L. Neumann, *After Victory* (1969). Thomas G. Paterson, *Soviet-American Confrontation* (1974); *On Every Front: The Making of the Cold War* (1979); *Meeting the Communist Threat* (1988). Robert A. Pollard, *Economic Security and the Origins of the Cold War* (1985). Martin Sherwin, *A World Destroyed* (1975). Gaddis Smith, *American Diplomacy During the Second World War* (1965); *Dean Acheson* (1972). John L. Snell, *Illusion and Necessity* (1967). William Taubman, *Stalin's American Policy* (1982). Athan G. Theoharis, *The Yalta Myths* (1970). Adam Ulam, *The Rivals: America and Russia Since World War II* (1971). Bernard Weisberger, *Cold War, Cold Peace* (1984). Lawrence Wittner, *American Intervention in Greece, 1943–1949* (1982). Daniel Yergin, *Shattered Peace* (1977).

Truman's Foreign Policy. Dean Acheson, *Present at the Creation* (1970). Hadley Arkes, *Bureaucracy, the Marshall Plan and National Interest* (1973). Richard J. Barnet, *The Alliance* (1983). Robert M. Blum, *Drawing the Line: The Origin of the American Containment Policy in East Asia* (1982). Russell D. Buhite, *Soviet-American Relations in Asia, 1945–1954* (1982). Warren I. Cohen, *America's Response to China* (rev. ed. 1980).

Robert Donovan, *Conflict and Crisis* (1977); *Tumultuous Years* (1982). John King Fairbank, *The United States and China* (rev. ed. 1971). Lloyd Gardner, *Architects of Illusion* (1970). Fraser J. Harbutt, *The Iron Curtain: Churchill, America, and the Origins of the Cold War* (1986). Michael Hogan, *The Marshall Plan* (1987). Akira Iriye, *The Cold War in Asia* (1974). Laurence Kaplan, *The United States and NATO* (1984). George F. Kennan, *American Diplomacy, 1900–1950* (1952); *Memoirs, 1925–1950* (1967). Joyce Kolko and Gabriel Kolko, *The Limits of Power* (1970). Bruce R. Koniholm, *The Origins of the Cold War in the Middle East* (1980). William R. Louis, *The British Empire in the Middle East* (1984). Gary May, *China Scapegoat* (1979). David Mayer, *George Kennan and the Dilemmas of U.S. Foreign Policy* (1988). Edwin O. Reischauer, *The United States and Japan* (rev. ed. 1965). Lisle Rose, *Roots of Tragedy* (1976). Michael Schaller, *The U.S. Crusade in China* (1979); *Communists* (1971); *The American Occupation of Japan: The Origins of the Cold War in Asia* (1985). Howard Schonberger, *Aftermath of War: Americans and the Remaking of Japan,* (1989). Anders Stephanson, *Kennan and the Art of Foreign Policy* (1989). Michael B. Stoff, *Oil, War, and American Security* (1980). Christopher Thorne, *Allies of a Kind* (1978). Imanuel Wexler, *The Marshall Plan Revisited* (1983).

Truman's Domestic Policies. Stephen K. Bailey, *Congress Makes a Law* (1950). Jack S. Ballard, *The Shock of Peace: Military and Economic Demobilization After World War II* (1983). William C. Berman, *The Politics of Civil Rights in the Truman Administration* (1970). Barton J. Bernstein, ed. , *Politics and Policies of the Truman Administration* (1970). Richard Dalfiume, *Desegregation of the U.S. Armed Forces* (1969). Richard O. Davies, *Housing Reform During the Truman Administration* (1966). John P. Diggins, *The Proud Decades* (1988). Robert Donovan, *Confict and Crisis* (1977); *Tumultuous Years* (1982). Andrew J. Dunar, *The Truman Scandals and the Politics of Morality* (1984). Robert H. Ferrell, *Harry S. Truman and the Modern American Presidency* (1983). Eric Goldman, *The Crucial Decade—and After: America, 1945–1960* (1961). Alonzo Hamby, *Beyond the New Deal: Harry S. Truman and American Liberalism* (1973). Susan Hartmann, *Truman and the 80th Congress* (1971). Roy Jenkins, *Truman* (1986). R. Alton Lee, *Truman and Taft-Hartley* (1967); *Truman and the Steel Seizure Case*

(1977). Arthur F. McClure, *The Truman Administration and the Problems of Postwar Labor* (1969). Donald R. McCoy, *The Presidency of Harry S. Truman* (1984). Donald McCoy and Richard Ruetten, *Quest and Response* (1973). David McCullough, *Truman* (1992). Maeva Marcus, *Truman and the Steel Seizure* (1977). Allen J. Matusow, *Farm Policies and Politics in the Truman Years* (1967). Merle Miller, *Plain Speaking* (1980). Richard L. Miller, *Truman: The Rise to Power* (1986). William O'Neill, *American High* (1986). William E. Pemberton, *Harry S. Truman* (1989). Monte S. Poen, *Harry S. Truman Versus the Medical Lobby* (1979). Gary Reichard, *Politics as Usual: The Age of Truman and Eisenhower* (1988). Christopher L. Tomlins, *The State and the Unions* (1985).

Cold War Politics and Culture. John P. Diggins, *The Proud Decades, 1941–1960* (1989). Steven M. Gillon, *Politics and Vision: The ADA and American Liberalism, 1947–1985* (1987). David Goldfield, *Black, White, and Southern: Race Relations and Southern Culture* (1990). Maurice Isserman, *If I Had a Hammer. . . : The Death of the Old Left and the Birth of the New Left* (1987). Norman Markowitz, *The Rise and Fall of the People's Century: Henry A. Wallace and American Liberalism, 1941–1948* (1973). James T. Patterson, *Mr. Republican* (1972). Richard Pells, *The Liberal Mind in a Conservative Age: American Intellectuals in the 1940s and 1950s* (1985). Irwin Ross, *The Loneliest Campaign* (1968). Richard Norton Smith, *Thomas E. Dewey and His Times* (1982). Allen Yarnell, *Democrats and Progressives* (1974).

The Korean War. Carl Berger, *The Korean Knot* (1957). Ronald Caridi, *The Korean War and American Politics* (1969). Bruce Cumings, *The Origins of the Korean War* (1980); ed., *Child of Conflict: The Korean-American Relationship, 1943–1953* (1983). Charles W. Dobbs, *The Unwanted Symbol* (1981). Joseph C. Goulden, *Korea: The Untold Story of the War* (1982). John Halliday and Bruce Cumings, *Korea: The Unknown War* (1980).

Robert Leckie, *Conflict* (1962). Glenn D. Paige, *The Korean Decision* (1968). Michael Schaller, *Douglas MacArthur* (1989). Robert R. Simmons, *The Strained Alliance* (1975). John Spanier, *The Truman-MacArthur Controversy* (1959). Allen Whiting, *China Crosses the Yalu* (1960).

Countersubversion. Michael R. Belknap, *Cold War Political Justice: The Smith Act, the Communist Party, and American Civil Liberties* (1977). Eric Bentley, ed., *Thirty Years of Treason*. David Caute, *The Great Fear* (1978). Larry Ceplair and Steven Englund, *The Inquisition in Hollywood* (1983). Richard Freeland, *The Truman Doctrine and the Origins of McCarthyism* (1971). Richard Fried, *Men Against McCarthy* (1976); *Nightmare in Red* (1990). Robert Griffith, *The Politics of Fear* (1970). Robert Griffith and Athan Theoharis, eds., *The Specter: Original Essays on the Cold War and the Origins of McCarthyism* (1974). Alan Harper, *The Politics of Loyalty* (1969). Stanley Kutler, *The American Inquisition* (1982). Harvey Levenstein, *Communism, Anticommunism, and the CIO* (1981). Mary Sperling McAuliffe, *Crisis on the Left* (1978). Victor Navasky, *Naming Names* (1980). William O'Neill, *A Better World* (1983). David M. Oshinsky, *A Conspiracy So Immense: The World of Joe McCarthy* (1983). Richard Gid Powers, *Secrecy and Power: The Life of J. Edgar Hoover* (1987). Ronald Radosh and Joyce Milton, *The Rosenberg File* (1983). Thomas C. Reeves, *The Life and Times of Joe McCarthy* (1982). Michael Paul Rogin, *The Intellectuals and McCarthy* (1967). Richard Rovere, *Senator Joe McCarthy* (1959). Walter and Miriam Schneer, *Invitation to an Inquest* (rev. ed. 1983). Ellen Schrecker, *No Ivory Tower* (1986). Edward Shils, *The Torment of Secrecy* (1956). Joseph Starobin, *American Communism in Crisis* (1972). Athan Theoharis, *Seeds of Repression* (1971); *Spying on Americans* (1978). Athan Theoharis and John Stuart Cox, *The Boss: J. Edgar Hoover and the Great American Inquisition* (1988). Allen Weinstein, *Perjury: The Hiss-Chambers Case* (1978). Stephen J. Whitfield, *The Culture of the Cold War* (1991).

The reception committee for the new kid on the block!

JAMES DEAN

The overnight sensation of 'East of Eden'

Warner Bros. put
all the force of
the screen
into a challenging
drama of today's
juvenile violence!

"REBEL WITHOUT A CAUSE"

CinemaScope
and WarnerColor

...and they both come from 'good' families!

ALSO STARRING NATALIE WOOD WITH SAL MINEO · JIM BACKUS · ANN DORAN · COREY ALLEN · WILLIAM HOPPER · STEWART STERN · MUSIC BY DAVID WEISBART · NICHOLAS RAY

AN ICON OF THE 1950s
The actor James Dean became enormously popular in the 1950s for his portrayal of brooding, sensitive young men rebelling against the stifling conventions of middle-class life. *Rebel Without a Cause* was one of his most successful films, and it suggested something of the restiveness and discontent that lay just below the surface of the seemingly stable culture of the era. *(Warner Brothers)*

CHAPTER THIRTY

THE AFFLUENT SOCIETY

I F AMERICA WAS EXPERIENCING a golden age in the 1950s and early 1960s, as many Americans believed at the time and many continue to believe today, it was largely a result of two developments. One was a booming national prosperity, which profoundly altered the social, economic, and even physical landscape of the United States as well as the way many Americans thought about their lives and their world. The other was the continuing struggle against communism, a struggle that created considerable anxiety but that also encouraged some Americans to look even more approvingly at their own society.

But if these compelling realities created a widespread sense of national purpose and self-satisfaction, they also helped blind many Americans to serious problems plaguing much of their society. More than 30 million Americans, according to some estimates, continued to live in poverty in the 1950s. Significant minorities—most prominently the 10 percent of the American people who were black, but also Hispanics, Asians, Indians, gays and lesbians, and others—continued to suffer social, political, and economic discrimination. Many American women were beginning to chafe at the obstacles to their personal and professional fulfillment. The very things that made America seem so successful in the 1950s also contributed, in the end, to bringing the nation's social problems more sharply into focus.

Gunnar Myrdal, a Swedish sociologist who had spent years studying life in the United States, wrote in 1944: "American affluence is heavily mortgaged.

America carries a tremendous burden of debt to its poor people." The efforts to pay that debt, and others, would ultimately help move the nation into the more turbulent era of the 1960s.

THE ECONOMIC "MIRACLE"

Among the most striking features of American society in the 1950s and early 1960s was a booming, almost miraculous, economic growth that made even the heady 1920s seem pale by comparison. But although it was a better balanced and more widely distributed prosperity than that of thirty years earlier, it was not as universal as some Americans liked to believe.

Economic Growth

By 1949, despite the continuing problems of postwar reconversion, an economic expansion had begun that would continue with only brief interruptions for almost twenty years. Between 1945 and 1960, the gross national product grew by 250 percent, from $200 billion to over $500 billion—a striking refutation of the widespread predictions in 1945 that GNP would decline once the demands of war production ended. Unemployment, which during the Depression had averaged between 15 and 25 percent, remained throughout the 1950s and early 1960s at about 5 percent or lower. Inflation, in the meantime, hovered around 3 percent a year or less.

The causes of this growth were varied. Government spending, which had ended the Depression in the 1940s, continued to stimulate growth through public funding of schools, housing, veterans' benefits, welfare, and the $100 billion interstate highway program, which began in 1956. Above all, there was military spending. Economic growth was at its peak (averaging 4.7 percent a year) during the first half of the 1950s, when military spending was highest because of the Korean War. In the late 1950s, with spending on armaments in decline, the annual rate of growth declined by more than half, to 2.25 percent.

Technological progress also contributed to the boom. Because of advances in production techniques and mechanical efficiency, worker productivity increased more than 35 percent in the first decade after the war, a rate far higher than that of any previous era. And technological research and development itself became an increasingly important sector of the economy, expanding the demand for scientists, engineers, and other highly trained experts.

Among the fruits of this scientific and technological research was the development of electronic computers, which first became commercially available in the mid-1950s and which almost immediately began to improve the performance of some American corporations. The first modern computer (the Mark I, developed by the International Business Machines Corporation, or IBM, and scientists at Harvard) emerged as a result of efforts during World War II to decipher enemy codes. For several years after the war, computers continued to develop in response to military needs. By 1954, however, IBM and other companies were developing computers for use by other government agencies and, more important, for private business. Not until the 1980s did most Americans come into direct and regular contact with computers, but the new machines were having a substantial effect on the economy long before that.

The national birth rate reversed a long pattern of decline with the so-called baby boom, which had begun during the war and peaked in 1957. The nation's population rose almost 20 percent in the decade, from 150 million in 1950 to 179 million in 1960. The baby boom meant increased consumer demand and expanding economic growth.

The rapid expansion of suburbs—whose population grew 47 percent in the 1950s, more than twice as fast as the population as a whole—helped stimulate growth in several important sectors of the economy. The number of privately owned cars (more essential for suburban than for urban living) more than doubled in a decade, sparking a great boom in the automobile industry. Demand for new homes helped sustain a

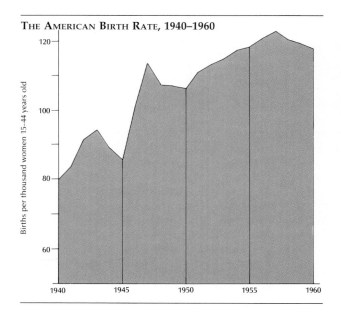

THE AMERICAN BIRTH RATE, 1940–1960

vigorous housing industry. The construction of roads, which was both a cause and a result of the growth of suburbs, stimulated the economy as well.

Because of this unprecedented growth, the economy grew nearly ten times as fast as the population in the thirty years after the war. And while that growth was far from equally distributed, it affected most of society. The average American in 1960 had over 20 percent more purchasing power than in 1945, and more than twice as much as during the prosperous 1920s. By 1960, per capita income (the average income for every individual man, woman, and child) was over $1,800–$500 more than it had been fifteen years before. Family incomes had risen even more. The American people had achieved the highest standard of living of any society in the history of the world.

The Rise of the Modern West

No region of the country experienced more dramatic changes as a result of the new economic growth than the American West. Its population expanded dramatically; its cities boomed; its industrial economy flourished. Before World War II, most of the West had been, economically at least, an appendage of the great industrial economy of the East—providing it with raw materials and agricultural goods. By the 1960s, some parts of the West were among the most important (and populous) industrial and cultural centers of the nation in their own right.

As during World War II, much of the growth of the West was a result of federal spending and investment—on the dams, power stations, highways, and other infrastructure projects that made economic development possible; and on the military contracts that continued to flow disproportionately to factories in California and Texas, many of them built with government funds during the war. But other factors played a role as well. The enormous increase in automobile use after World War II—a result, among other things, of suburbanization and improved highway systems—gave a large stimulus to the petroleum industry and contributed to the rapid growth of oil fields in Texas and Colorado, and of the metropolitan centers serving them: Houston, Dallas, and Denver. State governments in the West invested heavily in their universities. The University of Texas and University of California systems, in particular, became among the nation's largest and best; as centers of research, they helped attract technology-intensive industries to the region. Climate also contributed. Once they had the infrastructure (and, most important, the water supplies) to sustain large populations, southern California, Nevada, and Arizona, in particular, attracted many migrants from the East because of their warm, dry climates. The growth of Los Angeles after World War II was a remarkable phenomenon: more than 10 percent of all new businesses in the United States between 1945 and 1950 began in Los Angeles. Its population rose by over 50 percent between 1940 and 1960.

The New Economics

The exciting (and to some, surprising) discovery of the power of the American economic system was a major cause of the confident, even arrogant tone of much American political life in the 1950s. During the Depression, politicians, intellectuals, and others had often questioned the viability of capitalism. In the 1950s, such doubt virtually vanished. Two features in particular made the postwar economy a source of national confidence.

First was the belief that Keynesian economics made it possible for government to regulate and stabilize the economy without intruding directly into the private sector. The British economist John Maynard Keynes had argued as early as the 1920s that by varying the flow of government spending and managing the supply of currency, the state could stimulate the economy to cure recession, and dampen growth to prevent inflation. The experience of the last years of the Depression and the first years of the war had seemed to confirm this argument. And by the mid-1950s, Keynesian

theory was rapidly becoming a fundamental article of faith—not only among professional economists but among much of the public. The most popular economics textbook of the 1950s and 1960s, Paul Samuelson's *Economics*, imbued a generation of college students with Keynesian ideas. Armed with these fiscal and monetary tools, many economists now believed, it was possible for the government to maintain a permanent prosperity. The dispiriting boom-and-bust cycle long considered a permanent feature of industrial capitalism could now be banished forever. Never again would it be necessary for the nation to experience another Depression.

If any doubters remained, there was ample evidence to dispel their misgivings during the brief recessions the economy experienced during the era. When the economy slackened in late 1953, Secretary of the Treasury George M. Humphrey and the Federal Reserve Board worked to ease credit and make money more readily available. The economy quickly recovered, seeming to confirm the value of Keynesian tactics (even though Humphrey and the Board did not explicitly endorse them). A far more serious recession began late in 1957 and lasted more than a year. This time, the Eisenhower administration ignored the Keynesians and adopted such deflationary tactics as cutting the budget. The slow, halting pace of the recovery, in contrast with the rapid revival in 1954, seemed further to support the Keynesian philosophy. The new economics finally won official acceptance in 1963, when John Kennedy proposed a tax cut to stimulate economic growth. Although it took Kennedy's death and the political skills of Lyndon Johnson to win passage of the measure in 1964, the result seemed to be all that the Keynesians had predicted: an increase in private demand, which stimulated economic growth and reduced unemployment.

Accompanying the belief in the possibility of permanent economic stability was the equally exhilarating belief in permanent economic growth. As the economy continued to expand far beyond what any observer had predicted was possible only a few years before, more and more Americans assumed that such growth was now without bounds—that there were few effective limits to the abundance available to the nation. This was not only a comforting thought in itself; it also made possible a new outlook on social and economic problems. In the 1930s, many Americans had argued that the elimination of poverty and injustice would require a redistribution of wealth—a limitation on the fortunes of the rich and a distribution of wealth to the poor. By the mid-1950s, reformers concerned about economic deprivation were arguing that the solution lay in increased production. The affluent would not have to sacrifice in order to eliminate poverty; the nation would simply have to produce more abundance, thus raising the quality of life of even the poorest citizens to a level of comfort and decency.

The Keynesians never managed to remake federal economic policy entirely to their liking. Political obstacles consistently limited the ability of even the most committed Keynesians to use fiscal and monetary policies as they wished; and the increasingly complex modern economy did not always respond as quickly to Keynesian policies as the theory behind them suggested it should. Still, the new economics gave many Americans a confidence in their ability to solve economic problems that previous generations had never developed.

Capital and Labor

Over 4,000 corporate mergers took place in the 1950s; and more than ever before, a relatively small number of large-scale organizations controlled an enormous proportion of the nation's economic activity. This was particularly true in industries benefiting from government defense spending. As during World War II, the federal government tended to award military contracts to large corporations. In 1959, for example, half of all defense contracts went to only twenty firms. But the same pattern repeated itself in many other areas of the economy, as corporations changed from single-industry firms to diversified conglomerates. By the end of the decade, half the net corporate income in the nation was going to only slightly more than 500 firms, or one-tenth of 1 percent of the total number of corporations.

A similar consolidation was occurring in the agricultural economy. As increasing mechanization reduced the need for farm labor, the agricultural work force declined by more than half in the two decades after the war. Mechanization also endangered one of the most cherished American institutions: the family farm. By the 1960s, relatively few individuals could any longer afford to buy and equip a modern farm, and much of the nation's most productive land had been purchased by financial institutions and corporations.

Corporations enjoying booming growth were reluctant to allow strikes to interfere with their operations, and since the most important labor unions were now so large and entrenched that they could not easily be suppressed or intimidated, business leaders made important concessions to them. As early as 1948, Walter Reuther, president of the United Automobile Workers, obtained a contract from General Motors that included a built-in "escalator clause"—an automatic cost-of-living increase pegged to the consumer price

index. In 1955, Reuther received a guarantee from Ford Motor Company of continuing wages to auto workers even during layoffs. A few months later, steelworkers in several corporations won guarantees of an annual salary. By the mid-1950s, factory wages in all industries had risen substantially, to an average of $80 per week.

By the early 1950s, in other words, large labor unions had developed a new kind of relationship with employers, a relationship sometimes known as the "postwar contract." Workers in steel, automobiles, and other large unionized industries were receiving generous increases in wages and benefits; in return, the unions tacitly agreed to refrain from raising other issues—issues involving control of the workplace and a voice for workers in the planning of production. The postwar "contract" had the support of the National Labor Relations Board, whose mediators (many drawing from their experience in World War II) believed the purpose of labor relations was to maintain industrial peace and promote the general health of the economy, not to defend or expand the "rights" of workers. The contract served the corporations and the union leadership well, but many rank-and-file workers resented the abandonment of efforts to give them more control over the conditions of their labor. By the late 1960s and 1970s, workers in some unions (Teamsters, Mine Workers, and others) were forming dissident organizations in an effort to democratize the unions and increase the scope of their demands. In the meantime, the number of industrial jobs in some major industries was beginning to diminish as a result of new technologies that automated production. Even as the labor movement was enjoying impressive successes in winning better wages for its members, its share of the labor force dropped—from an all-time high of 36 percent in 1953 to 31 percent by the end of the decade.

The economic successes of the 1950s helped pave the way for a reunification of the labor movement. In December 1955, the American Federation of Labor and the Congress of Industrial Organizations ended their twenty-year rivalry and merged to create the AFL-CIO, under the leadership of George Meany.

But success also bred stagnation and corruption in some union bureaucracies. In 1957, the powerful Teamsters Union became the subject of a congressional investigation, and its president, David Beck, was charged with misappropriation of union funds. Beck ultimately stepped down to be replaced by Jimmy Hoffa, whom government investigators pursued for nearly a decade before finally winning a conviction against him (for tax evasion) in 1967. The United Mine Workers, the union that had spearheaded the industrial movement in the 1930s, similarly became tainted

WORKERS REPRESENTED BY UNIONS, 1920–1992

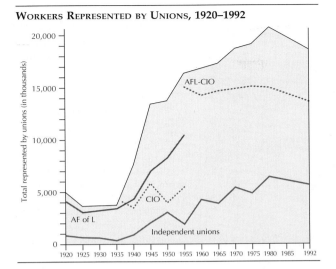

by suspicions of corruption and by violence. John L. Lewis's last years as head of the union were plagued with scandals and dissent within the organization. His successor, Tony Boyle, was ultimately convicted of complicity in the 1969 murder of Joseph ("Jock") Yablonski, the leader of a dissident faction within the union.

While the labor movement enjoyed significant success in winning better wages and benefits for workers already organized in strong unions, the majority of laborers who were as yet unorganized made fewer advances. Total union membership remained relatively stable throughout the 1950s, at about 16 million; and while this was in part a result of a shift in the work force from blue-collar to white-collar jobs, it was also a result of new obstacles to organization. The Taft-Hartley Act and the state right-to-work laws that it spawned made the creation of new unions powerful enough to demand recognition from employers more difficult.

In the American South, in particular, impediments to unionization were enormous. The CIO had launched a major organizing drive in the South shortly after World War II, targeting the poorly paid workers in textile mills in particular. But "Operation Dixie," as it was called, was a failure—as were most other organizing drives for at least thirty years after World War II. Anti-union sentiment was so powerful in the South—not just among employers, but also among politicians, the press, local police, and many others— that almost all organizing drives encountered crushing and usually fatal resistance.

PEOPLE OF PLENTY

Among the most striking social development of the postwar era was the rapid extension of a middle-class lifestyle and outlook to large groups of the population previously insulated from it. The new prosperity of social groups that had previously lived on the margins; the growing availability of consumer products at affordable prices and the rising public fascination with such products; and perhaps above all, the massive population movement from the cities to the suburbs— all helped make the American middle class a larger, more powerful, more homogeneous, and more dominant force than it had ever been before.

The new prosperity, in fact, inspired some Americans to see abundance as the key to understanding the American past and the American character. Leading intellectuals argued that American history had been characterized by a broad "consensus" about the value and necessity of competitive, capitalist growth. "However much at odds on specific issues," the historian Richard Hofstadter wrote in *The American Political Tradition* (1948), Americans have "shared a belief in the rights of property, the philosophy of economic individualism, the value of competition; they have accepted the economic virtues of capitalist culture as necessary qualities of man." David Potter, another leading American historian of the era, published an influential examination of "economic abundance and American character" in 1954. He called it *People of Plenty*. For the American middle class in the 1950s, at least, it seemed an appropriate label.

The Consumer Culture

At the center of middle-class culture in the 1950s, as it had been for many decades before, was a growing absorption with consumer goods. That was a result of increased prosperity, of the increasing variety and availability of products, and of advertisers' adeptness in creating a demand for those products. It was also a result of the growth of consumer credit, which increased by 800 percent between 1945 and 1957 through the development of credit cards, revolving charge accounts, and easy-payment plans. Prosperity fueled such long-time consumer crazes as the automobile, and Detroit responded to the boom with ever-flashier styling and accessories. Consumers also responded eagerly to the development of such new products as dishwashers, garbage disposals, television, hi-fis, and stereos. To a striking degree, the prosperity of the 1950s and 1960s was consumer driven (as opposed to investment driven).

Because consumer goods were so often marketed (and advertised) nationally, the 1950s were notable for the rapid spread of great national consumer crazes. For example, children, adolescents, and even some adults became entranced in the late 1950s with the hula hoop—a large plastic ring kept spinning around the waist. The popularity of the Walt Disney-produced children's television show *The Mickey Mouse Club* created a national demand for related products such as Mickey Mouse watches and hats. It also helped produce the stunning success of Disneyland, an amusement park near Los Angeles that re-created many of the characters and events of Disney entertainment programs. The Disney technique of turning an entertainment success into an effective tool for marketing consumer goods was not an isolated event. Many other entertainers and producers took note and did the same.

The Suburban Nation

By 1960 a third of the nation's population was living in suburbs. The growth of suburbs was a result not only of increased affluence, but of important innovations in home-building, which made single-family houses affordable to millions of new people. The most famous of the postwar suburban developers, William

CHICAGO'S ANNEXATIONS AND THE SUBURBAN NOOSE

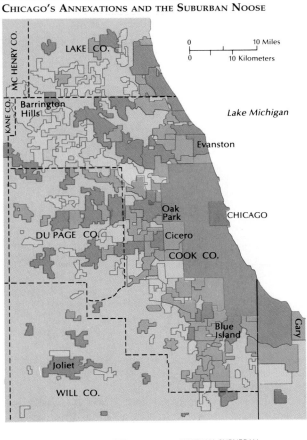

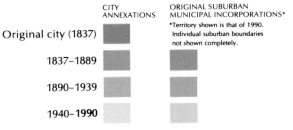

	CITY ANNEXATIONS	ORIGINAL SUBURBAN MUNICIPAL INCORPORATIONS*
Original city (1837)		*Territory shown is that of 1990. Individual suburban boundaries not shown completely.
1837–1889		
1890–1939		
1940–**1990**		

Levitt, came to symbolize the new suburban growth with his use of mass-production techniques to construct a large housing development on Long Island, near New York City. This first "Levittown" (there would later be others in New Jersey and Pennsylvania) consisted of several thousand two-bedroom Cape Cod-style houses, with identical interiors and only slightly varied facades, each perched on its own concrete slab (to eliminate excavation costs), facing curving, treeless streets. Levittown houses sold for under $10,000, and they helped meet an enormous demand

for housing that had been growing for more than a decade. Young couples—often newly married war veterans eager to start a family, assisted by low-cost, government-subsidized mortgages provided by the G.I. Bill (see p. 780)—rushed to purchase the inexpensive homes, not only in the Levittowns but in similar developments that soon began appearing throughout the country.

Why did so many Americans want to move to the suburbs? One reason was the enormous importance postwar Americans placed on family life after five years of war in which families had often been separated or otherwise disrupted. Suburbs provided families with larger homes than they could find (or afford) in the cities, and thus made it easier to raise larger numbers of children. They provided privacy. They provided security from the noise and dangers of urban living. They offered space for the new consumer goods—the cars, boats, appliances, outdoor furniture, and other products—that advertisers had helped persuade many middle-class Americans to crave.

For many Americans, suburban life also helped provide a sense of community that was sometimes difficult to develop in large, crowded, impersonal urban areas. In later years, the suburbs would come under attack for their supposed conformity, homogeneity, and isolation. But in the 1950s, many people were attracted by the idea of living in a community populated largely by people of similar age and background, and found it easier to form friendships and social circles there than in the city. Women in particular often valued the presence of other nonworking mothers living nearby to share the tasks of child raising.

Another factor motivating white Americans to move to the suburbs was race. There were some African-American suburbs. But most suburbs were restricted to whites—both because relatively few blacks could afford to live in them and because formal and informal barriers kept out even prosperous blacks. In an era when the black population of most cities was rapidly growing, many white families fled to the suburbs to escape the integration of urban neighborhoods and schools.

Suburban neighborhoods had many things in common with one another. But they were not uniform. A famous study of one Levittown revealed a striking variety of occupations, ethnic backgrounds, and incomes there. Still, the Levittowns and inexpensive developments like them ultimately became the homes of mainly lower-middle-class people one step removed from the inner city. Other, more affluent suburbs became enclaves of wealthy families. In virtually every city, a clear hierarchy emerged of upper-class suburban neighborhoods and more modest ones, just as such gradations had emerged years earlier among urban neighborhoods.

LEVITTOWN, NEW YORK, 1954
The mass-produced Levittowns in New York, New Jersey, and elsewhere were one version of the new suburbs that proliferated rapidly after World War II and created what became the dominant way of life for most members of the middle class. *(UPI/Bettmann)*

The Suburban Family

For professional men (who tended to work in the city, at some distance from their homes), suburban life generally meant a rigid division between their working and personal worlds. For many middle-class, married women, it meant an increased isolation from the workplace. The enormous cultural emphasis on family life in the 1950s strengthened popular prejudices against women entering the professions, or occupying any paid job at all. Many middle-class husbands considered it demeaning for their wives to be employed. And many women themselves shied away from the workplace when they could afford to, in part because of prevailing ideas about motherhood that seemed to require women to stay at home full-time with their children.

One of the most influential books in postwar American life was a famous guide to child rearing: Dr. Benjamin Spock's *Baby and Child Care*, first published in 1946 and reissued (and revised) repeatedly for decades thereafter. Dr. Spock's approach to raising babies was child-centered, as opposed to the parent-centered theories of many previous child-care experts. The purpose of motherhood, he taught, was to help children learn and grow and realize their potential. All other considerations, including the mother's own physical and emotional requirements, must be subordinated to the needs of the child. Dr. Spock at first envisioned only a very modest role for fathers in the process of child

rearing, although he changed his views on this (as on many other issues) over time.

Thus, women who could afford not to work faced heavy pressures—both externally and internally imposed—to remain in the home and concentrate on raising their children. Some women, however, had to balance these pressures against other, contradictory ones. As expectations of material comfort rose, many middle-class families needed a second income to maintain the standard of living they desired. As a result, the number of married women working outside the home actually increased in the postwar years—even as the social pressure for them to stay out of the workplace grew. By 1960, nearly a third of all married women were part of the paid work force.

The experiences of the 1950s worked in some ways to diminish the power of feminism, which for a time ebbed to its lowest point in nearly a century. But they also helped create conditions that only a decade later would create the most powerful feminist movement in American history. The increasing numbers of women in the workplace laid the groundwork for demands for equal treatment by employers that became an important part of the feminist crusades of the 1960s and 1970s. Some middle-class women who were not employed became deeply involved in the public world through work in such organizations as the League of Women Voters, the Red Cross, YWCAs, and PTAs, where they gained organizational and political skills that they would later be able to use in more explicitly feminist causes. And the growing frustrations of other women, who remained in the home, heightened the demand for female professional opportunities, a demand that would also soon help fuel the women's liberation movement.

The Birth of Television

Perhaps the most powerful medium of mass communication in history, television was central to the culture of the postwar era. Experiments in broadcasting pictures (along with sound) had begun as early as the 1920s, but commercial television began only shortly after World War II. Its growth was phenomenally rapid. In 1946, there were only 17,000 sets in the country; by 1957, there were 40 million television sets in use—almost as many sets as there were families. More people had television sets, according to one report, than had refrigerators (a statistic strikingly similar to one in the 1920s that had revealed more people owning radios than bathtubs).

The television industry emerged directly out of the radio industry, and all three of the major networks—The National Broadcasting Company, the Columbia Broadcasting System, and the American Broadcasting Company—had started as radio companies. Like radio, the television business was driven by advertising. The need to attract advertisers determined most programming decisions; and in the early days of television, sponsors often played a direct, powerful, and continuing role in determining the content of the programs they chose to sponsor. Many early television shows bore the names of the corporations that were paying for them: the *GE Television Theater*, the *Chrysler Playhouse*, the *Camel News Caravan*, and others. Some daytime serials (known as "soap operas," because their sponsors were almost always companies making household goods targeted at women) were actually written and produced by Procter and Gamble and other companies.

The impact of television on American life was rapid, pervasive, and profound. By the late 1950s, television news had replaced newspapers, magazines, and radios as the nation's most important vehicle of information. Television advertising helped create a vast market for new fashions and products. Televised athletic events gradually made professional and college sports one of the most important sources of entertainment (and one of the biggest businesses) in America. Television entertainment programming—almost all of it controlled by the three national networks and their corporate sponsors—replaced movies and radio as the principal source of diversion for American families.

Much of the programming of the 1950s and early 1960s created a common image of American life—an image that was predominantly white, middle-class, and suburban, and that was epitomized by such popular situation comedies as *Ozzie and Harriet* and *Leave It to Beaver*. Programming also reinforced the concept of gender roles that most men (and many women) unthinkingly embraced. Most situation comedies, in particular, showed families in which, as the title of one of the most popular put it, *Father Knows Best*, and in which most women were mothers and housewives striving to serve their children and please their husbands.

But television also conveyed other images: the gritty, urban working-class families in Jackie Gleason's *The Honeymooners*; the childless show-business family of the early *I Love Lucy*; the unmarried professional women in *Our Miss Brooks* and *My Little Margie*; the hapless African Americans in *Amos 'n Andy*. Television not only sought to create an idealized image of a homogeneous suburban America. It also sought to convey experiences at odds with that image—but to convey them in warm, unthreatening terms, taking social diversity and cultural conflict and domesticating them, turning them into something benign and even comic.

Yet television also, inadvertently, created conditions that could accentuate social conflict. Even those unable to share in the affluence of the era could, through television, acquire a vivid picture of how the rest of their society lived. Thus at the same time that television was reinforcing the homogeneity of the white middle class, it was also contributing to the sense of alienation and powerlessness among groups excluded from the world it portrayed.

Science and Space

In 1961, *Time* magazine chose as its "man of the year" not an individual but "the American Scientist." It was an indication of the widespread fascination with which Americans in the age of atomic weapons viewed science and technology. Major medical advances accounted for much of that fascination. Jonas Salk's vaccine to prevent polio, which the federal government provided free to the public beginning in 1955, virtually eliminated the disease from American life in a few short years. Other dread diseases such as diphtheria and tuberculosis also all but vanished from society (at least for a time) as new drugs and treatments emerged. Infant mortality declined by nearly 50 percent in the twenty-five years after the war; the death rate among young children declined significantly as well (although both such rates were lower in Western Europe). Average life expectancy in those same years rose by five years, to seventy-one.

But Americans were at least equally impressed by other scientific and technological innovations: the jet plane, the computer, synthetics, new types of commercially prepared foods. And nothing better illustrated the nation's veneration of scientific expertise than the popular enthusiasm for the American space program.

The program began in large part because of the Cold War. When the Soviet Union announced in 1957 that it had launched a satellite—*Sputnik*—which was orbiting the earth in outer space, the American government (and much of the public) reacted with alarm, as if the Soviet achievement was also a massive American failure. Strenuous efforts began to improve scientific education in the schools, to develop more research laboratories, and above all to speed the development of America's own exploration of outer space. The centerpiece of that exploration was the manned space program, established in 1958 with the selection of the first American space pilots, or "astronauts," who quickly became the nation's most revered heroes. On May 5, 1961, Alan Shepard became the first American launched into space (several months after a Soviet "cosmonaut," Yuri Gagarin, had made a similar, and longer, flight). On February 2, 1962, John Glenn (later a United States senator) became the first American to orbit the globe (again, only after Gagarin had already done so).

Interest in the space program remained high in the summer of 1969, when Neil Armstrong and Edwin Aldrin became the first men to walk on the surface of the moon. Not long after that, however, the government began to cut the funding for future missions, and popular enthusiasm for the program began to wane. In the late 1970s and 1980s, the National Aeronautics and Space Administration (NASA) managed to revive some of the earlier enthusiasm for space exploration with the development of a reusable "space shuttle," which performed various commercial functions (such as launching communications satellites) as well as research and military ones. Early in 1986, an explosion destroyed one of the shuttles, the *Challenger*, shortly after it took off. Seven astronauts (one of them a school teacher chosen in a national competition) died. The incident sparked a wave of national grief that made clear the degree to which the space program continued to embody some of the nation's most romantic hopes. But the disaster also revealed serious management problems within the program that stalled its further development.

Organized Society and Its Detractors

Large-scale organizations and bureaucracies increased their influence over American life in the postwar era, as they had been doing for many decades before.

White-collar workers came to outnumber blue-collar laborers for the first time, and an increasing proportion of them worked in corporate settings with rigid hierarchical structures. Industrial workers also confronted large bureaucracies, both in the workplace and in their own unions. Consumers discovered the frustrations of bureaucracy in dealing with the large national companies from whom they bought goods and services. More and more Americans were becoming convinced that the key to a successful future lay in acquiring the specialized training and skills necessary for work in large organizations, where every worker performed a particular, well-defined function.

The American educational system responded to the demands of this increasingly organized society by experimenting with changes in curriculum and philosophy. Elementary and secondary schools gave increased attention to the teaching of science, mathematics, and foreign languages—all of which educators considered important for the development of skilled, specialized professionals. The National Defense Education Act of 1958 (passed in response to the Soviet Union's *Sputnik* success) provided federal funding for development of programs in those areas. Universities in the meantime were expanding their curricula to provide more opportunities for students to develop specialized skills. The idea of the "multiversity"—a phrase first coined by the chancellor of the University of California at Berkeley to describe his institution's diversity—represented a commitment to making higher education a training ground for specialists in a wide variety of fields.

As in earlier eras, many Americans reacted to these developments with ambivalence, even hostility. The debilitating impact of bureaucratic life on the individual slowly became a central theme of popular and scholarly debate. William H. Whyte, Jr., produced one of the most widely discussed books of the decade: *The Organization Man* (1956), which attempted to describe the special mentality of the worker in a large, bureaucratic setting. Self-reliance, Whyte claimed, was losing place to the ability to "get along" and "work as a team" as the most valued trait in the modern character. Sociologist David Riesman had made similar observations in *The Lonely Crowd* (1950), in which he argued that the traditional "inner-directed" man, who judged himself on the basis of his own values and the esteem of his family, was giving way to a new "other-directed" man, more concerned with winning the approval of the larger organization or community.

The most derisive critics of bureaucracy, and of middle-class society generally, were a group of young poets, writers, and artists generally known as the "beats" (or, derisively, as "beatniks"). They wrote harsh critiques of what they considered the sterility and conformity of American life, the meaninglessness of American politics, and the banality of popular culture. Allen Ginsberg's dark, bitter poem *Howl* (1955) decried the "Robot apartments! invincible suburbs! skeleton treasuries! blind capitals! demonic industries!" of modern life. Jack Kerouac produced what may have been the bible of the Beat Generation in his novel *On the Road* (1957)—an account of a cross-country automobile trip that depicted the rootless, iconoclastic lifestyle of Kerouac and his friends.

Other, less starkly alienated writers also expressed misgivings in their work about the enormity and impersonality of modern society. Saul Bellow produced a series of novels—*The Adventures of Augie March* (1953), *Seize the Day* (1956), *Herzog* (1964), and others—that chronicled the difficulties American Jewish men had in finding fulfillment in modern urban America. J. D. Salinger wrote in *The Catcher in the Rye* (1951) of a prep-school student, Holden Caulfield, who was unable to find any area of society—school, family, friends, city—in which he could feel secure or committed.

THE "OTHER AMERICA"

It was relatively easy for white, middle-class Americans in the 1950s to believe that the world they knew—a world of economic growth, personal affluence, and cultural homogeneity—was the world virtually all Americans knew; that the values and assumptions they shared were ones that most other Americans shared too. But such assumptions were false. Even within the middle class, there was considerable restiveness—among women, intellectuals, young people, and others who found the middle-class consumer culture somehow unsatisfying, even stultifying. More importantly, large groups of Americans remained outside the circle of abundance and shared in neither the affluence of the middle class nor its values.

On the Margins of the Affluent Society

In 1962, the socialist writer Michael Harrington created a sensation by publishing a book called *The Other America*, in which he chronicled the continuing existence of poverty in America. The conditions he described were not new. Only the attention he was bringing to them was.

The great economic expansion of the postwar years reduced poverty dramatically but did not eliminate it. In 1960, at any given moment, more than a fifth of all American families (over 30 million people) continued to live below what the government defined as the poverty line (down from a third of all families fifteen years before). Many millions more lived just above the official poverty line, but with incomes that gave them little comfort and no security.

Most of the poor experienced poverty intermittently and temporarily. Eighty percent of those classified as poor at any particular moment were likely to have moved into poverty relatively recently and might move out of it again as soon as they found a job—an indication of how unstable employment could be at the lower levels of the job market. But approximately 20 percent of the poor were people for whom poverty was a continuous, debilitating reality, from which there was no easy escape. That included approximately half the nation's elderly and a large proportion of African Americans and Hispanics. Native Americans constituted the single poorest group in the country, a result of government policies that undermined the economies of the reservations and drove many Indians into cities, where some lived in a poverty worse than that they had left.

This "hard-core" poverty rebuked the assumptions of those who argued that economic growth would eventually lead everyone into prosperity; that, as many claimed, "a rising tide lifts all boats." It was a poverty that the growing prosperity of the postwar era seemed to affect hardly at all, a poverty, as Harrington observed, that appeared "impervious to hope."

Rural Poverty

Among those on the margins of the affluent society were many rural Americans. In 1948, farmers had received 8.9 percent of the national income; in 1956, they received only 4.1 percent. In part, this decline reflected the steadily shrinking farm population; in 1956 alone, nearly 10 percent of the rural population moved into or was absorbed by cities. But it also reflected declining farm prices. Because of enormous surpluses in basic staples, prices fell 33 percent in those years, even though national income as a whole rose 50 percent at the same time. Even most farmers who managed to survive experienced substantial losses of income at the same time that the prices of many consumer goods rose.

Not all farmers were poor. Some substantial landowners weathered, and even managed to profit from, the changes in American agriculture. Others moved from considerable to only modest affluence. But the agrarian economy did produce substantial numbers of genuinely impoverished people. Black sharecroppers and tenant farmers continued to live at or below subsistence level throughout the rural South—in part because of the mechanization of cotton picking beginning in 1944, in part because of the development of synthetic fibers that reduced demand for cotton generally. (Two-thirds of the cotton acreage of the South went out of production between 1930 and 1960.) Migrant farmworkers, a group concentrated especially in the West and Southwest and containing many Mexican-American and Asian-American workers, lived in similarly dire circumstances. In rural areas without much commercial agriculture—such as the Appalachian region in the East, where the decline of the coal economy reduced the one significant source of support for the region—whole communities lived in desperate poverty, increasingly cut off from the market economy. All these groups were vulnerable to malnutrition and even starvation.

The Inner Cities

As white families moved from cities to suburbs in vast numbers, more and more inner-city neighborhoods became vast repositories for the poor, "ghettos" from which there was no easy escape. The growth of these neighborhoods owed much to a vast migration of African Americans out of the countryside (where the cotton economy was in decline) and into industrial cities. More than 3 million black men and women moved from the South to northern cities between 1940 and 1960, many more than had made the same journey during the Great Migration during and after World War I. Chicago, Detroit, Cleveland, New York, and other eastern and midwestern industrial cities experienced a great expansion of their black populations—both in absolute numbers and, even more, as a percentage of the whole, since so many whites were leaving at the same time.

Similar migrations from Mexico and Puerto Rico expanded poor Hispanic neighborhoods in many American cities at the same time. Between 1940 and 1960, nearly a million Puerto Ricans moved into American cities (the largest group to New York). Mexican workers crossed the border in Texas and California and swelled the already substantial Latino communities of such cities as San Antonio, Houston, San Diego, and Los Angeles (which by 1960 had the largest Mexican-American population of any city, approximately 500,000 people).

Why these inner-city communities, populated largely by racial and ethnic minorities, remained so poor in the midst of growing affluence has been the subject of considerable, and very heated, debate. Some critics have argued that the new migrants were victims in part of their own pasts, that the work habits, values, and family structures they brought with them from their rural homes were poorly adapted to the needs of

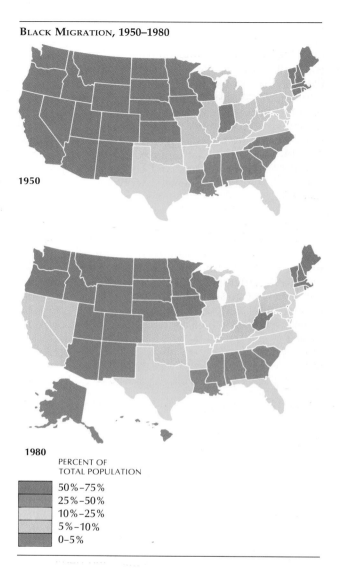

BLACK MIGRATION, 1950–1980

1950

1980

PERCENT OF
TOTAL POPULATION

50%–75%
25%–50%
10%–25%
5%–10%
0–5%

the modern industrial city. Others have argued that the inner city itself—its crippling poverty, its lack of strong educational or service institutions, its crime, its violence, its apparent hopelessness—created a "culture of poverty" that made it more difficult for individuals to advance.

Many others argue that a combination of declining blue-collar jobs, inadequate support for minority-dominated public schools, and barriers to advancement rooted in racism—and not the culture and values of the poor themselves—were the source of inner-city poverty. It is indisputable that inner cities were filling up with poor minority residents at the same time that the unskilled industrial jobs they were seeking were diminishing. Employers were relocating factories and mills from old industrial cities to new locations in suburbs, smaller cities, and even abroad—places where the cost of labor or other things were lower. Even in the factories that remained, automation was reducing the number of unskilled jobs. The economic opportunities that had helped earlier immigrant groups to rise up from poverty were unavailable to most of the postwar migrants. Nor can there be any doubt that historic patterns of racial discrimination in hiring, education, and housing doomed many members of these communities to continuing, and in some cases increasing, poverty.

For many years, the principal policy response to the poverty of inner cities was "urban renewal": the effort to tear down buildings in the poorest and most degraded areas. In the twenty years after World War II, urban renewal projects destroyed over 400,000 buildings, among them the homes of nearly 1.5 million people. In some cases, urban renewal provided new public housing for poor city residents. Some of it was considerably better than the housing they left; some of it was poorly designed and constructed, and deteriorated rapidly into dismal and dangerous slums. Urban renewal was, on the whole, better at eliminating "blights" than at helping the people who lived in them. In many cases, urban renewal projects replaced "slums" with middle- and upper-income housing (part of an often futile attempt to keep middle-class people from leaving), office towers, or commercial buildings; in Los Angeles, a baseball stadium for the Los Angeles Dodgers, recently relocated from Brooklyn, was erected on the site of a Mexican *barrio*.

One result of inner-city poverty was a rising rate of juvenile crime. Indeed, "juvenile delinquency" was one of the few results of poverty that middle-class Americans discussed and worried about with any consistency. A 1955 book, *One Million Delinquents*, called juvenile crime a "national epidemic" and described a troubling subculture of inner-city youth—embittered, rebellious adolescents with no hope of advancement and no sense of having a stake in the structure of their society.

THE RISE OF THE CIVIL RIGHTS MOVEMENT

After decades of skirmishes, an open battle began in the 1950s against racial segregation and discrimination, a battle that would prove to be one of the longest and most difficult of the century. Although white Americans played an important role in the civil-rights movement, pressure from African Americans themselves was the crucial element in raising the issue of race to prominence.

The Brown Decision and "Massive Resistance"

On May 17, 1954, the Supreme Court announced its decision in the case of *Brown v. Board of Education of Topeka*. In considering the legal segregation of a Kansas public school system, the Court rejected its own 1896 *Plessy* v. *Ferguson* decision, which had ruled that communities could provide blacks with separate facilities as long as the facilities were equal to those of whites.

The *Brown* decision was the culmination of many decades of effort by black opponents of segregation, and particularly by a group of talented NAACP lawyers, many of them trained at Howard University in Washington by the great legal educator Charles Houston. Thurgood Marshall, William Hastie, James Nabrit, and others spent years filing legal challenges to segregation in one state after another, nibbling at the edges of the system, and accumulating precedents to support their assault on the "separate but equal" doctrine itself. The same lawyers filed the suits against the school boards of Topeka, Kansas, and several other cities that became the basis for the *Brown* decision.

The Topeka suit involved the case of an African-American girl who had to travel several miles to a segregated public school every day even though she lived virtually next door to a white elementary school. When the case arrived before the Supreme Court, the justices examined it not simply in terms of legal precedent but in terms of history, sociology, and psychology. They concluded that school segregation inflicted unacceptable damage on those it affected, regardless of the relative quality of the separate schools. Chief Justice Earl Warren explained the unanimous opinion of his colleagues: "We conclude that in the field of public education the doctrine of 'separate but equal' has no place. Separate educational facilities are inherently unequal." The following year, the Court issued another decision (known as "*Brown II*") to provide rules for implementing the 1954 order. It ruled that communities must work to desegregate their schools "with all deliberate speed," but it set no timetable and left specific decisions up to lower courts.

In some communities—for example Washington, D.C.—compliance came relatively quickly and quietly. More often, however, strong local opposition (what came to be known in the South as "massive resistance") produced long delays and bitter conflicts. Some school districts ignored the ruling altogether.

Others attempted to circumvent it with purely token efforts to integrate. More than 100 southern members of Congress signed a "manifesto" in 1956 denouncing the *Brown* decision and urging their constituents to defy it. Southern governors, mayors, local school boards, and nongovernmental pressure groups (including hundreds of "White Citizens' Councils") all worked to obstruct desegregation. Many school districts enacted "pupil placement laws" allowing school officials to place students in schools according to their scholastic abilities and social behavior. Such laws were transparent devices for maintaining segregation; but in 1958, the Supreme Court (in *Shuttlesworth* v. *Birmingham Board of Education*) refused to declare them unconstitutional.

By the fall of 1957, only 684 of 3,000 affected school districts in the South had even begun to desegregate their schools. In those that had complied, white resistance often produced angry mob actions and other violence. Many white parents simply withdrew their children from the public schools and enrolled them in all-white "segregation academies"; some state and local governments diverted money from newly integrated public schools and used it to fund the new, all-white academies. The *Brown* decision, far from ending segregation, had launched a prolonged battle between federal authority and state and local governments, and between those who believed in racial equality and those who did not.

The Eisenhower administration was not eager to commit itself to that battle. The president himself had greeted the *Brown* decision with skepticism (and once said it had set back progress on race relations "at least fifteen years"). But in September 1957, he faced a case of direct state defiance of federal authority and felt compelled to act. Federal courts had ordered the desegregation of Central High School in Little Rock, Arkansas. An angry white mob tried to prevent implementation of the order by blockading the entrances to the school, and Governor Orval Faubus refused to do anything to stop the obstruction. President Eisenhower finally responded by federalizing the National Guard and sending troops to Little Rock to restore order and ensure that the court orders would be obeyed. Only then did Central High School admit its first black students.

The Expanding Movement

The *Brown* decision helped spark a growing number of popular challenges to segregation in the South. On December 1, 1955, Rosa Parks, a black woman, was arrested in Montgomery, Alabama, when she refused to give up her seat on a Montgomery bus to a white passenger (as required by the Jim Crow laws that regulated race relations in the city and throughout most of the South). Parks, an active civil rights leader in the community, had apparently decided spontaneously to resist the order to move. Her feet were tired, she later explained. But black leaders in Montgomery had been waiting for such an incident, which they wanted to use to challenge the segregation of the buses. The arrest of this admired woman produced outrage in the city's African-American community and helped local leaders organize a successful boycott of the bus system to demand an end to segregated seating.

The bus boycott owed much of its success to the prior existence of well-organized black citizens' groups. A black women's political caucus had, in fact, been developing plans for a boycott of the segregated buses for some time. They seized on Rosa Parks as a symbol of the movement. Once launched, the boycott was almost completely effective. Black workers who needed to commute to their jobs (of whom the largest group consisted of female domestic servants) formed car pools to ride back and forth to work, or simply walked, even at times over long distances. The boycott put economic pressure not only on the bus company (a private concern) but on many Montgomery merchants. The bus boycotters found it difficult to get to downtown stores and tended to shop instead in their own neighborhoods. Still the boycott might well have failed had it not been for a Supreme Court decision late in 1956, inspired in part by the protest, that declared segregation in public transportation to be illegal. The buses in Montgomery abandoned their discriminatory seating policies, and the boycott came to a close.

More important than the immediate victories of the Montgomery boycott was its success in establishing a new form of racial protest and in elevating to prominence a new figure in the movement for civil rights. The man chosen to head the boycott movement after its launching was a local Baptist pastor, Martin Luther King, Jr., the son of a prominent Atlanta minister, a powerful orator, and a gifted leader. At first King was reluctant to accept responsibility for the movement. But once he accepted the role, he became consumed by it.

King's approach to black protest was based on the doctrine of non-violence—that is, of passive resistance even in the face of direct attack. He drew from the teachings of Mahatma Gandhi, the Indian nationalist leader; from Henry David Thoreau and his doctrine of civil disobedience; and from Christian doctrine. And he produced an approach to racial struggle that captured the moral high ground for his supporters. He urged African Americans to engage in peaceful demon-

ROSA PARKS IN THE FRONT OF THE BUS
In December 1955 Rosa Parks was arrested in Montgomery, Alabama, for refusing to obey a law that required her to give up her seat to a white passenger and move to the back of the bus. Her defiance sparked an almost total boycott of Montgomery's transit system by black citizens. Just over a year later, the U.S. Supreme Court ruled that racial segregation of public transit systems was unconstitutional, and Mrs. Parks proudly posed for photographers sitting near the front of a city bus. *(UPI/Bettmann)*

strations; to allow themselves to be arrested, even beaten, if necessary; and to respond to hate with love. For the next thirteen years—as leader of the Southern Christian Leadership Conference, an interracial group he founded shortly after the bus boycott—he was the most influential and most widely admired black leader in the country. The popular movement he came to represent soon spread throughout the South and throughout the country.

Pressure from the courts, from northern liberals, and from blacks themselves also speeded the pace of racial change in other areas. One important color line had been breached as early as 1947, when the Brooklyn Dodgers signed the great Jackie Robinson as the first black to play major-league baseball. By the mid-1950s, blacks had established themselves as a powerful force in almost all professional sports. Within the government, President Eisenhower completed the integration of the armed forces, attempted to desegregate the federal work force, and in 1957 signed a civil rights act (passed, without active support from the White House, by a Democratic Congress) providing federal protection for blacks who wished to register to vote. It was a weak bill, with few mechanisms for enforcement, but it was the first civil rights bill of any kind to win passage since the end of Reconstruction, and it served as a signal that the executive and leg-islative branches were beginning to join the judiciary in the federal commitment to the "Second Reconstruction."

Causes of the Civil Rights Movement

Why did a civil rights movement begin to emerge at this particular moment? The injustices it challenged and the goals it promoted were hardly new; in theory, African Americans could have launched the same movement fifty or a hundred years earlier, or decades later. Why did they do so in the 1950s and 1960s?

Several factors contributed to the rise of African-American protest in these years. The legacy of World War II was one of the most important. Millions of black men and women had served in the military or worked in war plants during the war and had derived from the experience a broader view of the world, and of their place in it, than they had been able to develop in their relatively isolated lives prior to the 1940s.

Another factor was the growth of an urban black middle class, which had been developing for decades but which began to flourish after the war. Much of the impetus for the civil rights movement came from the leaders of urban black communities—ministers, educators, professionals—and much of it came as well from students at black colleges and universities, which had expanded significantly in the previous decades.

Men and women with education and a stake in society were often more aware of the obstacles to their advancement than poorer and more oppressed people, to whom the possibility of advancement may have seemed too remote even to consider. And urban blacks had considerably more freedom to associate with one another and to develop independent institutions than did rural blacks, who were often under the very direct supervision of white landowners.

Television and other forms of popular culture were another factor in the rising consciousness of racism among blacks. More than any previous generation, postwar blacks had constant, vivid reminders of how the white majority lived—of the world from which they were effectively excluded. Television also conveyed the activities of demonstrators to a national audience, ensuring that activism in one community would inspire similar protests in others.

In addition to the forces that were inspiring African Americans to mobilize, other forces were at work mobilizing many white Americans to support the movement once it began. One was the Cold War, which made racial injustice an embarrassment to Americans trying to present their nation as a model to the world. Another was the political mobilization of northern blacks, who were now a substantial voting bloc within the Democratic Party; politicians from northern industrial states could not ignore their views. Labor unions with substantial black memberships also played an important part in supporting (and funding) the civil rights movement.

This great and largely spontaneous social movement emerged, in short, out of an unpredictable combination of broad social changes and specific local grievances. Whatever its causes, it quickly took on a momentum that, by the early 1960s, had made it one of the most powerful forces in America.

EISENHOWER REPUBLICANISM

Dwight D. Eisenhower was the least experienced politician to serve in the White House in the twentieth century. He was also among the most politically successful presidents of the postwar era. At home, he pursued essentially moderate policies, avoiding most new initiatives but accepting the work of earlier reformers. Abroad, he continued and even intensified American commitments to oppose communism, but brought to some of those commitments a measure of restraint that his successors did not always match.

"What's Good for . . . General Motors"

The first Republican administration in twenty years was staffed mostly with men drawn from the same quarter as those who had staffed Republican administrations in the 1920s: the business community. But by the 1950s much of the American business community had acquired a very different social and political outlook from that of their predecessors of earlier decades. Above all, many of the nation's leading businessmen and financiers had reconciled themselves to at least the broad outlines of the Keynesian welfare state the New Deal had launched and, indeed, had come to see it as something that actually benefited them—by helping maintain social order, by increasing mass purchasing power, and by stabilizing labor relations.

To his cabinet, Eisenhower appointed wealthy corporate lawyers and business executives, who were not apologetic about their backgrounds—"eight millionaires and a plumber," the liberal *New Republic* magazine caustically remarked. (The plumber was Secretary of Labor Martin Durkin, president of the plumbers' union, who soon resigned.) Charles Wilson, president of General Motors, assured senators considering his nomination to be secretary of defense that he foresaw no conflict of interest because he was certain that "what was good for our country was good for General Motors, and vice versa." Missing from most members of this business-oriented administration was the deep hostility to "government interference" that had so dominated corporate attitudes three decades before.

Eisenhower's leadership style, which stressed delegation of authority to subordinates, helped enhance the power of his cabinet officers and others. Secretary of State John Foster Dulles was widely believed to be running American foreign policy almost single-handedly (although it has since become clear that the president was far more deeply involved in international decisions than was often apparent at the time). The White House chief of staff, former New Hampshire governor Sherman Adams, exercised broad authority over relations with Congress and strictly controlled access to the president—until he left office in disgrace, near the end of Eisenhower's presidency, after he was discovered to have accepted gifts from a wealthy businessman.

Eisenhower's consistent inclination was to limit federal activities and encourage private enterprise. He supported the private rather than public development of natural resources (and once talked about selling the Tennessee Valley Authority to a private company). To the chagrin of farmers, he lowered federal support for farm prices. He also removed the last limited wage and price controls maintained by the Truman administration. He opposed the creation of new social service programs such as national health insurance and strove constantly to reduce federal expenditures (even during the recession of 1958) and to balance the budget. He ended 1960, his last full year in office, with a $1 billion surplus.

The Survival of Social Welfare

The president took few new initiatives in domestic policy. But he resisted pressure from the right wing of his party and refused to dismantle those welfare policies of the New Deal that had survived the conservative assaults of the war years and after. Indeed, during his term, he agreed to extend the Social Security system to an additional 10 million people and unemployment compensation to an additional 4 million people; and he agreed to increase the minimum hourly wage from 75 cents to $1. Perhaps the most significant legislative accomplishment of the Eisenhower administration was the Federal Highway Act of 1956, which authorized $25 billion for a ten-year effort to construct over

40,000 miles of interstate highways. The program was to be funded through a highway "trust fund," whose revenues would come from new taxes on the purchase of fuel, automobiles, trucks, and tires.

In 1956, Eisenhower ran for a second term, even though he had suffered a serious heart attack the previous year. With Adlai Stevenson opposing him once again, he won by another, even greater landslide, receiving nearly 57 percent of the popular vote and 442 electoral votes to Stevenson's 89. Still, Democrats retained the control of both houses of Congress they had won back in 1954. And in 1958—during a serious recession—they increased that control by substantial margins.

The Decline of McCarthyism

In its first years in office the Eisenhower administration did little to discourage the anticommunist furor that had gripped the nation. Indeed, in many ways it helped sustain it. The president intensified the search for subversives in the government which Truman had begun several years earlier. More than 2,220 federal

THE ARMY-MCCARTHY HEARINGS
Senator Joseph McCarthy uses a map to show the supposed distribution of communists throughout the United States during the televised 1954 Senate hearings to mediate the dispute between McCarthy and the U.S. Army. Joseph Welch, chief counsel for the army, remains conspicuously unimpressed. *(UPI/Bettmann)*

employees resigned or were dismissed as a result of security investigations. Among them were most of the leading Asian experts in the State Department, many of whom were harried from office because they had shown inadequate enthusiasm for the now-exiled regime of Chiang Kai-shek.

Among the most celebrated controversies of the new administration's first year was the case of J. Robert Oppenheimer, director of the Manhattan Project during the war and one of the nation's most distinguished and admired physicists. Although Oppenheimer was now out of government service, he continued as a consultant to the Atomic Energy Commission. But he had angered some officials by his public opposition to development of the new, more powerful hydrogen bomb, which Truman had approved toward the end of his presidency. In 1953, the FBI distributed a dossier within the administration detailing Oppenheimer's prewar association with various left-wing groups. The president responded by ordering a "blank wall" to be placed between Oppenheimer and government secrets. A federal investigation, requested by Oppenheimer himself and conducted in an inflamed and confused atmosphere, revealed no evidence of disloyalty but nevertheless confirmed the decision to deny him a security clearance.

But by 1954, such policies were beginning to produce significant popular opposition—an indication that the anticommunist passions of several years earlier were beginning to abate. The clearest signal of that change was the political demise of Senator Joseph McCarthy.

During the first year of the Eisenhower administration, McCarthy continued to operate with impunity. The president, who privately loathed him, refused to speak out against him in public. Relatively few others —in the political world or in the press—were any more courageous. But McCarthy finally overreached himself in January 1954 when he attacked Secretary of the Army Robert Stevens and the armed services in general. At that point, the administration and influential members of Congress organized a special investigation of the charges, which became known as the Army-McCarthy hearings. They were among the first congressional hearings to be nationally televised.

The result was devastating to McCarthy. Watching McCarthy in action—bullying witnesses, hurling groundless (and often cruel) accusations, evading issues—much of the public began to see him as a villain, even a buffoon. In December 1954, the Senate voted 67 to 22 to condemn him for "conduct unbecoming a senator." Three years later, with little public support left, he died—a victim, apparently, of complications arising from alcoholism.

EISENHOWER, DULLES, AND THE COLD WAR

The threat of nuclear war with the Soviet Union created a sense of high anxiety in international relations in the 1950s. But the nuclear threat had another effect as well. With the potential costs of war now so enormous, both superpowers began to edge away from direct confrontations. The attention of both the United States and the Soviet Union began to turn to the rapidly escalating instability in the nations of the Third World.

Dulles and "Massive Retaliation"

Eisenhower's secretary of state, and (except for the president himself) the dominant figure in the nation's foreign policy in the 1950s, was John Foster Dulles, an aristocratic corporate lawyer with a stern moral revulsion to communism. He entered office denouncing the containment policies of the Truman years as excessively passive, arguing that the United States should pursue an active program of "liberation," which would lead to a "rollback" of communist expansion. Once in power, however, Dulles had to defer to the far more moderate views of the president himself, and he began to develop a new set of doctrines that reflected the impact of nuclear weapons on the world.

The most prominent of those doctrines was the policy of "massive retaliation," which Dulles announced early in 1954. The United States would, he explained, respond to communist threats to its allies not by using conventional forces in local conflicts (a policy that had led to so much frustration in Korea) but by relying on "the deterrent of massive retaliatory power" (by which he clearly meant nuclear weapons).

In part, the new doctrine reflected Dulles's inclination for tense confrontations, an approach he once defined as "brinksmanship"—pushing the Soviet Union to the brink of war in order to exact concessions. But the real force behind the massive-retaliation policy was economics. With pressure growing both in and out of government for a reduction in American military expenditures, an increasing reliance on atomic weapons seemed to promise, as some advocates put it, "more bang for the buck."

At the same time, Dulles intensified the efforts of Truman and Acheson before him to "integrate" the entire noncommunist world into a system of mutual defense pacts modeled on NATO. The new alliances were, without exception, far weaker than the European pact. By the end of the decade, the United States had become a party to almost a dozen such treaties in all areas of the world.

Korea and Vietnam

The most troubling foreign policy concern of the Truman years—the war in Korea—plagued the Eisenhower administration only briefly. On July 27, 1953, negotiators at Panmunjom finally signed an agreement ending the hostilities. Each antagonist was to withdraw its troops a mile and a half from the existing battle line, which ran roughly along the 38th parallel, the prewar border between North and South Korea. A conference in Geneva was to consider means by which to reunite the nation peacefully—although in fact the 1954 meeting produced no agreement and left the cease-fire line as the apparently permanent border between the two countries.

Almost simultaneously, however, the United States faced a difficult choice in Southeast Asia, where France was fighting to retain control of its onetime colony Vietnam. Opposing the French were the powerful nationalist forces of Ho Chi Minh (who was both a committed nationalist and a committed communist), which were determined to win independence for their nation. The Truman administration had supported the French, one of America's most important Cold War allies, and at first the Eisenhower administration did the same.

Early in 1954, however, 12,000 French troops became surrounded in a disastrous siege at the city of Dien Bien Phu. Only American intervention, it was clear, could prevent the total collapse of the French military effort. Yet despite the urgings of Secretary of State Dulles, Vice President Nixon, and others, Eisenhower refused to permit direct American military intervention in Vietnam, claiming that neither Congress nor America's other allies would support such action. Without American aid, the French defense of Dien Bien Phu finally collapsed on May 7, 1954; and France quickly agreed to a settlement of the conflict at a conference in Geneva that summer—the same conference that was considering the settlement of the Korean War. The agreement marked the end of the French commitment to Vietnam and the beginning of an expanded

EISENHOWER AND DULLES
Although President Eisenhower himself was a somewhat colorless television personality, his was the first administration to make extensive use of the new medium to promote its policies and dramatize its actions. The president's press conferences were frequently televised, and on several occasions Secretary of State John Foster Dulles reported to the president in front of the cameras. Dulles is shown here in the Oval Office on May 17, 1955, reporting on the occasion of his return from Europe, where he had signed the treaty restoring sovereignty to Austria. *(AP/Wide World Photos)*

American presence there. (See pp. 834–838 for a more detailed account of the early history of the Vietnam War.)

Israel and the Crises of the Middle East

The establishment of a Jewish state in Palestine had been the dream of a powerful international Zionist movement for more than half a century before World War II. The plight of the homeless Jews uprooted by the war, and the international horror at exposure of the full extent of the Holocaust, gave new strength to Zionist demands in the late 1940s. So did the enormous immigration of European Jews into Palestine after 1945, despite the efforts of Britain (which had governed the region since World War I) to limit them.

THE STATE OF ISRAEL
The prime minister of Israel, David Ben-Gurion, watches the departure of the last British troops from Palestine shortly after the United Nations approved (and the United States recognized) the existence of a new Jewish state in part of the region.   *(UPI/Bettmann)*

Finally, Britain brought the problem to the United Nations, which responded by recommending the partition of Palestine into a Jewish state and an Arab state. On May 14, 1948, British rule ended, and Jews proclaimed the existence of the nation of Israel. President Truman recognized the new government the following day. But the creation of Israel, while it resolved some conflicts, created others. Palestinian Arabs, unwilling to accept being displaced from what they considered their own country, rejected the partition and fought determinedly, if unsuccessfully, against the new state in 1948—the first of several Arab-Israeli wars.

Its support of Israel notwithstanding, America was deeply concerned about the stability and friendliness of the Arab regimes in the area. The reason was simple: the region contained the richest oil reserves in the world, reserves in which American companies had already invested heavily, and on which the health of the American (and world) economy would ultimately come to depend. Thus the United States reacted with alarm as it watched Mohammed Mossadegh, the nationalist prime minister of Iran, begin to resist the presence of Western corporations in his nation in the early 1950s. In 1953, the American CIA joined forces with conservative Iranian military leaders to engineer a coup that drove Mossadegh from office. To replace him, the CIA helped elevate the young Shah of Iran, Mohammed Reza Pahlavi, from his position as token constitutional monarch to that of virtually absolute ruler. The Shah remained closely tied to the United States for the next twenty-five years.

American policy was less effective in dealing with the nationalist government of Egypt, under the leadership of General Gamal Abdel Nasser, which in the early 1950s began to develop a trade relationship with the Soviet Union. In 1956, to punish Nasser for his friendliness toward the communists, Dulles withdrew American offers to assist in building the great Aswan Dam across the Nile. A week later, Nasser retaliated by seizing control of the Suez Canal from the British, saying that he would use the income from it to build the dam himself. The repercussions of that seizure were quick and profound.

On October 29, 1956, Israeli forces struck a preemptive blow against Egypt. The next day the British and French landed troops in the Suez to drive the Egyptians from the canal. Dulles and Eisenhower feared that the Suez crisis would drive the Arab states toward the Soviet Union and precipitate a new world war. By refusing to support the invasion, and by joining in a United Nations denunciation of it, the United States helped pressure the French and British to withdraw and helped persuade Israel to agree to a truce with Egypt.

Nasser's continuing flirtation with the Soviet

S. ll.

Union, which offered to assist in building the Aswan Dam once the United States withdrew from the project, strengthened American resolve to resist the growth of communist influence in the Middle East. It also increased the tendency of American officials to equate Arab nationalism with communism. In 1958, as pan-Arab forces loyal to Nasser challenged the government of Lebanon, Eisenhower ordered 5,000 American marines to land on the beaches of Beirut to protect the existing regime; British troops entered Jordan at about the same time to resist a similar threat there. The effect of the interventions was negligible. The governments of both countries managed to stabilize their positions on their own, and within months both the American and British forces withdrew.

Latin America and "Yankee Imperialism"

World War II and the Cold War had eroded the limited initiatives of the Good Neighbor Policy toward Latin America, as American economic aid now flowed increasingly to Europe. Latin American animosity toward the United States grew steadily during the 1950s, as more people in the region came to view the expanding influence of American corporations in their countries as a form of imperialism. Such concerns deepened in 1954, when the Eisenhower administration ordered the CIA to help topple the new, leftist government of Jacobo Arbenz Guzman in Guatemala, a regime that Dulles (responding to the entreaties of the United Fruit Company, a major investor in Guatemala fearful of Arbenz) argued was potentially communist. Four years later, the depths of anti-American sentiment became clear when Vice President Richard Nixon visited the region and was greeted in city after city by angry, hostile, occasionally dangerous mobs.

No nation in the region had been more closely tied to America than Cuba. Its leader, Fulgencio Batista, had ruled as a military dictator since 1952, when with American assistance he had toppled a more moderate government. Cuba's relatively prosperous economy had become a virtual fiefdom of American corporations, which controlled almost all the island's natural resources and had cornered over half the vital sugar crop, and of American organized crime, which controlled much of the lucrative tourist industry. Beginning in 1957, a popular movement of resistance to the Batista regime began to gather power under the leadership of Fidel Castro. By late 1958, the Batista forces were in almost total disarray. And on January 1, 1959, with Batista now in exile in Spain, Castro marched into Havana and established a new government.

At first, the American government reacted warmly to Castro, relieved to be rid of the corrupt and inef-

CASTRO IN MOSCOW, 1963
Fidel Castro, premier of Cuba since the 1959 revolution there, visited Moscow in 1963 to receive public assurances from Soviet premier Khrushchev that the USSR would come to his aid if the United States were to invade the islands again. Khrushchev announced that any American attack on Cuba would be treated as if it were an attack on the Soviet Union. Part of the settlement of the Cuban missile crisis the previous fall involved an American promise not to launch such an attack. *(UPI/Bettmann)*

fective Batista and hopeful that Castro would be a moderate, democratic reformer who would allow American economic activity to continue in Cuba unchallenged. But once Castro began implementing significant land reforms and expropriating foreign-owned businesses and resources, Cuban-American relations rapidly deteriorated. Of particular concern to Eisenhower and Dulles was the Cuban regime's growing interest in communist ideas and tactics. When Castro began accepting assistance from the Soviet Union in 1960, the United States cut back the "quota" by which Cuba could export sugar to America at a favored price. Early in 1961, as one of its last acts, the Eisenhower administration severed diplomatic relations with Castro. The American CIA had already begun secretly training Cuban expatriates for an invasion of the island to topple the new regime. Isolated by the United States, Castro soon cemented an alliance with the Soviet Union.

Europe and the Soviet Union

Although the problems of the Third World were moving slowly to the center of American foreign policy, the direct relationship with the Soviet Union and the effort to resist communist expansion in Europe remained the principal concerns of the Eisenhower administration.

Even as the United States was strengthening NATO and rearming West Germany, however, many Americans continued to hope for negotiated solutions to some of the remaining problems dividing the superpowers. Such hopes grew after the death of Josef Stalin in 1953, especially when the Soviet Union extended a peace overture to the rebellious Tito government in Yugoslavia, returned a military base to Finland, signed a peace treaty with Japan, and ended its long military occupation of Austria by allowing that nation to become an independent, neutral state. In 1955, Eisenhower and other NATO leaders met with the Soviet premier, Nikolai Bulganin, at a cordial summit conference in Geneva. But when a subsequent conference of foreign ministers met to try to resolve specific issues, they could find no basis for agreement.

Relations between the Soviet Union and the West soured further in 1956 in response to the Hungarian Revolution. Inspired by riots in Poland a year earlier, Hungarian dissidents had launched a popular uprising in November 1956 to demand democratic reforms. For several days, they had control of the Hungarian government. But before the month was out, Soviet tanks and troops entered Budapest to crush the uprising and restore an orthodox, pro-Soviet regime. The Eisenhower administration refused to intervene. But the suppression of the uprising convinced many American leaders that Soviet policies had not softened as much as the events of the previous two years had suggested.

The failure of conciliation brought renewed vigor to the Cold War and, among other things, greatly intensified the Soviet-American arms race. Both nations engaged in extensive nuclear testing. Both nations redoubled efforts to develop effective intercontinental ballistic missiles, which could deliver atomic warheads directly from one continent to another. The American military, in the meantime, developed a new breed of atomic-powered submarines, capable of launching missiles from under water anywhere in the world.

The arms race not only increased tensions between the United States and Russia; it increased tensions within each nation as well. In America, public concern about nuclear war was becoming a pervasive national nightmare, a preoccupation never far from popular thought. Movies, television programs, books, popular songs—all expressed the concern. Fear of communism, therefore, combined with fear of atomic war to create a persistent national anxiety.

The U-2 Crisis

In this tense and fearful atmosphere, the Soviet Union raised new challenges to the West in Berlin. The continuing existence of an anticommunist West Berlin inside communist East Germany remained an irritant and embarrassment to the Soviets. In November 1958, Nikita Khrushchev, who had succeeded Bulganin as Soviet premier and Communist Party chief earlier that year, renewed his predecessors' demands that the NATO powers abandon the city. The United States and its allies refused.

Khrushchev declined to force the issue. Instead, he suggested that he and Eisenhower discuss the issue personally, both in visits to each other's countries and at a summit meeting in Paris in 1960. The United States agreed. Khrushchev's 1959 visit to America produced a cool but polite response, and plans proceeded for the summit conference and for Eisenhower's visit to Moscow shortly thereafter. Only days before the scheduled beginning of the Paris meeting, however, the Soviet Union announced that it had shot down an American U-2, a high-altitude spy plane, over Russian territory. Its pilot, Francis Gary Powers, was in captivity. The Eisenhower administration responded clumsily, at first denying the allegations and then, when confronted with proof of them, awkwardly admitting that they were true. Khrushchev lashed back angrily, breaking up the Paris summit almost before it could begin and withdrawing his invitation to Eisenhower to visit the Soviet Union. But the U-2 incident was probably only a pretext. By the spring of 1960, Khrushchev—under heavy pressure from hardliners within his own government—knew that no agreement was possible on the Berlin issue; the U-2 incident may simply have been an excuse to avoid what he believed would be fruitless negotiations.

The events of 1960 provided a somber backdrop for the end of the Eisenhower administration. After eight years in office, Eisenhower had failed to eliminate the tensions between the United States and the Soviet Union. He had failed to end the costly and dangerous armaments race. And he had presided over a transformation of the Cold War from a relatively limited confrontation with the Soviet Union in Europe to a global effort to resist communist subversion. Yet Eisenhower had brought to these matters his own sense of the limits of American power. He had resisted military intervention in Vietnam. And he had placed a measure of restraint on those who urged the creation of an enormous American military establishment, warning in his farewell address in January 1961 of the "unwarranted influence" of a vast "military-industrial complex." His caution, in both domestic and international affairs, stood in marked contrast to the attitudes of his successors, who argued that the United States must act more boldly and aggressively on behalf of its goals at home and abroad.

SIGNIFICANT EVENTS

1946 Dr. Benjamin Spock publishes *Baby and Child Care*

1947 Jackie Robinson becomes first black to play in major leagues

Construction begins on Levittown, New York

1948 UAW and General Motors agree to automatic cost-of-living increases for auto workers

United Nations votes to partition Palestine and create state of Israel

1950 David Riesman publishes *The Lonely Crowd*

1951 J. D. Salinger publishes *The Catcher in the Rye*

1952 Eisenhower elected president

1953 Economic recession begins

Saul Bellow publishes *The Adventures of Augie March*

Department of Health, Education, and Welfare established

Earl Warren becomes chief justice

Truce ends Korean War

CIA helps engineer coup in Iran

Oppenheimer denied security clearance

Stalin dies

1954 Supreme Court rules on *Brown* v. *Board of Education*

Democrats regain control of Congress

Army-McCarthy hearings; Senate censures McCarthy

France surrenders at Dien Bien Phu; Geneva agreement partitions Vietnam

United States helps topple Arbenz regime in Guatemala

1955 Labor organizations reconcile and form AFL-CIO

Supreme Court Announces *"Brown II"* decision

Montgomery bus boycott begins

Ngo Dinh Diem becomes president of South Vietnam

Eisenhower and Bulganin meet in Geneva

1956 Federal Highway Act passed

Eisenhower reelected president

Suez crisis

Hungarian revolution crushed

1957 Postwar baby boom peaks

Economic recession begins

Labor racketeering investigations focus on Teamsters

Soviet Union launches *Sputnik*

Jack Kerouac publishes *On the Road*

Little Rock school desegregation crisis

Civil rights act passed

Germany joins NATO

1958 American manned space program founded

National Defense Education Act passed

American marines land in Lebanon

1959 Castro seizes power in Cuba

Nikita Khrushchev visits United States

1960 U-2 incident precedes collapse of Paris summit

1961 Yuri Gagarin of Soviet Union becomes first man in space

Alan Shepard becomes first American in space

United States breaks diplomatic relations with Cuba

Eisenhower gives farewell address

1962 Michael Harrington publishes *The Other America*

1969 Americans land on moon

UMW president "Jock" Yablonski murdered

SUGGESTED READINGS

General Studies. John Brooks, *The Great Leap* (1966). William Chafe, *The Unfinished Journey* (1986). Carl Degler, *Affluence and Anxiety* (1968). John P. Diggins, *The Proud Decades* (1989). Eric Goldman, *The Crucial Decade and After* (1960). David Halberstam, *The Fifties* (1993). Godfrey Hodgson, *America in Our Time* (1976). William Leuchtenburg, *A Troubled Feast* (1979). Douglas T. Miller and Marion Novak, *The Fifties* (1977). William O'Neill, *American High* (1986).

The Postwar Economy. David P. Calleo, *The Imperious Economy* (1982). Gilbert C. Fite, *American Farmers* (1981). John K. Galbraith, *The Affluent Society* (1958); *The New Industrial State* (1967). Mark I. Gelfand, *A Nation of Cities* (1975). Robert Heilbroner, *The Limits of American Capitalism* (1965). John Hutchinson, *The Imperfect Union* (1970). C. Wright Mills, *The Power Elite* (1956). Loren J. Okroi, *Galbraith, Harrington, Heilbroner* (1986). Joel Seidman, *American Labor from Defense to Reconversion* (1953). Harold G. Vatter, *The U.S. Economy in the 1950s* (1963).

Culture and Ideas. Daniel Bell, *The End of Ideology* (1960); ed., *the Radical Right* (1963). Peter Biskind, *Seeing is Believing: How Hollywood Taught Us to Stop Worrying and Love the Fifties* (1983). Paul Boyer, *By the Bomb's Early Light* (1986). Howard Brick, *Daniel Bell and the Decline of Intellectual Radicalism* (1986). Paul A. Carter, *Another Part of the Fifties* (1983). Ann Charters, *Kerouac* (1973). Bruce Cook, *The Beat Generation* (1971). Edward J. Epstein, *News from Nowhere* (1973). Herbert Gans, *The Levittowners* (1967). William Graebner, *The Age of Doubt: American Thought and Culture in the 1940s* (1991). David Halberstam, *The Powers That Be* (1979). Jeffrey Hart, *When the Going Was Good: American Life in the Fifties* (1982). Dolores Hayden, *Redesigning the American Dream* (1984). Kenneth T. Jackson, *The Crabgrass Frontier: The Suburbanization of the United States* (1985). Marty Jezer, *The Dark Ages: Life in the U.S. 1945–1960* (1982). Landon Y. Jones, *Great Expectations: America and the Baby Boom Generation* (1980). Neil Jumonville, *Critical Crossings: The New York Intellectuals in Postwar America* (1991). George Lipsitz, *Class and Culture in Cold War America* (1981). Mary Sperling McAuliffe, *Crisis on the Left* (1978). Walter A. McDougall, *. . . the Heavens and the Earth: A Political History of the Space Age* (1985). Dennis McNally, *Desolate Angel* (1979). Margaret Marsh, *Suburban Lives* (1990). Douglas T. Miller and Marion Novak, *The Fifties* (1977). Zane L. Miller, *Suburb: Neighborhood and Community in Forest Park, Ohio, 1935–1976* (1981). C. Wright Mills, *White Collar* (1956). Richard H. Pells, *The Liberal Mind in a Conservative Age: American Intellectuals in the 1940s and 1950s* (1985). David Potter, *People of Plenty* (1954). David Riesman, *The Lonely Crowd* (1950). Leila Rupp and Verta Taylor, *Survival in the Doldrums* (1987). Arthur M. Schlesinger, Jr., *The Vital Center* (1949). Lynn Spigel, *Make Room for TV* (1992). Walter Sullivan, ed., *America's Race for the Moon* (1962). John Tytell, *Naked Angels* (1976). Alan M. Wald, *The New York Intellectuals* (1987). Stephen J. Whitfield, *The Culture of the Cold War* (1991). William Whyte, *The Organization Man* (1956). Tom Wolfe, *The Right Stuff* (1979).

Gwendolyn Wright, *Building the American Dream: A Social History of Housing in America* (1981).

Women and Families. William Chafe, *The American Woman: Her Changing Social, Economic, and Political Roles, 1920–1970*, rev. ed. (1988). Ruth Cowan, *More Work for Mother: The Irony of Household Technology* (1983). Eugenia Kaledin, *Mothers and More: American Women in the 1950s* (1984). Susan Estabrook Kennedy, *If All We Did Was to Weep at Home: A History of White Working-Class Women in America* (1979). Alice Kessler-Harris, *Out to Work: A History of Wage-Earning Women in the United States* (1982). Elaine Tyler May, *Homeward Bound: American Families in the Cold War* (1988). Susan Strasser, *Never Done: A History of American Housework* (1982).

Politics in the Eisenhower Years. Sherman Adams, *Firsthand Report* (1961). Charles C. Alexander, *Holding the Line* (1975). Stephen Ambrose, *Eisenhower the President* (1984). Brian Balogh, *Chain Reaction: Expert Debate and Public Participation in American Nuclear Commercial Power, 1945–1975* (1991). Piers Brendon, *Ike* (1986). Jeff Broadwater, *Eisenhower and the Anti-Communist Crusade* (1992). Robert F. Burk, *Dwight D. Eisenhower* (1986). Barbara B. Clowse, *Brainpower for the Cold War: The Sputnik Crisis and the National Defense Education Act of 1958* (1981). Dwight D. Eisenhower, *The White House Years*, 2 vols. (1963–1965). Fred Greenstein, *The Hidden-hand Presidency* (1982). Emmet John Hughes, *The Ordeal of Power* (1963). Peter Lyon, *Eisenhower: Portrait of a Hero* (1974). Richard Nixon, *Six Crises* (1962). Herbert S. Parmet, *Eisenhower and the American Crusades* (1972). Nicol C. Rae, *The Decline and Fall of the Liberal Republicans* (1989). Gary Reichard, *The Reaffirmation of Republicanism* (1975); *Politics as Usual* (1988). David W. Reinhard, *The Republican Right Since 1945* (1983). Elmo Richardson, *The Presidency of Dwight D. Eisenower* (1979). Mark H. Rose, *Interstate: Express Highway Politics, 1941–1956* (1979). R. L. Rosholt, *An Administrative History of NASA* (1966).

Foreign Policy. Stephen Ambrose, *Ike's Spies* (1981). David L. Anderson, *Trapped by Success: The Eisenhower Administration and Vietnam, 1953–1961* (1991). Howard Ball, *Justice Downwind: America's Nuclear Testing Program in the 1950s* (1986). Michael Beschloss, *MAYDAY* (1986). Henry W. Brands, *Cold Warriors* (1988); *The Specter of Neutralism: The United States and the Emergence of the Third World, 1947–1960* (1989). Blanche W. Cooke, *The Declassified Eisenhower* (1981). Chester Cooper, *Lost Crusade* (1970); *The Lion's Last Roar* (1978). Cecil Currey, *Edward Lansdale: The Unquiet American* (1988). Robert A. Divine, *Foreign Policy and U.S. Presidential Elections*, 2 vols. (1974); *Blowing in the Wind: The Nuclear Test Ban Debate, 1954–1960* (1978); *Eisenhower and the Cold War* (1981). Frances Fitzgerald, *Fire in the Lake* (1972). Steven Z. Freiberger, *Dawn over Suez: The Rise of American Power in the Middle East, 1953–1957* (1992). Louis Gerson, *John Foster Dulles* (1967). Gregg Herken, *Counsels of War* (1985). George Herring, *America's Longest War* (1979). Richard G. Hewlett and Jack M. Hall,

Atoms for Peace and War, 1953–1961 (1989). Townsend Hoopes, *The Devil and John Foster Dulles* (1973). Richard Immerman, *The CIA in Guatemala* (1982). Burton Kaufman, *The Oil Cartel Case* (1978). Gabriel Kolko, *Confronting the Third World* (1988). Walter LaFeber, *Inevitable Revolutions* (1983). John T. McAlister, Jr., *Vietnam: The Origins of Revolution* (1969). Richard A. Melanson and David A. Mayers, ed., *Reevaluating Eisenhower* (1986). Stephen G. Rabe, *Eisenhower and Latin America* (1988). Kermit Roosevelt, *Counter-coup* (1980). Andrew Rotter, *The Path to Vietnam* (1987). Richard Smoke, *National Security and the Nuclear Dilemma* (1988). Hugh Thomas, *Suez* (1967). Mira Wilkins, *The Maturing of Multinational Enterprise* (1974).

Legal and Constitutional Issues. Alexander Bickel, *Politics and the Warren Court* (1965); *The Supreme Court and the Idea of Progress* (1970). Phillip Kurland, *Politics, the Constitution, and the Warren Court* (1970). Paul Murphy, *The Constitution in Crisis Times* (1972). Bernard Schwartz, *Super Chief: Earl Warren and His Supreme Court* (1983). Philip Stern, *The Oppenheimer Case* (1969). Michael Straight, *Trial by Television* (1954). John Weaver, *Earl Warren* (1967).

Civil Rights. John W. Anderson, *Eisenhower, Brownell, and the Congress* (1964). Numan V. Bartley, *The Rise of Massive Resistance* (1969). Taylor Branch, *Parting the Waters* (1988). Robert F. Burk, *The Eisenhower Administration and Black Civil Rights* (1984). William Chafe, *Civilities and Civil Rights* (1980).

David Garrow, ed., *The Montgomery Bus Boycott and the Women Who Started It: A Memoir of Jo Ann Gibson Robinson* (1987); *Bearing the Cross* (1986). Elizabeth Huckaby, *Crisis at Central High* (1980). Martin Luther King, Jr., *Stride Toward Freedom* (1958). Richard H. King, *Civil Rights and the Idea of Freedom* (1992). Richard Kluger, *Simple Justice* (1975). Steven Lawson, *Running for Freedom* (1991). Anthony Lewis, *Portrait of a Decade* (1964). Robert J. Norrell, *Reaping the Whirlwind: The Civil Rights Movement in Tuskegee* (1985). Howell Raines, *My Soul Is Rested* (1977). Harvard Sitkoff, *The Struggle for Black Equality, 1954–1980* (1981). Abigail Thernstrom, *Whose Votes Count? Affirmative Action and Minority Voting Rights* (1987). Nancy J. Weiss, *Whitney M. Young, Jr., and the Struggle for Civil Rights* (1989).

Minorities and the Poor. Rodolfo Acuña, *Occupied America: A History of Chicanos* (1981). Larry W. Burt, *Tribalism in Crisis: Federal Indian Policy, 1953–1961* (1982). Donald Fixico, *Termination and Relocation: Federal Indian Policy, 1945–1970* (1986). J. Wayne Flint, *Dixie's Forgotten People: The South's Poor Whites* (1979). Michael Harrington, *The Other America* (1962). Jacqueline Jones, *The Dispossessed: America's Underclasses from the Civil War to the Present* (1992). Nicholas Lemann, *The Promised Land: The Great Black Migration and How It Changed America* (1991). Elena Padilla, *Up from Puerto Rico* (1958). Linda Reed, *Simple Decency and Common Sense* (1992).

"In Country"
This grim 1968 photograph of an American G.I. conveys something of the unhappy character of the nation's military experience in Vietnam. Soldiers serving "in country" (as assignment to Vietnam itself was called) experienced both physical hardship, as they patrolled difficult and unfamiliar territory, and the demoralization of fighting in a confusing, frustrating, and ultimately unsuccessful war. *(John Olson/Black Star)*

CHAPTER THIRTY-ONE

THE ORDEAL OF LIBERALISM

B Y THE LATE 1950s, a growing restlessness was becoming apparent beneath the placid surface of American society. Anxiety about America's position in the world, growing pressures from African Americans and other minorities, the increasing visibility of poverty, the rising frustrations of women, and other long-suppressed discontents were beginning to make themselves felt in the nation's public life. Ultimately, that restlessness would make the 1960s one of the most turbulent eras of the twentieth century. But at first, it contributed to a bold and confident effort by political leaders to attack social and international problems within the framework of conventional liberal politics.

EXPANDING THE LIBERAL STATE

Those who yearned for a more active government in the late 1950s, and who accused the Eisenhower administration of allowing the nation to "drift," looked above all to the presidency for leadership. The political scientist Richard Neustadt, for example, published an influential book in 1960 entitled *Presidential Power*, which stressed the importance of presidential action in confronting national problems. Presidents faced many constraints, he argued, but effective presidents must learn to break free of them. The two men who served in the White House through most of the 1960s—John Kennedy and Lyndon Johnson—seemed for a time to be the embodiment of these liberal hopes.

John Kennedy

The campaign of 1960 produced two young candidates who claimed to offer the nation active leadership. The Republican nomination went almost uncontested to Vice President Richard Nixon, who abandoned the strident anticommunism that had characterized his earlier career and adopted a centrist position in favor of moderate reform. The Democrats, in the meantime, emerged from a hotly contested primary campaign united, somewhat uneasily, behind John Fitzgerald Kennedy, an attractive and articulate senator from Massachusetts who had narrowly missed being the party's vice presidential candidate in 1956.

John Kennedy grew up in a world of ease and privilege, although he himself suffered from a series of grave physical ailments throughout his life. He was the son of the wealthy and powerful Joseph P. Kennedy, controversial American ambassador to Britain at the beginning of World War II. After graduating from Harvard, he served in the navy during World War II, was decorated for bravery, and returned to Massachusetts in 1946 to run for office. By making liberal use of both his own war record and his family's money, he won a seat in Congress. Six years later, he was elected to the United States Senate, and in 1958 was reelected by a record margin. Within days of his triumph, he was planning his campaign for the White House. He premised his campaign, he said, "on the single assumption that the American people are uneasy at the present drift in our national course." But his appealing, and carefully crafted, public image was at least as important as his political positions in attracting his popular support.

A vigorous effort on behalf of Nixon by President Eisenhower in the closing days of the campaign, combined with continuing doubts about Kennedy's youth (he turned forty-three in 1960) and religion (he was a Catholic), almost enabled the Republicans to close what had at one time been a substantial Democratic lead. But Kennedy's strong performance in a series of televised presidential debates helped overcome the doubts. And in the end, he held on to win a tiny plurality of the popular vote—49.9 percent to Nixon's 49.6 percent—and only a slightly more comfortable electoral majority—303 to 219. If a few thousand voters in a few strategic states had voted differently, Nixon would have won.

Kennedy had campaigned promising a program of domestic legislation more ambitious than any since the New Deal, a program he described as the "New Frontier." But the narrowness of his victory limited his political effectiveness, and throughout his brief presidency he had serious problems with Congress. Although Democrats remained in control of both houses, the party's majorities were dependent on conservative southerners, who were far more likely to vote with the Republicans than with Kennedy. Many of those same southerners occupied powerful committee chairmanships. One after another of Kennedy's legislative proposals found themselves hopelessly stalled.

As a result, the president had to look elsewhere for opportunities to display positive leadership. One area where he believed he could do that was the economy. Economic growth was sluggish in 1961 when Kennedy entered the White House, with unemployment hovering at about 6 percent of the work force. Kennedy initiated a series of tariff negotiations with foreign governments—the "Kennedy Round"—in an effort to stimulate American exports. He began to consider an expanded use of Keynesian fiscal and monetary tools—culminating in his 1962 proposal for a substantial federal tax cut to stimulate the economy. And he used his personal prestige to battle inflation. In 1962, several steel companies, led by U.S. Steel, announced that they were raising their prices by $6 a ton, a move certain to trigger similar action by the rest of the steel industry. Kennedy put heavy pressure on U.S. Steel president Roger Blough and other steel executives to rescind the increase. The steel companies soon relented. But it was a fleeting victory. Kennedy's relationship with the corporate community was now permanently strained, and when the steel companies quietly raised prices again a few months later, the president did not protest.

More than any other president of the century (excepting perhaps the two Roosevelts and, later, Ronald Reagan), Kennedy made his own personality an integral part of his presidency and a central focus of national attention. Nothing illustrated that more clearly than the popular reaction to the tragedy of November 22, 1963. Kennedy had traveled to Texas with his wife and Vice President Lyndon Johnson for a series of political appearances. While the presidential motorcade rode slowly through the streets of Dallas, shots rang out. Two bullets struck the president—one in the throat, the other in the head. He was sped to a nearby hospital, where minutes later he was pronounced dead. Lee Harvey Oswald, who appeared to be a confused and embittered Marxist, was arrested for the crime later that day, and then mysteriously murdered by a Dallas nightclub owner, Jack Ruby, two days later as he was being moved from one jail to another.

The popular assumption at the time was that both Oswald and Ruby had acted alone, an assumption endorsed by a federal commission, chaired by Chief Justice Earl Warren, that was appointed to investigate the assassination. In later years, however, many Ameri-

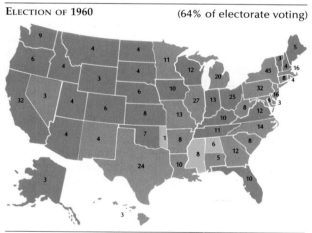

ELECTION OF 1960   (64% of electorate voting)

	ELECTORAL VOTE	POPULAR VOTE (%)
John F. Kennedy (Democratic)	303	34,227,096 (49.9)
Richard M. Nixon (Republican)	219	34,108,546 (49.6)
Harry F. Byrd (Dixiecrat)	15	501,643 (0.7)
Other candidates (Socialist Labor; Prohibition; National States Rights, Socialist Workers, Constitution)	—	197,029

for four days to watch the televised events surrounding the presidential funeral. Images of Kennedy's widow, his small children, his funeral procession, his grave site at Arlington Cemetery with its symbolic eternal flame—all became deeply embedded in the public mind. In later years, when Americans looked back at the optimistic days of the 1950s and early 1960s and wondered how everything had subsequently seemed to unravel, many would think of November 22, 1963, as the beginning of the change.

Lyndon Johnson

At the time, however, much of the nation took comfort in the personality and performance of Kennedy's successor in the White House, Lyndon Baines Johnson. Johnson was a native of the poor "hill country" of central Texas and had risen to eminence by dint of extraordinary, even obsessive effort and ambition. He entered public life in the 1930s as an aide to a Texas congressman, became the Texas director of the New Deal's National Youth Administration, and then, in 1937, was elected to Congress himself, fervently committed to Franklin Roosevelt. He rose steadily in Congress by working hard and by cultivating the favor of party leaders. In 1948, he narrowly won election to the United States Senate; a few years later he became the Senate majority leader, a job in which he displayed a legendary ability to persuade and cajole his colleagues into following his lead. Having failed to win the Democratic nomination for president in 1960, he surprised many who knew him by agreeing to accept the second position on the ticket with Kennedy. The events in Dallas thrust him into the White House.

Johnson's rough-edged, even crude, personality could hardly have been more different from Kennedy's. But like Kennedy, Johnson was a man who believed in the active use of power. And in the end, he proved more effective than his predecessor in translating his goals into reality. Between 1963 and 1966, he compiled the most impressive legislative record of any president since Franklin Roosevelt. He was aided by the tidal wave of emotion that followed the Kennedy assassination, which helped win support for many New Frontier proposals. But Johnson also constructed a remarkable reform program of his own, one that he ultimately labeled the "Great Society." And he won approval of much of it through the same sort of skillful congressional lobbying that had made him an effective majority leader.

Johnson envisioned himself, as well, as a great "coalition builder." He wanted the support of everyone, and for a time he very nearly got it. His first year

JOHN KENNEDY
The new president and his wife, Jacqueline, attend one of the five balls in Washington marking Kennedy's inauguration in 1961. *(Paul Schutzer,* Life *Magazine, © 1961 Time Warner, Inc.)*

cans—and in 1978 a congressional subcommittee—claimed that the Warren Commission report had not revealed the full story. *JFK,* a popular 1991 film by the director Oliver Stone, endorsed one of the many conspiracy theories advanced over the previous decades to explain the assassination. But no solid evidence has ever appeared to confirm any such theories, and many informed observers continue to believe that the Warren Commission Report (hasty and incomplete as it undoubtedly was) had the story essentially right.

The death of President Kennedy was one of several traumatic public episodes in national history that have left a permanent mark on all who experienced it. Millions of Americans suspended their normal activities

RETROACTIVE I, 1964
Within months of his death, John Kennedy had become transformed in the American imagination to a figure larger than life, a symbol of the nation's thwarted aspirations. The artist Robert Rauschenberg gave evidence of Kennedy's new mythological importance by making him the centerpiece of this evocation of contemporary American society. *(Wadsworth Atheneum, Hartford)*

in office was, by necessity, dominated by the campaign for reelection. There was little doubt that he would win—particularly after the Republican Party fell under the sway of its right wing and nominated the conservative Senator Barry Goldwater of Arizona. Liberal Republicans abandoned Goldwater and openly supported Johnson. In the November election, the president received a larger plurality, over 61 percent, than any candidate before or since. Goldwater managed to carry only his home state of Arizona and five states in the Deep South. Record Democratic majorities in both houses of Congress, many of whose members had been

swept into office only because of the margin of Johnson's victory, ensured that the president would be able to fulfill many of his goals. Johnson seemed well on his way to achieving his cherished aim of becoming the most successful reform president of the century.

The Assault on Poverty

The domestic programs of the Kennedy and Johnson administrations had two basic goals: maintaining the strength of the American economy and expanding the

THE "JOHNSON TREATMENT"
Lyndon Johnson was legendary for his powers of persuasion, a combination of charm and intimidation that often worked on even the most experienced politicians. He is shown here meeting in his office with Senate Minority Leader Everett Dirksen of Illinois, who became an ally of the president in 1964 in ending a filibuster against the Civil Rights Act of that year. *(Lyndon Baines Johnson Library)*

responsibilities of the federal government for the general social welfare. In the first, the two presidents were largely continuing a commitment that had been central to virtually every administration since early in the century. In the second, however, they were responding to a marked change in public assumptions. In particular, they were responding to what some described as the "discovery of poverty" in the late 1950s and early 1960s—the realization by Americans who had been glorying in prosperity that there were substantial portions of the population that remained destitute.

For the first time since the 1930s, the federal government took steps in the 1960s to create important new social welfare programs. The largest and probably the most important of these was Medicare: a program to provide federal aid to the elderly for medical expenses. Its enactment in 1965 came after a bitter, twenty-year debate between those who believed in the concept of national health assistance and those who denounced it as "socialized medicine." But the program as crafted by the Kennedy and Johnson administrations removed many objections. For one thing, it avoided the stigma of "welfare" by making Medicare benefits available to all elderly Americans, regardless of need (just as Social Security had done with pensions). That created a large middle-class constituency for the program. The program also defused the opposition of the medical community by allowing doctors serving Medicare patients to practice privately and, in the beginning, to charge their normal fees; Medicare simply shifted responsibility for paying those fees from the patient to the government. In 1966, Johnson steered to passage the Medicaid program, which extended federal medical assistance to welfare recipients of all ages. Criticism of both programs grew in subsequent years, both from those who thought Medicare and Medicaid were inadequate and from those who thought they were too expensive. But broad public support ensured their survival, and many liberals continued to hope for genuinely universal national health insurance. Not until the 1990s, however, would there be any serious effort to expand the system further.

Medicare and Medicaid were the first steps in a much larger assault on poverty—one that Kennedy had been contemplating in the last months of his life and one that Johnson launched only weeks after taking office. It emerged out of a long debate within the administration, and within Congress, about the nature of poverty and the best way to fight it. And it reflected the views of those who believed that poverty was a result of more than lack of money; it was a product of the institutional and cultural deficiencies of poor communities. By attacking those deficiencies, the planners of the antipoverty effort believed, government would help the poor to help themselves. That, in the end, was the key to the war on poverty: the effort to train the poor to be more successful. It was, as Johnson once put it, a "hand up, not a handout."

The centerpiece of this "war on poverty," as Johnson called it, was the Office of Economic Opportunity (OEO), which created an array of new educational, employment, housing, and health-care programs. But the OEO was controversial from the start, in part because of its commitment to the idea of "community action." Community action was an effort to involve members of poor communities themselves in the planning and administration of the programs designed to help them, to promote what some of its advocates called "maximum feasible participation." The community action programs provided some important benefits. In particular, they provided jobs for many poor people and gave them important experience in administrative and political work.

The community-action programs were also important to Native Americans. They allowed tribal leaders to design and run programs for themselves and to apply for funds from the federal government on an equal basis with state and municipal authorities. Administering these programs helped produce a new generation of tribal leaders who learned much about political and bureaucratic power from the experience.

But despite its achievements, the community-action approach proved impossible to sustain. Many programs fell victim to mismanagement or to powerful opposition from the local governments with which they were at times competing. Some activists in community-action agencies employed tactics that mainstream politicians considered frighteningly radical. The apparent excesses of a few agencies damaged the popular image of the community action program as a whole. And even though community action was a relatively small part of the war on poverty, its growing unpopularity undermined support for the larger program as well.

The OEO spent nearly $3 billion during its first two years of existence, and it helped reduce poverty significantly in certain areas. But it fell far short of eliminating poverty altogether. That was in part because of the weaknesses of the programs themselves and in part because funding for them, inadequate from the beginning, dwindled as the years passed and a costly war in Southeast Asia became the nation's first priority. Still, the war on poverty left a number of significant legacies. A generation of minority men and women became politically active in the community-action programs, and some of them continued to play a major role in public life for many years after. A series of programs—Head Start, a preschool enrichment program to help the children of poor families prepare for their educations; Food Stamps, which provided cash assistance to allow poor families to buy food; and others—were genuinely successful and had a permanent impact on poverty.

Cities, Schools, and Immigration

Closely tied to the antipoverty program were federal efforts to promote the revitalization of decaying cities and to strengthen the nation's schools. The Housing Act of 1961 offered $4.9 billion in federal grants to cities for the preservation of open spaces, the development of mass transit systems, and the subsidization of middle-income housing. In 1966, Johnson established a new cabinet agency, the Department of Housing and Urban Development (whose first secretary, Robert Weaver, was the first African American ever to serve in a presidential cabinet). Johnson also inaugurated the Model Cities program, which offered federal subsidies for urban redevelopment.

Kennedy had fought long and hard for federal aid to public education, but he had failed to overcome two important obstacles. Many Americans feared aid to education as the first step toward federal control of the schools. Many Catholics insisted federal assistance must extend to parochial as well as public schools, a demand that raised serious constitutional issues and one that Kennedy (a Catholic himself) refused to consider. Johnson managed to circumvent both objections with the Elementary and Secondary Education Act of 1965 and a series of subsequent measures. The bills extended aid to both private and parochial schools and based the aid on the economic conditions of their students, not the needs of the schools themselves. Total federal expenditures for education and technical training rose from $5 billion to $12 billion between 1964 and 1967.

The Johnson administration also supported the Immigration Act of 1965, one of the most important pieces of legislation of the 1960s, even if relatively unnoticed at the time. The law maintained a strict limit on the number of newcomers admitted to the country each year (170,000), but it eliminated the "national origins" system established in the 1920s, which had given preference to immigrants from northern Europe over those from other parts of the world. It continued to restrict immigration from some parts of Latin America, but it allowed people from all parts of Europe, Asia, and Africa to enter the United States on an equal basis. It meant that large new categories of immigrants—and especially large numbers of Asians—would begin entering the United States by the early 1970s and changing the character of the American population. Prior to the 1965 act, 90 percent of immigrants to the United States each year came from European countries; after the act, only 10 percent did.

Legacies of the Great Society

The great surge of reform of the Kennedy-Johnson years reflected a new awareness of social problems in America. It also reflected the confident belief of liberals that America's resources were virtually limitless and that purposeful public effort could surmount any obstacle. By the time Johnson left office, legislation had been either enacted or initiated to deal with a remarkable number of social issues: poverty, health care, education, cities, transportation, the environment, consumer protection, agriculture, science, the arts.

Taken together, the Great Society reforms meant a significant increase in federal spending. For a time, rising tax revenues from the growing economy nearly compensated for the new expenditures. In 1964, Johnson managed to win passage of the $11.5 billion tax cut that Kennedy had first proposed in 1962. The cut increased the federal deficit, but it helped produce substantial economic growth over the next several years that made up for much of the revenue initially lost. As Great Society programs began to multiply, however, and particularly as they began to compete with the escalating costs of America's military ventures, the federal budget rapidly outpaced increases in revenues. In 1961, the federal government had spent $94.4 billion. By 1970, that sum had risen to $196.6 billion.

The high costs of the Great Society programs and the inability of the government to find the revenues to pay for them contributed to a growing disillusionment in later years with the idea of federal efforts to solve social problems. By the 1980s, many Americans had become convinced that the Great Society efforts had not worked and that, indeed, government programs to solve social problems could not work. Others, however, argued equally fervently that social programs had made important contributions both to the welfare of the groups they were designed to help and to the health of the economy as a whole.

Whether because of economic growth or because of government antipoverty efforts—or, as seems most likely, because of both—the decade of the 1960s saw the most substantial decrease in poverty in the United States of any period in the nation's history. In 1959, according to the most widely accepted estimates, 21 percent of the American people lived below the officially established poverty line. By 1969, only 12 percent remained below that line. The improvements affected blacks and whites in about the same proportion: 56 percent of the black population had lived in poverty in 1959, while 32 percent did so ten years later—a 42 percent reduction; 18 percent of all whites had been poor in 1959, but only 10 percent were poor a decade later—a 44 percent reduction.

THE BATTLE FOR RACIAL EQUALITY

The nation's most important domestic initiative in the 1960s was the effort to provide justice and equality to African Americans. It was the most difficult commitment, the one that produced the severest strains on American society. It was also unavoidable. Black Americans were themselves ensuring that the nation would have to deal with the problem of race.

MAJOR ACHIEVEMENTS OF THE GREAT SOCIETY

1964 Civil Rights Act (prohibiting discrimination in public accommodations and hiring)
Twenty-fourth Amendment (abolishing poll tax)
Tax Reduction Act
Urban Mass Transportation Act (subsidizing urban mass transit)
Economic Opportunity Act (creating OEO, Job Corps, VISTA)
Wilderness Preservation Act
1965 Elementary and Secondary Education Act (providing aid to schools)
Medicare
Civil Rights Act (protecting voting rights)
Omnibus Housing Act (providing rent supplements to the poor)

1965 Department of Housing and Urban Development
National Endowments of the Arts and Humanities
Water Quality Act
Immigration law reform
Air Quality Act
Higher Education Act (offering federally financed scholarships)
1966 Medicaid
National Traffic and Motor Vehicle Safety Act
Highway Safety Act
Minimum wage increase
Department of Transportation
Model Cities
1967 Food Stamps
Corporation for Public Broadcasting

Expanding Protests

John Kennedy had long been vaguely sympathetic to the cause of racial justice, but he was hardly a committed crusader. His intervention during the 1960 campaign to help win the release of Martin Luther King, Jr., from a Georgia prison won him a large plurality of the black vote. But like many presidents before him, he feared alienating southern Democratic voters and powerful southern Democrats in Congress. His administration set out to contain the racial problem by expanding enforcement of existing laws and supporting litigation to overturn existing segregation statutes, hoping to make modest progress without creating politically damaging divisions.

But the pressure for more fundamental change could not be contained. In February 1960, black college students in Greensboro, North Carolina, staged a sit-in at a segregated Woolworth's lunch counter; and in the following weeks, similar demonstrations spread throughout the South, forcing many merchants to integrate their facilities. In the fall of 1960, some of those who had participated in the sit-ins formed the Student Nonviolent Coordinating Committee (SNCC), which worked to keep the spirit of resistance alive.

Sitting In

Black students stage a sit-in at a Woolworth's lunch counter in Charlotte, North Carolina, in 1960, after being refused service by the waitresses there. A similar demonstration at a Woolworth's in Greensboro several weeks earlier sparked a wave of sit-ins across the South. *(Bruce Roberts/Rapho-Photo Researchers)*

In 1961, an interracial group of students, working with the Congress of Racial Equality (CORE), began what they called "freedom rides" (reviving a tactic CORE had tried, without much success, in the 1940s). Traveling by bus throughout the South, the freedom riders tried to force the desegregation of bus stations. In some places, they met with such savage violence at the hands of enraged whites that the president finally dispatched federal marshals to help keep the peace. Kennedy also ordered the integration of all bus and train stations. In the meantime, SNCC workers began fanning out through black communities and even into remote rural areas to encourage blacks to challenge the obstacles to voting that the Jim Crow laws had created and that powerful social custom sustained. The Southern Christian Leadership Conference (SCLC) also created citizen-education and other programs—many of them organized by the remarkable Ella Baker, one of the great grassroots leaders of the movement—to mobilize black workers, farmers, housewives, and others to challenge segregation, disenfranchisement, and discrimination.

Continuing judicial efforts to enforce the integration of public education increased the pressure on national leaders to respond to the civil rights movement. In October 1962, a federal court ordered the University of Mississippi to enroll its first black student, James Meredith; Governor Ross Barnett, a strident segregationist, refused to enforce the order. When angry whites in Oxford, Mississippi, began rioting to protest the court decree, President Kennedy sent federal troops to the city to restore order and protect Meredith's right to attend the university.

Events in Alabama in 1963 helped bring the growing movement to something of a climax. In April, Martin Luther King, Jr., helped launch a series of nonviolent demonstrations in Birmingham, Alabama, a city unsurpassed in the strength of its commitment to segregation. Police Commissioner Eugene "Bull" Connor personally supervised a brutal effort to break up the peaceful marches, arresting hundreds of demonstrators and using attack dogs, tear gas, electric cattle prods, and fire hoses—at times even against small children—as much of the nation watched televised reports in horror. Two months later, Governor George Wallace—who had won election in 1962 pledging staunch resistance to integration—pledged to stand in the doorway of a building at the University of Alabama to prevent the court-ordered enrollment of several black students. Only after the arrival of federal marshals and a visit from Attorney General Robert Kennedy did Wallace give way. His stand won him wide popularity among whites throughout the nation who were growing uncomfortable with the pace of integration. That same night, NAACP official Medgar Evers was murdered in Mississippi.

A National Commitment

The events in Alabama and Mississippi were a warning to the president that he could no longer contain or avoid the issue of race. In an important television address the night of the University of Alabama confrontation (and the murder of Evers), Kennedy spoke eloquently of the "moral issue" facing the nation. "If an American," he asked, "because his skin is dark, . . . cannot enjoy the full and free life which all of us want, then who among us would be content to have the color of his skin changed and stand in his place? Who among us would then be content with the counsels of patience and delay?" Days later, he introduced a series of new legislative proposals prohibiting segregation in "public accommodations" (stores, restaurants, theaters, hotels), barring discrimination in employment, and increasing the power of the government to file suits on behalf of school integration.

To generate support for the legislation, and to dramatize the power of the growing movement, more than 200,000 demonstrators marched down the Mall in Washington, D.C., in August 1963 and gathered before the Lincoln Memorial for the greatest civil rights demonstration in the nation's history. President Kennedy, who had at first opposed the idea of the march, in the end gave it his open support after receiving pledges from organizers that speakers would not criticize the administration. Martin Luther King, Jr., in one of the greatest speeches of his distinguished oratorical career, roused the crowd with a litany of images prefaced again and again by the phrase "I have a dream." The march was the highwater mark of the peaceful, interracial civil rights movement—and one of the last moments of real harmony within it.

The assassination of President Kennedy three months later gave new impetus to the battle for civil rights legislation. The ambitious measure that Kennedy had proposed in June 1963 had stalled in the Senate after having passed through the House of Representatives with relative ease. Early in 1964, after Johnson applied both public and private pressure, supporters of the measure finally mustered the two-thirds majority necessary to close debate and end a filibuster by southern senators; and the Senate passed the most comprehensive civil rights bill in the nation's history.

The Battle for Voting Rights

Having won a significant victory in one area, the civil rights movement shifted its focus to another: voting rights. During the summer of 1964, thousands of civil rights workers, black and white, northern and southern, spread out through the South, but primarily in Mississippi, to work on behalf of black voter registration and participation. The campaign was known as "freedom summer," and it produced a violent response from some southern whites. Three of the first freedom workers to arrive in the South—two whites, Andrew Goodman and Michael Schwerner, and one black, James Chaney—were murdered by local police and others.

The "freedom summer" also produced the Mississippi Freedom Democratic Party (MFDP), an integrated alternative to the regular state party organiza-

KING MARCHES THROUGH SELMA
Martin Luther King, Jr., and his wife, Coretta (right), lead demonstrators on a march through Selma, Alabama, during his turbulent campaign for black voting rights in 1965. Selma was one of the last of the great interracial crusades on behalf of civil rights. Subsequent campaigns, such as King's frustrated effort in Chicago in 1966, attracted much less support from northern whites and far less attention in the media. *(Bruce Davidson/Magnum)*

tion. Under the leadership of Fannie Lou Hamer and others, the MFDP challenged the regular party's right to its seats at the Democratic National Convention that summer. President Johnson, eager to avoid antagonizing anyone (even southern white Democrats who seemed likely to support his Republican opponent), enlisted King's help to broker a compromise. It permitted the MFDP to be seated as observers, with promises of party reforms later on, while the regular party retained its official standing. Both sides grudgingly accepted the agreement. Both were embittered by it.

A year later, in March 1965, King helped organize a major demonstration in Selma, Alabama, to press the demand for the right of blacks to register to vote. Selma sheriff Jim Clark led local police in a brutal attack on the demonstrators—which, as in Birmingham, received graphic television coverage and horrified many viewers across the nation. Two northern whites participating in the Selma march were murdered in the course of the effort there—one, a minister, beaten to death in the streets of the town; the other, a Detroit housewife, shot as she drove along a highway at night with a black passenger in her car. The national outrage that followed the events in Alabama helped push Lyndon Johnson to propose and win passage of the Civil Rights Act of 1965, better known as the Voting Rights Act, which provided federal protection to blacks attempting to exercise their right to vote.

But important as such gains were, they failed to satisfy the rapidly rising expectations of African Americans as the focus of the movement began to move from political to economic issues.

The Changing Movement

For decades, the nation's African-American population had been undergoing a major demographic shift; and by the 1960s, the problem of racial injustice was no longer primarily southern and rural, as it had been earlier in the century. By 1966, 69 percent of American blacks were living in metropolitan areas and 45 percent outside the South. Although the economic condition of much of American society was improving, in the poor urban communities in which the black population was concentrated, things were getting significantly worse. Well over half of all American nonwhites lived in poverty at the beginning of the 1960s; black unemployment was twice that of whites. (See pp. 803–805.)

By the mid-1960s, therefore, the issue of race was moving out of the South and into the rest of the nation. The battle against school desegregation had moved beyond the initial assault on de jure segregation (seg-

regation by law) to an attack on de facto segregation (segregation in practice, as through residential patterns), thus carrying the fight into northern cities. Many African-American leaders (and their white supporters) were demanding, similarly, that the battle against job discrimination move to a new level. Employers should not only abandon negative measures to deny jobs to blacks; they should adopt positive measures to recruit minorities, thus compensating for past injustices. Lyndon Johnson gave his tentative support to the concept of "affirmative action" in 1965. Over the next decade, affirmative action guidelines gradually extended to virtually all institutions doing business with or receiving funds from the federal government (including schools and universities)—and to many others as well.

A symbol of the movement's new direction, and of the problems it would cause, was a major campaign in the summer of 1966 in Chicago, in which King played a prominent role. Organizers of the Chicago campaign hoped to direct national attention to housing and employment discrimination in northern industrial cities in much the same way similar campaigns had exposed legal racism in the South. But the Chicago campaign not only evoked vicious and at times violent opposition from white residents of that city; it failed to arouse the national conscience in the way events in the South had done. It did produce a weak agreement with the city government to end housing discrimination, but little changed as a result. The Chicago campaign was, on the whole, an exercise in frustration.

Urban Violence

Well before the Chicago campaign, the problem of urban poverty had thrust itself into national attention when riots broke out in black neighborhoods in major cities. There were a few scattered disturbances in the summer of 1964, most notably in New York City's Harlem. The first large race riot since the end of World War II occurred the following summer in the Watts section of Los Angeles. In the midst of a seemingly routine traffic arrest, a white police officer struck a protesting black bystander with his club. The incident triggered a storm of anger and a week of violence (and revealed how deeply blacks in Los Angeles, and in other cities, resented their treatment at the hands of local police). As many as 10,000 people were estimated to have participated in the violence—attacking white motorists, burning buildings, looting stores, and sniping at policemen. Thirty-four people died during the Watts uprising, which was eventually quelled by the National Guard; twenty-eight of the dead were black. In the summer of 1966, there were forty-three additional outbreaks, the most serious of them in Chicago and Cleveland. And in the summer of 1967, there were eight major riots, including the largest of them all—a racial clash in Detroit in which forty-three people (thirty-three of them black) died.

Televised reports of the violence alarmed millions of Americans and created both a new sense of urgency and a growing sense of doubt among many of those whites who had embraced the cause of racial justice only a few years before. A special Commission on Civil Disorders, created by the president in response to the riots, issued a celebrated report in the spring of 1968 recommending massive spending to eliminate the abysmal conditions of the ghettoes. "Only a commitment to national action on an unprecedented scale," the commission concluded, "can shape a future compatible with the historic ideals of American society." To many white Americans, however, the lesson of the riots was the need for stern measures to stop violence and lawlessness.

Black Power

Disillusioned with the ideal of peaceful change in co-operation with whites, an increasing number of African Americans were turning to a new approach to the racial issue: the philosophy of "black power." Black power could mean many different things. But in all its forms, it suggested a move away from interracial co-operation and toward increased awareness of racial distinctiveness. It was part of a long nationalist tradition among African Americans that extended back into slavery and that had its most visible twentieth-century expression in the Garvey movement.

Perhaps the most enduring impact of the black-power ideology was a social and psychological one: instilling racial pride in African Americans, who lived in a society whose dominant culture generally portrayed blacks as inferior to whites. It encouraged the growth of black studies in schools and universities. It helped stimulate important black literary and artistic movements. It produced a new interest among many blacks in their African roots. It led to a rejection by some blacks of certain cultural practices borrowed from white society: "Afro" hairstyles began to replace artificially straightened hair; some blacks began to adopt African styles of dress, even to change their names.

But black power had political manifestations as well, most notably in creating a deep schism within the civil rights movement. Traditional black organizations that had emphasized cooperation with sympathetic whites—groups such as the NAACP, the Urban League, and King's Southern Christian Leadership Conference—now faced competition from more radical groups. The Student Nonviolent Coordinating Committee and the Congress of Racial Equality had both begun as relatively moderate, interracial organizations; SNCC, in fact, was originally a student branch of the SCLC. By the mid-1960s, however, these and other groups were calling for more radical and occasionally even violent action against the racism of white society and were openly rejecting the approaches of older, more established black leaders.

Particularly alarming to many whites (and to some African Americans as well) were organizations that existed entirely outside the mainstream civil rights movement. In Oakland, California, the Black Panther Party (founded by Huey Newton and Bobby Seale) promised to defend black rights even if that required violence. Black Panthers organized along semimilitary lines and wore weapons openly and proudly. They were, in fact, more the victims of violence from the police than they were practitioners of violence themselves. But they created an image, quite deliberately, of militant blacks willing to fight for justice, in Newton's words, "through the barrel of a gun."

In Detroit, a once-obscure black nationalist group, the Nation of Islam, gained new prominence. Founded in 1931 by Elijah Poole (who converted to Islam and renamed himself Elijah Muhammed), the movement taught blacks to take responsibility for their own lives, to be disciplined, to live by strict codes of behavior, and to reject any dependence on whites.

The most celebrated of the Black Muslims, as whites often termed them, was Malcolm Little, a former drug addict and pimp who had spent time in prison and had rebuilt his life once joining the movement. He adopted the name Malcolm X ("X" to denote his lost African surname). And he became one of the movement's most influential spokesmen, particularly among younger blacks, as a result of his intelligence, his oratorical skills, and his harsh, uncompromising opposition to all forms of racism and oppression. He did not advocate violence, as his critics often claimed; but he insisted that black people had the right to defend themselves, violently if necessary, from those who assaulted them. Malcolm died in 1965 when black gunmen, presumably under orders from rivals within the Nation of Islam, assassinated him in New York. But a book he had been working on before his death with the writer Alex Haley (*The Autobiography of Malcolm X*) attracted wide attention after its publication in 1965. Malcolm remained an influential figure in many black communities long after his death—as important and revered a symbol to many African Americans as Martin Luther King, Jr.

Malcolm X
Malcolm X, a leader of the militant Black Muslims, arrives in Washington, D.C., in May 1963 to set up a headquarters for the organization there. Malcolm was hated and feared by many whites during his lifetime. He was assassinated in 1965. In subsequent years, he became a widely revered hero among African Americans.   *(UPI/Bettmann)*

"Flexible Response" and the Cold War

In international affairs as much as in domestic reform, the optimistic liberalism of the Kennedy and Johnson administrations dictated a more positive, more active approach to dealing with the nation's problems than in the past. And just as the new activism in domestic reform proved more difficult and divisive than liber-

als had imagined, so too it created frustrations and failures in foreign policy.

Diversifying Foreign Policy

John Kennedy's forceful inaugural address was a clear indication of how central opposition to communism was to his and the nation's thinking. "In the long history of the world," he proclaimed, "only a few generations have been granted the role of defending freedom in its hour of maximum danger. I do not shrink from this responsibility; I welcome it." Yet the speech—which, significantly, made no mention whatever of domestic affairs—was also an indication of Kennedy's belief that the United States was not doing enough to counter the communist threat, that it needed to be able to resist aggression in more flexible ways than the atomic weapons-oriented defense strategy of the Eisenhower years permitted.

Kennedy remained committed to the nation's atomic weapons program. Indeed, he ran for president criticizing the Eisenhower administration for allowing an imbalance of nuclear weapons (a "missile gap") to develop between the United States and the Soviet Union. In fact, as Kennedy discovered even before the election, whatever missile gap there was favored the United States. But Kennedy insisted on proceeding with an expansion of the nation's atomic arsenal nevertheless—and the Soviet Union, which several years earlier had slowed the growth of its own nuclear weapons stockpile, responded in kind.

Kennedy's unhappiness with the Eisenhower foreign policy was not that it relied on nuclear weapons; it was that it developed too few other tools and thus had little capacity to respond to problems for which nuclear weapons were inappropriate solutions. In particular, he was unsatisfied with the nation's ability to meet communist threats in "emerging areas" of the Third World. In 1959, the Soviet Union had directed communist movements around the world to shift attention away from direct confrontations with the industrial powers of the West and toward "wars of national liberation" in less developed nations. Kennedy, similarly, concluded that the Third World would be the arena in which the real struggle against communism would be waged in the future. He gave enthusiastic support to the growth of the Special Forces, a small branch of the army created in the 1950s to wage guerrilla warfare in limited conflicts. Kennedy expanded the unit, allowed its members to wear distinctive headgear (thus giving them the informal name "the Green Berets"), and gave them an elite status within the military they had never had before.

Kennedy also favored expanding American influence through peaceful means. To repair the badly deteriorating relationship with Latin America, he proposed an "Alliance for Progress": a series of projects undertaken cooperatively by the United States and Latin American governments for peaceful development and stabilization of the nations of that region. Its purpose was both to spur social and economic development and to inhibit the rise of Castro-like movements in other Central or South American countries. Kennedy also inaugurated the Agency for International Development (AID) to coordinate foreign aid. And he established what became one of his most popular innovations: the Peace Corps, which sent young American volunteers abroad to work in developing areas.

The Bay of Pigs Fiasco

Among the first foreign policy ventures of the Kennedy administration was a disastrous assault on the Castro government in Cuba. The Eisenhower administration had launched the project, and by the time Kennedy took office, the CIA had been working for months in Central America to train a small army of anti-Castro Cuban exiles to invade Cuba and overthrow the Castro regime.

Kennedy had misgivings about the project. But he believed that "communist domination in this hemisphere can never be negotiated" and that Castro represented a threat to the stability of other Latin American nations, and so he accepted the CIA's optimistic assessments of the chances for success and approved the invasion. On April 17, 1961, 2,000 of the armed exiles landed at the Bay of Pigs in Cuba, expecting first American air support and then a spontaneous uprising by the Cuban people on their behalf. They received neither. At the last minute, Kennedy withdrew the air support, fearful of involving the United States too directly in the invasion. (Air support would not likely have changed the result in any case.) And the expected uprising did not occur. Instead, well-armed Castro forces easily crushed the invaders, and within two days the entire mission had collapsed.

Kennedy somberly took responsibility for the fiasco. But he refused to rule out further measures against the

---

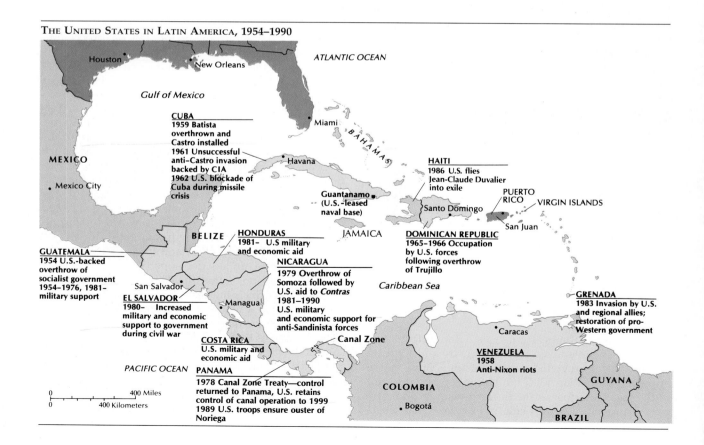

THE UNITED STATES IN LATIN AMERICA, 1954–1990

ATLANTIC OCEAN

Houston
New Orleans
Gulf of Mexico

CUBA
1959 Batista overthrown and Castro installed
1961 Unsuccessful anti-Castro invasion backed by CIA
1962 U.S. blockade of Cuba during missile crisis

MEXICO

Mexico City

Miami

BAHAMAS

Havana

HAITI
1986 U.S. flies Jean-Claude Duvalier into exile

PUERTO RICO   VIRGIN ISLANDS

Santo Domingo

San Juan

Guantanamo (U.S.-leased naval base)

BELIZE

HONDURAS
1981– U.S military and economic aid

JAMAICA

DOMINICAN REPUBLIC
1965–1966 Occupation by U.S. forces following overthrow of Trujillo

GUATEMALA
1954 U.S.-backed overthrow of socialist government 1954–1976, 1981– military support

San Salvador

NICARAGUA
1979 Overthrow of Somoza followed by U.S. aid to *Contras*
1981–1990 U.S. military and economic support for anti-Sandinista forces

Caribbean Sea

GRENADA
1983 Invasion by U.S. and regional allies; restoration of pro-Western government

EL SALVADOR
1980– Increased military and economic support to government during civil war

Managua

Caracas

COSTA RICA
U.S. military and economic aid

Canal Zone

VENEZUELA
1958 Anti-Nixon riots

GUYANA

PACIFIC OCEAN   PANAMA

PANAMA
1978 Canal Zone Treaty—control returned to Panama, U.S. retains control of canal operation to 1999
1989 U.S. troops ensure ouster of Noriega

COLOMBIA

Bogotá

BRAZIL

0   400 Miles
0   400 Kilometers

Castro regime. "We do not intend to abandon Cuba to the communists," he said only three days after the Bay of Pigs.

Confrontations with the Soviet Union

In the grim aftermath of the Bay of Pigs, Kennedy traveled to Vienna in June 1961 for his first meeting with Soviet Premier Nikita Khrushchev. Their frosty and at times angry exchange of views did little to reduce tensions between the two nations. Nor did Khrushchev's continuing irritation over the existence of a noncommunist West Berlin in the heart of East Germany.

In Vienna, Khrushchev had threatened war if the West did not abandon its defense of the city. Later in the summer, however, he settled on a less dangerous approach to the problem. Particularly embarrassing to the communists was the mass exodus of residents of East Germany to the West through the easily traversed border in the center of Berlin. Before dawn on August 13, 1961, the Soviet Union stopped the exodus by directing East Germany to construct a wall between East and West Berlin. Guards fired on those who continued to try to escape. For nearly thirty years, the Berlin Wall stood as the most potent physical symbol of the conflict between the communist and non-communist worlds.

The rising tensions culminated the following October in the most dangerous and dramatic crisis of the Cold War. During the summer of 1962, American intelligence agencies had become aware of the arrival of a new wave of Soviet technicians and equipment in Cuba and of military construction in progress. On October 14, aerial reconnaissance photos produced clear evidence that the Soviets were constructing sites on the island for offensive nuclear weapons. To the Soviets, placing missiles in Cuba probably seemed a reasonable, and relatively inexpensive, way to counter the presence of American missiles in Turkey (and a way to deter any future American invasion of Cuba). But to Kennedy and most other Americans, the missile sites represented an act of aggression by the Soviets toward the United States. Almost immediately, the president decided that the weapons could not be allowed to remain.

On October 22, after nearly a week of tense deliberations by a special task force in the White House, Kennedy ordered a naval and air blockade around Cuba, a "quarantine" against all offensive weapons. Soviet ships bound for the island slowed down or stopped before reaching the point of confrontation. But work on the missile sites continued. Preparations were under way for an American air attack on Cuba when, late in the evening of October 26, Kennedy received a message from Khrushchev implying that the Soviet

REPAIRING THE BERLIN WALL
First erected in 1961, the Berlin Wall became steadily higher and more elaborately fortified over the next several years. This 1963 photograph shows West Germans, at right, watching East German workers repair a section of wall after an East German mechanic rammed into it with an armored car as he escaped into West Berlin. He was shot by East German police but survived. *(UPI/Bettmann)*

Union would remove the missile bases in exchange for an American pledge not to invade Cuba. Ignoring other, tougher Soviet messages, the president agreed. Privately, he also promised to remove American missiles from Turkey, a decision he had already reached months earlier but had not yet implemented. The crisis was over.

The Cuban missile crisis brought the world closer to nuclear war than at any time since World War II. Both the United States and the Soviet Union had been forced to confront the momentous consequences of war. And in the following months, both seemed ready to move toward a new accommodation. In June 1963, President Kennedy spoke at American University in Washington, D.C., and seemed for the first time to offer hope for a peaceful rapprochement with the Soviet Union. That same summer, the United States and the Soviet Union concluded years of negotiation by agreeing to a treaty to ban the testing of nuclear weapons in the atmosphere—the first step toward mutual arms reduction since the beginning of the Cold War.

In the longer run, however, the missile crisis had more ominous consequences. The humiliating retreat the United States forced upon the Soviet leadership undermined the position of Nikita Khrushchev and contributed to his fall from power a year later. His replacement, Leonid Brezhnev, was a much more orthodox party figure, less interested in reform than Khrushchev had been. Perhaps more important, the graphic evidence the crisis gave the Soviets of their military inferiority helped produce a dramatic Soviet arms buildup over the next two decades, a buildup that contributed to a comparable increase in the United States in the early 1980s and that for a time undermined American support for a policy of rapprochement.

Johnson and the World

Lyndon Johnson entered the presidency lacking even John Kennedy's limited prior experience with international affairs. He was eager, therefore, not only to continue the policies of his predecessor but to prove quickly that he too was a strong and forceful leader.

An internal rebellion in the Dominican Republic gave him an early opportunity to do so. A 1961 assassination had toppled the repressive dictatorship of General Rafael Trujillo, and for the next four years various factions in the country had struggled for dominance. In the spring of 1965, a conservative military regime began to collapse in the face of a revolt by a broad range of groups on behalf of the nationalist reformer Juan Bosch, who had been elected president in

1962 and deposed by the military after only seven months in office. Arguing (without any evidence) that Bosch planned to establish a pro-Castro, communist regime, Johnson dispatched 30,000 American troops to quell the disorder. Only after a conservative candidate defeated Bosch in a 1966 election were the forces withdrawn.

From Johnson's first moments in office, however, his foreign policy was almost totally dominated by the bitter civil war in Vietnam and by the expanding involvement of the United States there. In many respects, Johnson was on this issue simply the unfortunate legatee of commitments initiated by his predecessors. But the determination of the new president, and of others within his administration, to prove their resolve in the battle against communism helped produce the final, decisive steps toward a full-scale commitment.

Vietnam

George Kennan, who helped devise the containment doctrine in whose name America went to war in Vietnam, once called the conflict "the most disastrous of all America's undertakings over the whole 200 years of its history." In retrospect, few would now disagree. Yet at first, the Vietnam War seemed simply one more Third World struggle on the periphery of the Cold War, a struggle in which the United States would try to tip the balance against communism without becoming too deeply or directly engaged. No president really decided to go to war in Vietnam. Rather, the American involvement there emerged from years of gradually increasing commitments that slowly and imperceptibly expanded.

The First Indochina War

Vietnam had a long history both as an independent kingdom and major power in its region, and as a subjugated province of China; its people were both proud of their past glory and painfully aware of their many years of subjugation. In the mid-nineteenth century, Vietnam became a colony of France. And like other European possessions in Asia, it fell under the control of Japan during World War II. After the defeat of Japan, the question arose of what was to happen to Vietnam in the postwar world. There were two opposing forces attempting to answer that question, both of them appealing to the United States for help. The French wanted to reassert their control over Vietnam. Challenging them was a powerful nationalist movement within Vietnam committed to creating an independent nation. The nationalists were organized into a political party, the Vietminh, which had been created in 1941 and led ever since by Ho Chi Minh, a communist educated in Paris and Moscow, and a fervent Vietnamese nationalist. The Vietminh had fought against Japan throughout World War II (unlike the French colonial officials who had remained in Vietnam during the war—as representatives of the Vichy regime—and had collaborated with the Japanese). In the fall of 1945, after the collapse of Japan and before the Western powers had time to return, the Vietminh declared Vietnam an independent nation and set up a nationalist government under Ho Chi Minh in Hanoi.

Ho had worked closely during the war with American intelligence forces in Indochina in fighting the Japanese; he apparently considered the United States something like an ally. When the war ended in 1945, he began writing President Truman asking for support in his struggle against the French. He received no reply to his letters, probably because no one in the State Department had heard of him. At the same time, Truman was under heavy pressure from both the British and the French to support France in its effort to reassert its control over Vietnam. The French argued that without Vietnam, their domestic economy would collapse. And since the economic revival of Western Europe was quickly becoming one of the Truman administration's top priorities, the United States did nothing to stop (although, at first, also relatively little to encourage) the French as they moved back into Vietnam in 1946 and began a struggle with the Vietminh to reestablish control over the country.

At first, the French had little difficulty reestablishing control. They drove Ho Chi Minh out of Hanoi and into hiding in the countryside; and in 1949, they established a nominally independent national government under the leadership of the former emperor, Bao Dai—an ineffectual, westernized playboy unable to assert any real independent authority. The real power remained in the hands of the French. But the Vietminh continued to challenge the French-dominated regime and slowly increased its control over large areas of the countryside. The French appealed to the United States for support; and in February 1950, the Truman administration formally recognized the Bao Dai regime and agreed to provide it with direct military and economic aid.

For the next four years, during what has become known as the First Indochina War, Truman and then Eisenhower continued to support the French military campaign against the Vietminh; by 1954, by some calculations, the United States was paying 80 percent of France's war costs. But the war went badly for the French anyway. Finally, late in 1953, Vietminh forces engaged the French in a major battle in the far northwest corner of the country, at Dien Bien Phu, an isolated and almost indefensible site. The French were surrounded, and the battle turned into a prolonged and horrible siege, with the French position steadily deteriorating. It was at this point that the Eisenhower administration decided not to intervene to save the French (see pp. 811–812). The defense of Dien Bien Phu collapsed and the French government decided the time had come to get out. The First Indochina War had come to an end.

Geneva and the Two Vietnams

An international conference at Geneva, planned many months before to settle the Korean dispute and other controversies, now took up the fate of Vietnam as well. The United States was only indirectly involved in the Vietnam phase of the Geneva conference. Secretary of State Dulles, who did not really believe in negotiating with communists, reluctantly attended (described by one observer as a "puritan in a house of ill repute") but left early; the United States never signed the accords. Even so, the Geneva conference produced an agreement to end the Vietnam conflict. There would be an immediate cease-fire in the war; Vietnam would be temporarily partitioned along the 17th parallel, with the Vietminh in control of North Vietnam, and a pro-Western regime in control of the South. In 1956, elections would be held to reunite the country under a single government.

The partition of Vietnam was, therefore, an essentially artificial one. But there were, in fact, real and important differences between North and South Vietnam. North Vietnam, the area now to be controlled by the Vietminh, was the heart of traditional Vietnamese society, the area where French influence had been the weakest. Hence the North had remained a reasonably stable, reasonably homogeneous culture, most of whose people lived in very close-knit, traditional villages. Northern Vietnam was also the poorest region of the country—overpopulated, plagued by a serious maldistribution of scarce land, and hit by a serious famine at the end of the war. The Vietminh had worked effectively to alleviate the great famine and had won strong popular allegiance to the regime as a result. (Later, in the early 1950s, it launched a disastrous land reform policy, which it soon repudiated.) The Hanoi government was also strengthened by the mass exodus, in 1954, at the time of the partition, of many of the Catholics and others in the north who might have opposed them had they stayed. The North Vietnamese were passionately committed to the unification of the

THE WAR IN VIETNAM AND INDOCHINA, 1964–1975

CHINA

Lao Cai

Than Uyen

Yen Bay

Dienbienphu

NORTH VIETNAM

BURMA

Hanoi

Haiphong

Red River
Delta

Pak Seng

Luang Prabang

Ban Ban

Plain of Jars

Vang Vieng

L A O S

Vinh

Gulf of Tonkin

Hainan

Vientiane

Mekong River

Udon Thani

Phanom

Dong Hoi

Partition Line 1954

Vinh Linh

DMZ (Demilitarized Zone)

QUANG TRI
PROVINCE

Khesanh

Hue

Phu Bai

Da Nang

Hoi An

Tamky

Chulai

My Lai

Quang Ngai

FRIENDSHIP HIGHWAY

THAILAND

Udon Ratchathani

Takhli

Don Muang

Lop Buri

Ratchasima

Dak To

Kontum

*Plateau of
Kontum*

Pleiku

Ankhe

Quinhon

South China Sea

Bangkok

Angkor Wat

Battambang

Tonle Sap

CAMBODIA

Mekong River

*Plateau of
Darlac*

Ban Me Thout

Sattahip

Nhatrang

Kompong
Cham

Bo Duc

Da Lat

Camranh Bay

Phanrang

Phnom
Penh

Prey Veng

**1970:
U.S. and South
Vietnam troops
entered Viet Cong
strongholds
inside Cambodia**

Tay Ninh

Ben Cat

Bienhua

Saigon

**SOUTH
VIETNAM**

Gulf of Thailand

Sihanoukville

Tan Son Nhut
Airbase

Vung Tau

Rach Gia

Cantho

Mekong Delta

Quan Long

*Ca Mau
Peninsula*

Con Son

| | 0 | 150 Miles |
| 0 | 150 Kilometers | |

■ U.S. bases

➡ U.S. and South Vietnam
invasion of Cambodia

→ Ho Chi Minh Trail
(communist supply route)

nation, a commitment with deep roots in Vietnamese history.

South Vietnam, by contrast, was a much more recently settled area. Until the early nineteenth century, in fact, very few Vietnamese had lived there; most of the sparse population had consisted of Khmer (Cambodians). Even in the 1950s, most of its people had been there only three generations or less. For many years it had been something like the American West in the nineteenth century—the place where adventurous, or opportunistic, or disenchanted people from the poor, overpopulated North would move in search of a new beginning, and in search of land (which was scarce in the north but plentiful in the south). It was a looser, more heterogeneous, more individualistic society. It was highly factionalized—religiously, politically, and ethnically—with powerful sects (and even a powerful mafia) all competing for power. It was also more prosperous and fertile than the North. It was not overpopulated. It had experienced no famine. It was the only region of the country producing a surplus for export.

South Vietnam had no legacy of strong commitment to the Vietminh and much less fervent commitment to national unification. It was the area where the influence of the French (their language, culture, and values) had been strongest and where there was a substantial, westernized middle class. It was, in other words, a society much more difficult to unite and to govern than the society of the North.

America and Diem

As soon as the Geneva Accords established the partition, the French finally left Vietnam altogether. The United States almost immediately stepped into the vacuum and became the principal benefactor of the new government in the South, led by Ngo Dinh Diem. Diem was an aristocratic Catholic from central Vietnam, an outsider in the South. But he was also a nationalist, uncontaminated by collaboration with the French. And he was, for a time, apparently successful. With the help of the American CIA, Diem waged an effective campaign against some of the powerful religious sects and the South Vietnamese mafia, which had challenged the authority of the central government. As a result, the United States came to regard Diem as a powerful and impressive alternative to Ho Chi Minh. Lyndon Johnson once called him the "Churchill of Southeast Asia."

The American government supported Diem's refusal in 1956 to permit the elections called for by the Geneva Accords, reasoning, almost certainly correctly,

that Ho Chi Minh would easily win any such election. Ho could count on 100 percent of the vote in the north, with its much larger population, and at least some support in the south. In the meantime, the United States poured military and economic aid into South Vietnam. By 1956, it was the second largest recipient of American military aid in the world, after Korea.

Diem's early successes in suppressing the sects in Vietnam led him in 1959 to begin a similar campaign to eliminate the Vietminh supporters who had stayed behind in the south after the partition. He was quite successful for a time, so successful in fact that the North Vietnamese found it necessary to respond. A new policy emanating from Moscow beginning in 1959, emphasizing communist wars of national liberation (as opposed to direct Soviet confrontations with the United States and NATO), also encouraged Ho Chi Minh to resume his armed struggle for national unification. In 1959, the Vietminh cadres in the south created the National Liberation Front (NLF), known to many Americans as the Viet Cong—an organization closely allied with the North Vietnamese government. It was committed to overthrowing the "puppet regime" of Diem and reuniting the nation. In 1960, under orders from Hanoi, and with both material and manpower support from North Vietnam, the NLF began military operations in the South. This marked the beginning of the Second Indochina War.

By 1961, NLF forces were very successfully destabilizing the Diem regime. They were killing over 4,000 government officials a year (mostly village leaders) and establishing effective control over many areas of the countryside. Diem was also by now losing the support of many other groups in South Vietnam, and he was even losing support within his own military. In 1963, the Diem regime precipitated a major crisis by trying to discipline and repress the South Vietnamese Buddhists in an effort to make Catholicism the dominant religion of the country. The Buddhists began to stage enormous antigovernment demonstrations; and after Diem launched a series of heavy-handed military and police actions against them—which included several massacres of demonstrators and violent government raids on their sacred pagodas—the demonstrations grew much larger. Several Buddhist monks doused themselves with gasoline, sat cross-legged in the streets of downtown Saigon, and set themselves on fire—in view of photographers and television cameras.

The Buddhist crisis was alarming and embarrassing to the Kennedy administration. It caused the American government to reconsider its commitment to Diem—although not to the survival of South Vietnam. Kennedy had greatly increased the number of American personnel and the level of American assis-

THE VIETNAM COMMITMENT

IN 1965 THE DEPARTMENT of Defense released a film intended for American soldiers about to embark for service in Vietnam and designed to explain why the United States had found it necessary to commit so many lives and resources to the defense of a small and distant land. The film was entitled *Why Vietnam?*—a question many Americans have pondered and debated in the three decades since. The debate has proceeded on two levels. At one level is an effort to assess the broad objectives Americans believed they were pursuing in Vietnam. At another is an effort to explain how and why policymakers made the specific decisions that led to the American commitment.

The Defense Department film itself offered one answer to the question of America's broad objectives, an answer that for a time most Americans tended to accept: The United States was fighting in Vietnam to defend freedom and stop aggression; and it was fighting in Vietnam to prevent the spread of communism into a new area of the world, to protect not only Vietnam but also the other nations of the Pacific that would soon be threatened if Vietnam itself were to fall. This explanation—that America intervened in Vietnam to defend its ideals and its legitimate interests—continued to attract support well after the war ended. Journalist Norman Podhoretz's 1982 book *Why We Were in Vietnam* argued that America was in Vietnam "to save the Southern half of that country from the evils of communism" and that the tragic events in Indochina since 1975

have proven the essential morality of the American cause. Political scientist Guenter Lewy contended, in *America in Vietnam* (1978), that the United States entered Vietnam to help an ally combat "foreign aggression." R. B. Smith argued that Vietnam was a vital American interest, that the global concerns of the United States required a commitment there. And historian Ernest R. May stated: "The paradox is that the Vietnam War, so often condemned by its opponents as hideously immoral, may well have been the most moral or at least the most selfless war in all of American history. For the impulse guiding it was not to defeat an enemy or to serve a national interest; it was simply not to abandon friends."

Others argued that America's broad objectives in Vietnam were less altruistic, that the intervention was a form of imperialism—part of a larger effort by the United States after World War II to impose a particular political and economic order on the world. "The Vietnam War," historian Gabriel Kolko wrote in *Anatomy of a War* (1985), "was for the United States the culmination of its frustrating postwar effort to merge its arms and politics to halt and reverse the emergence of states and social systems opposed to the international order Washington sought to establish." Economist Robert Heilbroner, writing in 1967, saw the American intent as somewhat more defensive; the intervention in Vietnam was a response to "a fear of losing our place in the sun," to a fear that a communist victory "would signal the end of capitalism as the dominant world order and would force the acknowledgment that America no longer constituted the model on which the future of world civilization would be mainly based."

---

tance to the anticommunist regime, and he was unwilling to permit South Vietnam to fall. American officials pressured Diem to reform his government, but Diem made no significant concessions. As a result, in the fall of 1963, Kennedy gave his tacit approval to a plot by a group of South Vietnamese generals to topple Diem. In early November 1963, the generals staged

the coup, assassinated Diem and his brother and principal adviser, Ngo Dinh Nhu (killings the United States had not wanted or expected), and established the first of a series of new governments, which were, for over three years, even less stable than the one they had overthrown. A few weeks after the coup, John Kennedy too was dead.

WHERE HISTORIANS DISAGREE

Those who looked less at the nation's broad objectives than at the internal workings of the policymaking process likewise produced competing explanations. Journalist David Halberstam's *The Best and the Brightest* (1972) argued that policymakers deluded themselves into thinking they could achieve their goals in Vietnam by ignoring, suppressing, or dismissing the information that might have suggested otherwise. The foreign policy leaders of the Kennedy and Johnson administrations were so committed to the idea of American activism and success that they refused to consider the possibility of failure; the Vietnam disaster was thus, at least in part, a result of the arrogance of the nation's leaders.

Larry Berman, a political scientist, offered a somewhat different view in *Planning a Tragedy* (1982). Lyndon Johnson never believed that American prospects in Vietnam were bright or that a real victory was within sight, Berman argued. Johnson was not misled by his advisers. He committed American troops to the war in Vietnam in 1965 not because he expected to win but because he feared that allowing Vietnam to fall would ruin him politically. To do otherwise, Johnson believed, would destroy his hopes for winning approval of his Great Society legislation at home.

Leslie H. Gelb (who as an official in the Defense Department in the 1960s directed the writing of the official study of the war that became known as the Pentagon Papers) produced another, related explanation for American intervention, which saw the roots of the involvement in the larger imperatives of the American foreign policy system. In *The Irony of Vietnam: the System Worked*, published in 1979 and written in collaboration with political scientist Richard K. Betts, Gelb argued that intervention in Vietnam was the logical perhaps even inevitable result of a political and bureaucratic order shaped by certain ideological assumptions. The American foreign policy system was wedded to the doctrine of containment and operated, therefore, in response to a single, overriding imperative: the need to prevent the expansion of communism.

The United States, Gelb maintained, stumbled into a commitment to a shaky government in South Vietnam in the 1950s, and the unvarying policy of every subsequent administration until 1975 was to do what was necessary to prevent the collapse of that government. They were doing so not because they anticipated victory but because they saw no alternative. However high the costs of intervention, they believed, the costs of not intervening, of allowing South Vietnam to fall, would be higher. At every step, American presidents did the minimum they thought necessary to stave off the collapse of South Vietnam. In the 1950s and early 1960s, that meant modest economic and military assistance. In the mid-1960s, as the military situation worsened, the same commitment required the introduction of American troops in large numbers. Only when the national and international political situation had shifted to the point where it was possible for American policymakers to reassess the costs of the commitment—to conclude that the costs of allowing Vietnam to fall were less than the costs of continuing the commitment (a shift that began to occur in the early 1970s)—was it possible for the United States to begin disengaging.

From Aid to Intervention

Lyndon Johnson thus inherited what was already a substantial American commitment to the survival of an anticommunist South Vietnam. During his first two years in office, he expanded that commitment into a full-scale American war. Why he did so has long been a subject of debate. (See "Where Historians Disagree," above.)

Many factors played a role in Johnson's decision. But the most obvious explanation is that the new president faced many pressures to expand the American involvement and only a very few to limit it. As the untested successor to a revered and martyred president, he felt obliged to prove his worthiness for the office by continuing the policies of his predecessor. Aid to South Vietnam had been one of the most prominent of those policies. Johnson also felt it necessary to retain in his administration many of the important figures of the Kennedy years. In doing so, he surrounded himself with a group of foreign policy advisers—Secretary of State Dean Rusk, Secretary of Defense Robert McNamara, National Security Adviser McGeorge Bundy, and others—who firmly believed that the United States had an obligation to resist communism in Vietnam. A compliant Congress raised little protest to, and indeed at one point openly endorsed, Johnson's use of executive powers to lead the nation into war. And for several years at least, public opinion remained firmly behind him—in part because Barry Goldwater's bellicose remarks about the war during the 1964 campaign made Johnson seem by comparison to be a moderate on the issue.

Above all, intervention in South Vietnam was fully consistent with nearly twenty years of American foreign policy. An anticommunist ally was appealing to the United States for assistance; all the assumptions of the containment doctrine, as it had come to be defined by the 1960s, seemed to require the nation to oblige. Vietnam, Johnson believed, was a test of American willingness to fight communist aggression, a test he was determined not to fail.

During his first months in office, Johnson expanded the American involvement in Vietnam only slightly, sending an additional 5,000 military advisers there and preparing to send 5,000 more. Then, early in August 1964, the president announced that American destroyers on patrol in international waters in the Gulf of Tonkin had been attacked by North Vietnamese torpedo boats. Later information raised serious doubts as to whether the administration reported the attacks accurately. At the time, however, virtually no one questioned Johnson's portrayal of the incident as a serious act of aggression, or his insistence that the United States must respond. By a vote of 416 to 0 in the House and 88 to 2 in the Senate, Congress hurriedly passed the Gulf of Tonkin Resolution, which authorized the president to "take all necessary measures" to protect American forces and "prevent further aggression" in Southeast Asia. The resolution became, in Johnson's view at least, an open-ended legal authorization for escalation of the conflict.

With the South Vietnamese leadership still in disarray, more and more of the burden of opposition to the Viet Cong fell on the United States. In February 1965, seven marines died when communist forces attacked an American military base at Pleiku. Johnson retaliated by ordering American bombings of the north, which attempted to destroy the depots and transportation lines responsible for the flow of North Vietnamese soldiers and supplies into South Vietnam. The bombing continued intermittently until 1972. A month later, in March 1965, two battalions of American marines landed at Da Nang in South Vietnam. There were now more than 100,000 American troops in Vietnam.

Four months later, the president finally admitted that the character of the war had changed. American soldiers would now, he announced, begin playing an active combat role in the conflict. By the end of the year, there were more than 180,000 American combat troops in Vietnam; in 1966, that number doubled; and by the end of 1967, there were over 500,000 American soldiers there—along with a considerable number of civilian personnel working in various capacities and many American women (some enlisted, some not) who worked as nurses in military hospitals. In the meantime, the air war had intensified; ultimately the tonnage of bombs dropped on North Vietnam would exceed that in all theaters during World War II. And American casualties were mounting. In 1961, 14 Americans had died in Vietnam. By the spring of 1966, more than 4,000 Americans had been killed.

Yet the gains resulting from the carnage were negligible. The United States had finally succeeded in 1965 in creating a reasonably stable government in the south under General Nguyen Van Thieu. But the new regime was hardly less corrupt or brutal than its predecessors, and no more able than they to establish its authority in its own countryside. The Viet Cong, not the Thieu regime, controlled the majority of South Vietnam's villages and hamlets.

The Quagmire

For more than seven years, American combat forces remained bogged down in a war that the United States was never able either to win or fully to understand. Combating a foe whose strength lay less in weaponry than in its infiltration of the population, the United States responded with heavy-handed technological warfare designed for conventional battles against conventional armies. American forces succeeded in winning most of the major battles in which they became engaged. There were astounding (if not always reliable) weekly casualty figures showing that far more communists than Americans were dying in combat. There was a continuous stream of optimistic reports from American military commanders, government officials, and others—including a famous statement of Secretary of Defense McNamara that he could see the

ON PATROL IN VIETNAM
A platoon of American soldiers tries to locate its position as it patrols the Vietnamese countryside in 1966. Among the many things that distinguished the Vietnam War from other conflicts in which Americans have fought was the difficulty of deciphering a terrain unlike any in the United States and the difficulty in locating, or even identifying, the enemy. *(Jim Pickerell/ Black Star)*

light at the end of the tunnel." But if the war was not actually being lost, neither was it being won.

Central to the American war effort was a commitment to what the military called "attrition," a strategy premised on the belief that the United States could inflict so many casualties and so much damage on the enemy that eventually they would be unable and unwilling to continue the struggle. But the attrition strategy failed because the North Vietnamese proved willing to commit many more soldiers to the conflict than the United States had expected (and many more than America itself was willing to send).

It failed, too, because the United States relied heavily on its bombing of the north to eliminate the communists' war-making capacity. American bombers struck at strategic targets (factories, bridges, railroads, shipyards, oil storage depots, etc.) in North Vietnam to weaken the material capacity of the communists to continue the war; and they bombed jungle areas of Vietnam, Laos, and Cambodia to cut off the "Ho Chi Minh Trail," the infiltration routes by which Hanoi sent troops and supplies into the south. In addition, the Americans hoped bombing would weaken the will of North Vietnam to continue the war.

By the end of 1967, virtually every identifiable target of any strategic importance in North Vietnam had been destroyed. The bombing had badly damaged the North Vietnamese economy, killed many soldiers and civilians, and made life difficult for those who survived, but it had produced none of the effects that the United States had expected. North Vietnam was not a modern, industrial society; it had few of the sorts of targets against which bombing is effective. And in any case, the North Vietnamese responded to the air raids with enormous ingenuity: they created a great network of underground tunnels, shops, and factories. They also secured increased aid from the Soviet Union and China. Infiltration of the south was unaffected; the North Vietnamese just kept moving the Ho Chi Minh Trail. Nor did the bombing weaken North Vietnam's will to continue fighting. On the contrary, it seemed to increase the nation's resolve and strengthen its hatred of the United States. As one North Vietnamese leader later explained: "There was extraordinary fervor then. The Americans thought that the more bombs they dropped, the quicker we would fall to our knees and surrender. But the bombs heightened rather than dampened our spirit."

Another crucial part of the American strategy was the "pacification" program, whose purpose was to push the Viet Cong from particular regions and then "pacify" those regions by winning the "hearts and minds" of the people. Routing the Viet Cong was often possible, but the subsequent pacification was more difficult. American forces were not adept at establishing the same kind of rapport with provincial Vietnamese that the Viet Cong had created; and the American military never gave that part of the program a very high priority in any case. Gradually, the pacification program gave way to a more heavy-handed relocation strategy, through which American troops uprooted villagers from their homes, sent them fleeing to refugee camps or into the cities (producing by 1967 more than 3 million refugees), and then destroyed the vacated villages and surrounding countryside. Saturation bombings (using conventional weapons and such inflammatory devices as napalm), bulldozing of settlements, chemical defoliation of fields and jungles—all were designed to eliminate possible Viet Cong sanctuaries. But the Viet Cong responded by moving to new sanctuaries elsewhere. The futility of the United States effort was suggested by the statement of an American officer after flattening one such hamlet that it had been "necessary to destroy [the village] in order to save it."

As the war dragged on and victory remained elusive, some American officers and officials began to urge the president to expand the military efforts. Some argued for heavier bombing and increased troop strength; others insisted that the United States attack communist enclaves in surrounding countries; a few began to urge the use of nuclear weapons. The Johnson administration, however, resisted. Unwilling to abandon its commitment to South Vietnam for fear of destroying American "credibility" in the world, the government was also unwilling to expand the war too far, for fear of provoking direct intervention by the Chinese, the Soviets, or both. In the meantime, the president began to encounter additional obstacles and frustrations at home.

The War at Home

As late as the end of 1965, few Americans, and even fewer influential ones, had protested the American involvement in Vietnam. But as the war dragged on and its futility began to become apparent, political support for it began to erode. A series of "teach-ins" on university campuses, beginning at the University of Michigan in 1965, sparked a national debate over the war before such debate developed inside the government itself. Such pacifist organizations as the American Friends Service Committee and the Women's International League for Peace and Freedom organized early protests. By the end of 1967, American students opposed to the war had become a significant political force. Enormous peace marches in New York, Washington, D.C., and other cities drew broad public attention to the antiwar movement. In the meantime, a growing number of journalists, particularly reporters who had spent time in Vietnam, helped sustain the movement with their frank revelations about the brutality and apparent futility of the war.

The growing chorus of popular protest soon began to stimulate opposition to the war from within the government. Senator J. William Fulbright of Arkansas, chairman of the powerful Senate Foreign Relations Committee, turned against the war and in January 1966 began to stage highly publicized and occasionally televised congressional hearings to air criticisms of it. Distinguished figures such as George F. Kennan and retired General James Gavin testified against the conflict,

giving opposition to the war greater respectability in the minds of many Americans generally unwilling to question the government or the military. Other members of Congress joined Fulbright in opposing Johnson's policies—including, in 1967, Robert F. Kennedy, brother of the slain president, now a senator from New York. Even within the administration, the consensus seemed to be crumbling. Robert McNamara, who had done much to help extend the American involvement in Vietnam, quietly left the government, disillusioned, in 1968. His successor as secretary of defense, Clark Clifford, became a quiet but powerful voice within the administration on behalf of a cautious scaling down of the commitment.

In the meantime, the American economy was beginning to suffer. Johnson's commitment to fighting the war while continuing his Great Society reforms—his promise of "guns and butter"—proved impossible to maintain. The inflation rate, which had remained at 2 percent through most of the early 1960s, rose to 3 percent in 1967, 4 percent in 1968, and 6 percent in 1969. In August 1967, Johnson asked Congress for a tax increase—a 10 percent surcharge that was widely labeled a "war tax"—which he knew was necessary if the nation was to avoid even more ruinous inflation. In return, congressional conservatives demanded and received a $6 billion reduction in the funding for Great Society programs.

THE TRAUMAS OF 1968

By the end of 1967, the twin crises of the war in Vietnam and the deteriorating racial situation at home, crises that fed upon and inflamed each other, had produced profound social and political tensions. In the course of 1968, those tensions seemed suddenly to burst to the surface and to threaten the nation with genuine chaos. Not since World War II had the United States experienced so profound a sense of crisis.

The Tet Offensive

On January 31, 1968, the first day of the Vietnamese New Year (Tet), communist forces launched an enormous, concerted attack on American strongholds throughout South Vietnam. A few cities, most notably Hue, fell to the communists. Others suffered major disruptions. But what made the Tet offensive so shocking to the American people, who saw vivid reports of it on television, was the sight of communist forces in the heart of Saigon, setting off bombs, shooting down

South Vietnamese officials and troops, and holding down fortified areas (including, briefly, the grounds of the American embassy).

The Tet offensive also suggested to the American public something of the brutality of the war in Vietnam. In the midst of the fighting, television cameras recorded the sight of a captured Viet Cong soldier being led up to a South Vietnamese officer in the streets of Saigon. Without a word, the officer pulled out his pistol and shot the young man in the head, leaving him lying dead in the street, his blood pouring onto the pavement. No single event did more to undermine support for the war in the United States.

American forces soon dislodged the Viet Cong from most of the positions they had seized, and the Tet offensive in the end cost the communists such appalling casualties that they were significantly weakened for months to come. Indeed, the Tet defeats permanently depleted the ranks of the NLF and forced North Vietnamese troops to take on a much larger share of the subsequent fighting. But all that had little impact on American opinion. Tet may have been a military victory for the United States; but it was a political defeat for the administration, a defeat from which it would never fully recover.

In the following weeks, opposition to the war grew substantially. Leading newspapers and magazines, television commentators, and mainstream politicians began taking public stands in favor of de-escalation of the conflict. Within weeks of the Tet offensive, public opposition to the war had almost doubled. And Johnson's personal popularity rating had slid to 35 percent, the lowest of any president since Harry Truman.

The Political Challenge

Beginning in the summer of 1967, dissident Democrats (led by the talented activist Allard Lowenstein) tried to mobilize support behind an antiwar candidate who would challenge Lyndon Johnson in the 1968 primaries. When Robert Kennedy declined their invitation, they turned to Senator Eugene McCarthy of Minnesota. A brilliantly orchestrated campaign by Lowenstein and thousands of young volunteers in the New Hampshire primary produced a startling showing by McCarthy in March; he nearly defeated the president.

A few days later, Robert Kennedy finally entered the campaign, embittering many McCarthy supporters, but bringing his own substantial strength among blacks, poor people, and workers to the antiwar cause. Polls showed the president trailing badly in the next scheduled primary, in Wisconsin. Indeed, public animosity toward the president was now so intense that Johnson did not even dare leave the White House to

campaign. On March 31, Johnson went on television to announce a limited halt in the bombing of North Vietnam—his first major concession to the antiwar forces—and, much more surprising, his withdrawal from the presidential contest.

For a moment, it seemed as though the antiwar forces had won. Robert Kennedy quickly established himself as the champion of the Democratic primaries, winning one election after another. In the meantime, however, Vice President Hubert Humphrey, with the support of President Johnson, entered the contest and began to attract the support of party leaders and of the many delegations that were selected not by popular primaries but by state party organizations. He soon appeared to be the front-runner in the race.

The King and Kennedy Assassinations

In the midst of this bitter political battle, in which the war had been the dominant issue, attention suddenly turned back to the nation's bitter racial conflicts. On April 4, Martin Luther King, Jr., who had traveled to Memphis, Tennessee, to lend his support to striking black sanitation workers in the city, was shot and killed while standing on the balcony of his motel. The assassin, James Earl Ray, who was captured days later in London and eventually convicted, had no apparent motive. Later evidence suggested that he had been hired by others to do the killing, but he himself has never revealed the identity of his employers.

King's tragic death produced an outpouring of grief matched in recent memory only by the reaction to the death of John Kennedy. Among American blacks, it also produced anger. In the days after the assassination, major riots broke out in more than sixty American cities. Forty-three people died; more than 3,000 suffered injuries; as many as 27,000 people were arrested.

For two months following the death of King, Robert Kennedy continued his campaign for the presidential nomination. Late in the night of June 6, he appeared in the ballroom of a Los Angeles hotel to acknowledge his victory in that day's California primary. As he left the ballroom after his victory statement, Sirhan Sirhan, a young Palestinian apparently enraged by pro-Israeli remarks Kennedy had recently made, emerged from a crowd and shot him in the head. Early the next morning, Kennedy died.

By the time of his death, Robert Kennedy—who earlier in his career had been widely considered a cold, ruthless agent of his more appealing brother—had emerged as a figure of enormous popular appeal. More than John Kennedy, Robert identified his hopes with the American "underclass"—with blacks, Hispanics, Indians, the poor—and with the many American liberals who were coming to believe that the problems of such groups demanded attention. Indeed, Robert Kennedy, much more than John, shaped what some would later call the "Kennedy legacy," a set of ideas that would for a time become central to American liberalism: the fervent commitment to using government to help the powerless. In addition, Robert had an impassioned following among many people who saw in him (and his family) the kind of glamour and hopefulness they had come, at least in retrospect, to identify with the martyred president. His campaign appearances inspired outbursts of public enthusiasm rarely seen in political life. The passions Kennedy had aroused made his violent death a particularly shattering experience for many Americans.

The presidential campaign continued gloomily during the last weeks before the convention. Hubert Humphrey, who had seemed likely to win the nomination even before Robert Kennedy's death, now faced only minor opposition—despite the embittered claims of many Democrats that Humphrey would simply continue the bankrupt policies of the Johnson administration. The approaching Democratic Convention, therefore, began to take on the appearance of an exercise in futility; and antiwar activists, despairing of winning any victories within the convention, began to plan major demonstrations outside it.

When the Democrats finally gathered in Chicago in August, even the most optimistic observers were predicting a turbulent convention. Inside the hall, delegates bitterly debated an antiwar plank in the party platform that both Kennedy and McCarthy supporters favored. Miles away, in a downtown park, thousands of antiwar protesters were staging demonstrations. On the third night of the convention, as the delegates were beginning their balloting on the now virtually inevitable nomination of Hubert Humphrey, demonstrators and police clashed in a bloody riot in the streets of Chicago. Hundreds of protesters were injured as police attempted to disperse them with tear gas and billy clubs. Aware that the violence was being televised to the nation, the demonstrators taunted the authorities with the chant, "The whole world is watching!" And Hubert Humphrey, who had spent years dreaming of becoming his party's candidate for president, received a nomination that appeared at the time to be almost worthless.

The Conservative Response

The turbulent events of 1968 persuaded many observers that American society was in the throes of revolutionary change. In fact, however, the response of most Americans to the turmoil was a conservative one.

CHICAGO, 1968
Demonstrators climb on a statue in a Chicago park during the 1968 Democratic National Convention, protesting both the Vietnam War and the harsh treatment they themselves had received from Mayor Richard Daley's Chicago police.
(Dennis Brack/Black Star)

The most visible sign of the conservative backlash was the surprising success of the campaign of George Wallace for the presidency. Wallace had established himself in 1963 as one of the nation's leading spokesmen for the defense of segregation when, as governor of Alabama, he had attempted to block the admission of black students to the University of Alabama. In 1964, he had run in a few Democratic presidential primaries and had done surprising well, even in several states outside the South. In 1968, he became a third-party candidate for president, basing his campaign on a host of conservative grievances, not all of them connected to race. He denounced the forced busing of students, the proliferation of government regulations and social

SIGNIFICANT EVENTS

1959 Soviet Comintern urges wars of "national liberation" in the Third World

National Liberation Front (NLF) created in Vietnam

1960 John F. Kennedy elected president

Greensboro sit-ins

War resumes in Vietnam

1961 Freedom rides

United States supports failed invasion of Bay of Pigs

Kennedy meets Khrushchev in Vienna

Berlin Wall erected

Peace Corps established

Alliance for Progress established

1962 Steel price increase provokes controversy

Kennedy proposes tax cut to stimulate economy

Desegregation crisis at University of Mississippi

Cuban missile crisis

1963 Martin Luther King, Jr., begins Birmingham campaign

Desegregation crisis at University of Alabama

Kennedy proposes civil rights bill

March on Washington

Test ban treaty signed

Buddhist crisis in Vietnam; Diem toppled by coup

Kennedy assassinated; Lyndon B. Johnson becomes president

1964 Johnson launches war on poverty

Congress passes tax cut

"Freedom summer" campaign in Mississippi

Congress passes Civil Rights Act

Gulf of Tonkin Resolution passed

United States begins bombing of North Vietnam

Johnson elected president by record margin

1965 Medicare enacted

Elementary and Secondary Education Act passed

Selma campaign for voting rights

Race riot breaks out in Watts, Los Angeles

Malcolm X publishes *Autobiography*

Malcolm X assassinated

Congress passes Voting Rights Act

United States intervenes in Dominican Republic

American combat troops sent to Vietnam

Antiwar activities begin on university campuses

Immigration Reform Act passed

1966 Medicaid enacted

King leads Chicago campaign

Senate Foreign Relations Committee holds hearings on Vietnam

1967 Johnson requests tax increase

Race riot breaks out in Detroit

Antiwar movement intensifies

1968 Department of Labor issues affirmative action rules

Viet Cong launch Tet offensive

Johnson withdraws from presidential contest

Martin Luther King, Jr., assassinated

Racial violence breaks out in American cities

Robert Kennedy assassinated

Demonstrators clash with police at Democratic National Convention

George Wallace launches third-party presidential campaign

Richard M. Nixon elected president

programs, and the permissiveness of authorities toward race riots and antiwar demonstrations. There was never any serious chance that Wallace would win the election; but his standing in the polls at times rose to over 20 percent.

A more effective effort to mobilize the "silent majority" in favor of order and stability was under way within the Republican Party. Richard Nixon, whose political career had seemed at an end after his losses in the presidential race of 1960 and a California gubernatorial campaign two years later, reemerged as the preeminent spokesman for what he called "Middle America." Nixon recognized that many Americans were tired of hearing about their obligations to the poor, tired of hearing about the sacrifices necessary to achieve racial justice, tired of judicial reforms that seemed designed to help criminals. By offering a vision of stability, law and order, government retrenchment, and "peace with honor" in Vietnam, he easily captured the nomination of his party for the presidency. And after the spectacle of the Democratic Convention, he enjoyed a commanding lead in the polls as the November election approached.

That lead diminished greatly in the last weeks before the voting. Old doubts about Nixon's character continued to haunt the Republican candidate. A skillful last-minute surge by Hubert Humphrey, who managed to restore a tenuous unity to the Democratic Party, narrowed the gap further. And the Wallace campaign appeared to be hurting the Republicans more than the Democrats. In the end, however, Nixon eked out a victory almost as narrow as his defeat in 1960. He received 43.4 percent of the popular vote to Humphrey's 42.7 percent (a margin of only about 500,000 votes), and 301 electoral votes to Humphrey's 191. George Wallace, who like most third-party candidates faded in the last weeks of the campaign, still managed to poll 13.5 percent of the popular vote

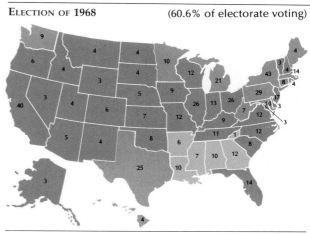

ELECTION OF 1968 (60.6% of electorate voting)

	ELECTORAL VOTE	POPULAR VOTE (%)
Richard M. Nixon (Republican)	301	31,770,237 (43.4)
Hubert H. Humphrey (Democratic)	191	31,270,533 (42.7)
George C. Wallace (American Independence)	46	9,906,141 (13.5)
Other candidates (Socialist Labor; D. Gregory; Socialist Workers; Peace and Freedom; McCarthy; Prohibition)	—	218,347

and to carry five southern states with a total of 46 electoral ballots—the best showing by a third-party candidate since the 1920s. Nixon had not won a decisive personal mandate. But the election made clear that a majority of the American electorate was more interested in restoring stability than in promoting social change.

SUGGESTED READINGS

General Studies. William Chafe, *The Unfinished Journey: America Since World War II*, rev. ed. (1991). Godfrey Hodgson, *America in Our Time* (1976). Allen J. Matusow, *The Unraveling of America: A History of Liberalism in the 1960s* (1984). Charles R. Morris, *A Time of Passion* (1984). Theodore H. White, *America in Search of Itself* (1982).

Kennedy and Johnson. Vaughn D. Bornet, *The Presidency of Lyndon B. Johnson* (1983). Thomas Brown, *JFK: The History of an Image* (1988). David Burner, *John F. Kennedy and a New Generation* (1988). Robert Caro, *The Years of Lyndon B. Johnson: The Path to Power* (1982); *Means of Ascent* (1990). Paul K. Conkin, *Big Daddy from the Pedernales* (1986). Robert Dallek, *Lone Star Rising: Lyndon Johnson and His Times, 1908–1960* (1991). Ronnie Dugger, *The Politician* (1982). Edward J. Epstein, *Inquest* (1966); *Legend* (1978). Henry Fairlie, *The Kennedy Promise: The Politics of Expectation* (1973). Eric Goldman, *The Tragedy of Lyndon Johnson* (1968). Richard N. Goodwin, *Remembering America* (1988). Jim Heath, *Decade of Disillusionment* (1975). Henry Hurt, *Reasonable Doubt* (1985). Lyndon B. Johnson, *Vantage Point* (1971). Doris Kearns, *Lyndon Johnson and the American Dream* (1976). Donald Lord, *John F. Kennedy: The Politics of Confrontation and Conciliation* (1977). William Manchester, *The Death of a President* (1967). Bruce Miroff, *Pragmatic Illusions: The Presidential Politics of JFK* (1976). Lewis Paper, *The Promise and the Performance* (1975). Herbert Parmet, *Jack* (1980); *JFK* (1983). George

Reedy, *The Twilight of the Presidency* (1970). Richard Reeves, *President Kennedy* (1992). Thomas Reeves, *A Question of Character: The Life of John F. Kennedy in Image and Reality* (1991). Arthur M. Schlesinger, Jr. , *A Thousand Days* (1965). Theodore Sorensen, *Kennedy* (1965). Anthony Summers, *Conspiracy* (1980). Warren Commission, *The Report of the Warren Commission* (1964). Theodore H. White, *The Making of the President, 1960* (1961). Garry Wills, *The Kennedy Imprisonment* (1982).

Domestic Policies and Politics.   Henry J. Aaron, *Politics and the Professors* (1978). Greg J. Duncan, *Years of Poverty, Years of Plenty* (1984). Mark Gelfand, *A Nation of Cities* (1975). James Giglio, *The Presidency of John F. Kennedy* (1991). Hugh Davis Graham, *Uncertain Trumpet* (1984). Robert H. Haveman, ed. , *A Decade of Federal Antipoverty Programs* (1977). Jim Heath, *John F. Kennedy and the Business Community* (1969). Daniel Knapp and Kenneth Polk, *Scouting the War on Poverty* (1971). Sar Levitan, *The Great Society's Poor Law* (1969). Sar Levitan and Robert Taggart, *The Promise of Greatness* (1976). Allen J. Matusow, *The Unraveling of America: A History of Liberalism in the 1960s* (1984). Charles Morris, *A Time of Passion* (1984). Charles Murray, *Losing Ground* (1984). Victor Navasky, *Kennedy Justice* (1971). James T. Patterson, *America's Struggle Against Poverty, 1900–1980* (1981). Frances Fox Piven and Richard Cloward, *Regulating the Poor* (1971). John E. Schwarz, *America's Hidden Success* (1983). James L. Sundquist, *Politics and Policy: The Eisenhower, Kennedy, and Johnson Years* (1968). Tom Wicker, *JFK and LBJ* (1968).

Race Relations.   Taylor Branch, *Parting the Waters: America in the King Years* (1988). Carl Brauer, *John F. Kennedy and the Second Reconstruction* (1977). Paul Burstein, *Discrimination, Jobs, and Politics* (1985). James Button, *Black Violence: Political Impact of the 1960s Race Riots* (1978). Stokely Carmichael and Charles Hamilton, *Black Power* (1967). Clayborne Carson, *In Struggle: SNCC and the Black Awakening of the 1960s* (1981). William Chafe, *Civilities and Civil Rights: Greensboro, North Carolina, and the Black Struggle for Freedom* (1980). Joe R. Feagin and Harlan Hahn, *Ghetto Revolts* (1973). Robert Fogelson, *Violence as Protest* (1971). David Garrow, *Protest at Selma* (1978); *The FBI and Martin Luther King* (1981); *Bearing the Cross* (1986). Hugh Davis Graham, *The Civil Rights Era* (1990). Alex Haley, *The Autobiography of Malcolm X* (1966). Martin Luther King, Jr., *Why We Can't Wait* (1964). Steven Lawson, *Black Ballots: Voting Rights in the South, 1966–1969* (1976). Nicholas Lemann, *The Promised Land: The Great Black Migration and How It Changed America* (1991). David L. Lewis, *King: A Critical Biography* (1970). Doug McAdam, *Freedom Summer* (1988). Benjamin Muse, *The American Negro Revolution* (1969). *Report of the National Advisory Commission on Civil Disorders* (1968). Stephen Oates, *Let the Trumpet Sound* (1982). Harvard Sitkoff, *The Struggle for Black Equality, 1954–1992* (1992). Mark Stern, *Calculating Visions: Kennedy, Johnson and Civil Rights* (1992). Abigail Thernstrom, *Whose Votes Count? Affirmative Action and Minority Voting Rights* (1987). Harris Wofford, *Of Kennedy and Kings* (1980). Eugene Wolfenstein, *The Victims of Democracy: Malcolm X and the Black Revolution* (1981).

Foreign Policy.   Elie Abel, *The Missile Crisis* (1966). Graham Allison, *Essence of Decision* (1971). Richard Barnet, *Intervention and Revolution* (1968). Michael Bechloss, *The Crisis Years* (1990).

McGeorge Bundy, *Danger and Survival* (1989). Warren Cohen, *Dean Rusk* (1980). Herbert Dinerstein, *The Making of a Missile Crisis* (1976). Bernard Firestone, *The Quest for Nuclear Stability* (1982). Louise Fitzsimmons, *The Kennedy Doctrine* (1972). Philip Geyelin, *Lyndon B. Johnson and the World* (1966). John Girling, *America and the Third World* (1980). Trumbull Higgins, *The Perfect Failure: Kennedy, Eisenhower, and the CIA at the Bay of Pigs* (1987). Roger Hilsman, *To Move a Nation* (1965). Haynes Johnson, *The Bay of Pigs* (1964). Robert Kennedy, *Thirteen Days* (1969). Dan Kurzman, *Santo Domingo* (1966). Walter LaFeber, *Inevitable Revolutions: The United States in Central America* (1985). Thomas J. McCormick, *America's Half Century: United States Foreign Policy in the Cold War* (1989). Richard D. Mahoney, *JFK: Ordeal in Africa* (1983). Gerald T. Rice, *The Bold Experiment: JFK's Peace Corps* (1985). Jerome Slater, *Intervention and Negotiation* (1970). Richard Walton, *Cold War and Counterrevolution* (1972). Peter Wyden, *Bay of Pigs* (1969).

Vietnam.   Mark Baker, *Nam* (1982). Lawrence Baskir and William Strauss, *Chance and Circumstance* (1978). Larry Berman, *Planning a Tragedy* (1982); *Lyndon Johnson's War* (1989). Peter Braestrup, *Big Story* (1977; abridged ed. 1978). William Broyles, Jr. , *Brothers in Arms: A Journey from War to Peace* (1986). Philip Davidson, *Vietnam at War* (1991). Gloria Emerson, *Winners and Losers* (1976). Frances Fitzgerald, *Fire in the Lake* (1972). John Galloway, *The Gulf of Tonkin Resolution* (1970). Leslie Gelb and Richard Betts, *The Irony of Vietnam: The System Worked* (1979). David Halberstam, *The Best and the Brightest* (1972). Michael Herr, *Dispatches* (1977). George C. Herring, *America's Longest War*, rev. ed. (1986). George McT. Kahin, *Intervention* (1986). Stanley Karnow, *Vietnam* (1983). Alexander Kendrick, *The Wound Within* (1974). Gabriel Kolko, *The Anatomy of a War* (1985). Robert W. Komer, *Bureaucracy at War* (1986). David Levy, *The Debate over Vietnam* (1991). Guenter Lewy, *America in Vietnam* (1978). Don Oberdorfer, *Tet* (1971). Bruce C. Palmer, Jr., *The 25-Year War* (1984). *The Pentagon Papers*, Senator Gravel edition (1975). Norman Podhoretz, *Why We Were in Vietnam* (1982). Thomas Powers, *Vietnam: The War at Home* (1973). Al Santoli, *Everything We Had* (1981). Herbert Schandler, *The Unmaking of a President: Lyndon Johnson and Vietnam* (1977). Neil Sheehan, *A Bright Shining Lie* (1988). R. B. Smith, *An International History of the Vietnam War: The Kennedy Strategy* (1985). Ronald Spector, *Advice and Support* (1983). Col. Harry Summers, *On Strategy* (1981). Wallace Terry, *Bloods* (1984). Thomas C. Thayer, *War Without Fronts* (1985). Wallace J. Thies, *When Governments Collide* (1980). James Thompson, *Rolling Thunder* (1980). Kathleen J. Turner, *Lyndon Johnson's Dual War: Vietnam and the Press* (1981). Irwin Unger, *The Movement* (1974). Marilyn Young, *The Vietnam Wars* (1991).

1968.   David Caute, *The Year of the Barricades* (1988). Lewis Chester, Godfrey Hodgson, and Lewis Page, *American Melodrama* (1969). David Farber, *Chicago '68* (1988). Marshall Frady, *Wallace*, rev. ed. (1976). Godfrey Hodgson, *America in Our Time* (1976). Charles Kaiser, *1968 in America* (1988). Norman Mailer, *Miami and the Siege of Chicago* (1968). Arthur M. Schlesinger, Jr., *Robert Kennedy and His Times* (1978). Ben Stavis, *We Were the Campaign* (1969). Theodore White, *The Making of the President, 1968* (1969).

THE CAMBODIAN INVASION, 1970
Richard Nixon precipitated one of the biggest crises of his turbulent presidency in the spring
of 1970 when he announced that American troops were invading Cambodia in search of
North Vietnamese sanctuaries there. In the days after the president's television address,
antiwar protests reached their highest (and most violent) levels ever. *(Dennis Brack/Black Star)*

CHAPTER THIRTY-TWO

THE CRISIS OF AUTHORITY

R ICHARD NIXON'S ELECTION IN 1968 was the result of more than the unpopularity of Lyndon Johnson and the war. It was the result, too, of a strong public reaction against what many Americans considered a frontal assault on the foundations of their culture. Throughout the late 1960s and early 1970s, new interest groups were mobilizing to demand protections and benefits. New values and assumptions were emerging to challenge traditional patterns of thought and behavior. The United States was in the throes, some believed, of a genuine cultural revolution.

Some Americans welcomed the changes. But the 1968 election returns suggested that more feared them. There was growing resentment against the attention directed toward minorities and the poor, against the federal social programs that were funneling billions of dollars into the inner cities to help the poor and unemployed, against the increasing tax burden on the middle class, against the "hippies" and radicals who were dominating public discourse with their bitter critiques of values most middle-class Americans held dear. It was time, many men and women believed, for a restoration of stability and a relegitimation of traditional centers of authority.

In Richard Nixon they found a man who seemed to match their mood perfectly. Himself a product of a hardworking, middle-class family, he had risen to prominence on the basis of his own unrelenting efforts, and he projected an image of stern dedication to traditional values. Yet the presidency of Richard Nixon, far from returning calm and stability to American politics, coincided with, and in many ways helped to produce, more years of crisis.

THE YOUTH CULTURE

Perhaps most alarming to conservative Americans in the 1960s and 1970s was a pattern of social and cultural protest that was emerging from younger Americans, who were giving vent to two related impulses. One was the impulse, originating with the political left, to create a great new community of "the people," which would rise up to break the power of elites and force the nation to end the war, pursue racial and economic justice, and transform its political life. The other at least equally powerful impulse was related to, but not entirely compatible with the first: the vision of individual "liberation." It found expression, in part, through the efforts of particular groups—African Americans, Indians, Hispanics, women, gay people, and others—to define and assert themselves and make demands on the larger society. It also found expression through the efforts of individuals to create a new culture—one that would allow them to escape from what they considered the dehumanizing pressures of what some called the modern "technocracy."

The New Left

In retrospect, it seems unsurprising that young Americans became so assertive and powerful in American

849

culture and politics in the 1960s. The postwar baby boom, the unprecedented number of people born in a few years just after World War II, was growing up. By 1970, more than half the American population was under thirty years old; more than 8 million Americans—eight times the number in 1950—were attending college. This was the largest generation of youth in American history, and it was coming to maturity in a time of unprecedented affluence, opportunity, and—for many—frustration. Relatively few of these young people embraced radical political causes or rebelled in any fundamental way against their culture. But those who did were numerous enough, and assertive enough, to have a disproportionate impact on both the cultural and the political climate.

One of the most visible results of the increasingly assertive youth movement was a radicalization of many American college and university students, who in the course of the 1960s formed what became known as the New Left—a large, diverse group of men and women energized by the polarizing developments of their time to challenge the political system. The New Left embraced the cause of African Americans and other minorities, but its own ranks consisted overwhelmingly of white people. Blacks and minorities formed political movements of their own.

The New Left drew from many sources. Some of its members were the children of radical parents (members of the so-called Old Left of the 1930s and 1940s), and had grown up with a critical view of society and politics. Indeed, the New Left drew considerable support, and guidance, from groups and individuals from the Old Left; it was not as entirely "new" as its champions liked to claim. The New Left drew as well from the writings of some of the important social critics of the 1950s—among them C. Wright Mills, a sociologist at Columbia University who wrote a series of scathing and brilliant critiques of modern bureaucracies. And while relatively few members of the New Left were communists, many were drawn to the writings of Karl Marx and such other Marxist theorists as Antonio Gramsci and Herbert Marcuse. Some came to revere Third World Marxists such as Che Guevara, Mao Zedong, and Ho Chi Minh. For a while, left-leaning figures in the labor movement helped nurture the New Left—although relations between the two movements soon deteriorated beyond repair over the New Left's unwillingness to embrace the anti-communism of the AFL-CIO.

But the New Left drew from nothing so much as the civil rights movement, in which many idealistic young white Americans had become involved in the early 1960s. Racism, oppression, and violence were nothing new to the many African Americans fighting for civil rights. But to white college students from mid-dle-class backgrounds, the exposure to social injustice (and personal danger) in the South was shocking and disillusioning, and it led many of them to question their assumptions about the basic values and institutions of American life. Within a few years, some white civil rights activists were beginning to consider broader political commitments.

In 1962, a group of students, most of them from prestigious universities, gathered in Michigan (at a conference center owned by the United Auto Workers) to form an organization to give voice to their demands: Students for a Democratic Society (SDS). Their declaration of beliefs, the Port Huron Statement, expressed their disillusionment with the society they had inherited and their determination to build a new politics. "Many of us began maturing in complacency," the statement (most of it the work of student activist Tom Hayden) declared. "As we grew, however, our comfort was penetrated by events too troubling to dismiss." In the following years, SDS became the principal organization of student radicalism.

Some members of SDS moved into inner-city neighborhoods and tried for a time, without notable success, to mobilize poor, working-class people politically. But most members of the New Left were students, and their radicalism centered for a time on issues related to the modern university. A 1964 dispute at the University of California at Berkeley over the rights of students to engage in political activities on campus gained national attention. The Free Speech Movement, as it called itself, created turmoil at Berkeley as students challenged campus police, occupied administrative offices, and produced a strike in which nearly three quarters of the Berkeley students participated. The immediate issue was the right of students to pass out literature and recruit volunteers for political causes on campus. But the protest quickly became as well an expression of a more basic critique of the university, and the society it seemed to represent. Mario Savio, a Berkeley graduate student and one of the leaders of the Free Speech Movement, captured something of the political anguish in a famous speech on campus, in which he said:

> There is a time when the operation of the machine becomes so odious, makes you so sick at heart, that you can't take part; you can't even passively take part, and you've got to put your bodies upon the gears and upon the wheels, upon the levers, upon all the apparatus and you've got to make it stop. And you've got to indicate to the people who run it, to the people who own it, that unless you're free, the machine will be prevented from working at all.

The revolt at Berkeley was the first outburst of what was to be nearly a decade of campus turmoil.

Students at Berkeley and elsewhere protested the impersonal character of the modern university, and they denounced the role of educational institutions in sustaining what they considered corrupt or immoral public policies. The antiwar movement greatly inflamed and expanded the challenge to the universities; and beginning in 1968, campus demonstrations, riots, and building seizures became almost commonplace. At Columbia University in New York, students seized the offices of the president and other members of the administration and occupied them for days until local police forcibly ejected them. Harvard University had a similar, and even more violent, experience a year later.

Also in 1969, Berkeley became the scene of perhaps the most prolonged and traumatic conflict of any American college campus in the 1960s: a battle over the efforts of a few students to build a "People's Park" on land the university planned to use to build a parking garage. This seemingly minor event precipitated weeks of impassioned and often violent conflicts between the university administration and its students and between students and police.

By the end of the People's Park battle, which lasted for more than a week, the Berkeley campus was completely polarized; even students who had not initially supported or even noticed the People's Park (the great majority) were, by the end, committed to its defense; 85 percent of the 15,000 students voted in a referendum to leave the park alone. Student radicals were, for the first time, winning large audiences for their extravagant rhetoric linking together university administrators, the police, and the larger political and economic system, describing them all as part of one united, oppressive force. As one Berkeley activist said in the midst of the battle: "You've pushed us to the end of your civilization here, against the sea in Berkeley. Then you pushed us into a square-block area called People's Park. It was the last thing we had to defend, this square block of sanity amid all your madness. . . . We are now homeless in your civilized world. We have become the great American gypsies, with only our mythology for a culture." Over the next several years, hardly any major university was immune to some level of disruption.

Most campus radicals were rarely if ever violent (except at times in their rhetoric). But the image of student radicalism in mainstream culture was one of chaos and disorder, based in part on the disruptive actions of relatively small groups of militants. As time went on, moreover, the fringes of the students became increasingly militant. Small numbers of especially dogmatic radicals—among them the "Weathermen," a violent offshoot of SDS—were responsible for a few cases of arson and bombing that destroyed campus buildings and claimed several lives.

Not many people, not even many students, ever accepted the radical political views that lay at the heart of the New Left. But many supported the position of SDS and other groups on particular issues, and above all on the Vietnam War. Student activists tried to drive training programs for military officers (ROTC) and bar military recruiters from college campuses. They attacked the laboratories and corporations that were producing weapons for the war. And between 1967 and 1969, they organized some of the largest political demonstrations in American history. The march on the Pentagon of October 1967, where demonstrators were met by a solid line of armed troops; the "spring mobilization" of April 1968, which attracted hundreds of thousands of demonstrators in cities around the country; the Vietnam "moratorium" of the fall of 1969, during which millions of opponents of the war gathered in major rallies across the nation; and countless other demonstrations, large and small—all helped thrust the issue of the war into the center of American politics.

Closely related to opposition to the war—and another issue that helped fuel the New Left—was opposition to the military draft. The gradual abolition of many traditional deferments—for graduate students, teachers, husbands, fathers, and others—swelled the ranks of those faced with conscription (and thus likely to oppose it). Draft card burnings became common features of antiwar rallies on college campuses. Many draft-age Americans simply refused induction, accepting what occasionally were long terms in jail as a result. Thousands of others fled to Canada, Sweden, and elsewhere (where they were joined by many deserters from the armed forces) to escape conscription. Not until 1977, when President Jimmy Carter issued a general pardon to draft resisters and a far more limited amnesty for deserters, did the Vietnam exiles begin to return to the country in substantial numbers.

The Counterculture

Closely related to the New Left was a new youth culture openly scornful of the values and conventions of middle-class society. The most visible characteristic of the counterculture, as it became known, was a change in lifestyle. As if to display their contempt for conventional standards, young Americans flaunted long hair, shabby or flamboyant clothing, and a rebellious disdain for traditional speech and decorum, which they replaced with their own "hippie" idiom. Also central to the counterculture were drugs: marijuana smoking—which after 1966 became almost as common a youthful diversion as beer drinking—and the less widespread but still substantial use of other, more potent hallucinogens, such as LSD.

WOODSTOCK
In the summer of 1969, more than 400,000 people gathered for a rock concert on a farm in Bethel, New York. Despite mostly terrible weather, the gathering was remarkably peaceful— sparking rapturous talk among some enthusiasts of the new youth culture about the "Woodstock nation." *(Shelly Rustin/Black Star)*

There was also a new, more permissive view of sexual behavior—the beginnings of what some called a "sexual revolution." To some degree, the emergence of more relaxed approaches to sexuality was a result less of the counterculture than of the new accessibility of effective contraceptives, most notably the birth control pill and, after 1973, legalized abortion. Fear of unwanted pregnancy, a powerful force inhibiting female sexuality, declined. But the new sexuality also reflected the counterculture's belief that individuals should strive for release from inhibitions and give vent to their instincts—including the instinct for sensual pleasure.

The counterculture's iconoclasm and hedonism sometimes masked its philosophy, which offered a fundamental challenge to the American middle-class mainstream. Like the New Left, with which it in many ways overlapped, the counterculture challenged the structure of modern American society, attacking its banality, its hollowness, its artificiality, its materialism, its isolation from nature. The most committed adherents of the counterculture—the hippies, who came to dominate the Haight-Ashbury neighborhood of San Francisco and other places, and the social dropouts, many of whom retreated to rural communes—rejected modern society altogether and attempted to find refuge in a simpler, more "natural" existence. But even those whose commitment to the counterculture was less dramatic shared a commitment to the idea of personal fulfillment through rejecting the inhibitions and conventions of middle-class culture. In a corrupt and alienating society, the new creed seemed to suggest, the first responsibility of the individual is cultivation of the self, the unleashing of one's own full potential for pleasure and fulfillment.

Theodore Roszak, whose book *The Making of a Counter Culture* (1969) became a central document of the era, captured much of the spirit of the movement in his frank admission that "the primary project of our counter culture is to proclaim a new heaven and a new earth so vast, so marvelous that the inordinate claims of technical expertise must of necessity withdraw to a subordinate and marginal status in the lives of men." Charles Reich's *The Greening of America* (1970) created a short-lived sensation with its argument that the individual should strive for a new form of consciousness—"Consciousness III," as he called it—in which the self would be the only reality.

The effects of the counterculture reached out to the larger society and helped create a new set of social norms that many young people (and some adults) chose to imitate. Long hair and freakish clothing became the badge not only of hippies and radicals but of an entire generation. The use of marijuana, the freer attitudes toward sex, the iconoclastic (and sometimes obscene) language—all spread far beyond the realm of the true devotees of the counterculture. And perhaps the most pervasive element of the new youth society was one that even the least radical members of the generation embraced: rock music. Rock'n'roll first achieved wide popularity in the 1950s, on the strength of such early performers as Buddy Holly and, above all, Elvis Presley. Early in the 1960s, its influence began to spread, a result in large part of the phenomenal popularity of the Beatles, the English group whose first visit to the United States in 1964 created a remarkable sensation, "Beatlemania." For a time, most rock musicians—like most popular musicians before them—concentrated largely on uncontroversial romantic themes. One of the first great hits of the Beatles was a song with the innocuous title "I Want to Hold Your Hand." By the late 1960s, however, rock had begun to reflect many of the new iconoclastic values of its time. The Beatles, for example, abandoned their once simple and seemingly innocent style for a new, experimental, even mystical approach that reflected the growing popular fascination with drugs and Eastern religions. Other groups, such as the Rolling Stones, turned even more openly to themes of anger, frustration, and rebelliousness. Many popular musicians used their music to express explicit political radicalism as well—especially some of the leading folk singers of the era, such as Bob Dylan and Joan Baez. Rock's driving rhythms, its undisguised sensuality, its often harsh and angry tone—all made it an appropriate vehicle for expressing the themes of the social and political unrest of the late 1960s.

A powerful symbol of the fusion of rock music and the counterculture was the great music festival at Woodstock, New York, in the summer of 1969, where 400,000 people gathered on a farm for nearly a week. Despite heavy rain, mud, inadequate facilities, and impossible crowding, the crowd remained peaceful and harmonious. Champions of the counterculture spoke rhapsodically at the time of how Woodstock represented the birth of a new youth nation, the "Woodstock nation." The Beat poet Allen Ginsberg, revered by many enthusiasts of the counterculture and himself a champion of the "new consciousness," wrote an ecstatic poem proclaiming that at Woodstock "a new kind of man has come to his bliss/to end the cold war he has borne/against his own kind of flesh."

Virtually no Americans could avoid seeing how rapidly the norms of their society were changing in the late 1960s. Those who attended movies saw a gradual

ABORIGINAL TERRITORIES AND MODERN RESERVATIONS OF WESTERN INDIAN TRIBES

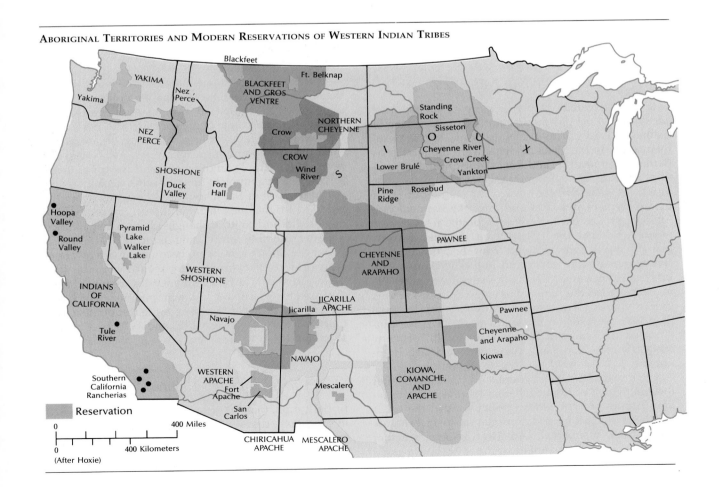

disappearance of the banal, conventional messages that had dominated films since the 1920s. Instead, they saw explorations of political issues, of new sexual mores, of violence, of social conflict. Television too began to turn (even if more slowly than the other media) to programming that reflected social and cultural conflict—as exemplified by the enormously popular *All in the Family*, whose protagonist, Archie Bunker, was a lower-middle-class bigot.

THE MOBILIZATION OF MINORITIES

The growth of African-American protest, and of a significant white response to it, both preceded the political and cultural upheavals of the 1960s and helped produce them. It also encouraged other minorities to assert themselves and demand redress of their grievances. For Indians, Hispanic Americans, gay men and women, and others, the late 1960s and 1970s were a time of growing self-expression and political activism.

Seeds of Indian Militancy

Few minorities had deeper or more justifiable grievances against the prevailing culture than American Indians—or Native Americans, as some began to call themselves in the 1960s. Indians were the least prosperous, least healthy, and least stable group in the nation. Average annual family income for Indians was $1,000 less than that for blacks. The Native American unemployment rate was ten times the national rate. Joblessness was particularly high on the reservations, where nearly half the Indians lived. But even most Indians living in cities suffered from their limited education and training and could find only menial jobs. Life expectancy among Indians was more than twenty years less than the national average. Suicides among Indian youths were a hundred times more frequent than among white youths. And while black Americans attracted the attention (for good or for ill) of many whites, Indians for many years remained largely ignored.

For much of the postwar era, and particularly after the resignation of John Collier as commissioner of Indian Affairs in 1946, federal policy toward the tribes had been shaped by a determination to incorporate Indians into mainstream American society, whether Indians wanted to assimilate or not. Two laws passed in 1953 established the basis of a new policy, which

became known as "termination." Through termination, the federal government withdrew all official recognition of the tribes as legal entities, administratively separate from state governments, and made them subject to the same local jurisdictions as white residents. At the same time, the government encouraged Indians to assimilate into the larger society and worked to funnel Native Americans into cities, where, presumably, they would adapt themselves to the white world and lose their cultural distinctiveness.

To some degree, the termination and assimilation policies achieved their objectives. The tribes grew weaker as legal and political entities. Many Native Americans adapted to life in the cities, at least to a degree. On the whole, however, the new policies were a disaster for the tribes and a failure for the reformers who had promoted them. Termination led to widespread corruption and abuse. And Indians themselves fought so bitterly against it that in 1958 the Eisenhower administration barred further "terminations" without the consent of the affected tribes. In the meantime, the struggle against termination had mobilized a new generation of Indian militants and had breathed life into the principal Native American organization, the National Congress of American Indians (NCAI), which had been created in 1944.

The Democratic administrations of the 1960s, though they did not disavow the termination policy, made no effort to revive it. Instead, they made modest efforts to restore at least some degree of tribal autonomy. The funneling of OEO money to tribal organizations through the community action program was one prominent example. In the meantime, the tribes themselves were beginning to fight for self-determination—partly because of the inspiration they drew from the black civil rights movement and partly in response to other social and cultural changes (among them, the expanding mobility and rising educational levels of younger Indians, who were becoming more aware of the world around them and of their own anomalous place within it). The new militancy also benefited from the rapid increase in the Indian population, which was growing much faster than that of the rest of the nation (nearly doubling between 1950 and 1970, to a total of about 800,000).

The Indian Civil Rights Movement

In 1961, more than 400 members of 67 tribes gathered in Chicago to discuss ways of bringing all Indians together in an effort to redress common wrongs. The manifesto they issued, the Declaration of Indian Purpose, stressed the "right to choose our own way of life" and

WOUNDED KNEE
Wounded Knee, South Dakota, had been the site of a conflict between American soldiers and Teton Sioux in 1890. The soldiers had attempted to suppress Indian religious rites ("Ghost Dances"), which whites considered threatening. The result had been a substantial massacre of the tribespeople. In 1973 armed members of the new American Indian Movement seized the village of Wounded Knee (now part of a Sioux reservation) and occupied it for over two months to press their demands for reform in federal Indian policy and tribal government. *(Michael Abramson/Black Star)*

the "responsibility of preserving our precious heritage."

The 1961 meeting was only one example of a growing Indian self-consciousness. Indians and others began writing books (for example, Vine Deloria, Jr.'s *Custer Died for Your Sins* and Dee Brown's *Bury My Heart at Wounded Knee*) and otherwise drawing renewed attention to the wrongs inflicted on the tribes by white people in past generations. One result was a gradual change in the way popular culture depicted Indians. By the 1970s, almost no films or television westerns any longer portrayed Indians as brutal savages attacking peaceful white people. And Indian activists even persuaded some white institutions to abandon what they considered demeaning references to them; Dartmouth College, for example, ceased referring to its athletic teams as the "Indians." The National Indian Youth Council, created in the aftermath of the 1961 Chicago meeting, promoted the idea of Indian nationalism and intertribal unity. In 1968, a group of

young militant Indians established the American Indian Movement (AIM), which drew its greatest support from those Indians who lived in urban areas but soon established a significant presence on the reservations as well.

The new activism had some immediate political results. In 1968, Congress passed the Indian Civil Rights Act, which guaranteed reservation Indians many of the protections accorded other citizens by the Bill of Rights, but which also recognized the legitimacy of tribal laws within the reservations. But leaders of AIM and other insurgent groups were not satisfied and turned increasingly to direct action. In 1968, Indian fishermen, citing old treaty rights, clashed with Washington State officials on the Columbia River and in Puget Sound. The following year, members of several tribes occupied the abandoned federal prison on Alcatraz Island in San Francisco Bay, claiming the site "by right of discovery."

In response to the growing pressure, the new Nixon administration appointed a Mohawk-Sioux to the position of commissioner of Indian Affairs in 1969; and in 1970, the president promised both increased tribal self-determination and an increase in federal aid. But the protests continued. In November 1972, nearly a thousand demonstrators, most of them Sioux, forcibly occupied the building of the Bureau of Indian Affairs in Washington, D.C., for six days. A more celebrated protest occurred later that winter at Wounded Knee, South Dakota, the site of the 1890 massacre of Sioux by federal troops.

In the early 1970s, Wounded Knee was part of a large Sioux reservation, two-thirds of which had been leased to white ranchers for generations as an outgrowth of the Dawes Act. Conditions for the Indian residents were desperate, and passions grew quickly in 1972 in response to the murder of a Sioux by a group of whites, who were not, many Indians believed, adequately punished. In February 1973, members of AIM seized and occupied the town of Wounded Knee for two months, demanding radical changes in the administration of the reservation and insisting that the government honor its long-forgotten treaty obligations. A brief clash between the occupiers and federal forces left one Indian dead and another wounded. Shortly thereafter the siege came to an end.

More immediately effective than these militant protests were the victories that various tribes were achieving in the 1970s in the federal courts. In *United States* v. *Wheeler* (1978), the Supreme Court confirmed that tribes had independent legal standing and could not be "terminated" by Congress. Other decisions ratified the authority of tribes to impose taxes on businesses within their reservations and to perform other sovereign functions. In 1985, the U.S. Supreme Court, in *County of Oneida* v. *Oneida Indian Nation*, supported Indian claims to 100,000 acres in upstate New York that the Oneida tribe claimed by virtue of treaty rights long forgotten by whites.

The Indian civil rights movement, like other civil rights movements of the same time, fell far short of winning full justice and equality for its constituents. Nor did it ever resolve its own internal conflicts—conflicts similar to those facing other minority groups at the same time. To some Indians, the principal goal was to defend tribal autonomy, to protect the right of Indians (and, more to the point, individual tribal groups) to remain separate and distinct. To others, the goal was equality—to win for Indians a place in society equal to that of other groups of Americans. This latter goal helped produce a new spirit of "pan-Indianism," an effort to persuade Indians to transcend tribal divisions and work together as "a Greater Indian America." But because there was no single Indian culture or tradition in America, pan-Indianism did not flourish.

For all its limits, however, the Indian civil rights movement helped the tribes win a series of new legal rights and protections that gave them a stronger position than they had enjoyed at any previous time in the twentieth century. It helped many Indians gain a renewed awareness of and pride in their identity as Indians and as part of distinct communities within the larger United States. And it challenged patterns of discrimination that had prevented many Native Americans from advancing in the world outside the tribes.

Hispanic-American Activism

More numerous and more visible than Indians were Hispanic-Americans (also known as Latinos), the fastest-growing minority group in the United States. They were no more a single, cohesive group than the Indians were. Some—including the descendants of early Spanish settlers in New Mexico—had roots as deep in American history as those of any other group. Others were men and women who had immigrated since World War II.

Large numbers of Puerto Ricans had migrated to eastern cities, particularly New York. South Florida's substantial Cuban population began with a wave of middle-class refugees fleeing the Castro regime in the early 1960s. These first Cuban migrants quickly established themselves as a successful and increasingly assimilated part of Miami's middle class. In 1980, a second, much poorer wave of Cuban immigrants—the so-called Marielitos, named for the port from which they left Cuba—arrived in Florida when Castro temporarily relaxed exit restrictions. (This group included a large number of criminals, whom Castro had, in effect, expelled from the country.) This second wave was less easily assimilated. Later in the 1980s, large numbers of immigrants (both legal and illegal) began to arrive from the troubled nations of Central and South America—from Guatemala, Nicaragua, El Salvador, Peru, and others. But the most numerous and important Hispanic group in the United States was Mexican Americans.

There had been a significant Mexican-American population in the West throughout the nineteenth and early twentieth centuries—descendants of Spanish and Mexican people who had settled in lands that once belonged to the Spanish Empire and the Republic of Mexico. But their numbers grew rapidly and substantially during and after World War II. Large numbers of Mexican Americans had entered the country during the war in response to the labor shortage, and many had

STRIKING GRAPEWORKERS
Cesar Chavez, founder and leader of the United Farm
Workers of America, leads striking Chicano farmworkers
in 1978, one of many actions that led to the recognition of
the union by most growers in California.   *(George Ballis/Black
Star)*

remained in the cities of the Southwest and the Pacific
Coast. After the war, when the legal agreements that
had allowed Mexican contract workers to enter the
country expired, large numbers of immigrants continued to move to the United States illegally. In 1953, the
government launched what it called Operation Wet-
back to deport the illegals, but the effort failed to stem
the flow of new arrivals. By 1960, there were substantial Mexican-American neighborhoods (barrios) in
American cities from El Paso to Detroit. The largest
(with more than 500,000 people, according to Census
figures) was in Los Angeles, which by then had a bigger Mexican population than any place except Mexico
City.

But the greatest expansion in the Mexican-American population was yet to come. In 1960, the Census
reported slightly more than 3 million Hispanics living
in the United States (the great majority of them Mexican Americans). In 1970, that number had grown to 9
million, and by 1990 to 20 million. Hispanics constituted more than a third of all legal immigrants to the
United States after 1960. Since there was also an uncounted but very large number of illegal immigrants
in those years (estimates ranged from 7 million to 12
million), the real percentage of Hispanic immigrants
was undoubtedly much larger.

By the late 1960s, therefore, Mexican Americans
were one of the largest population groups in the West—
outnumbering African Americans—and had established communities in most other parts of the nation as
well. They were also among the most urbanized groups
in the population; almost 90 percent lived and worked
in cities. Many of them (particularly members of the
oldest and most assimilated families of Mexican descent) were affluent and successful people. Wealthy
Cubans in Miami filled influential positions in the professions and local government; in the Southwest, Mexican Americans elected their own leaders to seats in
Congress and to governorships.

But most newly arrived Mexican Americans and
other Hispanics were less well educated than either
"Anglo" or black Americans and hence less well prepared for high-paying jobs. The fact that many spoke
English poorly or not at all further limited their employment prospects. Some of them found good industrial jobs in unionized industries, and some Mexican
Americans became important labor organizers in the
AFL-CIO. But many more (including the great majority of illegal immigrants) worked in low-paying service jobs, with few if any benefits and no job security.
And like African Americans and other minorities,
Mexican Americans encountered almost impossible
obstacles when they attempted to move out of blue-
collar or low-status service jobs. Almost nowhere were
they able to establish themselves as managers or executives in the companies in which they worked; few
were able to pursue successful professional careers.

Partly because of language barriers, partly because
the family-centered culture of many Hispanic communities discouraged effective organization, and
partly because of discrimination, Mexican Americans
and others were slower to develop political influence
than some other minorities. But some did respond to
the highly charged climate of the 1960s by strengthening their ethnic identification and organizing for political and economic power. Young Mexican-American
activists began to call themselves "Chicanos" (once a
term of derision used by whites) as a way of emphasizing the shared culture of Spanish-speaking Americans; and the term quickly moved into widespread
(although never universal) use among Mexican Americans. Some Chicanos advocated a form of nationalism
not unlike the ideas of black power advocates. The
Texas leaders of *La Raza Unida*, a Chicano political
party in the Southwest, called for the creation of something like an autonomous Mexican-American state
within a state; it demonstrated significant strength at
the polls in the 1970s.

One of the most visible efforts to organize Mexican
Americans occurred in California, where an Arizona-
born Chicano farmworker, Cesar Chavez, created an
effective union of itinerant farmworkers. His United
Farm Workers (UFW), a largely Chicano organization,
launched a prolonged strike in 1965 against growers to
demand, first, recognition of their union and, second,

increased wages and benefits. When employers resisted, Chavez enlisted the cooperation of college students, churches, and civil rights groups (including CORE and SNCC) and organized a nationwide boycott, first of table grapes and then of lettuce. In 1968, Chavez campaigned openly for Robert Kennedy. Two years later, he won a substantial victory when the growers of half of California's table grapes signed contracts with his union.

Hispanic Americans were at the center of another controversy of the 1970s and beyond: the issue of bilingualism. It was a question that aroused the opposition not only of many whites but of some Hispanics as well. Supporters of bilingualism in education (which included not just Hispanics, but Asians and others as well) argued that non-English-speaking Americans were entitled to schooling in their own language, that otherwise they would be at a grave disadvantage in comparison with native English speakers. Bilingualism, they argued, was the only way to overcome the language barrier that kept many students from making even minimal academic progress. The United States Supreme Court confirmed the right of non-English-speaking students to schooling in their native language in 1974. Opponents cited not only the cost and difficulty of bilingualism but the dangers it posed to students' ability to assimilate into the mainstream of American culture. Even many Hispanics feared that bilingualism might isolate their communities further from the rest of America and increase resentments toward them.

Challenging the "Melting Pot" Ideal

The efforts of blacks, Hispanics, Indians, Asians, and others to forge a clearer group identity seemed to challenge a longstanding premise of American political thought—the idea of the "melting pot." Older, European immigrant groups liked to believe that they had advanced in American society by adopting the values and accepting the rules of the world to which they had moved and by advancing within it on its own terms. The newly assertive ethnic groups of the 1960s and after were less willing to accept the standards of the larger society and more likely to demand recognition of their own ethnic identity. African Americans, Indians, Hispanics, and Asians all challenged the assimilationist idea. They advocated instead a culturally pluralistic society, in which racial and ethnic groups would preserve a sense of their own heritage and their own social and cultural norms.

To a large degree, the advocates of cultural pluralism succeeded. Recognition of the special character of particular groups was embedded in federal law through a wide range of affirmative action programs, which ex-

tended not only to blacks, but to Indians, Hispanics, Asians, and others as well. Ethnic studies programs proliferated in schools and universities. Eventually, this impulse led to an even more assertive (and highly controversial) cultural movement that in the 1980s and 1990s became known as "multiculturalism," which, among other things, challenged the "Eurocentric" basis of American education and culture and demanded that non-European civilizations be accorded equal attention.

Gay Liberation

The last important liberation movement to emerge in the 1960s, and the most surprising to many Americans, was the effort by homosexuals to win political and economic rights and, equally important, social acceptance. Homosexuality had been an unacknowledged reality throughout American history; not until many years after their deaths did many Americans know, for example, that revered cultural figures such as Walt Whitman and Horatio Alger were homosexuals. Non-heterosexual men and women had long been forced either to suppress their sexual preferences, to express them surreptitiously, or to live within isolated and often persecuted communities. But by the late 1960s, the liberating impulses that had affected other groups helped mobilize gay men and lesbians to fight for their own rights.

On June 27, 1969, police officers raided the Stonewall Inn, a gay nightclub in New York City's Greenwich Village, and began arresting patrons simply for frequenting the place. The raid was not unusual; police had been harassing gay bars (and homosexual men and women) for years. It was, in fact, the accumulated resentment of this long history of assaults and humiliations that caused the extraordinary response that summer night. Gay onlookers taunted the police, then attacked them. Someone started a blaze in the Stonewall Inn itself, almost trapping the policemen inside. Rioting continued throughout Greenwich Village (the center of New York's gay community) through much of the night.

The "Stonewall Riot" marked the beginning of the gay liberation movement—one of the most controversial challenges to traditional values and assumptions of its time. New organizations—among them the Gay Liberation Front, founded in New York in 1969—sprang up around the country. Public discussion and media coverage of homosexuality, long subject to an unofficial taboo, quickly and dramatically increased. Gay and lesbian activists had some success in challenging the longstanding assumption that homosexuality was "aberrant" behavior and argued that no sexual preference was any more "normal" than another.

Most of all, however, the gay liberation movement transformed the outlook of gay men and lesbians themselves. It helped them to "come out," to express their preferences openly and unapologetically, and to demand from society a recognition that gay relationships could be as significant and worthy of respect as heterosexual ones. Some gays advocated not only an acceptance of homosexuality as a valid and "normal" preference, but a change in the larger society as well: a redefinition of personal identity to give much greater importance to erotic impulses. There was much resistance to such efforts. But by the early 1980s, the gay liberation movement had made remarkable strides. Even the ravages of the AIDS epidemic (see pp. 912–913), which affected the gay community more disastrously than it affected any other group, failed to halt the growth of gay liberation. In many ways, it strengthened it.

By the early 1990s, gay men and lesbians were achieving some of the same milestones that other oppressed minorities had attained in earlier decades. Some openly gay politicians won election to public office. Universities were establishing gay and lesbian studies programs. And laws prohibiting discrimination on the basis of sexual preference were making slow, halting progress at the local level. But gay liberation produced a powerful backlash as well, as became evident when President Bill Clinton's 1993 effort to lift the ban on gays and lesbians serving in the military met a storm of criticism from members of Congress and from within the military itself.

THE NEW FEMINISM

American women constituted 51 percent of the population. But during the 1960s and 1970s, many women began to identify with minority groups and to demand a liberation of their own. Sexual discrimination was so deeply embedded in the fabric of society that when feminists began to denounce it, many men (and even many women) responded with bafflement and anger. By the 1970s, however, public awareness of the issue had increased dramatically, and the role of women in American life had changed more dramatically than that of any other group in the nation.

The Rebirth

Feminism had been a weak and often embattled force in American life for more than forty years after the adoption of the woman suffrage amendment in 1920. A few determined women kept feminist political demands alive in the National Woman's Party and other organizations. Many more women expanded the acceptable bounds of female activity by entering new areas of the workplace or engaging in political activities. Nevertheless, through the 1950s and early 1960s, active feminism was often difficult to detect. Yet within a very few years, it evolved from an almost invisible remnant to one of the most powerful social movements in American history.

The 1963 publication of Betty Friedan's *The Feminine Mystique* is often cited as the first event of contemporary women's liberation. Friedan had traveled around the country interviewing the women who had graduated with her from Smith College in 1947. Most of these women were living out the dream that postwar American society had created for them: they were affluent wives and mothers living in comfortable suburbs. And yet many of them were deeply frustrated and unhappy. The suburbs, Friedan claimed, had become a "comfortable concentration camp," providing the women who inhabited them with no outlets for their intelligence, talent, and education. The "feminine mystique" was responsible for "burying millions of women alive." The only escape was for them to begin to fulfill "their unique possibilities as separate human beings." By chronicling their unhappiness and frustration, Friedan's book had a powerful impact. But it did not so much cause the revival of feminism as help give voice to a movement that was already stirring.

By the time *The Feminine Mystique* appeared, John Kennedy had established the President's Commission on the Status of Women; and although the president's motives in creating it probably had more to do with deflecting more substantive feminist demands than with real commitment to women's goals, the commission brought national attention to sexual discrimination and helped create important networks of feminist activists who would lobby for legislative redress. Also in 1963, the Kennedy administration helped win passage of the Equal Pay Act, which barred the pervasive practice of paying women less than men for equal work. A year later, Congress incorporated into the Civil Rights Act of 1964 an amendment—Title VII—that extended to women many of the same legal protections against discrimination that were being extended to blacks.

The events of the early 1960s helped expose a contradiction that had been developing for decades between the image and the reality of women's roles in America. The image was what Friedan had called the "feminine mystique"—the ideal of women living happy, fulfilled lives in purely domestic roles. The reality was that increasing numbers of women (including, by 1963, over a third of all married women) had already entered the workplace and were encountering

WOMEN'S HISTORY

THE REVIVAL OF FEMINISM as a powerful social and political force in the 1960s and 1970s brought with it a dramatic rise of interest in women's history. Indeed, the field of women's history and women's studies has probably been the fastest-growing area of scholarship since the late 1970s. With it has come an effort to make gender a basic category of analysis for history of any kind.

But women's history was not new to the 1960s. Just as women had been challenging traditional gender norms long before the 1960s, so too have women (and some men) been writing women's history for many years. In the nineteenth century, such scholarship generally stressed the unrecognized contributions of women to history—for example, Sarah Hale's 1853 "Record of All Distinguished Women from 'the Beginning' till A.D. 1850." Work of the same sort continued into the twentieth century and, indeed, continues today. But after 1900, people committed to progressive reform movements began to produce a different kind of women's scholarship, in many ways more sociological than historical. It revealed, above all, ways in which women were victimized by a harsh new system of industrialism. In the process, it attempted to raise popular support for reform. Feminist scholars such as Edith Abbott, Margaret Byington, and Katherine Anthony examined the impact of economic change on working-class families, with a special focus on women; and they looked at the often terrible conditions in which women worked in factories, mills, and other people's homes. Their goal was less to celebrate women's contributions than to direct attention to the oppression of women by a rapacious capitalist system.

Feminism receded from prominence after the victory of the suffrage movement in 1920, and women's history entered a half century of relative inactivity as well. Women continued to write important histories in many fields, and some—for example, Eleanor Flexner, whose *Century of Struggle* (1959) became a classic history of the suffrage crusade—wrote explicitly about women. Mary Beard, best known for her work in collaboration with her husband Charles Beard on sweeping historical narratives, published a book of her own in 1946 that suggested some of the directions women's history would later take. In *Women as a Force in History*, she argued for the historical importance of ordinary women as shapers of society.

As modern feminism began to sweep across society in the 1960s and 1970s, interest in women's history revived as well. Gerda Lerner, one of the pioneers of the new women's history, once wrote of the impact of feminism on historical studies: "The recognition that we had been denied our history came to many of us as a staggering insight, which altered our consciousness irretrievably." For a time, the new women's history replicated the pattern of earlier studies of women. Much of the early work was in the "contributionist" tradition, stressing the way in which women had played more notable roles in major historical events than men had usually acknowledged. Other work stressed ways in which women had been victimized by their subordination to men and by their powerlessness within the industrial economy. Many scholars developed their feminist sensibilities under the influence of the civil rights movement; and in the 1960s and 1970s they tended to emphasize the artificiality of gender distinctions, just as early civil rights activists emphasized the artificiality of racial distinctions. The difference between women and men, they argued, was "socially constructed." It was also superficial

WHERE HISTORIANS DISAGREE

and (in the public world, at least) unimportant. The history of women was, therefore, the history of how men (with the unwitting help of many women) had created and maintained a set of fictions about women's capacities that late-twentieth-century women were now attempting to shatter.

By the late 1970s, however, many feminists were beginning to argue that there *were* basic differences between women and men—not just biological differences, but differences in values, sensibilities, and culture. This, of course, is what most men and many women had believed for decades (indeed centuries) before the feminist revolution. But the feminists of the 1970s and 1980s did not see these differences as evidence of women's incapacities. They saw them, rather, as evidence of an alternative female culture capable of challenging (and improving) the male-dominated world. Historians of women, therefore, began exploring areas of female experience that revealed the special character of women's culture and values: family, housework, motherhood, women's clubs and organizations, female literature, the social lives of working-class women, women's sexuality, and many other subjects that suggested "difference" more than "contributions" or "victimization." Partly in response, some historians began to make the same argument about men—that understanding "masculinity" and its role in shaping men's lives is as important as understanding notions of "femininity" in explaining the history of women.

The notion of gender as a source of social and cultural difference was responsible for the most powerful challenge women's history raised to the way in which scholars viewed the past. Gender, they argued, was a critical element of the explanation for many kinds of historical experiences, not just women's experiences. It is not enough simply to expand the existing story to make room for women, Joan Scott, one of the most influential theorists of gender studies, has written. Feminist history is, rather, a way of reconceptualizing the past to incorporate "ways in which hierarchies of difference—inclusions and exclusions—have been constituted."

There are many examples of the way historians have used gender to reinterpret not just the experience of women, but also the experiences of society as a whole. Carol Karlsen has argued that witchcraft in the seventeenth century was not (as earlier scholars argued) a result simply of religious superstition or of economic tensions within communities. It was an expression of assumptions about gender, and it targeted mostly women who violated the community's beliefs in what was appropriate for women to do. Labor historians such as Alice Kessler-Harris have shown the ways in which women were always present in the work force—despite popular myths to the contrary—and always a force in shaping the workplace, even as male ideas about gender limited their opportunities. Ann Scott, Linda Gordon, Theda Skocpol, and others have revealed ways in which women's political organizations and crusades crucially shaped the character of progressive and New Deal reform.

At the same time, historians of women—like historians in many other fields—have confronted other kinds of "difference": racial, ethnic, religious, regional, class. Many historians believe that these categories (race and class in particular) have in fact been more important in shaping the lives of men and women than has gender. Most women's historians, however, continue to believe that understanding concepts of gender is an essential part of understanding women's (and men's) lives, even if it is not the only, or even always the most important, part.

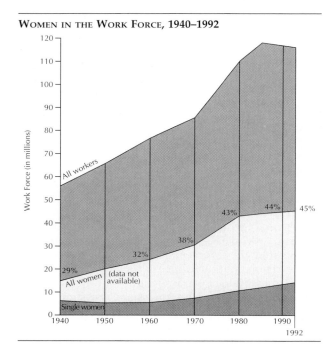

WOMEN IN THE WORK FORCE, 1940–1992

other areas of American life because of prejudices about women's proper role. It decried legal and economic discrimination, including the practice of paying women less than men for equal work (a practice the Equal Pay Act had not eliminated). The organization called for "a fully equal partnership of the sexes, as part of the worldwide revolution of human rights." By the end of the decade, its membership had expanded to 15,000.

Women's Liberation

By the late 1960s, new and more radical feminist demands were also attracting a large following, especially among younger, affluent, white, educated women—although generally not among the older women whose lives Friedan had studied. The new feminists were mostly younger, the vanguard of the baby-boom generation. Many of them drew inspiration from the New Left and the counterculture. Some were involved in the civil rights movement, others in the antiwar crusade. Many had found that even within those movements, they faced discrimination and exclusion or subordination to male leaders.

By the early 1970s, a significant change was visible in the tone and direction of the organization and of the women's movement as a whole. New books by younger feminists expressed a harsher critique of American society than Friedan had offered. Kate Millett's *Sexual Politics* (1969) signaled the new direction by complaining that "every avenue of power within the society is entirely within male hands." The answer to women's problems, in other words, was not, as Friedan had suggested, for individual women to search for greater personal fulfillment; it was for women to band together to assault the male power structure. Shulamith Firestone's *The Dialectic of Sex* (1970) was subtitled "The Case for Feminist Revolution."

In its most radical form, the new feminism rejected the whole notion of marriage, family, and even heterosexual intercourse (a vehicle, some women claimed, of male domination). Not many women, not even many feminists, embraced such extremes. But by the early 1970s large numbers of women were coming to see themselves as an exploited group organizing against oppression and developing a culture and communities of their own. The women's liberation movement inspired the creation of grassroots organizations and activities through which women not only challenged sexism and discrimination but created communities of their own. In cities and towns across the country, feminists opened women's bookstores, bars, and coffee shops. They founded feminist news-

widespread discrimination there; and that many other women were finding their domestic lives suffocating and frustrating. The conflict between the ideal and the reality was crucial to the rebirth of feminism.

In 1966, Friedan joined with other feminists to create the National Organization for Women (NOW), which was to become the nation's largest and most influential feminist organization. "The time has come," the founders of NOW maintained, "to confront with concrete action the conditions which now prevent women from enjoying the equality of opportunity and freedom of choice which is their right as individual Americans and as human beings." Like other movements for liberation, feminism drew much of its inspiration from the black struggle for freedom. "There is no civil rights movement to speak for women," the NOW organizers claimed, "as there has been for Negroes and other victims of discrimination."

The new organization reflected the varying constituencies of the emerging feminist movement. It responded to the complaints of the women Friedan's book had examined—affluent suburbanites with no outlet for their interests—by demanding greater educational opportunities for women and denouncing the domestic ideal and the traditional concept of marriage. But the heart of the movement, at least in the beginning, was directed toward the needs of women in the workplace. NOW denounced the exclusion of women from professions, from politics, and from countless papers and magazines. They created centers to assist victims of rape and abuse, women's health clinics (and, particularly after 1973, abortion clinics), and day-care centers.

Expanding Achievements

By the early 1970s, the public and private achievements of the women's movement were already substantial. In 1971, the government extended its affirmative action guidelines to include women—linking sexism with racism as an officially acknowledged social problem. In the meantime, women were making rapid progress in their efforts to move into the economic and political mainstream. The nation's major all-male educational institutions began to open their doors to women. (Princeton and Yale did so in 1969, and most other all-male colleges and universities soon followed.) Some women's colleges, in the meantime, began accepting male students—although some others remained committed to single-sex education, arguing for the value of the women's communities their campus created.

Women were also becoming an important force in business and the professions. Nearly half of all married women held jobs by the mid-1970s, and almost nine-tenths of all women with college degrees worked. The two-career family, in which both husband and wife maintained active professional lives, was becoming a widely accepted norm; many women were postponing marriage or motherhood for the sake of their careers. There were also important symbolic changes, such as the refusal of many women to adopt their husbands' names when they married and the use of the term "Ms." in place of "Mrs." or "Miss" to denote the irrelevance of a woman's marital status in the public world.

In politics, women were beginning to compete effectively with men by the early 1970s for both elected and appointive positions. By the early 1990s, women were serving in both houses of Congress, in numerous federal cabinet positions, as governors of several states, and in many other positions. Ronald Reagan named the first female Supreme Court Justice, Sandra Day O'Connor, in 1981; in 1993, Bill Clinton named the second, Ruth Bader Ginsburg. In 1984, the Democratic Party chose a woman, Representative Geraldine Ferraro of New York, as its vice presidential candidate. In academia, women were expanding their presence in traditional scholarly fields; they were also creating a field of their own—women's studies, which in the 1980s and early 1990s was the fastest-growing area of American scholarship.

MARCHING FOR WOMEN'S RIGHTS
By the end of the 1960s, the struggle for individual rights—which the African-American civil rights movement had helped push to the center of national consciousness—had helped inspire a broad range of movements. Perhaps the most important in the long run was the drive for women's rights, which was already formidable in the summer of 1970, when thousands of women joined this march through New York City. *(Werner Wolff/Black Star)*

In professional athletics, in the meantime, women were beginning to compete with men both for attention and for an equal share of prize money. Billie Jean King spearheaded the most effective female challenge to male domination of sports. Under her leadership, professional women tennis players established their own successful tours and demanded equal financial incentives when they played in the same tournaments as men. By the late 1970s, the federal government was pressuring colleges and universities to provide women with athletic programs equal to those available to men. Women even joined what had previously been the most celebrated all-male fraternity in American culture: the space program. Sally Ride became the first woman astronaut to travel in space in 1983.

In 1972, Congress approved the Equal Rights Amendment to the Constitution, which some feminists had been promoting since the 1920s, and sent it to the states. For a while ratification seemed almost certain. By the late 1970s, however, the momentum behind the amendment had died. The ERA was in trouble not because of indifference but because of a rising chorus of objections to it from people (including many antifeminist women) who feared it would disrupt traditional social patterns. In 1982, the amendment finally died when the time allotted for ratification expired.

The Abortion Controversy

A vital element of American feminism since the 1920s has been women's effort to win greater control of their own sexual and reproductive lives. In its least controversial form, this impulse helped produce an increasing awareness in the 1960s and 1970s of the problems of rape, sexual abuse, and wife beating. There continued to be some controversy over the dissemination of contraceptives and birth-control information; but that issue, at least, seemed to have lost much of the explosive character it had had in the 1920s, when Margaret Sanger had become a heroine to some and a figure of public scorn to others for her efforts on its behalf. A related issue, however, stimulated as much popular passion as any question of its time: abortion.

Abortion had once been legal in much of the United States, but by the beginning of the twentieth century it was banned by statute in most of the country and remained so into the 1960s (although many abortions continued to be performed quietly, and often dangerously, out of sight of the law). But the women's movement created strong new pressures on behalf of legalizing abortion. Several states had abandoned restrictions on abortion by the end of the 1960s. And in 1973, the Supreme Court's decision in *Roe* v. *Wade*, based on a relatively new theory of a constitutional "right to privacy" first recognized by the Court only a few years earlier in *Griswold* v. *Connecticut* (1965), invalidated all laws prohibiting abortion during the "first trimester"—the first three months of pregnancy. The issue seemed to be settled. But it soon became clear that it was not.

Although in many ways feminism was much like other liberation movements of the 1960s and 1970s, it differed from them in one fundamental respect: its success. The women's movement may not have fulfilled all its goals. But it achieved fundamental and permanent changes in the position of women in American life and promised to do much more.

NIXON, KISSINGER, AND THE WAR

Richard Nixon assumed office in 1969 committed not only to restoring stability at home but to creating a new and more stable order in the world. Central to Nixon's hopes for international stability was a resolution of the stalemate in Vietnam. Yet the new president felt no freer than his predecessor to abandon the American commitment there. He realized that the endless war was undermining both the nation's domestic stability and its position in the world. But he feared that a precipitous retreat would destroy American honor and "credibility."

During the 1968 campaign, Nixon claimed to have formulated a plan to bring "peace with honor" in Vietnam. He had refused to disclose its details. Once in office, however, he soon made clear that the plan consisted of little more than a vague set of general principles, not of any concrete measures to extricate the United States from the quagmire. American involvement in Indochina continued for four more years, during which the war expanded both in its geographic scope and in its bloodiness. And when a settlement finally emerged early in 1973, it produced neither peace nor honor. It succeeded only in removing the United States from the wreckage.

Vietnamization

Despite Nixon's own passionate interest in international affairs, he brought with him into government a man who ultimately seemed to overshadow him in the conduct of diplomacy: Henry Kissinger, a Harvard professor whom the president appointed as his special assistant for national security affairs. Kissinger quickly established dominance over both the secretary of state, William Rogers, and the secretary of defense, Melvin Laird, who were both more experienced in public life. That was in part a result of Nixon's passion for concentrating decision making in the White House. But Kissinger's keen intelligence, his bureaucratic skills, and his success in handling the press were at least equally important. Together, Nixon and Kissinger set out to find an acceptable solution to the stalemate in Vietnam.

The new Vietnam policy moved along several fronts. One was an effort to limit domestic opposition to the war so as to permit the administration more political space in which to maneuver. Aware that the military draft was one of the most visible targets of dissent, the administration devised a new "lottery" system, through which only a limited group—those nineteen-year-olds with low lottery numbers—would be subject to conscription. Later, the president urged the creation of an all-volunteer army. By 1973, the Selective Service System was on its way to at least temporary extinction.

More important in stifling dissent, however, was the new policy of "Vietnamization" of the war—the training and equipping of the South Vietnamese military to assume the burden of combat in place of American forces. In the fall of 1969, Nixon announced the withdrawal of 60,000 American ground troops from Vietnam, the first reduction in U.S. troop strength since the beginning of the war. The withdrawals continued steadily for more than three years, so that by the fall of 1972 relatively few American soldiers remained in Indochina. From a peak of more than 540,000 in 1969, the number had dwindled to about 60,000.

Vietnamization did help quiet domestic opposition to the war. But it did nothing to break the stalemate in the negotiations with the North Vietnamese in Paris. The new administration quickly decided that new military pressures would be necessary to do that.

Escalation

By the end of their first year in office, Nixon and Kissinger had concluded that the most effective way to tip the military balance in America's favor was to destroy the bases in Cambodia from which the American military believed the North Vietnamese were launching many of their attacks. Very early in his presidency, Nixon ordered the air force to begin bombing Cambodian territory to destroy the enemy sanctuaries. He kept the raids secret from Congress and the public. In the spring of 1970, possibly with U.S. encouragement and support, conservative military leaders overthrew the neutral government of Cambodia and established a new, pro-American regime under General Lon Nol. Lon Nol quickly gave his approval to American incursions into his territory; and on April 30, Nixon went on television to announce that he was ordering American troops across the border into Cambodia to "clean out" the bases that the enemy had been using for its "increased military aggression."

Literally overnight, the Cambodian invasion restored the dwindling antiwar movement to vigorous life. The first days of May saw the most widespread and vocal antiwar demonstrations ever. Hundreds of thousands of protesters gathered in Washington to denounce the president's policies. Millions, perhaps, participated in countless smaller demonstrations on campuses nationwide. Antiwar frenzy was reaching so high a level that it was possible briefly for some Americans to believe (incorrectly) that a genuine revolution was imminent. The mood of crisis intensified greatly on May 4, when four college students were killed and nine others injured when members of the National Guard opened fire on antiwar demonstrators at Kent State University in Ohio. Ten days later, police killed two black students at Jackson State University in Mississippi during a demonstration there.

The clamor against the war quickly spread into the government and the press. Congress angrily repealed the Gulf of Tonkin Resolution in December, stripping the president of what had long served as the legal basis for the war. Nixon ignored the action. Then, in June 1971, first the *New York Times* and later other newspapers began publishing excerpts from a secret study of the war prepared by the Defense Department during the Johnson administration. The so-called Pentagon Papers, leaked to the press by former Defense official Daniel Ellsberg, provided confirmation of what many had long believed: that the government had been dishonest, both in reporting the military progress of the war and in explaining its own motives for American involvement. The administration went to court to suppress the documents, but the Supreme Court finally ruled that the press had the right to publish them.

Particularly troubling, both to the public and to the government itself, were signs of decay within the American military. Morale and discipline among U.S. troops in Vietnam, who had been fighting a savage and inconclusive war for more than five years, was rapidly deteriorating. The trial and conviction in 1971 of Lieutenant William Calley, who was charged with overseeing a massacre of more than 100 unarmed South Vietnamese civilians, attracted wide public attention to the dehumanizing impact of the war on those who fought it—and to the terrible consequences for the Vietnamese people of that dehumanization. Less publicized were other, more widespread problems among American troops in Vietnam: desertion, drug addiction, racial hostilities, refusal to obey orders, even the killing of unpopular officers by enlisted men.

The continuing carnage, the increasing savagery, and the social distress at home had largely destroyed public support for the war. By 1971, nearly two-thirds of those interviewed in public opinion polls were urging American withdrawal from Vietnam. But from Richard Nixon there came no sign of retreat. On the contrary, the events of the spring of 1970 left him more convinced than ever of the importance of resisting those who opposed his military policies. With the approval of the White House, both the FBI and the CIA intensified their surveillance and infiltration of antiwar and radical groups, often resorting to blatant illegalities. Administration officials sought to discredit prominent critics of the war by leaking damaging personal information about them. At one point, White House agents broke into the office of a psychiatrist in an unsuccessful effort to steal files on Daniel Ellsberg, the former Defense Department official who had leaked a secret study of the origins of the war (the Pentagon Papers) to the press in 1971. During the congressional campaign of 1970, Vice President Spiro Agnew, using the acid rhetoric that had already made him the hero of many conservatives, stepped up his attack on the "effete" and "impudent" critics of the administration. The president himself once climbed on top of an automobile to taunt a crowd of angry demonstrators.

Meanwhile, the fighting in Indochina raged on. In February 1971, the president ordered the air force to assist the South Vietnamese army in an invasion of Laos—a test, as he saw it, of his Vietnamization program. Within weeks, the South Vietnamese scrambled back across the border in defeat. American bombing in Vietnam and Cambodia increased, despite its apparent ineffectiveness. In March 1972, the North Vietnamese mounted their biggest offensive since 1968 (the so-called Easter Offensive). American and South Vietnamese forces managed to halt the communist advance, but it was clear that without American support the offensive would have succeeded. At the same time, Nixon ordered American planes to bomb targets near Hanoi, the capital of North Vietnam, and Haiphong, its principal port, and called for the mining of seven North Vietnamese harbors (including Haiphong) to stop the flow of supplies from China and the Soviet Union.

"Peace with Honor"

As the 1972 presidential election approached, the administration stepped up its efforts to produce a breakthrough in negotiations with the North Vietnamese. In April 1972, the president dropped his longtime insistence on a removal of North Vietnamese troops from the south before any American withdrawal. Meanwhile, Henry Kissinger was meeting privately in Paris with the North Vietnamese foreign secretary, Le Duc Tho, to work out terms for a cease-fire. On October 26, only days before the presidential election, Kissinger announced that "peace is at hand."

Several weeks later (after the election), negotiations broke down once again. Although both the American and the North Vietnamese governments were ready to accept the Kissinger-Tho plan for a cease-fire, the Thieu regime balked, still insisting on a full withdrawal of North Vietnamese forces from the south. Kissinger tried to win additional concessions from the communists to meet Thieu's objections, but on December 16 talks broke off.

The next day, December 17, American B-52s began the heaviest and most destructive air raids of the entire war on Hanoi, Haiphong, and other North Vietnamese targets. Civilian casualties were high. And fifteen American B-52s were shot down by the North Vietnamese; in the entire war to that point, the United States had lost only one of the giant bombers. On December 30, Nixon terminated the "Christmas bombing." The United States and the North Vietnamese returned to the conference table. And on January 27, 1973, they signed an "agreement on ending the war and restoring peace in Vietnam." Nixon claimed that the Christmas bombing had forced the North Vietnamese to relent. At least equally important, however, was the enormous American pressure on Thieu to accept the cease-fire.

The terms of the Paris accords were little different from those Kissinger and Tho had accepted in principle a few months before. There would be an immediate cease-fire. The North Vietnamese would release several hundred American prisoners of war, whose fate had become an emotional issue of great importance within the United States. After that the agreement descended into murky and plainly unworkable arrangements. The Thieu regime would survive for the moment—the principal North Vietnamese concession to the United States—but North Vietnamese forces already in the South would remain there. An undefined committee would work out a permanent settlement.

Defeat in Indochina

American forces were hardly out of Indochina before the Paris accords collapsed. During the first year after the cease-fire, the contending Vietnamese armies suffered greater battle losses than the Americans had absorbed during ten years of fighting. Finally, in March 1975, the North Vietnamese launched a full-scale offensive against the now greatly weakened forces of the south. Thieu appealed to Washington for assistance; the president (now Gerald Ford) appealed to Congress for additional funding; Congress refused. Late in April 1975, communist forces marched into Saigon, shortly after officials of the Thieu regime and the staff of the American embassy had fled the country in humiliating disarray. Communist forces quickly occupied the capital, renamed it Ho Chi Minh City, and began the process of reuniting Vietnam under the harsh rule of Hanoi. At about the same time, the Lon Nol regime in Cambodia fell to the murderous communists of Pol Pot and the Khmer Rouge—whose genocidal policies led to the deaths of more than a third of the country's people over the next several years.

That was the dismal end of over a decade of direct American military involvement in Vietnam. More than 1.2 million Vietnamese soldiers had died in combat, along with countless civilians throughout the region. A beautiful land had been ravaged, its agrarian economy left in ruins; for many years after, Vietnam remained one of the poorest and most politically oppressive nations in the world. The United States had paid a heavy price as well. The war had cost the

THE FALL OF SAIGON
Americans and other foreigners scramble to board U.S. he-
licopters for evacuation from Saigon, only hours before
North Vietnamese troops arrive to seize control of the city.
Many South Vietnamese officials struggled to find a place
on the boats and helicopters as well. *(UPI/Bettmann)*

nation almost $150 billion in direct costs and much
more indirectly. It had resulted in the deaths of over
55,000 young Americans and the injury of 300,000
more. And the nation had suffered a blow to its confidence and self-esteem from which it would not soon
recover.

NIXON, KISSINGER, AND THE WORLD

The continuing war in Vietnam provided a dismal
backdrop to what Nixon considered his larger mission
in world affairs: the construction of a new international
order. The president had become convinced that old
assumptions of a "bipolar" world—in which the
United States and the Soviet Union were the only truly
great powers—were now obsolete. America must
adapt to the new "multipolar" international structure,
in which China, Japan, and Western Europe were becoming major, independent forces. "It will be a safer
world and a better world," he said in 1971, "if we have
a strong, healthy United States, Europe, Soviet Union,
China, Japan—each balancing the other, not playing
one against the other, an even balance."

Nixon and Kissinger believed it was possible to construct something like the "balance of power" that had

permitted nineteenth-century Europe to experience
nearly a century of relative stability. To do so, however, required a major change in several longstanding
assumptions of American foreign policy.

China and the Soviet Union

For more than twenty years, ever since the fall of
Chiang Kai-shek in 1949, the United States had treated
China, the second largest nation on earth, as if it did
not exist. Instead, America recognized the forlorn
regime-in-exile on Taiwan as the legitimate government of mainland China. Nixon and Kissinger wanted
to forge a new relationship with the Chinese communists—in part to strengthen them as a counterbalance
to the Soviet Union. The Chinese, for their part, were
eager to forestall the possibility of a Soviet-American
alliance against China and to end China's own isolation from the international arena.

In July 1971, Nixon sent Henry Kissinger on a secret mission to Beijing. When Kissinger returned, the
president made the startling announcement that he
would visit China himself within the next few months.
That fall, with American approval, the United Nations
admitted the communist government of China and expelled the representatives of the Taiwan regime, whose
claim to be the legitimate government of all China had
been a major obstacle to western recognition of the
communist regime. Finally, in February 1972, Nixon
paid a formal visit to China and, in a single stroke,
erased much of the deep American animosity toward
the Chinese communists. Nixon did not yet formally
recognize the communist regime, but in 1972 the
United States and China began low-level diplomatic
relations.

The initiatives in China coincided with (and probably assisted) an effort by the Nixon administration to
improve relations with the Soviet Union. In 1969,
American and Soviet diplomats met in Helsinki, Finland, to begin talks on limiting nuclear weapons. In
1972, they produced the first Strategic Arms Limitation Treaty (SALT I), which froze the nuclear missiles
(ICBMs) of both sides at present levels. In May of that
year, the president traveled to Moscow to sign the
agreement. The next year, the Soviet premier, Leonid
Brezhnev, visited Washington, and the two leaders
pledged renewed efforts to speed the next phase of
arms control negotiations.

The Problems of Multipolarity

The policies of rapprochement with communist China
and detente with the Soviet Union reflected Nixon's
and Kissinger's belief in the importance of stable

Détente at High Tide
The visit of Soviet Premier Leonid Brezhnev to Washington in 1973 was a high-water mark in the search for détente between the two nations, a search that had begun as early as 1962, that continued through parts of five presidential administrations, and that collapsed in disarray in the late 1970s. Here, Brezhnev and Nixon share friendly words while standing on the White House balcony. *(J. P. Laffont/Sygma)*

what became known as the Nixon Doctrine, by which the United States would "participate in the defense and development of allies and friends" but would leave the "basic responsibility" for the future of those "friends" to the nations themselves. In practice, the Nixon Doctrine meant a declining American interest in contributing to Third World development; a growing contempt for the United Nations, where less-developed nations were gaining influence through their sheer numbers; and increasing support to authoritarian regimes attempting to withstand radical challenges from within.

In 1970, for example, the CIA poured substantial funds into Chile to help support the established government against a communist challenge. When the Marxist candidate for president, Salvador Allende, came to power through an honest election, the United States began funneling more money to opposition forces in Chile to help "destabilize" the new government. In 1973, a military junta seized power from Allende, who was subsequently murdered. The United States developed a friendly relationship with the new, repressive military government of General Augusto Pinochet.

In the Middle East, conditions were growing more volatile in the aftermath of the 1967 "Six-Day War," in which Israel routed Egyptian, Syrian, and Jordanian forces, gained control of the whole of the long-divided city of Jerusalem, and occupied substantial new territories: on the west bank of the Jordan River, the Gaza Strip, the Golan Heights, and elsewhere. The war also increased the number of refugee Palestinians—Arabs who claimed the lands now controlled by Israel and who, dislodged from their homes, became a source of considerable instability in Jordan, Lebanon, and the other surrounding countries into which they now moved. Jordan's ruler, King Hussein, was particularly alarmed by the influx of Palestinians and by the activities of the Palestinian Liberation Organization (PLO) and other radical groups, which he feared would threaten Jordan's important relationship with the United States. After a series of uprisings in 1970, Hussein ordered the Jordanian army to expel the Palestinians. Many of them moved to Lebanon, where they became part of many years of instability and civil war.

In October 1973, on the Jewish High Holy Day of Yom Kippur, Egyptian and Syrian forces attacked Israel. For ten days, the Israelis struggled to recover from the surprise attack; finally, they launched an effective counteroffensive against Egyptian forces in the Sinai. At that point, the United States intervened, placing heavy pressure on Israel to accept a cease-fire rather than press its advantage.

relationships among the great powers. But great-power relationships could not alone ensure international stability, for the "Third World" remained the most volatile and dangerous source of international tension.

Central to the Nixon-Kissinger policy toward the Third World was the effort to maintain a stable status quo without involving the United States too deeply in local disputes. In 1969 and 1970, the president described

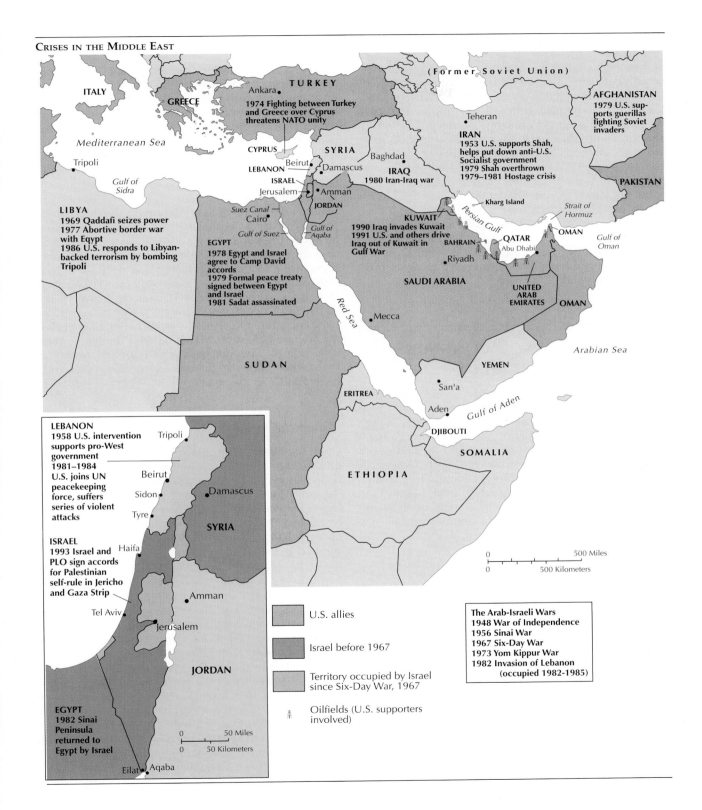

CRISES IN THE MIDDLE EAST

TURKEY
1974 Fighting between Turkey and Greece over Cyprus threatens NATO unity

AFGHANISTAN
1979 U.S. supports guerillas fighting Soviet invaders

IRAN
1953 U.S. supports Shah, helps put down anti-U.S. Socialist government
1979 Shah overthrown
1979–1981 Hostage crisis

IRAQ
1980 Iran-Iraq war

KUWAIT
1990 Iraq invades Kuwait
1991 U.S. and others drive Iraq out of Kuwait in Gulf War

LIBYA
1969 Qaddafi seizes power
1977 Abortive border war with Eqypt
1986 U.S. responds to Libyan-backed terrorism by bombing Tripoli

EGYPT
1978 Egypt and Israel agree to Camp David accords
1979 Formal peace treaty signed between Egypt and Israel
1981 Sadat assassinated

(Former Soviet Union)

ITALY
GREECE
Ankara
CYPRUS
SYRIA
LEBANON
Beirut
Damascus
Baghdad
Teheran
PAKISTAN
ISRAEL
Jerusalem
Amman
JORDAN
Suez Canal
Cairo
Gulf of Suez
Gulf of Aqaba
Kharg Island
Strait of Hormuz
QATAR
BAHRAIN
Abu Dhabi
OMAN
Gulf of Oman
UNITED ARAB EMIRATES
OMAN
Persian Gulf
Riyadh
SAUDI ARABIA
Mecca
Red Sea
SUDAN
YEMEN
San'a
Aden
Gulf of Aden
ERITREA
DJIBOUTI
ETHIOPIA
SOMALIA
Arabian Sea
Mediterranean Sea
Tripoli
Gulf of Sidra

LEBANON
1958 U.S. intervention supports pro-West government
1981–1984 U.S. joins UN peacekeeping force, suffers series of violent attacks

ISRAEL
1993 Israel and PLO sign accords for Palestinian self-rule in Jericho and Gaza Strip

EGYPT
1982 Sinai Peninsula returned to Egypt by Israel

Tripoli
Beirut
Sidon
Tyre
Haifa
SYRIA
Damascus
Amman
Tel Aviv
Jerusalem
JORDAN
Eilat
Aqaba

0   50 Miles
0   50 Kilometers

0   500 Miles
0   500 Kilometers

U.S. allies

Israel before 1967

Territory occupied by Israel since Six-Day War, 1967

Oilfields (U.S. supporters involved)

The Arab-Israeli Wars
1948 War of Independence
1956 Sinai War
1967 Six-Day War
1973 Yom Kippur War
1982 Invasion of Lebanon
        (occupied 1982-1985)

The imposed settlement of the Yom Kippur War demonstrated the growing dependence of the United States and its allies on Arab oil. Permitting Israel to continue its drive into Egypt might have jeopardized the ability of the United States to purchase needed petroleum from the Arab states. A brief but painful embargo by the Arab governments on the sale of oil to supporters of Israel (including America) in 1973 provided an ominous warning of the costs of losing access to the region's resources. The lesson of the Yom Kippur War, therefore, was that the United States could not ignore the interests of the Arab nations in its efforts on behalf of Israel.

A larger lesson of 1973 was that the nations of the Third World could no longer be expected to act as passive, cooperative "client states." The United States could no longer depend on cheap, easy access to raw materials as it had in the past.

POLITICS AND ECONOMICS UNDER NIXON

For a time in the late 1960s, it had seemed to many Americans that the forces of chaos and radicalism were taking control of the nation. The domestic policy of the Nixon administration was an attempt to restore balance: between the needs of the poor and the desires of the middle class, between the power of the federal government and the interests of local communities. In the end, however, economic and political crises—some beyond the administration's control, some of its own making—sharply limited Nixon's ability to fulfill his domestic goals.

Domestic Initiatives

Many of Nixon's domestic policies were a response to what he believed to be the demands of his own constituency—conservative, middle-class people whom he liked to call the "silent majority" and who wanted to reduce federal "interference" in local affairs. He tried, unsuccessfully, to persuade Congress to pass legislation prohibiting the use of forced busing to achieve school desegregation. He forbade the Department of Health, Education, and Welfare to cut off federal funds from school districts that had failed to comply with court orders to integrate. At the same time, he began to reduce or dismantle many of the social programs of the Great Society and the New Frontier. In 1973, for example, he abolished the Office of Economic Oppor-

tunity, the centerpiece of the antipoverty program of the Johnson years.

Yet Nixon's domestic efforts were not entirely negative. One of the administration's boldest efforts was an attempt to overhaul the nation's enormous welfare system. Nixon proposed replacing the existing system, which almost everyone agreed was cumbersome, expensive, and inefficient, with what he called the Family Assistance Plan. It would in effect have created a guaranteed annual income for all Americans: $1,600 in federal grants, which could be supplemented by outside earnings up to $4,000. Even many liberals applauded the proposal as an important step toward expanding federal responsibility for the poor. Nixon, however, presented the plan in conservative terms: as something that would reduce the supervisory functions of the federal government and transfer to welfare recipients themselves daily responsibility for their own lives. Although the FAP won approval in the House in 1970, concerted attacks by welfare recipients (who considered the benefits inadequate), members of the welfare bureaucracy (whose own influence stood to be sharply diminished by the bill), and conservatives (who opposed a guaranteed income on principle) helped kill it in the Senate.

From the Warren Court to the Nixon Court

Of all the liberal institutions that had aroused the enmity of the "silent majority" in the 1950s and 1960s, none had evoked more anger and bitterness than the Supreme Court. Not only had its rulings on racial matters disrupted traditional social patterns in both the North and the South, but its staunch defense of civil liberties had, in the eyes of many Americans, contributed to the increase in crime, disorder, and moral decay. In *Engel* v. *Vitale* (1962), the Court had ruled that prayers in public schools were unconstitutional, sparking outrage among religious fundamentalists and others. In *Roth* v. *United States* (1957), the Court had sharply limited the authority of local governments to curb pornography. In a series of other decisions, the Court had greatly strengthened the civil rights of criminal defendants and, in the eyes of many Americans, had greatly weakened the power of law enforcement officials to do their jobs. For example, in *Gideon* v. *Wainwright* (1963), the Court had ruled that every felony defendant was entitled to a lawyer regardless of his or her ability to pay. In *Escobedo* v. *Illinois* (1964), it had ruled that a defendant must be allowed access to a lawyer before questioning by police. In *Miranda* v. *Arizona* (1966), the Court had confirmed the obligation of authorities to inform a criminal suspect of his or her rights. By 1968, the Warren Court had become the target of Americans of all kinds who felt the balance of power in the United States had shifted too far toward the poor and dispossessed at the expense of the middle class, and toward criminals at the expense of law-abiding citizens.

One of the most important decisions of the Warren Court in the 1960s was *Baker* v. *Carr* (1962), which required state legislatures to apportion electoral districts so that all citizens' votes would have equal weight. In dozens of states, systems of legislative districting had given disproportionate representation to sparsely populated rural areas, hence diminishing the voting power of urban residents. The reapportionment that the decision required greatly strengthened the voting power of African Americans, Hispanics, and other groups concentrated in cities.

Nixon was determined to use his judicial appointments to give the Court a more conservative cast. His first opportunity came almost as soon as he entered office. When Chief Justice Earl Warren resigned early in 1969, Nixon replaced him with a federal appeals court judge of known conservative leanings, Warren Burger. A few months later, Associate Justice Abe Fortas resigned after allegations of financial improprieties. To replace him, Nixon named Clement F. Haynsworth, a respected federal circuit court judge from South Carolina. But Haynsworth came under fire from Senate liberals, black organizations, and labor unions for his conservative record on civil rights and for what some claimed was a conflict of interest in several of the cases on which he had sat. The Senate rejected him. Nixon's next choice was G. Harrold Carswell, a judge of the Florida federal appeals court almost entirely lacking in distinction and widely considered unfit for the Supreme Court. The Senate rejected his nomination too.

Nixon angrily denounced the votes, calling them expressions of prejudice against the South. But he was careful thereafter to choose men of standing within the legal community to fill vacancies on the Supreme Court: Harry Blackmun, a moderate jurist from Minnesota; Lewis F. Powell, Jr., a respected judge from Virginia; and William Rehnquist, a member of the Nixon Justice Department. In the process, he transformed the Warren Court into what some called the "Nixon Court" and others the "Burger Court."

The new Court, however, fell short of what the president and many conservatives had expected. Rather than retreating from its commitment to social reform, the Court in many areas actually moved further. In *Swann* v. *Charlotte-Mecklenburg Board of Education* (1971), it ruled in favor of the use of forced busing to achieve racial balance in schools. Not even the intense

and occasionally violent opposition of local communities such as Boston and Louisville, Kentucky, was able to weaken the judicial commitment to integration. In *Furman* v. *Georgia* (1972), the Court overturned existing capital punishment statutes and established strict new guidelines for such laws in the future. In *Roe* v. *Wade* (1973), it struck down laws forbidding abortions.

In other decisions, however, the Burger Court was more moderate. Although the justices approved busing as a tool for achieving integration, they rejected, in *Milliken* v. *Bradley* (1974), a plan to transfer students across district lines (in this case, between Detroit and its suburbs) to achieve racial balance. While the Court upheld the principle of affirmative action in its celebrated 1978 decision *Bakke* v. *Board of Regents of California*, it established restrictive new guidelines for such programs in the future. In *Stone* v. *Powell* (1976), the Court agreed to certain limits on the right of a defendant to appeal a state conviction to the federal judiciary.

The Election of 1972

However unsuccessful his administration may have been in achieving some of its specific goals, Nixon entered the presidential race in 1972 with a substantial reserve of strength. The events of that year improved his position immeasurably. His energetic reelection committee collected enormous sums of money to support the campaign. The president himself used the powers of incumbency with great effect, refraining from campaigning and concentrating on highly publicized international decisions and state visits. Agencies of the federal government dispensed funds and favors to strengthen Nixon's political standing in critical areas.

Nixon was most fortunate in 1972, however, in his opposition. The return of George Wallace to the presidential fray caused some early concern. Nixon was delighted to see Wallace run in the Democratic primaries and quietly encouraged him to do so. But he feared that Wallace would again launch a third-party campaign; Nixon's own reelection strategy rested on the same appeals to the troubled middle class that Wallace was expressing. The possibility of such a campaign vanished in May, when a would-be assassin shot the Alabama governor during a rally at a Maryland shopping center. Paralyzed from the waist down, Wallace was unable to continue campaigning.

The Democrats, in the meantime, were making their own contributions to the Nixon cause by nominating for president a representative of their most liberal wing: Senator George S. McGovern of South Dakota.

An outspoken critic of the war, a forceful advocate of advanced liberal positions on virtually every social and economic issue, McGovern seemed to embody those aspects of the turbulent 1960s that middle-class Americans were most eager to reject. McGovern profited greatly from party reforms (which he himself had helped to draft) that reduced the power of party leaders and gave increased influence to women, blacks, and young people in the selection of the Democratic ticket. But those same reforms helped make the Democratic Convention of 1972 an unappealing spectacle to much of the public. The candidate then disillusioned even some of his own supporters by his indecisive reaction to revelations that his running mate, Senator Thomas Eagleton of Missouri, had undergone treatment for an emotional disturbance. Eagleton finally withdrew from the ticket. The remainder of the Democratic presidential campaign was an exercise in futility.

On election day, Nixon won reelection by one of the largest margins in history: 60.7 percent of the popular vote compared with 37.5 percent for the forlorn McGovern, and an electoral margin of 520 to 17. The Democratic candidate had carried only Massachusetts and the District of Columbia. The new commitments that Nixon had so effectively expressed—to restraint in social reform, to decentralization of political power, to the defense of traditional values, and to a new balance in international relations—had clearly won the approval of the American people. But other problems were already lurking in the wings.

The Troubled Economy

Although it was political scandal that would ultimately destroy the Nixon presidency, the most important national crisis of the early 1970s was the decline of the American economy. For three decades, the American economy had been the envy of the world. It had produced as much as a third of the world's industrial goods and had dominated international trade. The American dollar had been the strongest currency in the world, and the American standard of living had risen steadily from its already substantial heights. Many Americans assumed that this remarkable prosperity was the normal condition of their society. In fact, however, it rested in part on several artificial conditions that were rapidly disappearing by the late 1960s: above all, the absence of significant foreign competition and easy access to raw materials in the Third World.

Inflation, which had been creeping upward for several years when Richard Nixon took office, soon be-

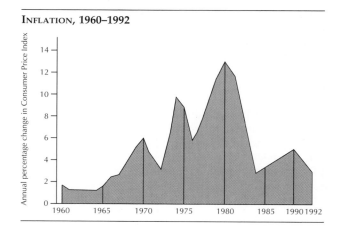

INFLATION, 1960–1992

gan to soar; it would be the most disturbing economic problem of the 1970s. Its most visible cause was a significant increase in federal deficit spending in the 1960s, when the Johnson administration tried to fund the war in Vietnam and its ambitious social programs without raising taxes. But there were other, equally important causes of the inflation and of the economic problems that lay behind it. No longer did the United States have exclusive access to cheap raw materials around the globe; not only were other industrial nations now competing for increasingly scarce raw materials; but Third World suppliers of those materials were beginning to realize their value and to demand higher prices for them.

The greatest immediate blow to the American economy was the increasing cost of energy. More than any nation on earth, the United States based its economy on the easy availability of cheap and plentiful fossil fuels. No society was more dependent on the automobile; none was more wasteful in its use of oil and gas in its homes, schools, and factories. Domestic petroleum reserves were no longer sufficient to meet this demand, and the nation was heavily dependent on imports from the Middle East and Africa.

For many years, the Organization of Petroleum Exporting Countries (OPEC) had operated as an informal bargaining unit for the sale of oil by Third World nations, but had seldom managed to exercise any real strength. But in the early 1970s, OPEC began to assert itself, to use its oil both as an economic tool and as a political weapon. In 1973, in the midst of the Yom Kippur War, Arab members of OPEC announced that they would no longer ship petroleum to nations supporting Israel—which meant the United States and its allies in Western Europe. At about the same time, the OPEC nations agreed to raise their prices 400 percent.

These twin shocks produced momentary economic chaos in the West. The United States suffered its first fuel shortage since World War II. And although the boycott ended a few months later, the price of energy continued to skyrocket both because of OPEC's new militant policies and because of the weakening competitive position of the dollar in world markets. No single factor did more to produce the soaring inflation of the 1970s.

But inflation was only one of the new problems facing the American economy. The other, and more important in the long run, was the decline of the nation's manufacturing sector. American industry had flourished in the immediate aftermath of World War II, in part because of the new plant capacity the war had created, in part because the country faced almost no competition from other industrial nations. American workers in unionized industries had profited from this postwar success by winning some of the most generous wage and benefits packages in the world.

By the 1970s, however, the climate for American manufacturing had changed significantly. Many of the great industrial plants were now many decades old, much less efficient than the newer plants that Japan and European industrial nations had constructed after the war. In some industries (notably steel and automobiles), management had become complacent and stultifyingly bureaucratic. Most important, U.S. manufacturing now faced major competition from abroad—not only in world trade (which still constituted only a small part of the American economy) but also at home. Automobiles, steel, and many other manufactured goods from Japan and Europe established major footholds in the United States markets. Some of America's new competitors benefited from lower labor costs than their U.S. counterparts; but that was only one of many reasons for their success.

Thus the 1970s marked the beginning of a long, painful process of deindustrialization, during which thousands of factories across the country closed their gates and millions of workers lost their jobs. New employment opportunities were becoming available in other, growing areas of the economy: technology, information systems, and many other more "knowledge-based" industries. But many industrial workers were poorly equipped to move into those jobs. The result was a growing pool of unemployed and underemployed workers; the virtual disappearance of industrial jobs from many inner cities, where large numbers of minorities lived; and the impoverishment of communities dependent on particular industries. Some of the nation's manufacturing sectors ultimately revived, but few regained the size and dominance they had enjoyed in the 1950s and 1960s; and few employed a work force as large or as relatively well paid as they once had.

The Nixon Response

The Nixon administration responded to these mounting economic problems by focusing on the one thing it thought it could control: inflation. The government moved first to reduce spending and raise taxes. But those policies produced both congressional and popular protest, and Nixon turned increasingly to an economic tool more readily available to him: control of the currency. Placing conservative economists at the head of the Federal Reserve Board, he ensured sharply higher interest rates and a contraction of the money supply. But the tight money policy did little to curb inflation: the cost of living rose a cumulative 15 percent during Nixon's first two and a half years in office. Economic growth, in the meantime, declined. The United States was encountering a new and puzzling dilemma: "stagflation," a combination of rising prices and general economic stagnation.

In the summer of 1971, Nixon imposed a ninety-day freeze on all wages and prices at their existing levels. Then, in November, he launched what he called Phase II of his economic plan: mandatory guidelines for wage and price increases, to be administered by a federal agency. Inflation subsided temporarily, but the recession continued. Fearful that the recession would be more damaging than inflation in an election year, the administration reversed itself late in 1971: interest rates were allowed to drop sharply, and government spending was increased—producing the largest budget deficit since World War II. The new tactics helped revive the economy in the short term, but inflation rose substantially—particularly after the administration abandoned the strict Phase II controls and replaced them with a set of voluntary, and almost entirely ineffective, guidelines. In 1973, prices rose 9 percent; in 1974, after the Arab oil embargo and the OPEC price increases, they rose 12 percent—the highest rate since the relaxation of price controls shortly after World War II. The value of the dollar continued to slide, and the nation's international trade continued to decline. In the meantime, the energy crisis was quickly becoming a national preoccupation. But while Nixon talked often about the need to achieve "energy independence," he offered few concrete proposals.

The erratic economic programs of the Nixon administration were a sign of a broader national confusion about the prospects for American prosperity. The Nixon pattern—of lurching from a tight money policy to curb inflation at one moment, to a spending policy to cure recession at the next—repeated itself during the two administrations that followed.

THE WATERGATE CRISIS

Although economic problems greatly concerned the American people in the 1970s, another stunning development almost entirely preoccupied the nation beginning early in 1973: the fall of Richard Nixon. The president's demise was a result, in part, of his own personality. Defensive, secretive, resentful of his critics, he brought to his office an element of mean-spiritedness that helped undermine even his most important accomplishments. But the larger explanation lay in Nixon's view of American society and the world, and of his own role in both. The president believed the United States faced grave dangers from the radicals and dissidents who were challenging his policies. He came increasingly to consider any challenge to his policies a threat to "national security." By identifying his own political fortunes with those of the nation, Nixon was creating a climate in which he and those who served him could justify almost any tactics to stifle dissent and undermine opposition.

The Scandals

Nixon's outlook was in part a culmination of long-term changes in the presidency. Public expectations of the president had increased dramatically in the years since World War II; yet the constraints on the authority of the office from Congress, the courts, interest groups, the media and elsewhere had grown as well. In response, a succession of presidents had sought new methods for the exercise of power, often stretching the law, occasionally breaking it.

Nixon not only continued but greatly accelerated these trends. Facing a Democratic Congress hostile to his goals, he attempted to find ways to circumvent the legislature whenever possible. Saddled with a federal bureaucracy unresponsive to his wishes, he constructed a hierarchy of command in which virtually all executive power became concentrated in the White House. Operating within a rigid, even autocratic staff structure, the president became a solitary, at times brooding figure, whose contempt for his opponents and impatience with obstacles to his policies festered and grew. Unknown to all but a few intimates, he also became mired in a pattern of illegalities and abuses of power that in late 1972 began to break through to the surface.

Early on the morning of June 17, 1972, police arrested five men who had broken into the offices of the Democratic National Committee in the Watergate office building in Washington, D.C. Two others were seized a short time later and charged with supervising the break-in. When reporters for the *Washington Post* began researching the backgrounds of the culprits, they discovered that among those involved in the burglary were former employees of the Committee for the Re-Election of the President (CRP). One of them had worked in the White House itself. Moreover, they had been paid for the break-in from a secret fund of the re-election committee, a fund controlled by members of the White House staff.

Public interest in the disclosures grew slowly in the last months of 1972. Few Americans questioned the president's assurances that neither he nor his staff had any connection with what he called "this very bizarre incident." Early in 1973, however, the Watergate burglars went on trial; and under relentless prodding from federal judge John J. Sirica, one of the defendants, James W. McCord, agreed to cooperate both with the grand jury and with a special Senate investigating committee recently established under Senator Sam J. Ervin of North Carolina. McCord's testimony opened a floodgate of confessions, and for months a parade of White House and campaign officials exposed one illegality after another. Foremost among them was a member of the inner circle of the White House, counsel to the president John Dean, who leveled allegations against Nixon himself.

Two different sets of scandals were emerging from the investigations. One was a general pattern of abuses of power involving both the White House and the Nixon campaign committee, which included, but was not limited to, the Watergate break-in. The other scandal, and the one that became the major focus of public attention for nearly two years, was the way in which the administration tried to manage the investigations of the Watergate break-in and other abuses—a pattern of behavior that became known as the "cover-up." There was never any conclusive evidence that the president had planned or approved the burglary in advance. But there was mounting evidence that he had been involved in illegal efforts to obstruct investigations of and withhold information about the episode. Testimony before the Ervin committee provided evidence of the complicity of Dean, Attorney General John Mitchell, top White House assistants H. R. Haldeman and John Ehrlichman, and others. As interest in the case grew to something approaching a national obsession, the investigation focused increasingly on a single question: in the words of Senator Howard Baker of Tennessee, a member of the Ervin committee, "What did the President know and when did he know it?"

Nixon accepted the departure of those members of his administration implicated in the scandals. But he continued to insist that he himself was innocent. There the matter might have rested, had it not been for the disclosure during the Senate hearings of a White House taping system that had recorded virtually every conversation in the president's office during the period in question. All the groups investigating the scandals sought access to the tapes; Nixon, pleading "executive privilege," refused to release them. A special prosecutor appointed by the president to handle the Watergate cases, Harvard law professor Archibald Cox, took Nixon to court in October 1973 in an effort to force him to relinquish the recordings. Nixon, clearly growing desperate, then fired Cox and suffered the humiliation of watching both Attorney General Elliot Richardson and his deputy resign in protest. This "Saturday night massacre" made the president's predicament infinitely worse. Not only did public pressure force him to appoint a new special prosecutor, Texas attorney Leon Jaworski, who proved just as determined as Cox to subpoena the tapes; but the episode precipitated an investigation by the House of Representatives into the possibility of impeachment.

The Fall of Richard Nixon

Nixon's situation deteriorated further in the following months. Late in 1973, Vice President Spiro Agnew be-

came embroiled in a scandal of his own when evidence surfaced that he had accepted bribes and kickbacks while serving as governor of Maryland and even as vice president. In return for a Justice Department agreement not to press the case, Agnew pleaded no contest to a lesser charge of income-tax evasion and resigned from the government. With the controversial Agnew no longer in line to succeed to the presidency, the prospect of removing Nixon from the White House became less worrisome to his opponents. The new vice president (the first appointed under the terms of the Twenty-fifth Amendment, which had been adopted in 1967) was House minority leader Gerald Ford, an amiable and popular Michigan congressman.

The impeachment investigation quickly gathered pace. In April 1974, in an effort to head off further subpoenas of the tapes, the president released transcripts of a number of relevant conversations, claiming that they proved his innocence. Investigators and much of the public felt otherwise. Even these edited tapes seemed to suggest Nixon's complicity in the cover-up. In July, the crisis reached a climax. First the Supreme Court ruled unanimously, in *United States* v. *Richard M. Nixon*, that the president must relinquish the tapes to Special Prosecutor Jaworski. Days later, the House Judiciary Committee voted to recommend three articles of impeachment, charging that Nixon had, first, obstructed justice in the Watergate cover-up; second, misused federal agencies to violate the rights of citizens; and third, defied the authority of Congress by refusing to deliver tapes and other materials subpoenaed by the committee.

NIXON'S FAREWELL
Only moments before, Nixon had been in tears saying goodbye to his staff in the East Room of the White House. But as he boarded a helicopter to begin his trip home to California shortly after resigning as president, he flashed his trademark "victory" sign to the crowd on the White House Lawn. *(Bettmann)*

SIGNIFICANT EVENTS

1961 Representatives of sixty-seven tribes draft Declaration of Indian Purpose

1962 Students for a Democratic Society formed at Port Huron, Michigan

Supreme Court decides *Baker* v. *Carr*

1963 Betty Friedan publishes *The Feminine Mystique*

1964 Free Speech Movement begins at UC Berkeley

Beatles come to America

1965 United Farm Workers strike

1966 National Organization for Women (NOW) formed

Miranda v. *Arizona* expands rights of criminal suspects

1967 Antiwar protesters march on Pentagon

Israel and Arabs clash in Six-Day War

1968 Campus riots break out at Columbia University and elsewhere

Antiwar "mobilization" day

American Indian Movement (AIM) launched

Nuclear nonproliferation treaty signed

1969 Antiwar movement stages Vietnam "moratorium"

Theodore Roszak publishes *The Making of a Counter Culture*

People's Park uprising at Berkeley

Nixon orders secret bombing of Cambodia

Nixon begins withdrawing American troops from Vietnam

"Stonewall Riot" in New York City launches gay liberation movement

400,000 people attend rock concert in Woodstock, N.Y.

1970 American troops enter Cambodia

Antiwar protests increase

Students killed at Kent State and Jackson State universities

Palestinians expelled from Jordan

Charles Reich publishes *The Greening of America*

Even without additional evidence, Nixon might well have been impeached by the full House and convicted by the Senate. Early in August, however, he provided at last the "smoking gun"—the concrete proof of his guilt that his defenders had long contended was missing from the case against him. Among the tapes that the Supreme Court compelled Nixon to relinquish were several that offered apparently incontrovertible evidence of his involvement in the Watergate cover-up. Only days after the burglary, the recordings disclosed, the president had ordered the FBI to stop investigating the break-in. Impeachment and conviction now seemed inevitable.

For several days, Nixon brooded in the White House, on the verge, some claimed, of a breakdown. Finally, on August 8, 1974, he announced his resignation—the first president in American history ever to

do so. At noon the next day, while Nixon and his family were flying west to their home in California, Gerald Ford took the oath of office as president.

Many Americans expressed relief and exhilaration that, as the new president put it, "Our long national nightmare is over." Many were relieved to be rid of Richard Nixon, who had lost virtually all the wide popularity that had won him his landslide reelection victory only two years before. And many were also exhilarated that, as some boasted, "the system had worked." But the wave of good feeling could not obscure the deeper and more lasting damage of the Watergate crisis. In a society in which distrust of leaders and institutions of authority was already widespread, the fall of Richard Nixon seemed to confirm the most cynical assumptions about the character of American public life.

SIGNIFICANT EVENTS

1971   Pentagon Papers published

Supreme Court decides *Swann* v. *Charlotte-Mecklenburg Board of Education*

Nixon imposes wage-price freeze and controls

1972   Congress approves Equal Rights Amendment

Nixon visits China

SALT I treaty signed

United States mines Haiphong harbor in North Vietnam

Nixon orders "Christmas bombing" of North Vietnam

Supreme Court decides *Furman* v. *Georgia*

Burglary interrupted in Watergate office building

Nixon reelected president

1973   Indians demonstrate at Wounded Knee

Supreme Court decides *Roe* v. *Wade*

Paris accords produce cease-fire; America withdraws from Vietnam

Israel and Arabs clash in Yom Kippur War

Arab oil embargo produces first American energy crisis

Watergate scandal expands

1974   Impeachment proceedings begin against Nixon

Vice President Spiro Agnew resigns; Gerald Ford appointed to replace him

Nixon resigns; Ford becomes president

1975   South Vietnam falls

Khmer Rouge seize control of Cambodia

1977   President Carter pardons Vietnam draft resisters

1978   Vietnam invades Cambodia

Supreme Court hands down *Bakke* decision

1980   Large numbers of Cubans ("Marielitos") migrate to Florida

1982   Equal Rights Amendment fails to be ratified

SUGGESTED READINGS

General Studies.   John Morton Blum, *Years of Discord: American Politics and Society, 1961–1974* (1991). Peter N. Carroll, *It Seemed Like Nothing Happened* (1982). Allen J. Matusow, *The Unraveling of America* (1984). Kim McQuaid, *The Anxious Years* (1989). William O'Neill, *Coming Apart* (1971).

The New Left and the Counterculture.   Edward Bacciocco, Jr., *The New Left in America* (1974). Ronald Berman, *America in the Sixties* (1968). Wini Breines, *Community and Organization in the New Left* (1983). Peter Clecak, *Radical Paradoxes* (1973). Peter Collier and David Horowitz, *Destructive Generation: Second Thoughts About the Sixties* (1989). Morris Dickstein, *Gates of Eden* (1977). Joan Didion, *Slouching Towards Bethlehem* (1967); *The White Album* (1979). John Diggins, *The American Left in the Twentieth Century* (1973). Sara Evans, *Personal Politics* (1979). Lewis Feuer, *The Conflict of Generations* (1969). Richard Flacks, *Youth and Social Change* (1971). Todd Gitlin, *The Whole World Is Watching* (1981); *The Sixties: Years of Hope, Days of Rage* (1987). Paul Goodman, *Growing Up Absurd* (1960). David Harris, *Dreams Die Hard* (1983). Maurice Isserman, *"If I Had a Hammer. . . ": The Death of the Old Left and the Birth of the New Left* (1987). Joseph Kelner and James Munves, *The Kent State Coverup* (1980). Kenneth Keniston, *Young Radicals* (1968); *Youth and Dissent* (1971). Richard King, *The Party of Eros* (1972). James Kunen, *The Strawberry Statement* (1968). Lawrence Lader, *Power on the Left* (1979). Klaus Mehnert, *Twilight of the Young* (1978). James Miller, *"Democracy in the Streets": From Port Huron to the Siege of Chicago* (1987). Charles Reich, *The Greening of America* (1970). W. J. Rorabaugh, *Berkeley at War* (1989). Theodore Roszak, *The*

Making of a Counter Culture (1969). Kirkpatrick Sale, *SDS* (1973). Irwin Unger, *The Movement* (1974). Milton Viorst, *Fire in the Streets* (1979). Jon Wiener, *Come Together: John Lennon in His Time* (1984).

Indians, Hispanics, Asians. Rodolfo Acuña, *Occupied America*, 2nd ed. (1981). Larry W. Burt, *Tribalism in Crisis: Federal Indian Policy, 1953–1961* (1982). Vine Deloria, Jr., *Behind the Trail of Broken Treaties* (1974); *Custer Died for Your Sins* (1969). Ronald Dewing, *Wounded Knee: The Meaning and Significance of the Second Incident* (1985). Douglas E. Foley, *From Peones to Politicos: Class and Ethnicity in a South Texas Town, 1900–1987* (1988). Peter Iverson, *The Navajo Nation* (1981). Oscar Lewis, *La Vida* (1969). D'Arcy McNickle, *Native American Tribalism* (1973). Matt Meier and Feliciano Rivera, *The Chicanos* (1972). David M. Reimers, *Still the Golden Door: The Third World Comes to America* (1985). Julian Samora, *Los Mojados* (1971). Stan Steiner, *The New Indians* (1968). Ronald Takaki, *Strangers from a Distant Shore: A History of Asian Americans* (1989); *A Different Mirror: A History of Multicultural America* (1993). Ronald Taylor, *Chavez and the Farm Workers* (1975). Wilcomb Washburn, *Red Man's Land/White Man's Land* (1971). Charles F. Wilkinson, *American Indians, Time, and the Law* (1987).

Feminism. William Chafe, *The American Woman* (1972). Nancy Cott, *The Grounding of Modern Feminism* (1987). Marian Faux, *Roe v. Wade* (1988). Jo Freeman, *The Politics of Women's Liberation* (1975). Betty Friedan, *The Feminine Mystique* (1963). Carol Gilligan, *In A Different Voice* (1982). Cynthia Harrison, *On Account of Sex: The Politics of Women's Issues, 1945–1968* (1988). Susan M. Hartmann, *From Margin to Mainstream: Women and American Politics Since 1960* (1989). Alice Kessler-Harris, *Out to Work: A History of Wage-Earning Women in the United States* (1982). Ethel Klein, *Gender Politics* (1984). Kristin Luker, *Abortion and the Politics of Motherhood* (1984). Robin Morgan, ed., *Sisterhood Is Powerful* (1970). Rosalind Petchesky, *Abortion and Women's Choice* (1984). Sheila Rothman, *Woman's Proper Place* (1978). Winifred Wandersee, *On the Move: American Women in the 1970s* (1988). Gayle Yates, *What Women Want* (1975).

Nixon and the World. Seyom Brown, *The Crisis of Power* (1979). Lloyd Gardner, *A Covenant with Power* (1984); *The Great Nixon Turnaround* (1973). Seymour Hersh, *The Price of Power* (1983). Roger Hilsman, *The Crouching Future* (1975). Arnold Isaacs, *Without Honor: Defeat in Vietnam and Cambodia* (1983). Walter Isaacson, *Kissinger* (1992). Marvin Kalb and Bernard Kalb, *Kissinger* (1974). Henry A. Kissinger, *White House Years* (1979); *Years of Upheaval* (1982); *Diplomacy* (1994). David Landau, *Kissinger: The Uses of Power* (1972). Robert S. Litwak, *Detente and the Nixon Doctrine: American Foreign Policy and the Pursuit of Stability* (1984). Timothy Lomperis, *The War Nobody Lost—and Won* (1984). Roger Morris, *Uncertain Greatness* (1977). Harland Moulton, *From Superiority to Parity* (1973). John Newhouse, *Cold Dawn* (1973). Michael Oksenberg and Robert Oxnam, eds., *Dragon and Eagle* (1978). Gareth Porter, *A Peace Denied* (1975); *Vietnam* (1979). Thomas Powers, *The Man Who Kept the Secrets* (1979). William Quandt, *Decade of Decision* (1977). Franz Schurman, *The Foreign Policies of Richard Nixon* (1987). William Shawcross, *Sideshow: Nixon, Kissinger, and the Destruction of Cambodia* (1978). Richard Stevenson, *The Rise and Fall of Detente* (1985). John Stockwell, *In Search of Enemies* (1977). Robert Stookey, *America and the Arab States* (1975). Robert D. Schulzinger, *Henry Kissinger: Doctor of Diplomacy* (1989). Tad Szulc, *The Illusion of Peace* (1978).

Nixon and His Presidency. Stephen Ambrose, *Nixon: The Triumph of a Politician, 1962–1972* (1989). Richard Barnet, *The Lean Years* (1980). Fawn Brodie, *Richard Nixon: The Shaping of His Character* (1981). Vincent Burke and Vee Burke, *Nixon's Good Deed* (1974). John Ehrlichman, *Witness to Power* (1982). H.R. Haldeman, *The Haldeman Diaries: Inside the Nixon White House* (1994). Joan Hoff, *Nixon Reconsidered* (1994). J. C. Hurewitz, ed., *Oil, the Arab-Israeli Dispute, and the Industrial World* (1976). R. L. Miller, *The New Economics of Richard Nixon* (1972). Daniel P. Moynihan, *The Politics of a Guaranteed Income* (1973). R. P. Nathan et al., *Monitoring Revenue Sharing* (1975). Richard Nixon, *RN: The Memoirs of Richard Nixon* (1978). Herbert Parmet, *Richard Nixon and His America* (1989). Raymond Price, *With Nixon* (1977). James Reichley, *Conservatives in an Age of Change: The Nixon and Ford Administrations* (1981). William Safire, *Before the Fall* (1975). Joan Edelman Spero, *The Politics of International Economic Relations* (1977). Michael Tanzer, *The Energy Crisis* (1974). Theodore H. White, *The Making of the President, 1972* (1973). Bob Woodward and Scott Armstrong, *The Brethren* (1980).

Nixon and Watergate. Fawn Brodie, *Richard Nixon* (1981). Richard Cohen and Jules Witcover, *A Heartbeat Away* (1974). Len Colodny and Robert Gettlin, *Silent Coup* (1991). John Dean, *Blind Ambition* (1976). James Doyle, *Not Above the Law* (1977). Fred Emery, *Watergate: The Corruption of American Politics* (1994). Stanley J. Kutler, *The Wars of Watergate* (1990). J. Anthony Lukas, *Nightmare: The Underside of the Nixon Years* (1976). Bruce Mazlish, *In Search of Nixon* (1972). Richard M. Nixon, *RN: The Memoirs of Richard Nixon* (1978). Jonathan Schell, *The Time of Illusion* (1975). Arthur M. Schlesinger, Jr., *The Imperial Presidency* (1973). William Sirica, *To Set the Record Straight* (1979). Maurice Stans, *The Terrors of Justice* (1984). Theodore H. White, *Breach of Faith* (1975). Garry Wills, *Nixon Agonistes* (1970). Bob Woodward and Carl Bernstein, *All the President's Men* (1974); *The Final Days* (1976).

LINING UP FOR FUEL
Motorists line up outside a Virginia gas station in 1979 during one of a series of gasoline shortages that plagued American society during the 1970s. *(Dennis Brack/Black Star)*

CHAPTER THIRTY-THREE

THE "AGE OF LIMITS"

HE FRUSTRATIONS OF THE early 1970s—the defeat in Vietnam, the Watergate crisis, the decay of the American economy—inflicted damaging blows to the confident, optimistic nationalism that had characterized so much of the postwar era. At first many Americans responded to these problems by announcing the arrival of an "age of limits," in which America would have to learn to live with increasingly constricted expectations. By the end of the decade, however, the contours of another response to the challenges had become visible in both American culture and American politics. It was a response that combined a conservative retreat from some of the heady visions of the 1960s with a reinforced commitment to the idea of economic growth, international power, and American exceptionalism.

POLITICS AND DIPLOMACY
AFTER WATERGATE

In the aftermath of Richard Nixon's ignominious departure from office, many wondered whether faith in the presidency, and in the government as a whole, could easily be restored. The administrations of the two presidents who succeeded Nixon did little to answer those questions.

The Ford Custodianship

Gerald Ford inherited the presidency under unenviable circumstances. He had to try to rebuild confidence in government in the face of the widespread cynicism the Watergate scandals had produced. And he had to try to restore prosperity in the face of major domestic and international challenges to the American economy. He enjoyed some success in the first of these efforts but very little in the second.

The new president's effort to establish himself as a symbol of political integrity suffered a setback only a month after he took office, when he granted Richard Nixon "a full, free, and absolute pardon" for any crimes he may have committed during his presidency. Ford explained that he was attempting to spare the nation the ordeal of years of litigation and to spare Nixon himself any further suffering. But much of the public suspected a secret deal with the former president. The pardon caused a decline in Ford's popularity from which he never fully recovered. Nevertheless, most Americans considered him a decent man; his honesty and amiability did much to reduce the bitterness and acrimony of the Watergate years.

The Ford administration enjoyed less success in its effort to solve the problems of the American economy. In his efforts to curb inflation, the president rejected the idea of wage and price controls and called instead for largely ineffective voluntary efforts. After supporting high interest rates, opposing increased federal spending (through liberal use of his veto power), and resisting pressures for a tax reduction, Ford had to deal with a serious recession in 1974 and 1975. Central to the economic problems was the continuing energy crisis. In the aftermath of the Arab oil embargo of 1973, the OPEC cartel began to raise the price of oil—by 400 percent in 1974 alone. Even so, American dependence on OPEC supplies continued to grow—one of the principal reasons why inflation reached 11 percent in 1976.

At first it seemed that the new administration's foreign policy would differ little from that of its predecessor. Ford retained Henry Kissinger as secretary of state and continued the general policies of the Nixon years. Late in 1974, Ford met with Leonid Brezhnev at Vladivostok in Siberia and signed an arms control accord that was to serve as the basis for SALT II, thus achieving a goal the Nixon administration had long sought. The following summer, after a European security conference in Helsinki, Finland, the Soviet Union and Western nations agreed to ratify the borders that had divided Europe since 1945; and the Soviets pledged to increase respect for human rights within their own country. Meanwhile, in the Middle East, Henry Kissinger helped produce a new accord by which Israel agreed to return large portions of the occupied Sinai to Egypt, and the two nations pledged not to resolve future differences by force. In China, finally, the death of Mao Zedong in 1976 brought to power a new, apparently more moderate government eager to expand its ties with the United States.

Nevertheless, as the 1976 presidential election approached, Ford's policies were coming under attack from both the right and the left. In the Republican primary campaign, Ford faced a powerful challenge from former California governor Ronald Reagan, leader of the party's conservative wing, who spoke for many on the right who were unhappy with any conciliation of communists. The president only barely survived the assault to win his party's nomination. The Democrats, in the meantime, were gradually uniting behind a new and, before 1976, almost entirely unknown candidate: Jimmy Carter, a former governor of Georgia who organized a brilliant primary campaign and appealed to the general unhappiness with Washington by offering honesty, piety, and an outsider's skepticism of the federal government. And while Carter's mammoth lead in opinion polls dwindled to almost nothing by election day, unhappiness with the economy and a general disenchantment with Ford enabled the Democrat to hold on for a narrow victory. Carter emerged with 50 percent of the popular vote to Ford's 47.9 percent and 297 electoral votes to Ford's 240.

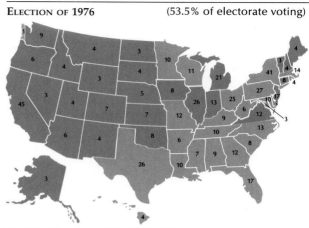

ELECTION OF 1976		(53.5% of electorate voting)

	ELECTORAL VOTE	POPULAR VOTE (%)
Jimmy Carter (Democratic)	297	40,828,587 (50.0)
Gerald R. Ford (Republican)	240	39,147,613 (47.9)
Ronald Reagan (Independent Republican)	1	—
Other candidates McCarthy (Ind.), Libertarian	—	1,575,459 (2.1)

The Trials of Jimmy Carter

Like Ford, Jimmy Carter assumed the presidency at a moment when the nation faced problems of staggering complexity and difficulty. Perhaps no leader could have thrived in such inhospitable circumstances. But Carter seemed at times to make his predicament worse by a style of leadership that many considered self-righteous and inflexible. He left office in 1981 one of the least popular presidents of the century.

Carter had campaigned for the presidency as an "outsider," representing Americans suspicious of entrenched bureaucracies and complacent public officials. He carried much of that suspiciousness with him to Washington. He surrounded himself in the White House with a group of close-knit associates from Georgia; and in the beginning, at least, he seemed deliberately to spurn assistance from more experienced political figures. Carter was among the most intelligent men ever to serve in the White House, but his critics charged that he provided no overall vision or direction to his government. His ambitious legislative agenda included major reforms of the tax and welfare systems; Congress passed virtually none of it.

Carter devoted much of his time to the problems of energy and the economy. Entering office in the midst of a recession, he moved first to reduce unemployment by raising public spending and cutting federal taxes. Unemployment declined, but inflation soared—less because of the fiscal policies he implemented than because of the continuing, sharp increases in energy prices imposed on the West by OPEC. During Carter's last two years in office, prices rose at well over a 10

JIMMY AND ROSALYNN CARTER, JANUARY 20, 1977
Jimmy Carter startled the crowds (and alarmed the Secret Service) on his Inauguration Day by walking down Pennsylvania Avenue from the Capitol to the White House after taking the oath of office. Not since Jefferson, whose effort to identify with the "common man" Carter hoped to emulate, had a president walked in his inaugural parade. *(Owen Franken/Sygma)*

percent annual rate. Like Nixon and Ford before him, Carter responded with a combination of tight money and calls for voluntary restraint. He appointed first G. William Miller and then Paul Volcker, both conservative economists, to head the Federal Reserve Board, thus ensuring a policy of high interest rates and reduced currency supplies. By 1980, interest rates had risen to the highest levels in American history; at times, they exceeded 20 percent.

The problem of energy also grew steadily more troublesome in the Carter years. In the summer of 1979, instability in the Middle East produced a second major fuel shortage in the United States. In the midst of the crisis, OPEC announced another major price increase, clouding the economic picture still further. Faced with increasing pressure to act (and with public opinion polls showing his approval rating at a dismal 26 percent, lower than Richard Nixon's lowest figures), Carter retreated to Camp David, the presidential retreat in the Maryland mountains. Ten days later, he emerged to deliver a remarkable television address. It included a series of proposals for resolving the energy crisis. But it was most notable for Carter's bleak assessment of the national condition. Speaking with unusual fervor, he complained of a "crisis of confidence" that had struck "at the very heart and soul of our national will." The address became known as the "malaise" speech (although Carter himself had never used that word), and it helped fuel charges that the president was trying to blame his own problems on the American people. Carter's sudden firing of several members of his cabinet a few days later deepened his political problems.

Human Rights and National Interests

Among Jimmy Carter's most frequent campaign promises was a pledge to build a new basis for American foreign policy, one in which the defense of "human rights" would replace the pursuit of "selfish interests." Carter spoke out sharply and often about violations of human rights in many countries (including, most prominently, the Soviet Union). Beyond that general commitment, the Carter administration focused on several more traditional concerns. Carter completed negotiations begun several years earlier on a pair of treaties to turn over control of the Panama Canal to the government of Panama. Domestic opposition to the treaties was intense, especially among conservatives who viewed the new arrangements as part of a general American retreat from international power. But the administration argued that relinquishing the canal was the best way to improve relations with Latin America and avoid violence in Panama. After an acrimonious debate, the Senate ratified the treaties by 68 to 32, only one vote more than the necessary two-thirds majority.

Less controversial, within the United States at least, was Carter's stunning success in arranging a peace treaty between Egypt and Israel—the crowning accomplishment of his presidency. Middle East negotiations had seemed hopelessly stalled when a dramatic breakthrough occurred in November 1977. The Egyptian president, Anwar Sadat, accepted an invitation from Prime Minister Menachem Begin to visit Israel. In Tel Aviv, he announced that Egypt was now willing to accept the state of Israel as a legitimate political entity. But translating these good feelings into an actual peace treaty proved more difficult.

When talks between Israeli and Egyptian negotiators stalled, Carter invited Sadat and Begin to a summit conference at Camp David in September 1978, and held them there for two weeks while he and others helped mediate the disputes between them. On September 17, Carter escorted the two leaders into the White House to announce agreement on a "framework" for an Egyptian-Israeli peace treaty. Carter intervened again several months later, when talks stalled once more, and helped produce a compromise on the most sensitive issue between the two parties: the Palestinian refugee issue. On March 26, 1979, Begin and Sadat returned together to the White House to sign a formal peace treaty between their two nations.

In the meantime, Carter continued trying to improve relations with China and the Soviet Union and to complete a new arms agreement. He responded eagerly to the overtures of Deng Xiaoping, the new Chinese leader who was attempting to open his nation to the outside world. On December 15, 1978, Washington and Beijing announced the resumption of formal diplomatic relations between the two nations. A few months later, Carter traveled to Vienna to meet with the aging and visibly ailing Brezhnev to finish drafting the new SALT II arms control agreement. The treaty set limits on the number of long-range missiles, bombers, and nuclear warheads on each side. Almost immediately, however, SALT II met with fierce conservative opposition in the United States. Central to the arguments was a fundamental distrust of the Soviet Union that nearly a decade of detente had failed to destroy; but specific provisions of the treaty—which even some supporters of detente felt were too favorable to the Soviets—also fueled the opposition. By the fall of 1979, with the Senate scheduled to begin debate over the treaty shortly, ratification was already in jeopardy. Events in the following months would provide a final blow, both to the treaty and to the larger framework of detente.

The Year of the Hostages

Ever since the early 1950s, the United States had provided political support and, more recently, massive

SIGNING THE CAMP DAVID ACCORDS
Jimmy Carter experienced many frustrations during his presidency, but his successful efforts in 1978 to negotiate a peace treaty between Israel and Egypt was undoubtedly his finest hour. Egyptian President Anwar Sadat and Israel Prime Minister Menachem Begin join Carter here in the East Room of the White House to sign the accords they had hammered out during two weeks at the president's retreat at Camp David. *(D. B. Owen/Black Star)*

military assistance to the government of the Shah of Iran, hoping to make his nation a bulwark against Soviet expansion in the Middle East. By 1979, however, the Shah was in deep trouble with his own people. Many Iranians resented the repressive, authoritarian tactics through which the Shah had maintained his autocratic rule. At the same time, Islamic clergy (and much of the fiercely religious populace) opposed his efforts to modernize and westernize a fundamentalist society. The combination of resentments produced a powerful revolutionary movement. In January 1979, the Shah fled the country.

The United States made cautious efforts in the first months after the Shah's abdication to establish cordial relations with the succession of increasingly militant regimes that followed. By late 1979, however, revolutionary chaos in Iran was making any normal relations impossible. What power there was resided with a zealous religious leader, the Ayatollah Ruhollah Khomeini, whose hatred of the West in general and the United States in particular was intense.

In late October 1979, the deposed Shah arrived in New York to be treated for cancer. Days later, on November 4, an armed mob invaded the American embassy in Teheran, seized the diplomats and military personnel inside, and demanded the return of the Shah to Iran in exchange for their freedom. Fifty-three Americans remained hostages in the embassy for over a year. Coming after years of international humiliations and defeats, the hostage seizure released a deep well of anger and emotion in the United States.

Only weeks after the hostage seizure, on December 27, 1979, Soviet troops invaded Afghanistan, the mountainous Islamic nation lying between the USSR and Iran. The Soviet Union had in fact been a power in Afghanistan for years, and the dominant force since April 1978, when a coup had established a Marxist government there with close ties to the Kremlin. But while some observers claimed that the Soviet invasion was a Russian attempt to secure the status quo, others—most notably the president—claimed it was a Russian "stepping stone to their possible control over much of the world's oil supplies." It was also the "gravest threat to world peace since World War II." Carter angrily imposed a series of economic sanctions on the Russians, canceled American participation in the 1980 summer Olympic Games in Moscow, and announced the withdrawal of SALT II from Senate consideration.

The combination of domestic economic troubles and international crises created widespread anxiety, frustration, and anger in the United States—damaging President Carter's already low standing with the public, and giving added strength to an alternative political force that had already made great strides.

THE RISE OF THE AMERICAN RIGHT

Much of the anxiety that pervaded American life in the 1970s was a result of jarring public events that left many men and women shaken and uncertain about their leaders and their government. But much of it was a result, too, of significant changes in the character of America's economy, society, and culture. Together these changes disillusioned many liberals, perplexed the already weakened left, and provided the right with its most important opportunity in generations to seize a position of authority in American life.

The Sunbelt and Its Politics

The most widely discussed demographic phenomenon of the 1970s was the rise of what became known as the "Sunbelt"—a term coined by the political analyst Kevin Phillips to describe a collection of regions that together emerged in the postwar era to become the most dynamically growing parts of the country. The Sunbelt included the Southeast (particularly Florida), the Southwest (particularly Texas), and above all, California, which became the nation's most populous state, surpassing New York, in 1964, and continued to grow in the years that followed. By 1980, the population of the Sunbelt had risen to exceed that of the industrial regions of the North and East, which were experiencing not only a relative, but in some cases an absolute, decline in population.

In addition to shifting the nation's economic focus from one region to another, the rise of the Sunbelt helped produce a change in the political climate. The strong populist traditions in the South and the West were capable of producing progressive and even radical politics; but more often in the late twentieth century, they produced a strong opposition to the growth of government and a resentment of the proliferating regulations and restrictions that the liberal state was producing. Many of those regulations and restrictions—environmental laws, land-use restrictions, even the fifty-five-mile-per-hour speed limit created during the energy crisis to force motorists to conserve fuel—affected the West more than any other region. Both the South and the West, moreover, embraced myths about their own pasts that reinforced the hostility to

GROWTH OF THE SUNBELT: POPULATION AND URBAN CENTER SHIFTS, 1970–1990

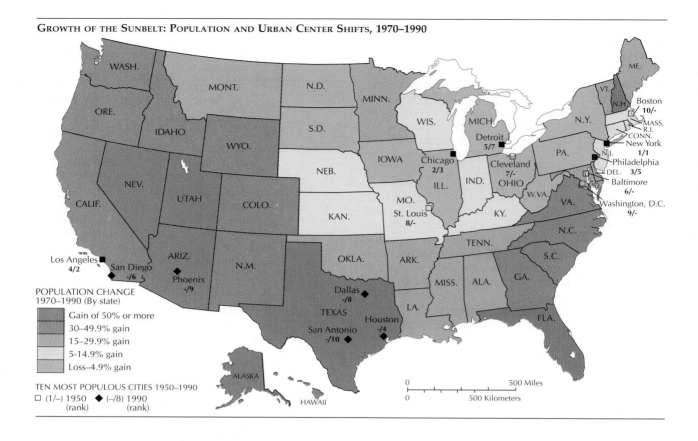

POPULATION CHANGE
1970–1990 (By state)

- Gain of 50% or more
- 30–49.9% gain
- 15–29.9% gain
- 5–14.9% gain
- Loss–4.9% gain

TEN MOST POPULOUS CITIES 1950–1990
□ (1/–) 1950   ◆ (–/8) 1990
   (rank)   (rank)

the liberal government of the mid- and late-twentieth century. White southerners equated the federal government's effort to change racial norms in the region with what they believed was the tyranny of Reconstruction. Westerners embraced an image of their region as a refuge of "rugged individualism" and resisted what they considered efforts by the government to impose new standards of behavior on them. Thus, the same impulses and rhetoric that populists had once used to denounce banks and corporations, the new conservative populists of the postwar era used to attack the government—and the liberals, radicals, and minorities whom they believed were driving its growth.

If anything, the growth of the Sunbelt seemed to strengthen the hostility toward government in the politics of the regions. In the 1970s and early 1980s, the boom mentality of some of these rapidly growing areas (especially south Florida, Texas, and southern California) conflicted sharply with the concerns of the older industrial states of the Northeast and Midwest. Saddled with declining economic bases, highly congested, home to large, impoverished minority groups, they remained more committed to social programs and

more interested in regulated growth than the relatively wide-open areas of the Sunbelt.

The so-called Sagebrush Rebellion, which emerged in parts of the West in the late 1970s, mobilized conservative opposition to environmental laws and restrictions on development. It also sought to portray the West (which had probably benefited more than any other region from federal investment) as a victim of government control. Its members complained about the very large amounts of land the federal government owned in many western states and demanded that they be opened for development.

The South as a whole was considerably more conservative than other parts of the nation, and its growth served to increase the power of the right in the 1960s and 1970s. The West was not, on the whole, a more conservative region than others; but its rise in the postwar period did help produce some of the most numerous and powerful conservative movements in the nation—particularly in southern California, where Orange County (a large suburban area south of Los Angeles) emerged as one of the most important centers of right-wing politics in the country. When the right rose to power in the 1970s and 1980s, westerners were among its most important leaders and constituents.

Religious Revivalism

In the 1960s, many social critics had predicted the virtual extinction of religious influence in American life. *Time* magazine had reported such assumptions in 1966 with a celebrated cover emblazoned with the question, "Is God Dead?" But religion in America was far from dead. Indeed, in the 1970s the United States experienced the beginning of a major religious revival, perhaps the most powerful since the Second Great Awakening of the early nineteenth century. It continued in various forms into the 1990s.

Some of the new religious enthusiasm found expression in the rise of various cults and pseudo-faiths: the Church of Scientology; the Unification Church of the Reverend Sun Myung Moon; even the tragic People's Temple, whose members committed mass suicide in their jungle retreat in Guyana in 1978. But the most important impulse of the religious revival was the growth of evangelical Christianity.

Evangelicism is the basis of many forms of Christian faith. But evangelicals have in common a belief in personal conversion through direct communication with God. Evangelical religion had been the dominant form of Christianity in America through much of its history, and a substantial subculture since the late nineteenth century. In its modern form, it had been increasingly visible since at least the early 1950s, when evangelicals such as Billy Graham and Pentecostals such as Oral Roberts had begun to attract huge national (and international) followings for their energetic revivalism.

For many years, the evangelicals had gone largely unnoted by much of the media and the secular public, which had dismissed them as a limited, provincial phenomenon. By the early 1980s, it was no longer possible to do so. Earlier in the century, many (although never all) evangelicals had been relatively poor rural people, largely isolated from the mainstream of American culture. But the great capitalist expansion after World War II had lifted many of these people out of poverty and into the middle class, where they were more visible and more assertive. More than 70 million Americans now described themselves as "born-again" Christians—men and women who had established a "direct personal relationship with Jesus." Christian evangelicals owned their own newspapers, magazines, radio stations, and television networks. They operated their own schools and universities. They occupied positions of eminence in the worlds of entertainment and professional sports. And one of their number ultimately occupied the White House itself—Jimmy Carter,

who during the 1976 campaign had talked proudly of his own "conversion experience" and who continued openly to proclaim his "born-again" Christian faith during his years in office.

For Jimmy Carter and for some others, evangelical Christianity had formed the basis for a commitment to racial and economic justice and to world peace. For many evangelicals, however, the message of the new religion was very different—but no less political. In the 1970s, some Christian evangelicals became active on the political and cultural right. They were alarmed by what they considered the spread of immorality and disorder in American life; and they were concerned about the way a secular and, as they saw it, godless culture was intruding into their communities and families—through popular culture, through the schools, and through government policies. Many evangelical men and women feared the growth of feminism and the threat they believed it posed to the traditional family, and they resented the way in which government policies advanced the goals of the women's movement. Particularly alarming to them were Supreme Court decisions eliminating all religious observance from schools and, later, the decision guaranteeing women the right to an abortion.

By the late 1970s, the "Christian right" had become a visible and increasingly powerful political force. Jerry Falwell, a fundamentalist minister in Virginia with a substantial television audience, launched a movement he called the Moral Majority, which attacked the rise of "secular humanism" in American culture. The Moral Majority and other organizations of similar inclination opposed federal interference in local affairs, denounced abortion, divorce, feminism, and homosexuality, defended unrestricted free enterprise, and supported a strong American posture in the world. Some evangelicals reopened issues that had long seemed closed. For example, many fundamentalist Christians denied the scientific doctrine of evolution and instead urged the teaching in schools of the biblical story of the Creation. Others demanded various forms of censorship or control of television, movies, rock music, books, magazines, and newspapers. Their goal was a new era in which Christian values once again dominated American life.

The Emergence of the New Right

Evangelical Christians were an important part, but only a part, of what became known as the New Right—a diverse but powerful movement that enjoyed rapid growth in the 1970s and early 1980s. It had begun to take shape after the 1964 election, in which Barry Goldwater had suffered his shattering defeat. Richard

Viguerie, a remarkable conservative activist and organizer, took a list of 12,000 contributors to the Goldwater campaign and used it to develop a formidable conservative communications and fund-raising organization. By the mid-1970s, he had gathered a list of 4 million contributors and 15 million supporters. Conservative campaigns had for many years been less well funded and organized than those of their rivals. Beginning in the 1970s, largely because of these and other organizational advances, conservatives found themselves almost always better funded and organized than their opponents. Gradually these direct-mail operations helped create a much larger conservative infrastructure, designed to match and even exceed what the right saw as the powerful liberal infrastructure. By the late 1970s, there were right-wing think tanks, consulting firms, lobbyists, foundations, and scholarly centers.

Another factor in the revival of the right was the emergence of a credible right-wing leadership in the late 1960s and early 1970s to replace the discredited conservative hero of the 1950s, Barry Goldwater. Chief among this new generation of conservative leaders was Ronald Reagan. Reagan had grown up in modest circumstances in the Midwest and attended a small college in Illinois. In 1937, at the age of 26, he went to Hollywood and became a moderately successful actor, in westerns at times, but mostly in light romantic comedies. A liberal and a fervent admirer of Franklin Roosevelt as a young man, he moved decisively to the right after his second marriage, to Nancy Davis, a woman of strong conservative convictions; and after, as president of the Screen Actors Guild, he became embroiled in battles with communists in the union. In the early 1950s, he became a corporate spokesman for General Electric and won a wide following on the right with his smooth, eloquent speeches in defense of individual freedom and private enterprise.

In 1964, Reagan delivered a memorable television speech on behalf of Goldwater. After Goldwater's defeat, he worked quickly not only to seize the leadership of the conservative wing of the party but to denounce those Republicans who had repudiated Goldwater. "I don't think we should turn the high command over to leaders who were traitors during the battle just ended," Reagan said in 1965, when other Republicans were trying to push anti-Goldwater moderates into positions of leadership in the party. In 1966, with the support of a group of wealthy conservatives, he won the first of two terms as governor of California—which gave him a much more visible platform for promoting himself and his ideas.

The presidency of Gerald Ford also played an important role in the rise of the right, by destroying the fragile equilibrium that had enabled the right wing and the moderate wing of the Republican Party to coexist. Ford, probably without realizing it, touched on some of the right's rawest nerves. He appointed as vice president Nelson Rockefeller, the liberal Republican governor of New York and an heir to one of America's great fortunes; many conservatives had been demonizing Rockefeller and his family for more than twenty years. (Viguerie attributed the birth of the New Right to this event alone.) Ford proposed an amnesty program for draft resisters, embraced and even extended the hated Nixon-Kissinger policies of detente, presided over the fall of Vietnam, and agreed to cede the Panama Canal to Panama. When Reagan challenged Ford in the 1976 Republican primaries, the president survived, barely, only by dumping Nelson Rockefeller from the ticket, replacing him with Senator Robert Dole of Kansas, and agreeing to a platform largely written by one of Reagan's principal allies, Senator Jesse Helms of North Carolina. Reagan hailed that platform by saying that the party "must raise a banner of no pale pastels, but bold colors which make it unmistakably clear where we stand on all the issues troubling the people."

The Tax Revolt

At least equally important to the success of the new right was a new and potent conservative issue: the tax revolt. It had its public beginnings in 1978, when Howard Jarvis, a conservative activist in California, launched the first successful major citizens' tax revolt in California with Proposition 13, a referendum question on the state ballot rolling back property tax rates. Similar antitax movements soon began in other states and eventually spread to national politics.

The tax revolt became the solution to one of the right's biggest problems. For more than thirty years after the New Deal, Republican conservatives had struggled to halt and even reverse the growth of the federal government. Most of those efforts had ended in futility. Attacking government programs directly, as right-wing politicians from Robert Taft to Barry Goldwater discovered, was not the way to attract majority support. Every federal program had a political constituency. The biggest and most expensive programs had the broadest support. (Goldwater was plagued throughout the 1964 campaign by fears he would dismantle Social Security.)

In Proposition 13 and similar initiatives, members of the right found a better way to undermine government than by attacking specific programs: attacking taxes. By separating the issue of taxes from the issue of what taxes supported, the right found a way to achieve the most controversial elements of its own agenda (eroding the government's ability to expand and launch new programs) without openly antagonizing the millions of voters who supported specific programs. Virtually no one liked to pay taxes, and as the economy grew weaker and the relative burden of paying taxes grew heavier, that resentment naturally rose. The right exploited that resentment and, in the process, expanded its constituency far beyond anything it had known before. The 1980 presidential election propelled it to a historic victory.

The Campaign of 1980

By the time of the crises in Iran and Afghanistan, Jimmy Carter was in desperate political trouble—his standing in popularity polls lower than that of any president in history. Senator Edward Kennedy, younger brother of John and Robert Kennedy and one of the most magnetic (and controversial) figures in the Democratic Party, was preparing to challenge him in the primaries. For a short while, the seizure of the hostages and the stern American response to the Soviet invasion revived Carter's candidacy. But as the hostage crisis dragged on, public impatience grew. Kennedy won a series of victories over the president in the later primaries. Carter managed in the end to stave off Kennedy's challenge and win his party's nomination. But it was an unhappy convention that heard the president's listless call to arms, and Carter's campaign aroused little popular enthusiasm as he prepared to face a powerful challenge.

The Republican Party, in the meantime, had rallied enthusiastically behind the man who, four years earlier, had nearly stolen the nomination from Gerald Ford. Ronald Reagan was a sharp critic of the excesses of the federal government. He linked his campaign to the spreading tax revolt (something to which he had paid relatively little attention in the past) by promising substantial tax cuts. Equally important, he championed a restoration of American "strength" and "pride" in the world. Although he refrained from discussing the issue of the hostages, Reagan clearly benefited from the continuing popular frustration at Carter's inability to resolve the crisis. In a larger sense, he benefited as well from the accumulated frustrations of more than a decade of domestic and international disappointments.

On election day 1980, the anniversary of the seizure of the hostages in Iran, Reagan swept to victory, winning 51 percent of the vote to 41 percent for Jimmy Carter, and 7 percent for John Anderson—a moderate Republican congressman from Illinois who had mounted

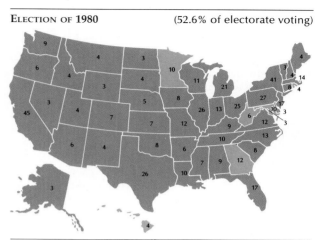

ELECTION OF 1980	(52.6% of electorate voting)

	ELECTORAL VOTE	POPULAR VOTE (%)
Ronald Reagan (Republican)	489	43,901,812 (50.7)
Jimmy Carter (Democratic)	49	35,483,820 (41.0)
John B. Anderson (Independent)	—	5,719,722 (6.6)
Other candidates (Libertarian)	—	921,299 (1.1)

an independent campaign. Carter carried only five states and the District of Columbia, for a total of 49 electoral votes to Reagan's 489. The Republican Party won control of the Senate for the first time since 1952; and although the Democrats retained a modest majority in the House, the lower chamber too seemed firmly in the hands of conservatives.

On the day of Reagan's inauguration, the American hostages in Iran were released after their 444-day ordeal. Jimmy Carter, in the last hours of his presidency, had concluded months of negotiations by agreeing to release several billion dollars in Iranian assets that he had frozen in American banks shortly after the seizure of the embassy. The government of Iran, desperate for funds to support its floundering war against neighboring Iraq, had ordered the hostages freed in return. Americans welcomed the hostages home with demonstrations of joy and patriotism not seen since the end of World War II. But while the celebration in 1945 had marked a great American triumph, the euphoria in 1981 marked something quite different—a troubled nation grasping for reassurance. Ronald Reagan set out to provide it.

THE "REAGAN REVOLUTION"

Ronald Reagan assumed the presidency in January 1981 promising a change in government more fundamental than any since the New Deal of fifty years before. While his eight years in office produced a significant shift in public policy, they brought nothing so fundamental as many of his supporters had hoped or his opponents had feared. But there was no ambiguity about its purely political achievements. Reagan succeeded brilliantly in making his own engaging personality the central fact of American politics in the 1980s.

The Reagan Coalition

Reagan owed his election to widespread disillusionment with Carter and to the crises and disappointments that many voters, perhaps unfairly, associated with him. But he owed it as well to the emergence of a powerful coalition of conservative groups. That coalition was not a single, cohesive movement. It was an uneasy and generally temporary alliance among several very different movements.

The Reagan coalition included a small but highly influential group of wealthy Americans associated with the corporate and financial world—the kind of people who had dominated American politics and government through much of the nation's history until the New Deal began to challenge their preeminence. What united this group was a firm commitment to capitalism and to unfettered economic growth; a deep hostility to most (although not all) government interference in markets; and a belief that most of what is valuable in American life depends on the health and strength of the corporate world, and thus that the corporate world is entitled to a special position of influence and privilege in society. Central to this group's agenda in the 1980s was opposition to what it considered the "redistributive" politics of the federal government (and especially its highly progressive tax structure) and hostility to the rise of what they believed were "antibusiness" government regulations. Reagan courted them carefully and effectively.

A second element of the Reagan coalition was even smaller, but also disproportionately influential: a group of intellectuals commonly known as "neo-conservatives," who gave to the right something it had not had in many years—a firm base among "opinion leaders," people with access to the most influential public forums for ideas. Many of these people had once been liberals and, before that, socialists. But during the turmoil of the 1960s, they had become alarmed by what

RONALD AND NANCY REAGAN
The president and the first lady greet guests at a White House social event. Nancy Reagan was most visible in her efforts to make the White House, and her husband's presidency, seem more glamorous than those of most recent administrations. But she also played an important, if quiet, policy role in the administration. *(Dirck Halstead/ Gamma Liaison)*

they considered a dangerous and destructive radicalism that was destabilizing American life, and by the weakening of liberal ardor in the battle against communism. Neo-conservatives were sympathetic to the complaints and demands of capitalists, but their principal concern was to reassert legitimate authority and reaffirm Western democratic, anticommunist values and commitments. They considered themselves engaged in a battle to regain control of the marketplace of ideas—to "win back the culture"—from the crass, radical ideas that had polluted it. Some neo-conservative intellectuals went on to become important figures in the battle against multi-culturalism and "political correctness" within academia.

These two groups joined in an uneasy alliance in 1980 with the vast and growing movement known as the "New Right" (or, to some, the populist right). Several things differentiated the New Right from the corporate conservatives and the neo-conservatives. Perhaps the most important was a fundamental distrust of the "eastern establishment": a suspicion of its motives and goals; a sense that it exercised a dangerous, secret power in American life; a fear of the hidden influence of such establishment institutions and people as the Council on Foreign Relations, the Trilateral Commission, Henry Kissinger, and the Rockefellers.

These "populist" conservatives expressed the kinds of concerns that outsiders, non-elites, have traditionally voiced in American society: an opposition to centralized power and influence, a fear of living in a world where distant, hostile forces are controlling society and threatening individual freedom and community autonomy. It was a testament to Ronald Reagan's political skills, and personal charm that he was able to generate enthusiastic support from these populist conservatives while at the same time appealing to more elite conservative groups whose concerns were in many ways antithetical to those of the New Right.

Reagan in the White House

Even many people who disagreed with Reagan's policies found themselves drawn to his attractive and carefully honed public image. Reagan was a master of television, a gifted public speaker, and—in public at least—rugged, fearless, and seemingly impervious to danger or misfortune. He turned seventy weeks after taking office and was the oldest man ever to serve as president. But through most of his presidency, he seemed vigorous, resilient, even youthful. He spent his many vacations on a California ranch, where he chopped wood and rode horses. When he was wounded in an assassination attempt in 1981, he joked with doctors on his way into surgery and appeared to bounce back from the ordeal with remarkable speed. Four years later, he seemed to rebound from cancer surgery with similar zest. He had few visible insecurities. Even when things went wrong, as they often did, the blame seldom seemed to attach to Reagan himself (inspiring some Democrats to begin referring to him as the "Teflon president").

Reagan was not much involved in the day-to-day affairs of running the government; he surrounded himself with tough, energetic administrators who insulated him from many of the pressures of the office and who apparently relied on him largely for general guidance, not specific decisions. At times, the president revealed a startling ignorance about the nature of his own policies or the actions of his subordinates. But Reagan did make active use of his office to generate support for his administration's programs, by appealing repeatedly to the public over television and by fusing his proposals with a highly nationalistic rhetoric.

"Supply-Side" Economics

Reagan's 1980 campaign for the presidency had promised, among other things, to restore the economy to health by a bold experiment that became known as "supply-side" economics or, to some, "Reaganomics." Supply-side economics operated from the assumption that the woes of the American economy were in large part a result of excessive taxation, which left inadequate capital available to investors to stimulate growth. The solution, therefore, was to reduce taxes, with particularly generous benefits to corporations and wealthy individuals, in order to encourage new investments. The result would be a general economic revival that would help everyone. Because a tax cut would reduce government revenues (at least at first), it would also be necessary to reduce government expenses. A cornerstone of the Reagan economic program, therefore, was a dramatic cut in the federal budget.

In its first months in office, accordingly, the new administration hastily assembled a legislative program based on the supply-side idea. It proposed $40 billion in budget reductions and managed to win congressional approval of almost all of them. In addition, the president proposed a bold, three-year rate reduction of 30 percent on both individual and corporate taxes. In the summer of 1981, Congress passed it too, after lowering the reductions slightly, to 25 percent. Not since Lyndon Johnson had a president compiled so impressive a legislative record in his first months in office. Reagan was successful because he had a disciplined Republican majority in the Senate, and because the Democratic majority in the House was weak and riddled with defectors. Shaken by the results of the 1980 election, dozens of Democrats from relatively conservative districts (mostly in the South) deserted the party's leadership; the defectors became known as "boll weevils."

Men and women whom Reagan appointed fanned out through the executive branch of government committed to reducing the role of government in American economic life. "Deregulation," an idea many Democrats had begun to embrace in the Carter years, became the religion of the Reagan administration. Secretary of the Interior James Watt had been a major figure in the Sagebrush Rebellion, a movement among western conservatives to fight federal environmental regulations, which they believed had a particularly devastating effect on their region's economy. Watt opened up public lands and water to development. The Environmental Protection Agency (before its directors were indicted for corruption) relaxed or entirely eliminated enforcement of critical environmental laws and regulations. The Civil Rights Division of the Justice Department eased enforcement of civil rights laws. The Department of Transportation slowed implementation of new rules limiting automobile emissions and imposing new safety standards on cars and trucks. By getting government "out of the way," Reagan officials promised, they were ensuring economic revival.

By early 1982, however, the nation had sunk into the most severe recession since the 1930s. The Reagan economic program was not directly to blame for the problems. It was more a result of the high interest rates the Federal Reserve Board (run by Carter appointee William Volcker) had maintained since the late 1970s as an antidote to inflation. The high interest rates made it difficult for businesses and individuals to borrow money for investment or consumer purchases. They also made the dollar attractive to overseas investors and significantly raised its value—thus making American products more expensive abroad and significantly reducing exports. By 1984, the U.S. trade deficit was $111 billion; in 1980, there had been a $25 billion surplus. The effects of the recession were particularly devastating on American industry, which had already been experiencing serious problems for a decade. Industrialists closed some plants, reduced the labor force in others, and eliminated millions of manufacturing jobs. In 1982 unemployment reached 11 percent, its highest level in over forty years. Farmers, even more dependent than manufacturers on the export trade, fared even worse. Hundreds of thousands of them lost so much money in the early 1980s that they lost their farms.

The recession convinced many people, including some conservatives, that the Reagan economic program (and thus the Reagan presidency) had failed. In fact, however, the economy recovered more rapidly and impressively than almost anyone had expected. By late 1983, unemployment had fallen to 8.2 percent, and it declined steadily for several years after that. The gross national product had grown 3.6 percent in a year, the largest increase since the mid-1970s. Inflation had fallen below 5 percent. The economy continued to grow, and both inflation and unemployment remained

low (at least by the new and more pessimistic standards the nation seemed now to have accepted) through most of the decade.

The recovery was a result of many things. The years of tight money policies by the Federal Reserve Board, however painful and destructive they may have been in other ways, had helped lower inflation; equally important, the Board had lowered interest rates early in 1983 in response to the recession. A worldwide "energy glut" and the virtual collapse of the OPEC cartel had produced at least a temporary end to the inflationary pressures of spiraling fuel costs. And stagger-

FEDERAL BUDGET AND SURPLUS/DEFICIT, 1940–1993

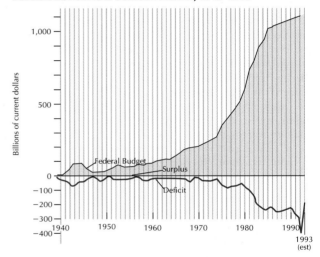

GROSS NATIONAL PRODUCT, 1940–1992

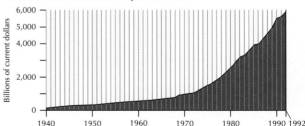

BUDGET AND SURPLUS/DEFICIT AS PERCENT OF GNP, 1940–1992

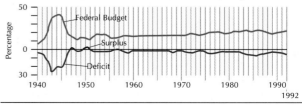

ing federal budget deficits were pumping billions of dollars into the flagging economy. As a result, consumer spending and business investment both increased. And the stock market rose up from the doldrums of the late 1970s and began a sustained and historic boom. In August 1982, the Dow Jones Industrial Average stood at 777. Five years later it had passed 2,000. Despite a frightening crash in the fall of 1987, the market continued to grow: by 1994, the Dow Jones average was nearing 4,000.

The Fiscal Crisis

The economic revival did little, however, to reduce the staggering, and to many Americans alarming, deficits in the federal budget. By the mid-1980s, this growing fiscal crisis had become one of the central issues in American politics. Having entered office promising a balanced budget within four years, Reagan presided over record budget deficits and accumulated more debt in his eight years in office than the American government had accumulated in its entire previous history. Before the 1980s, the highest single-year budget deficit in American history had been $66 billion (in 1976). Throughout the 1980s, the annual budget deficit consistently exceeded $100 billion (and in 1991 peaked at $268 billion). The national debt rose from $907 billion in 1980 to nearly $3.5 trillion by 1991.

The enormous deficits had many causes, some of them stretching back over decades of American public policy decisions. In particular, the budget suffered from enormous increases in the costs of "entitlement" programs (especially Social Security and Medicare), a result of the aging of the population and dramatic increases in the cost of health care. But some of the causes of the deficit lay in the policies of the Reagan administration. The 1981 tax cuts, the largest in American history, eroded the revenue base of the federal government and accounted for a significant percentage of the deficit. The massive increase in military spending (a proposed $1.6 trillion over five years) on which the Reagan administration insisted added more to the federal budget than its cuts in domestic spending removed.

In the face of these deficits, the administration refused to consider raising income taxes (although it did agree to a major increase in the Social Security tax). It would not agree to reductions in military spending. It could not much reduce the costs of entitlement programs, and it could do nothing to reduce interest payments on the massive (and growing) debt. Its answer to the fiscal crisis, therefore, was further cuts in "discretionary" domestic spending, which included many

programs aimed at the poorest (and politically weakest) Americans. There were reductions in funding for food stamps; a major cut in federal subsidies for low-income housing (which became one of many factors contributing to the radical increase in homelessness that by the late 1980s was plaguing virtually all American cities); strict new limitations on Medicare and Medicaid payments; reductions in student loans, school lunches, and other educational programs; and an end to many forms of federal assistance to the states and cities—which helped precipitate years of local fiscal crises as well.

By the end of Reagan's third year in office, funding for domestic programs had been cut nearly as far as Congress (and, apparently, the public) was willing to tolerate, and still no end to the rising deficits was in sight. Congress responded with the so-called Gramm-Rudman bill, passed late in 1985, which mandated major deficit reductions over five years and provided for automatic budget cuts in all areas of government spending should the president and Congress fail to agree on an alternative solution. Under Gramm-Rudman, the budget deficit did decline for several years from its 1983 high. But much of that decline was a result of a substantial surplus in the Social Security trust fund (which the sharply increased Social Security taxes had produced), not of the provisions of the law. By the late 1980s, many fiscal conservatives were calling for a constitutional amendment mandating a balanced budget—a provision the president himself claimed to support. (Congress came within a few votes of passing such an amendment in 1994.)

Reagan and the World

Reagan encountered a similar combination of triumphs and difficulties in international affairs. Determined to restore American pride and prestige in the world, he argued that the United States should once again become active and assertive in opposing communism and in supporting friendly governments whatever their internal policies.

Relations with the Soviet Union, which had been steadily deteriorating in the last years of the Carter administration, grew still more chilly in the first years of the Reagan presidency. The president spoke harshly of the Soviet regime (which he once called the "evil empire"), accusing it of sponsoring world terrorism and declaring that any armaments negotiations must be linked to negotiations on Soviet behavior in other areas. Relations with the Russians deteriorated further after the government of Poland (under strong pressure from

S I G N I F I C A N T   E V E N T S

1965   Richard Viguerie launches conservative direct-mail operations

1966   Ronald Reagan elected governor of California

1974   OPEC raises oil prices

"Stagflation" (recession and inflation together) begins

Ford pardons Nixon

Ford meets Brezhnev at Vladivostok summit

1976   Reagan challenges Ford in Republican presidential primaries

Jimmy Carter elected president

Mao Zedong dies

1977   Panama Canal treaties signed

1978   Camp David accords signed

Panama Canal treaties ratified

Voters in California approve Proposition 13, launching tax revolt

1979   Energy crisis jolts United States

U.S. and China restore diplomatic relations

Iranian revolution overthrows Shah

American diplomats taken hostage in Iran

Soviet Union invades Afghanistan

Sandinista revolution triumphs in Nicaragua

SALT II treaty signed

1980   U.S. boycotts Moscow Olympics

Attempt to rescue American hostages in Iran fails; Secretary of State Cyrus Vance resigns in protest

Edward Kennedy challenges Carter in Democratic primaries

Ronald Reagan elected president

1981   American hostages in Iran released

Reagan wins major tax and budget cuts

U.S. military buildup begins

Soviet Union forces imposition of martial law in Poland

United States begins supporting contra rebellion in Nicaragua

Reagan survives assassination attempt

1982   Severe recession

Inflation and interest rates decline

Israel invades Lebanon

1983   U.S. Marines killed in terrorist attack in Beirut

United States invades Grenada

Nuclear freeze movement expands in United States

Unemployment reaches 10.2 percent

Economic recovery begins

1984   Jesse Jackson campaigns for Democratic presidential nomination

Democrats nominate Geraldine Ferraro for vice president

Reagan defeats Walter Mondale in presidential election

Moscow) imposed martial law on the country in the winter of 1981 to crush a growing challenge from an independent labor organization, Solidarity.

Although the president had long denounced the SALT II arms control treaty as unfavorable to the United States, he continued to honor its provisions. But the Reagan administration at first made little progress toward arms control in other areas. In fact, the presi-

dent proposed the most ambitious (and potentially most expensive) new military program in many years: the so-called Strategic Defense Initiative (SDI), widely known as "Star Wars" (after a popular movie of that name). Reagan claimed that SDI, through the use of lasers and satellites, could provide an effective shield against incoming missiles and thus make nuclear war obsolete. The Soviet Union claimed that the new program would elevate the arms race to new and more dangerous levels (a complaint many domestic critics of SDI shared) and insisted that any arms control agreement begin with an American abandonment of SDI.

The escalation of Cold War tensions and the slowing of arms control initiatives helped produce an important popular movement in Europe and the United States calling for an end to nuclear weapons buildups. In America, the principal goal of the movement was a "nuclear freeze," an agreement between the two superpowers not to expand their atomic arsenals. In what many believed was the largest mass demonstration in American history, nearly a million people rallied in New York City's Central Park in 1982 to support the freeze. Perhaps partly in response to this growing pressure, the administration began tentative efforts to revive arms control negotiations in 1983.

It also began, rhetorically at least, to support opponents of communism anywhere in the world, whether or not the regimes or movements they were challenging had any direct connection to the Soviet Union. This new policy became known as the Reagan Doctrine, and it meant, above all, a new American activism in the Third World. The most conspicuous examples of the new activism came in Latin America. In October 1982, the administration sent American soldiers and Marines into the tiny Caribbean island of Grenada to oust an anti-American Marxist regime that showed signs of forging a relationship with Moscow. In El Salvador, where first a repressive military regime and later a moderate civilian one were engaged in murderous struggles with left-wing revolutionaries (who were supported, according to the Reagan administration, by Cuba and the Soviet Union), the president provided increased military and economic assistance. In neighboring Nicaragua, a pro-American dictatorship had fallen to the revolutionary "Sandinistas" in 1979; the new government had grown increasingly anti-American (and increasingly Marxist) throughout the early 1980s. The administration gave both rhetorical and material support to the so-called contras, a guerrilla movement drawn from several antigovernment groups and fighting (without great success) to topple the Sandinista regime. Indeed, support of the contras became a mission of special importance to the president, and later the source of some of his greatest difficulties.

In other parts of the world, the administration's bellicose rhetoric seemed to hide an instinctive restraint. In June 1982, the Israeli army launched an invasion of Lebanon in an effort to drive guerrillas of the Palestinian Liberation Organization from the country. The United States supported the Israelis rhetorically but also worked to permit PLO forces to leave Lebanon peacefully. An American peacekeeping force entered Beirut to supervise the evacuation. American marines then remained in the city, apparently to protect the fragile Lebanese government, which was embroiled in a vicious civil war. Now identified with one faction in the struggle, Americans became the targets in 1983 of a terrorist bombing of a U.S. military barracks in Beirut that left 241 marines dead. Rather than become more deeply involved in the Lebanese struggle, Reagan withdrew American forces.

The tragedy in Lebanon was an example of the changing character of Third World struggles: an increasing reliance on terrorism by otherwise powerless groups to advance their political aims. A series of terrorist acts in the 1980s—attacks on airplanes, cruise ships, commercial and diplomatic posts; the seizing of American and other Western hostages—alarmed and frightened much of the Western world. The Reagan administration spoke bravely about its resolve to punish terrorism; and at one point in 1986, the president ordered American planes to bomb sites in Tripoli, the capital of Libya, whose controversial leader Muammar al-Qaddafi was widely believed to be a leading sponsor of terrorism. In general, however, terrorists remained difficult to identify or control.

The Election of 1984

Reagan approached the campaign of 1984 at the head of a united Republican Party firmly committed to his candidacy. The Democrats, as had become their custom, followed a more fractious course. Former vice president Walter Mondale established an early and commanding lead in the race by soliciting support from a wide range of traditional Democratic interest groups, and survived challenges from Senator Gary Hart of Colorado (who claimed to represent a "new generation" of leadership) and the magnetic Jesse Jackson, who had established himself as the nation's most prominent spokesman for minorities and the poor. Mondale captured the nomination and brought momentary excitement to the Democratic campaign by selecting a woman, Representative Geraldine Ferraro of New York, to be his running mate and the first female candidate ever to appear on a national ticket.

The Republican Party rallied comfortably behind its revered leader, whose triumphant campaign that fall scarcely took note of his opponents and spoke instead of what he claimed was the remarkable revival of American fortunes and spirits under his leadership. His campaign emphasized such phrases as "It's Morning in America" and "America Is Back." Reagan's victory in 1984 was decisive. He won approximately 59 percent of the vote, and carried every state but Mon-

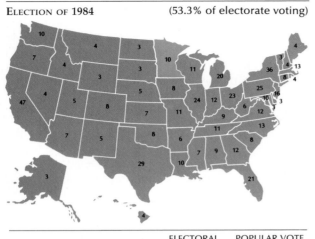

ELECTION OF 1984   (53.3% of electorate voting)

	ELECTORAL VOTE	POPULAR VOTE (%)
Ronald Reagan (Republican)	525	54,455,075 (59)
Walter Mondale (Democratic)	13	37,577,185 (41)

dale's native Minnesota and the District of Columbia. But Reagan was much stronger than his party. Democrats gained a seat in the Senate and maintained only slightly reduced control of the House of Representatives.

The triumphant reelection of Ronald Reagan was the high-water mark of conservative, and Republican, fortunes in the postwar era. It reflected satisfaction with the impressive performance of the economy under the Republican economic program, and pride in the new assertiveness the United States was showing in the world. To many Reagan supporters, the 1984 election seemed to be the dawn of a new conservative era. But almost no one anticipated the revolutionary changes that would change the world, and the United States's place in it, within a very few years. The election of 1984, therefore, was not so much the first of a new era as the last of an old one. It was the final campaign of the Cold War.

SUGGESTED READINGS

The Ford Presidency. James M. Cannon, *Time and Chance: Gerald Ford's Appointment with History* (1994); Gerald Ford, *A Time to Heal* (1979). John R. Greene, *The Limits of Power: The Nixon and Ford Administrations* (1992). Robert T. Hartmann, *Palace Politics* (1980). Gerald Ter Horst, *Gerald Ford* (1975). Richard Reeves, *A Ford Not a Lincoln* (1976). A. James Reichley, *Conservatives in an Age of Change: The Nixon and Ford Administrations* (1981). Edward and Frederick Schapsmeier, *Gerald R. Ford's Date with Destiny: A Political Biography* (1989). James L. Sundquist, *The Decline and Resurgence of Congress* (1981).

The Carter Presidency. Jack Bass and Walter Devries, *The Transformation of Southern Politics* (1976). James Bill, *The Eagle and the Lion* (1988). Zbigniew Brzezinski, *Power and Principle* (1983). Jimmy Carter, *Why Not the Best?* (1975); *Keeping Faith* (1982). Rosalynn Carter, *First Lady from Plains* (1984). Steven Gillon, *The Democrats' Dilemma: Walter Mondale and the Liberal Legacy* (1992). Betty Glad, *Jimmy Carter* (1980). Erwin Hargrove, *Jimmy Carter as President* (1989). Steven B. Hunt, *The Energy Crisis* (1978). Haynes Johnson, *In the Absence of Power* (1980). Charles O. Jones, *The Trusteeship Presidency* (1988). Hamilton Jordan, *Crisis* (1982). Walter LaFeber, *Panama Canal* (1978). Clark Mollenhoff, *The President Who Failed* (1980). A. Glenn Mower, Jr. , *Human Rights and American Foreign Policy* (1987). William B. Quandt, *Decade of Decisions* (1977); *Camp David* (1986). Barry Rubin, *Paved with Good Intentions* (1983). Lars Schoultz, *Human Rights and U.S. Policy Toward Latin America* (1981). Gaddis Smith, *Morality, Reason, and Power* (1986). Strobe Talbott, *Endgame* (1979). Jules Witcover, *Marathon* (1977). James Wooten, *Dasher* (1978). Cyrus Vance, *Hard Choices* (1983).

The New Right. Sidney Blumenthal, *The Rise of the Counter-Establishment* (1986). George Nash, *The Conservative Intellectual Movement in America Since 1945* (1979). Burton Yale Pines, *Back to Basics* (1982). David W. Reinhard, *The Republican Right Since 1945* (1983). Kirkpatrick Sale, *Power Shift: The Rise of the Southern Rim and Its Challenge to the Eastern Establishment* (1975). Peter Steinfels, *The Neo-Conservatives* (1979). John K. White, *The New Politics of Old Values* (1988). John Woodridge, *The Evangelicals* (1975).

The Reagan Presidency. Frank Ackerman, *Reaganomics* (1982). Laurence I. Barrett, *Gambling with History* (1984). Bill Boyarsky, *The Rise of Ronald Reagan* (1968). Paul Boyer, ed. , *Reagan as President: Contemporary Views of the Man, His Politics, and His Policies* (1990). William J. Broad, *Teller's War: The Top-Secret Story Behind the Star Wars Deception* (1992). Lou Cannon, *Reagan* (1982); *President Reagan: The Role of a Lifetime* (1990). Joan Claybrook, *Retreat from Safety: Reagan's Attack on American Health* (1984). Robert Dallek, *Ronald Reagan: The Politics of Symbolism* (1984). Ronnie Dugger, *On Reagan* (1983). Thomas Byrne Edsall, *The New Politics of Inequality* (1984). Anne Edwards, *Early Reagan* (1987). Rowland Evans and Robert Novak, *The Reagan Revolution* (1981). Benjamin

Friedman, *Day of Reckoning: The Consequences of American Economic Policy Under Reagan and After* (1988). Jack Germond and Jules Witcover, *Blue Smoke and Mirrors: How Reagan Won and Why Carter Lost the Election of 1980* (1981); *Wake Us When It's Over: Presidential Politics of 1984* (1985). George Gildner, *Wealth and Poverty* (1981). Fred I. Greenstein, ed., *The Reagan Presidency* (1983). William Greider, *The Education of David Stockman and Other Americans* (1982). Haynes Johnson, *Sleepwalking Through History: America in the Reagan Years* (1991). Jonathan Lash, *A Season of Spoils: The Story of the Reagan Administration's Attack on the Environment* (1984). Robert Lekachman, *Greed Is Not Enough: Reaganomics* (1982). Jane Mayer and Doyle McManus, *Landslide: The Unmaking of the President, 1984–1988* (1988). Charles Noble, *Liberalism at Work: The Rise and Fall of OSHA* (1986). Peggy Noonan, *What I Saw at the Revolution: A Political Life in the Reagan Era* (1990). John L. Palmer and Isabel V. Sawhill, eds., *The Reagan Experiment* (1982). Michael J. Piore and Charles F. Sabel, *The Second Industrial Divide* (1984). Frances Fox Piven and Richard A. Cloward, *The New Class War: Reagan's Attack on the Welfare State and Its Consequences* (1982). Nancy Reagan, *My Turn* (1989). Richard Reeves, *The Reagan Detour* (1985). Donald T. Regan, *For the Record* (1988). Michael Rogin, *Ronald Reagan: The Movie* (1987). Michael Schaller, *Reckoning with Reagan: America and Its President in the 1980s* (1992). C. Brant Short, *Ronald Reagan and the Public Lands: America's Conservation Debate, 1979–1984* (1989). Hedrick Smith, *The Power Game* (1988). Hedrick Smith et al., *Reagan: The Man, the President* (1980). David A. Stockman, *The Triumph of Politics* (1986). Sidney Weintraub and Marvin Goodstein, eds., *Reaganomics in the Stagflation Economy* (1983). F. Clifton White and William Gil, *Why Reagan Won* (1982). Theodore H. White, *America in Search of Itself* (1982). Garry Wills, *Reagan's America* (1987).

Reagan and the World.   Seweryn Bialer and Michael Mandelbaum, eds., *Gorbachev's Russia and American Foreign Policy* (1988). Raymond Bonner, *Weakness and Deceit: U.S. Policy and El Salvador* (1984). Tom Buckley, *Violent Neighbors* (1984). Steven Emerson, *Secret Warriors: Inside the Covert Military Operations of the Reagan Era* (1988). Thomas L. Friedman, *From Beirut to Jerusalem* (1989). Alexander Haig, *Caveat: Realism, Reagan and Foreign Policy* (1984). Jane Hunter et al., *The Iran-Contra Connection* (1987). David E. Kyvig, ed., *Reagan and the World* (1990). Walter LaFeber, *Inevitable Revolutions,* rev. ed. (1984). Richard A. Melanson, *Reconstructing Consensus: American Foreign Policy Since the Vietnam War* (1991). John Newhouse, *War and Peace in the Nuclear Age* (1989). Robert O. Pastor, *Condemned to Repetition: The United States and Nicaragua* (1987). Charles D. Smith, *Palestine and the Arab-Israeli Conflict,* 2nd ed. (1992). Strobe Talbott, *Deadly Gambits* (1984); *The Master of the Game: Paul Nitze and the Nuclear Peace* (1988). Daniel Wirls, *Buildup: The Politics of Defense in the Reagan Era* (1992). Bob Woodward, *Veil: The Secret Wars of the CIA* (1987).

THE SECOND RUSSIAN REVOLUTION
Supporters of Russian President Boris Yeltsin march through Red Square in August 1991 carrying an enormous Russian flag—a symbol of defiance aimed at the Soviet regime, some of whose hardliners were attempting a coup to restore traditional communist rule. Within a few months, the Soviet Union had ceased to exist and its various republics, including Russia, had become independent nations. *(Reuters/Bettmann)*

CHAPTER THIRTY-FOUR

BEYOND THE COLD WAR

N NOVEMBER 8, 1989, East German soldiers stood guard at the Berlin Wall—keeping westerners out and easterners in—as they had done every day for more than twenty-eight years. The next day they were gone. Within hours, thousands of citizens of both sides of the divided city were swarming over the wall in celebration. Within weeks, bulldozers were tearing it down. Within a year, East and West Germany—divided by the Cold War for forty-five years—had reunited.

The breaching of the Berlin Wall and the reunification of Germany were among the most dramatic of a series of changes between 1986 and 1991 that radically transformed the world order. The Cold War, which as late as 1985 had seemed a permanent fact of international life, came to an end. A new world order, the outlines of which were still only dimly visible, was in the process of being born.

The Cold War had shaped the foreign policy and many aspects of the domestic life of the United States for nearly half a century. Its sudden end changed the character of national politics, economics, and culture. But America in the late 1980s and early 1990s was also encountering a series of other important social and economic changes, many of them unrelated to the Cold War. As the end of the twentieth century approached,

most Americans were uncertain whether the changes would bring a better, safer world or a harsher and more dangerous one.

AMERICA AND THE WANING OF THE COLD WAR

In the midst of the turbulent changes that enveloped the world beginning in the late 1980s, it was difficult to identify the point at which it had all begun. Some pointed to the upheavals in Poland in 1981, the first broad challenge to communist rule in Eastern Europe in over a decade. Some pointed to the Soviet war in Afghanistan, a long, stalemated conflict that ultimately proved more disastrous to the Soviet economy and the Soviet government than the Vietnam War had been to the United States. Some pointed to the long-term economic troubles of the Eastern-bloc nations; by the late 1980s, some were experiencing something close to collapse, and even the most successful were falling further and further behind the dynamically expanding economies of Western Europe.

The most frequent explanation, however, centered on a single man: Mikhail Gorbachev, who succeeded to the leadership of the Soviet Union in 1985 and, to the surprise of almost everyone, very quickly became the most revolutionary figure in world politics in at least four decades.

The Fall of the Soviet Union

Benefiting from widespread frustration with the rigid and ineffective policies of the preceding twenty years (which reformers began to call the "time of stagnation"), Gorbachev transformed Soviet politics with two dramatic new initiatives. The first he called *glasnost* (openness). *Glasnost* meant the dismantling of many of the repressive mechanisms that had been among the most conspicuous features of Soviet life for over half a century. Suddenly it became possible for Soviet citizens to express themselves more freely, to criticize the government, even to organize politically in opposition to official policy. The other policy Gorbachev called *perestroika* (reform, or restructuring). Through it, he attempted to remake the rigid and unproductive Soviet economy by introducing, among other things, such elements of capitalism as private ownership and the profit motive. He also began to transform Soviet foreign policy.

The severe economic problems at home evidently convinced Gorbachev that the Soviet Union could no longer sustain its extended commitments around the world. As early as 1987, he began reducing Soviet influence in Eastern Europe. And in 1989, in the space of a few months, the government of every nation in the so-called Soviet bloc—Poland, Hungary, Czechoslovakia, Bulgaria, Romania, and East Germany—was either overthrown or forced to transform itself into an essentially noncommunist (and in some cases, actively anticommunist) regime. The Communist Parties of Eastern Europe all but collapsed. And in every case, Gorbachev and the Soviet Union not only refused to oppose, but actively encouraged, the changes.

The challenges to communism were not successful everywhere. In May 1989, students in China had begun staging large demonstrations calling for greater democratization, which the post-Mao government had long been promising but had never delivered. A visit by Gorbachev to Beijing in late May inspired even greater demonstrations. By the beginning of June, the demonstrations had grown so large and widespread, and had attracted the support of so much of the population, that it seemed possible the communist regime might topple. Instead, hard-line leaders seized control and sent military forces to crush the uprising. The result was a bloody massacre on June 3, 1989, in Tiananmen Square in Beijing, in which a still-unknown number of demonstrators—perhaps several thousand—died. The assault crushed the democracy movement, restored the hard-liners to power, and inaugurated a period of repression and international ostracism. It did not, however, stop China's efforts to modernize and even westernize its economy.

The events in China had no counterpart in the rest of the communist world. The attempt by the Romanian

TIANANMEN SQUARE, 1989
The democracy movement in China accelerated rapidly in the spring of 1989 and was most visible through the vast crowds of students who began demonstrating in Tiananmen Square in Beijing. Some of them fashioned a rough replica of the American Statue of Liberty, which they called the "Goddess of Liberty," an act particularly galling to the conservative leadership of the communist regime. On June 3, the government sent troops into the Square to clear out and arrest the demonstrating students. Hundreds, perhaps thousands, were killed in the violence that resulted from that decision. *(Forrest Anderson/Gamma Liaison)*

dictator Nicolae Ceausescu to crush a dissident revolt in his country in December 1989 produced a popular revolution that drove him from power, led to his capture and execution, and culminated in the installation of a new, noncommunist (although still authoritarian) regime. In all other Eastern European nations, the toppling of communist regimes was remarkably peaceful.

There were even signs of democratization in parts of the world far removed from the Soviet empire. Early in 1990, the government of South Africa, long an international pariah for its rigid enforcement of white supremacy through the "apartheid" system, began a cautious retreat from its traditional policies. Among other things, it legalized the major black opposition movements, most prominently the African National Congress, which had been banned for decades. And on February 11, 1990, it released from prison the leader of the ANC, Nelson Mandela, a revered hero to black South Africans who had been in jail for twenty-seven years. Over the next several years, the South African government repealed its apartheid laws. And in 1994, there were national elections in which all South Africans could participate. As a result, Nelson Mandela became the first black president of South Africa.

In 1991, communism began to collapse at the site of its birth: the Soviet Union itself. An unsuccessful coup by hard-line Soviet leaders on August 19 precipitated a dramatic unraveling of communist power. Within days, not only did the coup itself collapse in the face of resistance from the public and, more important, crucial elements within the military; not only did Mikhail Gorbachev return to power; but the forces of disunion that had been gathering strength for several years made a great leap forward. It soon became evident that the legitimacy of both the Communist Party and the central Soviet government had been fatally injured. By the end of August, almost every republic in the Soviet Union had declared independence; the Soviet government was clearly powerless to stop the fragmentation. At the same time, Boris Yeltsin, the president of the Russian Republic, in effect outlawed the Communist Party—barring it from owning property or playing any significant role in the life of the largest and most important republic in the Soviet Union. Gorbachev himself finally resigned as leader of the now virtually powerless communist party and Soviet government, and the Soviet Union ceased to exist.

Reagan and Gorbachev

In the face of these dramatic changes, American foreign policy, which for over four decades had remained securely tied to the premises of "containment," suddenly seemed obsolete. And while a new strategic doctrine to replace containment did not quickly emerge, the pattern of American international behavior began inevitably to change. The last years of the Reagan administration coincided with the first years of the Gorbachev regime; and while Reagan was skeptical of Gorbachev at first, he gradually became convinced (by, among others, British Prime Minister Margaret Thatcher) that the Soviet leader was sincere in his desire for reform.

That the Gorbachev regime was committed to a new relationship with the West had been clear almost from the start, when the new leader began reaching out to Washington for major arms control agreements. At a summit meeting with Reagan in Reykjavik, Iceland, in 1986, Gorbachev proposed reducing the nuclear arsenals of both sides by 50 percent or more, although continuing disputes over Reagan's commitment to the SDI program derailed agreements. But in 1988, after Reagan and Gorbachev exchanged cordial visits to each other's capitals, the two superpowers signed a treaty eliminating American and Soviet intermediate-range nuclear forces (INF) from Europe—the most significant arms control agreement of the nuclear age. At about the same time, Gorbachev ended the Soviet Union's long and frustrating military involvement in Afghanistan, removing one of the principal irritants in the relationship between Washington and Moscow.

The Fading of the Reagan Revolution

For a time, the dramatic changes around the world and Reagan's personal popularity deflected attention from a series of scandals that might well have destroyed another administration. Top officials in the Environmental Protection Agency resigned when it was disclosed that they were flouting the laws they had been appointed to enforce. Officials of the CIA and the Defense Department resigned after revelations of questionable stock transactions. Reagan's secretary of labor left office after being indicted for racketeering (although he was later acquitted). Edwin Meese, the White House counsel and later attorney general, finally resigned in 1988 after years of attacks for controversial financial arrangements that many believed had compromised his office.

Unnoticed at first were several larger scandals that surfaced only as Reagan was about to leave office. One involved misuse of funds by the Department of Housing and Urban Development, abuses so widespread that by 1990 the survival of the agency itself was in question. Another, more serious scandal involved the savings and loan industry. The Reagan administration had sharply reduced regulatory controls over the troubled savings and loans. Many savings banks responded by rapidly, often recklessly, and sometimes corruptly, expanding. By the end of the decade the industry was in chaos, and the government was forced to step in to prevent a complete collapse. The government insured the assets of most savings and loan depositors; and as the banks failed, it found itself saddled with large debts. Predictions of eventual cost to the public of the debacle ran to more than half a trillion dollars.

But the most politically damaging scandal of the Reagan years came to light in November 1986. After reports of the episode had begun appearing in foreign newspapers, the White House conceded that it had sold weapons to the revolutionary government of Iran, apparently as part of a largely unsuccessful effort to secure the release of several Americans being held hostage by radical Islamic groups in the Middle East. Even more damaging was the administration's revelation that some of the money from the arms deal with Iran had been covertly and illegally funneled into a fund to aid the contras in Nicaragua.

In the months that followed, aggressive reporting and a highly publicized series of congressional hearings exposed a remarkable and previously unsuspected feature of the Reagan White House: the existence within it of something like a "secret government," largely unknown to the State Department, the Defense Department, even parts of the CIA, dedicated to advancing the administration's foreign policy aims through secret and at times illegal means. The principal figure in this covert world appeared at first to be an obscure marine lieutenant colonel assigned to the staff of the National Security Council, Oliver North. But gradually it became clear that North was acting in concert with other, more powerful figures in the administration. The Iran-contra scandal, as it became known, did serious damage to the Reagan presidency—even though the investigations were never able decisively to tie the president himself to the most serious violations of the law.

There were other signs in the late 1980s that the glow of the "Reagan Revolution" was beginning to fade. In October 1987, the American stock market—whose spectacular success had been one of the most conspicuous features of the economic boom—experienced the greatest single-day decline in its history; and although stock prices recovered and continued to rise over the next two years, the crash eroded confidence in the financial markets. At about the same time, one of the most popular financial innovations of the 1980s, the "leveraged buyout," which had permitted a wave of corporate takeovers financed by huge loans (many of them in the form of risky "junk bonds"), began to unravel. Some of the nation's largest corporations, un-

able to carry the enormous debt they had acquired in their takeover efforts, began to flounder or collapse. And some of the financial managers who had engineered the buyouts and takeovers were convicted of insider trading and other fraudulent activities.

The Election of 1988

The fraying of the Reagan administration helped the Democrats regain control of the United States Senate in 1986 and fueled hopes in the party for a presidential victory in 1988. Even so, several of the most popular figures in the Democratic Party refused to run. The early favorite, Senator Gary Hart of Colorado,

THE BUSH CAMPAIGN, 1988
Vice President George Bush had never been an effective campaigner, but in 1988 he helped his candidacy revive with an unabashed attack on his opponent's values and patriotism. Bush himself missed no chance to surround himself with patriotic symbols, including this red, white, and blue hot-air balloon in Kentucky. *(L. Johnson/Gamma Liaison)*

ELECTION OF 1988

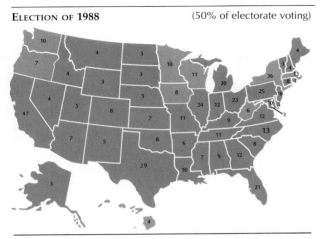

(50% of electorate voting)

	ELECTORAL VOTE	POPULAR VOTE (%)
George Bush (Republican)	426	54
Michael Dukakis (Democratic)	112	46

withdrew from the race in May 1987 after embarrassing revelations of an extramarital relationship with a young model. That left the field to a group of lesser-known candidates and to the civil rights leader Jesse Jackson, whose fervent support among African Americans made him a major force in the party.

The man who emerged victorious from the crowded field was relatively little known: Michael Dukakis, a three-term governor of Massachusetts who claimed to have helped produce a dramatic revival in the New England economy (a revival frequently described as "the Massachusetts miracle"). Dukakis was a dry, even dull campaigner. But Democrats remained optimistic about their prospects in 1988, largely because of the identity of their opponent, Vice President George Bush—who had been an ineffective campaigner in 1980 when he ran unsuccessfully for president, and who had attracted derision for his performance in the 1984 campaign, when he was running for reelection as vice president. Bush captured the Republican nomination without great difficulty, but he entered the last months of the campaign substantially behind Dukakis.

Beginning at the Republican convention, however, Bush staged a remarkable turnaround by making his campaign into a long, relentless attack on Dukakis, tying him to all the unpopular social and cultural stances Americans had come to identify with "liberals." Indeed, the Bush campaign was almost certainly the most savage of the twentieth century. It was also,

apparently, one of the most effective, although the listless, indecisive character of the Dukakis effort contributed to the Republican cause as well. Bush won a substantial victory in November: 54 percent of the popular vote to Dukakis's 46, and 426 electoral votes to Dukakis's 111. But Bush carried few Republicans into office with him; the Democrats retained secure majorities in both houses of Congress.

The Bush Presidency

The Bush presidency was notable for a series of dramatic developments in international affairs and an almost complete absence of initiatives or ideas on domestic issues. For a time, Bush's achievements in foreign policy managed to obscure the absence of a domestic agenda. By early 1992, however, with the nation in the second year of a serious recession, the president's once overwhelming popularity had begun to fray.

The broad popularity Bush enjoyed during his first three years in office was partly because of his subdued, unthreatening public image. But it was primarily because of the wonder and excitement with which Americans viewed the dramatic events in the rest of the world. Bush profited both passively and actively from the nation's satisfaction at having "won" the Cold War. He took credit for the international changes, even though he had played a relatively small role in most of them. But he also launched initiatives of his own. Late in 1989, he dispatched American troops to Panama to overthrow the unpopular military leader Manuel Noriega, who was under indictment in the United States for drug trafficking and whose contemptuous defiance of American pressures had embarrassed the government in Washington for two years. The Panama invasion—which installed an elected, pro-American, civilian government in Panama—was highly popular within the United States.

Bush moved cautiously at first in dealing with the changes in the Soviet Union. But like Reagan, he eventually embraced Gorbachev and reached a series of significant agreements with the Soviet Union in its waning years. The Gorbachev regime had all but repudiated the arms race with the United States in the late 1980s and had been working energetically to produce arms control agreements well before Bush entered office. In the three years after the INF agreement in 1988, the United States and the Soviet Union moved rapidly toward even more far-reaching arms reduction agreements, including major troop reductions in Europe and the dismantling of new categories of strategic weapons. At the same time, the Soviet Union and the new, noncommunist governments in Eastern Europe were appealing to the West for economic assistance through subsidies, loans, and investments; the United States, beset with its own fiscal and economic difficulties, was slow to respond.

On domestic issues, the Bush administration was less successful—partly because the president himself seemed to have little interest in promoting a domestic agenda and partly because he faced serious obstacles. His administration inherited a staggering burden of debt and a federal deficit that had been out of control for nearly a decade. Any domestic agenda that required significant federal spending was, therefore, incompatible with the president's pledge to reduce the deficit and his 1988 campaign promise of "no new taxes." President Bush also faced a Democratic Congress, which was not, on the whole, disposed to cooperate with him. And while the president himself was at heart a nonideological pragmatist, he was deeply concerned about the right wing of his own party and, in his eagerness to ingratiate himself with them, took divisive positions on such cultural issues as abortion and affirmative action that further damaged his ability to work with Congress.

Despite this political stalemate, Congress and the White House managed on occasion to agree on significant measures. They cooperated in producing a plan to salvage the floundering savings and loan industry. In 1990, the president bowed to congressional pressure and agreed to a significant tax increase as part of a multiyear "budget package" designed to reduce the deficit. In 1991, after almost two years of acrimonious debate, the president and Congress agreed on a civil rights bill to combat job discrimination.

But the most serious domestic problem facing the Bush administration was one to which neither the president nor Congress had any answer: a recession that began late in 1990 and slowly increased its grip on the national economy in 1991 and 1992. Because of the enormous level of debt that corporations (and individuals) had accumulated in the 1980s, the recession caused an unusual number of bankruptcies. It also created growing fear and frustration among middle- and working-class Americans and increasing pressure on the government to address such problems as the rising cost of health care.

The Gulf War

The events of 1989–1991 had left the United States in the unanticipated position of being the only real superpower in the world. The Soviet Union was too embroiled in its own problems to play a major international role any longer. Germany and Japan, the new economic superpowers, had no significant military strength. China remained largely isolated in international affairs. The Bush administration, therefore, had to consider what to do with America's formidable political and military power in a world in which the major justification for that power—the Soviet threat—was now gone.

The events of 1990–1991 suggested two possible answers, both of which had some effect on policy. One was that the United States would reduce its military strength dramatically and concentrate its energies and resources on pressing domestic problems. And, indeed, there was considerable movement in that direction both in Congress and within the administration. The other was that America would continue to use its power actively, not to fight communism but to defend its economic interests. Once again, that drew the United States into the turbulent politics of the Middle East.

On August 2, 1990, the armed forces of Iraq invaded and quickly overwhelmed their small, oil-rich neighbor, the emirate of Kuwait. Saddam Hussein, the militaristic leader of Iraq, soon announced that he was annexing Kuwait and set out to entrench his forces there. After some initial indecision, the Bush administration agreed to join with other nations to force Iraq out of Kuwait—through the pressure of economic sanctions if possible, through military force if necessary. Within a few weeks, Bush had persuaded virtually every important government in the world, including the Soviet Union and almost all the Arab and Islamic states, to join in a United Nations-sanctioned trade embargo of Iraq. That meant the Iraqis, whose economy was already weak, would be unable to sell any oil on world markets and would be unable to buy any products from abroad or generate hard currency with which to pay their massive debts.

At the same time, the United States and its allies (including the British, French, Egyptians, and Saudis) began deploying a massive military force along the border between Kuwait and Saudi Arabia, a force that ultimately reached 690,000 troops (425,000 of them American) and that assembled the largest and most sophisticated collection of military technology ever used in warfare.

By late 1990, the Bush administration was clearly losing patience with the sanctions and was preparing for war. On November 29, the United Nations, at the request of the United States, voted to authorize military action to expel Iraq from Kuwait if Iraq did not leave by January 15, 1991. On January 12, both houses of Congress voted to authorize the use of force against Iraq, although many Democrats opposed the resolution, arguing that sanctions should be given more time to work. And on January 16, American and allied air forces began a massive bombardment of Iraqi forces in Kuwait and of military and industrial installations in Iraq itself.

The allied bombing continued for six weeks, meeting only token resistance from the small Iraqi air force and Iraqi ground defenses. And on February 23, allied (primarily American) forces under the command of General Norman Schwarzkopf began a major ground offensive—not primarily against the heavily entrenched Iraqi forces along the Kuwait border, as expected, but into Iraq itself. The allied armies encountered almost no resistance and suffered only light casualties (141 fatalities). There were no reliable figures for the number of Iraqi military casualties, but some estimates of deaths (most as a result of the bombing) ranged as high as 100,000. There were also a significant, if unverifiable, number of civilian casualties. On February 28, Iraq announced its acceptance of allied terms for a cease-fire, and the brief war came to an end.

The quick and (for America) relatively painless victory over Iraq was highly popular in the United States. But the longer-range results of the Gulf War were more difficult to assess. The tyrannical regime of Saddam Hussein survived, in a weakened form but showing no signs of retreat from its militaristic ambitions. And Kuwait returned to the control of its prewar government, an undemocratic monarchy increasingly unpopular with its own people.

The Election of 1992

President Bush's popularity reached a record high in the immediate aftermath of the Gulf War. For a time, over 90 percent of those polled claimed to approve of the way he was handling his office, the highest approval rating in the history of opinion surveys. But the president received much lower approval ratings for his handling of domestic issues. As the recession worsened in late 1991, and as the administration declined to propose any policies for combatting it, the president's popularity rapidly eroded.

Because the early maneuvering for the 1992 presidential election occurred when President Bush's popularity remained high, many leading Democrats declined to run. That gave Bill Clinton, the young and energetic five-term governor of Arkansas, the opportunity to emerge early as the front-runner, as a result of a skillful campaign that emphasized broad economic issues over the racial and cultural questions that had so divided the Democrats in the past. Clinton survived a bruising primary campaign and a series of damaging personal controversies to win his party's nomination. And George Bush withstood an embarrassing primary challenge from the conservative journalist Pat Buchanan to become the Republican nominee again.

Complicating the campaign was the emergence of Ross Perot, a blunt, forthright Texas billionaire who became an independent candidate by tapping popular resentment of the federal bureaucracy and by promising tough, uncompromising leadership to deal with the fiscal crisis and other problems of government. Particularly appealing to many voters were Perot's attacks on corruption in the political system and his insistence that his own campaign (funded by his personal fortune, not by special-interest lobbies) was a

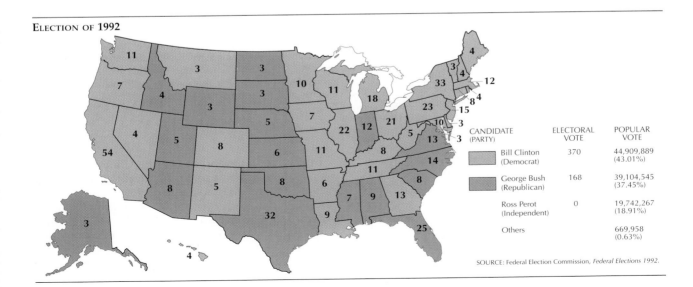

ELECTION OF 1992

CANDIDATE (PARTY)	ELECTORAL VOTE	POPULAR VOTE
Bill Clinton (Democrat)	370	44,909,889 (43.01%)
George Bush (Republican)	168	39,104,545 (37.45%)
Ross Perot (Independent)	0	19,742,267 (18.91%)
Others		669,958 (0.63%)

SOURCE: Federal Election Commission, *Federal Elections 1992.*

pure reflection of the will of the people. At several moments in the spring, Perot led both Bush and Clinton in public opinion polls. In July, as he began to face hostile scrutiny from the media, he abruptly withdrew from the race. But early in October, he reentered and soon regained much (although never all) of his early support.

After a campaign in which the economy and the president's unpopularity were the principal issues, Clinton won a clear, but hardly overwhelming, victory over Bush and Perot. He received 43 percent of the vote in the three-way race, to the president's 38 percent and Perot's 19 percent (the best showing for a third-party or independent candidate since Theodore Roosevelt in 1912). Clinton won 370 electoral votes to Bush's 168; Perot won none. Democrats retained control of both houses of Congress.

Launching the Clinton Presidency

Bill Clinton was the first Democratic president since Jimmy Carter, and the first liberal activist to be president since Lyndon Johnson. He entered office carrying the extravagant expectations of liberals who had spent a generation in exile. He also had significant political weaknesses. Having won the votes of well under half the electorate, he enjoyed no powerful mandate. Democratic majorities in Congress were frail, and Democrats in any case had grown unaccustomed to bowing to presidential leadership. The Republican leadership in Congress was highly adversarial and opposed the president with unusual unanimity on many issues.

The new administration compounded its problems with a series of missteps and misfortunes in its first months. The president's effort to end the longtime ban on gay men and women serving in the military met with ferocious resistance from the armed forces themselves and from many conservatives in both parties. He was forced to settle for a pallid compromise. Several of his early appointments—to the Justice Department, in particular—became sources of controversy and were eventually withdrawn. A longtime friend of the president from Arkansas serving in the office of the White House counsel committed suicide in the summer of 1993. His death helped spark an escalating inquiry into some banking and real estate ventures involving the President and his wife in the early 1980s; and the clumsy actions of some administration officials raised suspicions that the White House was attempting to interfere with the investigation into what became known as the Whitewater affair. A special prosecutor began investigating these issues in 1993. His first reports (on the actions of figures in President Clinton's administration accused of trying to cover up evidence) revealed no evidence of illegality.

BILL AND HILLARY CLINTON
Hillary Clinton quickly established herself as the most active and powerful first lady in American history—as she demonstrated by her stewardship of the president's most important domestic initiative: health care reform. President and Mrs. Clinton often appeared together to speak to citizen and student groups about their health plan and other initiatives. *(Brad Markel/Gamma Liaison)*

Despite its many problems, the Clinton administration could boast of some significant achievements in its first year. The president narrowly (by a single vote in the Senate) won approval of a budget that marked a significant turn away from the policies of the Reagan-Bush years. It included a substantial tax increase on the wealthiest Americans, a significant reduction in many areas of government spending, and a major expansion of tax credits to low-income families, designed to help lift many struggling families out of poverty. Clinton also signed legislation requiring employers to give both male and female employees unpaid leaves to deal with such urgent family responsibilities as the birth of a child or the illness of a relative. And after a long and difficult battle against, among others, Ross Perot, the AFL-CIO, and most Democrats in Congress, he won approval of the North American Free Trade Agreement, which eliminated most trade barriers among the United States, Canada, and Mexico.

The fate of the president's most ambitious initiatives remained unclear well into his second year. A task force chaired by the president's wife, Hillary Rodham Clinton, proposed a sweeping reform of the nation's health-care system designed to guarantee coverage to every American and hold down the costs of medical care. (In the process of heading the task force, Mrs. Clinton emerged as the most important figure in the administration after the president, and the most powerful First Lady in American history). Opposition from (among others) insurance companies, drug companies, doctors, and small businesses—who balked at the proposed requirement that they provide insurance to their employees—clouded the prospects for reform. By late 1994, the prospects for any comprehensive reform seemed dim.

The foreign policy of the Clinton administration was, on the whole, cautious and even tentative—a reflection, perhaps, of the president's relative inexperience in international affairs, but also of the rapidly changing character of the world order. Clinton presided over (although his administration had played a small role in creating) a historic agreement between Israel and the Palestinian Liberation Organization to end their long struggle over the lands Israel had occupied in 1967. His administration reached an agreement with Ukraine for an elimination of the nuclear weapons that had been positioned there when the republic had been part of the Soviet Union. And after months of resisting involvement in a bloody civil war in Bosnia (part of the former Yugoslavia), he agreed early in 1994 to NATO air strikes and other military actions against the aggressors in the conflict. But there was as yet no clear outline for a new American foreign policy to replace containment.

MODERN TIMES

The widespread popular suspicion of politics and government that characterized American life in the 1980s and 1990s was in part a result of decades of crises and scandals in public life. But it reflected, too, a series of major changes in the character and behavior of the American economy and American society, which were changing more rapidly—and more jarringly—than at any time in the twentieth century.

The New Economy

Foremost among the changes that challenged and perplexed Americans in the last years of the twentieth century was a difficult transformation of the national economy. The changes had begun in earnest in the early 1970s, when the Arab oil embargo and the rapid increase in energy prices first shook the stability of the American economy. But the energy crisis was only one of many changes that affected the United States. More important in the long run was the rise of powerful economic competitors in Western Europe (especially Germany) and Asia (above all, Japan), who successfully challenged the United States in world trade and penetrated deeply into the American domestic market. Automobiles, steel, and other manufactured goods imported from abroad—often priced lower than their American counterparts—cut into the market share of major industries in the United States and contributed to the contraction of heavy manufacturing (and hence of industrial jobs) that characterized the nation's economy in the 1980s and 1990s.

The result of these and other factors was a series of fundamental changes in the behavior of the economy. Economic growth continued, but at a much slower rate. In the twenty years after World War II, the Gross National Product grew, on average, by 3.8 percent a year. In the last two decades, the GNP has grown by an average of less than 2.6 percent. Productivity grew 2.6 percent a year in the 1950s and 1960s; in the 1970s and 1980s it grew by less than 1 percent. The national savings rate—the rate at which individuals and institutions saved income, which then became available for investment—peaked at around 10 percent between 1948 and 1973. In the 1980s, at its highest, the rate was 3.2 percent.

For families and individuals, the results of these contractions were often devastating. In the first twenty years after World War II, it was possible for many, perhaps most, Americans, to sustain themselves on a single (usually male) income. In later years, more and more families required two incomes to sustain their standards of living, and even that was often not enough. In the 1950s and 1960s, most Americans could expect to live more comfortably as adults than their parents had; in the 1980s and 1990s, increasing numbers of Americans were finding it impossible even to live as well as the generation before them. From 1973 to 1989, median family income increased less than 2 percent (from $33,656 a year to $34,213), even though many families added a second income in those years. Poverty in America declined steadily and at times dramatically in the years after World War II, so that by the end of the 1960s the percentage of people living in poverty had declined to 12 percent (from about 20 percent in preceding decades). By the late 1980s, the poverty rate had climbed back to its old levels—and beyond—to over 24 percent. As always, this increase in poverty affected women, children, and minorities far more than any other groups.

The increasingly unequal distribution of wealth and income in the United States accentuated these changes. Over 94 percent of the new wealth created by the American economy in the 1980s went to the wealthiest 20 percent of the population; over 50 percent went to the top 1 percent. In the meantime, the middle 40 percent of the population experienced an actual decline in wealth. It was little wonder that the economic anxieties of the middle class became one of the central issues in American politics in the late 1980s and early 1990s.

The Graying of America

One of the most fundamental changes in American life in the post-liberal era was the new profile of the American population. After decades of steady growth, the nation's birth rate began to decline in the 1970s and remained low through the 1980s and early 1990s. In 1970, there were 18.4 births for every 1,000 people in the population. By 1975, the rate had declined to 14.6, the lowest in the twentieth century. And despite a modest increase in the 1980s, the rate remained below 16

throughout the decade. The declining birth rate and a significant rise in life expectancy produced a substantial increase in the proportion of elderly citizens. Over 12 percent of the population was more than sixty-five years old by 1990, as compared with 8 percent in 1970. That figure was projected to rise to over 20 percent by the end of the century. In 1990 the median age was 32.9 years, as compared with 28.0 in 1970.

The aging of the population had important, if not entirely predictable, implications. It was, for example, a cause of the increasing costliness of Social Security pensions. It meant rapidly increasing health costs, both for the federal Medicare system and for private hospitals and insurance companies. It also ensured that the elderly, who already formed one of the most powerful interest groups in America, would remain politically formidable well into the twenty-first century.

The Changing Profile of Immigration

Perhaps the most striking demographic change in America in the 1970s and 1980s, and the one likely to have the farthest-reaching consequences, was the enormous change in both the extent and the character of

THE AMERICAN BIRTH RATE, 1960–1990

Births per thousand women 15–44 years old

120 · 100 · 80 · 60 · 0

1960 1965 1970 1975 1980 1985 1990

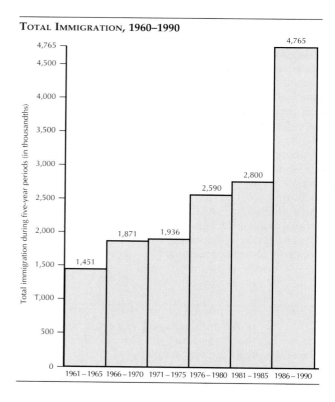

TOTAL IMMIGRATION, 1960–1990

Total immigration during five-year periods (in thousandths)

1961–1965	1,451
1966–1970	1,871
1971–1975	1,936
1976–1980	2,590
1981–1985	2,800
1986–1990	4,765

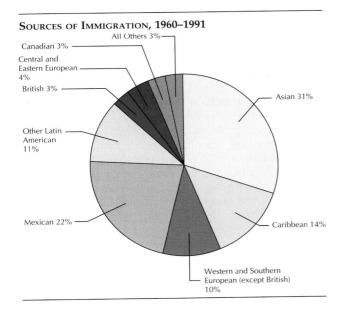

SOURCES OF IMMIGRATION, 1960–1991

All Others 3%
Canadian 3%
Central and Eastern European 4%
British 3%
Other Latin American 11%
Mexican 22%
Western and Southern European (except British) 10%
Asian 31%
Caribbean 14%

immigration. The nation's immigration quotas expanded significantly in those years (partly to accommodate refugees from Southeast Asia and other nations), allowing more newcomers to enter the United States legally than at any point since the beginning of the twentieth century. In the 1970s, more than 4 million legal immigrants entered the United States. In the 1980s, that number rose to more than 6 million. When the uncounted but very large numbers of illegal immigrants in those years are included, the wave of immigration in the twenty years after 1970 is the largest of the twentieth century.

Equally striking was the character of the new immigration. The Immigration Reform Act of 1965 (see p. 824) had eliminated quotas based on national origin; from then on, newcomers from regions other than Latin America were generally admitted on a first-come, first-served basis. In 1965, 90 percent of the immigrants to the United States came from Europe. Twenty years later, only 10 percent of the new arrivals were Europeans. The extent and character of the new immigration was causing a dramatic change in the composition of the American population. Already by the early 1990s, people of white European background constituted under 80 percent of the population (as opposed to 90 percent a half century before). It seemed likely that by the middle of the twenty-first century, whites of European heritage would constitute less than 50 percent of the population.

Particularly important to the new immigration were two groups: Hispanics and Asians. Both had been significant segments of the American population for many decades—Hispanics since the very beginning of the nation's history, Asians since the waves of Chinese and Japanese immigration in the nineteenth century. But both groups experienced enormous, indeed unprecedented, growth after 1965.

People from Latin America constituted more than a third of the total number of legal immigrants to the United States in every year since 1965—and a much larger proportion of the total number of illegal immigrants. In California and the Southwest, in particular, they became an increasingly important presence. There were also substantial Hispanic populations in Illinois, New York, and Florida. High birth rates among Hispanic communities already in the United States further increased their numbers. In the 1980 census, 6 percent of the population was listed as being of Hispanic origin. The 1990 census showed an increase to 9 percent—or 20 million people. (Twenty years earlier, the number had been 7 million.) Economic problems and political repression in Mexico and other Latin American and Caribbean nations propelled the new immigrants to the United States; but in most of the areas to which they moved, opportunities were also hard to find. Mexican Americans had an official poverty rate of 20 percent in 1990 (and a real poverty rate that was probably much higher, given the number of illegal immigrants who evaded official statistics). The poverty rate among Puerto Ricans was 30 percent. For illegal immigrants, conditions were particularly dire. Because they were subject to deportation if they came to the attention of the government, they had no legal recourse to being exploited by employers. Most worked for subsistence wages in menial jobs, constantly fearful of exposure.

The growing Hispanic presence became a political issue of increasing importance in the 1980s and 1990s, both to "Anglos" and, of course, to Hispanics themselves. The Immigration Reform and Control (or Simpson-Mazzoli) Act of 1987 reflected the political power of both groups. Its principal goal was to respond to the demands of whites in the Southwest and California by stemming the flow of illegal immigrants (mostly from Mexico). To that end, it placed the burden on employers for the first time to confirm the legal status of their employees. Those who failed to do so faced economic and even criminal penalties. Hispanics charged that the bill would increase discrimination in hiring, and in the first years after its passage there was considerable evidence that such charges were well founded. At the same time, the act responded to the growing political influence of Hispanics by offering amnesty to all undocumented workers who had entered the country before 1982. By the early 1990s, however, it seemed clear that the law was failing. Illegal immigration from Mexico and elsewhere was continuing at near record levels.

White residents of areas in which the Hispanic populations were growing rapidly often reacted with alarm, fearing that they would soon become a minority in what they considered their own cities. Such fears lay behind efforts to bar the use of the Spanish language in public schools and other measures to force Hispanic immigrants to assimilate more quickly and completely. And while the strenuous effort to combat Hispanic street gangs in Los Angeles and other cities was motivated mainly by the desire to fight crime, it was also an effort to halt the creation of an "alien" culture within America (much like the efforts to eliminate the "zoot-suiters" in the 1940s; see p. 755). These white fears prompted angry and defiant responses from many Hispanics. "You hear all the ravings and complaints like, 'In the year 2000 Los Angeles is going to become a minority city! The Mexicans are going to take over!'" a Mexican-American film producer said in 1989. "I'd like to remind them that we're just going to reinstate the original composition of the city—like it was a hundred years ago, before they showed up."

In the 1980s and early 1990s, Asian immigrants arrived in even greater numbers than Hispanics, constituting more than 40 percent of the total of legal newcomers. They swelled the already substantial Chinese and Japanese communities in California and elsewhere. And they created substantial new communities of immigrants from Vietnam, Thailand, Cambodia, Laos, the Philippines, Korea, and India. By 1990, there were more than 7 million Asian Americans in the United States, more than twice the number of ten years before. Like Hispanics, they were concentrated mainly in large cities and in the West.

Many of the new Asian immigrants were refugees, including Vietnamese driven from their homes in the aftermath of the disastrous war in which the United States had so long been involved. Large numbers of "boat people"—Vietnamese refugees who put to sea in crowded boats without any clear destination—ultimately found their way to the United States, usually after enduring terrible dangers and hardships. But many Asian immigrants were highly educated professionals seeking greater opportunities in the United States.

Like most new immigrant groups, Asian Americans found adjustment to the very different culture of the United States difficult and disorienting. "When I think how lonely I am in America," a Vietnamese immigrant wrote in the late 1980s, "I wonder why I am here, and what I have to live for." They also experienced resentment and discrimination. Whites feared Asian competition in economic activities that they had been accustomed to controlling. For example, there were heated disputes between white and Vietnamese shrimpers on the Gulf Coast in Texas, Mississippi, and Louisiana. Some African Americans resented the success of Asian merchants in black neighborhoods (as the black filmmaker Spike Lee noted in his 1989 film *Do the Right Thing*). In New York, racial tensions led to a black boycott of some Korean grocery stores in African American neighborhoods in 1990. Resentment of Asian-Americans may have been a result, in part, of their remarkable success. Indeed, some Asian groups (most notably Indians, Japanese, and Chinese) were by the 1980s earning larger average annual incomes than whites. Chinese and Japanese Americans consistently ranked at or near the top of high school and college classes in the 1980s. That was in part because Asian-American communities contained significant numbers of people who had been involved in business and the professions before coming to America and had arrived with a high degree of expertise. They also placed an unusually high value on education.

Black America in the Post-Liberal Era

The civil rights movement and the other liberal efforts of the 1960s had two very different effects on African Americans. On the one hand, there were increased opportunities for advancement available to those in a position to take advantage of them. On the other hand, as the industrial economy declined and government services dwindled, there was a growing sense of helplessness and despair among the large groups of nonwhites who continued to find themselves barred from upward mobility.

For the black middle class, which by the late 1970s constituted nearly a third of the entire black population of America, the progress was at times astonishing. Economic disparities between black and white professionals did not vanish, but they diminished substantially. Black families moved into more affluent urban communities and, in many cases, into suburbs—at times as neighbors of whites, more often into predominantly black communities. The number of blacks attending college rose by 350 percent in the decade following the passage of the civil rights acts (in contrast to a 150 percent increase among whites); African Americans made up 12 percent of the college population in 1990 (up from 5 percent twenty-five years earlier). The percentage of black high-school graduates going on to college was by then virtually the same as that of white high-school graduates (although a far smaller proportion of blacks than whites managed to complete high school). And African Americans were making rapid strides in many professions from

Comparison of Black and White Occupational Distribution, 1992

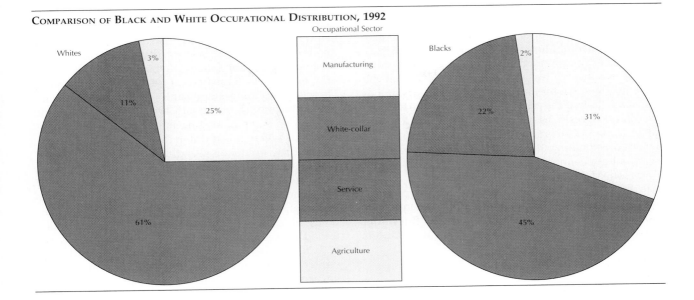

which, a generation earlier, they had been barred or within which they had been segregated. They were becoming partners in major law firms, joining the staffs of major hospitals and the faculties of major universities. Nearly half of all employed blacks in the United States had white-collar jobs. There were few areas of American life from which blacks were any longer entirely excluded. Middle-class blacks, in other words, had realized great gains from the legislation of the 1960s, from the changing national mood on race, and from the creation of controversial affirmative action programs.

But the rise of a black middle class also accentuated (and perhaps even helped cause) the increasingly desperate plight of other black Americans, whom many of the liberal programs of the 1960s had never reached. This growing "underclass" made up about a third of the nation's black population. It felt the impact of the economic troubles of the 1970s and 1980s with special force. And as more successful blacks moved out of the inner cities, the poor were left virtually alone in their decaying neighborhoods. By the late 1980s, more than one-third of all black families lived in poverty; at the same time, just under 11 percent of white families could be officially classified as poor. Fewer than half of young inner-city blacks finished high school; more than 60 percent were unemployed.

The black family structure suffered as well from the dislocations of urban poverty. There was a radical increase in the number of single-parent, female-headed black households in the 1970s and 1980s. In the early 1990s, over 60 percent of all black children were born into single-parent families, as opposed to only 15 percent of white children. In 1960, only 20 percent of black children had lived in single-parent homes.

Nonwhites were disadvantaged by many things in the changing social and economic climate of the 1980s. Among them was a growing impatience with affirmative action and other programs designed to advance their fortunes, as symbolized by the Bakke case in 1978 and by a growing reluctance among federal officials after 1980 to move aggressively to enforce affirmative action guidelines. Nonwhites suffered as well from a steady decline in the number of unskilled jobs in the economy. They suffered from the deterioration of public education and of other social services, which made it more difficult for them to find opportunities for advancement. And they suffered, in some cases, from a sense of futility and despair, born of years of entrapment in brutal urban ghettoes.

By the early 1990s, whole generations of nonwhites had grown to maturity living in destitute neighborhoods where welfare, drug dealing, and other crimes were virtually the only means of support for many people. Violence was increasingly a part of daily life. While rates of violent crime were declining nationally in the late 1980s and early 1990s, violence (much of it entirely random) was escalating in many inner-city communities—a result of the drug trade, gang wars, and the proliferation of guns.

The anger and despair such conditions were creating among inner-city residents became clear in the summer of 1992 in Los Angeles. The previous year, a bystander had videotaped several Los Angeles police officers beating an apparently helpless black man whom they had captured after an auto chase. Broadcast repeatedly around the country, the tape evoked outrage among whites and blacks alike. But an all-white jury in a suburban community just outside Los Angeles acquitted the officers when they were tried for assault. Black residents of South Central Los Angeles, one of the poorest communities in the city, erupted in anger—precipitating the largest racial disturbance of the twentieth century. There was widespread looting and arson. More than fifty people died.

In the 1960s, urban uprisings had helped produce a major (if ultimately inadequate) government effort to deal with the problems of the inner city. But in the fiscally starved 1990s, the Los Angeles riot produced no such response.

Modern Plagues: Drugs, AIDS, and Homelessness

The new immigrants of the 1980s and 1990s arrived in cities being ravaged not just by economic decline but by two new and deadly epidemics. One was a dramatic increase in drug use, which penetrated nearly every community in the nation. The enormous demand for drugs, and particularly for "crack" cocaine, spawned what was in effect a multibillion-dollar industry; and those reaping the enormous profits of the illegal trade fought strenuously and often savagely to protect their positions.

Political figures of both parties spoke heatedly about the need for a "war on drugs"; but in the absence of significant funding for such programs, government efforts appeared to be having little effect. Drug use declined significantly among middle-class people beginning in the late 1980s, but the epidemic showed no signs of abating in the poor urban neighborhoods where it was doing the most severe damage.

The drug epidemic was directly related to another scourge of the 1980s and 1990s: the epidemic spread of a new and lethal disease first documented in 1981 and soon named AIDS (acquired immune deficiency syndrome). AIDS is the product of the HIV virus, which is transmitted by the exchange of bodily fluids (blood or semen). The virus gradually destroys the body's immune system and makes its victims highly vulnerable to a number of diseases (particularly to various forms of cancer and pneumonia) to which they would otherwise have a natural resistance. Although those infected with the virus (i.e., HIV positive) can live for many years without developing AIDS, once they do become ill they are virtually certain to die. The first American victims of AIDS, (and in the early 1990s the group among whom cases remained the most numerous) were homosexual men. But by the late 1980s, as the gay community began to take preventive measures, the most rapid increase in the spread of the disease occurred among heterosexuals, many of them intravenous drug users, who spread the virus by sharing contaminated hypodermic needles. By the early 1990s,

U.S. government agencies were estimating that between 1 and 1.5 million Americans were infected with the HIV virus. (Worldwide, the figure was approximately 10 million). Over 200,000 Americans had actually contracted AIDS, and over 130,000 had died. Although by the 1990s researchers had discovered several drugs that could delay or limit the effects of AIDS, neither a cure nor a vaccine seemed imminent. Governments and private groups, in the meantime, began promoting AIDS awareness in increasingly visible and graphic ways—urging young people, in particular, to avoid "unsafe sex" through abstinence or the use of latex condoms.

The spread of AIDS had a chilling effect on the sexual revolution that had transformed behavior beginning in the 1960s. Fear of infection caused many people to avoid casual sexual relations; but the more puritanical sexual standards against which many Americans had rebelled in the 1960s did not return.

The increasing scarcity of housing for low-income people contributed to another urban crisis of the 1980s and 1990s: homelessness. There had always been homeless men and women in most major cities; but their numbers were clearly increasing at an alarming rate in the face of rising housing costs, severe cutbacks in federal support for public housing, reduced welfare assistance, deinstitutionalization of the mentally ill, the declining availability of unskilled jobs, and the increasing weakness of family structures. The phenomenon of tens of thousands of homeless people at large in the cities put pressure on municipal governments to provide shelter and assistance for the indigent; but in an age of fiscal stringency and greatly reduced federal aid, cities found it difficult to respond adequately to the dimensions of the crisis.

Battles Against Feminism and Abortion

Among the principal goals of the New Right as it became more powerful and assertive in the 1980s and 1990s was to challenge feminism and its achievements. Leaders of the New Right had campaigned successfully against the proposed Equal Rights Amendment to the Constitution. And they played a central role in the most divisive issue of the late 1980s and early 1990s: the controversy over abortion rights.

For those who favored allowing women to choose to terminate unwanted pregnancies, the Supreme Court's decision in *Roe* v. *Wade* (1973) had seemed to settle the question. By the 1980s, abortion was the most commonly performed surgical procedure in the country. But at the same time, opposition to abortion was creating a powerful grassroots movement. The right-

to-life movement, as it called itself, found its most fervent supporters among Catholics; and indeed, the Catholic Church itself lent its institutional authority to the battle against legalized abortion. Religious doctrine also motivated the anti-abortion stance of Mormons, fundamentalist Christians, and other groups. The opposition of some other anti-abortion activists had less to do with religion than with their commitment to traditional notions of family and gender relations. To them, abortion was a particularly offensive part of a much larger assault by feminists on the role of women as wives and mothers. It was also, many foes contended, a form of murder. Fetuses, they claimed, were human beings who had a "right to life" from the moment of conception.

Although the right-to-life movement was persistent in its demand for a reversal of *Roe* v. *Wade* or, barring that, a constitutional amendment banning abortion, it also attacked abortion in more limited ways, at its most vulnerable points. In the 1970s, Congress and many state legislatures began barring the use of public funds to pay for abortions, thus making them almost inaccessible for many poor women. The Reagan and Bush administrations imposed further restrictions on federal funding and even on the right of doctors in federally funded clinics to give patients any information on abortion. Extremists in the right-to-life movement began picketing, occupying, and at times bombing abortion clinics. One anti-abortion activist murdered a doctor in Florida who performed abortions; other physicians were subject to campaigns of terrorism and harassment—part of an effort to force them to abandon serving women who wanted abortions.

The changing composition of the Supreme Court in the 1980s to early 1990s (when five new conservative justices were named by Presidents Reagan and Bush) renewed the right-to-life movement's hopes for a reversal of *Roe* v. *Wade*. In *Webster* v. *Reproductive Health Services* (1989), the Court upheld a Missouri law that forbade any institution receiving state funds from performing abortions, whether or not those funds were used to finance the abortions. But the Court stopped short of overturning its 1973 decision.

Through much of the 1970s and 1980s, defenders of abortion had remained confident that *Roe* v. *Wade* protected their right to choose abortion and that the anti-abortion movement was unlikely to prevail. But the changing judicial climate of the late 1980s mobilized defenders of abortion as never before. They called themselves the "pro-choice" movement, because they were defending not so much abortion itself as every woman's right to choose whether and when to bear a child. It quickly became clear that the pro-choice movement was in many parts of the country at least as strong as, and in some areas much stronger than, the right-to-life movement. With the election of President Clinton in 1992, the immediate threat to *Roe* v. *Wade* seemed to fade. In his first two years in office, Clinton named two pro-choice justices to the Court—Ruth Bader Ginsburg and Stephen Breyer.

At times the pro-choice campaign overshadowed other efforts by feminists to protect and expand the rights of women. But such efforts continued. Women's organizations and many individual women worked strenuously in the 1980s and 1990s to improve access to child care for poor women, and to win the right to caregiver leaves for parents. They also worked to raise awareness of sexual harassment in the workplace, with considerable success. Colleges, universities, government agencies, even many corporations established strict new standards of behavior for their employees in dealing with members of the opposite sex and created grievance procedures for those who believed they had been harassed.

Both the achievements and the limits of their progress on this issue were evident in the sensational controversy in 1991 over Judge Clarence Thomas, President Bush's nominee for a seat on the Supreme Court. Late in the confirmation proceedings, accusations of sexual harassment from Anita Hill, a law professor and former employee of Thomas, became public. Hill's testimony before the Senate Judiciary Committee dramatically polarized both the Senate and the nation. Feminists and others tended to believe the accusations and hailed the accuser for drawing national attention to the issue of harassment; but many Americans (and most members of the virtually all-male Senate) apparently did not believe her—or at least concluded that the alleged activities should not disqualify Thomas from serving on the Court. Thomas was ultimately confirmed by a narrow margin.

The Changing Left and the New Environmentalism

The New Left of the 1960s and early 1970s did not disappear after the end of the war in Vietnam, but it faded rapidly. Many of the students who had fought in its battles grew up, left school, and entered conventional careers. Some radical leaders, disillusioned by the unresponsiveness of American society to their demands, resignedly gave up the struggle and chose instead to work "within the system." Marxist critiques continued to flourish in academic circles, but to much of the public they came to appear dated and irrelevant—particularly as, beginning in 1989, Marxist governments collapsed in disrepute.

PRINCE WILLIAM SOUND, ALASKA
The giant oil tanker *Exxon Valdez* hit a reef in Prince William Sound in April 1989, and the result was the largest oil spill in American history. In this photograph, a tugboat pulls the tanker across the sound after it finally floated off the reef thirteen days after running aground. *(UPI/Bettmann)*

Yet a left of sorts did survive, giving evidence in the process of how greatly the nation's political climate had changed. Where 1960s activists had rallied to protest racism, poverty, and war, their counterparts in the 1980s and 1990s more often fought to stop the proliferation of nuclear weapons and power plants, to save the wilderness, to protect endangered species, to limit reckless economic development, and to otherwise protect the environment.

Public concerns about the environment had arisen intermittently since the beginning of the industrial era and had been growing in intensity since 1962, when the publication of Rachel Carson's *Silent Spring* aroused widespread public concern about the effect of insecticides on the natural world. (See "The American Environment," pp. 919–922.) Several highly visible environmental catastrophes in the 1960s and 1970s greatly increased that concern. Among them were a major oil spill off Santa Barbara, California, in 1969; the discovery of large deposits of improperly disposed toxic wastes in a residential community in upstate New York in 1978; and a frightening accident at the nuclear power plant on Three Mile Island, Pennsylvania in 1979. These and other revelations of the extent to which human progress threatened the natural world helped produce a major popular movement.

In the spring of 1970, a nationwide "Earth Day" signaled the beginning of the environmental movement. It differed markedly from the "conservation" movements of earlier years. Modern environmentalists shared the concerns of such earlier figures as John Muir and Gifford Pinchot about preserving some areas of the wilderness and carefully managing the exploitation of resources. But the new activists went much further, basing their positions on the developing field of ecology, the study of the interconnections among all components of an environment. Toxic wastes, air and water pollution, the destruction of forests, the extinction of species—these were not separate, isolated problems. All elements of the earth's environment were intimately and delicately linked, ecologists claimed. Damaging any one of those elements risked damaging all the others. Only by adopting a new social ethic, in which economic growth became less important than ecological health, or a new economics, in which environmental costs were factored into economic analyses, could the human race hope to survive in a healthy world.

In the twenty years after the first Earth Day, environmental issues gained increasing attention and support. Although the federal government generally displayed limited interest in the subject, environmentalists won a series of significant battles, mostly at the local level. They blocked the construction of roads, airports, and other projects (including American development of the supersonic transport airplane, or SST) that they claimed would be ecologically dangerous. By the end of the decade, the sense of urgency had grown, as scientists began warning that the release of certain industrial pollutants (most notably chlorofluorocarbons) into the atmosphere was depleting the ozone layer of the earth's atmosphere, which protects the globe from the sun's most dangerous rays. They warned, too, of the related danger of global warming, a rise in the earth's temperature as a result of emissions from the burning of fossil fuels (coal and oil).

The concern for the environment, the opposition to nuclear power, the resistance to economic development—all were reflections of a more fundamental characteristic of the post-Vietnam left. In a sharp break from the nation's long commitment to growth and progress, many dissidents argued that only by limiting growth and curbing traditional forms of progress could society hope to survive. Some of these critics of the "idea of progress" expressed a gloomy resignation, urging a lowering of social expectations and predicting an inevitable deterioration in the quality of life. Other advocates of restraint believed that change did not require decline: human beings could live more comfortably and more happily if they learned to respect the limits imposed on them by their environment. But in either case, such arguments evoked strong opposition from conservatives and others, who ridiculed the no-growth ideology as an expression of defeat-

ism and despair. Ronald Reagan, in particular, made an attack on the idea of "limits" central to his political success.

Turning Inward

For many Americans, the answer to the dilemmas of living in uncertain times lay not in religion or politics but in the cultivation of the self. No aspect of the culture of the 1980s and early 1990s aroused more comment than this tendency of individuals to "turn inward," that is, to replace social concerns with personal ones. Among affluent Americans, at least, there emerged

ELECTRONIC LEARNING
These students at the Clara Barton School in Minneapolis, photographed in 1991, were among millions of young people throughout the nation whose educational experience was being transformed by the proliferation of computers and other electronic devices. Among other things, the computer revolution increased the gulf separating affluent schools from poor ones; many schools in underfunded districts lacked the money to purchase the new equipment. *(Ed Bock/Stock Market)*

SIGNIFICANT EVENTS

1979   Nuclear accident at Three Mile Island

1981   Existence of AIDS reported in United States

   Solidarity movement leads revolt against communist regime in Poland

1985   Mikhail Gorbachev chosen as leader of the Soviet Union

   Reagan and Gorbachev meet in Geneva

   Congress passes Gramm-Rudman bill to limit deficits

   Homeless crisis worsens

   Crack cocaine appears in American cities

1986   U.S. planes bomb targets in Libya

   Reagan and Gorbachev meet in Reykjavik, Iceland

   Insider trading scandals on Wall Street

   Democrats regain control of U.S. Senate

   Iran-contra scandal revealed

   Glasnost and perestroika expand in Soviet Union

1987   Gorbachev visits Reagan in Washington

   Congress investigates Iran-contra scandal

   Stock market falls by record 508 points

   Televangelist scandals begin

   Congress passes Immigration Reform and Control Act

1988   INF Treaty signed

   Gorbachev announces Soviet troop reductions in Europe

   George Bush elected president

1989   Berlin Wall dismantled, German reunification begins

   Communist regimes collapse throughout Eastern Europe

   Chinese government suppresses student uprising with assault on demonstrators in Tiananmen Square

   American troops invade Panama

   Supreme Court's *Webster* decision limits, but does not overturn, *Roe* v. *Wade*

1990   South Africa begins dismantling *apartheid* system

   Bush agrees to tax increase

   Recession begins

   Iraq invades Kuwait; United Nations imposes sanctions

1991   Failed coup precipitates collapse of Soviet regime and disintegration of Soviet Union

   Civil rights bill reinforces laws against job discrimination

   United States drives Iraq out of Kuwait in Gulf War

   Controversy surrounds confirmation of Clarence Thomas to Supreme Court

1992   Bill Clinton elected president

   Ross Perot polls 19 percent of popular vote in independent campaign for presidency

   Major race riot in Los Angeles

1993   Congress approves tax increase as part of deficit reduction

   Congress ratifies North American Free Trade Agreement

   Clinton proposes national health care system

1994   U.S. participates in air strikes in Bosnia

a pervasive concern with personal "lifestyles." In the booming 1980s, which greatly increased the affluence of the upper middle class, such concerns became a central theme of popular culture. The "yuppie"—the young, urban professional with a large disposable income, intent on ever greater material comforts—became a common image of the Reagan years (often as a contrast to the ever more desperate poverty that was becoming visible in the same urban communities the "yuppies" were "gentrifying").

The American Future

The American people had suffered many trials and disappointments since the heady days at the end of World War II, when an "American Century" seemed about to dawn; and since the mid-1950s, when the country appeared poised for a prolonged era of domestic tranquility, economic abundance, and international preeminence. By the mid-1990s, America, like many other nations, was faced with the problems of a changing industrial economy, an increasingly diverse and contentious population, growing dangers to the environment that threatened the health of the entire world, and a declining popular faith in the ability of the nation's leaders and institutions to deal with these problems.

The dramatically different world order that was emerging from the upheavals of the late twentieth century was filled with dangers, both at home and abroad. But the United States, despite its many problems, remained what it had been for over two centuries: one of the stablest, wealthiest, and most resilient societies in modern history. At the dawn of a new millennium and a new era, the United States—whose example had done much to fuel the forces of change—was challenged with preserving and extending its own democracy in the face of major new perils and great new opportunities.

SUGGESTED READINGS

The Post Cold-War World. Bernard Gwertzman and Michael T. Kaufman, eds., *The Collapse of Communism* (1990). Paul Kennedy, *The Rise and Fall of the Great Powers* (1987). Robert Kuttner, *The End of Laissez Faire: National Purpose and the Global Economy After the Cold War* (1991). Henry R. Nau, *The Myth of America's Decline: Leading the World Economy in the 1990s* (1990). Joseph Nye, *Bound to Lead: The Changing Nature of American Power* (1990). H. Norman Schwarzkopf, *It Doesn't Take a Hero* (1992).

Politics After Reagan. E. J. Dionne, *Why Americans Hate Politics* (1991). Thomas Ferguson and Joel Rogers, *Right Turn* (1986). William Greider, *Who Will Tell the People?* (1992). Robert S. McElvaine, *The End of the Conservative Era: Liberalism After Reagan* (1987). Kevin Phillips, *The Politics of Rich and Poor: Wealth and the American Electorate in the Reagan Aftermath* (1990). Adolph L. Reed, Jr., *The Jesse Jackson Phenomenon (1986).* Bob Woodard, *The Agenda* (1994)

Post-Liberal Culture. Peter N. Carroll, *It Seemed Like Nothing Happened* (1982). Peter Clecak, *America's Quest for the Ideal Self* (1983). Jim Hougan, *Decadence: Radical Nostalgia, Narcissism, and Decline in the Seventies* (1975). Christopher Lasch, *The Culture of Narcissism* (1978). Edwin Schur, *The Awareness Trap* (1976). Daniel Yankelovich, *New Rules: Search for Self-Fulfillment in a World Turned Upside Down* (1981).

Economy and Society. Carl Abbott, *The New Urban America: Growth and Politics in the Sunbelt Cities* (1981). Michael A. Bernstein and David E. Adler, *Understanding American Economic Decline* (1994). Barry Bluestone and Bennett Harrison, *The Deindustrializing of America* (1982). Connie Bruck, *The Predator's Ball: The Junk Bond Raiders and the Man Who Staked Them* (1988). Bryan Burroughs and John Helyar, *Barbarians at the Gate: The Fall of RJR Nabisco* (1990). Elizabeth Fee and Daniel M. Fox, eds., *AIDS: The Burdens of History* (1988); *AIDS: The Making of a Chronic Disease* (1992). Gerald N. Grob, *From Asylum to Community: Mental Health Policy in Modern Amer-*

ica (1991). Robert Heilbroner and Lester Thurow, *Five Economic Challenges* (1983). John Langone, *AIDS: the Facts* (1988). Frank Levy, *Dollars and Dreams: The Changing American Income Distribution* (1987). Michael Lewis, *Liar's Poker* (1989). Eric Marcus, *Making History: The Struggle for Gay and Lesbian Equal Rights, 1945–1990* (1992). Robert Reich, *The Work of Nations: Preparing Ourselves for Twenty-first-Century Capitalism* (1991). Kirkpatrick Sale, *Power Shift* (1975). Jonathan Schell, *The Fate of the Earth* (1982). Bruce J. Schulman, *From Cotton Belt to Sunbelt: Federal Policy, Economic Development, and the Transformation of the South, 1938–1980* (1991). Randy Shilts, *And the Band Played On: Politics, People, and the AIDS Epidemic* (1987). James B. Stewart, *Den of Thieves* (1991). Studs Terkel, *The Great Divide* (1988). John Woodridge, *The Evangelicals* (1975). Daniel Yergin, *The Prize* (1991).

Gender and Family. Mary Francis Berry, *Why ERA Failed* (1986). Susan M. Bianchi, *American Women in Transition* (1987). Nancy Caraway, *Segregated Sisterhood: Racism and the Politics of American Feminism* (1991). Andrea Dworkin, *Right-Wing Women* (1983). Barbara Ehrenreich, *The Hearts of Men: American Dreams and the Flight from Commitment* (1983). Jonathan Kozol, *Rachel and Her Children: Homeless Families in America* (1988). Kristin Luker, *Abortion and the Politics of Motherhood* (1984). Jane Mansbridge, *Why We Lost the ERA* (1986). Donald G. Mathews and Jane Sherron De Hart, *Sex, Gender, and the Politics of E.R.A.: A State and the Nation* (1990). Rosalind Pechesky, *Abortion and Woman's Choice* (1984). Harrell R. Rodgers, Jr., *Poor Women, Poor Families* (1986). Hilda Scott, *Working Your Way to the Bottom: The Feminization of Poverty* (1985). Ruth Sidel, *Women and Children Last* (1986). Suzanne Staggenborg, *The Pro-Choice Movement: Organization and Activism in the Abortion Conflict* (1991). Winifred D. Wandersee, *On the Move: American Women in the 1970s* (1988).

Nonwhites in the 1970s and 1980s. Ken Auletta, *The Underclass* (1981). Frank D. Bean and Marta Tienda, *The Hispanic Population of the United States* (1987). Derrick Bell, *And We Are*

Not Saved: The Elusive Quest for Racial Justice (1987). James D. Cockcroft, *Outlaws in the Promised Land: Mexican Immigrant Workers and America's Future* (1986). John Crewden, *The Tarnished Door: The New Immigrants and the Transformation of America* (1983). Vine Deloria, Jr., *American Indian Policy in the Twentieth Century* (1985). Leslie W. Dunbar, ed., *Minority Report* (1984). Marian Wright Edelman, *Families in Peril* (1987). Douglas Glasgow, *The Black Underclass* (1980). Andrew Hacker, *Two Nations: Black and White, Separate, Hostile, Unequal* (1992). Michael Katz, *The Undeserving Poor: From the War on Poverty to the War on Welfare* (1989). Nicholas Lemann, *The Promised Land: The Great Black Migration and How It Changed America* (1989). David M. Reimers, *Still the Golden Door* (1985). Carol B. Stack, *All Our Kin: Strategies for Survival in a Black Community* (1975). Stan Steiner, *The New Indians* (1968). William Julius Wilson, *The Truly Disadvantaged* (1987).

THE AMERICAN ENVIRONMENT

SILENT SPRING

ONE SUMMER DAY IN 1957, a small plane flew over the nature sanctuary behind Olga Huckins's house in Duxbury, Massachusetts. It sprayed the land below with an oily mist and then vanished. The next day, Huckins found seven dead songbirds, their beaks gaping in apparent agony. She was so furious that she wrote an angry letter to a local paper; as an afterthought, she sent a copy to her friend Rachel Carson. It was one of those small events that alters the course of history.

Carson was a biologist and a gifted writer. Educated at Johns Hopkins University at a time when few women became scientists, she had gone to work for the government as an aquatic biologist. Although she was extremely shy, her skills as a writer quickly led her colleagues to rely on her to communicate their work to a wider public. Even-

---

PESTICIDE SPRAYING
When pesticides first became available to farmers, they proved so effective against agricultural pests that soon they were being sprayed on most crops. Although scientists and consumers have raised many questions about the safety of such chemicals, they continue to play an important role in the farm economy. Most foods grown in the United States are still treated with pesticides to some degree, although the growing popularity of organic foods (cultivated without artificial fertilizers or pesticides) testifies to the durability of the concerns Carson raised. *(Bettmann)*

THE AMERICAN ENVIRONMENT

tually, in 1949, she became chief editor for the U.S. Fish and Wildlife Service. In the meantime, she began to write popular essays about her special love, the ocean. A first book proved only marginally successful, but in 1951 she published *The Sea Around Us*. It instantly became an international best seller, bringing Carson a fame she never imagined and enough income to retire. By 1957, she was one of the most popular nature writers of her generation. Huckins's letter would turn her life onto an entirely new path.

The mist that the plane had sprayed behind Huckins's house was a mixture of ordinary fuel oil and a chemical called dicholoro-diphenyl-trichloroethane: DDT. In 1939, a Swiss chemist named Paul Muller had discovered that although DDT seemed harmless to human beings and other mammals, it was extremely toxic to insects. American scientists learned of Muller's discovery in 1942, just as the army was grappling with the special problems of tropical warfare. Unless something could be done to exterminate the mosquitoes that carried malaria and the lice that carried typhus, thousands of soldiers seemed likely to die from disease.

Under these circumstances, DDT seemed a godsend. It was first used on a large scale in Italy in 1943–1944 during a typhus outbreak, which it quickly helped end. Soon it was being sprayed in mosquito-infested areas of Pacific islands where American troops were fighting the Japanese. No soldiers suffered any apparent ill effects from the sprayings, and the incidence of malaria dropped precipitously. DDT quickly gained a reputation as a miraculous tool for controlling insects, and it undoubtedly saved thousands of lives. For its discovery, Paul Muller was awarded the Nobel Prize in medicine in 1948.

With so many benefits and no obvious drawbacks, the new chemical was first released for public use in 1945. Scientists in the Food and Drug Administration noted only one disturbing fact about DDT: it tended to accumulate in the fatty tissues of large animals, including humans, and was passed on in the milk of cows and humans alike. In large doses, it damaged the central nervous system. But data on the effects of chronic exposure were lacking, and the FDA could not legally restrict its use while waiting for further research. DDT thus entered the marketplace billed as an extraordinarily safe and effective poison, the ultimate weapon against destructive insects.

For the next decade, the new chemical continued to live up to its early billing. It helped farmers eliminate chronic pests and was widely used to control mosquitoes. One of its most impressive successes was against the gypsy moth, a voracious insect that had been stripping the leaves from northeastern forests ever since being accidentally introduced to the Boston area in 1868. All previous efforts to control the destructive moth had come to naught, but it virtually vanished from forests that were sprayed with DDT.

By the time Rachel Carson received Olga Huckins's letter, however, signs of trouble were beginning to appear in areas that had been sprayed with the chemical. For one, its effectiveness against certain insects declined as they developed resistance to its effects, so that higher doses were needed to produce the same lethal effect. A resistant housefly had appeared as early as 1948, and a resistant mosquito by 1949.

More worrisome were the chemical's effects on larger animals. Some were killed outright, like the birds in Olga Huckins's back yard. But DDT also seemed to inhibit some animals' ability to reproduce. It would later be learned that the eggshells of certain birds

THE AMERICAN ENVIRONMENT

RACHEL CARSON
Rachel Carson, who began her career as a marine biologist,
became the world's best-selling author about the ocean environment in the 1950s. Carson's abiding love for the creatures
of shore and surf led to her concern about the harm pesticides might do them.   *(Bettmann)*

were so thinned by the chemical that young birds were crushed in their nests even before they hatched. The extraordinary persistence of DDT in the environment, and its
tendency to accumulate in fatty tissues, meant that animals could concentrate surprising quantities in their flesh. This was especially true of those at the top of food chains—
eagles, trout, and, not least, people. What this meant remained unclear, but many bird
lovers were noting a general reduction in bird populations, and people who fished were
catching fewer fish. As the woods became emptier and more silent, DDT seemed the
mostly likely culprit.

THE AMERICAN ENVIRONMENT

Rachel Carson had worried about pesticides for years, but it was not until reading Olga Huckins's letter that she decided to do something about them. Meticulously gathering the best available data, she wrote a book that was published in 1962, *Silent Spring*. In it, she warned that the indiscriminate use of pesticides was wreaking havoc with the web of life, destroying wildlife populations, and even threatening human health. She wrote of a landscape in which sickness and death threatened animals and people alike, and "a strange stillness" had replaced the familiar songs of birds. Her eloquence was made all the more urgent by her private knowledge as she finished the book that she herself was dying of cancer.

Silent Spring became one of the most controversial books of the 1960s. It sold nearly half a million copies within six months of its publication and was discussed everywhere. The chemical industry responded with cries of outrage. After first trying to suppress the book's publication altogether and threatening lawsuits against its author and publisher, pesticide manufacturers began a long campaign to discredit Carson and repair the damage her book had done. They attacked her, often unfairly, for being unscientific, for distorting facts, and for being hostile to technological progress. In the end, though, Carson won at least a partial victory: the U.S. finally banned the sale of DDT in 1972. More important, her book raised public awareness about the threats human activities pose to the natural environment. Although she died in 1964, no single person would be more important in shaping environmental policies over the next thirty years.

APPENDICES

THE UNITED STATES

CANADA

WASHINGTON
- ■ Seattle
- □ Tacoma
- ⊡ Olympia
- ○ Spokane

OREGON
- ■ Portland
- ○ Salem
- ○ Eugene

MONTANA
- ○ Helena
- ○ Billings

NORTH DAKOT
- ○ Bismarck

IDAHO
- ⊙ Boise

SOUTH DAKO
- ★ Pierre
- ○ Rapid City

WYOMING
- ○ Casper
- ○ Laramie
- ★ Cheyenne

NEBRA

NEVADA
- ○ Reno
- ○ Carson City
- ○ Las Vegas

CALIFORNIA
- ■ Sacramento
- Berkeley
- ■ Oakland
- San Francisco
- ○ Stockton
- ○ Sunnyvale
- ■ San Jose
- ○ Modesto
- ⊡ Fresno
- ⊡ Bakersfield
- ○ Oxnard
- Glendale
- ○ Pasadena
- ⊡ Los Angeles
- Torrance
- San Bernardino
- ○ Riverside
- Long Beach
- ○ Anaheim
- Huntington Beach
- ○ Santa Ana
- ○ San Diego

UTAH
- ■ Salt Lake City
- ○ Provo

COLORADO
- ○ Boulder
- ■ Denver
- Lakewood
- ○ Aurora
- ○ Colorado Springs
- ○ Pueblo

ARIZONA
- ■ Phoenix
- ○ Tempe
- ○ Mesa
- ○ Tucson

NEW MEXICO
- ○ Taos
- ★ Santa Fe
- ○ Albuquerque
- ⊡ El Paso

- ○ Amarillo
- ○ Lubb
- **TEXA**
- San Anto

PACIFIC OCEAN

HAWAII
- *Kauai*
- *Oahu* Honolulu
- Ewa
- *Maui*
- *Hawaii*

0   100 Miles
0   100 Kilometers

RUSSIA

ALASKA
- ○ Fairbanks
- Anchorage
- ★ Juneau

CANADA

MEXICO

0   100 Miles
0   100 Kilometers

CANADA

Lake Superior

MINNESOTA

Minneapolis • St. Paul

Lake Huron

MICHIGAN

Lake Michigan

WISCONSIN

Milwaukee

Madison •

Grand
Rapids   Flint
        Sterling Heights
Lansing   Warren
          Detroit
          Livonia
     Ann Arbor   Cleveland

Lake Ontario

Rochester

Buffalo

Lake Erie

Erie

NEW YORK

Albany
Syracuse
Springfield
Hartford

Worcester   Boston
            Providence
MASSACHUSETTS
CONNECTICUT   Manchester
RHODE ISLAND

New Haven
Bridgeport
Stamford

MAINE

Augusta
VERMONT   Portland
Burlington
Montpelier   NEW
HAMPSHIRE
Concord

Manchester

IOWA

Des Moines •

Cedar
Rapids
Davenport

Rockford
Chicago   Gary   South
                  Bend
          Fort Wayne

Toledo

Akron

PENNSYLVANIA

Youngstown

Harrisburg

Allentown

Trenton
Newark   New York
         Jersey City

Peoria •

Urbana •

Springfield •

OHIO

Columbus

Pittsburgh

Baltimore

Philadelphia
NEW JERSEY

Dover
DELAWARE

kansas City
Kansas City
Topeka •

MISSOURI

Independence

Jefferson City •

St. Louis

ILLINOIS

INDIANA

Indianapolis

Dayton
Cincinnati

Louisville
Evansville

Frankfort •
Lexington •

WEST
VIRGINIA

Charleston

WASHINGTON
D.C.
Alexandria

Annapolis
MARYLAND

VIRGINIA

Richmond

Hampton
Newport News
Portsmouth

Norfolk
Virginia Beach
Chesapeake

Springfield •

KENTUCKY

Roanoke •

Greensboro   Durham
Winston-
Salem   Raleigh

ATLANTIC OCEAN

ARKANSAS

Little Rock

Memphis

Knoxville

Nashville

TENNESSEE

Chattanooga

Asheville •   Charlotte

NORTH CAROLINA

Greenville •

Columbia

OMA

Huntsville

Birmingham

Atlanta

SOUTH CAROLINA

Augusta •

Charleston

ving
arland
allas
ngton

Shreveport •

MISSISSIPPI

Jackson •

ALABAMA

Montgomery •

GEORGIA

Macon •

Columbus

Savannah

URBAN POPULATION CENTERS

◾ Over 5,000,000

■ 1,000,000-5,000,000

▣ 500,000-1,000,000

○ 100,000-500,000

• Less than 100,000

☆ State capitals

LOUISIANA

Baton Rouge

Beaumont

Houston

Galveston •

New Orleans

Mobile   Pensacola

Biloxi

Tallahassee

Jacksonville

FLORIDA

Gulf of Mexico

Orlando

Tampa
St. Petersburg

us Christi

Fort Lauderdale
Hialeah   Hollywood
Miami

0   300 Miles

0   300 Kilometers

TOPOGRAPHICAL MAP OF THE UNITED STATES

Puget Sound

Ranges

Columbia Range

Columbia R.

Cascade

Coast

Willamette R.

Columbia Plateau

Snake R.

Owyhee

Snake R.

Kootenai R.

Marias R.

Milk R.

Missouri R.

R O C K Y   M O U N T A I N S

Yellowstone R.

Bighorn R.

Tongue R.

Powder R.

Belle Fourche R.

Assiniboine R.

Red River

G R E A T

Little Missouri R.

Black Hills

Cheyenne R.

James R.

Missouri

Niobrara R.

Loup R.

Sacramento R.

Humboldt R.

Great Salt Lake

GREAT BASIN

Sierra Nevada

Central Valley

San Joaquin R.

Death Valley

Virgin R.

Sevier R.

Green R.

Colorado R.

White R.

Gunnison

Yampa R.

N. Platte R.

Laramie R.

S. Platte

Lodgepole Cr.

N. Platte R.

Platte R.

Republican R.

Smoky Hill R.

Kans

Arkansas R.

P L A I N S

Coast

Ranges

Mohave Desert

Colorado R.

Verde R.

Gila R.

Colorado Plateau

Rio Grande R.

Pecos R.

Cimarron R.

Canadian R.

N. Canadian R.

Red

Colorado R.

Trinity

Brazos R.

PACIFIC OCEAN

Rio Grande

Pecos R.

Nueces R.

Rio Grande R.

G

125°

120°

115°

110°

105°

100°

Lake Superior

Lake Huron

Lake Michigan

Lake Ontario

Lake Erie

Mississippi R.

St. Croix R.

Des Moines R.

Iowa R.

Cedar R.

Rock R.

Fox R.

Illinois R.

Kankakee

Wabash R.

CENTRAL PLAINS

Missouri R.

Osage R.

Ozark Plateau

White R.

Arkansas R.

S. Francis R.

Ouachita R.

Yazoo R.

Mississippi R.

Tombigbee R.

Pearl R.

Red R.

Sabine R.

Alabama R.

Chattahoochee R.

C O A S T A L   P L A I N

Galveston Bay

Gulf of Mexico

Scioto R.

Ohio R.

Kanawha R.

Mts.

Allegheny

Cumberland R.

Tennessee R.

APPALACHIAN MOUNTAINS

Blue Ridge Mountains

Saluda R.

Savannah R.

Altamaha R.

Allegheny R.

APPALACHIAN MOUNTAINS

Shenandoah Valley

Potomac R.

James R.

Roanoke R.

Susquehanna R.

Delaware R.

Hudson R.

Mohawk R.

Adirondack Mts.

St. Lawrence R.

Kennebeck R.

Connecticut R.

C O A S T A L   P L A I N

Chesapeake Bay

A T L A N T I C   O C E A N

ATLANTIC OCEAN

50°

45°

40°

35°

30°

25°

65°

70°

75°

80°

85°

90°

THE WORLD

United States and
its possessions

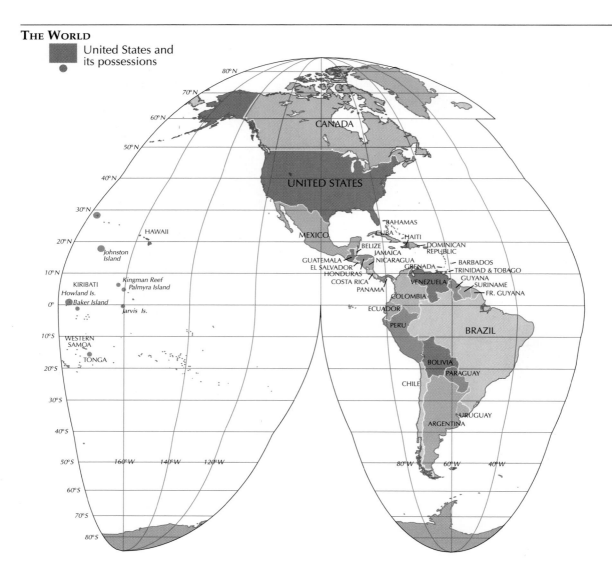

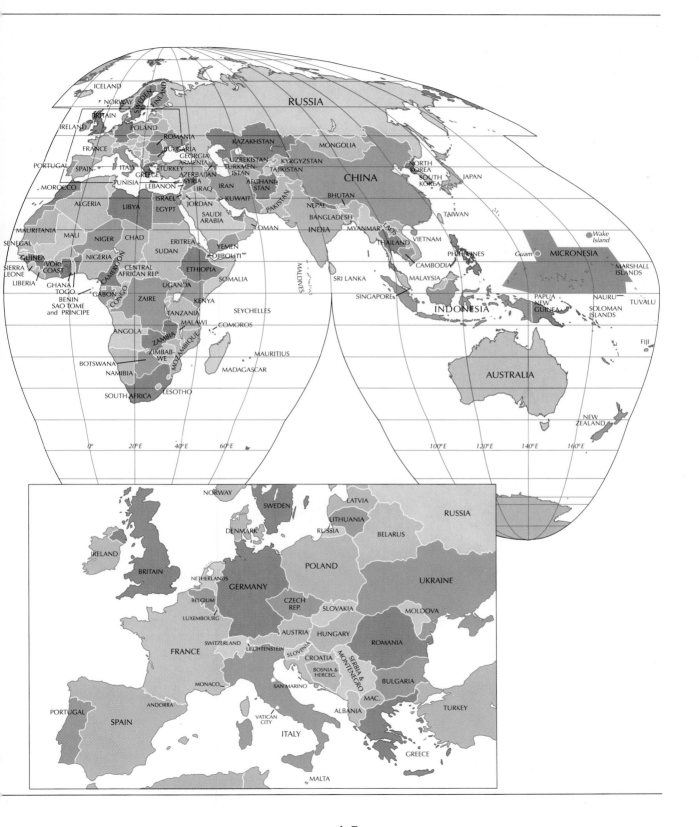

ICELAND
NORWAY
SWEDEN
FINLAND
BRITAIN
IRELAND
POLAND
ROMANIA
FRANCE
BULGARIA
GEORGIA
KAZAKHSTAN
MONGOLIA
PORTUGAL
SPAIN
ITALY
GREECE
TURKEY
ARMENIA
AZERBAIJAN
UZBEKISTAN
TURKMEN-
ISTAN
KYRGYZSTAN
TAJIKISTAN
CHINA
NORTH
KOREA
SOUTH
KOREA
JAPAN
RUSSIA
TUNISIA
LEBANON
SYRIA
IRAN
AFGHANI-
STAN
MOROCCO
ISRAEL
IRAQ
KUWAIT
JORDAN
PAKISTAN
NEPAL
BHUTAN
TAIWAN
ALGERIA
LIBYA
EGYPT
SAUDI
ARABIA
BANGLADESH
INDIA
MYANMAR
LAOS
MAURITANIA
OMAN
THAILAND
VIETNAM
Wake
Island
SENEGAL
MALI
NIGER
CHAD
ERITREA
YEMEN
MALDIVES
PHILIPPINES
Guam
MICRONESIA
GUINEA
SUDAN
DJIBOUTI
SRI LANKA
CAMBODIA
MARSHALL
ISLANDS
SIERRA
LEONE
IVORY
COAST
NIGERIA
CAMEROON
CENTRAL
AFRICAN REP.
ETHIOPIA
SOMALIA
MALAYSIA
LIBERIA
GHANA
TOGO
BENIN
GABON
CONGO
ZAIRE
UGANDA
KENYA
SINGAPORE
INDONESIA
PAPUA
NEW
GUINEA
NAURU
SOLOMAN
ISLANDS
TUVALU
SAO TOME
and PRINCIPE
TANZANIA
MALAWI
SEYCHELLES
COMOROS
ANGOLA
ZAMBIA
ZIMBAB-
WE
MOZAMBIQUE
MAURITIUS
FIJI
BOTSWANA
NAMIBIA
MADAGASCAR
AUSTRALIA
SOUTH AFRICA
LESOTHO
NEW
ZEALAND

0°   20°E   40°E   60°E   100°E   120°E   140°E   160°E

NORWAY
SWEDEN
LATVIA
RUSSIA
DENMARK
LITHUANIA
RUSSIA
BELARUS
IRELAND
BRITAIN
NETHERLANDS
POLAND
GERMANY
BELGIUM
CZECH
REP.
UKRAINE
LUXEMBOURG
SLOVAKIA
MOLDOVA
AUSTRIA
HUNGARY
SWITZERLAND
LIECHTENSTEIN
SLOVENIA
ROMANIA
FRANCE
CROATIA
SERBIA &
MONTENEGRO
MONACO
BOSNIA &
HERCEG.
BULGARIA
ANDORRA
SAN MARINO
MAC.
PORTUGAL
SPAIN
VATICAN
CITY
ALBANIA
TURKEY
ITALY
GREECE
MALTA

A-7

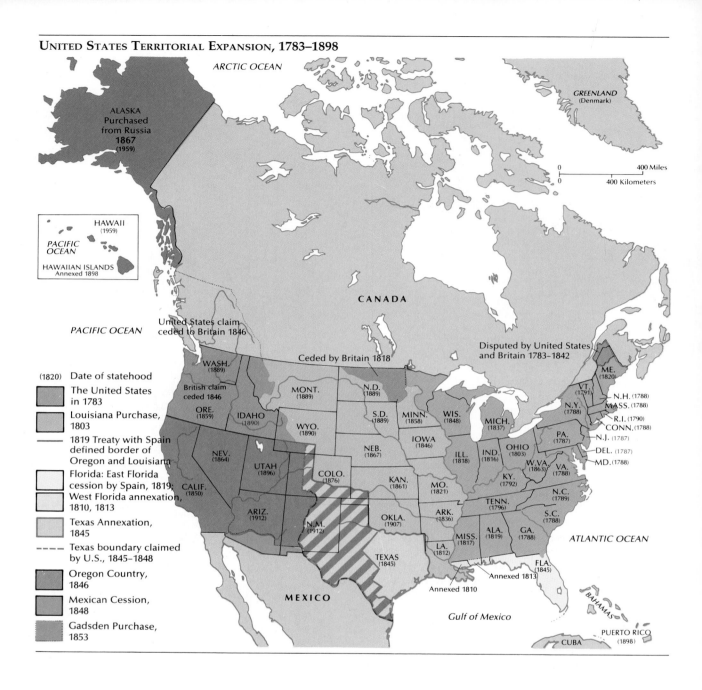

United States Territorial Expansion, 1783–1898

ARCTIC OCEAN

ALASKA
Purchased
from Russia
1867
(1959)

GREENLAND
(Denmark)

0 ___ 400 Miles
0 ___ 400 Kilometers

HAWAII
(1959)

PACIFIC
OCEAN

HAWAIIAN ISLANDS
Annexed 1898

PACIFIC OCEAN

CANADA

United States claim
ceded to Britain 1846

Ceded by Britain 1818

Disputed by United States
and Britain 1783–1842

ME.
(1820)

WASH.
(1889)

British claim
ceded 1846

MONT.
(1889)

N.D.
(1889)

VT.
(1791)

N.H. (1788)

ORE.
(1859)

IDAHO
(1890)

S.D.
(1889)

MINN.
(1858)

WIS.
(1848)

MICH.
(1837)

N.Y.
(1788)

MASS. (1788)

R.I. (1790)

CONN. (1788)

WYO.
(1890)

IOWA
(1846)

PA.
(1787)

N.J. (1787)

NEV.
(1864)

NEB.
(1867)

ILL.
(1818)

IND.
(1816)

OHIO
(1803)

W.VA.
(1863)

VA.
(1788)

DEL. (1787)

MD. (1788)

UTAH
(1896)

COLO.
(1876)

KAN.
(1861)

MO.
(1821)

KY.
(1792)

CALIF.
(1850)

N.C.
(1789)

ARIZ.
(1912)

N.M.
(1912)

OKLA.
(1907)

ARK.
(1836)

TENN.
(1796)

S.C.
(1788)

MISS.
(1817)

ALA.
(1819)

GA.
(1788)

ATLANTIC OCEAN

TEXAS
(1845)

LA.
(1812)

FLA.
(1845)

Annexed 1813

Annexed 1810

MEXICO

Gulf of Mexico

BAHAMAS

PUERTO RICO
(1898)

CUBA

Legend:

(1820) Date of statehood

The United States
in 1783

Louisiana Purchase,
1803

1819 Treaty with Spain
defined border of
Oregon and Louisiana

Florida: East Florida
cession by Spain, 1819;
West Florida annexation,
1810, 1813

Texas Annexation,
1845

Texas boundary claimed
by U.S., 1845–1848

Oregon Country,
1846

Mexican Cession,
1848

Gadsden Purchase,
1853

THE DECLARATION OF INDEPENDENCE

In Congress, July 4, 1776,

THE UNANIMOUS DECLARATION OF THE THIRTEEN UNITED STATES OF AMERICA

When, in the course of human events, it becomes necessary for one people to dissolve the political bands which have connected them with another, and to assume, among the powers of the earth, the separate and equal station to which the laws of nature and of nature's God entitle them, a decent respect to the opinions of mankind requires that they should declare the causes which impel them to the separation.

We hold these truths to be self-evident, that all men are created equal; that they are endowed by their Creator with certain unalienable rights; that among these, are life, liberty, and the pursuit of happiness. That, to secure these rights, governments are instituted among men, deriving their just powers from the consent of the governed; that, whenever any form of government becomes destructive of these ends, it is the right of the people to alter or to abolish it, and to institute a new government, laying its foundation on such principles, and organizing its powers in such form, as to them shall seem most likely to effect their safety and happiness. Prudence, indeed, will dictate that governments long established, should not be changed for light and transient causes; and, accordingly, all experience hath shown, that mankind are more disposed to suffer, while evils are sufferable, than to right themselves by abolishing the forms to which they are accustomed. But, when a long train of abuses and usurpations, pursuing invariably the same object, evinces a design to reduce them under absolute despotism, it is their right, it is their duty, to throw off such government and to provide new guards for their future security. Such has been the patient sufferance of these colonies, and such is now the necessity which constrains them to alter their former systems of government. The history of the present King of Great Britain is a history of repeated injuries and usurpations, all having, in direct object, the establishment of an absolute tyranny over these States. To prove this, let facts be submitted to a candid world:

He has refused his assent to laws the most wholesome and necessary for the public good.

He has forbidden his governors to pass laws of immediate and pressing importance, unless suspended in their operation till his assent should be obtained; and, when so suspended, he has utterly neglected to attend to them.

He has refused to pass other laws for the accommodation of large districts of people, unless those people would relinquish the right of representation in the legislature; a right inestimable to them, and formidable to tyrants only.

He has called together legislative bodies at places unusual, uncomfortable, and distant from the depository of their public records, for the sole purpose of fatiguing them into compliance with his measures.

He has dissolved representative houses repeatedly for opposing, with manly firmness, his invasions on the rights of the people.

He has refused, for a long time after such dissolutions, to cause others to be elected; whereby the legislative powers, incapable of annihilation, have returned to the people at large for their exercise; the state remaining, in the meantime, exposed to all the danger of invasion from without, and convulsions within.

He has endeavored to prevent the population of these States; for that purpose, obstructing the laws for naturalization of foreigners, refusing to pass others to encourage their migration hither, and raising the conditions of new appropriations of lands.

He has obstructed the administration of justice, by refusing his assent to laws for establishing judiciary powers.

He has made judges dependent on his will alone, for the tenure of their officers, and the amount and payment of their salaries.

He has erected a multitude of new offices, and sent hither swarms of officers to harass our people, and eat out their substance.

He has kept among us, in time of peace, standing armies, without the consent of our legislatures.

He has affected to render the military independent of, and superior to, the civil power.

He has combined, with others, to subject us to a jurisdiction foreign to our Constitution, and unacknowledged by our laws; giving his assent to their acts of pretended legislation:

For quartering large bodies of armed troops among us:

For protecting them by a mock trial, from punishment, for any murders which they should commit on the inhabitants of these States:

For cutting off our trade with all parts of the world:

For imposing taxes on us without our consent:

For depriving us, in many cases, of the benefit of trial by jury:

For transporting us beyond seas to be tried for pretended offences:

For abolishing the free system of English laws in a neighboring province, establishing therein an arbitrary government, and enlarging its boundaries, so as to render it at once an example and fit instrument for introducing the same absolute rule into these colonies:

For taking away our charters, abolishing our most valuable laws, and altering, fundamentally, the powers of our governments:

For suspending our own legislatures, and declaring themselves invested with power to legislate for us in all cases whatsoever.

He has abdicated government here, by declaring us out of his protection, and waging war against us.

He has plundered our seas, ravaged our coasts, burnt our towns, and destroyed the lives of our people.

He is, at this time, transporting large armies of foreign mercenaries to complete the works of death, desolation, and tyranny, already begun, with circumstances of cruelty and perfidy scarcely paralleled in the most barbarous ages, and totally unworthy the head of a civilized nation.

He has constrained our fellow citizens, taken captive on the high seas, to bear arms against their country, to become the executioners of their friends, and brethren, or to fall themselves by their hands.

He has excited domestic insurrections amongst us, and has endeavored to bring on the inhabitants of our frontiers, the merciless Indian savages, whose known rule of warfare is an undistinguished destruction of all ages, sexes, and conditions.

In every stage of these oppressions, we have petitioned for redress, in the most humble terms; our repeated petitions have been answered only by repeated injury. A prince, whose character is thus marked by every act which may define a tyrant, is unfit to be the ruler of a free people.

Nor have we been wanting in attention to our British brethren. We have warned them, from time to time, of attempts made by their legislature to extend an unwarrantable jurisdiction over us. We have reminded them of the circumstances of our emigration and settlement here. We have appealed to their native justice and magnanimity, and we have conjured them, by the ties of our common kindred, to disavow these usurpations, which would inevitably interrupt our connections and correspondence. They, too, have been deaf to the voice of justice and consanguinity. We must, therefore, acquiesce in the necessity, which denounces our separation, and hold them as we hold the rest of mankind, enemies in war, in peace, friends.

We, therefore, the representatives of the United States of America, in general Congress assembled, appealing to the Supreme Judge of the world for the rectitude of our intentions, do, in the name, and by the authority of the good people of these colonies, solemnly publish and declare, that these united colonies are, and of right ought to be, free and independent states: that they are absolved from all allegiance to the British Crown, and that all political connection between them and the state of Great Britain is, and ought to be, totally dissolved; and that, as free and independent states, they have full power to levy war, conclude peace, contract alliances, establish commerce, and to do all other acts and things which independent states may of right do. And, for the support of this declaration, with a firm reliance on the protection of Divine Providence, we mutually pledge to each other our lives, our fortunes, and our sacred honor.

The foregoing Declaration was, by order of Congress, engrossed, and signed by the following members:

JOHN HANCOCK

New Hampshire
Josiah Bartlett
William Whipple
Matthew Thornton

New York
William Floyd
Philip Livingston
Francis Lewis
Lewis Morris

Delaware
Caesar Rodney
George Read
Thomas McKean

North Carolina
William Hooper
Joseph Hewes
John Penn

Massachusetts Bay
Samuel Adams
John Adams
Robert Treat Paine
Elbridge Gerry

New Jersey
Richard Stockton
John Witherspoon
Francis Hopkinson
John Hart
Abraham Clark

Maryland
Samuel Chase
William Paca
Thomas Stone
Charles Carroll,
   of Carrollton

South Carolina
Edward Rutledge
Thomas Heyward, Jr.
Thomas Lynch, Jr.
Arthur Middleton

Rhode Island
Stephen Hopkins
William Ellery

Pennsylvania
Robert Morris
Benjamin Rush
Benjamin Franklin
John Morton
George Clymer
James Smith
George Taylor
James Wilson
George Ross

Virginia
George Wythe
Richard Henry Lee
Thomas Jefferson
Benjamin Harrison
Thomas Nelson, Jr.
Francis Lightfoot Lee
Carter Braxton

Georgia
Button Gwinnett
Lyman Hall
George Walton

Connecticut
Robert Sherman
Samuel Huntington
William Williams
Oliver Wolcott

Resolved, That copies of the Declaration be sent to the several assemblies, conventions, and committees, or councils of safety, and to the several commanding officers of the continental troops; that it be proclaimed in each of the United States, at the head of the army.

THE CONSTITUTION OF THE UNITED STATES OF AMERICA[1]

We the People of the United States, in Order to form a more perfect Union, establish Justice, insure domestic Tranquility, provide for the common defence, promote the general Welfare, and secure the Blessings of Liberty to ourselves and our Posterity, do ordain and establish this CONSTITUTION for the United States of America.

Article 1

Section 1.

All legislative Powers herein granted shall be vested in a Congress of the United States, which shall consist of a Senate and House of Representatives.

Section 2.

The House of Representatives shall be composed of Members chosen every second Year by the People of the several States, and the Electors in each State shall have the Qualifications requisite for Electors of the most numerous Branch of the State Legislature.

No Person shall be a Representative who shall not have attained to the Age of twenty-five Years, and been seven Years a Citizen of the United States, and who shall not, when elected, be an Inhabitant of that State in which he shall be chosen.

[Representatives and direct Taxes[2] shall be apportioned among the several States which may be included within this Union, according to their respective Numbers, which shall be determined by adding to the whole Number of free Persons, including those bound to Service for a Term of Years, and excluding Indians not taxed, three fifths of all other Persons.][3] The actual Enumeration shall be made within three Years after the first Meeting of the Congress of the United States, and within every subsequent Term of ten Years, in such Manner as they shall by Law direct. The Number of Representatives shall not exceed one for every thirty Thousand, but each State shall have at Least one Representative; and until such enumeration shall be made, the State of New Hampshire shall be entitled to chuse three, Massachusetts eight, Rhode-Island and Providence Plantations one, Connecticut five, New

York six, New Jersey four, Pennsylvania eight, Delaware one, Maryland six, Virginia ten, North Carolina five, South Carolina five, and Georgia three.

When vacancies happen in the Representation from any State, the Executive Authority thereof shall issue Writs of Election to fill such Vacancies.

The House of Representatives shall chuse their Speaker and other Officers; and shall have the sole Power of Impeachment.

Section 3.

The Senate of the United States shall be composed of two Senators from each State, chosen by the Legislature thereof, for six Years; and each Senator shall have one Vote.

Immediately after they shall be assembled in Consequence of the first Election, they shall be divided as equally as may be into three Classes. The Seats of the Senators of the first Class shall be vacated at the Expiration of the second Year, of the second Class at the Expiration of the fourth Year, and of the third Class at the Expiration of the sixth Year, so that one-third may be chosen every second Year; and if Vacancies happen by Resignation, or otherwise, during the Recess of the Legislature of any State, the Executive thereof may make temporary Appointments until the next Meeting of the Legislature, which shall then fill such Vacancies.

No Person shall be a Senator who shall not have attained to the Age of thirty Years, and been nine Years a Citizen of the United States, and who shall not, when elected, be an Inhabitant of that State for which he shall be chosen.

The Vice President of the United States shall be President of the Senate, but shall have no vote, unless they be equally divided.

The Senate shall chuse their other Officers, and also a President pro tempore, in the absence of the Vice President, or when he shall exercise the office of President of the United States.

The Senate shall have the sole Power to try all Impeachments. When sitting for that purpose they shall be on Oath or Affirmation. When the President of the United States is tried, the Chief Justice shall preside: And no person shall be convicted without the Concurrence of two thirds of the Members present.

Judgment in Cases of Impeachment shall not extend further than to removal from Office, and disqualification to hold and enjoy any Office of honor, Trust, or Profit under the United States: but the Party

---

[1] This version, which follows the original Constitution in capitalization and spelling, was published by the United States Department of the Interior, Office of Education, in 1935.
[2] Altered by the Sixteenth Amendment.
[3] Negated by the Fourteenth Amendment.

convicted shall nevertheless be liable and subject to Indictment, Trial, Judgment, and Punishment, according to Law.

Section 4.

The Times, Places and Manner of holding Elections for Senators and Representatives, shall be prescribed in each State by the Legislature thereof; but the Congress may at any time by Law make or alter such Regulations, except as to the Places of Chusing Senators.

The Congress shall assemble at least once in every Year, and such Meeting shall be on the first Monday in December, unless they shall by Law appoint a different day.

Section 5.

Each House shall be the Judge of the Elections, Returns and Qualifications of its own Members, and a Majority of each shall constitute a Quorum to do Business; but a smaller number may adjourn from day to day, and may be authorized to compel the Attendance of absent Members, in such Manner, and under such Penalties, as each House may provide.

Each House may determine the Rules of its Proceedings, punish its Members for disorderly Behaviour, and, with the Concurrence of two thirds, expel a Member.

Each House shall keep a Journal of its Proceedings, and from time to time publish the same, excepting such Parts as may in their Judgment require Secrecy; and the Yeas and Nays of the Members of either House on any question shall, at the Desire of one fifth of those Present, be entered on the Journal.

Neither House, during the Session of Congress, shall, without the Consent of the other, adjourn for more than three days, nor to any other Place than that in which the two Houses shall be sitting.

Section 6.

The Senators and Representatives shall receive a Compensation for their Services, to be ascertained by Law, and paid out of the Treasury of the United States. They shall in all Cases, except Treason, Felony, and Breach of the Peace, be privileged from Arrest during their Attendance at the Session of their respective Houses, and in going to and returning from the same; and for any Speech or Debate in either House, they shall not be questioned in any other Place.

No Senator or Representative shall, during the Time for which he was elected, be appointed to any civil Office under the Authority of the United States, which shall have been created, or the Emoluments whereof shall have been increased, during such time; and no Person holding any Office under the United States shall be a Member of either House during his continuance in Office.

Section 7.

All Bills for raising Revenue shall originate in the House of Representatives; but the Senate may propose or concur with Amendments as on other bills.

Every Bill which shall have passed the House of Representatives and the Senate, shall, before it become a Law, be presented to the President of the United States; If he approve he shall sign it, but if not he shall return it, with his Objections, to that House in which it shall have originated, who shall enter the Objections at large on their Journal, and proceed to reconsider it. If after such Reconsideration two thirds of that House shall agree to pass the bill, it shall be sent, together with the objections, to the other House, by which it shall likewise be reconsidered, and if approved by two thirds of that House, it shall become a Law. But in all such Cases the Votes of both Houses shall be determined by Yeas and Nays, and the Names of the Persons voting for and against the Bill shall be entered on the Journal of each House respectively. If any Bill shall not be returned by the President within ten Days (Sundays excepted) after it shall have been presented to him, the Same shall be a Law, in like Manner as if he had signed it, unless the Congress by their Adjournment prevent its Return, in which Case it shall not be a Law.

Every Order, Resolution, or Vote to which the Concurrence of the Senate and House of Representatives may be necessary (except on a question of Adjournment) shall be presented to the President of the United States; and before the Same shall take Effect, shall be approved by him, or being disapproved by him, shall be repassed by two thirds of the Senate and House of Representatives, according to the Rules and Limitations prescribed in the Case of a Bill.

Section 8.

The Congress shall have Power To lay and collect Taxes, Duties, Imposts and Excises, to pay the Debts and provide for the common Defence and general Welfare of the United States; but all Duties, Imposts and Excises shall be uniform throughout the United States;

To borrow money on the credit of the United States;

To regulate Commerce with foreign Nations, and among the several States, and with the Indian Tribes;

To establish an uniform rule of Naturalization, and uniform Laws on the subject of Bankruptcies throughout the United States;

To coin Money, regulate the Value thereof, and of foreign Coin, and fix the Standard of Weights and Measures;

To provide for the Punishment of counterfeiting the Securities and current Coin of the United States;

To establish Post Offices and post Roads;

To promote the Progress of Science and useful Arts, by securing for limited Times to Authors and Inventors the exclusive Right to their respective Writings and Discoveries;

To constitute Tribunals inferior to the Supreme Court;

To define and punish Piracies and Felonies committed on the high Seas, and Offenses against the Law of Nations;

To declare War, grant Letters of Marque and Reprisal, and make Rules concerning Captures on Land and Water;

To raise and support Armies, but no Appropriation of Money to that Use shall be for a longer Term than two Years;

To provide and maintain a Navy;

To make Rules for the Government and Regulation of the land and naval forces;

To provide for calling forth the Militia to execute the Laws of the Union, suppress Insurrections and repel Invasions;

To provide for organizing, arming, and disciplining the Militia, and for governing such Part of them as may be employed in the Service of the United States, reserving to the States respectively, the Appointment of the Officers, and the Authority of training the Militia according to the discipline prescribed by Congress;

To exercise exclusive Legislation in all Cases whatsoever, over such District (not exceeding ten Miles square) as may, by Cession of particular States, and the acceptance of Congress, become the Seat of the Government of the United States, and to exercise like Authority over all Places purchased by the Consent of the Legislature of the State in which the Same shall be, for the Erection of Forts, Magazines, Arsenals, Dockyards, and other needful Buildings;—And

To make all Laws which shall be necessary and proper for carrying into Execution the foregoing Powers, and all other Powers vested by this Constitution in the Government of the United States, or in any Department or Officer thereof.

Section 9.

The Migration or Importation of such Persons as any of the States now existing shall think proper to admit, shall not be prohibited by the Congress prior to the Year one thousand eight hundred and eight, but a tax or duty may be imposed on such Importation, not exceeding ten dollars for each Person.

The privilege of the Writ of Habeas Corpus shall not be suspended, unless when in Cases of Rebellion or Invasion the public Safety may require it.

No bill of Attainder or ex post facto Law shall be passed.

No capitation, or other direct, Tax shall be laid unless in Proportion to the Census or Enumeration herein before directed to be taken.

No Tax or Duty shall be laid on Articles exported from any State.

No Preference shall be given by any Regulation of Commerce or Revenue to the Ports of one State over those of another: nor shall Vessels bound to, or from, one State, be obliged to enter, clear, or pay Duties in another.

No Money shall be drawn from the Treasury, but in Consequence of Appropriations made by Law; and a regular Statement and Account of the Receipts and Expenditures of all public Money shall be published from time to time.

No Title of Nobility shall be granted by the United States: And no Person holding any Office of Profit or Trust under them, shall, without the Consent of the Congress, accept of any present, Emolument, Office, or Title, of any kind whatever, from any King, Prince, or foreign State.

Section 10.

No State shall enter into any Treaty, Alliance, or Confederation; grant Letters of Marque and Reprisal; coin Money; emit Bills of Credit; make any Thing but gold and silver Coin a Tender in Payment of Debts; pass any Bill of Attainder, ex post facto Law, or Law impairing the Obligation of Contracts, or grant any Title of Nobility.

No State shall, without the Consent of the Congress, lay any Imposts or Duties on Imports or Exports, except what may be absolutely necessary for executing its inspection Laws; and the net Produce of all Duties and Imposts, laid by any State on Imports or Exports, shall be for the use of the Treasury of the United States; and all such Laws shall be subject to the Revision and Control of the Congress.

No state shall, without the Consent of Congress, lay any duty of Tonnage, keep Troops, or Ships of War in time of Peace, enter into any Agreement or Compact with another State, or with a foreign Power, or engage in War, unless actually invaded, or in such imminent Danger as will not admit of delay.

Article II

Section 1.

The executive Power shall be vested in a President of the United States of America. He shall hold his Office during the Term of four years, and, together with the Vice President, chosen for the same Term, be elected, as follows:

Each State shall appoint, in such Manner as the Legislature thereof may direct, a Number of Electors, equal to the whole Number of Senators and Representatives to which the State may be entitled in the Congress: but no Senator or Representative, or Person holding an Office of Trust or Profit under the United States, shall be appointed an Elector.

[The Electors shall meet in their respective States, and vote by Ballot for two persons, of whom one at least shall not be an Inhabitant of the same State with themselves. And they shall make a List of all the Persons voted for, and of the Number of Votes for each; which List they shall sign and certify, and transmit sealed to the Seat of the Government of the United States, directed to the President of the Senate. The President of the Senate shall, in the Presence of the Senate and House of Representatives, open all the Certificates, and the Votes shall then be counted. The Person having the greatest Number of Votes shall be the President, if such Number be a Majority of the whole Number of Electors appointed; and if there be more than one who have such Majority, and have an equal Number of Votes, then the House of Representatives shall immediately chuse by Ballot one of them for President; and if no Person have a Majority, then from the five highest on the list the said House shall in like Manner chuse the President. But in chusing the President, the Votes shall be taken by States, the Representation from each State having one Vote; a quorum for this Purpose shall consist of a Member or Members from two-thirds of the States, and a Majority of all the States shall be necessary to a Choice. In every Case, after the Choice of the President, the Person having the greatest Number of Votes of the Electors shall be the Vice President. But if there should remain two or more who have equal votes, the Senate shall chuse from them by Ballot the Vice President.][4]

---

[4] Revised by the Twelfth Amendment.

The Congress may determine the Time of chusing the Electors, and the Day on which they shall give their Votes; which Day shall be the same throughout the United States.

No person except a natural-born Citizen, or a Citizen of the United States, at the time of the Adoption of this Constitution, shall be eligible to the Office of President; neither shall any Person be eligible to that Office who shall not have attained to the Age of thirty-five years, and been fourteen Years a Resident within the United States.

In Case of the Removal of the President from Office, or of his Death, Resignation, or Inability to discharge the Powers and Duties of the said Office, the same shall devolve on the Vice President, and the Congress may by Law provide for the Case of Removal, Death, Resignation, or Inability, both of the President and Vice President, declaring what Officer shall then act as President, and such Officer shall act accordingly, until the disability be removed, or a President shall be elected.

The President shall, at stated Times, receive for his Services a Compensation, which shall neither be increased nor diminished during the Period for which he shall have been elected, and he shall not receive within that Period any other Emolument from the United States, or any of them.

Before he enter on the execution of his Office, he shall take the following Oath or Affirmation:—"I do solemnly swear (or affirm) that I will faithfully execute the Office of President of the United States, and will, to the best of my Ability, preserve, protect, and defend the Constitution of the United States."

Section 2.

The President shall be Commander in Chief of the Army and Navy of the United States, and of the Militia of the several States, when called into the actual Service of the United States; he may require the Opinion, in writing, of the principal Officer in each of the executive Departments, upon any subject relating to the Duties of their respective Offices, and he shall have Power to Grant Reprieves and Pardons for Offenses against the United States, except in Cases of Impeachment.

He shall have Power, by and with the Advice and Consent of the Senate, to make Treaties, provided two-thirds of the Senators present concur; and he shall nominate, and by and with the Advice and Consent of the Senate, shall appoint Ambassadors, other public Ministers and Consuls, Judges of the supreme Court, and all other Officers of the United States, whose

Appointments are not herein otherwise provided for, and which shall be established by Law: but the Congress may by Law vest the Appointment of such inferior Officers, as they think proper, in the President alone, in the Courts of Law, or in the Heads of Departments.

The President shall have Power to fill up all Vacancies that may happen during the Recess of the Senate, by granting Commissions which shall expire at the End of their next Session.

Section 3.

He shall from time to time give to the Congress Information of the State of the Union, and recommend to their Consideration such Measures as he shall judge necessary and expedient; he may, on extraordinary occasions, convene both Houses, or either of them, and in Case of Disagreement between them, with respect to the Time of Adjournment, he may adjourn them to such Time as he shall think proper; he shall receive Ambassadors and other public Ministers; he shall take care that the Laws be faithfully executed, and shall Commission all the Officers of the United States.

Section 4.

The President, Vice President and all civil Officers of the United States, shall be removed from Office on Impeachment for, and Conviction of, Treason, Bribery, or other high Crimes and Misdemeanors.

Article III

Section 1.

The judicial Power of the United States, shall be vested in one supreme Court, and in such inferior Courts as the Congress may from time to time ordain and establish. The Judges, both of the supreme and inferior Courts, shall hold their Offices during good Behaviour, and shall, at stated Times, receive for their Services, a Compensation, which shall not be diminished during their Continuance in Office.

Section 2.

The judicial Power shall extend to all Cases, in Law and Equity, arising under this Constitution, the Laws of the United States, and Treaties made, or which shall be made, under their Authority;—to all Cases affecting ambassadors, other public ministers and consuls;—to all cases of admiralty and maritime Jurisdiction;—to Controversies to which the United States shall be a Party;—to Controversies between two or more States;—between a State and Citizens of another State;[5]—between Citizens of different States—between Citizens of the same State claiming Lands under Grants of different States, and between a State, or the Citizens thereof, and foreign States, Citizens, or Subjects.

In all Cases affecting Ambassadors, other public Ministers and Consuls, and those in which a State shall be Party, the supreme Court shall have original Jurisdiction. In all the other Cases before mentioned, the supreme Court shall have appellate Jurisdiction, both as to Law and Fact, with such Exceptions, and under such Regulations as the Congress shall make.

The trial of all Crimes, except in Cases of Impeachment, shall be by Jury; and such Trial shall be held in the State where the said Crimes shall have been committed; but when not committed within any State, the Trial shall be at such Place or Places as the Congress may by Law have directed.

Section 3.

Treason against the United States, shall consist only in levying War against them, or in adhering to their Enemies, giving them Aid and Comfort. No Person shall be convicted of Treason unless on the Testimony of two Witnesses to the same overt Act, or on Confession in open Court.

The Congress shall have power to declare the Punishment of Treason, but no Attainder of Treason shall work Corruption of Blood, or Forfeiture except during the Life of the Person attained.

Article IV

Section 1.

Full Faith and Credit shall be given in each State to the public Acts, Records, and judicial Proceedings of every other State. And the Congress may by general Laws prescribe the Manner in which such Acts, Records and Proceedings shall be proved, and the Effect thereof.

Section 2.

The Citizens of each State shall be entitled to all Privileges and Immunities of Citizens in the several States.

A Person charged in any State with Treason, Felony, or other Crime, who shall flee from Justice, and be found in another State, shall on demand of the

---

[5] Qualified by the Eleventh Amendment.

executive Authority of the State from which he fled, be delivered up, to be removed to the State having Jurisdiction of the crime.

No Person held to Service or Labour in one State, under the Laws thereof, escaping into another, shall, in Consequence of any Law or Regulation therein, be discharged from such Service or Labour, but shall be delivered up on Claim of the Party to whom such Service or Labour may be due.

Section 3.

New States may be admitted by the Congress into this Union; but no new State shall be formed or erected within the Jurisdiction of any other State; nor any State be formed by the Junction of two or more States, or parts of States, without the Consent of the Legislatures of the States concerned as well as of the Congress.

The Congress shall have Power to dispose of and make all needful Rules and Regulations respecting the Territory or other Property belonging to the United States; and nothing in this Constitution shall be so construed as to Prejudice any Claims of the United States, or of any particular State.

Section 4.

The United States shall guarantee to every State in this Union a Republican Form of Government, and shall protect each of them against Invasion; and on Application of the Legislature, or of the Executive (when the Legislature cannot be convened) against domestic violence.

Article V

The Congress, whenever two-thirds of both Houses shall deem it necessary, shall propose Amendments to this Constitution, or, on the Application of the Legislatures of two-thirds of the several States, shall call a Convention for proposing Amendments, which, in either Case, shall be valid to all Intents and Purposes, as part of this Constitution, when ratified by the Legislatures of three-fourths of the several States, or by Conventions in three-fourths thereof, as the one or the other Mode of Ratification may be proposed by the Congress; Provided that no Amendment which may be made prior to the Year One thousand eight hundred and eight shall in any Manner affect the first and fourth Clauses in the Ninth Section of the first Article; and that no State, without its Consent, shall be deprived of its equal Suffrage in the Senate.

Article VI

All Debts contracted and Engagements entered into, before the Adoption of this Constitution, shall be as valid against the United States under this Constitution, as under the Confederation.

This Constitution, and the Laws of the United States which shall be made in Pursuance thereof; and all Treaties made, or which shall be made, under the Authority of the United States, shall be the supreme Law of the Land; and the Judges in every State shall be bound thereby, any Thing in the Constitution or Laws of any State to the Contrary notwithstanding.

The Senators and Representatives before mentioned, and the Members of the several State Legislatures, and all executive and judicial Officers, both of the United States and of the several States, shall be bound by Oath or Affirmation to support this Constitution; but no religious Tests shall ever be required as a qualification to any Office or public Trust under the United States.

Article VII

The Ratification of the Conventions of nine States shall be sufficient for the Establishment of this Constitution between the States so ratifying the same.

Done in Convention by the Unanimous Consent of the States present the Seventeenth Day of September in the Year of our Lord one thousand seven hundred and Eighty seven, and of the Independence of the United States of America the Twelfth. In Witness whereof We have hereunto subscribed our Names.[6]

George Washington
President and deputy from Virginia

New Hampshire
John Langdon
Nicholas Gilman

Massachusetts
Nathaniel Gorham
Rufus King

Connecticut
William Samuel
  Johnson
Roger Sherman

New York
Alexander Hamilton

New Jersey
William Livingston
David Brearley
William Paterson
Jonathan Dayton

---

[6] These are the full names of the signers, which in some cases are not the signatures on the document.

Pennsylvania
Benjamin Franklin
Thomas Mifflin
Robert Morris
George Clymer
Thomas FitzSimons
Jared Ingersoll
James Wilson
Gouverneur Morris

Delaware
George Read
Gunning Beford, Jr.
John Dickinson
Richard Bassett
Jacob Broom

Maryland
James McHenry
Daniel of St. Thomas
    Jenifer
Daniel Carroll

Virginia
John Blair
James Madison, Jr.

North Carolina
William Blount
Richard Dobbs
    Spaight
Hugh Williamson

South Carolina
John Rutledge
Charles Cotesworth
    Pinckney
Charles Pinckney
Pierce Butler

Georgia
William Few
Abraham Baldwin

Articles in Addition to, and Amendment of, the Constitution of the United States of America, Proposed by Congress, and Ratified by the Legislatures of the Several States, Pursuant to the Fifth Article of the Original Constitution[7]

[Article I]

Congress shall make no law respecting an establishment of religion, or prohibiting the free exercise thereof; or abridging the freedom of speech, or of the press; or the right of the people peaceably to assemble, and to petition the Government for a redress of grievances.

[Article II]

A well regulated Militia, being necessary to the security of a free State, the right of the people to keep and bear Arms shall not be infringed.

[Article III]

No Soldier shall, in time of peace, be quartered in any house, without the consent of the Owner, nor in time of war, but in a manner to be prescribed by law.

---

[7] This heading appears only in the joint resolution submitting the first ten amendments.

[Article IV]

The right of the people to be secure in their persons, houses, papers, and effects, against unreasonable searches and seizures, shall not be violated, and no Warrants shall issue, but upon probable cause, supported by Oath or affirmation, and particularly describing the place to be searched, and the persons or things to be seized.

[Article V]

No person shall be held to answer for a capital or otherwise infamous crime, unless on a presentment or indictment of a Grand Jury, except in cases arising in the land or naval forces, or in the Militia, when in actual service in time of War or public danger; nor shall any person be subject for the same offence to be twice put in jeopardy of life or limb; nor shall be compelled in any criminal case to be a witness against himself, nor be deprived of life, liberty, or property, without due process of law; nor shall private property be taken for public use, without just compensation.

[Article VI]

In all criminal prosecutions, the accused shall enjoy the right to a speedy and public trial, by an impartial jury of the State and district wherein the crime shall have been committed, which district shall have been previously ascertained by law, and to be informed of the nature and cause of the accusation; to be confronted with the witnesses against him; to have compulsory process for obtaining witnesses in his favour, and to have the Assistance of Counsel for his defence.

[Article VII]

In suits at common law, where the value in controversy shall exceed twenty dollars, the right of trial by jury shall be preserved, and no fact tried by a jury, shall be otherwise reexamined in any Court of the United States, than according to the rules of the common law.

[Article VIII]

Excessive bail shall not be required, nor excessive fines imposed, nor cruel and unusual punishments inflicted.

[Article IX]

The enumeration of the Constitution, of certain rights, shall not be construed to deny or disparage others retained by the people.

[Article X]

The powers not delegated to the United States by the Constitution, nor prohibited by it to the States, are reserved to the States respectively, or to the people.
     [Amendments I-X, in force 1791.]

[Article XI][8]

The Judicial power of the United States shall not be construed to extend to any suit in law or equity, commenced or prosecuted against one of the United States by Citizens of another State, or by Citizens or Subjects of any Foreign State.

[Article XII][9]

The Electors shall meet in their respective States and vote by ballot for President and Vice-President, one of whom, at least, shall not be an inhabitant of the same State with themselves; they shall name in their ballots the person voted for as President, and in distinct ballots the person voted for as Vice-President, and they shall make distinct lists of all persons voted for as President, and of all persons voted for as Vice-President, and of the number of votes for each, which lists they shall sign and certify, and transmit sealed to the seal of the government of the United States, directed to the President of the Senate;—The President of the Senate shall, in the presence of the Senate and House of Representatives, open all the certificates and the votes shall then be counted;—The person having the greatest number of votes for President, shall be the President, if such number be a majority of the whole number of Electors appointed; and if no person have such majority, then from the persons having the highest numbers not exceeding three on the list of those voted for as President, the House of Representatives shall choose immediately, by ballot, the President. But in choosing the President, the votes shall be taken by states, the representation from each state having one vote; a quorum for this purpose shall consist of a member or members from two-thirds of the states, and a majority of all the states shall be necessary to a choice. And if the House of Representatives shall not choose a President whenever the right of choice shall devolve upon them, before the fourth day of March next following, then the Vice-President shall act as President, as in the case of the death or other constitutional disability of the President.—The person having the greatest number of votes as Vice-President, shall be the Vice-President, if such number be a majority of the whole number of Electors appointed, and if no person have a majority, then from the two highest numbers on the list, the Senate shall choose the Vice-President; a quorum for the purpose shall consist of two-thirds of the whole number of Senators, and a majority of the whole number shall be necessary to a choice. But no person constitutionally ineligible to the office of President shall be eligible to that of Vice-President of the United States.

[Article XIII][10]

Section 1.

Neither slavery nor involuntary servitude, except as a punishment for crime whereof the party shall have been duly convicted, shall exist within the United States, or any place subject to their jurisdiction.

Section 2.

Congress shall have power to enforce this article by appropriate legislation.

[Article XIV][11]

Section 1.

All persons born or naturalized in the United States, and subject to the jurisdiction thereof, are citizens of the United States and of the State wherein they reside. No State shall make or enforce any law which shall abridge the privileges or immunities of citizens of the United States; nor shall any State deprive any person of life, liberty, or property, without due process of law; nor deny to any person within its jurisdiction the equal protection of the laws.

---

[8] Adopted in 1798.
[9] Adopted in 1804.

[10] Adopted in 1865.
[11] Adopted in 1868.

Section 2.

Representatives shall be apportioned among the several States according to their respective numbers, counting the whole number of persons in each State, excluding Indians not taxed. But when the right to vote at any election for the choice of electors for President and Vice-President of the United States, Representatives in Congress, the Executive and Judicial officers of a State, or the members of the Legislature thereof, is denied to any of the male inhabitants of such State, being twenty-one years of age, and citizens of the United States, or in any way abridged, except for participation in rebellion, or other crime, the basis of representation therein shall be reduced in the proportion which the number of such male citizens shall bear to the whole number of male citizens twenty-one years of age in such State.

Section 3.

No person shall be a Senator or Representative in Congress, or elector of President and Vice-President, or hold any office, civil or military, under the United States, or under any State, who, having previously taken an oath, as a member of Congress, or as an officer of the United States, or as a member of any State legislature, or as an executive or judicial officer of any State, to support the Constitution of the United States, shall have engaged in insurrection or rebellion against the same, or given aid or comfort to the enemies thereof. But Congress may by a vote of two-thirds of each House, remove such disability.

Section 4.

The validity of the public debt of the United States, authorized by law, including debts incurred for payment of pensions and bounties for services in suppressing insurrection or rebellion, shall not be questioned. But neither the United States nor any State shall assume or pay any debts or obligation incurred in aid of insurrection or rebellion against the United States, or any claim for the loss or emancipation of any slave; but all such debts, obligations, and claims shall be held illegal and void.

Section 5.

The Congress shall have the power to enforce, by appropriate legislation, the provisions of this article.

[Article XV][12]

Section 1.

The right of citizens of the United States to vote shall not be denied or abridged by the United States or by any State on account of race, color, or previous condition of servitude—

Section 2.

The Congress shall have power to enforce this article by appropriate legislation.

[Article XVI][13]

The Congress shall have power to lay and collect taxes on incomes, from whatever source derived, without apportionment among the several States, and without regard to any census or enumeration.

[Article XVII][14]

The Senate of the United States shall be composed of two Senators from each State, elected by the people thereof, for six years; and each Senator shall have one vote. The electors in each State shall have the qualifications requisite for electors of the most numerous branch of the State legislatures.

When vacancies happen in the representation of any State in the Senate, the executive authority of such State shall issue writs of election to fill such vacancies: *Provided,* That the legislature of any State may empower the executive thereof to make temporary appointments until the people fill the vacancies by election as the legislature may direct.

This amendment shall not be so constructed as to affect the election or term of any Senator chosen before it becomes valid as part of the Constitution.

[Article XVIII][15]

Section 1.

After one year from the ratification of this article the manufacture, sale, or transportation of intoxicating liquors within, the importation thereof into, or the

---

[12] Adopted in 1870.
[13] Adopted in 1913.
[14] Adopted in 1913.
[15] Adopted in 1918.

exportation thereof from the United States and all territory subject to the jurisdiction thereof for beverage purposes is hereby prohibited.

Section 2.

The Congress and the several States shall have concurrent power to enforce this article by appropriate legislation.

Section 3.

This article shall be inoperative unless it shall have been ratified as an amendment to the Constitution by the legislatures of the several States, as provided in the Constitution, within seven years from the date of the submission hereof to the States by the Congress.

[Article XIX][16]

The right of citizens of the United States to vote shall not be denied or abridged by the United States or by any State on account of sex.

Congress shall have power to enforce this article by appropriate legislation.

[Article XX][17]

Section 1.

The terms of the President and Vice-President shall end at noon on the 20th day of January, and the terms of Senators and Representatives at noon on the 3d day of January, of the years in which such terms would have ended if this article had not been ratified; and the terms of their successors shall then begin.

Section 2.

The Congress shall assemble at least once in every year, and such meeting shall begin at noon on the 3d day of January, unless they shall by law appoint a different day.

Section 3.

If, at the time fixed for the beginning of the term of the President, the President elect shall have died, the Vice-President elect shall become President. If a President shall not have been chosen before the time fixed for the beginning of his term or if the President elect shall

have failed to qualify, then the Vice-President elect shall act as President until a President shall have qualified; and the Congress may by law provide for the case wherein neither a President elect nor a Vice-President elect shall have qualified, declaring who shall then act as President, or the manner in which one who is to act shall be selected, and such person shall act accordingly until a President or Vice-President shall have qualified.

Section 4.

The Congress may by law provide for the case of the death of any of the persons from whom the House of Representatives may choose a President whenever the right of choice shall have devolved upon them, and for the case of the death of any of the persons from whom the Senate may choose a Vice-President whenever the right of choice shall have devolved upon them.

Section 5.

Sections 1 and 2 shall take effect on the 15th day of October following the ratification of this article.

Section 6.

This article shall be inoperative unless it shall have been ratified as an amendment to the Constitution by the legislatures of three-fourths of the several States within seven years from the date of its submission.

[Article XXI][18]

Section 1.

The eighteenth article of amendment to the Constitution of the United States is hereby repealed.

Section 2.

The transportation or importation into any State, Territory, or possession of the United States for delivery or use therein of intoxicating liquors, in violation of the laws thereof, is hereby prohibited.

Section 3.

This article shall be inoperative unless it shall have been ratified as an amendment to the Constitution by conventions in the several States, as provided in the Constitution, within seven years from the date of the submission hereof to the States by the Congress.

---

[16] Adopted in 1920.
[17] Adopted in 1933.

[18] Adopted in 1933.

[Article XXII][19]

No person shall be elected to the office of the President more than twice, and no person who has held the office of President, or acted as President, for more than two years of a term to which some other person was elected President shall be elected to the office of the President more than once.

But this Article shall not apply to any person holding the office of President when this Article was proposed by the Congress, and shall not prevent any person who may be holding the office of President, or acting as President, during the term within which this Article becomes operative from holding the office of President or acting as President during the remainder of such term.

This article shall be inoperative unless it shall have been ratified as an amendment to the Constitution by the legislatures of three-fourths of the several states within seven years from the date of its submission to the states by the Congress.

[Article XXIII][20]

Section 1.

The District constituting the seat of Government of the United States shall appoint in such manner as the Congress may direct:

A number of electors of President and Vice-President equal to the whole number of Senators and Representatives in Congress to which the District would be entitled if it were a State, but in no event more than the least populous State; they shall be in addition to those appointed by the States, but they shall be considered, for the purposes of the election of President and Vice-President, to be electors appointed by a State; and they shall meet in the District and perform such duties as provided by the twelfth article of amendment.

Section 2.

The Congress shall have power to enforce this article by appropriate legislation.

[Article XXIV][21]

Section 1.

The right of citizens of the United States to vote in any primary or other election for President or Vice President, for electors for President or Vice President, or for Senator or Representative in Congress, shall not be denied or abridged by the United States or any state by reason of failure to pay any poll tax or other tax.

Section 2.

The Congress shall have the power to enforce this article by appropriate legislation.

[Article XXV][22]

Section 1.

In case of the removal of the President from office or of his death or resignation, the Vice President shall become President.

Section 2.

Whenever there is a vacancy in the office of the Vice President, the President shall nominate a Vice President who shall take office upon confirmation by a majority vote of both Houses of Congress.

Section 3.

Whenever the President transmits to the President Pro Tempore of the Senate and the Speaker of the House of Representatives his written declaration that he is unable to discharge the powers and duties of his office, and until he transmits to them a written declaration to the contrary, such powers and duties shall be discharged by the Vice President as Acting President.

Section 4.

Whenever the Vice President and a majority of either the principal officers of the executive departments or of such other body as Congress may by law provide, transmit to the President Pro Tempore of the Senate

---

[19] Adopted in 1961.
[20] Adopted in 1961.

[21] Adopted in 1964.
[22] Adopted in 1967.

and the Speaker of the House of Representatives their written declaration that the President is unable to discharge the powers and duties of his office, the Vice President shall immediately assume the powers and duties of the office as Acting President.

Thereafter, when the President transmits to the President Pro Tempore of the Senate and the Speaker of the House of Representatives his written declaration that no inability exists, he shall resume the powers and duties of his office unless the Vice President and a majority of either the principal officers of the executive departments or of such other body as Congress may by law provide, transmit within four days to the President Pro Tempore of the Senate and the Speaker of the House of Representatives their written declaration that the President is unable to discharge the powers and duties of his office. Thereupon Congress shall decide the issue, assembling within forty-eight hours for that purpose if not in session. If the Congress, within twenty-one days after receipt of the latter written declaration, or, if Congress is not in session, within twenty-one days after Congress is required to assemble, determines by two-thirds vote of both Houses that the President is unable to discharge the powers and duties of his office, the Vice President shall continue to discharge the same as Acting President; otherwise, the President shall resume the powers and duties of his office.

[Article XXVI][23]

Section 1.

The right of citizens of the United States, who are eighteen years of age or older, to vote shall not be denied or abridged by the United States or by any State on account of age.

Section 2.

The Congress shall have power to enforce this article by appropriate legislation.

---

[23] Adopted in 1971.

[Amendment XXVII][24]

No law varying the compensation for the services of Senators and Representatives shall take effect until an election of Representatives shall have intervened.

PRESIDENTIAL ELECTIONS

Year	Candidates	Parties	Popular Vote	Percentage of Popular Vote	Electoral Vote	Percentage of Voter Participation
1789	**GEORGE WASHINGTON (Va.)***				69	
	John Adams				34	
	Others				35	
1792	**GEORGE WASHINGTON (Va.)**				132	
	John Adams				77	
	George Clinton				50	
	Others				5	
1796	**JOHN ADAMS (Mass.)**	Federalist			71	
	Thomas Jefferson	Democratic-Republican			68	
	Thomas Pinckney	Federalist			59	
	Aaron Burr	Dem.-Rep.			30	
	Others				48	
1800	**THOMAS JEFFERSON (Va.)**	Dem.-Rep.			73	
	Aaron Burr	Dem.-Rep.			73	
	John Adams	Federalist			65	
	C. C. Pinckney	Federalist			64	
	John Jay	Federalist			1	
1804	**THOMAS JEFFERSON (Va.)**	Dem.-Rep.			162	
	C. C. Pinckney	Federalist			14	
1808	**JAMES MADISON (Va.)**	Dem.-Rep.			122	
	C. C. Pinckney	Federalist			47	
	George Clinton	Dem.-Rep.			6	
1812	**JAMES MADISON (Va.)**	Dem.-Rep.			128	
	De Witt Clinton	Federalist			89	
1816	**JAMES MONROE (Va.)**	Dem.-Rep.			183	
	Rufus King	Federalist			34	
1820	**JAMES MONROE (Va.)**	Dem.-Rep.			231	
	John Quincy Adams	Dem.-Rep.			1	
1824	**JOHN Q. ADAMS (Mass.)**	Dem.-Rep.	108,740	30.5	84	26.9
	Andrew Jackson	Dem.-Rep.	153,544	43.1	99	
	William H. Crawford	Dem.-Rep.	46,618	13.1	41	
	Henry Clay	Dem.-Rep.	47,136	13.2	37	
1828	**ANDREW JACKSON (Tenn.)**	Democratic	647,286	56.0	178	57.6
	John Quincy Adams	National Republican	508,064	44.0	83	
1832	**ANDREW JACKSON (Tenn.)**	Democratic	687,502	55.0	219	55.4
	Henry Clay	National Republican	530,189	42.4	49	
	John Floyd	Independent			11	
	William Wirt	Anti-Mason	33,108	2.6	7	
1836	**MARTIN VAN BUREN (N.Y.)**	Democratic	765,483	50.9	170	57.8
	W. H. Harrison	Whig			73	
	Hugh L. White	Whig	739,795	49.1	26	
	Daniel Webster	Whig			14	
	W. P. Magnum	Independent			11	

*State of residence at time of election.

Year	Candidates	Parties	Popular Vote	Percentage of Popular Vote	Electoral Vote	Percentage of Voter Participation
1840	**WILLIAM H. HARRISON (Ohio)**	Whig	1,274,624	53.1	234	80.2
	Martin Van Buren	Democratic	1,127,781	46.9	60	
	J. G. Birney	Liberty	7,069		—	
1844	**JAMES K. POLK (Tenn.)**	Democratic	1,338,464	49.6	170	78.9
	Henry Clay	Whig	1,300,097	48.1	105	
	J. G. Birney	Liberty	62,300	2.3	—	
1848	**ZACHARY TAYLOR (La.)**	Whig	1,360,967	47.4	163	72.7
	Lewis Cass	Democratic	1,222,342	42.5	127	
	Martin Van Buren	Free-Soil	291,263	10.1	—	
1852	**FRANKLIN PIERCE (N.H.)**	Democratic	1,601,117	50.9	254	69.6
	Winfield Scott	Whig	1,385,453	44.1	42	
	John P. Hale	Free-Soil	155,825	5.0	—	
1856	**JAMES BUCHANAN (Pa.)**	Democratic	1,832,955	45.3	741	78.9
	John C. Frémont	Republican	1,339,932	33.1	114	
	Millard Fillmore	American	871,731	21.6	8	
1860	**ABRAHAM LINCOLN (Ill.)**	Republican	1,865,593	39.8	180	81.2
	Stephen A. Douglas	Democratic	1,382,713	29.5	12	
	John C. Breckinridge	Democratic	848,356	18.1	72	
	John Bell	Union	592,906	12.6	39	
1864	**ABRAHAM LINCOLN (Ill.)**	Republican	2,213,655	55.0	212	73.8
	George B. McClellan	Democratic	1,805,237	45.0	21	
1868	**ULYSSES S. GRANT (Ill.)**	Republican	3,012,833	52.7	214	78.1
	Horatio Seymour	Democratic	2,703,249	47.3	80	
1872	**ULYSSES S. GRANT (Ill.)**	Republican	3,597,132	55.6	286	71.3
	Horace Greeley	Democratic; Liberal Republican	2,834,125	43.9	66	
1876	**RUTHERFORD B. HAYES (Ohio)**	Republican	4,036,298	48.0	185	81.8
	Samuel J. Tilden	Democratic	4,300,590	51.0	184	
1880	**JAMES A. GARFIELD (Ohio)**	Republican	4,454,416	48.5	214	79.4
	Winfield S. Hancock	Democratic	4,444,952	48.1	155	
1884	**GROVER CLEVELAND (N.Y.)**	Democratic	4,874,986	48.5	219	77.5
	James G. Blaine	Republican	4,851,981	48.2	182	
1888	**BENJAMIN HARRISON (Ind.)**	Republican	5,439,853	47.9	233	79.3
	Grover Cleveland	Democratic	5,540,309	48.6	168	
1892	**GROVER CLEVELAND (N.Y.)**	Democratic	5,556,918	46.1	277	74.7
	Benjamin Harrison	Republican	5,176,108	43.0	145	
	James B. Weaver	People's	1,041,028	8.5	22	
1896	**WILLIAM McKINLEY (Ohio)**	Republican	7,104,779	51.1	271	79.3
	William J. Bryan	Democratic-People's	6,502,925	47.7	176	
1900	**WILLIAM McKINLEY (Ohio)**	Republican	7,207,923	51.7	292	73.2
	William J. Bryan	Dem.-Populist	6,358,133	45.5	155	
1904	**THEODORE ROOSEVELT (N.Y.)**	Republican	7,623,486	57.9	336	65.2
	Alton B. Parker	Democratic	5,077,911	37.6	140	
	Eugene V. Debs	Socialist	402,283	3.0	—	
1908	**WILLIAM H. TAFT (Ohio)**	Republican	7,678,908	51.6	321	65.4
	William J. Bryan	Democratic	6,409,104	43.1	162	
	Eugene V. Debs	Socialist	420,793	2.8	—	

Year	Candidates	Parties	Popular Vote	Percentage of Popular Vote	Electoral Vote	Percentage of Voter Participation
1912	**WOODROW WILSON (N.J.)**	Democratic	6,293,454	41.9	435	58.8
	Theodore Roosevelt	Progressive	4,119,538	27.4	88	
	William H. Taft	Republican	3,484,980	23.2	8	
	Eugene V. Debs	Socialist	900,672	6.0	—	
1916	**WOODROW WILSON (N.J.)**	Democratic	9,129,606	49.4	277	61.6
	Charles E. Hughes	Republican	8,538,221	46.2	254	
	A. L. Benson	Socialist	585,113	3.2	—	
1920	**WARREN G. HARDING (Ohio)**	Republican	16,152,200	60.4	404	49.2
	James M. Cox	Democratic	9,147,353	34.2	127	
	Eugene V. Debs	Socialist	919,799	3.4	—	
1924	**CALVIN COOLIDGE (Mass.)**	Republican	15,725,016	54.0	382	48.9
	John W. Davis	Democratic	8,386,503	28.8	136	
	Robert M. LaFollette	Progressive	4,822,856	16.6	13	
1928	**HERBERT HOOVER (Calif.)**	Republican	21,391,381	58.2	444	56.9
	Alfred E. Smith	Democratic	15,016,443	40.9	87	
	Norman Thomas	Socialist	267,835	0.7	—	
1932	**FRANKLIN D. ROOSEVELT (N.Y.)**	Democratic	22,821,857	57.4	472	56.9
	Herbert Hoover	Republican	15,761,841	39.7	59	
	Norman Thomas	Socialist	881,951	2.2	—	
1936	**FRANKLIN D. ROOSEVELT (N.Y.)**	Democratic	27,751,597	60.8	523	61.0
	Alfred M. Landon	Republican	16,679,583	36.5	8	
	William Lemke	Union	882,479	1.9	—	
1940	**FRANKLIN D. ROOSEVELT (N.Y.)**	Democratic	27,244,160	54.8	449	62.5
	Wendell L. Willkie	Republican	22,305,198	44.8	82	
1944	**FRANKLIN D. ROOSEVELT (N.Y.)**	Democratic	25,602,504	53.5	432	55.9
	Thomas E. Dewey	Republican	22,006,285	46.0	99	
1948	**HARRY S. TRUMAN (Mo.)**	Democratic	24,105,695	49.5	304	53.0
	Thomas E. Dewey	Republican	21,969,170	45.1	189	
	J. Strom Thurmond	State-Rights Democratic	1,169,021	2.4	38	
	Henry A. Wallace	Progressive	1,156,103	2.4	—	
1952	**DWIGHT D. EISENHOWER (N.Y.)**	Republican	33,936,252	55.1	442	63.3
	Adlai E. Stevenson	Democratic	27,314,992	44.4	89	
1956	**DWIGHT D. EISENHOWER (N.Y.)**	Republican	35,575,420	57.6	457	60.6
	Adlai E. Stevenson	Democratic	26,033,066	42.1	73	
	Other	—	—		1	
1960	**JOHN F. KENNEDY (Mass.)**	Democratic	34,227,096	49.9	303	62.8
	Richard M. Nixon	Republican	34,108,546	49.6	219	
	Other	—	—		15	
1964	**LYNDON B. JOHNSON (Tex.)**	Democratic	43,126,506	61.1	486	61.7
	Barry M. Goldwater	Republican	27,176,799	38.5	52	
1968	**RICHARD M. NIXON (N.Y.)**	Republican	31,770,237	43.4	301	60.6
	Hubert H. Humphrey	Democratic	31,270,533	42.7	191	
	George Wallace	American Indep.	9,906,141	13.5	46	
1972	**RICHARD M. NIXON (N.Y.)**	Republican	47,169,911	60.7	520	55.2
	George S. McGovern	Democratic	29,170,383	37.5	17	
	Other	—	—		1	
1976	**JIMMY CARTER (Ga.)**	Democratic	40,828,587	50.0	297	53.5
	Gerald R. Ford	Republican	39,147,613	47.9	241	
	Other	—	1,575,459	2.1	—	
1980	**RONALD REAGAN (Calif.)**	Republican	43,901,812	50.7	489	52.6
	Jimmy Carter	Democratic	35,483,820	41.0	49	
	John B. Anderson	Independent	5,719,722	6.6	—	
	Ed Clark	Libertarian	921,188	1.1	—	

Year	Candidates	Parties	Popular Vote	Percentage of Popular Vote	Electoral Vote	Percentage of Voter Participation
1984	**RONALD REAGAN (Calif.)**	Republican	54,455,075	59.0	525	53.3
	Walter Mondale	Democratic	37,577,185	41.0	13	
1988	**GEORGE BUSH (Texas)**	Republican	47,946,422	54.0	426	50.2
	Michael S. Dukakis	Democratic	41,016,429	46.0	112	
1992	**WILLIAM J. CLINTON (Ark.)**	Democratic	44,908,233	43.3	370	55.2
	George Bush	Republican	39,102,282	37.7	168	
	Ross Perot	Independent	19,721,433	19.0	—	

VICE PRESIDENTS AND CABINET MEMBERS

The Washington Administration (1789–1797)

Vice President	John Adams	1789–1797
Secretary of State	Thomas Jefferson	1789–1793
	Edmund Randolph	1794–1795
	Timothy Pickering	1795–1797
Secretary of Treasury	Alexander Hamilton	1789–1795
	Oliver Wolcott	1795–1797
Secretary of War	Henry Knox	1789–1794
	Timothy Pickering	1795–1796
	James McHenry	1796–1797
Attorney General	Edmund Randolph	1789–1793
	William Bradford	1794–1795
	Charles Lee	1795–1797
Postmaster General	Samuel Osgood	1789–1791
	Timothy Pickering	1791–1794
	Joseph Habersham	1795–1797

The John Adams Administration (1797–1801)

Vice President	Thomas Jefferson	1797–1801
Secretary of State	Timothy Pickering	1797–1800
	John Marshall	1800–1801
Secretary of Treasury	Oliver Wolcott	1797–1800
	Samuel Dexter	1800–1801
Secretary of War	James McHenry	1797–1800
	Samuel Dexter	1800–1801
Attorney General	Charles Lee	1797–1801
Postmaster General	Joseph Habersham	1797–1801
Secretary of Navy	Benjamin Stoddert	1798–1801

The Jefferson Administration (1801–1809)

Vice President	Aaron Burr	1801–1805
	George Clinton	1805–1809
Secretary of State	James Madison	1801–1809
Secretary of Treasury	Samuel Dexter	1801
	Albert Gallatin	1801–1809
Secretary of War	Henry Dearborn	1801–1809
Attorney General	Levi Lincoln	1801–1805
	Robert Smith	1805
	John Breckinridge	1805–1806
	Caesar Rodney	1807–1809
Postmaster General	Joseph Habersham	1801
	Gideon Granger	1801–1809
Secretary of Navy	Robert Smith	1801–1809

The Madison Administration (1809–1817)

Vice President	George Clinton	1809–1813
	Elbridge Gerry	1813–1817
Secretary of State	Robert Smith	1809–1811
	James Monroe	1811–1817
Secretary of Treasury	Albert Gallatin	1809–1813
	George Campbell	1814
	Alexander Dallas	1814–1816
	William Crawford	1816–1817
Secretary of War	William Eustis	1809–1812
	John Armstrong	1813–1814
	James Monroe	1814–1815
	William Crawford	1815–1817
Attorney General	Caesar Rodney	1809–1811
	William Pinkney	1811–1814
	Richard Rush	1814–1817
Postmaster General	Gideon Granger	1809–1814
	Return Meigs	1814–1817
Secretary of Navy	Paul Hamilton	1809–1813
	William Jones	1813–1814
	Benjamin Crowninshield	1814–1817

The Monroe Administration (1817–1825)

Vice President	Daniel Tompkins	1817–1825
Secretary of State	John Quincy Adams	1817–1825
Secretary of Treasury	William Crawford	1817–1825
Secretary of War	George Graham	1817
	John C. Calhoun	1817–1825
Attorney General	Richard Rush	1817
	William Wirt	1817–1825
Postmaster General	Return Meigs	1817–1823
	John McLean	1823–1825

Secretary of Navy	Benjamin Crowninshield	1817–1818
	Smith Thompson	1818–1823
	Samuel Southard	1823–1825

The John Quincy Adams Administration (1825–1829)

Vice President	John C. Calhoun	1825–1829
Secretary of State	Henry Clay	1825–1829
Secretary of Treasury	Richard Rush	1825–1829
Secretary of War	James Barbour	1825–1828
	Peter Porter	1828–1829
Attorney General	William Wirt	1825–1829
Postmaster General	John McLean	1825–1829
Secretary of Navy	Samuel Southard	1825–1829

The Jackson Administration (1829–1837)

Vice President	John C. Calhoun	1829–1833
	Martin Van Buren	1833–1837
Secretary of State	Martin Van Buren	1829–1831
	Edward Livingston	1831–1833
	Louis McLane	1833–1834
	John Forsyth	1834–1837
Secretary of Treasury	Samuel Ingham	1829–1831
	Louis McLane	1831–1833
	William Duane	1833
	Roger B. Taney	1833–1834
	Levi Woodbury	1834–1837
Secretary of War	John H. Eaton	1829–1831
	Lewis Cass	1831–1837
	Benjamin Butler	1837
Attorney General	John M. Berrien	1829–1831
	Roger B. Taney	1831–1833
	Benjamin Butler	1833–1837
Postmaster General	William Barry	1829–1835
	Amos Kendall	1835–1837
Secretary of Navy	John Branch	1829–1831
	Levi Woodbury	1831–1834
	Mahlon Dickerson	1834–1837

The Van Buren Administration (1837–1841)

Vice President	Richard M. Johnson	1837–1841
Secretary of State	John Forsyth	1837–1841
Secretary of Treasury	Levi Woodbury	1837–1841
Secretary of War	Joel Poinsett	1837–1841
Attorney General	Benjamin Butler	1837–1838
	Felix Grundy	1838–1840
	Henry D. Gilpin	1840–1841
Postmaster General	Amos Kendall	1837–1840
	John M. Niles	1840–1841
Secretary of Navy	Mahlon Dickerson	1837–1838
	James Paulding	1838–1841

The William Harrison Administration (1841)

Vice President	John Tyler	1841
Secretary of State	Daniel Webster	1841
Secretary of Treasury	Thomas Ewing	1841
Secretary of War	John Bell	1841
Attorney General	John J. Crittenden	1841
Postmaster General	Francis Granger	1841
Secretary of Navy	George Badger	1841

The Tyler Administration (1841–1845)

Vice President	None	
Secretary of State	Daniel Webster	1841–1843
	Hugh S. Legaré	1843
	Abel P. Upshur	1843–1844
	John C. Calhoun	1844–1845
Secretary of Treasury	Thomas Ewing	1841
	Walter Forward	1841–1843
	John C. Spencer	1843–1844
	George Bibb	1844–1845
Secretary of War	John Bell	1841
	John C. Spencer	1841–1843
	James M. Porter	1843–1844
	William Wilkins	1844–1845
Attorney General	John J. Crittenden	1841
	Hugh S. Legaré	1841–1843
	John Nelson	1843–1845
Postmaster General	Francis Granger	1841
	Charles Wickliffe	1841
Secretary of Navy	George Badger	1841
	Abel P. Upshur	1841
	David Henshaw	1843–1844
	Thomas Gilmer	1844
	John Y. Mason	1844–1845

The Polk Administration (1845–1849)

Vice President	George M. Dallas	1845–1849
Secretary of State	James Buchanan	1845–1849
Secretary of Treasury	Robert J. Walker	1845–1849
Secretary of War	William L. Marcy	1845–1849
Attorney General	John Y. Mason	1845–1846
	Nathan Clifford	1846–1848
	Isaac Toucey	1848–1849
Postmaster General	Cave Johnson	1845–1849
Secretary of Navy	George Bancroft	1845–1846
	John Y. Mason	1846–1849

The Taylor Administration (1849–1850)

Vice President	Millard Fillmore	1849–1850
Secretary of State	John M. Clayton	1849–1950
Secretary of Treasury	William Meredith	1849–1850
Secretary of War	George Crawford	1849–1850
Attorney General	Reverdy Johnson	1849–1850
Postmaster General	Jacob Collamer	1849–1850
Secretary of Navy	William Preston	1849–1850
Secretary of Interior	Thomas Ewing	1849–1850

The Fillmore Administration (1850–1853)

Vice President	None	
Secretary of State	Daniel Webster	1850–1852
	Edward Everett	1852–1853
Secretary of Treasury	Thomas Corwin	1850–1853
Secretary of War	Charles Conrad	1850–1853
Attorney General	John J. Crittenden	1850–1853
Postmaster General	Nathan Hall	1850–1852
	Sam D. Hubbard	1852–1853
Secretary of Navy	William A. Graham	1850–1852
	John P. Kennedy	1852–1853

Secretary of Interior	Thomas McKennan	1850
	Alexander Stuart	1850–1853

The Pierce Administration (1853–1857)

Vice President	William R. King	1853–1857
Secretary of State	William L. Marcy	1853–1857
Secretary of Treasury	James Guthrie	1853–1857
Secretary of War	Jefferson Davis	1853–1857
Attorney General	Caleb Cushing	1853–1857
Postmaster General	James Campbell	1853–1957
Secretary of Navy	James C. Dobbin	1853–1857
Secretary of Interior	Robert McClelland	1853–1857

The Buchanan Administration (1857–1861)

Vice President	John C. Breckinridge	1857–1861
Secretary of State	Lewis Cass	1857–1860
	Jeremiah S. Black	1860–1861
Secretary of Treasury	Howell Cobb	1857–1860
	Philip Thomas	1860–1861
	John A. Dix	1861
Secretary of War	John B. Floyd	1857–1861
	Joseph Holt	1861
Attorney General	Jeremiah S. Black	1857–1860
	Edwin M. Stanton	1860–1861
Postmaster General	Aaron V. Brown	1857–1859
	Joseph Holt	1859–1861
	Horatio King	1861
Secretary of Navy	Isaac Toucey	1857–1861
Secretary of Interior	Jacob Thompson	1857–1861

The Lincoln Administration (1861–1865)

Vice President	Hannibal Hamlin	1861–1865
	Andrew Johnson	1865
Secretary of State	William H. Seward	1861–1865
Secretary of Treasury	Samuel P. Chase	1861–1864
	William P. Fessenden	1864–1865
	Hugh McCulloch	1865
Secretary of War	Simon Cameron	1861–1862
	Edwin M. Stanton	1862–1865

Attorney General	Edward Bates	1861–1864
	James Speed	1864–1865
Postmaster General	Horatio King	1861
	Montgomery Blair	1861–1864
	William Dennison	1864–1865
Secretary of Navy	Gideon Welles	1861–1865
Secretary of Interior	Caleb B. Smith	1861–1863
	John P. Usher	1863–1865

The Andrew Johnson Administration (1865–1869)

Vice President	None	
Secretary of State	William H. Seward	1865–1869
Secretary of Treasury	Hugh McCulloch	1865–1869
Secretary of War	Edwin M. Stanton	1865–1867
	Ulysses S. Grant	1867–1868
	Lorenzo Thomas	1868
	John M. Schofield	1868–1869
Attorney General	James Speed	1865–1866
	Henry Stanbery	1866–1868
	William M. Evarts	1868–1869
Postmaster General	William Dennison	1865–1866
	Alexander Randall	1866–1869
Secretary of Navy	Gideon Welles	1865–1869
Secretary of Interior	John P. Usher	1865
	James Harlan	1865–1866
	Orville H. Browning	1866–1869

The Grant Administration (1869–1877)

Vice President	Schuyler Colfax	1869–1873
	Henry Wilson	1873–1877
Secretary of State	Elihu B. Washburne	1869
	Hamilton Fish	1869–1877
Secretary of Treasury	George S. Boutwell	1869–1873
	William Richardson	1873–1874
	Benjamin Bristow	1874–1876
	Lot M. Morrill	1876–1877
Secretary of War	John A. Rawlins	1869
	William T. Sherman	1869
	William W. Belknap	1869–1876
	Alphonso Taft	1876
	James D. Cameron	1876–1877
Attorney General	Ebenezer Hoar	1869–1870
	Amos T. Ackerman	1870–1871
	G. H. Williams	1871–1875
	Edwards Pierrepont	1875–1876
	Alphonso Taft	1876–1877

Postmaster General	John A. J. Creswell	1869–1874
	James W. Marshall	1874
	Marshall Jewell	1874–1876
	James N. Tyner	1876–1877
Secretary of Navy	Adolph E. Borie	1869
	George M. Robeson	1869–1877
Secretary of Interior	Jacob D. Cox	1869–1870
	Columbus Delano	1870–1875
	Zachariah Chandler	1875–1877

The Hayes Administration (1877–1881)

Vice President	William A. Wheeler	1877–1881
Secretary of State	William M. Evarts	1877–1881
Secretary of Treasury	John Sherman	1877–1881
Secretary of War	George W. McCrary	1877–1879
	Alex Ramsey	1879–1881
Attorney General	Charles Devens	1877–1881
Postmaster General	David M. Key	1877–1880
	Horace Maynard	1880–1881
Secretary of Navy	Richard W. Thompson	1877–1880
	Nathan Goff, Jr.	1881
Secretary of Interior	Carl Schurz	1877–1881

The Garfield Administration (1881)

Vice President	Chester A. Arthur	1881
Secretary of State	James G. Blaine	1881
Secretary of Treasury	William Windom	1881
Secretary of War	Robert T. Lincoln	1881
Attorney General	Wayne MacVeagh	1881
Postmaster General	Thomas L. James	1881
Secretary of Navy	William H. Hunt	1881
Secretary of Interior	Samuel J. Kirkwood	1881

The Arthur Administration (1881–1885)

| Vice President | None | |
| Secretary of State | F. T. Frelinghuysen | 1881–1885 |

Secretary of Treasury	Charles J. Folger	1881–1884
	Walter Q. Gresham	1884
	Hugh McCulloch	1884–1885
Secretary of War	Robert T. Lincoln	1881–1885
Attorney General	Benjamin H. Brewster	1881–1885
Postmaster General	Timothy O. Howe	1881–1883
	Walter Q. Gresham	1883–1884
	Frank Hatton	1884–1885
Secretary of Navy	William H. Hunt	1881–1882
	William E. Chandler	1882–1885
Secretary of Interior	Samuel J. Kirkwood	1881–1882
	Henry M. Teller	1882–1885

The Cleveland Administration (1885–1889)

Vice President	Thomas A. Hendricks	1885–1889
Secretary of State	Thomas F. Bayard	1885–1889
Secretary of Treasury	Daniel Manning	1885–1887
	Charles S. Fairchild	1887–1889
Secretary of War	William C. Endicott	1885–1889
Attorney General	Augustus H. Garland	1885–1889
Postmaster General	William F. Vilas	1885–1888
	Don M. Dickinson	1888–1889
Secretary of Navy	William C. Whitney	1885–1889
Secretary of Interior	Lucius Q. C. Lamar	1885–1888
	William F. Vilas	1888–1889
Secretary of Agriculture	Norman J. Colman	1889

The Benjamin Harrison Administration (1889–1893)

Vice President	Levi P. Morton	1889–1893
Secretary of State	James G. Blaine	1889–1892
	John W. Foster	1892–1893
Secretary of Treasury	William Windom	1889–1891
	Charles Foster	1891–1893
Secretary of War	Redfield Proctor	1889–1891
	Stephen B. Elkins	1891–1893
Attorney General	William H. H. Miller	1889–1891
Postmaster General	John Wanamaker	1889–1893

Secretary of Navy	Benjamin F. Tracy	1889–1893
Secretary of Interior	John W. Noble	1889–1893
Secretary of Agriculture	Jeremiah M. Rush	1889–1893

The Cleveland Administration (1893–1897)

Vice President	Adlai E. Stevenson	1893–1897
Secretary of State	Walter Q. Gresham	1893–1895
	Richard Olney	1895–1897
Secretary of Treasury	John G. Carlisle	1893–1897
Secretary of War	Daniel S. Lamont	1893–1897
Attorney General	Richard Olney	1893–1895
	James Harmon	1895–1897
Postmaster General	Wilson S. Bissell	1893–1895
	William L. Wilson	1895–1897
Secretary of Navy	Hilary A. Herbert	1893–1897
Secretary of Interior	Hoke Smith	1893–1896
	David R. Francis	1896–1897
Secretary of Agriculture	Julius S. Morton	1893–1897

The McKinley Administration (1897–1901)

Vice President	Garret A. Hobart	1897–1901
	Theodore Roosevelt	1901
Secretary of State	John Sherman	1897–1898
	William R. Day	1898
	John Hay	1898–1901
Secretary of Treasury	Lyman J. Gage	1897–1901
Secretary of War	Russell A. Alger	1897–1899
	Elihu Root	1899–1901
Attorney General	Joseph McKenna	1897–1898
	John W. Griggs	1898–1901
	Philander C. Knox	1901
Postmaster General	James A. Gary	1897–1898
	Charles E. Smith	1898–1901
Secretary of Navy	John D. Long	1897–1901

Secretary of Interior	Cornelius N. Bliss	1897–1899
	Ethan A. Hitchcock	1899–1901
Secretary of Agriculture	James Wilson	1897–1901

The Theodore Roosevelt Administration (1901–1909)

Vice President	Charles Fairbanks	1905–1909
Secretary of State	John Hay	1901–1905
	Elihu Root	1905–1909
	Robert Bacon	1909
Secretary of Treasury	Lyman J. Gage	1901–1902
	Leslie M. Shaw	1902–1907
	George B. Cortelyou	1907–1909
Secretary of War	Elihu Root	1901–1904
	William H. Taft	1904–1908
	Luke E. Wright	1908–1909
Attorney General	Philander C. Knox	1901–1904
	William H. Moody	1904–1906
	Charles J. Bonaparte	1906–1909
Postmaster General	Charles E. Smith	1901–1902
	Henry C. Payne	1902–1904
	Robert J. Wynne	1904–1905
	George B. Cortelyou	1905–1907
	George von L. Meyer	1907–1909
Secretary of Navy	John D. Long	1901–1902
	William H. Moody	1902–1904
	Paul Morton	1904–1905
	Charles J. Bonaparte	1905–1906
	Victor H. Metcalf	1906–1908
	Truman H. Newberry	1908–1909
Secretary of Interior	Ethan A. Hitchcock	1901–1907
	James R. Garfield	1907–1909
Secretary of Agriculture	James Wilson	1901–1909
Secretary of Labor and Commerce	George B. Cortelyou	1903–1904
	Victor H. Metcalf	1904–1906
	Oscar S. Straus	1906–1909
	Charles Nagel	1909

The Taft Administration (1909–1913)

Vice President	James S. Sherman	1909–1913
Secretary of State	Philander C. Knox	1909–1913
Secretary of Treasury	Franklin MacVeagh	1909–1913
Secretary of War	Jacob M. Dickinson	1909–1911
	Henry L. Stimson	1911–1913

Attorney General	George W. Wickersham	1909–1913
Postmaster General	Frank H. Hitchcock	1909–1913
Secretary of Navy	George von L. Meyer	1909–1913
Secretary of Interior	Richard A. Ballinger	1909–1911
	Walter L. Fisher	1911–1913
Secretary of Agriculture	James Wilson	1909–1913
Secretary of Labor and Commerce	Charles Nagel	1909–1913

The Wilson Administration (1913–1921)

Vice President	Thomas R. Marshall	1913–1921
Secretary of State	William J. Bryan	1913–1915
	Robert Lansing	1915–1920
	Bainbridge Colby	1920–1921
Secretary of Treasury	William G. McAdoo	1913–1918
	Carter Glass	1918–1920
	David F. Houston	1920–1921
Secretary of War	Lindley M. Garrison	1913–1916
	Newton D. Baker	1916–1921
Attorney General	James C. McReynolds	1913–1914
	Thomas W. Gregory	1914–1919
	A. Mitchell Palmer	1919–1921
Postmaster General	Albert S. Burleson	1913–1921
Secretary of Navy	Josephus Daniels	1913–1921
Secretary of Interior	Franklin K. Lane	1913–1920
	John B. Payne	1920–1921
Secretary of Agriculture	David F. Houston	1913–1920
	Edwin T. Meredith	1920–1921
Secretary of Commerce	William C. Redfield	1913–1919
	Joshua W. Alexander	1919–1921
Secretary of Labor	William B. Wilson	1913–1921

The Harding Administration (1921–1923)

Vice President	Calvin Coolidge	1921–1923
Secretary of State	Charles E. Hughes	1921–1923
Secretary of Treasury	Andrew Mellon	1921–1923
Secretary of War	John W. Weeks	1921–1923

Attorney General	Harry M. Daugherty	1921–1923
Postmaster General	Will H. Hays	1921–1922
	Hubert Work	1922–1923
	Harry S. New	1923
Secretary of Navy	Edwin Denby	1921–1923
Secretary of Interior	Albert B. Fall	1921–1923
	Hubert Work	1923
Secretary of Agriculture	Henry C. Wallace	1921–1923
Secretary of Commerce	Herbert C. Hoover	1921–1923
Secretary of Labor	James J. Davis	1921–1923

The Coolidge Administration (1923–1929)

Vice President	Charles G. Dawes	1925–1929
Secretary of State	Charles E. Hughes	1923–1925
	Frank B. Kellogg	1925–1929
Secretary of Treasury	Andrew Mellon	1923–1929
Secretary of War	John W. Weeks	1923–1925
	Dwight F. Davis	1925–1929
Attorney General	Harry M. Daugherty	1923–1924
	Harlan F. Stone	1924–1925
	John G. Sargent	1925–1929
Postmaster General	Harry S. New	1923–1929
Secretary of Navy	Edwin Derby	1923–1924
	Curtis D. Wilbur	1924–1929
Secretary of Interior	Hubert Work	1923–1928
	Roy O. West	1928–1929
Secretary of Agriculture	Henry C. Wallace	1923–1924
	Howard M. Gore	1924–1925
	William M. Jardine	1925–1929
Secretary of Commerce	Herbert C. Hoover	1923–1928
	William F. Whiting	1928–1929
Secretary of Labor	James J. Davis	1923–1929

The Hoover Administration (1929–1933)

Vice President	Charles Curtis	1929–1933
Secretary of State	Henry L. Stimson	1929–1933
Secretary of Treasury	Andrew Mellon	1929–1932
	Ogden L. Mills	1932–1933

Secretary of War	James W. Good	1929
	Patrick J. Hurley	1929–1933
Attorney General	William D. Mitchell	1929–1933
Postmaster General	Walter F. Brown	1929–1933
Secretary of Navy	Charles F. Adams	1929–1933
Secretary of Interior	Ray L. Wilbur	1929–1933
Secretary of Agriculture	Arthur M. Hyde	1929–1933
Secretary of Commerce	Robert P. Lamont	1929–1932
	Roy D. Chapin	1932–1933
Secretary of Labor	James J. Davis	1929–1930
	William N. Doak	1930–1933

The Franklin D. Roosevelt Administration (1933–1945)

Vice President	John Nance Garner	1933–1941
	Henry A. Wallace	1941–1945
	Harry S. Truman	1945
Secretary of State	Cordell Hull	1933–1944
	Edward R. Stettinius, Jr.	1944–1945
Secretary of Treasury	William H. Woodin	1933–1934
	Henry Morgenthau, Jr.	1934–1945
Secretary of War	George H. Dern	1933–1936
	Henry A. Woodring	1936–1940
	Henry L. Stimson	1940–1945
Attorney General	Homer S. Cummings	1933–1939
	Frank Murphy	1939–1940
	Robert H. Jackson	1940–1941
	Francis Biddle	1941–1945
Postmaster General	James A. Farley	1933–1940
	Frank C. Walker	1940–1945
Secretary of Navy	Claude A. Swanson	1933–1940
	Charles Edison	1940
	Frank Knox	1940–1944
	James V. Forrestal	1944–1945
Secretary Interior	Harold L. Ickes	1933–1945
Secretary of Agriculture	Henry A. Wallace	1933–1940
	Claude R. Wickard	1940–1945
Secretary of Commerce	Daniel C. Roper	1933–1939
	Harry L. Hopkins	1939–1940
	Jesse Jones	1940–1945
	Henry A. Wallace	1945
Secretary of Labor	Frances Perkins	1933–1945

The Truman Administration (1945–1953)

Vice President	Alben W. Barkley	1949–1953
Secretary of State	Edward R. Stettinius, Jr.	1945
	James F. Byrnes	1945–1947
	George C. Marshall	1947–1949
	Dean G. Acheson	1949–1953
Secretary of Treasury	Fred M. Vinson	1945–1946
	John W. Snyder	1946–1953
Secretary of War	Robert P. Patterson	1945–1947
	Kenneth C. Royall	1947
Attorney General	Tom C. Clark	1945–1949
	J. Howard McGrath	1949–1952
	James P. McGranery	1952–1953
Postmaster General	Frank C. Walker	1945
	Robert E. Hannegan	1945–1947
	Jesse M. Donaldson	1947–1953
Secretary of Navy	James V. Forrestal	1945–1947
Secretary of Interior	Harold L. Ickes	1945–1946
	Julius A. Krug	1946–1949
	Oscar L. Chapman	1949–1953
Secretary of Agriculture	Clinton P. Anderson	1945–1948
	Charles F. Brannan	1948–1953
Secretary of Commerce	Henry A. Wallace	1945–1946
	W. Averell Harriman	1946–1948
	Charles W. Sawyer	1948–1953
Secretary of Labor	Lewis B. Schwellenbach	1945–1948
	Maurice J. Tobin	1948–1953
Secretary of Defense	James V. Forrestal	1947–1949
	Louis A. Johnson	1949–1950
	George C. Marshall	1950–1951
	Robert A. Lovett	1951–1953

The Eisenhower Administration (1953–1961)

Vice President	Richard M. Nixon	1953–1961
Secretary of State	John Foster Dulles	1953–1959
	Christian A. Herter	1959–1961
Secretary of Treasury	George M. Humphrey	1953–1957
	Robert B. Anderson	1957–1961
Attorney General	Herbert Brownell, Jr.	1953–1958
	William P. Rogers	1958–1961
Postmaster General	Arthur E. Summerfield	1953–1961
Secretary of Interior	Douglas McKay	1953–1956
	Freed A. Seaton	1956–1961

Secretary of Agriculture	Ezra T. Benson	1953–1961
Secretary of Commerce	Sinclair Weeks	1953–1958
	Lewis L. Strauss	1958–1959
	Frederick H. Mueller	1959–1961
Secretary of Labor	Martin P. Durkin	1953
	James P. Mitchell	1953–1961
Secretary of Defense	Charles E. Wilson	1953–1957
	Neil H. McElroy	1957–1959
	Thomas S. Gates Jr.	1959–1961
Secretary of Health, Education, and Welfare	Oveta Culp Hobby	1953–1955
	Marion B. Folsom	1955–1958
	Arthur S. Flemming	1958–1961

The Kennedy Administration (1961–1963)

Vice President	Lyndon B. Johnson	1961–1963
Secretary of State	Dean Rusk	1961–1963
Secretary of Treasury	C. Douglas Dillon	1961–1963
Attorney General	Robert F. Kennedy	1961–1963
Postmaster General	J. Edward Day	1961–1963
	John A. Gronouski	1963
Secretary of Interior	Stewart L. Udall	1961–1963
Secretary of Agriculture	Orville L. Freeman	1961–1963
Secretary of Commerce	Luther H. Hodges	1961–1963
Secretary of Labor	Arthur J. Goldberg	1961–1962
	W. Willard Wirtz	1962–1963
Secretary of Defense	Robert S. McNamara	1961–1963
Secretary of Health, Education, and Welfare	Abraham A. Ribicoff	1961–1962
	Anthony J. Celebrezze	1962–1963

The Lyndon Johnson Administration (1963–1969)

Vice President	Hubert H. Humphrey	1965–1969
Secretary of State	Dean Rusk	1963–1969
Secretary of Treasury	C. Douglas Dillon	1963–1965
	Henry H. Fowler	1965–1969

Attorney General	Robert F. Kennedy	1963–1964
	Nicholas Katzenbach	1965–1966
	Ramsey Clark	1967–1969
Postmaster General	John A. Gronouski	1963–1965
	Lawrence F. O'Brien	1965–1968
	Marvin Watson	1968–1969
Secretary of Interior	Stewart L. Udall	1963–1969
Secretary of Agriculture	Orville L. Freeman	1963–1969
Secretary of Commerce	Luther H. Hodges	1963–1964
	John T. Connor	1964–1967
	Alexander B. Trowbridge	1967–1968
	Cyrus R. Smith	1968–1969
Secretary of Labor	W. Willard Wirtz	1963–1969
Secretary of Defense	Robert F. McNamara	1963–1968
	Clark Clifford	1968–1969
Secretary of Health, Education, and Welfare	Anthony J. Celebrezze	1963–1965
	John W. Gardner	1965–1968
	Wilbur J. Cohen	1968–1969
Secretary of Housing and Urban Development	Robert C. Weaver	1966–1969
	Robert C. Wood	1969
Secretary of Transportation	Alan S. Boyd	1967–1969

The Nixon Administration (1969–1974)

Vice President	Spiro T. Agnew	1969–1973
	Gerald R. Ford	1973–1974
Secretary of State	William P. Rogers	1969–1973
	Henry A. Kissinger	1973–1974
Secretary of Treasury	David M. Kennedy	1969–1970
	John B. Connally	1971–1972
	George P. Shultz	1972–1974
	William E. Simon	1974
Attorney General	John N. Mitchell	1969–1972
	Richard G. Kleindienst	1972–1973
	Elliot L. Richardson	1973
	William B. Saxbe	1973–1974
Postmaster General	Winton M. Blount	1969–1971
Secretary of Interior	Walter J. Hickel	1969–1970
	Rogers Morton	1971–1974

Secretary of Agriculture	Clifford M. Hardin	1969–1971
	Earl L. Butz	1971–1974
Secretary of Commerce	Maurice H. Stans	1969–1972
	Peter G. Peterson	1972–1973
	Frederick B. Dent	1973–1974
Secretary of Labor	George P. Shultz	1969–1970
	James D. Hodgson	1970–1973
	Peter J. Brennan	1973–1974
Secretary of Defense	Melvin R. Laird	1969–1973
	Elliot L. Richardson	1973
	James R. Schlesinger	1973–1974
Secretary of Health, Education, and Welfare	Robert H. Finch	1969–1970
	Elliot L. Richardson	1970–1973
	Caspar W. Weinberger	1973–1974
Secretary of Housing and Urban Development	George Romney	1969–1973
	James T. Lynn	1973–1974
Secretary of Transportation	John A. Volpe	1969–1973
	Claude S. Brinegar	1973–1974

The Ford Administration (1974–1977)

Vice President	Nelson A. Rockefeller	1974–1977
Secretary of State	Henry A. Kissinger	1974–1977
Secretary of Treasury	William E. Simon	1974–1977
Attorney General	William Saxbe	1974–1975
	Edward Levi	1975–1977
Secretary of Interior	Rogers Morton	1974–1975
	Stanley K. Hathaway	1975
	Thomas Kleppe	1975–1977
Secretary of Agriculture	Earl L. Butz	1974–1976
	John A. Knebel	1976–1977
Secretary of Commerce	Frederick B. Dent	1974–1975
	Rogers Morton	1975–1976
	Elliot L. Richardson	1976–1977
Secretary of Labor	Peter J. Brennan	1974–1975
	John T. Dunlop	1975–1976
	W. J. Usery	1976–1977
Secretary of Defense	James R. Schlesinger	1974–1975
	Donald Rumsfeld	1975–1977
Secretary of Health, Education, and Welfare	Caspar Weinberger	1974–1975
	Forrest D. Mathews	1975–1977

Secretary of Housing and Urban Development	James T. Lynn	1974–1975
	Carla A. Hills	1975–1977
Secretary of Transportation	Claude Brinegar	1974–1975
	William T. Coleman	1975–1977

The Carter Administration (1977–1981)

Vice President	Walter F. Mondale	1977–1981
Secretary of State	Cyrus R. Vance	1977–1980
	Edmund Muskie	1980–1981
Secretary of Treasury	W. Michael Blumenthal	1977–1979
	G. William Miller	1979–1981
Attorney General	Griffin Bell	1977–1979
	Benjamin R. Civiletti	1979–1981
Secretary of Interior	Cecil D. Andrus	1977–1981
Secretary of Agriculture	Robert Bergland	1977–1981
Secretary of Commerce	Juanita M. Kreps	1977–1979
	Philip M. Klutznick	1979–1981
Secretary of Labor	F. Ray Marshall	1977–1981
Secretary of Defense	Harold Brown	1977–1981
Secretary of Health, Education and Welfare	Joseph A. Califano	1977–1979
	Patricia R. Harris	1979
Secretary of Health and Human Services	Patricia R. Harris	1979–1981
Secretary of Education	Shirley M. Hufstedler	1979–1981
Secretary of Housing and Urban Development	Patricia R. Harris	1977–1979
	Moon Landrieu	1979–1981
Secretary of Transportation	Brock Adams	1977–1979
	Neil E. Goldschmidt	1979–1981
Secretary of Energy	James R. Schlesinger	1977–1979
	Charles W. Duncan	1979–1981

The Reagan Administration (1981–1989)

Vice President	George Bush	1981–1989
Secretary of State	Alexander M. Haig	1981–1982
	George P. Shultz	1982–1989
Secretary of Treasury	Donald Regan	1981–1985
	James A. Baker III	1985–1988
	Nicholas F. Brady	1988–1989
Attorney General	William F. Smith	1981–1985
	Edwin A. Meese III	1985–1988
	Richard Thornburgh	1988–1989
Secretary of Interior	James Watt	1981–1983
	William P. Clark, Jr.	1983–1985
	Donald P. Hodel	1985–1989
Secretary of Agriculture	John Block	1981–1986
	Richard E. Lyng	1986–1989
Secretary of Commerce	Malcolm Baldrige	1981–1987
	C. William Verity, Jr.	1987–1989
Secretary of Labor	Raymond Donovan	1981–1985
	William Brock	1985–1987
	Ann D. McLaughlin	1987–1989
Secretary of Defense	Caspar Weinberger	1981–1987
	Frank C. Carlucci	1987–1989
Secretary of Health and Human Services	Richard Schweiker	1981–1983
	Margaret Heckler	1983–1985
	Otis R. Bowen	1985–1989
Secretary of Education	Terrel H. Bell	1981–1985
	William J. Bennett	1985–1988
	Laura F. Cavazos	1988–1989
Secretary of Housing and Urban Development	Samuel Pierce	1981–1989
Secretary of Transportation	Drew Lewis	1981–1983
	Elizabeth Dole	1983–1987
	James H. Burnley	1987–1989
Secretary of Energy	James Edwards	1981–1982
	Donald P. Hodel	1982–1985
	John S. Herrington	1984–1989

The Bush Administration (1989–1993)

Vice President	J. Danforth Quayle	1989–1993
Secretary of State	James A. Baker III	1989–1992
	Lawrence S. Eagleburger	1992–1993
Secretary of Treasury	Nicholas F. Brady	1989–1993

Attorney General	Richard Thornburgh	1989–1991
	William P. Barr	1991–1993
Secretary of Interior	Manuel Lujan	1989–1993
Secretary of Agriculture	Clayton K. Yeutter	1989–1991
	Edward Madigan	1991–1993
Secretary of Commerce	Robert A. Mosbacher	1989–1992
	Barbara H. Franklin	1992–1993
Secretary of Labor	Elizabeth Dole	1989–1991
	Lynn M. Martin	1991–1993
Secretary of Defense	Richard B. Cheney	1989–1993
Secretary of Health and Human Services	Louis W. Sullivan	1989–1993
Secretary of Education	Laura F. Cavazos	1989–1991
	Lamar Alexander	1991–1993
Secretary of Housing and Urban Development	Jack F. Kemp	1989–1993
Secretary of Transportation	Samuel K. Skinner	1989–1992
	Andrew H. Card	1992–1993
Secretary of Energy	James D. Watkins	1989–1993
Secretary of Veterans Affairs	Edward J. Derwinski	1989–1993

The Clinton Administration (1993–)		
Vice President	Albert Gore, Jr.	1993–
Secretary of State	Warren M. Christopher	1993–
Secretary of Treasury	Lloyd M. Bentsen, Jr.	1993–

Attorney General	Janet Reno	1993–
Secretary of Interior	Bruce Babbitt	1993–
Secretary of Agriculture	Mike Espy	1993–
Secretary of Commerce	Ronald H. Brown	1993–
Secretary of Labor	Robert B. Reich	1993–
Secretary of Defense	Les Aspin	1993–1994
	William Perry	1994–
Secretary of Health and Human Services	Donna E. Shalala	1993–
Secretary of Education	Richard W. Riley	1993–
Secretary of Housing and Urban Development	Henry G. Cisneros	1993–
Secretary of Energy	Hazel R. O'Leary	1993–
Secretary of Transportation	Federico Pena	1993–
Secretary of Veterans Affairs	Jesse Brown	1993–

Population of the United States, 1790–1993

Year	Population	Percent Increase	Population per Square Mile	Percent Urban/ Rural	Percent White/ Nonwhite	Median Age
1790	3,929,214		4.5	5.1/94.9	80.7/19.3	NA
1800	5,308,483	35.1	6.1	6.1/93.9	81.1/18.9	NA
1810	7,239,881	36.4	4.3	7.3/92.7	81.0/19.0	NA
1820	9,638,453	33.1	5.5	7.2/92.8	81.6/18.4	16.7
1830	12,866,020	33.5	7.4	8.8/91.2	81.9/18.1	17.2
1840	17,069,453	32.7	9.8	10.8/89.2	83.2/16.8	17.8
1850	23,191,876	35.9	7.9	15.3/84.7	84.3/15.7	18.9
1860	31,443,321	35.6	10.6	19.8/80.2	85.6/14.4	19.4
1870	39,818,449	26.6	13.4	25.7/74.3	86.2/13.8	20.2
1880	50,155,783	26.0	16.9	28.2/71.8	86.5/13.5	20.9
1890	62,947,714	25.5	21.2	35.1/64.9	87.5/12.5	22.0
1900	75,994,575	20.7	25.6	39.6/60.4	87.9/12.1	22.9
1910	91,972,266	21.0	31.0	45.6/54.4	88.9/11.1	24.1
1920	105,710,620	14.9	35.6	51.2/48.8	89.7/10.3	25.3
1930	122,775,046	16.1	41.2	56.1/43.9	89.8/10.2	26.4
1940	131,669,275	7.2	44.2	56.5/43.5	89.8/10.2	29.0
1950	150,697,361	14.5	50.7	64.0/36.0	89.5/10.5	30.2
1960	179,323,175	18.5	50.6	69.9/30.1	88.6/11.4	29.5
1970	203,302,031	13.4	57.4	73.5/26.5	87.6/12.4	28.0
1980	226,545,805	11.4	64.0	73.7/26.3	86.0/14.0	30.0
1990	248,709,873	9.8	70.3	77.5/22.5	80.3/19.7	32.9
1993	259,383,000	4.3	73.3	NA/NA	NA/NA	NA

NA = Not Available.

Employment, 1870–1992

Year	Number of Workers (in millions)	Male/Female Employment Ratio	Percentage of Workers in Unions
1870	12.5	85/15	—
1880	17.4	85/15	—
1890	23.3	83/17	—
1900	29.1	82/18	3
1910	38.2	79/21	6
1920	41.6	79/21	12
1930	48.8	78/22	7
1940	53.0	76/24	27
1950	59.6	72/28	25
1960	69.9	68/32	26
1970	82.1	63/37	25
1980	108.5	58/42	23
1985	108.9	57/43	19
1992	117.6	55/45	16

PRODUCTION, TRADE, AND FEDERAL SPENDING/DEBT, 1790–1992

Year	Gross National Product (GNP) (in billions $)	Balance of Trade (in millions $)	Federal Budget (in billions $)	Federal Surplus/Deficit (in billions $)	Federal Debt (in billions $)
1790	—	−3	.004	+0.00015	.076
1800	—	−20	.011	+0.0006	.083
1810	—	−18	.008	+0.0012	.053
1820	—	−4	.018	−0.0004	.091
1830	—	+3	.015	+0.100	.049
1840	—	+25	.024	−0.005	.004
1850	—	−26	.040	+0.004	.064
1860	—	−38	.063	−0.01	.065
1870	7.4	−11	.310	+0.10	2.4
1880	11.2	+92	.268	+0.07	2.1
1890	13.1	+87	.318	+0.09	1.2
1900	18.7	+569	.521	+0.05	1.2
1910	35.3	+273	.694	−0.02	1.1
1920	91.5	+2,880	6.357	+0.3	24.3
1930	90.7	+513	3.320	+0.7	16.3
1940	100.0	−3,403	9.6	−2.7	43.0
1950	286.5	+1,691	43.1	−2.2	257.4
1960	506.5	+4,556	92.2	+0.3	286.3
1970	992.7	+2,511	196.6	+2.8	371.0
1980	2,631.7	+24,088	579.6	−59.5	914.3
1985	4,087.7	−148,480	946.3	−212.3	1,827.5
1990	5,524.5	−101,012	1,251.8	−220.5	3,233.3
1992	5,961.9	−84,501	1,381.9	−290.2	4,064.6

ILLUSTRATIONS

MAPS

CHARTS

INDEX